THE VATICAN

ALL THE PAINTINGS

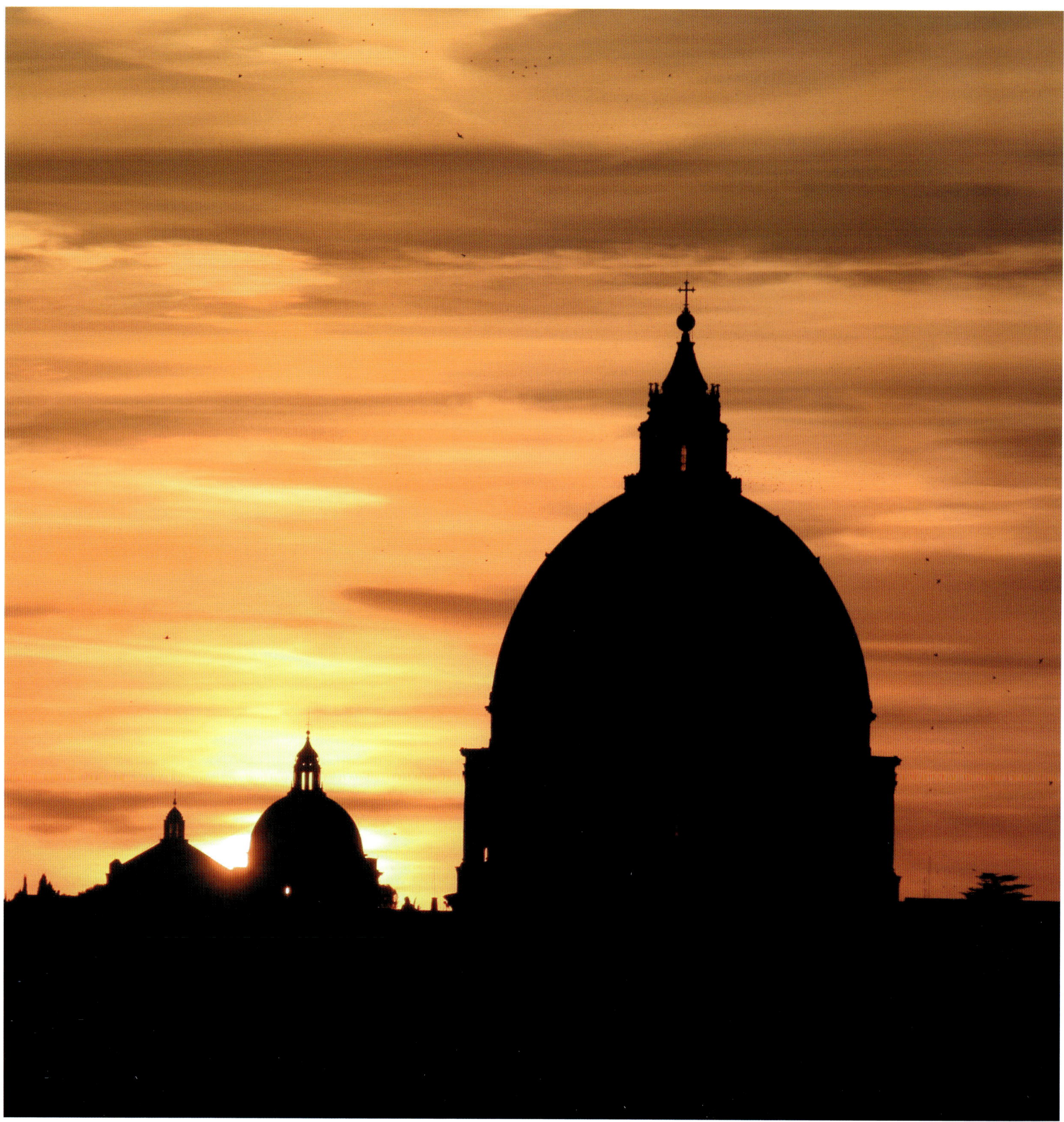

THE VATICAN

ALL THE PAINTINGS

The Complete Collection of Old Masters
Plus More than 300 Sculptures, Maps, Tapestries,
and Other Artifacts

ANJA GREBE

INTRODUCTION BY ROSS KING

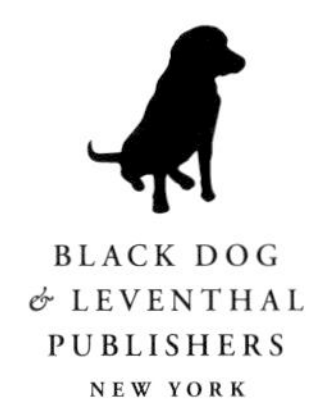

BLACK DOG
& LEVENTHAL
PUBLISHERS
NEW YORK

Translated by Richard Elliott

Cover design by Katie Benezra

Black Dog & Leventhal Publishers
Hachette Book Group
1290 Avenue of the Americas
New York, NY 10104

www.hachettebookgroup.com
www.blackdogandleventhal.com

Originally published in 2013 as a hardcover and ebook by Black Dog & Leventhal Publishers

First trade paperback edition: March 2020

Black Dog & Leventhal Publishers is an imprint of Perseus Books, LLC, a subsidiary of Hachette Book Group, Inc. The Black Dog & Leventhal Publishers name and logo are trademarks of Hachette Book Group, Inc.

Print book interior design by Liz Dreisbach
Images courtesy of Endeavour London Ltd.
Picture research: Jennifer Jeffrey
See page 525 for additional image credits
ISBNs: 978-1-57912-943-9 (hardcover); 978-0-7624-7065-5 (trade paperback)

Printed in China

IM

10 9 8 7 6 5 4 3

CONTENTS

INTRODUCTION

If geography is destiny, it is only appropriate that the Vatican Museums hold one of the world's greatest art collections. Now home to masterpieces by Leonardo da Vinci, Michelangelo, Raphael, and Titian, the Vatican has always been a place sacred to the arts. The poetic and creative impulses of the hill beside the Tiber are revealed in its name: The ancient Romans called this modest eminence the Mons Vaticanus, a reference to the poets and seers, or vates, who dwelled there, and whose writings, the *vaticinia*, were scrutinized for clues to the future. According to the Roman scholar Varro, the word vates came from *vi mentis*, meaning "a force of the mind," or what today we might call the creative imagination. The Vatican therefore made an auspicious home for the fine arts.

The Early Christians believed that for the ancient Romans the presiding deity of the Vatican had been Apollo, the god of poetry and music. An old tradition held that a temple dedicated to Apollo stood on the site. A history of the popes begun in the sixth century, the *Liber pontificalis*, stated that Peter was buried "in the temple of Apollo, near the place where he was crucified… in the Vatican." In all likelihood, Peter was indeed executed and then buried in the precincts of the Vatican. In 1940 a necropolis was uncovered on the southern slope of the Vatican, complete with rows of mausolea and, as Pope Pius XII announced to the world in 1950, an ancient shrine to St. Peter. However, excavations have discovered no temple dedicated to Apollo or anyone else.

Still, myth is often more coercive and compelling than facts. The story of the temple of Apollo became firmly entrenched in Vatican lore, taking on its own reality. In 1511 Raphael painted his famous fresco, known as *Parnassus*, in the Room of Signature in the Vatican Palace, showing Apollo gathered on Mount Parnassus with a who's who of the literary arts, from Homer through to Petrarch and Boccaccio. He painted his scene around and above a north-facing window that, in his day, offered a view of the south slope of the Vatican hill. This pairing of Raphael's fresco with the Vatican hill beyond the window was no coincidence. There may never have been a temple of Apollo on the slopes of the Vatican, but the Vatican became a kind of modern Parnassus, with many popes and cardinals assembling and supporting artists and writers and becoming truly Apollonian in their patronage of the fine arts.

To give what is perhaps the most conspicuous example, Pope Julius II was not only the man who commissioned Raphael to decorate the papal apartments and Michelangelo to paint the vault of the Sistine Chapel; he was also the founder of the Vatican Museums, whose nucleus is the set of ancient statues that he assembled in the courtyard garden of the Villa del Belvedere. One of the first acquisitions was, fittingly, the ancient sculpture now known as the *Apollo Belvedere*, rediscovered sometime in the 1480s and owned by Julius when he was still a cardinal. A poem composed during Julius's papacy by a man named Capodiferro imagined this statue coming to life and declaring that, thanks to the pope, the Vatican, and not Delos or Delphi, was now the true home of Apollo.

Capodiferro was writing ingratiating propaganda for Julius. But there was much truth in what he said, and the Vatican has become a sanctuary of the arts. Julius was only one of numerous enlightened ecclesiastical patrons whose commissions now grace the rooms of the Vatican Pinacoteca as well as the walls and vault of the Sistine Chapel and the Vatican Apartments. For many centuries, popes, cardinals, and the religious orders were responsible for the realization of dozens of masterpieces. The point is made none too subtly in the clever painting-within-a-painting in Giotto's majestic *Stefaneschi Polyptych*, done for the high altar of the old basilica of St. Peter's and now on resplendent display in the Vatican Pinacoteca. On the reverse of the altarpiece, Giotto's patron, Cardinal Stefaneschi, is shown proudly presenting St. Peter with Giotto's finished altarpiece. Michelangelo would pay a similar tribute to Pope Julius in the figure of the Prophet Zechariah, who is found above the door of the Sistine Chapel, depicted in profile with the unmistakable features of Julius.

It was not merely popes and wealthy cardinals who commissioned work from artists. Sometime around the year 1200, a pair of painters named Giovanni and Nicolò were hired to do a painting of a Last Judgment for a Benedictine monastery in Rome. One of the many intriguing things about this work, now in the Vatican Pinacoteca, is that the patrons were, according to its inscription, "Lady Benedetta, handmaid of God, and the Abbess Costanza." The two nuns are depicted in the painting—naturally, among the saved. In contracting with the two Roman painters, Benedetta and Costanza participated in a long and distinguished tradition of Church patronage.

Painted on a circular wooden panel with a rectangular add-on beneath, the Last Judgment painted for Benedetta and Costanza looks like a giant keyhole through which we can peer to glimpse another world teeming inside, vibrant and vivid. And Giovanni and Nicolò's painting offers a through-the-keyhole view into a world of beauty and faith. So many of the treasures in the collections of the Vatican Museums—gorgeously reproduced in this volume, and clearly and succinctly described by Anja Grebe—depict this same vitality. Nowhere is it more forcefully expressed than in Michelangelo's figures in the Sistine Chapel, where the figure of the Prophet Jonah, rearing back as if to gaze in wonder at the frescoed vault, reflects the amazement of the thousands of visitors who flock into the chapel each day.

Walking through the Vatican, or turning these pages, we get an incomparable lesson in the history of art. But we also receive a profound impression of the skill and passion of the artists, and of their wonderful "force of mind."

— Ross King
Oxford, 2013

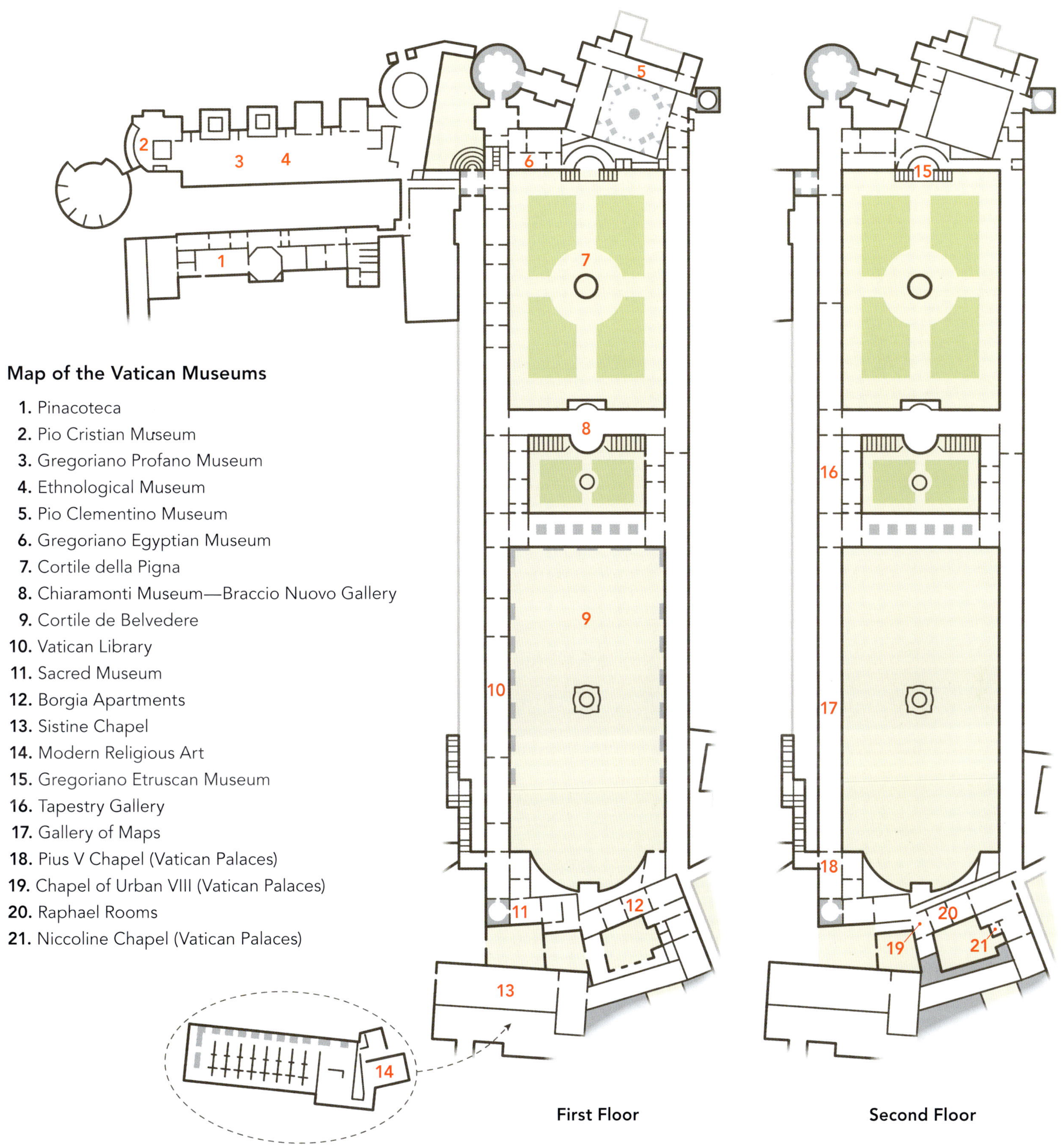
Map of the Vatican Museums
1. Pinacoteca
2. Pio Cristian Museum
3. Gregoriano Profano Museum
4. Ethnological Museum
5. Pio Clementino Museum
6. Gregoriano Egyptian Museum
7. Cortile della Pigna
8. Chiaramonti Museum—Braccio Nuovo Gallery
9. Cortile de Belvedere
10. Vatican Library
11. Sacred Museum
12. Borgia Apartments
13. Sistine Chapel
14. Modern Religious Art
15. Gregoriano Etruscan Museum
16. Tapestry Gallery
17. Gallery of Maps
18. Pius V Chapel (Vatican Palaces)
19. Chapel of Urban VIII (Vatican Palaces)
20. Raphael Rooms
21. Niccoline Chapel (Vatican Palaces)
First Floor
Second Floor

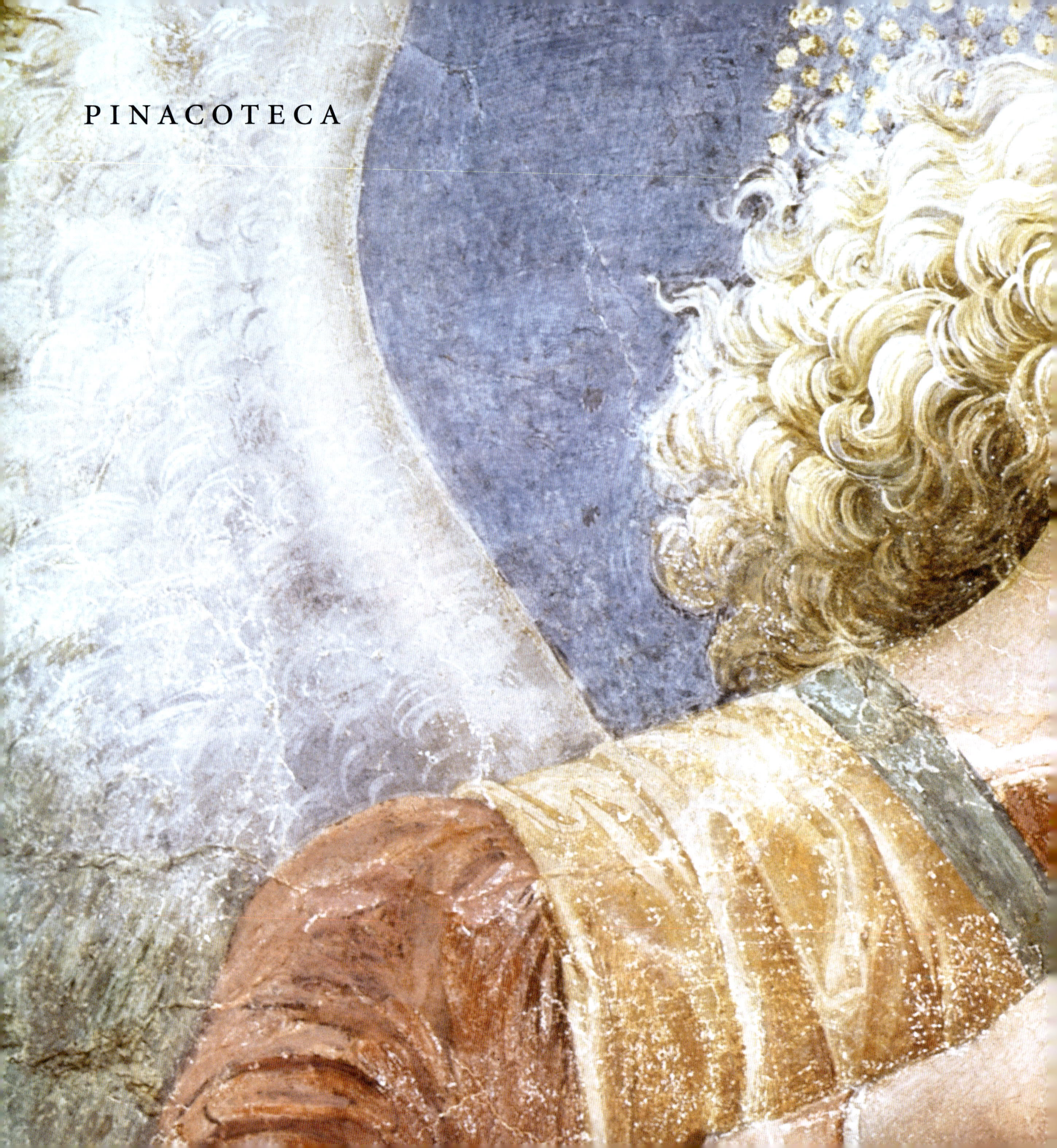

PINACOTECA

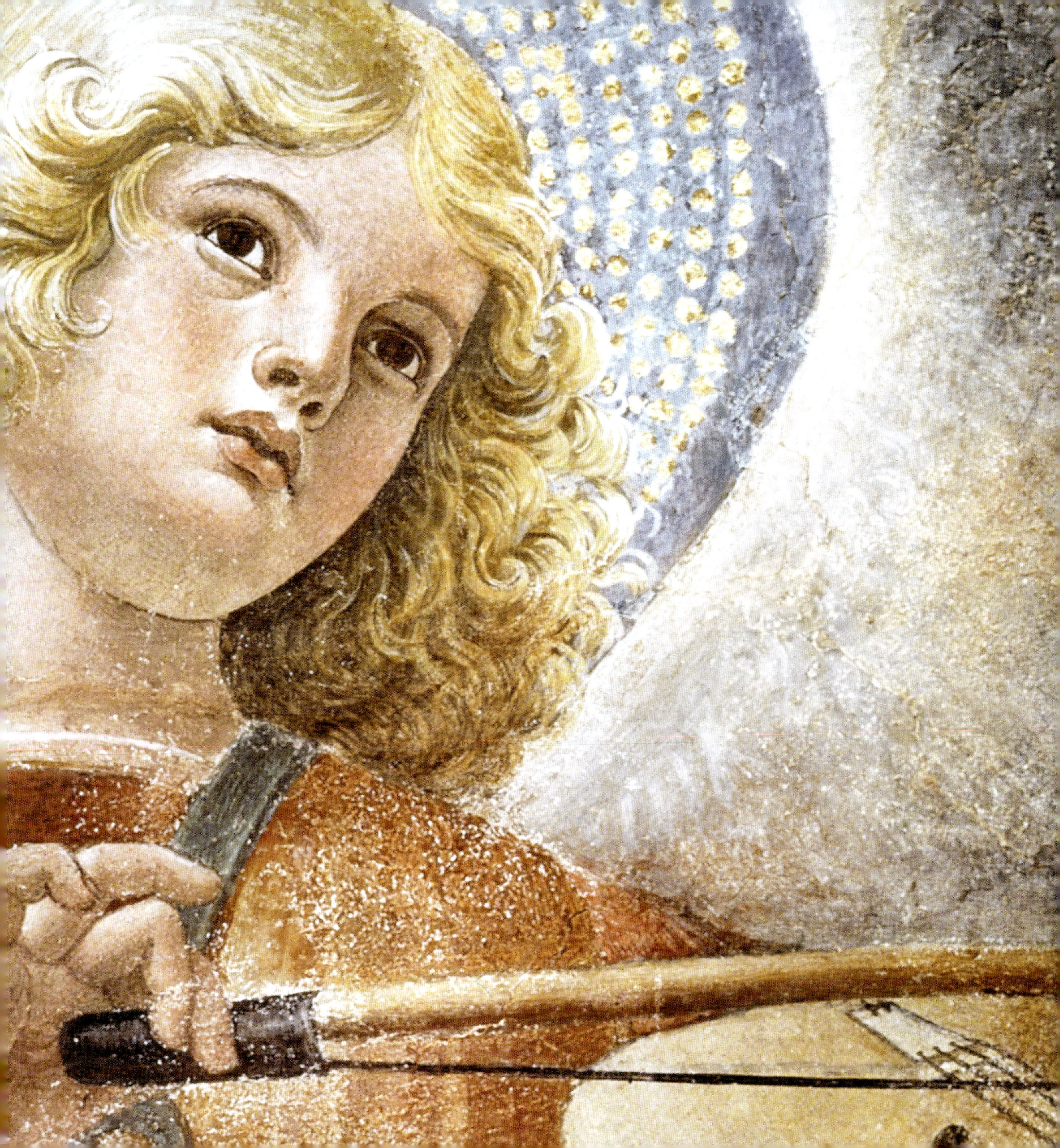

PINACOTECA

The Pinacoteca Vaticana is one of the most magnificent museums in the world. Its extraordinary collection of Italian art includes the most comprehensive collection of large altarpieces by the Renaissance painter Raphael and numerous masterworks by the likes of Leonardo, Titian, Caravaggio, Giotto, Giovanni Bellini, Guido Reni, Filippo Lippi, and Veronese. Non-Italian artists, such as the Frenchman Nicolas Poussin, the German Lucas Cranach, the Fleming Daniel Seghers, and the Englishman Sir Thomas Lawrence, are also represented here with major works.

Although popes had previously commissioned painters to create works intended for their foundations elsewhere, collecting for the purposes of art appreciation and prestige did not begin until the seventeenth century. In the Baroque era it became fashionable to collect paintings, and in addition to the pope, leaders both sacred and secular began to accumulate artwork.

The Pinacoteca Vaticana did not actually begin in the Vatican. Rather, the collection was originally housed in the Quirinal Palace, built by Pope Gregory XIII (1502–1585, reigned from 1572) as a summer residence on the Quirinal Hill, one of the Seven Hills of Rome, at the northeast of the city center. Many of the later popes also preferred the large Baroque palace complex on the Quirinal, with its architecural nooks and crannies, to the Vatican, and extended the palace according to their taste.

The Pinacoteca collection originally comprised paintings gifted to or purchased by the popes as well as paintings removed from altars during the renovation of St. Peter's Basilica and other churches during the course of the eighteenth century. Among the gifted and bequeathed works, the most noteworthy is Ludovico Carracci's *Holy Trinity* (ca. 1590), left to Pope Innocent XII by Cardinal Flavio I Chigi when he died in 1693. Those that came from St. Peter's include such important altarpieces as the *Martyrdom of St. Erasmus* by Nicolas Poussin and *St. Petronilla* by Guercino. Guido Reni's masterpiece the *Crucifixion of St. Peter* found its way into the papal collection from the church of San Paolo alle Tre Fontane in Rome. Other acquisitions came from churches outside Rome, including *St. George and the Dragon* by Paris Bordone, brought from the Minorite church of San Francesco in Noale, and Titian's *Virgin and Child with Saints* from San Nicoletto della Lattuga in Venice.

In the middle of the eighteenth century, Pope Benedict XIV (1675–1758, reigned from 1740) grew the collection to include works directed at the broader public, in addition to the older, more private part of the collection held in the Quirinal Palace. Benedict XIV supported the new intellectual current of the Enlightenment and did much for the cultural renewal of Rome. As well as expanding cultural academies, libraries, and theaters, Benedict XIV also promoted the arts and artistic taste. To this end, in 1748 he acquired a total of 187 paintings from the estate of Marchese Giovanni Battista Sacchetti, which the marchese had collected at his palace on Via Giulia. Benedict XIV's aim was to establish a public art gallery on the capitol, called the Capitoline galleries, where the paintings would "be preserved on the one hand in order to adorn and serve the greater glory of our city of Rome and on the other to offer instruction and an example to those young people interested in studying the liberal arts."

By 1750, the Sacchetti collection, consisting mainly of masterpieces from the sixteenth and seventeenth centuries, had been supplemented by a large number of works from the collection of Prince Giberto Pio di Savoia. Before moving to Madrid, the prince had asked Benedict XIV for permission to export his art collection. The pontiff duly gave his approval in exchange for "a few works...for our favor." As a result, the papal gallery added 126 paintings.

Besides his interest in the masters of the Renaissance and Baroque, Benedict XIV also collected the so-called "primitives," or medieval art. In addition to founding the Capitoline galleries, Benedict XIV also established the Museo Sacro in the Vatican Library. There, he gathered not only works by Italian masters of the thirteenth and fourteenth centuries but Byzantine icons too, which would be key elements of the Pinacoteca Vaticana collection.

The Pinacoteca Vaticana was formally founded in 1790. In July of that year, Pius VI (1717–1799, reigned from 1775) decreed that the papal picture collection at the Quirinal Palace was to be brought to the Vatican with the aim of establishing a permanent gallery there. The "extensive and exquisite collection of paintings, consisting of originals by the most famous old and new masters," reported the Italian periodical *Diario Ordinario* on June 10, 1790, was intended to supplement the existing collection of antique sculptures in the Museo Pio-Clementino. The 118 paintings at Quirinal, including the aforementioned masterpieces by Guido Reni, Poussin, and Vasari, were displayed in three rooms of what is now the Galleria degli Arazzi.

In 1796 the Pinacoteca Vaticana project came to an abrupt end when the Papal States were occupied during Napoleon's Italian campaign. As he did everywhere else, Napoleon confiscated important works of art and transported them to France in order to enrich the Musée Napoléon in the Louvre. In addition to selected works from the Pinacoteca, numerous altarpieces and paintings from churches in Rome and the pontifical possessions in other parts of Italy were taken to Paris, including Caravaggio's *Deposition*, Raphael's *Transfiguration*, *Coronation of the Virgin*, and *Madonna di Foligno*, and Perugino's *Decemviri Altarpiece*. When they were restored to Italy after the fall of Napoleon in 1815, these works were not returned to their original sites but housed in the Vatican, where they were put on display alongside the collections from the Capitoline gallery and new accessions, such as Thomas Lawrence's *Portrait of George IV* (1816), in five rooms of the Appartamento Borgia.

Over subsequent decades the Pinacoteca Vaticana switched locations a number of times within the Vatican Palace, but the size of the ever-growing collection and the limited amount of available space remained a problem. After moving to the apartments of Pius V on the second floor of the palace in 1833, for example, only thirty-five paintings could be exhibited. Larger-format Quattrocento works such as Filippo Lippi's *Coronation of the Virgin*, Antonio Vivarini's *St. Antony Abbot* polyptych, and Carlo Crivelli's *Virgin and Child* were housed in three rooms of the Lateran Pinacoteca in the Lateran Palace, a former papal residence. A few works, such as Paris Bordone's *St. George and the Dragon*, continued to be held at the Quirinal Palace.

This scattering of the collection over different locations, which in many cases had inadequate lighting, proved unsatisfactory over the long term. Only during the pontificate of St. Pius X (1835–1914, reigned from 1903) was the collection allocated adequate rooms on the ground floor of the Biblioteca. This new Pinacoteca Vaticana, comprising 277 paintings gathered from various locations and including for the first time the 181 medieval paintings and icons of the Museo Sacro, was dedicated by Pius X on March 28, 1909.

In 1929 foreign affairs once again affected the Pinacoteca. Article 18 of the Lateran Treaty between the Holy See and the Kingdom of Italy, under which the political and territorial sovereignty of the Vatican State was established, confirmed the Holy See's ownership of its collections. There was just one condition: that the art treasures be made accessible to the public on a permanent basis. This was impossible to fulfill at the collection's existing location in the library wing, and so another move was initiated, accompanied by extensive building plans.

On October 27, 1932, Pius XI (1857–1939, reigned from 1922) dedicated a new building in the neo-Renaissance style designed by the architect Luca Beltrami (1854–1933), which remains the home of the Pinacoteca Vaticana to this day. For the first time in its history, the collection finally had a display space designed specifically for this purpose, with sufficient room and appropriate lighting. In addition to the Pinacoteca building, a new entrance to the Vatican Museums was built that afforded visitors direct access from Viale Vaticano, without first having to cross through the Vatican Palace. For the new entrance area, which remained the Vatican Museums' main visitor entrance until the year 2000, architect Giuseppe Momo (1875–1940) and sculptor Antonio Maraini designed the famous double staircase that now serves as an exit and is one of Rome's best-known works of architectural art.

An important element of the reorganization of 1932 was the rehanging of the paintings, which were presented for the first time in chronological order and by school. With a few modifications, this rehanging has survived to the present day. The first two rooms are dedicated to work ranging from the "primitives" of the Middle Ages to the masters of the early Renaissance, particularly Giotto, Simone Martini, Bernardo Daddi, and Antonio Veneziano. This early work is followed by five rooms given over to masterpieces of fifteenth-century Italian art, with altars and paintings by Fra Angelico, Filippo Lippi, Benozzo Gozzoli, Carlo Crivelli, Antonio Vivarini, Pinturicchio, and Perugino. Room VIII, dedicated to Raphael, is a particular highlight of the collection. In addition to major altarpieces and predellas, it contains a collection of tapestries after Raphael's designs. The next three rooms contain masterpieces of sixteenth-century Italian art, including pictures by Leonardo, artists of the Raphael school, and Venetian masters such as Titian and Veronese. Further highlights are displayed in the three rooms devoted to works of the seventeenth century, from Caravaggio to Poussin, Sassoferrato, and Carlo Maratta. Next come two rooms containing artworks of the eighteenth and nineteenth centuries. The penultimate room features models by Gianlorenzo Bernini for the Cathedra Petri (St. Peter's Throne), and the collection concludes with a room containing icons from the fifteenth to eighteenth centuries.

The Pinacoteca Vaticana collection offers viewers a kind of tour of the history of European art, especially Italian art. The fame of the Vatican picture gallery—now totaling over 450 paintings—rests on the variety and quality of the works, representing every era. Given that this is the pontifical collection, the focus is on sacred art, a category that encompasses some of the most important works of the last several centuries. Within this context, the range of subjects is extremely wide: images of the Mother of God are exhibited next to stories of the saints and episodes from the life of Christ. Precisely because of this contiguity of similar motifs, the Pinacoteca Vaticana—perhaps more than any other collection—enables viewers to compare, and acquaint themselves with, the characteristics and peculiarities of individual artists from the Middle Ages to the beginnings of modernism.

ROOM 1

M
O
Y
SES
TOBIS SVS
TENTRIB

A
MO
S
ECCE DNS EXERCITV
VM GRA DI ENS

Roman School, first half of 12th century
***Moses*, ca. 1120–1130**
Diameter: 59.5 cm; Detached fresco
Pinacoteca; Room I; Inv. 40508

Roman School, first half of 12th century
***Amos*, ca. 1120–1130**
Diameter: 59.5 cm; Detached fresco
Pinacoteca; Room I; Inv. 40513

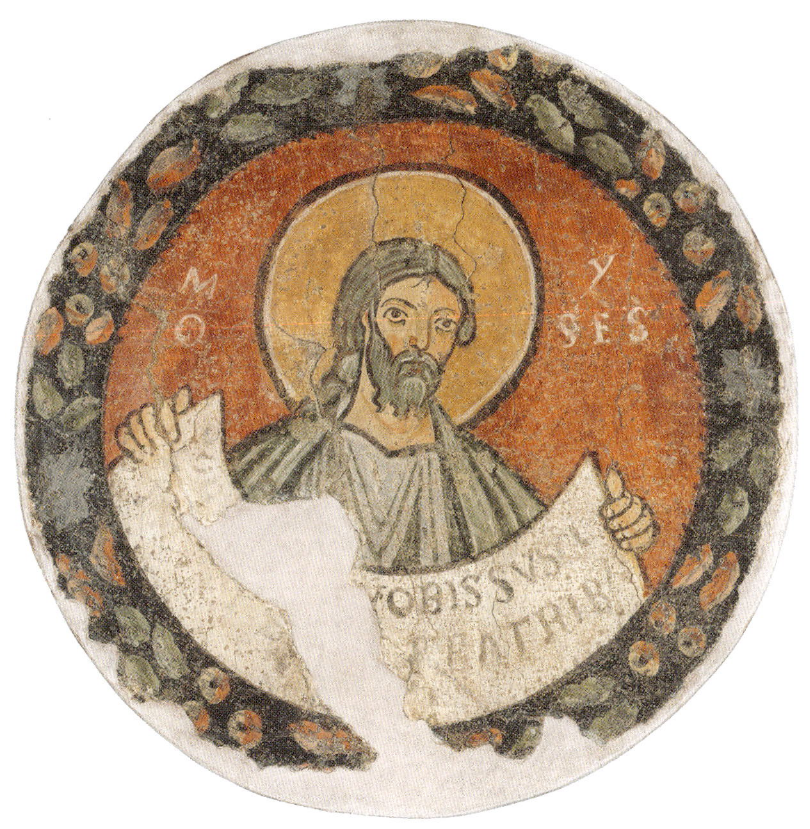

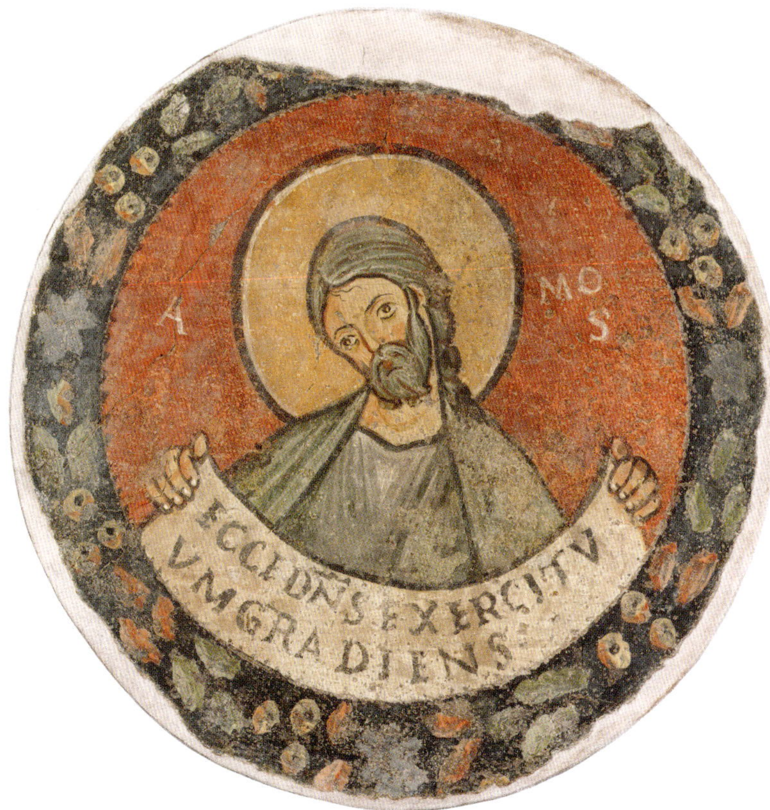

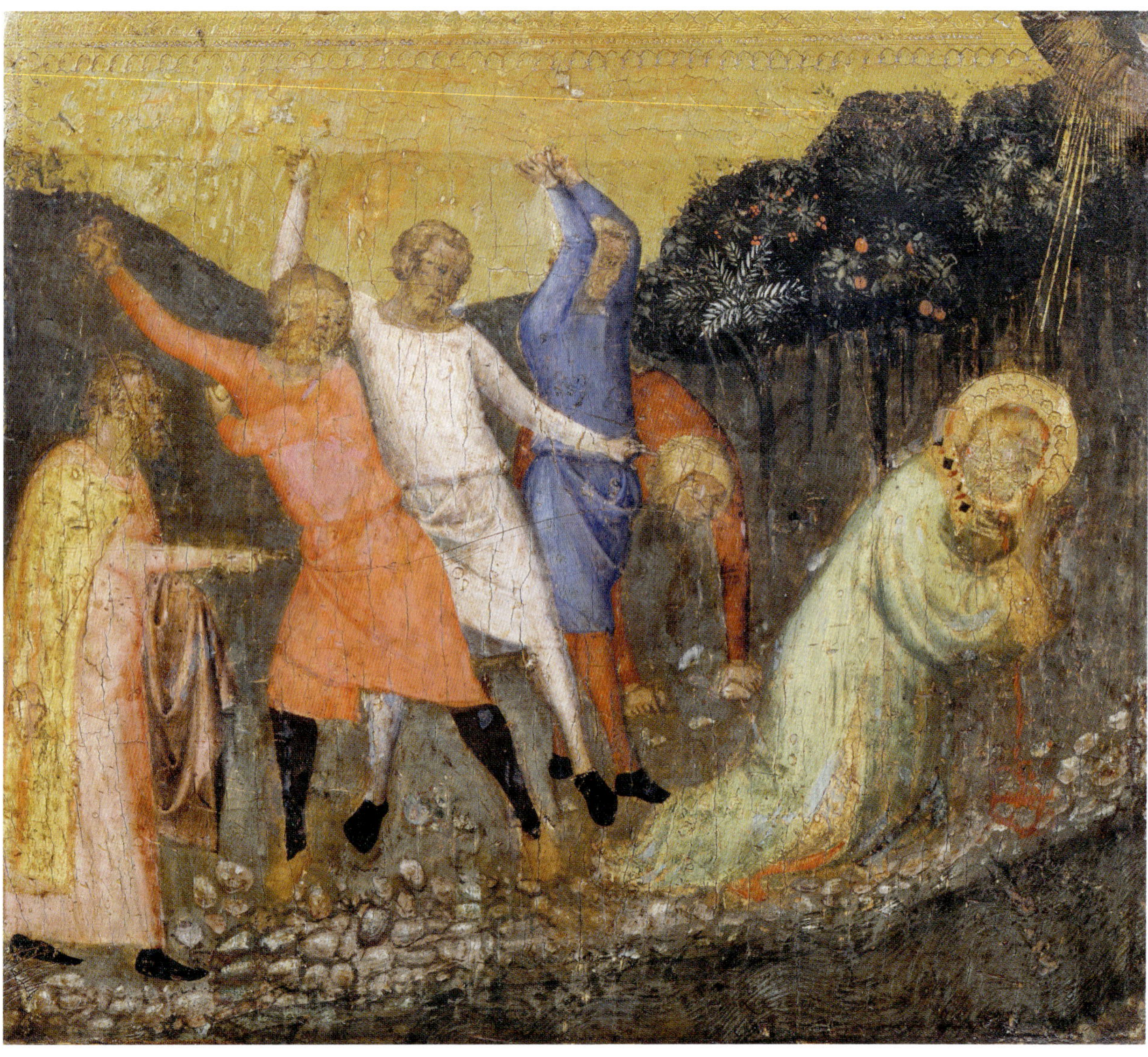

Bernardo Daddi

Story of St. Stephen: Martyrdom

This small panel depicting the stoning of St. Stephen is by the Florentine painter Bernardo Daddi, who inherited Giotto's sense of drama and emotion. It is the first of a series of eight small predella panels illustrating the life of the saint, who was the first Christian. On the right-hand side we see St. Stephen streaming with blood, having sunk to his knees under the hail of stones from his tormentors. Spurred on by a member of the Supreme Council, four young henchmen continue with undiminished vigor to rain stones on the collapsing saint. Variety was important to Daddi, and each of the henchmen is shown employing a different throwing technique and wearing clothes of a different color. The man at the back is even depicted in a complicated foreshortened pose as he bends down to eagerly search for stones. The panel, which is badly damaged in places, stands out for its sophisticated composition. Daddi lines up the saint's torturers diagonally, starting with the High Priest in the foreground, thereby lending the picture a sense of depth. The peaceful orchard in the background also alludes to the martyrdom with the red of its fruit. The saint's imminent end is announced by the hand of God, which touches him with its rays as Stephen, even in the moment of death, asks for forgiveness for his tormentors.

Bernardo Daddi, ca. 1290– ca. 1348
***Story of St. Stephen: Martyrdom*, ca. 1348**
26.7 x 30.5 cm; Tempera on wood panel
Pinacoteca; Room I; Inv. 40148

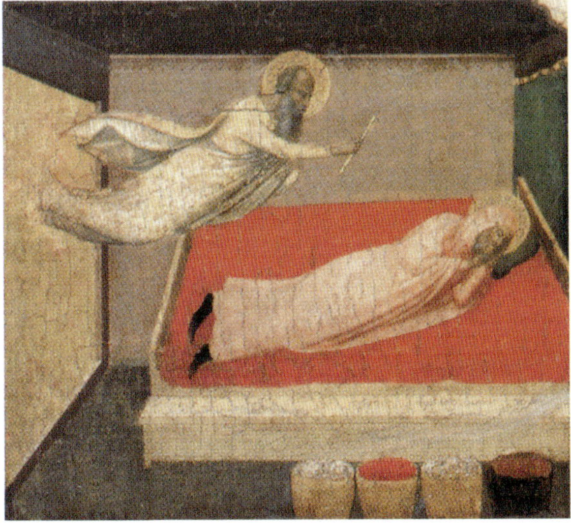
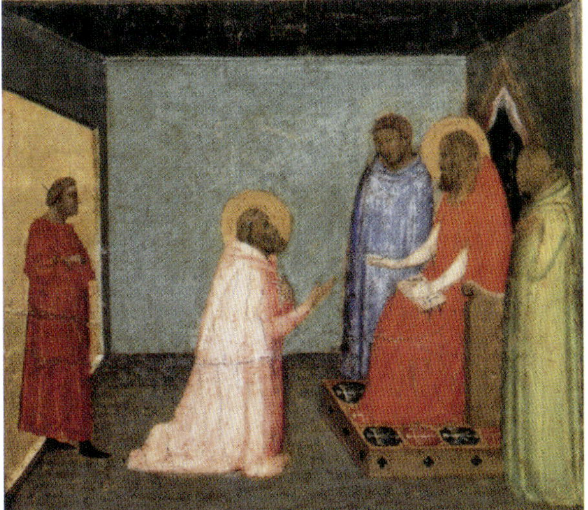
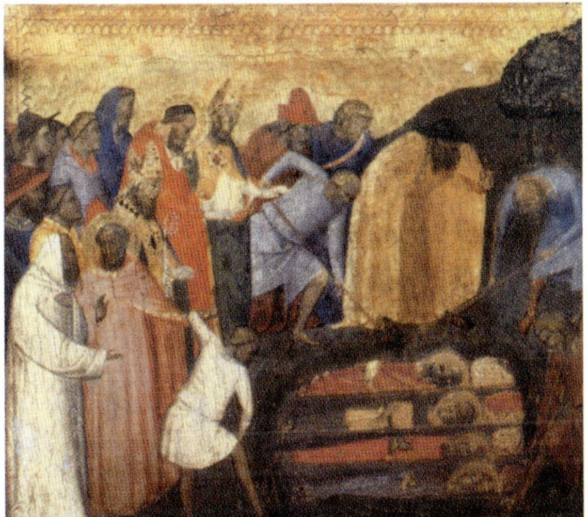
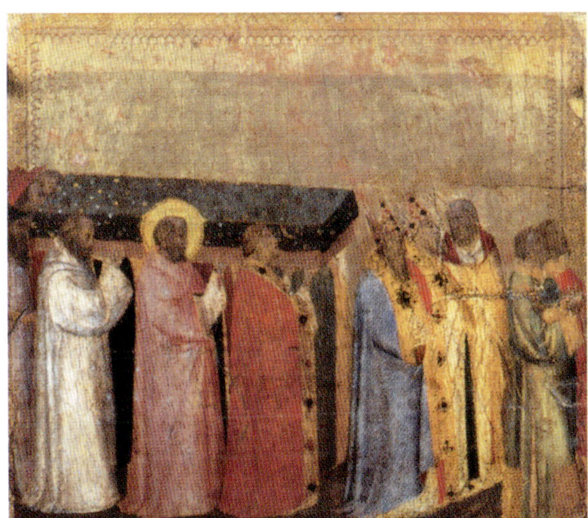
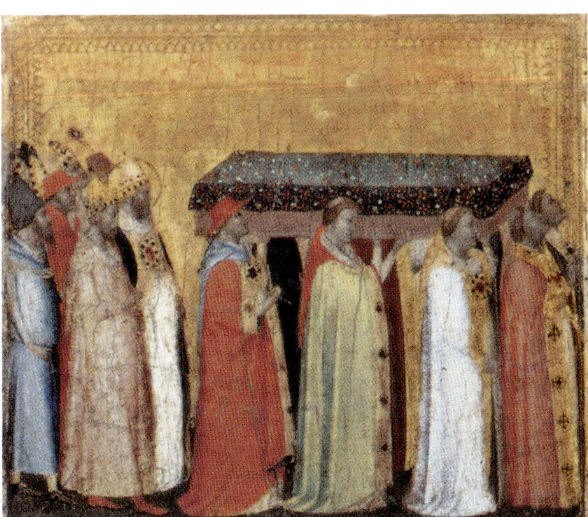
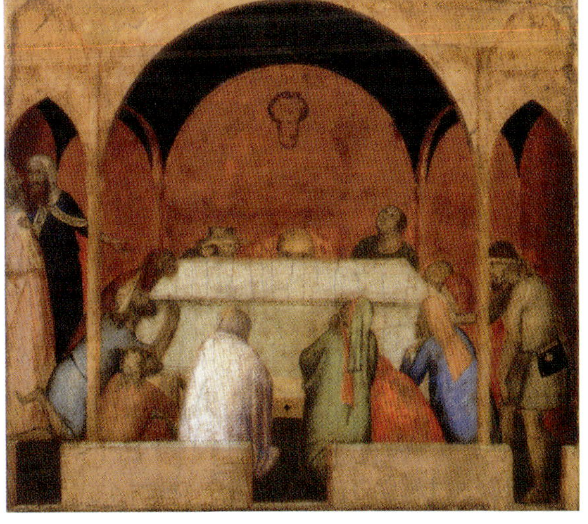

Bernardo Daddi, ca. 1290– ca. 1348
***Story of St. Stephen: St. Gemaiele Appears to St. Luciano*, ca. 1345**
26.7 x 30.4 cm; Tempera on wood panel
Pinacoteca; Room I; Inv. 40147

Bernardo Daddi, ca. 1290– ca. 1348
***Story of St. Stephen: St. Luciano Tells His Vision to the Patriarch of Jerusalem*, ca. 1345**
26.5 x 30 cm; Tempera on wood panel
Pinacoteca; Room I; Inv. 40158

Bernardo Daddi, ca. 1290– ca. 1348
***Story of St. Stephen: Finding of the Tomb of St. Stephen*, ca. 1345**
26.5 x 30.5 cm; Tempera on wood panel
Pinacoteca; Room I; Inv. 40149

Bernardo Daddi, ca. 1290– ca. 1348
***Story of St. Stephen: Second Translation of the Corpses*, ca. 1345**
26.5 x 30 cm; Tempera on wood panel
Pinacoteca; Room I; Inv. 40160

Bernardo Daddi, ca. 1290– ca. 1348
***Story of St. Stephen: St. Stephen's Corpse Is Brought to Rome*, ca. 1345**
26.5 x 30 cm; Tempera on wood panel
Pinacoteca; Room I; Inv. 40159

Bernardo Daddi, ca. 1290– ca. 1348
***Story of St. Stephen: Pilgrims at the Tomb of the Saint*, ca. 1345**
26.5 x 30.4 cm; Tempera on wood panel
Pinacoteca; Room I; Inv. 40161

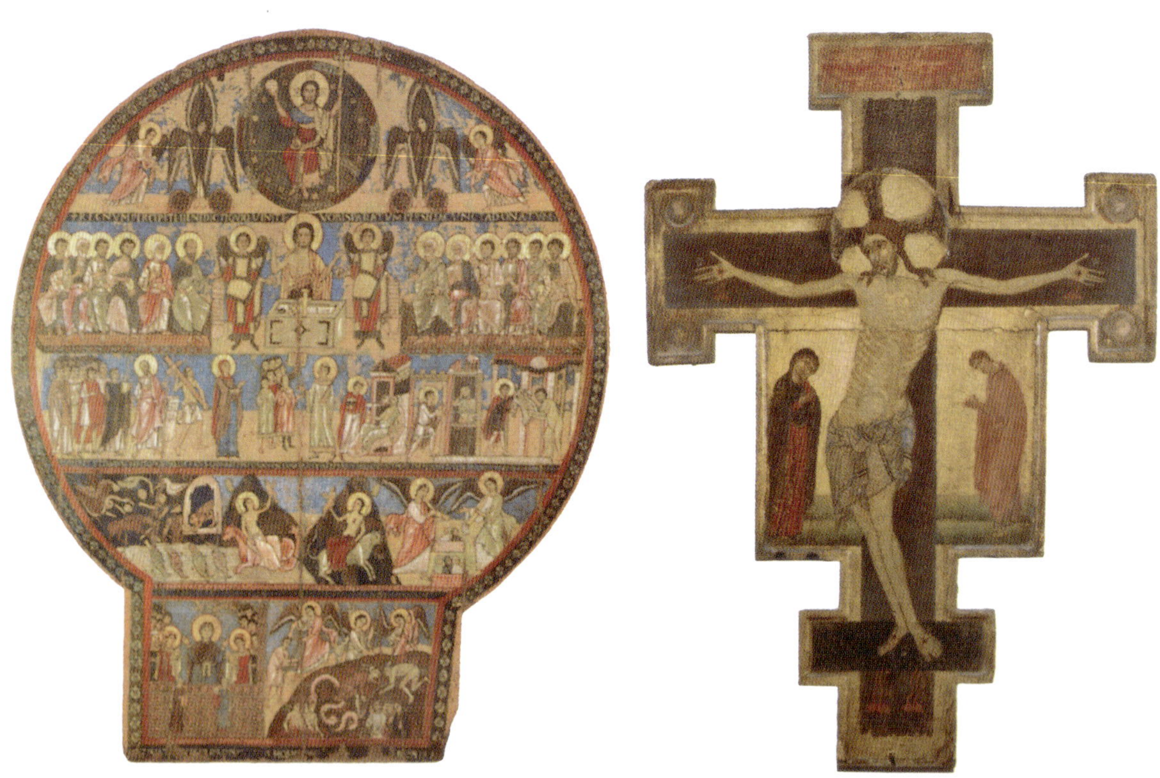

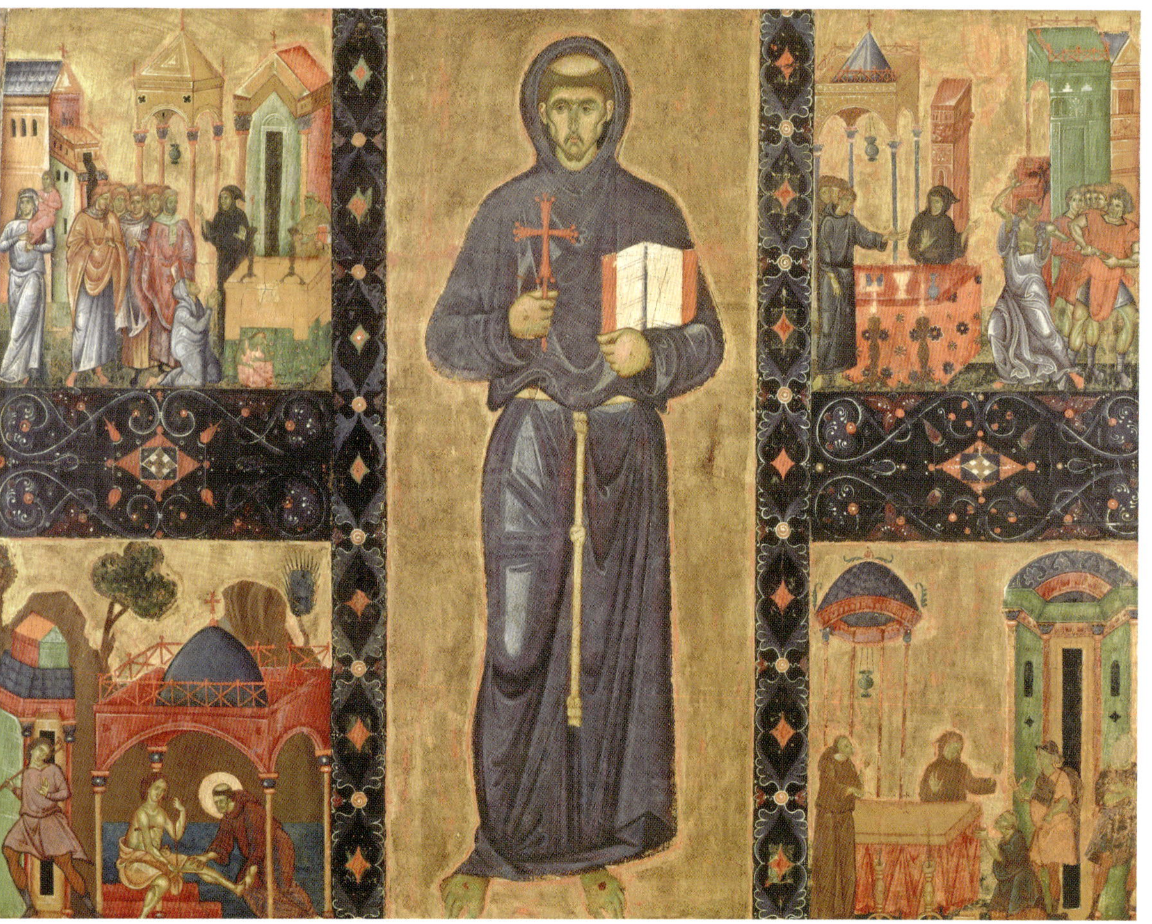

Giovanni e Nicolò, late 12th century
***Last Judgment*, undated**
288 x 243 cm; Tempera on wood panel
Pinacoteca; Room I; Inv. 40526

Umbrian School, 13th century
***Processional Cross*, ca. 1260–1270**
104 x 74 cm; Tempera on wood panel
Pinacoteca; Room I; Inv. 40005

Giunta Pisano, school of, active 1236–1254
***St. Francis and Four Scenes from His Life*, 1260–1270**
67 x 86.5 cm; Tempera on wood panel
Pinacoteca; Room I; Inv. 40023

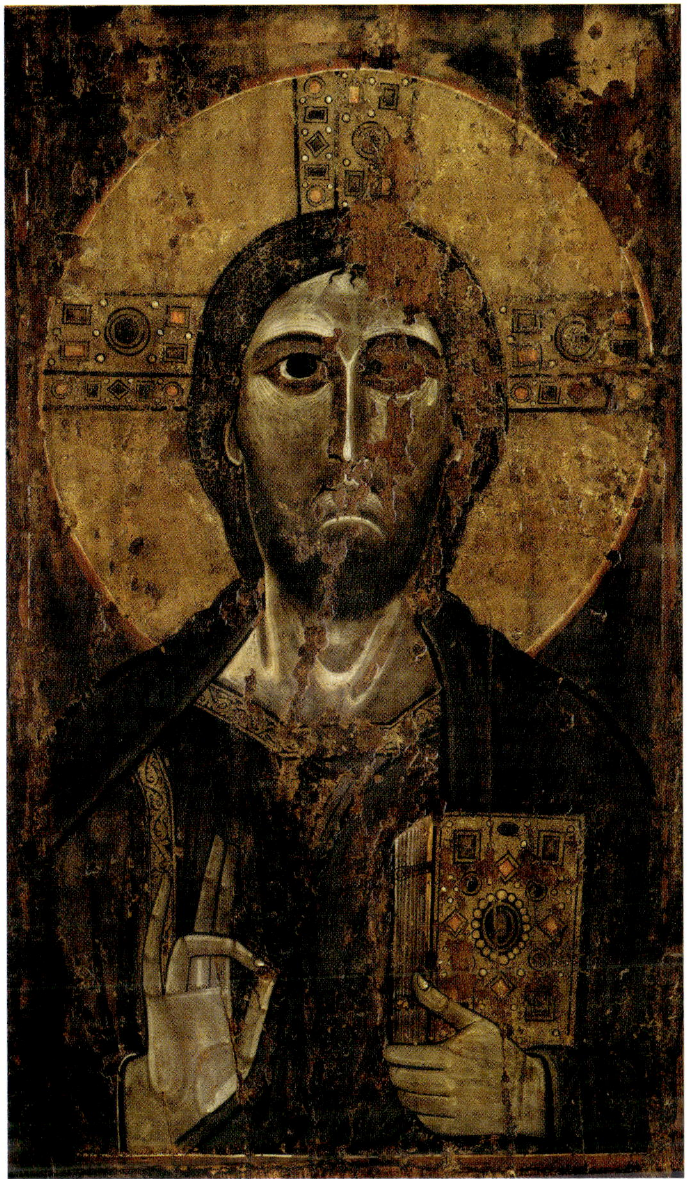

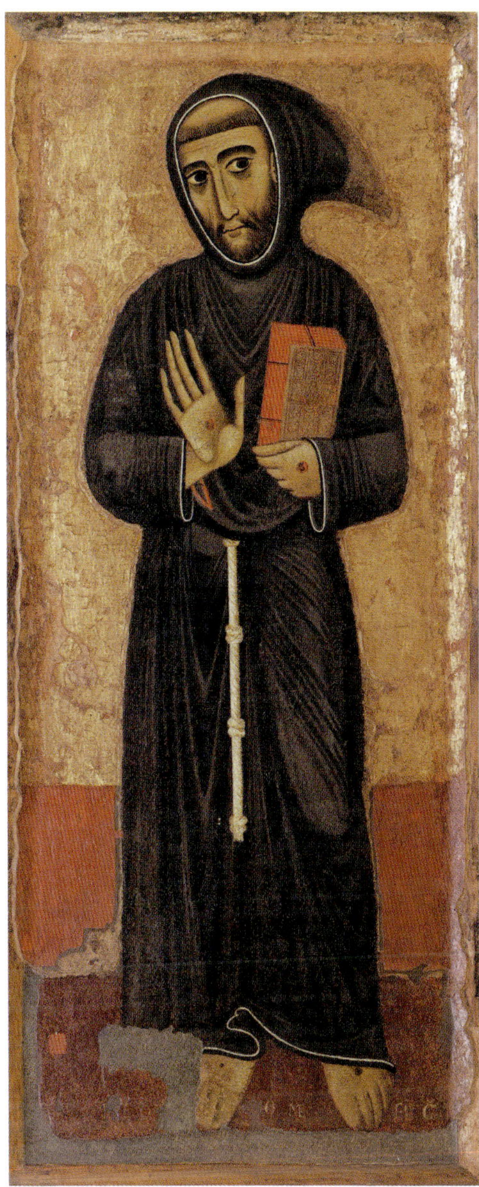

Roman School, second half of 12th century
***Christ*, undated**
98.2 x 58.6 cm; Tempera on canvas
Pinacoteca; Room I; Inv. 40020

Margaritone d'Arezzo, ca. 1240–1290
***St. Francis of Assisi*, 1270–1280**
127.2 x 53.9 cm; Oil on wood panel
Pinacoteca; Room I; Inv. 40002

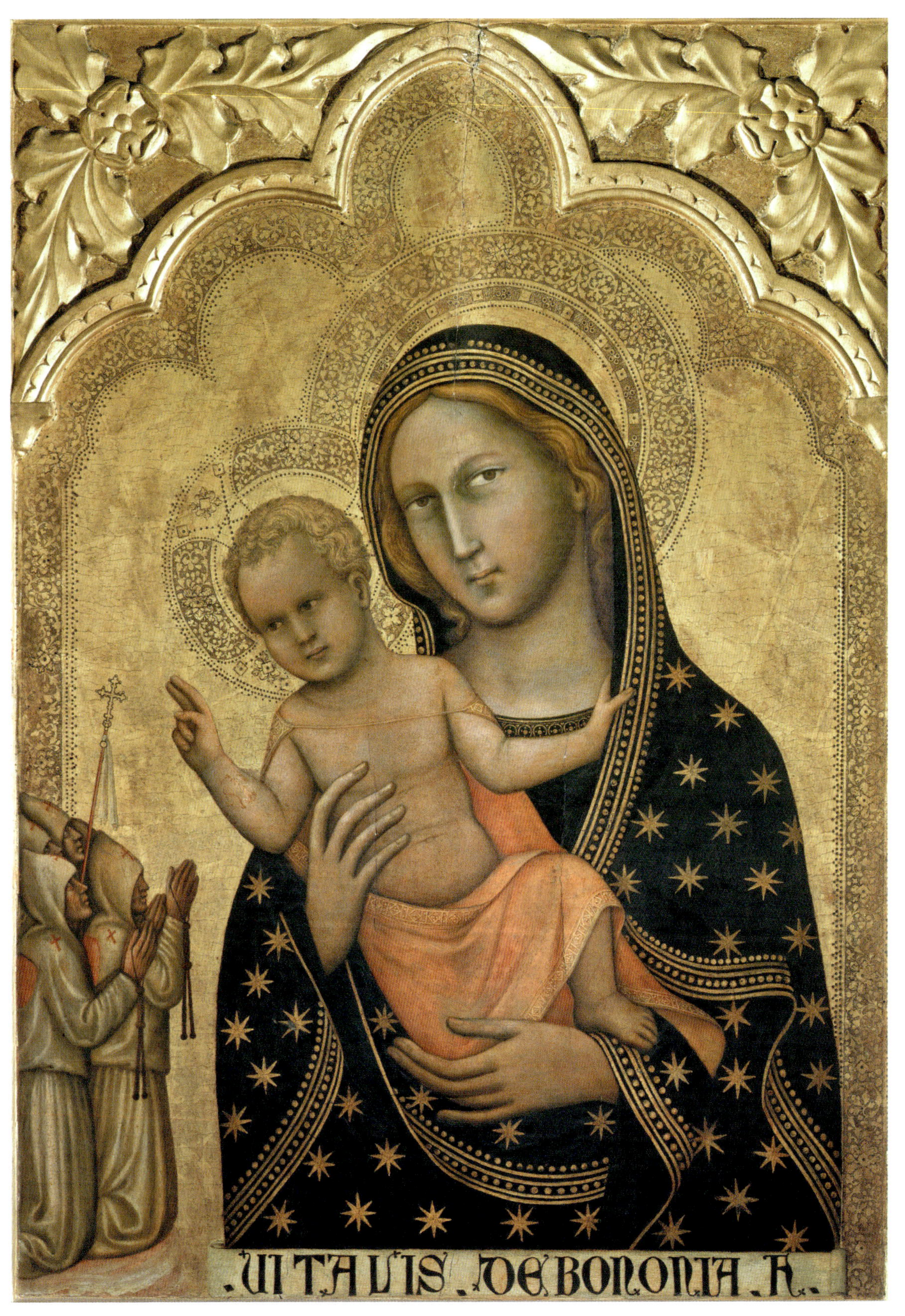
.VITALIS .DE BONONIA .F.

Vitale da Bologna

The Virgin and Child, known as the Madonna dei Battuti

This panel of the Virgin and Child is regarded as one of Vitale da Bologna's most beautiful paintings. The artist's proud signature "VITALIS DE BONONIA F." ("Vitalis of Bologna made this") is inscribed in a banner that runs along the lower edge of the painting. The ends of the banner curl realistically around the body of the Virgin, who seems to grow up and out of the inscription. Draped in a star-studded cloak, the Virgin appears here in the guise of the Queen of Heaven. The model for Vitale da Bologna's depiction of the Mother of God as a half-length figure holding in her arms the Infant Jesus, shown making a sign of blessing, goes back to a medieval icon design. The dark flesh tones and almond-shaped eyes derive from the same model. The Virgin, with her head slightly bowed, fixes the viewer with a somewhat solemn gaze while Jesus turns toward the group of small figures on the left with a gentle smile on his face. The figures, drapped in white hooded habits decorated with red crosses, have scourges in their hands and are members of an order of flagellants known as the Battuti, a radical community of penitents who reenacted the Passion of Christ on their own bodies. The Ospedale dei Battuti Bianchi in Ferrara, for whom Vitale da Bologna painted this expensive gilded panel, was founded in 1343, allowing the work to be dated to around that time.

Vitale da Bologna, before 1309–1359/61
***The Virgin and Child: Madonna dei Battuti,* ca. 1340**
95.6 x 68 cm; Tempera on wood panel
Pinacoteca; Room I; Inv. 40017

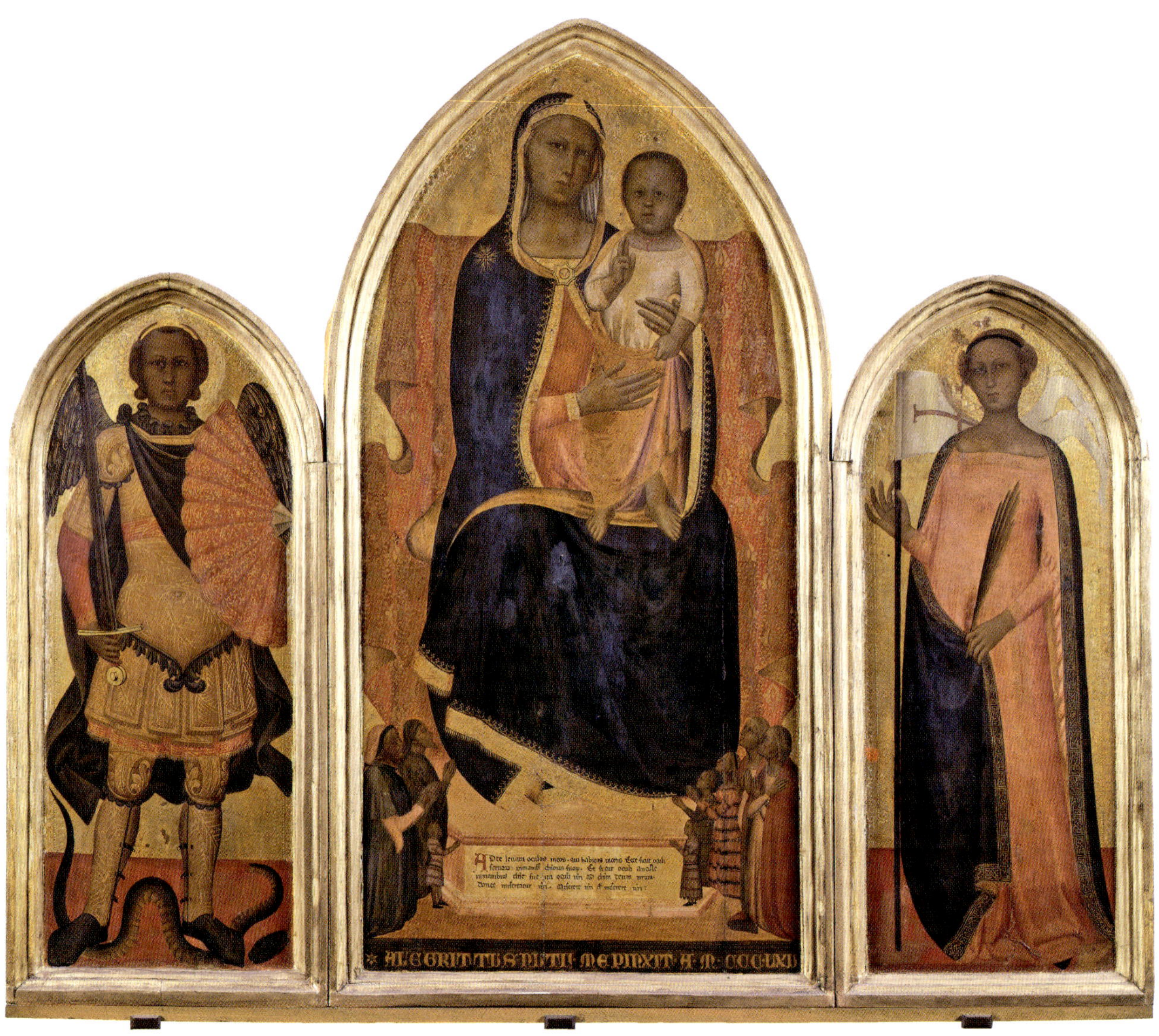

Allegretto Nuzi

The Virgin and Child Enthroned with SS. Michael and Ursula

This unusually shaped triptych once adorned the chapel dedicated to SS. Michael and Ursula in the Church of Santa Lucia in Fabriano (Marche), the hometown of the painter Allegretto Nuzi. Nuzi signed his name and recorded the date of completion along the bottom edge of the central panel. The work depicts the enthroned Virgin Mary holding the Infant Jesus, with members of the donor family kneeling at her feet. The smaller side panels present full-length figures of the chapel's patrons: Archangel Michael in the guise of the armored dragon slayer and St. Ursula with her martyr's palm and banner of the cross. When the triptych was closed, the Mother of God and the Infant Jesus, shown making the sign of blessing, would have soared up icon-like out of the lower section. In terms of color, the panels coordinate harmoniously with one another through the consistent use of red, blue and gold. The gold ground and gold pattern of the cloth of honor behind the Virgin heighten the sense of preciousness. Mary gently holds on to the Infant Jesus, whose coral necklace, with its teardrop shape and red hue, alludes to Christ's Passion and his future role as redeemer. Similarly, the small donor figures are shown turning to Christ as the Savior. Their bearing reflects the prayer of supplication on the plinth of the throne with its verses from Psalm 122: "Unto Thee lift I up mine eyes, O thou that dwellest in the heavens. [...] Have mercy upon us O Lord, have mercy upon us!"

Allegretto Nuzi, 1315–1373
***The Virgin and Child with SS. Michael and Ursula*, 1365**
123.2 x 65.8 cm; Tempera on wood panel
Pinacoteca; Room I; Inv. 40204

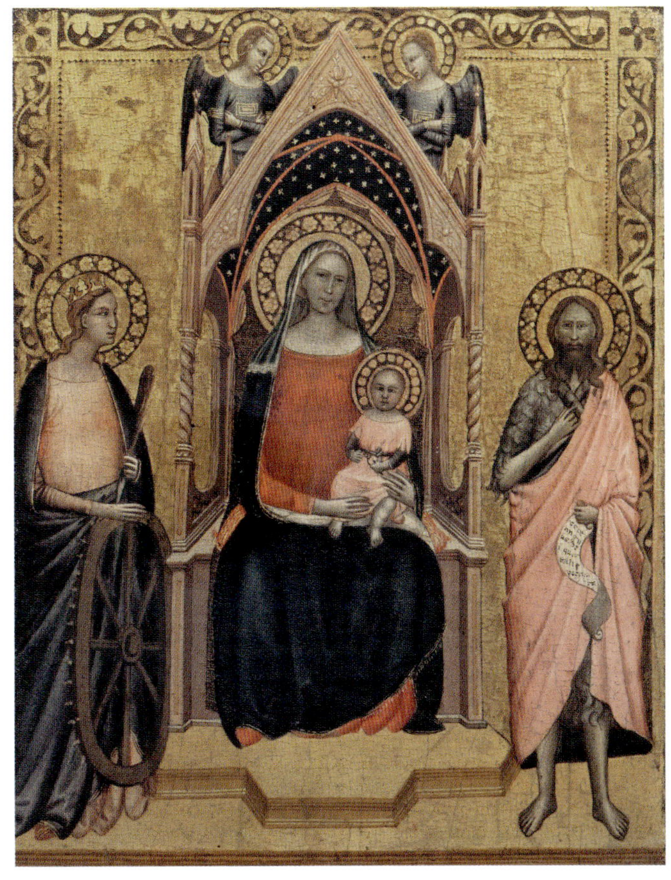

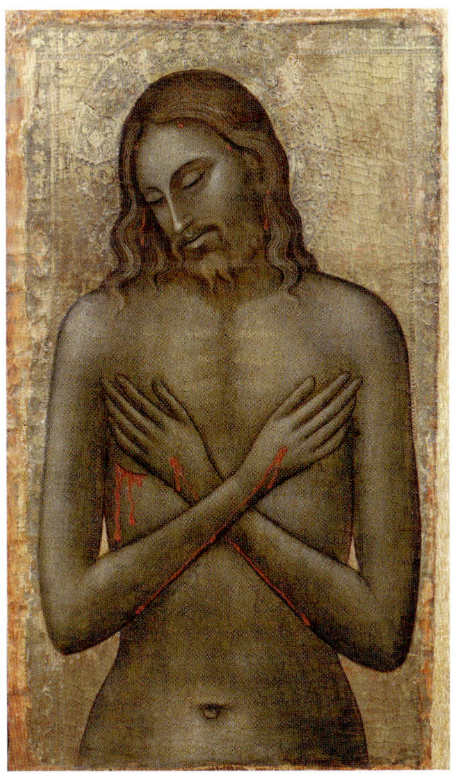

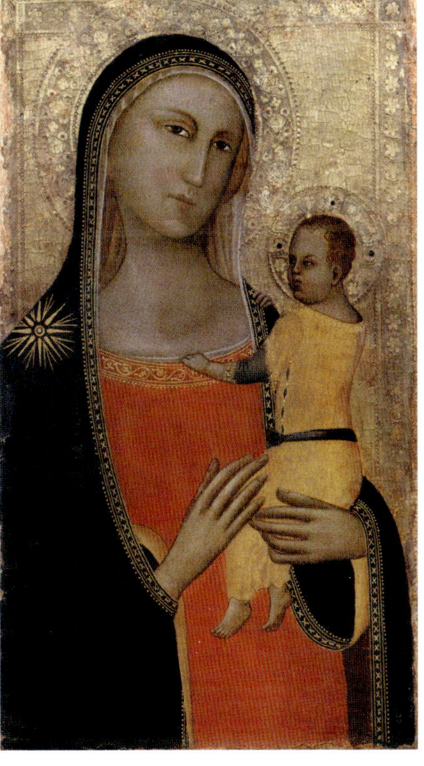

Allegretto Nuzi, Workshop of, 1315–1373
The Virgin and Child Enthroned with SS. Michael and Ursula,
1380–1390
36.4 cm x 28.7 cm; Tempera on wood panel
Pinacoteca; Room I; Inv. 40209

Allegretto Nuzi, Workshop of, 1315–1373
***Dead Christ*, ca. 1365**
34.6 x 19.9 cm; Tempera on wood panel
Pinacoteca; Room I; Inv. 40210

Allegretto Nuzi, Workshop of, 1315–1373
***Madonna and Child*, ca. 1365**
34.6 x 19.9 cm; Tempera on wood panel
Pinacoteca; Room I; Inv. 40208

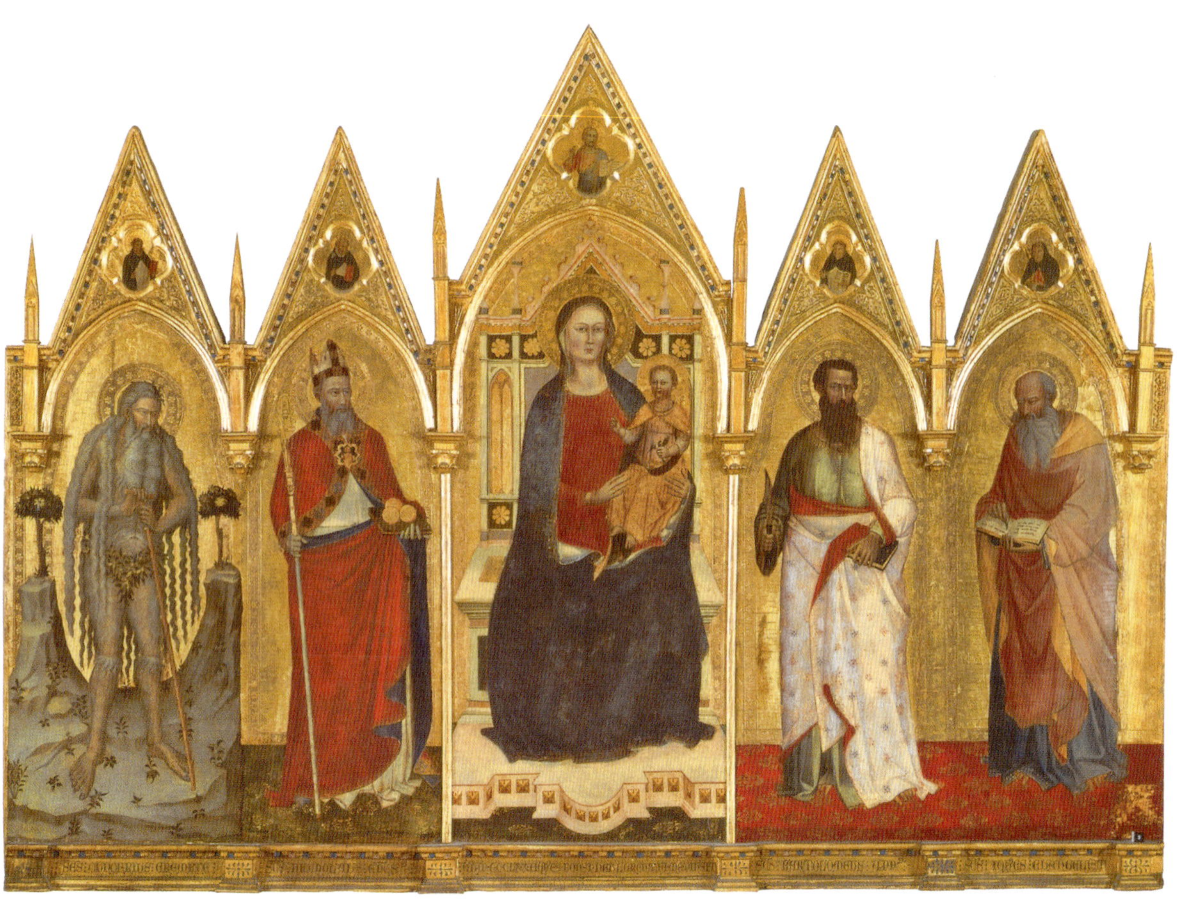

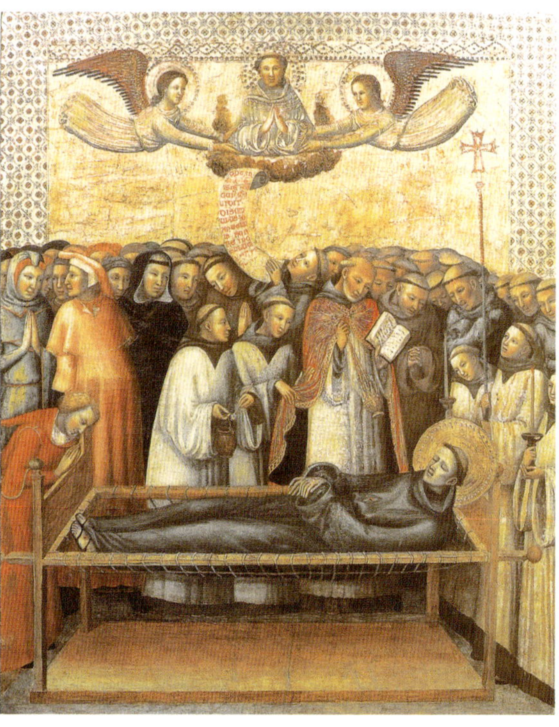

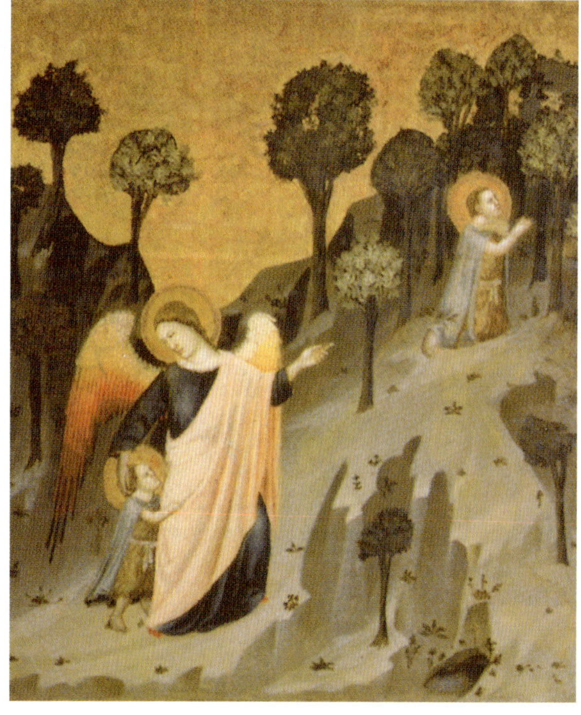

Giovanni Bonsi, active 1351–1371
***Madonna and Child with Saints*, 1371**
166 x 234 cm; Tempera on wood panel
Pinacoteca; Room I; Inv. 40009

Pseudo Jacopino di Francesco, 14th century
***Funeral of St. Francis*, ca. 1330**
88.6 x 70.7 cm; Tempera on wood panel
Pinacoteca; Room I; Inv. 40018

Master of the Life of St. John, first half of 14th century
***St. Giovanino with an Angel*, before 1340**
47.8 x 40.5 cm; Tempera and gold on wood panel
Pinacoteca; Room I; Inv. 40185

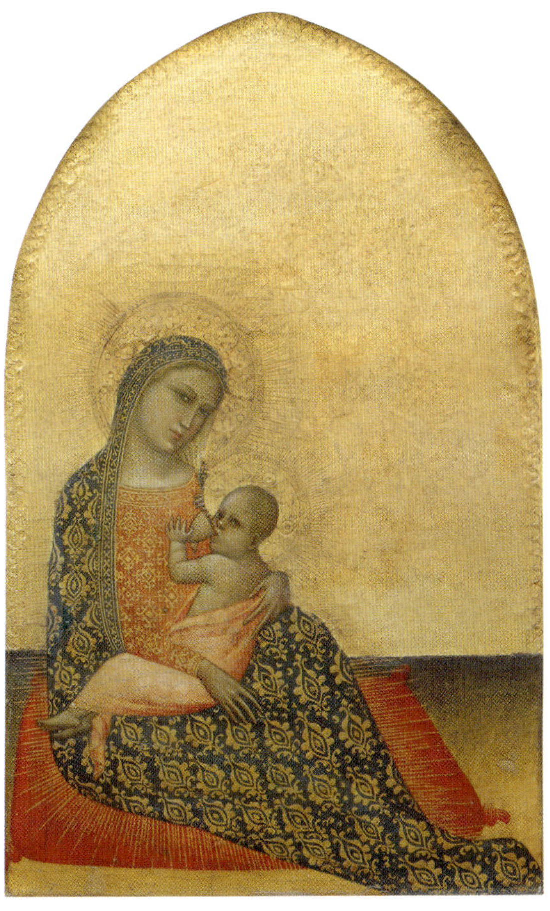
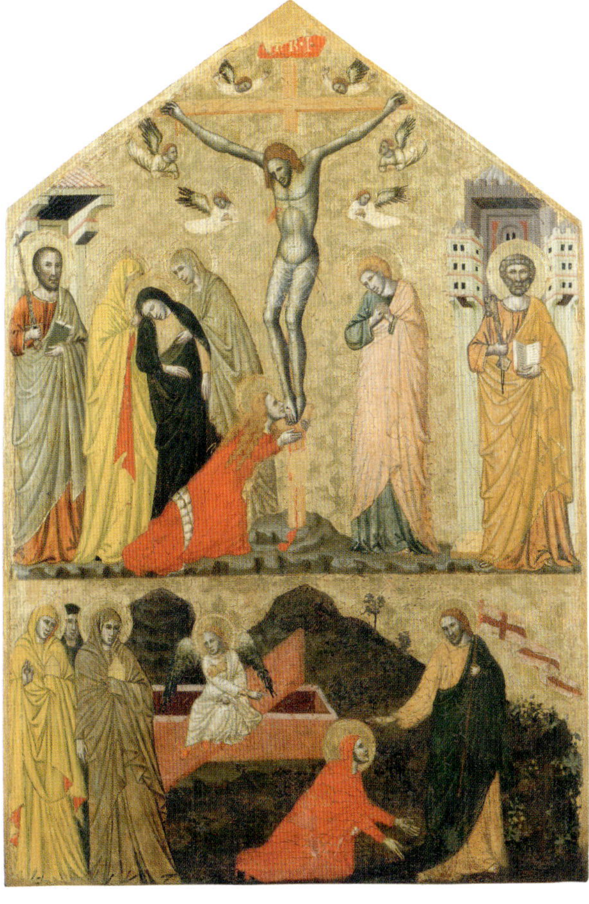
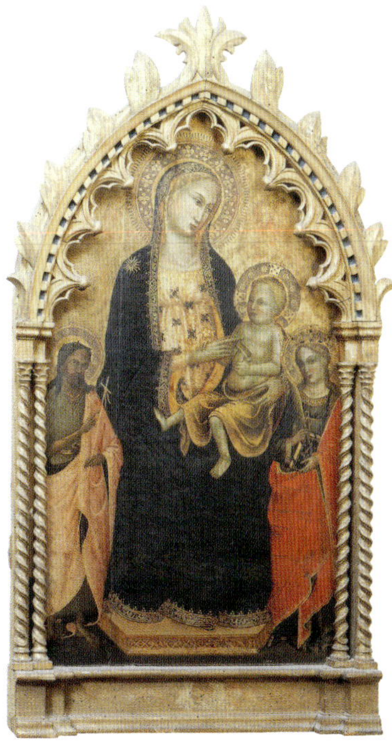
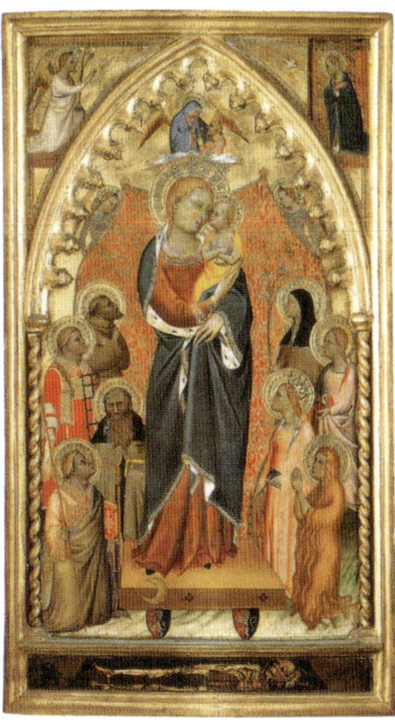
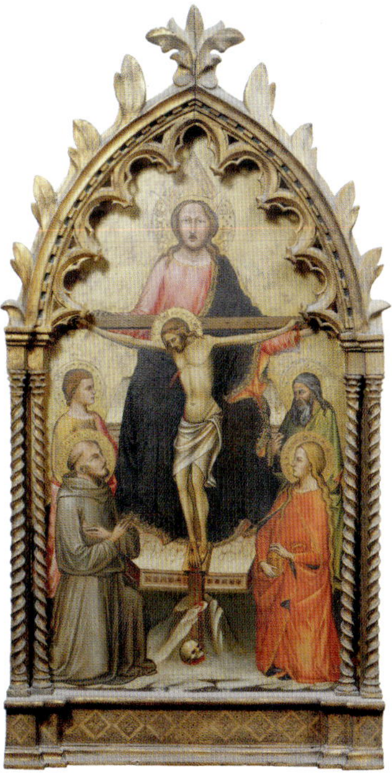

Francescuccio Ghissi, active 1345–1374
***Madonna Nursing the Child (Madonna del Latte)*, 1350–1355**
36.7 x 21.7 cm; Tempera and gold on wood panel
Pinacoteca; Room I; Inv. 40211

School of Rimini, mid-14th century
***Crucifixion*, 1356–1360**
56.1 x 37.7 cm; Tempera on wood panel
Pinacoteca; Room I; Inv. 40181

Master of St. Jacopo a Mucciana, active ca. 1390–1420
***Madonna with Saints*, undated**
86.5 x 45.8 cm; Tempera and gold on wood panel
Pinacoteca; Room I; Inv. 40004

Giovanni del Biondo, active 1356–1399
***Madonna and Child with Saints and Angels*, 1391**
75.4 x 43.4cm; Tempera on wood panel
Pinacoteca; Room I; Inv. 40014

Niccolò di Pietro Gerini, Workshop of, active 1368–1415
***Holy Trinity with Saints*, undated**
86 x 46.8 cm; Tempera and gold on wood panel
Pinacoteca; Room I; Inv. 40006

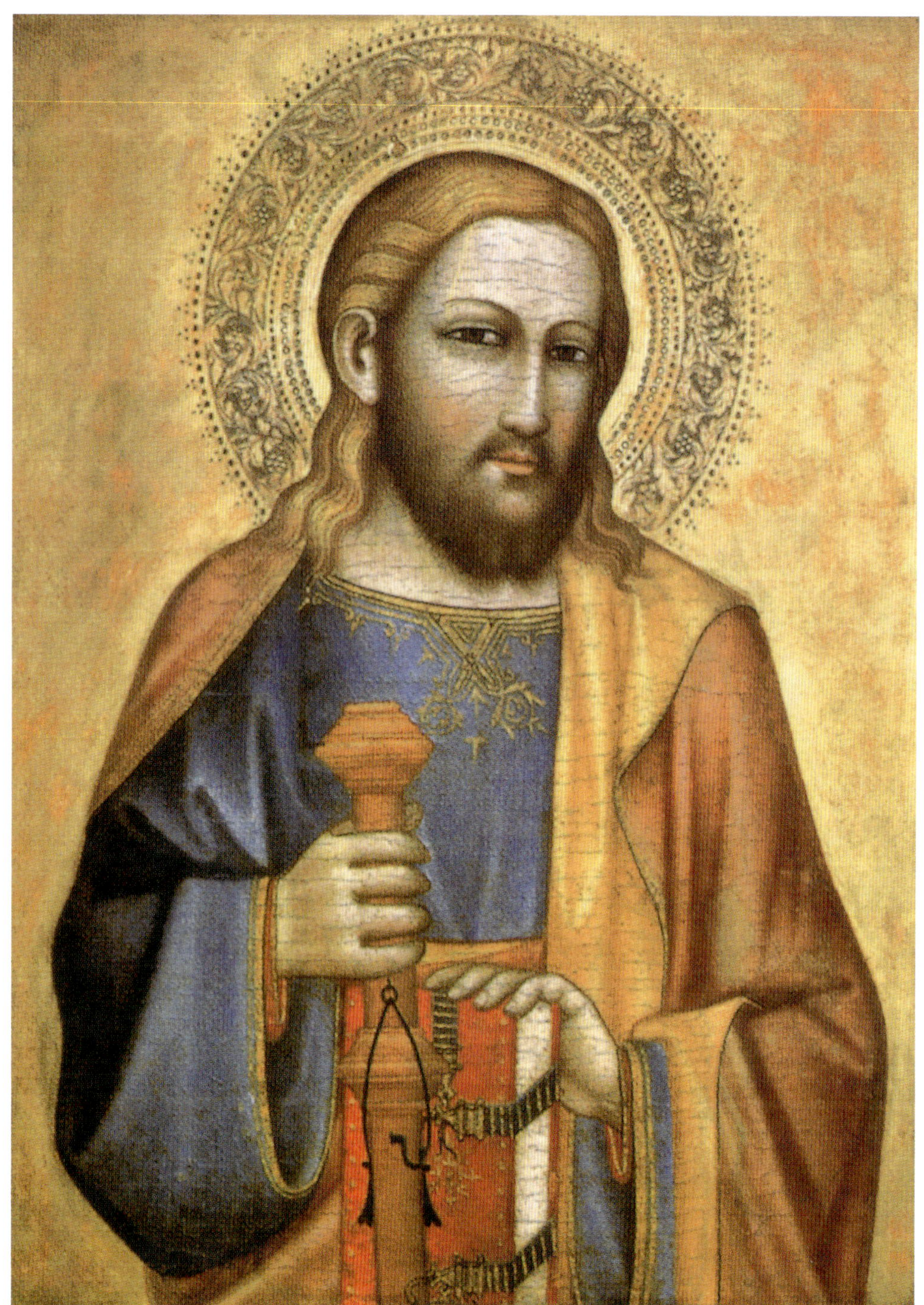

Antonio Veneziano (Antonio di Francesco)

St. James the Great

This painting with a gold background depicts a bearded man with Christ-like features. It is the apostle and pilgrim St. James the Great, as revealed by his attribute the pilgrim's staff, which he holds demonstratively before him. The book identifies him as a preacher of God's word. The painter shows a great love of detail in his rendering of the red book binding, the leather cover decorated with gold, and the tie. The head of the saint has been painted with similar care, allowing individual hairs to be distinguished in the beard. Another example of supreme skill is the finely punched halo—that looks as if it has been engraved—against which the saint's head stands out vividly. The work is thought to have once formed part of a larger polyptych, along with the panel of Mary Magdalene (Pinacoteca Vaticana, inv. 40019). It has been attributed to the painter Antonio Veneziano, originally from Venice, who was active mainly as a fresco painter in Pisa, Florence, and Siena during the final third of the fourteenth century. Giorgio Vasari, author of the *Lives of the Painters, Sculptors, and Architects*, praised the grace of Antonio Veneziano's paintings and his ability to makes his figures look alive, "as if they were speaking."

Antonio Veneziano (Antonio di Francesco), active 1369–1388
***St. James the Great*, undated**
57 x 43 cm; Tempera and gold on wood panel
Pinacoteca; Room I; Inv. 40016

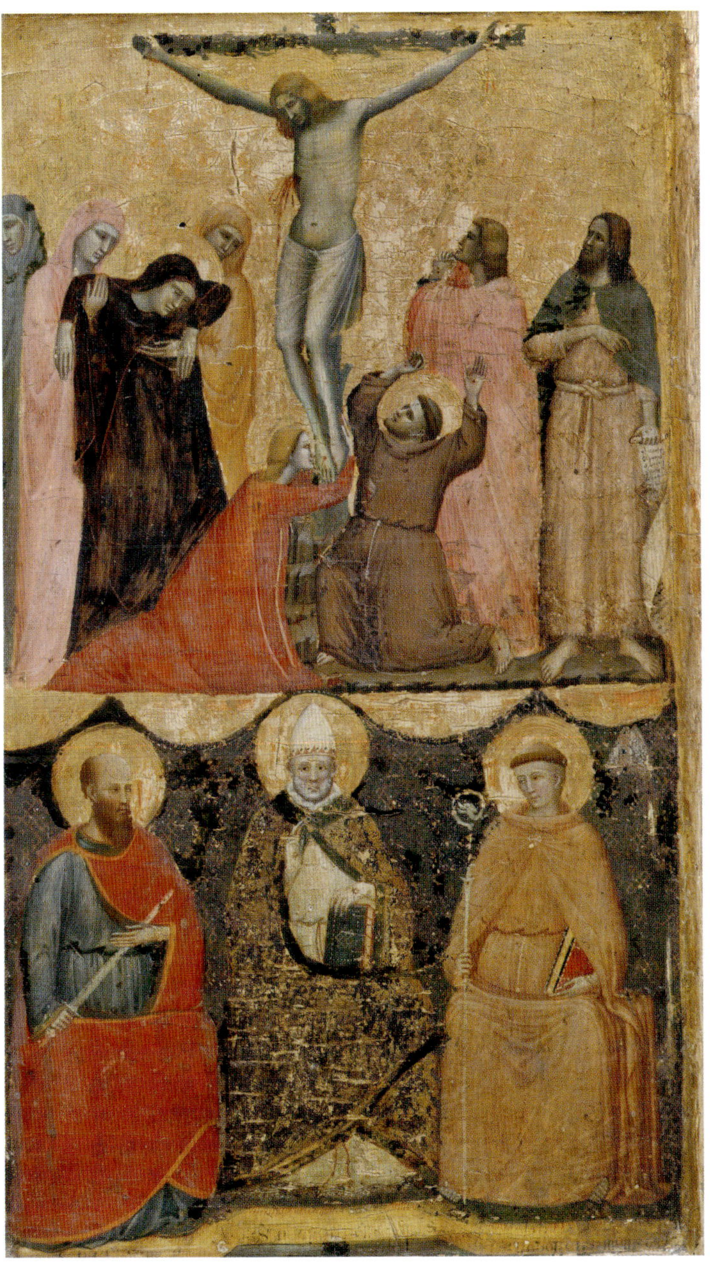

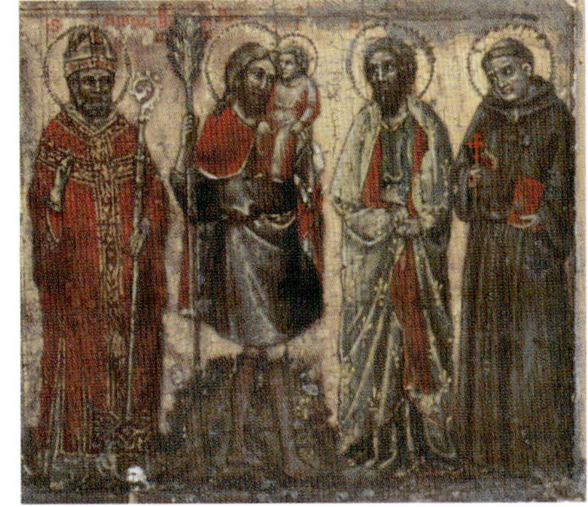

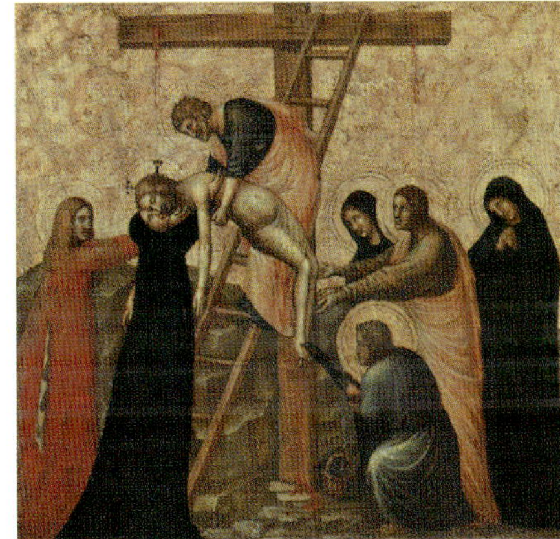

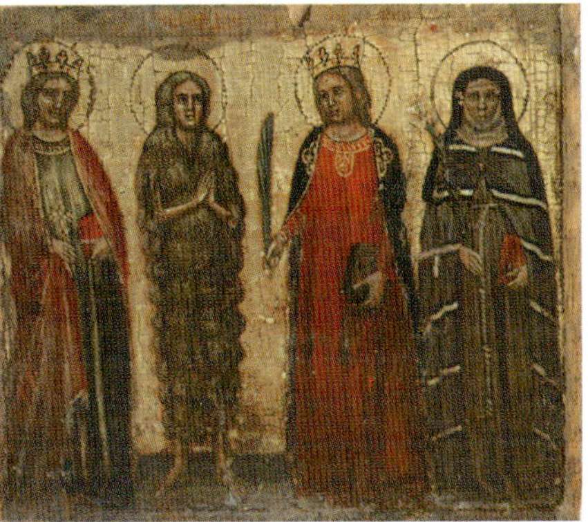

Pseudo Baronzio, mid-14th century
***Crucifixion*, ca. 1335**
39.8 x 23.5 cm; Tempera on wood panel
Pinacoteca; Room I; Inv. 40175

School of Rimini, mid-14th century
***St. Apollinare with other Saints*, before 1350**
12.5 x 14.8 cm; Tempera and gold on wood panel
Pinacoteca; Room I; Inv. 40173.2.2

Master of St. Maria in Porto Fuori, mid-14th century
***Deposition*, 1330-1340**
19.3 x 21.1 cm; Tempera on wood panel
Pinacoteca; Room I; Inv. 40167

School of Rimini, mid-14th century
***St. Margaret of Antiochia with other Saints*, before 1350**
12.3 x 14.5 cm; Tempera and gold on wood panel
Pinacoteca; Room I; Inv. 40173.2.1

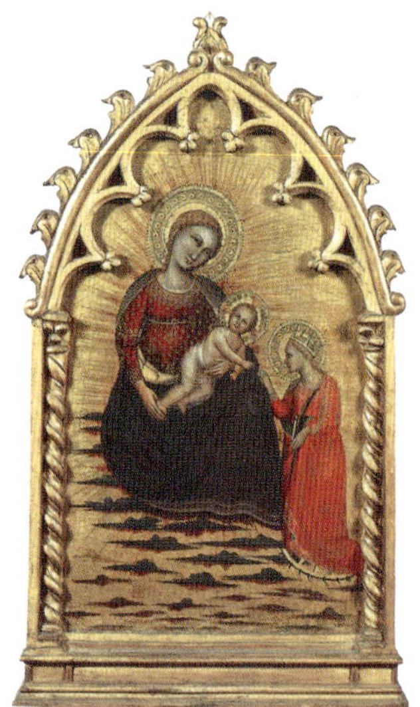

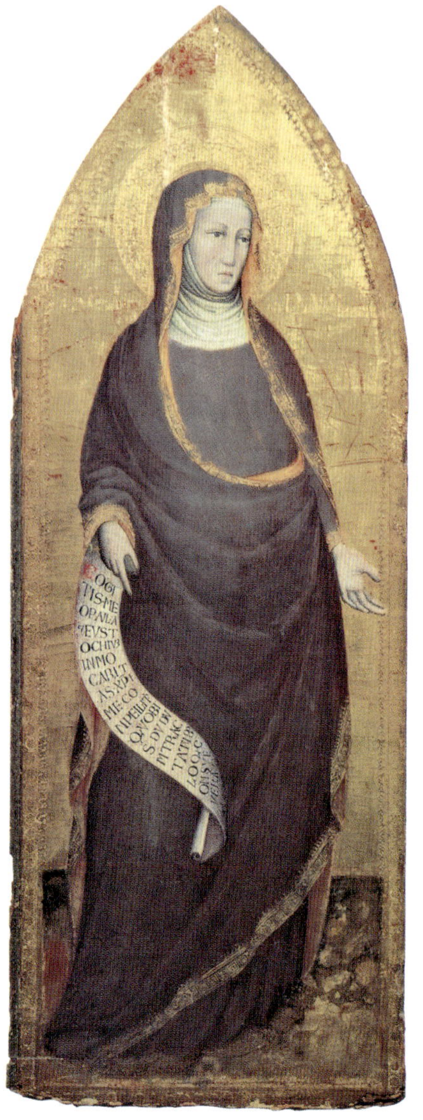

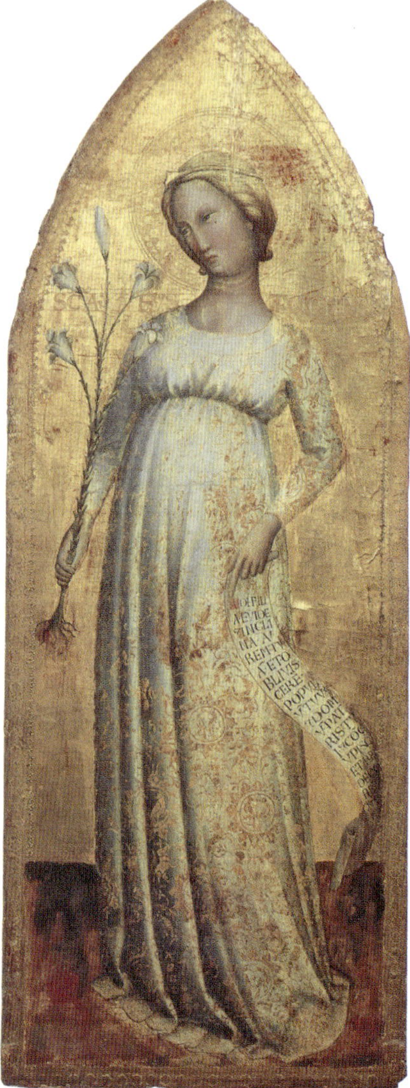

Olivuccio di Ciccarello, active 1388–1439
Mystical Marriage of St. Catherine,
late 14th century
55.7 x 32.7 cm; Tempera and gold on wood panel
Pinacoteca; Room I; Inv. 40207

Master of the Madonna Strauss, active 1390–1420
***St. Paola*, undated**
94 x 35 cm; Tempera and gold on wood panel
Pinacoteca; Room I; Inv. 40001

Master of the Madonna Strauss, active 1390–1420
***St. Eustachio*, undated**
95 x 36 cm; Tempera and gold on wood panel
Pinacoteca; Room I; Inv. 40003

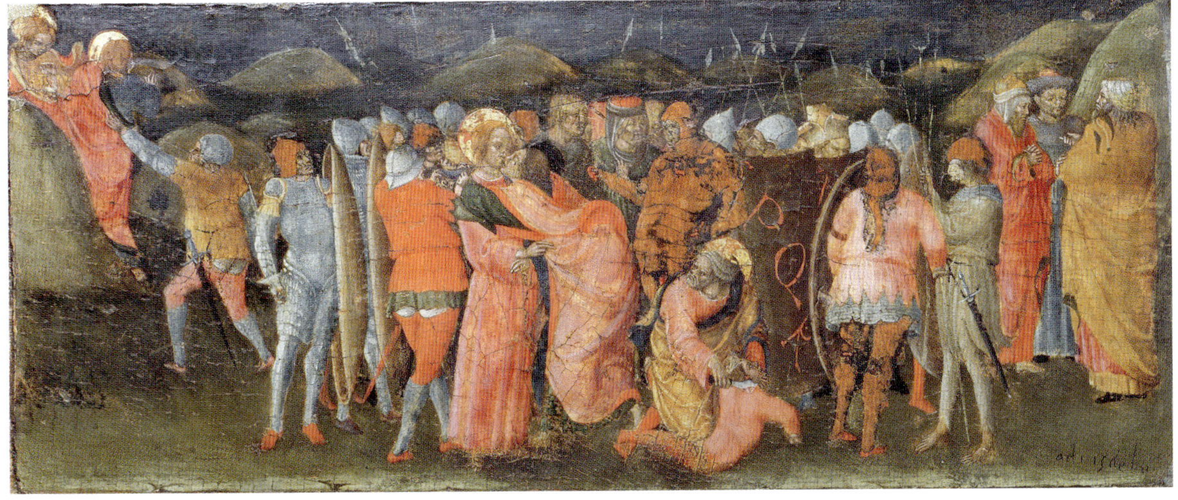

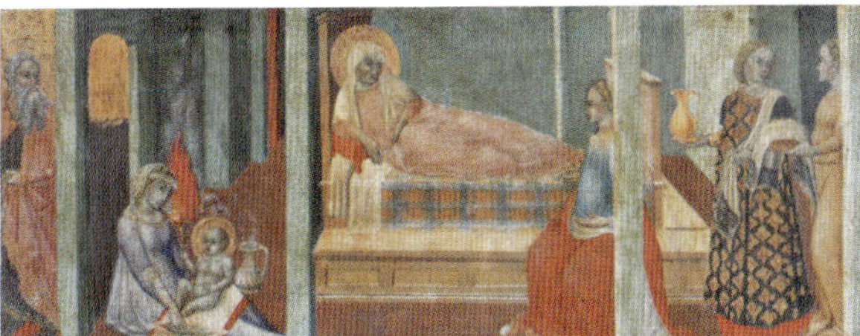

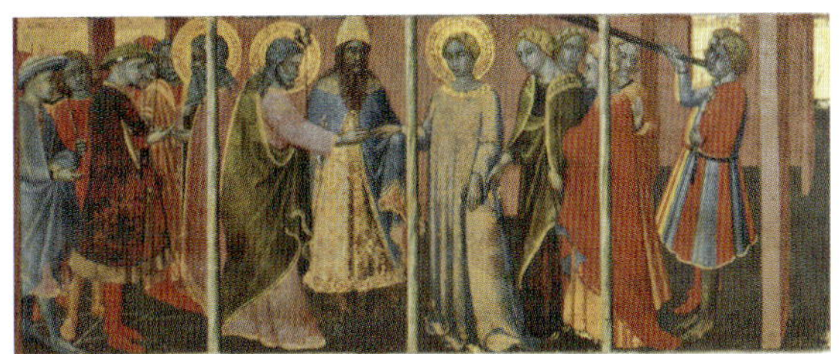

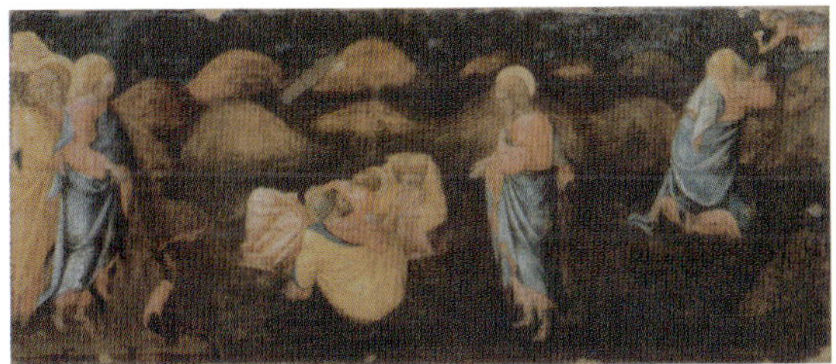

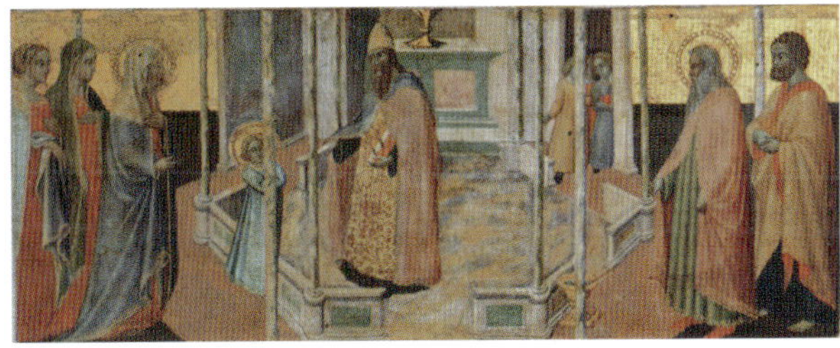

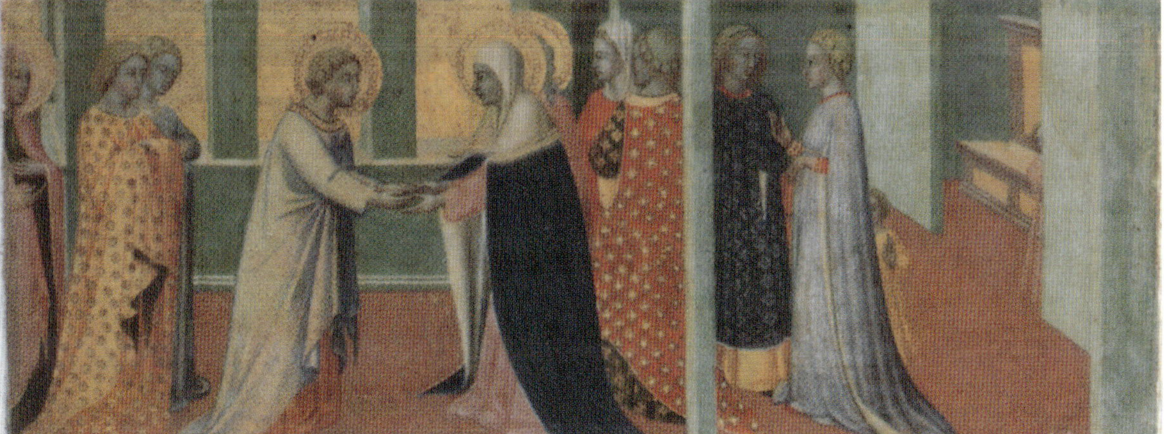

Bartolomeo di Tommaso, active 1425–1453
***The Arrest of Christ*, 1437**
23.2 x 52.2 cm; Tempera on wood panel
Pinacoteca; Room I; Inv. 40267

Sienese School, first half of 15th century
***Nativity*, first half of 15th century**
15.6 x 37.9 cm; Tempera on wood panel
Pinacoteca; Room I; Inv. 40237

Sienese School, first half of 15th century
***Marriage of the Virgin*, first half of 15th century**
15.3 x 37.8 cm; Tempera on wood panel
Pinacoteca; Room I; Inv. 40239

Bartolomeo di Tommaso, active 1425-1453
Christ in the Garden Gethsemane, 1432
22.6 x 50 cm; Tempera on wood panel
Pinacoteca; Room I; Inv. 40266

Bartolomeo di Tommaso, active 1425-1453
Presentation of the Virgin at the Temple, 1432
22.6 x 50 cm; Tempera on wood panel
Pinacoteca; Room I; Inv. 40266

Bartolomeo di Tommaso, active 1425-1453
***The Visitation*, 1432**
22.6 x 50 cm; Tempera on wood panel
Pinacoteca; Room I; Inv. 40266

SALA II

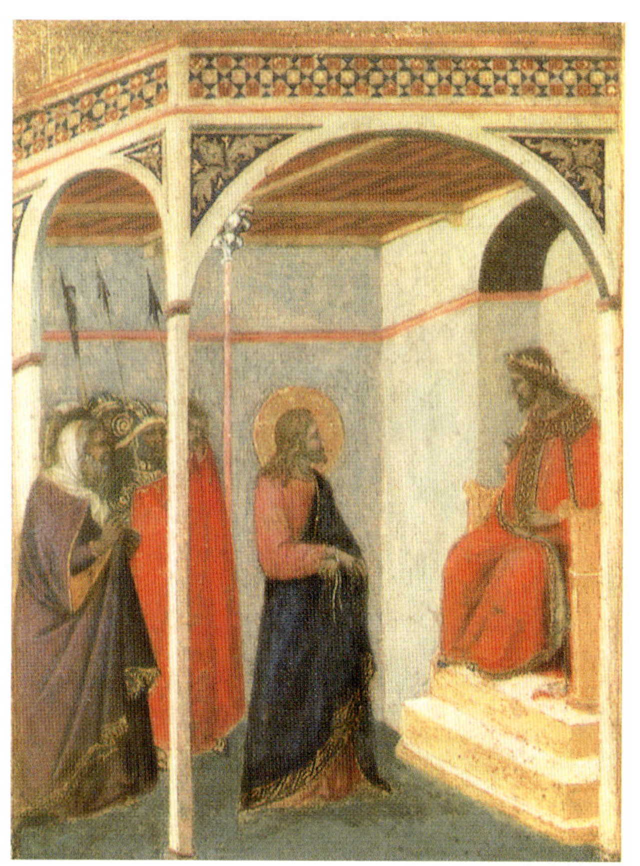

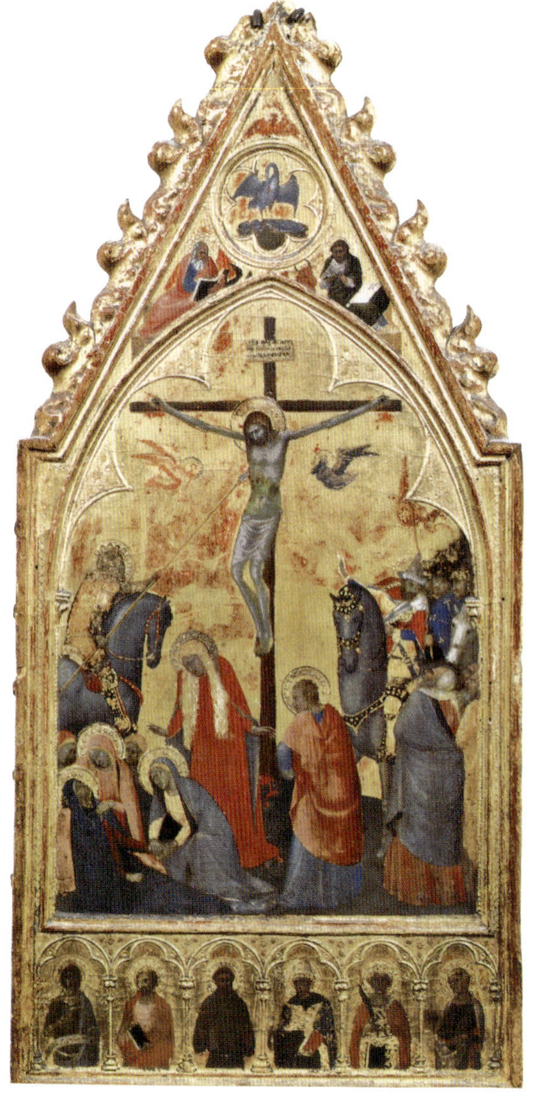

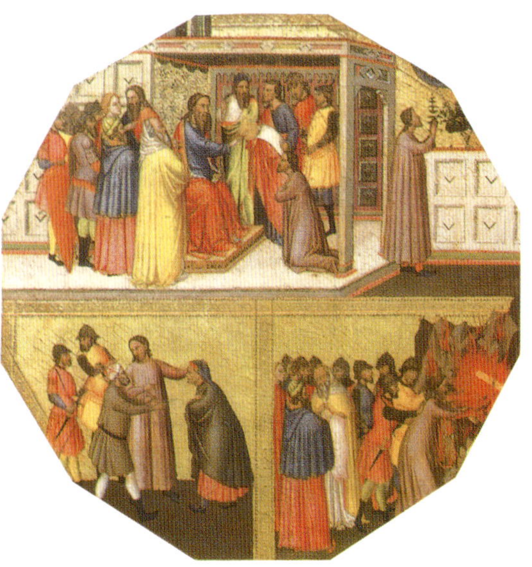

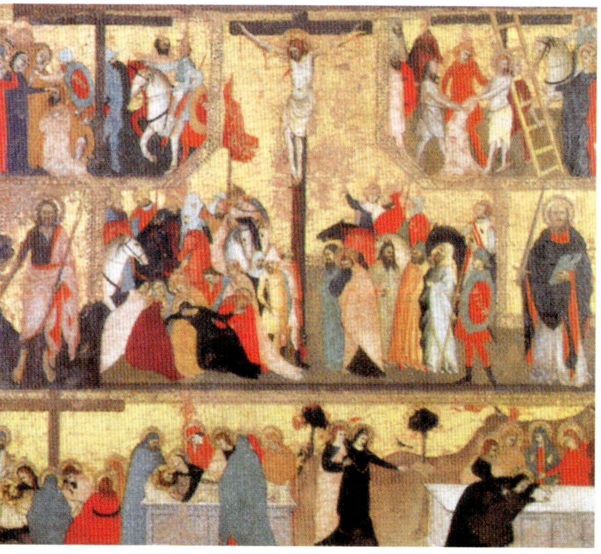

Pietro Lorenzetti, ca. 1280–1348
***Christ Before Pontius Pilate*, ca. 1335**
37.6 x 27.7 cm; Tempera on wood panel
Pinacoteca; Room II; Inv. 40168

Lippo Memmi, active 1317–1356
***Crucifixion*, before 1347**
58.8 x 28.3 cm; Tempera on wood panel
Pinacoteca; Room II; Inv. 40156

Florentine School, 14th century
***Story of a False Prophet*, before 1340**
56 x 55.5 cm; Tempera and gold on wood panel
Pinacoteca; Room II; Inv. 40223

Alesso di Andrea, active 1341–1347
***Crucifixion and Passion Scenes*, ca. 1345**
54 x 65.3 cm; Tempera and gold on wood panel
Pinacoteca; Room II; Inv. 40222

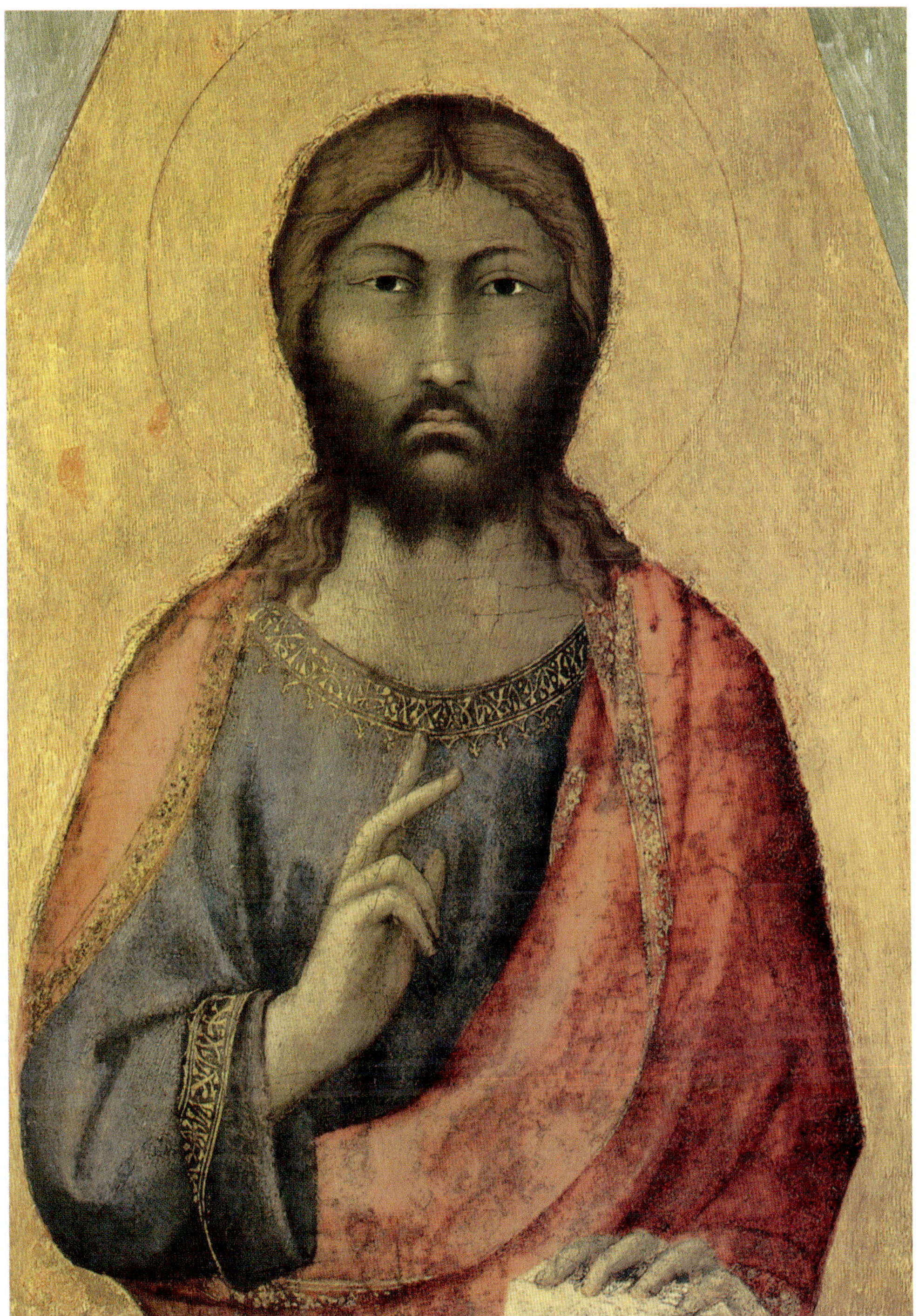

Simone Martini

Christ the Redeemer Conferring a Blessing

Simone Martini is one of the most important representatives of Sienese Early Renaissance painting. This small panel, thought to have formed the upper part of a polyptych, is a supreme example of his gentle, elegant style. Its subject is a half-length figure of Christ. The Redeemer holds up his right hand in a gesture of blessing, while his left rests on the Bible, embodying God's word. With its frontal pose, solemn gaze, almond-shaped eyes, and dark flesh tone, the Christ figure harks back to Byzantine icons, which were highly revered in Italy. The softly flowing robes with their gold filigree edging are, by contrast, characteristics of Simone Martini's work. Also typical of the Sienese master are the strong blue and red tones of Christ's cloak and undergarment, which the painter has modeled with great subtlety. Together with the gold ground, they give the work an inner light that emphasizes the majestic appearance of the Christ figure. Similar qualities can be observed in Martini's famous *Maestà* fresco (ca. 1315) in the Palazzo Pubblico in Siena, produced around the same time as this Christ panel in the Pinacoteca.

Simone Martini, 1284-1344
Christ the Redeemer Conferring a Blessing, ca. 1315-1320
38.3 x 28.5 cm; Tempera on wood panel
Pinacoteca; Room II; Inv. 40165

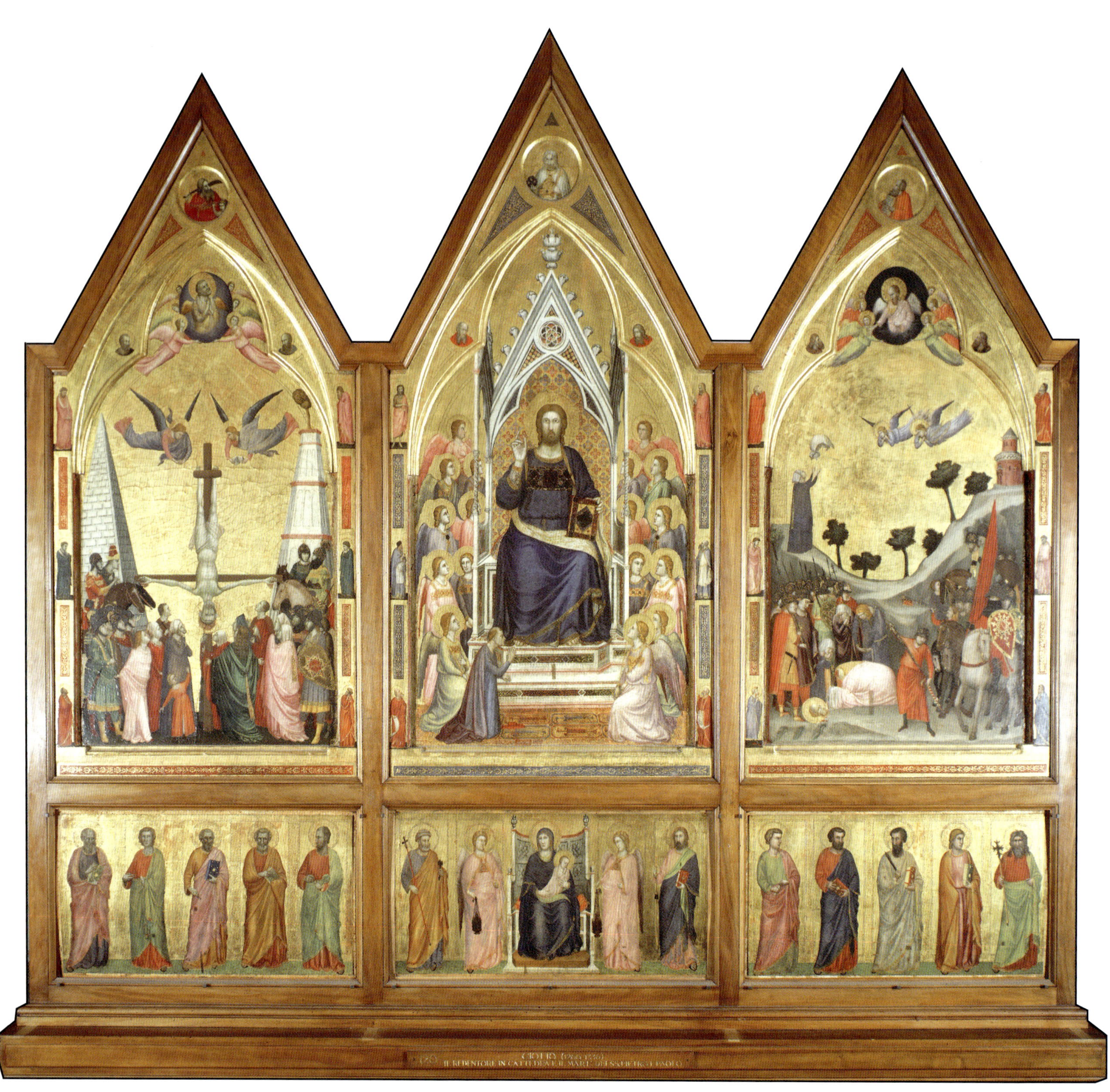

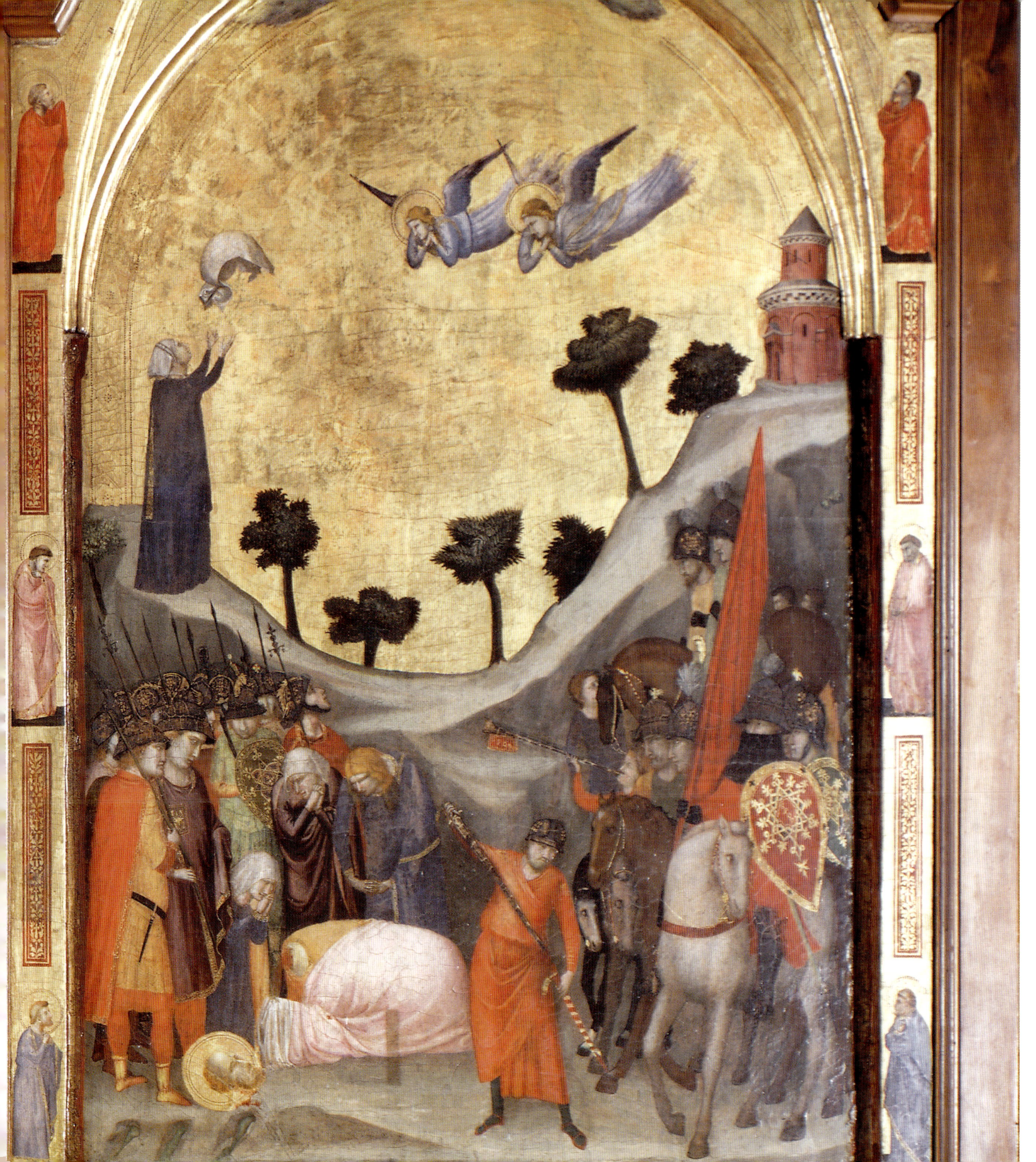

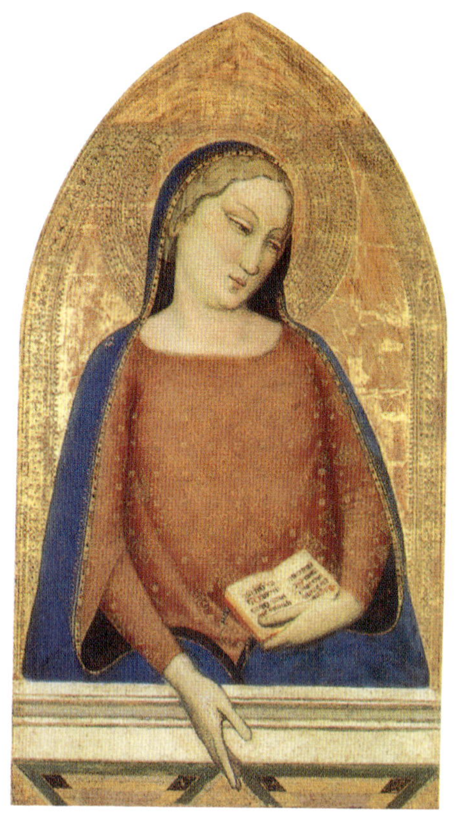

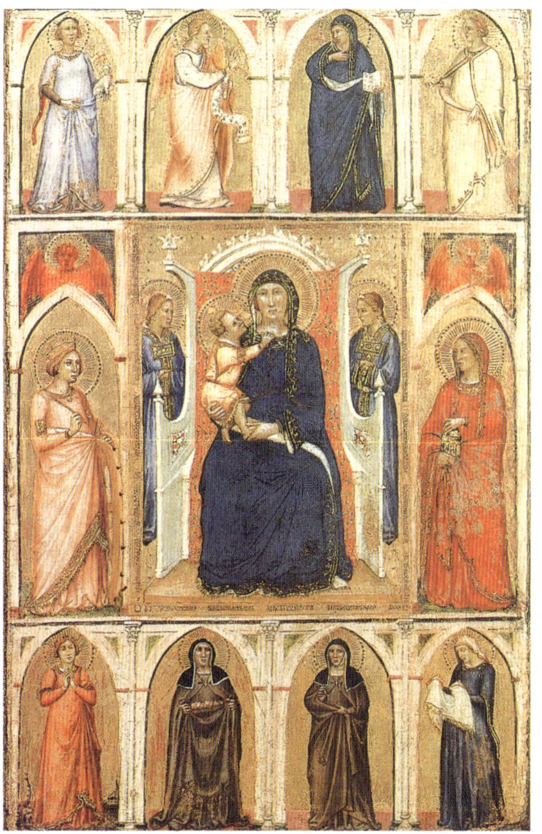

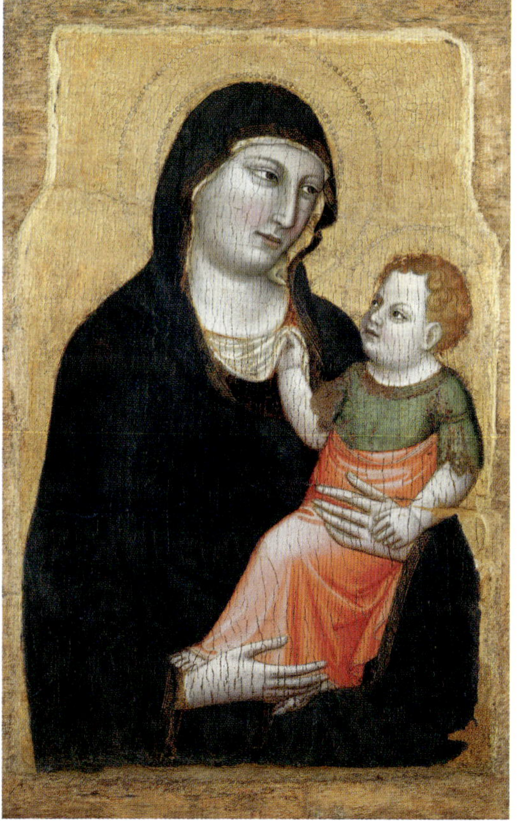

Bernardo Daddi, 1290–1350
***Madonna of the Magnificat*, 1335**
71 x 53 cm; Tempera on wood panel
Pinacoteca; Room II; Inv. 40174

Puccio Capanna, active 1325–1350
***Madonna and Child with Saints (Regina Virginum)*, ca. 1330**
36.5 x 24 cm; Tempera and gold on wood panel
Pinacoteca; Room II; Inv. 40170

Jacopo del Casentino (also called Jacopo Landini), 1297–1358
***Madonna and Child*, ca. 1320**
67 x 42.5 cm; Tempera on wood panel
Pinacoteca; Room II; Inv. 40179

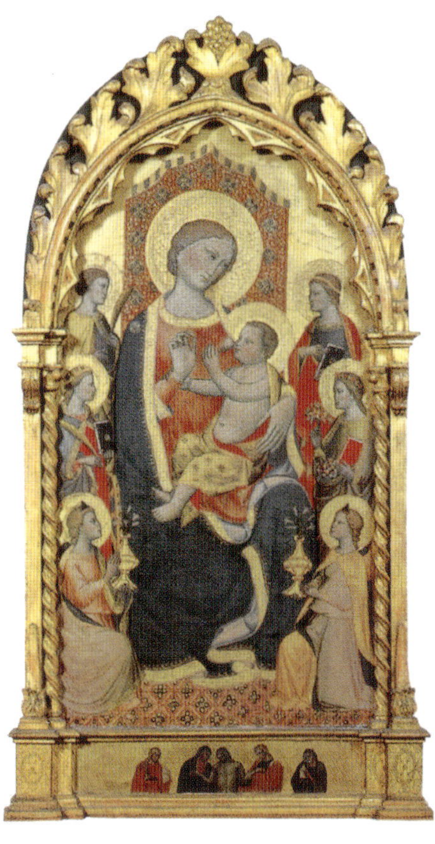

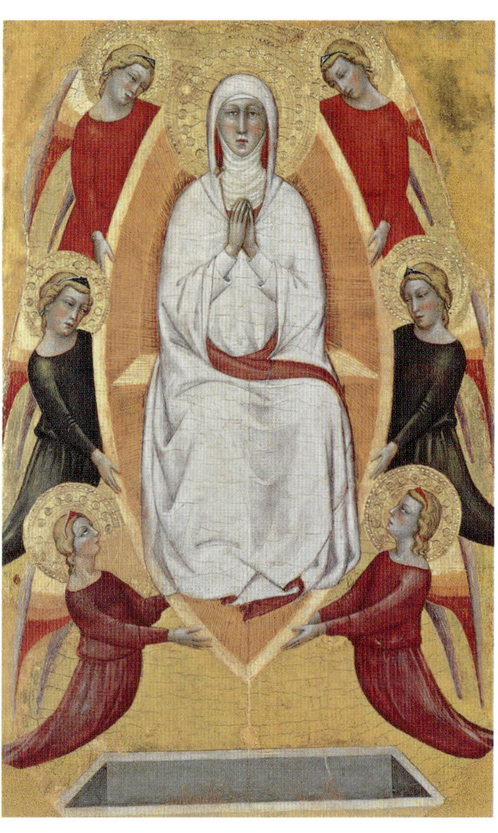

Florentine School, 14th century
***Madonna Nursing with Saints*, ca. 1380**
118.3 x 65 cm; Tempera and gold on wood panel
Pinacoteca; Room II; Inv. 40010

Don Silvestro dei Gherarducci, 1339–1399
***Assumption of Mary*, ca. 1356**
41.3 x 26.5 cm; Tempera on wood panel
Pinacoteca; Room II; Inv. 40116

Florentine School, 14th century
***Madonna and Child*, ca. 1320**
20.2 x 16.6 cm; Tempera and gold on wood panel
Pinacoteca; Room II; Inv. 40176

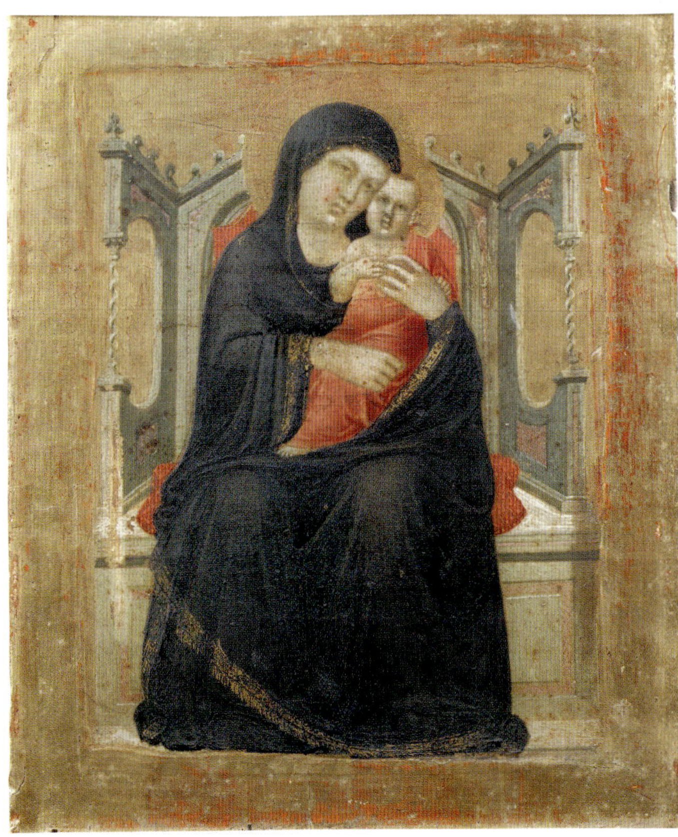

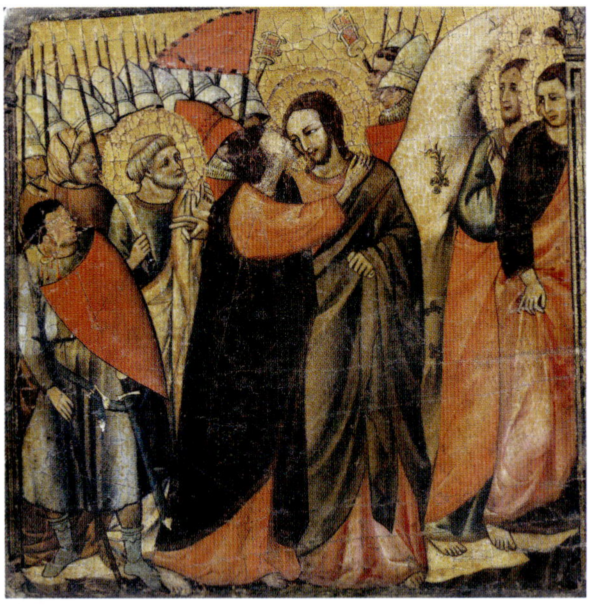

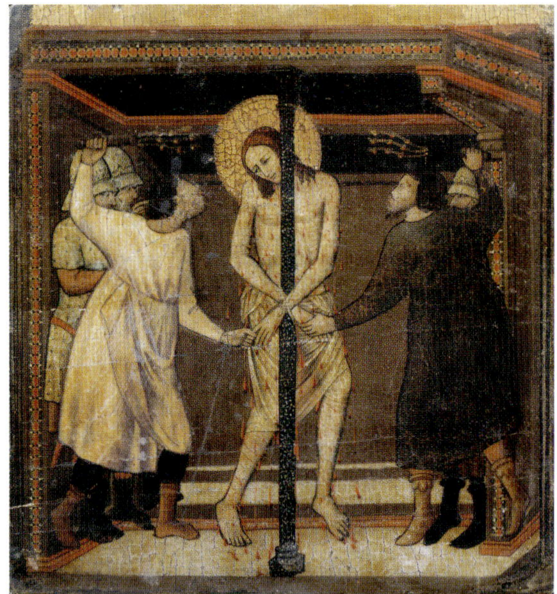

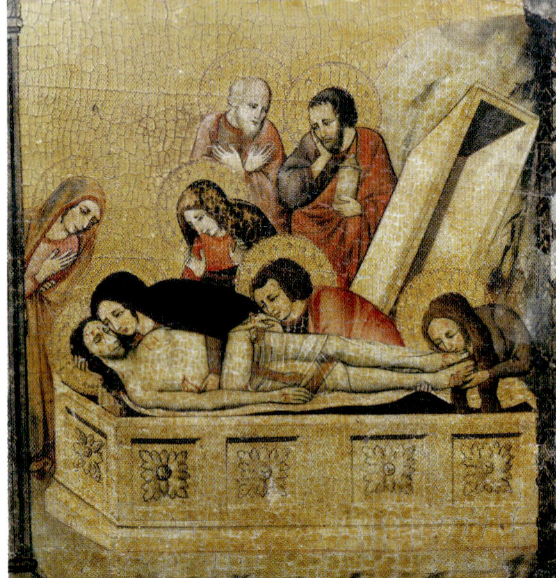

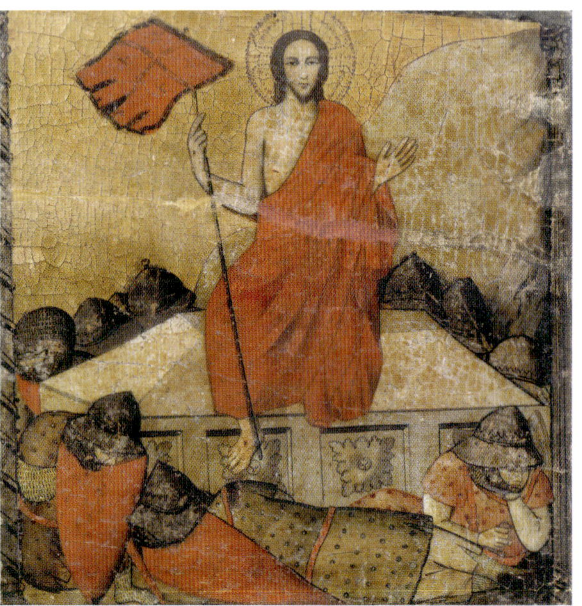

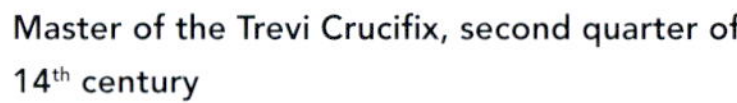

Master of the Trevi Crucifix, second quarter of 14th century
***Kiss of Judas (From Life of Christ)*, 1320–1330**
33.8 x 34.3 cm; Tempera on wood panel
Pinacoteca; Room II; Inv. 40108

Master of the Trevi Crucifix, second quarter of 14th century
***Flagellation (From Life of Christ)*, 1320–1330**
35.5 x 34 cm; Tempera on wood panel
Pinacoteca; Room II; Inv. 40109

Master of the Trevi Crucifix, second quarter of 14th century
***Deposition From Life of Christ*, 1320–1330**
36.6 x 34.9 cm; Tempera on wood panel
Pinacoteca; Room II; Inv. 40111

Master of the Trevi Crucifix, second quarter of 14th century
***Resurrection (From Life of Christ)*, 1320–1330**
34 x 33.4 cm; Tempera on wood panel
Pinacoteca; Room II; Inv. 40112

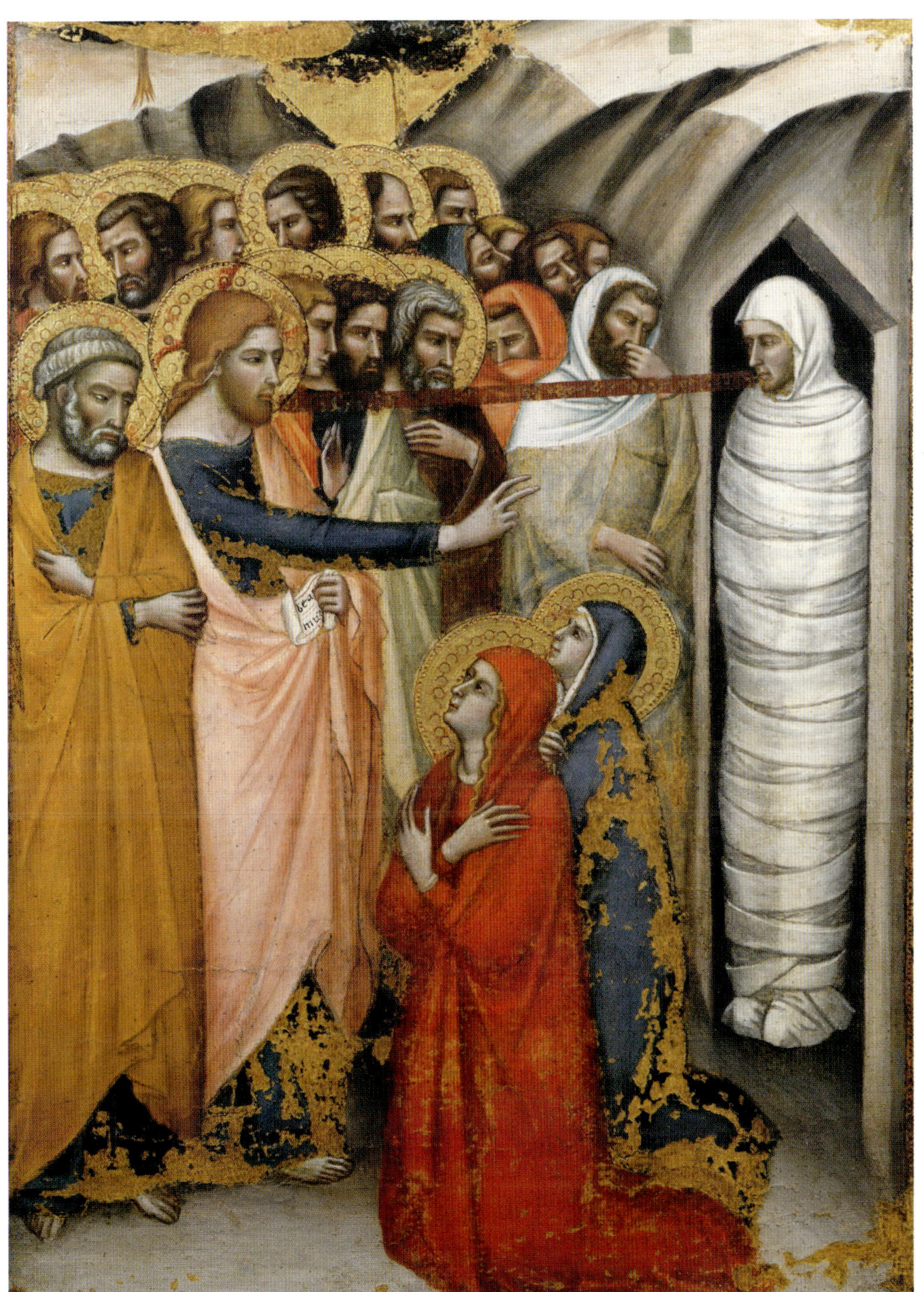

Luca di Tommè

The Resurrection of Lazarus

The resurrection of Lazarus is one of Christ's most remarkable miracles. In this predella panel the Sienese painter Luca di Tommè adheres closely to the account given in the Gospel of St. John (John 11: 32–44). The painting depicts the moment when Christ, moved by the laments of SS. Marie Magdalene and Martha, the sisters of the deceased, arrives in front of the tomb and recalls their brother to life with the words: "Lazarus, come forth!" This phrase was presumably once inscribed on the ribbon that links Christ's lips to Lazarus's mouth, which can also be seen as a symbol of the breath of life. As in the biblical account, Lazarus appears at the opening of the tomb upright and wrapped in graveclothes. A man holds his nose in order to fend off the smell. The reactions of Christ's disciples and the citizens of Bethany, who are crowded around, are also depicted with considerable psychological sophistication and range from incredulity to amazement and astonishment. Luca di Tommè based his work on a depiction of the same subject by the great Sienese master Duccio (ca. 1255–1319), whose composition he condenses, in terms of both narrative and design, lending his version a greater sense of balance.

Luca di Tommè, active 1355–1389
***The Resurrection of Lazarus*, 1362**
52 x 39 cm; Oil on wood panel
Pinacoteca; Room II ; Inv. 40221

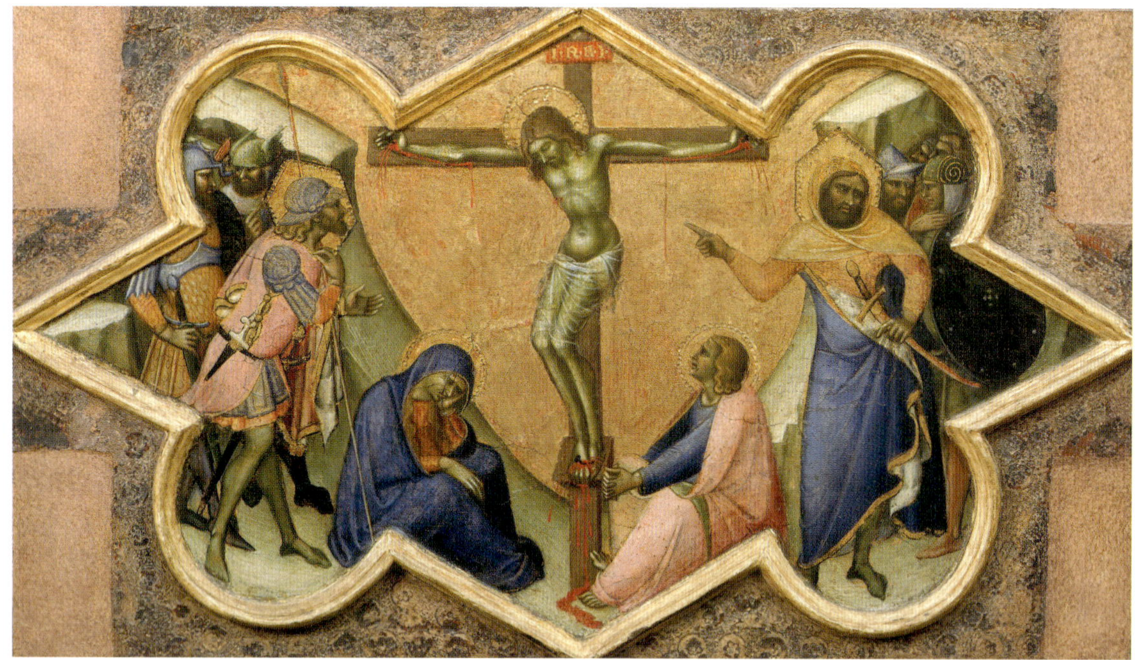

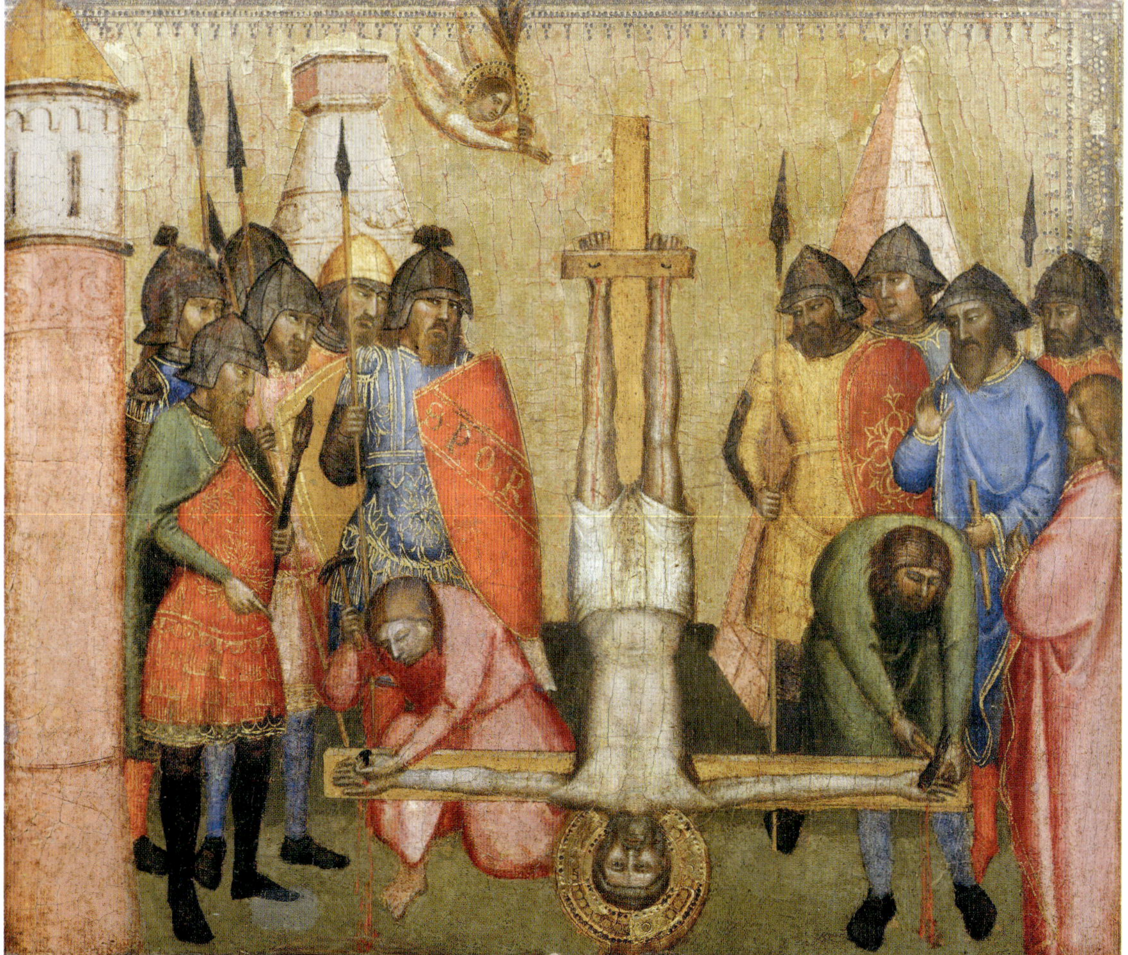

Luca di Tommè, active 1355–1389
***Crucifixion*, 1362**
32.8 x 56 cm; Oil on wood panel
Pinacoteca; Room II; Inv. 40195

Jacopo di Cione, active 1365–1398
***Martyrdom of St. Peter*, undated**
34.7 x 42.2 cm; Tempera on wood panel
Pinacoteca; Room II; Inv. 42104

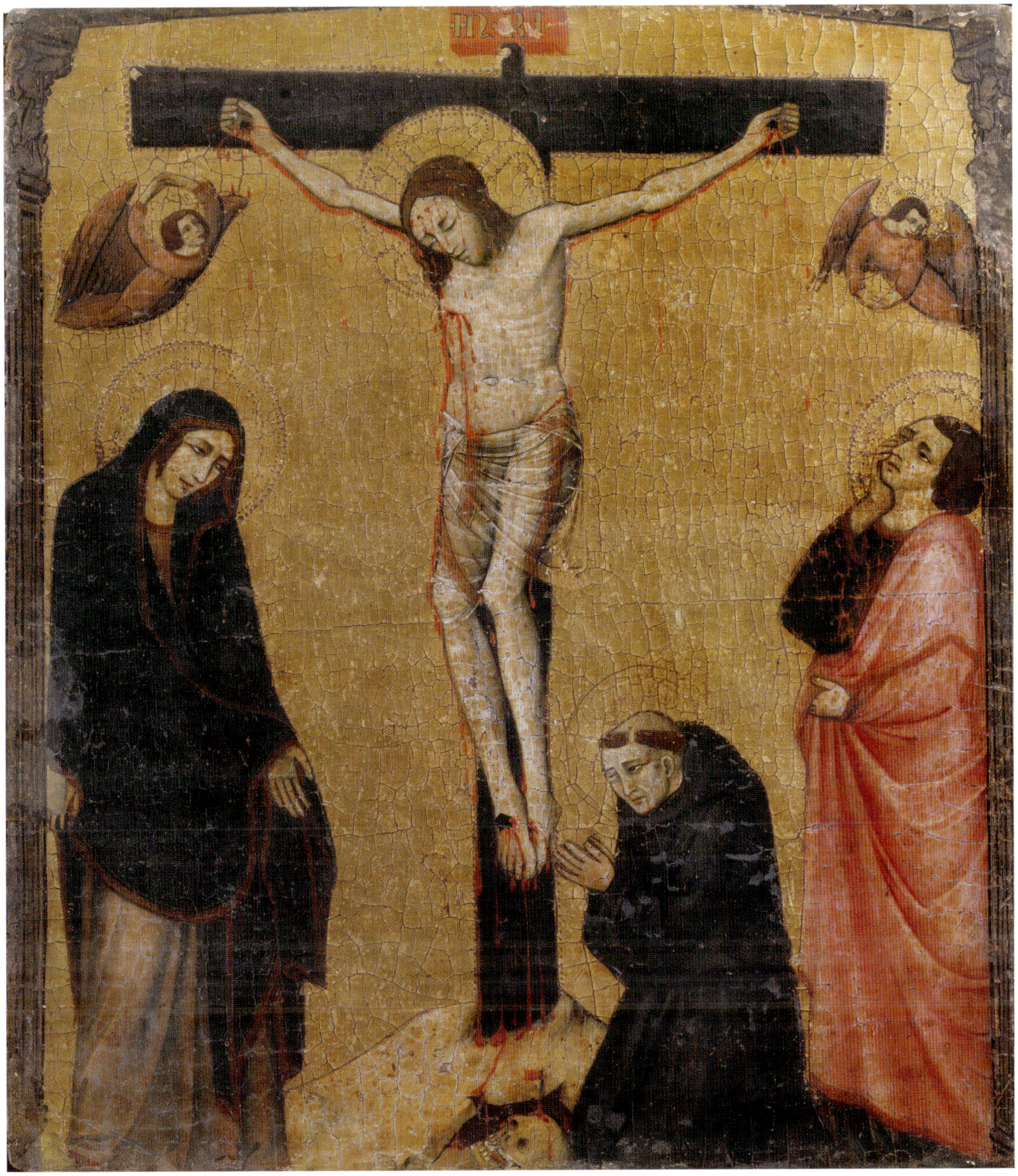

Master of the Trevi Crucifix, second quarter of 14th century
***Crucifixion (From Life of Christ)*, 1320–1330**
39 x 35 cm; Tempera on wood panel
Pinacoteca; Room II; Inv. 40110

Andrea da Firenze (Andrea Bonaiuti), ca. 1320–1377
***Crucifixion*, ca. 1370**
22.5 x 32.5 cm; Tempera on wood panel
Pinacoteca; Room II; Inv. 40118

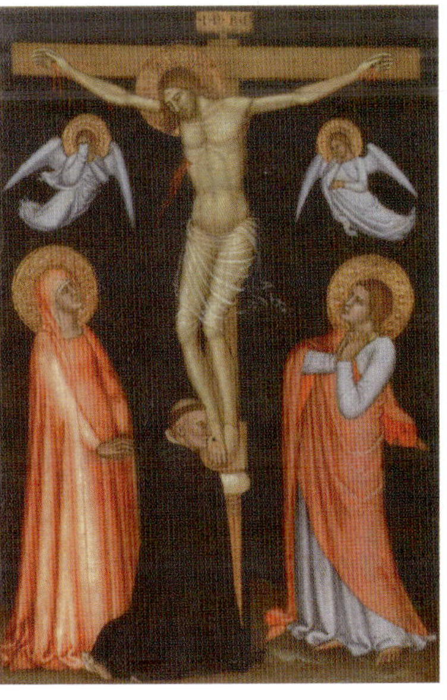

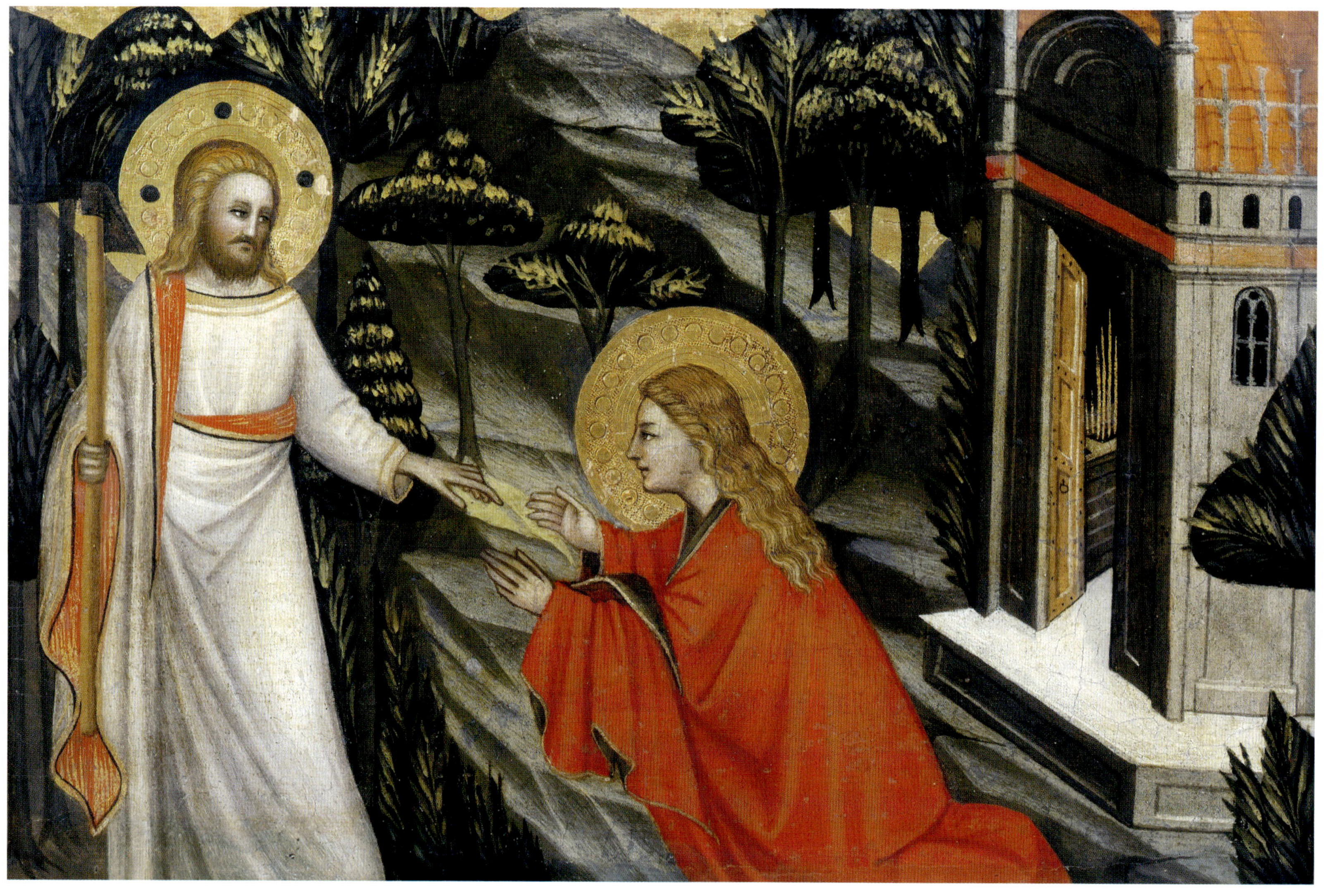

Cenni di Francesco

Noli Me Tangere

The painter Cenni di Francesco was one of the most active examples of the Florentine Early Renaissance around the turn of the fifteenth century. One of his earliest documented works is this small panel of Christ and Mary Magdalene in the Garden, once part of a predella featuring scenes from the life of Mary Magdalene which included two other small panels also in the Pinacoteca (*The Feast in the House of the Pharisee* and *The Crucifixion*). Depicted here is the saint's encounter with the resurrected Christ in the garden by the tomb, which Cenni di Francesco transforms into a kind of grove planted with trees of different types. According to the account in the Gospel of St. John (John 20:11–18), Mary sat weeping before Christ's empty tomb when Christ appeared to her in the figure of a gardener. With the words "Noli me tangere," from which this painting takes its name, Jesus instructed her not to touch him. Cenni has depicted this tension-filled moment with the greatest of subtlety, ingeniously conveying Mary Magdalene's desire to reach out and touch Christ by showing her straining forward with her upper body while stretching out her arms. Christ repudiates Mary regretfully with an outstretched arm. Its clear composition, the elegant movements of the figures and the luxuriant, gently flowing garments make this a characteristic work of the late Trecento between Late Gothic and the Early Renaissance.

Cenni di Francesco, active 1369–1415
***Noli Me Tangere*, 1370–1375**
23.7 x 34 cm; Tempera on wood panel
Pinacoteca; Room II; Inv. 40184

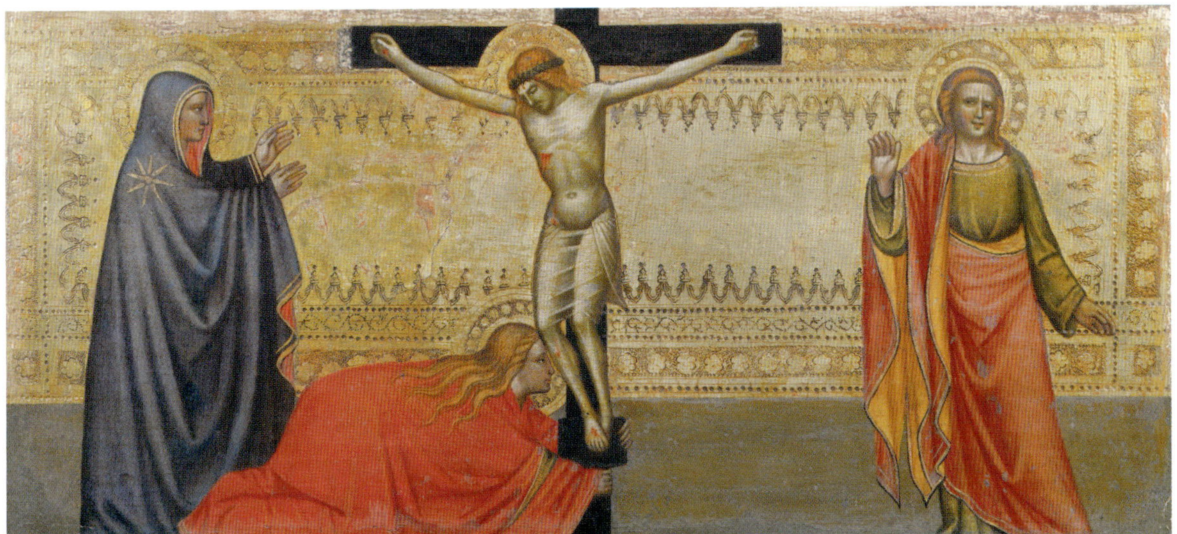

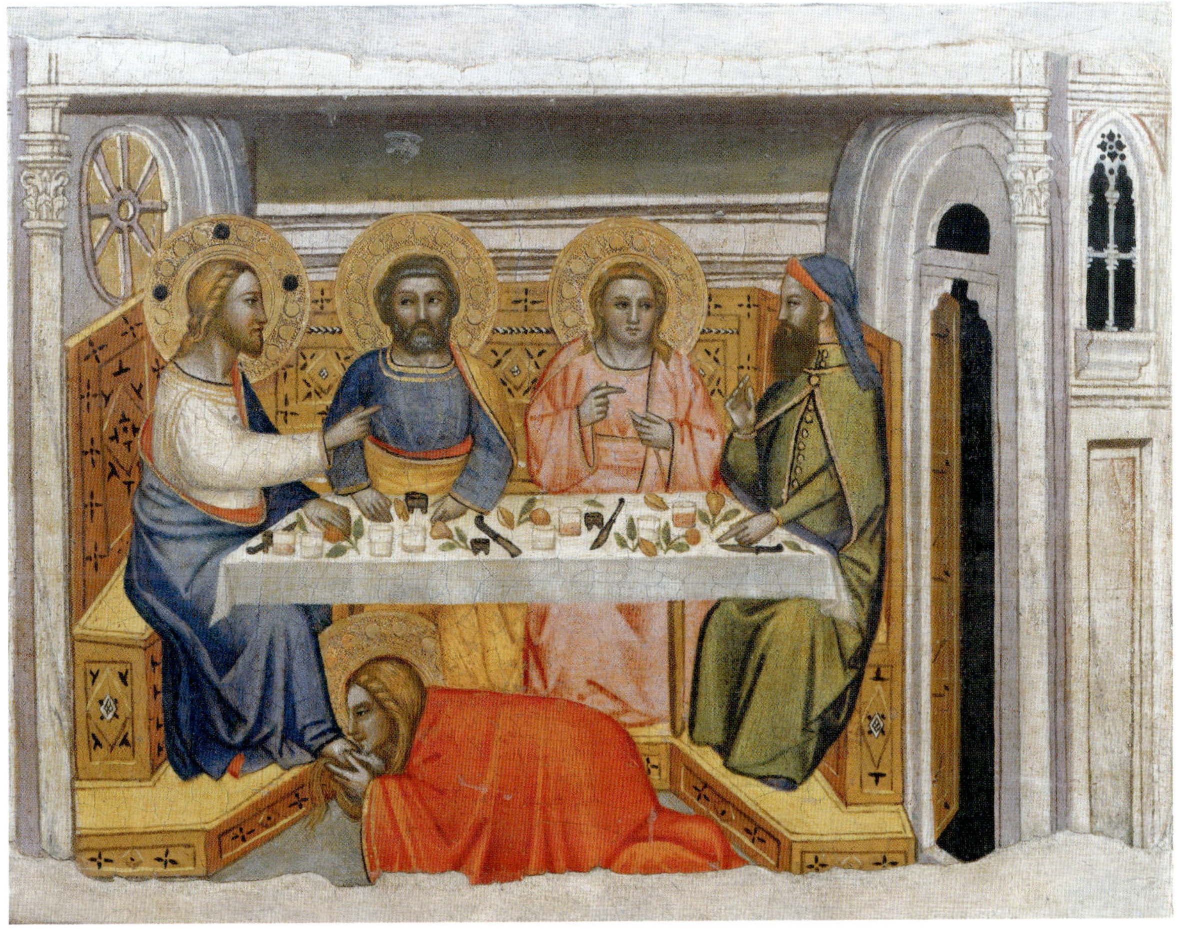

Cenni di Francesco, active 1369–1415
***Scene from the Life of Mary Magdalene: Crucifixion*, 1370–1375**
24 x 52 cm; Tempera on wood panel
Pinacoteca; Room II; Inv. 40183

Cenni di Francesco, active 1369–1415
***Scene from the Life of Mary Magdalene: At the House of the Pharisee*, 1370–1375**
23.7 x 31 cm; Tempera on wood panel
Pinacoteca; Room II; Inv. 40182

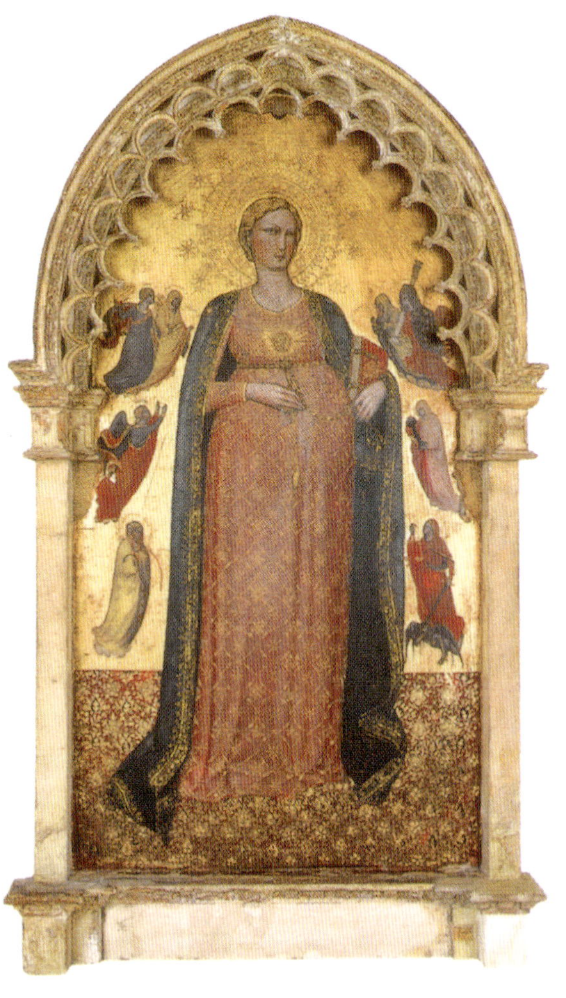

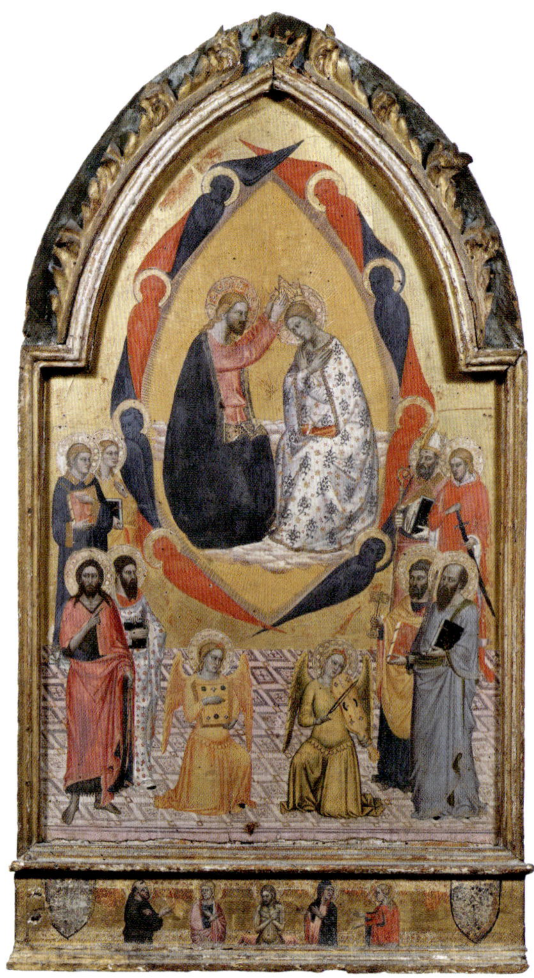

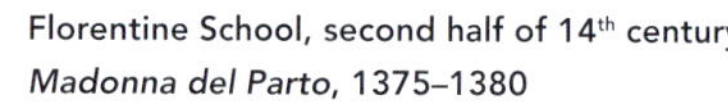

Florentine School, second half of 14th century
***Madonna del Parto*, 1375–1380**
106.5 x 58.5 cm; Tempera on wood panel
Pinacoteca; Room II; Inv. 40520

Jacopo di Cione (follower of), active 1365–1398
***Coronation of the Virgin*, ca. 1375**
115.8 x 63.5 cm; Tempera and gold on wood panel
Pinacoteca; Room II; Inv. 40008

Florentine School, 14th century
***Lamentation*, 1300–1320**
23.6 x 19.7 cm; Tempera on wood panel
Pinacoteca; Room II; Inv. 40171

Master of the Ashmolean Predella, active 1360–1390
***Flight into Egypt*, before 1370**
38 x 35 cm; Tempera on wood panel
Pinacoteca; Room II; Inv. 40103

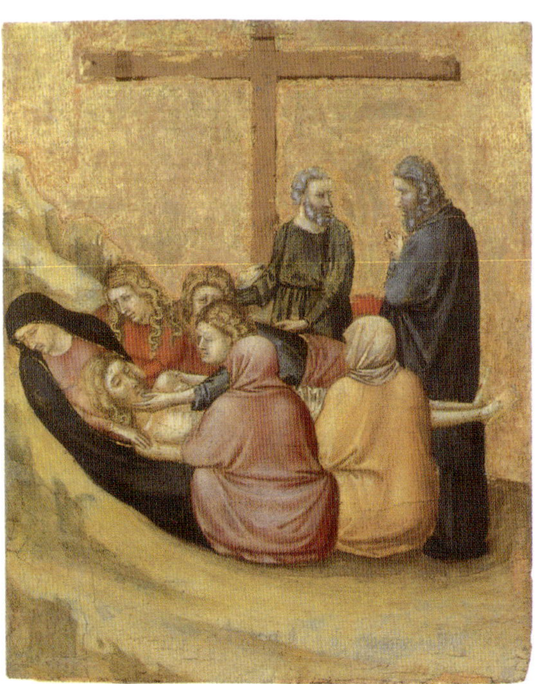

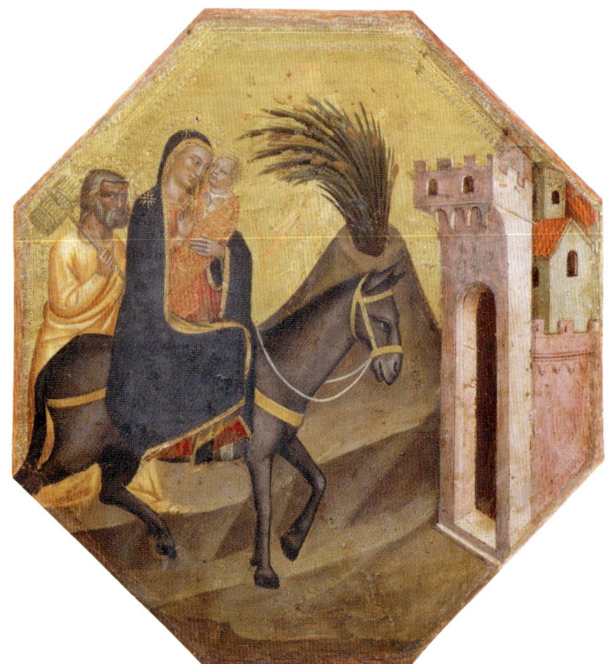

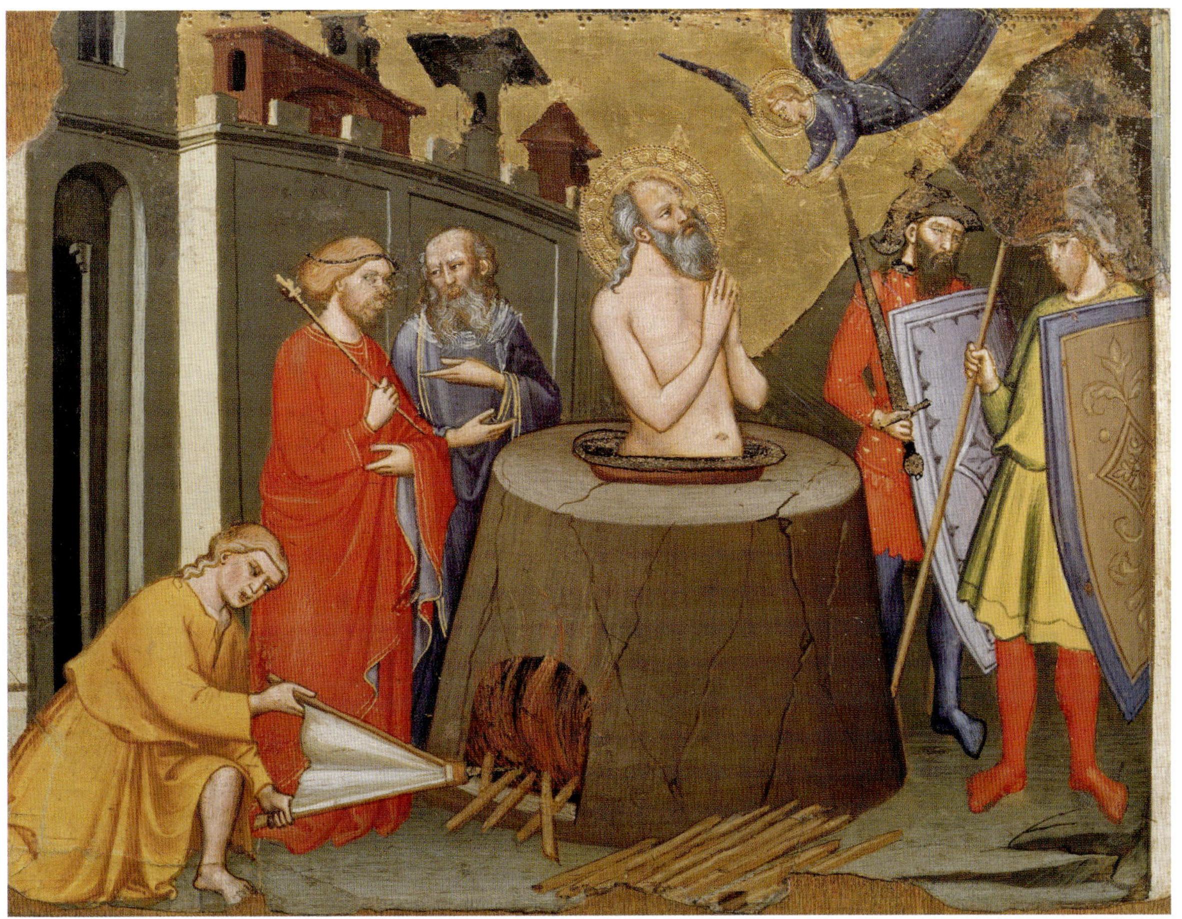

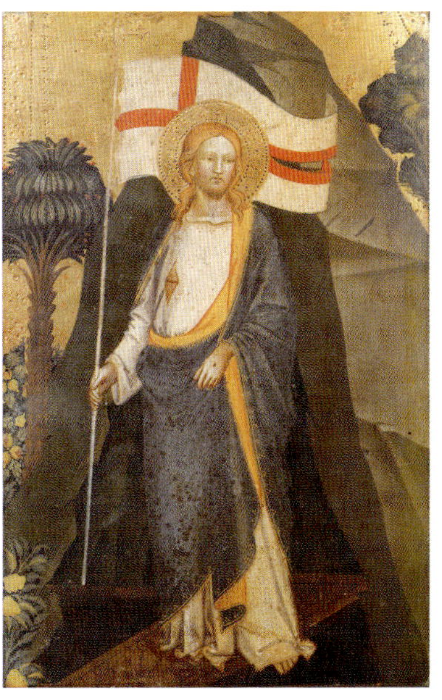

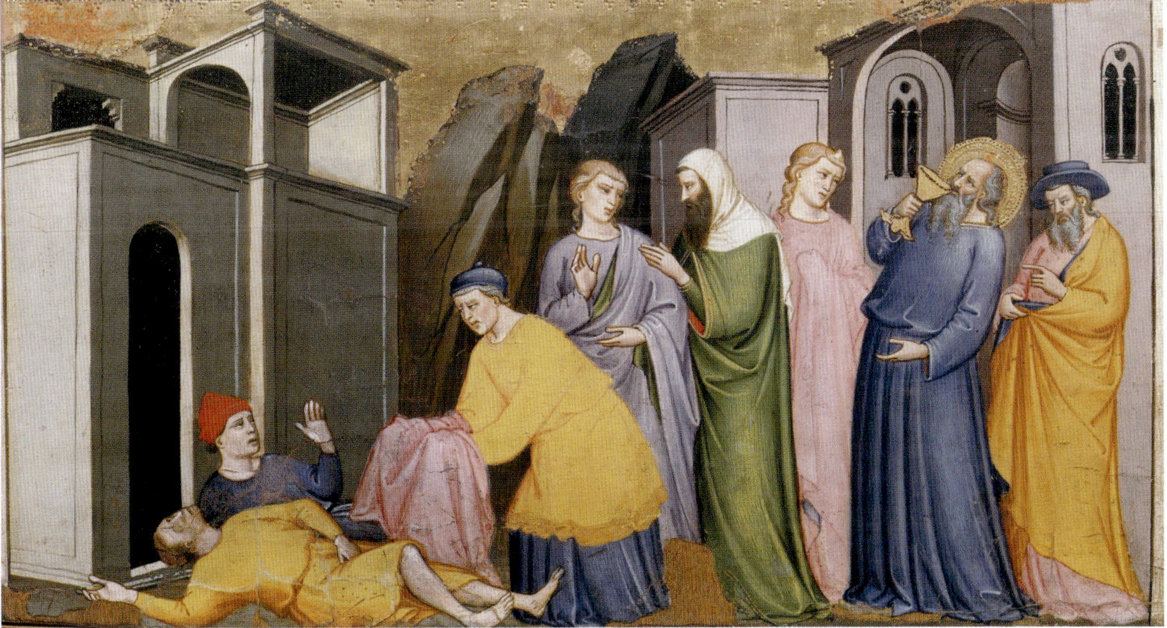

Agnolo Gaddi, 1350–1396
***Martyrdom of St. John*, 14th century**
38 x 26 cm; Tempera on wood panel
Pinacoteca; not on display; Inv. 40191

Master of the Misericordia and Agnolo Gaddi, active 1369–1396
***Resurrection*, 1390–1395**
38.2 x 26.2 cm; Tempera and gold on wood panel
Pinacoteca; Room II; Inv. 40114

Agnolo Gaddi, 1350–1396
***Pagan Priests Try to Poison St. John*, 14th century**
22.5 x 18.3 cm; Tempera on wood panel
Pinacoteca; Room II; Inv. 40190

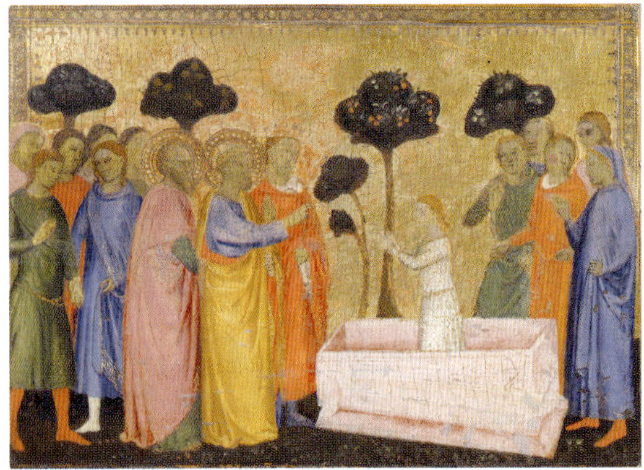

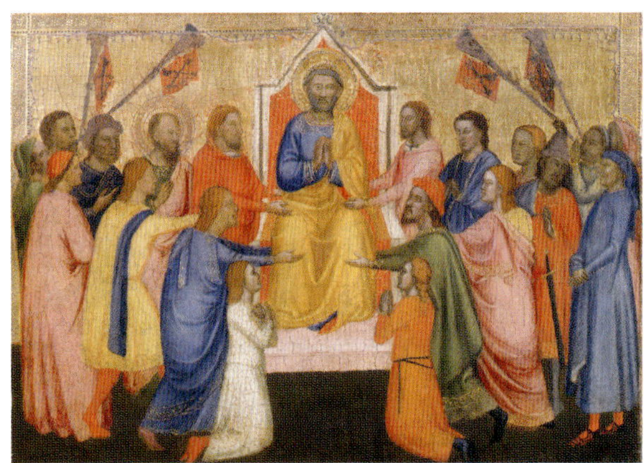

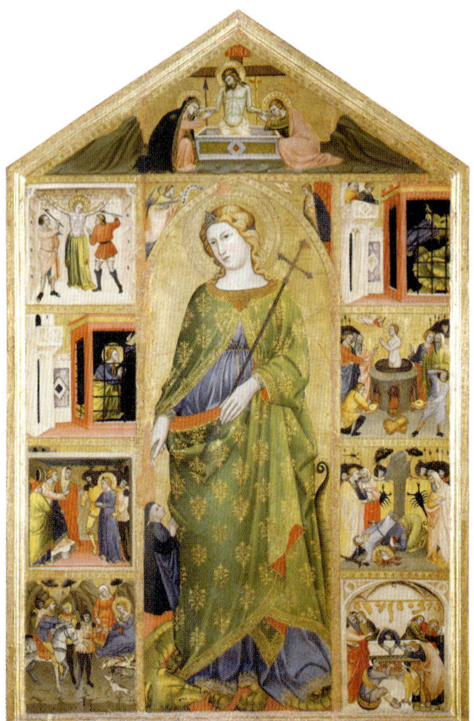

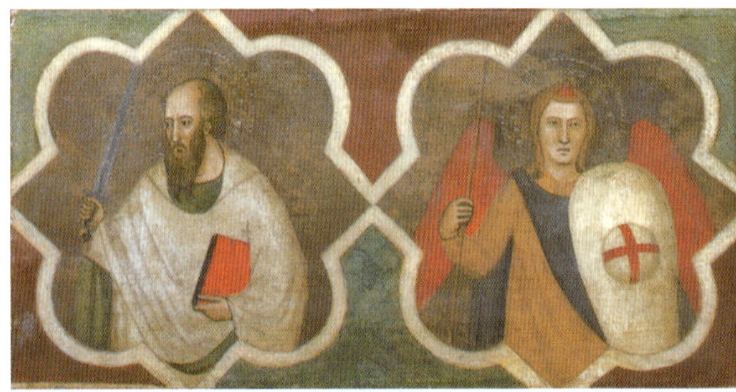

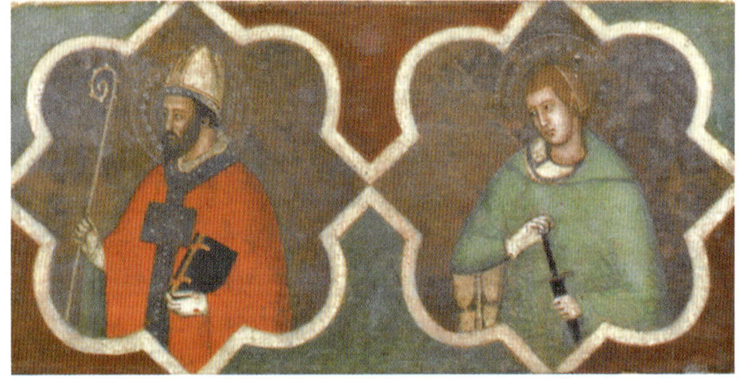

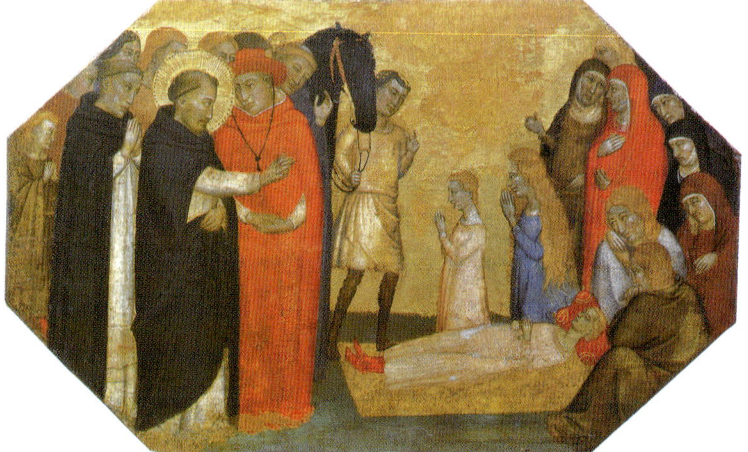

Jacopo di Cione, active 1365–1398
***St. Peter Rescues the Son of Teofilo*, undated**
39.4 x 53.5 cm; Tempera and gold on wood panel
Pinacoteca; Room II; Inv. 40113

Jacopo di Cione, active 1365–1398
***St. Peter Preaching*, undated**
39.3 x 53.7 cm; Tempera and gold on wood panel
Pinacoteca; Room II; Inv. 40107

Turino Vanni (in the style of), 1349–1438
***St. Margaret*, undated**
166 x 196.7 cm; Tempera on wood panel
Pinacoteca; Room II; Inv. 40007

Andrea da Firenze (Andrea Bonaiuti), 1320–1377
***St. Paul and Archangel Michael*, undated**
19.5 x 39.5 cm; Tempera on wood panel
Pinacoteca; Room II; Inv. 40115.2.1

Andrea da Firenze (Andrea Bonaiuti), 1320–1377
***St. Augustine and St. Julius*, undated**
19.5 x 39.5 cm; Tempera on wood panel
Pinacoteca; Room II; Inv. 40115.2.2

Jacopo di Cione (follower of), 14th century
***St. Dominic Bringing Napoleone Orsini Back to Life*, 1360–1370**
17.7 x 29.3 cm; Tempera on wood panel
Pinacoteca; Room II; Inv. 40192

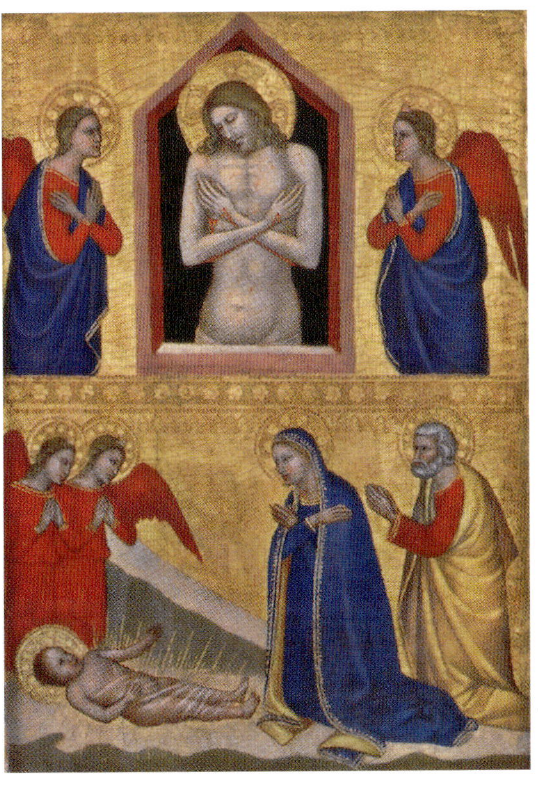

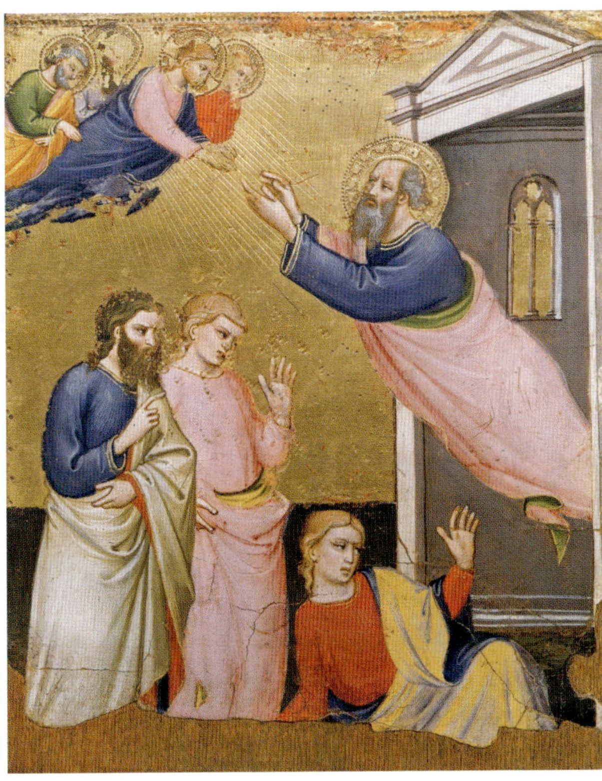

Francescuccio Ghissi, active 1345–1374
Christ Lamented by Angels, Adoration of the Child, ca. 1360
39.3 x 28.5 cm; Tempera and gold on wood panel
Pinacoteca; Room II; Inv. 40244

Ambrogio di Baldese, 1352–1429
Ascension of St. John, ca. 1390–1395
22.5 x 18.3 cm; Tempera and gold on wood panel
Pinacoteca; Room II; Inv. 40189

Niccolo di Tommaso, 1350–1380
St. Brigid and Nativity, before 1372
43.5 x 53.8 cm; Tempera and gold on wood panel
Pinacoteca; Room II; Inv. 40137

Master of the Ashmolean Predella, 1360–1390
Annunciation to Joachim, undated
38 x 34.9 cm; Tempera on wood panel
Pinacoteca; Room II; Inv. 40096

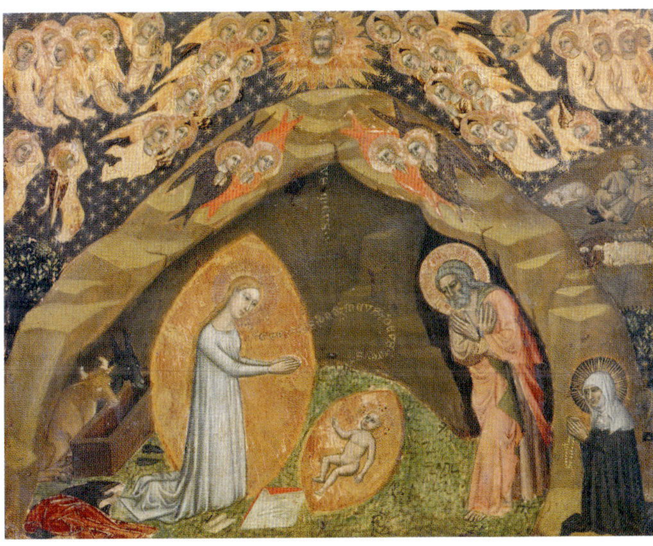

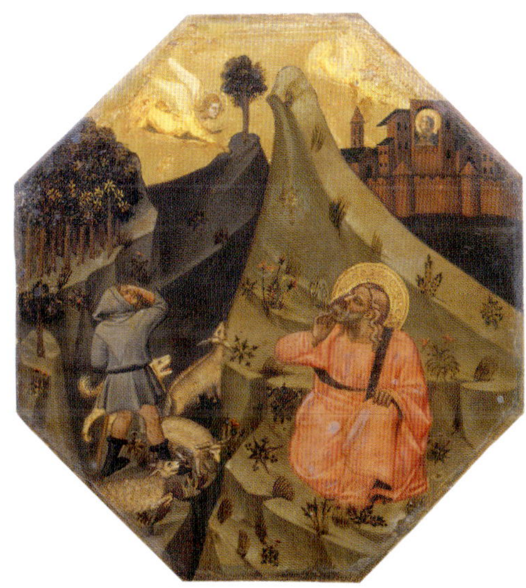

Lorenzo Monaco (Pietro di Giovanni)

Scenes from the Life of Saint Benedict

This small and narrow rectangular panel presents two episodes from the life of the founder of the Benedictine Order, St. Benedict of Nursia (ca. 480–547/560). On the left we see St. Benedict thwarting an attempt by Satan to lead a young monk into temptation. According to the Legenda Aurea, Benedict reported that this monk was seduced by a demon in the form of a small black child who pulled him out of the room by the hem of his garment. The saint recognized the demonic nature of the child and cast out the evil from the monk. The right half of the picture depicts the miraculous raising of a young brother killed by the collapse of a wall, again the work of the devil, during the building of the Benedictine abbey at Monte Cassino. This panel is thought to have once formed part of a larger altar dedicated to St. Benedict which was installed in the abbey of San Benedetto fuori di Porta a Pinti in Florence. The Florentine painter Lorenzo Monaco ("the Monk") was a member of the Camaldolese Order, which allied the Rule of St. Benedict to an eremitical existence. His works are remarkable for their realistic and unadorned, yet uniquely poetic, pictorial language whose emphasis is on clear communication of the pictorial content.

Lorenzo Monaco (Pietro di Giovanni), 1370–1423/24
***Scenes from the Life of St. Benedict*, before 1400–1415**
29.7 x 65 cm; Tempera on wood panel
Pinacoteca; Room II; Inv. 40193

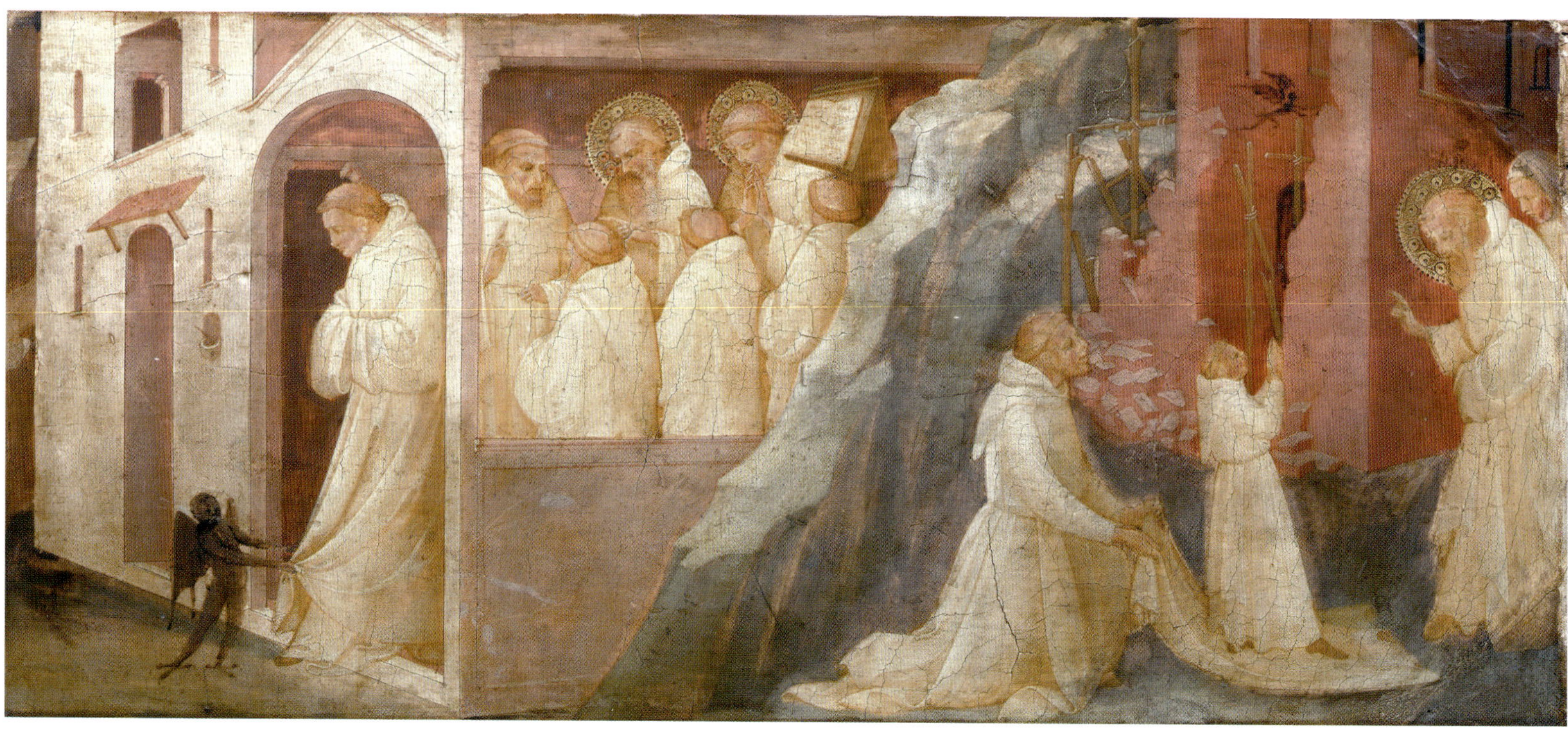

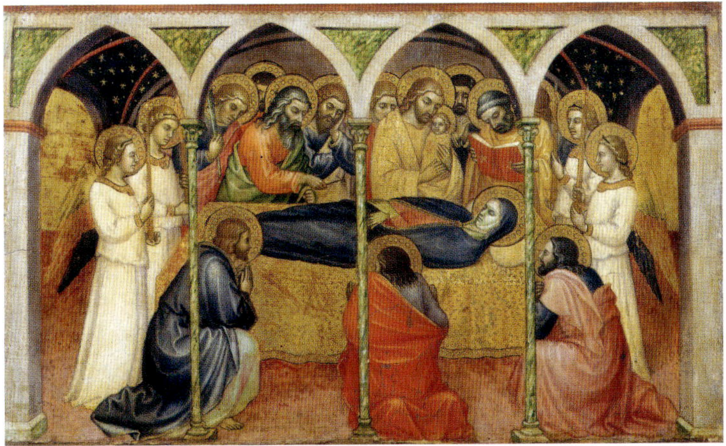

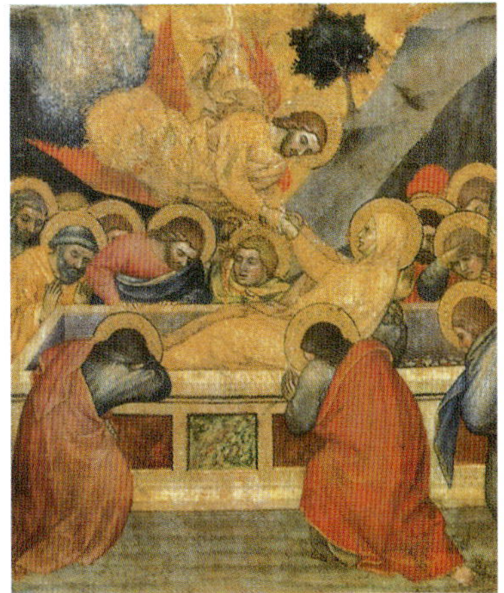

Taddeo di Bartolo, ca. 1362–1422
***Death of the Virgin*, ca. 1410**
34.5 x 56 cm; Tempera on wood panel
Pinacoteca; Room II; Inv. 40169

Taddeo di Bartolo, ca. 1362–1422
***Resurrection of the Virgin*, ca. 1410**
34 x 29.5 cm; Tempera on wood panel
Pinacoteca; Room II; Inv. 40155

Gentile da Fabriano, ca. 1370–1427
***Annunciation*, ca. 1425**
40. 6 x 48.4; Tempera on wood panel
Pinacoteca; Room II; Inv. 40601

Lorenzo Monaco (Pietro di Giovanni), 1370–1423/24
***St. Anthony and St. Paul*, before 1400–1410**
22.3 x 24.6; Tempera on wood panel
Pinacoteca; Room II; Inv. 40214

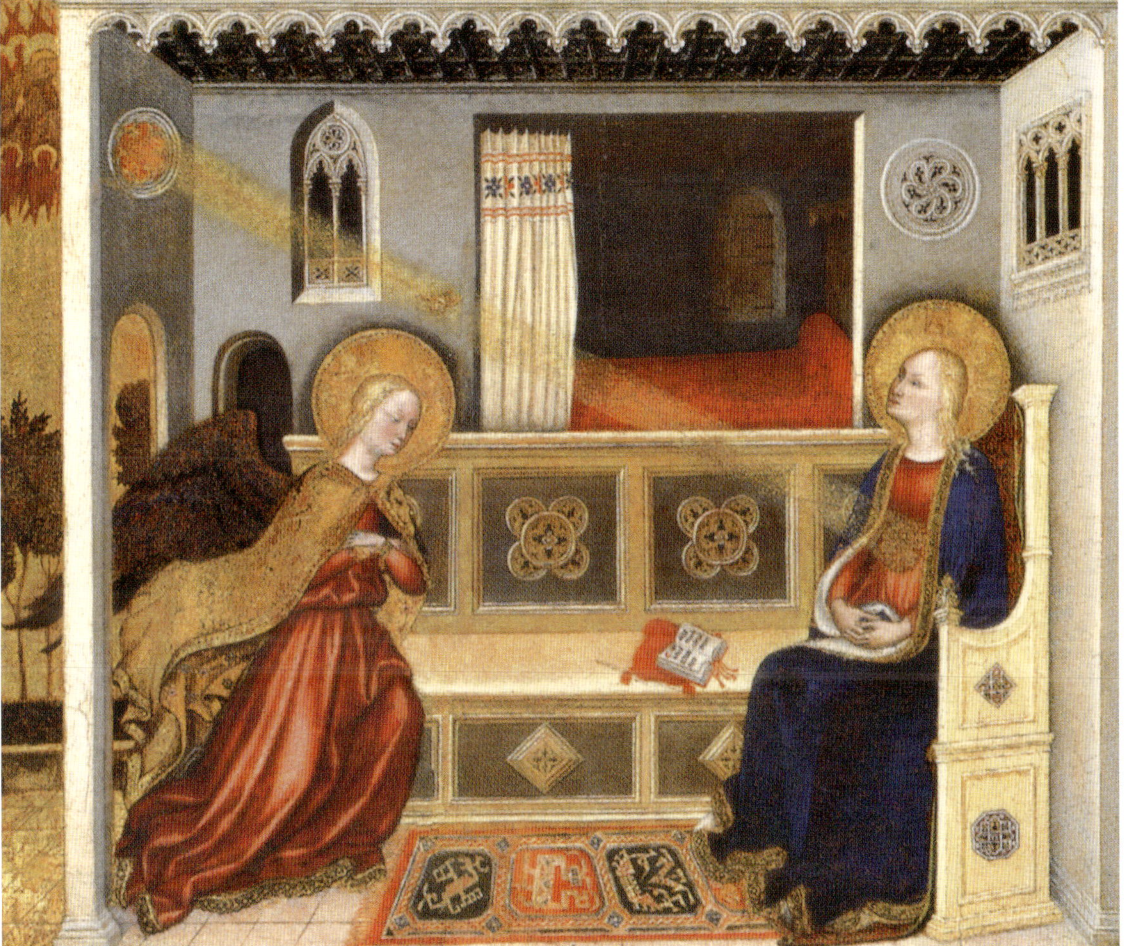

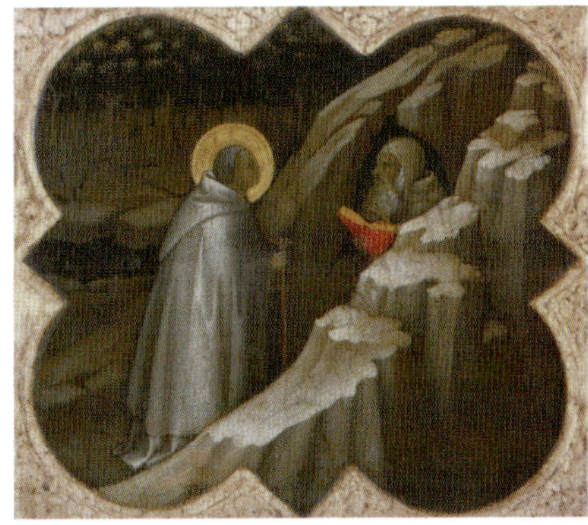

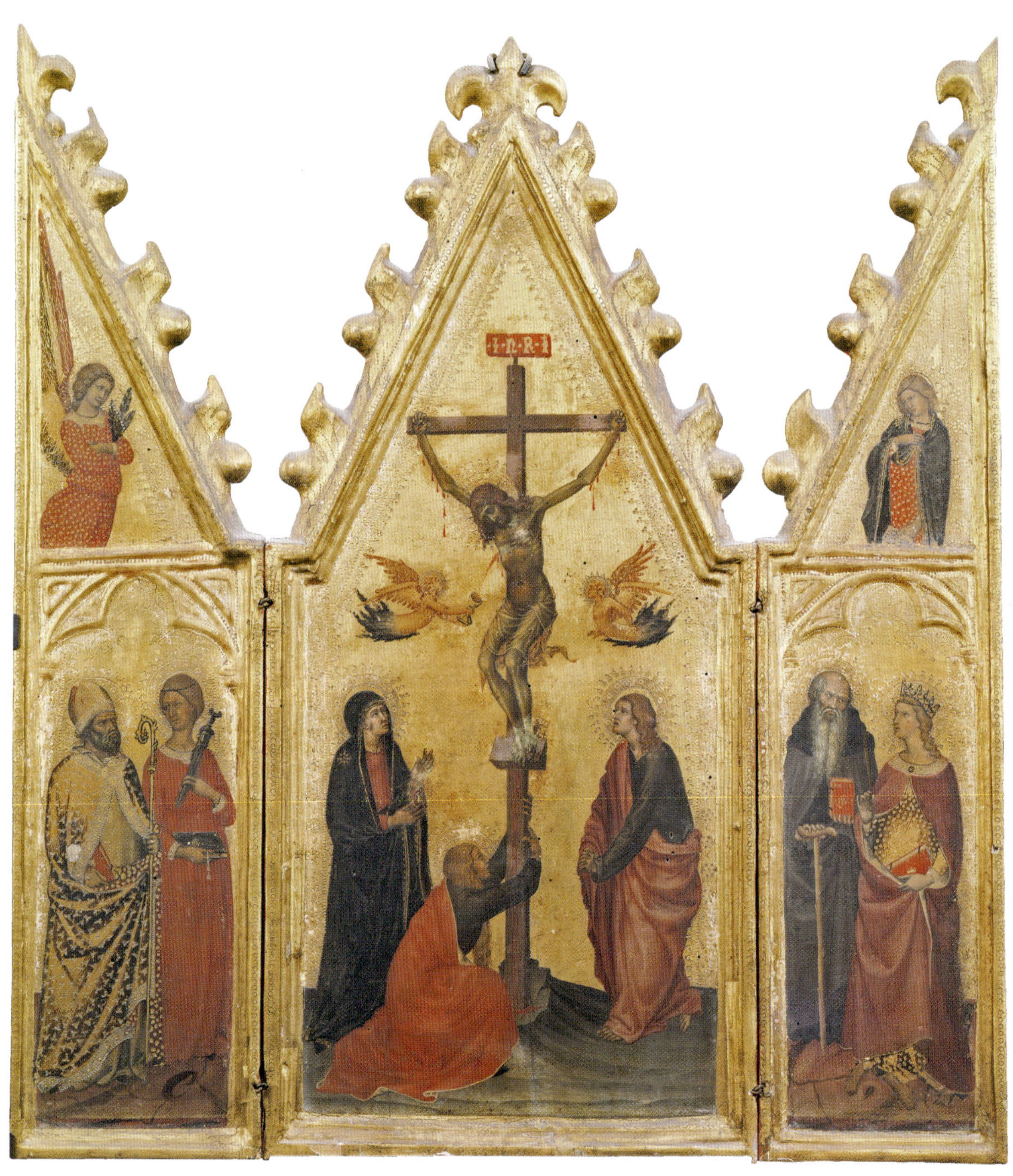

Paolo di Giovanni Fei, active 1372–1410
***Crucifixion and Saints and Annunciation*, 1375–1395**
65 x 29.7 cm; Tempera and oil on wood panel
Pinacoteca; Room II; Inv. 40220

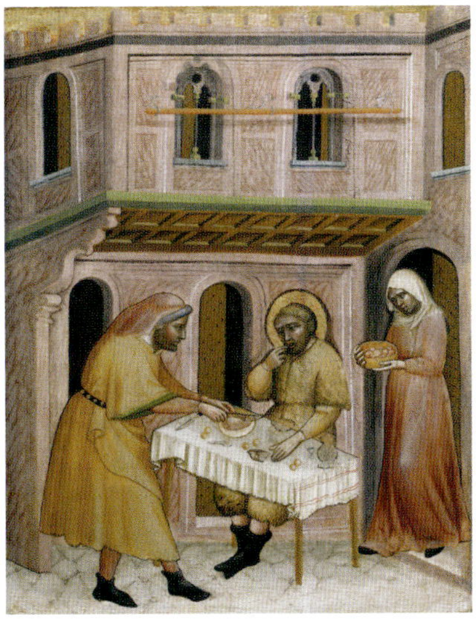

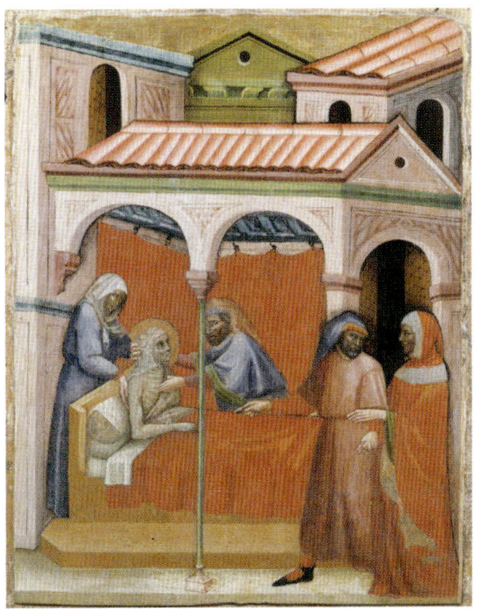

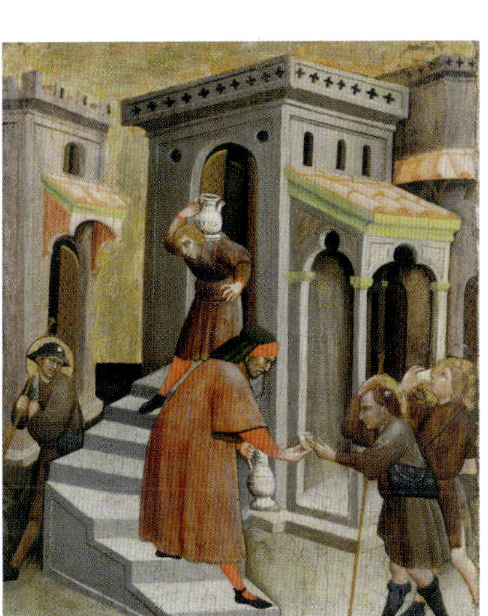

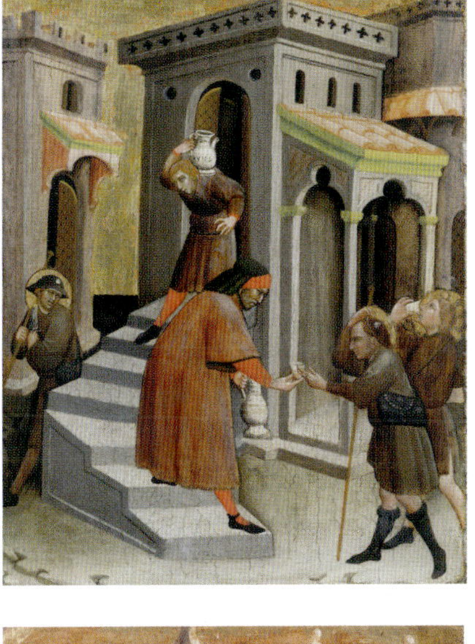

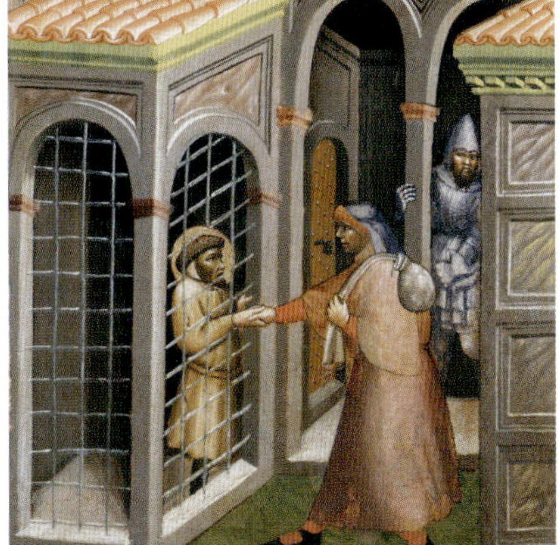

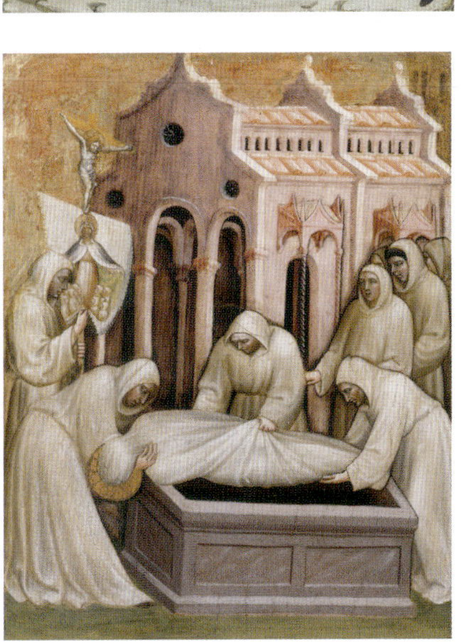

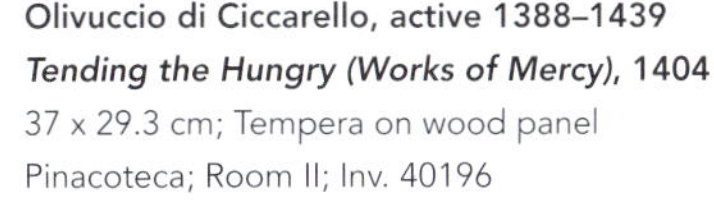

Olivuccio di Ciccarello, active 1388–1439
***Tending the Hungry (Works of Mercy)*, 1404**
37 x 29.3 cm; Tempera on wood panel
Pinacoteca; Room II; Inv. 40196

Olivuccio di Ciccarello, active 1388–1439
***Visiting the Sick (Works of Mercy)*, 1404**
37.4 x 29.5 cm; Tempera on wood panel
Pinacoteca; Room II; Inv. 40199

Olivuccio di Ciccarello, active 1388–1439
***Clothing the Naked (Works of Mercy)*, 1404**
37.5 x 29.3 cm; Tempera on wood panel
Pinacoteca; Room II; Inv. 40198

Olivuccio di Ciccarello, active 1388–1439
***Tending the Thirsty and Housing the Pilgrims (Works of Mercy)*, 1404**
36.6 x 29.3 cm; Tempera on wood panel
Pinacoteca; Room II; Inv. 40197

Olivuccio di Ciccarello, active 1388–1439
***Visiting the Prisoners (Works of Mercy)*, 1404**
37 x 29.2 cm; Tempera on wood panel
Pinacoteca; Room II; Inv. 40200

Olivuccio di Ciccarello, active 1388–1439
***Burying the Dead (Works of Mercy)*, 1404**
36.7 x 29.4 cm; Tempera on wood panel
Pinacoteca; Room II; Inv. 40201

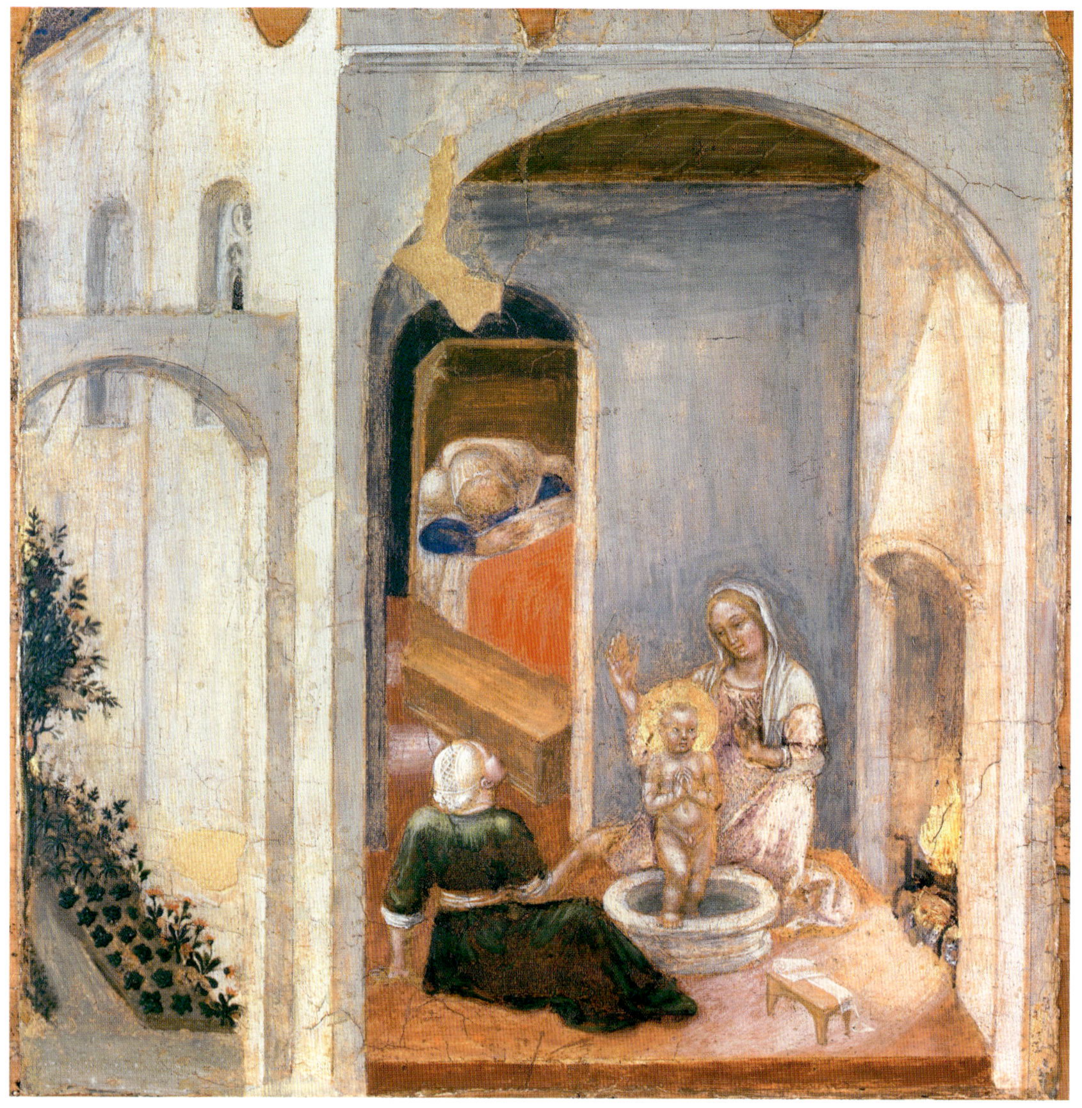

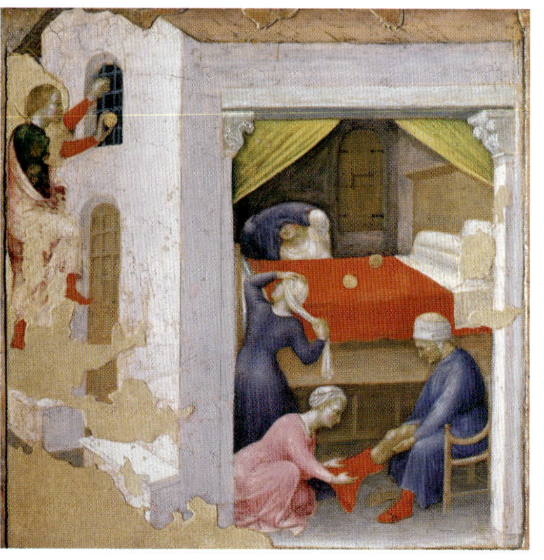

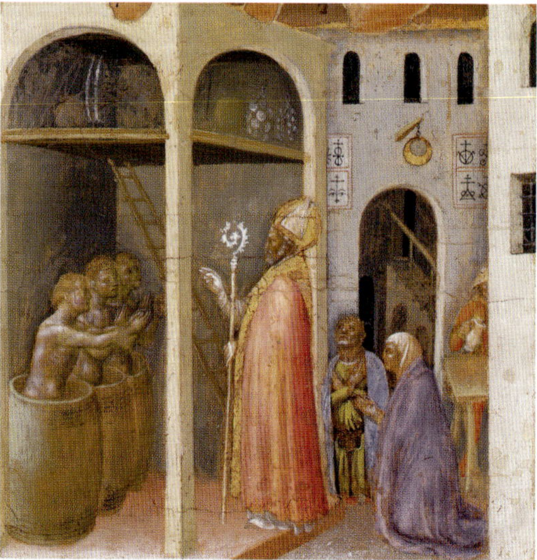

Gentile da Fabriano, ca. 1370–1427
***Quaratesi Polyptych: Birth of St. Nicholas of Bari*, 1425**
35.5 x 35.5 cm; Tempera on wood panel
Pinacoteca; Room II; Inv. 40247

Gentile da Fabriano, ca. 1370–1427
***Quaratesi Polyptych: The Miracle of the Three Maidens*, 1425**
35.8 x 36.1 cm; Tempera on wood panel
Pinacoteca; Room II; Inv. 40248

Gentile da Fabriano, ca. 1370–1427
***Quaratesi Polyptych: St. Nicholas of Bari Raising Three Boys from the Dead*, 1425**
36.5 x 36.5 cm; Tempera on wood panel
Pinacoteca; Room II; Inv. 40250

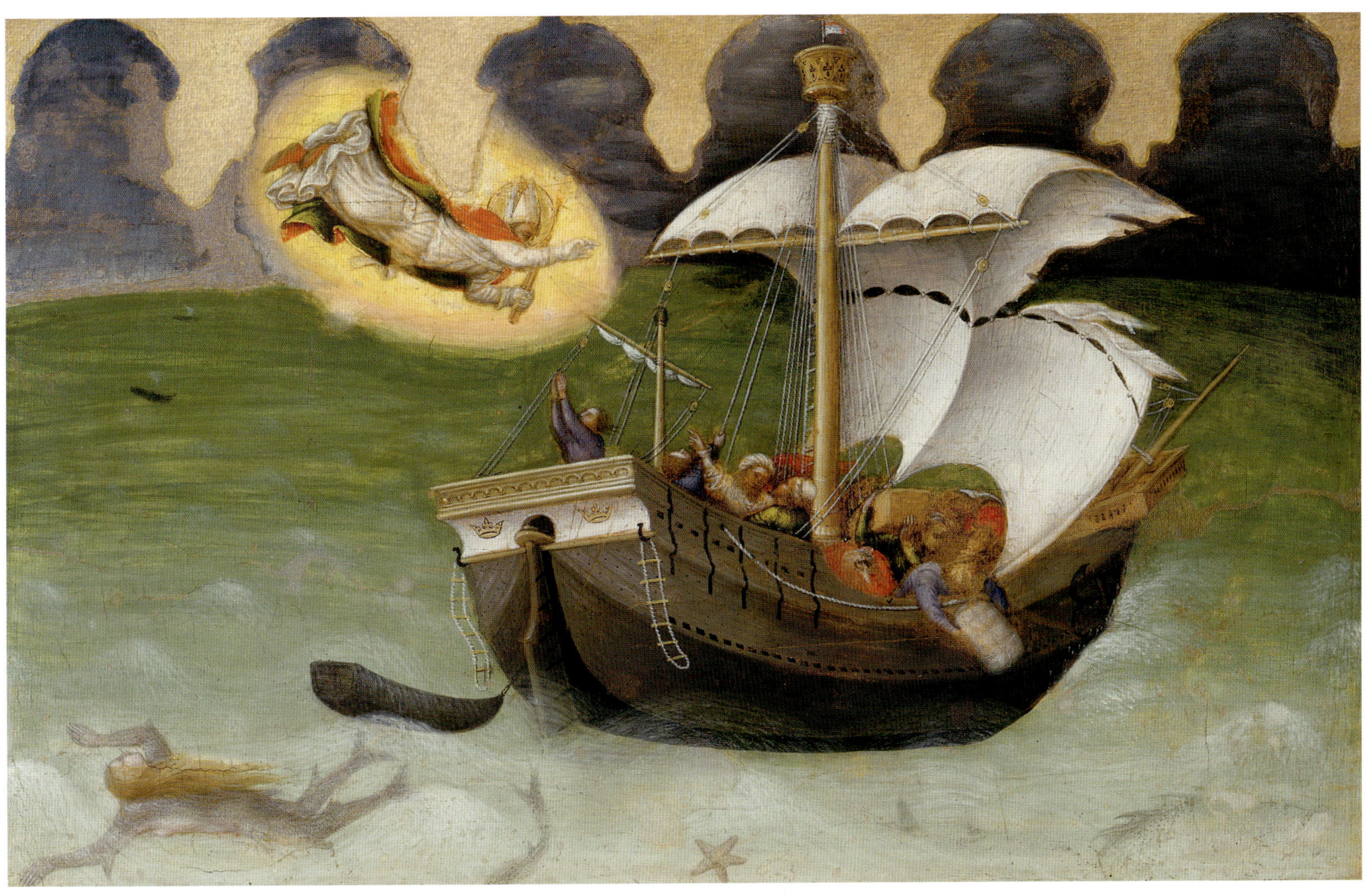

Gentile da Fabriano

Quaratesi Polyptch: St. Nicholas Appeases the Tempest of the Sea

Despite its small format, this panel is one of the best-known works by the Italian painter Gentile da Fabriano. This is due above all to the extremely vibrant and realistic manner in which Gentile tells the story of this miracle performed by St. Nicholas of Bari, the patron saint of sailors. Like the saint, the artist also had an extremely turbulent life, which took him from his hometown Fabriano via Venice, Brescia, Florence, Siena, and Orvieto to Rome, where he died just a few months after his arrival. Among Gentile's Florentine works is the Quaratesi Polyptych, so named after the family who commissioned it. This was completed in 1425 for the high altar of San Niccolò Oltrarno and is now split between several museums. One of the scenes from the predella depicts the miraculous rescue of a ship in distress. Gentile depicts the ship as a typical merchantman of the day being tossed about in the wildly foaming sea with a torn mainsail and listing heavily. The sailors are agitatedly trying to throw some of the precious cargo overboard while one of them grapples with the ropes in an attempt to stabilize the mast. Meanwhile a traveler appeals for help to St. Nicholas, who provides the longed-for assistance. The painter has added various small details of his own such as the ship's boat rocking in the water and the rope ladders. One rather magical touch is the mermaid swimming in the foreground who looks on with astonishment as the miracle unfolds.

Gentile da Fabriano, ca. 1370–1427
***Quaratesi Polyptych: St. Nicholas Saving a Ship from the Tempest*, 1425**
38.2 x 62 cm; Tempera on wood panel
Pinacoteca; Room II; Inv. 40249

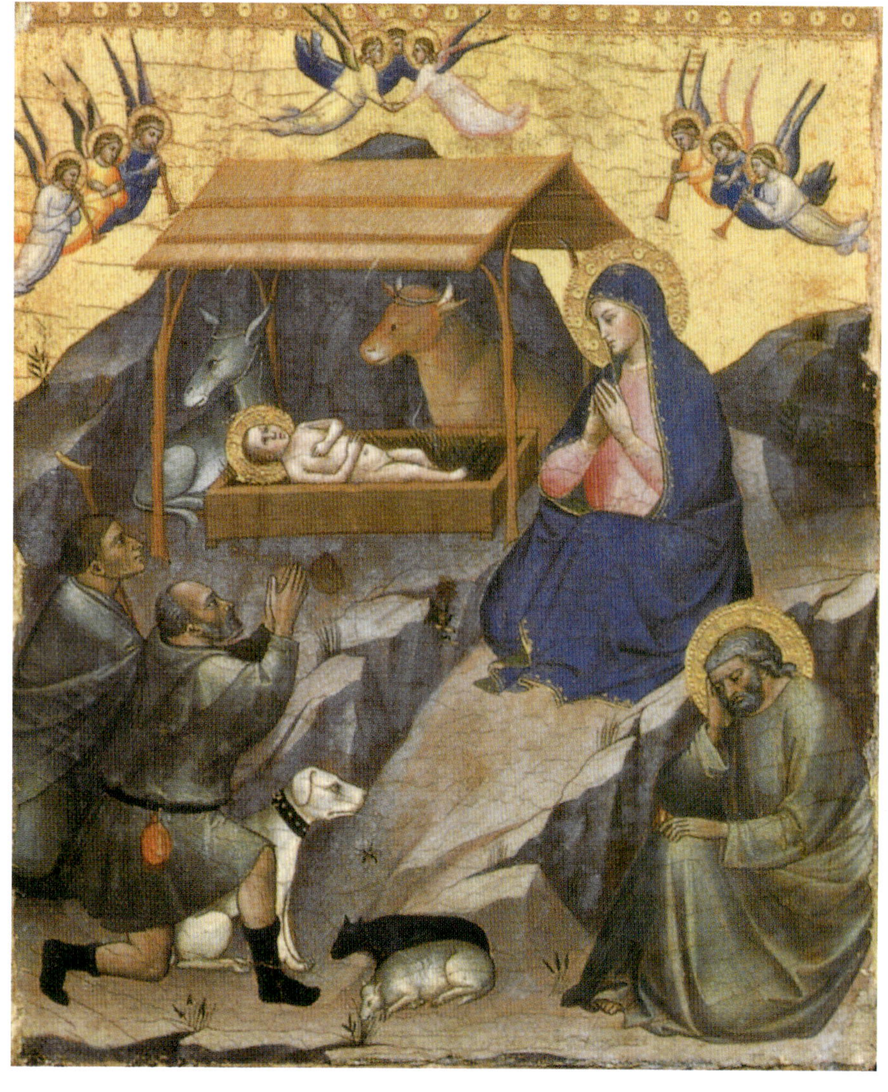

Mariotto di Nardo, active ca. 1389–1424
***Nativity*, ca. 1400**
34.3 x 28.5 cm; Tempera on wood panel
Pinacoteca; Room II; Inv. 40102

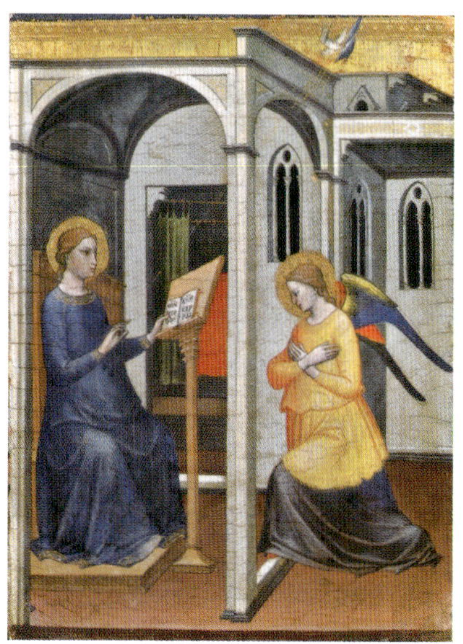

Mariotto di Nardo, active ca. 1389–1424
***Annunciation*, ca. 1400**
34.3 x 25.5 cm; Tempera on wood panel
Pinacoteca; Room II; Inv. 40101

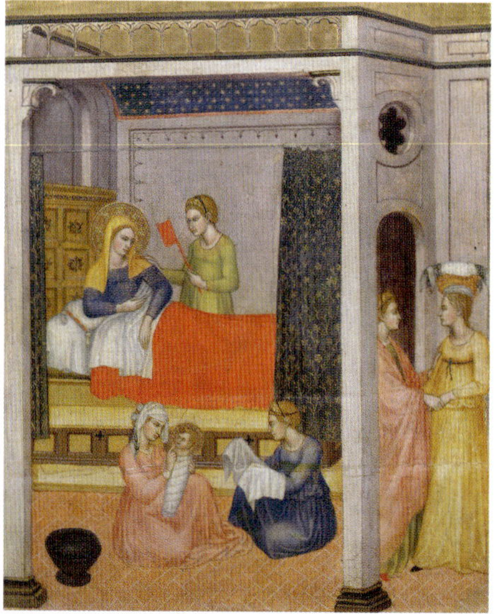

Gregorio di Cecco di Luca, early 14th century
***Nativity of the Virgin*, ca. 1400**
41 x 33.5 cm; Tempera and gold on wood panel
Pinacoteca; Room II; Inv. 40187

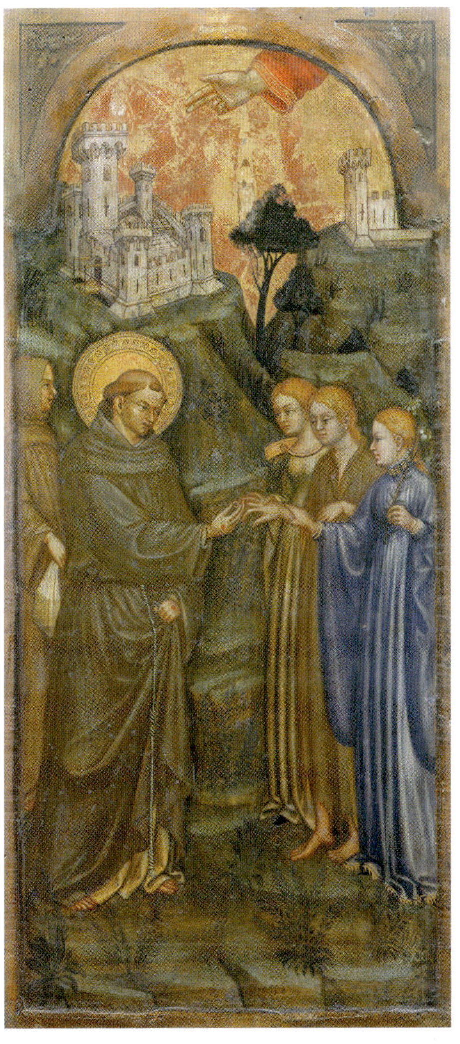

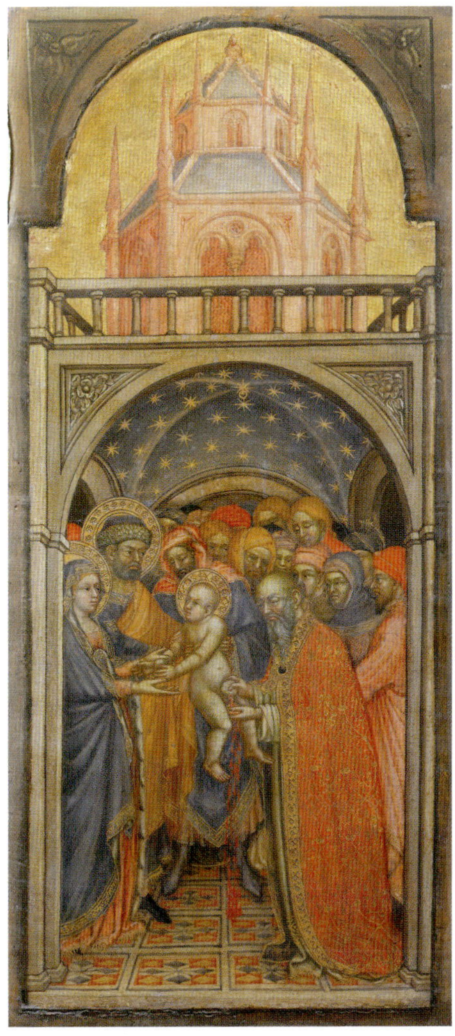

Ottaviano Nelli, 1375–1444
***Mystical Marriage of St. Francis*, ca. 1425**
70.1 x 31.8 cm; Tempera on cambered wood panel
Pinacoteca; Room II; Inv. 40213

Ottaviano Nelli, 1375–1444
***Circumcision*, ca. 1425**
70 x 31.9 cm; Tempera on cambered wood panel
Pinacoteca; Room II; Inv. 40218

Mariotto di Nardo, active ca. 1389–1424
***Miracle of St. Nicholas*, 1389–1424**
35.5 x 54.8 cm; Tempera on wood panel
Pinacoteca; Room II; Inv. 40097

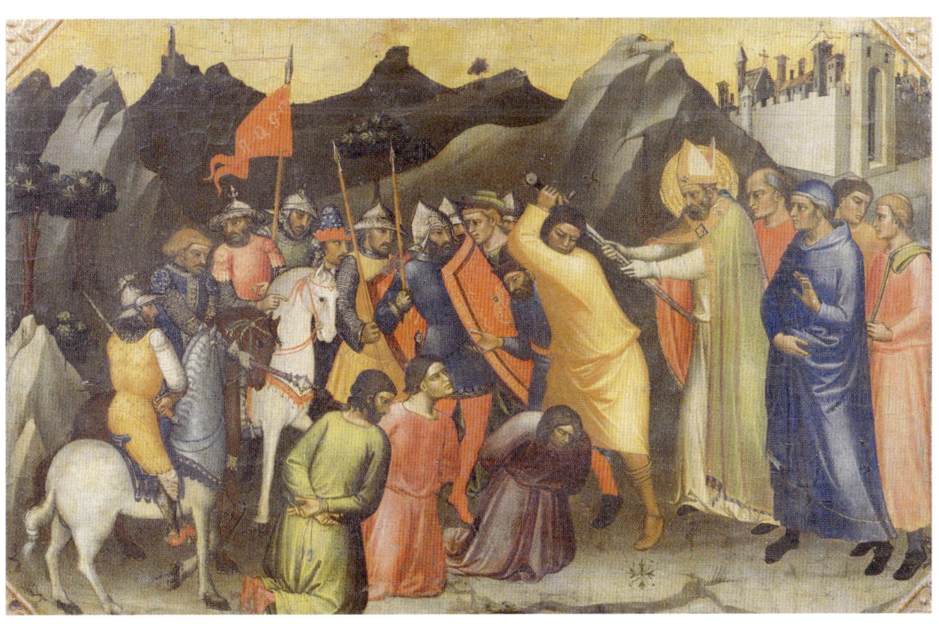

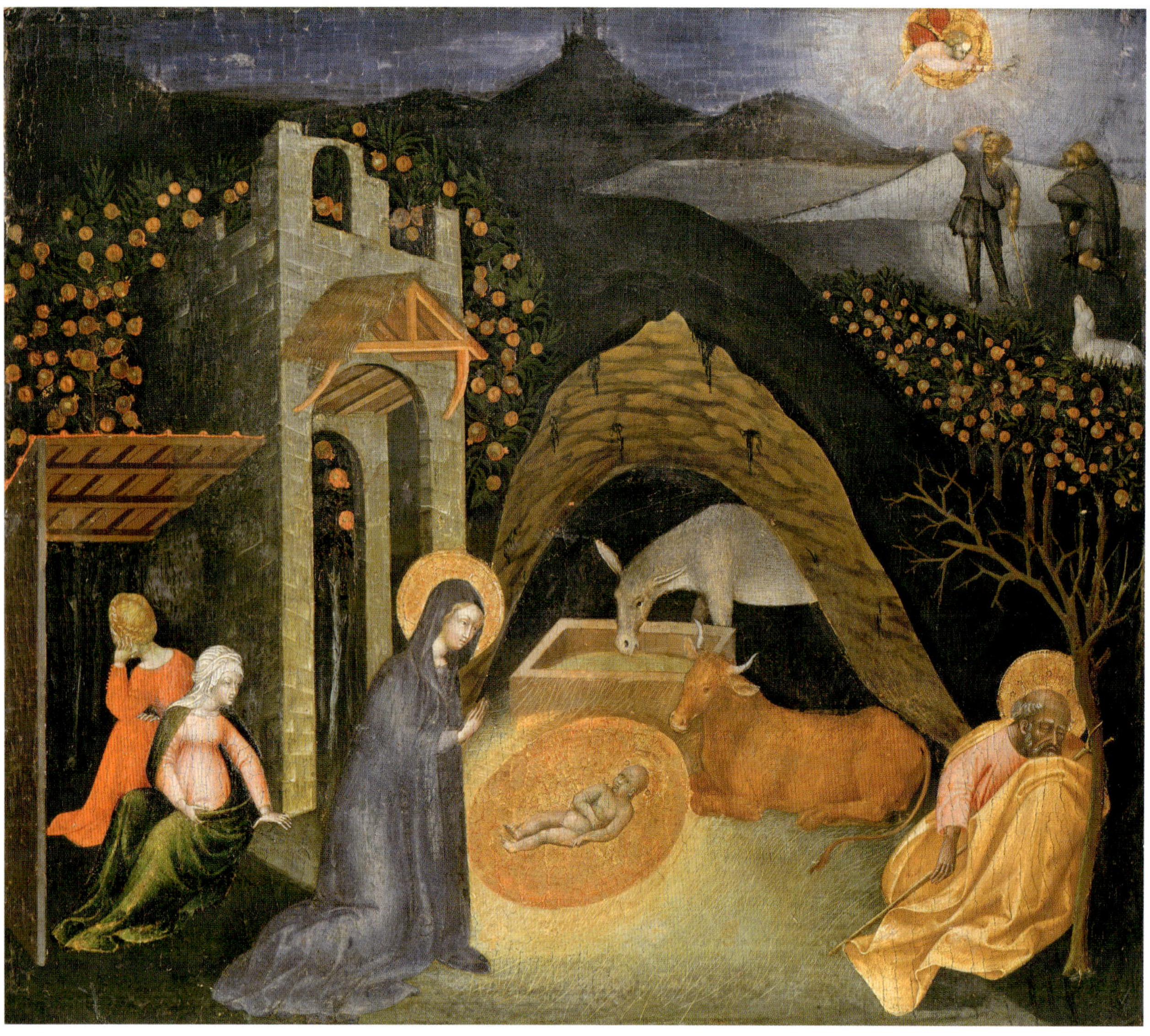

Giovanni di Paolo

The Nativity

Giovanni di Paolo stands out among painters of the Sienese school of the Quattrocento for his highly individual style evident in this panel of the birth of Christ. Once part of a polyptych, it was split up and is now distributed between museums all over the world. Giovanni di Paolo has given the Annunication scene a nocturnal setting, which is very unusual. It is illuminated solely by means of light sources intrinsic to the subject—the celestial rays emitted by the Infant Jesus and the bright opening of the skies around the angel as he announces the birth to the shepherds. This device has enabled the painter to lend the scene an otherworldly quality. Many of the realistically depicted elements in the picture also have symbolic connotations. The ox and the donkey are not just typical beasts of the stable but are also, according to the prophecies of Isaiah (Isaiah 1:3), specifically associated with the Savior. The thornless rosebushes that border the stable ruins and the entire clearing stand for Mary's virginity and, due to their red color, can also be interpreted as a symbol of Christ's Passion. Furthermore, roses flowering in December symbolize the birth of Christ. By contrast, the tree against which Joseph is sleeping is completely devoid of leaves. Among the witnesses to the miraculous birth of Christ are two midwives, one of who is shown, unusually, from the rear.

Giovanni di Paolo, 1395/1400–1482
***The Nativity*, ca. 1440**
38.8 x 45.7 cm; Tempera on wood panel
Pinacoteca; Room II; Inv. 40132

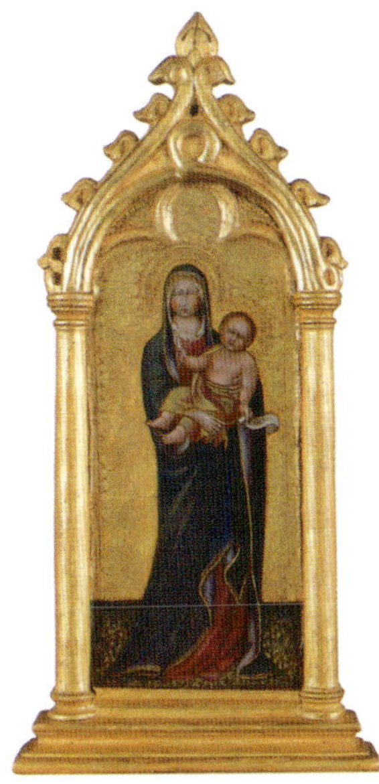

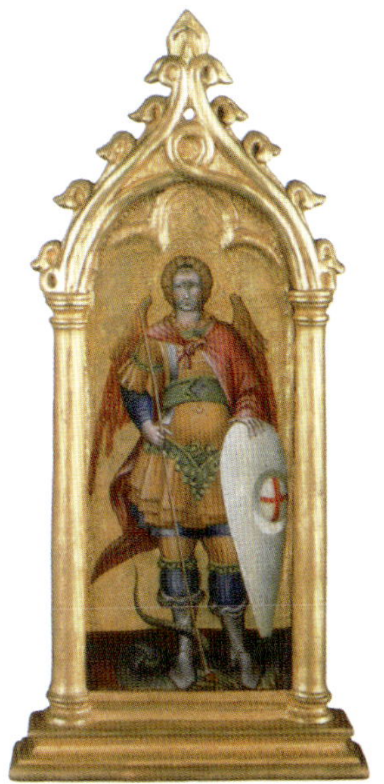

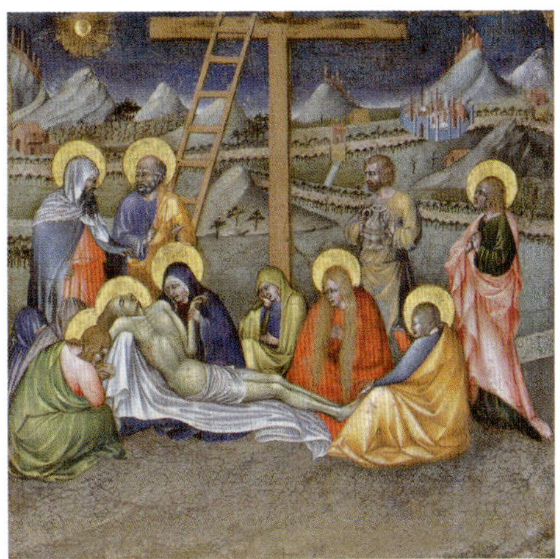

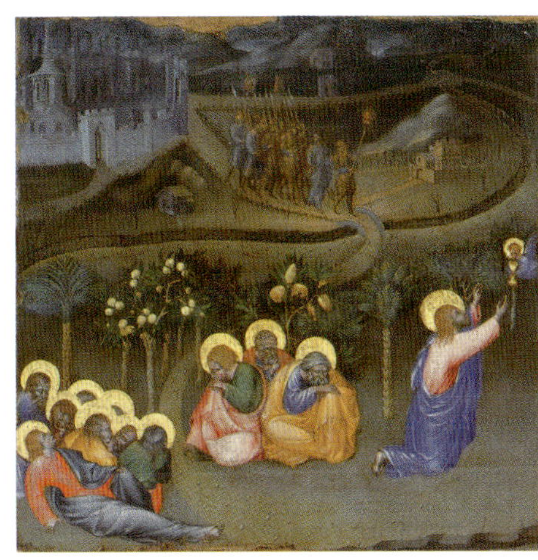

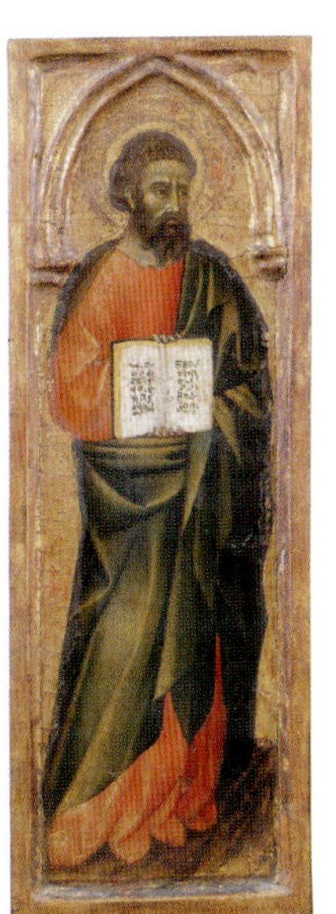

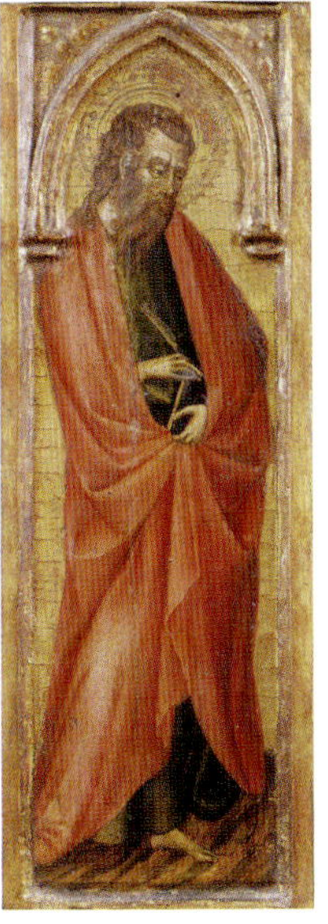

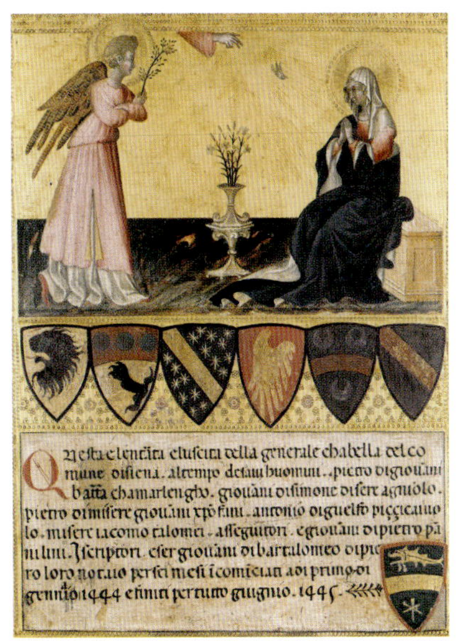

Giovanni di Paolo, 1395/1400–1482
***Madonna and Child*, ca. 1436–1440**
19 x 8.5 cm; Tempera on wood panel
Pinacoteca; Room II; Inv. 40125

Giovanni di Paolo, 1395/1400–1482
***Archangel Michael*, ca. 1436–1440**
18.5 x 8.2 cm; Tempera on wood panel
Pinacoteca; Room II; Inv. 40128

Giovanni di Paolo, 1395/1400–1482
***Lamentation*, ca. 1440–1445**
32.5 x 33.5 cm; Tempera on wood panel
Pinacoteca; Room II; Inv. 40124

Giovanni di Paolo, 1395/1400–1482
***Prayer in the Garden Gethsemane*, undated**
32 x 32.5 cm; Tempera on wood panel
Pinacoteca; Room II; Inv. 40129

Giovanni di Paolo, 1395/1400–1482
***St. Matthew*, ca. 1450–1460**
39.3 x 14.2 cm; Tempera and gold on wood panel
Pinacoteca; Room II; Inv. 40127

Giovanni di Paolo, 1395/1400–1482
***Evangelist*, ca. 1450–1460**
40 x 14.2 cm; Tempera and gold on wood panel
Pinacoteca; Room II; Inv. 40126

Giovanni di Paolo, 1395/1400–1482
***The Annunciation*, 1445**
48.5 x 35.5 cm; Tempera on wood panel
Pinacoteca; Room II; Inv. 40131

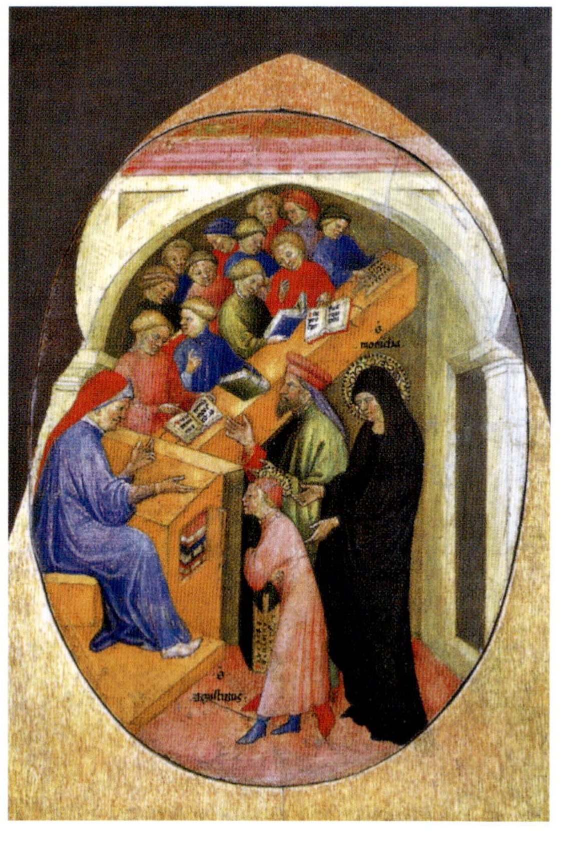

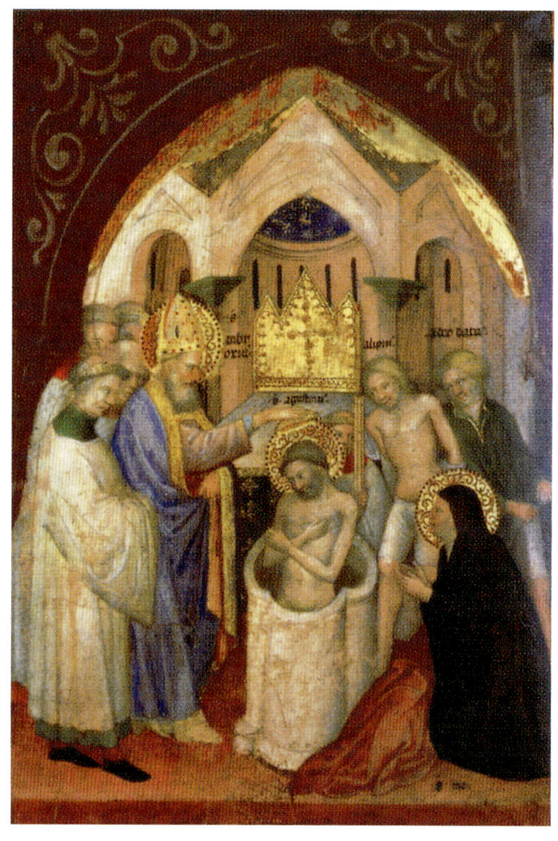

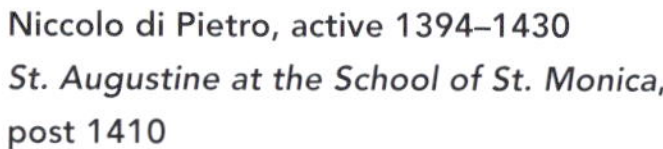

Niccolo di Pietro, active 1394–1430
***St. Augustine at the School of St. Monica*, post 1410**
40 x 27.6 cm; Tempera on wood panel
Pinacoteca; Room II; Inv. 40205

Niccolo di Pietro, active 1394–1430
***Baptism of St. Ambrogio*, post 1410**
39.8 x 27.4 cm; Tempera on wood panel
Pinacoteca; Room II; Inv. 40202

Niccolo di Pietro, active 1394–1430
***St. Augustine with Disciples*, post 1410**
39.7 x 27.4 cm; Tempera on wood panel
Pinacoteca; Room II; Inv. 40203

Niccolo di Pietro, active 1394–1430
***St. Augustine Teaching*, post 1410**
33.7 x 26 cm; Tempera on wood panel
Pinacoteca; Room II; Inv. 40206

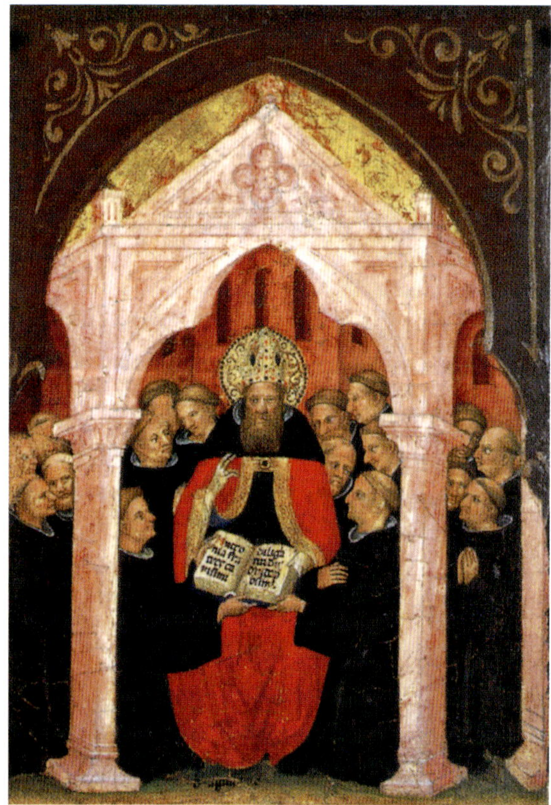

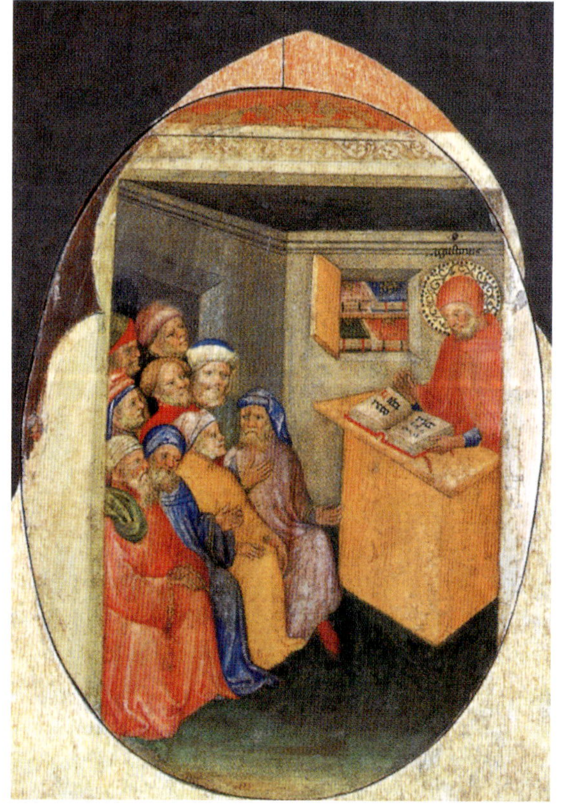

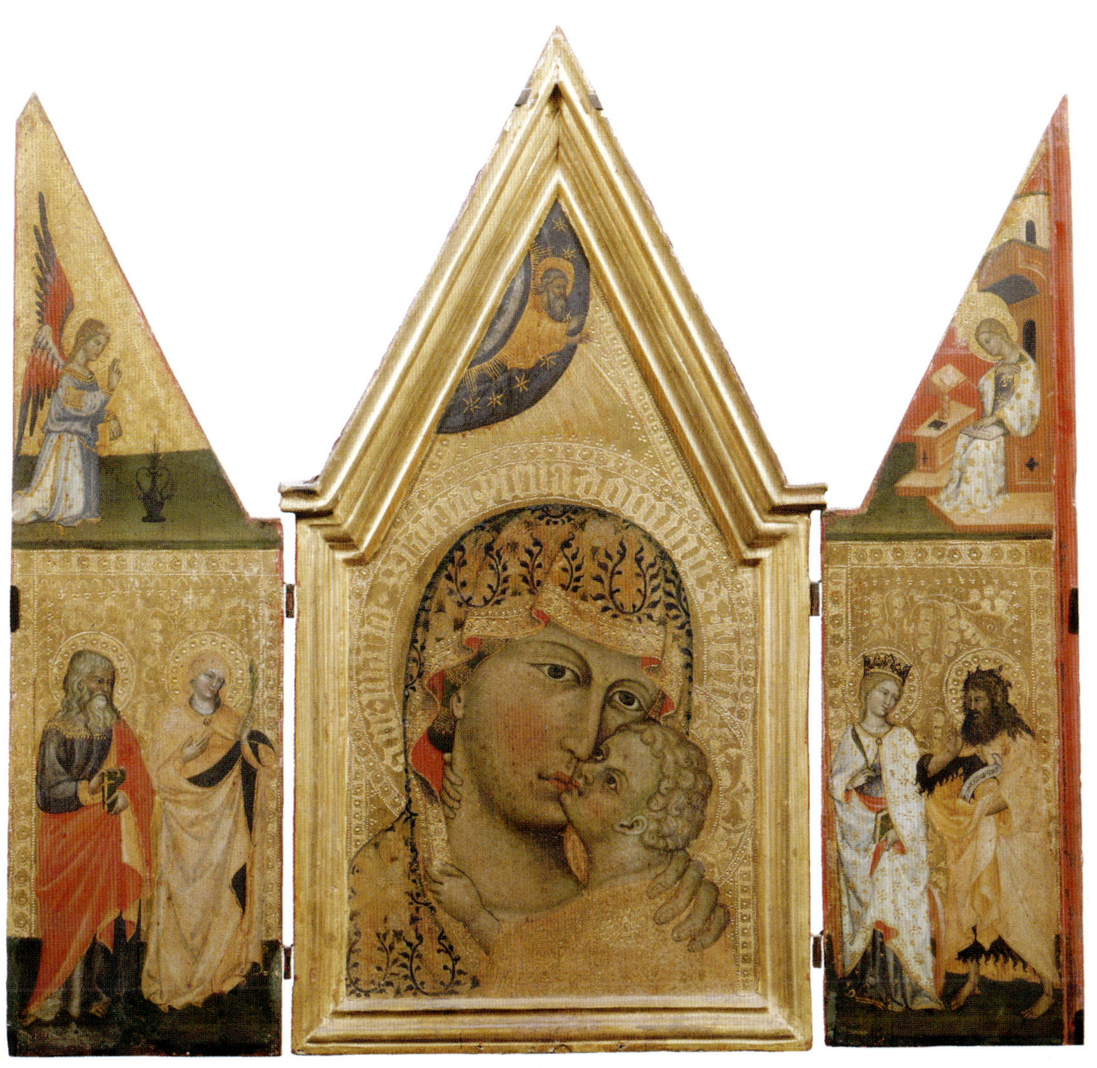

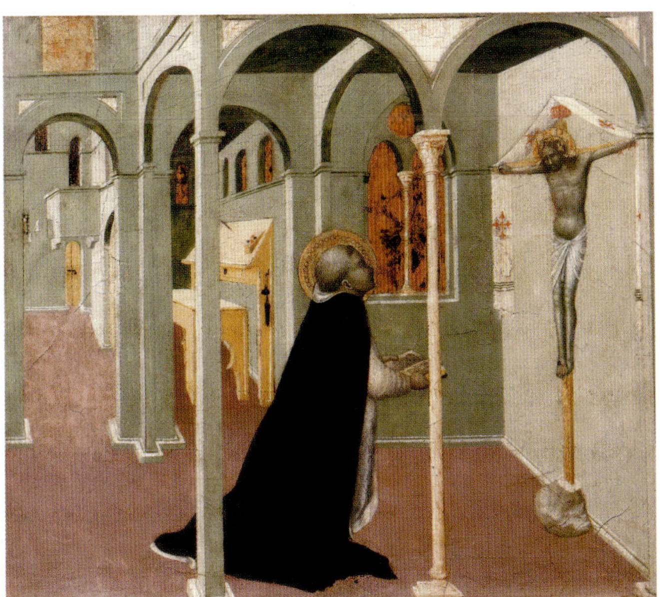

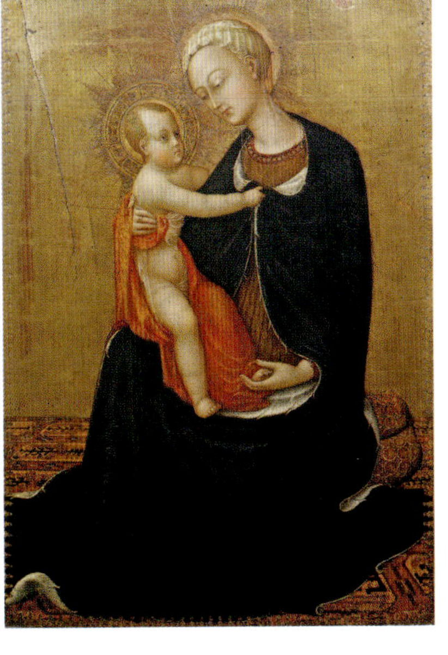

Master of the Brancacci Triptych, active early 15th century
***Madonna with Saints*, undated**
56.5 x 29.3 cm; Tempera and gold on wood panel
Pinacoteca; Room II; Inv. 40099

Sassetta (Stefano di Giovanni), ca. 1400–1450
***Vision of St. Thomas Aquinas*, 1423–1450**
25 x 28.8 cm; Tempera on wood panel
Pinacoteca; Room II; Inv. 40234

Sassetta (Stefano di Giovanni), ca. 1400–1450
***Madonna and Child*, ca. 1435**
73 x 54.5 cm; Tempera on wood panel
Pinacoteca; Room II; Inv. 42139

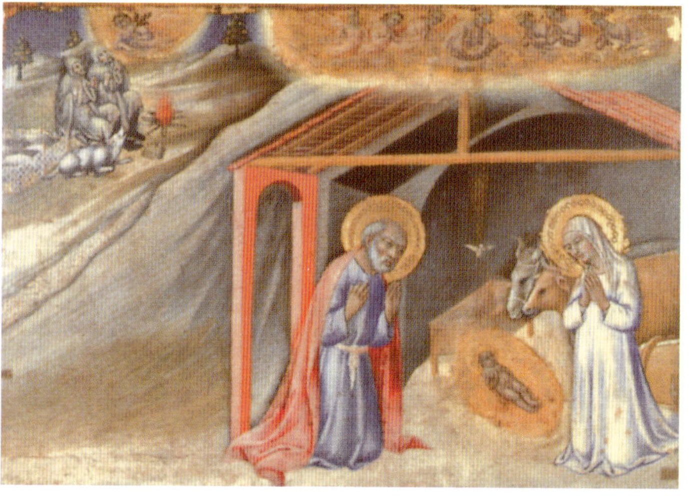

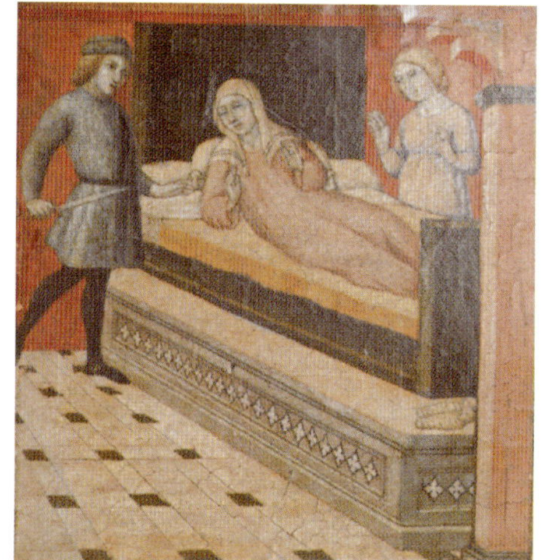

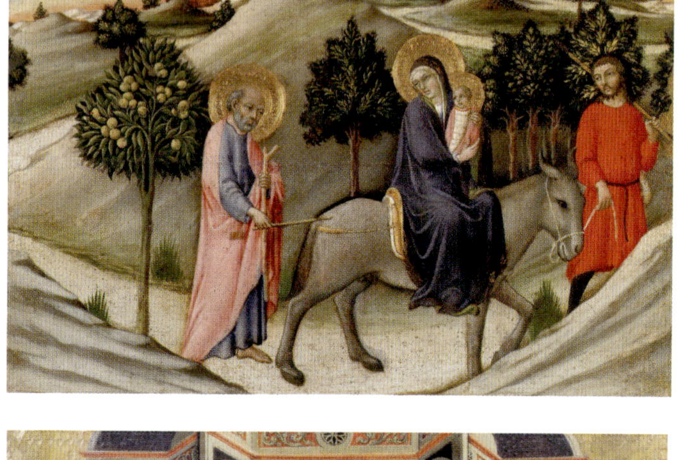

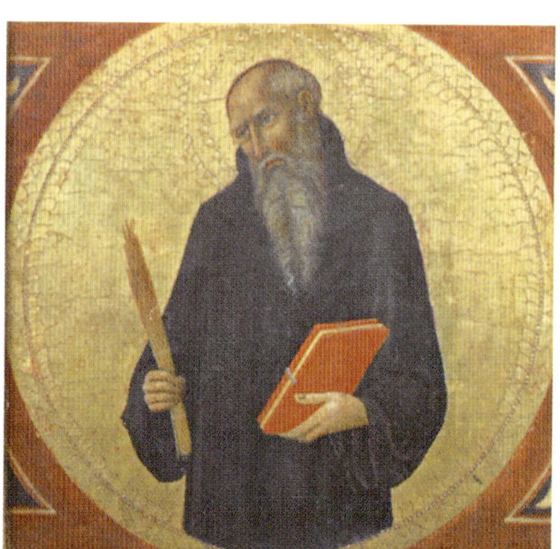

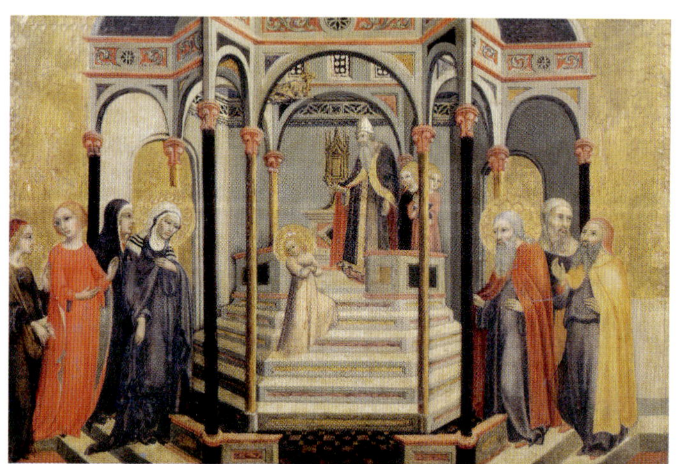

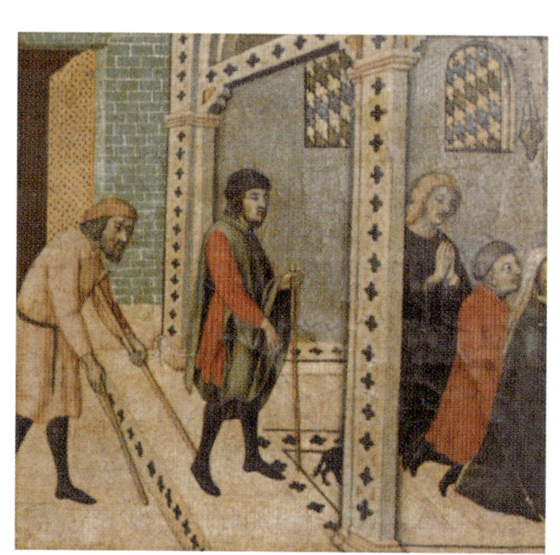

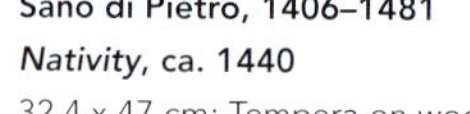

Sano di Pietro, 1406–1481
***Nativity*, ca. 1440**
32.4 x 47 cm; Tempera on wood panel
Pinacoteca; Room II; Inv. 40144

Sano di Pietro, 1406–1481
***Miracle of St. Peter*, before 1440**
23.2 x 21.7 cm; Tempera on wood panel
Pinacoteca; Room II; Inv. 40139

Sano di Pietro, 1406–1481
***Flight into Egypt*, ca. 1440**
33.2 x 49.7 cm; Tempera on wood panel
Pinacoteca; Room II; Inv. 40145

Sano di Pietro, 1406–1481
***St. Benedict*, before 1460**
36 x 33.5 cm; Tempera on wood panel
Pinacoteca; Room II; Inv. 40134

Sano di Pietro, 1406–1481
***The Virgin at the Temple*, before 1448**
31.5 x 47.5 cm; Tempera on wood panel
Pinacoteca; Room II; Inv. 40136

Sano di Pietro, 1406–1481
***Prayer at the Tomb of St. Peter*, before 1440**
23.3 x 22.8 cm; Tempera on wood panel
Pinacoteca; Room II; Inv. 40142

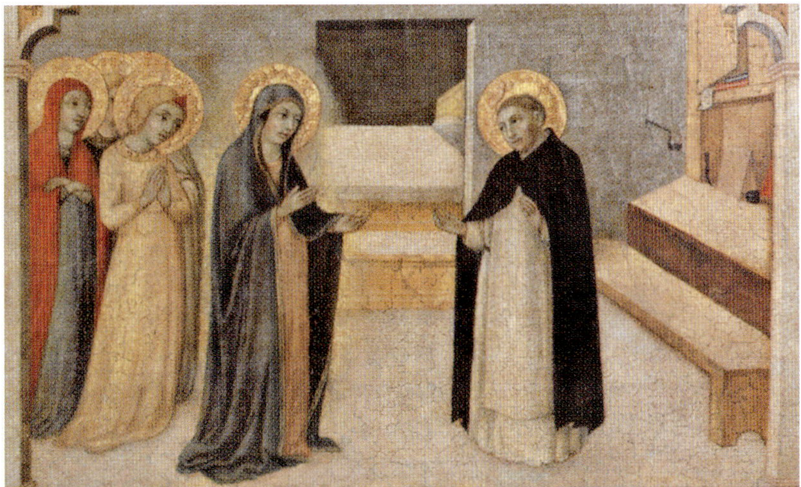

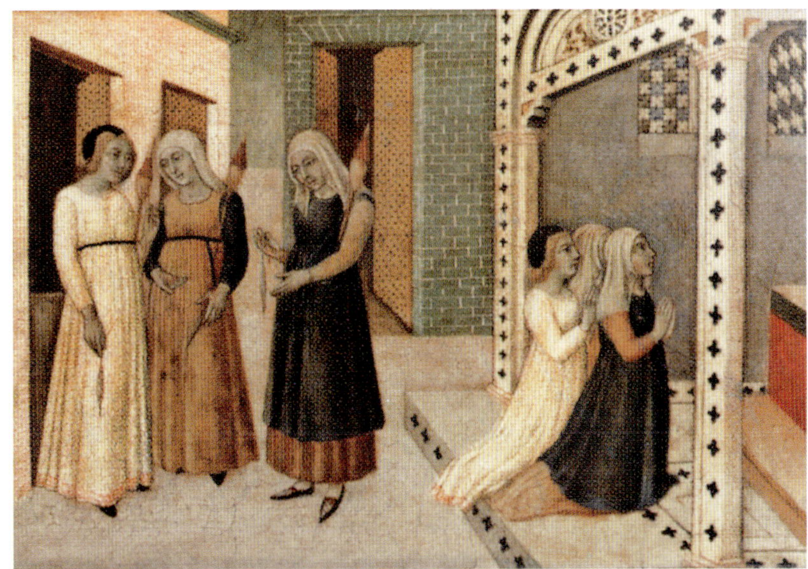

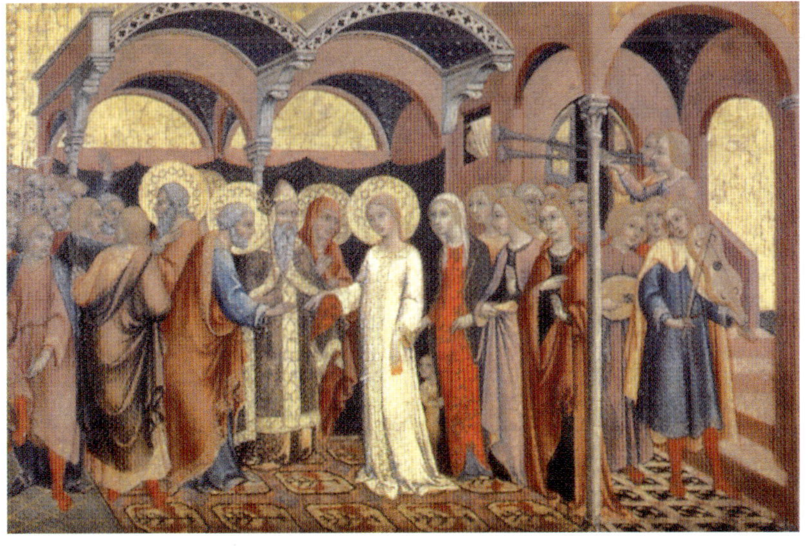

Sano di Pietro, 1406–1481
***The Virgin Appears to St. Peter*, before 1440**
22.7 x 36.7 cm; Tempera on wood panel
Pinacoteca; Room II; Inv. 40140

Sano di Pietro, 1406–1481
***Miracle of the Spindle*, before 1440**
23.3 x 36.7 cm; Tempera on wood panel
Pinacoteca; Room II; Inv. 40141

Sano di Pietro, 1406–1481
***Marriage of the Virgin*, before 1448**
32 x 46 cm; Tempera on wood panel
Pinacoteca; Room II; Inv. 40138

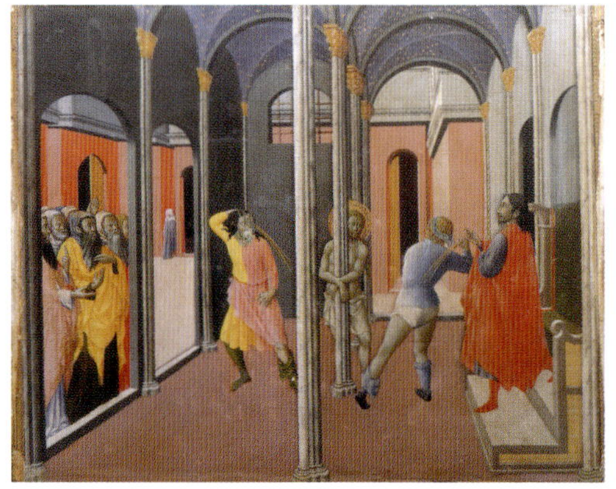

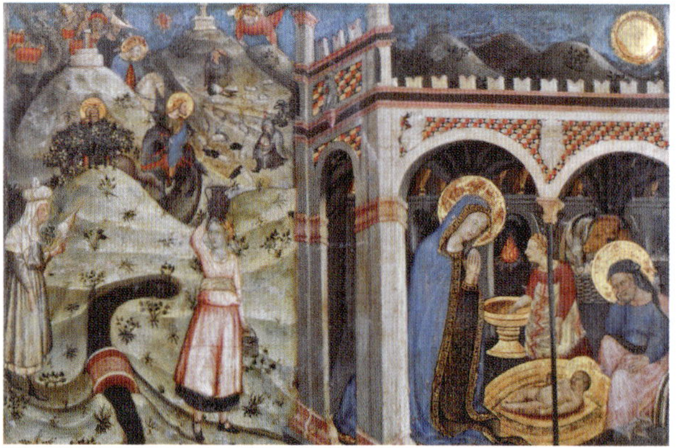

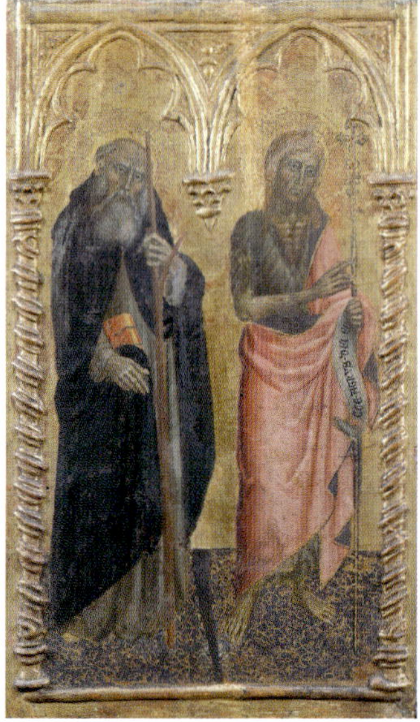

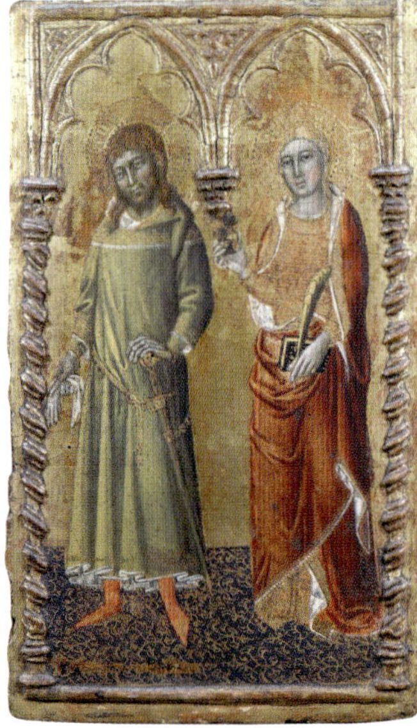

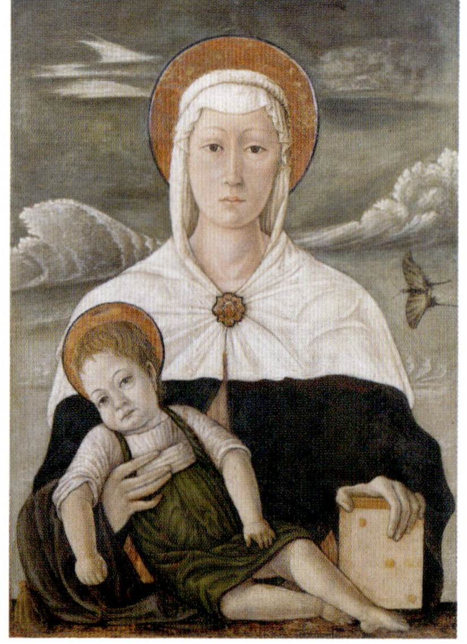

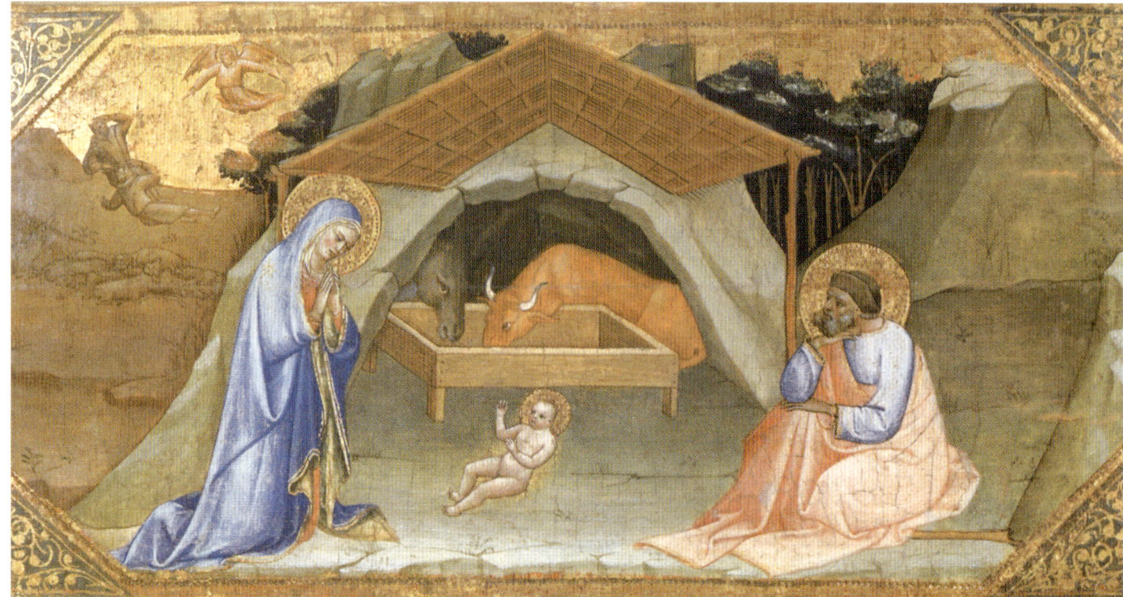

Master of the Osservanza, 1345–1440
***Flagellation*, ca. 1435**
36.7 x 46 cm; Tempera on wood panel
Pinacoteca; Room II; Inv. 40232

Marche School, mid-15th century
***Nativity*, ca. 1450**
31 x 47.2 cm; Tempera on wood panel
Pinacoteca; Room II; Inv. 40242

Policleto di Cola?, active 1400–1446
***St. Anthony the Abbot and St. John the Baptist*, ca. 1430**
43.1 x 25.8 cm; Tempera on wood panel
Pinacoteca; Room II; Inv. 40219

Policleto di Cola, active 1400–1446
***St. Jules and Mary Magdalene*, ca. 1430**
42.8 x 25.4 cm; Tempera on wood panel
Pinacoteca; Room II; Inv. 40212

Francesco di Gentile, 15th century
***Madonna and Child*, 15th century**
63 x 46 cm; Tempera on wood panel
Pinacoteca; Room II; Inv. 40263

Lippo d'Andrea, active early 15th century
***Nativity*, undated**
31.2 x 59.3 cm; Tempera and gold on wood panel
Pinacoteca; Room II; Inv. 40194

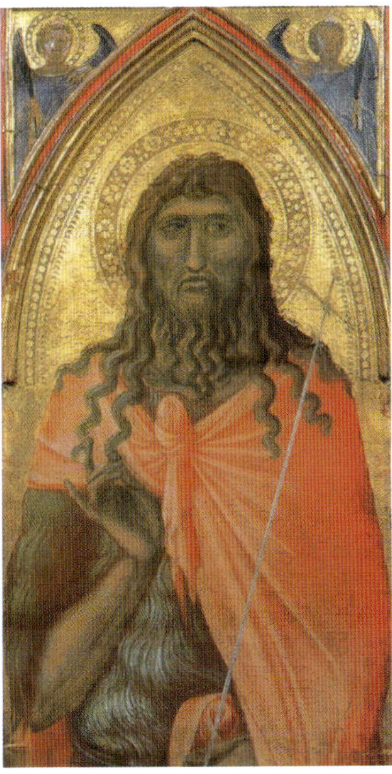

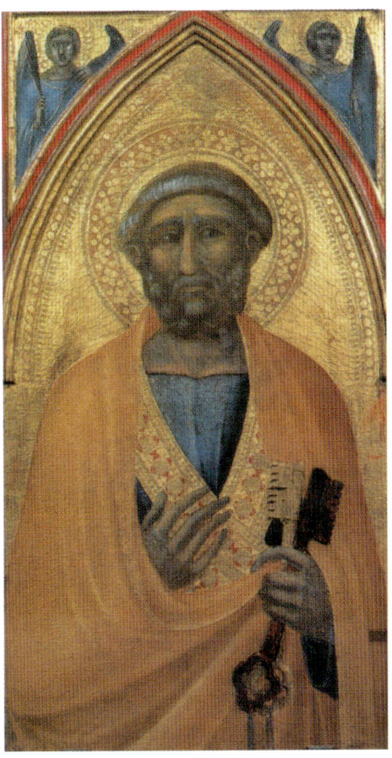

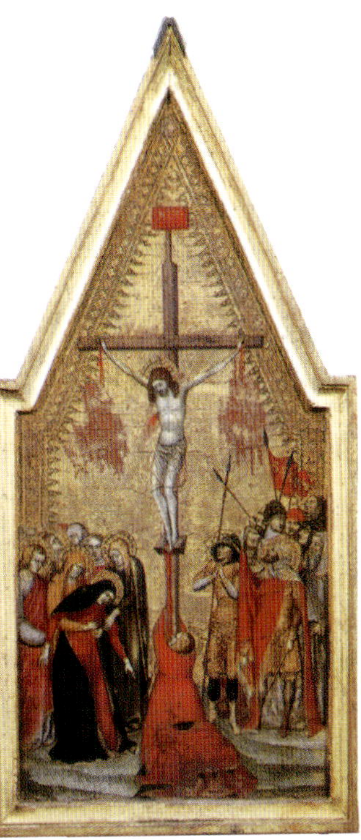

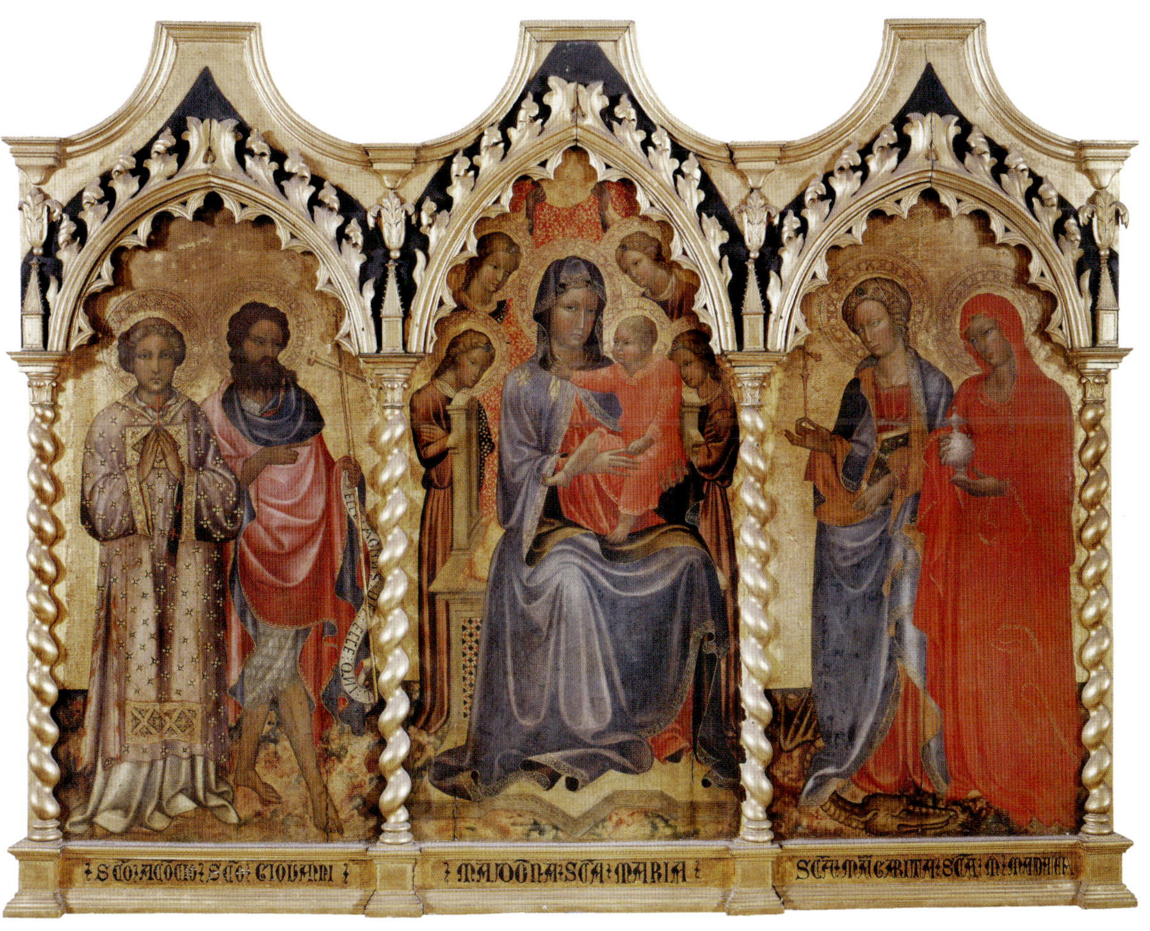

Pietro Lorenzetti, ca. 1280-1348
***St. John the Baptist*, undated**
80.2 x 42 cm; Tempera on wood panel
Pinacoteca; Room II; Inv. 40166

Pietro Lorenzetti, ca. 1280-1348
***St. Peter*, undated**
78 x 42 cm; Tempera on wood panel
Pinacoteca; Room II; Inv. 40163

Pietro Lorenzetti, Workshop of, first half of 14th century
***Crucifixion*, undated**
50.8 x 23.9 cm; Tempera and gold on wood panel
Pinacoteca; Room II; Inv. 40152

Master of Barga, first half of 15th century
***Madonna Enthroned with Saints*, ca. 1440**
139.9 x 66.6 cm; Tempera and gold on wood panel
Pinacoteca; Room II; Inv. 40246

ROOM III

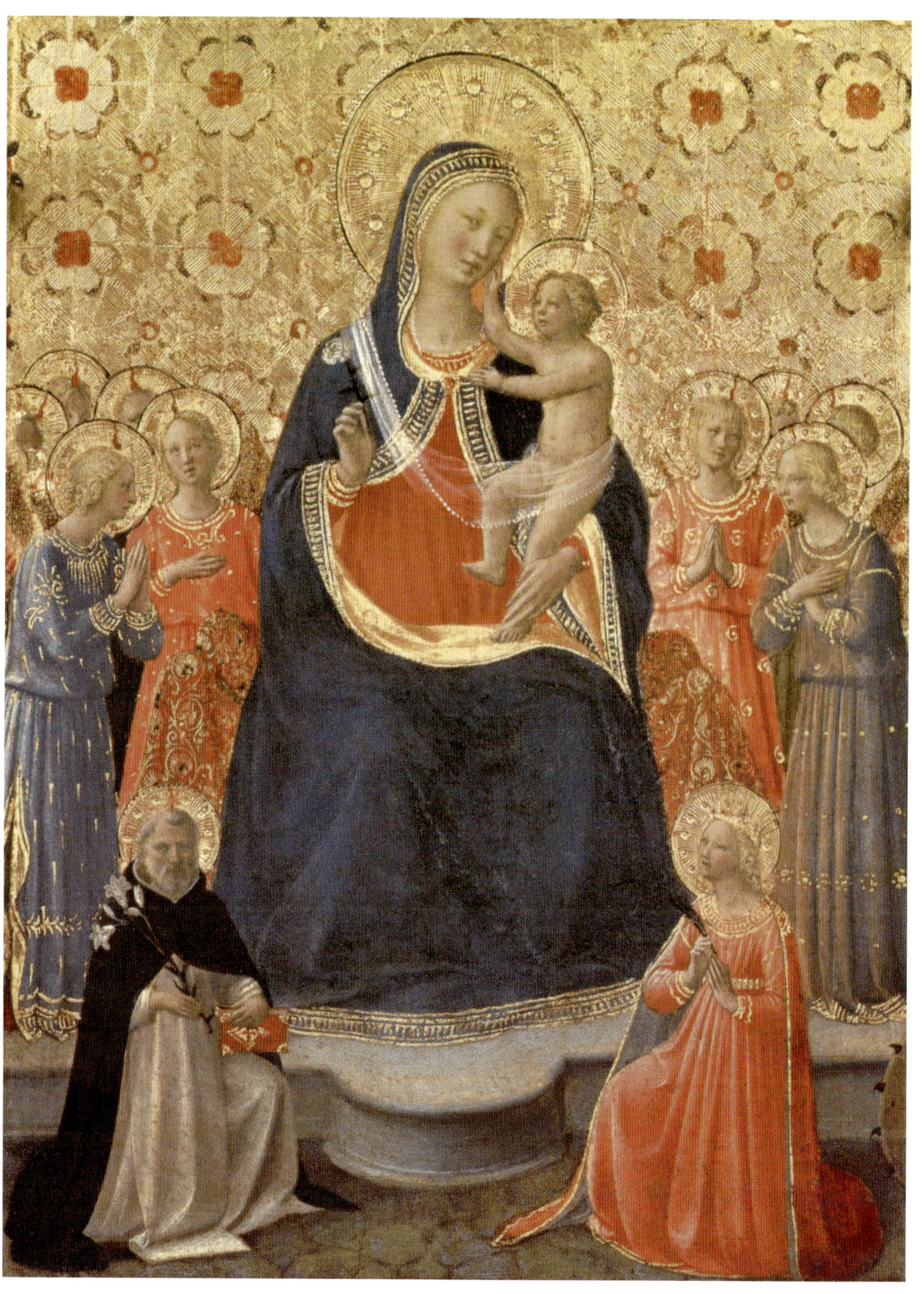

Fra Angelico (Guido di Pietro)

The Virgin and Child Enthroned with SS. Dominic and Catherine of Alexandria

The Virgin and Child Enthroned with SS. Dominic and Catherine of Alexandria is like an exquisite jewel. This effect derives above all from the harmony and balance of the three dominant colors red, blue, and gold, which come together in their purest form in the figure of the Holy Virgin. The dress of St. Catherine and the garments of the angels standing on either side of the throne have, by contrast, been lightened. The other main color values are black and white, most conspicuous in the clothing of St. Dominic, who kneels at the feet of the Virgin, but also visible in his lily branch, in Mary's white rose, and in St. Catherine's wheel (visible in the bottom right-hand corner of the panel) and martyr's palm frond. With their gold-trimmed robes, the close-standing angels form a kind of colorful tapestry behind the Virgin, who stands out all the more strongly against the red, gold-patterned throne covering. Gold and red are also the colors of the flower-studded background with its incised pattern, which makes a decisive contribution to the sparkling effect of the work as a whole. Another supreme achievement of Fra Angelico is the transparent veil, which descends in a gentle curve from Mary's shoulder to the Child's lap. In a gesture filled with tenderness, Jesus strokes the cheek of his mother, whose mild glance rests on the viewer. The inner connection between mother and child was an innovation of the art of the early Quattrocento, of which the Florentine friar Fra Angelico was one of the most important masters.

Fra Angelico (Guido di Pietro), 1395–1455
***The Virgin and Child Enthroned with SS. Dominic and Catherine of Alexandria*, ca. 1435**
24.4 x 18.7 cm; Tempera on wood panel
Pinacoteca; Room III; Inv. 40253

Fra Angelico (Guido di Pietro)

St. Francis Receiving the Stigmata

Fra Angelico is one of the most important exponents of the Florentine Early Renaissance. The Dominican monk (hence the title "Fra") combined a life of painting with a life of devotion to God. He is best known for scenes of a harmonious, classical beauty apparently bathed in divine light. In this depiction of the stigmatization of St. Francis, the divine light has itself become the subject of the painting. Fra Angelico's symmetrically constructed composition shows the saint, on the left-hand side of the panel, in a rocky wasteland. His hands and feet are pierced by red rays emanating from a Christ cherub on the right, hovering in an aureole of rays above a crevice in the rock. This fissure is like a torrent of light, directing and intensifying the rays that touch the Franciscan. The saint kneels with outstretched arms to receive God's grace. The radiant power of the light also illumines St. Francis's co-brother, seated on the ground on the right, who anxiously shields his face with his hand. This small panel once formed part of the St. Francis predella (other sections in Berlin and Altenburg/Thuringia), itself part of a larger altar whose main panels are now lost.

Fra Angelico (Guido di Pietro), 1395–1455
***St. Francis Receiving the Stigmata*, 1428-1429**
27.5 x 33 cm; Tempera on wood panel
Pinacoteca; Room III; Inv. 40258

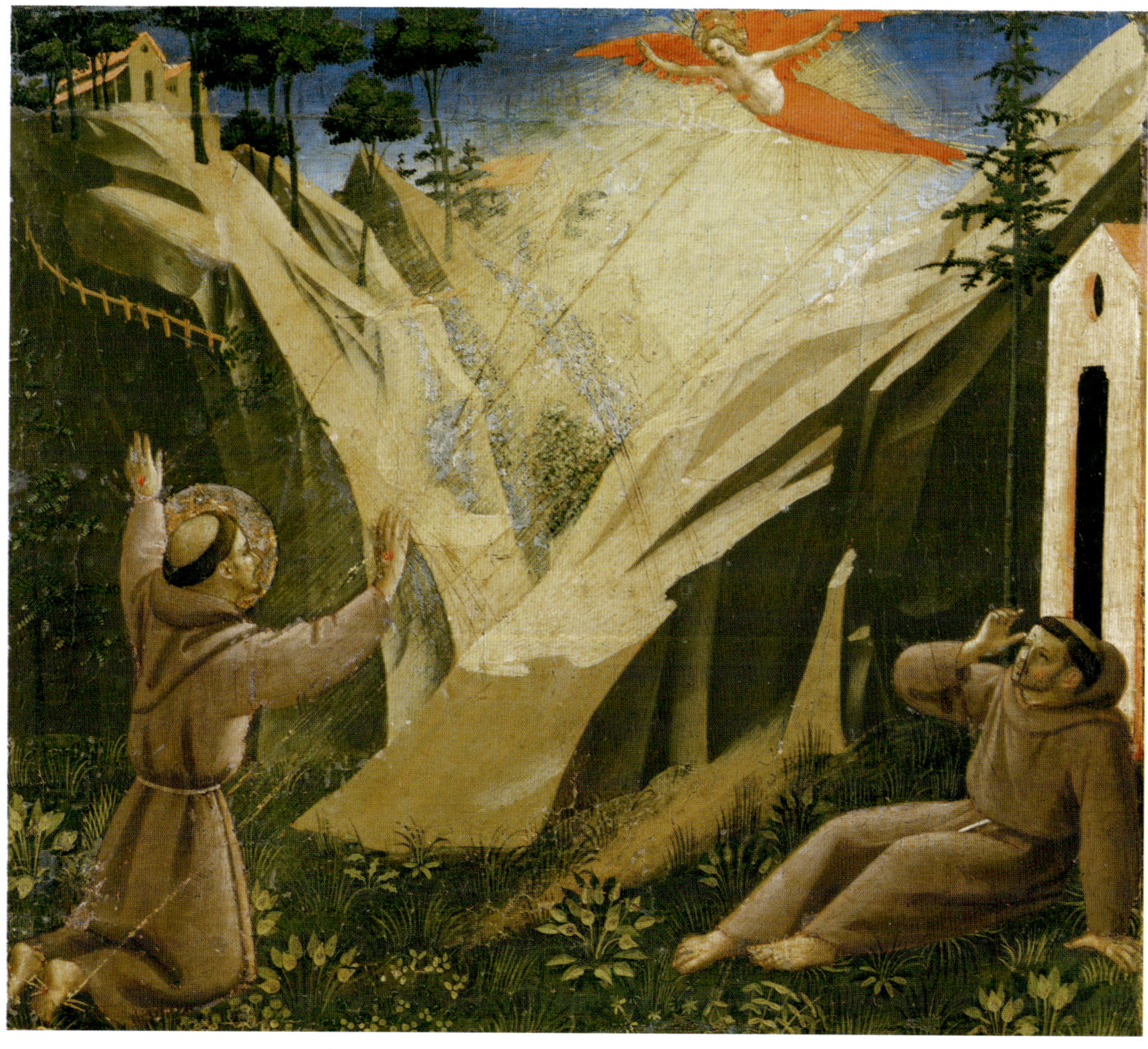

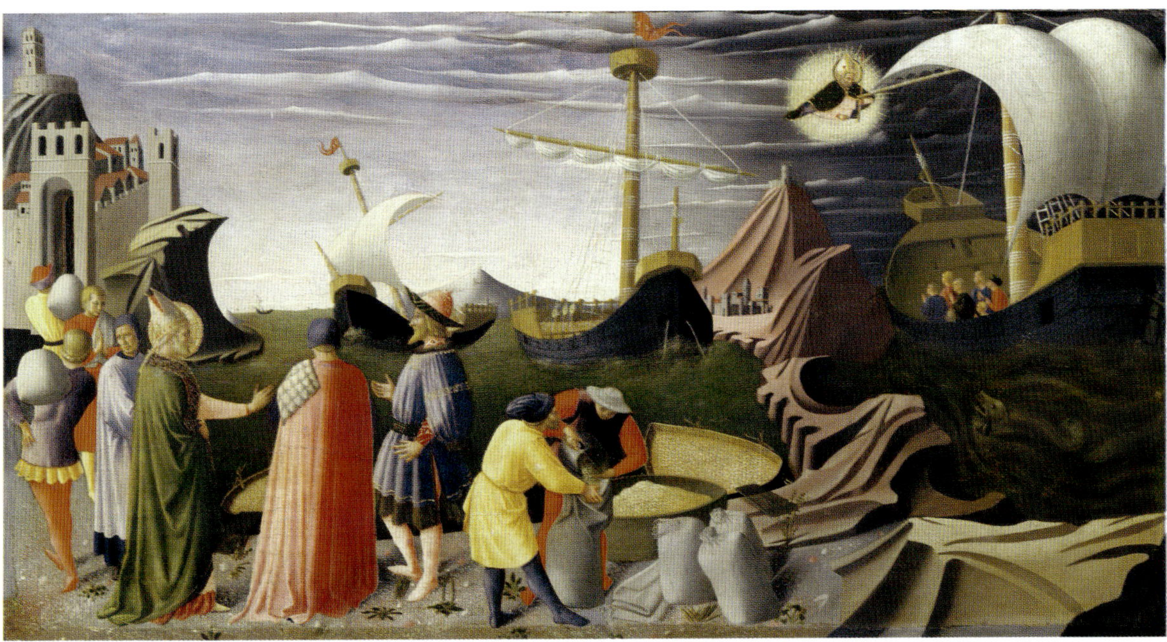

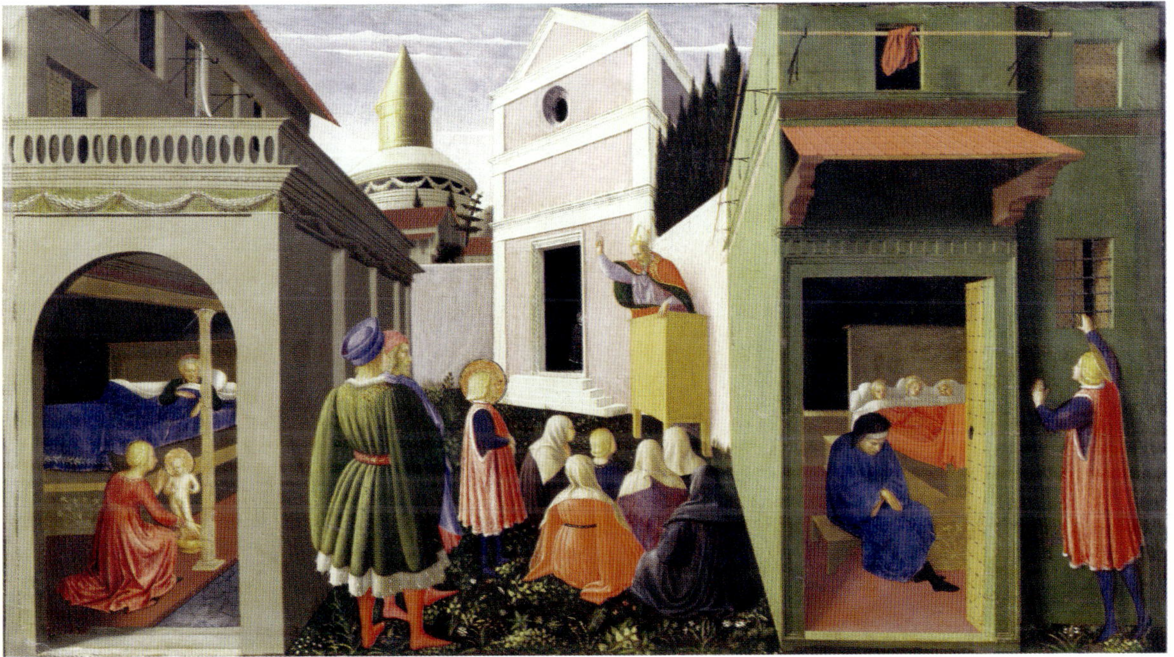

Fra Angelico (Guido di Pietro), 1395–1455
Perugia Triptych: The Meeting of St. Nicholas with the Imperial Messenger and the Miracle of the Salvage of the Ship with Grain,
ca. 1437
33 x 63 cm; Tempera and gold on wood panel
Pinacoteca; Room III; Inv. 40252

Fra Angelico (Guido di Pietro), 1395–1455
Perugia Triptych: Birth of St. Nicholas,
ca. 1437
33 x 63 cm; Tempera and gold on wood panel
Pinacoteca; Room III; Inv. 40252

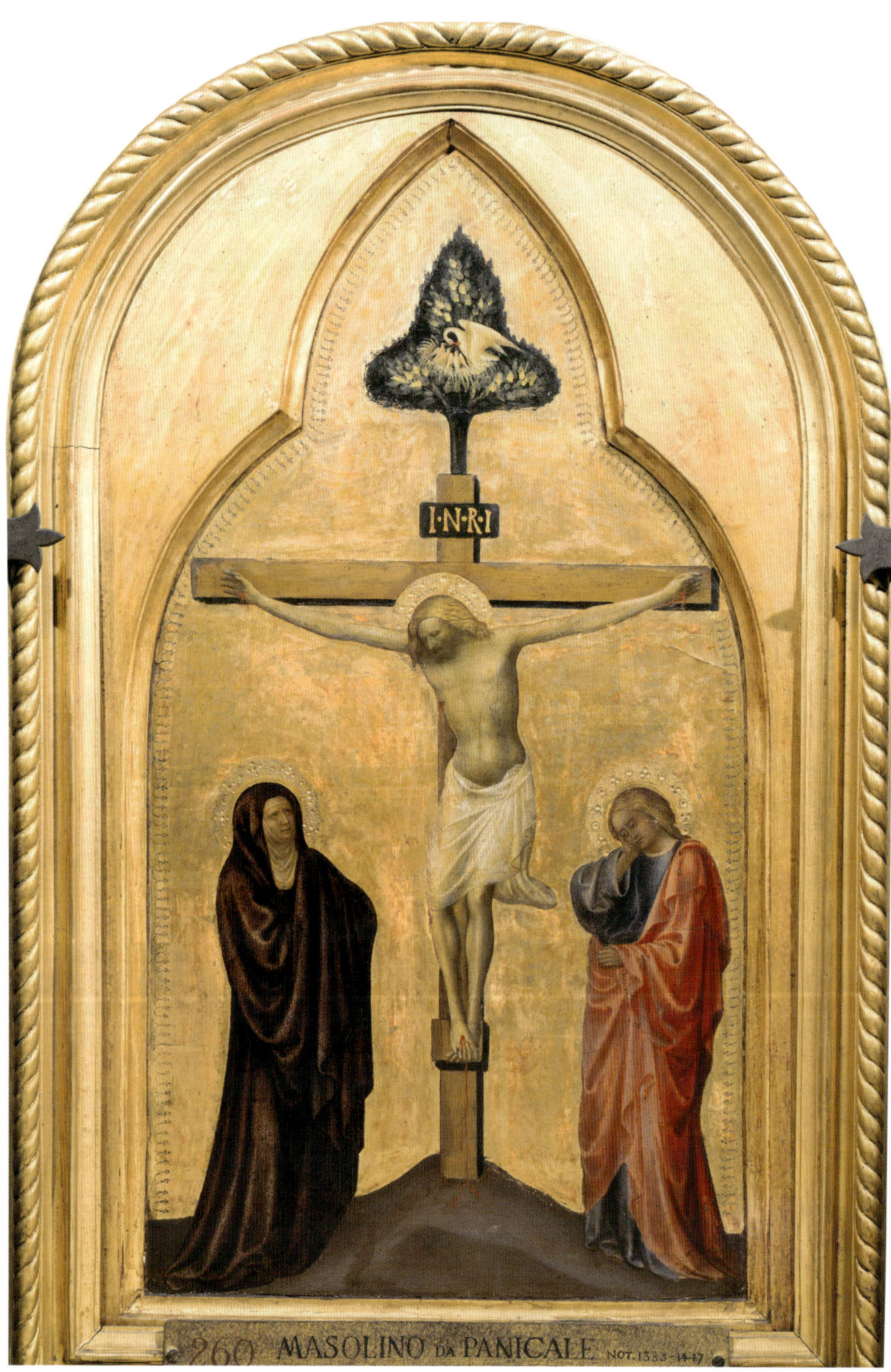

Masolino da Panicale (Tommaso di Cristoforo Fini), 1383–1440
Crucifixion, 1428–1431
53.1 x 31.6 cm; Oil on wood panel
Pinacoteca; Room III; Inv. 40260

Masolino da Panicale (Tommaso di Cristoforo Fini), 1383–1440
Burial of the Virgin, 1428–1431
19.7 x 48.4 cm; Oil on wood panel
Pinacoteca; Room III; Inv. 40245

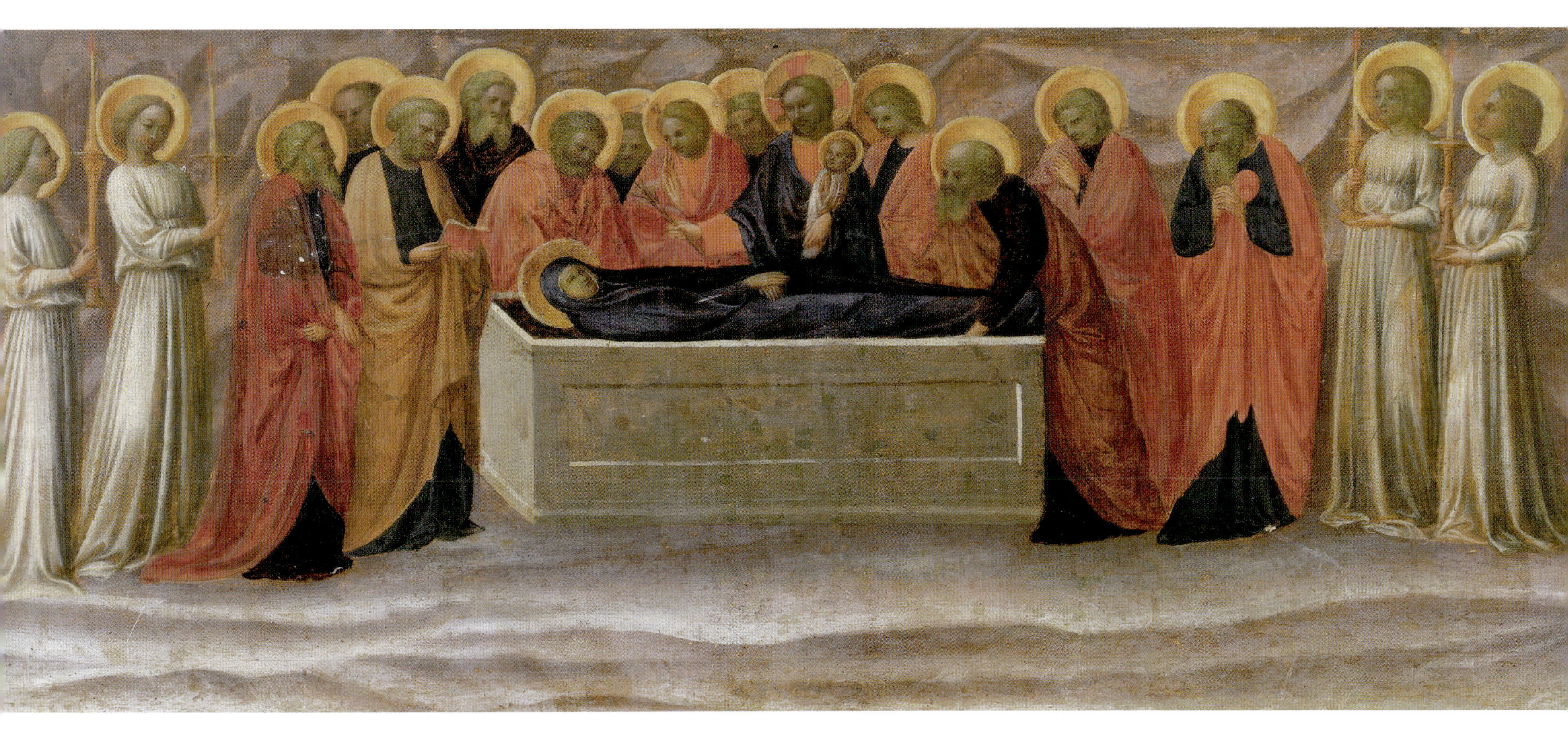

Fra Angelico (Guido di Pietro), 1395–1455
***Triptych with Virgin Enthroned*, ca. 1430**
30 x 15 cm (central panel), 34 x 9 cm (side panels);
Tempera on wood panel
Pinacoteca; Room III; Inv. 40254

Benozzo Gozzoli, Workshop of, 15th century
***Deposition*, 15th century**
22.5 x 91 cm; Tempera on wood panel
Pinacoteca; Room III; Inv. 40264

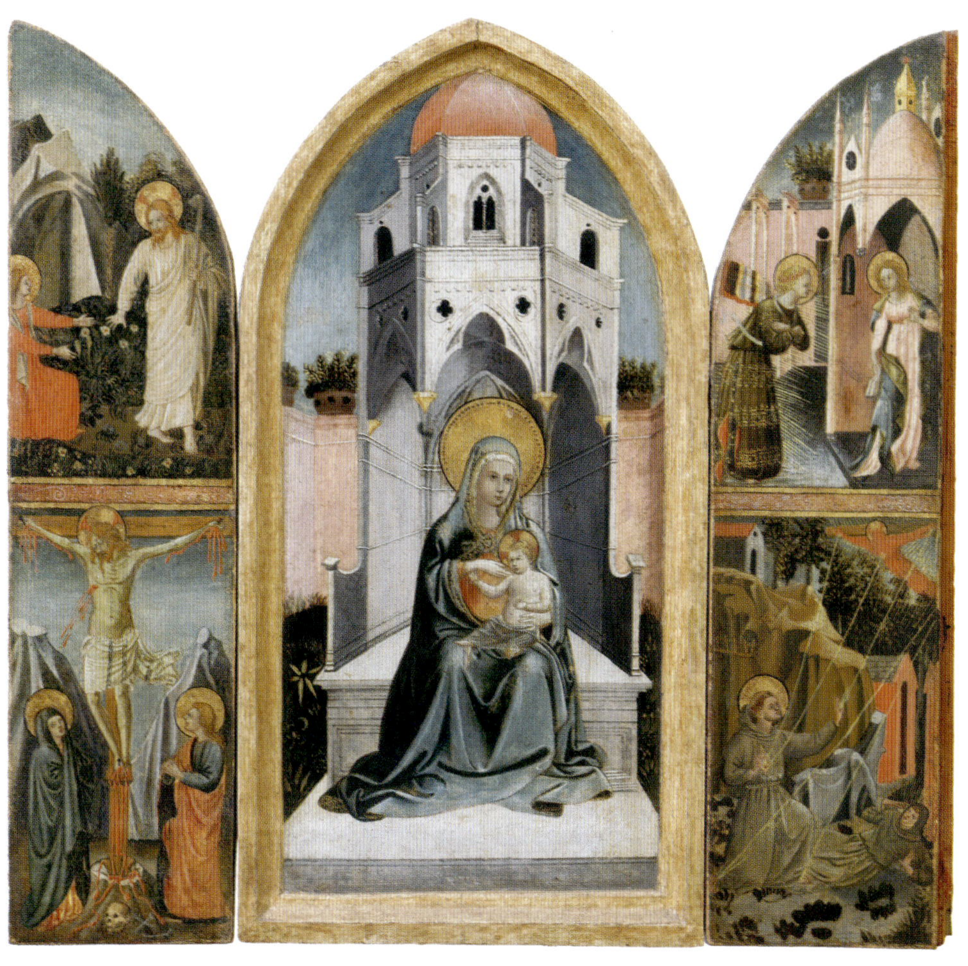

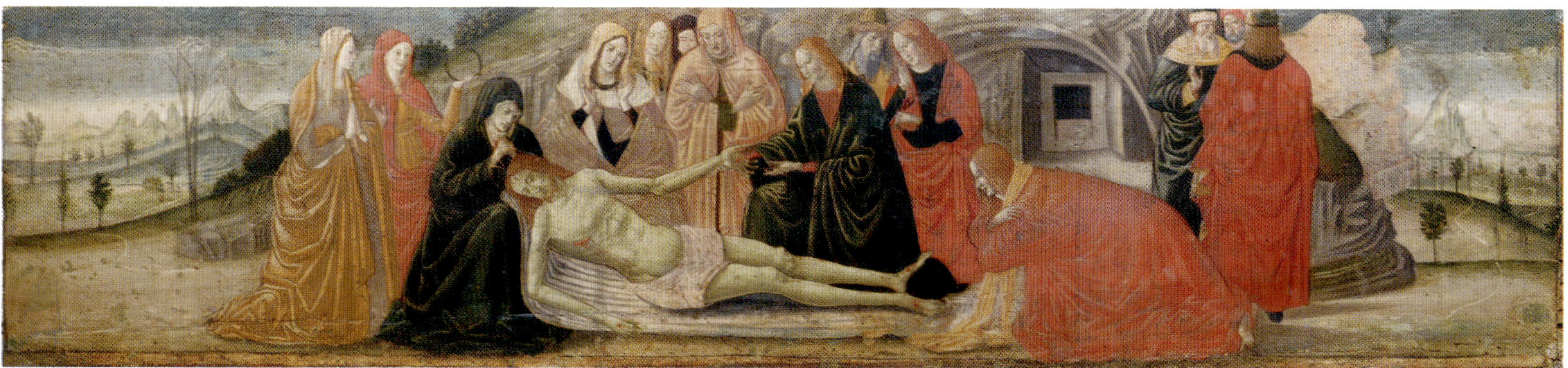

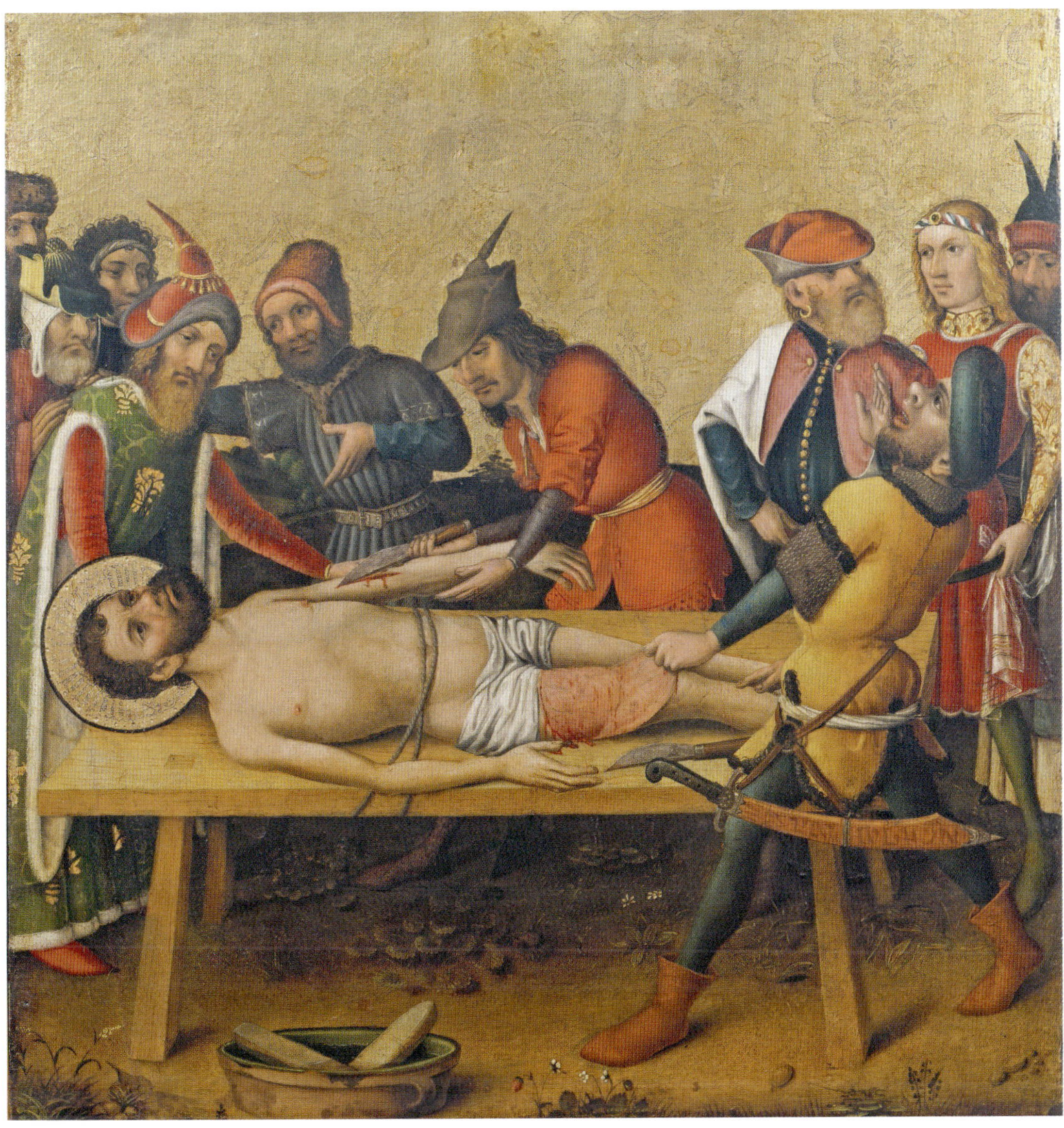

German School (Rhineland)

The Martyrdom of St. Bartholomew

This panel and the Martyrdom of SS. Simon and Judas (inv. 40593), which belong to the same altar setting, are two of the few non-Italian works in the Pinacoteca. They derive from the Benedictine abbey of Muri in Switzerland (dissolved in 1841), where they are thought to have formed part of a large altarpiece incorporating depictions of the martyrdom of various saints. They were painted by a Rhenish artist in the middle of the fifteenth century on the model of the martyrdom panels (ca. 1435) by the Cologne master Stephan Lochner (ca. 1400–1451). Bartholomew the Apostle endured an especially cruel martyrdom: he was flayed alive. The order for this torture is believed to have been given by the brother of King Polymius of Armenia, depicted, it is thought, as the bearded, richly clothed man by the left edge of the painting. While the executioners, whom the painter has endowed with coarse facial features, concentrate on carrying out the gruesome sentence, the bystanders seem merely to observe and comment inquisitively as the saint endures his suffering with composure. The graphic realism of the picture is typical of German art of the mid-fifteenth century and is designed to arouse the compassion of the viewer.

German School (Rhineland), 15th century
The Martyrdom of St. Bartholomew,
15th century
61 x 59 cm; Oil on wood panel
Pinacoteca; Room III; Inv. 40599

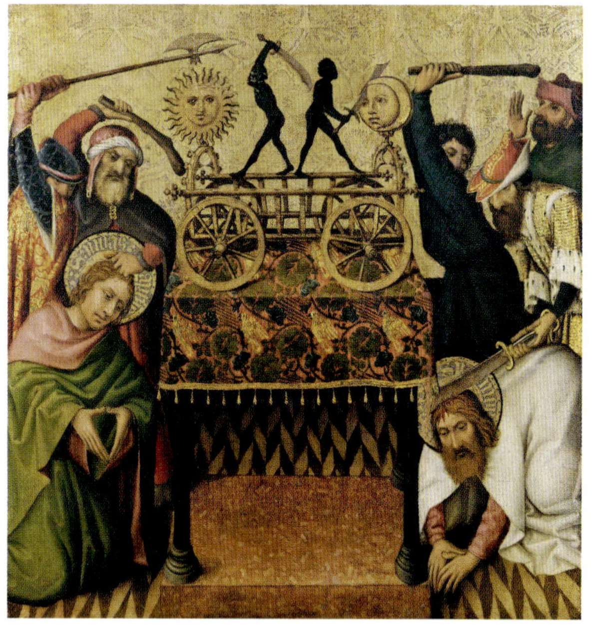

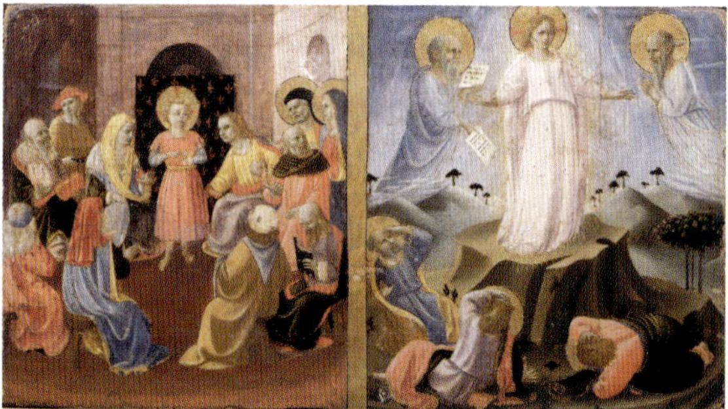

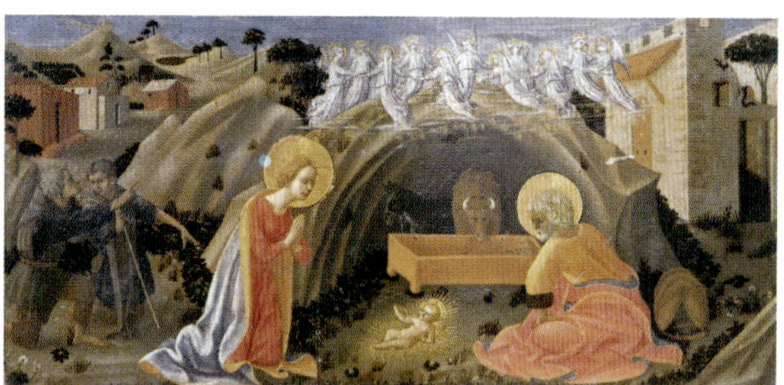

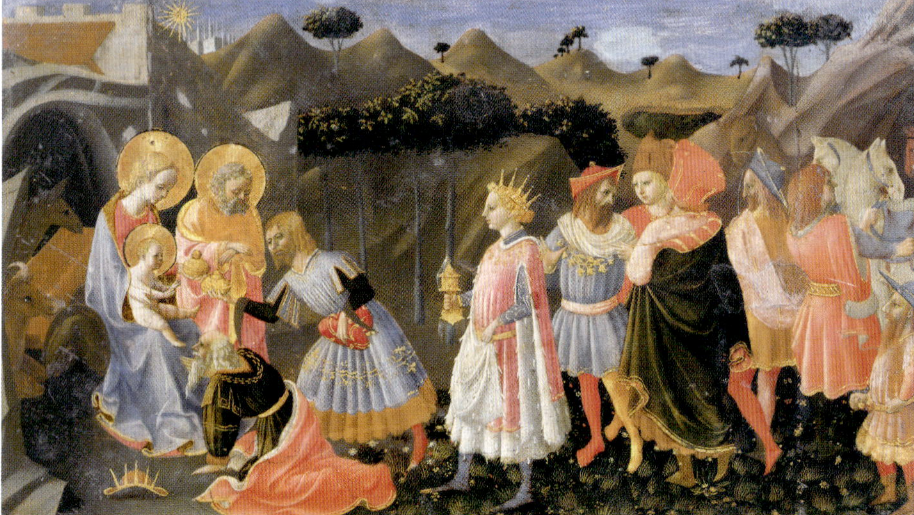

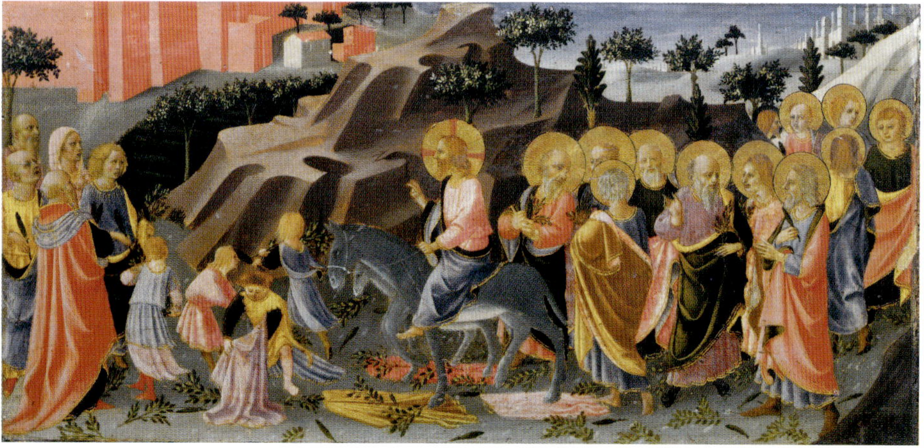

German School (Rhineland), 15th century
***Martyrdom of St. Simon and Giuda*, 15th century**
58 x 58 cm; Tempera on wood panel
Pinacoteca; Room III; Inv. 40593

Pseudo Domenico di Michelino, 1417-1491
***Christ Among the Doctors; The Transfiguration of Christ*, 15th century**
22.5 x 41 cm; Tempera on wood panel
Pinacoteca; Room III; Inv. 40259

Pseudo Domenico di Michelino, 1417-1491
***Nativity*, 15th century**
23.5 x 49 cm; Tempera on wood panel
Pinacoteca; Room III; Inv. 40255

Pseudo Domenico di Michelino, 1417-1491
***Adoration of the Magi*, 15th century**
22.5 x 41 cm; Tempera on wood panel
Pinacoteca; Room III; Inv. 40257

Pseudo Domenico di Michelino, 1417-1491
***Entry of Christ into Jerusalem*, 15th century**
23.5 x 49 cm; Tempera on wood panel
Pinacoteca; Room III; Inv. 40256

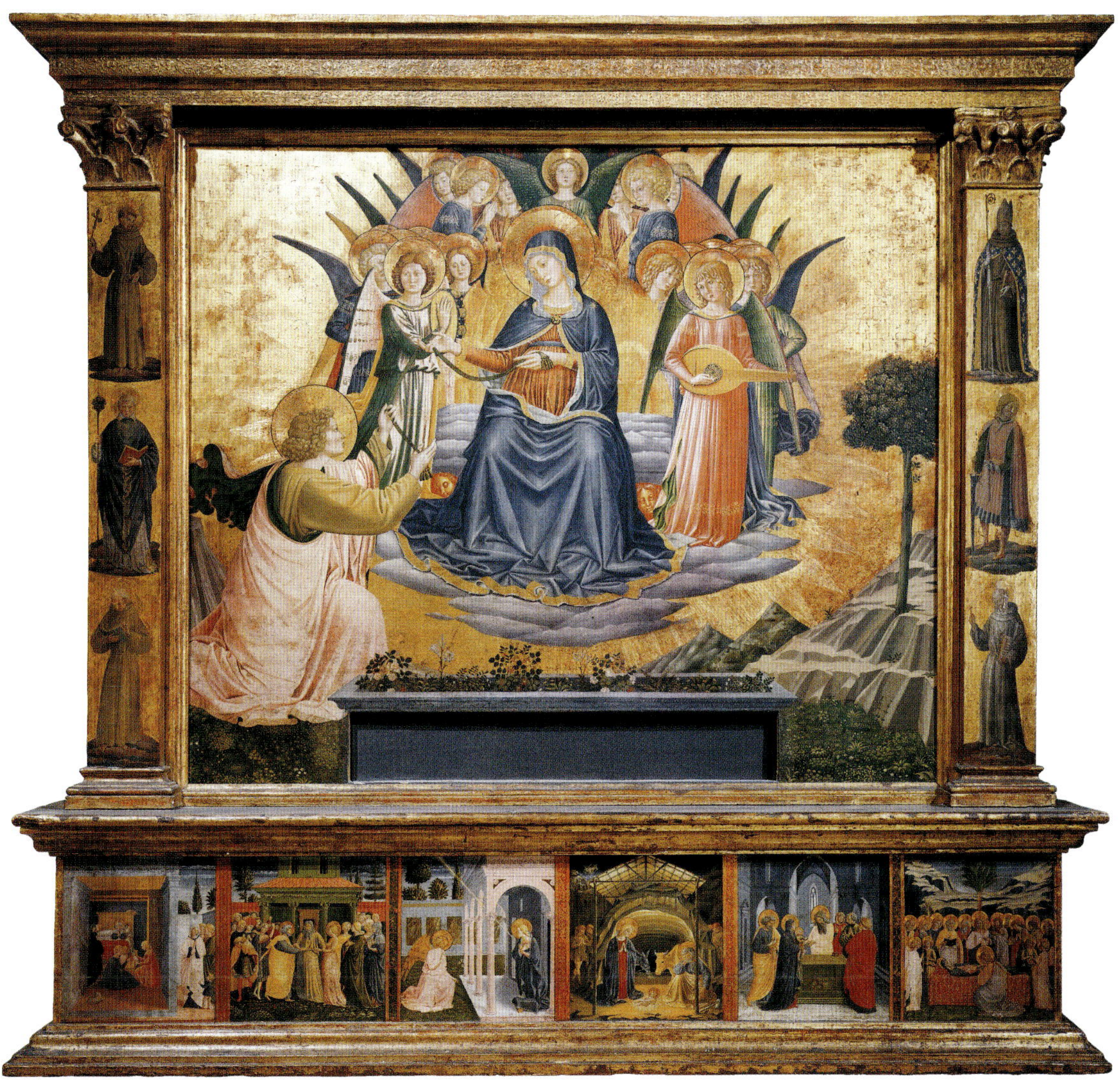

Benozzo Gozzoli

Madonna Presenting a Girdle to St. Thomas; Predella: The Life of the Virgin Mary

This altarpiece, which survives in a state of near-perfect preservation, with painted architectural framework and predella, depicts an unusual subject: the Virgin presenting her girdle to St. Thomas the Apostle. This scene derives from a legend according to which "doubting" Thomas was unable to be present at the death of the Virgin. In order to dispel his doubts regarding her Ascension, she gave him her girdle. In this version by Benozzo Gozzoli, one of the main exponents of the Florentine School in the fifteenth century, the Virgin is shown at the center of the panel floating on an ingeniously designed throne of clouds inside an aureole of angels. Immediately below her is a sarcophagus planted with red and white roses, lilies and cowslip (also known as "key of heaven"). These flowers, which are depicted with botanical precision, should also be seen as symbols of the Virgin Mary. On the left we see a kneeling St. Thomas receiving the gift of the girdle. His inner turmoil is revealed by his look of captivation as he gazes at Mary and the fluttering tip of his mantle behind his back. This central scene is bordered on either side by three small figures of saints. Further scenes from the life of the Virgin are presented in the predella. From left to right they are: the birth of the Virgin, the betrothal of the Virgin, the Annunciation, the birth of Christ, the presentation in the temple, and the death of the Virgin.

Benozzo Gozzoli, 1420–1497
Madonna Presenting a Girdle to St. Thomas; predella: The Life of the Virgin Mary,
ca. 1450–1452
133 x 164 cm; Tempera on wood panel
Pinacoteca; Room III; Inv. 40262

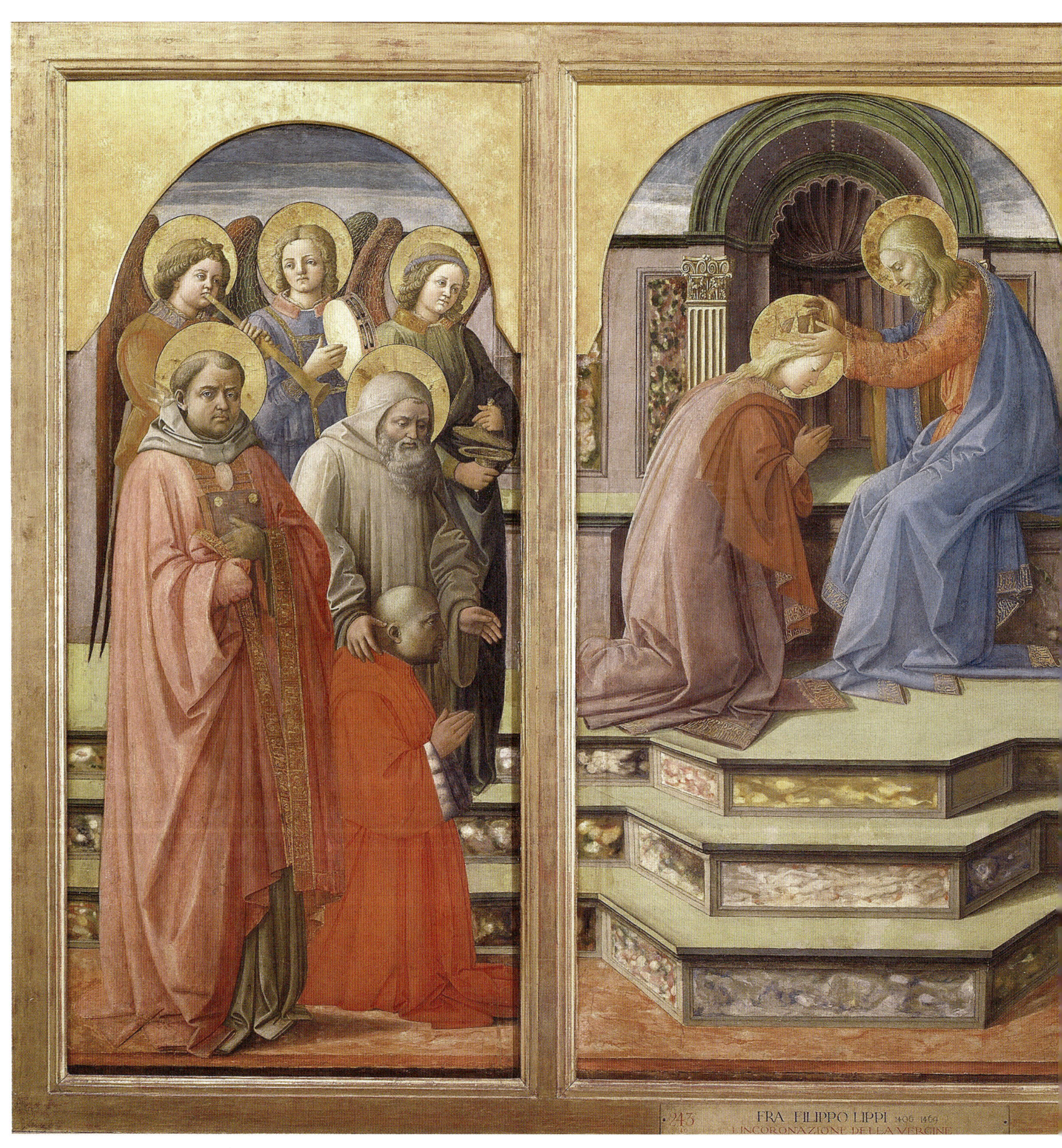
243
FRA FILIPPO LIPPI 1406 1469
L'INCORONAZIONE DELLA VERGINE

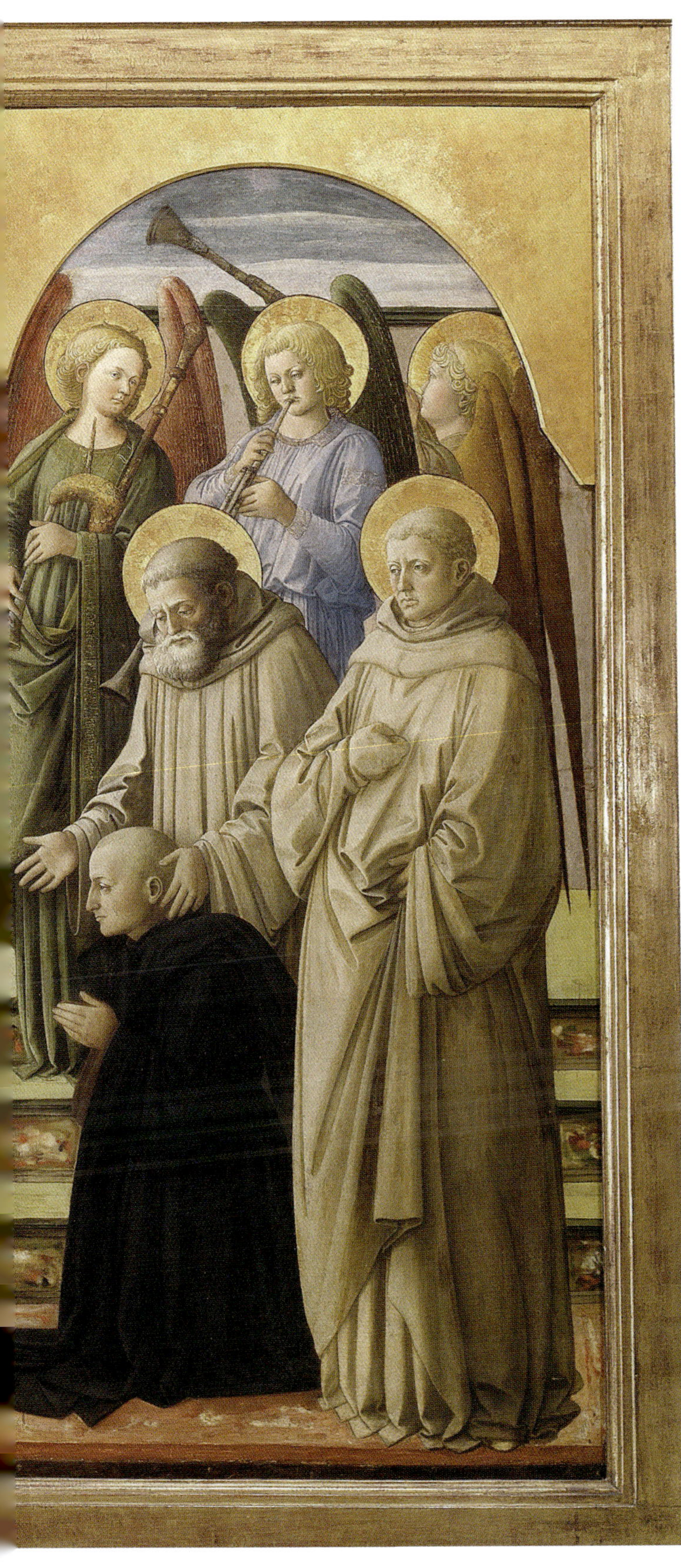

Fra Filippo Lippi and Workshop

The Coronation of the Virgin with Musical Angels and Saints

Among the painter-monks of the Florentine Quattrocento (15th century art), the Carmelite friar Filippo Lippi must surely occupy the foremost position. One of Lippi's key works is his *Coronation of the Virgin* in the Pinacoteca Vaticana, painted as an altarpiece for the chapel of St. Bernard at the abbey of San Bernardo in Arezzo. Carlo Marsuppini, a native of Arezzo and at that time chancellor of the Republic of Florence, commissioned the work in memory of his father Gregorio, who died in 1444 and is shown kneeling reverently in the left-hand panel of the triptych. Next to him stands his patron St. Pope Gregory the Great, a Father of the Church. On the opposite side we see Carlo Marsuppini in the company of two saintly founders of monastic orders who are commending him to the Virgin Mary (in the central panel). The Virgin is shown with humbly bowed head, receiving the crown from Christ. In attendance on either side are angels—some of them thought to have been painted by Lippi's assistants—with their music instruments. The scene is in perfect harmony with the spirit of the Renaissance. This is evident in the classical monumentality of the figures, the painter's adherence to the rules of proportion and perspective, and the classical-style throne architecture, the most obvious features of which are the central shell niche and the different colored marble facing of the throne steps and rear wall.

Fra Filippo Lippi and Workshop, 1406–1469
***The Coronation of the Virgin with Musical Angels and Saints*, ca. 1444**
164 x 83 cm; Tempera on wood panel
Pinacoteca; Room III; Inv. 40243

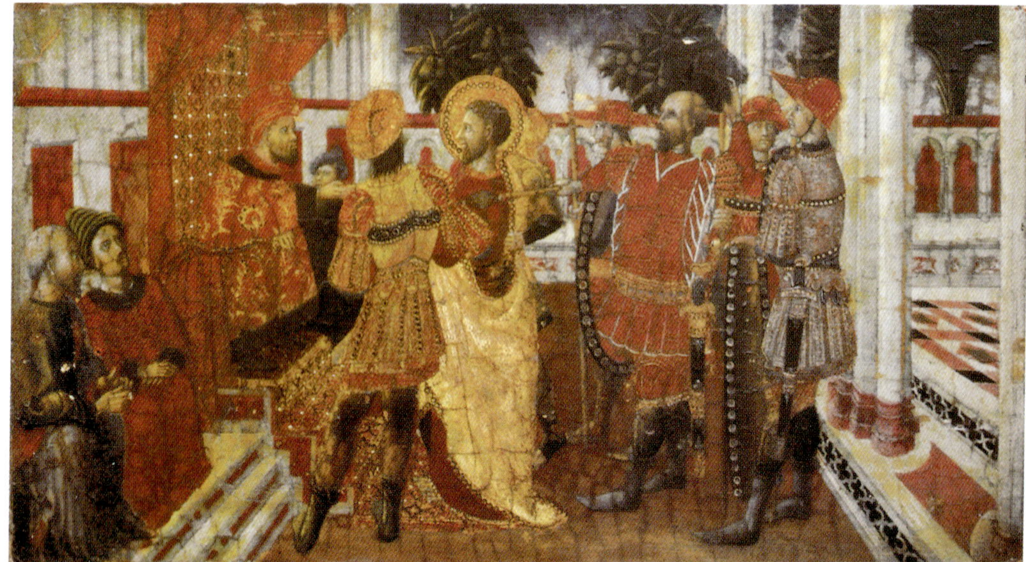

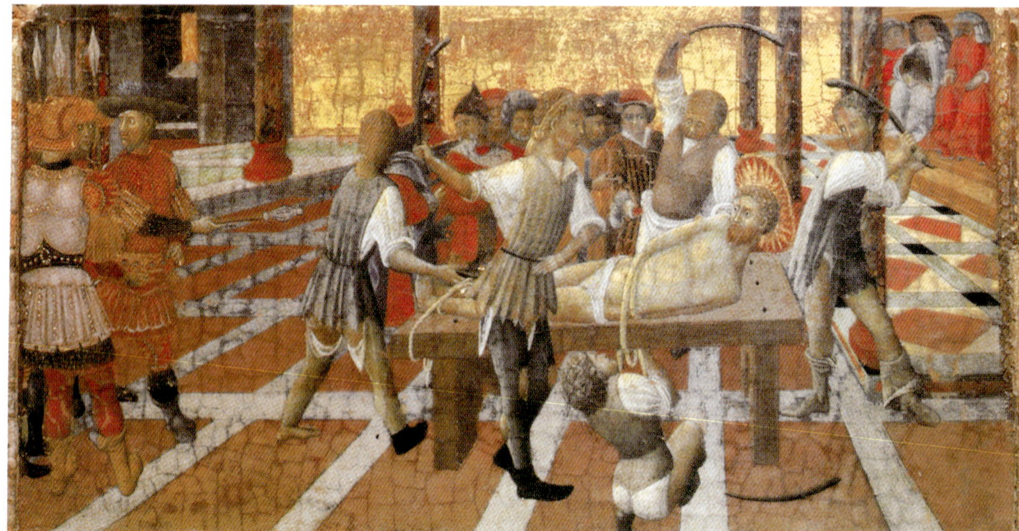

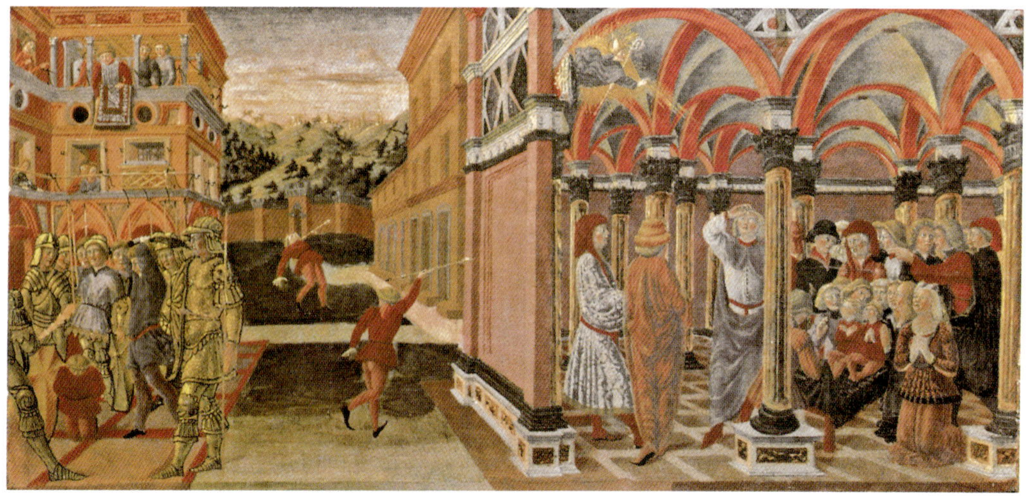

Pietro di Giovanni d'Ambrogio, 1410–1449
***St. Vittorino and the Emperor*, undated**
21.5 x 37.5 cm; Tempera on wood panel
Pinacoteca; Room III; Inv. 40235

Pietro di Giovanni d'Ambrogio, 1410–1449
***Martyrdom of St. Vittorino*, undated**
20.5 x 39.5 cm; Tempera on wood panel
Pinacoteca; Room III; Inv. 40236

Vecchietta (Lorenzo di Pietro), ca. 1412–1480
***Miracle of St. Ludovico of Tolosa*,**
ca. 1458–1460
31 x 64 cm; Tempera on wood panel
Pinacoteca; Room III; Inv. 40233

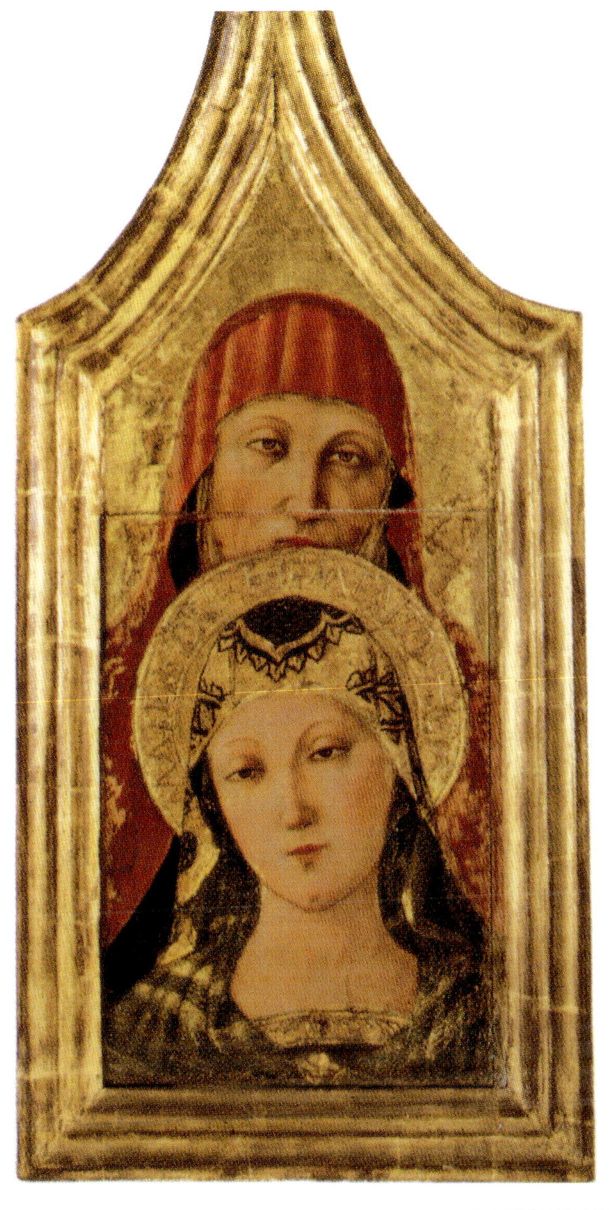

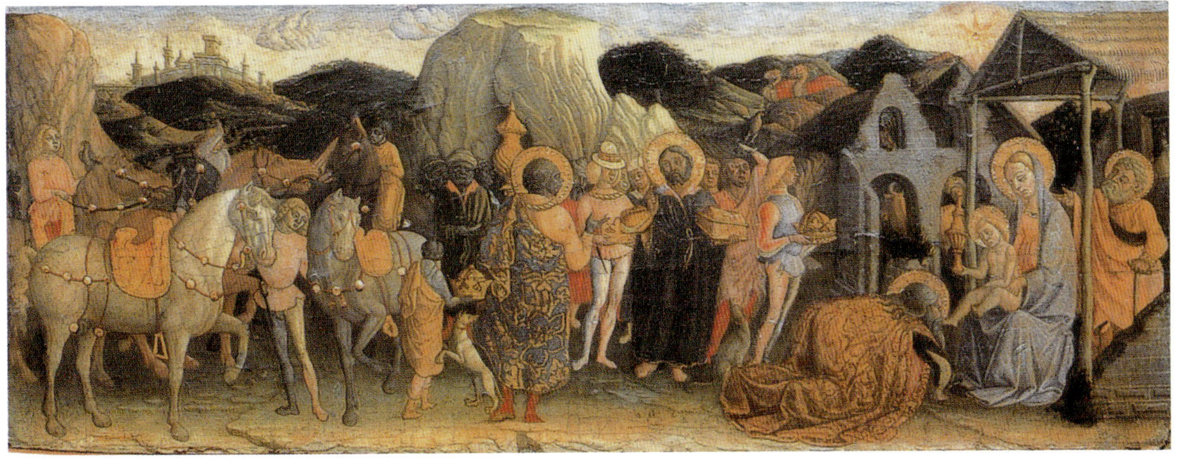

Lorenzo d'Alessandro, ca. 1445–1501
***Virgin Mary and St. Anne*, ca. 1490**
54 x 24 cm; Tempera and gold on wood panel
Pinacoteca; Room III; Inv. 40241

Ludovico Urbani, active 1460–1493
***Adoration of the Magi*, ca. 1477**
25 x 65 cm; Tempera on wood panel
Pinacoteca; Room III; Inv. 40261

ROOM IV

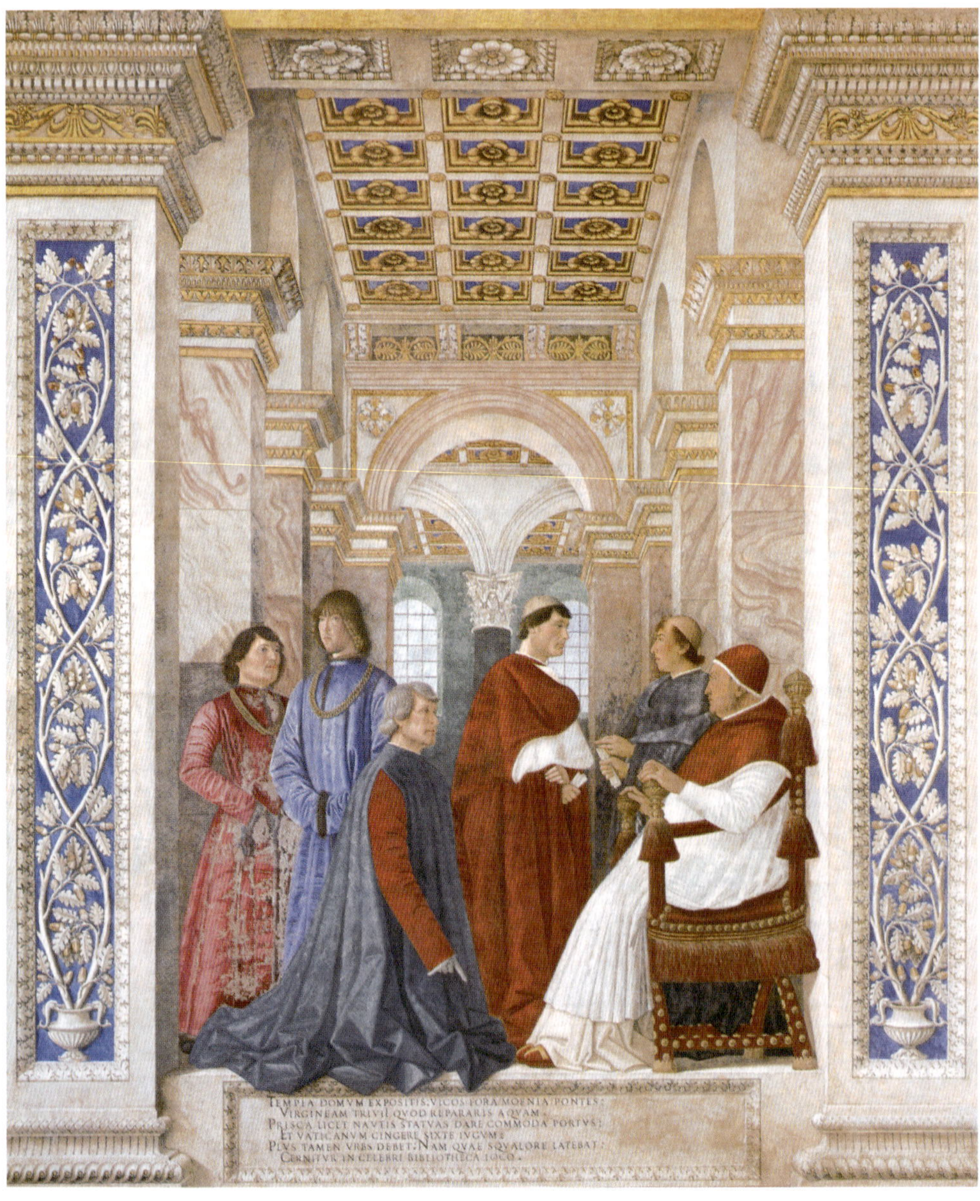

Melozzo da Forlì (Melozzo degli Ambrosi)

Pope Sixtus IV Founding the Vatican Library

Melozzo da Forlì's painting shows the appointment of scholar Bartolomeo Sacchi (Platina) to the position of prefect of the Vatican Library. The work was part of a vast fresco program commissioned by Sixtus IV (1414–1484, pope from 1471) from the best artists of the day for the furnishing of the Vatican Apostolic Library, which he inaugurated in 1475. This depiction of the founding act on June 15, 1475, once occupied a central position in the Sala Latina. In order to represent the simultaneously real and symbolic event, Melozzo da Forlì designed a complex arrangement of figures set in a magnificent illusionistic Renaissance architectural space. The figures are organized into two spatial ranks with the enthroned Sixtus IV and Platina, kneeling before him, in the forefront. Platina points to the inscription on the marble plinth praising the construction of the library and various other of the pope's building projects. Among the other dignitaries it is possible to identify Giuliano della Rovere (Pope Julius II from 1503 to 1513) in his red cardinal's tunic and, on the left, two non-ordained papal nephews. The lively facial expressions are a good example of Melozzo da Forlis's empathetic style of portraiture.

Melozzo da Forlì (Melozzo degli Ambrosi), 1438–1494
***Pope Sixtus IV Founding the Vatican Library*, ca. 1477**
370 x 315 cm; Detached fresco transferred onto canvas
Pinacoteca; Room IV; Inv. 40270

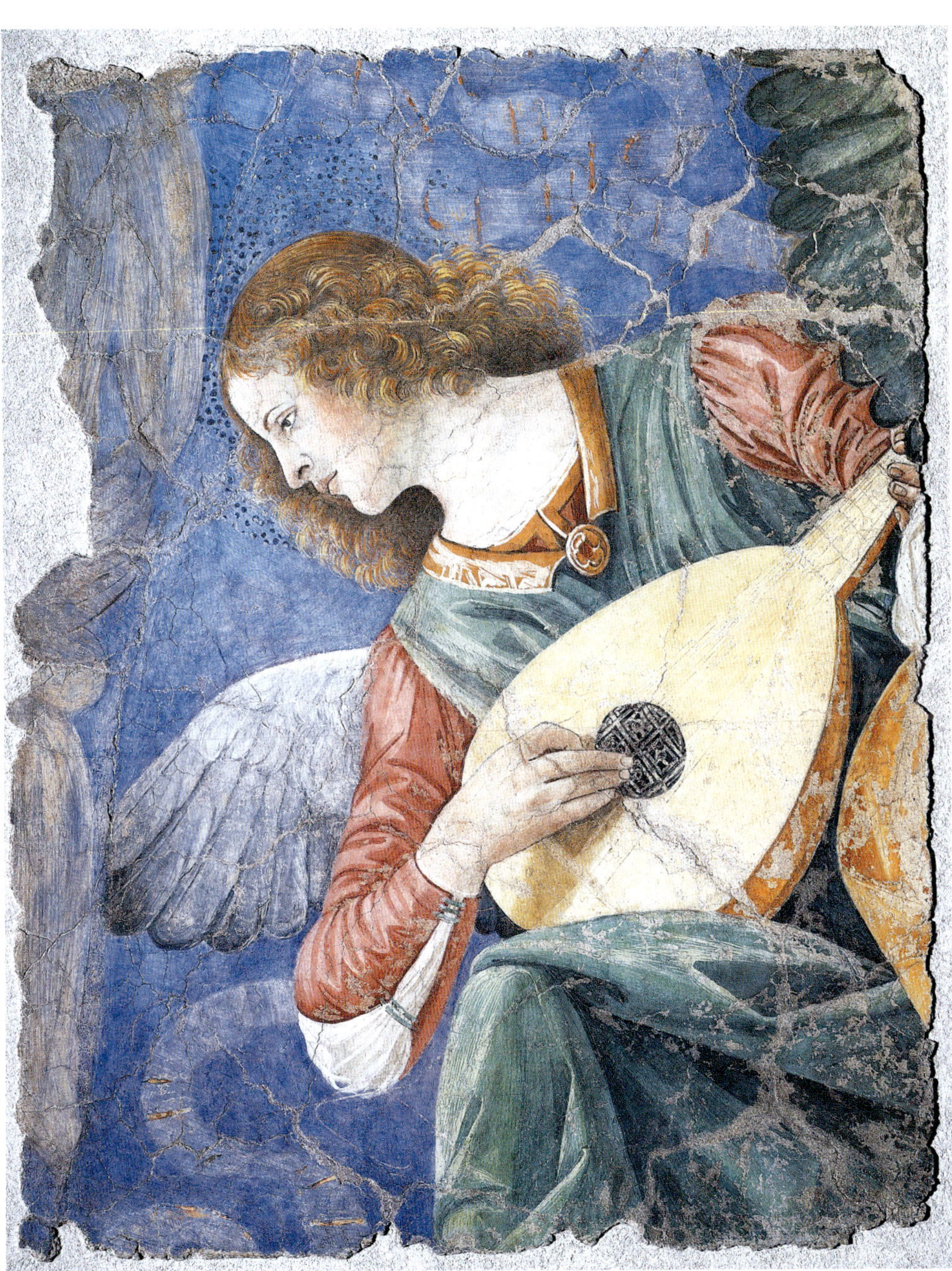

Melozzo da Forlì (Melozzo degli Ambrosi)

Angel Playing the Lute

Melozzo da Forlì, a native of Forlì in Emilia-Romagna, is known primarily as a fresco painter. In addition to his hometown, he worked, among other places, in Urbino, Loreto, and Rome, where he was commissioned around 1480 to paint the vault of the apse in the basilica of Santi Apostoli. The Angel Playing the Lute was once part of that work. The subject of the fresco, commissioned by Cardinal Girolamo Riari, the nephew of Pope Sixtus IV, was the Ascension of Christ surrounded by apostles and musician angels. Sadly, the work was destroyed in 1711 and only a few fragments survive. While the figure of Christ ascending to heaven is now in the Quirinal Palace, the angels and the heads of some of the apostles have found their way into the Pinacoteca Vaticana. All the figures, including the angel devoutly playing the lute, have been painted with consummate skill and are depicted in pronounced *di sotto in sù* perspective (looking up from below). The simultaneously elegant and monumental design of the painting shows the influence of the Paduan court painter Andrea Mantegna, who may have been one of Melozzo da Forlì's masters. However, whereas Mantegna's figures are distinguished by a certain severity, Melozzo's exude an ethereal lyricism that continues to enchant viewers today. It is not by accident that his angels are among the most popular motifs in the Vatican Museums.

Melozzo da Forlì (Melozzo degli Ambrosi), 1438–1494
***Angel Playing the Lute*, 15th century**
117 x 93.5 cm; Fragment of detached fresco
Pinacoteca; Room IV; Inv. 40269.14.10

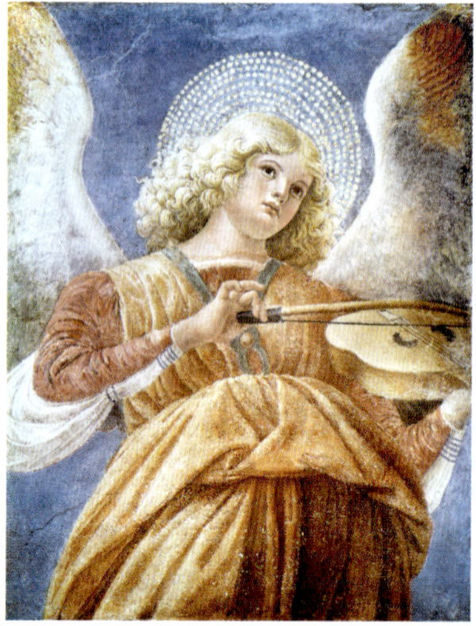

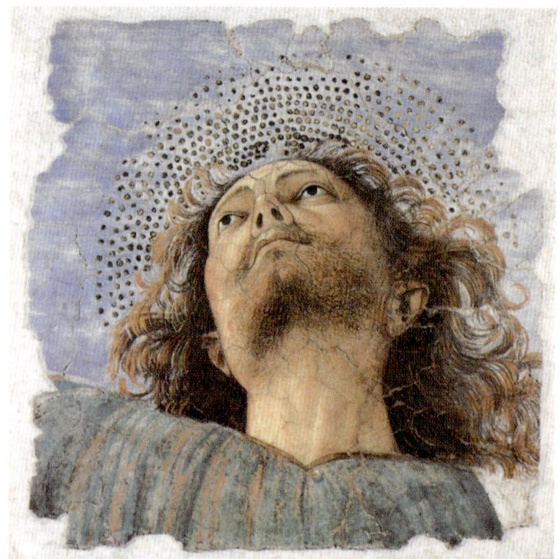

Melozzo da Forli (Melozzo degli Ambrosi), 1438–1494
***Angel Playing the Viola da Braccio*, 15th century**
113 x 91 cm; Fragment of detached fresco
Pinacoteca; Room IV; Inv. 40269.14.5

Melozzo da Forli (Melozzo degli Ambrosi), 1438–1494
***Head of an Apostle*, ca. 1480**
62.5 x 62.55 cm; Fragment of detached fresco
Pinacoteca; Room IV; Inv. 40269.14.3

Melozzo da Forli (Melozzo degli Ambrosi), 1438–1494
***Head of an Apostle*, ca. 1480**
74 x 72.5 cm; Fragment of detached fresco
Pinacoteca; Room IV; Inv. 40269.14.13

Melozzo da Forli (Melozzo degli Ambrosi), 1438–1494
***Musical Angel with Flute, Drum, and Fife*, 15th century**
98.5 x 199 cm; Fragment of detached fresco
Pinacoteca; Room IV; Inv. 40269.14.7

Melozzo da Forli (Melozzo degli Ambrosi), 1438–1494
***Detached Fresco of a Musical Angel with Ribeca*, ca. 1480**
102.5 x 73.5 cm; Fragment of detached fresco
Pinacoteca; Room IV; Inv. 40269.14.11

Melozzo da Forli (Melozzo degli Ambrosi), 1438–1494
***Head of an Apostle*, ca. 1480**
62.5 x 62.55 cm; Fragment of detached fresco
Pinacoteca; Room IV; Inv. 40269.14.2

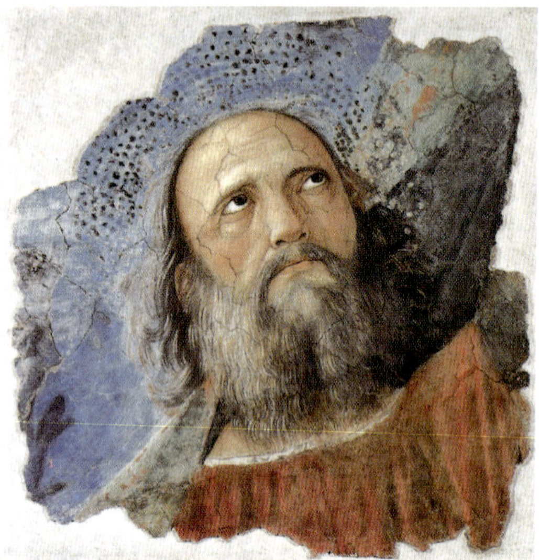

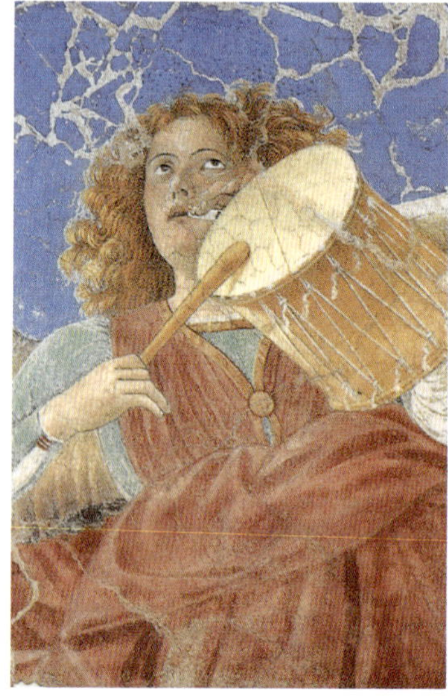

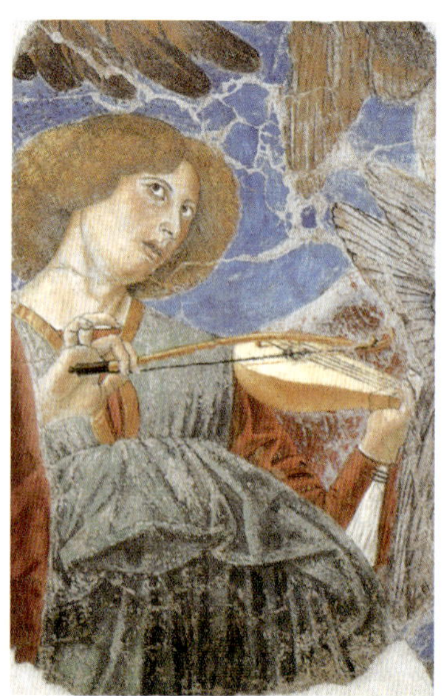

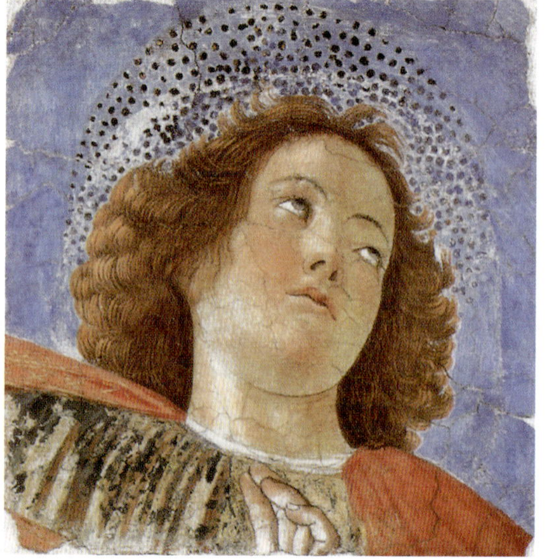

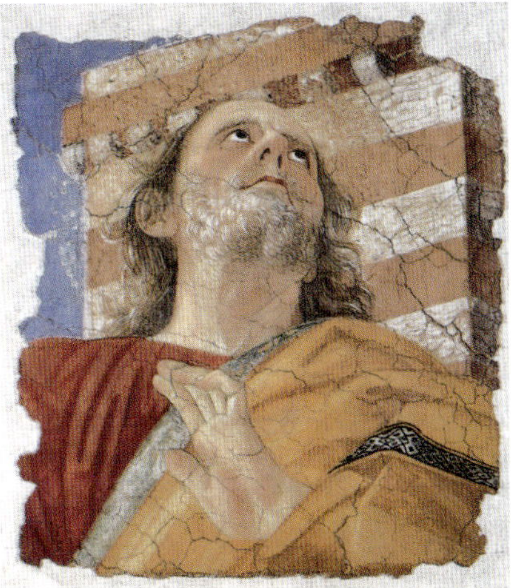

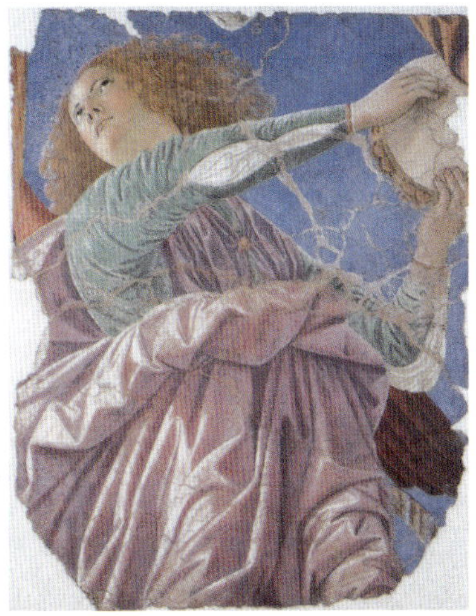

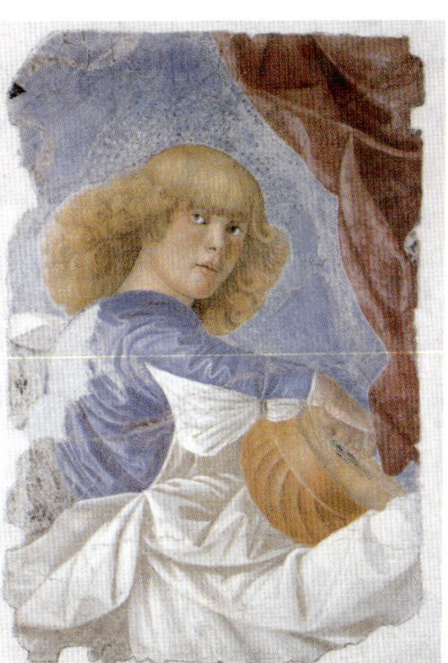

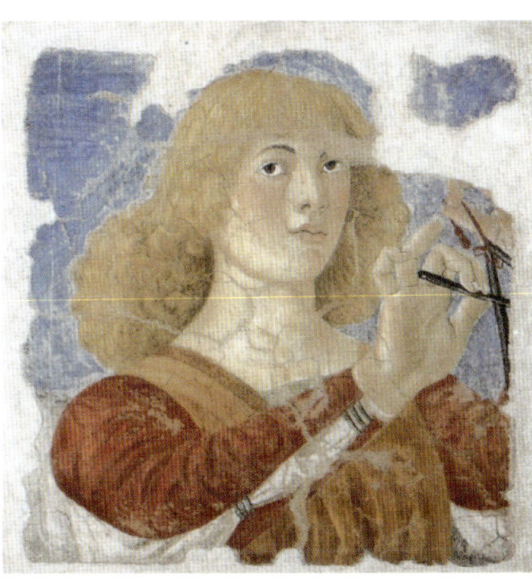

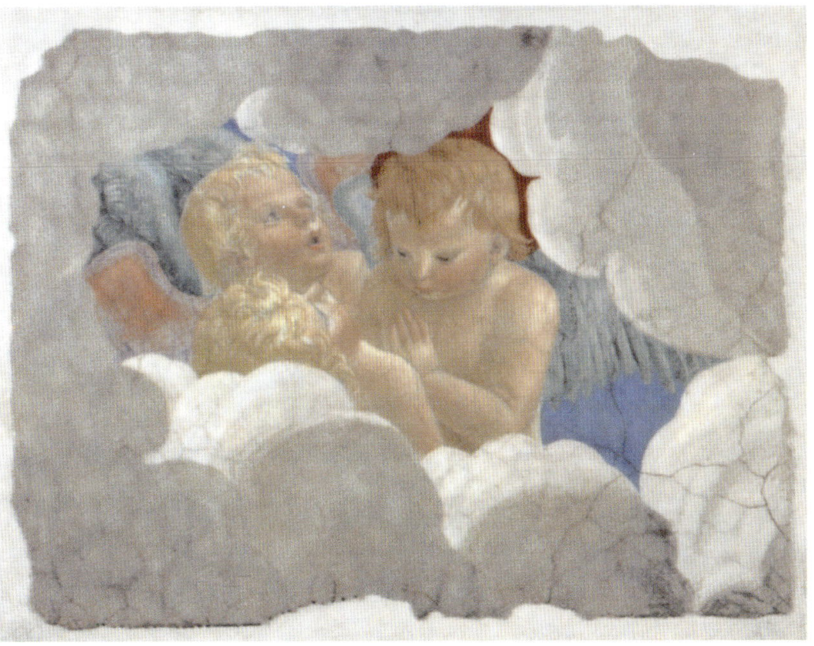

Melozzo da Forli (Melozzo degli Ambrosi), 1438–1494
***Head of an Apostle*, ca. 1480**
75.5 x 67.5 cm; Fragment of detached fresco
Pinacoteca; Room IV; Inv. 40269.14.12

Melozzo da Forli (Melozzo degli Ambrosi), 1438–1494
***Musical Angel with Tambour*, ca. 1480**
117.5 x 96.5 cm; Fragment of detached fresco
Pinacoteca; Room IV; Inv. 40269.14.8

Melozzo da Forli (Melozzo degli Ambrosi), 1438–1494
***Angel Playing the Lute*, ca. 1480**
101 x 70 cm; Fragment of detached fresco
Pinacoteca; Room IV; Inv. 40269.14.14

Melozzo da Forli (Melozzo degli Ambrosi), 1438–1494
***Angel with Triangle*, ca. 1480**
61.5 x 61.5 cm; Fragment of detached fresco
Pinacoteca; Room IV; Inv. 40269.14.9

Melozzo da Forli (Melozzo degli Ambrosi), 1438–1494
***Group of Angels Cherubim*, ca. 1480**
78.5 x 95.5 cm; Fragment of detached fresco
Pinacoteca; Room IV; Inv. 40269.14.1

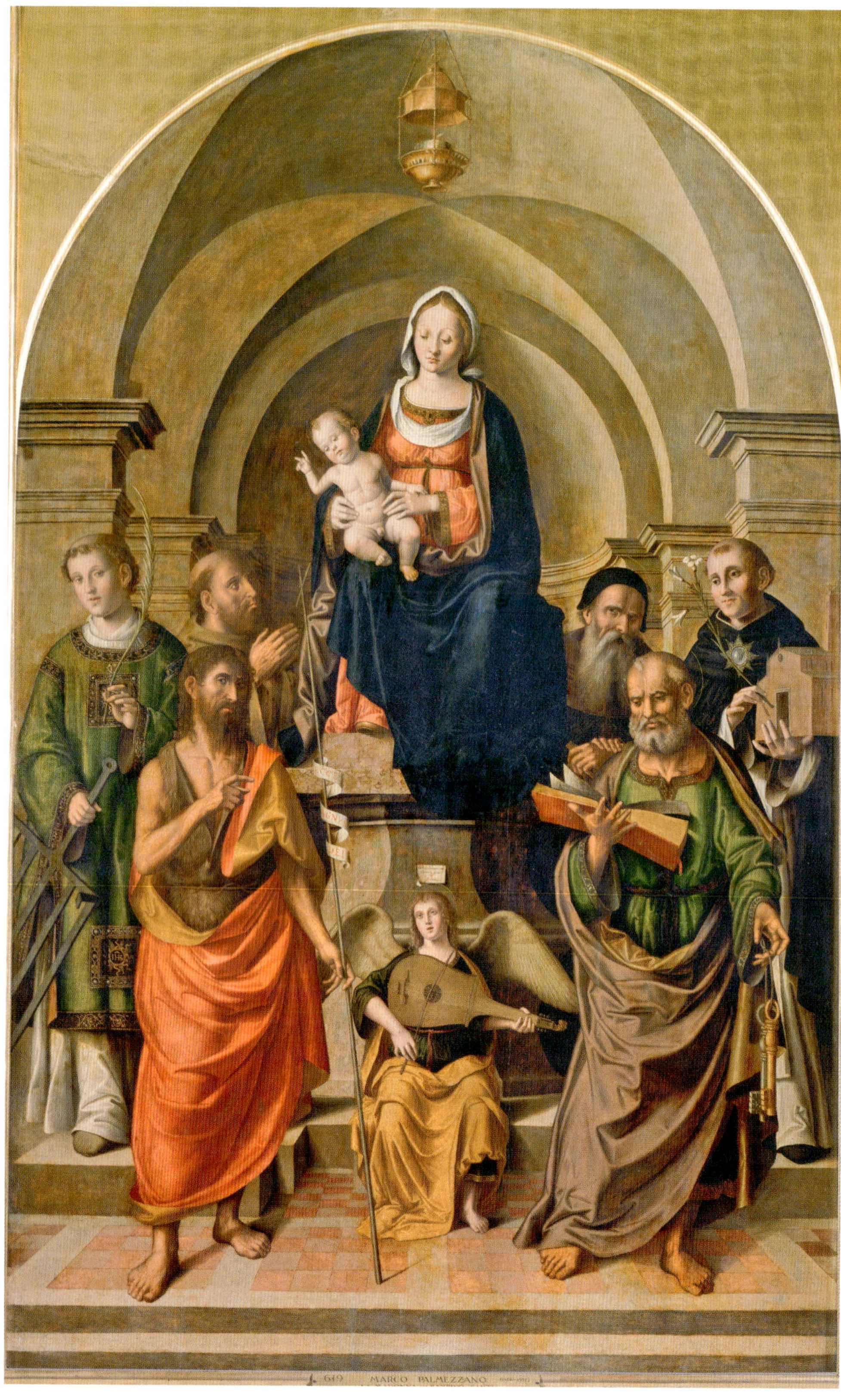

Marco Palmezzano

The Virgin and Child with Saints

Garments shimmering with color, perspective architectural settings, lively gestures and facial expressions, balanced compositions—these are some of the chief characteristics of Marco Palmezzano's paintings which are all present in his *Virgin and Child with Saints*. This large panel is from the church of the Carmelite convent in Cesena. It depicts the enthroned Virgin and Child accompanied by six male saints and a musician angel. In this Sacra Conversazione ("sacred conversation") the Infant Jesus, who makes a blessing, is shown as being especially close to the saints on his left. In addition to St. Francis, who received the stigmata from Christ, this group includes St. Lawrence and John the Baptist, who points to the ribbon around his staff bearing the inscription "Ecce Agnus Dei" ("Behold, the Lamb of God"). Assigned to Mary, as the embodiment of the Church (Ecclesia,) are important representatives of the Church and the monastic orders: in the foreground St. Peter, the Prince of Apostles, with St. Dominic and St. Anthony Abbot behind him. Although obliged to respect his patrons' choice of saints, Palmezzano was able to exploit his artistic talent to the full in his rendering of the clothing and design of the throne architecture. Worthy of particular note is the marble throne with its staggered levels. It is here that Palmezzano has chosen to sign the work.

Marco Palmezzano, 1456 or 1459–1539
***Madonna and Child with Saints*, 1537**
340 x 226.5 cm; Oil on wood panel
Pinacoteca; Room IV; Inv. 40619

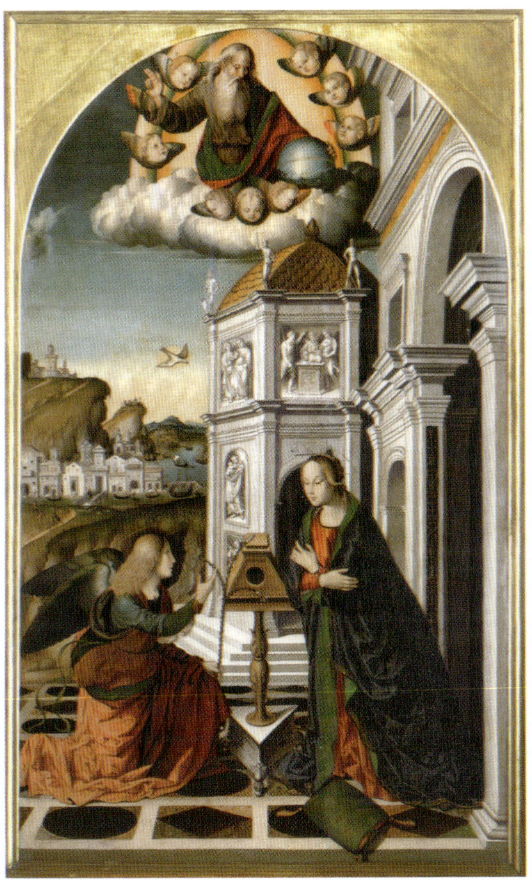

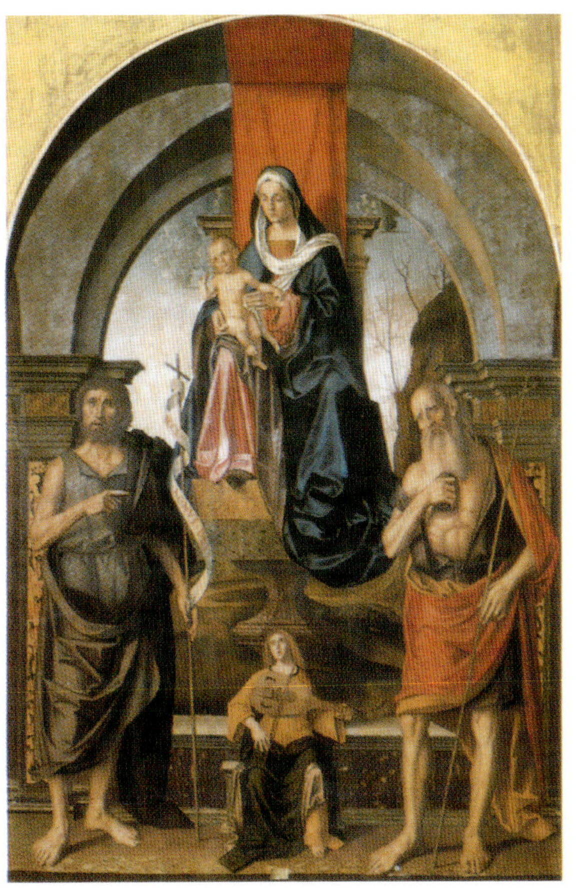

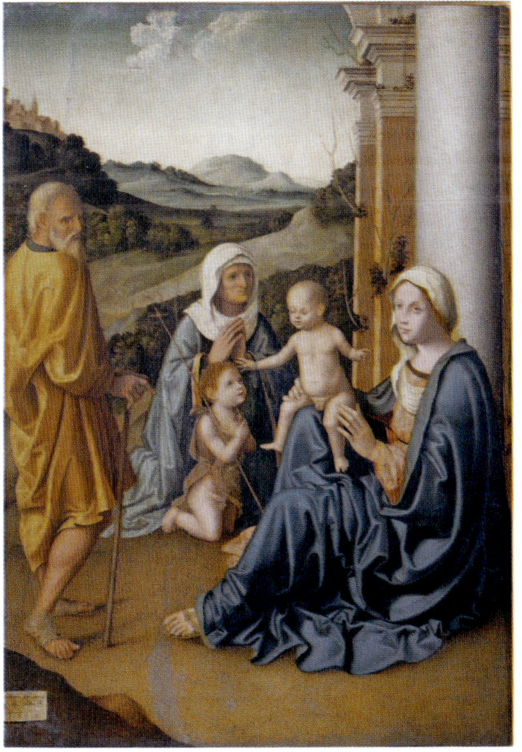

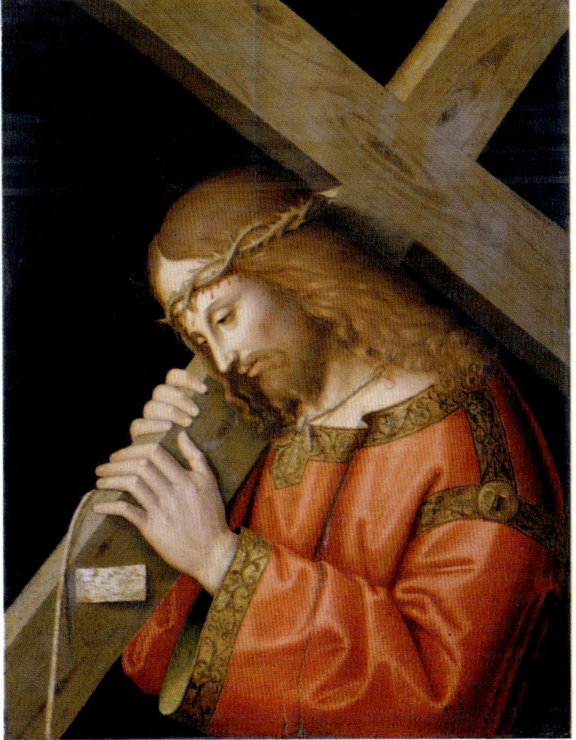

Marco Palmezzano, 1459–1539
***Annunciation*, ca. 1522–1524**
280 x 175 cm; Oil on wood panel
Pinacoteca; Room IV; Inv. 40272

Marco Palmezzano, 1459–1539
***The Virgin and Child with Saints*, 1510**
295 x 194 cm; Oil on wood panel
Pinacoteca; Room IV; Inv. 40273

Marco Palmezzano, 1459–1539
***Sacred Family*, 1515**
90 x 66 cm; Oil on wood panel
Pinacoteca; Room IV; Inv. 40274

Marco Palmezzano, 1459–1539
***Christ Carrying the Cross*, 1535**
54 x 42.3 cm; Oil on wood panel
Pinacoteca; Room IV; Inv. 40271

ROOM V

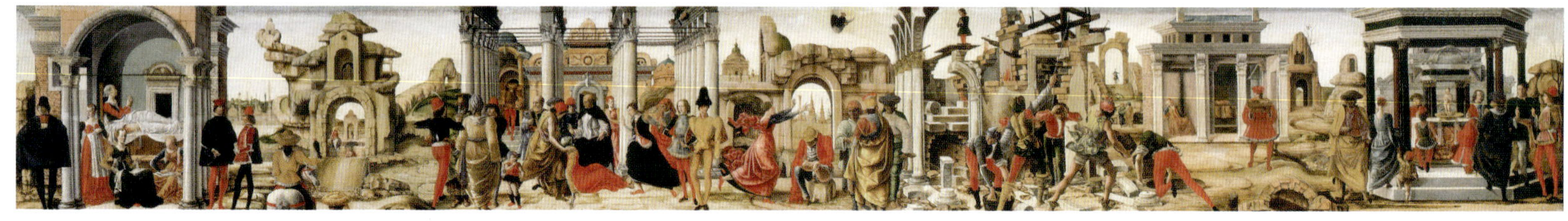

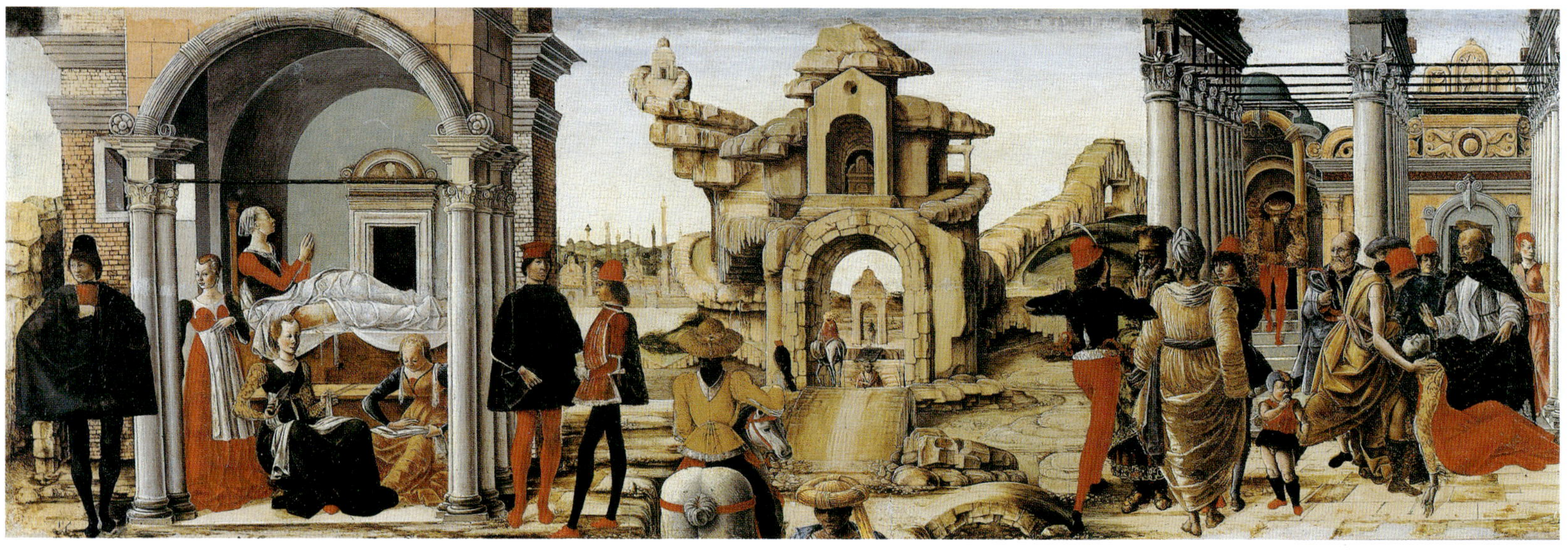

Ercole De'Roberti, ca. 1450–1496
***Four Miracles of St. Vincent Ferreri: The Saint Brings Back to Life a Child Killed by Its Mother*, 1473**
30 x 215 cm; Tempera on wood panel
Pinacoteca; Room V; Inv. 40286

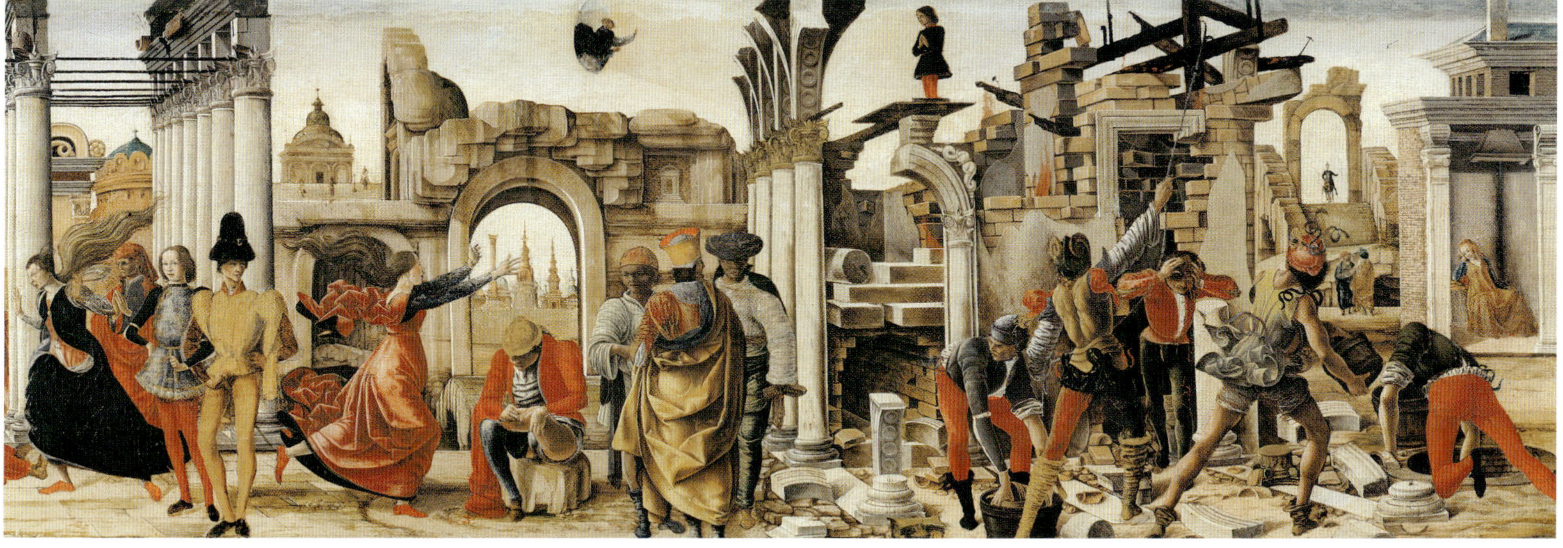

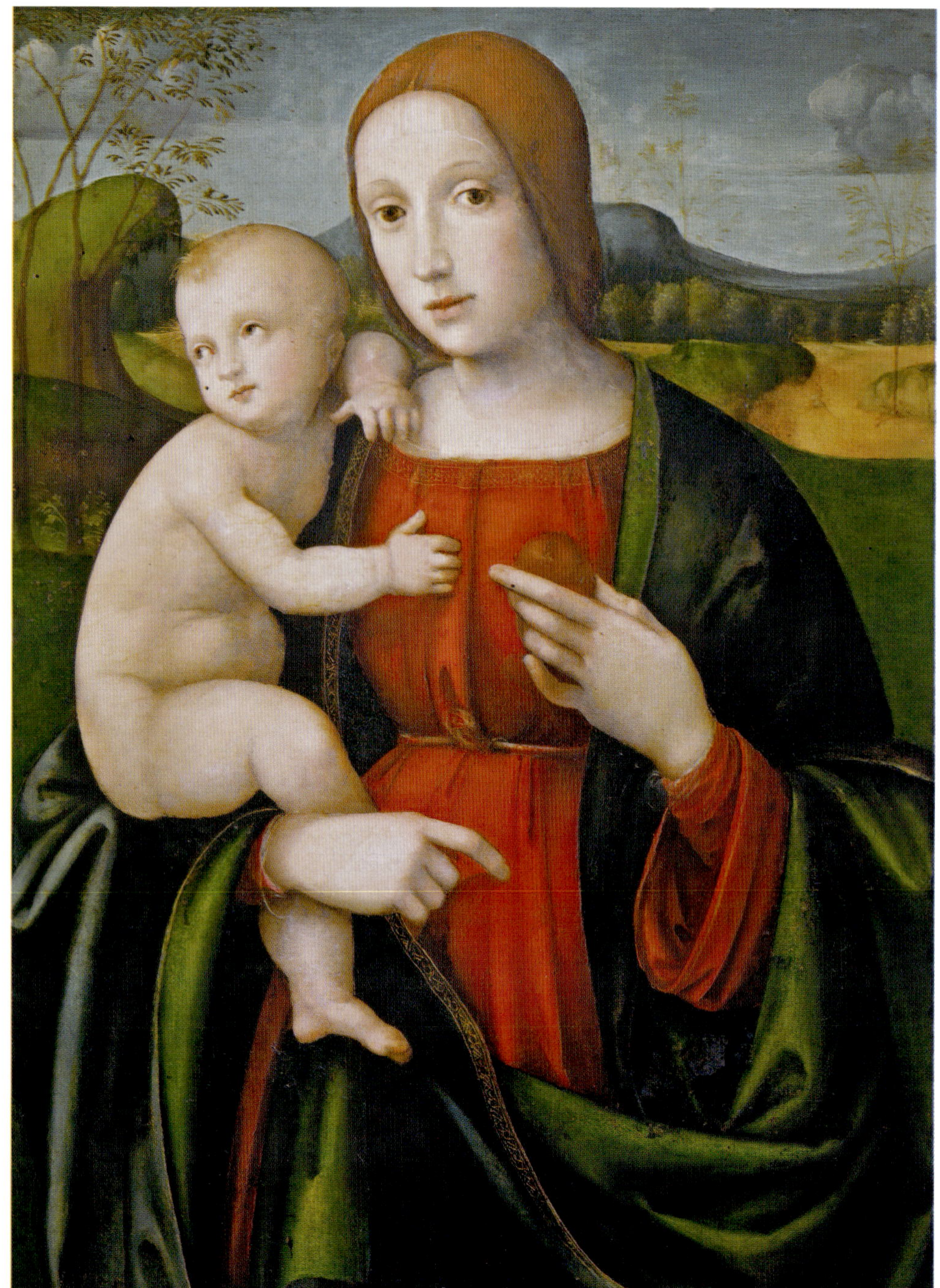

Francesco Francia (Francesco Raibolini), attributed to

The Virgin and Child

The Virgin and Child in front of a landscape was one of the favorite motifs of the Bolognese painter Francesco Francia. What is immediately striking about this particular panel is its simplicity of composition, which focuses entirely on the central figure group, the mother and child. Given the total absence of halos and attributes, this could at first glance be the portrait of a young noblewoman and her child. The Virgin Mary is precisely positioned on the central axis, with the vertical further emphasized by the brilliant red of her gown. The painting is dominated by Mary's green mantle, which falls in elaborate, sweeping folds. Both gown and cloak possess a shimmering texture that lends the largely unadorned garments a markedly luxurious note. In contrast to the sumptuous clothing of the Madonna, the Infant Jesus is completely naked. Whereas the mother fixes her gaze on an imaginary viewer before her, Jesus looks out of the picture to the left, full of yearning. It is possible that he is reflecting on his future role as redeemer of the world, a task to which the apple in Mary's hand, the only traditional attribute in the picture, symbolically alludes. Stylistically the panel is in keeping with the paintings of the Virgin and Child produced by Francia around 1495 and is therefore dated to this time.

Francesco Francia (Francesco Raibolini) attributed to, ca. 1450–1517
***The Virgin and Child*, ca. 1495**
64 x 49 cm; Oil on wood panel
Pinacoteca; Room V; Inv. 40643

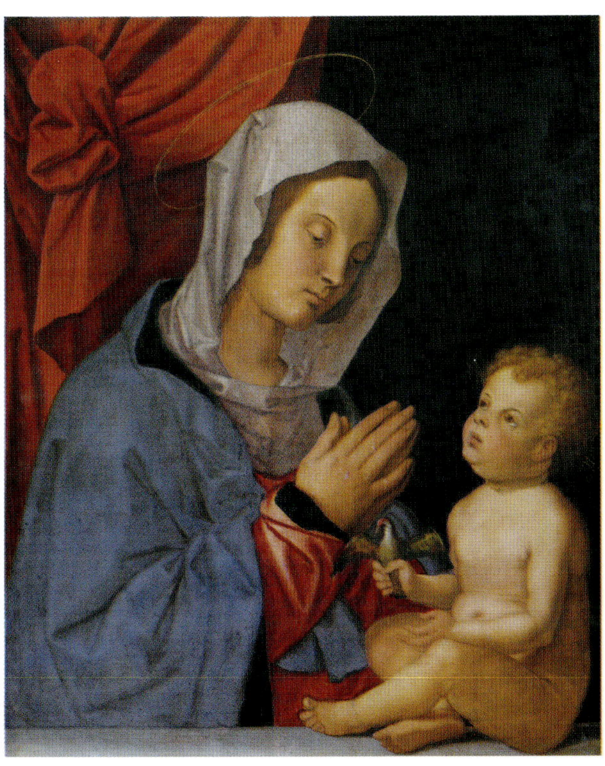

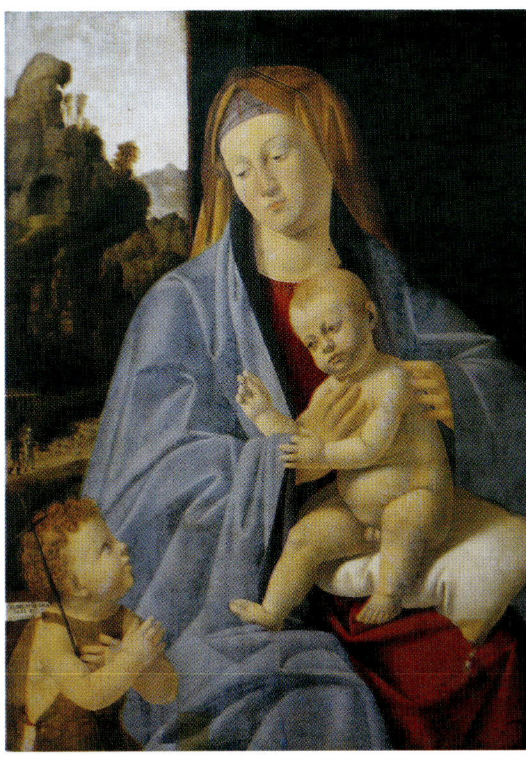

Bartolomeo Montagna, ca. 1450–1523
***Madonna and Child*, ca. 1503**
74 x 60 cm; Oil on wood panel
Pinacoteca; Room V; Inv. 40278

Marco Basaiti, active 1496–1530
***Madonna and Child*, undated**
74 x 54 cm; Tempera on wood panel
Pinacoteca; Room V; Inv. 40280

Giovanni Battista da Faenza, 1465/1470–1516
***Madonna and Child with Saints*, undated**
58 x 37 cm; Tempera on wood panel
Pinacoteca; Room V; Inv. 40294

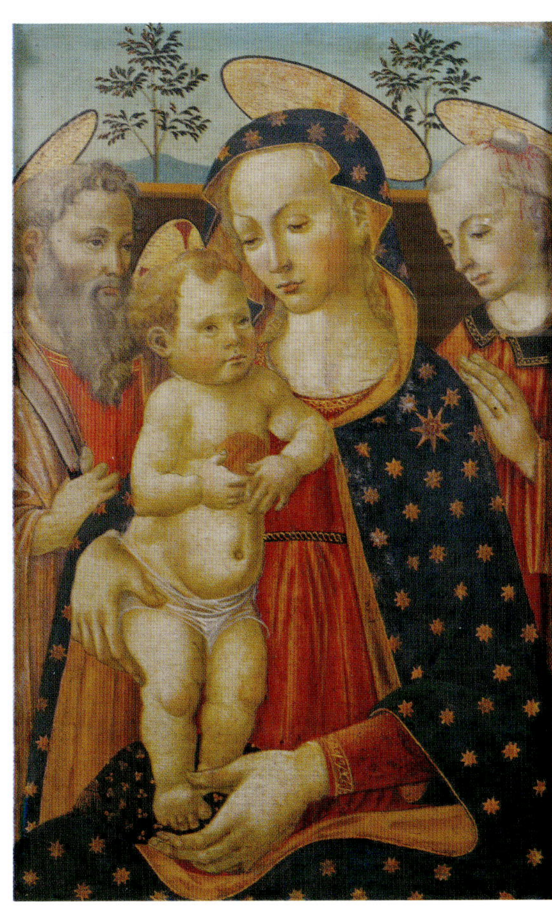

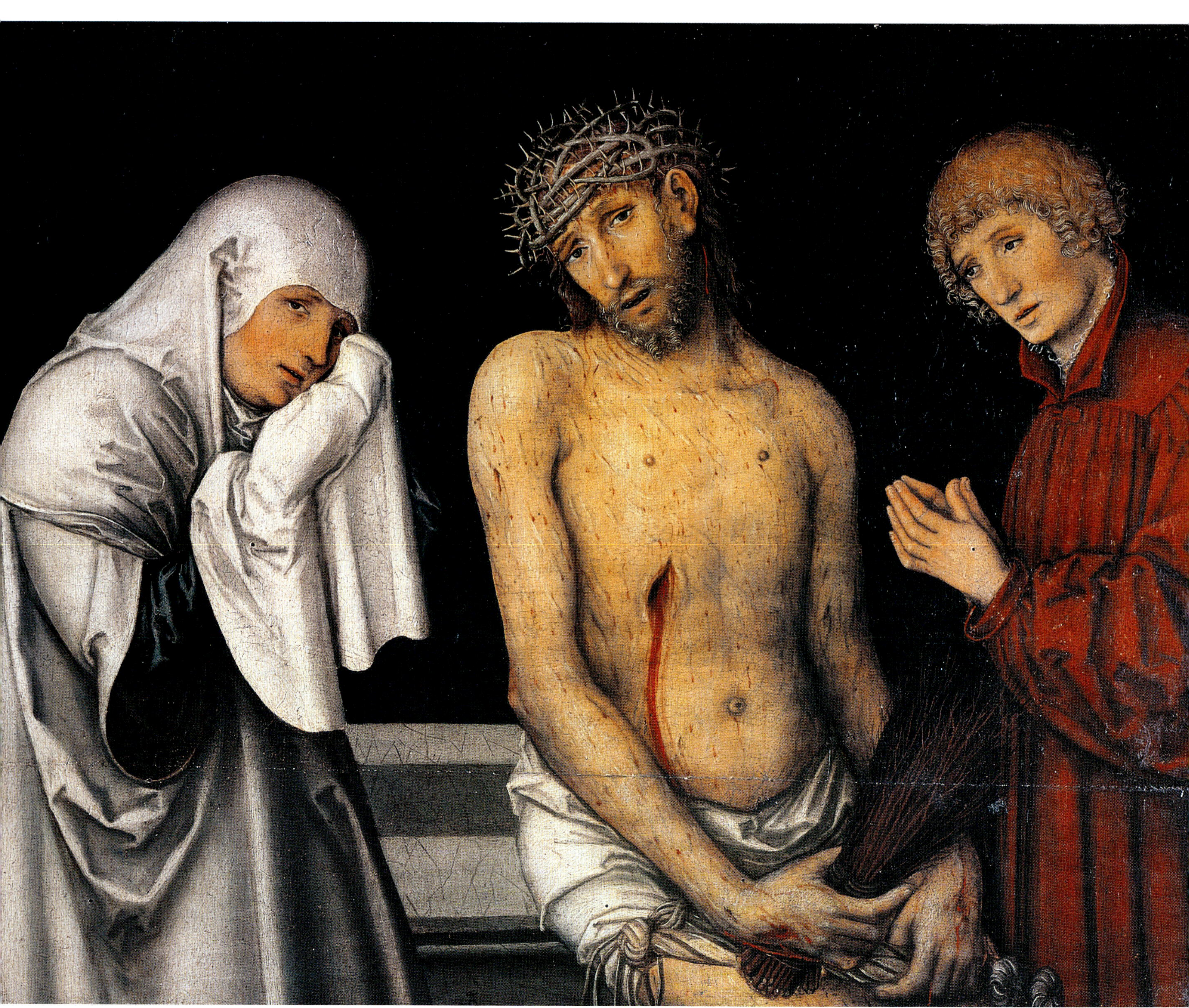

Lucas Cranach the Elder

Pietà

This painting by Lucas Cranach the Elder, perhaps the best-known German Renaissance painter after Albrecht Dürer, is one of the few works by non-Italian artists in the Pinacoteca. The art-loving Pope Pius IX acquired the panel in 1851 from the disposal of art treasures of the Augustinian monastery at Kreuzlingen in Switzerland. Through the addition of the grieving Virgin Mary and St. John, this landscape-format panel expands a common motif in Cranach's oeuvre, that of Christ as the Man of Sorrows, into a pietà. The aim of both types of image was to elicit the viewer's compassion for the suffering Christ, shown here seated on his sarcophagus at the center of the picture. Christ's maltreated body bears all the signs of the Passion: the crown of thorns on his bleeding head, the bloody, swollen weals from his scourging, the gaping wound in his side and the stigmata from the crucifixion nails. Christ's open mouth seems to emit a faint moan, and his pain-filled eyes rest on the viewer. His grieving mother Mary and beloved disciple St. John incline their heads toward him and appeal to the viewer to do the same. The black background has the effect of directing the viewer's attention to the figures while also lending them a portrait-like presence.

Lucas Cranach the Elder, 1472–1553
***Pietà*, undated**
54 x 74 cm; Oil on wood panel
Pinacoteca; Room V; Inv. 40275

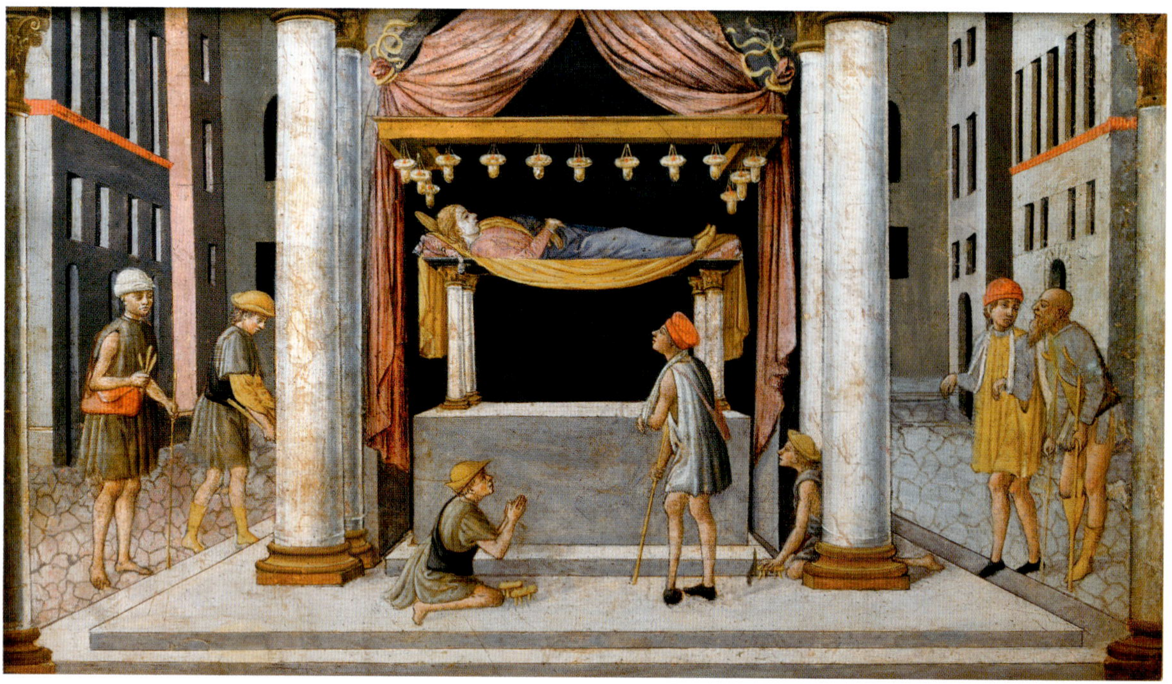

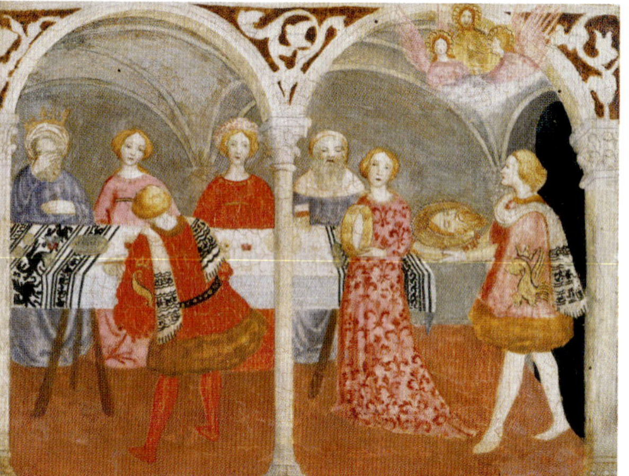

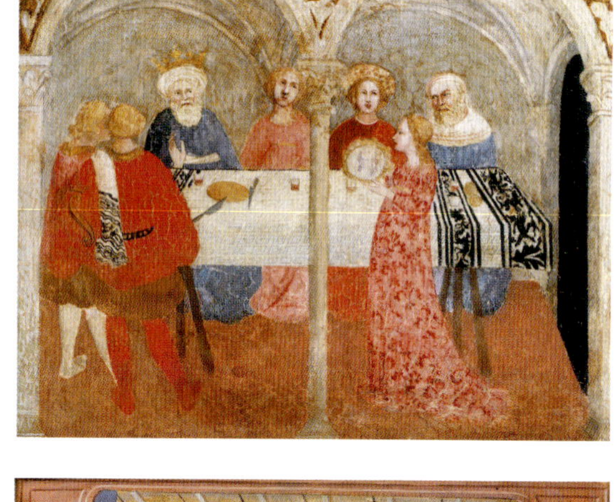

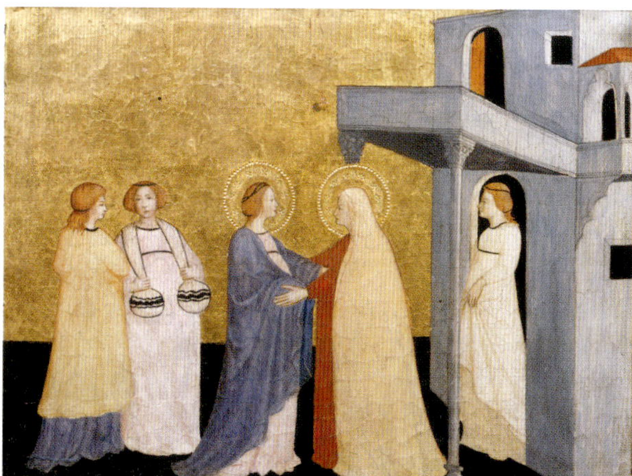

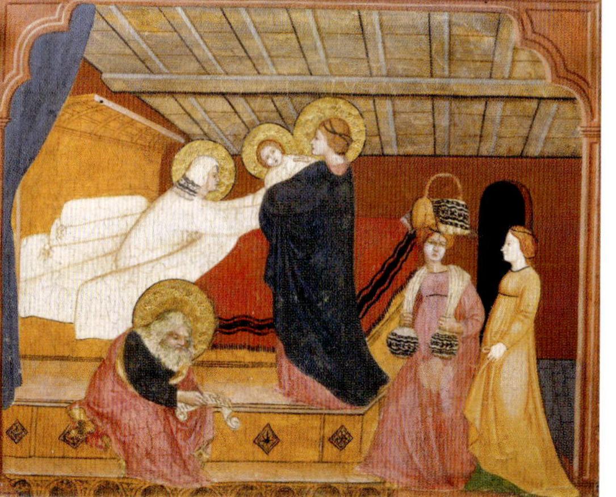

Florentine School, 15th century
***The Sick Pray before the Body of St. Barbara*, 15th century**
31.1 x 55.4 cm; Tempera on wood panel
Pinacoteca; Room V; Inv. 40284

Florentine School, first half of 15th century
***Salome with the Head of St. John the Baptist*, undated**
28.5 x 37 cm; Tempera on wood panel
Pinacoteca; Room V; Inv. 40289

Florentine School, first half of 15th century
***St. John and Herodes*, undated**
28.5 x 34 cm; Tempera on wood panel
Pinacoteca; Room V; Inv. 40287

Florentine School, first half of 15th century
***Visitation*, 15th century**
28 x 34.5 cm; Tempera on wood panel
Pinacoteca; Room V; Inv. 40283

Florentine School, 15th century
***Birth of St. John the Baptist*, 15th century**
28 x 34.5 cm; Tempera on wood panel
Pinacoteca; Room V; Inv. 40285

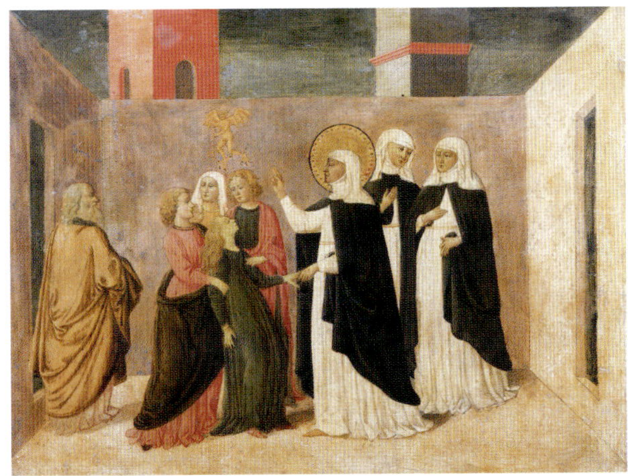

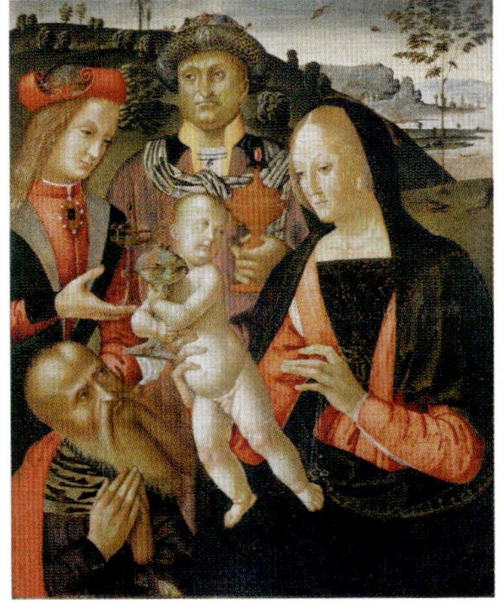

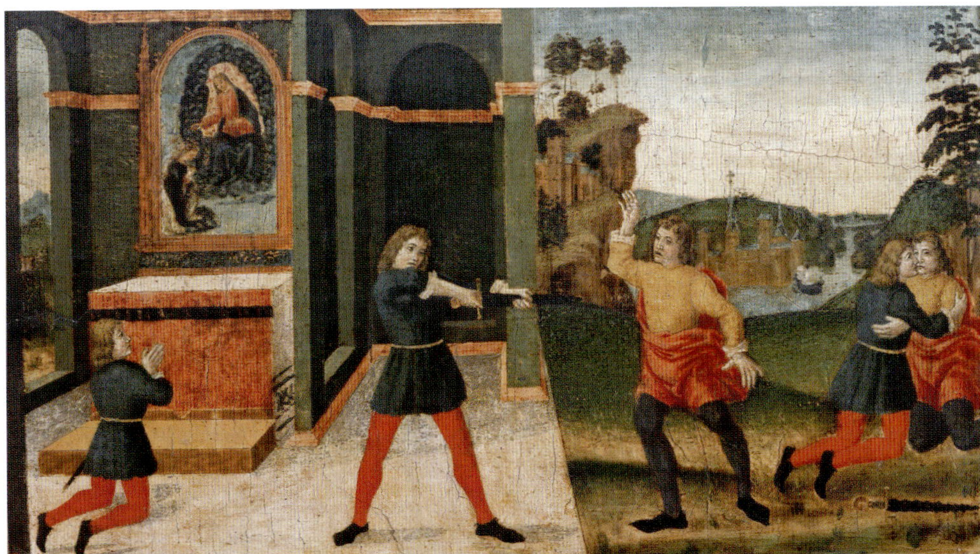

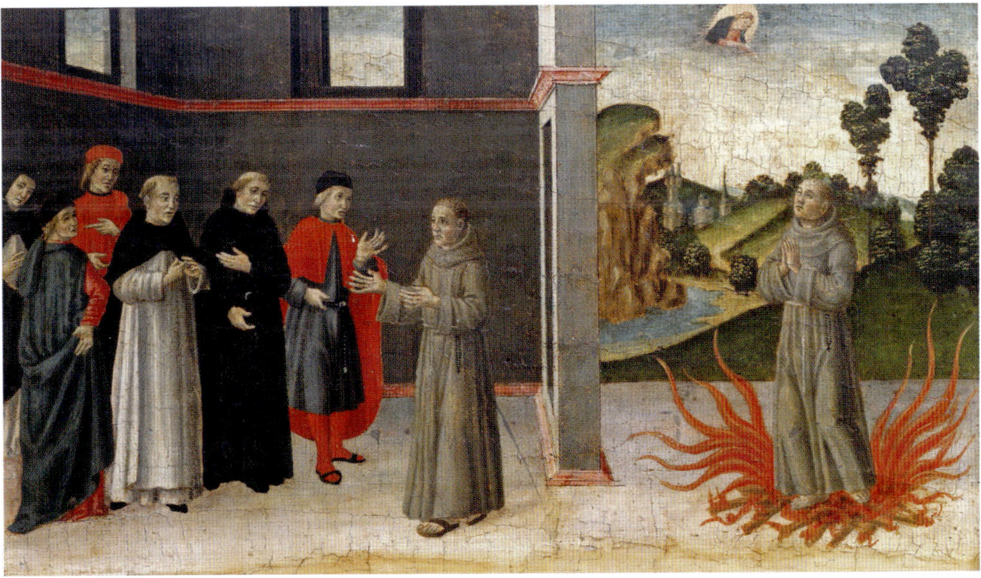

Florentine School, 15th century
***St. Catherine Excorcising a Possessed Woman*, 15th century**
34.5 x 46 cm; Tempera on wood panel
Pinacoteca; Room V; Inv. 40327

Bernardino di Mariotto, 1478–1566
***Adoration of the Magi*, undated**
54.4 x 44 cm; Tempera on wood panel
Pinacoteca; Room V; Inv. 40620

Lucchese Master of the Immaculate Conception, late 15th–early 16th century
***The Immaculate Virgin Reconciles Two Enemies*, 1505–1510**
23 x 39.4 cm; Tempera on wood panel
Pinacoteca; Room V; Inv. 40295

Lucchese Master of the Immaculate Conception, late 15th–early 16th century
***A Franciscan Submits Himself to an Ordeal by Fire*, 1505–1510**
22.5 x 39.5 cm; Tempera on wood panel
Pinacoteca; Room V; Inv. 40293

ROOM VI

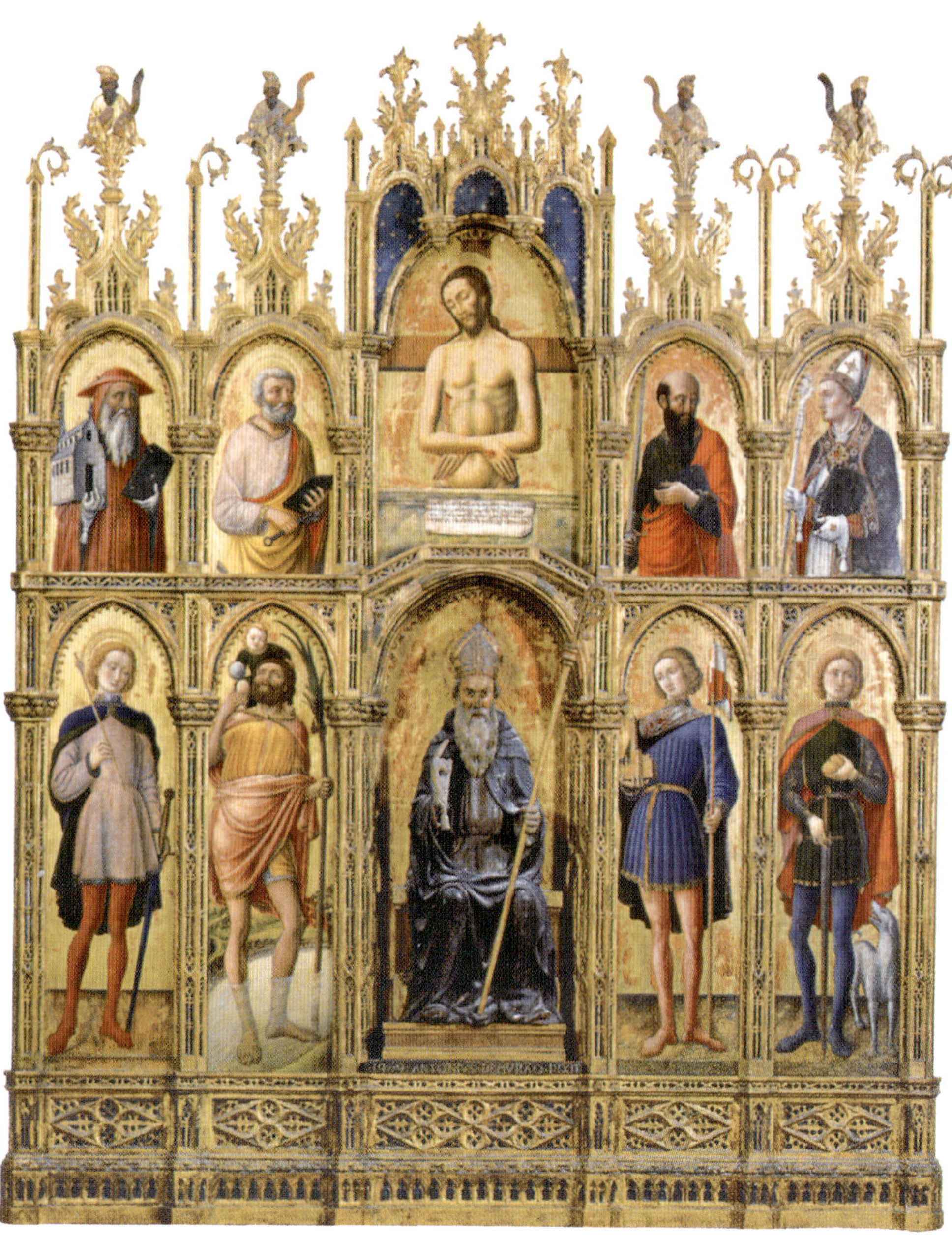

Antonio Vivarini

St. Anthony Abbot with Eight Saints and Christ

This altarpiece, with its original carved frame, is the last documented work of the Venetian painter Antonio Vivarini. Just as the architecture of the frame fluctuates between the Gothic pointed arch and the Renaissance rounded arch, so too the painting combines Gothic elements with formal features characteristic of the early modern period. Typically Gothic are the gently elongated figures of the saints, who exude a certain courtly elegance. On the other hand, they are standing in the classical contrapposto stance and seem to be modeled in space. The conscious realism with which they have been painted is also characteristic of the Renaissance. With his "classicizing Gothic," Vivarini appealed not merely to the tastes of Venetian art lovers, for the polyptych was made as an altarpiece for the oratory of the Confraternity of St. Anthony Abbot in the city of Pesaro. Enthroned at the center of the work is the figure of St. Anthony, who in the Late Middle Ages was invoked among other things as the patron saint of the disease St. Anthony's Fire (ergotism). His image has been executed in low relief but was probably only painted, not modeled, by Vivarini. Nevertheless, the artist has self-confidently signed the work "1464 Antonius de Murano pinxit" ("Painted by Antonius da Murano in 1464") below the rendering of the saint. Above St. Antony is the half-length figure of Christ in the guise of Man of Sorrows (imago pietatis), flanked by SS. Peter and Paul.

Antonio Vivarini, ca. 1418–1476/84
***St. Anthony Abbot with Eight Saints and Christ*, 1464**
105 x 130 cm; Tempera on wood panel
Pinacoteca; Room VI; Inv. 40303

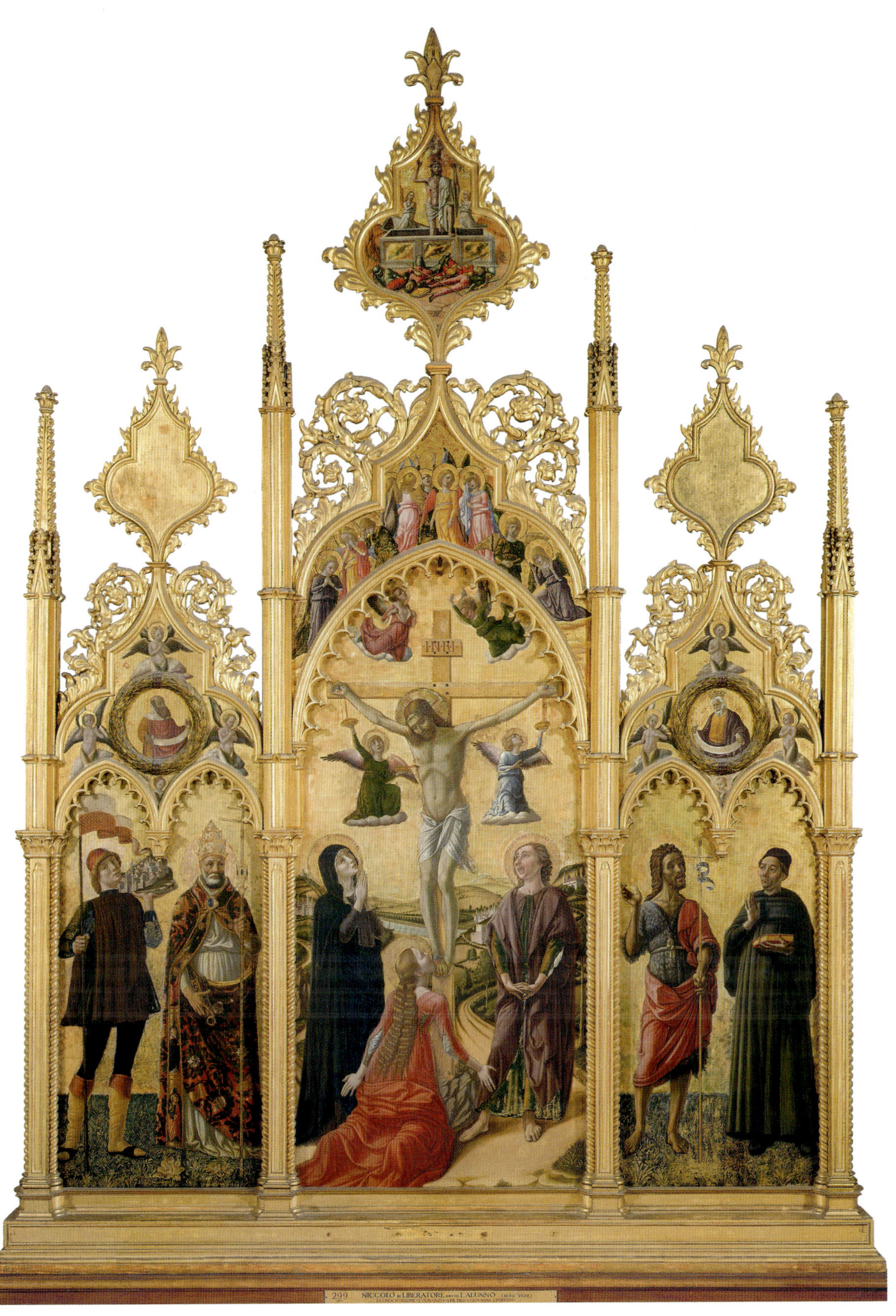

Niccolò di Liberatore (Niccolò Alunno), ca. 1430–1502
***Camerino Triptych*, undated**
250 x 117 cm; Tempera on wood panel
Pinacoteca; Room VI; Inv. 40299

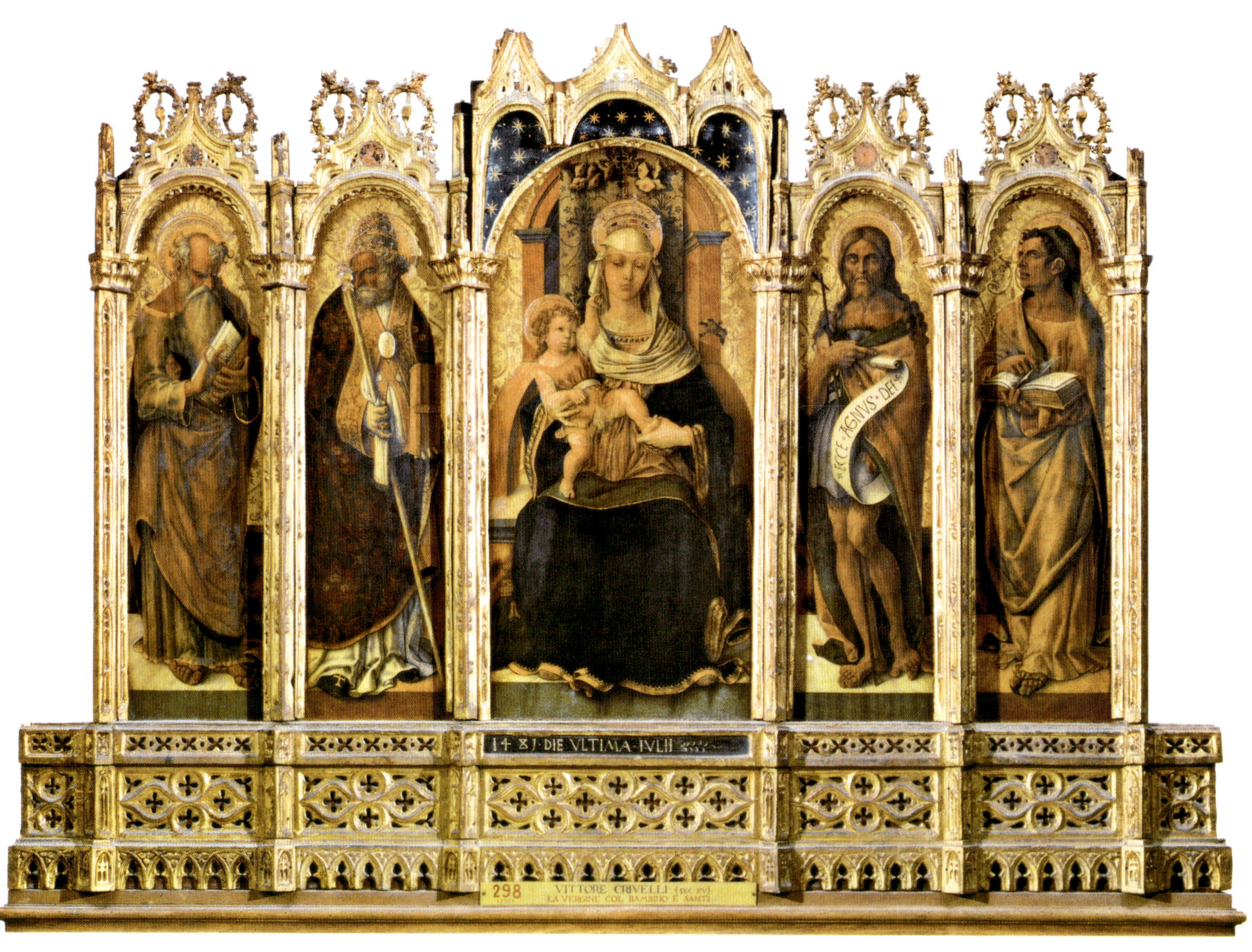

Vittorio Crivelli, ca. 1440–1501
***Madonna and Child with Saints*, 1481**
100 x 48; Tempera on wood panel
Pinacoteca; Room VI; Inv. 40298

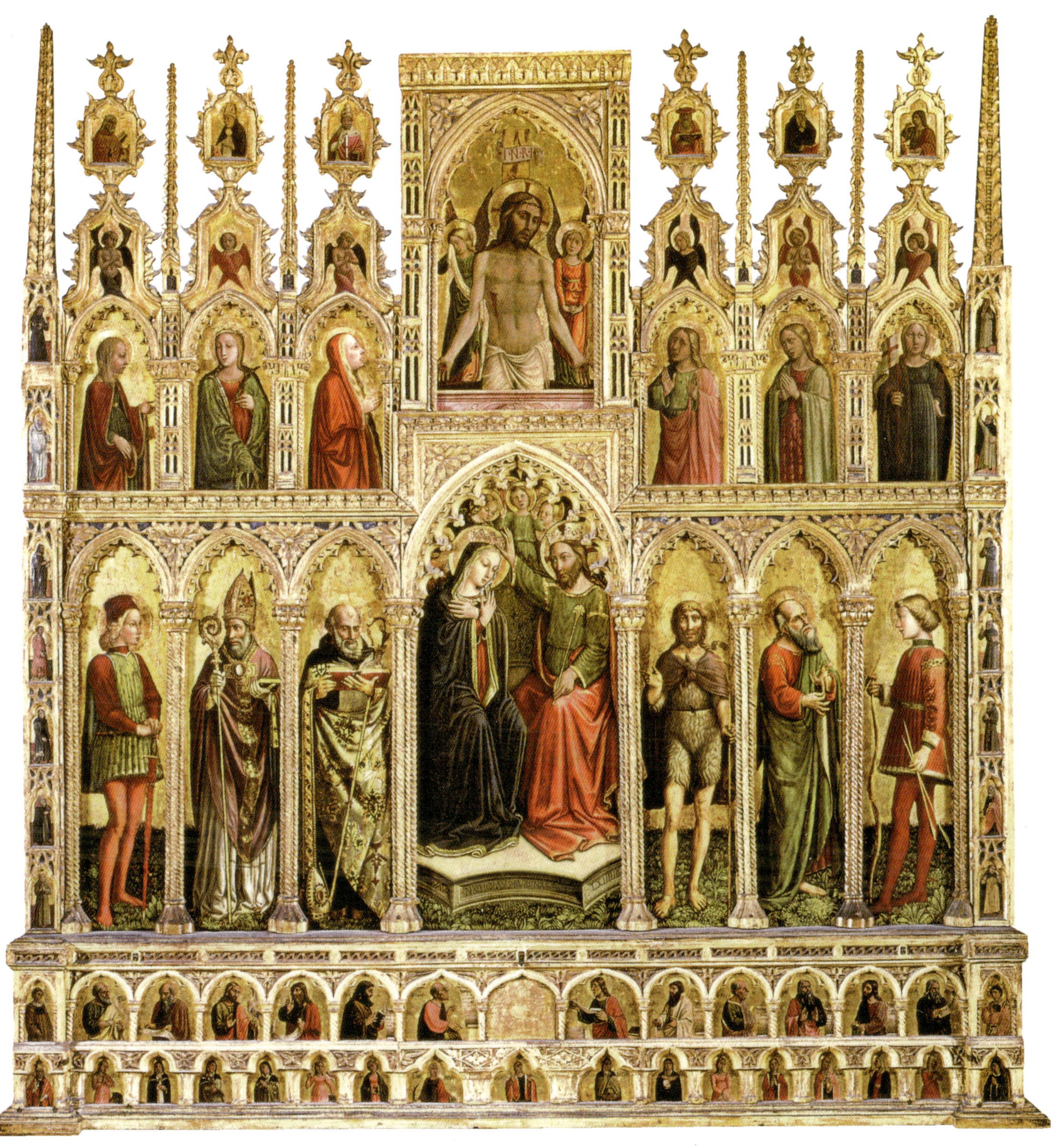

Niccolò di Liberatore (Niccolò Alunno), ca. 1430–1502
***Montelparo Polyptych*, ca. 1466**
291 x 280 cm; Tempera on panel
Pinacoteca; Room VI; Inv. 40307

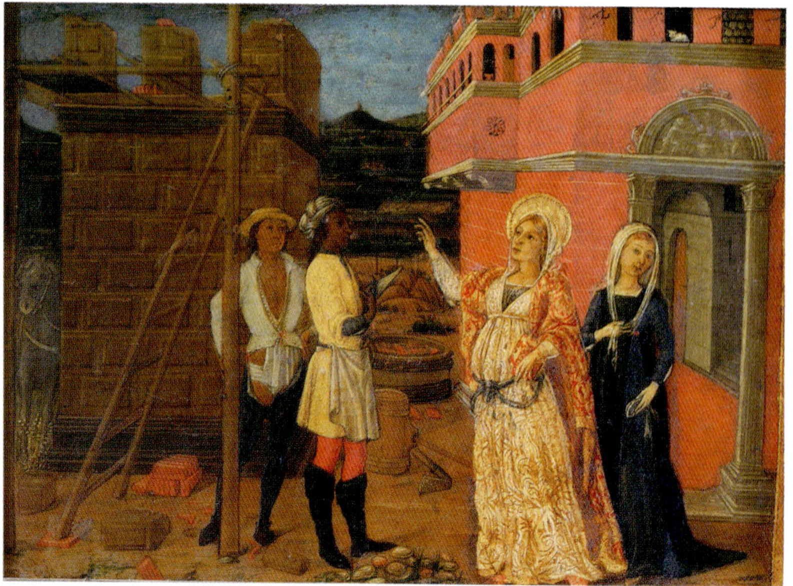

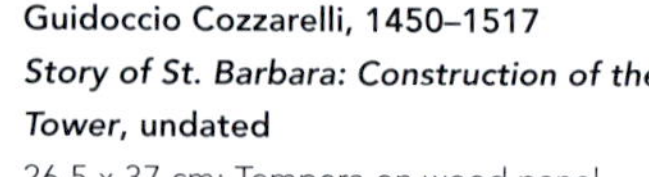

Guidoccio Cozzarelli, 1450–1517
***Story of St. Barbara: Construction of the Tower*, undated**
26.5 x 37 cm; Tempera on wood panel
Pinacoteca; Room VI; Inv. 40308.4.1

Guidoccio Cozzarelli, 1450–1517
***Story of St. Barbara: Flagellation*, undated**
26.5 x 37 cm; Tempera on wood panel
Pinacoteca; Room VI; Inv. 40308.4.2

Guidoccio Cozzarelli, 1450–1517
***Story of St. Barbara: The Saint with Her Father*, undated**
26.5 x 37 cm; Tempera on wood panel
Pinacoteca; Room VI; Inv. 40308.4.3

Guidoccio Cozzarelli, 1450–1517
***Story of St. Barbara: Decapitation*, undated**
26.5 x 37 cm; Tempera on wood panel
Pinacoteca; Room VI; Inv. 40408.4.4

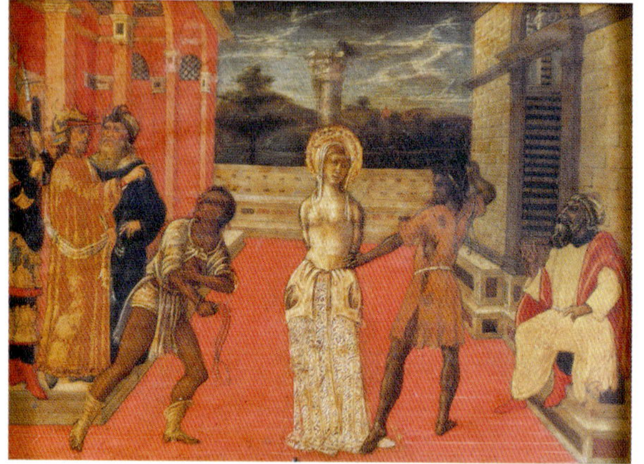

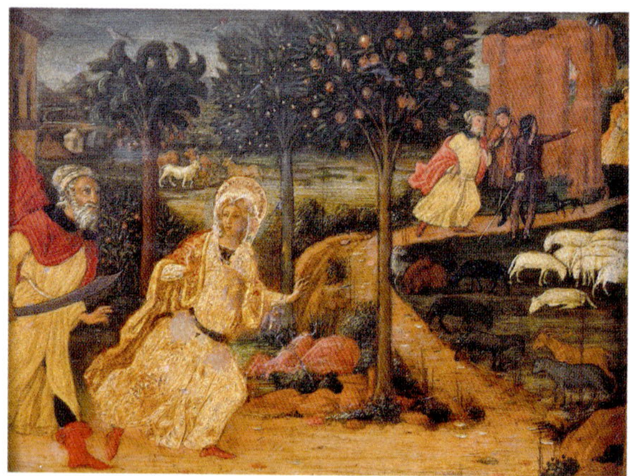

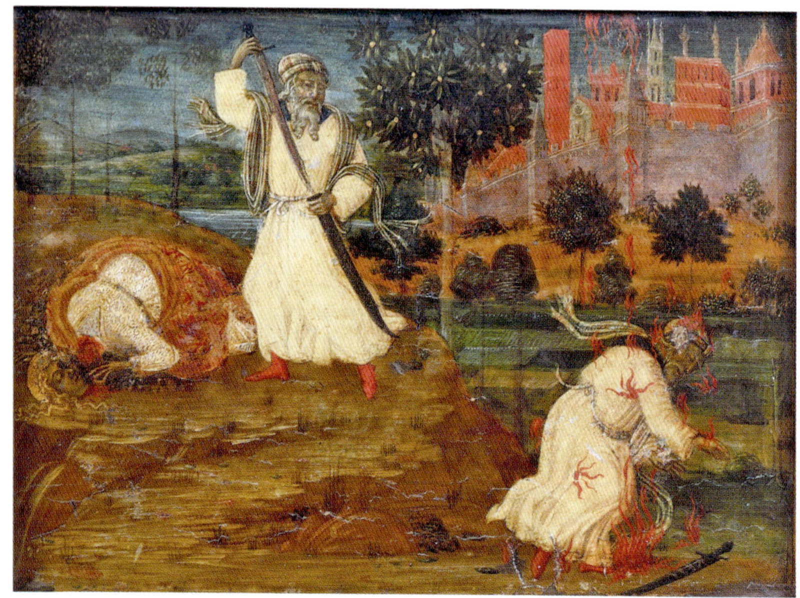

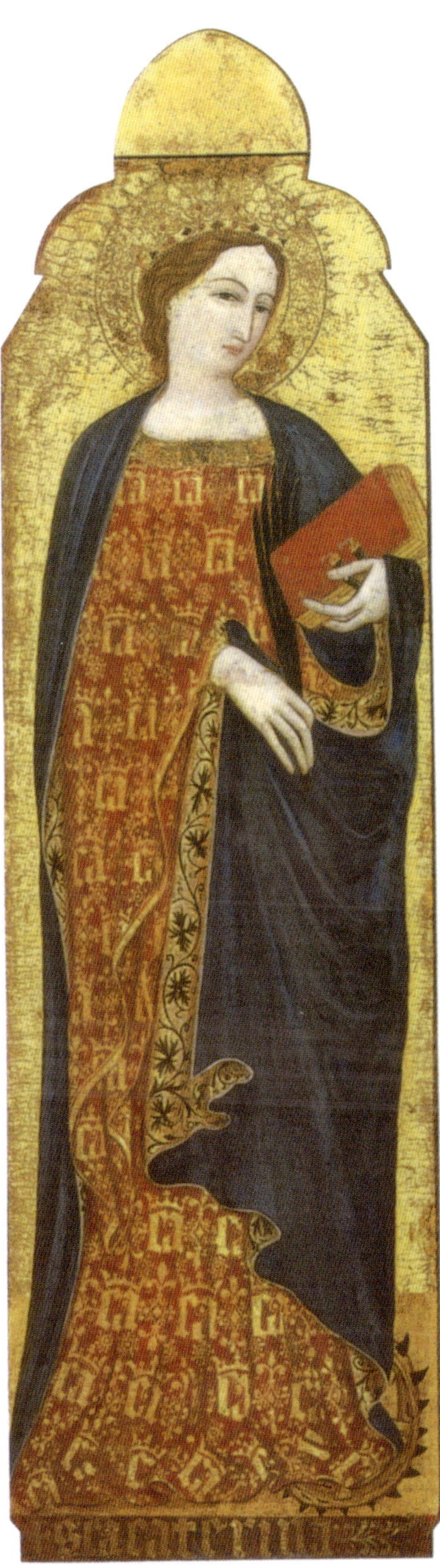

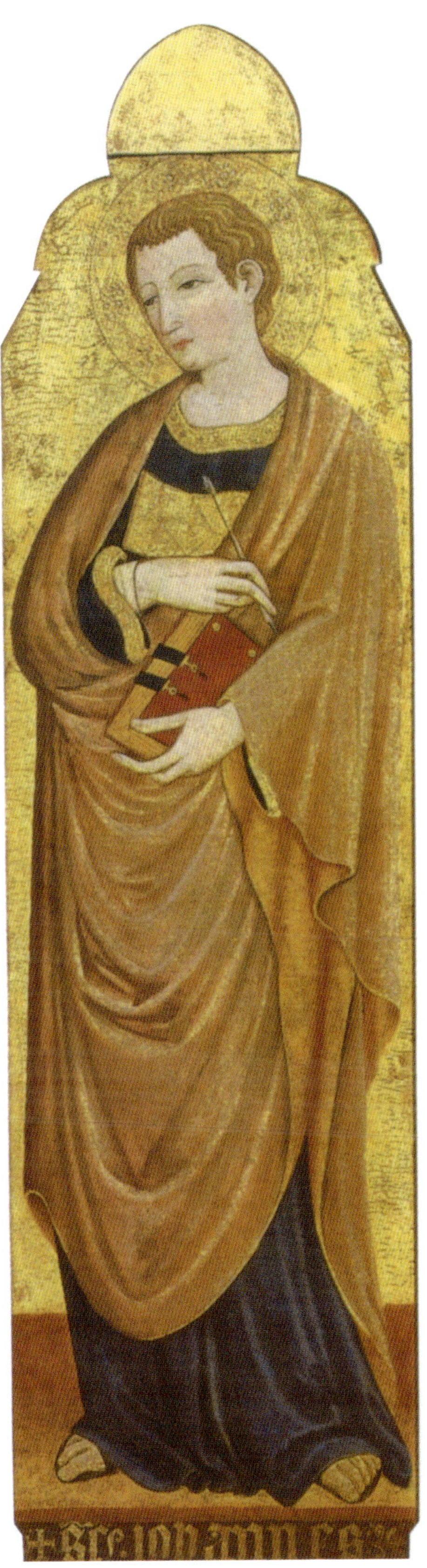

Master of Narni of 1409, early 15th century
***St. Catherine*, undated**
109 x 38.7 cm; Tempera and gold on wood panel
Pinacoteca; Room VI; Inv. 40302

Master of Narni of 1409, early 15th century
***St. John the Evangelist*, undated**
108.8 x 38.7 cm; Tempera and gold on wood panel
Pinacoteca; Room VI; Inv. 40304

Master of Narni of 1409, early 15th century
***St. Andrew*, undated**
108.8 x 38.7 cm; Tempera and gold on wood panel
Pinacoteca; Room VI; Inv. 40305

Master of Narni of 1409, early 15th century
***St. Augustine of Ippona*, undated**
108.8 x 38.7 cm; Tempera and gold on wood panel
Pinacoteca; Room VI; Inv. 40306

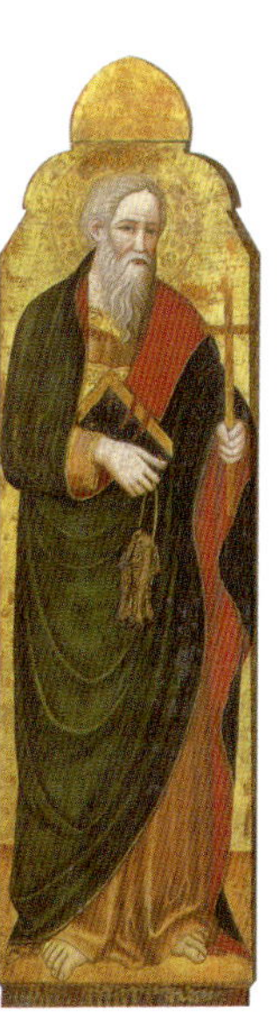

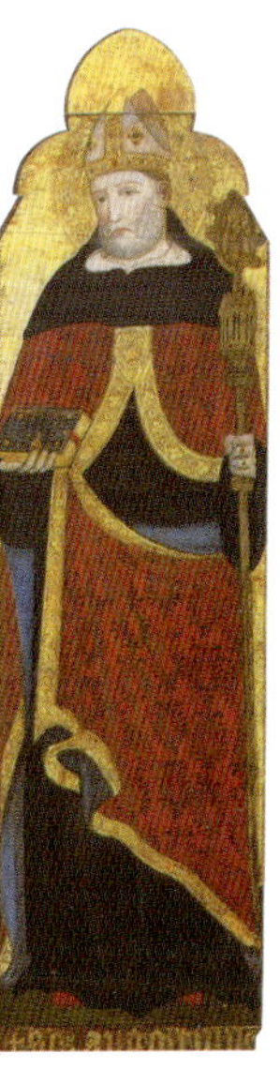

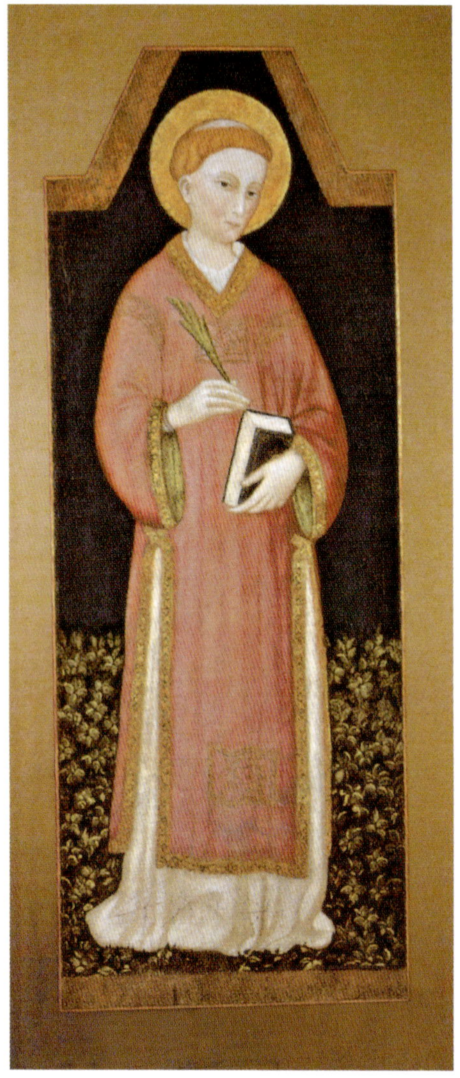

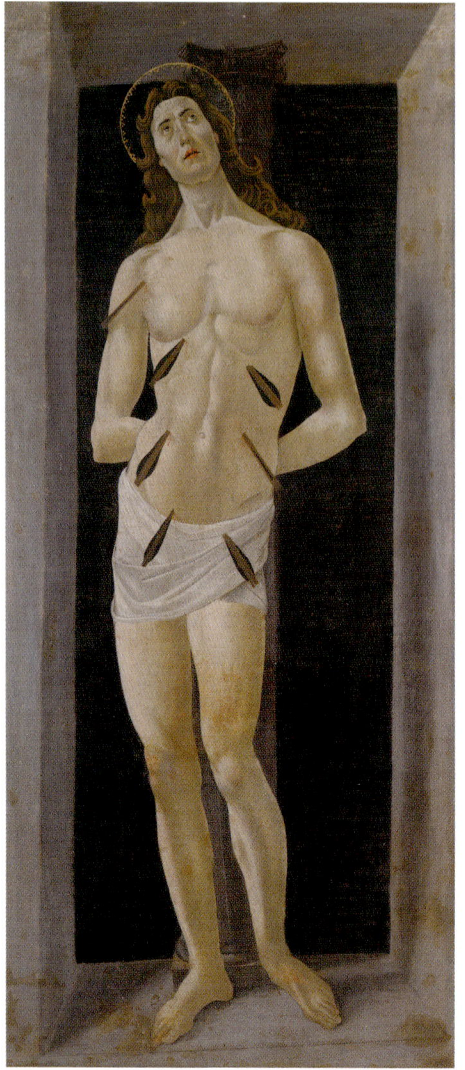

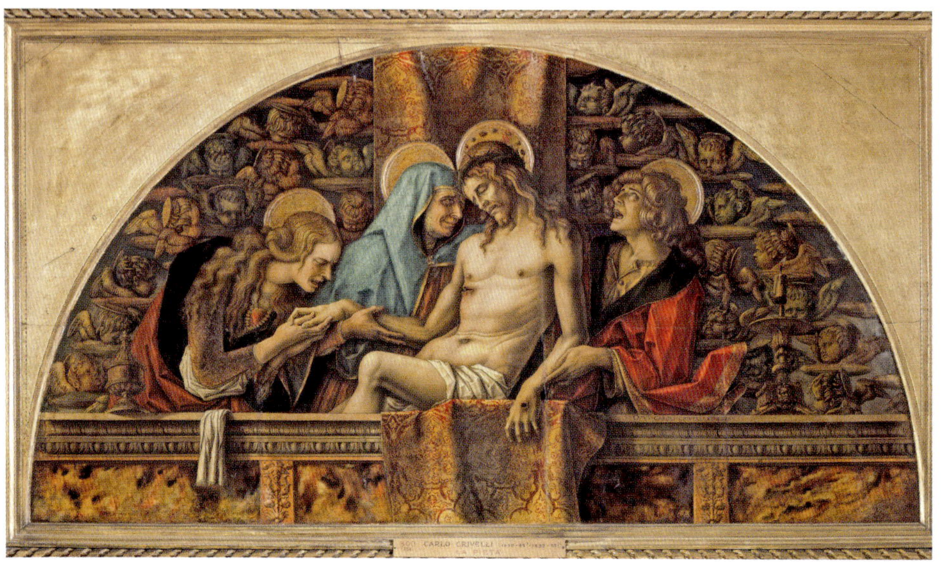

Master of St. Verecondo, early 15th century
***St. Stephen*, undated**
120.4 x 47.3 cm; Tempera on wood panel
Pinacoteca; Room VI; Inv. 41638

Sandro Botticelli (follower of), 1445–1510
***St. Sebastian*, undated**
162.1 x 74.5 cm; Tempera on wood panel
Pinacoteca; Room VI; Inv. 40301

Carlo Crivelli, ca. 1435–1494
***Pietà*, undated**
105 x 205 cm; Tempera on wood panel
Pinacoteca; Room VI; Inv. 40300

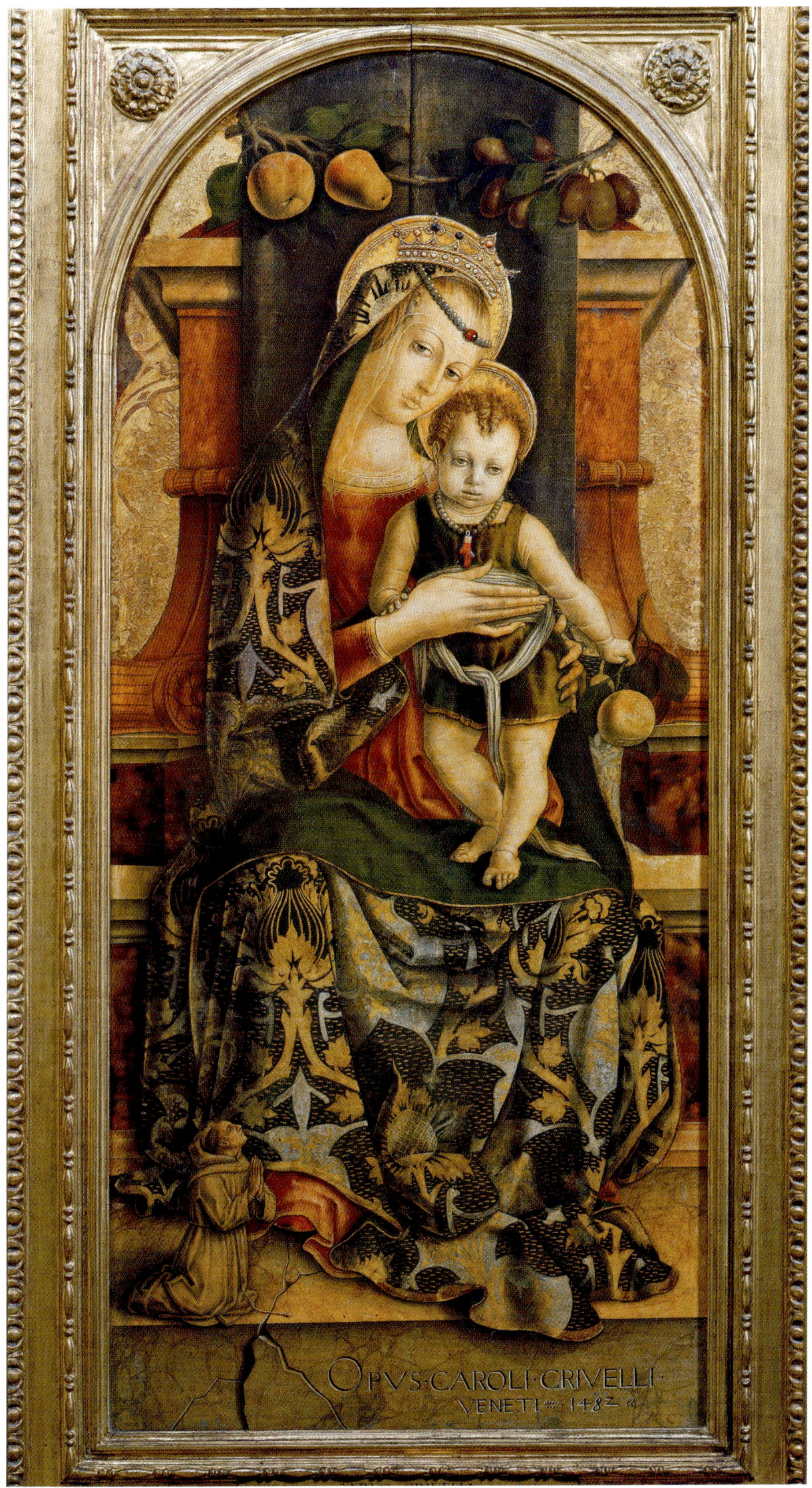

Carlo Crivelli

The Virgin and Child

Carlo Crivelli has a highly characteristic decorative style of painting and this panel of the Virgin and Child is one of his masterpieces. It was commissioned for the church of San Francesco at Force near Ascoli Piceno (Marche), where Crivelli was living at the time. The donor was the Franciscan monk depicted as the tiny figure kneeling at the feet of the Virgin. The larger-than-life-size Madonna is seated on a mighty marble throne, holding on her lap a chubby Infant Jesus. Her crown, set with precious stones, marks her out as the Queen of Heaven. The painting is dominated by the Virgin's exquisite mantle with its conspicuous pomegranate pattern in gold and silver. According to tradition, the pomegranate is a symbol of Mary as Mother of the Church. The apple held by the Infant Jesus, on the other hand, symbolizes victory over original sin by means of his self-sacrifice—alluded to by his red coral chain. Decorative effect and Christian symbolism are thus closely intertwined in this work. Mother and child both observe the viewer with a serious expression on their faces and with head slightly bowed, contributing to the powerful impression created by this image. Crivelli has signed the work "Opus Caroli Crivelli Veneti 1482" ("The work of Carlo Crivelli of Venice 1482") on the illusionistic painted stone plinth in the foreground.

Carlo Crivelli, ca. 1435–1494
***The Virgin and Child*, 1482**
148 x 67 cm; Tempera on wood panel
Pinacoteca; Room VI; Inv. 40297

ROOM VII

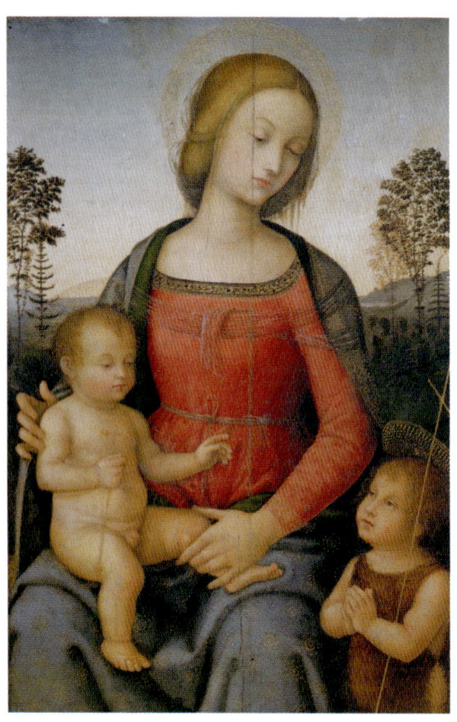

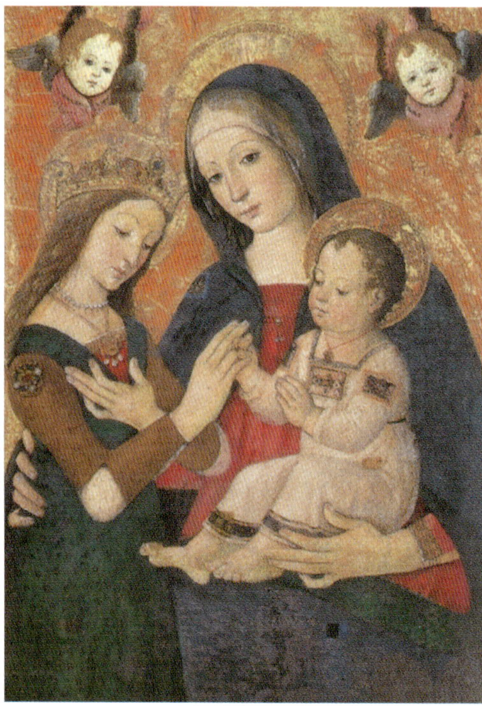

Umbrian School, 15th century
Madonna with St. John as Child, 15th century
57 x 38 cm; Tempera on wood panel
Pinacoteca; Room VII; Inv. 40313

Pinturicchio, School of, 1454–1513
Mystical Marriage of St. Catherine, undated
45 x 34 cm; Tempera on wood panel
Pinacoteca; Room VII; Inv. 40314

Pinturicchio (Bernardino di Betto), 1454–1513
Madonna and Child, ca. 1490
105 x 87 cm; Tempera on wood panel
Pinacoteca; Room VII; Inv. 40324

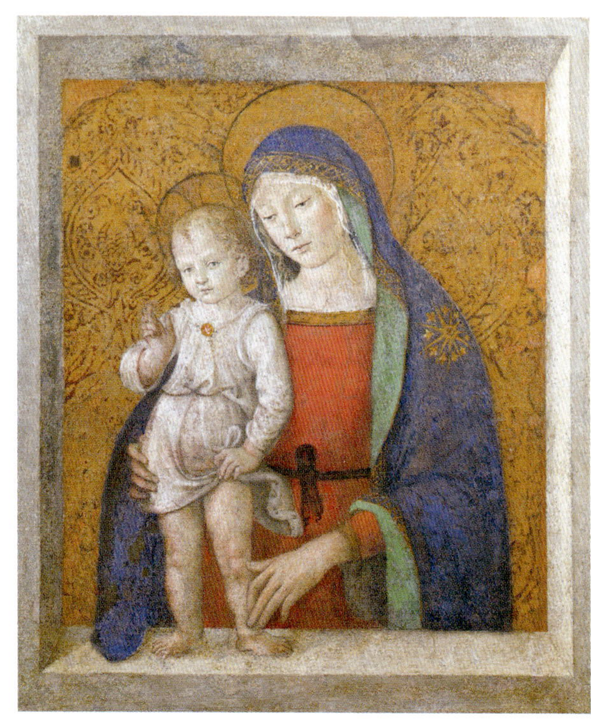

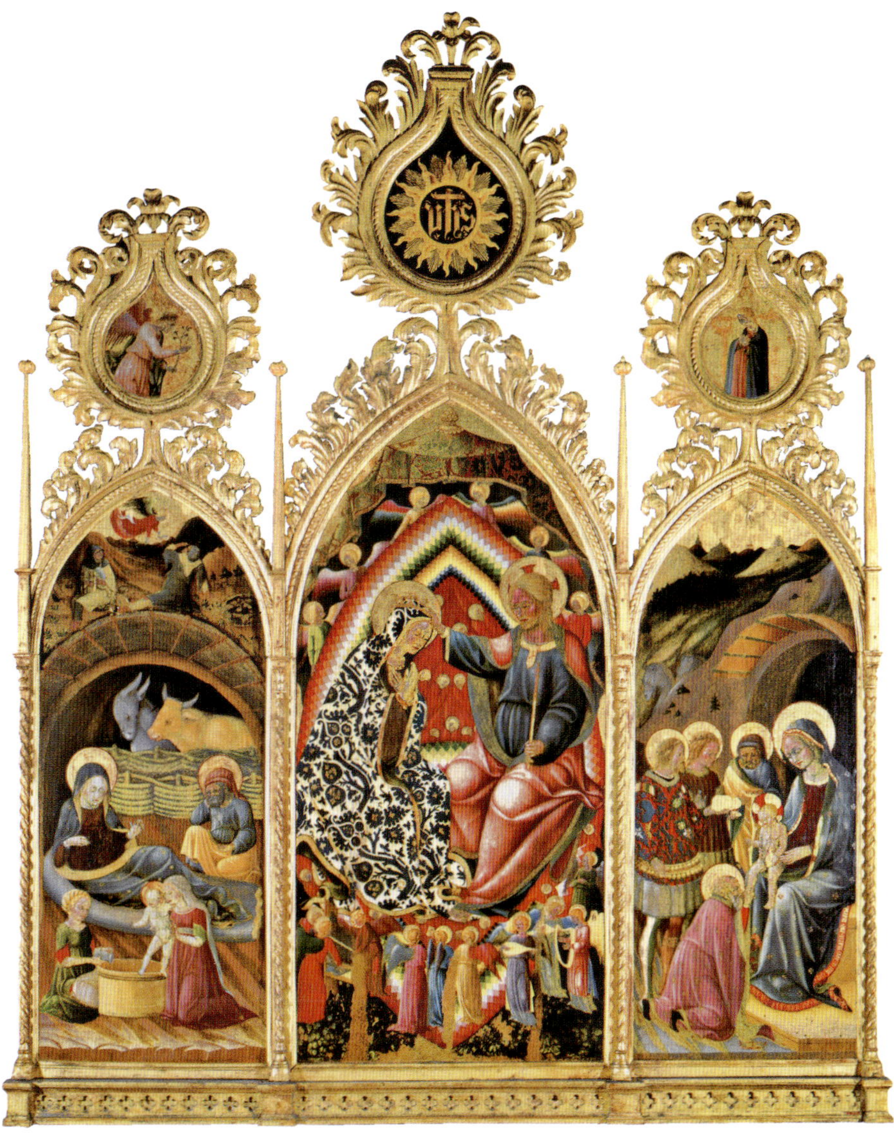

Bartolomeo di Tommaso

Nativity, Coronation of the Virgin, Adoration of the Magi (Rospigliosi Triptych)

This large-format triptych is the most important work of the panel and fresco painter Bartolomeo di Tommaso. Bartolomeo is thought to have trained in Ancona, although his decorative style also shows the influence of the Sienese painter Sassetta (ca. 1392–1450/51). This tripartite work was commissioned by Giulio Cesare da Varano (1430–1502), ruler from the age of fourteen of the small state of Camerino (Marche), as an altarpiece for the collegiate church of San Venanzio. The name "Rospigliosi Triptych," however, refers to the renowned Rospigliosi collection of art in Rome, which acquired the altarpiece in 1799. Depicted are three scenes from the life of the Virgin. In the central panel we see her being crowned by Christ in heaven, while the left panel shows the birth of Christ in the stable in Bethlehem the right panels shows the adoration of the three kings. Bartolomeo da Foligno is known for his combination of realism with a more stylized approach and for his preference for unusual patterns, such as the colorfully faceted mandorla and Mary's white, black, and gold brocade mantle. Bartolomeo's love of narrative is evident in the scene depicting the Infant Christ's first bath, in the bustling orchestra of angels in the central panel, and in the tête-à-tête between the ox and the donkey next to the crib.

Bartolomeo di Tommaso, active 1425–1455
Nativity, Coronation of the Virgin, Adoration of the Magi, **(Rospigliosi Triptych) ca. 1450**
284 x 234. 5; Tempera on wood panel
Pinacoteca; Room VII; Inv. 40296

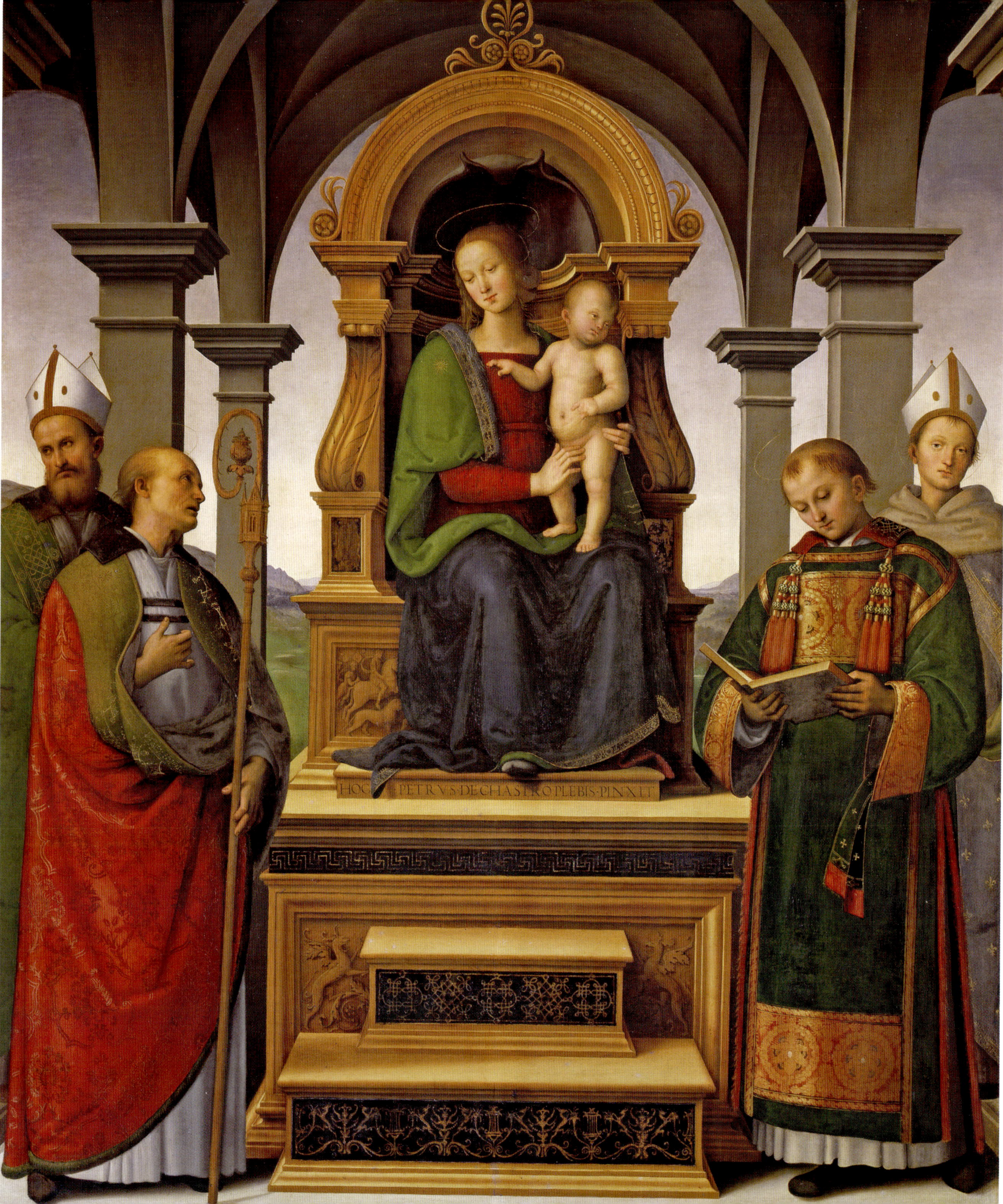
HOC PETRVS·DE CHASTRO PLEBIS·PINXIT

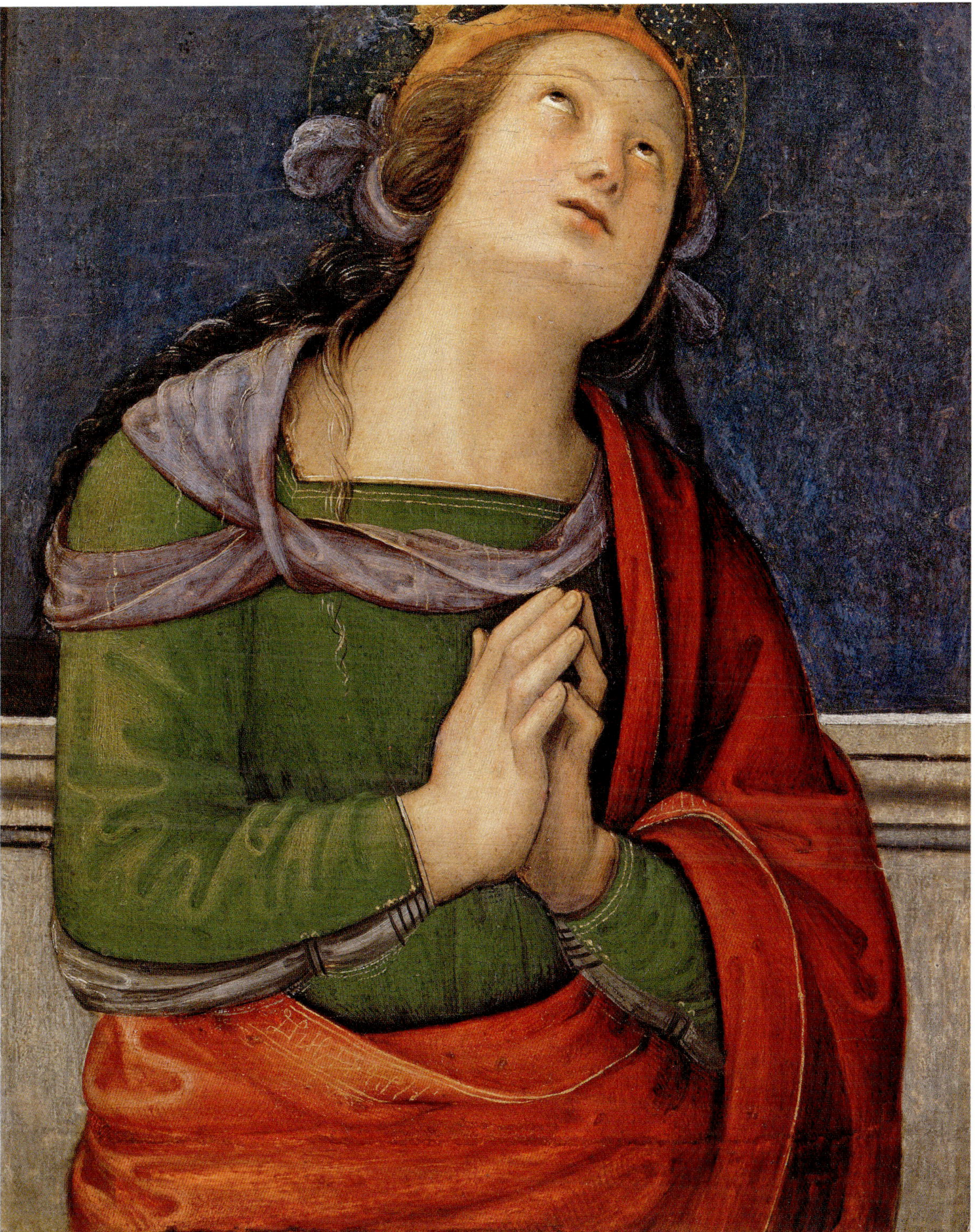

Pietro Perugino, ca. 1450–1523
***Madonna and Child with Saints*, 1495-1496**
193 x 165 cm; Tempera and oil on wood panel
Pinacoteca; Room VII; Inv. 40317

Pietro Perugino, ca. 1450–1523
***St. Flavia*, 1496**
33.5 x 26 cm; Tempera and oil on wood panel
Pinacoteca; Room VII; Inv. 40320

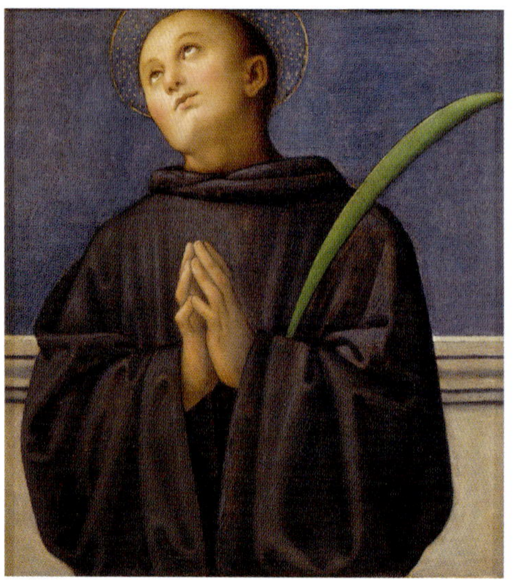

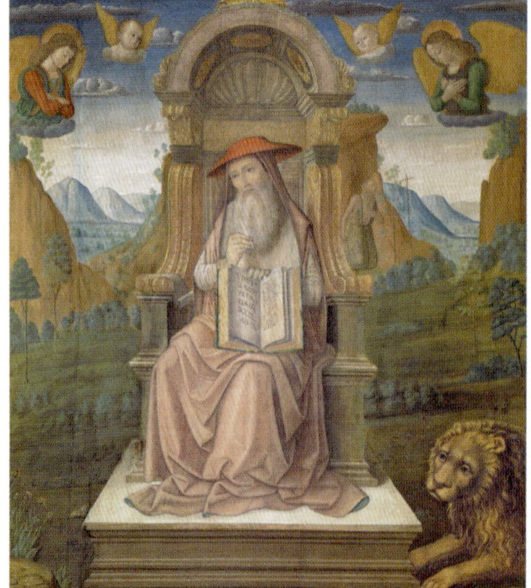

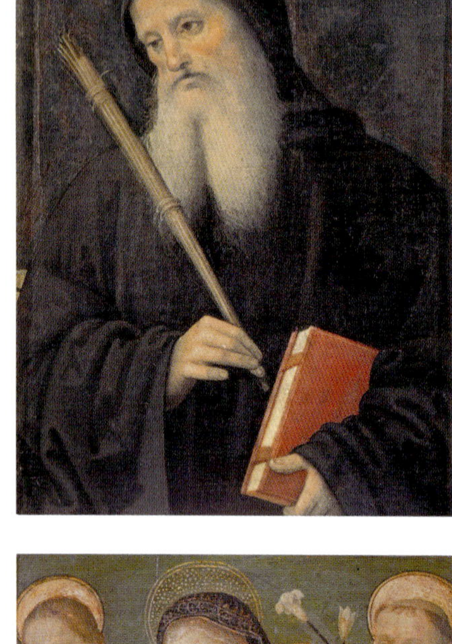

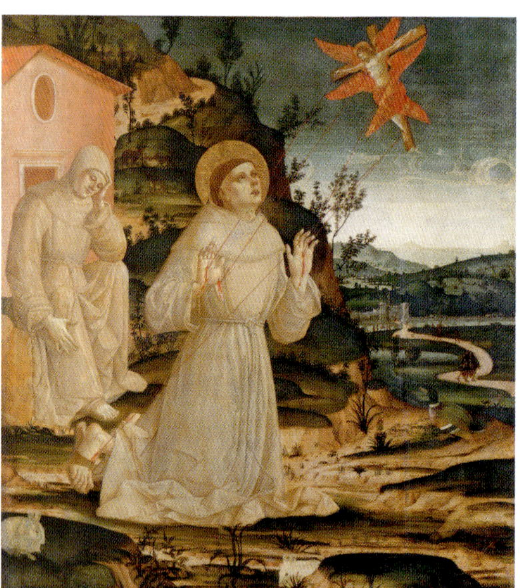

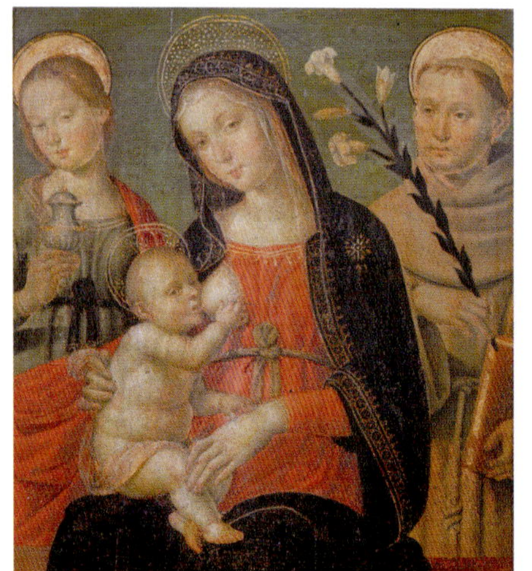

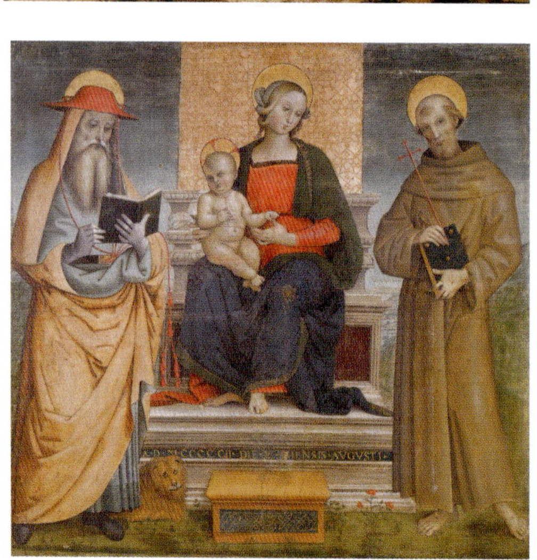

Pietro Perugino, ca. 1450–1523
***St. Placido*, 1496**
33.5 x 30 cm; Tempera and oil on wood panel
Pinacoteca; Room VII; Inv. 40321

Giovanni Santi, ca. 1440–1494
***St. Jerome Enthroned*, 1496-1499**
189 x 168 cm; Tempera on wood panel transferred onto canvas
Pinacoteca; Room VII; Inv. 40326

Pietro Perugino, ca. 1450–1523
***St. Benedict*, undated**
31 x 26 cm; Tempera and oil on wood panel
Pinacoteca; Room VII; Inv. 40319

Antoniazzo Romano, 1430–1510
***St. Francis Receiving the Stigmata*, undated**
152 x 140 cm; Tempera on wood panel
Pinacoteca; Room VII; Inv. 40322

Lo Spagna (Giovanni di Pietro), ca. 1450–1528
***Madonna and Child with SS. Mary Magdalene and Anthony of Padua*, undated**
49 x 45 cm; Tempera on wood panel
Pinacoteca; Room VII; Inv. 40311

Tiberio d'Assisi, ca. 1470–1524
***Madonna with Saints*, 1502**
128 x 134 cm; Tempera on wood panel
Pinacoteca; Room VII; Inv. 40315

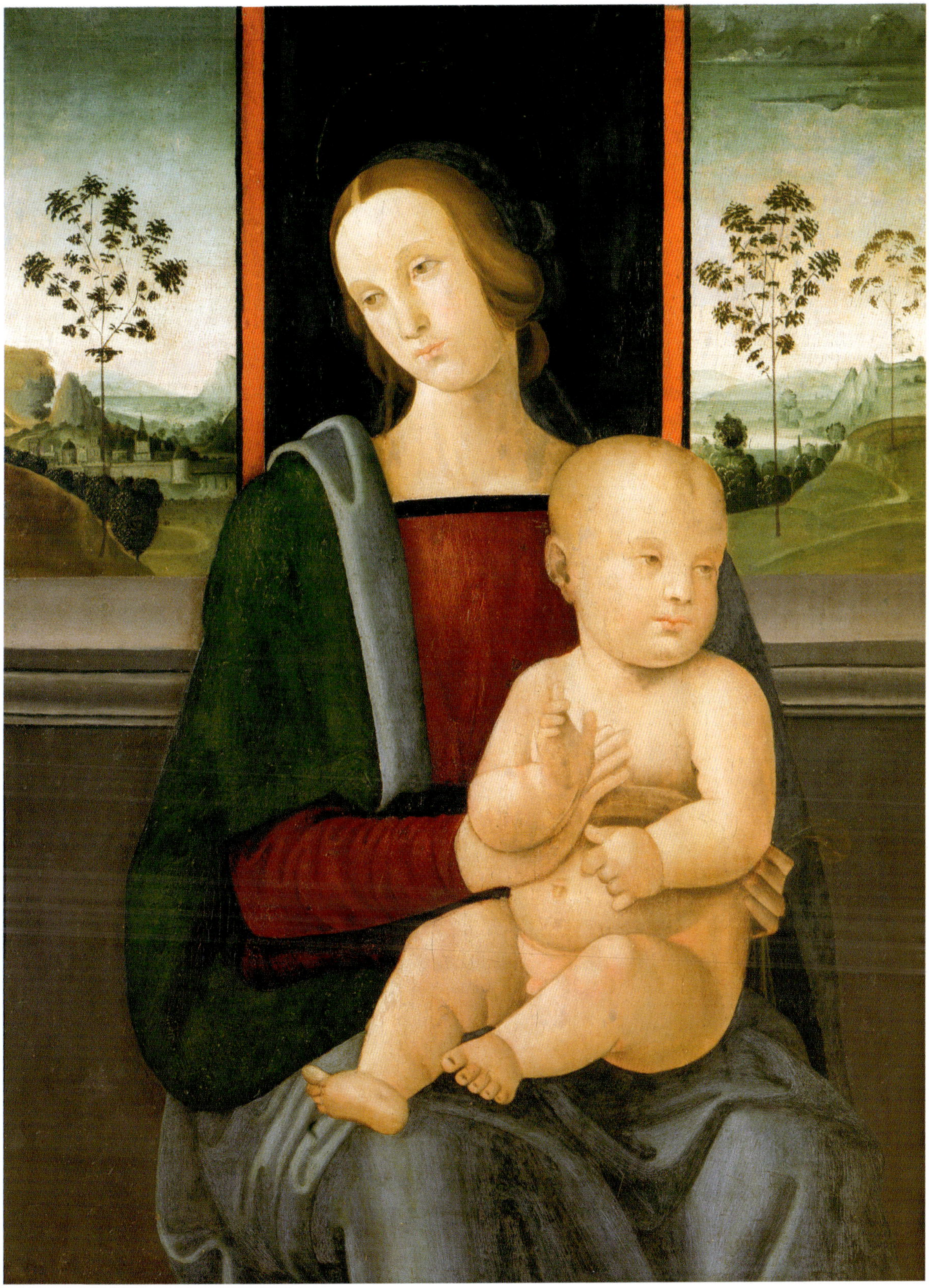

Andrea d'Assisi, 1484–1521
***Madonna*, undated**
64.5 x 49 cm; Tempera on wood panel
Pinacoteca; Room VII; Inv. 40310

Mariano di Ser Austerio da Perugia, 1470–ca. 1530
***Madonna with Saints*, ca. 1493**
190 x 171 cm; Oil on wood panel
Pinacoteca; Room VII; Inv. 40347

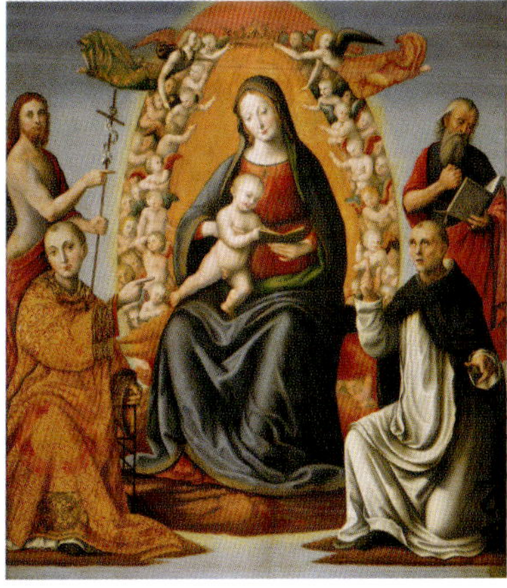

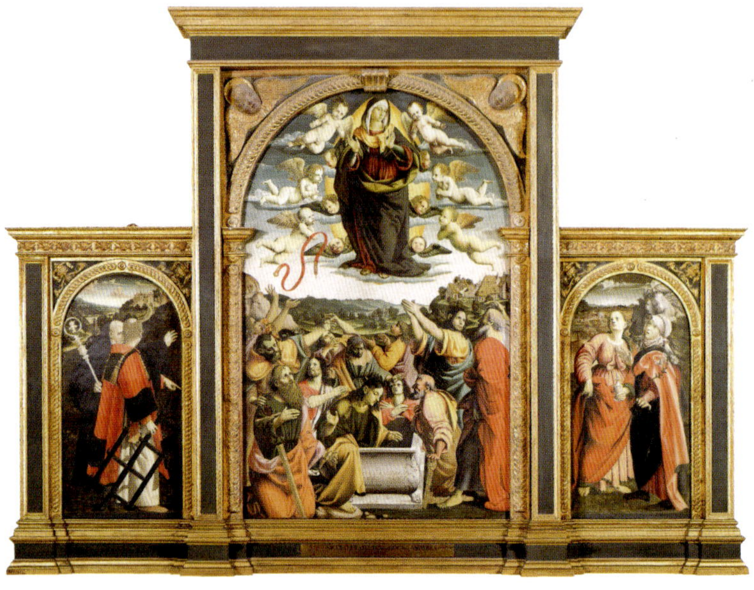

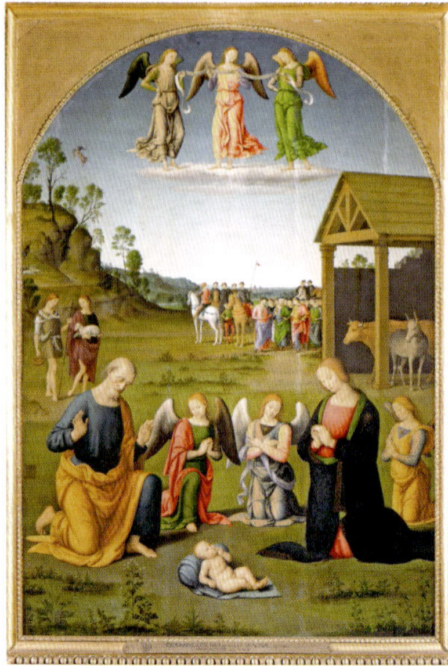

Cola dell'Amatrice, 1489–1555
***Assumption of the Virgin and SS. Lawrence, Benedict, Mary Magdalene, and Catherine of Siena*, 1515**
200 x 133 cm; Oil on wood panel
Pinacoteca; Room VII; Inv. 40372

Lo Spagna (Giovanni di Pietro), ca. 1450–1528
***Madonna della Spineta also known as Arrival of the Magi*, ca. 1507**
222 x 156 cm; Tempera on wood panel
Pinacoteca; Room VII; Inv. 40316

Pastura (Antonio del Massaro), ca. 1450–1516
***Miracle of St. Thomas, Mass of St. Gregory, St. Jerome Penitent*, 1497**
130 x 52 cm; Tempera on wood panel
Pinacoteca; Room VII; Inv. 40323

Bernardino di Mariotto, 1478–1566
***Madonna and Child with SS. Severino and Dominic*, undated**
50 x 34 cm; Tempera on canvas transferred from wood
Pinacoteca; Room VII; Inv. 40328

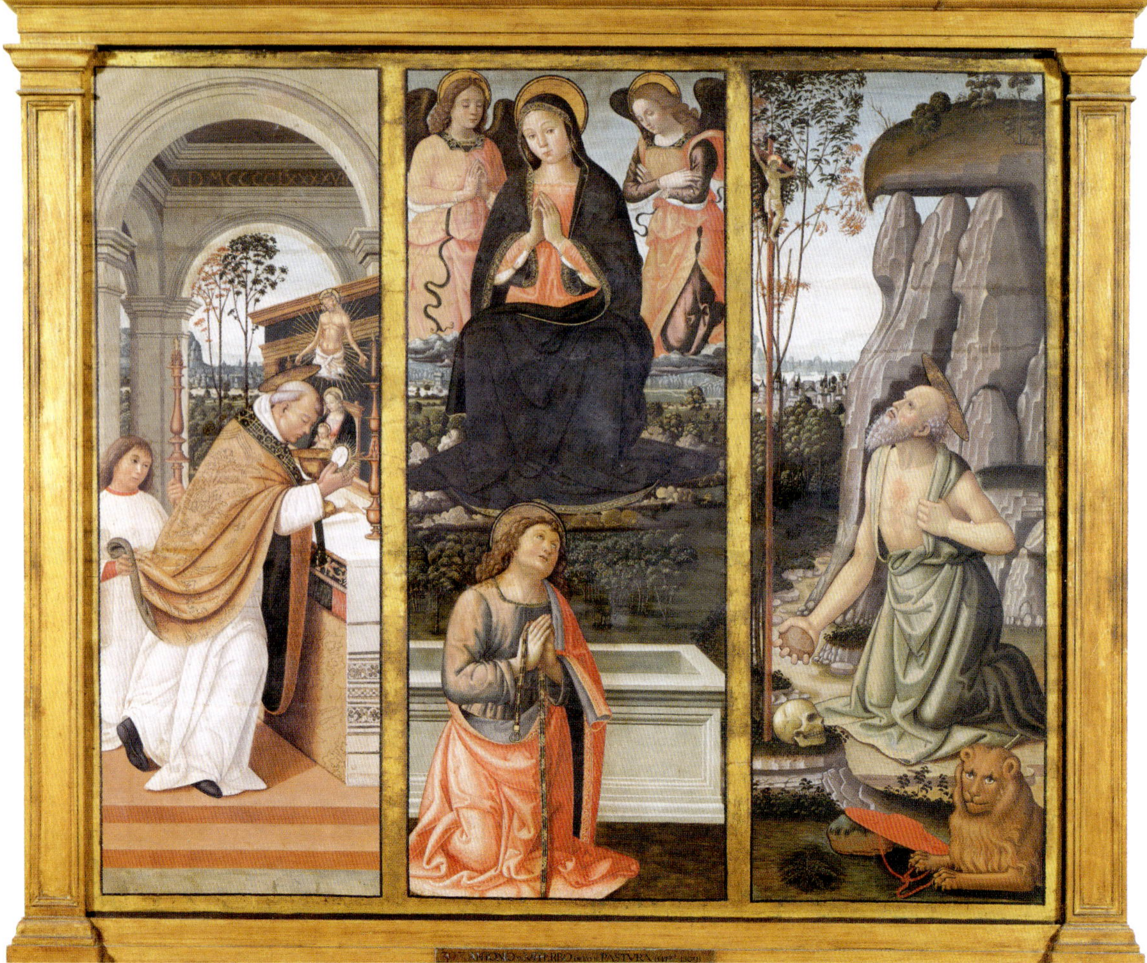

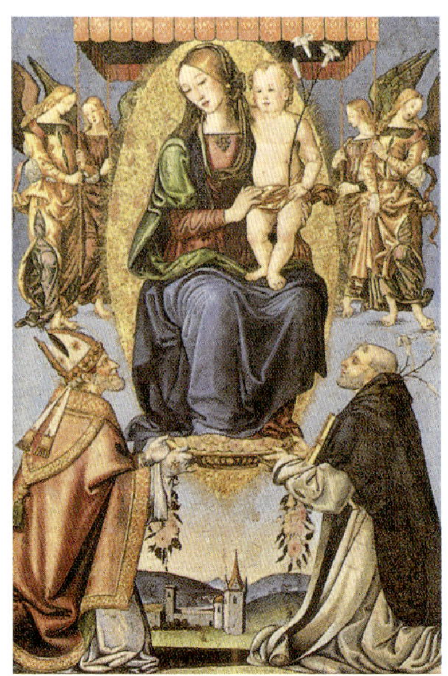

ROOM VIII

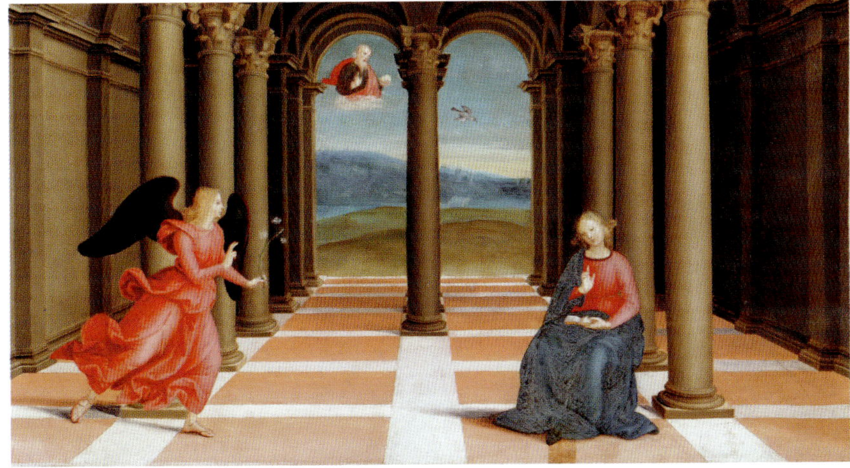

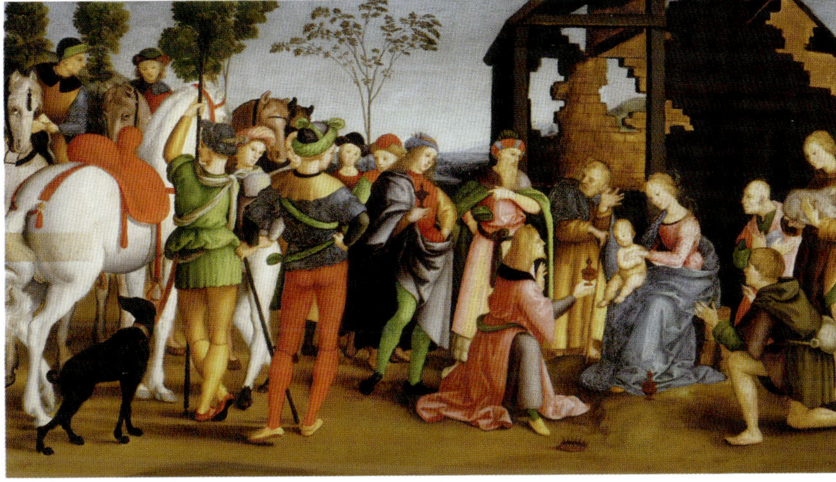

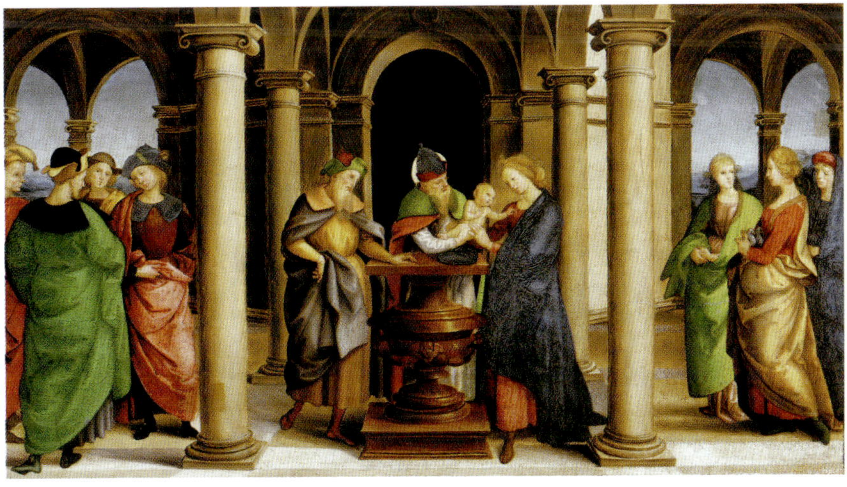

Raphael (Raffaello Sanzio), 1483–1520
***Predella panel with Annunciation, from The Coronation of the Virgin (Pala Oddi)*, ca. 1503**
39 x 63 cm; Tempera and oil on wood panel
Pinacoteca; Room VIII; Inv. 40335

Raphael (Raffaello Sanzio), 1483–1520
***Predella with Adoration of the Magi, from The Coronation of the Virgin (Pala Oddi)*, ca. 1503**
39 x 190 cm; Tempera and oil on wood panel
Pinacoteca; Room VIII; Inv. 40335

Raphael (Raffaello Sanzio), 1483–1520
***Predella with Presentation at the Temple (Pala Oddi)*, ca. 1503**
approx. 39 x 63 cm; Tempera and oil on wood panel
Pinacoteca; Room VIII; Inv. 40335

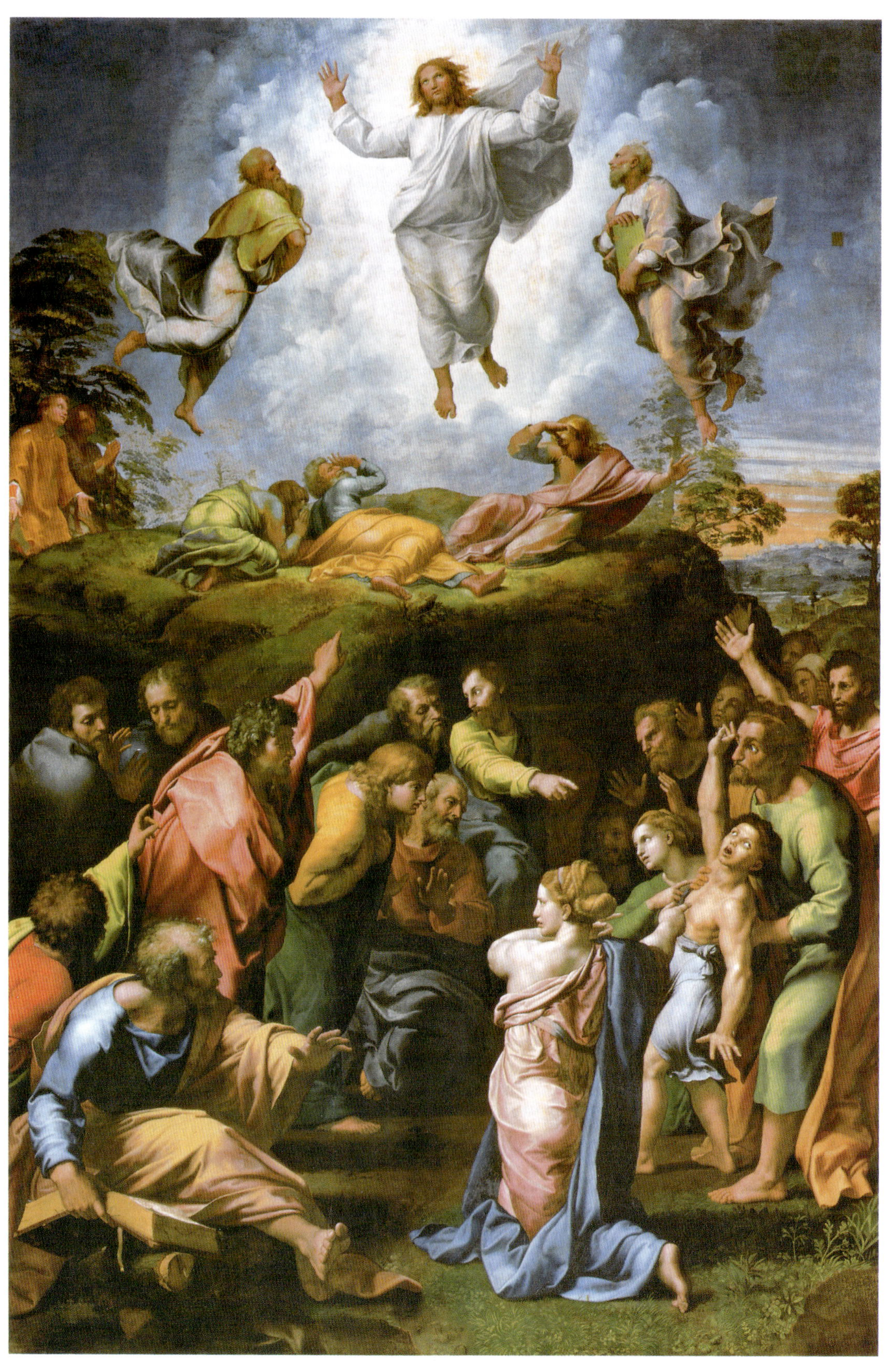

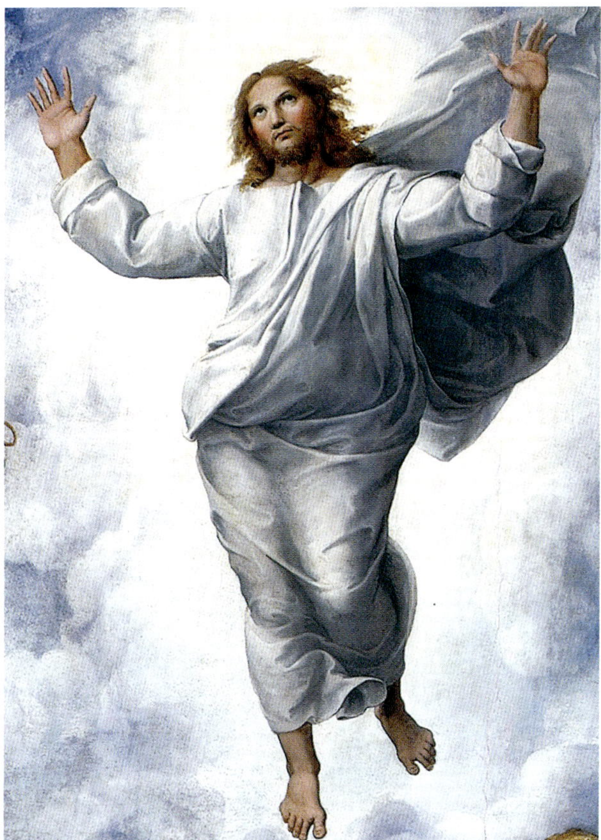

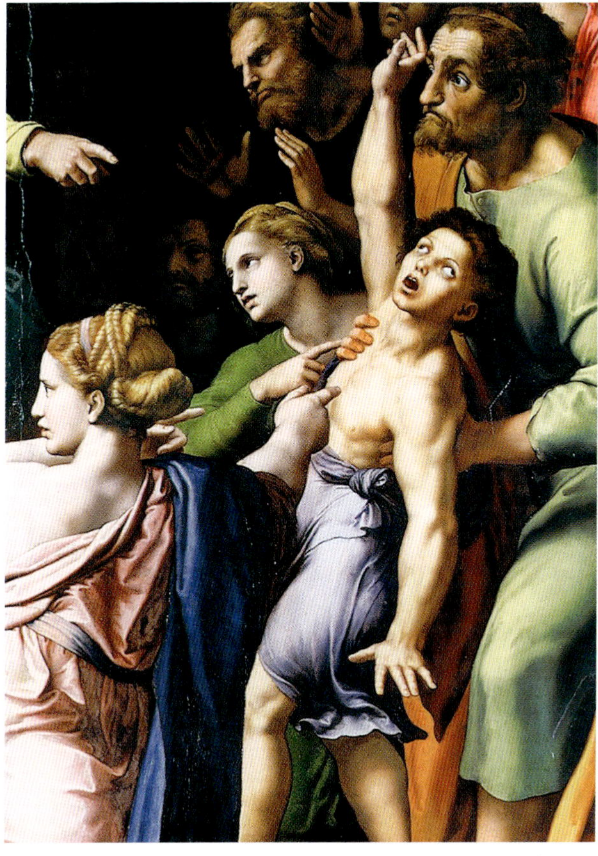

Raphael (Raffaello Santi)

Transfiguration

This dramatically lit scene depicts the transfiguration of Christ on Mount Tabor. After climbing the mountain with three of his disciples, Christ metamorphosed into a being of pure light: "His face did shine as the sun, and his raiment was white as the light" (Matthew 17: 2). Alongside him appeared the prophets Moses and Elijah, and the voice of God made itself heard. Raphael combines the transfiguration scene with an attempt by the disciples to heal a "possessed" boy. Only Christ, newly returned from Mount Tabor, was able to cure the boy of his lunacy. This enormous panel was the last picture painted by Raphael and is regarded as his artistic testament. It reveals his consummate skill in composition, the handling of light and color, the modeling of drapery, expressive gesture, and the combining of apparent opposites such as darkness and light, the heavenly and earthly spheres, and divine and human action. When Raphael died on April 6, 1520, the painting was placed at the head of his deathbed. Although commissioned by Cardinal Giulio de' Medici (Pope Clement VII from 1523) for his episcopal seat of Narbonne, the work was so admired by the artist's contemporaries that it remained in Rome, at the church of St. Pietro in Montorio.

Raphael (Raffaello Santi), 1483–1520
***Transfiguration*, ca. 1517–1520**
410 x 279 cm; Oil on wood panel
Pinacoteca; Room VIII; Inv. 40333

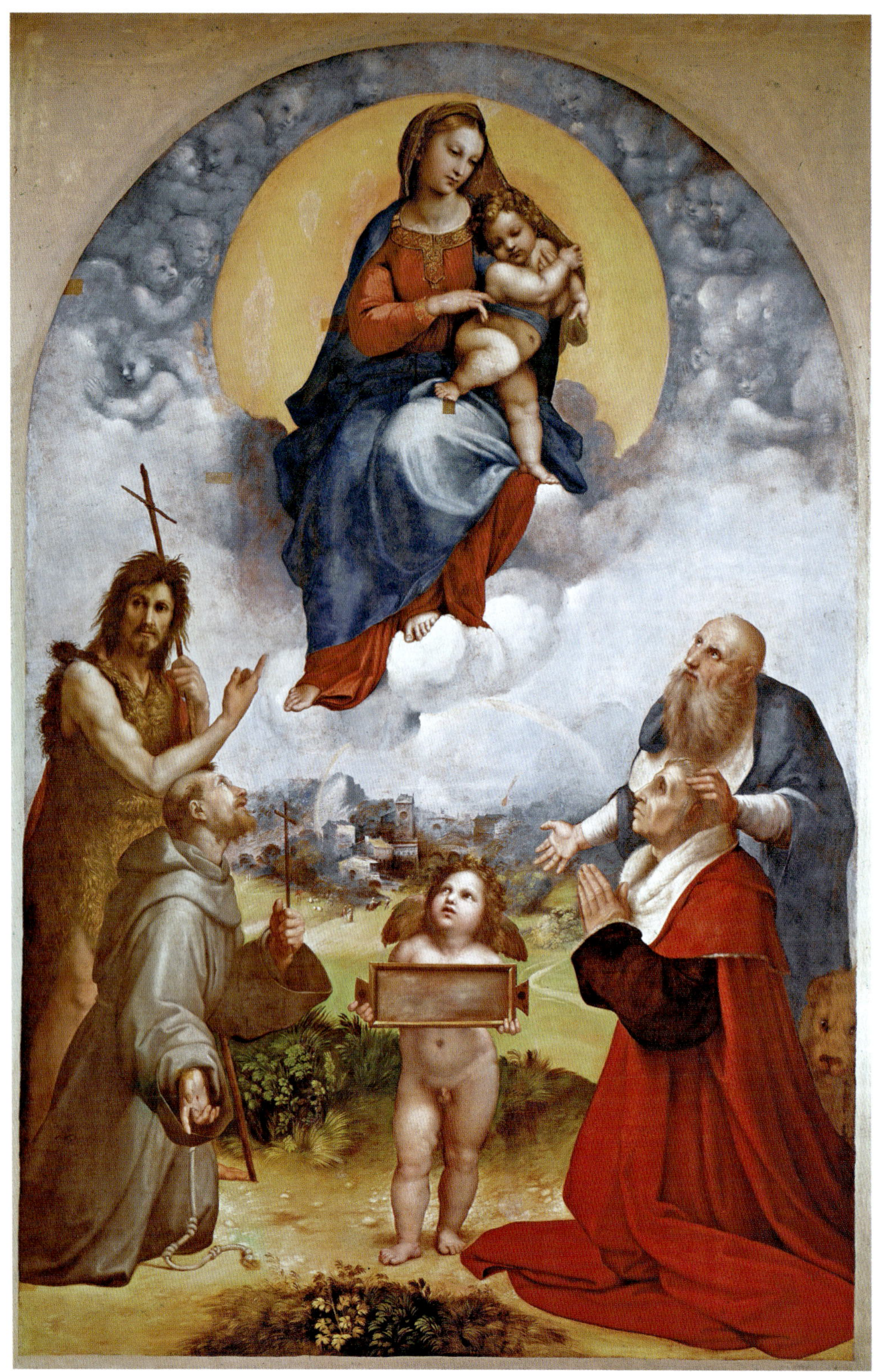

Raphael (Raffaello Santi)

The Madonna di Foligno

The Madonna di Foligno is named after its later home, the monastery of St. Anna delle Contesse in Foligno, the native town of the donor, Sigismondo de' Conti (1432–1512). De' Conti had commissioned the work for the high altar of the Franciscan church of Santa Maria in Aracoeli in Rome, which had originally been built to commemorate the appearance of the Blessed Virgin to the Roman emperor Augustus in a vision. Raphael's picture takes up this theme but shows the donor, accompanied by John the Baptist, St. Francis, and St. Jerome, in place of Emperor Augustus. The close connection between the donor group and the Virgin is underlined by the harmony in the color of their garments. The work is distinctive for its emotional power, a typical feature of Raphael's mature style, giving expression to the inner turmoil of the figures. The heavenly and earthly zones are no longer as clearly delineated as they were in the Pala Oddi. In the background, the vision of the Virgin Mary gives way to a dramatic stormy sky. This alludes to a severe storm over Foligno during which De' Conti's country seat survived a lightning strike thanks, it was claimed, to the intervention of the Madonna. This would also allow the painting to be seen as a votive picture. De' Conti died in 1512 shortly before the completion of the work, which is not thought to have been placed on the high altar of Santa Maria in Aracoeli until a year after the donor's burial in the church.

Raphael (Raffaello Santi), 1483–1520
***The Madonna di Foligno*, 1511-1512**
308 x 198 cm; Tempera and oil on wood panel
Pinacoteca; Room VIII; Inv. 40329

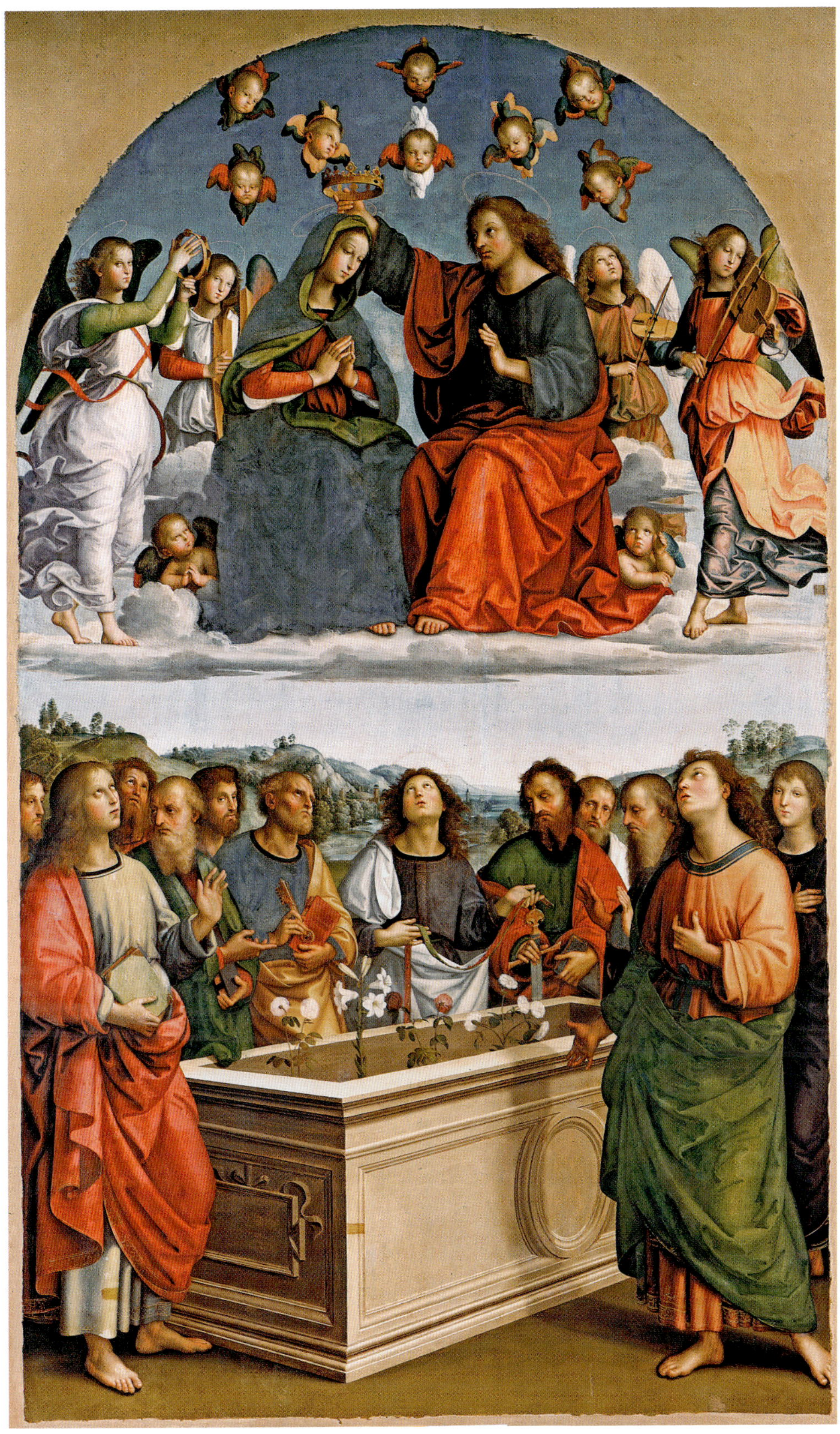

Raphael (Raffaello Santi)

The Coronation of the Virgin, also known as the Pala Oddi

The Coronation of the Virgin is the earliest of Raphael's large works held by the Pinacoteca and indeed one of the earliest of all his known altar paintings. It was painted around 1502–1504, shortly after he completed his apprenticeship with Perugino, whose harmonious, graceful figures and style of composition are still very much in evidence in places, leading Giorgio Vasari, in his *Lives of the Painters, Sculptors, and Architects* of 1550, to attribute the work to Perugino. However, the greater movement of the figures, the audacious diagonal positioning of the sarcophagus, the depth of the landscape, and the individual physiognomies of the figures point unambiguously to the young Raphael. With *The Coronation of the Virgin*, Raphael created his first masterpiece. The high panel is clearly divided into a heavenly zone, showing the coronation by Christ of the Virgin, attended by angels, and an earthly zone with the apostles standing around the empty tomb. Some of the heads of the apostles seem to have been worked up as portraits and express a range of different reactions to the event unfolding in heaven. The atmospheric landscape background reveals a Netherlandish influence. The name Pala Oddi ("Oddi Altarpiece") derives from the Oddi family who commissioned the altar for their sepulchral chapel in Perugia. In addition to the main image, the altar also comprised three predella scenes, which are also housed in the Pinacoteca (inv. 40335).

Raphael (Raffaello Santi), 1483–1520
***The Coronation of the Virgin, also known as Pala Oddi*, 1502–1504**
272 x 165 cm; Tempera on wood transferred onto canvas
Pinacoteca; Room VIII; Inv. 40334

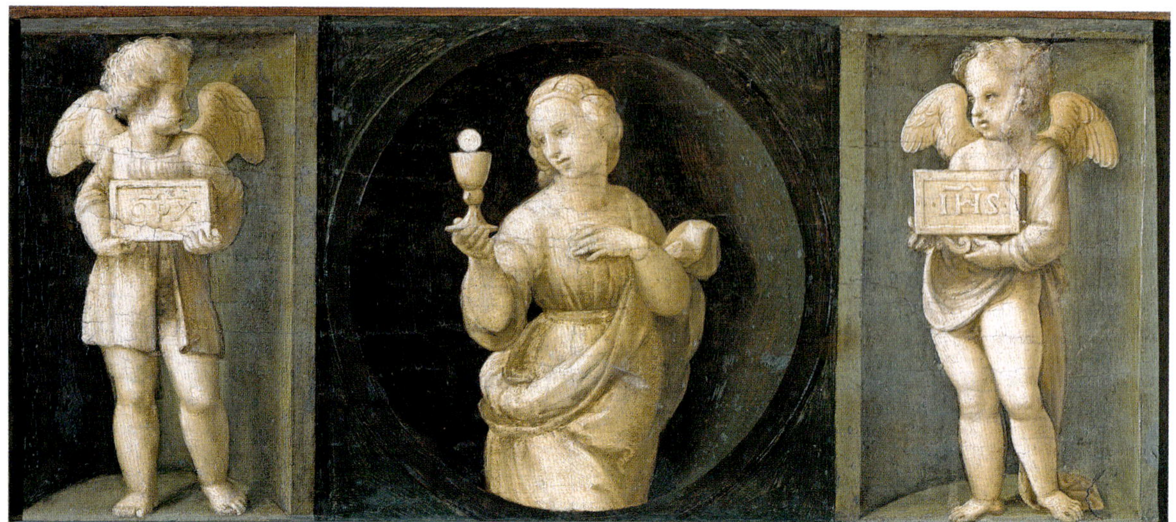

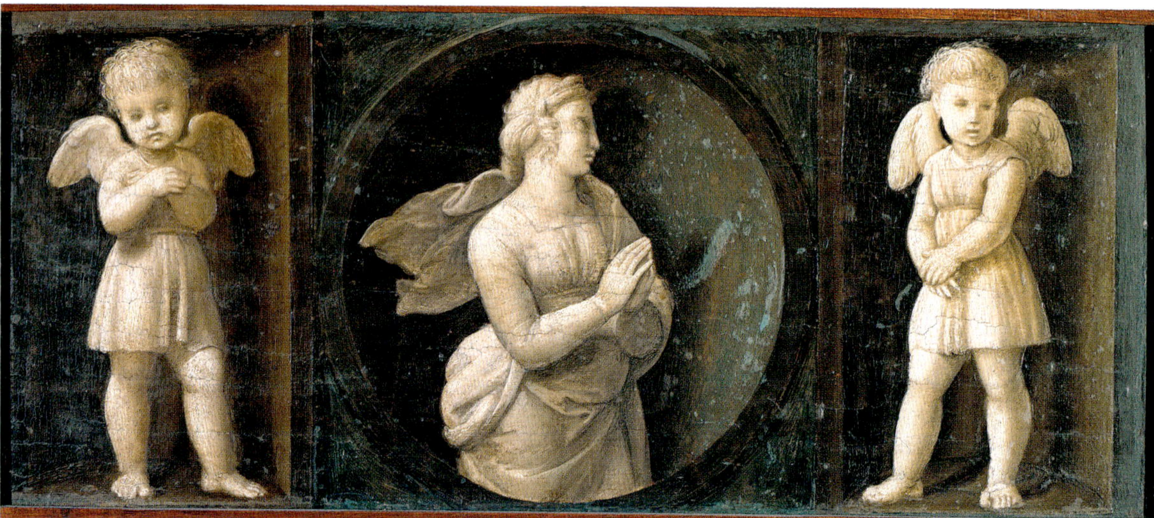

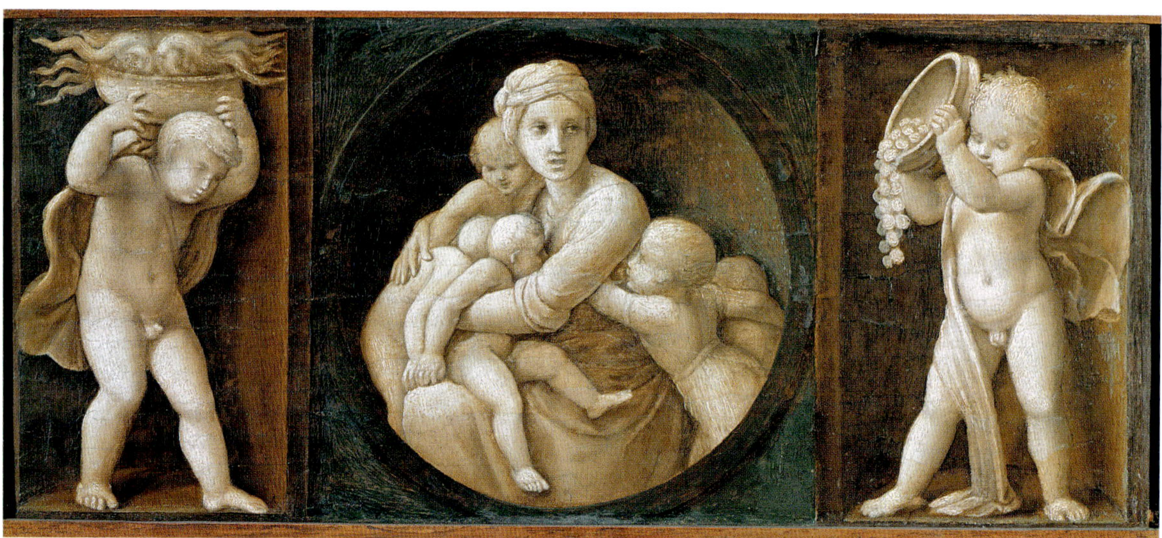

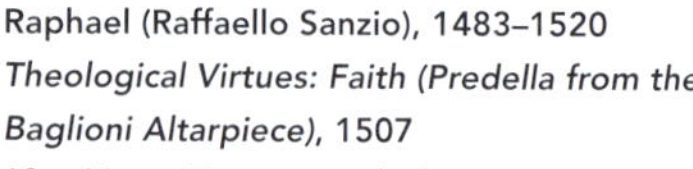

Raphael (Raffaello Sanzio), 1483–1520
***Theological Virtues: Faith (Predella from the Baglioni Altarpiece)*, 1507**
18 x 44 cm; Tempera and oil on wood panel
Pinacoteca; Room VIII; Inv. 40332

Raphael (Raffaello Sanzio), 1483–1520
***Theological Virtues: Hope (Predella from the Baglioni Altarpiece)*, 1507**
18 x 44 cm; Tempera and oil on wood panel
Pinacoteca; Room VIII; Inv. 40330

Raphael (Raffaello Sanzio), 1483–1520
***Theological Virtues: Charity (Predella from the Baglioni Altarpiece)*, 1507**
18 x 44 cm; Tempera and oil on wood panel
Pinacoteca; Room VIII; Inv. 40331

ROOM IX

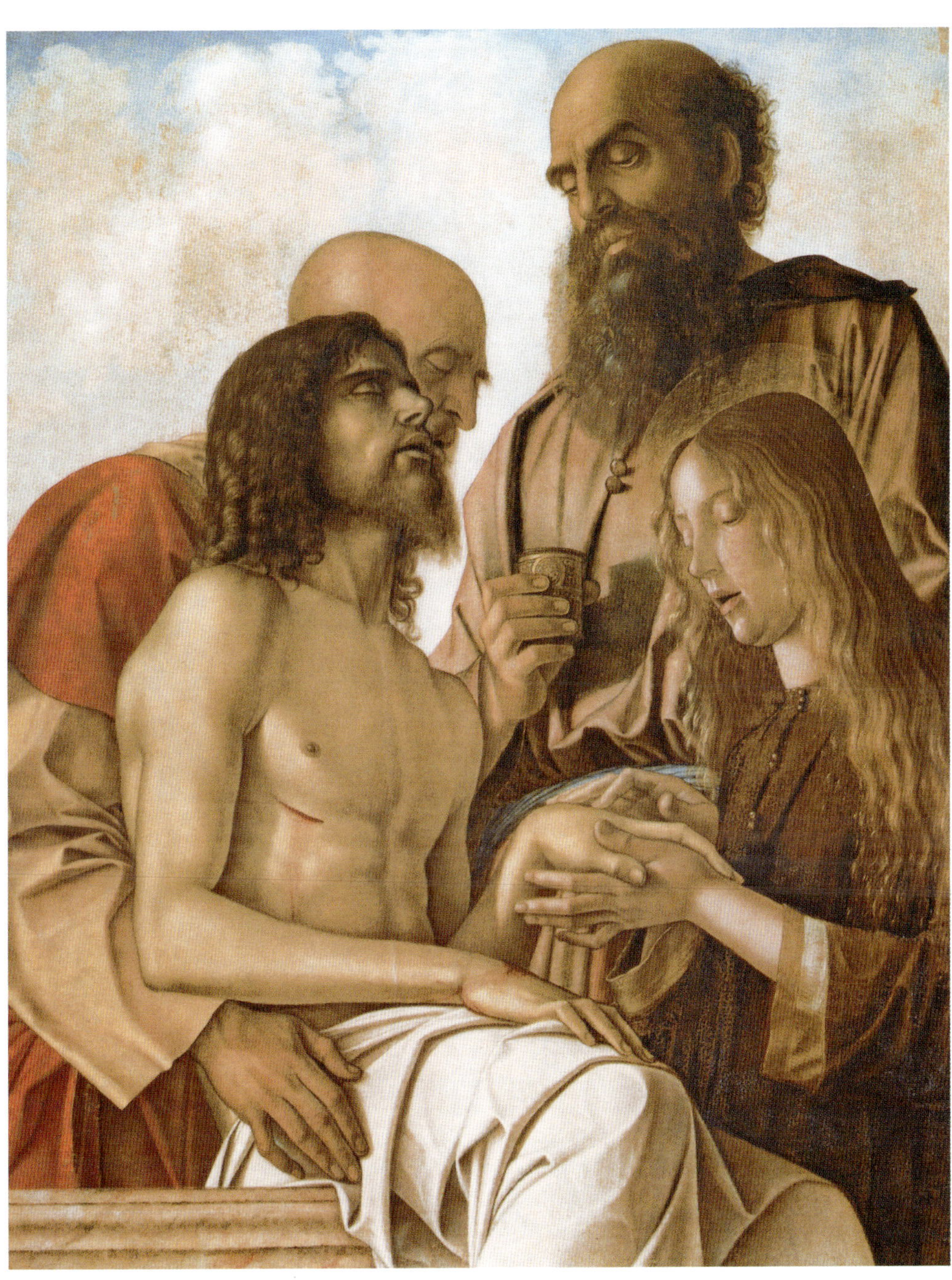

Giovanni Bellini

The Lamentation over the Dead Christ

Giovanni Bellini's *Lamentation* is one of the most powerful works in the Pinacoteca. It is thought to have once been the uppermost part of an altarpiece painted by Bellini around 1473 for the Franciscan church in Pesaro, Italy. This would certainly explain the emphatic "from below" perspective. The viewer sees Christ as if out of the depths of the grave. Christ's body is supported by Joseph of Arimathea, a wealthy Jew who, according the Gospels, donated the burial place for Christ. Beside him stands Nicodemus with a vessel containing precious myrrh and aloe, with which Mary Magdalene, kneeling before him, anoints the dead Christ. This detail of the anointing of Christ's hand offers an excellent example of the subtlety of Bellini's visual imagery. This scene, depicted in enthralling close-up, combines the traditional lamentation with the embalming of Christ. The main focus of the composition is on the presentation of the corpse, whose muscular upper body derives from classical models. Although depicted with restraint, it is impossible to overlook the bloody wounds on the chest and hands. Like the gently backward-falling head with its wan, half open lips, they invite the viewer to contemplate Christ's suffering. Despite its deeply distressing subject, this painting seems filled with an inner poetry, an effect that derives above all from Bellini's skillful handling of the light and subtle gradations of color.

Giovanni Bellini, ca. 1430–1516
***The Lamentation over the Dead Christ*, 1473–1476**
107 x 84 cm; Oil on wood panel
Pinacoteca; Room IX; Inv. 40290

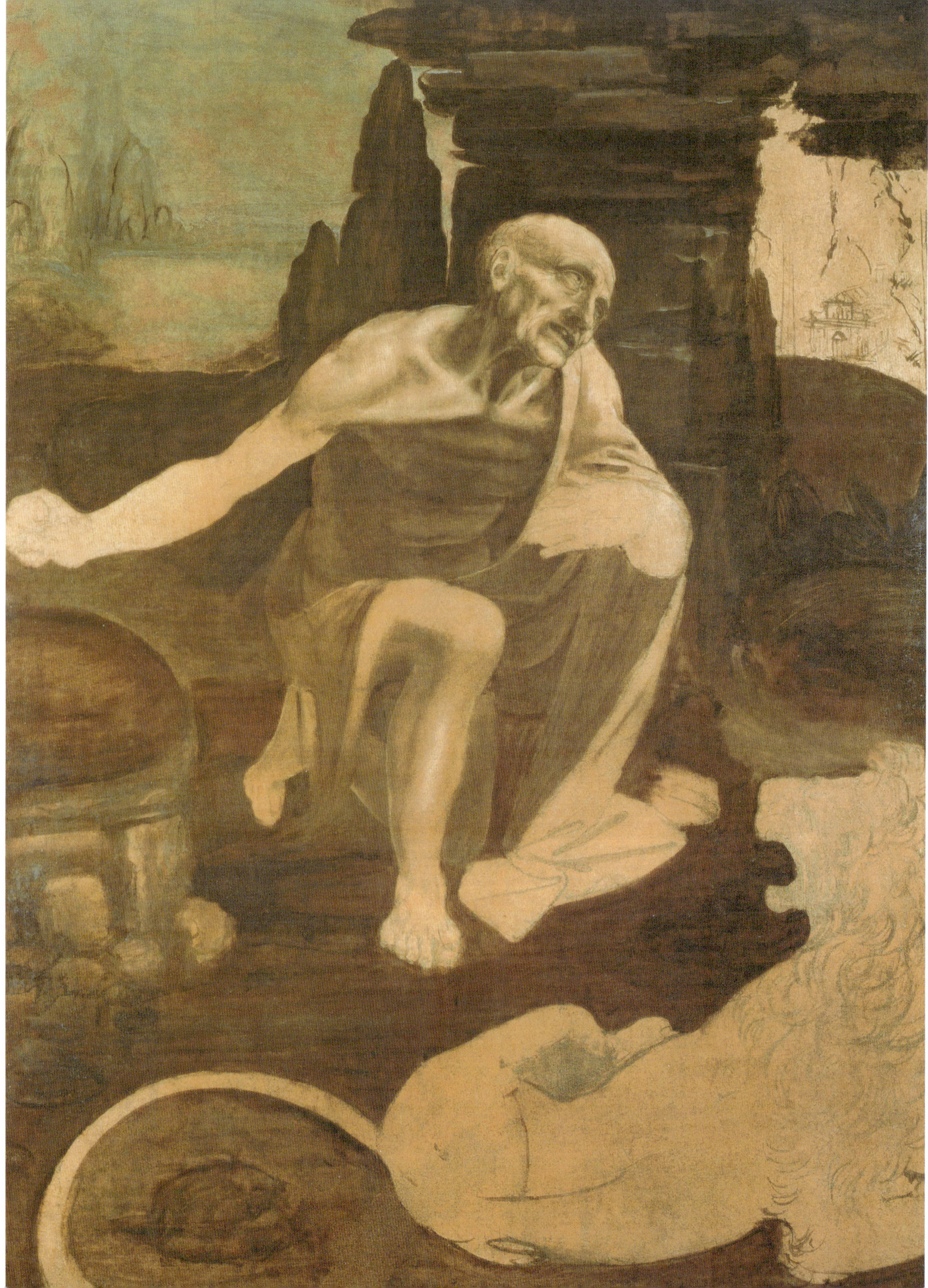

Leonardo da Vinci

St. Jerome

This panel of St. Jerome is one of Leonardo da Vinci's more enigmatic works. It was painted around 1482, the year Leonardo moved from Florence to the ducal court in Milan. It is not known why the highly innovative picture was never finished. It may be that the work failed to meet with the approval of a possible patron or that Leonardo's own perfectionism led him to abandon it. It seems that the artist worked on a number of different areas of the picture at the same time, rather than completing the central figure of the saint, the background, or the lion (St. Jerome's animal attribute) crouching in the foreground before moving on to another part. From a contemporary point of view, the work is fascinating precisely because of its sketch-like state, as this affords an insight into Leonardo's painting method. Da Vinci started by sketching the outlines of the individual elements of the picture with rapid brushstrokes, as is clearly evident in the case of the lion and the church in the background. He then began to fill in these outlines with one color tone at a time. There are only a few places where he started to model the final surface, like the rocks behind St. Jerome and the saint's emaciated upper body, which reveals his anatomical studies. The work was only identified in the early nineteenth century—by the painter Angelica Kauffmann—as the work of Leonardo. It was acquired by Pius IX for the Pinacoteca Vaticana in 1856.

Leonardo da Vinci, 1452–1519
***St. Jerome*, ca. 1482**
103 x 75 cm; Oil on wood panel
Pinacoteca; Room IX; Inv. 40337

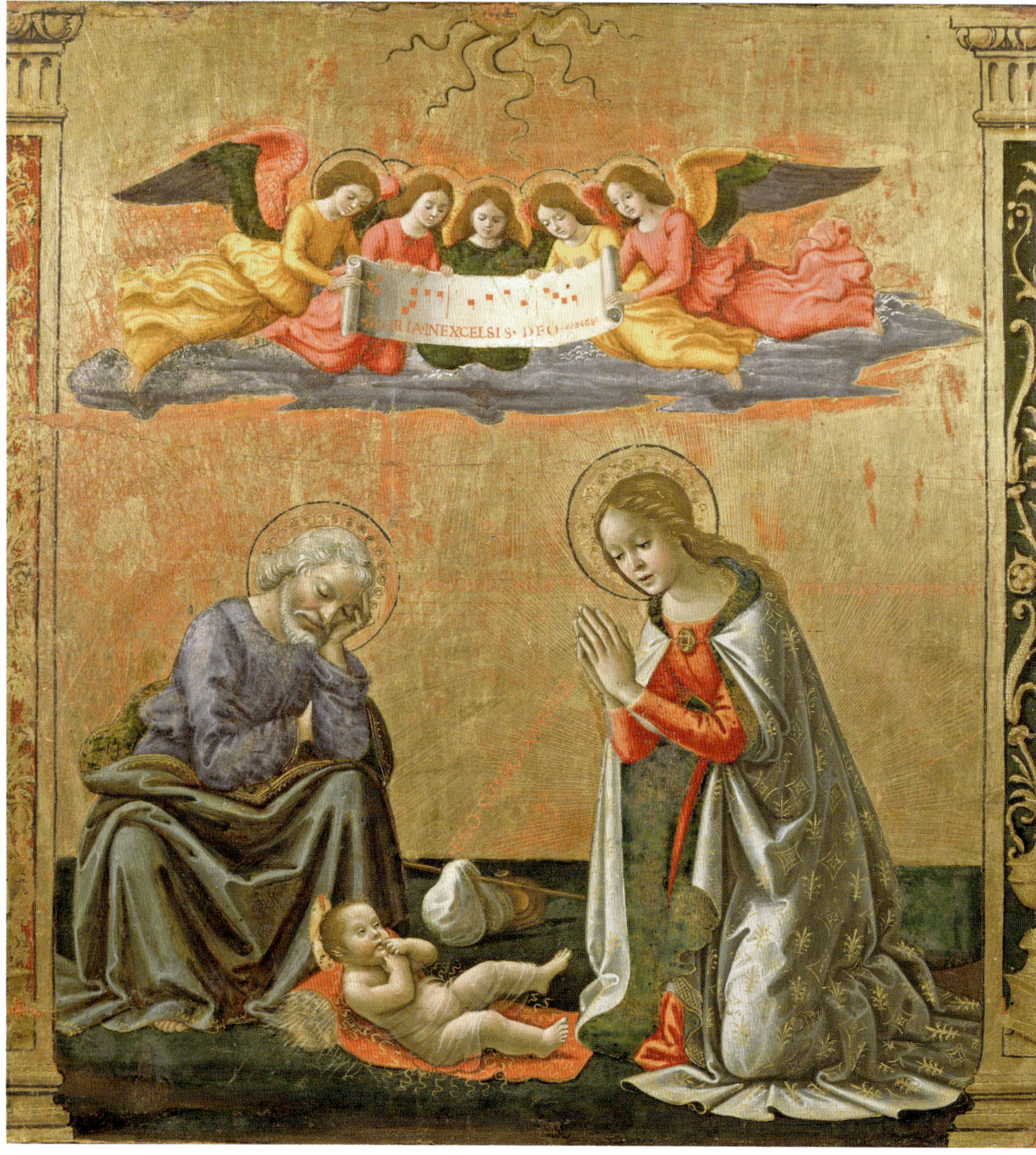

Domenico Ghirlandaio and Workshop, 1449–1494
***Nativity*, 15th century**
54 x 42 cm; Tempera on wood panel
Pinacoteca; Room IX; Inv. 40344

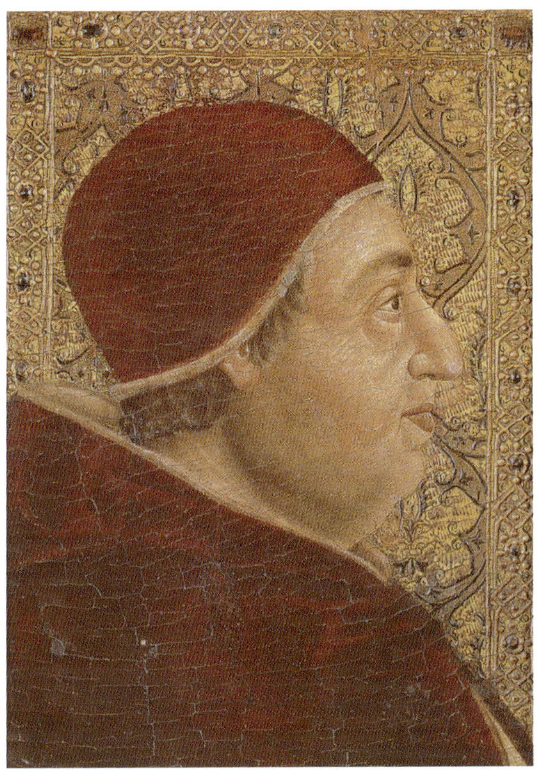

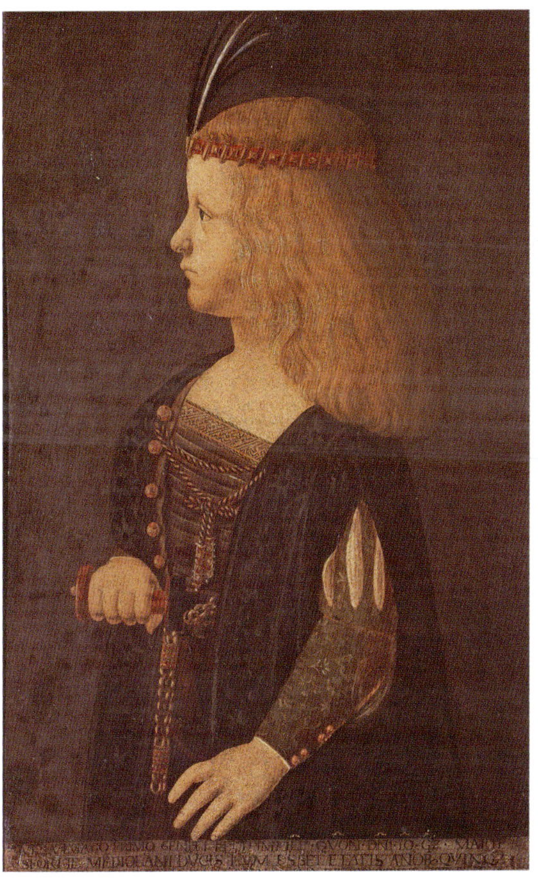

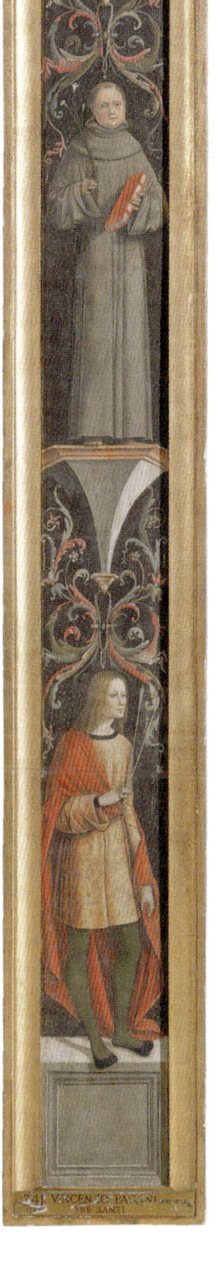

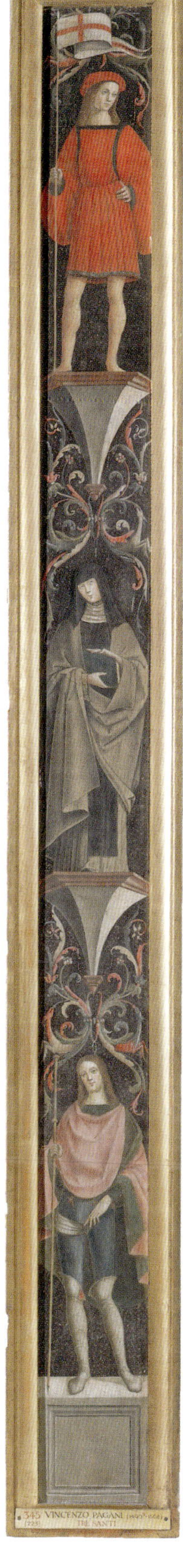

Pedro Berruguete, 1450–1504
***Portrait of Alessandro VI Borgia*, undated**
40 x 29 cm; Oil on wood panel
Pinacoteca; Room IX; Inv. 40463

Bernardino De'Conti, ca. 1470–1525
***Portrait of Francesco Sforza at the Age of 5*, 1496**
65 x 42 cm; Oil on wood panel
Pinacoteca; Room IX; Inv. 40446

Vincenzo Pagani, ca. 1490–1568
***St. Sebastian, St. Anthony of Padua, St. Nicholas*, undated**
215 x 17 cm; Tempera on wood panel
Pinacoteca; Room IX; Inv. 40341

Vincenzo Pagani, ca. 1490–1568
***St. Roch, St. Clara, St. Venanzio*, undated**
215 x 17 cm; Tempera on wood panel
Pinacoteca; Room IX; Inv. 40345

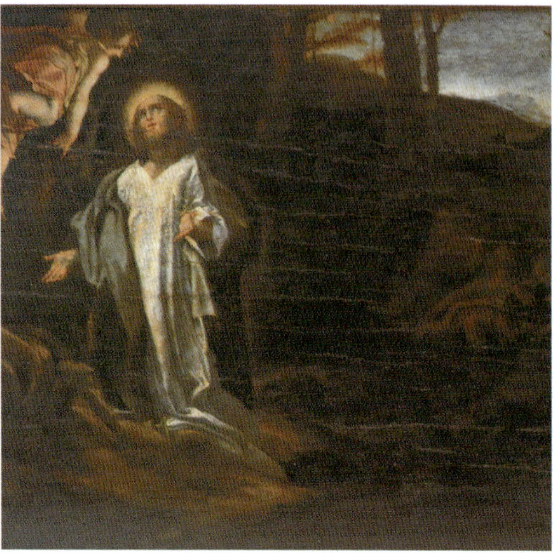
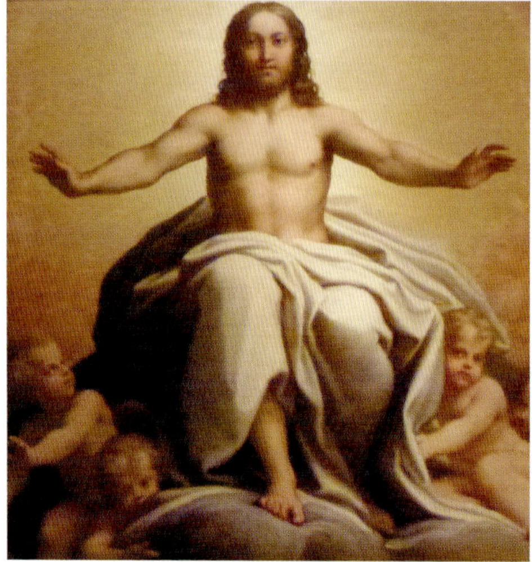
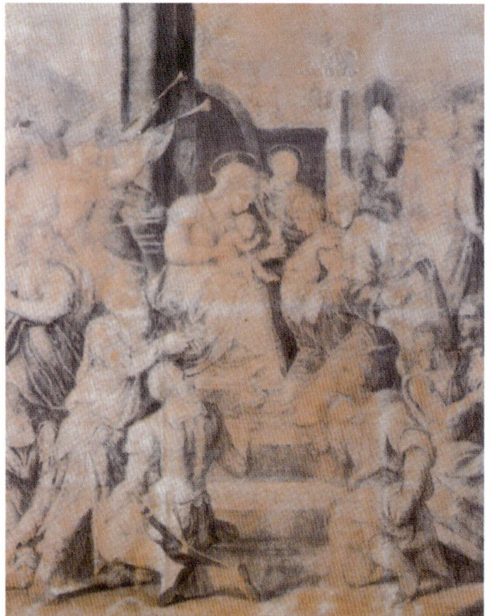
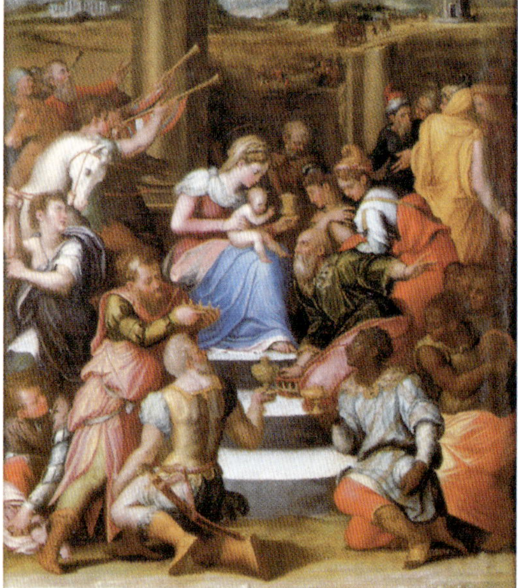
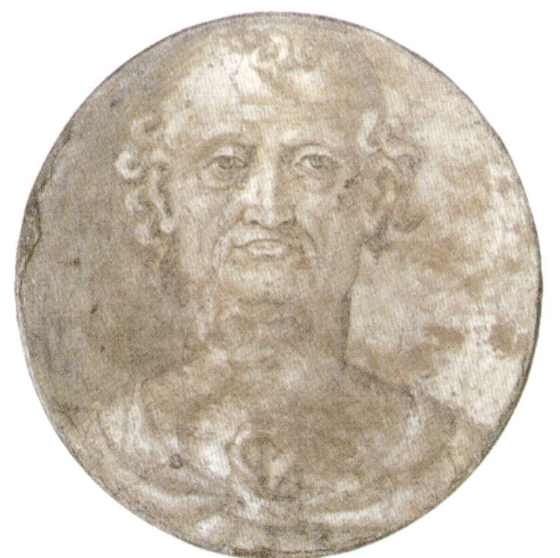

Antonio Allegri da Correggio, 1489–1534
***Christ in the Garden of Gethsemane*, undated**
37.5 x 43 cm; Oil on canvas
Pinacoteca; Room IX; Inv. 40762

Antonio Allegri da Correggio (follower of), 16th century
***Christ the Redeemer*, 16th century**
105 x 98 cm; Oil on canvas
Pinacoteca; Room IX; Inv. 40634

Raffaellino del Colle, ca. 1490–1566
***Adoration of the Magi*, mid-16th century**
163.5 x 132.5 cm; Pencil and white crayon on carton
Pinacoteca; Room IX; Inv. 56507

Raffaellino del Colle, ca. 1490–1566
***Nativity and Adoration of the Magi*, mid-16th century**
164 x 137 cm; Oil on wood panel transferred onto canvas
Pinacoteca; Room IX; Inv. 41138

Lombard School, 16th century
***So-called Portrait of Bramante*, 16th century**
51 cm (diameter); Fresco
Pinacoteca; Room IX; Inv. 40342

ROOM X

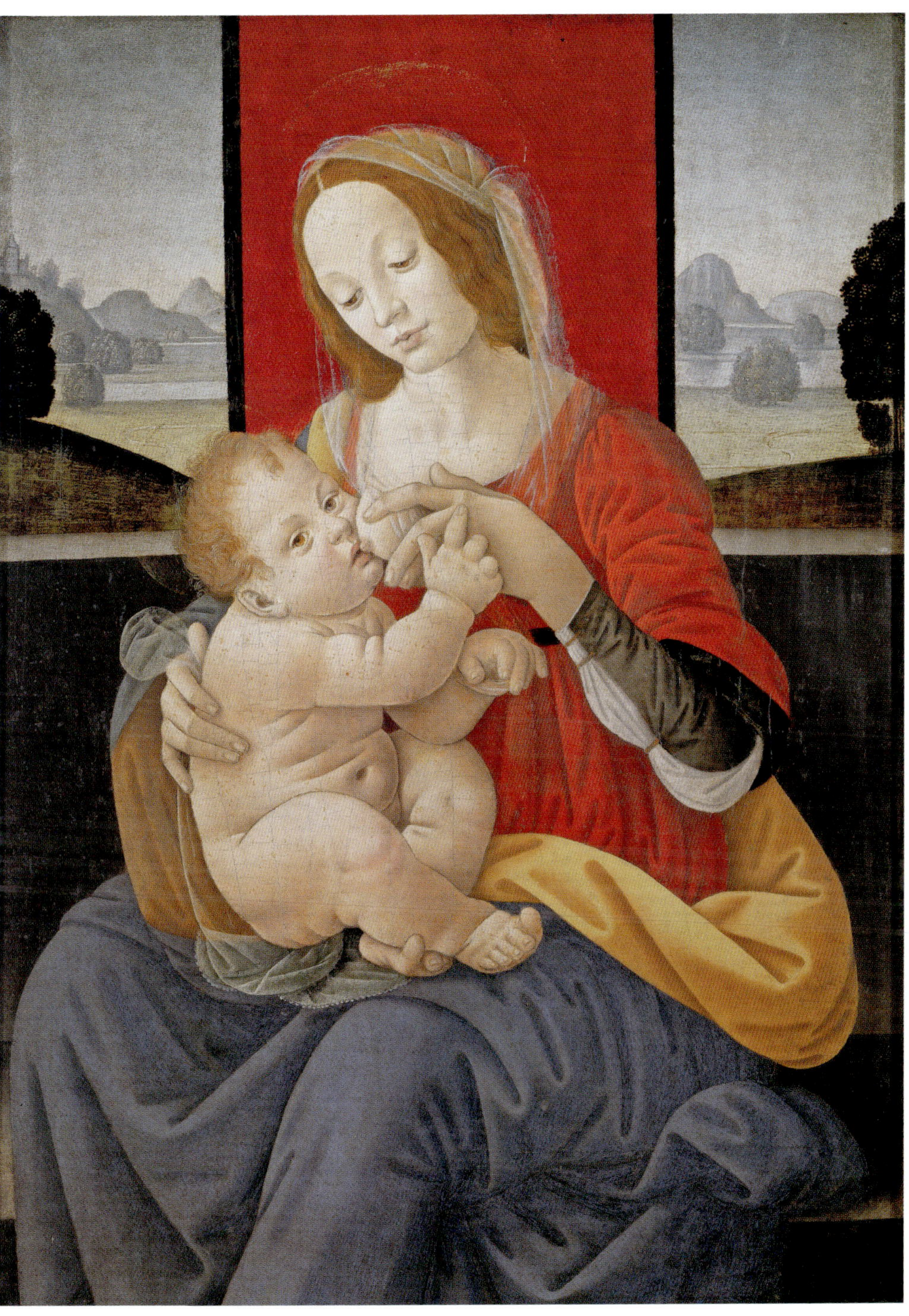

Lorenzo di Credi

Madonna Nursing the Christ Child

The picture type known as Madonna lactans, that is to say the Virgin Mary nursing her child, dates back to the Byzantine icon tradition of the Maria Galaktotrophousa. In the fifteenth century this type of devotional image enjoyed great popularity. From a theological point of view, it underlines Christ's human nature. The Florentine painter Lorenzo di Credi, a fellow pupil of Leonardo da Vinci's in the workshop of Andrea del Verocchio (ca. 1435–1488), emphasizes the intimacy between mother and child. Mary is shown bending down to the plump child in order to give him her breast. Jesus sits cross-legged on her lap and raises his right hand to the Madonna's left, dispensing the milk. His outstretched index finger enables the movement to be interpreted as a gesture of blessing on the part of the Christ Child. Jesus has turned his gaze on the viewer, thereby doing justice to his future role as the Redeemer. Mary, by contrast, devotes her entire attention to the feeding process. The radiant colors of the Virgin's clothing underscore the inner luminosity emitted by her. In its use of the sfumato technique, the background landscape visible on either side of the cloth of honor is reminiscent of the landscapes of Leonardo.

Lorenzo di Credi, 1456/60–1537
***Madonna Nursing the Christ Child*, undated**
78.1 x 57.4 cm; Oil on wood panel
Pinacoteca; Room X; Inv. 40340

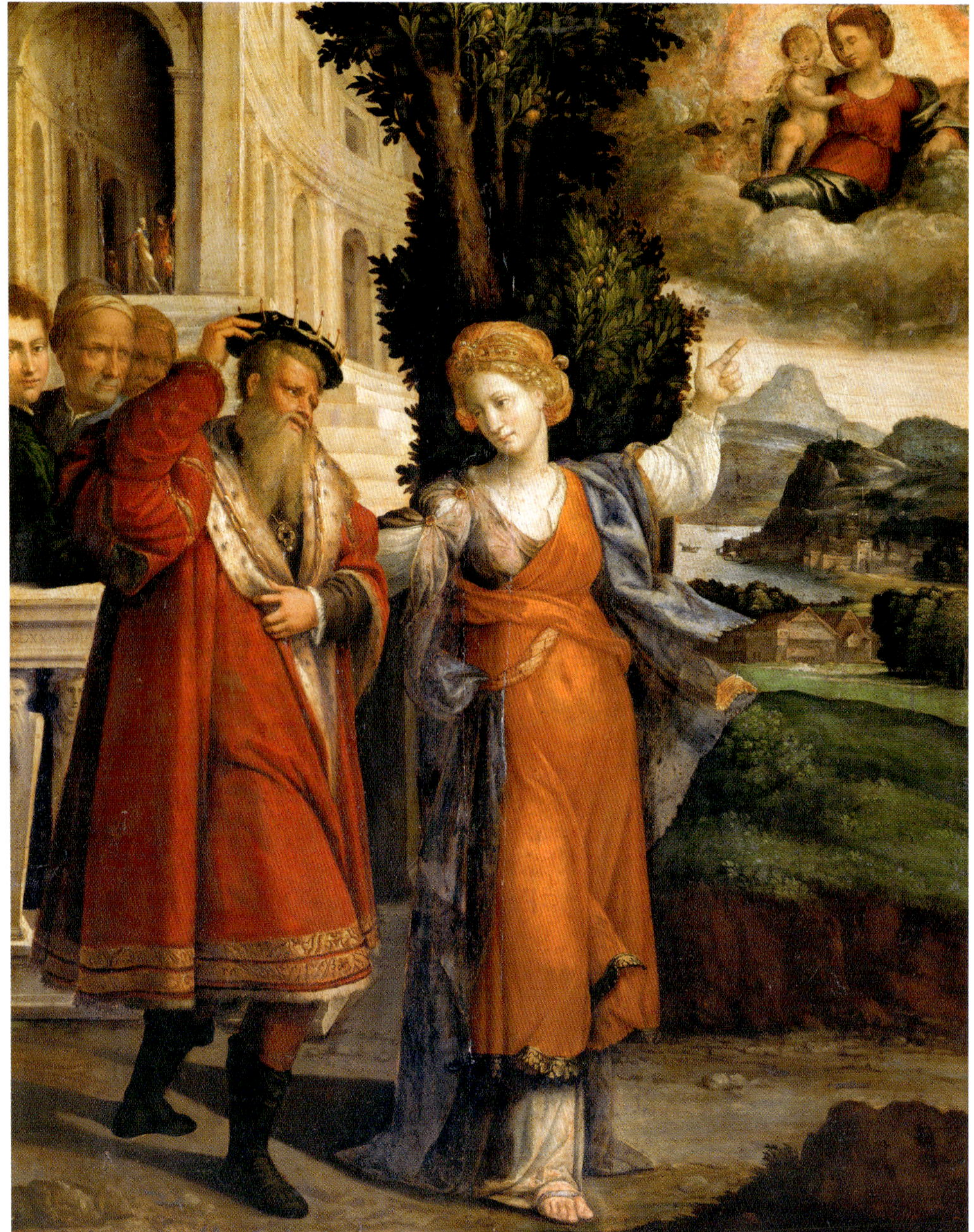

Il Garofalo (Benvenuto Tisi)

The Vision of Emperor Augustus

The Ferrarese painter Benvenuto Tisi, known as Il Garofalo, worked in Rome between 1509 and 1512, initially assisting Raphael on the decoration of the Stanza della Segnatura. Combining Raphael's classicism with Venetian painterliness and the Ferrarese School's decorative handling of color, Garofalo created a fascinating style of his own. *The Vision of Emperor Augustus* is one of the last works Garofalo produced before going completely blind in 1550. Particularly striking are the warm reds and oranges that cause the work to glow with an inner fire. They also link the two main mortals in the picture, the Roman emperor Augustus and the Tiburtine Sibyl, with the appearance of the Virgin Mary and Christ Child in the sky above. The scene is based on a legend stating that Augustus saw a vision of the Virgin and Child on the day of Christ's birth. This was interpreted by the sibyl as a sign of the coming of the Almighty. Augustus immediately forbade his adherents to worship him, the emperor, as a God. Garofalo sets the incident, which is reported as having occurred on the site of the present-day church of Santa Maria in Aracoeli on the Capitoline Hill, in front of an extensive, almost romantic landscape. The imperial palace on the left, out of which a number of courtiers have emerged to observe the scene, forms an imposing backdrop.

Il Garofalo (Benvenuto Tisi), 1481–1559
The Vision of Emperor Augustus, 1544
143 x 118 cm; Oil on wood panel
Pinacoteca; Room X; Inv. 40355

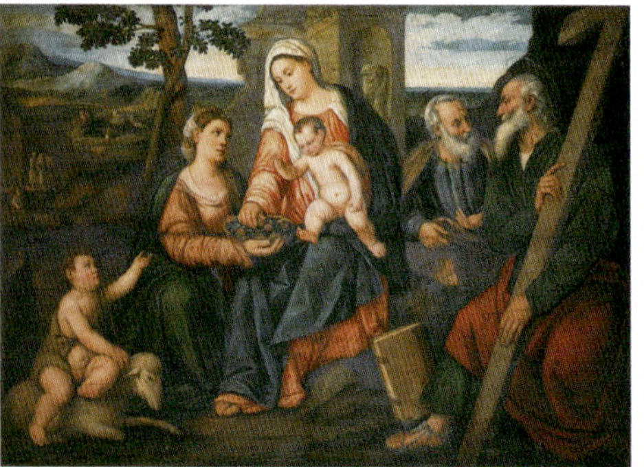

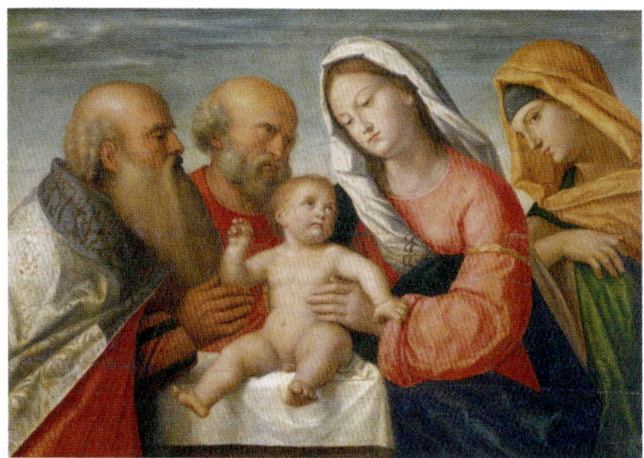

Bonifazio Veronese (Bonifacio de' Pitati), 1487–1553
Holy Family, undated
128 x 182 cm; Oil on canvas
Pinacoteca; Room X; Inv. 40353

Francesco Bissolo, 1470–1554
Presentation at the Temple, undated
62.4 x 91.7 cm; Oil on wood panel
Pinacoteca; Room X; Inv. 40361

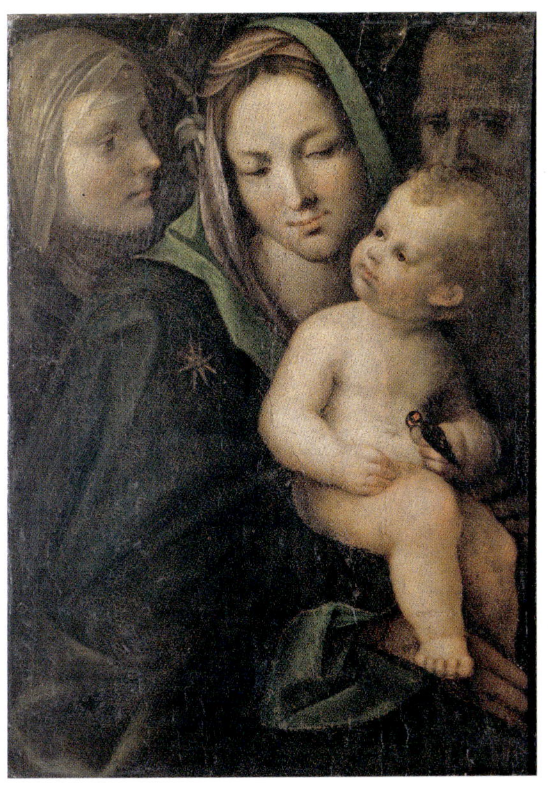

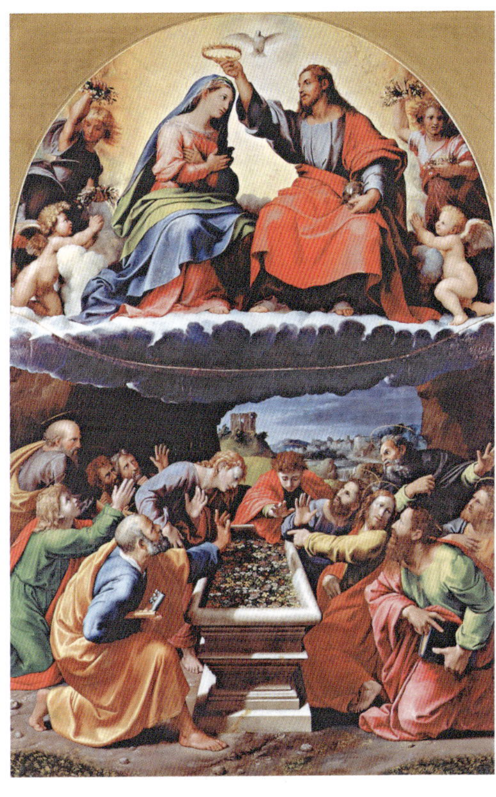

Girolamo del Pacchia, 1477–1535
***Madonna and Child*, undated**
71 x 52.8 cm; Oil on wood panel
Pinacoteca; Room X; Inv. 40338

Giulio Romano and Giovan Francesco Penni; 1490 or 1499–1546, ca. 1488–1528
***Coronation of the Virgin (Madonna di Monteluce)*, 1505–1525**
354 x 232 cm; Oil on wood panel
Pinacoteca; Room X; Inv. 40359

Il Garofalo (Benvenuto Tisi), 1481–1559
***Holy Family*, undated**
62 x 82 cm; Oil on wood panel
Pinacoteca; Room X; Inv. 40358

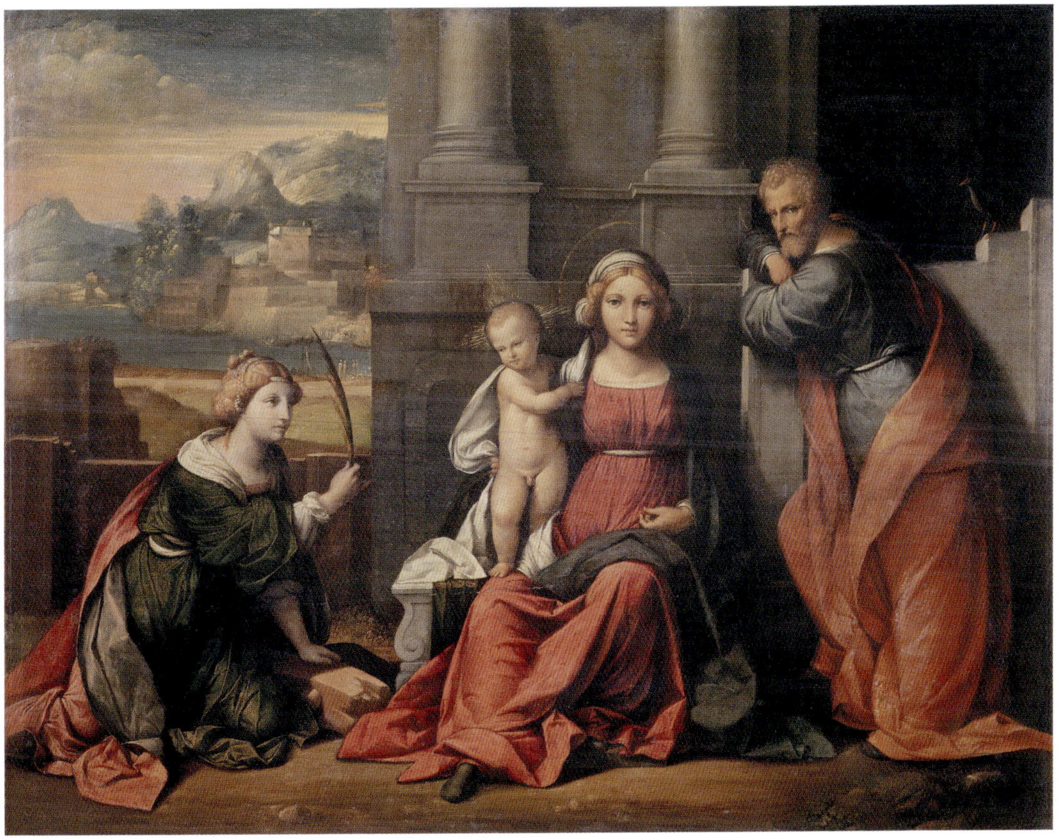

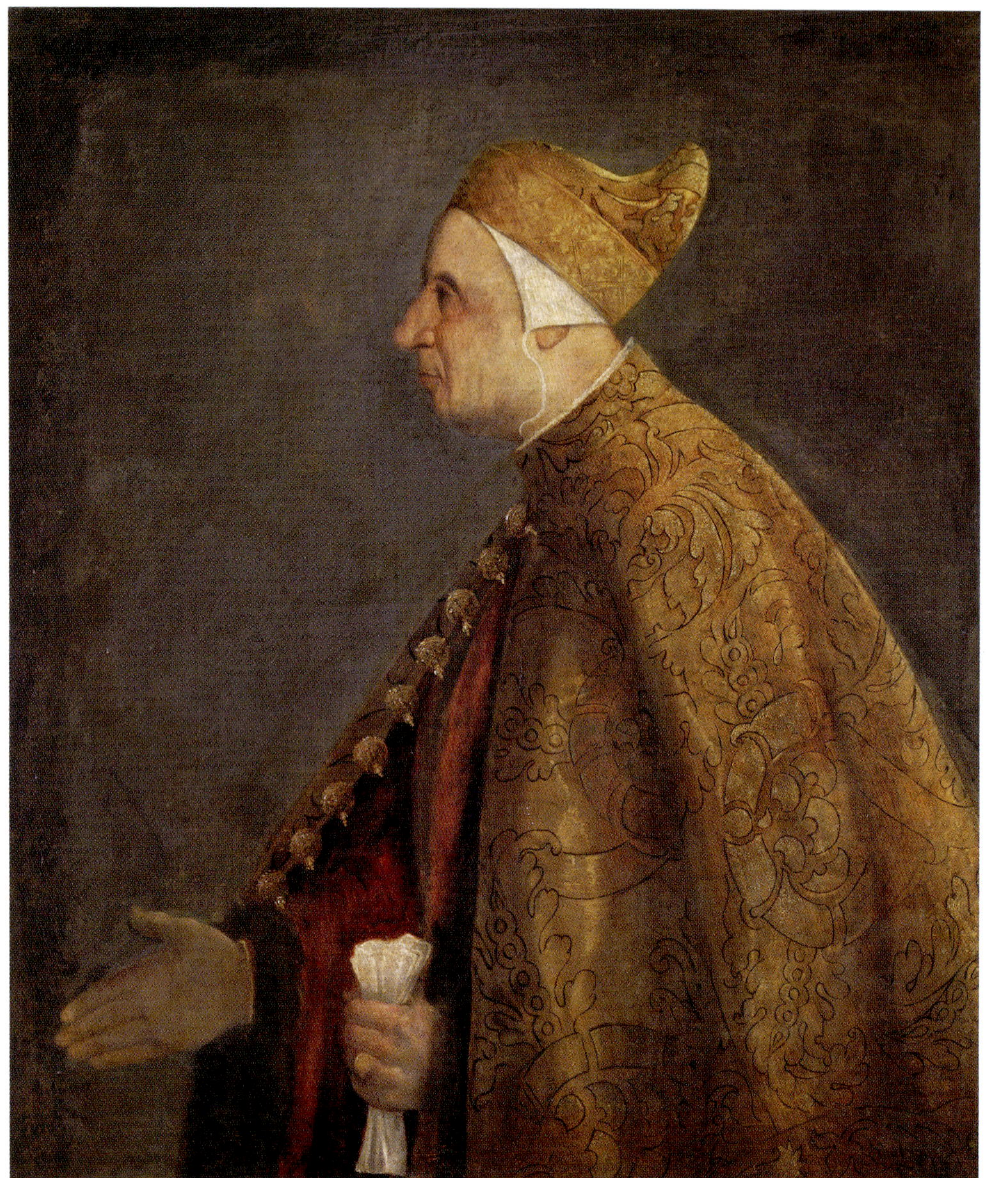

Titian (Tiziano Vecellio)

Portrait of the Doge Niccolò Marcello

The Venetian master Titian was one of the most sought-after portrait painters of his day. In the case of this highly lifelike portrait of Doge Niccolò Marcello (ca. 1399–1474), the challenge he faced was to portray a subject who had died before the artist was born. Titian is thought to have taken as his model a half-length portrait by Gentile Bellini (active 1460–1507) painted during the doge's lifetime (copy in the National Gallery, London). From this he adopted the antiquated profile view and facial features such as the prominent cheekbones, large nose, bulging brow, and protruding lower lip. Titian gave these features a softer treatment, however, endowing Marcello with an altogether more friendly facial expression. He also introduced aspects of his own, enlarging the field of view and showing the doge as he performs his duties. Marcello extends his right hand in a gesture of greeting or address. Through the opening in the doge's cloak, Titian provides a further demonstration of his artistry in his rendering of the exquisite gold buttons (campanoni d'oro) and gown of a golden-reddish hue, a color that would later be celebrated as "titian."

Titian (Tiziano Vecellio), ca. 1490–1576
***Portrait of the Doge Niccolò Marcello*, ca. 1542**
103 x 90 cm; Oil on canvas
Pinacoteca; Room X; Inv. 40445

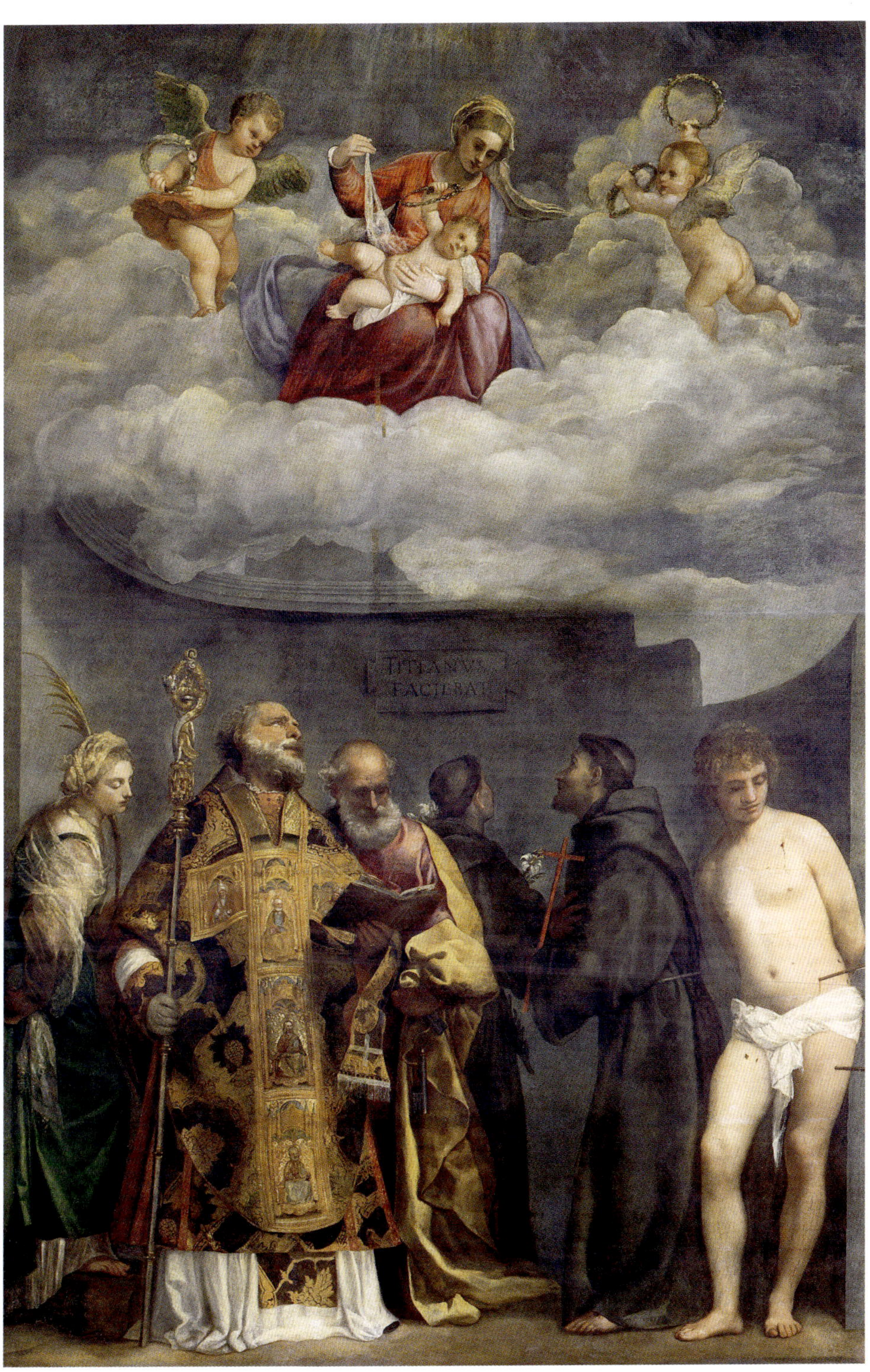

Titian (Tiziano Vecellio)

The Virgin and Child with Saints, also known as the Madonna di San Niccolò dei Frari

It is impossible to overlook the large plaque at the very center of this painting inscribed with the words "Titianus Faciebat" ("Made by Titian"). The enormous panel gives a new twist to the traditional motif of the Virgin and Child with saints. The leading master of the Venetian Renaissance was originally supposed to paint a traditional Sacra Conversazione ("sacred conversation," an enthroned Virgin flanked by saints) for the church of San Niccolò dei Frari. However, technical examinations have revealed that he changed his mind during the painting process and instead came up with a bizarre spatial arrangement, strictly divided into heavenly and earthly zones, which has lost none of its power to fascinate. The only connecting element between heaven and earth is Titian's proud signature on the dark skin of the wall that encloses SS. Catherine of Alexandria, Nicholas, Peter, Anthony of Padua, Francis, and Sebastian like prisoners in a dungeon. None of the saints look at the viewer; instead they direct their gaze at the floor or toward the vision of the Virgin and the Infant Jesus, who is preparing to hand out rosaries. From the opening in heaven divine light falls on the saints, causing their garments and attributes to shimmer. Titian's rendering of St. Catherine's glittering veil is particularly masterful. The rays of light at the upper edge of the painting emanate from the dove of the Holy Ghost, which was removed in the nineteenth century.

Titian (Tiziano Vecellio), ca. 1490–1576
The Virgin and Child with Saints:
***Madonna di San Niccolo dei Frari*, 1533–1535**
388 x 270 cm; Oil on wood panel
Pinacoteca; Room X; Inv. 40351

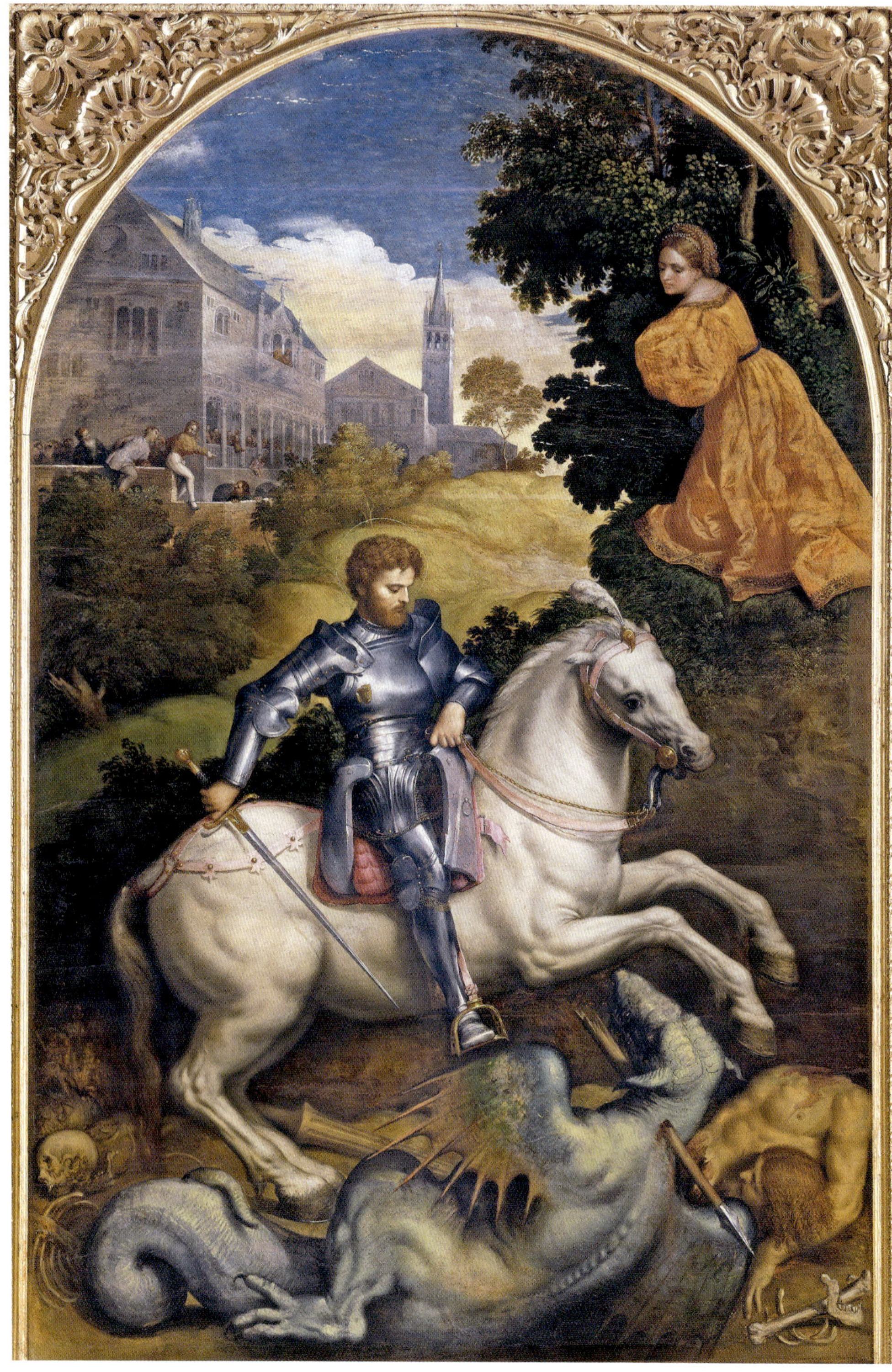

Paris Bordone

St. George and the Dragon

One of the most important examples of Venetian painting of the Cinquecento (sixteenth-century art) was Paris Bordone, a pupil of Titian from Treviso. Bordone acquired his teacher's love of shimmering colors but made far more emphatic use of them even than Titian in the dramatization of his pictures. The large-format *St. George and the Dragon*, painted by the twenty-five-year-old Bordone for the church of San Giorgio at the Minorite monastery of San Francesco in Noale (Vicenza), depicted in the background, is full of dramatic movement. The entire foreground is taken up with the scene of St. George fighting the dragon, which the saintly knight has pierced with his lance and is preparing to finish off with his sword. The figure of St. George mounted on his powerful white steed, which rears up on its hind legs, recalls antique equestrian statues. The drama of the scene is heightened by the chiaroscuro contrasts between the dragon's cave and the landscape above, but also by gruesome elements such as the bones and body parts in the foreground. With this noble deed, George saves the princess in the sumptuous orange-red gown, already chosen to be the next victim, whom we see kneeling above the cave. From the palace, agitated courtiers observe the battle scene, in which the young Bordone reveals his full artistic and narrative talent.

Paris Bordon, 1500–1571
***St. George and the Dragon*, ca. 1525**
290 x 189 cm; Oil on wood panel
Pinacoteca; Room X; Inv. 40354

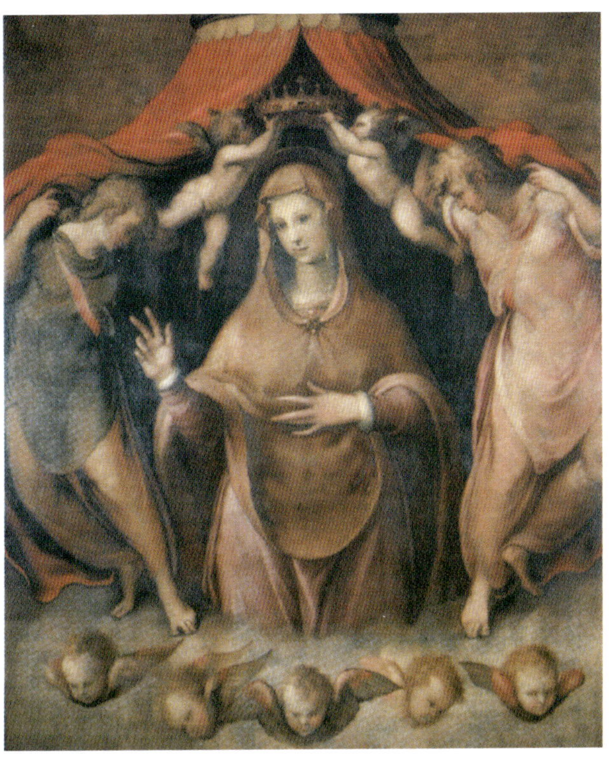

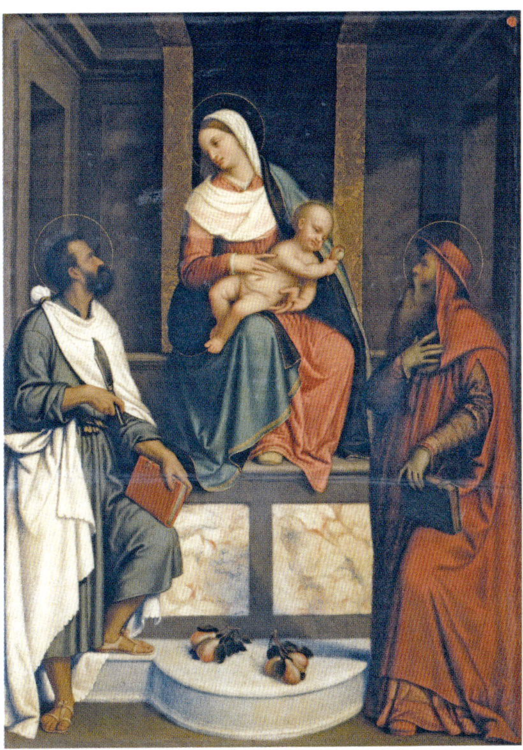

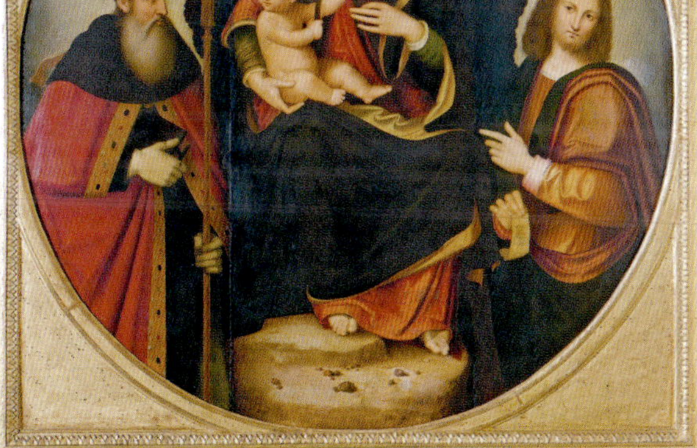

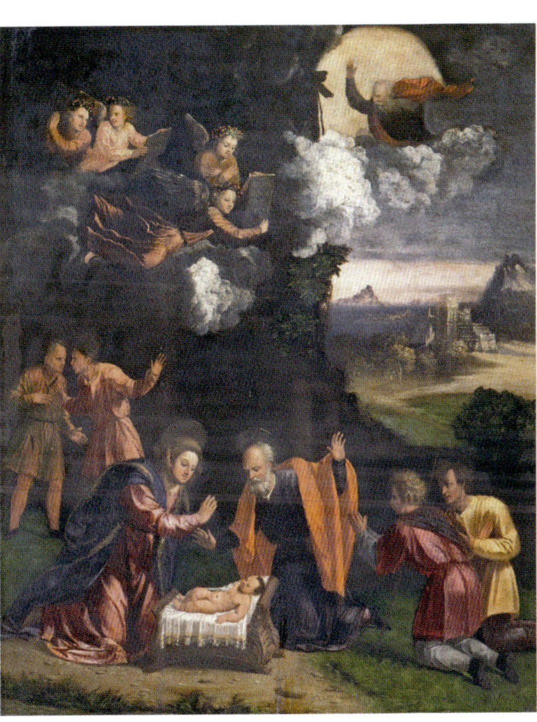

Francesco de'Rossi Salviati, 1510–1563
***Coronation of the Virgin*, ca. 1560–1563**
179.5 x 143 cm; Oil on canvas
Pinacoteca; Room X; Inv. 44942

Moretto da Brescia, ca. 1498–1554
***Madonna and Child enthroned with SS. Bartholomew and Jerome*, ca. 1550**
186 x 138 cm; Oil on canvas
Pinacoteca; Room X; Inv. 40349

Lombardi School, 16th century
***Madonna della Cintura*, 1521**
Diameter: 156 cm; Oil on wood panel
Pinacoteca; Room X; Inv. 40336

Camillo Filippi, ca. 1500–1574
***Adoration of the Shepherds*, undated**
80 x 64 cm; Oil on wood panel
Pinacoteca; Room X; Inv. 40357

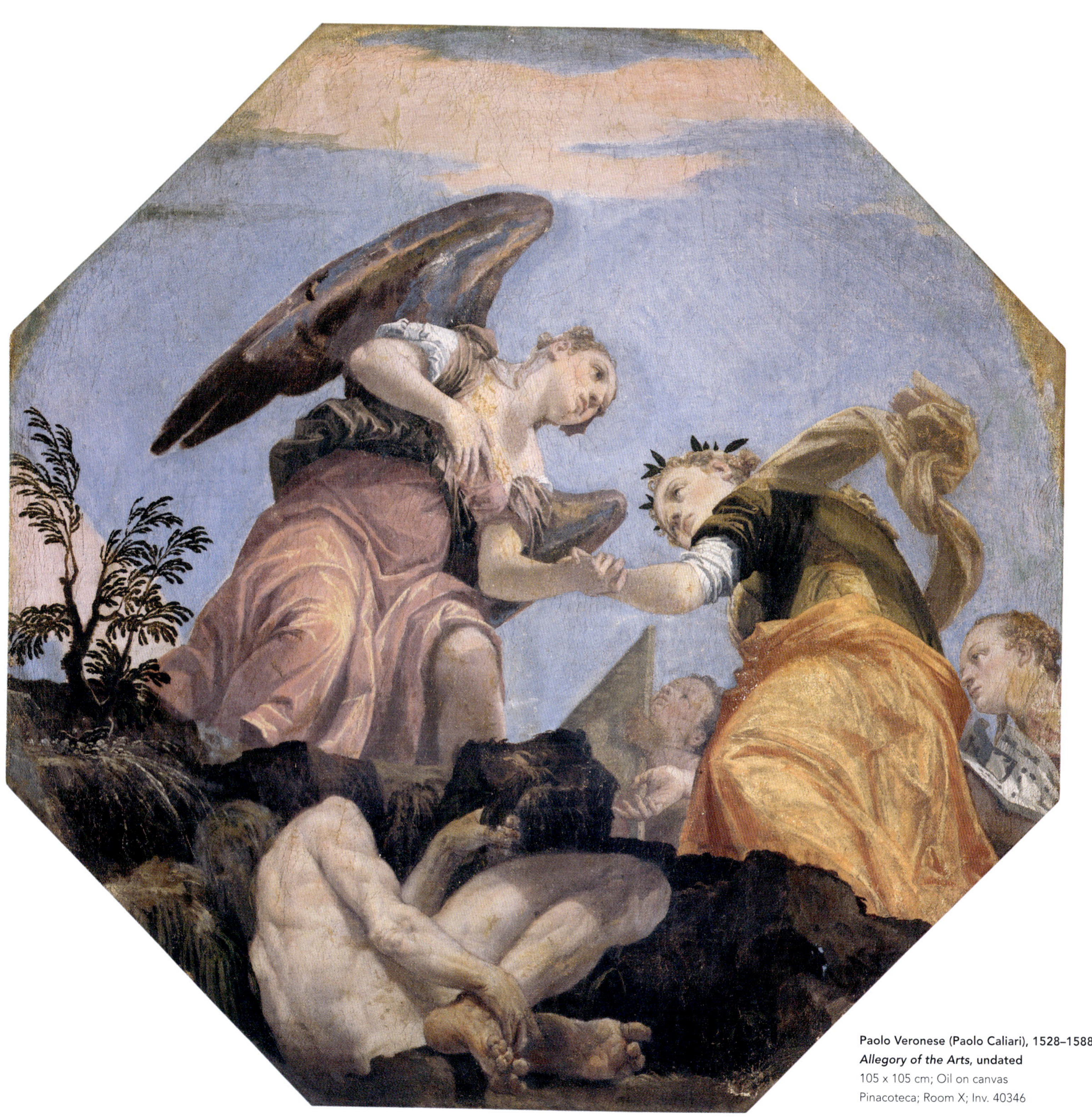

Paolo Veronese (Paolo Caliari), 1528–1588
***Allegory of the Arts*, undated**
105 x 105 cm; Oil on canvas
Pinacoteca; Room X; Inv. 40346

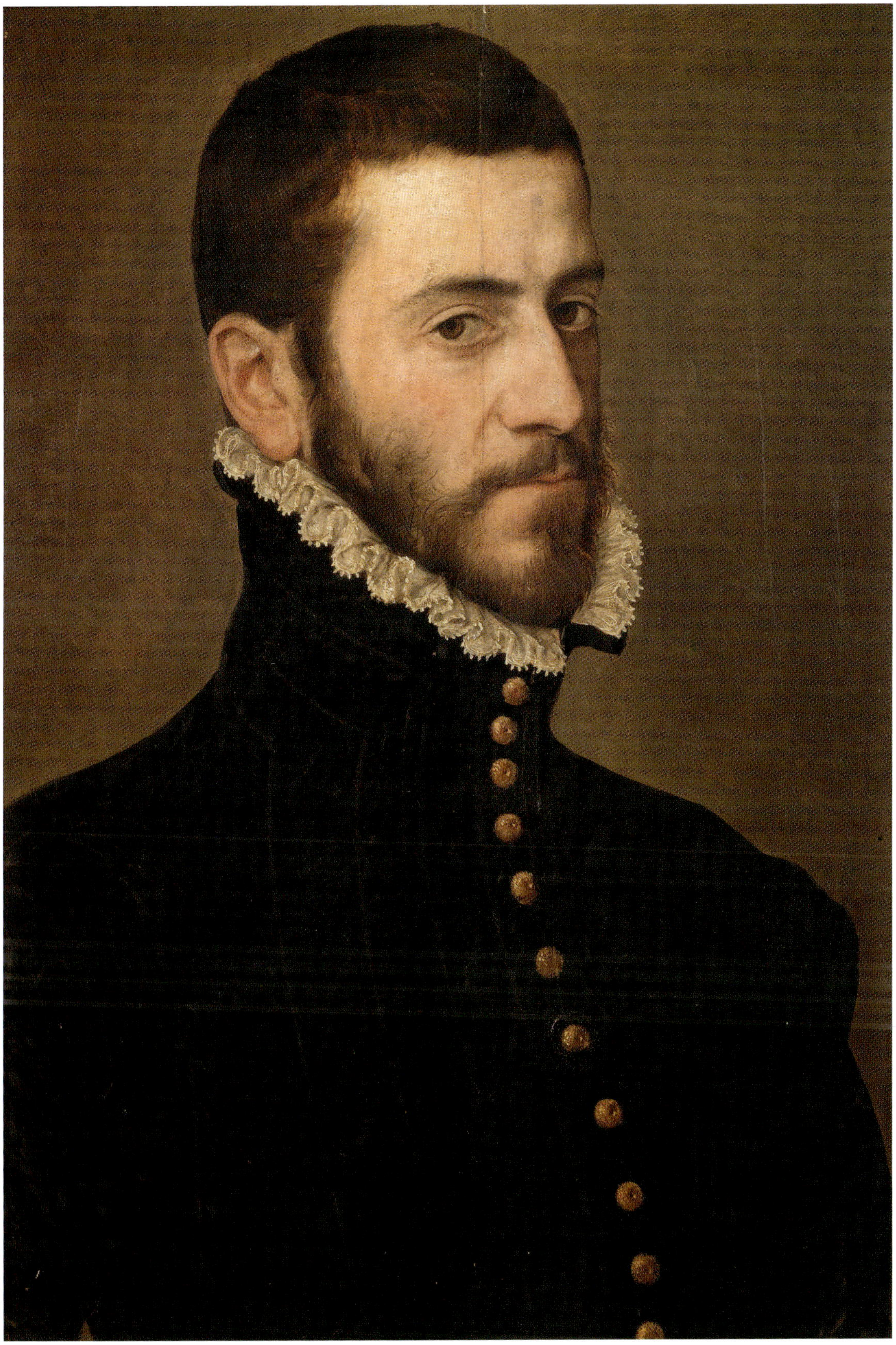

Antonio Moro, ca. 1520–1576/77
***Male Portrait*, undated**
50 x 35 cm; Oil on wood panel
Pinacoteca; Room X; Inv. 40444

Lombard School, 16th century
***Christ at the Column*, 16th century**
72 x 55 cm; Oil on wood panel
Pinacoteca; Room X; Inv. 40339

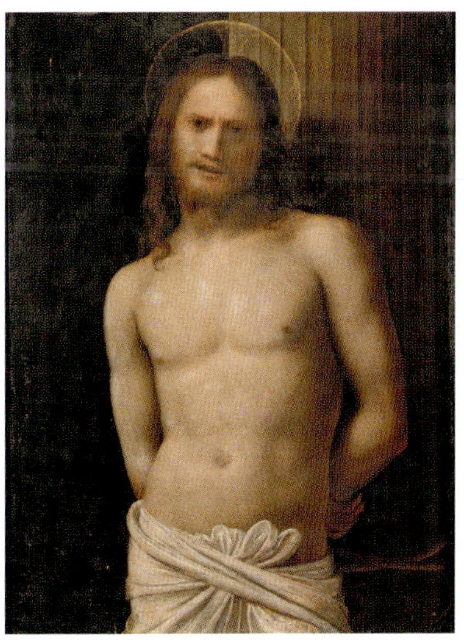

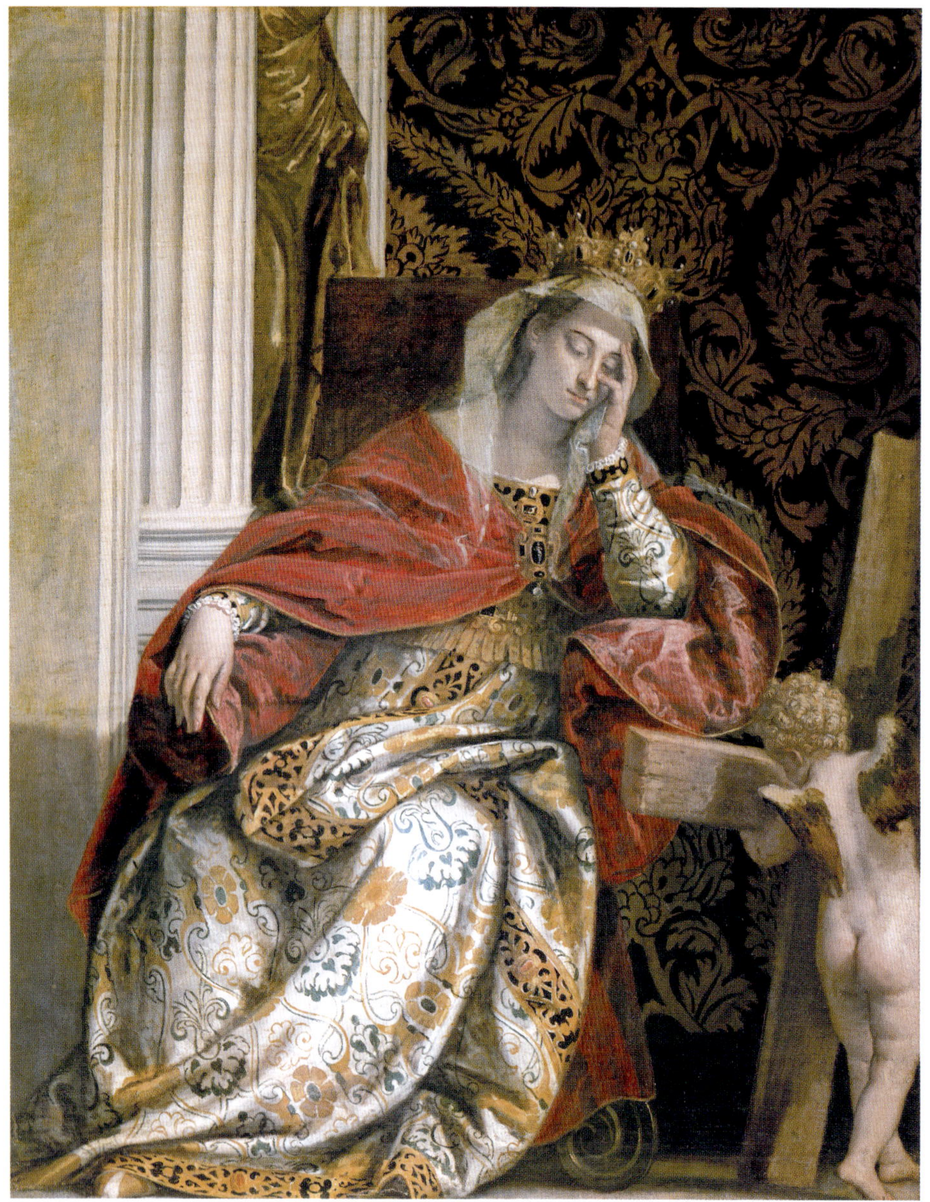

Paolo Veronese (Paolo Caliari)

The Vision of St. Helena

What could at first glance be taken to be the portrait of a noblewoman is in reality a scene from the life of St. Helena. The Venetian painter Veronese understood better than any other Renaissance artist how to combine religious motifs with worldly splendor. Helena (ca. 248/50–ca. 330), the mother of Emperor Constantine the Great, was the first Roman Augusta (wife or mother of the emperor) to be baptized. She saw a vision in which it was revealed that she would discover Christ's cross on Golgotha during a trip to Palestine. This vision is the subject of Veronese's painting. The canvas is almost filled by the richly appareled figure of Helena at rest on a throne. Her head is inclined to the right, where a winged putto supports the mighty upper portion of a cross. Although Helena's eyes are closed, the fingers of her left hand act as a kind of magnifying glass, making her inner vision visible to the viewer. In this late work, Veronese excels at the depiction of Helena's shimmering garments, which fall in heavy folds around the saint's body. The original purpose of the painting is unknown. It was acquired by the Pinacoteca Capitolina in 1750 from the collection of the princes of Pio di Savoia.

Paolo Veronese (Paolo Caliari), 1528–1588
***The Vision of St. Helen*, ca. 1580**
166 x 134 cm; Oil on canvas
Pinacoteca; Room X; Inv. 40352

Jacopo Boateri, mid-16th century
***Madonna and Child*, undated**
71 x 60 cm; Oil on wood panel
Pinacoteca; Room X; Inv. 40360

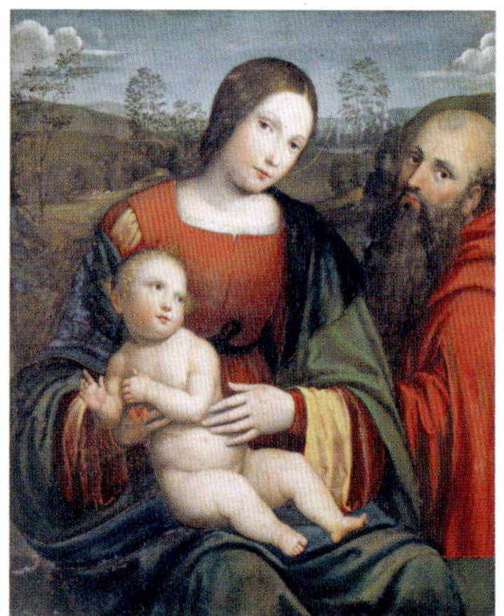

ROOM XI

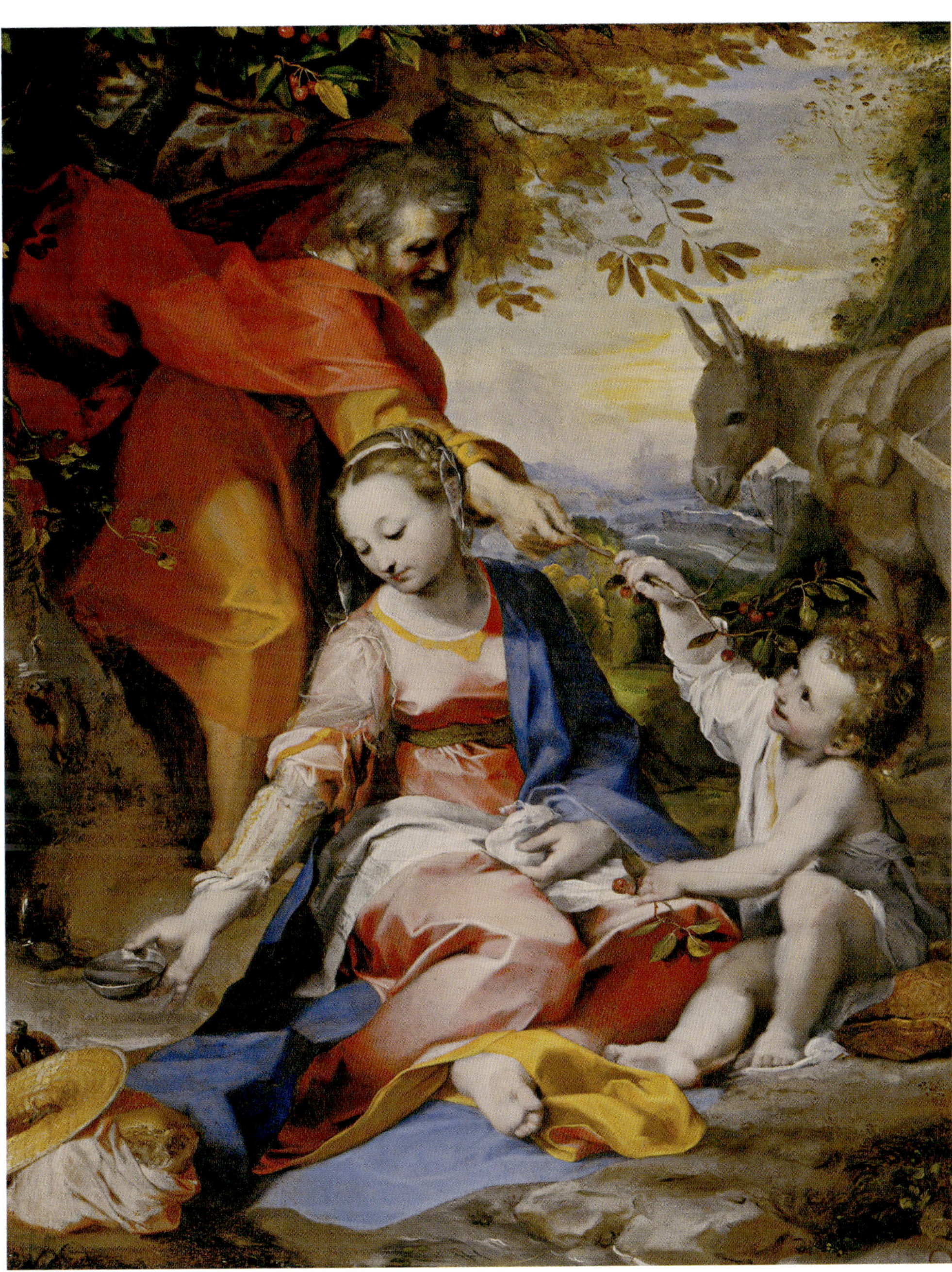

Federico Barocci

Rest on the Flight into Egypt, also known as *The Madonna of the Cherries*

This idyllic scene depicts the Holy Family at rest during the flight into Egypt. The Virgin has been placed center-stage, reposing on her blue mantle, while the Infant Jesus sits on a small golden brocade cushion by her side. Joseph thoughtfully passes him a branch of cherries freshly picked from a tree that also provides the resting travelers with shade. In the left of the foreground lies their modest baggage—a small bag containing bread, a straw hat, and a small container of water. Mary uses a shallow bowl to scoop water from a stream next to the clearing. From the middle distance a donkey patiently observes the intimate family scene unfolding beneath a glowing morning sky. A viewer with no knowledge of the biblical story of the flight into Egypt could be forgiven for interpreting this picture, dominated by bright pastel hues, as a young family's cheerful outing to the country. As a supporter of the Counter-Reformation, Barocci subscribed to the principle of representing religious content in a visually appealing, empathetic, and easily comprehensible manner. Paintings like the *Madonna of the Cherries* were designed to open the eyes and heart of the viewer. At the same time, Barocci's works, with their sophisticated composition and display of consummate skill, also became sought-after collectors' items.

Federico Barocci, 1528/35–1612
Rest on the Flight into Egypt, **also known as**
The Madonna of the Cherries, **1582–1584**
133 x 100 cm; Oil on canvas
Pinacoteca; Room XI; Inv. 40377

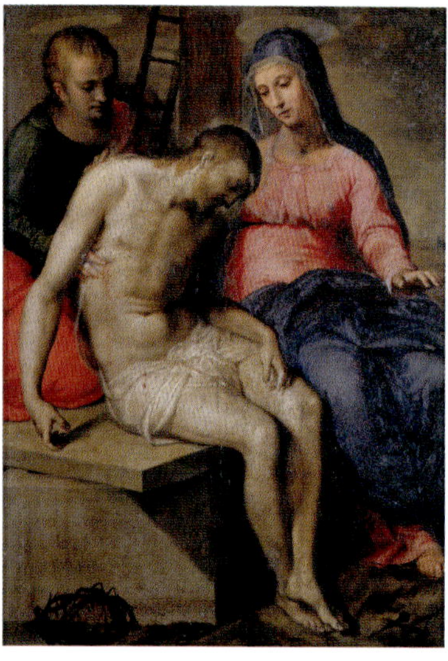
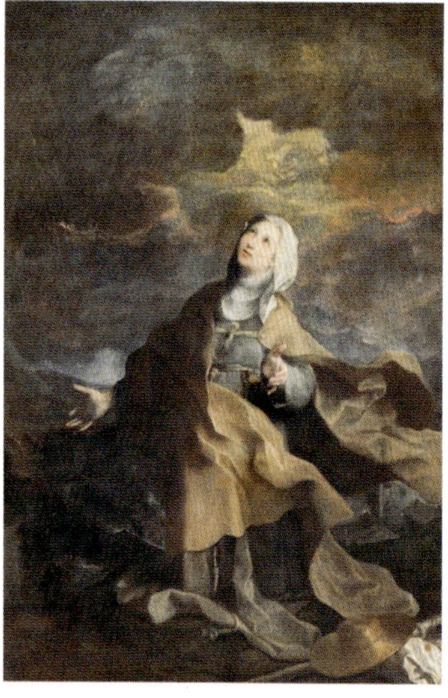
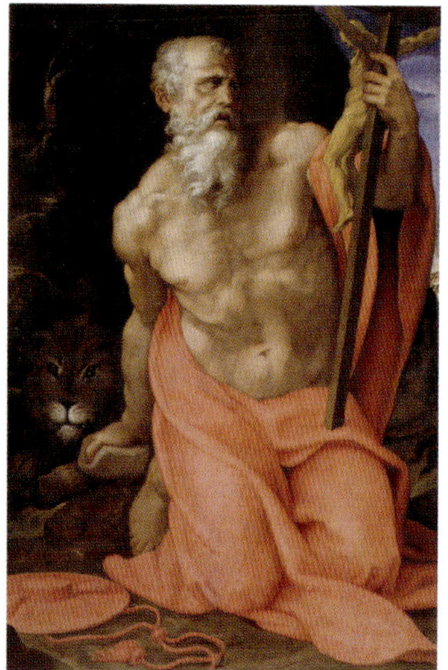
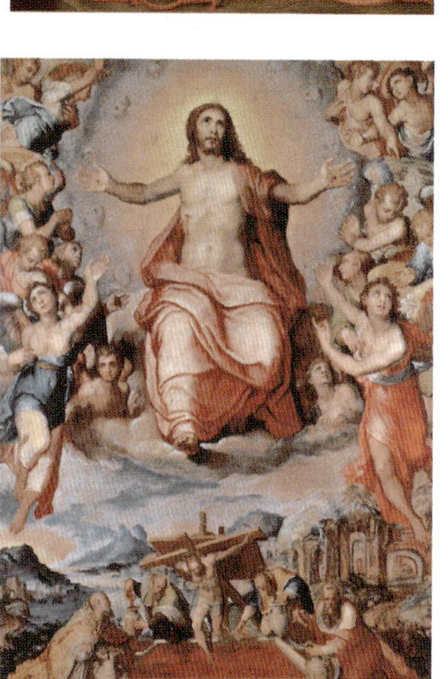
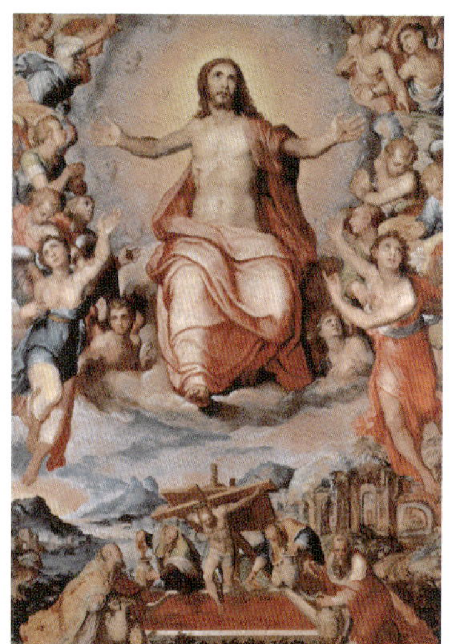
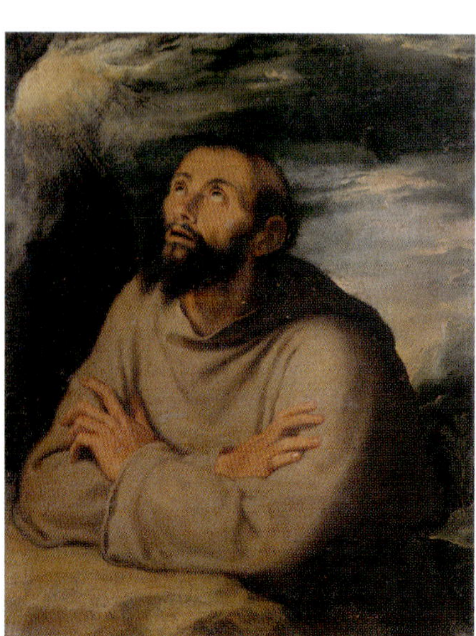
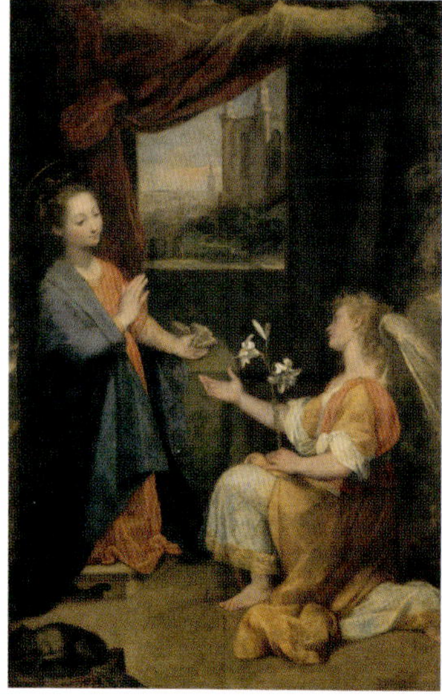
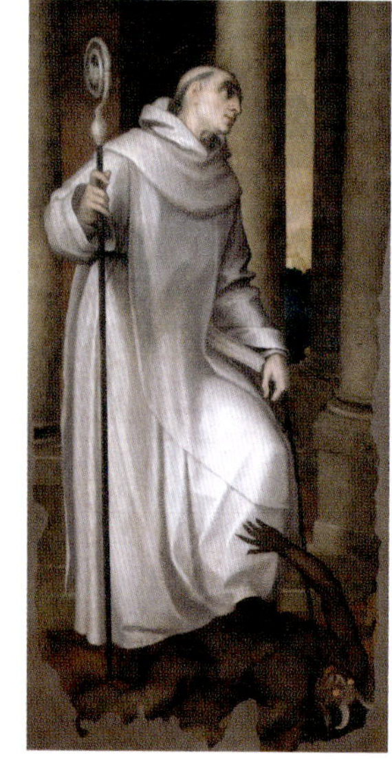

Marcello Venusti (school of), 1512/1515–1579
***Pietà*, undated**
46.5 x 34 cm; Oil on canvas
Pinacoteca; Room XI; Inv. 40379

Federico Barocci, 1528/35–1612
***Blessed Michelina*, ca. 1606**
252 x 171 cm; Oil on canvas
Pinacoteca; Room XI; Inv. 40378

Girolamo Muziano, 1528–1592
***St. Jerome*, ca. 1585–1592**
147 x 98 cm; Oil on wood panel transferred to canvas
Pinacoteca; Room XI; Inv. 40369

Federico Barocci, 1528/35–1612
***St. Francis Receiving the Stigmata*, ca. 1595**
169 x 119 cm; Oil on canvas
Pinacoteca; Room XI; Inv. 40380

Girolamo Muziano, 1528/32–1592
***St. Francis of Assisi Receives the Stigmata*, undated**
42 x 28 cm; Oil on wood panel transferred to canvas
Pinacoteca; Room XI; Inv. 40370

Marco da Pino da Siena, ca. 1525–ca. 1587
***Christ in Glory*, ca. 1571**
139 x 96 cm; Oil on wood panel
Pinacoteca; Room XI; Inv. 42179

Girolamo Muziano, 1528/32–1592
***St. Francis of Assisi*, undated**
85 x 69 cm; Oil on wood panel transferred to canvas
Pinacoteca; Room XI; Inv. 40371

Federico Barocci, 1528/35–1612
***Annunciation*, 1582–1584**
248 x 170 cm; Oil on canvas
Pinacoteca; Room XI; Inv. 40376

Marcello Venusti, 1512/1515–1579
***St. Bernard*, 1563–1564**
220 x 110 cm; Oil on wood panel
Pinacoteca; Room XI; Inv. 40350

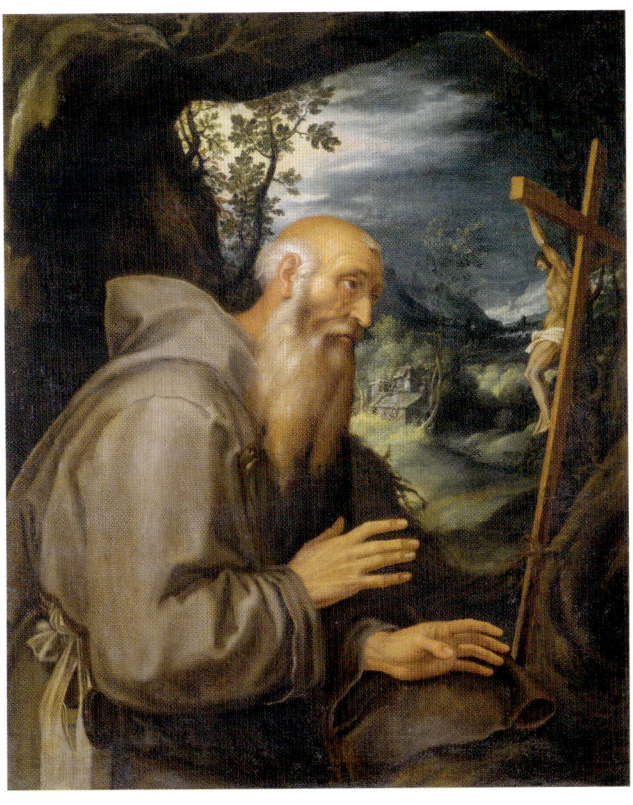

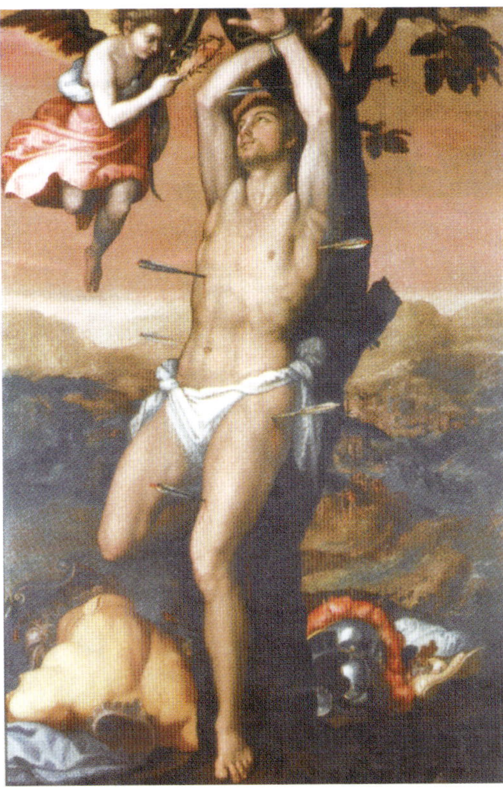

Girolamo Muziano, 1528/32–1592
***Hermit*, ca. 1590**
134.5 x 112 cm; Oil on canvas
Pinacoteca; Room XI; Inv. 40367

Girolamo Sermoneta da Siciolante, 1521–1575
***St. Sebastian*, undated**
234 x 147 cm; Oil on canvas
Pinacoteca; Room XI; Inv. 44275

Girolamo Muziano, 1528/32–1592
***Resurrection of Lazarus*, 1555**
295 x 440 cm; Oil on canvas
Pinacoteca; Room XI; Inv. 40368

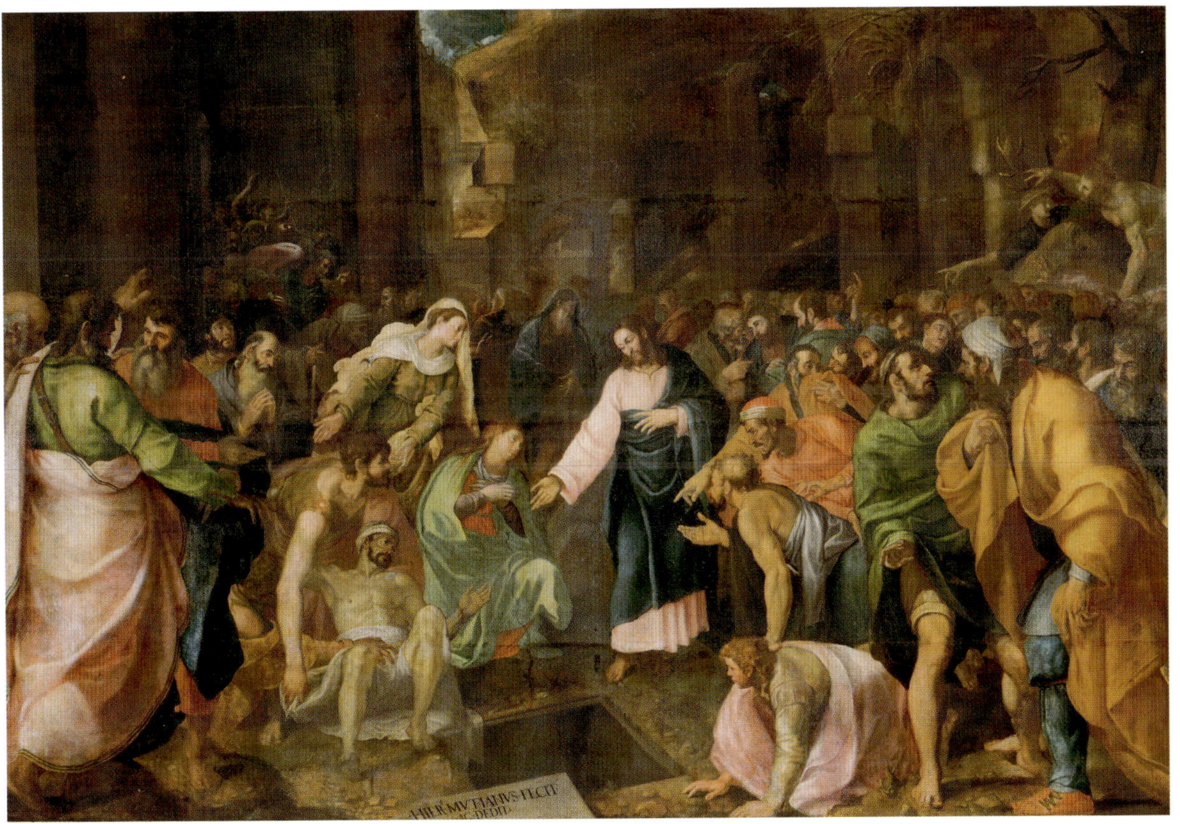

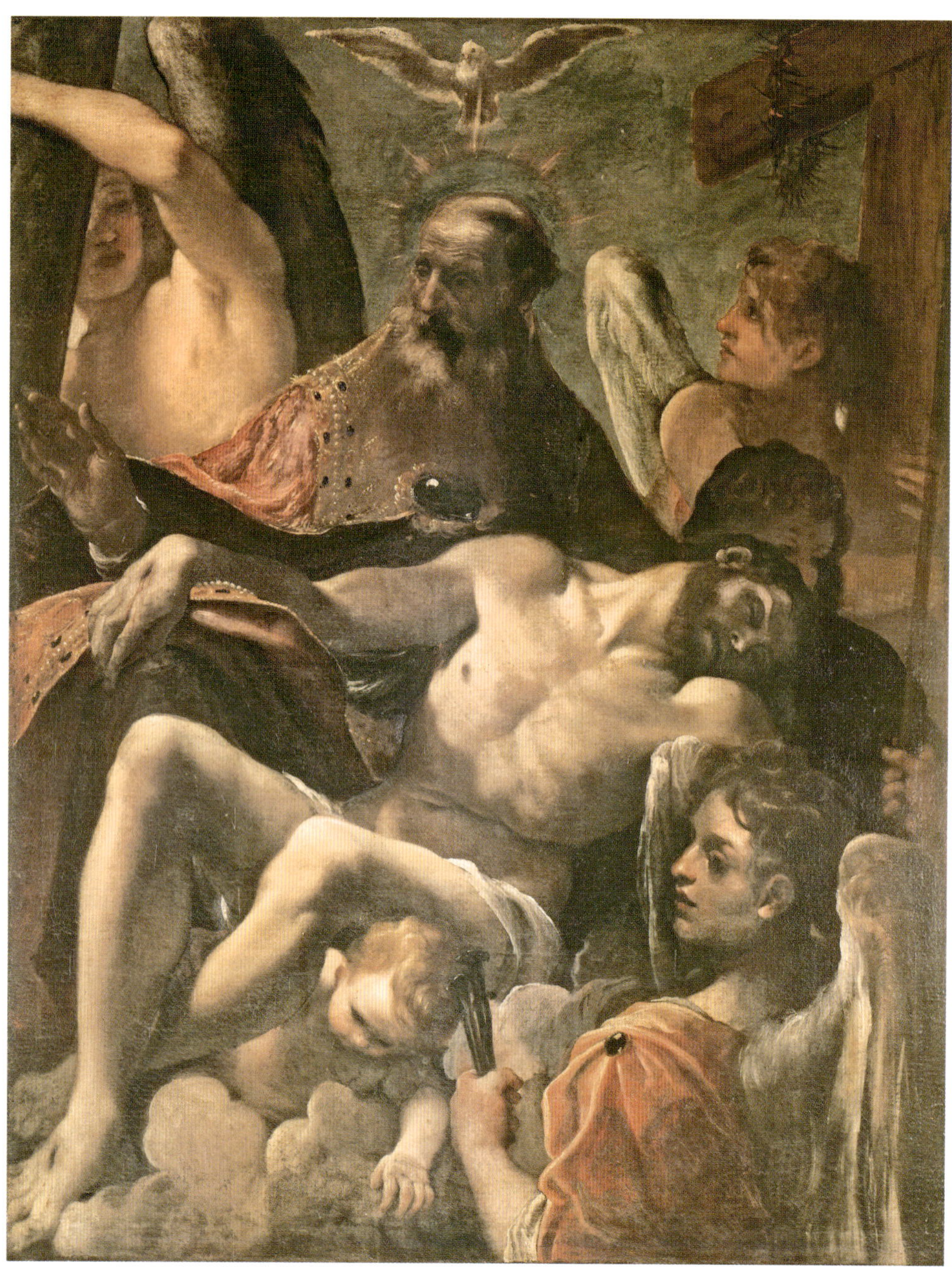

Ludovico Carracci

The Holy Trinity

The Bolognese painter Ludovico Carracci is regarded as one of the initiators of the Baroque style in Italy. The typical characteristics of this style—dramatic chiaroscuro created by shadows, an emphasis on diagonals, expressive gesture, and facial expressions—are present in Carracci's *Holy Trinity*. In the usual interpretation of this motif, sometimes referred to as the "Throne of Grace," God the Father holds Christ on his own lap. In this version, however, the corpse, cross, and instruments of Christ's suffering are supported by angels. The painter's innovative solution combines the pictorial motifs of the Throne of Grace and the Angel Pietà with the presentation of the instruments of the Passion by angels. Carracci interweaves the various iconographical elements, protagonists, and picture planes in a sophisticated web of bodies, garments, and artifacts. The unifying central element is the body of Christ, which rises from left of foreground to occupy almost the entire diagonal. This diagonal is counterbalanced by God the Father, forming a vertical extended further by the dove of the Holy Ghost and marking out the central axis. The Almighty is flanked by the two angels holding the pillar at which Christ was scourged and the crucifix with the bloody crown of thorns. While the putto underneath Christ's bent legs introduces a playful element into the scene, the angel in the bottom left of the painting invites the viewer to reflect on Christ's sacrificial death.

Lodovico Carracci, 1555–1619
***The Holy Trinity*, ca. 1590**
172.5 x 126.5 cm; Oil on canvas
Pinacoteca; Room XI; Inv. 41429

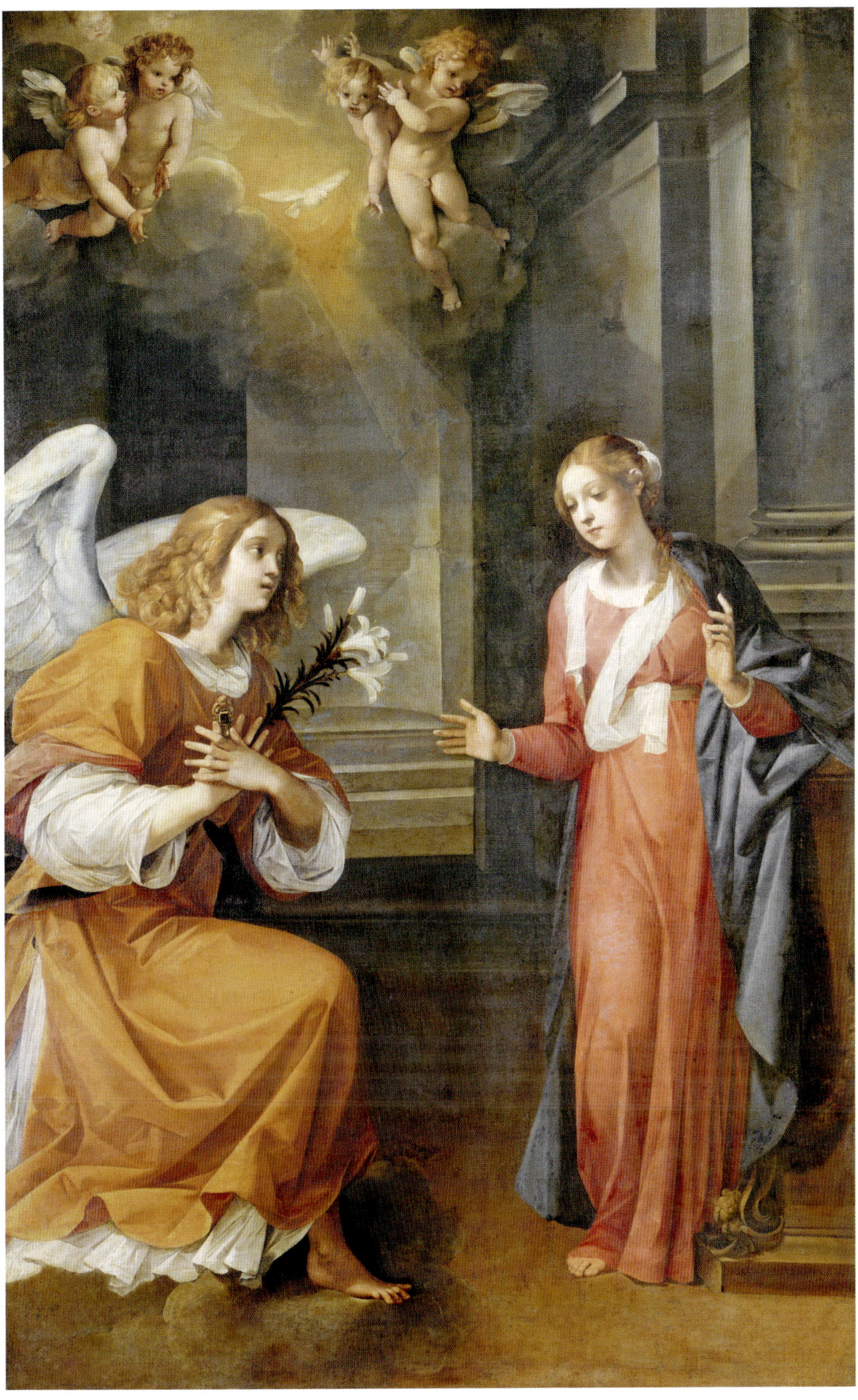

Cavaliere d'Arpino (Giuseppe Cesari)

The Annunciation

The son of a painter in the service of the pope, Giuseppe Cesari, known after his place of birth as Cavaliere d'Arpino, acquired attention as an enormously talented fourteen-year-old and rapidly made a successful career for himself in Rome. By the age of twenty-two he was at the head of a large workshop which Caravaggio entered as a journeyman in 1593. In addition to major fresco commissions, Cesari painted works on canvas, such as this *Annunciation*, whose original purpose is unknown. The painting is signed "Ioseph Arpinas F. 1606" on the bottom of the plinth on the right. Cesari places Mary and the angel in an empty stone hall resembling a church, with a few steps leading up to a shallow apse in the background. The warm tones of Mary's and the angel's robes stand out clearly against the dark and sober space. Mary, dressed in a flowing red gown with white veil and a blue mantle, leans against a lectern and turns with open arms and humbly bowed head toward the angel. The latter, in fluttering robes, kneels before her and, with an ardent gesture, announces the conception of the Son of God, who appears in the form of the dove of the Holy Ghost in the midst of a ray of divine light. With consummate skill, Cesari has blended typical Baroque spotlighting and divine light, lending a softness to the garments and facial features.

Cavalier d'Arpino (Giuseppe Cesari), 1568–1640
***The Annunciation*, 1606**
290 x 184 cm; Oil on canvas
Pinacoteca; Room XI; Inv. 40365

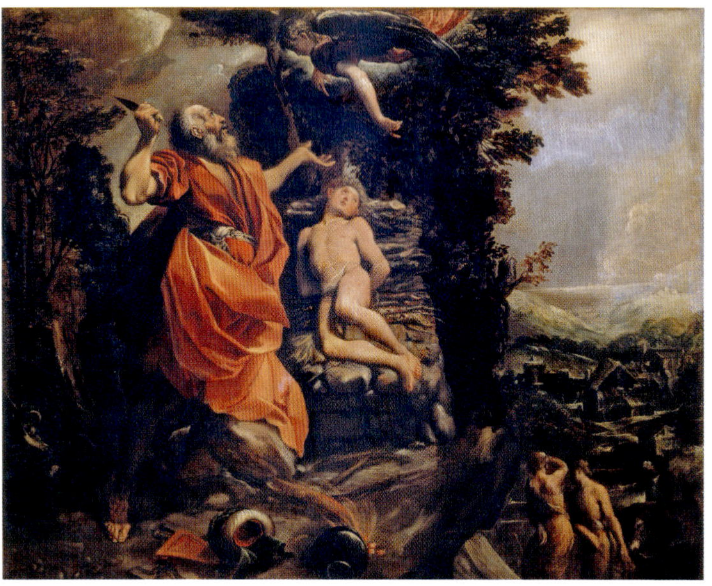

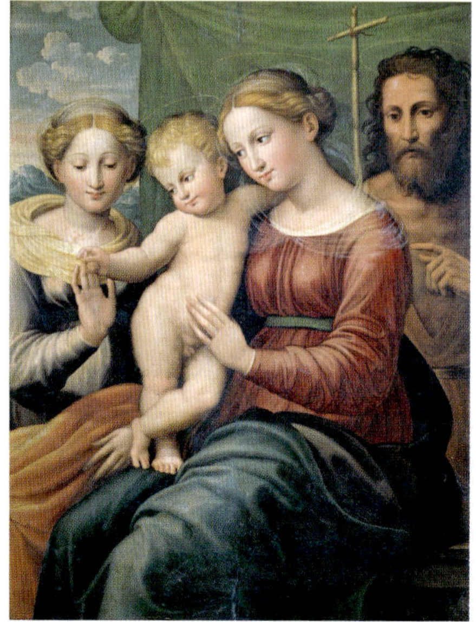

Ludovico Carracci, 1555–1619
***Sacrifice of Isaac*, undated**
107 x 133 cm; Oil on canvas
Pinacoteca; Room XI; Inv. 40669

Innocenzo da Imola, ca. 1484–1550
***Mystic Marriage of St. Catherine*, undated**
83 x 63 cm; Oil on wood panel
Pinacoteca; Room XI; Inv. 40373

Jacopo Zucchi, ca. 1541–1596
***Procession of St. Gregorio*, 1573–1575**
168 x 128 cm; Oil on wood panel
Pinacoteca; Room XI; Inv. 40374

Jacopo Zucchi, ca. 1541–1596
***Miracle of the Snow*, 1573–1575**
171 x 151 cm; Oil on wood panel
Pinacoteca; Room XI; Inv. 42157

Tommaso Laureti, ca. 1530–1602
***Miracle of St. Peter*, undated**
129 x 69 cm; Oil on canvas
Pinacoteca; Room XI; Inv. 55949

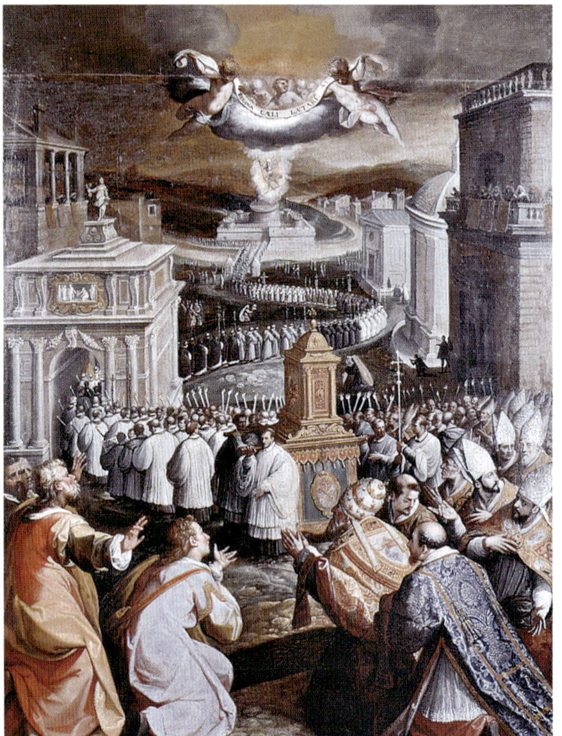

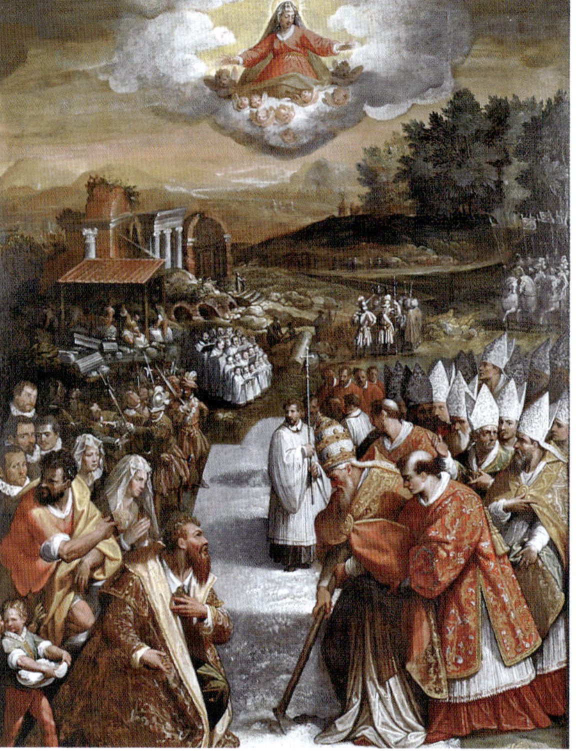

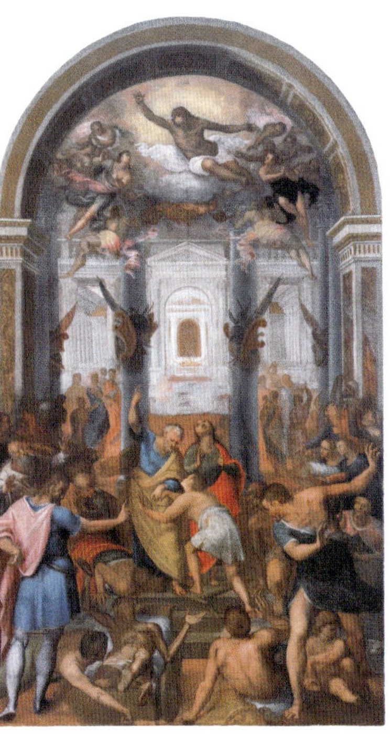

SALA XII

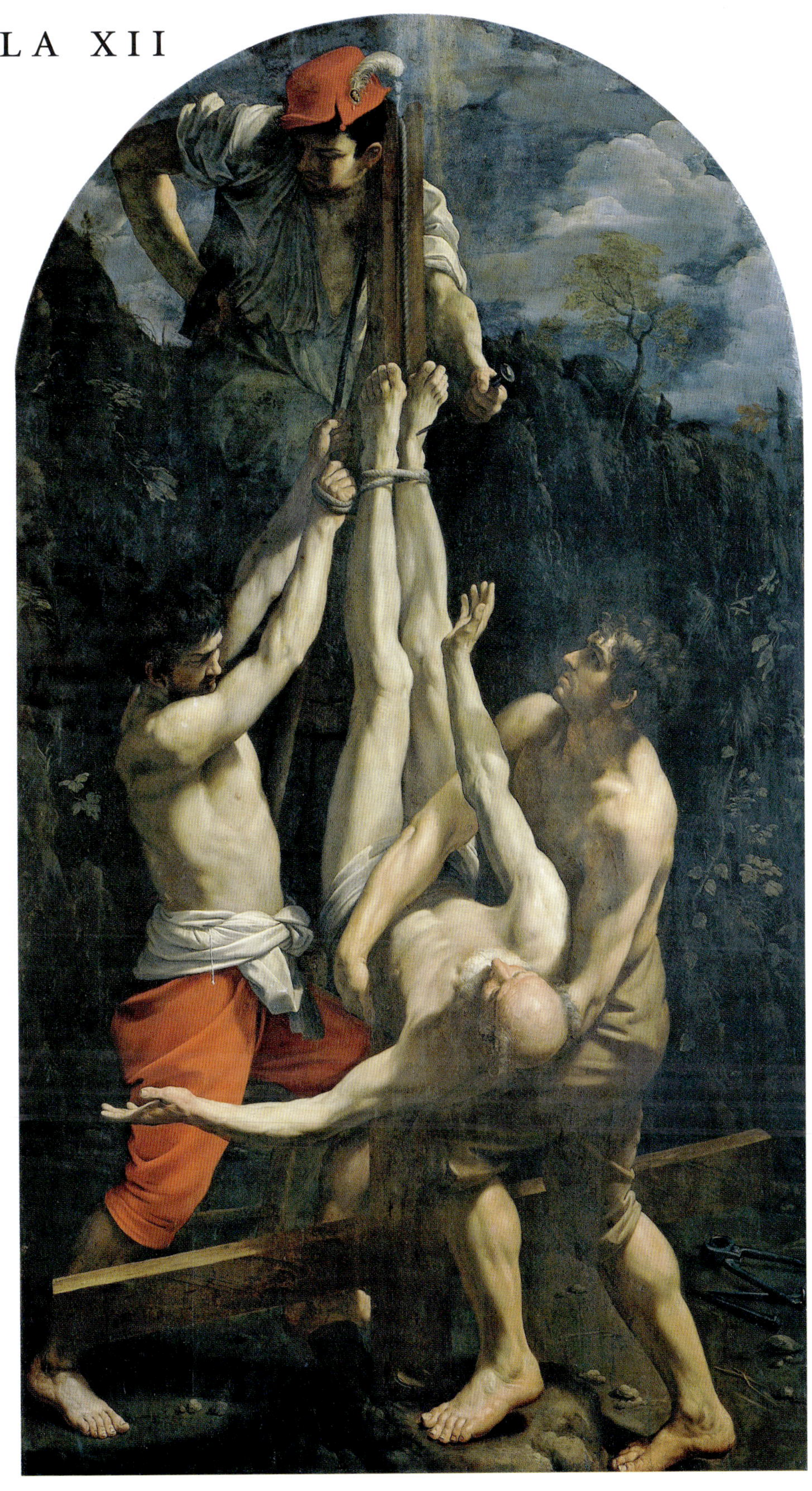

Guido Reni

The Crucifixion of St. Peter

According to legend, St. Peter, like Christ, was crucified. Believing himself unworthy to suffer the same death as Jesus, however, he asked his executioners to crucify him upside down. This painting by the Baroque artist Guido Reni, from Bologna, shows the setting up of the cross. Three executioners are shown securing St. Peter, wearing only a loincloth, to the cross as the saint appears to direct their actions with his arms. The foremost henchman supports St. Peter's upper body, a second stabilizes the cross with his knee while pulling the rope more tightly around his feet, and a third, standing on the ladder behind the cross, takes hold of a hammer in order to strike an enormous nail through Peter's right foot. This large panel, commissioned in 1604 by Cardinal Pietro Aldobrandini for the monastery church of San Paolo alle Tre Fontane outside the gates of Rome, combines Renaissance elements with the expressive power of the Baroque. Classical aspects include the symmetry around the central axis of the cross and the restrained depiction of emotion—the face of the saint, for example, is partially hidden. The dramatic chiaroscuro and slightly oblique postures of the figures lend the scene much of its tension and dynamism and are distinctly Baroque.

Guido Reni, 1575–1642
***The Crucifixion of St. Peter*, 1604–1605**
305 x 171 cm; Oil on wood
Pinacoteca; Room XII; Inv. 40387

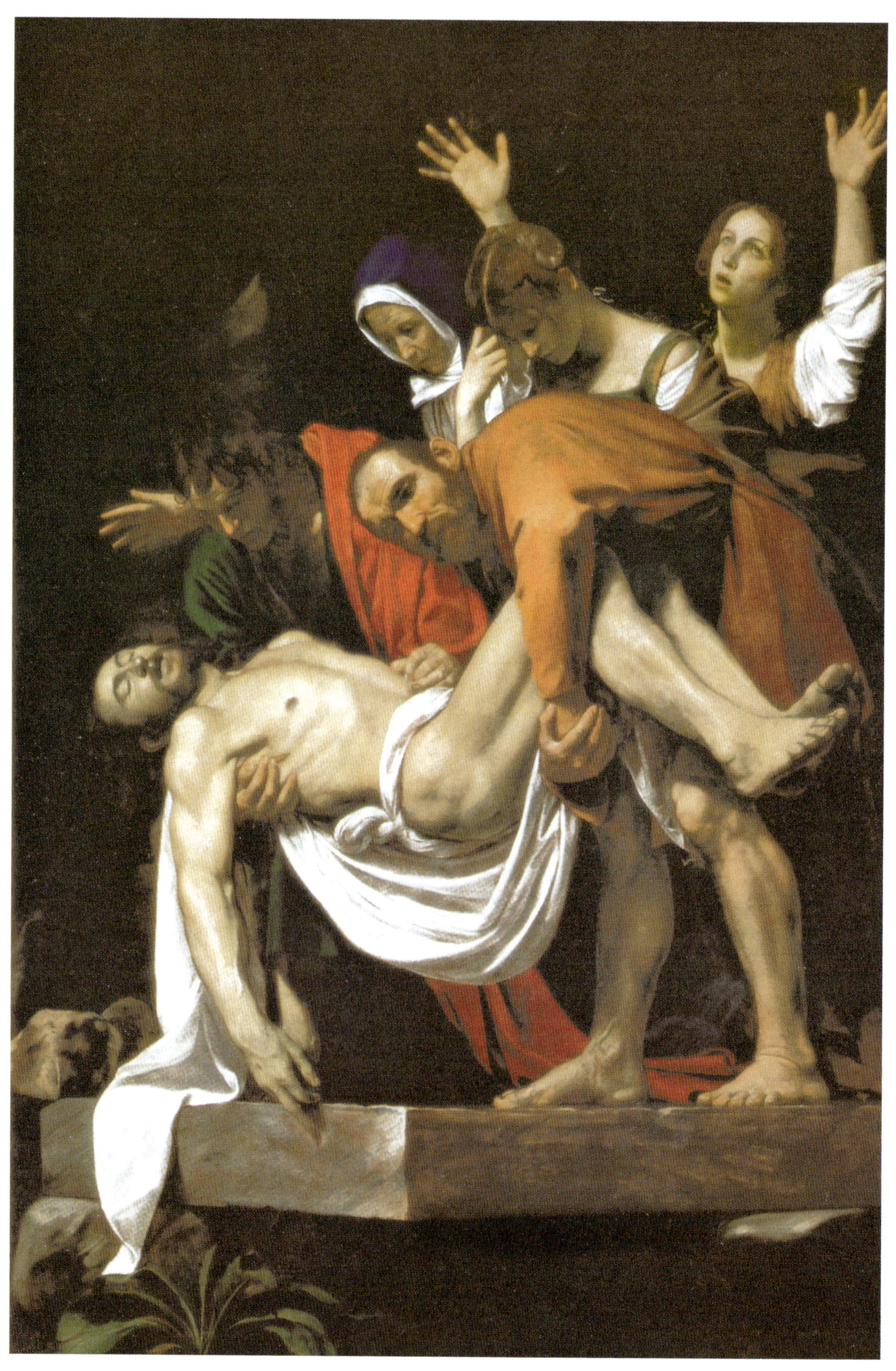

Caravaggio (Michelangelo Merisi da Caravaggio)

The Deposition

Caravaggio's *Deposition* is one of the most famous works in the Pinacoteca. It was commissioned around 1600 by Girolamo Vittrice for the sepulchral chapel of his uncle Pietro Vittrice in the Oratorian church of Santa Maria in Vallicella in Rome. The period from 1600 to 1604 was one of the most productive in the painter's life. For the Vittrice chapel, Caravaggio, who made a name for himself with audacious compositions and a lifestyle widely regarded as scandalous, devised a daring, fan-like composition that, moving from top to bottom, presents each stage in the bearing of Christ's body from the cross to the grave in a kind of time-lapse sequence. At the same time, the reactions of the mourners run the gamut of manifestations of grief from arms raised in lamentation all the way to quiet reflection, accentuated by the dramatic spotlighting. The latter also endows the fabrics of the garments, which glow forth out of the darkness, with a life of their own. Caravaggio's naturalism, as exemplified by the unadorned rendering of the corpse, the boorish-looking saints and details such as dirty fingernails, was admired and decried in equal measure. Viewed from below, this scene seems to be urging the beholder to catch the body of Christ in his or her own arms.

Caravaggio (Michelangelo Merisi da Caravaggio), 1571–1610
***The Deposition*, 1600–1604**
300 x 203 cm; Oil on canvas
Pinacoteca; Room XII; Inv. 40386

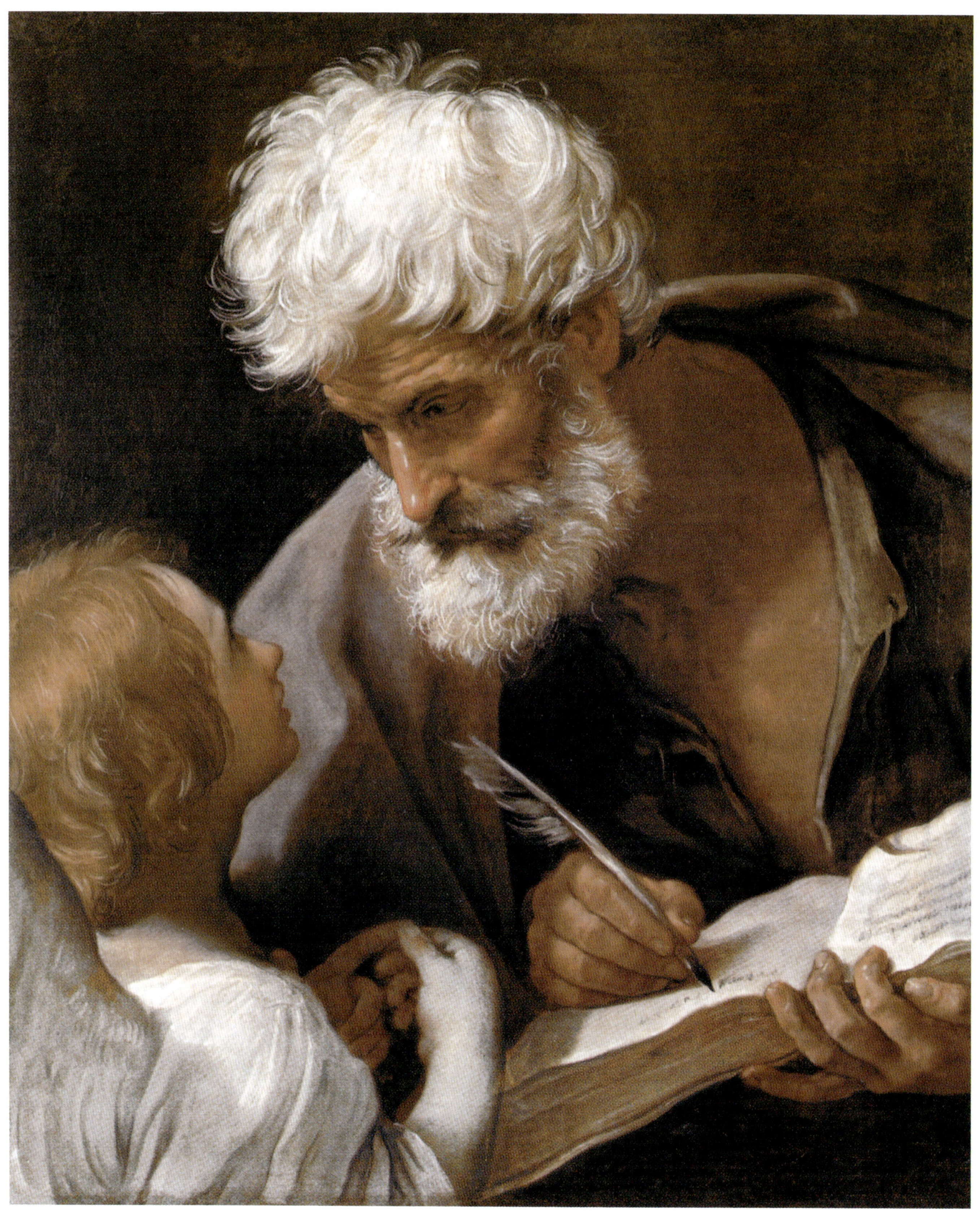

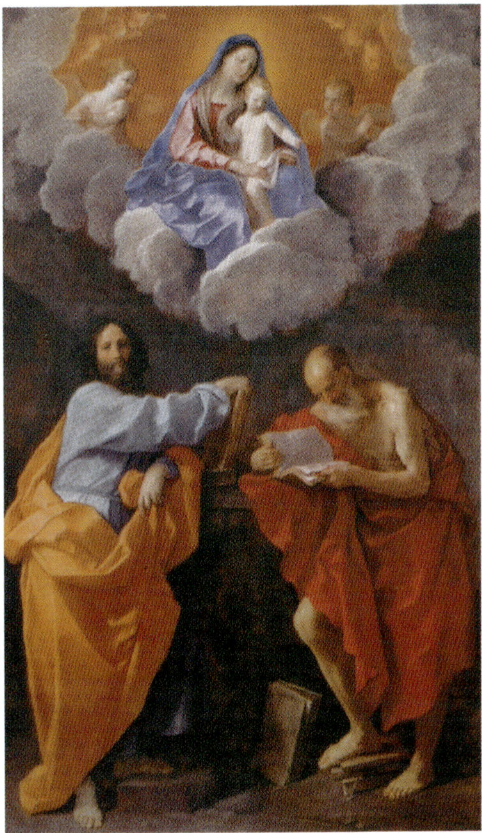

Guido Reni, 1575–1642
***Virgin Mary in Glory with SS. Thomas and Jerome*, 1634**
340 x 210 cm; Oil on canvas
Pinacoteca; Room XII; Inv. 40389

Guido Reni

St. Matthew and the Angel

Reni's depiction of the dialogue between St. Matthew the Evangelist and the angel is one of the of the Baroque master's most beautiful creations. The use of color, the close cropping of the picture, with its diagonal positioning of the Evangelist's upper body, the tension-filled chiaroscuro, and the careful highlighting of the hair and fingers are reminiscent of the work of Caravaggio, who was regarded at the time as Reni's artistic adversary. As in Caravaggio's St. Matthew cycle in the church of San Luigi dei Francesi, Reni represents the inspiration of the aged-looking Evangelist as an angel, who appears to be communicating the verses of the gospel via his hypnotic gaze rather than by means of the spoken word. The angel's hand gesture, however, indicates direct speech, which Matthew carefully records with a quill on the blank pages of his book. Numerous collectors apparently wanted this relatively small composition for their private art cabinets and Reni made with his own hand a number of copies of the original picture, which is in the collection of Bob Jones University in Greenville, South Carolina. The version in the Pinacoteca differs from the original only in its greater use of impasto and darker tones, typical of Reni's late works dating from 1635–40.

Guido Reni, 1575–1642
***St. Matthew and the Angel*, 1635–1640**
85 x 68 cm; Oil on canvas
Pinacoteca; Room XII; Inv. 40395

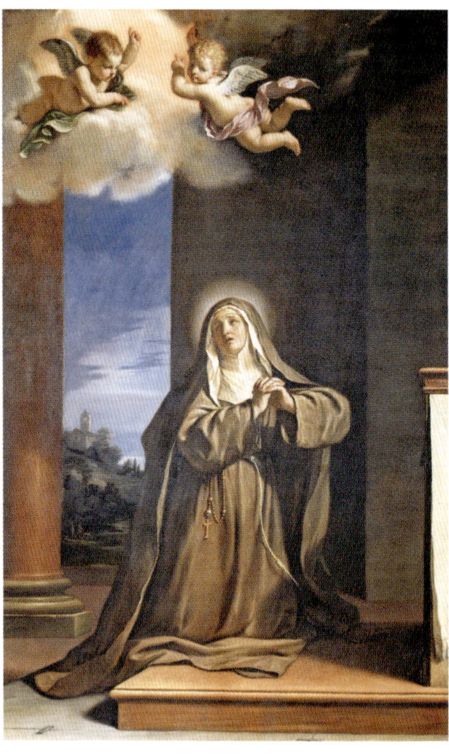

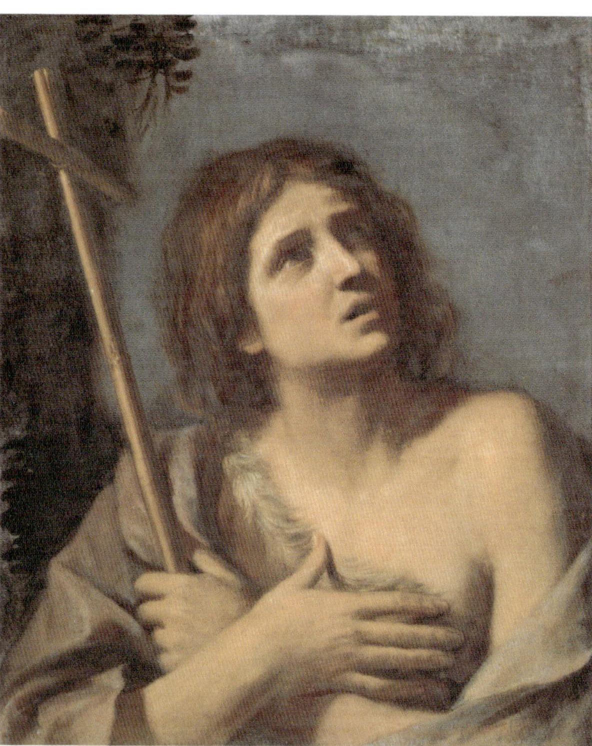

Giovanni Francesco Barbieri (Guercino), 1591–1666
***St. Margaret of Cortona*, undated**
255 x170 cm; Oil on canvas
Pinacoteca; Room XII; Inv. 40392

Giovanni Francesco Barbieri (Guercino), 1591–1666
***St. John the Baptist*, undated**
63 x 50 cm; Oil on canvas
Pinacoteca; Room XII; Inv. 40393

Giovanni Francesco Barbieri (Guercino), 1591–1666
***The Incredulity of St. Thomas*, undated**
120 x 143 cm; Oil on canvas
Pinacoteca; Room XII; Inv. 40383

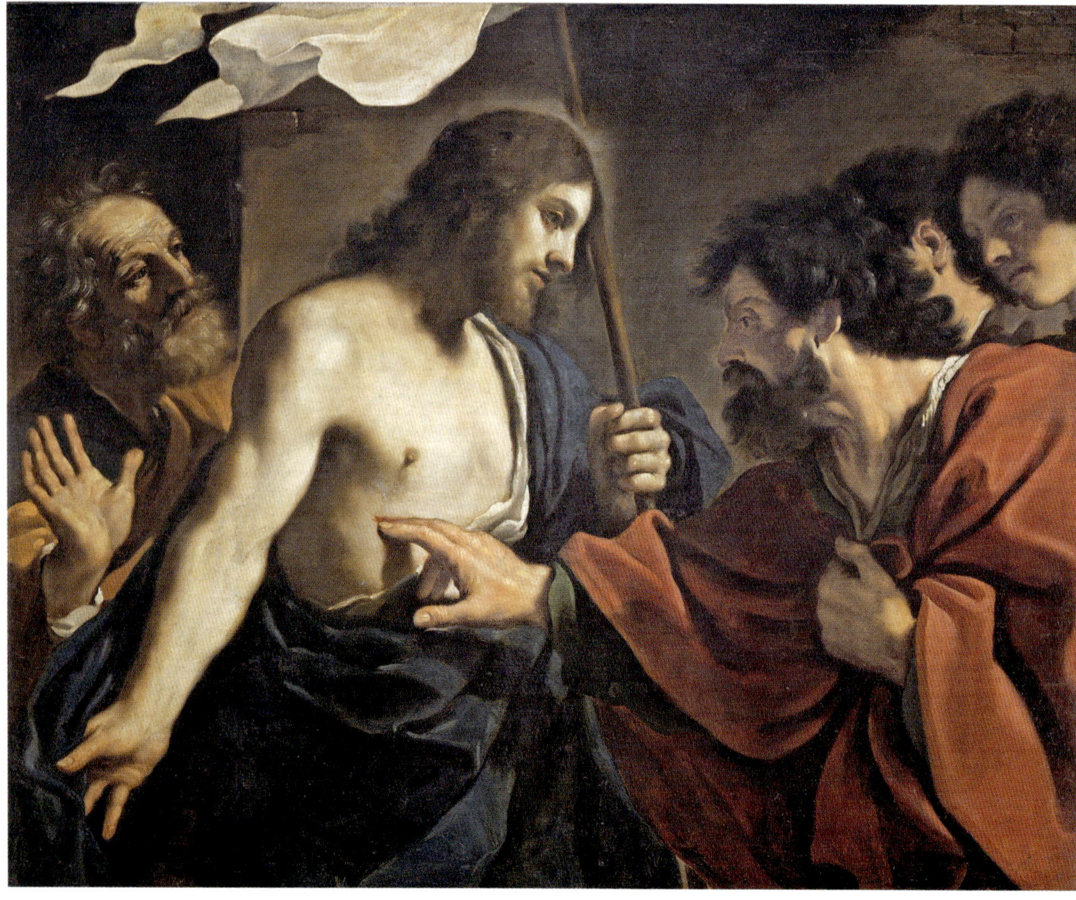

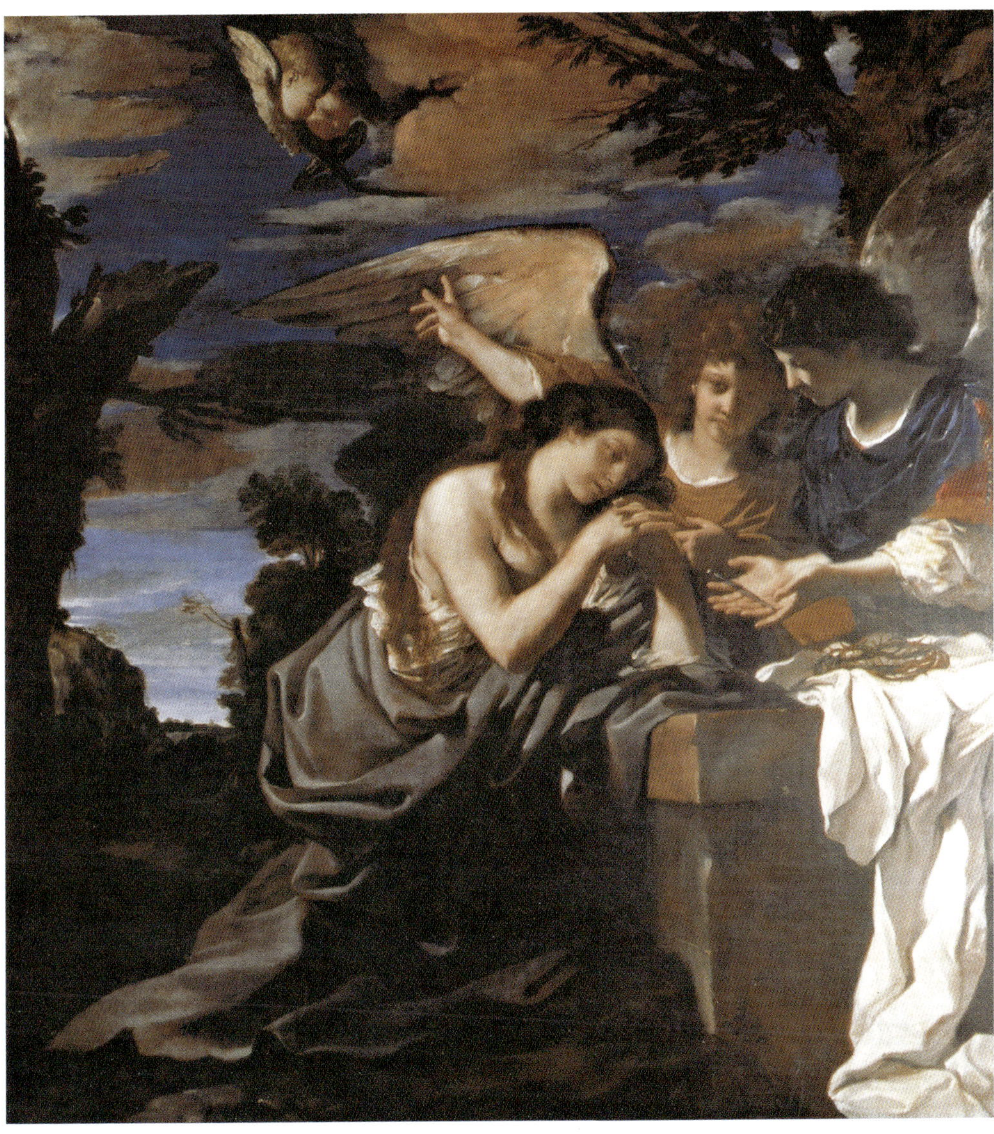

Guercino (Giovanni Francesco Barbieri)

The Penitent Mary Magdalene with Two Angels

Guercino was one of the most productive and independent of the Italian Baroque painters. He took ideas from Ludovico and Annibale Carracci, Caravaggio, and Guido Reni and fused them into a style all his own that came to be highly esteemed. During the two years or so that Guercino spent in Rome (1621–23) at the invitation of Pope Gregory XV, he produced this virtually square painting of the penitent Mary Magdalene for the main altar of the church of Maria Maddalena delle Convertite, destroyed in 1800, on the Corso in Rome. The identification of Christ's companion with the sinner who washed his feet (Luke 7: 38–39) derives from a sermon given by Pope Gregory the Great in 591. In the Late Middle Ages, "sinner" was narrowed down to "prostitute". Guercino's depiction of the saint, who reveals her voluptuous beauty to the gaze of the viewer, her upper body exposed and her hair loose, also plays on this identity. The handling of the light establishes a direct connection between the breast of the saint and the instruments of Christ's suffering—the nail, crown of thorns, and shroud—presented by the angels, who contemplate her with a deeply moved expression. Guercino's penitent saint was intended as a model and a figure of identification for the nuns of the convent, themselves former prostitutes.

Guercino (Giovanni Francesco Barbieri) 1591–1666
***The Penitent Mary Magdalene with Two Angels*, ca. 1622**
222 x 200; Oil on canvas
Pinacoteca; Room XII; Inv. 40391

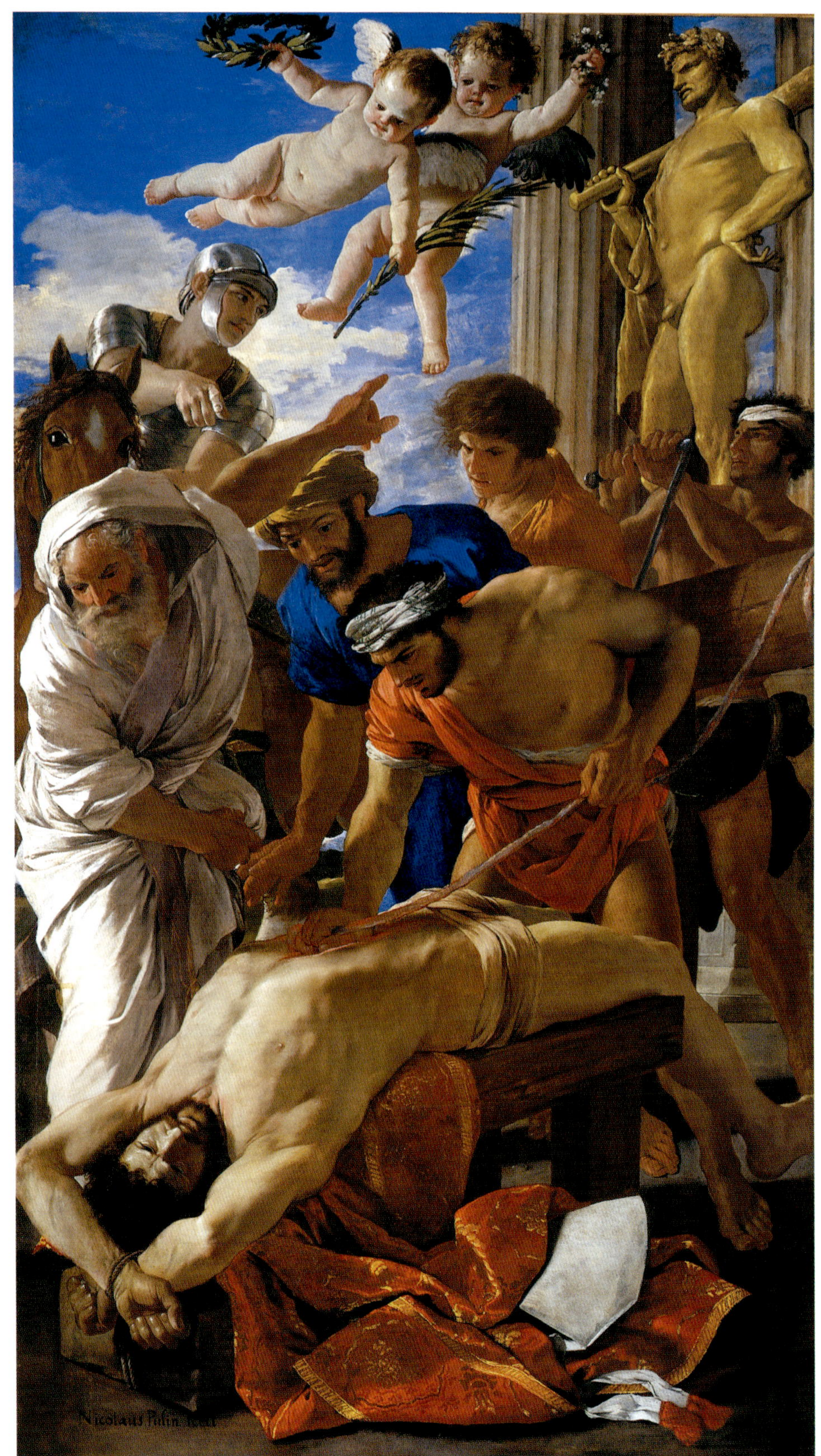

Nicolas Poussin

The Martyrdom of St. Erasmus

The Martyrdom of St. Erasmus by the Frenchman Nicolas Poussin is one of the few non-Italian paintings in the Pinacoteca. It was nevertheless painted in Rome, where Poussin spent most of his life and created his most important works. Produced for St. Peter's Basilica, the painting was Poussin's first major public commission. It depicts in unusual perspective the cruel martyrdom of the bishop-saint, who is being disemboweled while fully conscious. Erasmus lies with his head extended toward the viewer on a wooden bench that cuts across the painting from the lower left edge. While the executioners, commanded by a mounted soldier, busy themselves eviscerating the saint by winding his intestines onto a large winch, a white-clad priest tries to persuade Erasmus to adore a statue of Hercules. Two angels can already be seen descending from heaven with martyr's palm and laurel wreath. In spite of the cleverly planned, tension-filled composition, atmospheric lighting, masterly rendering of the nude, and appropriate depiction of emotions, the painting failed to please the Roman public, which no doubt considered the direct confrontation with the saint's pain-contorted face and gruesome suffering to be unseemly.

Nicolas Poussin, 1594–1665
***The Martyrdom of St. Erasmus*, ca. 1628–1629**
320 x 186 cm; Oil on canvas
Pinacoteca; Room XII; Inv. 40349

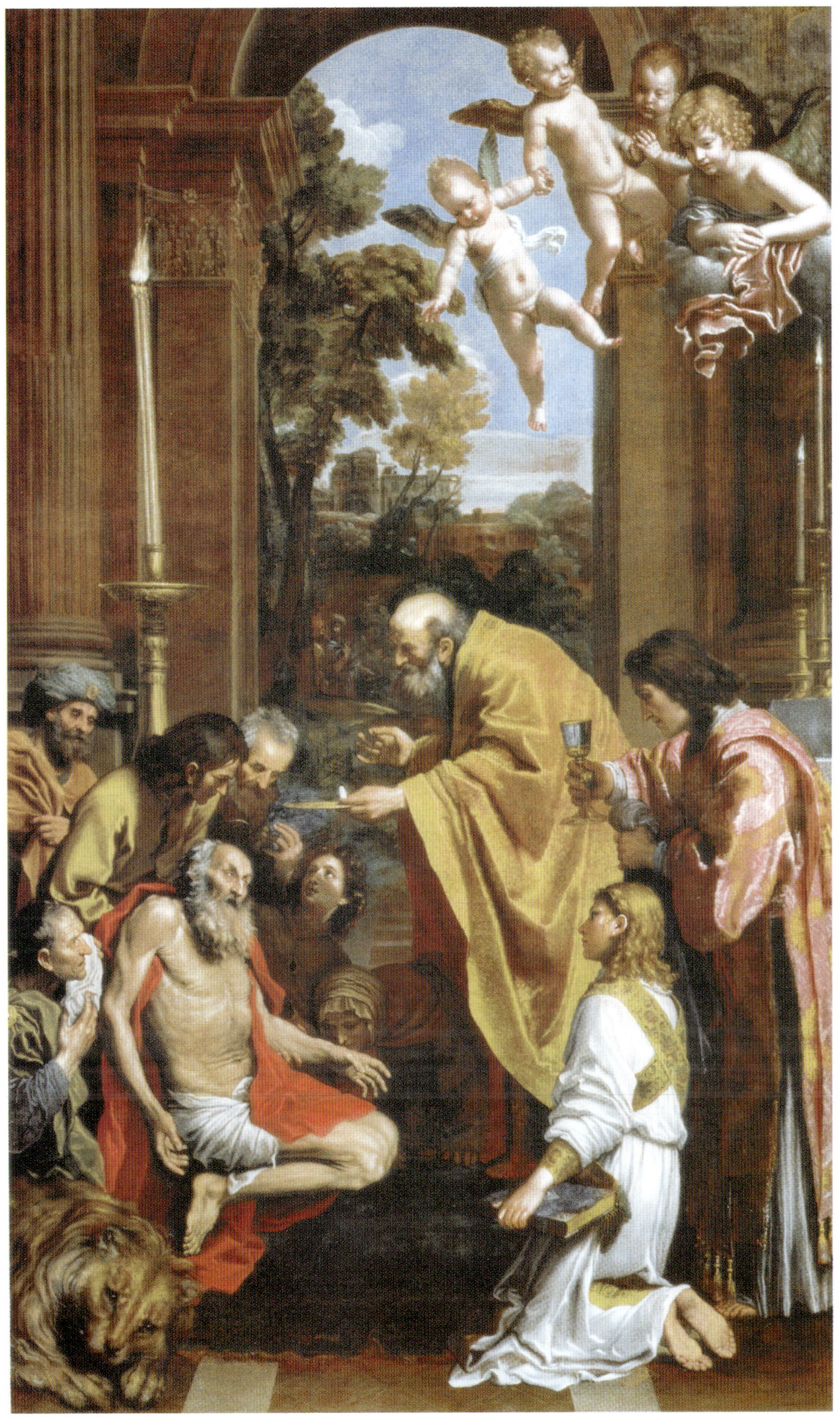

Domenichino (Domenico Zampieri)

The Last Communion of St. Jerome

The subject of this painting commissioned by the Congregation of St. Jerome for the church of St. Gerolamo della Carità in Rome is the rarely depicted last communion of the ninety-year-old saint. Jerome is shown virtually naked, as a penitent, and is supported by his followers as he summons up all his strength to receive the Host. Domenichino has taken his cue from a version of the subject by his teacher Agostino Carracci, improving on the clarity of the composition at the same time. The fragility and simultaneous strength of will of the saint and the affectionate concern of the bystanders are also more clearly expressed, but without appearing exaggerated. This early work by Domenichino, who hailed from Bologna, reveals for the first time his skillful rendering of shimmering color tones, which lend his works their much-admired sheen. The only pure colors are the red of St. Jerome's mantle and the dazzling white of the Host. The theological association between the saint and the symbolic body of Christ is thus emphasized through color as well. The Last Communion of St. Jerome helped Domenichino achieve a breakthrough in Rome in 1614. The work was praised above all for its balanced composition, appropriate expression, and well-thought-out use of color. Also admired were the choir of angels and the depiction of the landscape in the background.

Domenichino (Domenico Zampieri), 1581–1641
***The Last Communion of St. Jerome*, 1614**
419 x 256 cm; Oil on canvas
Pinacoteca; Room XII; Inv. 40384

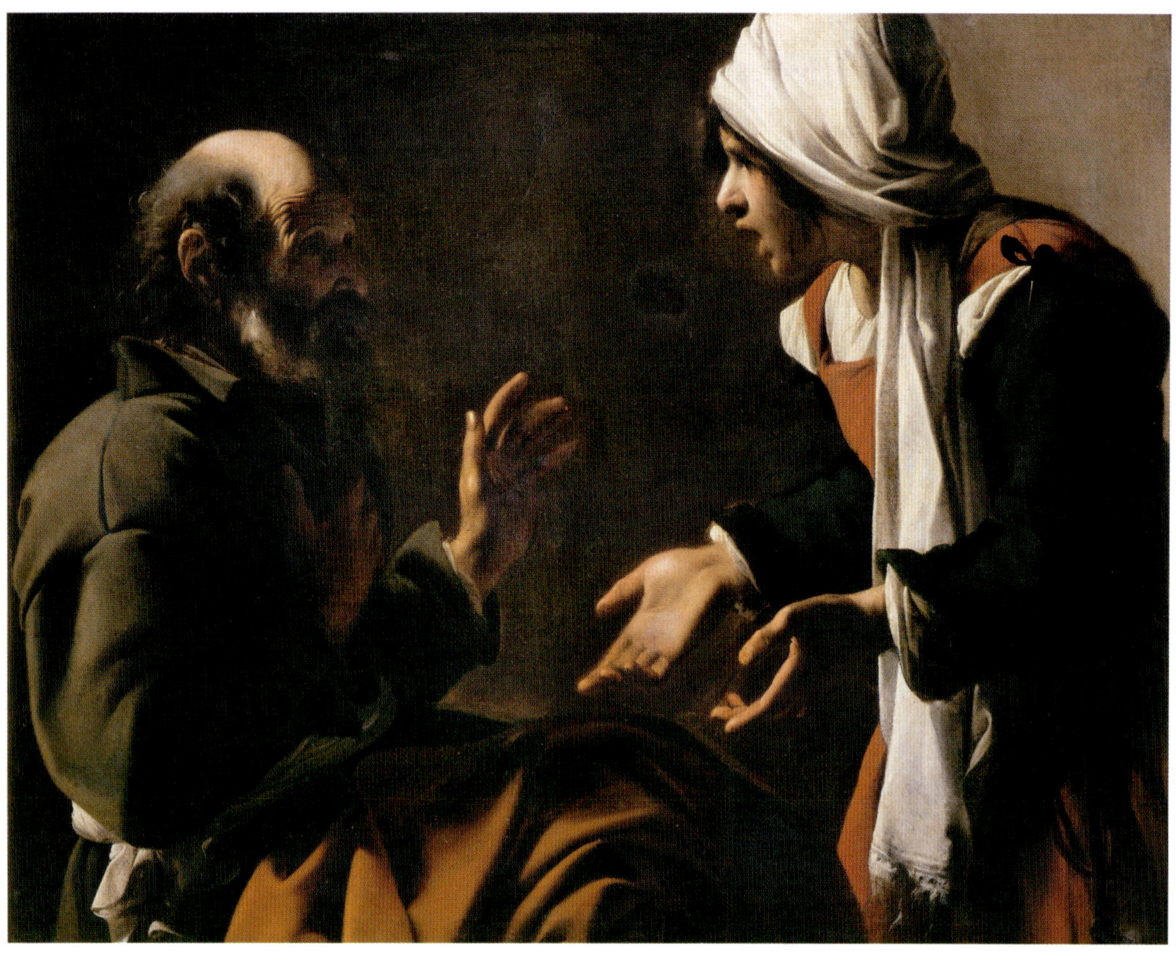

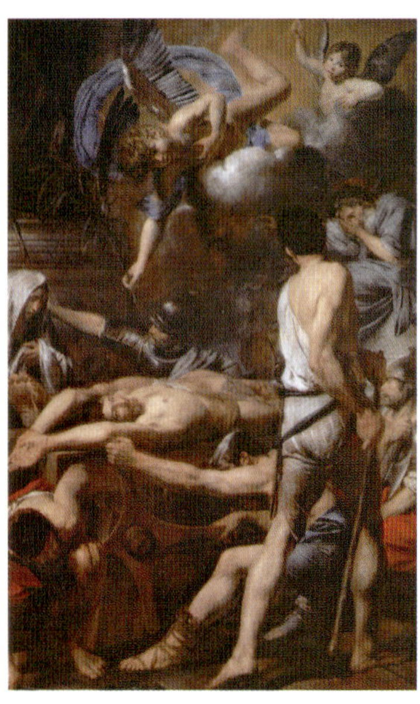

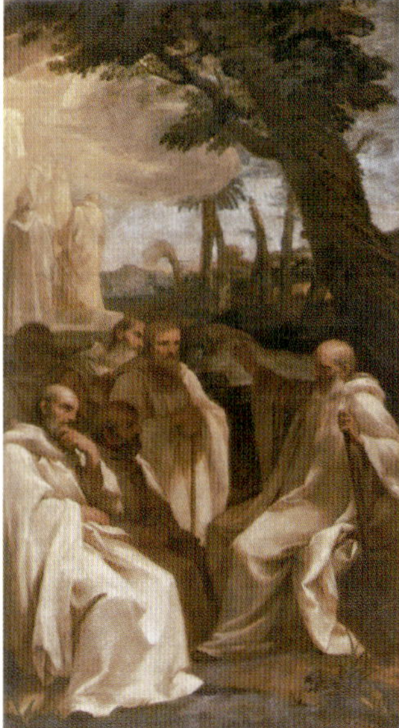

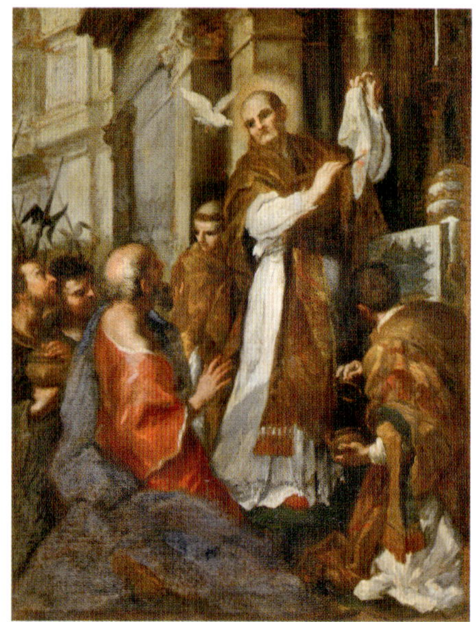

Pensionante del Saraceni, active 1610–1620
***Denial of St. Peter*, undated**
100 x 129 cm; Oil on canvas
Pinacoteca; Room XII; Inv. 40385

Valentin de Boulogne, 1594–1632
***Martyrdom of SS. Processus and Martinian*, 1629**
302 x 192 cm; Oil on canvas
Pinacoteca; Room XII; Inv. 40381

Andrea Sacchi, 1599–1661
***The Vision of St. Romuald*, before 1629**
310 x 175 cm; Oil on canvas
Pinacoteca; Room XII; Inv. 40382

Andrea Sacchi, 1599–1661
***Miracle of St. Gregory*, 1625**
47 x 37 cm; Oil on fabric
Pinacoteca; Room XII; Inv. 40760

ROOM XIII

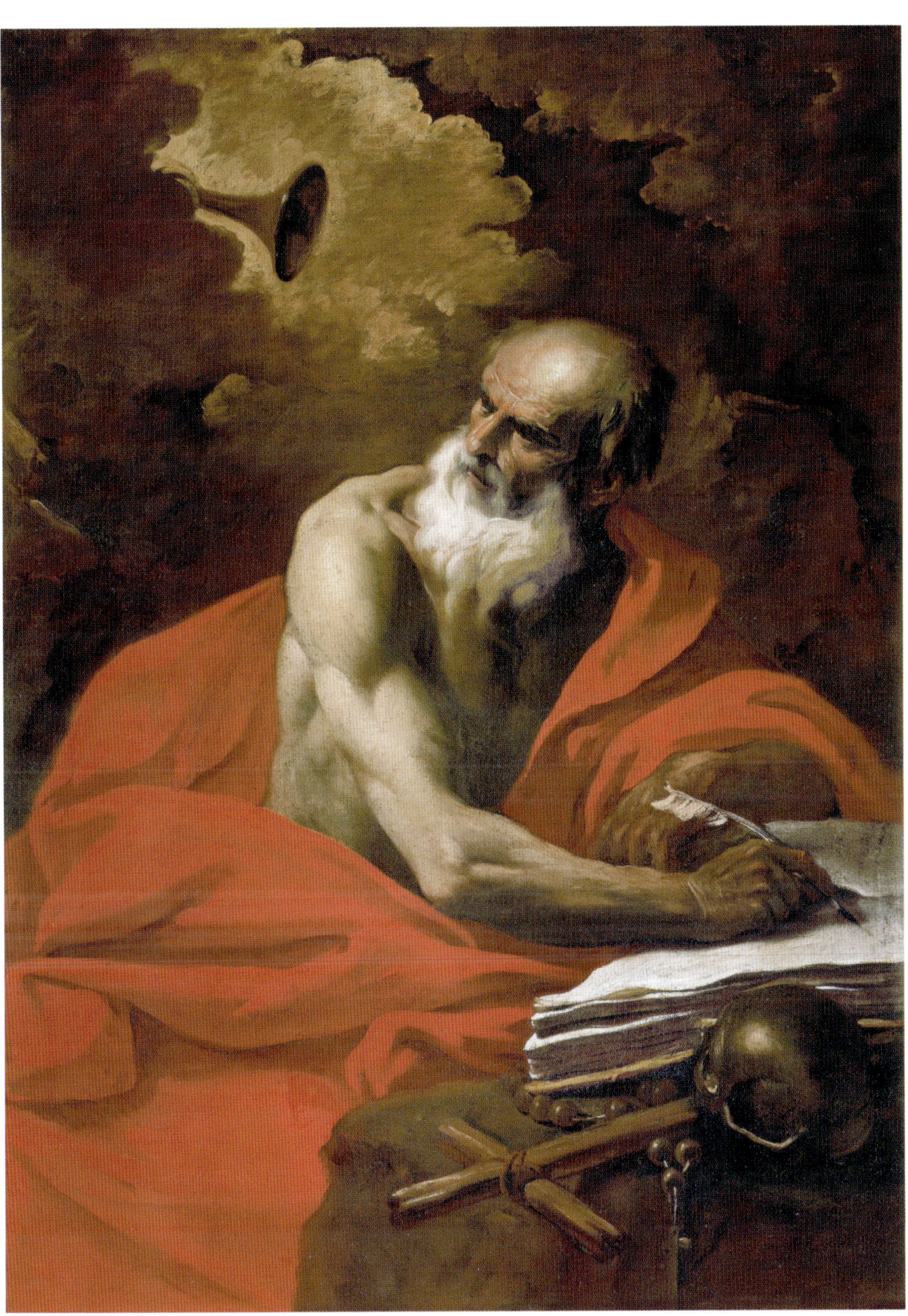

Pier Francesco Mola, attributed to

St. Jerome

This painting attributed to the Roman Baroque painter Pier Francesco Mola depicts the St. Jerome who is primarily known for translating the Bible into Latin (the Vulgate). Jerome's work as an author and translator is indicated by the book and quill. He is also depicted as a penitent, his naked upper body only loosely enveloped by his red cardinal's mantle. Disappointed at the worldly magnificence of the Church, the saint is supposed to have retreated to the desert to lead the life of an ascetica. On the rock serving St. Jerome as a desk lie two other symbols of his acts of penance: a skull and a rosary. The trumpet emerging from the clouds alludes to a legend whereby the saint suddenly and miraculously hears the trumpet of the Angel of the Apocalypse, an embodiment of the voice of God reminding him of the transience of the world. Mola's painting refers to a famous painting by the Spanish Baroque painter Jusepe Ribera, which nevertheless depicts the saint in an interior space. What is remarkable about Mola's version is the visual contrast between the generous folds of the radiant scarlet cloak and the muscular upper body of the saint, who seems to grow out of the sea of red folds.

Pier Francesco Mola, attributed to, 1612–1666
***St. Jerome*, undated**
135 x 98 cm; Oil on wood panel
Pinacoteca; Room XIII; Inv. 40403

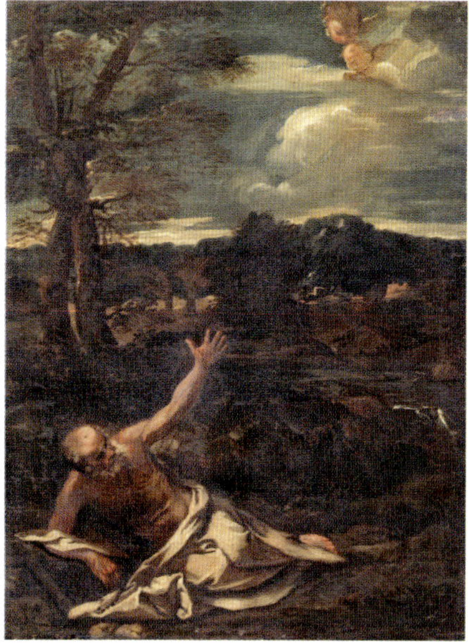

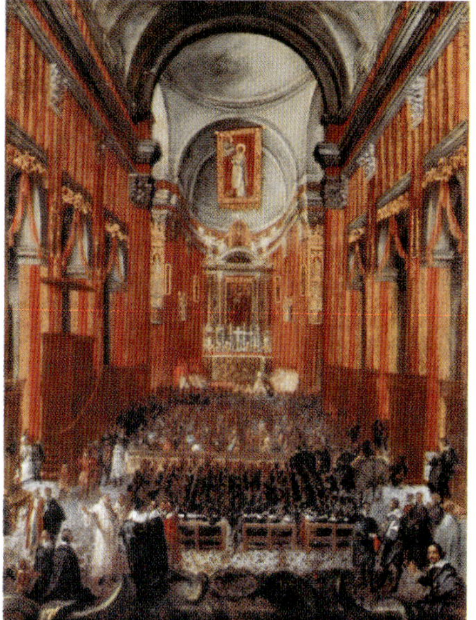

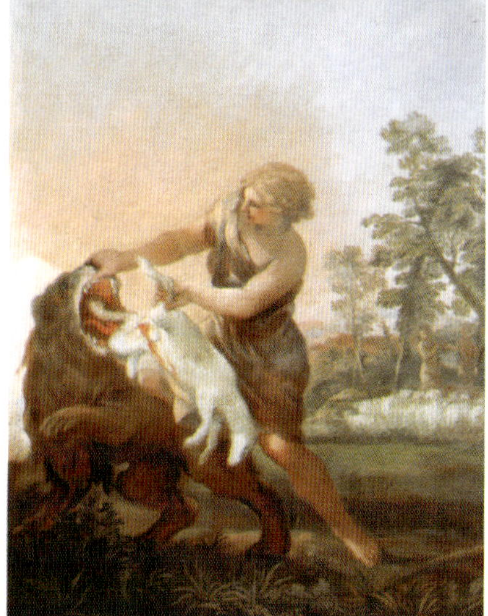

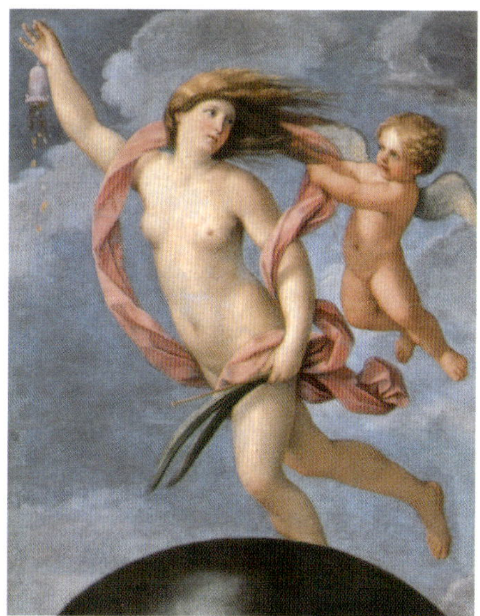

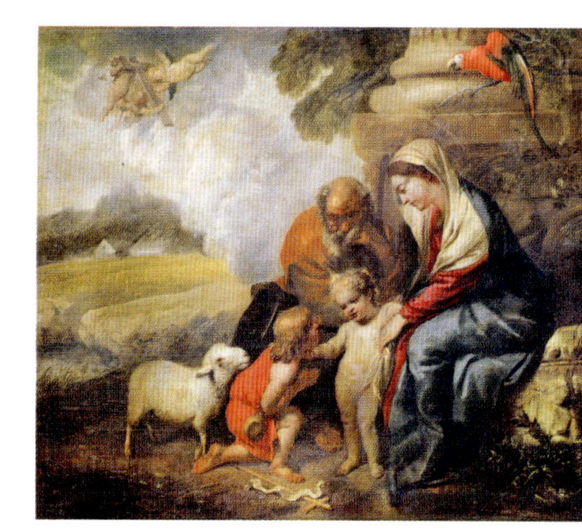

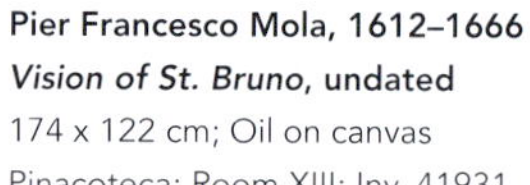

Pier Francesco Mola, 1612–1666
***Vision of St. Bruno*, undated**
174 x 122 cm; Oil on canvas
Pinacoteca; Room XIII; Inv. 41931

Andrea Sacchi, 1599–1661
***Interior of Santa Maria in Vallicella*, 1622**
98 x 74 cm; Oil on canvas
Pinacoteca; Room XIII; Inv. 42343

Pietro da Cortona, 1596–1669
***David and the Lion*, undated**
125 x 97 cm; Oil on canvas
Pinacoteca; Room XIII; Inv. 40410

Guido Reni (school of), 1575–1642
***Fortune and Amor*, ca. 1623**
188 x 155 cm; Oil on canvas
Pinacoteca; Room XIII; Inv. 40653

Pietro da Cortona, 1596–1669
***David Slaying Goliath*, undated**
125 x 97 cm; Oil on canvas
Pinacoteca; Room XIII; Inv. 40414

Giovanni Benedetto Castiglione, 1609–1664
***The Holy Family with St. John*, undated**
97 x 123 cm; Oil on canvas
Pinacoteca; Room XIII; Inv. 40413

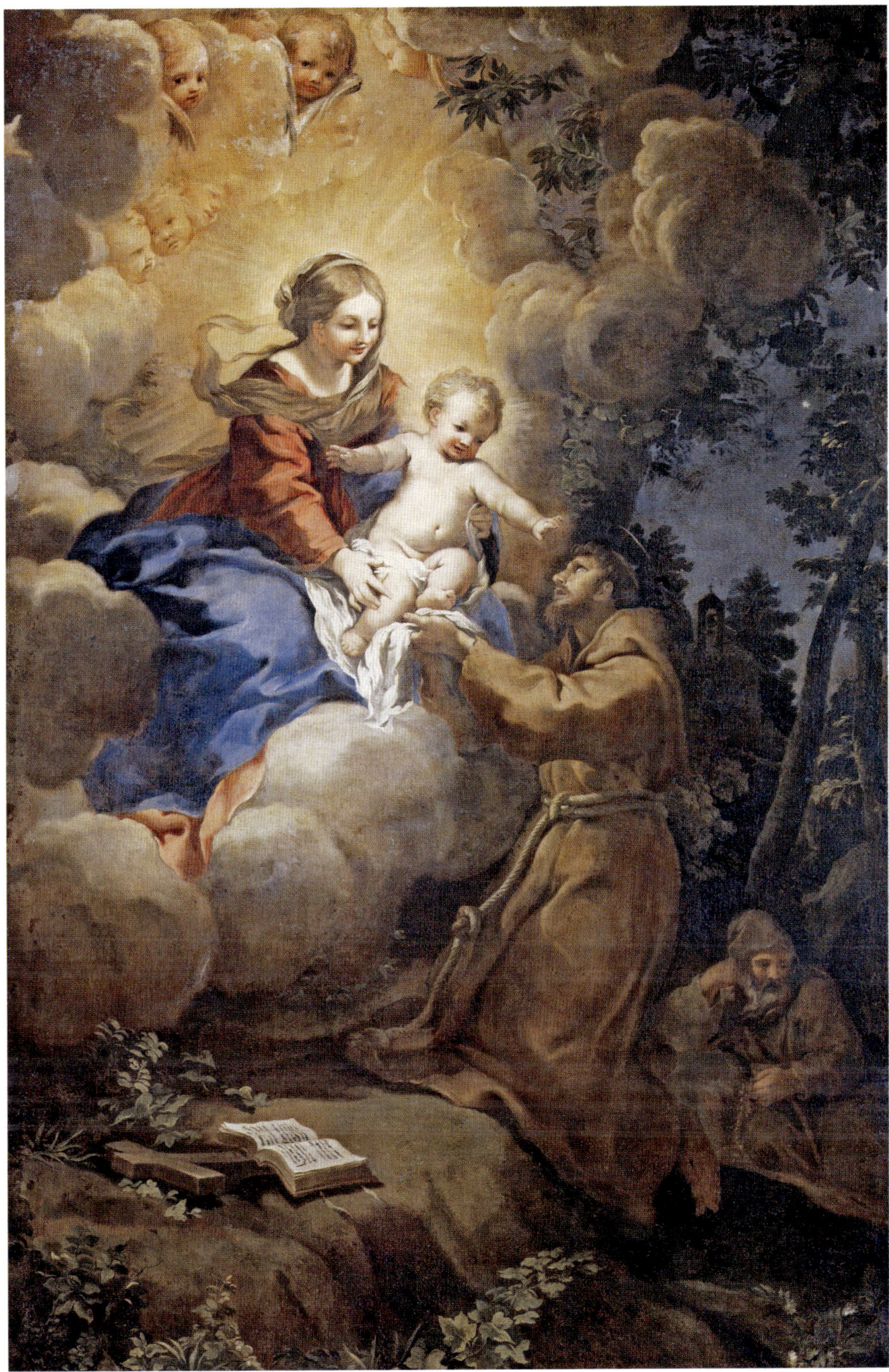

Pietro da Cortona (Pietro Berrettini)

The Virgin and Child Appearing to St. Francis of Assisi

Pietro Berrettini, known by his place of birth, Cortona, was one of the most sought-after artists of his day. He specialized in major fresco programs and illusionistic ceiling paintings. He also introduced a number of innovations into his altar paintings, including this vision of St. Francis, of which he had already produced a larger version for the Montauto chapel in the church of Santissima Annunziata in Arezzo. His attempt to create as perfect as possible an illusion of space is evident here in the opening of heaven behind Mary and the background landscape on the right. The dissolving of boundaries, which came to the forefront mainly in the Late Baroque, was initiated in part by Cortona. He achieved this effect by lighting the most distant points in a painting, rather than merely depicting the actual light sources. This lends his work a mysterious depth. The opening of heaven also symbolizes the brilliance of light that radiates from the Virgin and Child, with which St. Francis, during his vision, is also blessed. Thanks to his faith, expressed through prayer, he is able to take the Heavenly Child in his arms while his sleeping companion remains oblivious to the celestial happenings.

Pietro da Cortona (Pietro Berrettini), 1596–1669
***The Virgin and Child Appearing to St. Francis of Assisi*, ca. 1641**
227 x 151 cm; Oil on canvas
Pinacoteca; Room XIII; Inv. 40405

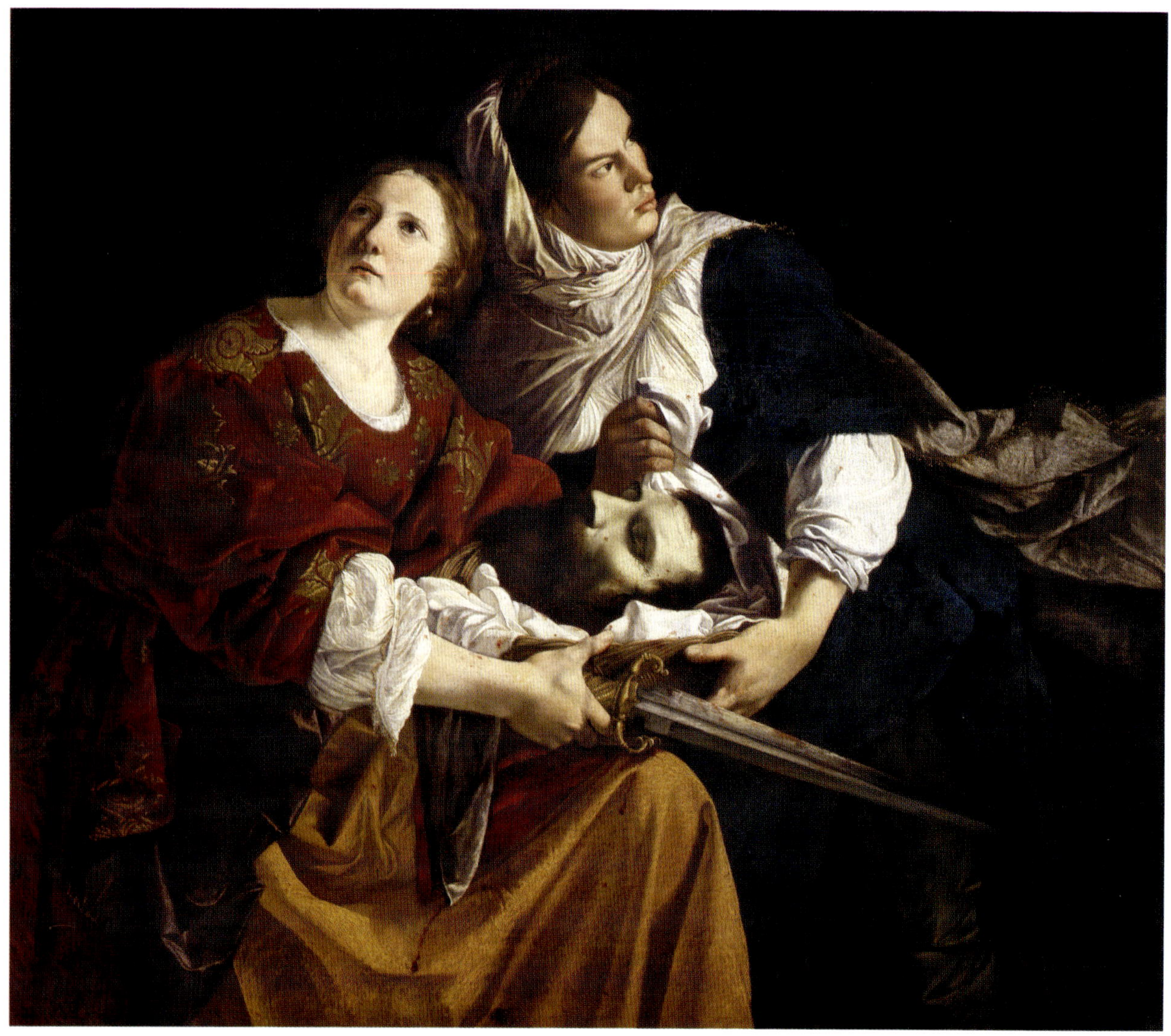

Orazio Gentileschi

Judith and Her Handmaid with the Head of Holofernes

The Pisan painter Orazio Gentileschi, father of the famous female painter Artemisia Gentileschi, was one of the first artists, around 1600, to adopt Caravaggio's new naturalistic style. However, as the example of *Judith and Her Handmaid with the Head of Holofernes* shows, he toned down the often extreme expressiveness of Caravaggio's pictures. The work depicts the Old Testament story of Judith, who saved her people by entering the camp of the enemy army and cutting off the head of its general, Holofernes, with his own sword. In Caravaggio's version of the story (Rome, Galleria Nazionale di Arte Antica, 1598/99), the moment of decapitation, in all its gruesomeness, is placed at the center of the composition. Gentileschi, on the other hand, chooses to depict the moment after the act, when the blood-spattered Judith passes the basket containing the head of Holofernes to her maid. The deep red of her outer garment denotes her as a murderer. She looks heavenward with an equally questioning and frightened gaze, as if seeking confirmation that she has done the right thing. Her handmaid, whose intricately folded headcloth and shirt are works of art in themselves, feistily takes hold of the basket containing the pallid, ghostly head and looks around for possible enemies. Although his handling of light and color are reminiscent of Caravaggio, Gentileschi goes further in his subtle psychological characterization of the figures.

Orazio Gentileschi, 1563–1639
***Judith and Her Handmaid with the Head of Holofernes*, 1611–1612**
123 x 142 cm; Oil on canvas
Pinacoteca; Room XIII; Inv. 41059

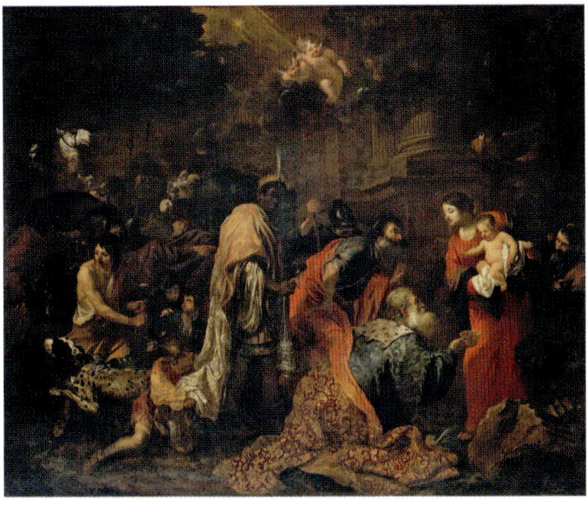
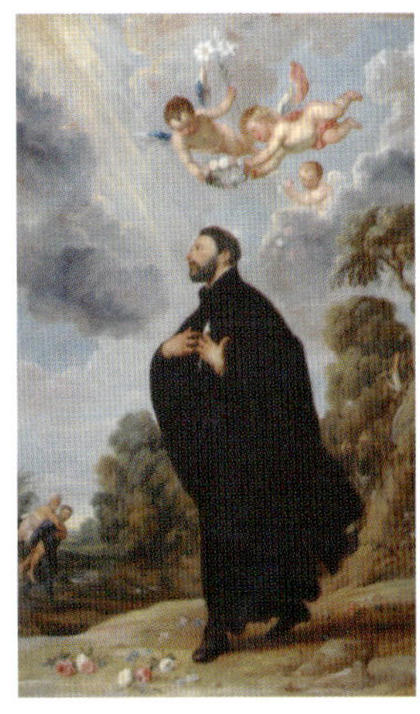
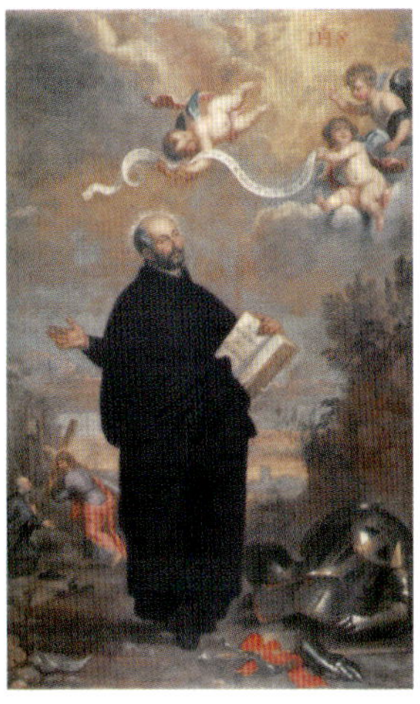
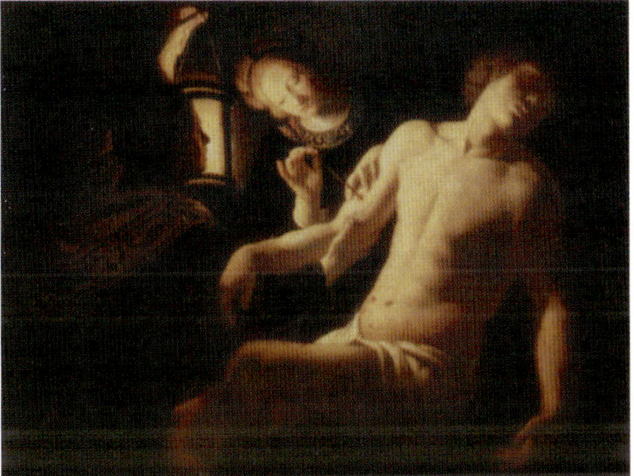
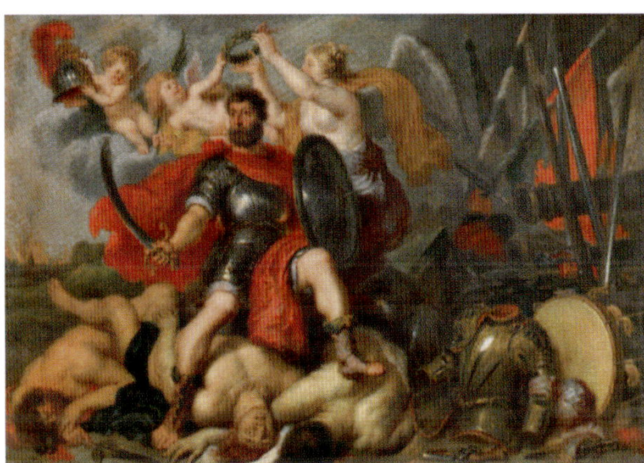
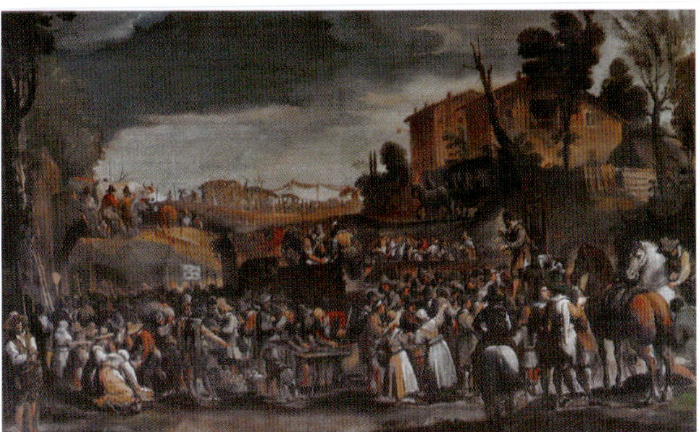
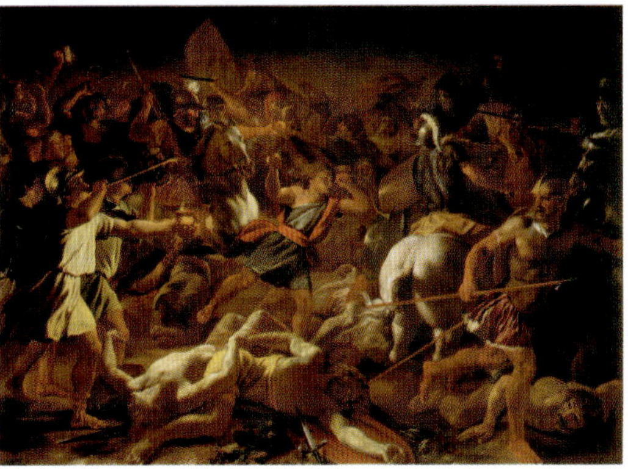

Vincent Malo, 1600–1644
***Adoration of the Magi*, undated**
324 x 396.5 cm; Oil on wood panel
Pinacoteca; Room XIII; Inv. 40401

Gerard Seghers and Jan Wildens, 1591–1651, ca. 1586–1653
***St. Francesco Saverino Xavier*, undated**
346 x 214 cm; Oil on canvas
Pinacoteca; Room XIII; Inv. 40775

Gerard Seghers and Jan Wildens, 1591–1651, ca. 1586–1653
***St. Ignatius*, undated**
345 x 213 cm; Oil on canvas
Pinacoteca; Room XIII; Inv. 40790

Trophime Bigot, 1579–1650
***St. Sebastian Healed by Irene*, undated**
98 x 137 cm; Oil on canvas
Pinacoteca; Room XIII; Inv. 42307

Peter Paul Rubens (school of), 17th century
***Apotheosis of Vincenzo I Gonzaga*, 17th century**
149 x 200 cm; Oil on canvas
Pinacoteca; Room XIII; Inv. 40784

Giovanni Francesco Barbieri (Guercino), 1591–1666
***Village Feast*, ca. 1620**
113 x 180 cm; Tempera on canvas
Pinacoteca; Room XIII; Inv. 40811

Nicolas Poussin, 1594–1665
***The Battle of Gideon*, 1624–1625**
98 x 137 cm; Oil on canvas
Pinacoteca; Room XIII; Inv. 40815

ROOM XIV

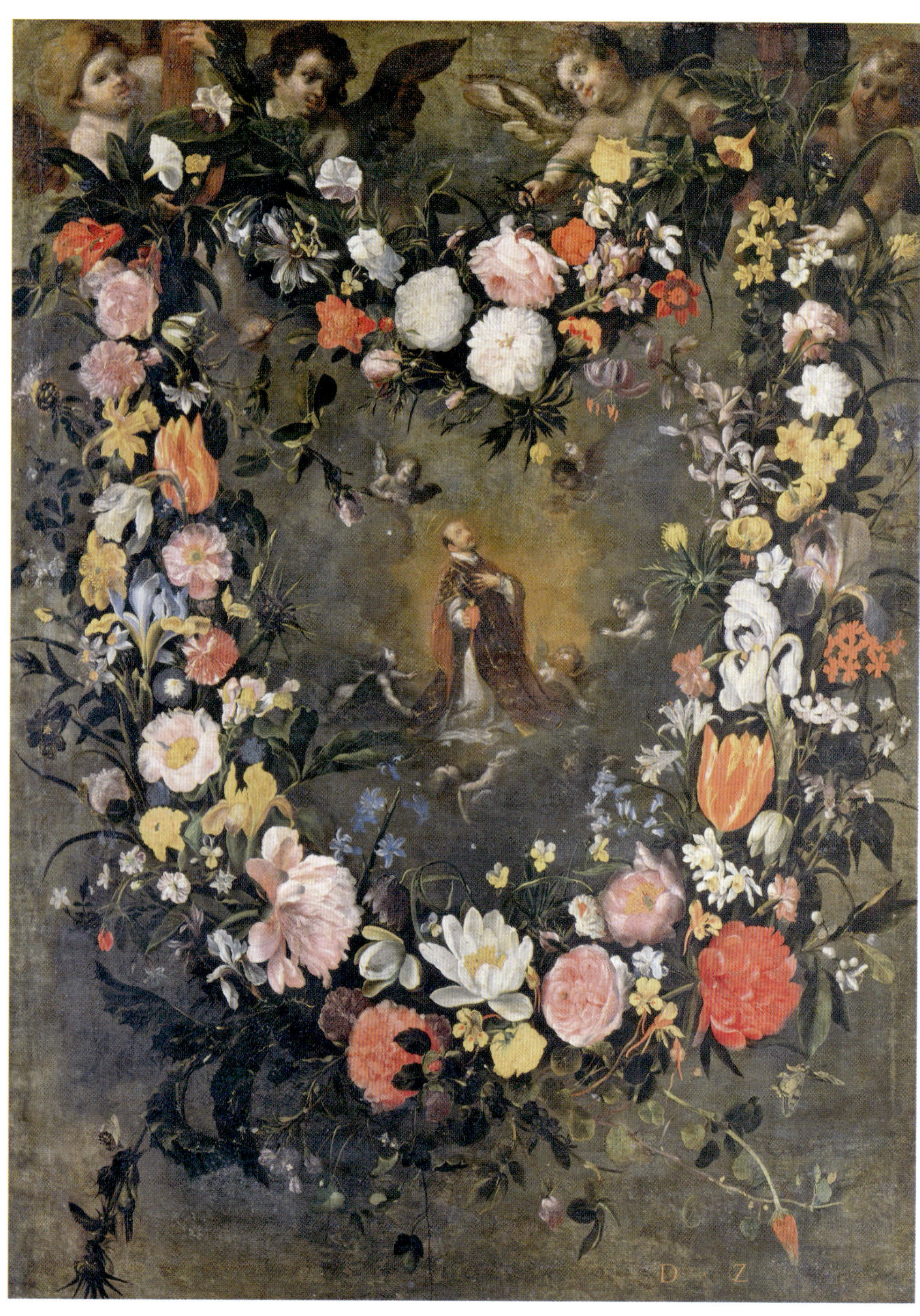

Daniel Seghers and Hendrik van Balen

Garland of Flowers with St. Ignatius

The flower garland paintings of the Flemish artist Daniel Seghers strike a surprising note within a Vatican collection otherwise dominated by Christian history paintings. However, rather than being unadulterated still-lifes they are quite literally religious at core. In the *Garland of Flowers with St. Ignatius* the flowers form a heart-shaped frame around St. Ignatius of Loyola (1491–1556), the founder of the Jesuit Order, who was canonized in 1622. The saint kneels with his attribute, a flaming heart symbolizing his fervent love of God, with his eyes raised devoutly to heaven and surrounded by adoring putti. The garland of flowers supported by four angels serves not merely a decorative function as an elaborate frame for the image of the saint; by means of shape and color it too constitutes a flaming heart, thereby giving expression to the saint's intense love of God through the language of flowers. The Antwerp flower painter Daniel Seghers, a pupil of Jan Brueghel the Elder, was himself a Jesuit. In this work, made during his sojourn in Rome between 1625 and 1627, Seghers painted only the garland himself. The image of the saint was painted by the Flemish artist Hendrik van Balen.

Daniel Seghers and Hendrik van Balen, 1590–1661, 1575–1632
***Garland of Flowers with St. Ignatius*, 17th century**
120 x 90 cm; Oil on canvas,
Pinacoteca; Room XIV; Inv. 40418

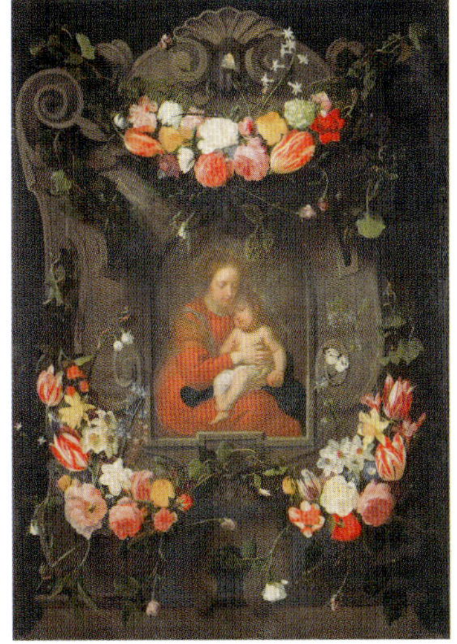

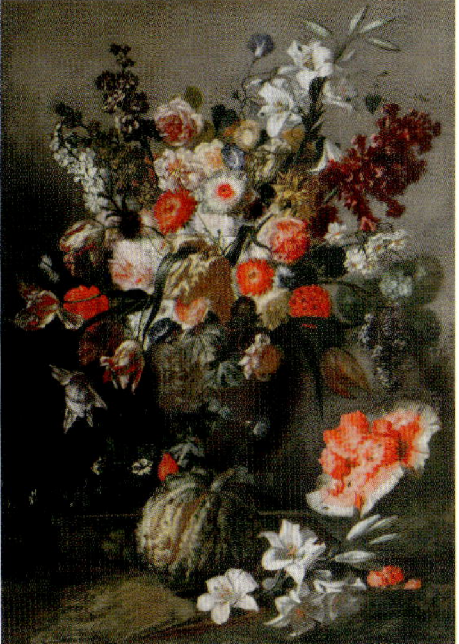

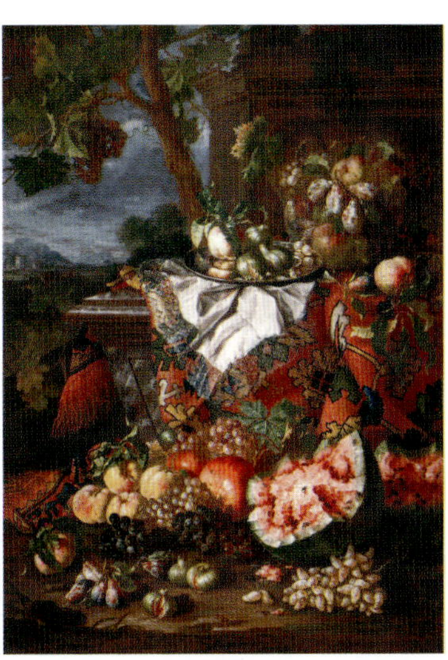

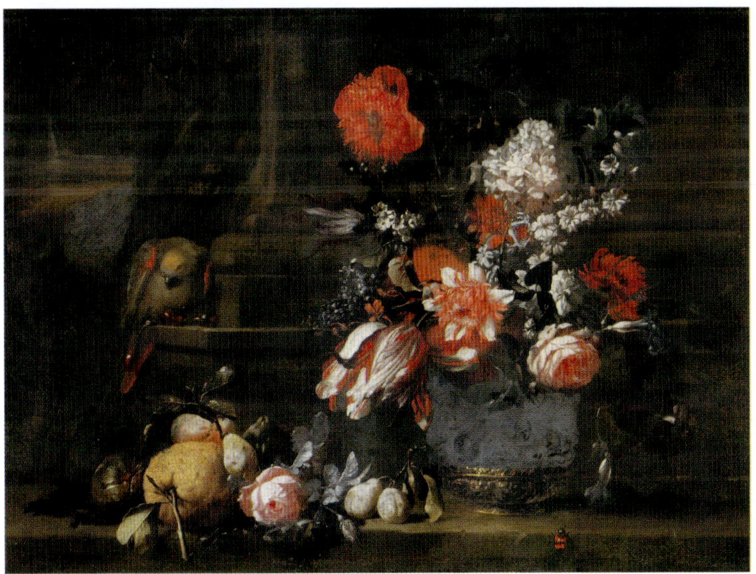

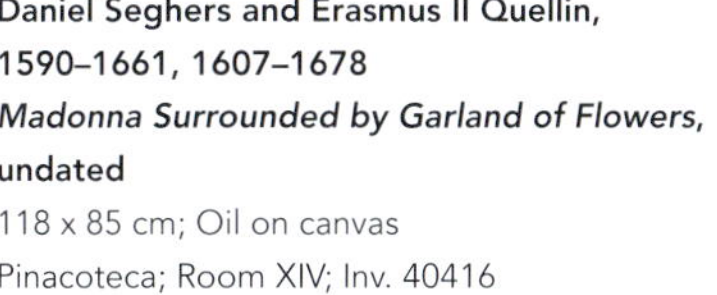

Daniel Seghers and Erasmus II Quellin, 1590–1661, 1607–1678
***Madonna Surrounded by Garland of Flowers,* undated**
118 x 85 cm; Oil on canvas
Pinacoteca; Room XIV; Inv. 40416

Franz Werner von Tamm, 1658–1724
***Fruits and Flowers,* undated**
130 x 98 cm; Oil on canvas
Pinacoteca; Room XIV; Inv. 40429

Andrea Belvedere, 1652–1732
***Flowers and Fruits,* undated**
131 x 98 cm; Oil on canvas
Pinacoteca; Room XIV; Inv. 40424

Pietro Navarra, late 17th century–early 18th century
***Flowers and Fruit,* undated**
135 x 98 cm; Oil on canvas
Pinacoteca; Room XIV; Inv. 40427

Roman School, late 17th century
***Flowers and Fruits,* undated**
82 x 105 cm; Oil on canvas
Pinacoteca; Room XIV; Inv. 41667

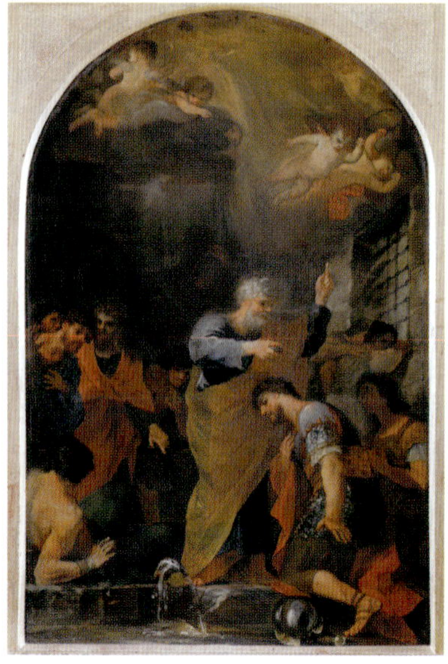

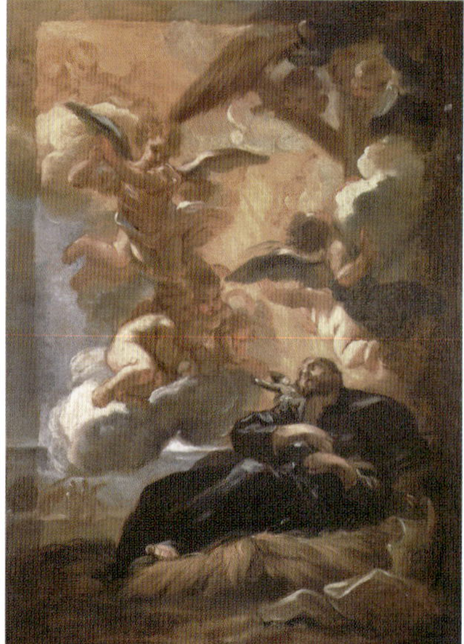

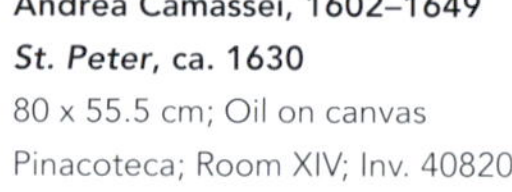

Andrea Camassei, 1602–1649
***St. Peter*, ca. 1630**
80 x 55.5 cm; Oil on canvas
Pinacoteca; Room XIV; Inv. 40820

Giovanni Battista Baciccia (Giovanni Battista Gaulli), 1639–1709
***Vision of St. Francesco Saverio (Xavier)*, ca. 1675**
64.5 x 46 cm; Oil on canvas
Pinacoteca; Room XIV; Inv. 41489

David Ryckaert III, 1612–1661
***L'Alchimista*, undated**
48 x 38 cm; Oil on canvas
Pinacoteca; Room XIV; Inv. 40451

Bartolomé Murillo, 1618–1682
***Martyrdom of St. Peter d'Arbues*, undated**
132.5 x 102 cm; Oil on canvas
Pinacoteca; Room XIV; Inv. 40746

Pietro Paolini, 1603–1681
***Portrait of an Actor*, 1630–1640**
74 x 98 cm; Oil on canvas
Pinacoteca; Room XIV; Inv. 40462

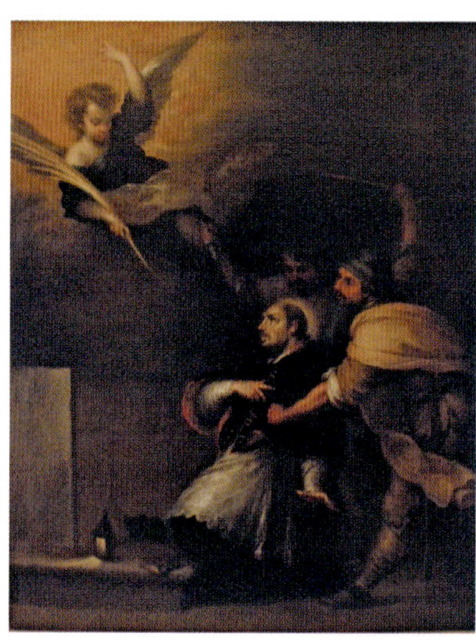

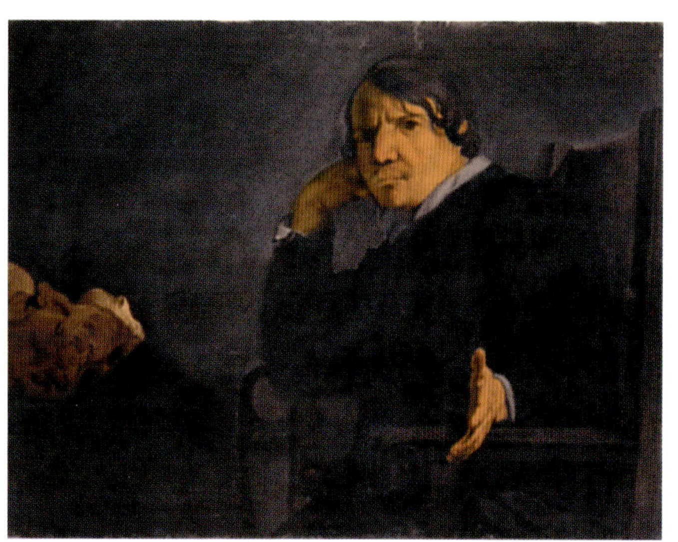

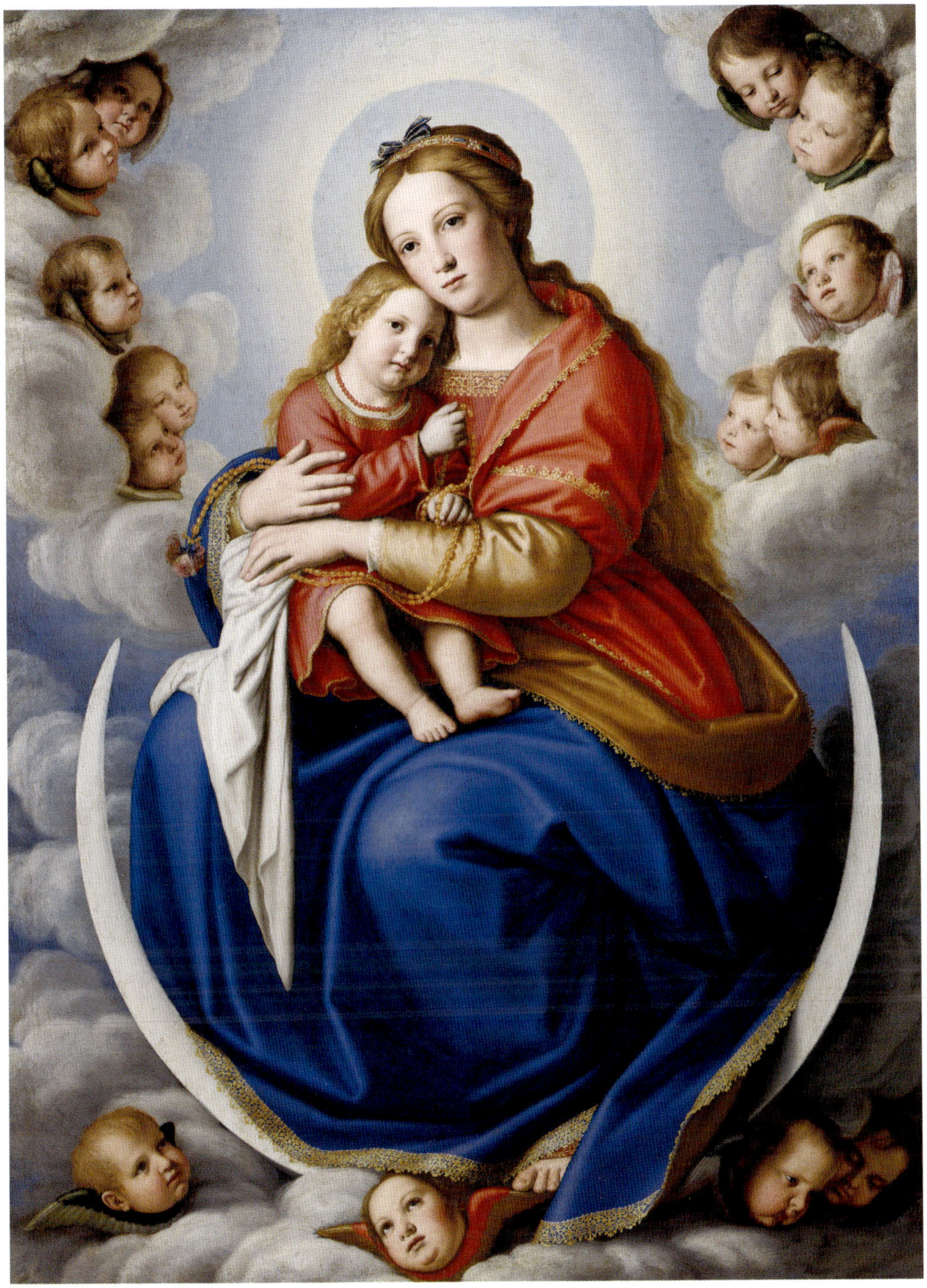

Sassoferrato (Giovanni Battista Salvi)

The Virgin and Child on a Crescent Moon

After his arrival in Rome in around 1635/40, the painter Giovanni Battista Salvi, known as Sassoferrato, devoted himself above all to the painting of private devotional pictures which were extremely popular during the Counter-Reformation. In addition to Raphael's holy figures, his models included the works of the German Renaissance artist Albrecht Dürer. *The Virgin and Child on a Crescent Moon* was inspired by Dürer's title woodcut for his Life of the Virgin series (1511), which was disseminated all over Europe. Sassoferrato adapted Dürer's motif of the breastfeeding Madonna to the requirements of the devotional image by directing the gaze of both Jesus and Mary toward the viewer. The Virgin, wrapped in shimmering red-blue-gold robes, is shown lovingly embracing the Christ Child as he leans against her breast. Jesus holds a long rosary and wears a coral necklace as a symbol of his future passion. The heartfelt expression of mother and child is intensified by the angels, who contemplate the divine pair from their garland of clouds. With their evident devotion, the angels also serve as models for the viewers. Queen Isabella II of Spain presented the painting to Pope Pius IX in around 1850, a time when Sassoferrato's somewhat saccharine style was highly favored.

Sassoferrato (Giovanni Battista Salvi), 1605–1685
***The Virgin and Child on a Crescent Moon*, ca. 1650**
133 x 98 cm; Oil on canvas
Pinacoteca; Room XIV; Inv. 40396

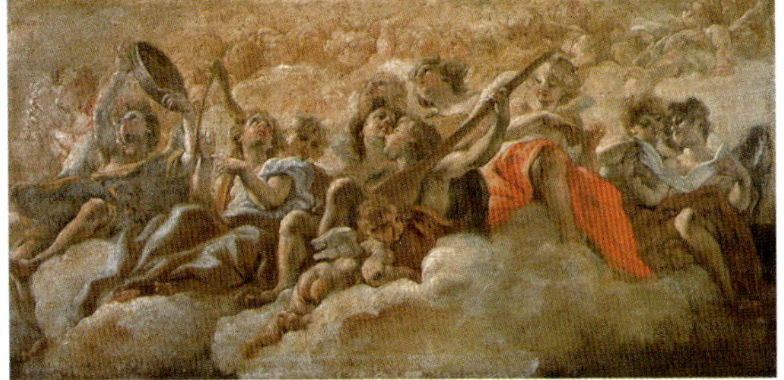

Giovanni Battista Baciccia (Giovanni Battista Gaulli), 1639–1709
***Music-Making Angels*, ca. 1672**
49 x 98 cm; Oil on canvas
Pinacoteca; Room XIV; Inv. 40752

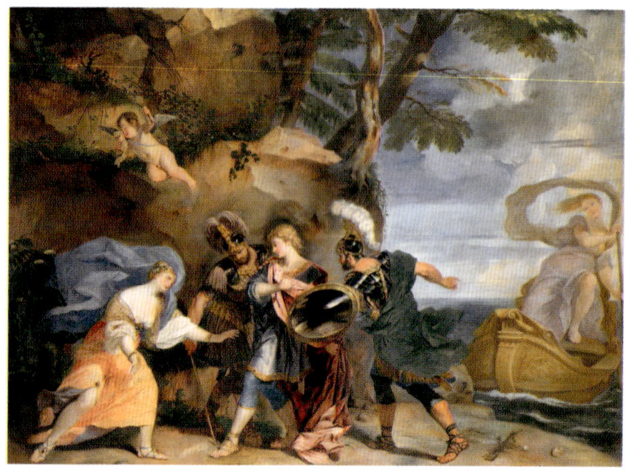
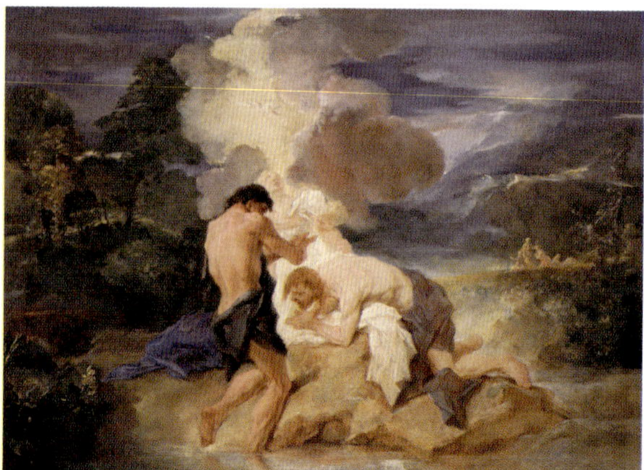
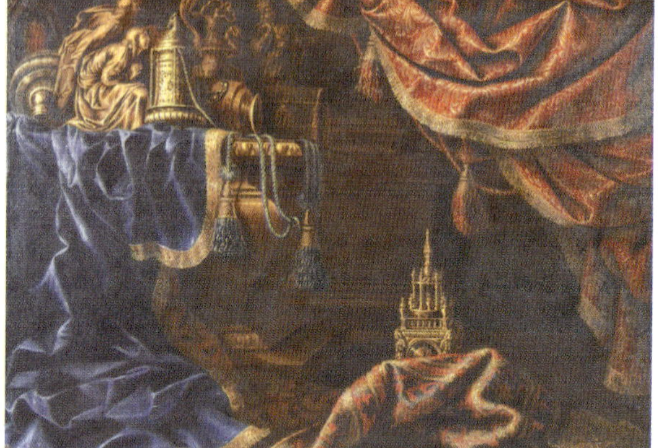
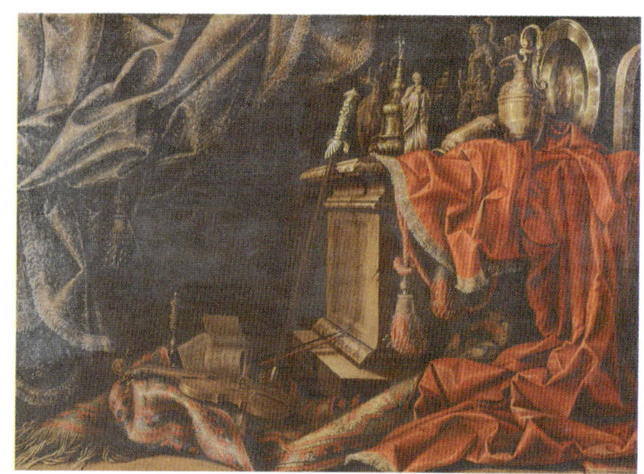
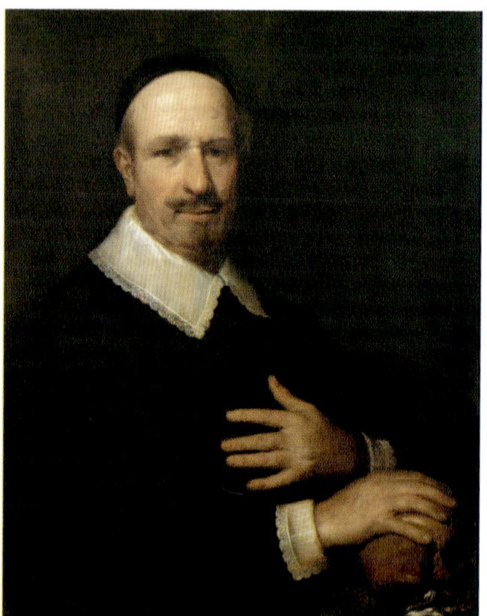
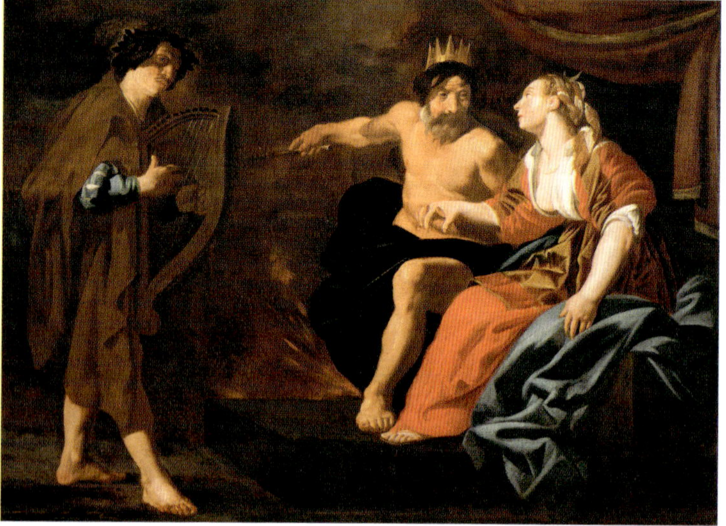

Giovanni Bonati (Giovanni Bonatti), 1635–1681
***Rinaldo and Armida*, ca. 1665**
235 x 327 cm; Oil on canvas
Pinacoteca; Room XIV; Inv. 40891

Pierre-Louis Cretey, 1635–1702
***Baptism of Christ*, undated**
96 x 134 cm; Oil on canvas
Pinacoteca; Room XIV; Inv. 40402

Francesco Fieravino, active 1650–1680
***Draperies*, undated**
95 x 132 cm; Oil on canvas
Pinacoteca; Room XIV; Inv. 41271

Francesco Fieravino, active 1650–1680
***Draperies with Musical Instruments*, undated**
95 x 132 cm; Oil on canvas
Pinacoteca; Room XIV; Inv. 41272

Pieter Meert, ca. 1620–1669
***Portrait of a Man*, undated**
80 x 64 cm; Oil on wood panel
Pinacoteca; Room XIV; Inv. 40447

Dutch School, first half of 17th century
***Orpheus, Pluto, and Proserpina*, first half of 17th century**
88 x 126 cm; Oil on canvas
Pinacoteca; Room XIV; Inv. 40419

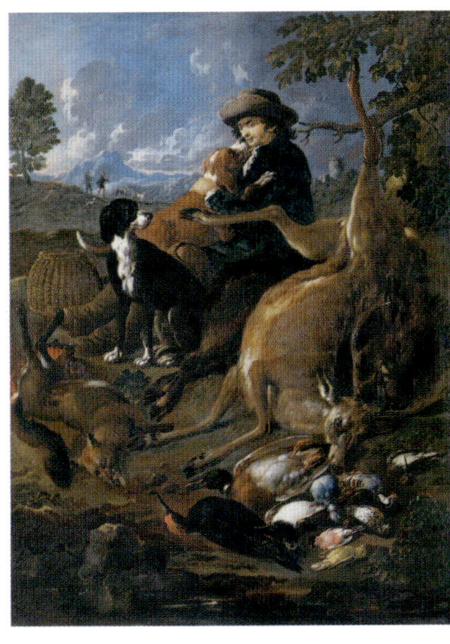

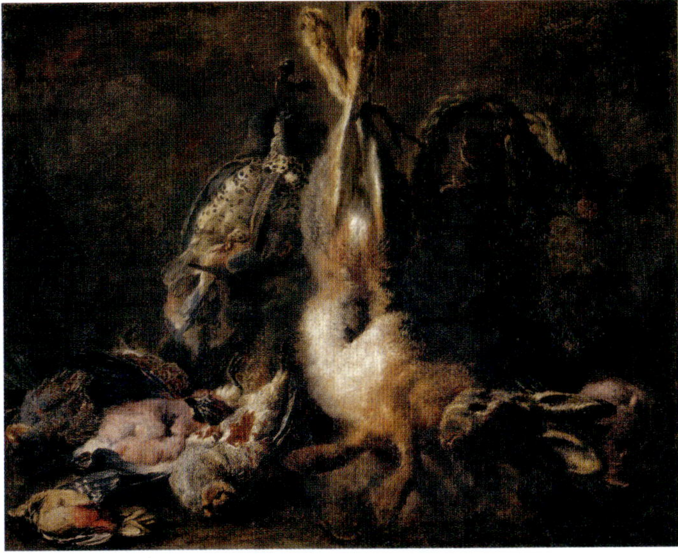

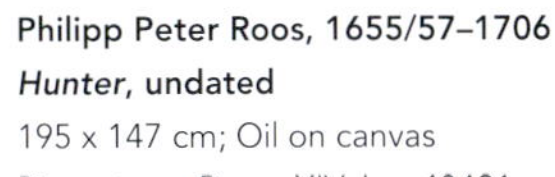

Philipp Peter Roos, 1655/57–1706
***Hunter*, undated**
195 x 147 cm; Oil on canvas
Pinacoteca; Room XIV; Inv. 40421

Baldassarre de Caro, 1689–1750
***Still Life with Dead Animals*, undated**
76 x 95 cm; Oil on canvas
Pinacoteca; Room XIV; Inv. 40417

Pieter van Bloemen, 1657–1720
***Horses*, undated**
61.5 x 96 cm; Oil on canvas
Pinacoteca; Room XIV; Inv. 40423

Anonymous Painter, late 17th century
***Hunter with Game*, late 17th century**
99.5 x 126 cm; Oil on canvas
Pinacoteca; Room XIV; Inv. 40420

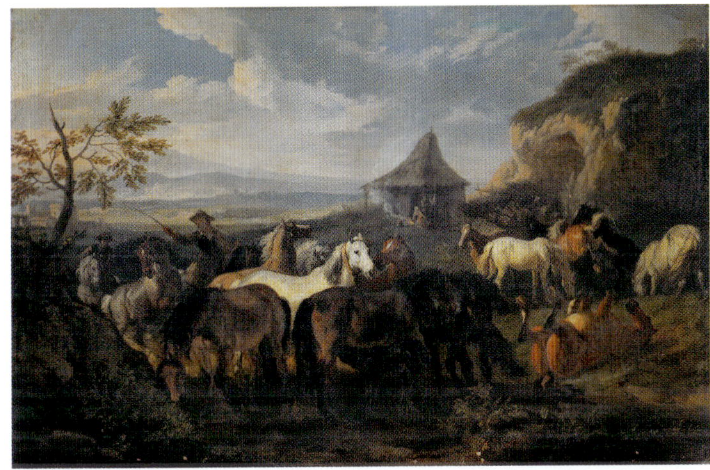

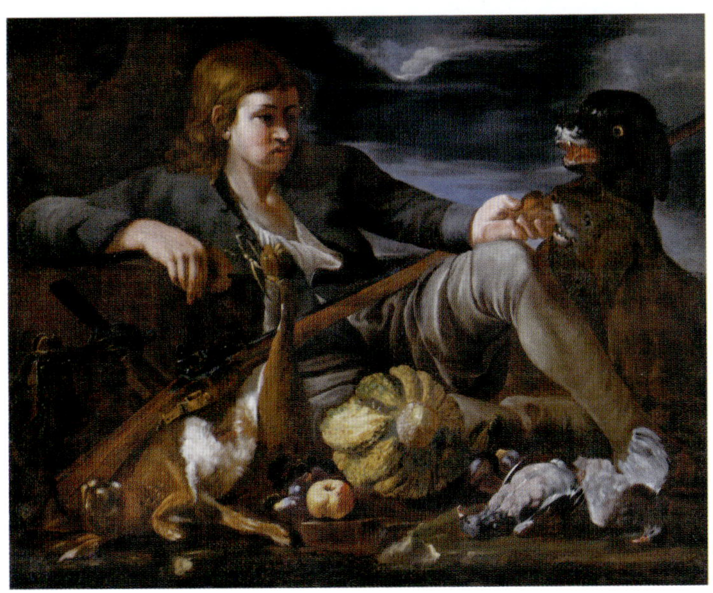

ROOM XV

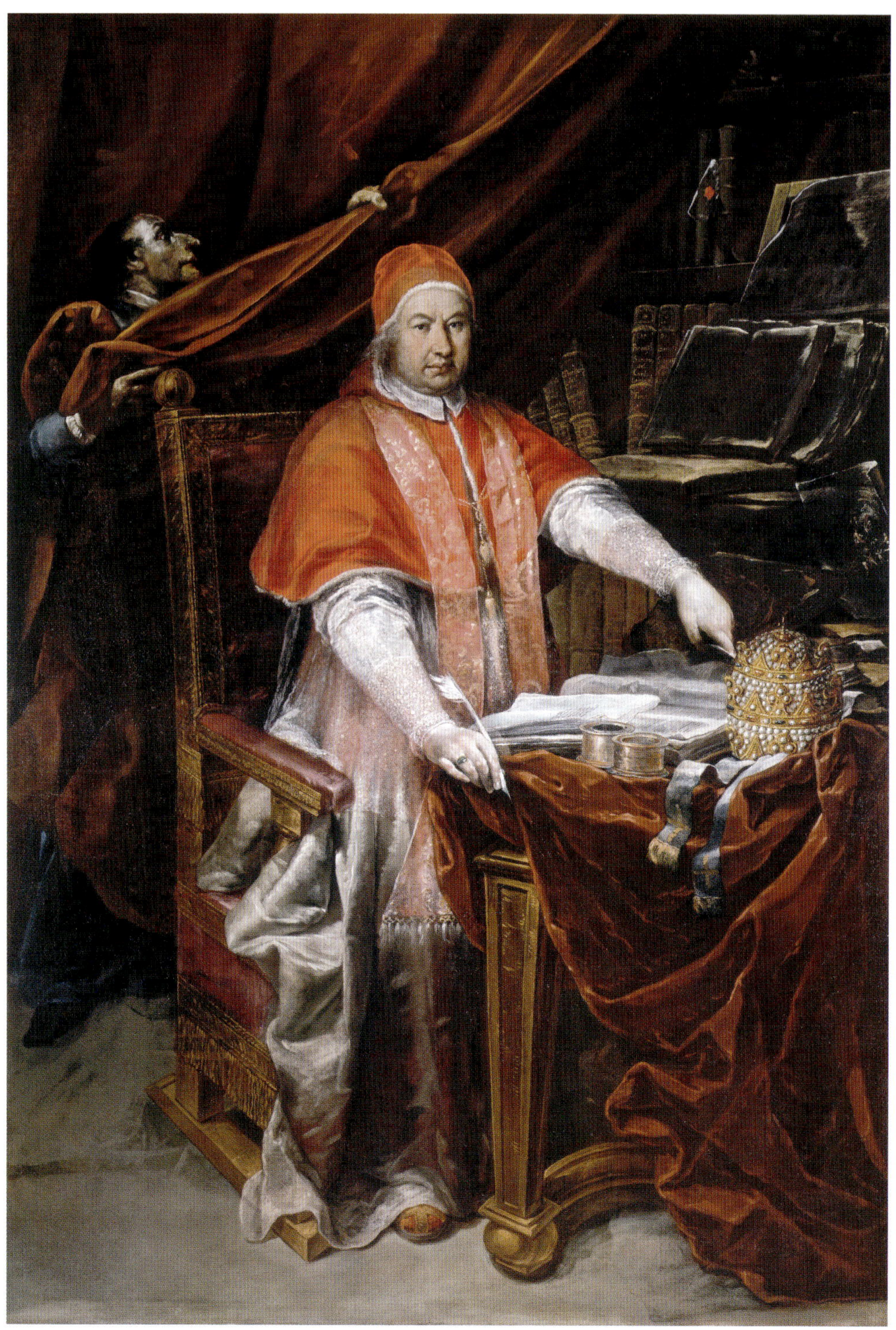

Giuseppe Maria Crespi

Pope Benedict XIV

This portrait of Benedict XIV is one of the late masterpieces of Bolognese artist Giuseppe Maria Crespi, who achieved fame above all as a painter of genre scenes. The work was beset by numerous difficulties and took around a year to complete. Benedict XIV commissioned the work in 1739 when, as Prospero Lambertini, he was still a cardinal and the archbishop of his hometown, Bologna. The portrait was almost finished when Lambertini was elected pope on August 17, 1740. Crespi had, in all haste, to replace the cardinal's vestments with papal vestments. No other changes were undertaken to the work, which, unusually for a papal likeness, combines two different types of portrait: that of a man of the cloth in the dignity of his religious office and that of the scholar in his study. Nevertheless, Prospero Lambertini pursued his scientific studies and continued to write theological texts as Benedict XIV. Crespi has introduced a personal note into the work with the genre-like figure of the servant who deliberately pulls back the curtain. Despite this caricatural touch, Benedict XIV was highly pleased with the portrait and bestowed high honors on Crespi.

Giuseppe Maria Crespi, 1665–1747
***Pope Benedict XIV*, 1740**
260 x 180 cm; Oil on canvas
Pinacoteca; Room XV; Inv. 40458

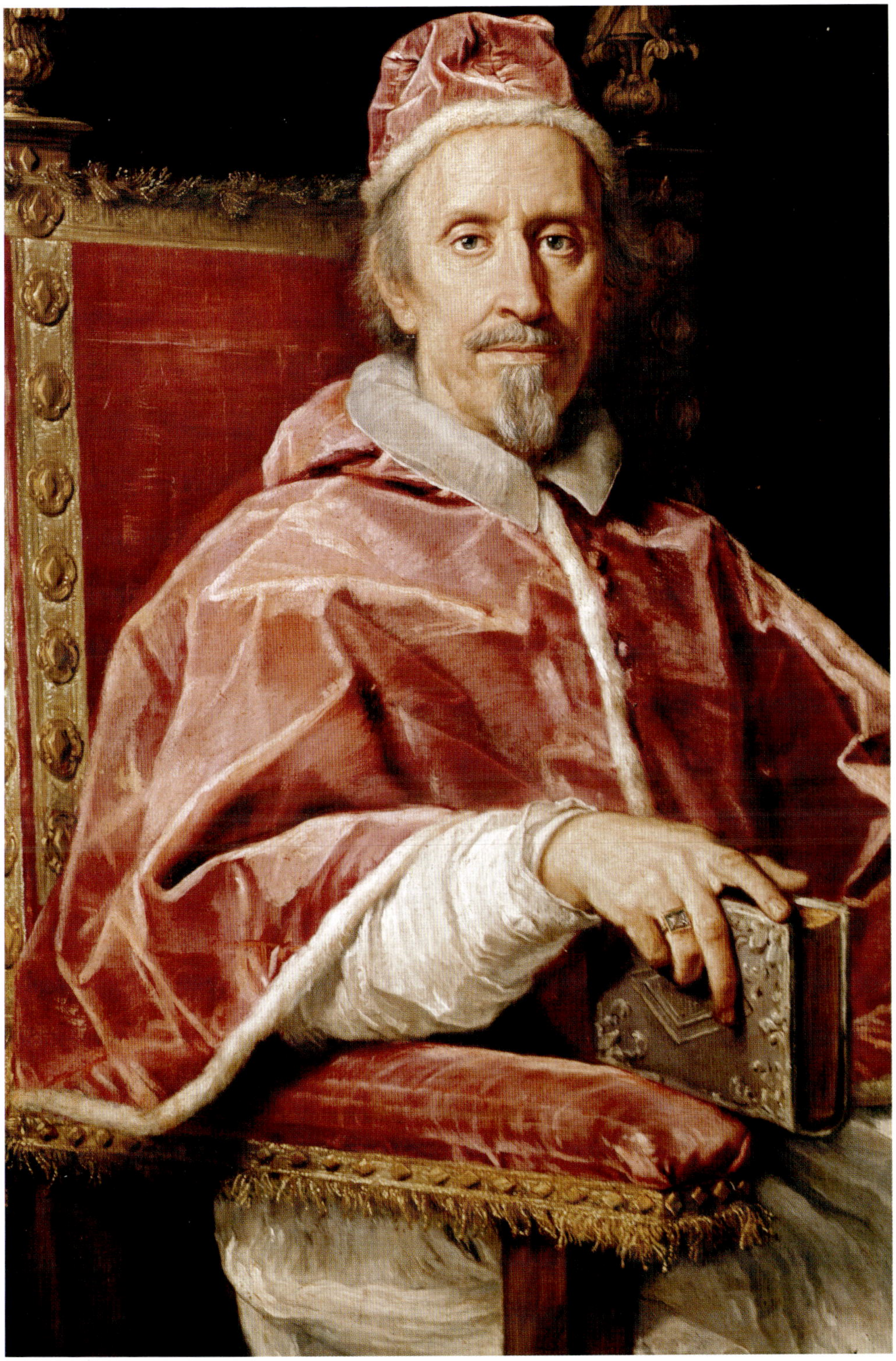

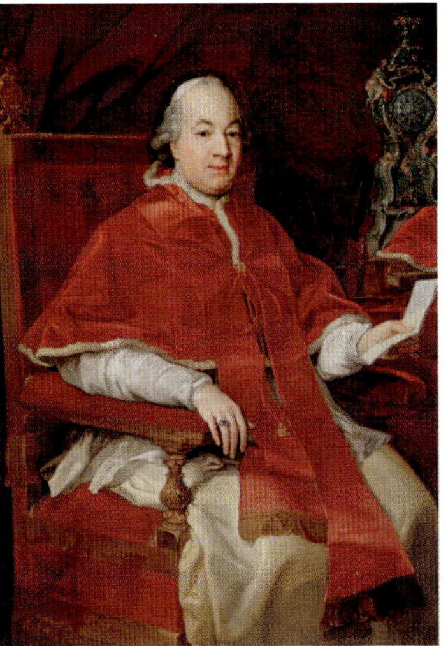

Pompeo Girolamo Batoni and Workshop, 1708–1787
***Portrait of Pius VI*, 1775**
137.7 x 98 cm; Oil on canvas
Pinacoteca; Room XV; Inv. 40455

Carlo Maratta

Portrait of Clement IX

The subject of this portrait, Clement IX (1600–1669), was only pope for a short time: from June 26, 1667 to his death on December 9, 1669. By the time Carlo Maratta was commissioned to paint his portrait, in 1669, the much-loved pope had already fallen ill, something not immediately apparent from the painting. An exponent of the classical tendency in Baroque art, Maratta was one of the most sought-after painters in Rome at this time. In keeping with his classical principles, he has portrayed Clement IX on the basis of a model developed by Raphael in 1511–12 for his portrait of Julius II, showing the pope seated as a half-length figure in three-quarter profile. Like Raphael, Maratta depicts the pontiff in white normal-wear vestments with a crimson cape and cap whose reflections bring a glow to his serious face. This sensitive character study of an art-loving pope considered to be particularly gentle is a kind of a snapshot taken as Clement interrupts his reading to fix the viewer with his attentive gaze. After Clement's death the portrait remained in his family until its acquisition by Louis Mendelssohn, a Detroit businessman of Jewish descent, who presented it to Pope Pius XI in 1931.

Carlo Maratta, 1625–1713
***Portrait of Clement IX*, ca. 1669**
145 x 116 cm; Oil on canvas
Pinacoteca; Room XV; Inv. 40460

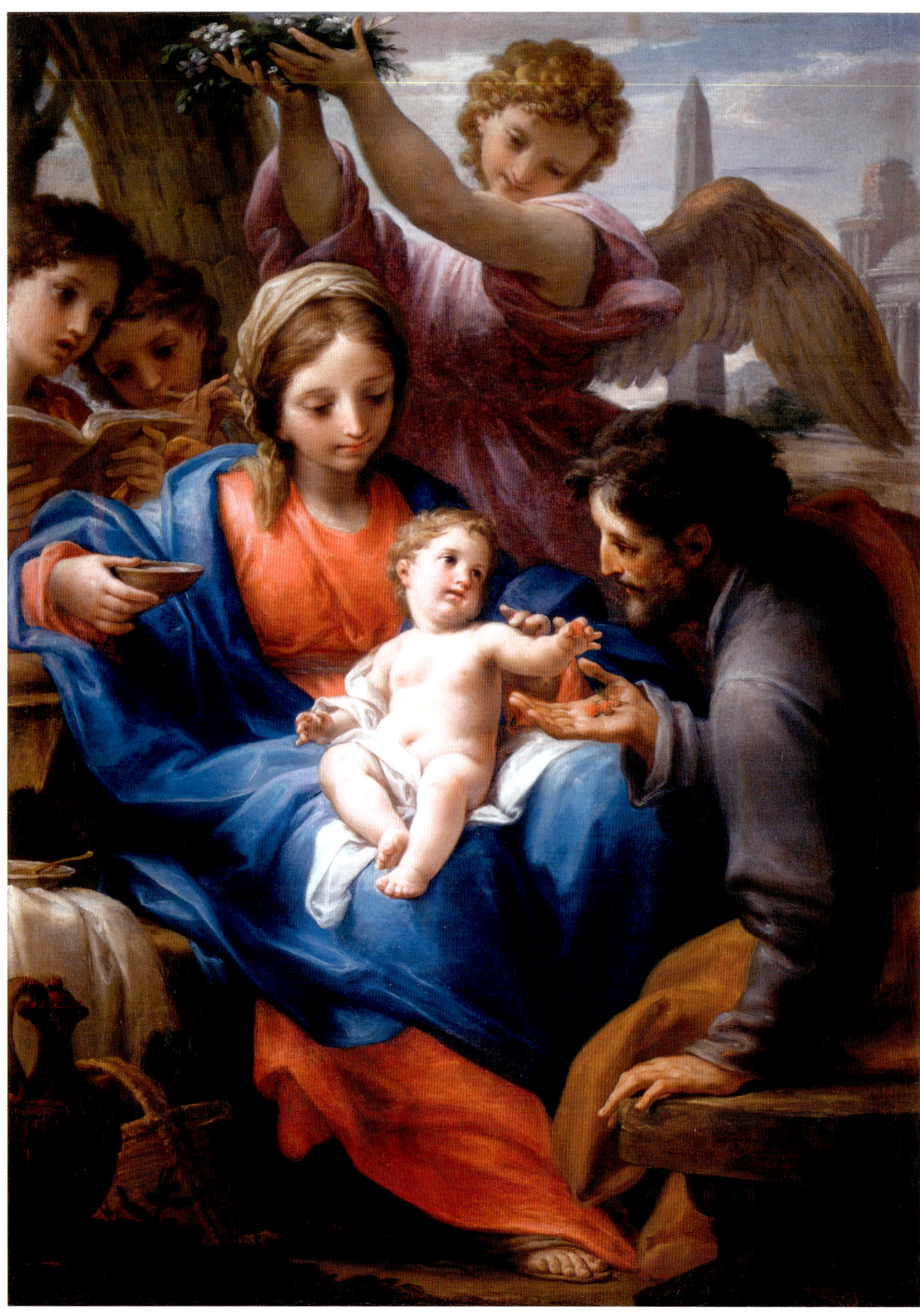

Francesco Mancini, 1679–1758
***Holy Family (Rest on the Flight into Egypt),* undated**
136 x 100 cm; Oil on canvas
Pinacoteca; Room XV; Inv. 40398

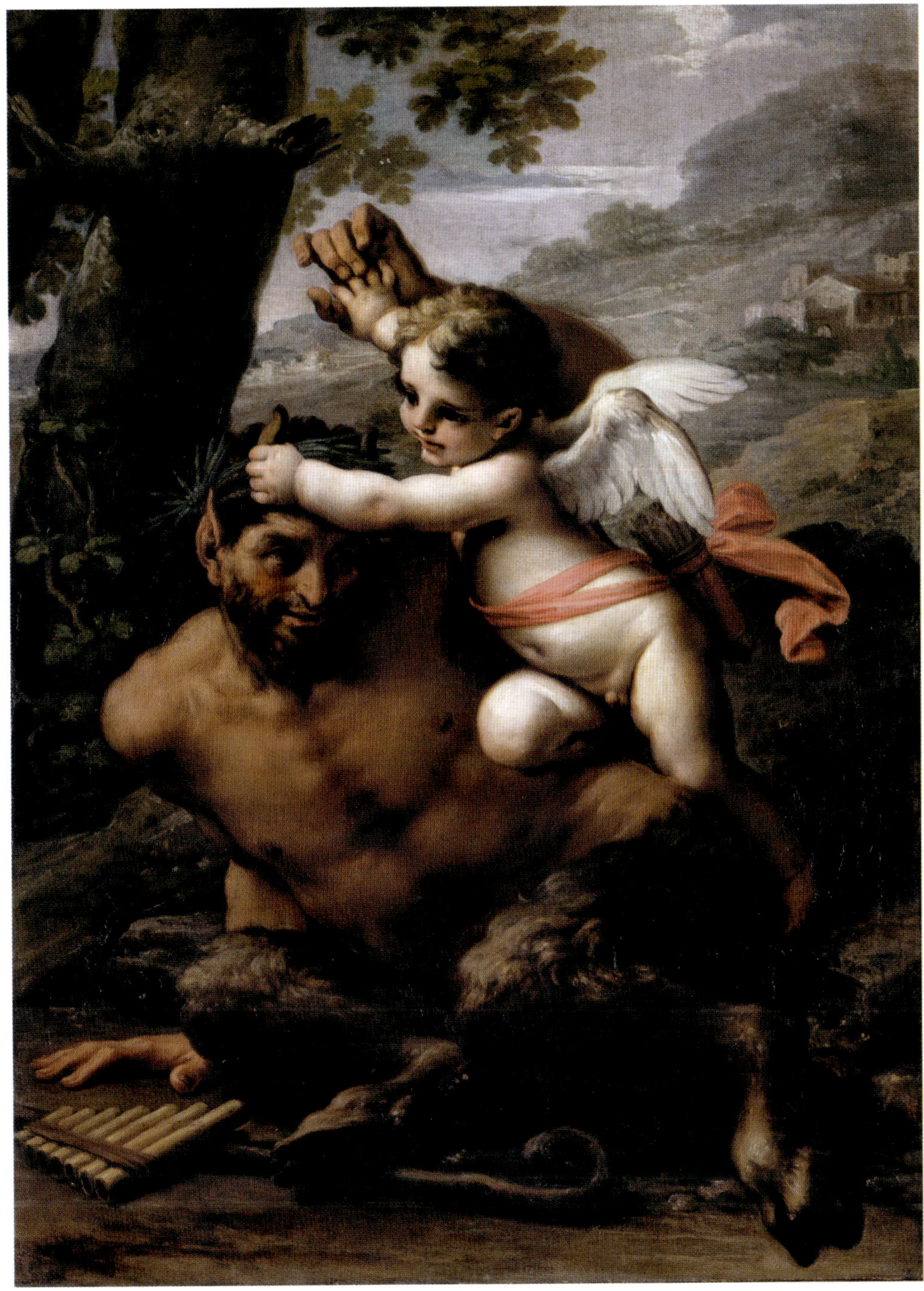

Francesco Mancini

Cupid and Pan

Cupid and Pan is one of the few mythological paintings in the Pinacoteca. It is also something of an exception within the oeuvre of Rococo painter Francesco Mancini, who in the eighteenth century was renowned above all for his sacred pictures. This canvas was acquired by Pope Clement XIV in 1772 along with a pendant depicting the victory of Chastity over Cupid (now in the Quirinale Palace) and Mancini's *Rest on the Flight into Egypt* (inv. 40398). Originally known as Cupid Conquering Nature, this work depicts the unequal battle between Cupid, the god of love, and Pan, the god of shepherds, the forest, and nature. Conventionally depicted as a hybrid creature with the body and horns of a goat, Pan, on the ground, defends himself against the assaults of the small boy Cupid, who has grasped hold of one of his horns. Situated in an idyllic undulating landscape, the scene is divided into dark and light halves, corresponding to the two adversaries. Mancini contrasts Pan's dark, muscular upper body with the porcelain-like surface of Cupid's plump flesh. This comic treatment conceals a serious moral message, however; namely, that free rein should not be given to the passions.

Francesco Mancini, 1679–1758
***Cupid and Pan*, undated**
125 x 92 cm; Oil on wood panel
Pinacoteca; Room XV; Inv. 40748

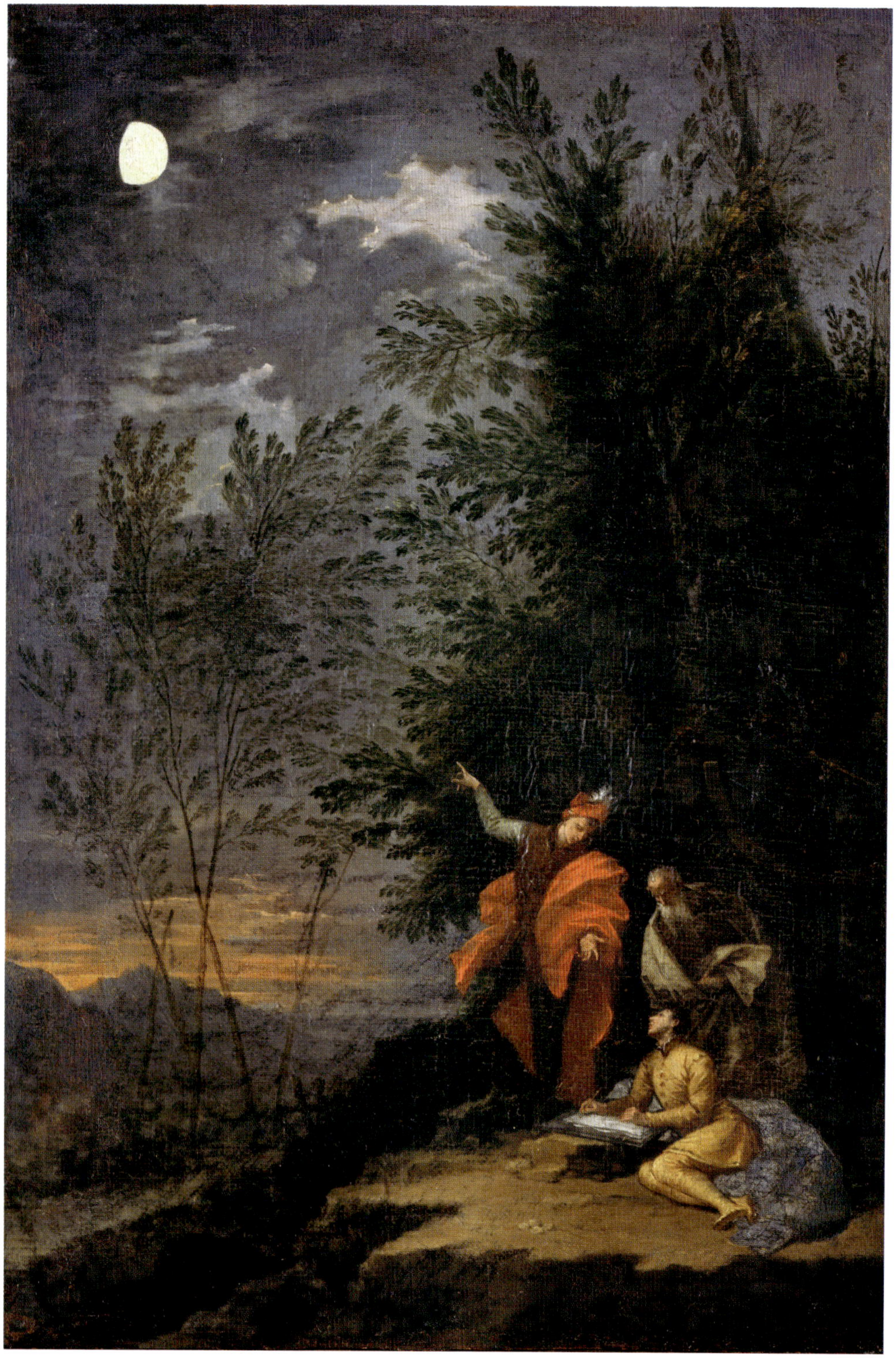

Donato Creti

Astronomical Observations: Mars

Creti's series of eight astronomical observations, painted in 1711, is one of the most unusual works in the Pinacoteca. That such a subject could become the subject of a multi-part work of art testifies to the close connection between art and science during the Age of Enlightenment. Creti's sequence of pictures shows the seven known planets (not including Uranus, which remained undiscovered until 1781) plus a comet. The observations of the planets are set outdoors at night, giving Creti an opportunity to demonstrate his talent as a painter of landscapes. In each of the paintings including the Mars picture, small figures in the foreground observe and comment on the planets. Their distinguished clothing indicates that they could be members of the nobility pursuing astronomy as a gallant leisure activity. Indeed the paintings were commissioned by one such noble dilettante, the Bolognese Count Luigi Ferdinando Marsigli. The Count presented the series to Clement XI in 1711 with the request that the pope establish an observatory of his own. In 1712 Clement XI responded by supporting the creation of Italy's first public observatory in Bologna.

Donato Creti, 1671–1749
***Astronomical Observations: Mars*, 1711**
51.2 x 35; Oil on canvas
Pinacoteca; Room XV; Inv. 40436

Donato Creti, 1671–1749
***Astronomical Observations: Comet*, 1711**
51 x 35.2; Oil on canvas
Pinacoteca; Room XV; Inv. 40435

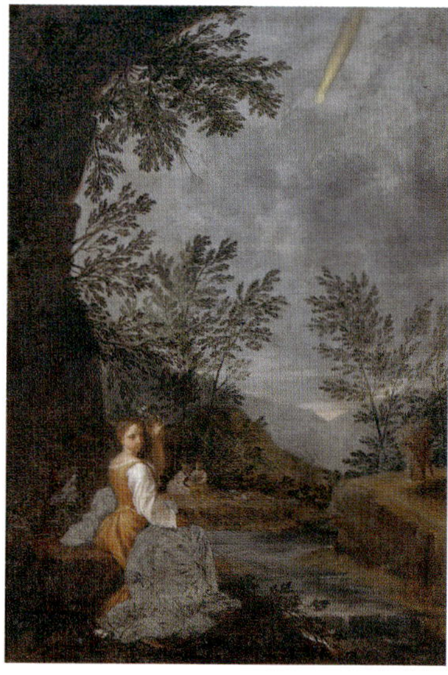

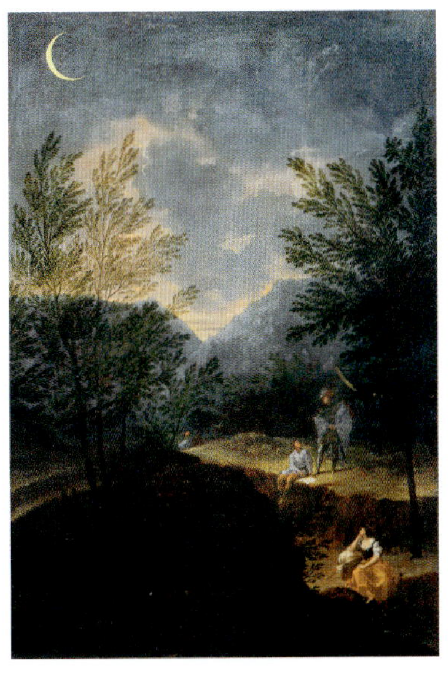
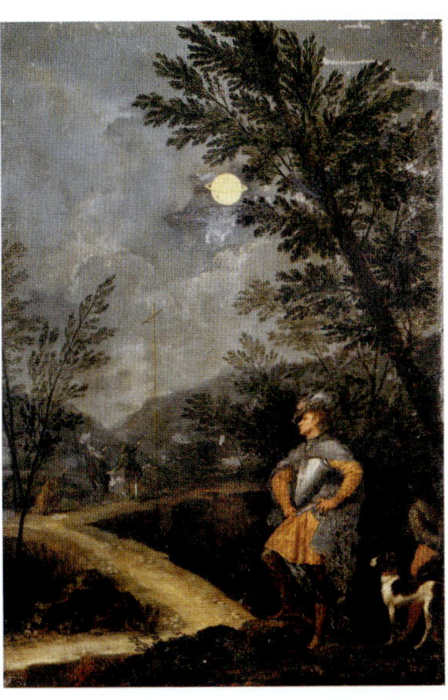
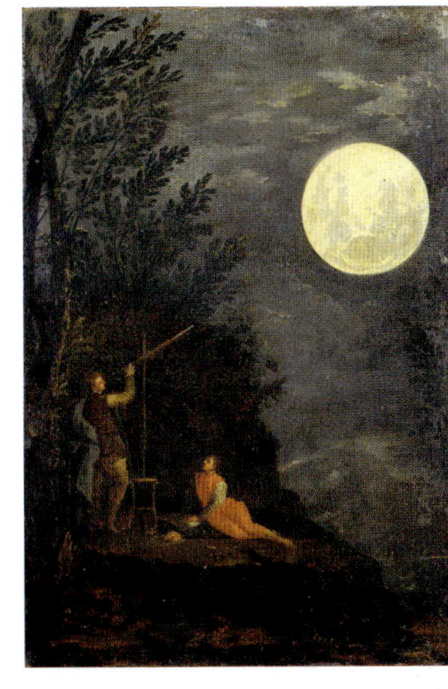
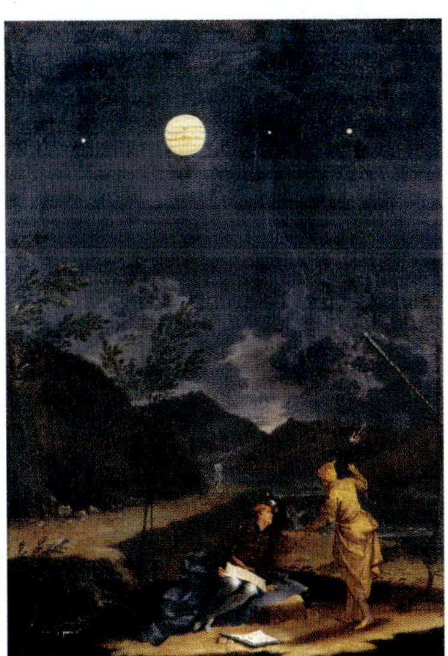
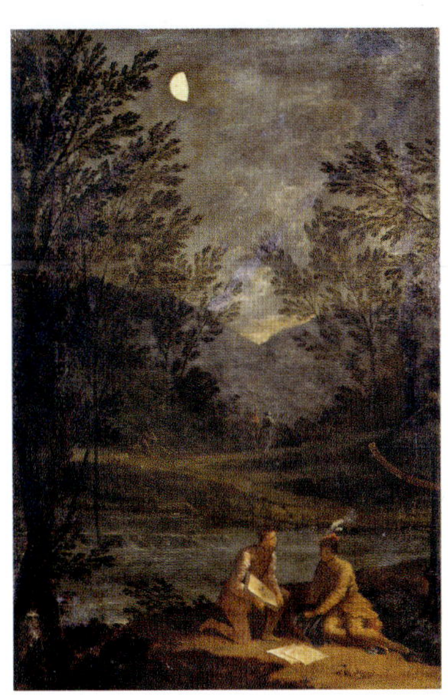

Donato Creti, 1671–1749
***Astronomical Observations: Venus*, 1711**
51 x 35.2; Oil on canvas
Pinacoteca; Room XV; Inv. 40435

Donato Creti, 1671–1749
***Astronomical Observations: Saturn*, 1711**
50.8 x 34.8 cm; Oil on canvas
Pinacoteca; Room XV; Inv. 40438

Donato Creti, 1671–1749
***Astronomical Observations: Luna*, 1711**
51 x 35 cm; Oil on canvas
Pinacoteca; Room XV; Inv. 40433

Donato Creti, 1671–1749
***Astronomical Observations: Sun*, 1711**
51 x 34.8 cm; Oil on canvas
Pinacoteca; Room XV; Inv. 40432

Donato Creti, 1671–1749
***Astronomical Observations: Jupiter*, 1711**
50.5 x 35 cm; Oil on canvas
Pinacoteca; Room XV; Inv. 40437

Donato Creti, 1671–1749
***Astronomical Observations: Mercury*, 1711**
50.6 x 35 cm; Oil on canvas
Pinacoteca; Room XV; Inv. 40434

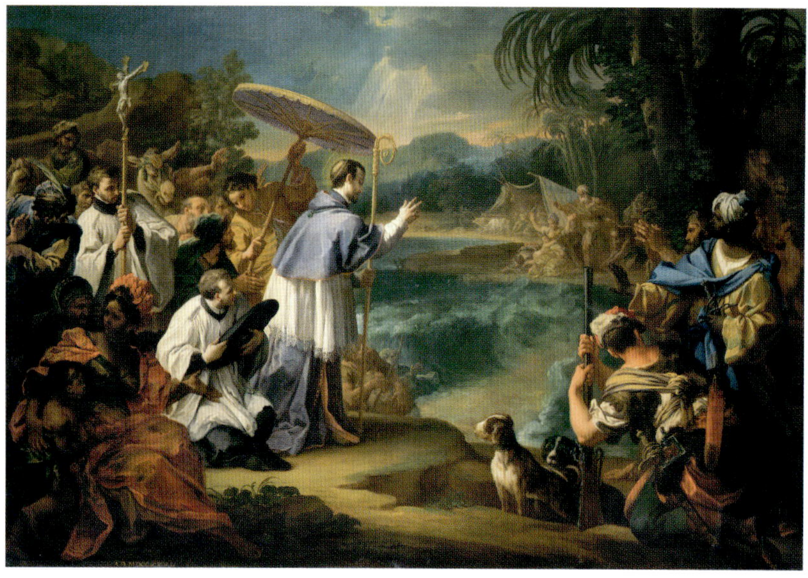

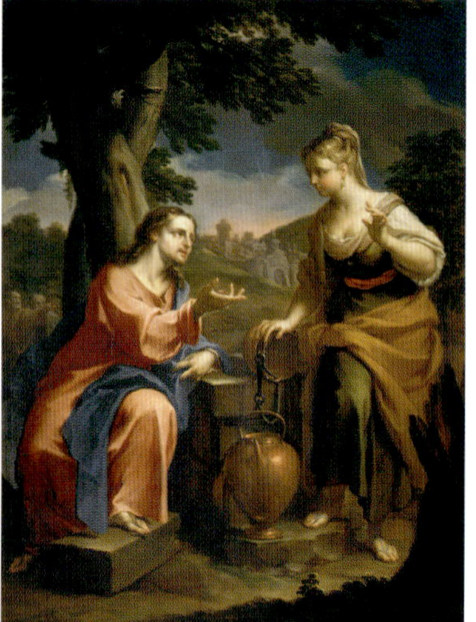

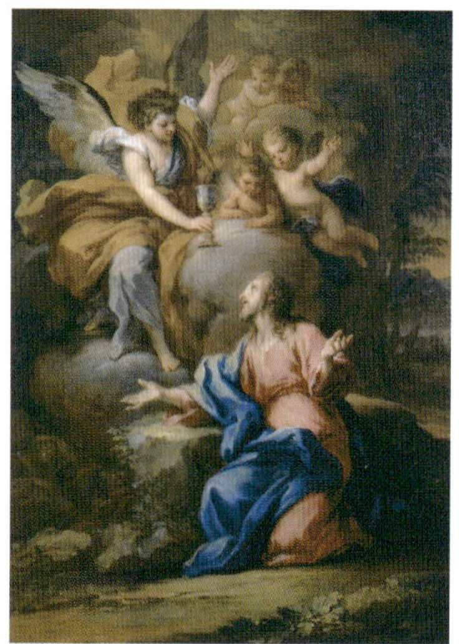

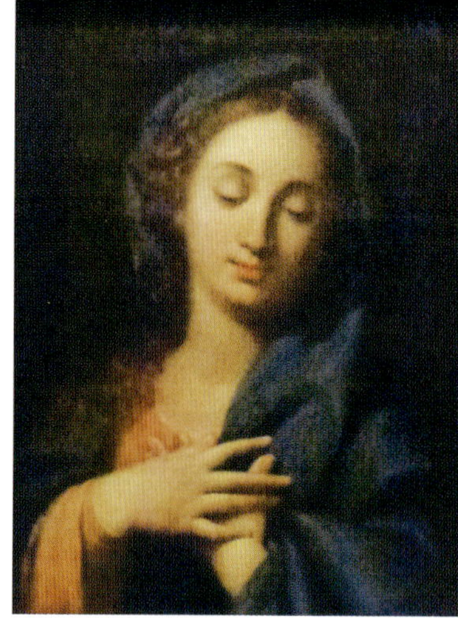

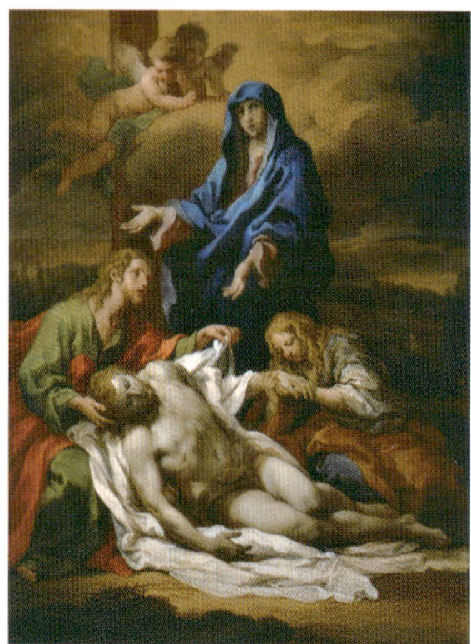

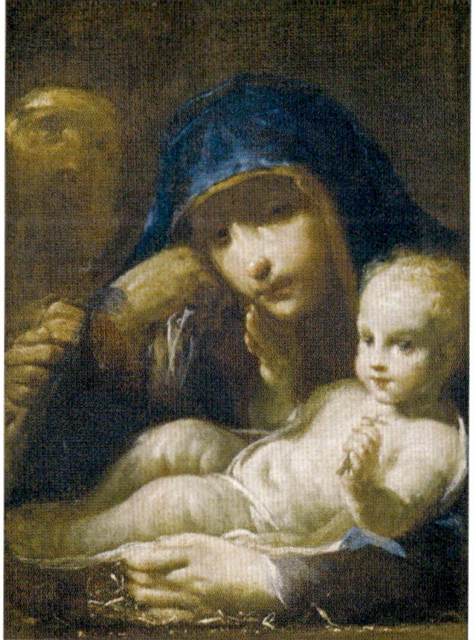

Sebastiano Conca, 1676/80–1764
***Miracle of St. Toribio*, 1726**
175 x 260 cm; Oil on canvas
Pinacoteca; Room XV; Inv. 40836

Francesco Trevisani, 1656–1746
***Christ and the Samaritan Woman*, undated**
258 x 192 cm; Oil on canvas
Pinacoteca; Room XV; Inv. 42018

Sebastiano Conca, 1680–1764
***Christ in the Garden Gethsemane*, 1746**
63 x 47 cm; Oil on canvas
Pinacoteca; Room XV; Inv. 40779

Sebastiano Conca, Workshop of, 1680–1764
***Madonna*, undated**
67 x 50.5 cm; Oil on canvas
Pinacoteca; Room XV; Inv. 41265

Sebastiano Conca, 1680–1764
***Deposition*, 1746**
63 x 47 cm; Oil on canvas
Pinacoteca; Room XV; Inv. 40774

Giuseppe Maria Crespi, 1665–1747
***Holy Family*, 1735–1740**
59.5 x 44.5 cm; Oil on canvas
Pinacoteca; Room XV; Inv. 40388

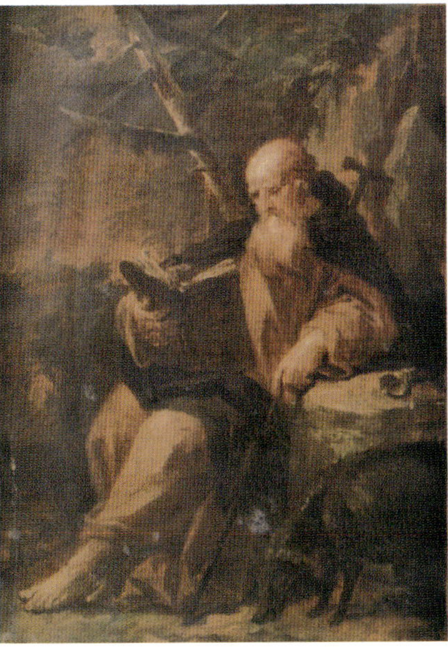
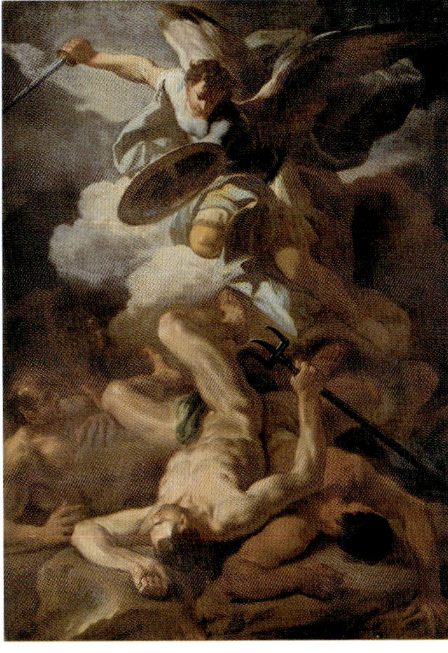
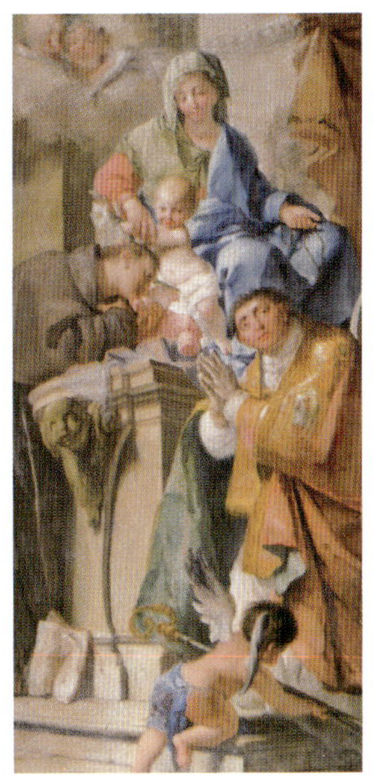
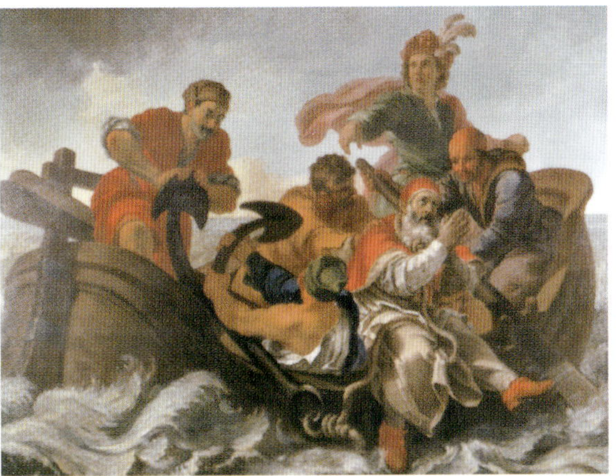
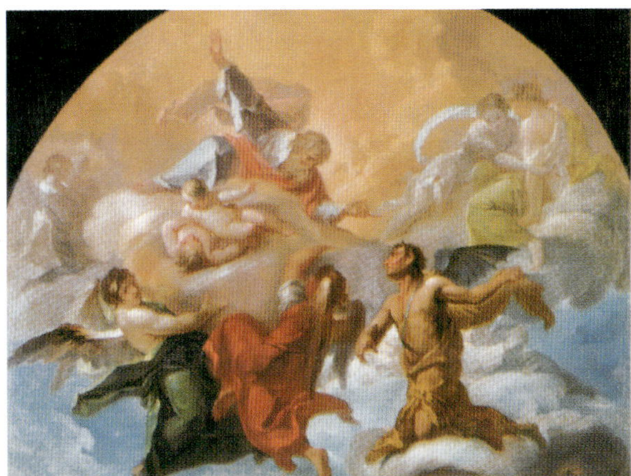
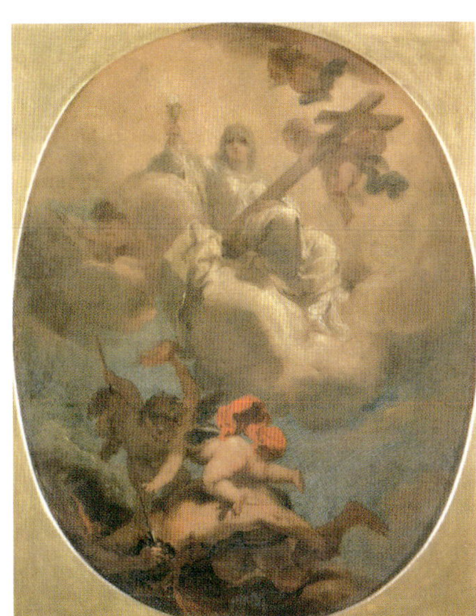
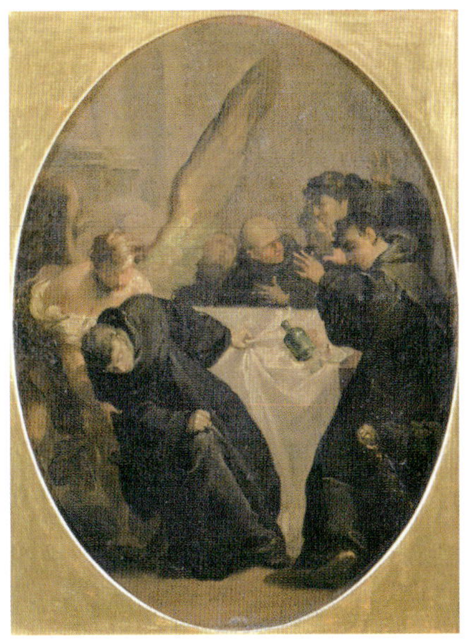

Alessandro Magnasco, 1667–1749
***St. Anthony*, undated**
41 x 31 cm; Oil on wood panel
Pinacoteca; Room XV; Inv. 40764

Corrado Giaquinto, 1703–1766
***Archangel Michael Fights the Devil*, 1720–1725**
135 x 98 cm.; Oil on canvas
Pinacoteca; Room XV; Inv. 40400

Giovanni Battista Crosato, 1686–1758
***Madonna with Child and Saints*, undated**
255 x 130 cm; Oil on canvas
Pinacoteca; Room XV; Inv. 40805

Pier Leone Ghezzi, 1674–1755
***Martyrdom of St. Clement*, ca. 1725**
230 x 307 cm; Oil on canvas
Pinacoteca; Room XV; Inv. 40840

Corrado Giaquinto, 1703–1766
***Satan and God the Father*, mid-18th century**
88 x 116.5 cm; Oil on canvas
Pinacoteca; Room XV; Inv. 40800

Gaetano Gandolfi, 1734–1802
***Triumph of Faith*, ca. 1774**
49.3 x 38.6 cm; Oil on canvas
Pinacoteca; Room XV; Inv. 40407

Gaetano Gandolfi, 1734–1802
***Death of St. Andrea Avellino*, ca. 1774**
49 x 37 cm; Oil on canvas
Pinacoteca; Room XV; Inv. 40409

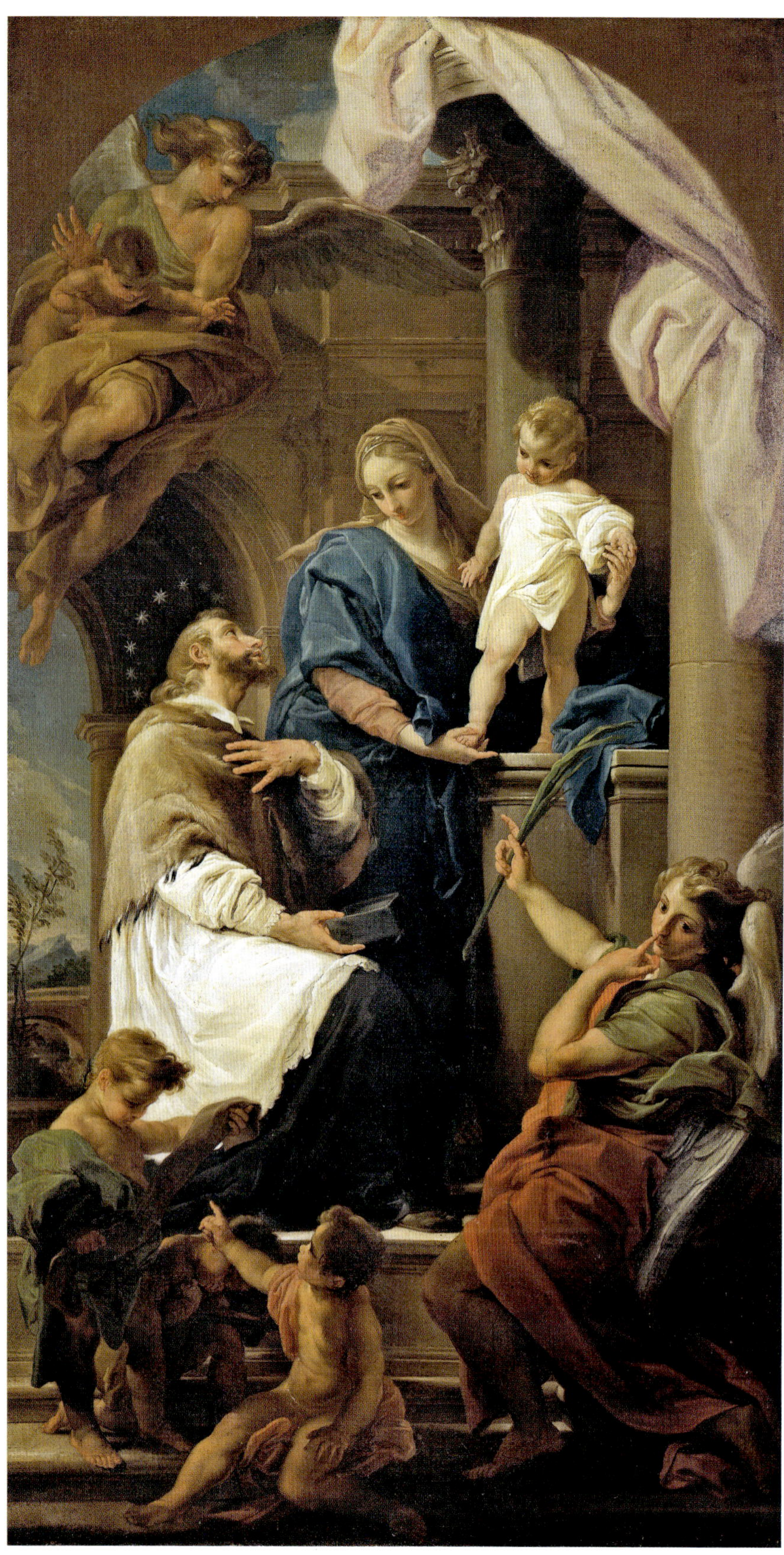

Pompeo Girolamo Batoni (1708–1787)

St. John of Nepomuk Before the Virgin Mary

Pompeo Girolamo Batoni, from Lucca, was one of the most successful painters in Rome in the eighteenth century. One of his largest works is *St. John of Nepomuk before the Virgin Mary* in the church of Santa Maria della Pace in Brescia (consecrated in 1746). For this important commission, which stands almost 4.5 meters high, Batoni painted a number of smaller-scale preliminary versions, of which the Pinacoteca picture is one. This work depicts the Bohemian martyr St. John Nepomuk (ca. 1350–1393), canonized in 1729, venerating the Infant Jesus, who stands on a kind of predella as he is presented to the saint by his mother. The angel in the foreground, clad in fluttering robes and pointing out the saint with the martyr's palm, is an important figure. His index finger raised to his mouth stands for St. John Nepomuk's defense of the seal of the confessional, for which he suffered death by drowning. The landscape with the bridge in the background may be an allusion to John's martyrdom. In his clear composition, which emphasizes the central diagonal, Batoni reveals himself to be a successor to the classical tendency in Baroque art. With their somewhat contrived poses, overlarge eyes, and small mouths, the figures correspond to a Rococo ideal of beauty. The classical architectural setting shares certain aspects with the church of Santa Maria della Pace, which was under construction in 1743.

Pompeo Girolamo Batoni, 1708–1787
***St. John of Nepomuk Before the Virgin Mary*, 1746**
120 x 63.5 cm; Oil on canvas
Pinacoteca; Room XV; Inv. 40415

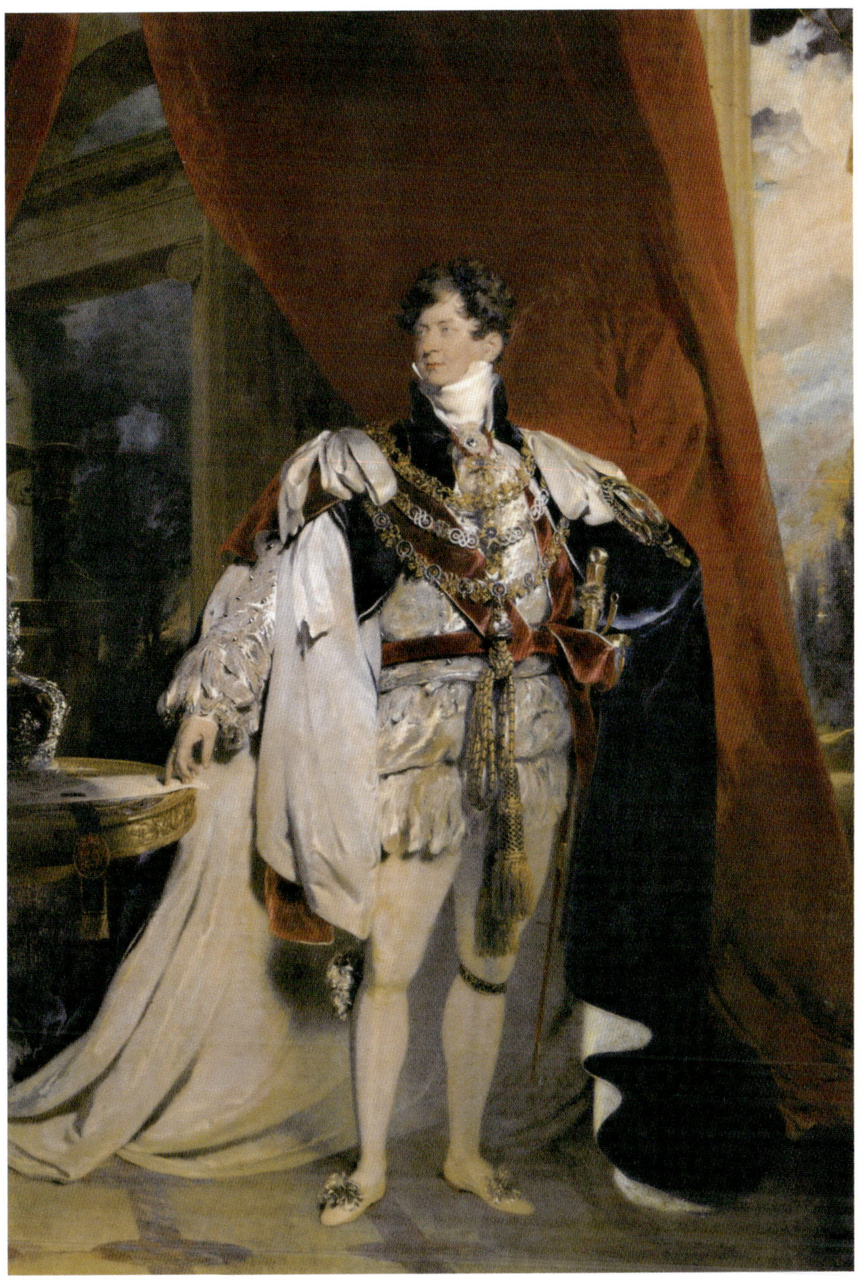

Thomas Lawrence

King George IV of England

This imposing work depicts King George IV of England (1762–1830) as Prince Regent. One of the most celebrated portraitists of his day, Thomas Lawrence, ennobled by George IV in 1815, has painted the king in front of a massive hanging of red velvet in a classic regal pose. George's ceremonial garb of shimmering silver stands strongly against the dark background. In its particular shape and lustrous surface it recalls the armor worn by the rulers of old. The blue velvet mantle, star and chain, and blue knee strap show the king to be a member of the Order of the Garter, the senior chivalric order of the United Kingdom. King George directs a resolute gaze toward an unknown person or object to his left, where the crown and the Regency Act of 1811 sit on the table. In reality, George IV was regarded as weak-willed and capricious. Lawrence has also idealized the physical appearance of the 50-year-old prince, hiding his heavy figure beneath the sumptuous regalia. The painting is thought to have been presented by George to Pope Pius VII (reigned 1800–1823) shortly after ascending the throne in 1820 in order to seal the good diplomatic relations between the United Kingdom and the Holy See.

Thomas Lawrence, 1769–1830
***King George IV of England*, 1816**
292 x 204; Oil on canvas
Pinacoteca; Room XV; Inv. 40448

Jean Hubert, 1721–1786
***Portrait of Voltaire*, ca. 1775**
41 x 35.5 cm; Oil on wood panel
Pinacoteca; Room XV; Inv. 40876

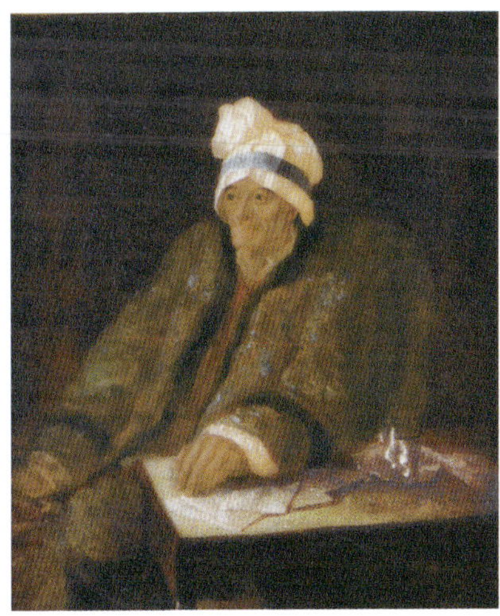

ROOM XVI

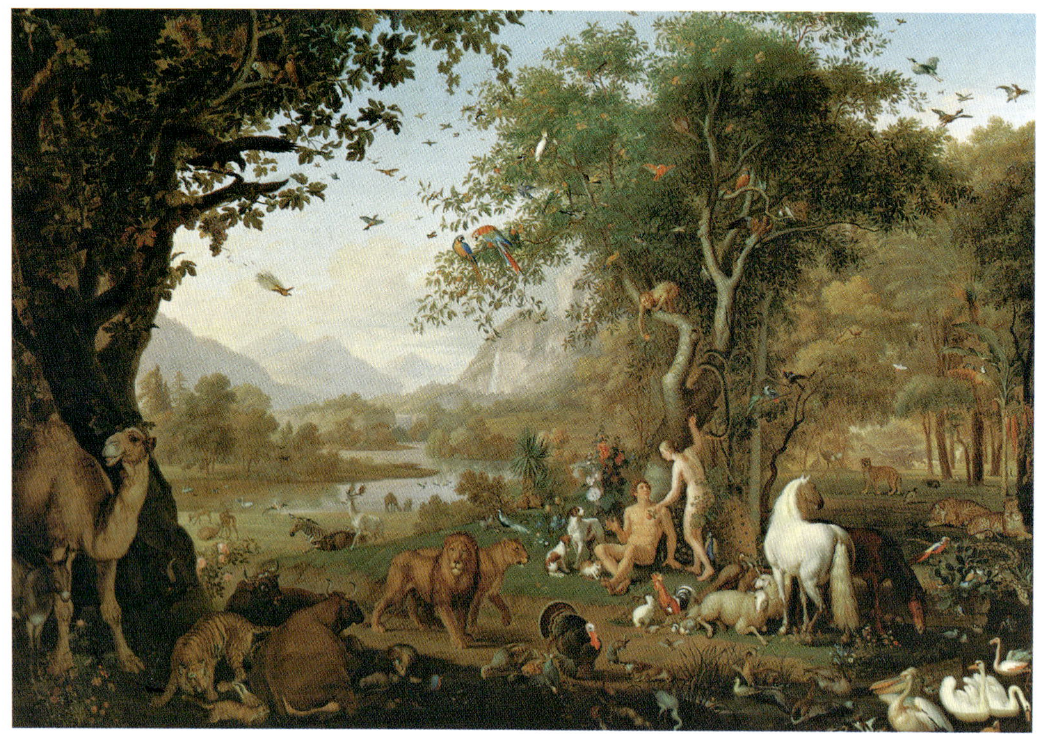

Wenzel Peter, 1745–1829
***Adam and Eve*, undated**
247 x 336 cm; Oil on canvas
Pinacoteca; Room XVI; Inv. 41266

Wenzel Peter, 1745–1829
***Eagle Owl with Prey in Landscape*, 1788**
99 x 72 cm; Oil on canvas
Pinacoteca; Room XVI; Inv. 41259

Wenzel Peter, 1745–1829
***Self-Portrait*, 1813**
75 x 71 cm; Oil on canvas
Pinacoteca; Room XVI; Inv. 40449

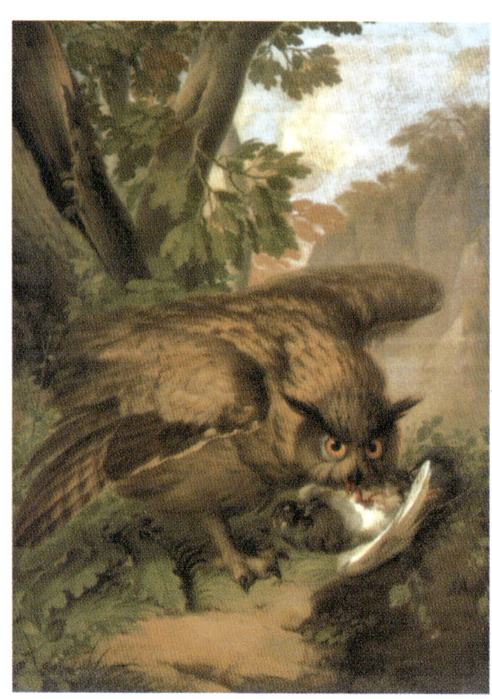

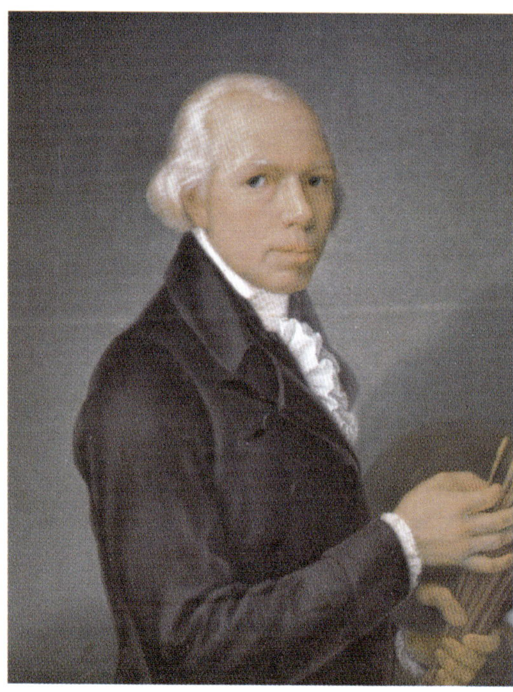

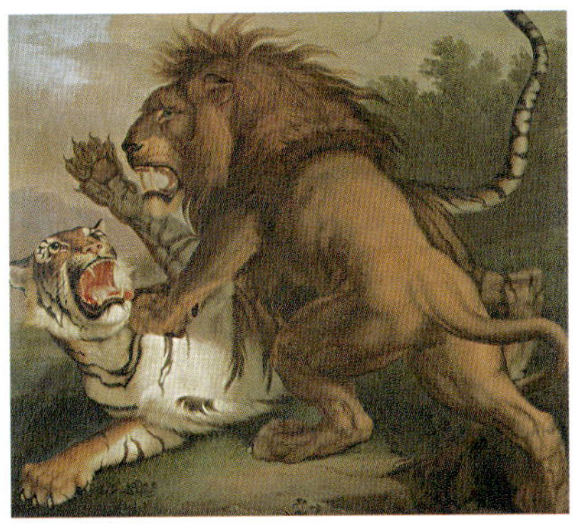

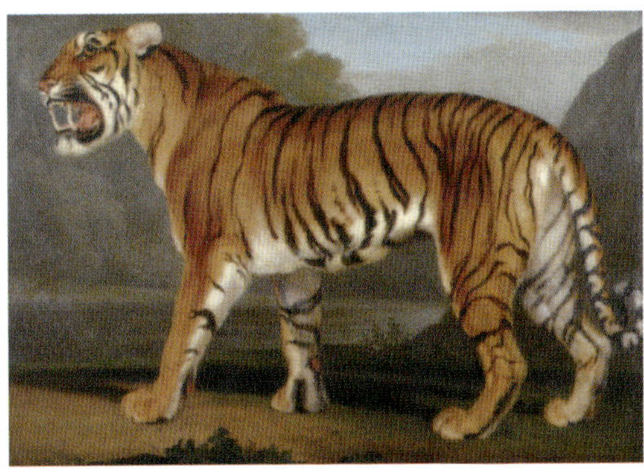

Wenzel Peter, 1745–1829
***Lion and Tiger Fighting*, undated**
136 x 130 cm; Oil on canvas
Pinacoteca; Room XVI; Inv. 41262

Wenzel Peter, 1745–1829
***Tiger*, undated**
124 x 172 cm; Oil on canvas
Pinacoteca; Room XVI; Inv. 41260

Wenzel Peter, 1745–1829
***Leopard and Zebra Fighting*, undated**
130 x 138 cm; Oil on canvas
Pinacoteca; Room XVI; Inv. 41256

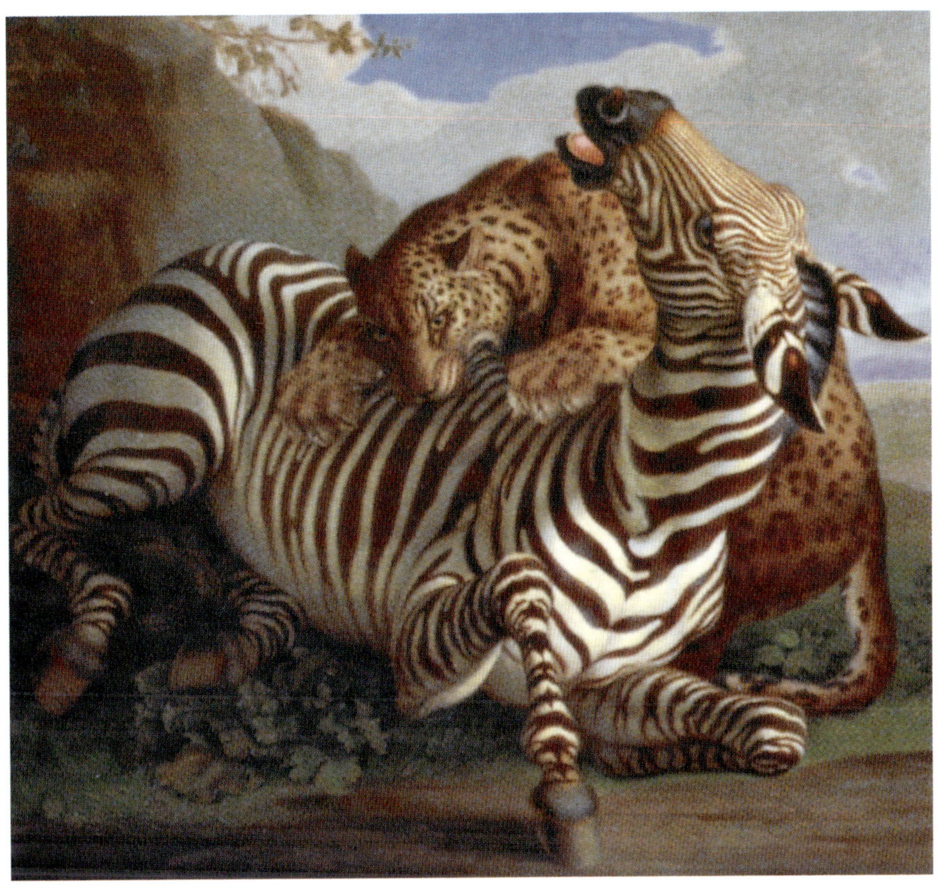

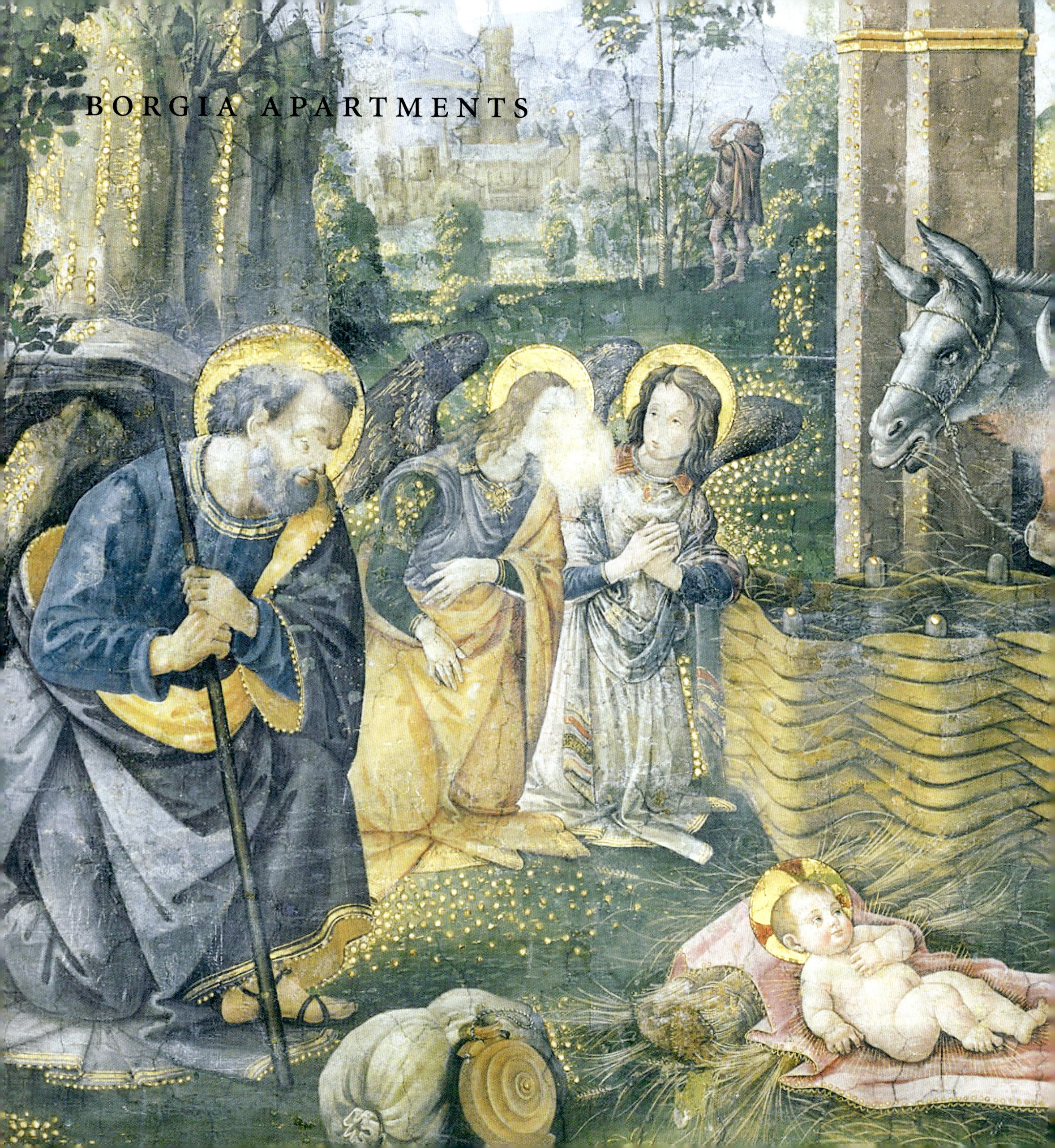

BORGIA APARTMENTS

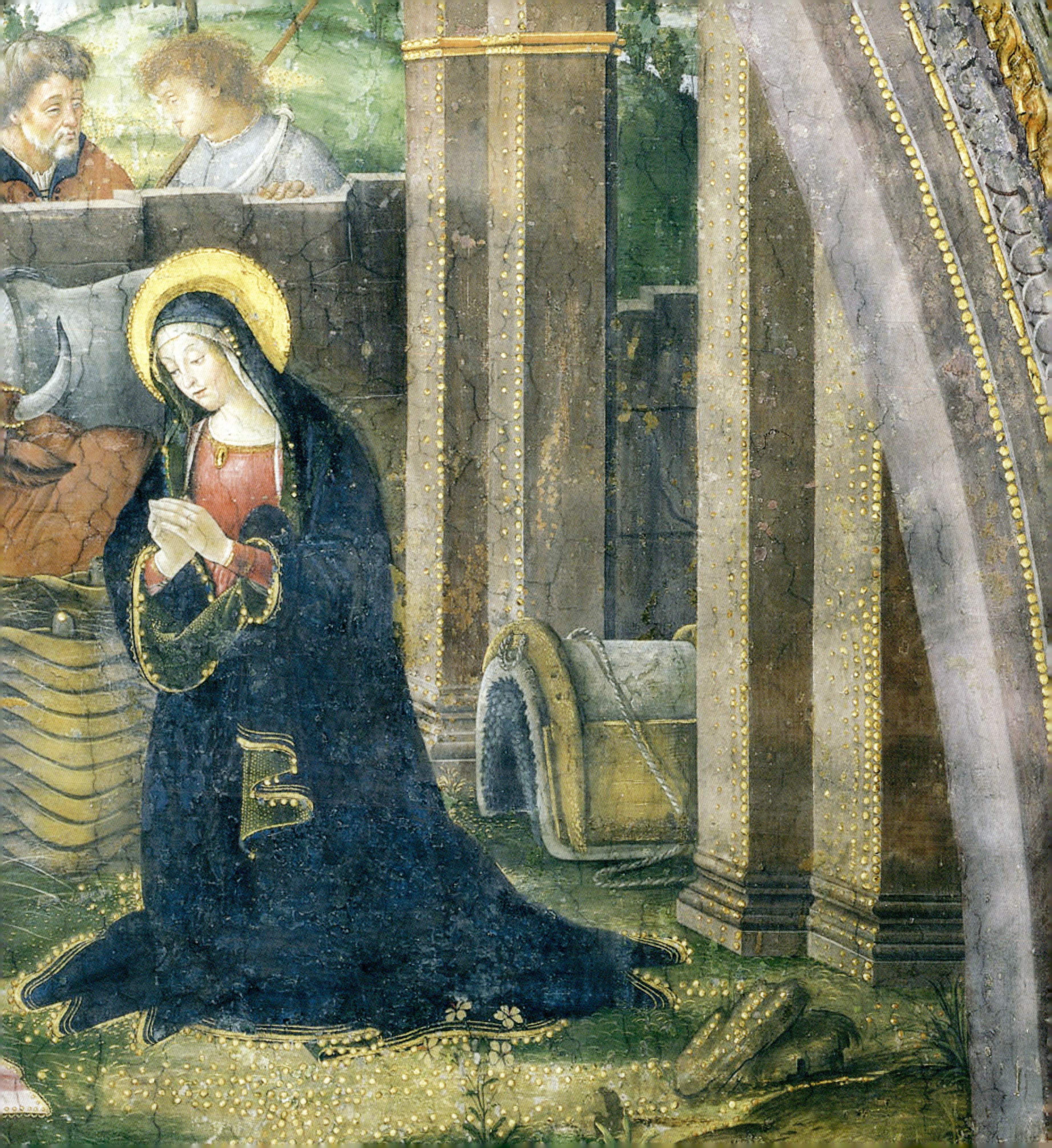

BORGIA APARTMENTS

On March 29, 1493, Pope Alexander VI (1431–1503, reigned from 1492) wrote a remarkable letter to the City of Orvieto in Umbria, Italy. In it he explained to the local citizens that the completion of their cathedral would have to be postponed because he needed the painter Pinturicchio, currently at work there, for the decoration of his private chambers in the Vatican. Known as the Borgia Apartments, these rooms are among the most extensively frescoed suites in the papal palace. Pinturicchio and his assistants decorated a total of five rooms with cycles of paintings that have remained largely unchanged to this day.

Despite being referred to as "private chambers," it should be pointed out that in earlier times these rooms were at least semi-official in character. Although Alexander VI had his bed chamber, living quarters, and treasure chamber here, the front areas in particular, those looking out on the Sistine Chapel and the Sala Regia, were used for official occasions such as diplomatic receptions, audiences, the annual washing of feet and blessing of the poor, consistories (meetings with cardinals), the signing of treaties, and even parties. In his diaries, the pope's master of ceremonies, Johannes Burchardus (1440–1506), distinguishes between the more public areas and the "secret rooms" (camere secrete) accessible as a rule to only a small number of religious and secular dignitaries. The pope also provided high-ranking visitors with guest rooms in the Borgia Apartments. Among his first guests were King Frederick I of Naples and Marquis Gianfrancesco II Gonzaga of Mantua, as well as the latter's adversary, Charles VIII of France, in January 1495. In response to the newly completed frescoes, the French king is reported to have declared that in no other palace had he seen "decoration of this kind."

Charles VIII's praise is by no means extravagant. With its combination of Christian, mythological, and allegorical subjects, as well as motifs relating to the pope himself, the apartment's pictorial program is tailored as much to Alexander VI as it is to the official function of the rooms. Alexander VI was known on the one hand as a power broker and on the other as a patron of the arts and sciences. He belonged to the influential Spanish noble family of Borgia (Spanish: Borja), which had already produced one pope (Callixtus III, reigned 1455–1458). As a cardinal, Alexander VI had led an extravagant and profligate lifestyle. Despite holding high religious office, he lived with the mother of four of his ten children, Giovanni, Cesare, Lucrezia, and Goffredo, several of whom were to achieve renown themselves, and his election as pope in 1492 had been preceded by corruption and intrigue, notably bribery and the buying and selling of the papal office. Shortly after he became pope, Alexander VI transformed the Vatican into a court of the muses, doing his utmost—and employing ruthless methods, as the Orvieto letter demonstrates—to bring the best artists, poets, and scholars to the Vatican. His approach is most evident in the Borgia Apartments.

The apartment comprises six rooms and side-rooms located on the first floor of the papal palace built by Nicholas V (1397–1455, reigned from 1447). However, only five of the rooms—the Room of the Faith (Sala dei Misteri della Fede), the Room of the Saints (Sala dei Santi), the Room of Liberal Arts (Sala delle Arti Liberali), the Room of Creed (Sala del Credo), and the Room of Sybils (Sala delle Sibille)—were decorated by Pinturicchio (ca. 1454–1513) and his workshop, the exception being the Sala die Pontefici, which served as an important reception and audience room. The room names were coined at the end of the nineteenth century by the art historians Franz Ehrle and Enrico Stevenson, based on the dominant decorative motifs, and were adopted internationally. The surviving pictorial decoration by Pinturicchio is confined mainly to the upper zones, taking the form of figurative and ornamental compositions in the lunettes and ceiling compartments. Only traces of his decoration of the lower wall areas, thought to have been largely ornamental, remain.

The pendentive spaces and ceilings throughout the rooms are linked by an elaborate decorative framework, which in many places makes symbolic reference to Pope Alexander VI and the Borgia family. Although the only portrait as such of Alexander VI appears in the Resurrection scene in the Sala dei Misteri della Fede, his position and role as donor are omnipresent. The dedication of the overall program of the Appartamento to the profession of the Catholic faith and the story of Christ's life and deeds enabled Alexander VI to write himself into that story. Furthermore, the frescoes' linking of Christian theology and mythology draws attention to his interest in, and promotion of, humanist learning, the aim of which was to revive the antique within the context of Christian doctrine. This principle of typology—the drawing of parallels between different layers of history, such as the Old and New Testaments, the antique world and the story of Christ's life and deeds, Christian and secular history—is the thematic and compositional underpinning of the Borgia Apartments. And Pinturicchio's formal organization of the program lives up to this thematic challenge thanks to the painter's exceptionally realistic presentation of the familiar stories against a backdrop of classical architectural and enchanting scenery. Furthermore, the large-format landscapes create the illusion that the space opens up beyond and to either side, giving Pinturicchio the occasion to develop sophisticated pictorial solutions. His artistry was insufficient, however, to convince Alexander VI's successor, Julius II (1443–1513, reigned from 1503), to continue to use the rooms as his private quarters. On the contrary, the new pope showed his disdain for the corrupt Alexander VI by moving into rooms (known as the Stanze) directly above the Borgia apartment and commissioning Raphael, an even more famous artist, to decorate them with frescoes.

The first room, known as the Sala dei Misteri della Fede (Room of the Mysteries of Faith), is decorated with scenes from the life of the Virgin Mary. A more descriptive name for the room would therefore be the Hall of the Life of the Virgin. The seven lunettes show various episodes from Mary's life: the *Annunciation*, the *Birth of Christ*, the *Adoration of the Magi*, *the Resurrection of Christ*, the *Ascension of Christ*, the *Descent of the Holy Spirit* at *Pentecost*, and the *Assumption of the Virgin*. Here, as in the other rooms, the events generally take place outdoors in front of extravagant architectural backdrops, revealing Pinturicchio's talent as a landscape painter. The lunette scenes and ceiling frescoes form part of the same program. In the case of the Sala dei Misteri della Fede, the Old Testament kings David and Solomon and prophets Isaiah and Jeremiah depicted in the vault all foretold in their prophesies the New Testament story of salvation through Christ.

The Sala dei Santi ("Room of the Saints") contains six pendentive frescoes illustrating scenes from the lives of the female saints Catherine, Barbara, Susanna, Mary, and Elizabeth, and the male saints Sebastian, Antony, and Paul, grouped by gender. The selection of these particular saints does not relate to any known program and remains the subject of dispute among art historians and theologians. An unusual element is the inclusion of the *Visitation* scene involving Mary and Elizabeth, which one would have expected to find among the scenes from the life of the Virgin in the Sala dei Misteri. Furthermore, representations of the Old Testament saint Susanna and SS. Antony and Paul in the wilderness were by no means common at the end of the fifteenth century. Even more unusual is the ceiling fresco, whose scenes from the legend of Isis, Osiris, and Apis take up a rare mythological theme that evidently alludes to the founding myth of the Borgia dynasty. The ancient myth is combined with images of Old Testament heroes David (doing battle with Goliath) and Judith (as the conqueror of Holofernes) as well as the classical figures Hercules and the ancient Roman sea god Neptune.

The significance of prophecies to Christ's future reign, a subject first approached in the Sala del Credo, is repeated in the final room of the Borgia Apartments, the Sala delle Sibille e dei Profeti ("Room of the Sibyls and Prophets"). Here, twelve small pendentive spaces are each occupied by both a sibyl and a prophet. The figures are depicted three-quarter-length against a blue background, with inscribed banners swirling around them. The ceiling medallions, by contrast, contain scenes depicting ancient sacrifices, whose meaning and connection to the frescoes below are not always clear.

The Sala delle Arti Liberali ("Room of the Liberal Arts") has a completely different theme than the other rooms of the Borgia Apartments. Here the pendentives contain female personifications of the seven liberal arts (rhetoric, music, arithmetic, geometry, astronomy, logic, and grammar) enthroned within a circle formed by exponents of each relevant science or "art." The ceiling program is dedicated to the cardinal virtue of justice. Various judgment scenes from classical history and the Old Testament, including Abraham and the Angels of the Lord and the justice of Hadrian, surround the central figure, a personification of justice.

The Sala del Credo ("Hall of the Creed") has twelve round-arched lunettes depicting the twelve apostles, each accompanied by an Old Testament prophet. Thick golden frames border the lunettes, and the men each hold an inscribed banner that swirls around their upper body. Although the lunettes all present the same theme, the sequence is far from monotonous as Pinturicchio has varied the individual figures in terms of age, clothing, and style of hair and beard, thereby infusing the cycle with vitality. The frescoes are arranged in order of the verses of the Creed inscribed on the apostles' banners.

THE ROOM OF THE MYSTERIES OF THE FAITH

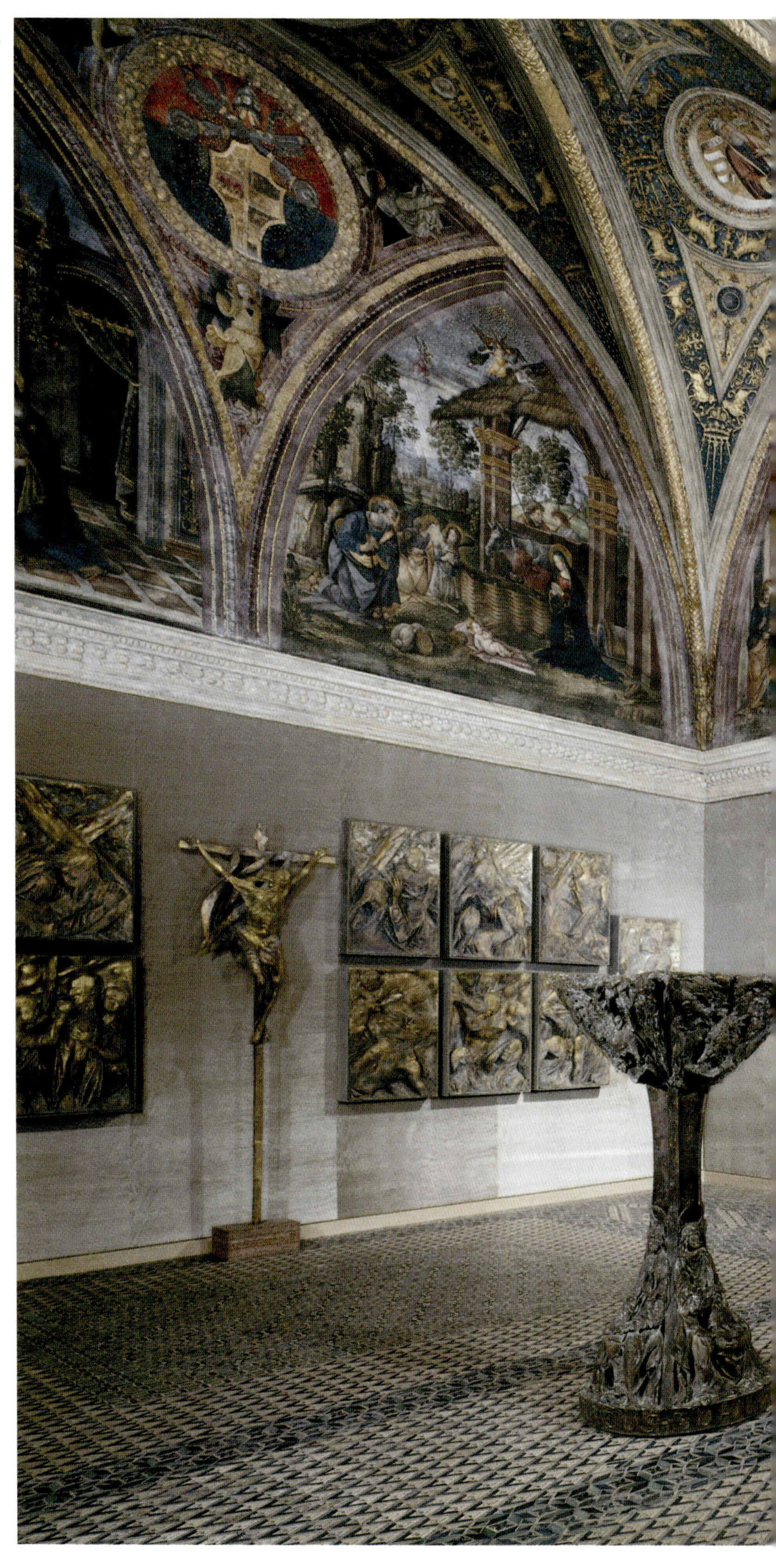

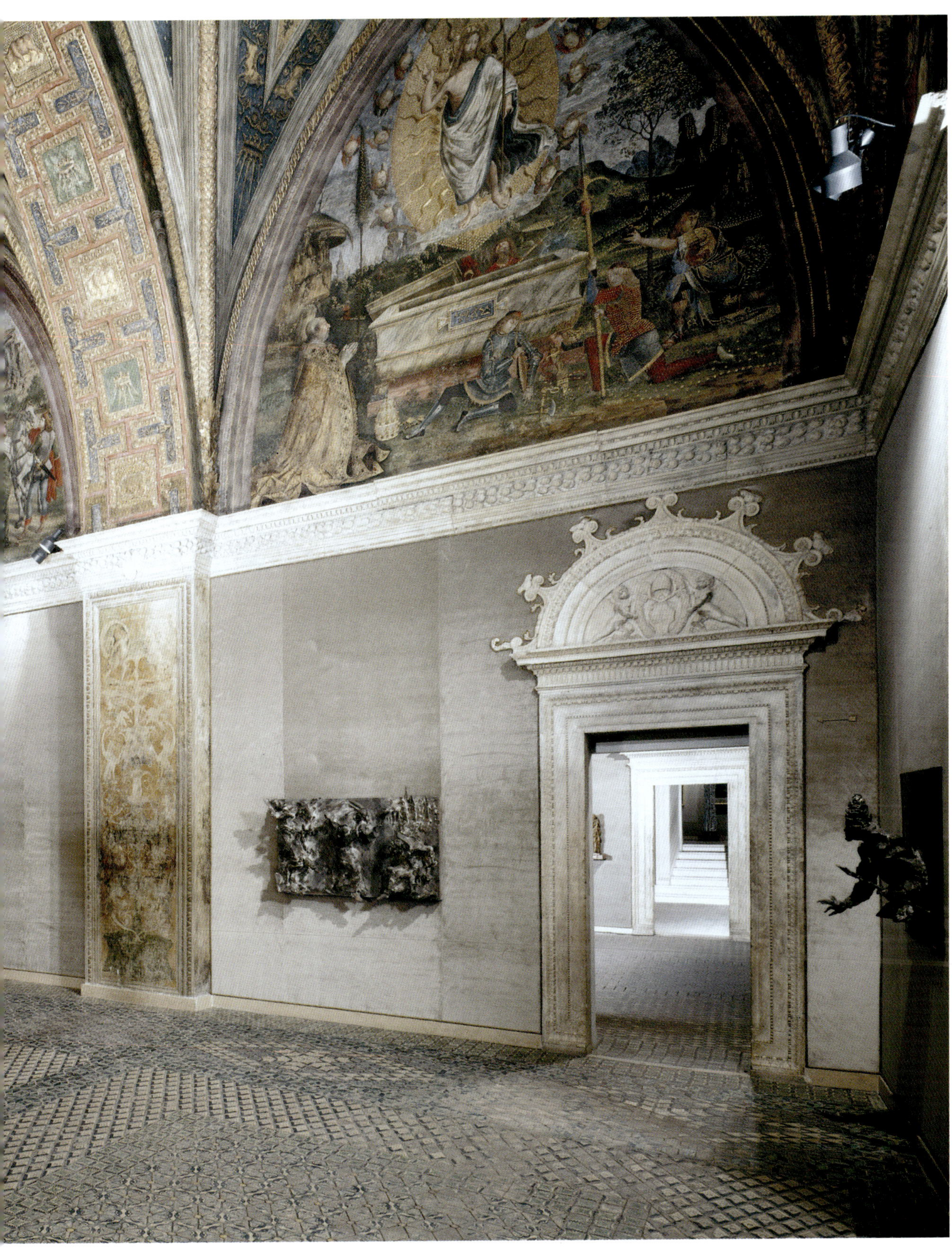

Pinturicchio (Bernardino di Betto), 1454–1513
View of Sala dei Misteri della Fede,
***Borgia Apartments*, 1492–1494**
Fresco
The Room of the Mysteries of the Faith,
Borgia Apartments

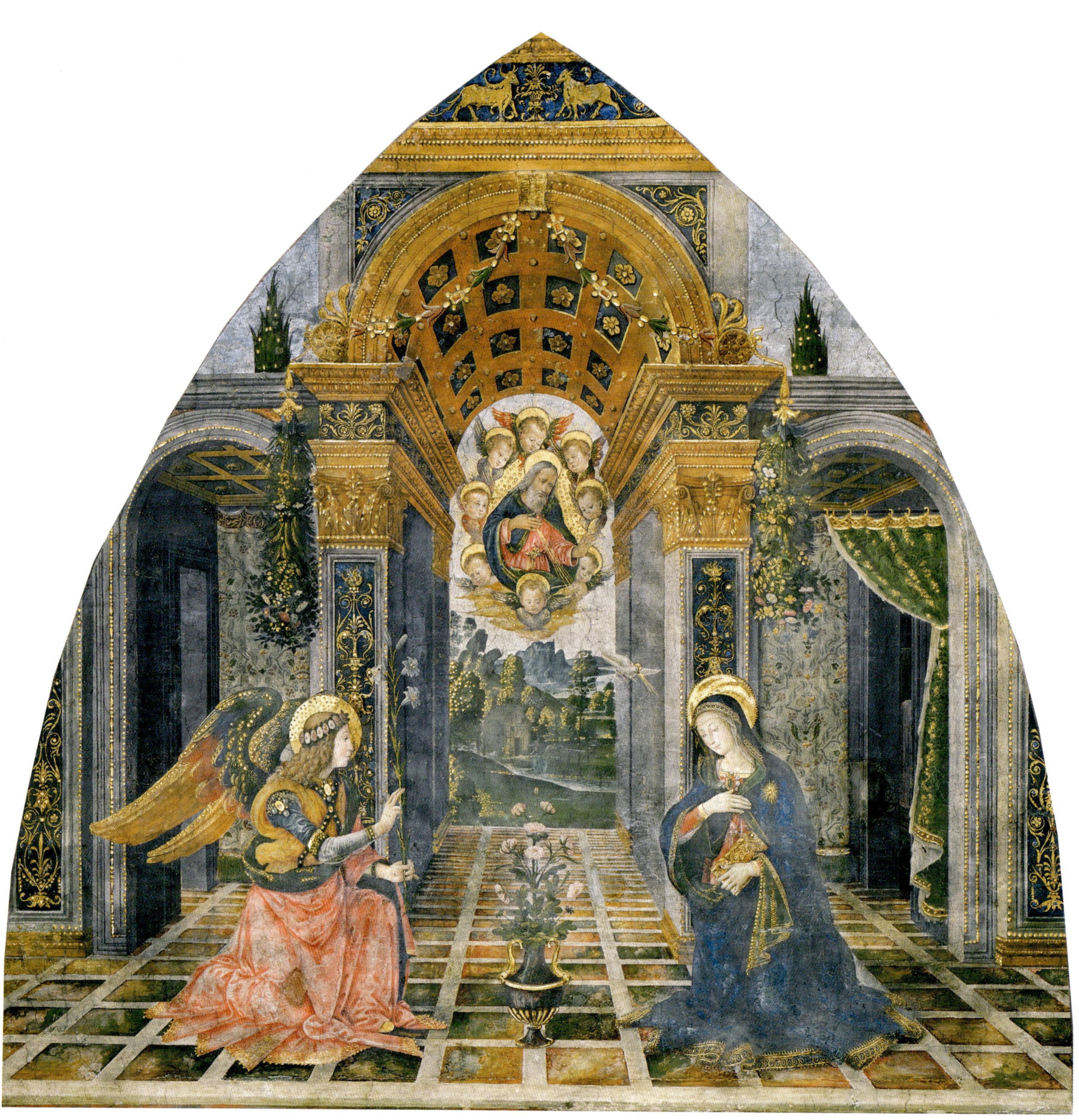

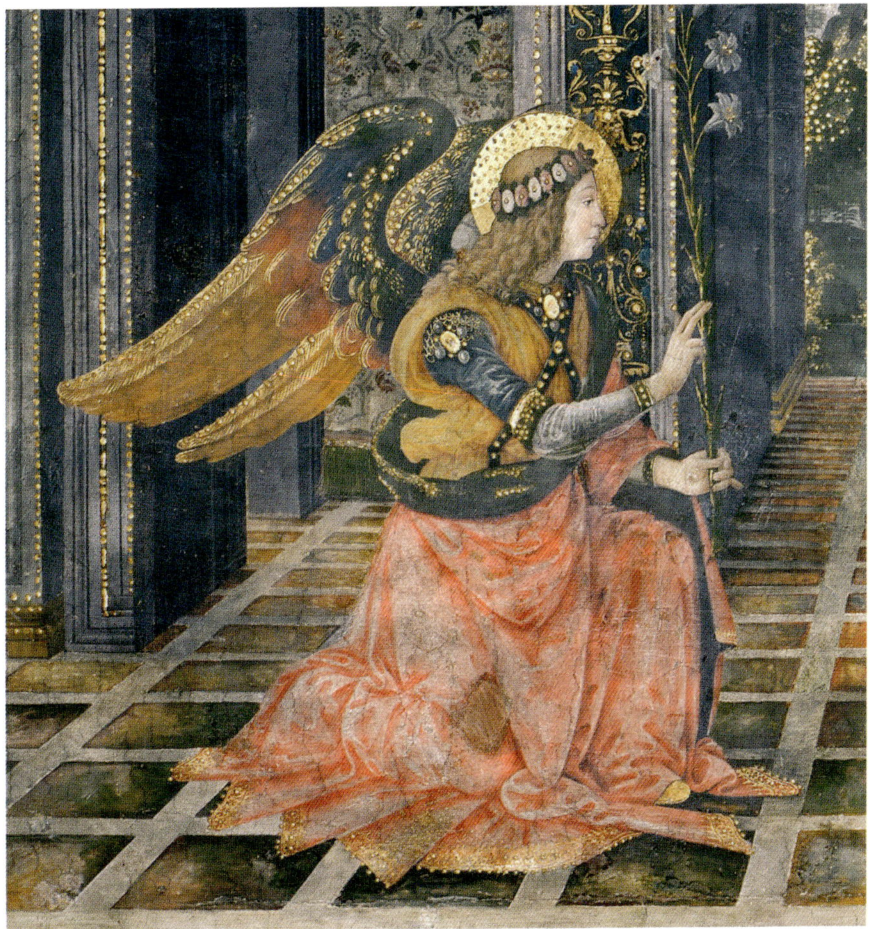

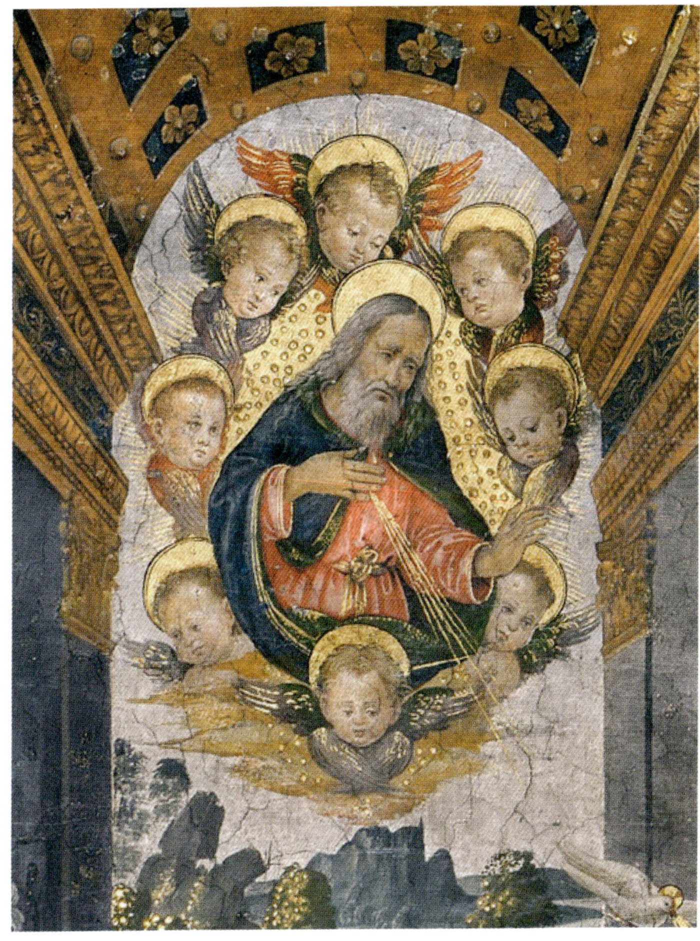

Pinturicchio (Bernardino di Betto)

The Annunciation

The *Annunciation of the Birth of Christ* forms a prelude to the scenes from the life of the Virgin Mary and Jesus. Pinturicchio has located the event, which according to the Gospel of St. Luke occurred in Mary's house, in a palatial Renaissance-style interior closed off at the back by an architectural element resembling a triumphal arch. Through the middle arch, the view opens onto a landscape. The Annunciation itself takes place in the foreground of this rigorously symmetrical fresco. Mary, wearing a blue mantle, kneels on the right and offers a humble gesture of greeting to the angel, who approaches her from the left holding a lily. Between the two, precisely aligned with the central axis, is a tall vase containing a magnificent spray of white thornless roses symbolizing, as does the lily, the purity of the Virgin Mary. Above the vase, at the exact center of the picture and framed by an aureole of angels, hovers God the Father, who sends down the Holy Spirit Dove to Mary, bearing the cross as a symbol of his future role as redeemer. The entablature above the middle arch is decorated with a pair of golden oxen on a blue background. These emblems of the Borgia family frame the papal coat of arms, establishing a clear connection between the Annunciation and Alexander VI.

Pinturicchio (Bernardino di Betto), 1454–1513
***The Annunciation*, 1492–1494**
Fresco
The Room of the Mysteries of the Faith,
Borgia Apartments

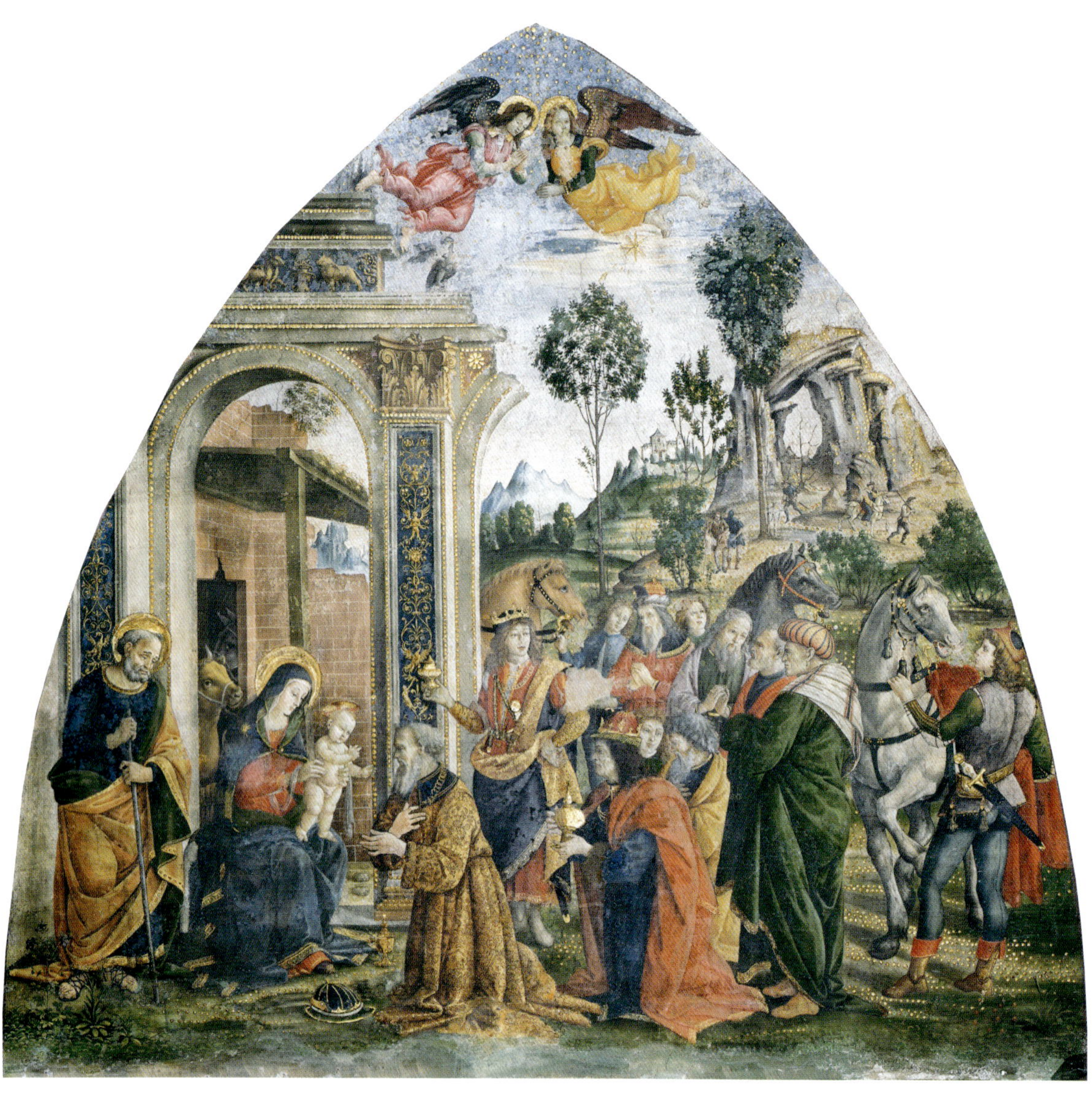

Pinturicchio (Bernardino di Betto)

The Adoration of the Magi

This fresco shows the adoration of the Christ Child by the three kings, who appear outside the Bethlehem stable with their followers. Pinturicchio has depicted the stable as a magnificent antique ruin that divides the picture space into two halves. On the left, Mary, accompanied by her husband Joseph, sits with the Child beneath a tall arcade. In the stable behind them an ox and a donkey can be seen. The eldest king kneels before the Holy Family and is visibly moved as he receives a blessing from the Child. The two younger kings with their precious gifts respectively stand and kneel behind him. The kings' magnificent garments harmonize chromatically with the clothes of the Holy Family, binding the group of figures closer together. Behind the kings, their followers press forward, many pausing to worship the Child. The grooms trying to calm the kings' mounts constitute another anecdotal element. In the background, above the rocky landscape, two angels hover next to the star of Bethlehem. Pinturicchio reveals his love of variety and talent for narrative in his depiction of the different reactions to the miracle in the stable at Bethlehem, and the scene radiates an aura of magnificence characteristic of his style.

Pinturicchio (Bernardino di Betto), 1454–1513
***The Adoration of the Magi*, 1492–1494**
Fresco
The Room of the Mysteries of the Faith,
Borgia Apartments

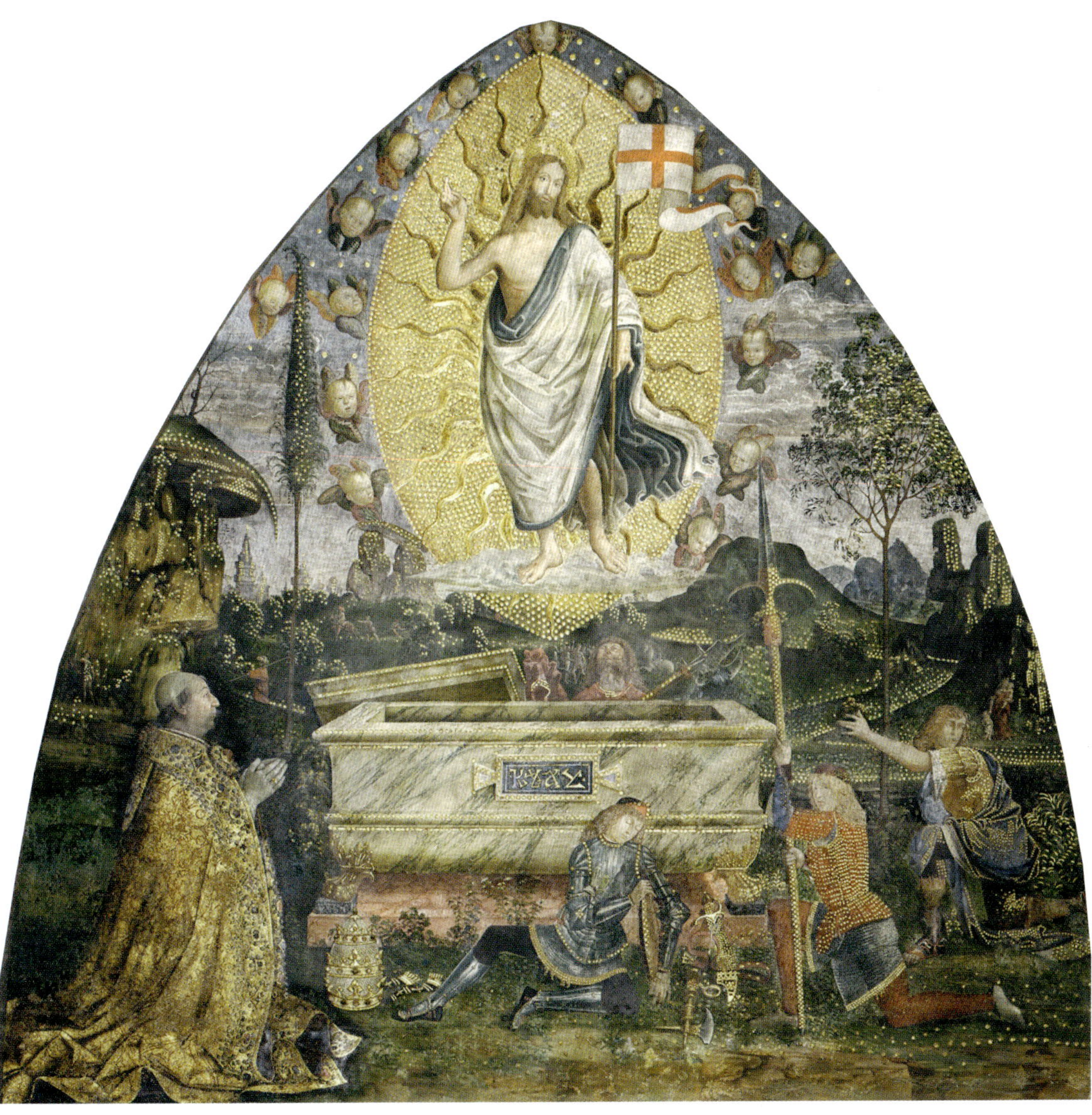

Pinturicchio (Bernardino di Betto)

The Resurrection of Christ

The *Resurrection*, which adorns a transverse wall, is the most famous fresco of the Sala dei Misteri della Fede. Before the eyes of the donor Alexander VI and framed by an aureole of angels, Christ, risen from the dead, floats above his open sarcophagus and its rocky setting. Pope Alexander VI kneels in the left foreground (on Christ's right-hand side), substantially larger than the guards grouped around the tomb. Unlike most of the watchmen and small figures in the landscape behind, the pope seems to be attentively following the miracle of the Resurrection. Alexander VI's golden cope, fastened with a brooch over the breast, links him chromatically with the golden mandorla around Christ. This fresco stands out for its rigorously symmetrical composition, emphasizing the majestic appearance of the resurrected Christ. The overall scene creates an impression of extreme preciousness, heightened further by the rows of gilt stucco studs that Pinturicchio has set into the mandorla and here and there in the landscape. At the same time, his depiction of the marble sarcophagus, the gleaming weapons and armor, and the rocky ledge in the foreground show the painter to be a master of realism.

Pinturicchio (Bernardino di Betto), 1454–1513
***The Resurrection of Christ*, 1492–1494**
Fresco
The Room of the Mysteries of the Faith,
Borgia Apartments

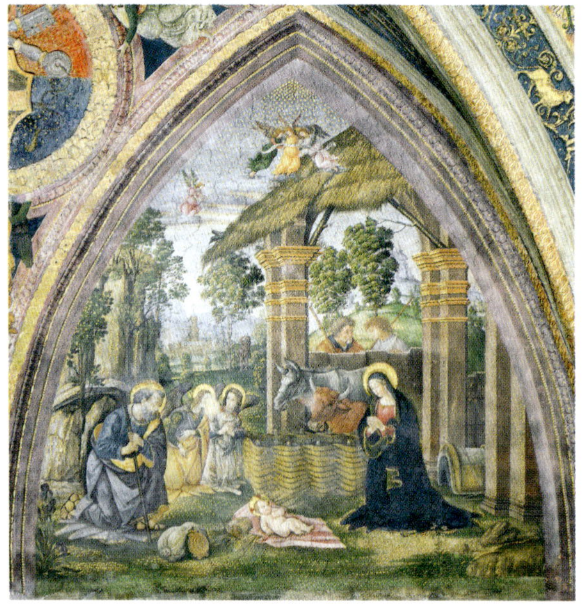

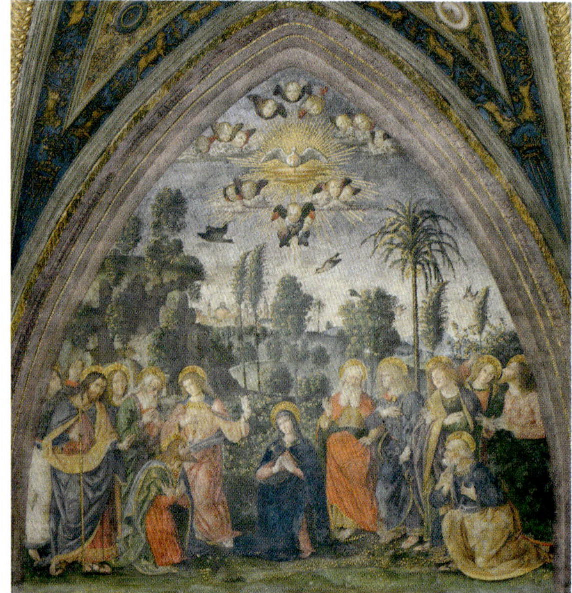

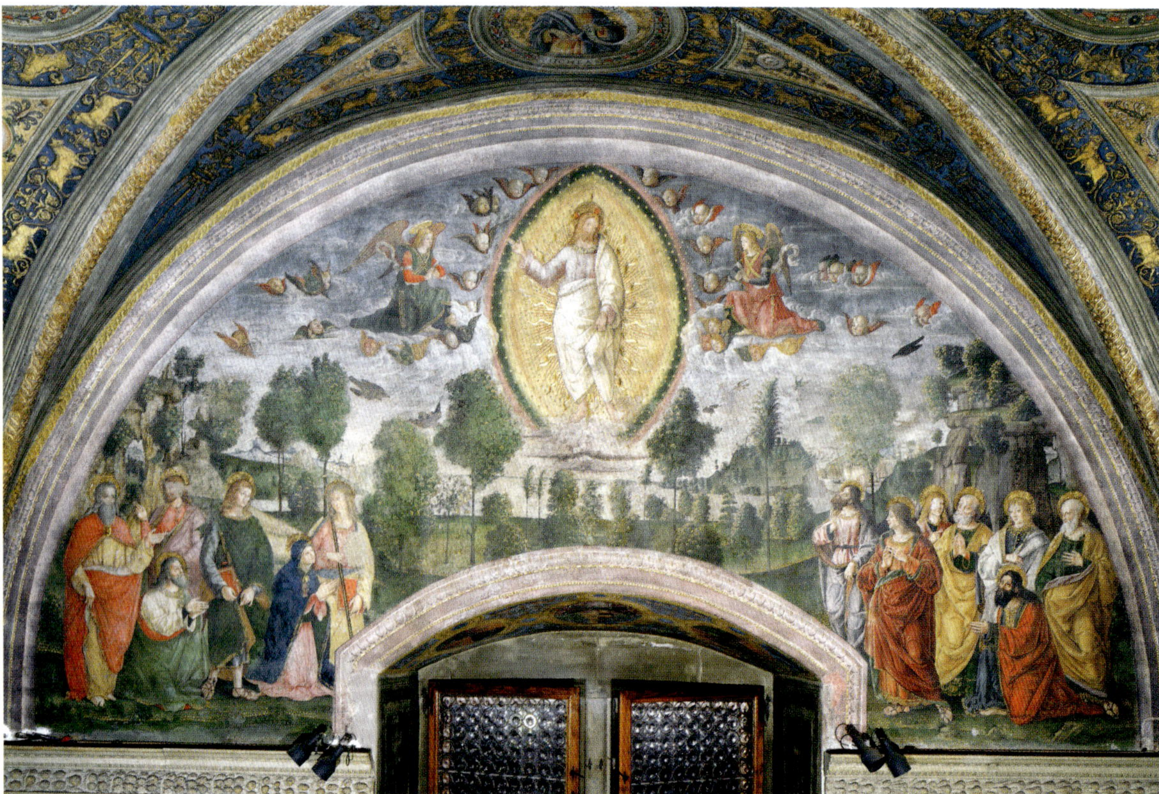

Pinturicchio (Bernardino di Betto), 1454–1513
***Nativity*, 1492–1494**
Fresco
The Room of the Mysteries of the Faith,
Borgia Apartments

Pinturicchio (Bernardino di Betto), 1454–1513
***Descent of the Holy Spirit*, 1492–1494**
Fresco
The Room of the Mysteries of the Faith,
Borgia Apartments

Pinturicchio (Bernardino di Betto), 1454–1513
***Ascension of Christ*, 1492–1494**
Fresco
The Room of the Mysteries of the Faith,
Borgia Apartments

Pinturicchio (Bernardino di Betto), 1454–1513
***Ascension of the Virgin*, 1492–1494**
Fresco
The Room of the Mysteries of the Faith,
Borgia Apartments

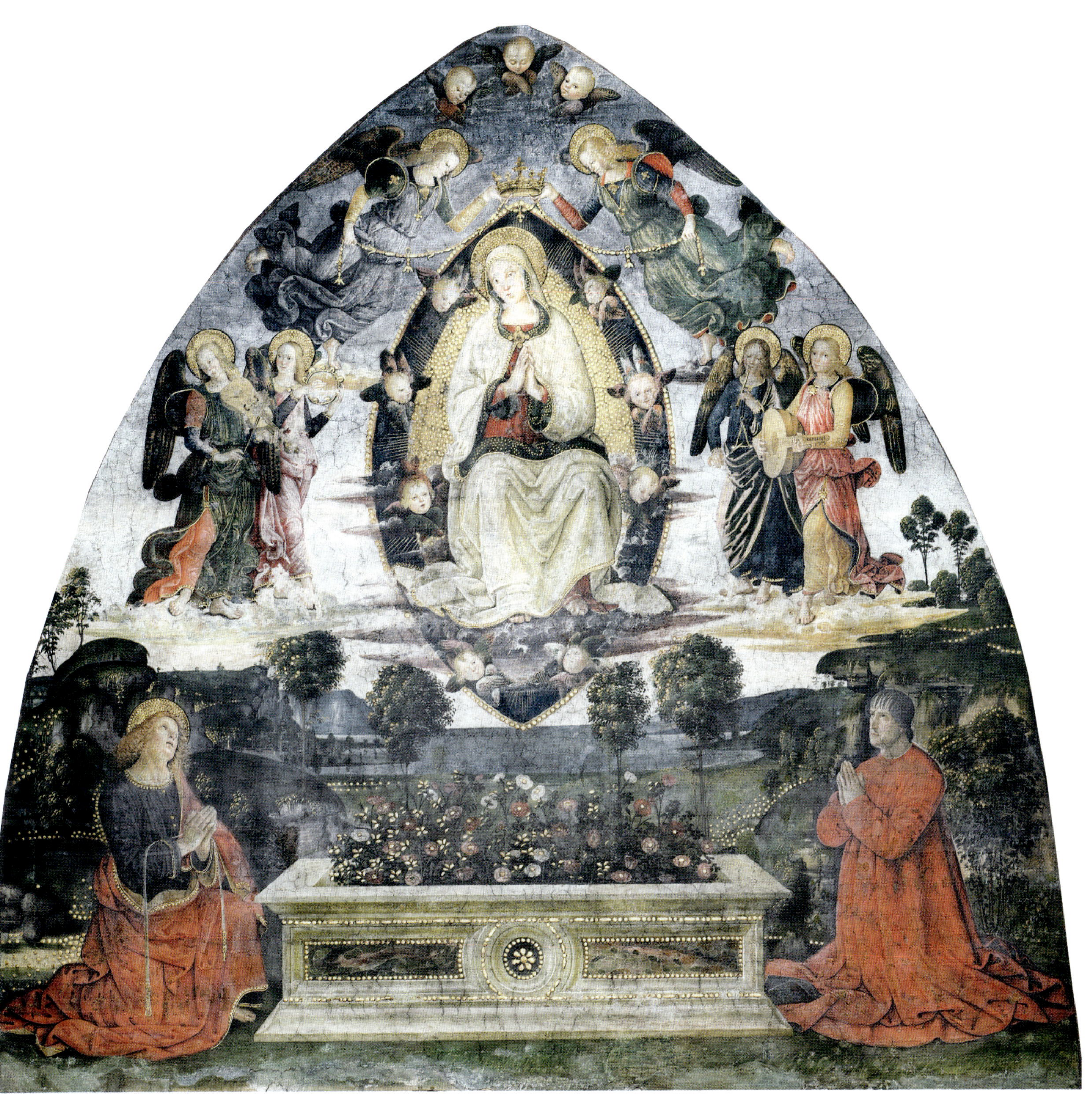

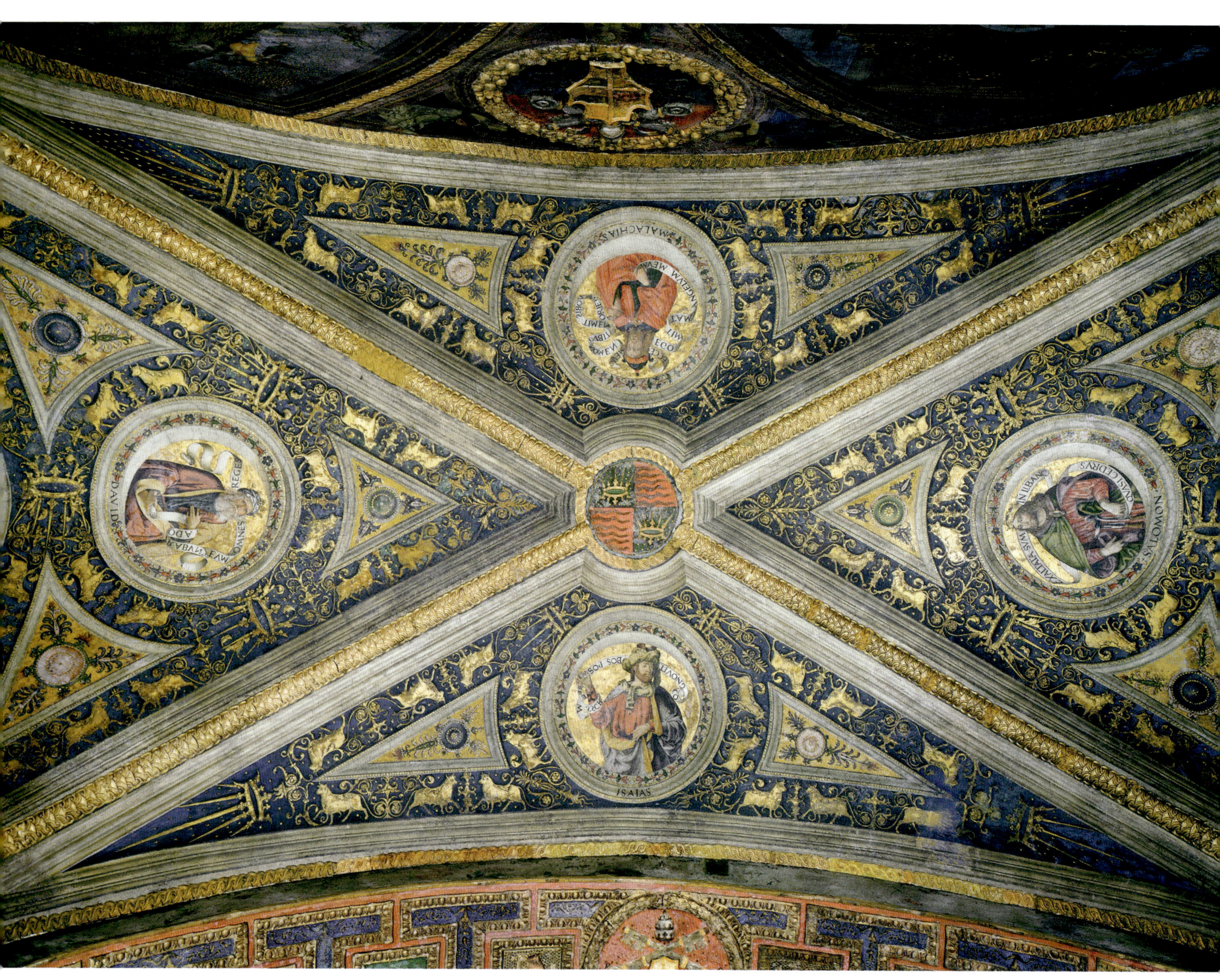
ISAIAS

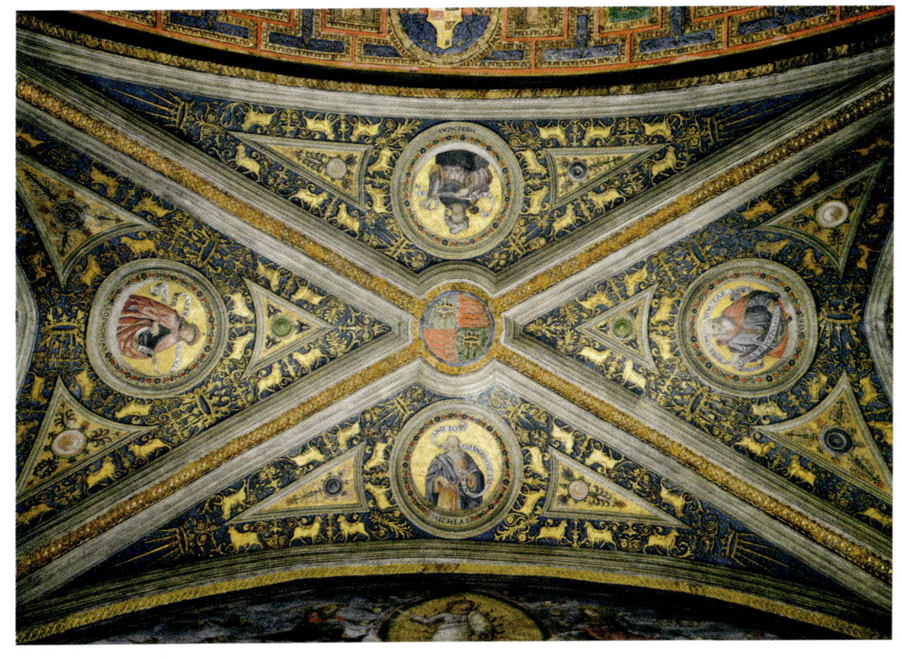

Pinturicchio (Bernardino di Betto)

The Ceiling of the Room of Faith

The walls of the Room of Faith are surmounted by two double-barrel vaults whose pictorial program is closely linked to the episodes from the life of Jesus and the Virgin Mary depicted in the lunettes. The medallions containing images of the saints are set against a blue background decorated with golden oxen, the emblem of the Borgia family. The rear vault contains the kings David and Solomon and prophets Isaiah and Malachi, portrayed as men of dignity dressed in long robes. The banners they hold are inscribed with verses from their books that relate to the pictures in the lunettes. The *Adoration of the Magi*, for example, has been allocated the medallion of the aged David, on whose banner are the words: "All kings shall fall down before him" (Psalms 72:11). Opposite David, above the *Ascension of Christ*, is his son Solomon as a young king. Isaiah occupies the vault compartment in the central arch not allocated to any specific lunette, his turban lending him an Oriental air. His banner bears the inscription: "The ox knoweth his owner" (Isaiah 1:3), which normally alludes to the ox present at the birth of Christ. In this case, however, it refers to the emblem of the Borgias and therefore to Alexander VI, who is clearly positioning himself as a disciple of Christ.

Pinturicchio (Bernardino di Betto), 1454–1513
***The Ceiling of the Room of Faith*, 1492–1494**
Fresco
The Room of the Mysteries of the Faith,
Borgia Apartments

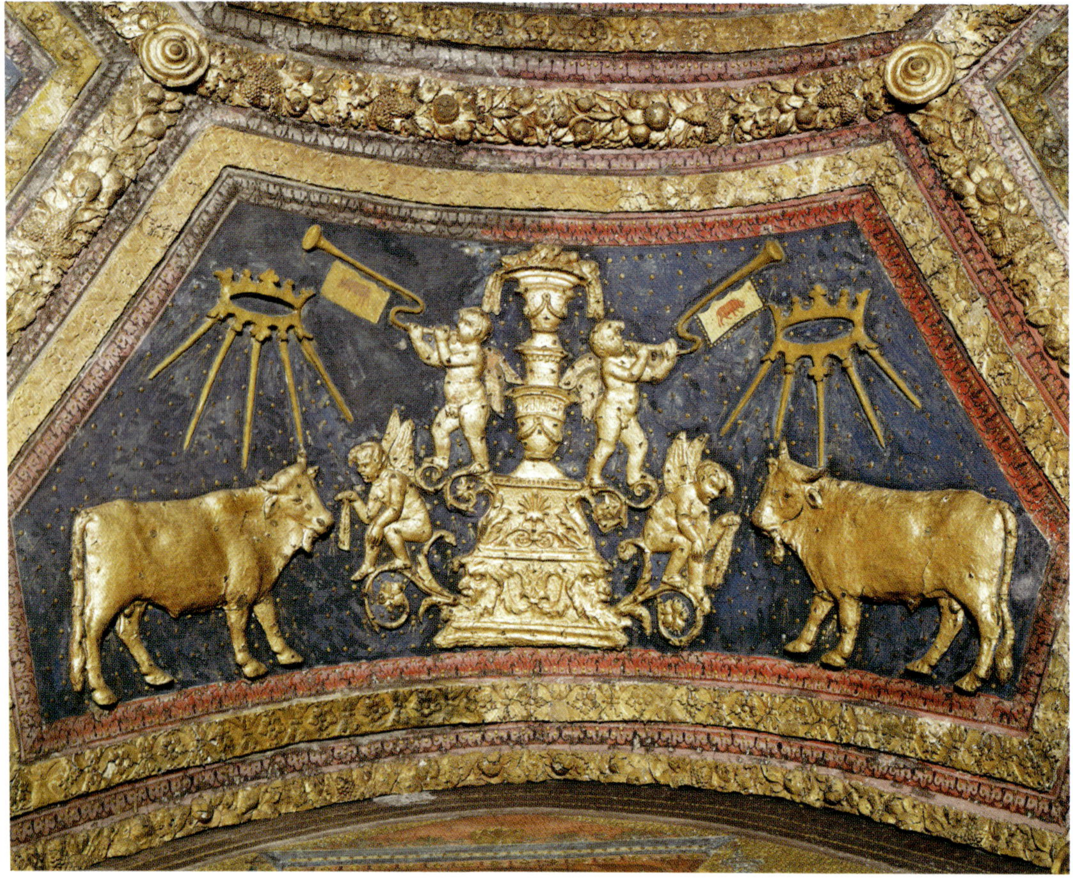

Pinturicchio (Bernardino di Betto), 1454–1513
***Emblem of the Borgia Family (ceiling detail)*, 1492–1494**
Fresco
The Room of the Mysteries of the Faith,
Borgia Apartments

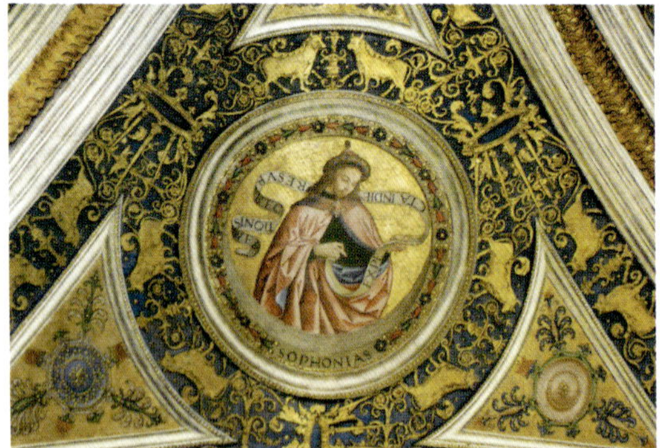

Pinturicchio (Bernardino di Betto), 1454–1513
***Medallion with the Prophet Sofonia (ceiling detail)*, 1492–1494**
Fresco
The Room of the Mysteries of the Faith,
Borgia Apartments

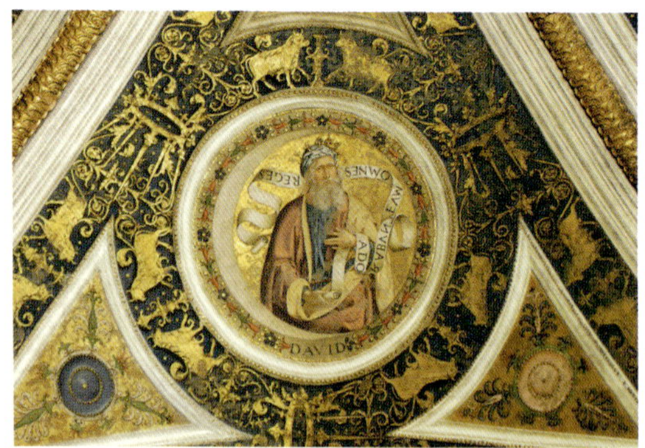

Pinturicchio (Bernardino di Betto), 1454–1513
***Medallion with the King David (ceiling detail)*, 1492–1494**
Fresco
The Room of the Mysteries of the Faith,
Borgia Apartments

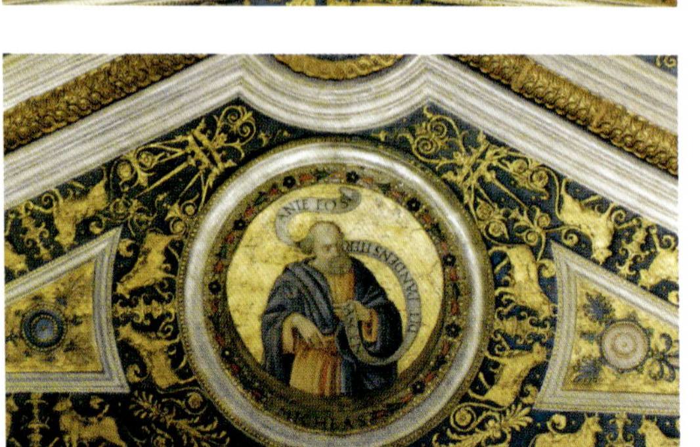

Pinturicchio (Bernardino di Betto), 1454–1513
***Medallion with the Prophet Micah (ceiling detail)*, 1492–1494**
Fresco
The Room of the Mysteries of the Faith,
Borgia Apartments

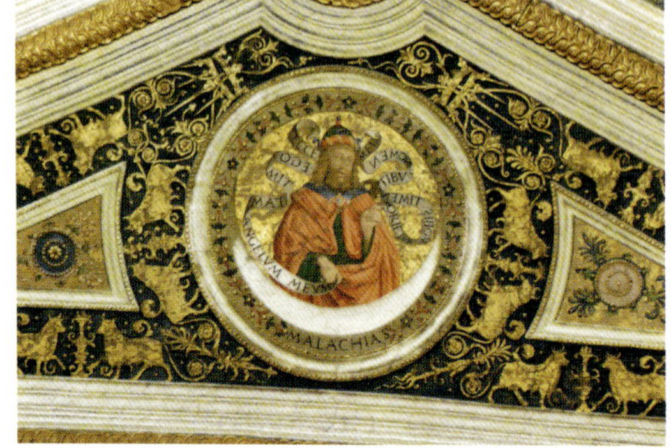

Pinturicchio (Bernardino di Betto), 1454–1513
***Medallion with the Prophet Malachi (ceiling detail)*, 1492–1494**
Fresco
The Room of the Mysteries of the Faith,
Borgia Apartments

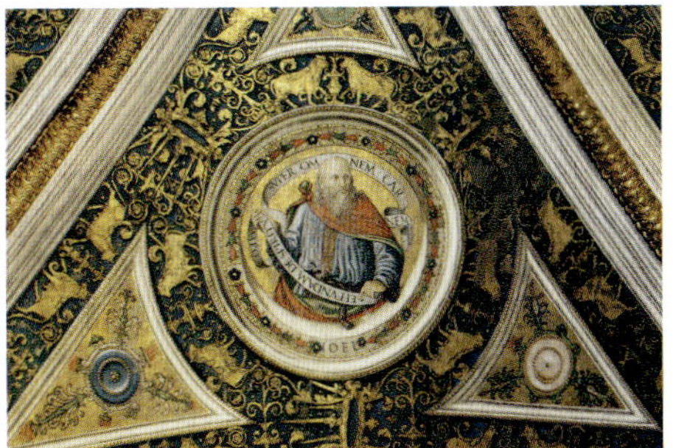

Pinturicchio (Bernardino di Betto), 1454–1513
***Medallion with the Prophet Joel (ceiling detail),* 1492–1494**
Fresco
The Room of the Mysteries of the Faith,
Borgia Apartments

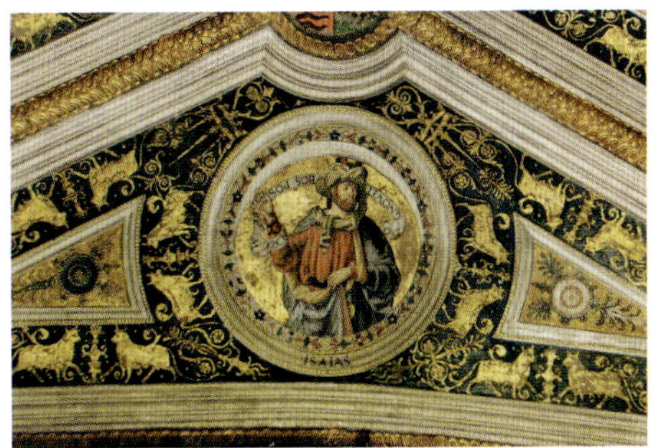

Pinturicchio (Bernardino di Betto), 1454–1513
***Medallion with Prophet Isaiah (ceiling detail),* 1492–1494**
Fresco
The Room of the Mysteries of the Faith,
Borgia Apartments

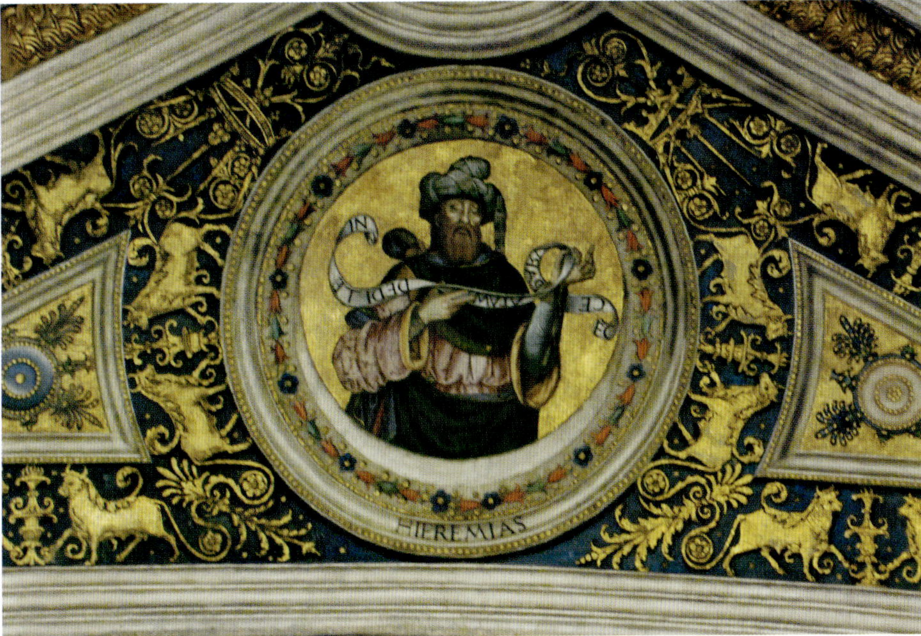

Pinturicchio (Bernardino di Betto), 1454–1513
***Medallion with Prophet Jeremiah (ceiling detail),* 1492–1494**
Fresco
The Room of the Mysteries of the Faith,
Borgia Apartments

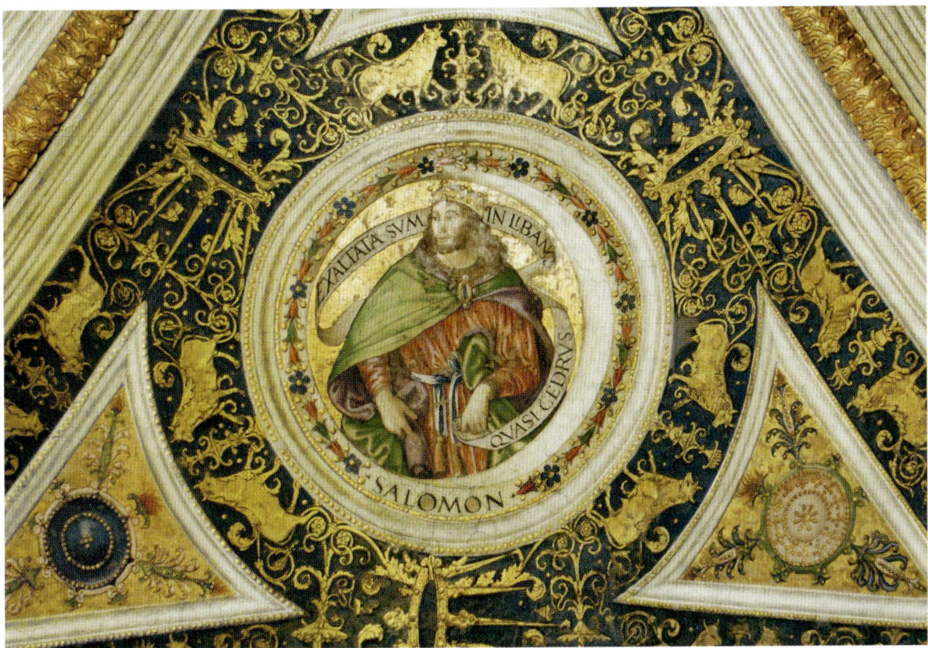

Pinturicchio (Bernardino di Betto), 1454–1513
***Medallion with the King Solomon (ceiling detail),* 1492–1494**
Fresco
The Room of the Mysteries of the Faith,
Borgia Apartments

THE ROOM OF SAINTS

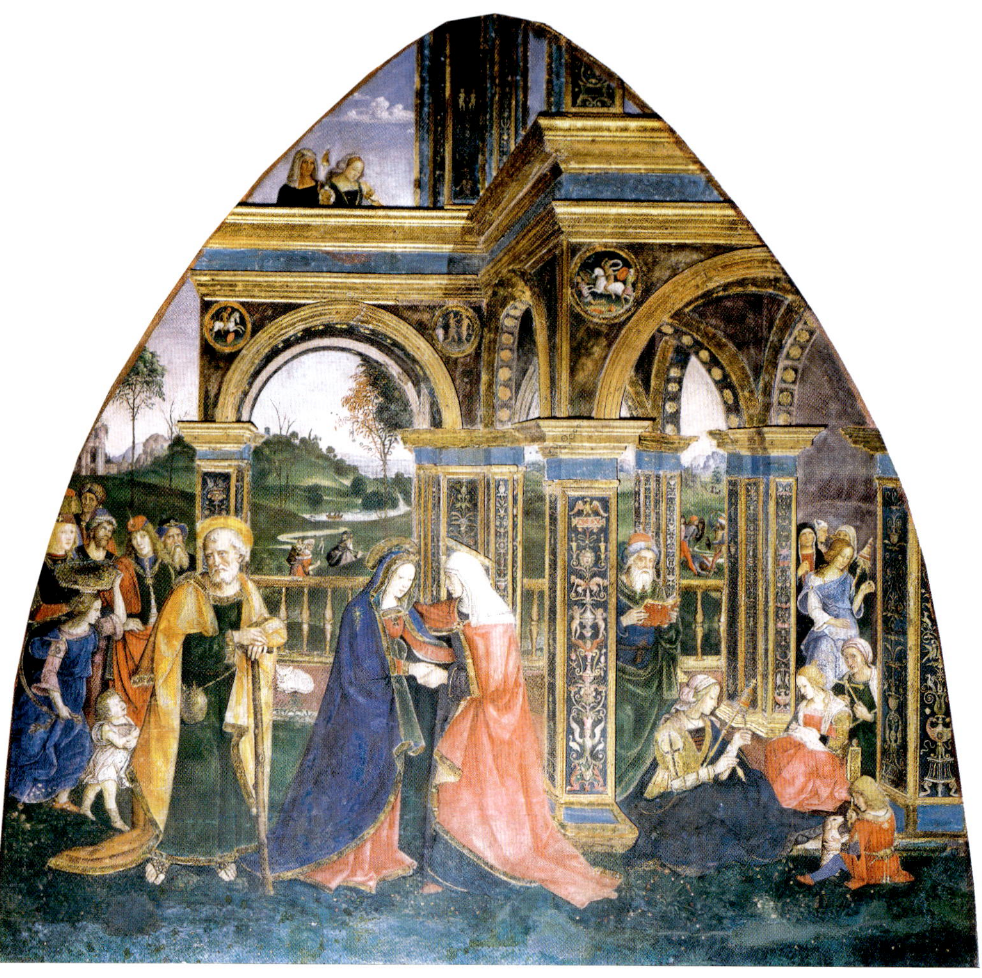

Pinturicchio (Bernardino di Betto)

The Visitation

In the story of Christ's birth, the Annunciation is followed by the Visitation. According to the Gospel of St. Luke (Luke 1:39–45), the Virgin visits her relative Elizabeth, who is pregnant with John the Baptist, full of joy about carrying Jesus. When the two women greet each other, Elizabeth realizes that Mary is carrying the future Redeemer and praises her relative and the fruit of her womb. Pinturicchio has set the meeting of the two holy women before a loggia-like Renaissance-style palace. Because Elizabeth is the main saint within the context of the Sala dei Santi, she occupies the middle axis while Mary, wearing the blue mantle of the Queen of Heaven, stands before her on the left. The Virgin is accompanied by Joseph, who waits for her with a detached air, leaning on his staff. Elizabeth's husband, Joachim, is the elderly man reading a book under the arcade on the right. Pinturicchio has populated the meeting of the cousins with numerous additional figures, who are observing from the background, doing handicrafts such as spinning and embroidery, or, in the case of the young boy in the right foreground, playing with a dog. Elizabeth's significance lies in her early recognition of Jesus as the Redeemer, which no doubt explains her unusual selection as one of the saints in this cycle.

Pinturicchio (Bernardino di Betto), 1454–1513
***The Visitation*, 1492–1494**
Fresco
The Room of Saints, Borgia Apartments

Pinturicchio (Bernardino di Betto)

The Martyrdom of St. Sebastian

In the lunette fresco of the Martyrdom of St. Sebastian, the saint stands more or less at the center of the picture chained to a plinth that is part of the ruins of a house. Behind him extends a deep landscape. This fresco is located above a window onto the courtyard, which accounts for its unusual composition. The saint's body has been pierced by arrows fired by the six archers distributed on each side of the window. Each archer is shown at a different stage of shooting or preparing his shot, revealing great versatility of the part of Pinturicchio. On the far right kneels a man in a splendid gold brocade coat and a tall red cap who gives the soldiers orders to shoot. The precise moment depicted here is the climax of St. Sebastian's martyrdom, as indicated by the appearance of an angel in the sky. The fresco shows Pinturicchio's interest in antique art, as the saint's contrapposto or off-balance stance and body, clad only in a loincloth, demonstrate the artist's knowledge of classical proportions. In addition, both the building fragments in the foreground and the two buildings in the background—the Colosseum and what may be a free portrait of the church of San Sebastiano in Rome—reference antique architecture.

Pinturicchio (Bernardino di Betto), 1454–1513
***The Martyrdom of St. Sebastian*, 1492–1494**
Fresco
The Room of Saints, Borgia Apartments

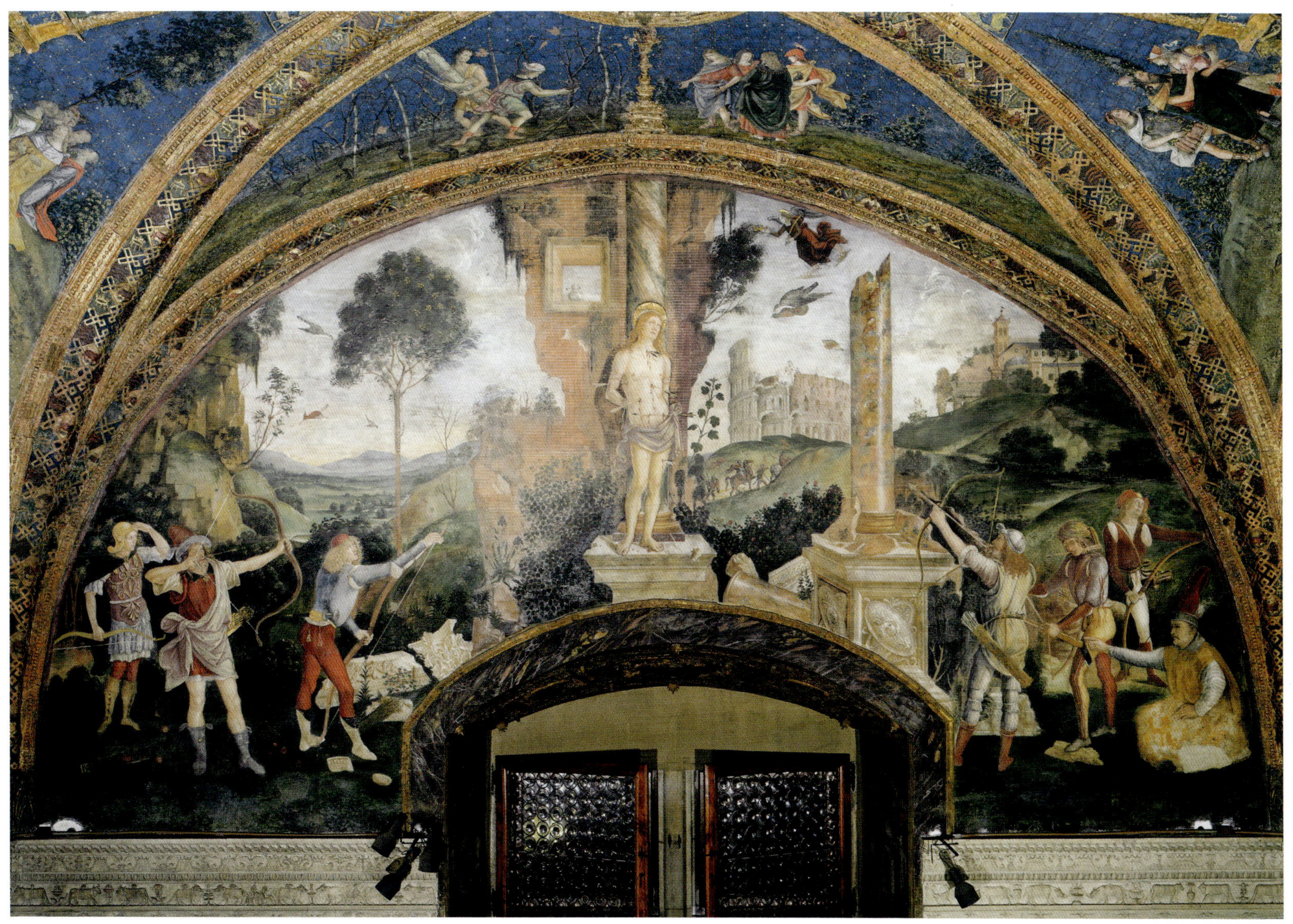

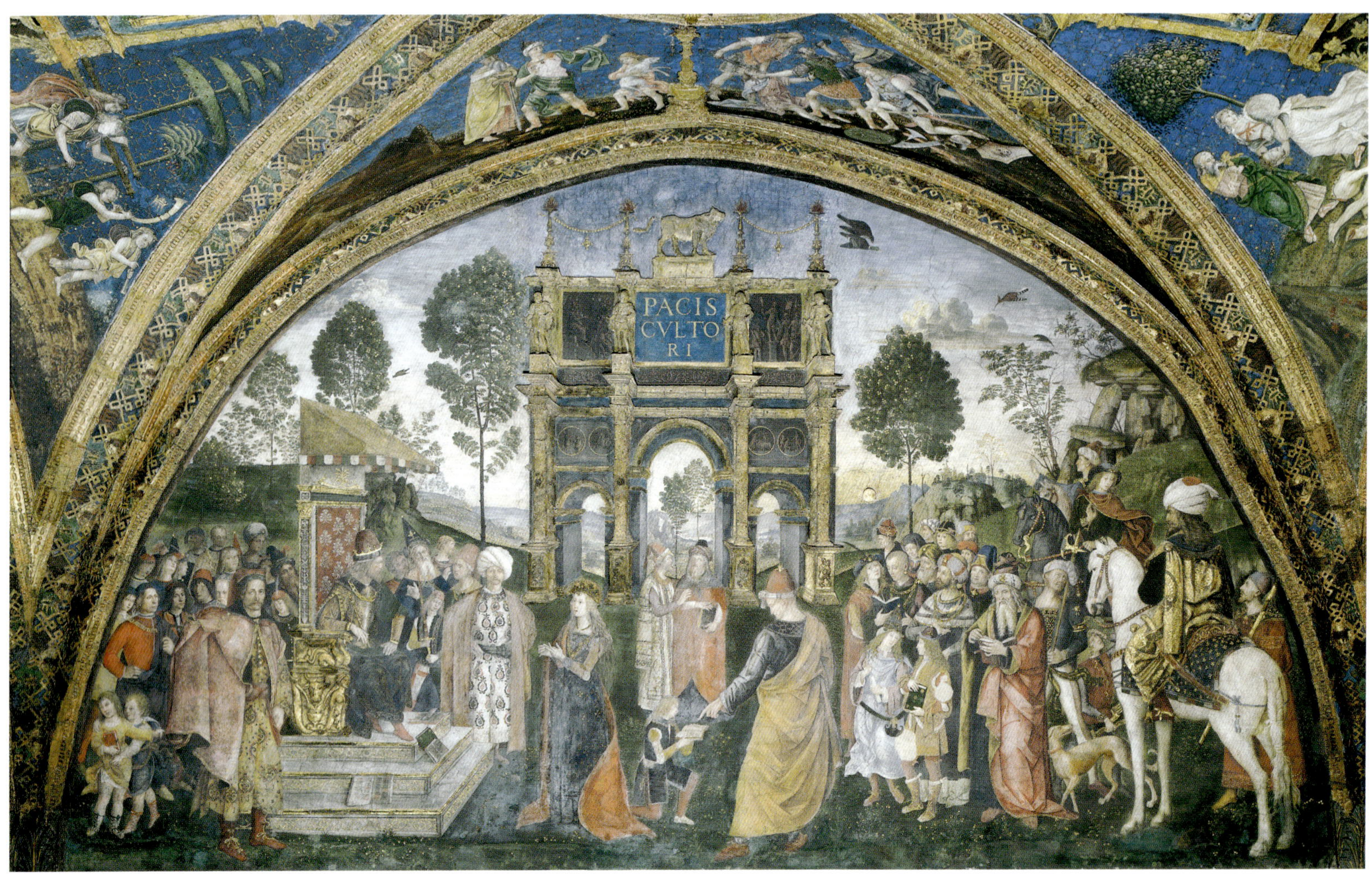

Pinturicchio (Bernardino di Betto)

The Dispute of St. Catherine

This fresco depicts the dispute of St. Catherine of Alexandria, in which the king's erudite daughter tested her knowledge against the philosophers of the Roman emperor Maxentius (reigned 306–312 AD). The *Golden Legend* describes how Catherine refused to renounce her Christian faith and was sentenced by the emperor to die a martyr's death. Following the account in the *Legend*, Pinturicchio has depicted her as a beautiful virgin who fearlessly pits herself against the emperor, his scholars, and the court. This wide painting is divided into two halves linked by a triumphal arch reminiscent of the Arch of Constantine in Rome, but inscribed with the words "Pacis Cultori" ("Guardian of the Peace"), the motto of Alexander VI, and crowned by an ox, the emblem of the Borgia family. To the left is the enthroned Maxentius and his court, while the right-hand side is taken up by the philosophers, who are shown disputing with Catherine. Pinturicchio brought his great love of variety to his depiction of the different characters, their attitudes, and the inexhaustibly inventive folds of their brightly colored garments. A number of especially lifelike figures are thought to be portraits of important officials and nuncios at the papal court.

Pinturicchio (Bernardino di Betto), 1454–1513
***The Dispute of St. Catherine*, 1492–1494**
Fresco
The Room of Saints, Borgia Apartments

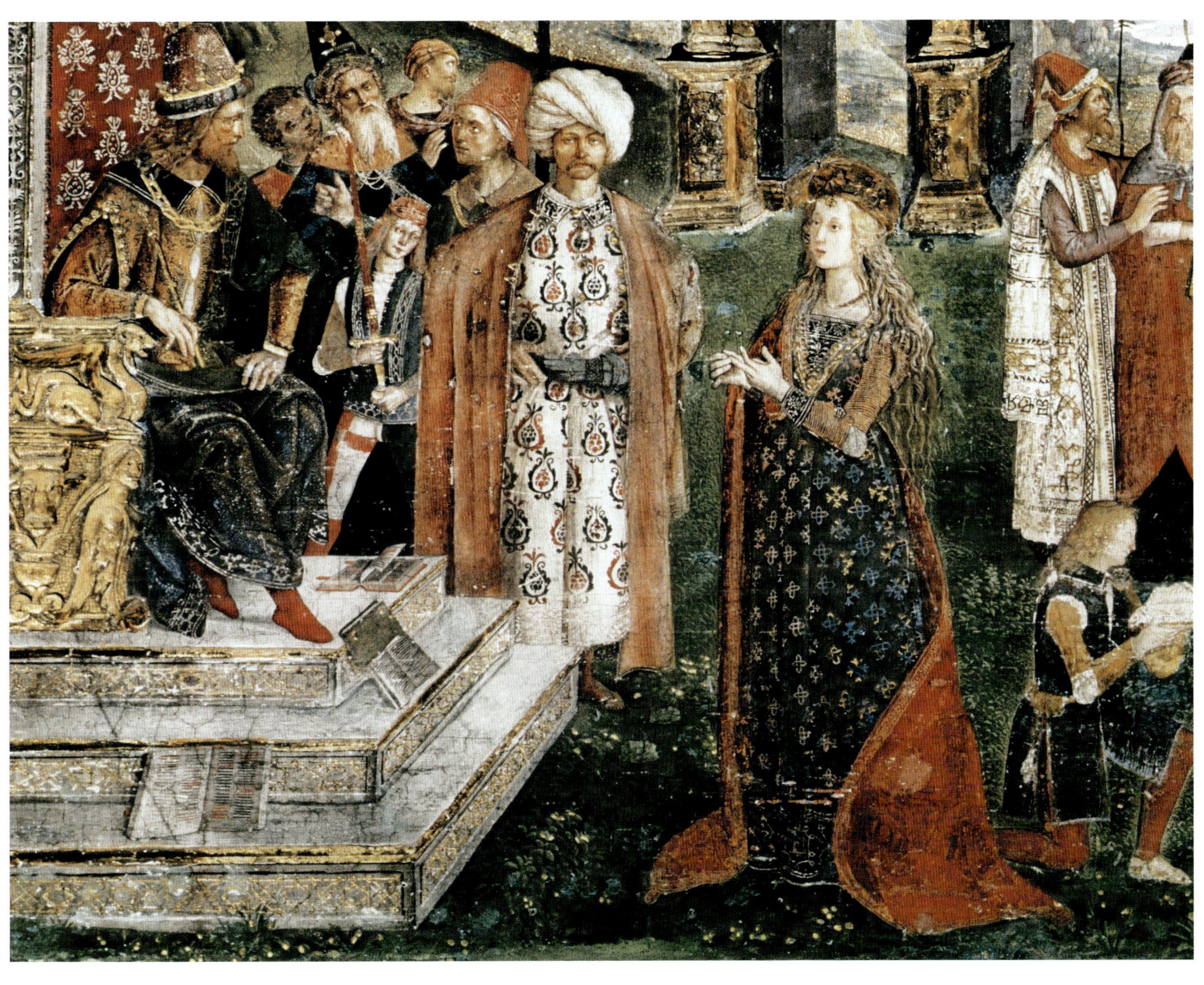

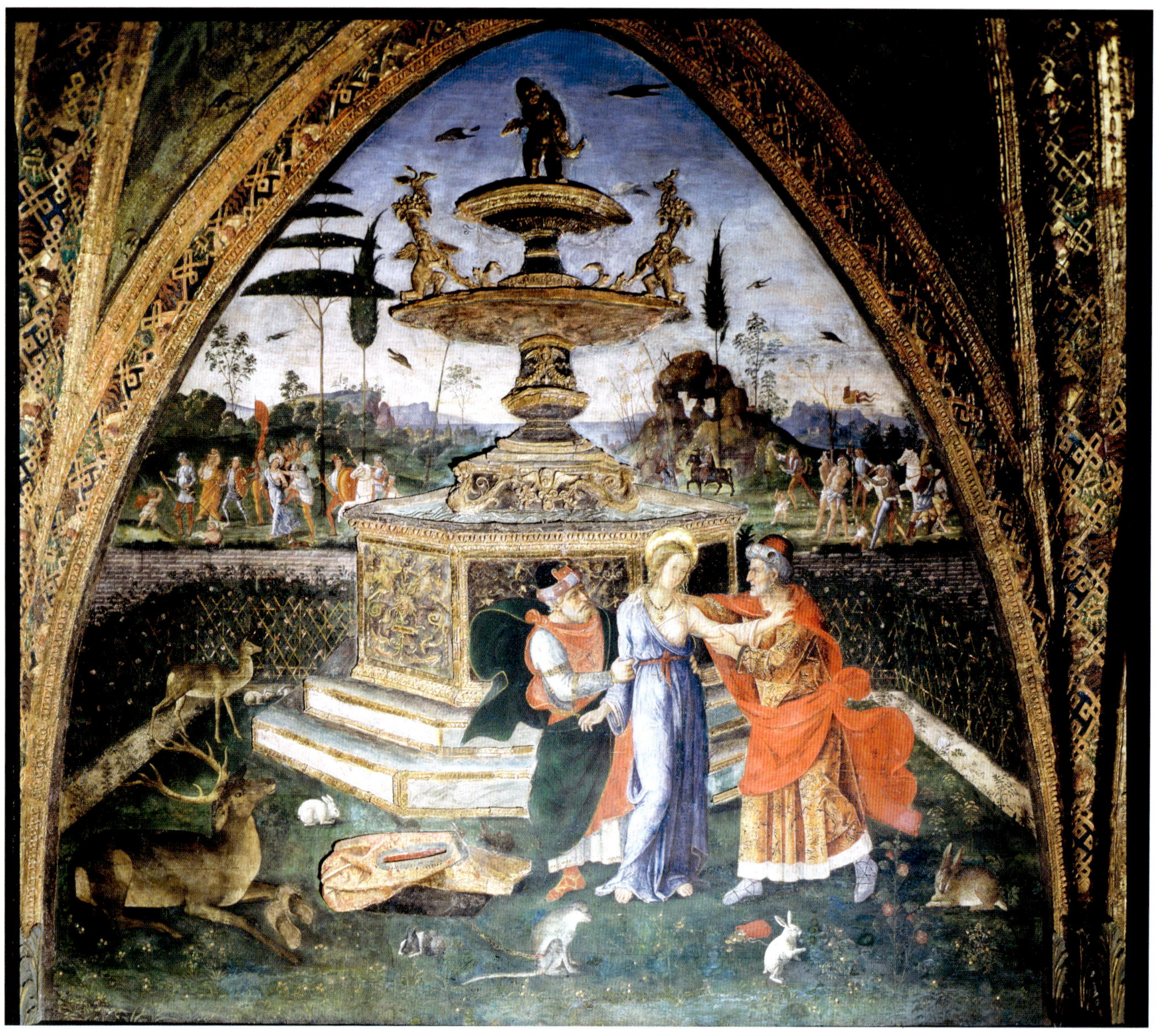

Pinturicchio (Bernardino di Betto)

Susanna and the Elders

The only Old Testament scene Pinturicchio included in the Sala dei Santi's cycle is *Susanna and the Elders*. This episode, also known as *Susanna at her Bath*, depicts two elderly judges accosting the beautiful wife of Joachim while she is bathing and attempting to violate her, before she is saved by young Daniel. Pinturicchio has positioned the action in the foreground, in front of an impressive fountain (standing in for the bath) that is richly decorated in the Renaissance style. The fountain stands in the middle of a grassy basin that is reminiscent of the Garden of Eden. The fauna—a hare, a monkey, a stag, and a roe deer—can be understood as symbols of carnality and chastity. The two old men have grasped hold of the struggling Susanna from either side and are trying to disrobe her. In the background, two later scenes from the story of Susanna are unfolding. On the left, the saint wrongly accused of adultery by the two old men is surrounded by a crowd intent on stoning her. On the right, justice is done as the old men are in turn stoned for their misdeed and subsequent slander.

Pinturicchio (Bernardino di Betto), 1454–1513
***Susanna and the Elders*, 1492–1494**
Fresco
The Room of Saints, Borgia Apartments

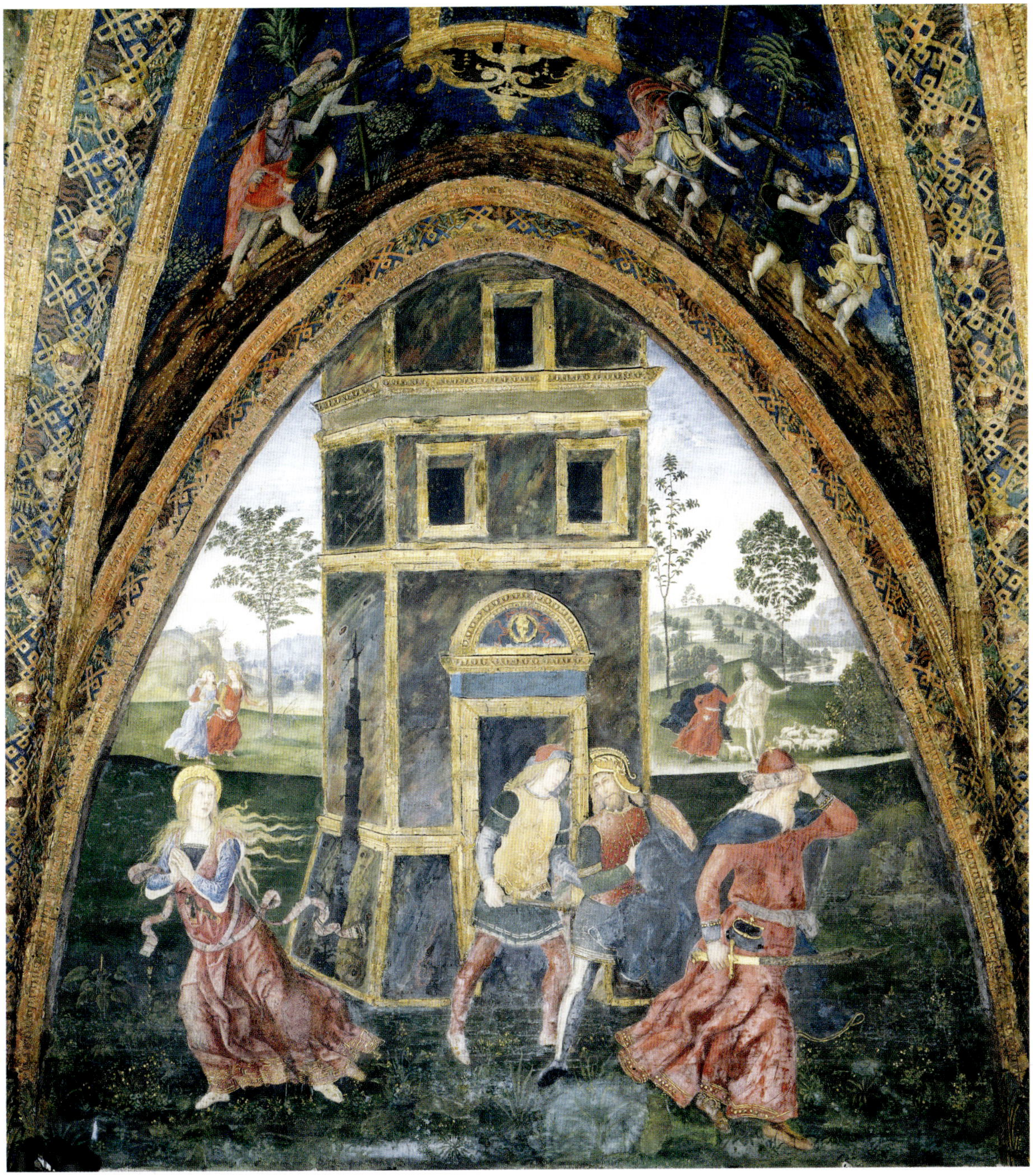

Pinturicchio (Bernardino di Betto), 1454–1513
***The Martyrdom of St. Barbara*, 1492–1494**
Fresco
The Room of Saints, Borgia Apartments

Pinturicchio (Bernardino di Betto), 1454–1513
***Sts. Anthony Abbot and Paul the Hermit*,**
1492–1494
Fresco
The Room of Saints, Borgia Apartments

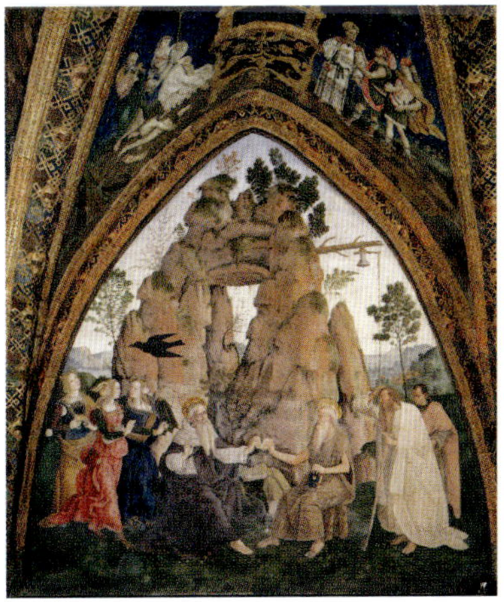

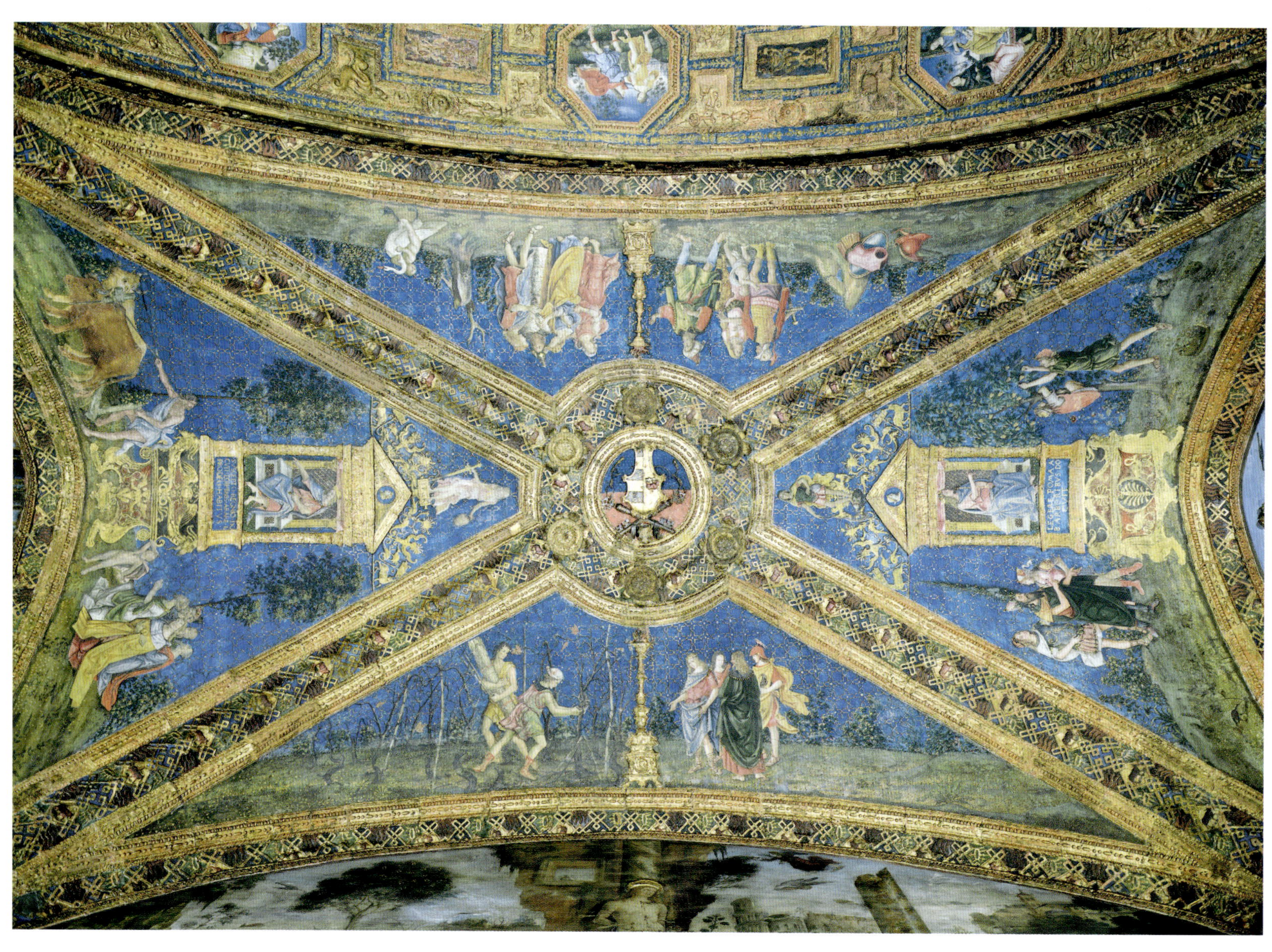

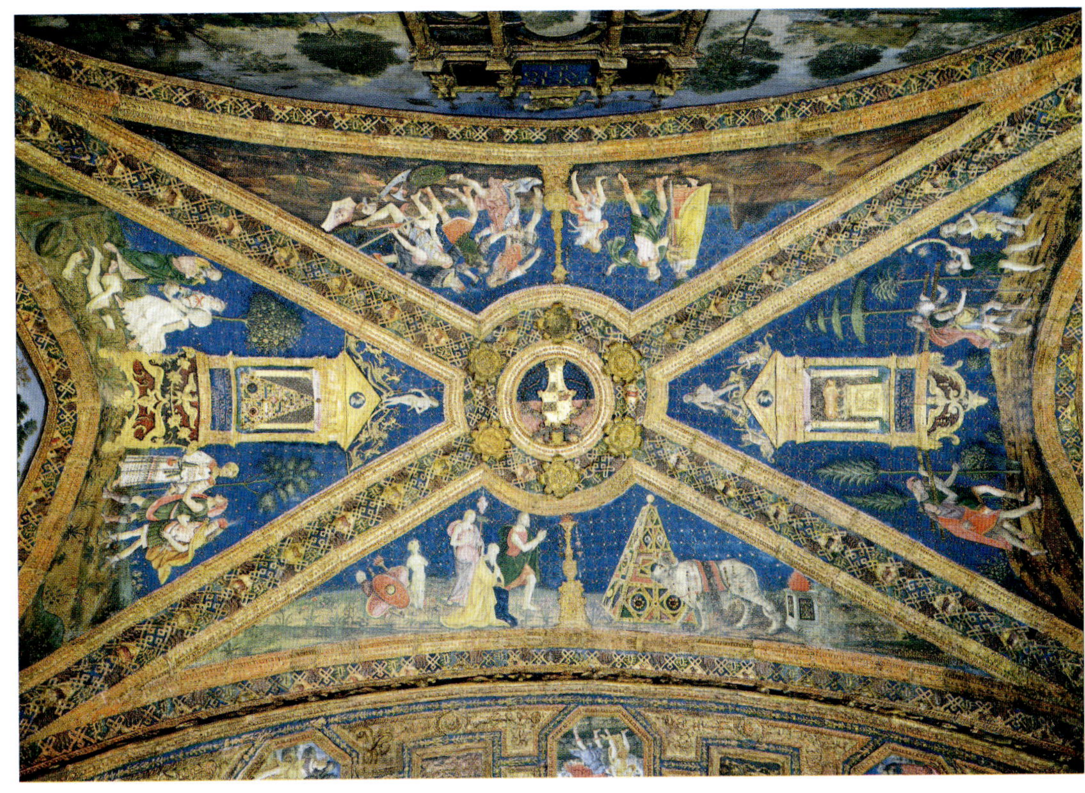

Pinturicchio (Bernardino di Betto)

The Ceiling of the Room of Saints

It may seem astonishing that in the apartment of the pope, Christ's representative on earth, and moreover in a room dedicated to the lives of the saints, a number of whom sacrificed their lives in the fight against paganism, the ceiling is decorated with episodes from classical mythology. The vault above the entrance features scenes from the legend of Isis and Osiris, with depictions of the Old Testament heroes David and Judith with the head of Holofernes in the narrower side compartments. An explanation for this unusual choice of decoration lies in its connection to Alexander VI, as the Borgia family, whose animal emblem was the ox, traced its origins back to the Egyptian king Osiris and his consort Isis. The transverse arch depicts the story of Isis as Io, whom Zeus transformed into a cow, and the ceiling compartment above the window goes on to show Io, now transformed back into a beautiful woman, assuming her place on the throne as the Egyptian queen Isis. The opposite ceiling compartment shows a high priest marrying Isis and Osiris. Despite the fact that the legend takes place in ancient Egypt, Pinturicchio depicts the figures in fifteenth-century dress.

Pinturicchio (Bernardino di Betto), 1454–1513
***The Ceiling of the Room of Saints*, 1492–1494**
Fresco
The Room of Saints, Borgia Apartments

THE ROOM OF LIBERAL ARTS

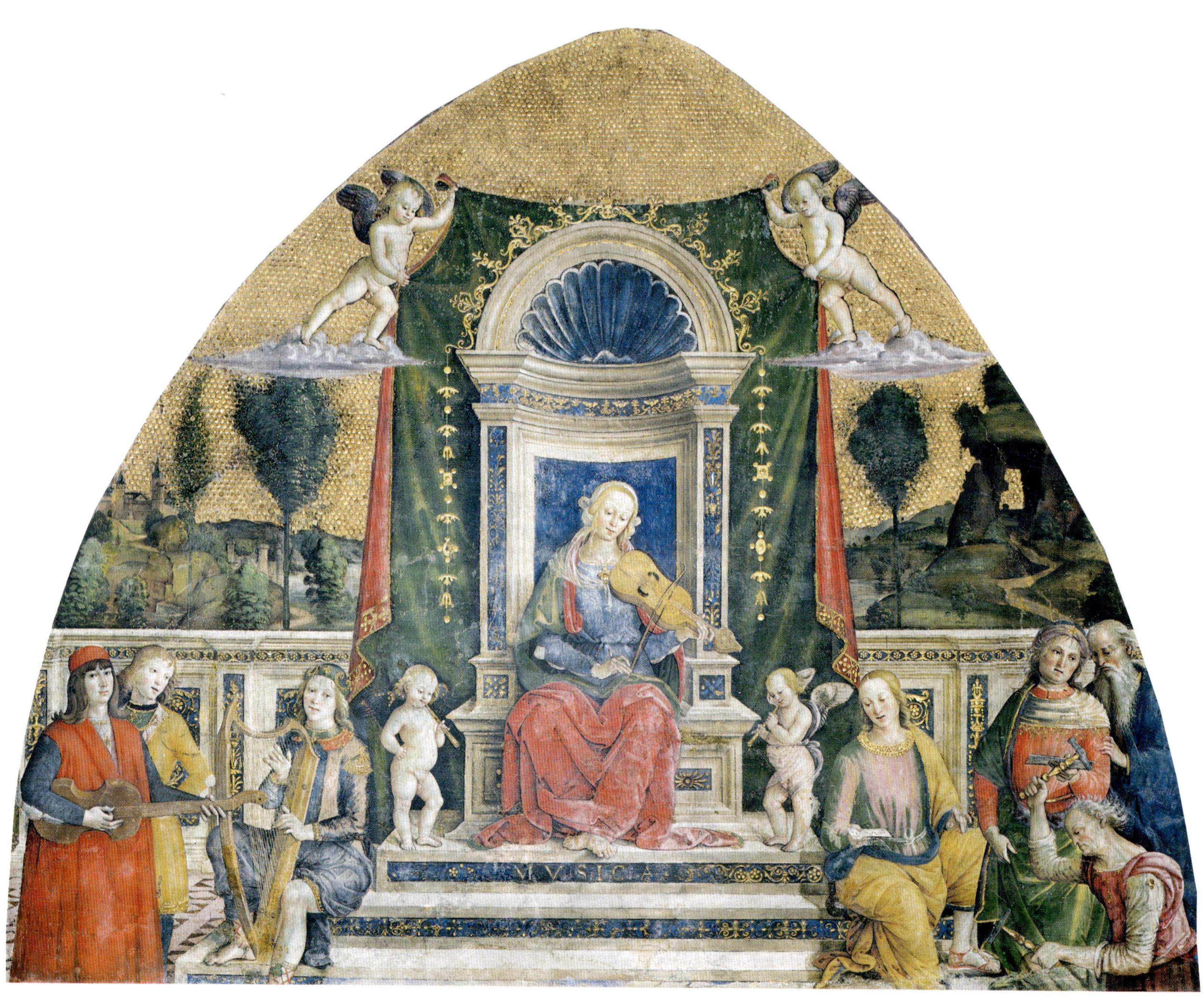

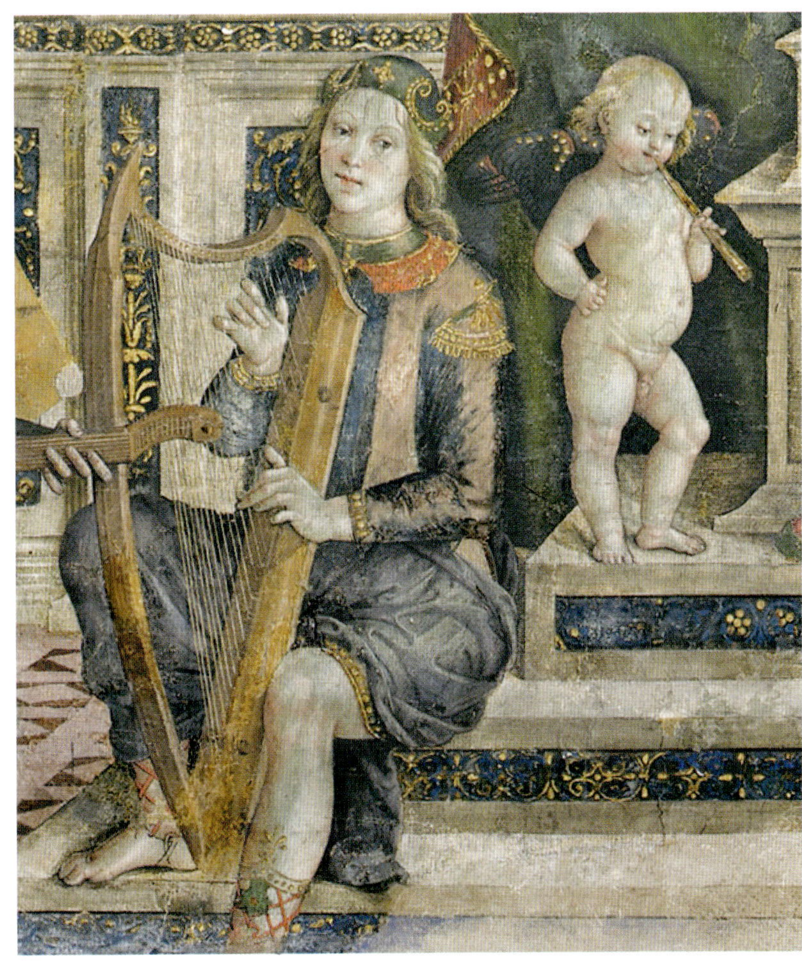

Pinturicchio (Bernardino di Betto)

Music

Pinturicchio (Bernardino di Betto), 1454–1513
Music, 1492–1494
Fresco
The Room of Liberal Arts, Borgia Apartments

Music had a special place among the seven liberal arts cultivated during late antiquity. Although by and large a performing art, due to the mathematical basis underlying the key system and principles of composition, it was once regarded as a science. Pinturicchio has personified music as a beautiful blonde woman on a raised marble throne surmounted by a shell niche and set against a green cloth of honor held up by two angels. She is playing a violin (*viola da braccio*) and is surrounded by men, women, and putti (child-angels) with musical instruments. The viewer is given the impression of standing in front of a small orchestra. The two putti play flutes and a harpist sits on the left while a singer is on the right, seated on the steps of the throne. The youth dressed in red in the left foreground is playing a guitar while one of the men on the right is availing himself of an anvil and hammers. This figure has been identified with the Old Testament progenitors of music, Tubal-Cain and Jubal, who represent the mythical association of music and the blacksmith's craft. A landscape with a lake extends into the background, surmounted by a sky punctuated with gilt stucco studs that lend the entire scene a celestial luster.

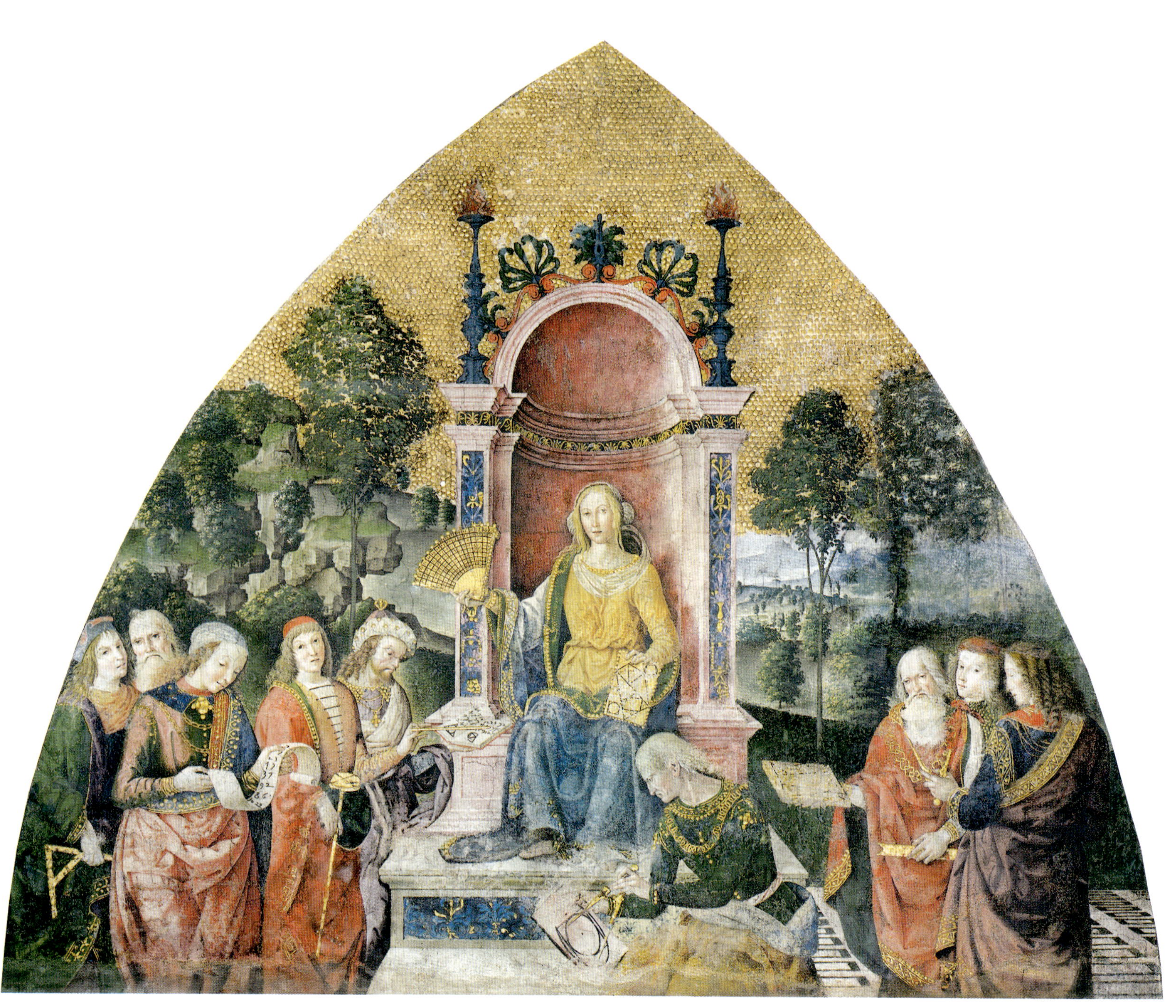

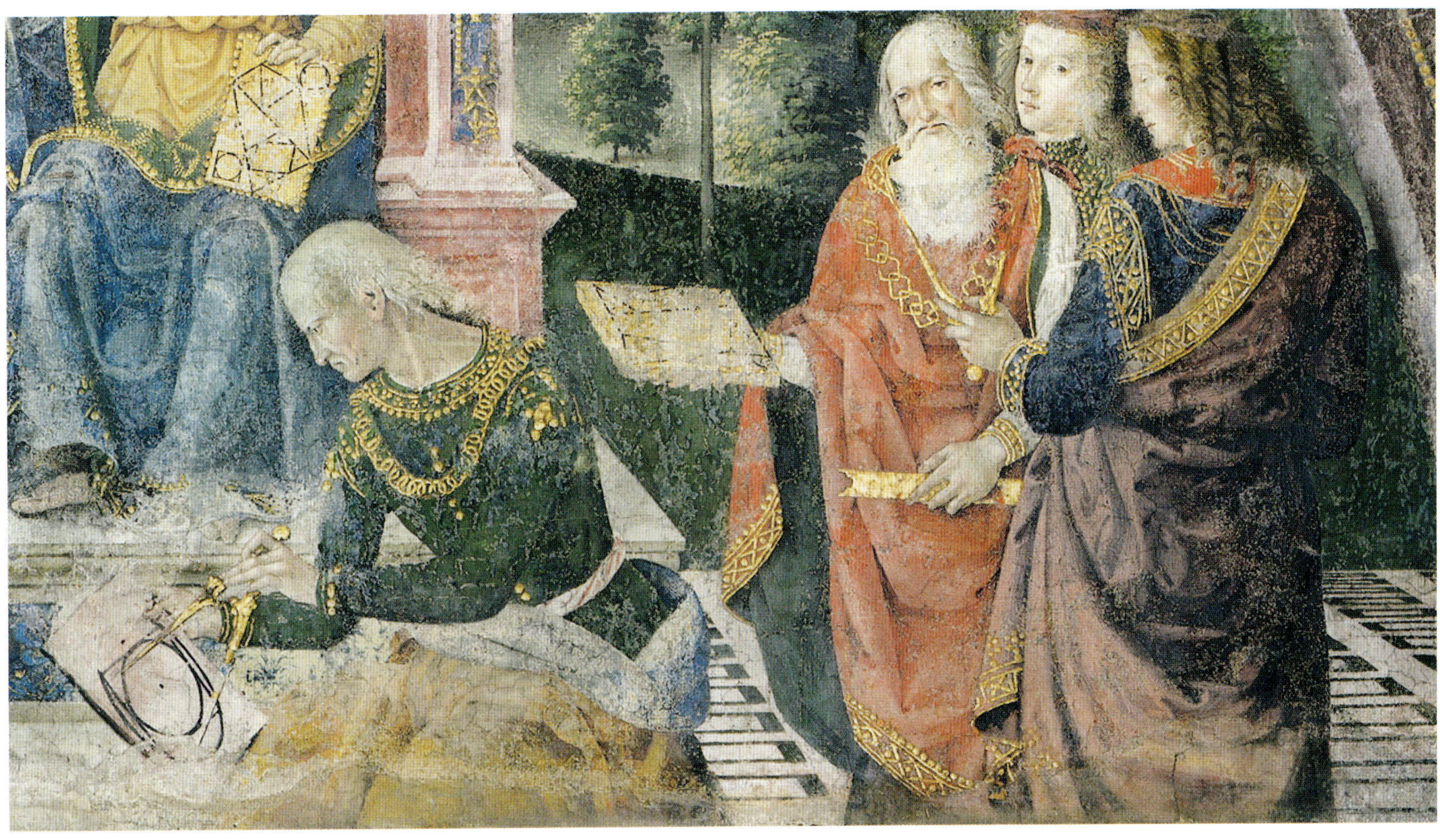

Pinturicchio (Bernardino di Betto)

Geometry

Within the seven liberal arts, geometry was classified as one of the four mathematical arts that make up the *quadrivium*. The object of this discipline was the calculation of points, lines, planes, and bodies, and their relationships with one another. Accordingly, Pinturicchio has given his personification of geometry an instrument for measuring angles and a chart of geometric shapes. Dressed magnificently in gold and blue, she is seated at the center of the picture on a high throne of red marble that is surmounted by torches and a voluted leaf decoration and set in front of a landscape. Scholars of different ages gather around the throne, holding measuring instruments or notes of geometric calculations. Some think that the elderly man in a green and gold tunic, who sits on the steps of the throne drawing circles on a piece of paper with a set of compasses, may be Euclid (ca. 320–270 BC), the father of geometry, who was much admired during the Renaissance. Like those of the other scholars, his clothes are a mixture of the contemporary and the antique. The rich gold braid combines with the studs of gilt stucco that form the sky to lend the painting an air of great resplendence.

Pinturicchio (Bernardino di Betto), 1454–1513
***Geometry*, 1492–1494**
Fresco
The Room of Liberal Arts, Borgia Apartments

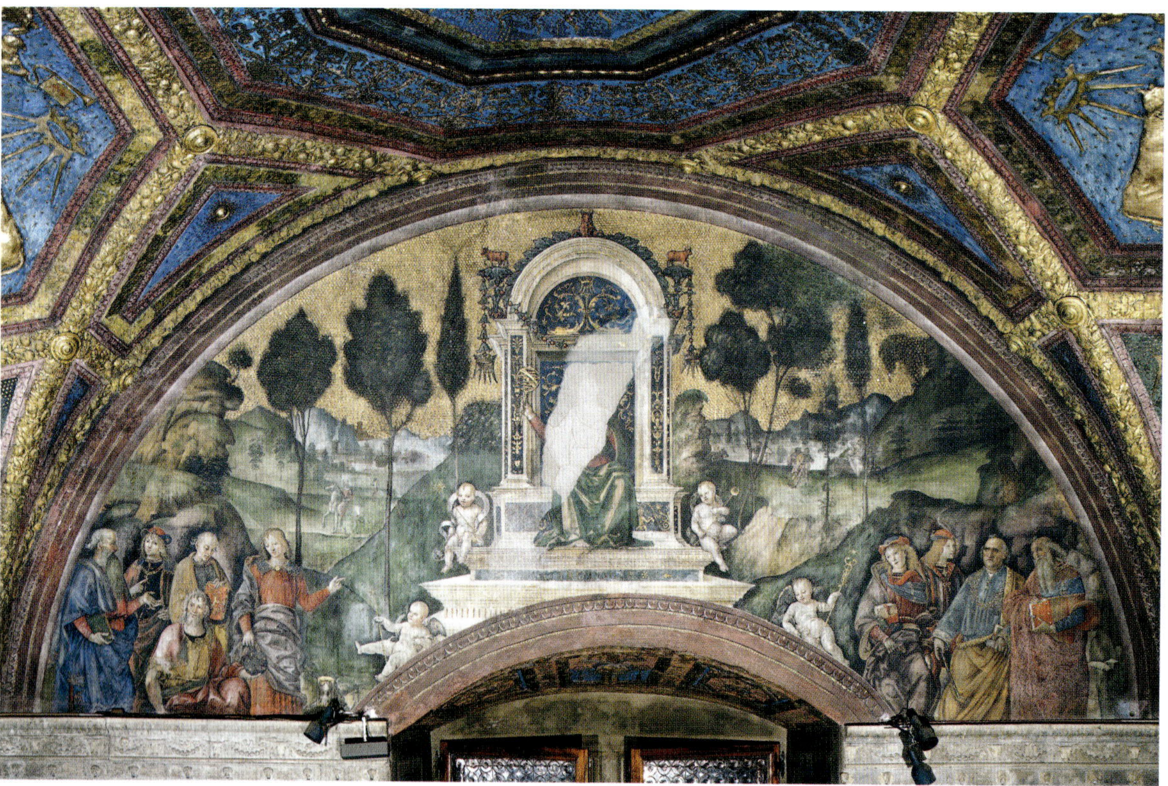

Pinturicchio (Bernardino di Betto), 1454–1513
***Astronomy*, 1492–1494**
Fresco
The Room of Liberal Arts, Borgia Apartments

Pinturicchio (Bernardino di Betto), 1454–1513
***Arithmetic*, 1492–1494**
Fresco
The Room of Liberal Arts, Borgia Apartments

Pinturicchio (Bernardino di Betto), 1454–1513
***Dialectic*, 1492–1494**
Fresco
The Room of Liberal Arts, Borgia Apartments

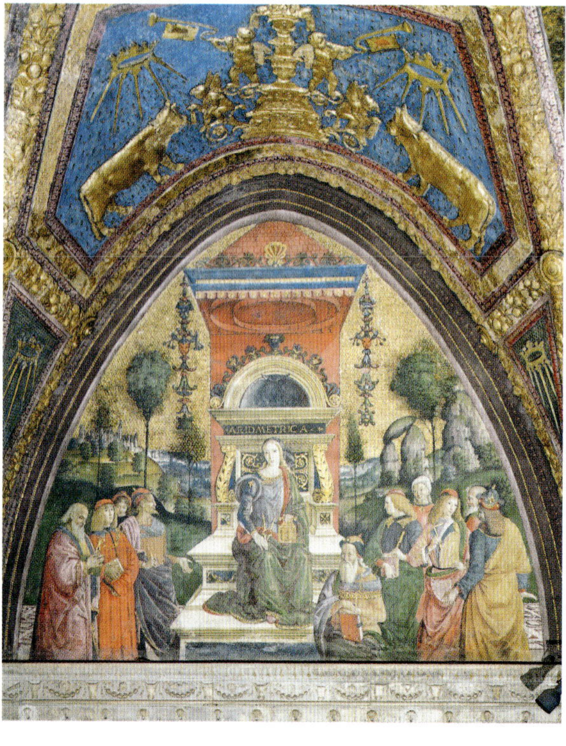

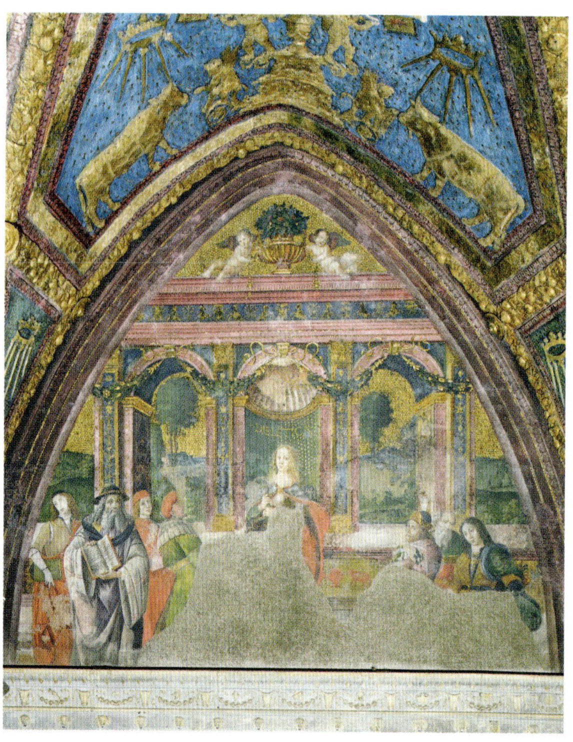

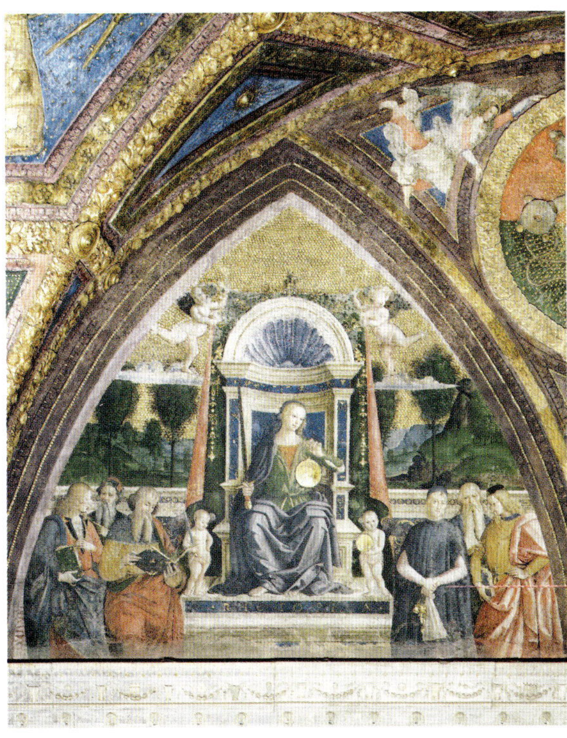

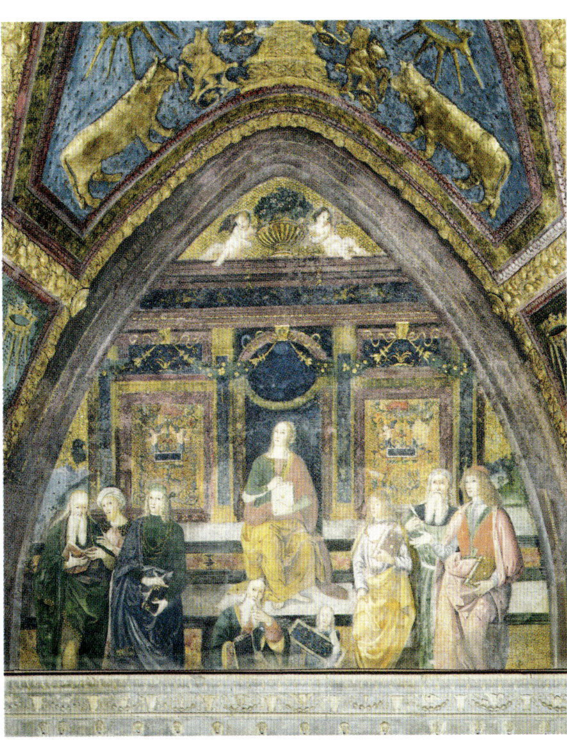

Pinturicchio (Bernardino di Betto), 1454–1513
***Rhetoric*, 1492–1494**
Fresco
The Room of Liberal Arts, Borgia Apartments

Pinturicchio (Bernardino di Betto), 1454–1513
***Grammar*, 1492–1494**
Fresco
The Room of Liberal Arts, Borgia Apartments

Pinturicchio (Bernardino di Betto), 1454–1513
***Borgia Arms, Ceiling: The Room of Liberal Arts, Borgia Apartments*, 1492–1494**
Fresco
The Room of Liberal Arts, Borgia Apartments

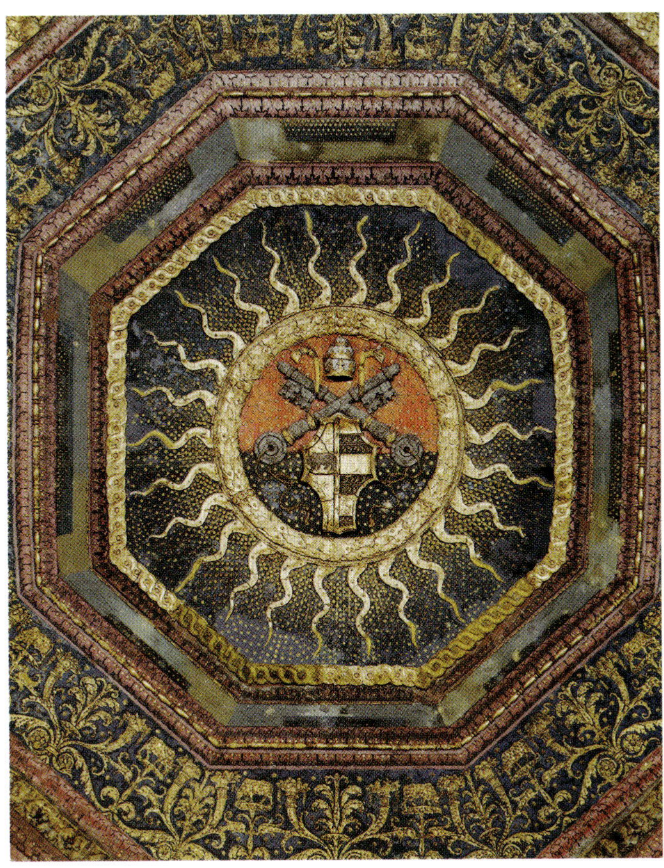

THE ROOM OF SIBYLS AND PROPHETS

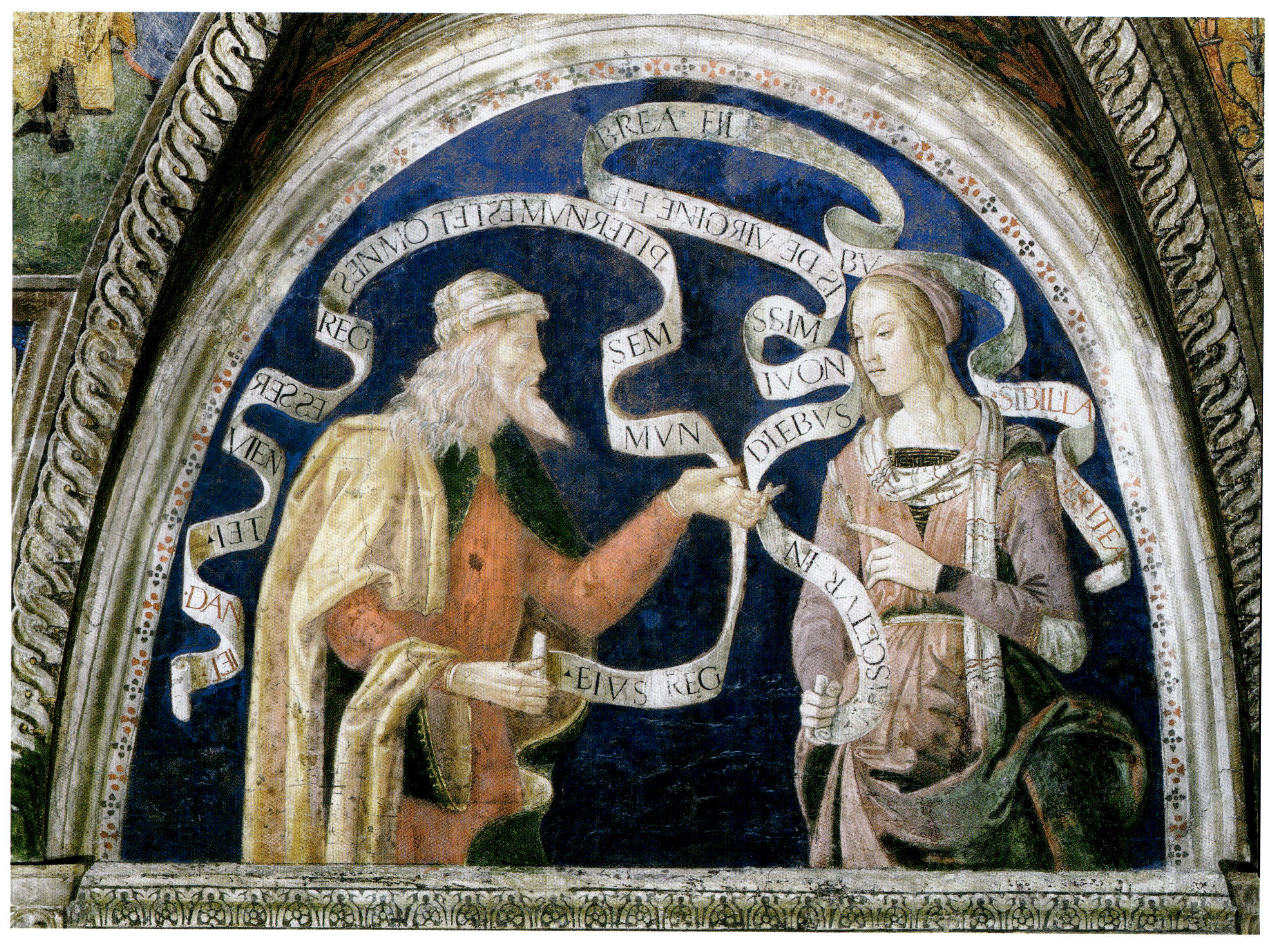

Pinturicchio (Bernardino di Betto)

Prophet Daniel and the Erythraean Sibyl

The Erythraean Sibyl and the prophet Daniel occupy one of the outer arch spaces above the window in the Sala delle Sibille e dei Profeti. While Daniel, characterized as a dignified old man with long hair and a pointed beard, appears in full profile, the sibyl with whom he is paired turns to him in three-quarter profile. Breaking with the medieval tradition, Pinturicchio has depicted her not as a wise old woman but as a beautiful young girl with loose hair and fluttering garments. The two figures seem to be engaged in a spirited debate, enlivened by their eloquent gestures. Their banners reveal the topic of their discussion to be the coming of Christ. Daniel's words are taken from the chapter of his book that deals with the Everlasting Dominion and prophecy that "all dominions shall serve and obey him" (Daniel 7:27). The Erythraean Sibyl, meanwhile, foretells, "In a new age a son to a Jewish Virgin will be born."

Pinturicchio (Bernardino di Betto)
Prophet Daniel and the Erythraean Sibyl,
1492–1494
Fresco
The Room of Sibyls and Prophets,
Borgia Apartments

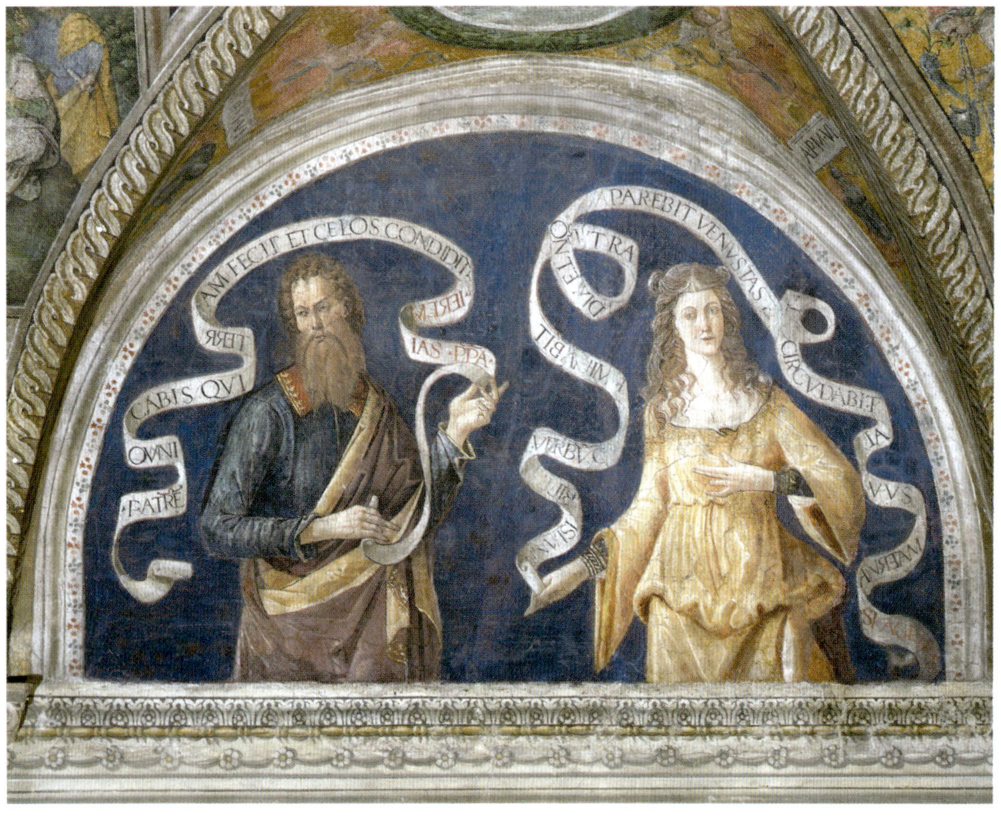

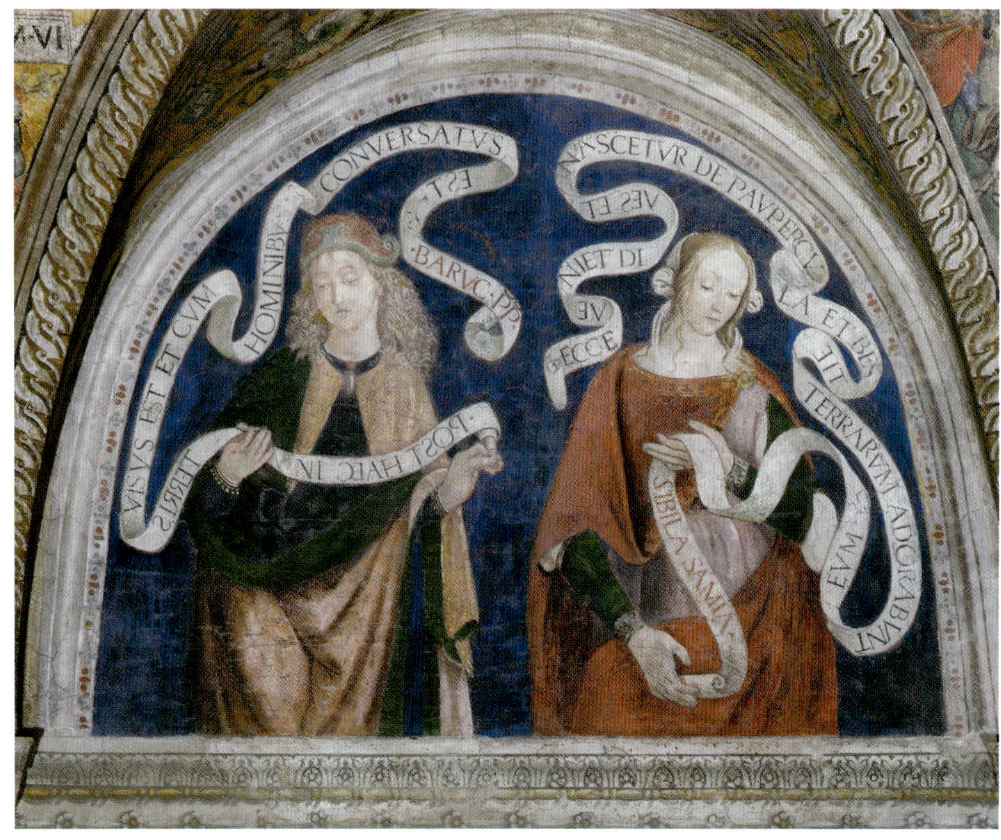

Pinturicchio (Bernardino di Betto), 1454–1513
***Jeremiah and the Agrippan Sibyl*, 1492–1494**
Fresco
The Room of Sibyls and Prophets,
Borgia Apartments

Pinturicchio (Bernardino di Betto), 1454–1513
***Baruch and the Samian Sibyl*, 1492–1494**
Fresco
The Room of Sibyls and Prophets,
Borgia Apartments

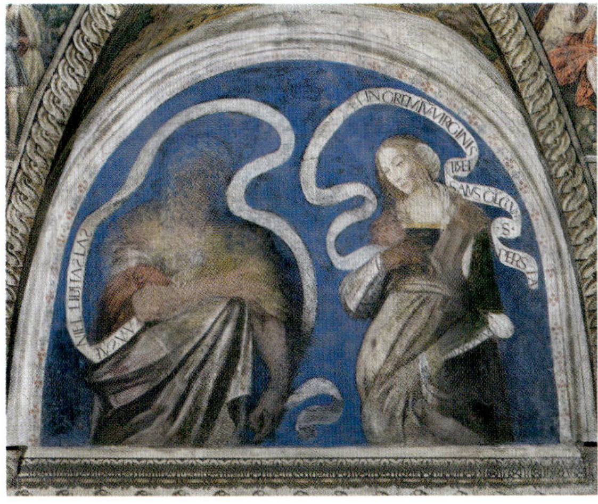

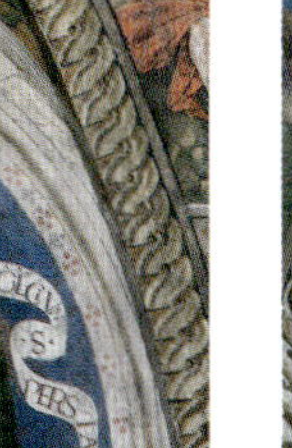

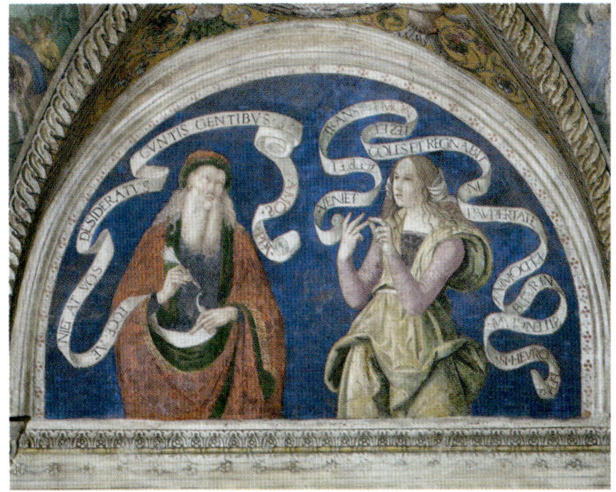

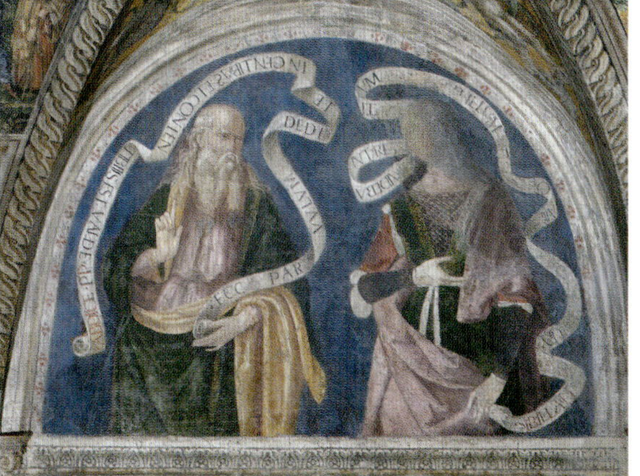

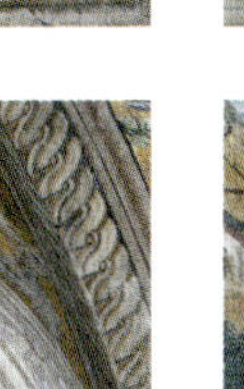

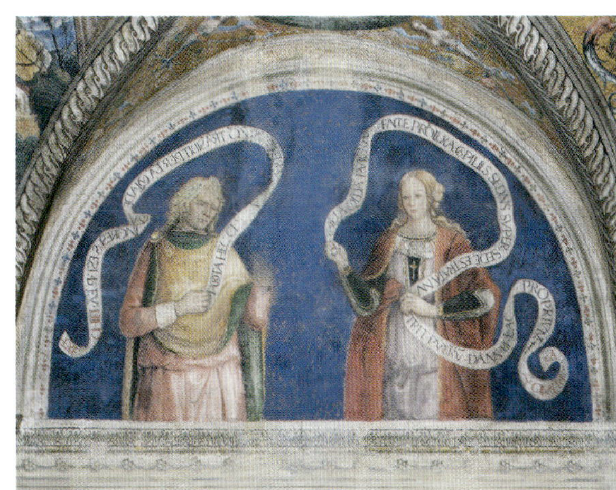

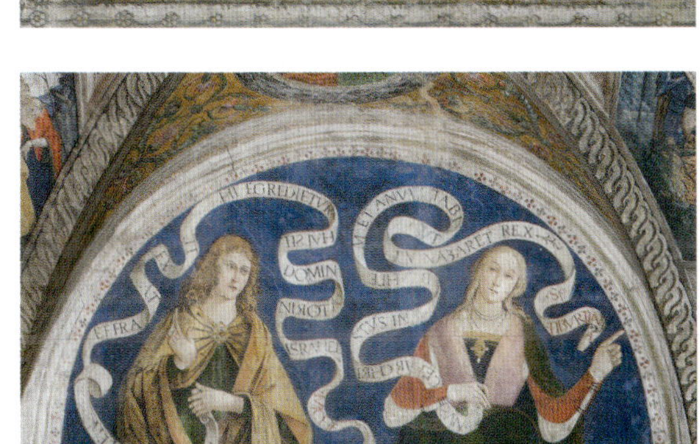

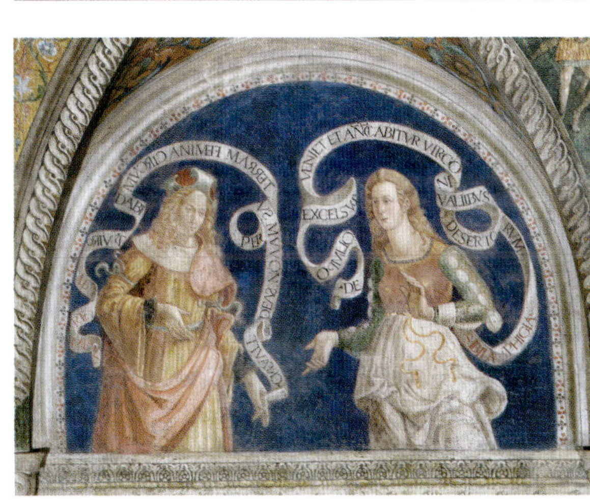

Pinturicchio (Bernardino di Betto), 1454–1513
***Zechariah and the Persian Sibyl*, 1492–1494**
Fresco
The Room of Sibyls and Prophets,
Borgia Apartments

Pinturicchio (Bernardino di Betto), 1454–1513
***Amos and the European Sibyl*, 1492–1494**
Fresco
The Room of Sibyls and Prophets,
Borgia Apartments

Pinturicchio (Bernardino di Betto), 1454–1513
***Obadiah and the Libyan Sibyl*, 1492–1494**
Fresco
The Room of Sibyls and Prophets,
Borgia Apartments

Pinturicchio (Bernardino di Betto), 1454–1513
***Ezekiel and the Cimmerian Sibyl*, 1492–1494**
Fresco
The Room of Sibyls and Prophets,
Borgia Apartments

Pinturicchio (Bernardino di Betto), 1454–1513
***Micah and the Tiburtine Sibyl*, 1492–1494**
Fresco
The Room of Sibyls and Prophets,
Borgia Apartments

Pinturicchio (Bernardino di Betto), 1454–1513
***Jeremiah and the Phrygian Sibyl*, 1492–1494**
Fresco
The Room of Sibyls and Prophets,
Borgia Apartments

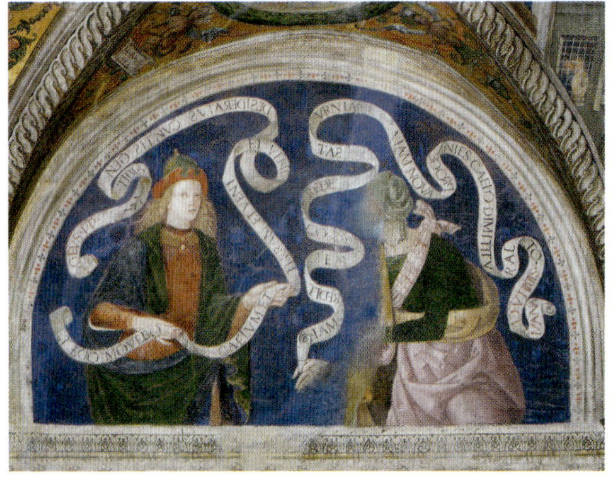

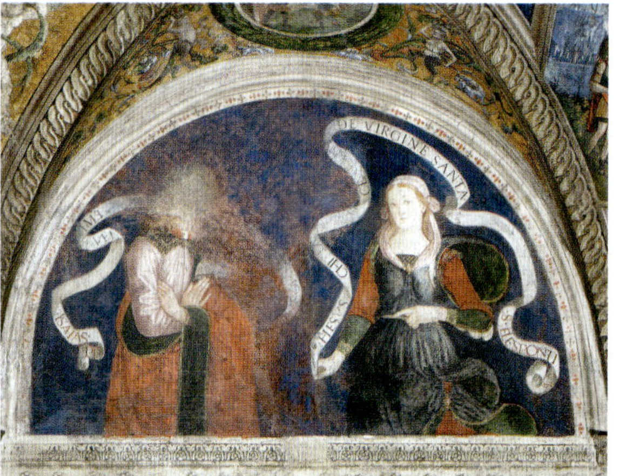

Pinturicchio (Bernardino di Betto), 1454–1513
***Haggai and the Cumaean Sibyl*, 1492–1494**
Fresco
The Room of Sibyls and Prophets,
Borgia Apartments

Pinturicchio (Bernardino di Betto), 1454–1513
***Isaiah and the Hellespontine Sibyl*, 1492–1494**
Fresco
The Room of Sibyls and Prophets,
Borgia Apartments

Pinturicchio (Bernardino di Betto), 1454–1513
***Moses and the Delphic Sibyl*, 1492–1494**
Fresco
The Room of Sibyls and Prophets,
Borgia Apartments

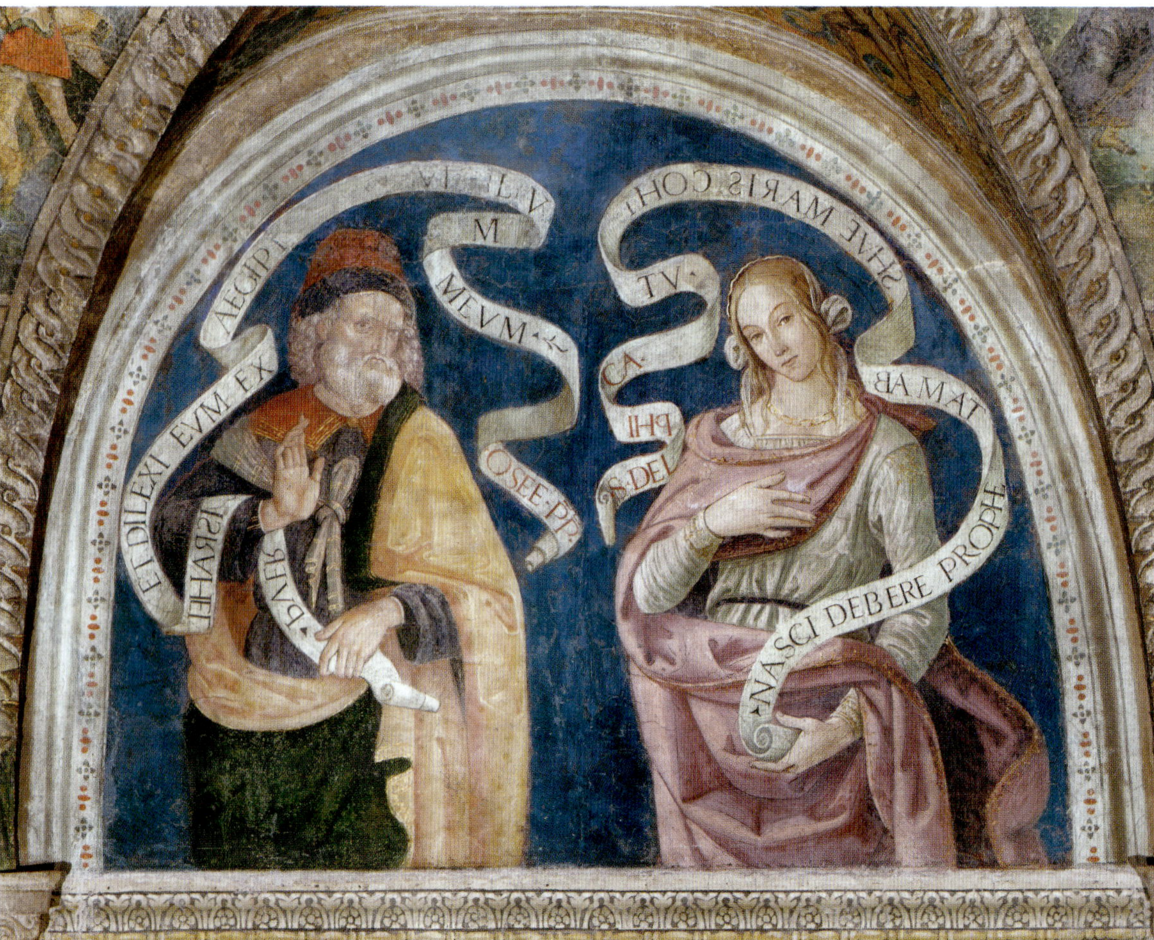

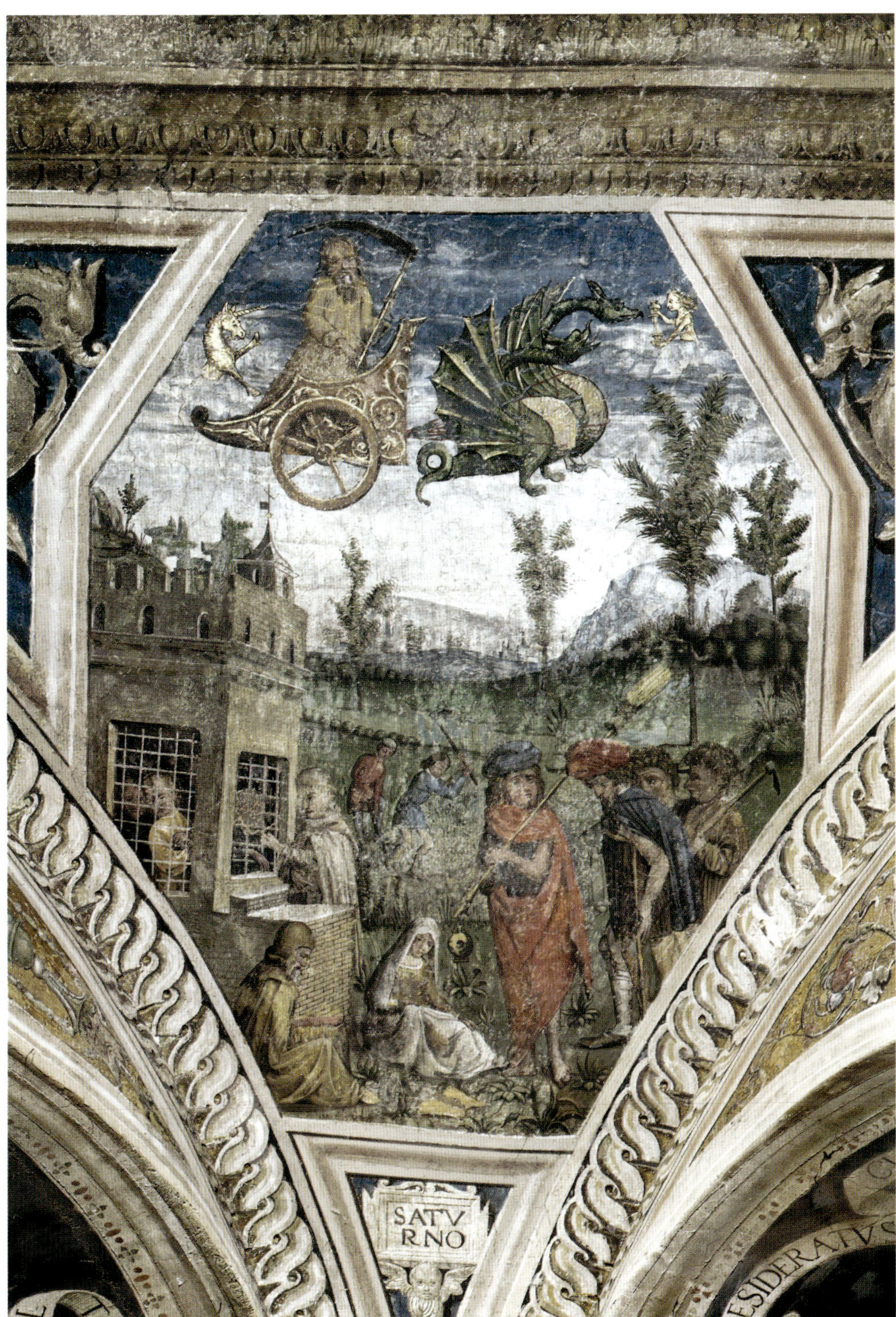

Pinturicchio (Bernardino di Betto)

Saturn

The Sala delle Sibille e dei Profeti is crowned with a richly ornamented flat vault decorated with gold stucco studs reproducing a starry sky. The broad frame of the vault is set with octagonal compartments containing symbolic representations of the seven known planets and the personifications of the astrological signs. The series begins with Saturn, above the entrance to the room. As the planet that takes the longest time to orbit the sun, Saturn was ranked highest in the hierarchy of the planets. The pictorial field is divided into two zones: In the celestial zone, Saturn, personified as an elderly man holding a scythe representing old age, rides in a chariot drawn by two dragons flying over a hilly wooded landscape. The two creatures to the left and right of the chariot are Saturn's constellations Capricorn, resembling a unicorn, and Aquarius. The earthly zone contains depictions of Saturn's so-called planet-children, a group of individuals whose characteristics and behavior were believed to be strongly influenced by Saturn. They are people associated with working the land, with poverty, and with old age and include farm laborers, cripples, and prisoners, to whom a monk, out of compassion, brings food.

Pinturicchio (Bernardino di Betto), (1454–1513)
***Saturn*, 1492–1494**
Fresco
The Room of Sibyls and Prophets, Borgia Apartments

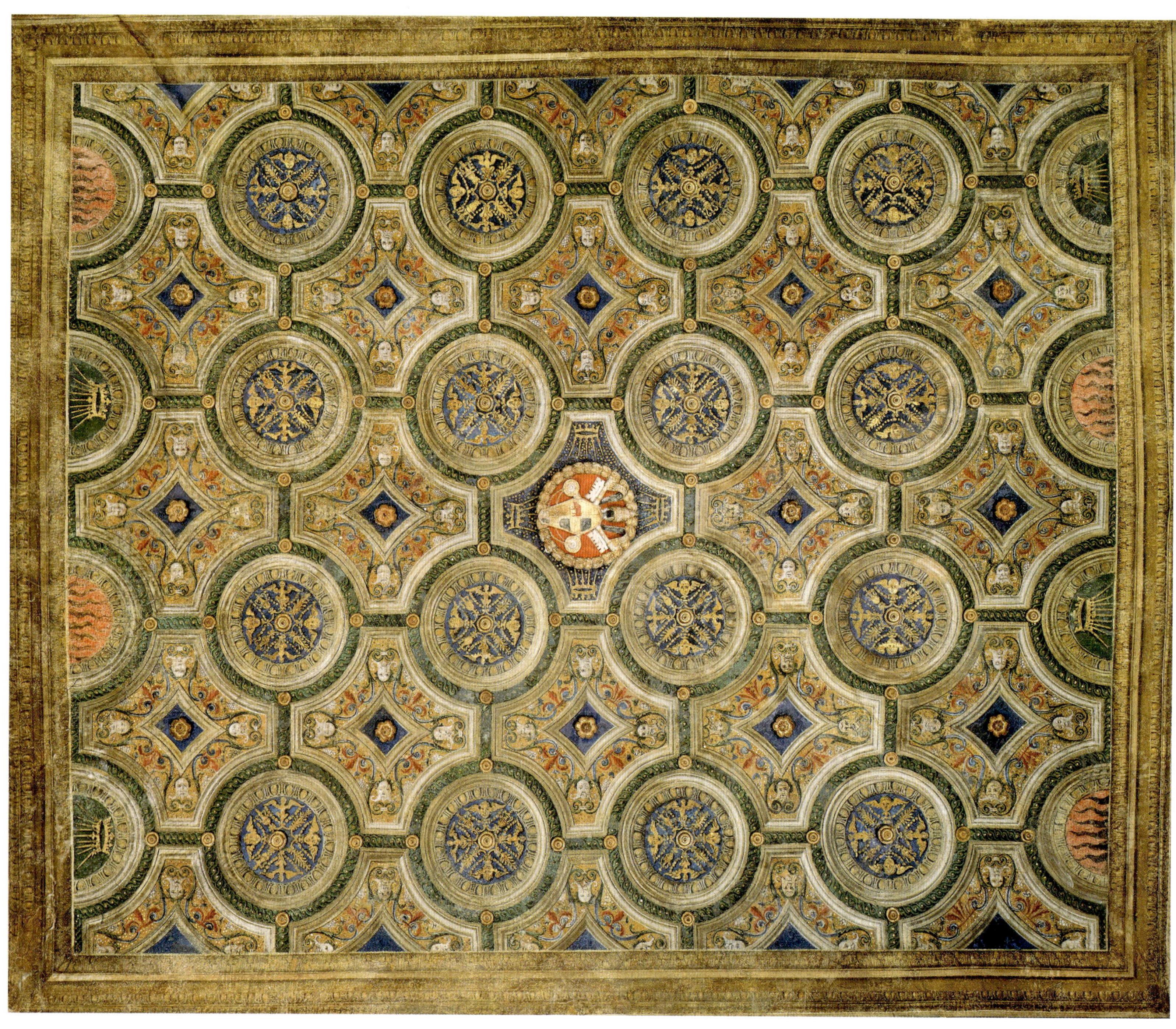

Pinturicchio (Bernardino di Betto), 1454–1513
***Ceiling: The Room of Sibyls and Prophets, Borgia Apartments*, 1492–1494**
Fresco
The Room of Sibyls and Prophets,
Borgia Apartments

THE ROOM OF CREED

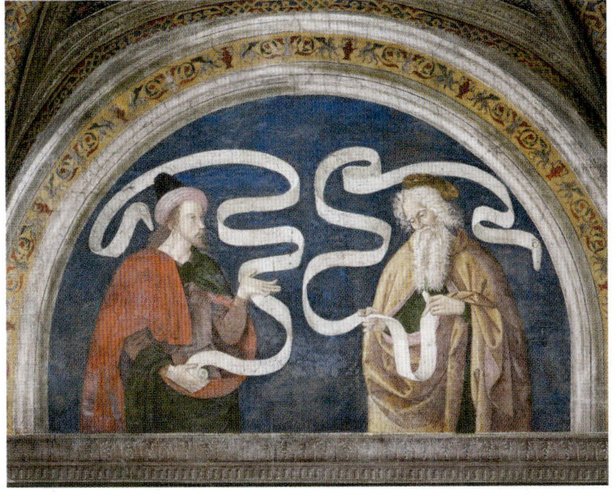

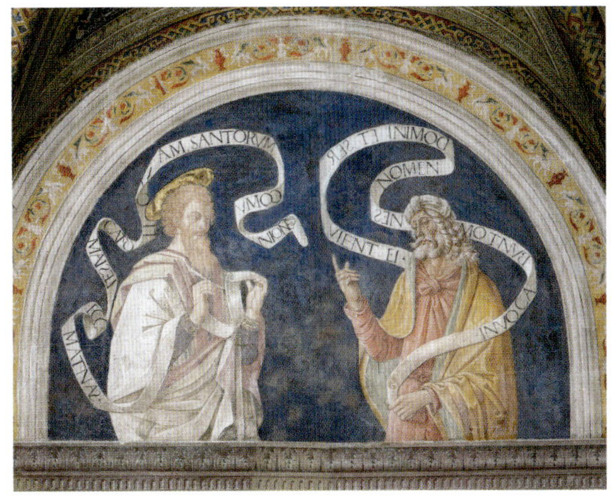

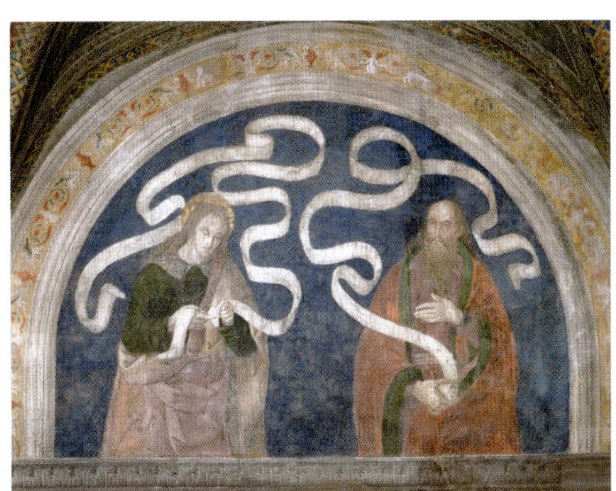

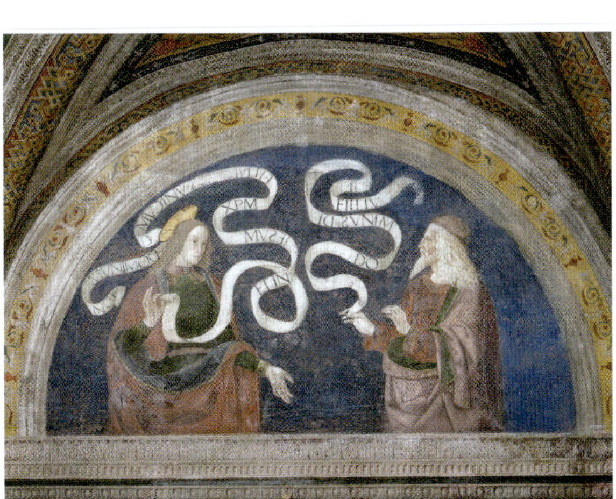

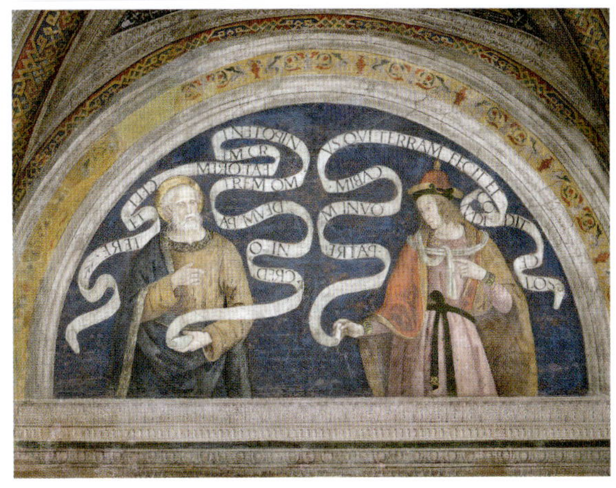

Pinturicchio (Bernardino di Betto), 1454–1513
***St. Matthew and Obadiah*, 1492–1494**
Fresco
The Room of Creed, Borgia Apartments

Pinturicchio (Bernardino di Betto), 1454–1513
***St. Thomas and Daniel*, 1492–1494**
Fresco
The Room of Creed, Borgia Apartments

Pinturicchio (Bernardino di Betto), 1454–1513
***St. Thaddeus and Zechariah*, 1492–1494**
Fresco
The Room of Creed, Borgia Apartments

Pinturicchio (Bernardino di Betto), 1454–1513
***St. Simon and Malachi*, 1492–1494**
Fresco
The Room of Creed, Borgia Apartments

Pinturicchio (Bernardino di Betto), 1454–1513
***St. John and David*, 1492–1494**
Fresco
The Room of Creed, Borgia Apartments

Pinturicchio (Bernardino di Betto), 1454–1513
***St. Peter and Jeremiah*, 1492–1494**
Fresco
The Room of Creed, Borgia Apartments

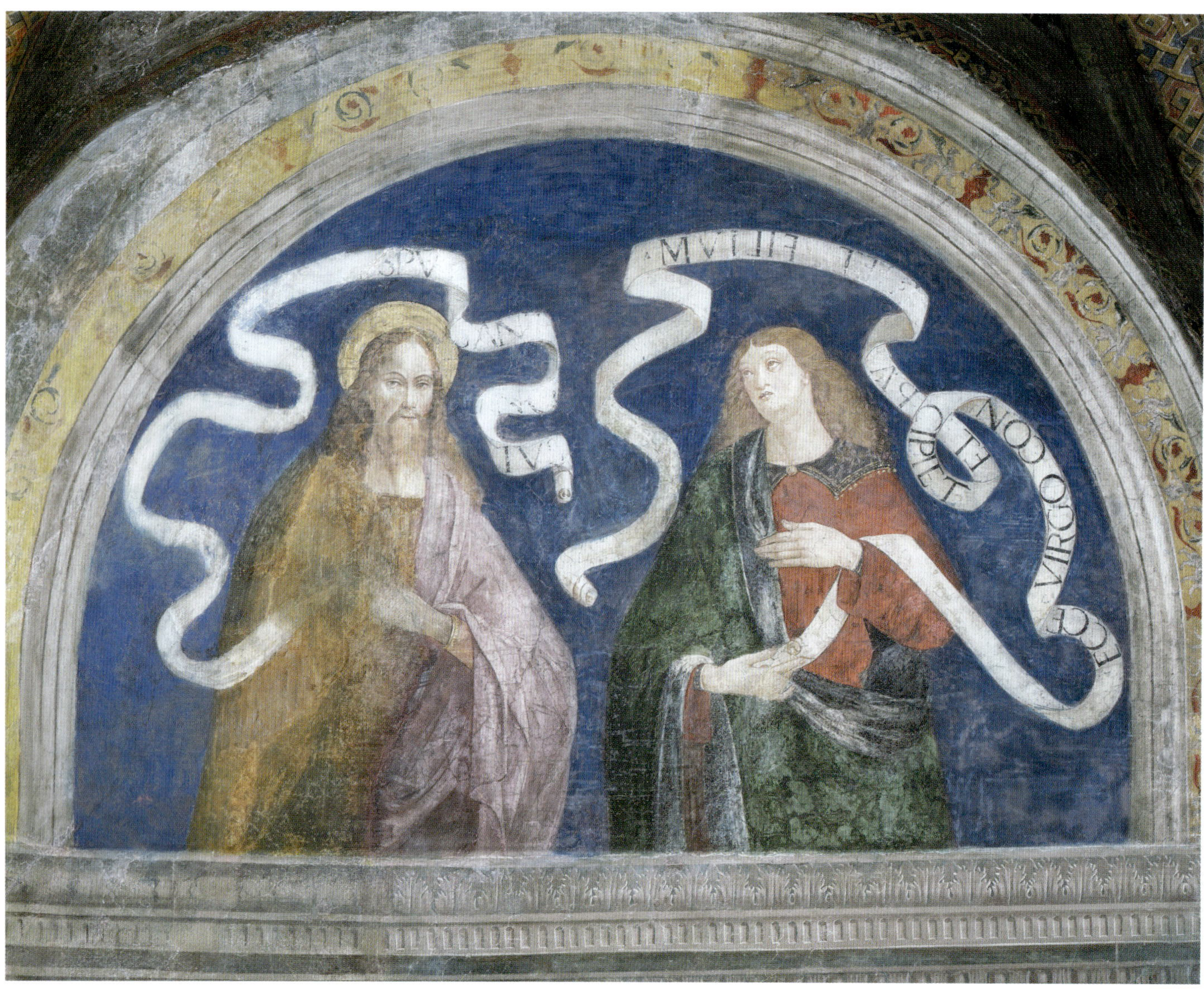

Pinturicchio (Bernardino di Betto)

St. Andrew and Isaiah

This lunette depicts St. Andrew with the prophet Isaiah. St. Andrew's banner contains the words "and conceived by the Holy Ghost," while the quotation on the youthful Isaiah's reads, "Behold, a virgin shall conceive, and bear a son" (Isaiah 7:14), prophesying the birth of Christ. The prophet is shown turning reverently toward St. Andrew. The figures are depicted with the utmost realism, an effect heightened by the skillful modeling of light and shadow in their garments, in which Pinturicchio also reveals himself to be a master of color.

Pinturicchio (Bernardino di Betto), 1454–1513
***St. Andrew and Isaiah*, 1492–1494**
Fresco
The Room of Creed, Borgia Apartments

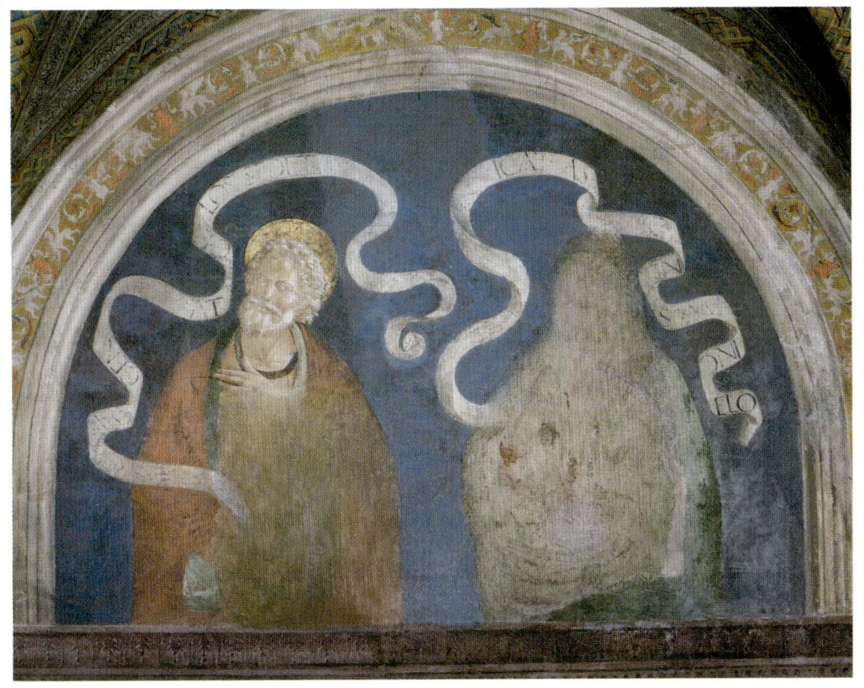

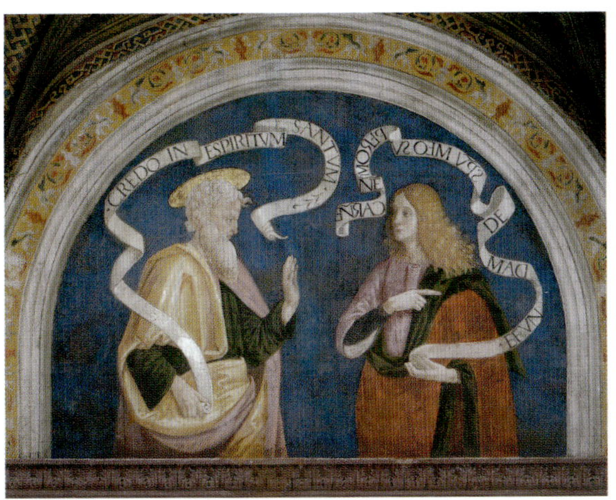

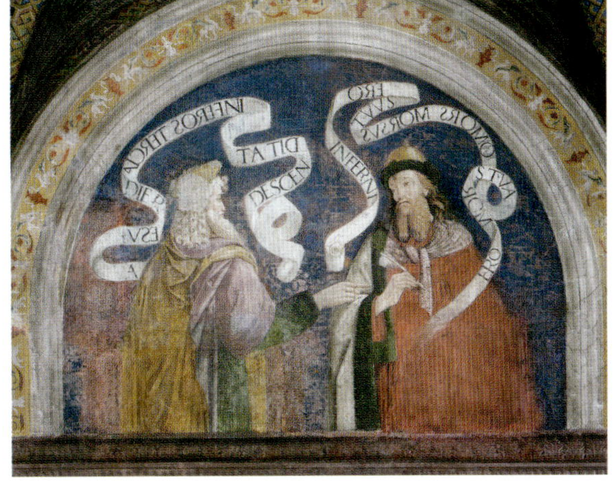

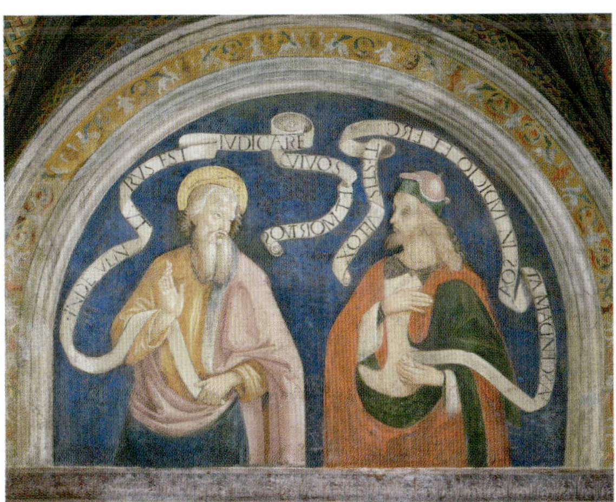

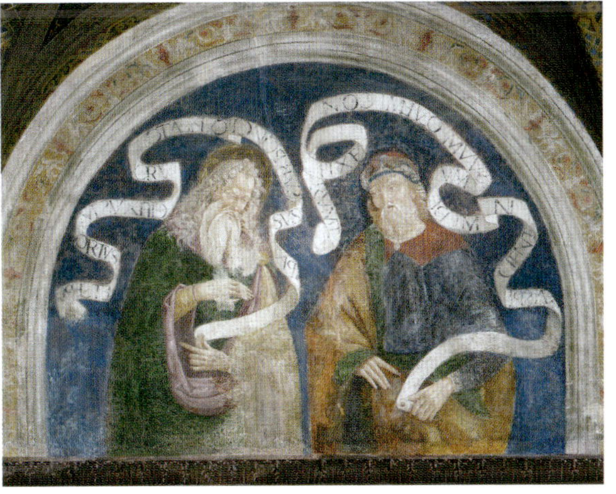

Pinturicchio (Bernardino di Betto), 1454–1513
***St. James the Lesser and Amos*, 1492–1494**
Fresco
The Room of Creed, Borgia Apartments

Pinturicchio (Bernardino di Betto), 1454–1513
***St. Bartholomew and Joel*, 1492–1494**
Fresco
The Room of Creed, Borgia Apartments

Pinturicchio (Bernardino di Betto), 1454–1513
***St. Matthew and Hosea*, 1492–1494**
Fresco
The Room of Creed, Borgia Apartments

Pinturicchio (Bernardino di Betto), 1454–1513
***Philip and Malachi*, 1492–1494**
Fresco
The Room of Creed, Borgia Apartments

Pinturicchio (Bernardino di Betto), 1454–15113
***James the Greater and Zechariah*, 1492–1494**
Fresco
The Room of Creed, Borgia Apartments

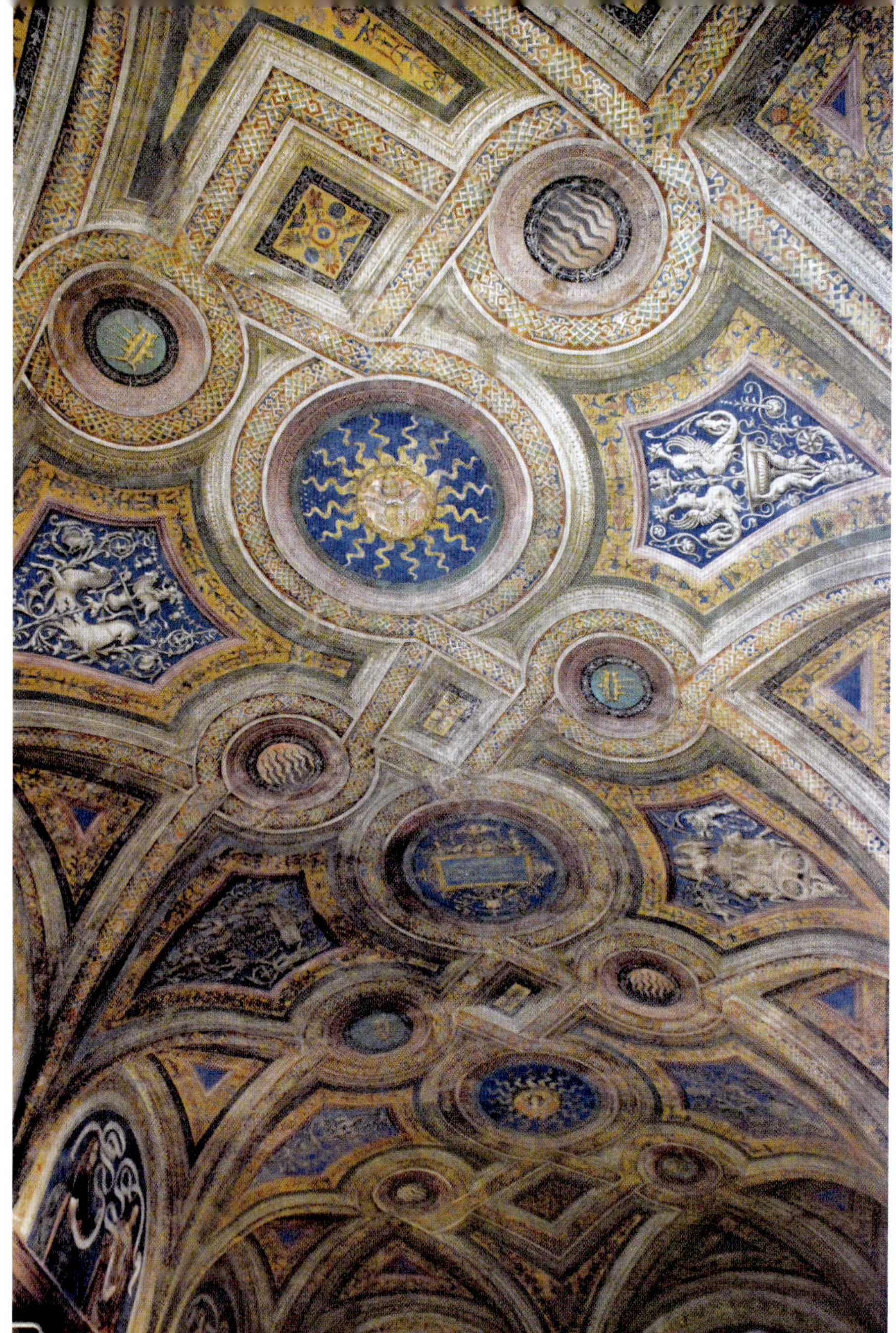

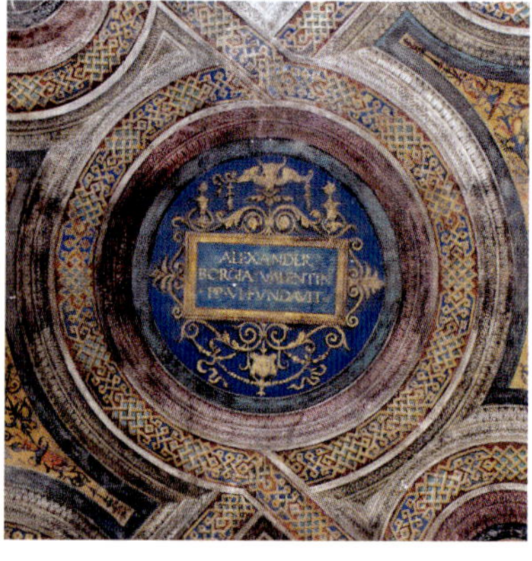

Pinturicchio (Bernardino di Betto)

Sala del Credo: ceiling

With its numerous subdivisions and lavish decoration, the ceiling of the Sala del Credo is the most sumptuous of the Borgia Apartments. Although tied to his patron's theological program for the room, comprising depictions of apostles and prophets, Pinturicchio nevertheless succeeded in showcasing his talent for decoration and knowledge of antique ornament. The ceiling's central axis is dominated by three large medallions with blue backgrounds, which are dedicated to the glorification of Alexander VI. A plaque with a frame in the grotesque style "set into" the central circular compartment names the pope as the donor of the fresco cycle. The two outer compartments show the papal coat of arms radiating golden tongues of flame. The broad frames around the lunettes and the hexagonal compartments that mark the transition from the ceiling to the lunette zone are also decorated with plentiful and highly imaginative figurative and ornamental grotesque motifs. In the two middle fields, Pinturicchio reiterates the inscription of the central medallion on one side and gives the date, 1494, on the other.

Pinturicchio (Bernardino di Betto), 1454–1513
***The Room of Creed: Ceiling, Borgia Apartments*, 1492–1494**
Fresco
The Room of Creed, Borgia Apartments

Pinturicchio (Bernardino di Betto), 1454–1513
***The Room of Creed: Ceiling detail*, 1492–1494**
Fresco
The Room of Creed, Borgia Apartments

THE HALL OF PONTIFFS

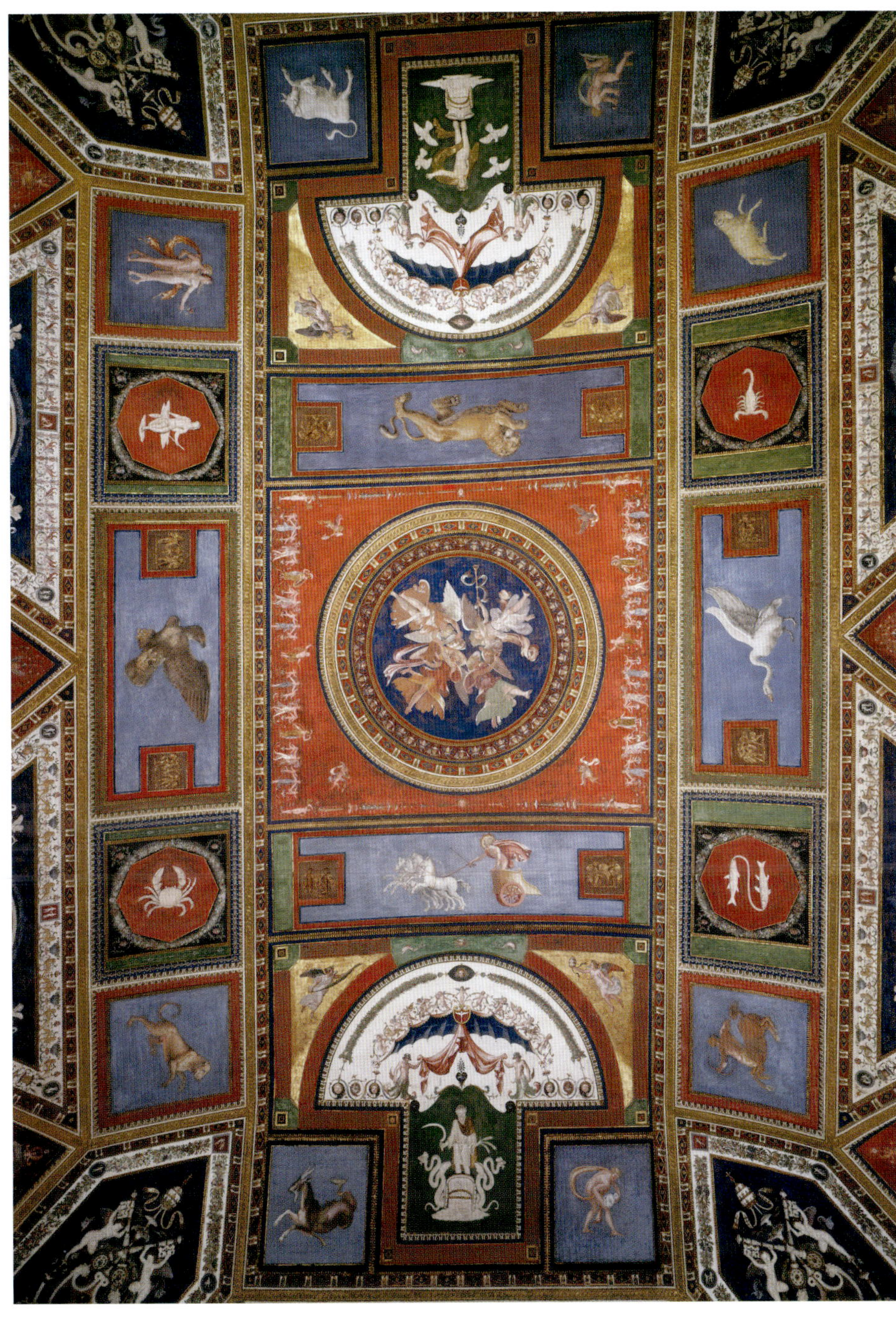

Lorenzo Sabbatini and followers, ca. 1530–1576
***Ceiling of the Hall of the Pontiffs*, 1492–1494**
Fresco
The Hall of the Pontiffs, Borgia Apartments

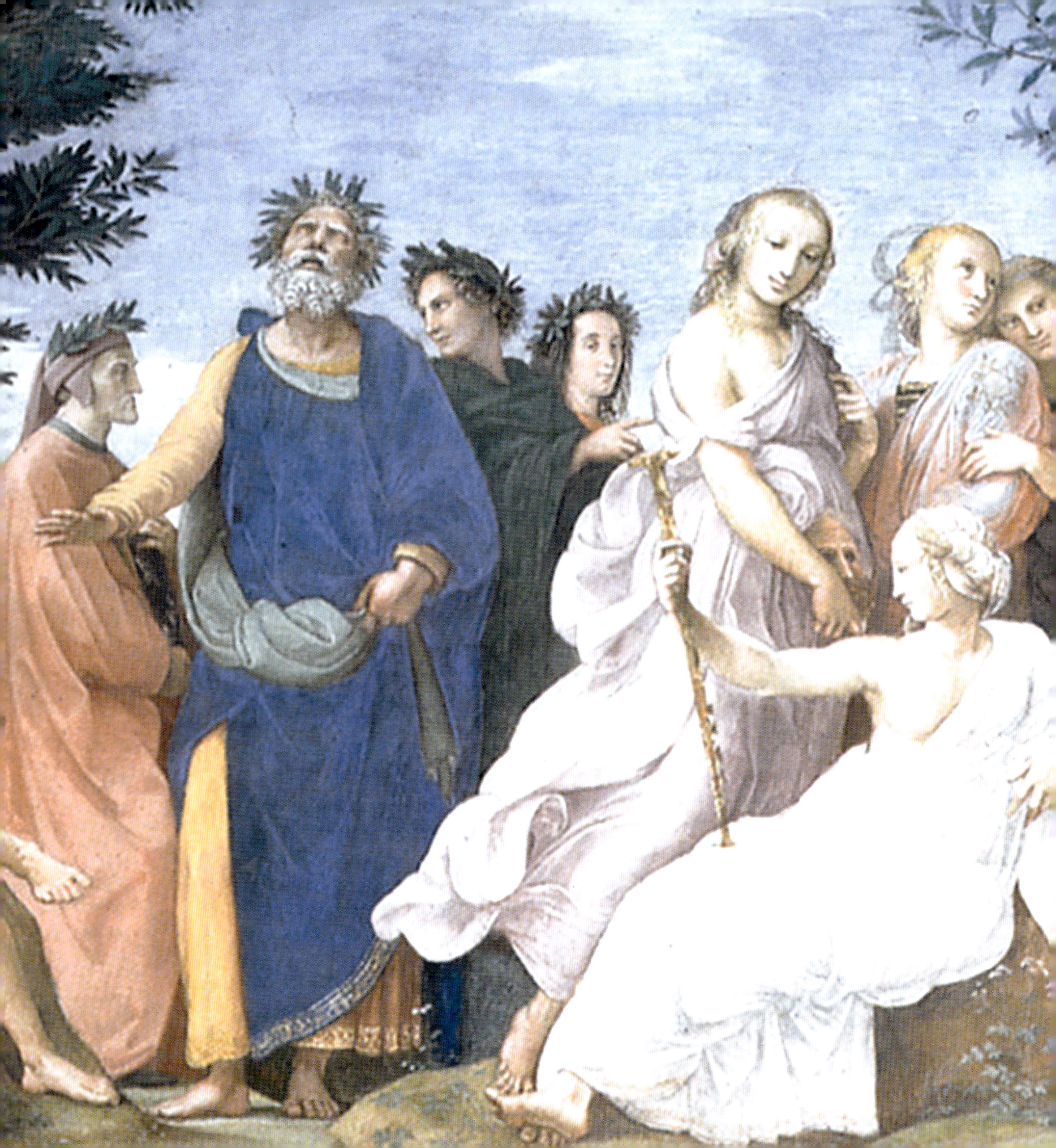

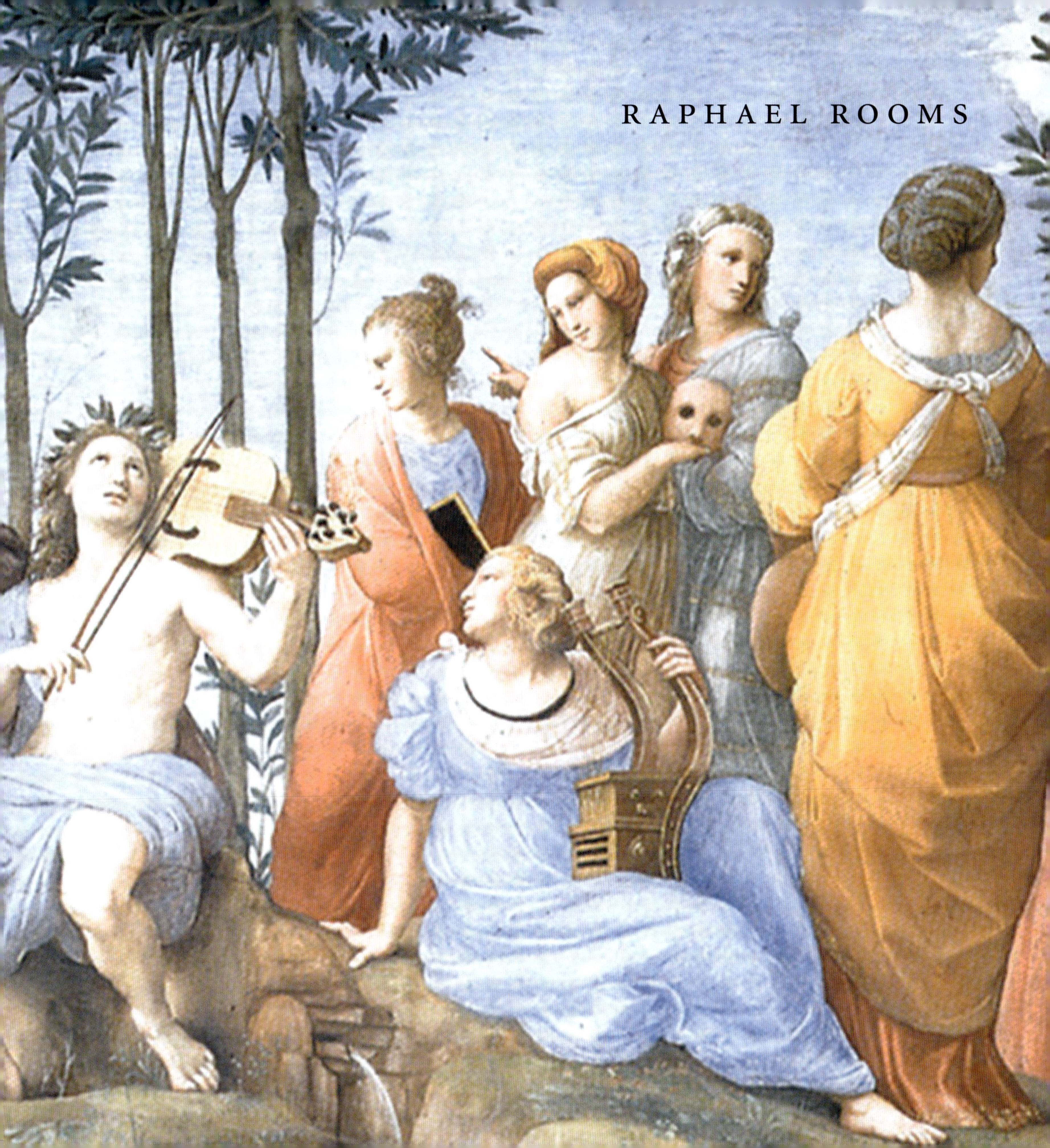

RAPHAEL ROOMS

RAPHAEL ROOMS

The four rooms famous throughout the world today as Raphael's Rooms were the private chambers of popes Julius II (1443–1513, reigned from 1503), Leo X Medici (1475–1521, reigned from 1513), and Clement VII Medici (1478–1534, reigned from 1523). In choosing these particular rooms in 1507, Julius II was to some extent making a political statement. The pope had no desire to reside in the chambers of Alexander VI Borgia (1431–1503, reigned from 1492), the predecessor he loathed, even though the apartment had been so magnificently decorated by Pinturicchio just a few years earlier. Instead, he chose the rooms on the second floor of the Vatican Palace immediately above the Appartamento Borgia that overlap to some extent with the chambers of popes Nicholas III (ca. 1212/16–1280, reigned from 1277) and Nicholas V (1397–1455, reigned from 1447).

Following in the footsteps of his relative and predecessor Sixtus IV della Rovere (1414–1484, pope from 1471), the builder of the Sistine Chapel, as a great patron of the arts, Julius II engaged Perugino and Luca Signorelli, two of the most famous Renaissance painters at his court, to decorate the Rooms. As young artists, both had worked on the Sistine Chapel between 1481 and 1484. Perugino and Signorelli had already completed parts of the Rooms frescoes when they were joined in 1508 by Raphael. According to Giorgio Vasari, the biographer of the artists, it was Julius II's court architect Bramante who had recommended the twenty-year-old painter—a fellow native of Urbino—to the pope. Julius II was so enthralled with Raphael's test piece that he handed him responsibility for the entire fresco decoration of the Rooms. In order to make way for Raphael, the pope ordered the destruction of Perugino's and Signorelli's wall paintings. Only Perugino's ceiling in the Room of Fire (Stanza dell'Incendio) was—at Raphael's request—retained and can still be admired today.

The paintings in the Rooms depicting historic events are framed by an abundance of painted decoration in the Renaissance style, which is thought to have been executed mainly by Raphael's assistants. The caryatids, grisaille work, and painted architectural elements relate to the antique motifs and humanist learning promoted by Julius II and subsequent popes. Papal coats of arms and heraldic figures are a recurrent theme and serve to immortalize the pontiffs as patrons of the arts. Another way of representing the popes was to portray them in historical roles, and Julius II, Leo X, and Clement VII all had themselves depicted as pontiffs from earlier times. Despite the wide range of motifs, the various artists who worked on the project, and the fifteen years that it took to complete the decoration, the Rooms present a unified whole. This harmony is due primarily to Raphael's supreme skill, which enabled him to create one of the most important of all Renaissance interiors.

THE ROOM OF CONSTANTINE

The largest room in the apartment, the Room of Constantine (Sala di Costantino), served as the venue for semiofficial audiences and festivities such as banquets and weddings of the pope's relatives. The room takes its name from its frescoes' depictions of scenes from the life of Constantine the Great (ca. 280–337, reigned from 306), the first Christian emperor of Rome. Planned by Raphael under Julius II and begun under Leo X, the decoration of the room was completed—by Giulio Romano and Giovanni Francesco Penni—at the beginning of the reign of Clement VII. The large pictorial spaces are designed to simulate tapestries and are interspersed with depictions of enthroned popes accompanied by female personifications of the virtues. The style of the frescoes differs markedly from that of the works executed by Raphael himself, exhibiting stronger Mannerist elements characteristic of Romano and Penni. The painterly vehemence and agitation of these works, mainly battle scenes, are well suited to their content.

The first scene chronologically is the *Vision of the Cross*, on the narrow wall. This describes the vision that helped Constantine vanquish the heathen anti-emperor Maxentius. The room's largest fresco is the *Battle of the Milvian Bridge*, which takes up virtually the entire long wall. This work depicts the victory of Constantine's troops over the army of Maxentius, which enabled Constantine to claim sole rule. Further events from the life of the emperor are the *Donation of Constantine* and the *Baptism of Constantine*, both of which played an important part in the founding of Christian imperial rule and the establishing of a close relationship between Church and state.

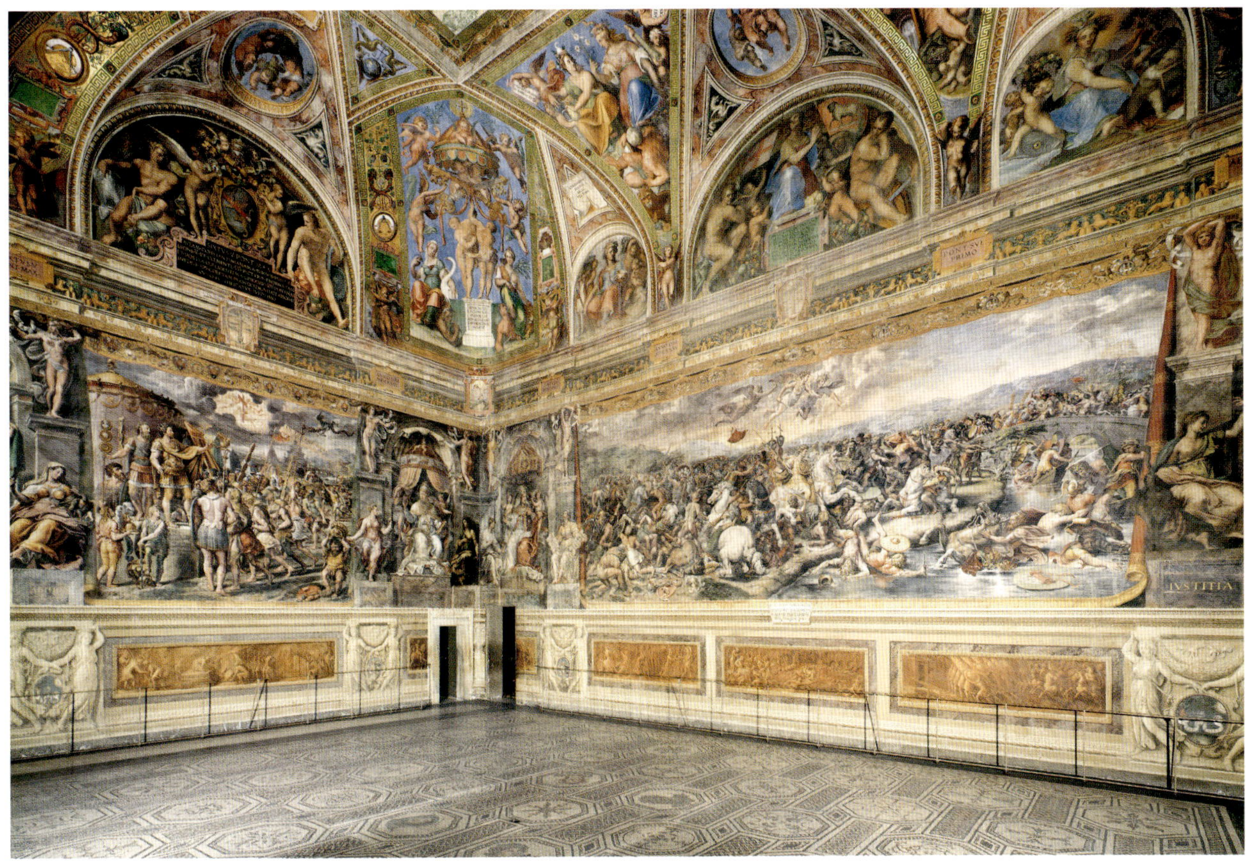

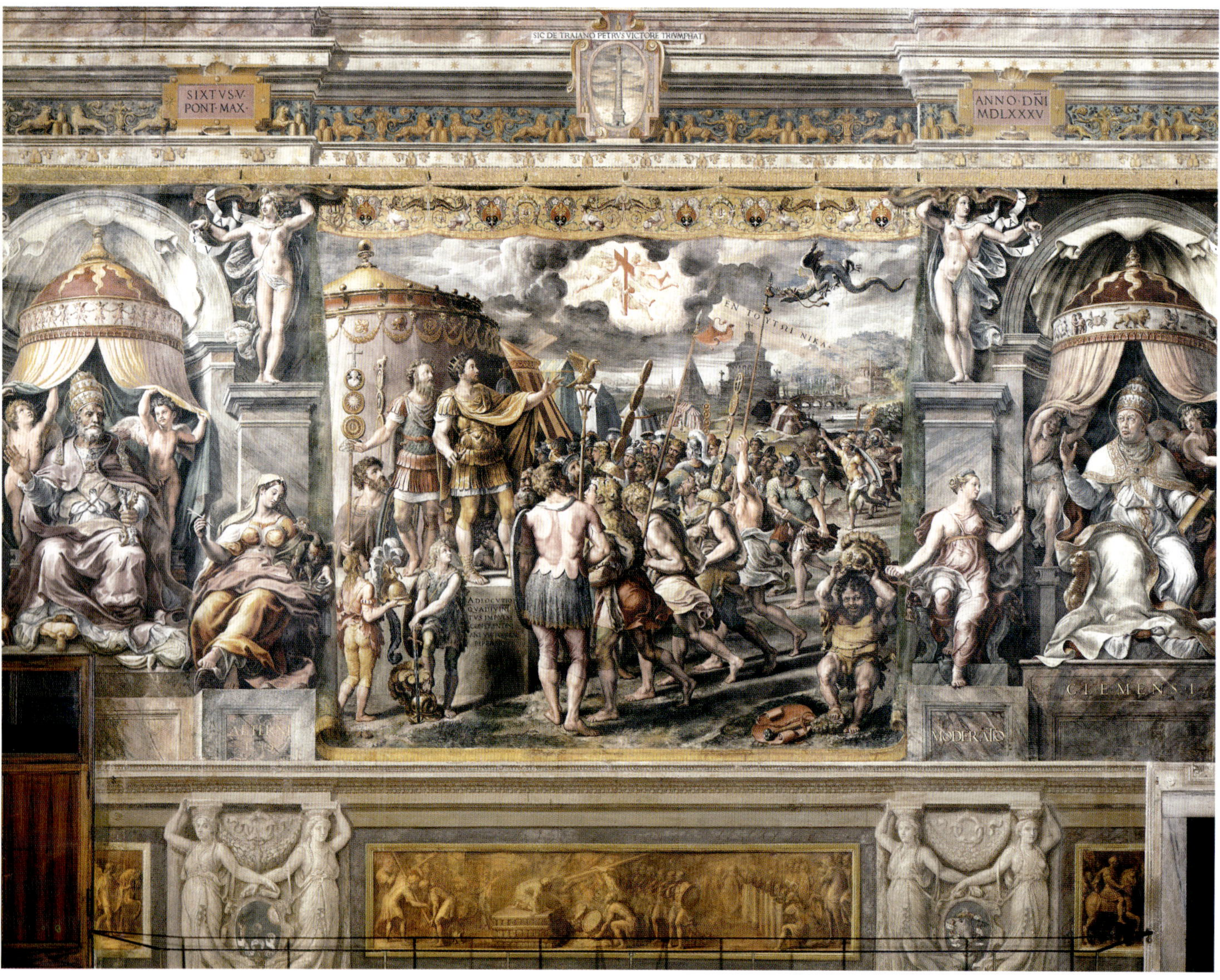

Raphael (Raffaello Sanzio) and Giulio Romano

Vision of the Cross

"In this sign will you conquer!" is one of the best-known phrases in history and lies at the heart of this fresco of Constantine's vision of the cross, executed by Giulio Romano after Raphael's designs. The scene unfolds in Emperor Constantine's military camp in advance of the battle of the Milvian Bridge. Constantine stands on a podium outside his massive round tent and addresses his soldiers, who can be seen rushing up to him with their standards. Suddenly, the dark clouds part and three angels appear holding a blood-red cross and accompanied by the announcement of victory (in Greek) quoted above. The inscription is positioned above a round, towerlike structure that has been identified as the Mausoleum of Hadrian, later the Castel Sant'Angelo, and alludes to Constantine's role as the first Christian emperor of Rome. Constantine stares, transfixed by the vision of the cross, while the army commander standing by his side holds a standard bearing the cross. In the agitation of the emperor and his soldiers, Romano reveals himself to be a master at conveying emotion, just as the squires standing below the podium holding Constantine's armor, the dwarf with the helmet in the right foreground, and the fluttering dragon standard demonstrate his talent for narrative.

Raphael (Raffaello Sanzio) and Giulio Romano, 1492 or 1499–1546
***Vision of the Cross*, 1520–1524**
Fresco
The Room of Constantine, Raphael Rooms

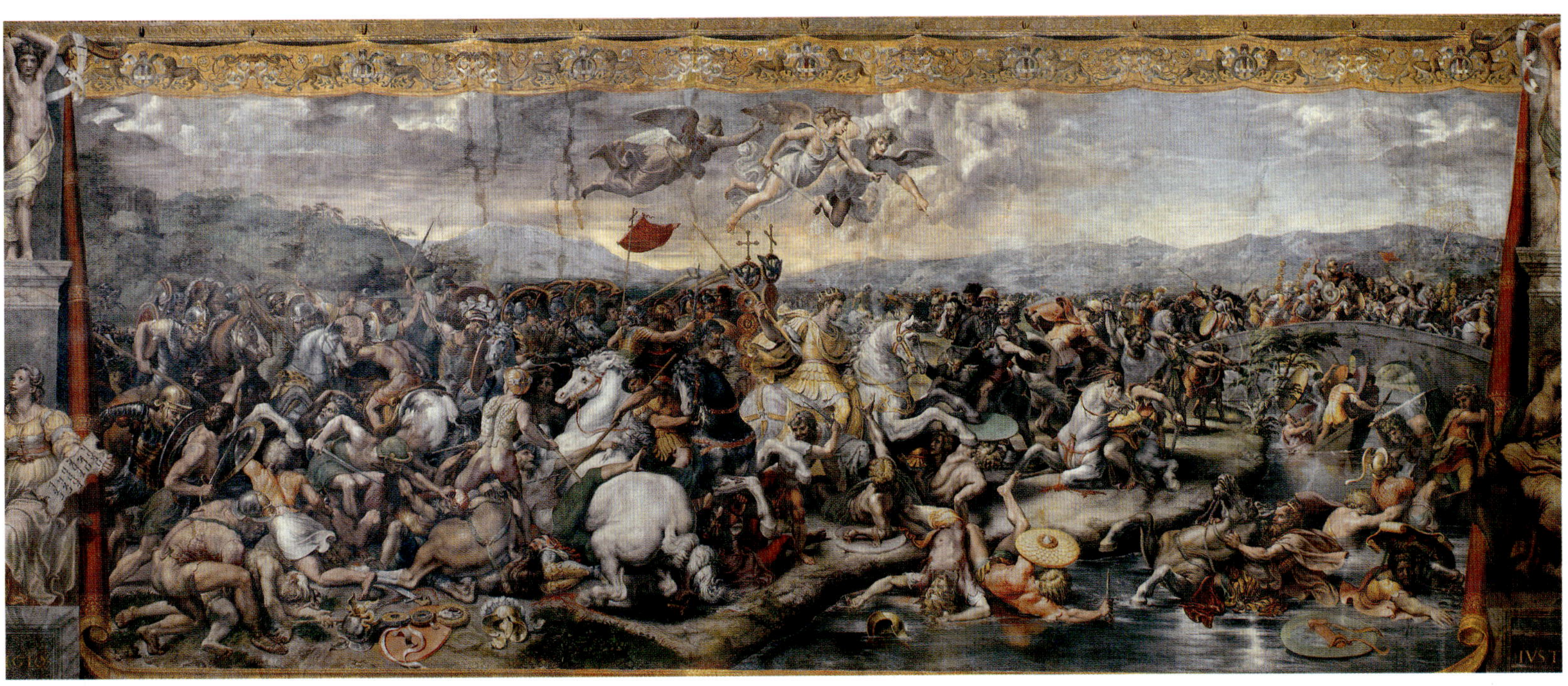

Raphael (Raffaello Sanzio) and Giulio Romano

Battle of the Milvian Bridge

The *Battle of the Milvian Bridge* is the largest and most famous fresco in this room. Fought in 312, this was the battle in which Constantine, despite the larger forces lined up against him, was able to achieve a definitive victory over his rival Maxentius and attain sole rule as the first Christian emperor. The wall painting by Giulio Romano after Raphael's designs depicts the climax of the battle—the death of Maxentius, shown on the right sinking into the waters of the Tiber with his horse. To the left, on the riverbank, Constantine thunders up on a white steed, a resplendent victor in gleaming golden armor accompanied by three angels. Behind him rise two standards surmounted by crosses, whose apparition predicted victory for Constantine. A tumultuous battle rages around the two rivals, so chaotic it is almost impossible to decipher what is going on, and inflamed further by trumpeters in the background blowing fanfares. On the right, the Milvian Bridge is crowded with fighting soldiers, both on horseback and on foot, who seem about to topple over the sides into the river. The background depicts the hilly landscape north of Rome; on the left is Villa Madama, a countryseat designed by Raphael for Clement VII.

Raphael (Raffaello Sanzio) and Giulio Romano
***Battle of the Milvian Bridge*, 1520–1524**
Fresco
The Room of Constantine, Raphael Rooms

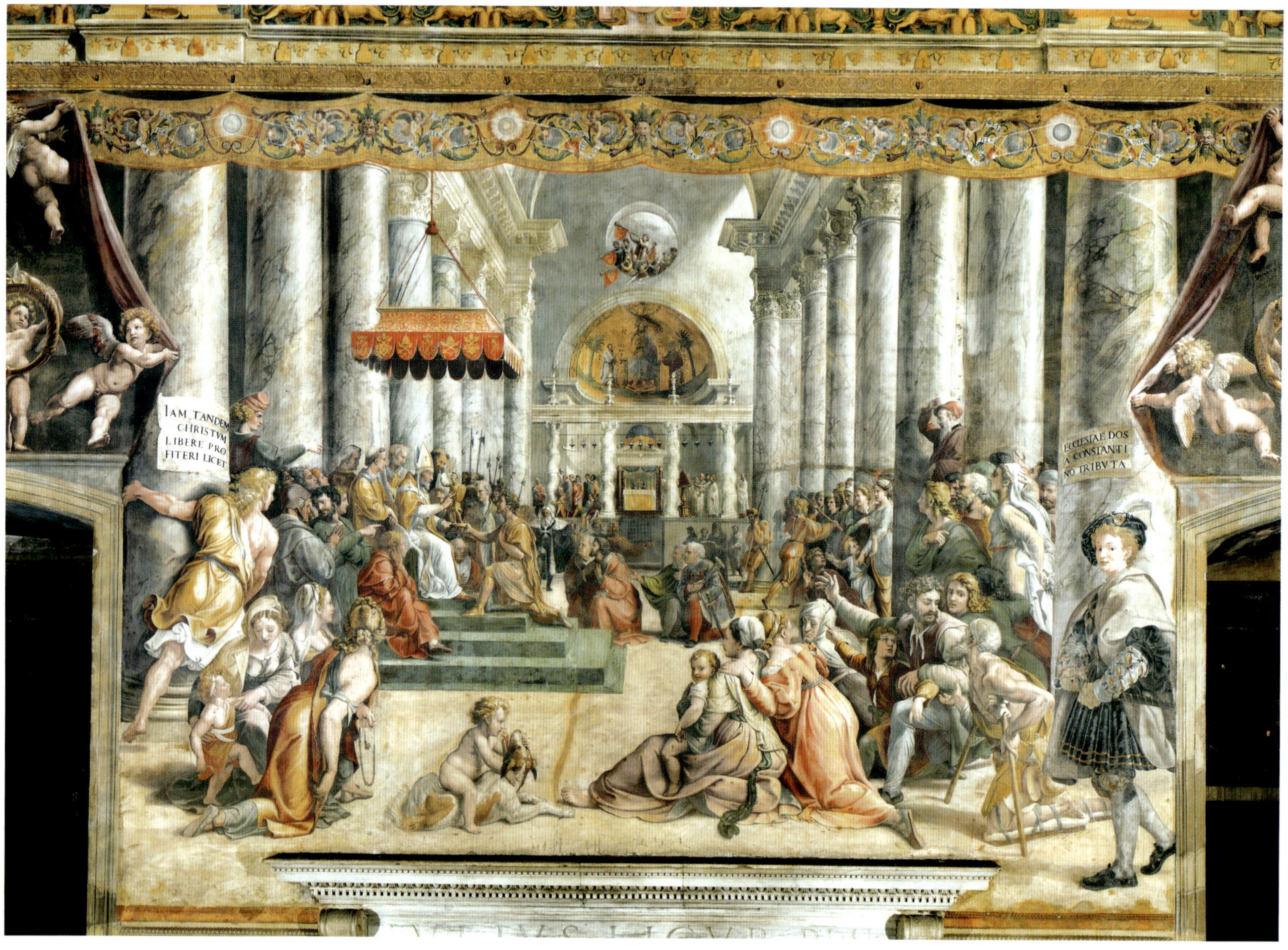

Raphael (Raffaello Sanzio) and Giovanni Francesco Penni

Donation of Constantine

After attaining sole rule over the Roman Empire, in around 313 Emperor Constantine supposedly promised Pope Sylvester I spiritual sovereignty over Rome, Italy, and the western half of the Roman Empire. The document known as the "Donation of Constantine," on which the medieval popes based claims for far-reaching spiritual and secular power, was revealed in the fifteenth century to be a forgery dating from around 800. Later popes continued to assert the validity of the act of donation, however, which this fresco in the Sala di Costantino also affirmed. In it, Constantine hands the pope, enthroned in the middle ground under a red baldachino and bearing the features of Clement VII, a golden statuette as a symbol of the city of Rome. This scene unfolds in the nave of Old St. Peter's Basilica and is remarkable for the precise depiction of the architecture of the church, which was destroyed in the sixteenth century. In addition to its importance as an art-historical document, Penni's depiction of the citizens of Rome, gathered in the basilica, camped in the foreground, and observing events from between the columns, is also worthy of appreciation.

Raphael (Raffaello Sanzio) and Giovanni Francesco Penni, 1483–1520
***Donation of Constantine*, 1520–1524**
Fresco
The Room of Constantine, Raphael Rooms

Raphael (Raffaello Sanzio) and Giovanni Francesco Penni

Baptism of Constantine

This fresco, painted by Raphael's pupil Giovanni Francesco Penni after designs by the master, depicts the baptism of Constantine, an event from the life of the emperor that is known only in legend. Although Constantine promoted Christianity and professed his faith, he is not known to have been officially baptized. The baptism depicted here takes place in the baptistry of the Lateran Basilica, which Constantine erected after his battle with Maxentius on the demolished campsite of his opponent's elite cavalry. Penni depicted the octagonal structure with its mighty Ionic pillars with great fidelity. At the center of the picture, Constantine kneels before Pope Sylvester I, who pours water over the emperor's head from a dish. Above stands a man dressed in blue holding a long cross that points to the sign of victory sent by God and is the symbol of Constantine's rule. The pope has been given the facial features of Clement VII, under whose pontificate the Sala di Costantino was painted. In addition to various clergy, a number of figures are depicted in Renaissance dress, among them, on the far left, a bearded courtier in a luxurious black-and-gray coat who points to the baptism scene.

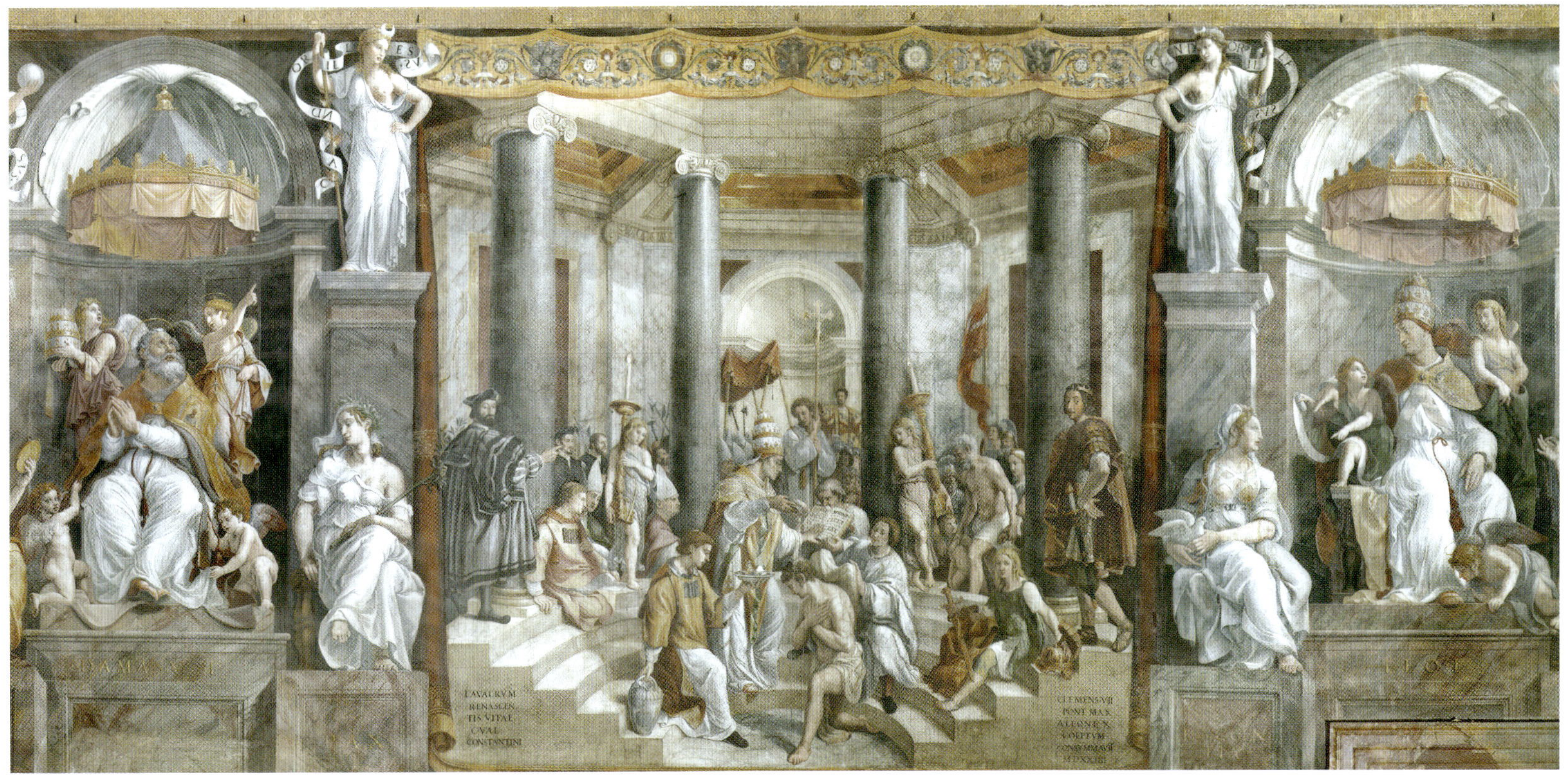

Raphael (Raffaello Sanzio) and Giovanni Francesco Penni, 1488–1520
***Baptism of Constantine*, 1517–1524**
Fresco
The Room of Constantine, Raphael Rooms

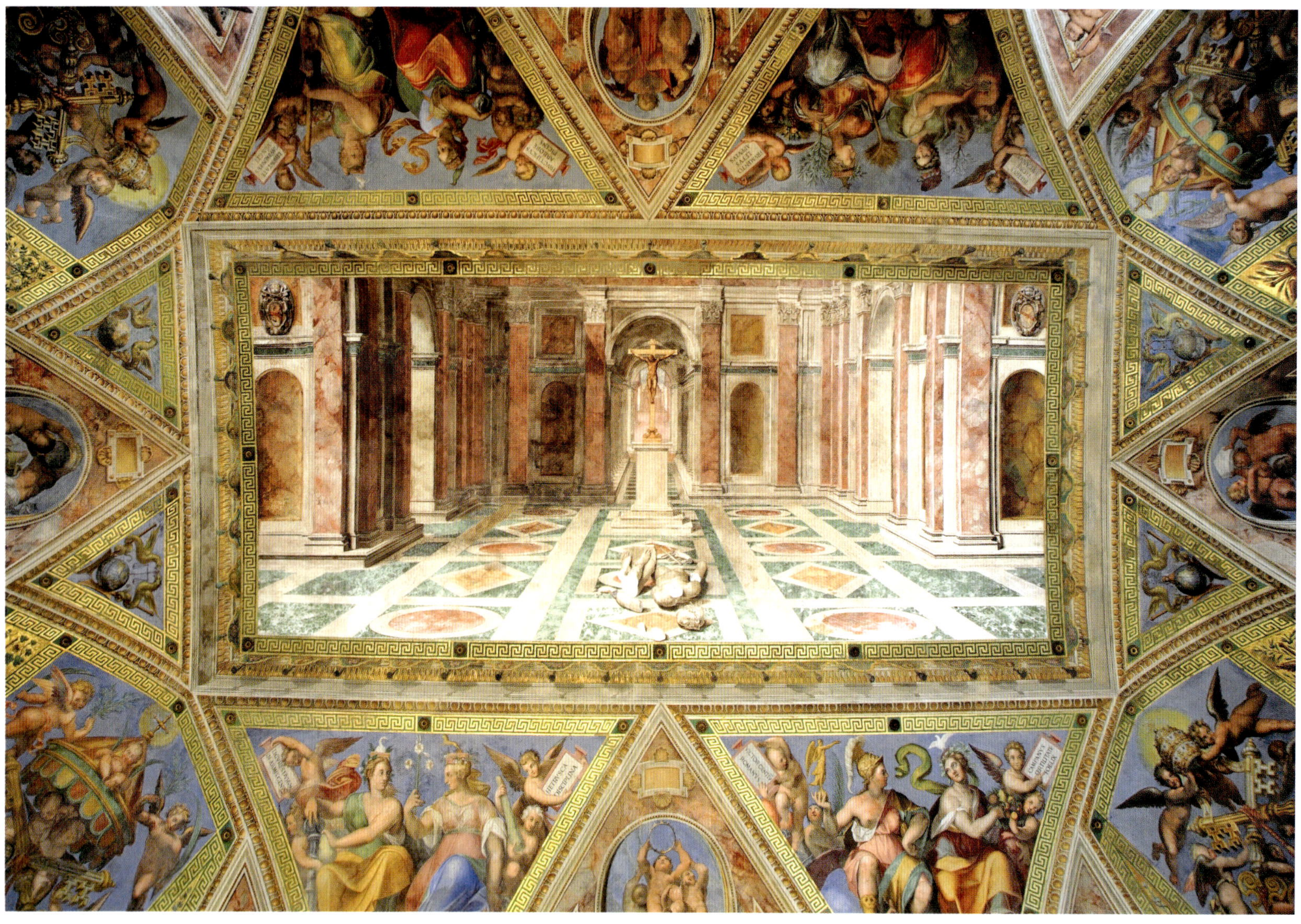

Tommaso Laureti

Triumph of Christian Religion, The Ceiling from the Room of Constantine

The monumental ceiling fresco of the Sala di Costantino depicts the triumph of Christianity and the Catholic faith. Gregory XIII (1502–1585, reigned from 1572) had the original plain wooden ceiling replaced with a painted vault, and commissioned the Sicilian artist Tommaso Laureti. Due to its grand dimensions, however, it would not be completed until the reign of Gregory's successor Sixtus V (1521–1590, reigned from 1585). Laureti was famous for his sophisticated illusionistic paintings of architecture, which this ceiling exemplifies. His principle of representation known as *di sotto in su* ("from below upwards") effectively expands the viewer's own space into the depicted space of the painting. In the case of the ceiling of the Sala di Costantino, the principle of dissolving boundaries served to vividly depict the triumph of Christianity over heathenism, in the form of the shattered statue of a god in the foreground. Behind the statue is a soaring crucifix on a stone plinth. The perspective marble floor directs attention on the few figurative elements, whose importance is also emphasized by optical means. This glorification of faith was in harmony with the objectives of the Catholic Counter-Reformation following the Council of Trent (1545–1563).

Tommaso Laureti, ca. 1530–1602
Triumph of Christian Religion, The Ceiling from the Room of Constantine, 1582-1585
Fresco
The Room of Constantine, Raphael Rooms

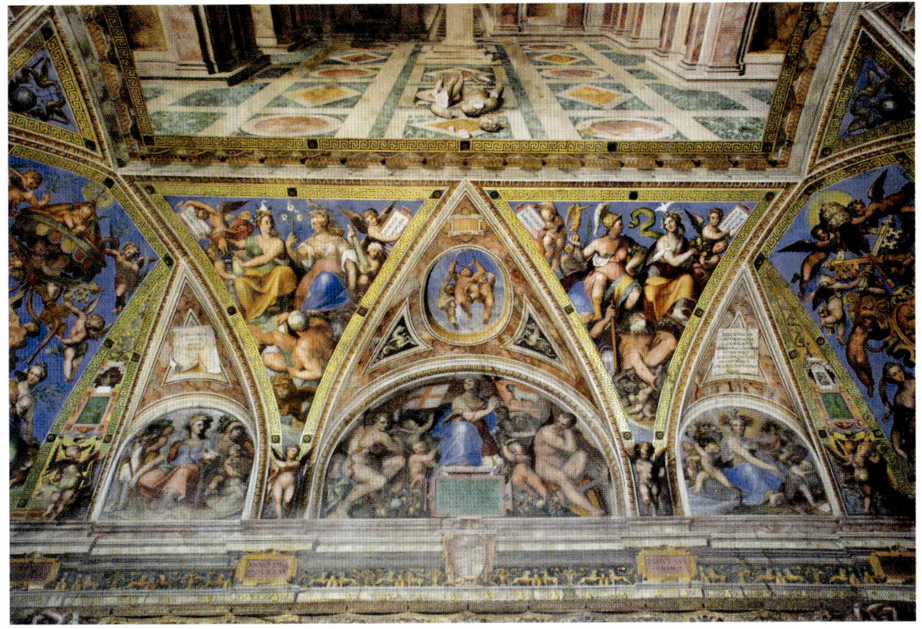

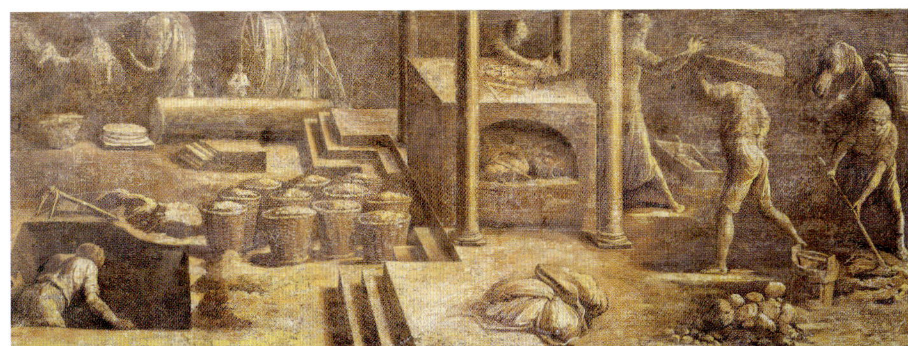

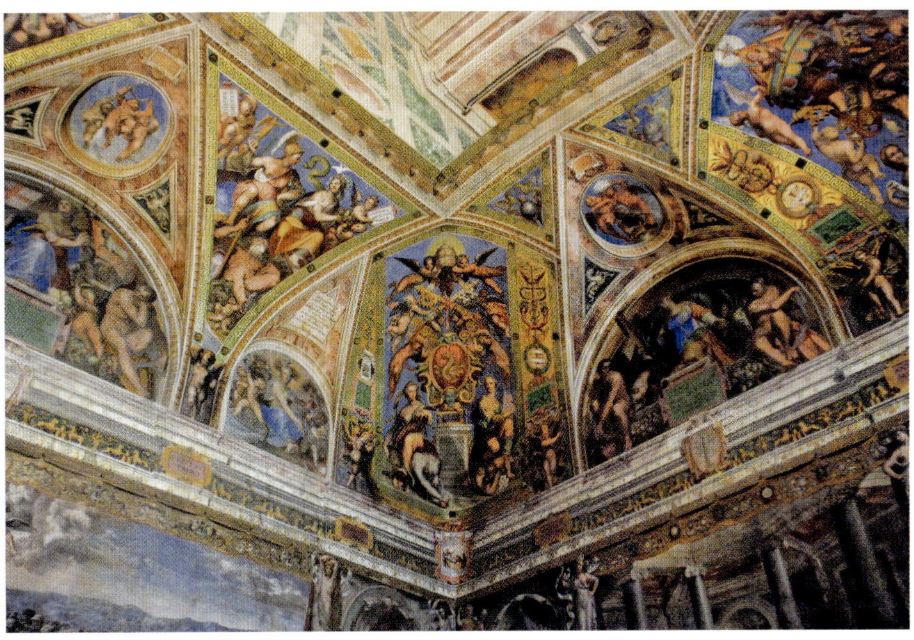

Tommaso Laureti, ca. 1530–1602
Northern Ceiling: The Provincia of Romana and Naples, Angels with the Motto of Clemens VII, and The Provincia of Liguria and Toscana
Fresco
The Room of Constantine, Raphael Rooms

Giulio Romano, 1499–1546
Fresco with the Foundation of Old St. Peter
Fresco
The Room of Constantine, Raphael Rooms

Tommaso Laurenti, ca. 1530–1602
Western Ceiling: Arms of Gregory XIII, Corner Fresco
Fresco
The Room of Constantine, Raphael Rooms

THE ROOM OF THE SIGNATURE

The first room to be painted was the Room of the Signature (Stanza della Segnatura), which Julius II had fitted out as his study and private library, though it also served as the occasional venue for meetings of the ecclesiastical tribunal. The fresco decoration, developed in consultation with the pope, brings together theology, philosophy, poetry, and justice as the pillars of Christian humanism, and these are represented in the ceiling roundels as female personifications. Each of these gold-backed roundels corresponds to a thematically related wall fresco. Below *Theology*, Raphael painted the *Disputation upon the Blessed Sacrament*, glorifying the mystery of the Trinity and the sacrament of the Eucharist. *Poetry* corresponds to the fresco depicting *Parnassus*, the mountain on which the god of poetry Apollo gathered with the Muses. *Justice* is illustrated by scenes of the origins of the two most important legal codes and personifications of virtue. The most famous fresco in this room is the *School of Athens*, which is positioned beneath *Philosophy*. This painting, whose sophisticated perspective opens up a deep vista in the small room, represents an idealized gathering of scholars and artists from the classical world, the Middle Ages, and the Renaissance, and constitutes one of Raphael's greatest achievements.

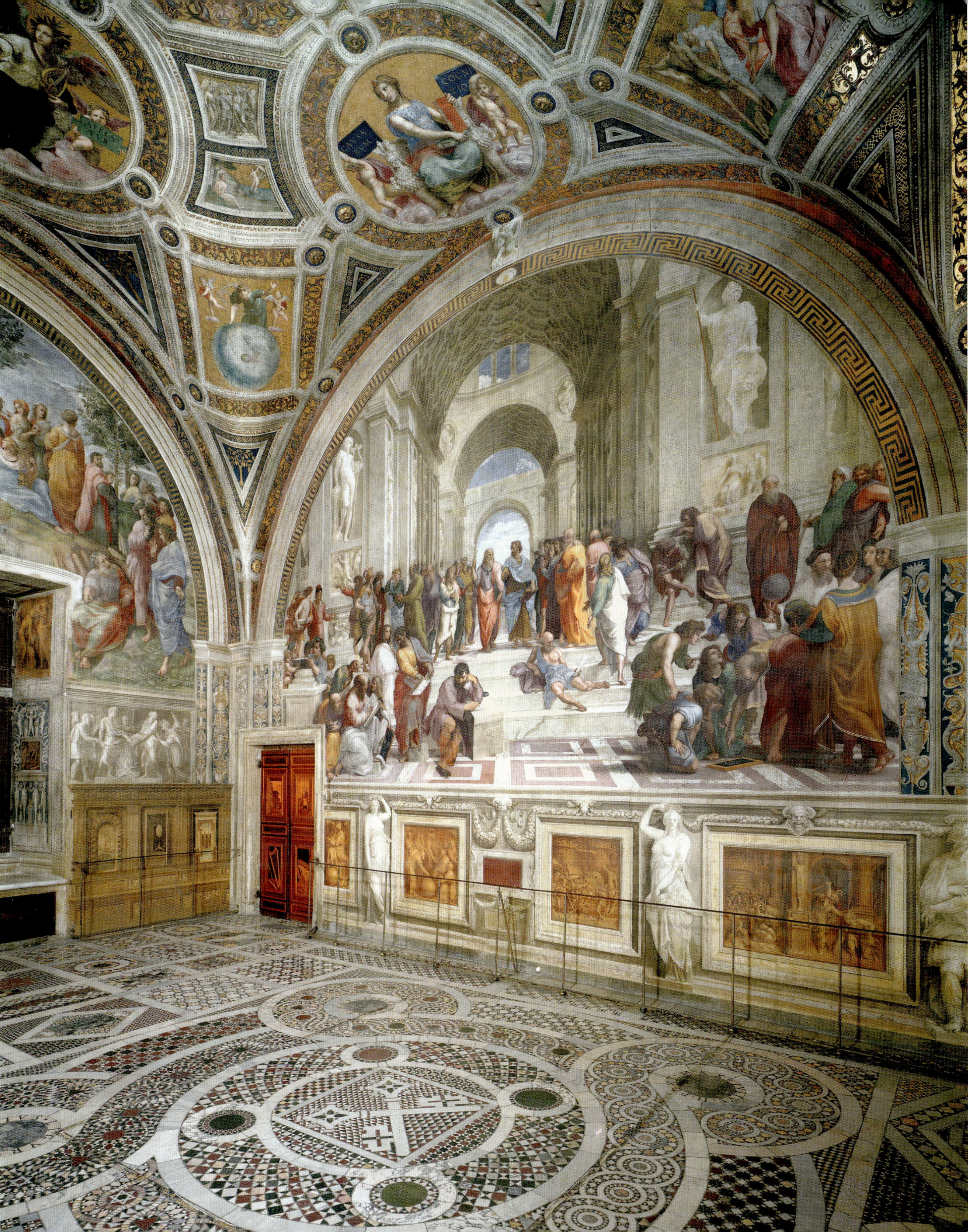

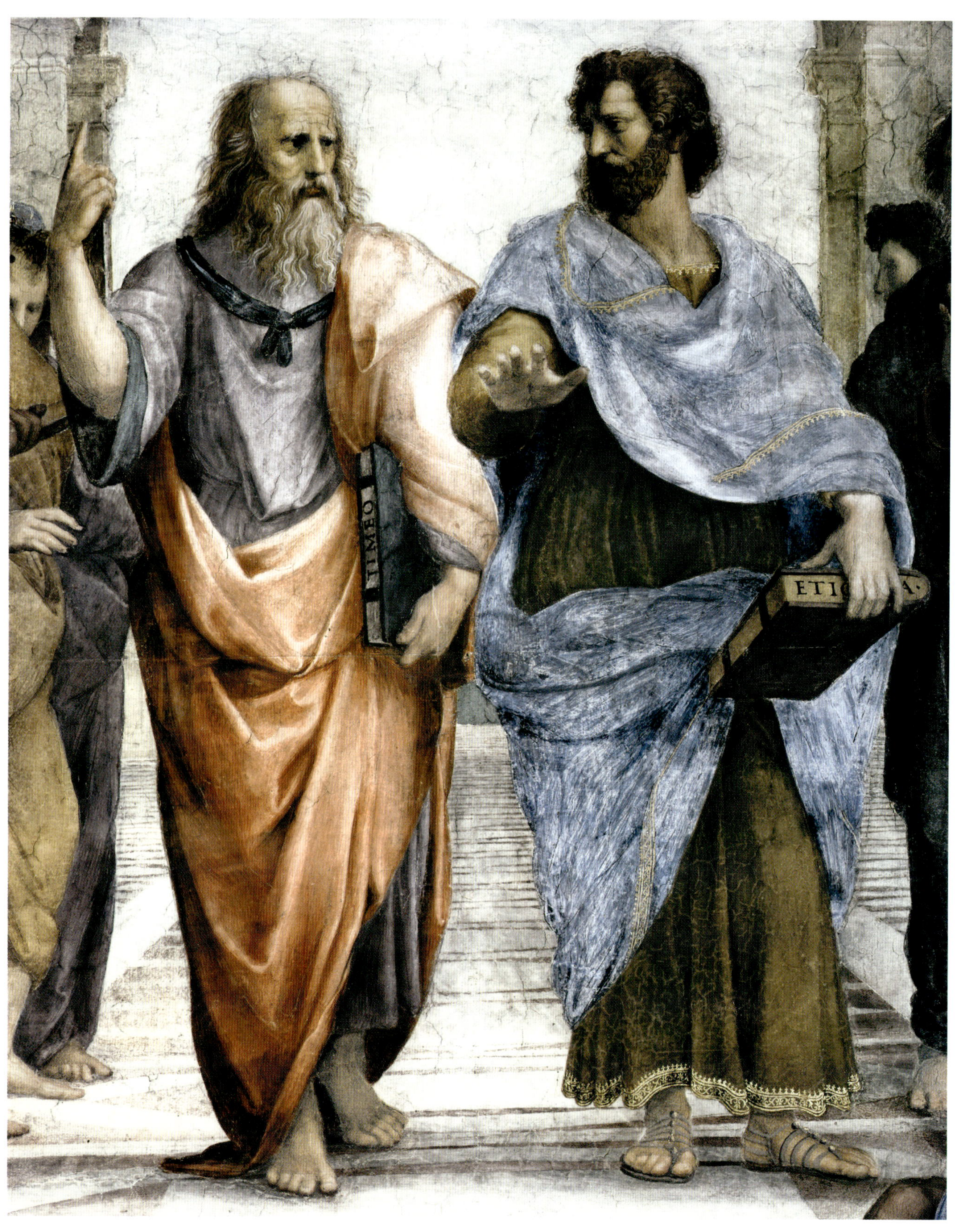
TIMEO

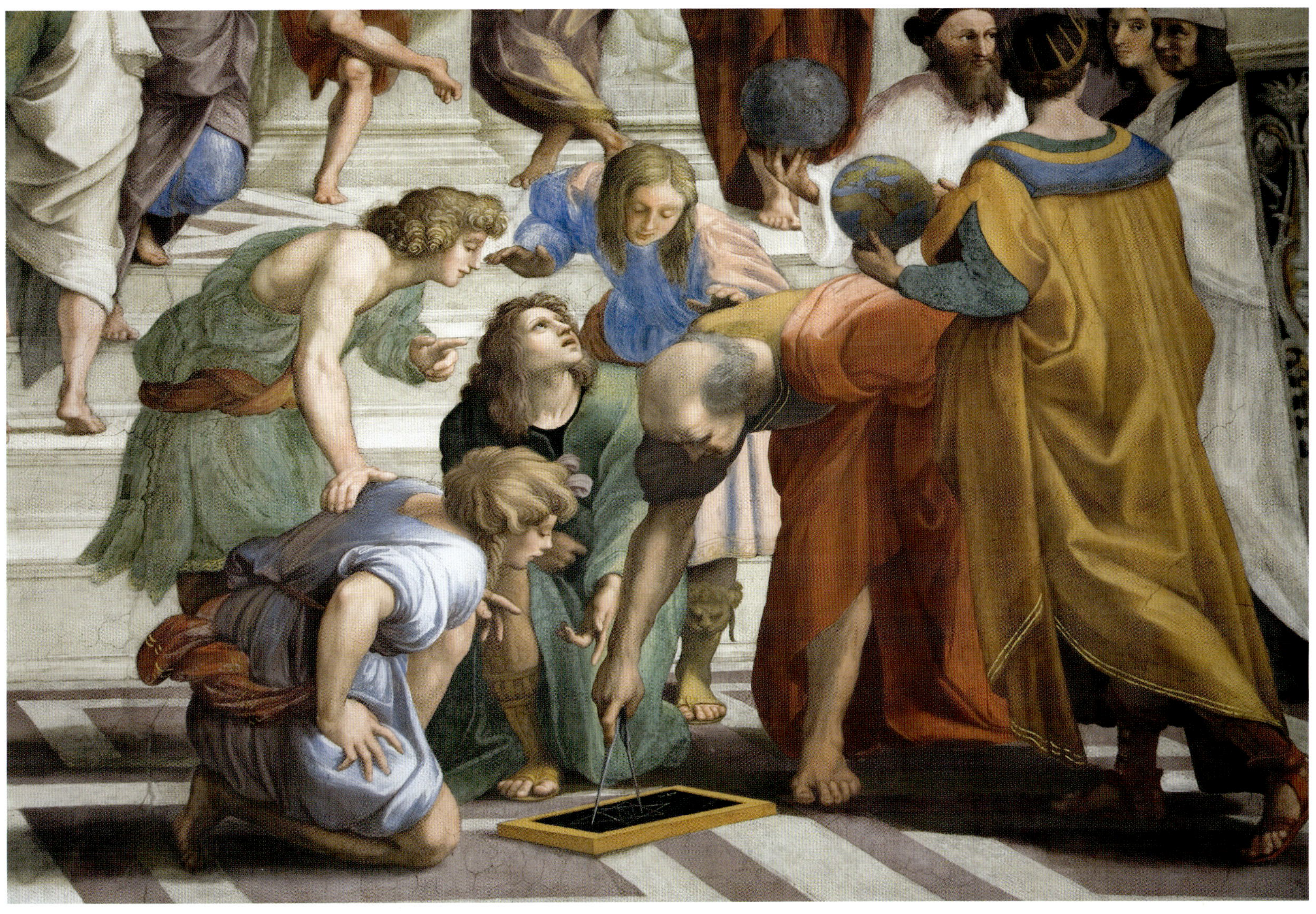

Raphael (Raffaello Sanzio)

The School of Athens

The most famous painting in the Room of the Signature is the *School of Athens* representing philosophy and science, disciplines in which Raphael includes painting and architecture. It is in part an homage to some of the most important artists and scholars active at the papal court at the beginning of the sixteenth century, most importantly the architect Bramante, to whom Raphael owed his recommendation to Julius II. The figures are gathered before monumental perspective architecture dominated by arches, reminiscent of Bramante's designs for the rebuilding of St. Peter's. This idealized meeting of thinkers is led by Plato and Aristotle, the most significant classical philosophers, who stand at the center of the painting. Conspicuous in the foreground are two scholars holding slates, on the left Pythagoras and on the right Euclid, with the features of Bramante. As the embodiments of arithmetic and geometry, these two figures also represent the connection between architecture and the art of perspective. While Raphael has portrayed himself as a simple onlooker in a black beret on the right-hand edge of the fresco, he has given the severe-looking figure of Heraclitus, seated in the foreground, the features of Michelangelo.

Raphael (Raffaello Sanzio), 1483–1520
***The School of Athens*, 1508–1511**
Fresco
The Room of the Signature, Raphael Rooms

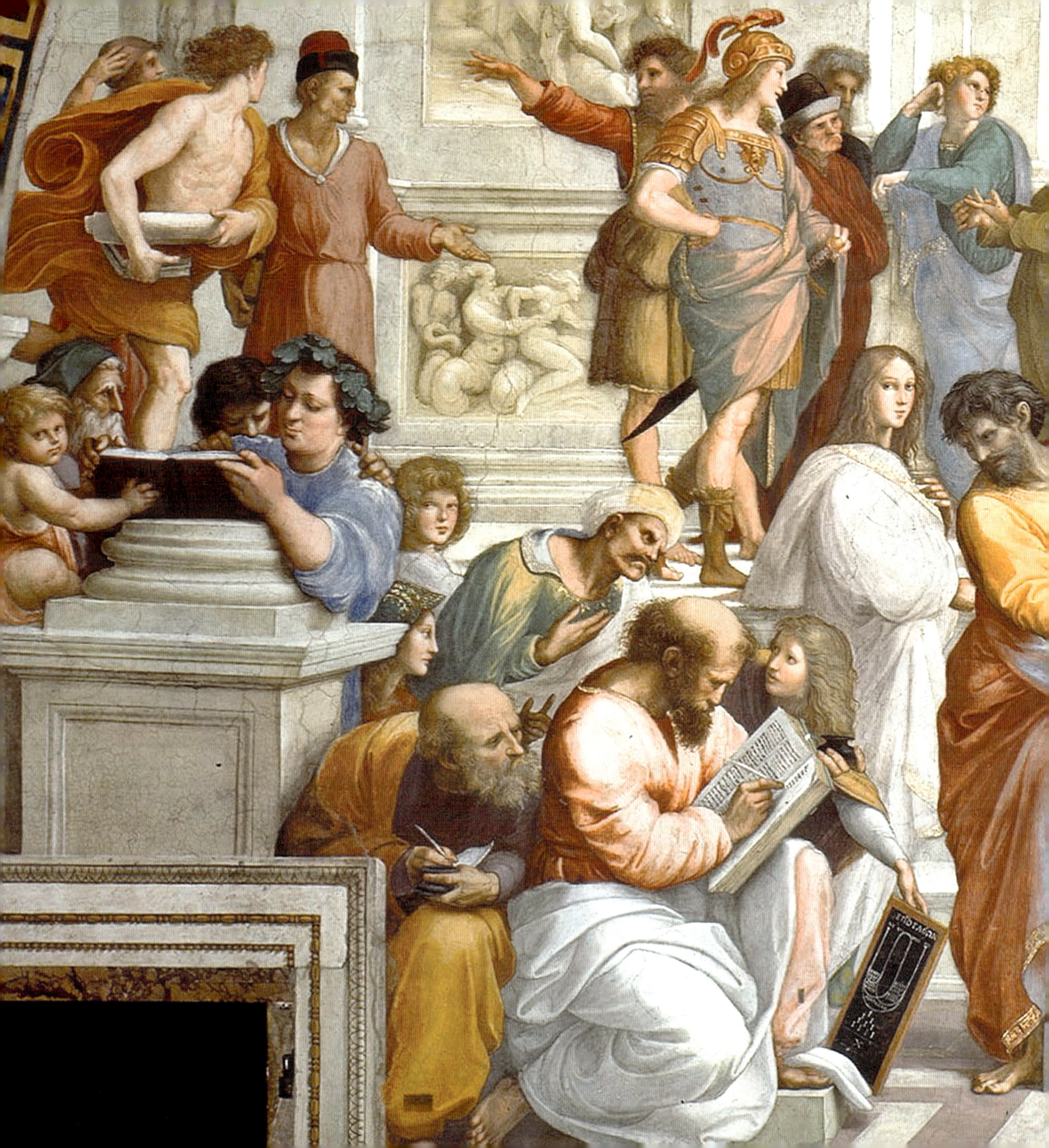

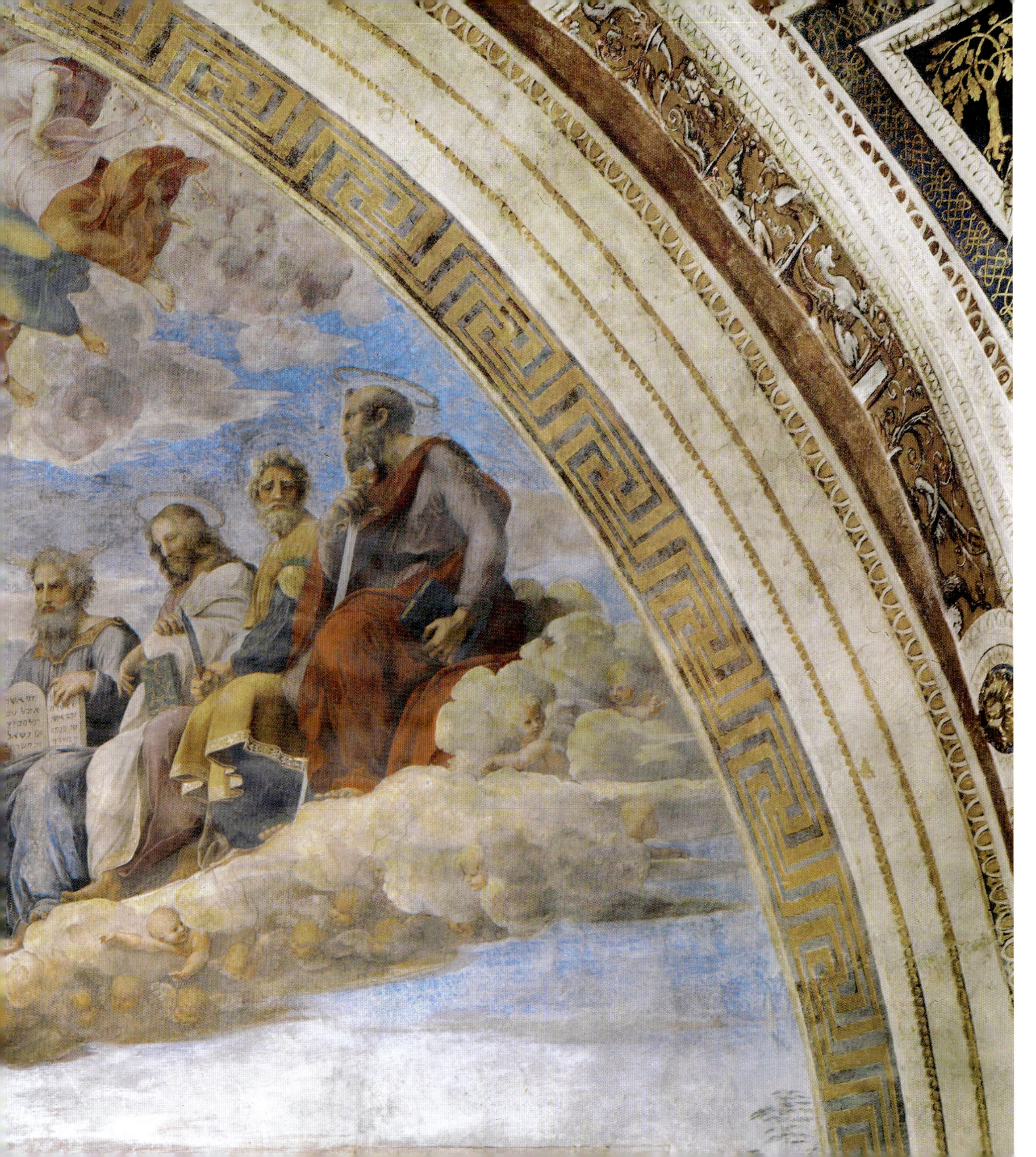

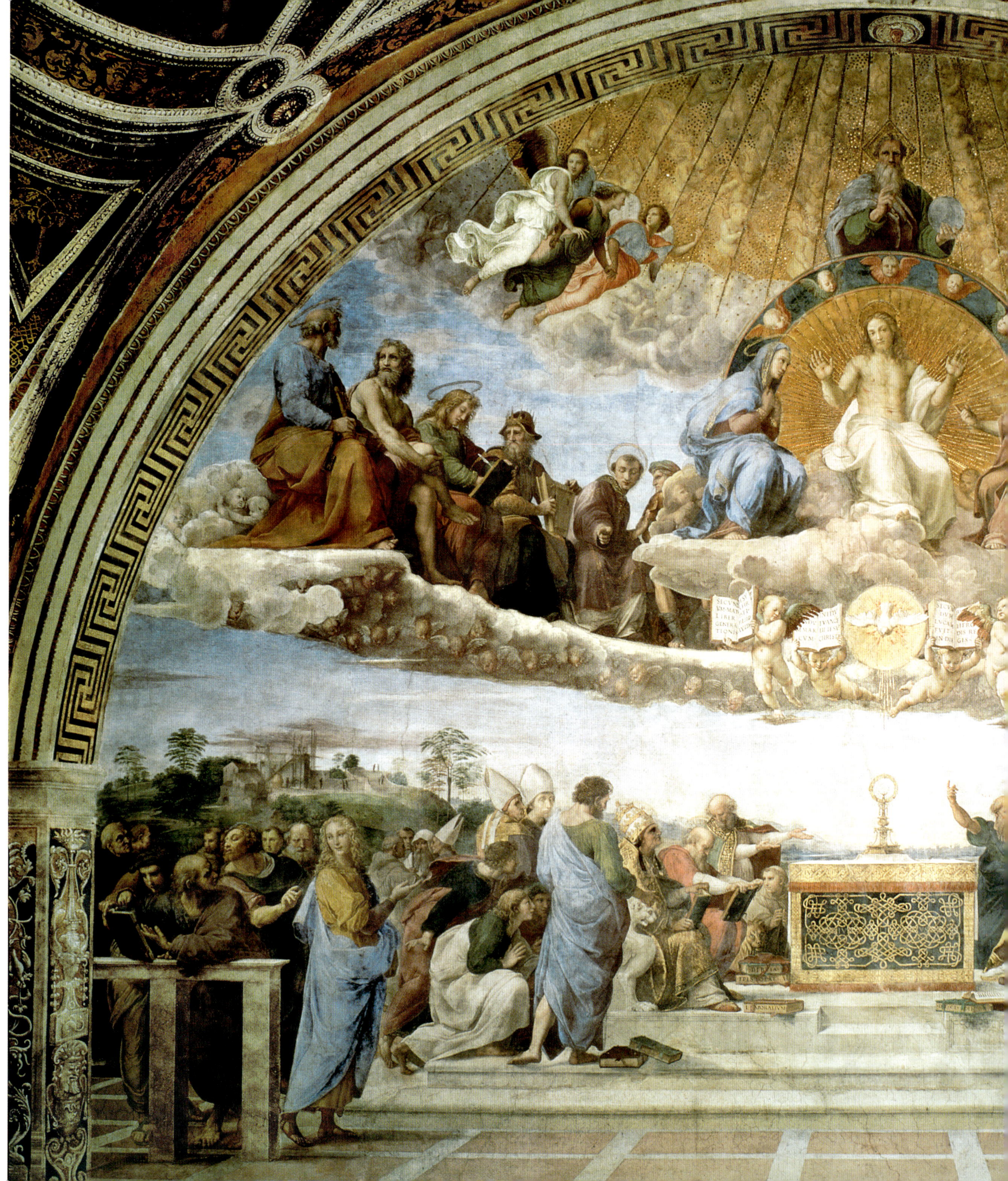

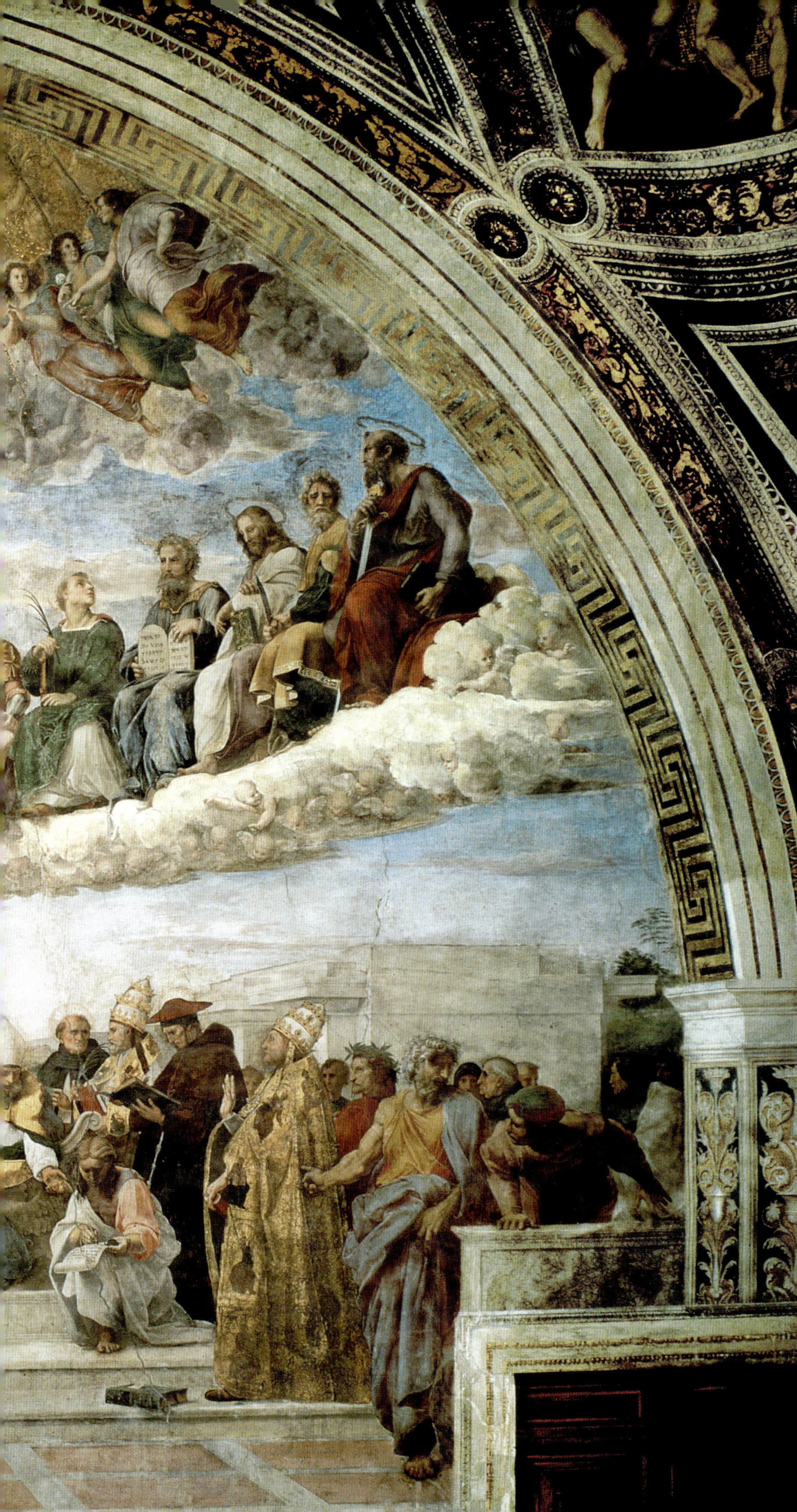

Raphael (Raffaello Sanzio), 1483–1520
***Disputation Over the Blessed Sacrament*, 1508–1511**
Fresco
The Room of the Signature, Raphael Rooms

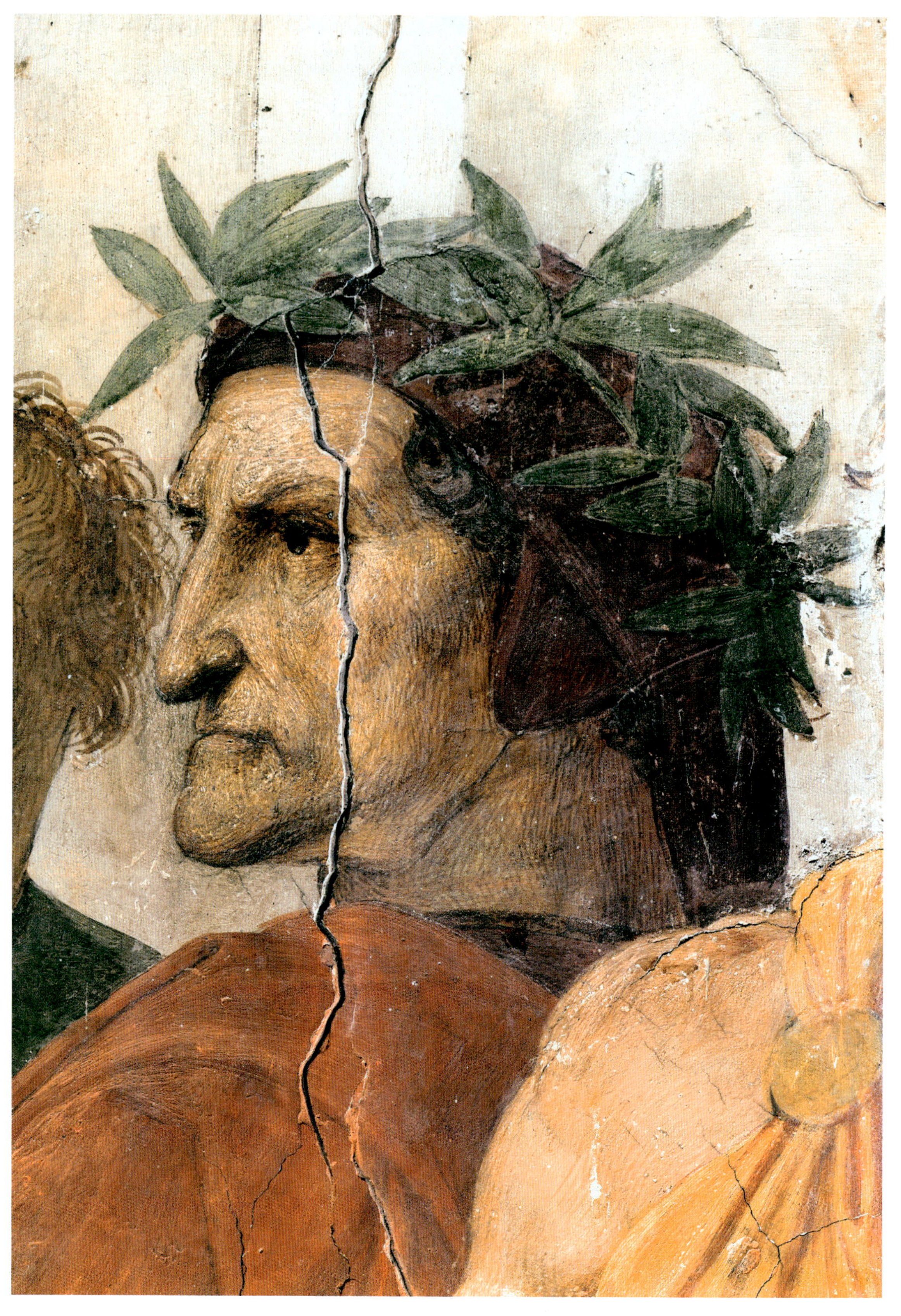

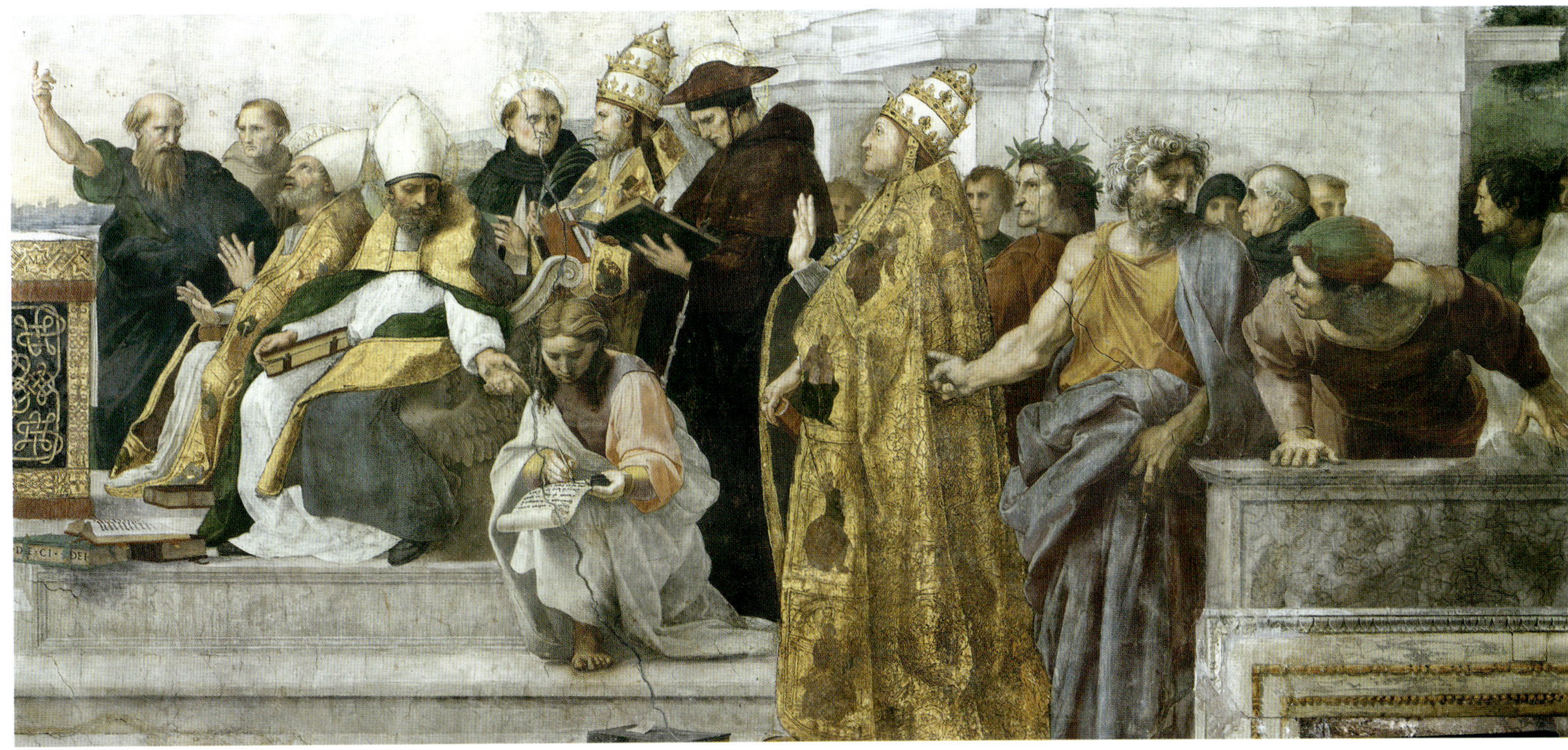

Raphael (Raffaello Sanzio)

Disputation over the Blessed Sacrament

This large painting depicts the glorification of the Christian faith and the sacrament of the Eucharist. The mystery of God made flesh and the real presence of Christ in the Host is the subject of the central axis of the picture. In the celestial zone we see the Holy Trinity with God the Father in the golden firmament giving a blessing; Christ accompanied by the Virgin Mary and John the Baptist (the Deësis); and the dove of the Holy Ghost. Christ, wearing white robes, appears against a medallion of golden rays, and with raised arms displays the wounds he sustained during his sacrificial death on the cross. The white dove of the Holy Ghost is also shown before a golden medallion. There is an explicit chromatic and formal relationship between these two roundels and the Host, which is placed in a monstrance on an altar and is the real center of the painting. It is toward the Host that the attention of the saints in heaven and the theologians, scholars, and representatives of the Church on the altar steps is directed as they debate the mysteries of the Eucharist with expressive gestures. Around the altar sit the Church Fathers St. Jerome, St. Ambrose, and St. Gregory the Great, who has been given the features of Julius II. The tall pope on the right is Sixtus IV; next to him, in profile, is the head of Dante crowned with a laurel wreath.

Raphael (Raffaello Sanzio), 1483–1520
***Disputation over the Blessed Sacrament*, 1508–1511**
Fresco
The Room of the Signature, Raphael Rooms

Raphael (Raffaello Sanzio), 1483–1520
***The Cardinal and Theological Virtues,* 1508–1511**
Fresco
The Room of the Signature, Raphael Rooms

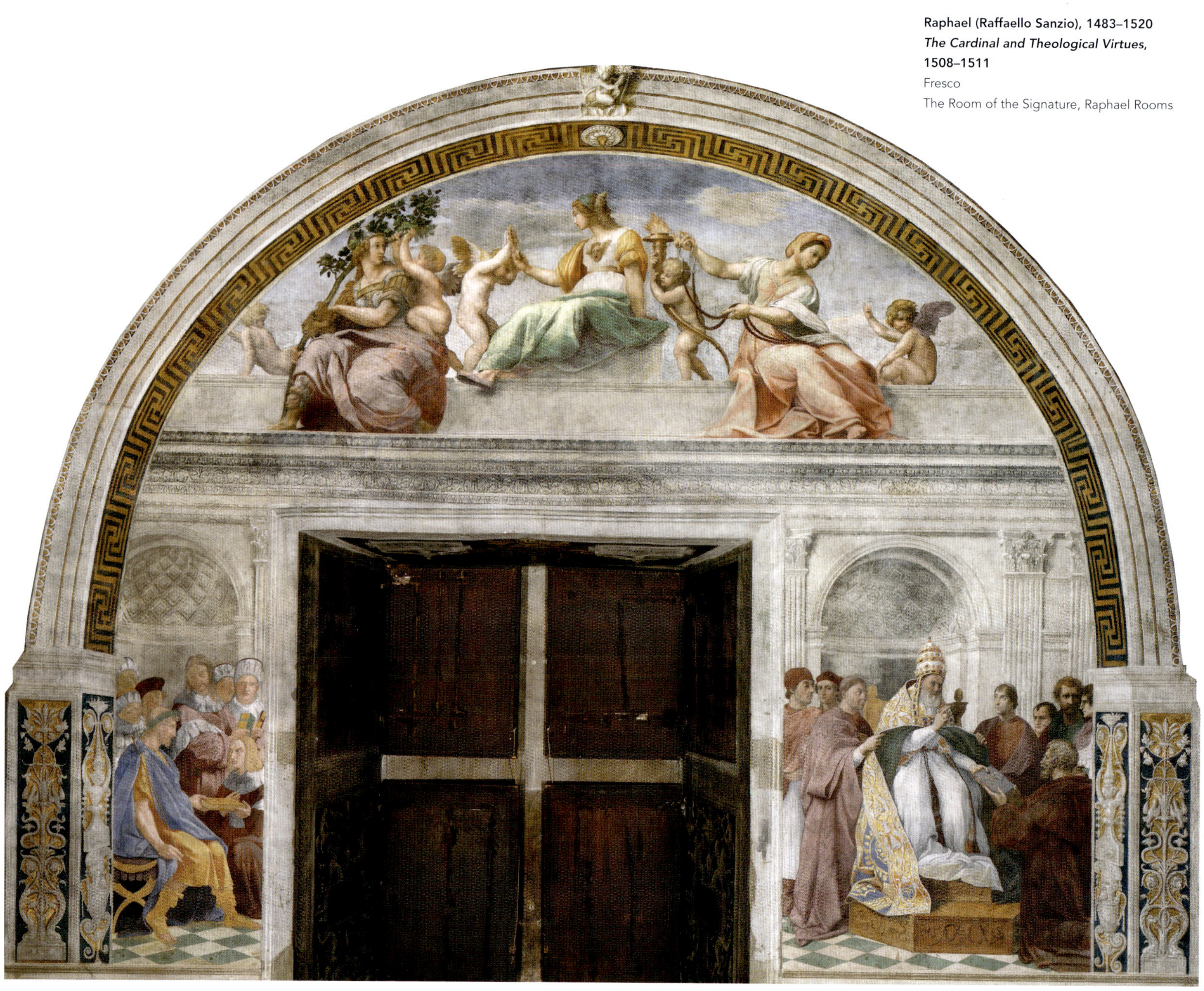

Raphael (Raffaello Sanzio)

Parnassus

Parnassus is a mountain in central Greece regarded in ancient times as the home of Apollo, the god of poetry, and the Muses. Raphael's fresco depicts the summit of the mountain as the setting for an idealized gathering of Apollo, the Muses, and artists from different centuries. Raphael has cleverly incorporated the doorway into his composition, as the substructure of the mountain. The god is seated at the center of the picture beneath a laurel tree (symbolizing poetic glory), playing a *viola da braccio*. His gaze is directed toward the personification of poetry on the ceiling vault. He is surrounded by the Muses in the guise of beautiful maidens holding objects representing their attributes. On the left and right are groups of male figures wearing laurel wreaths and the ancient Greek poet Sappho with a lyre. Like Apollo, she embodies the association in the ancient world between music and poetry. Among the poets assembled on Mount Parnassus is the blind Homer, on the left between Virgil and Dante (shown in profile), and the Renaissance poets Ariosto and Boccaccio, standing next to the Muses on the right. The three figures in the right foreground have been identified as the ancient authors Horace and Ovid and the humanist Sannazaro.

Raphael (Raffaello Sanzio), 1483–1520
***Parnassus*, 1508– 1511**
Fresco
The Room of the Signature, Raphael Rooms

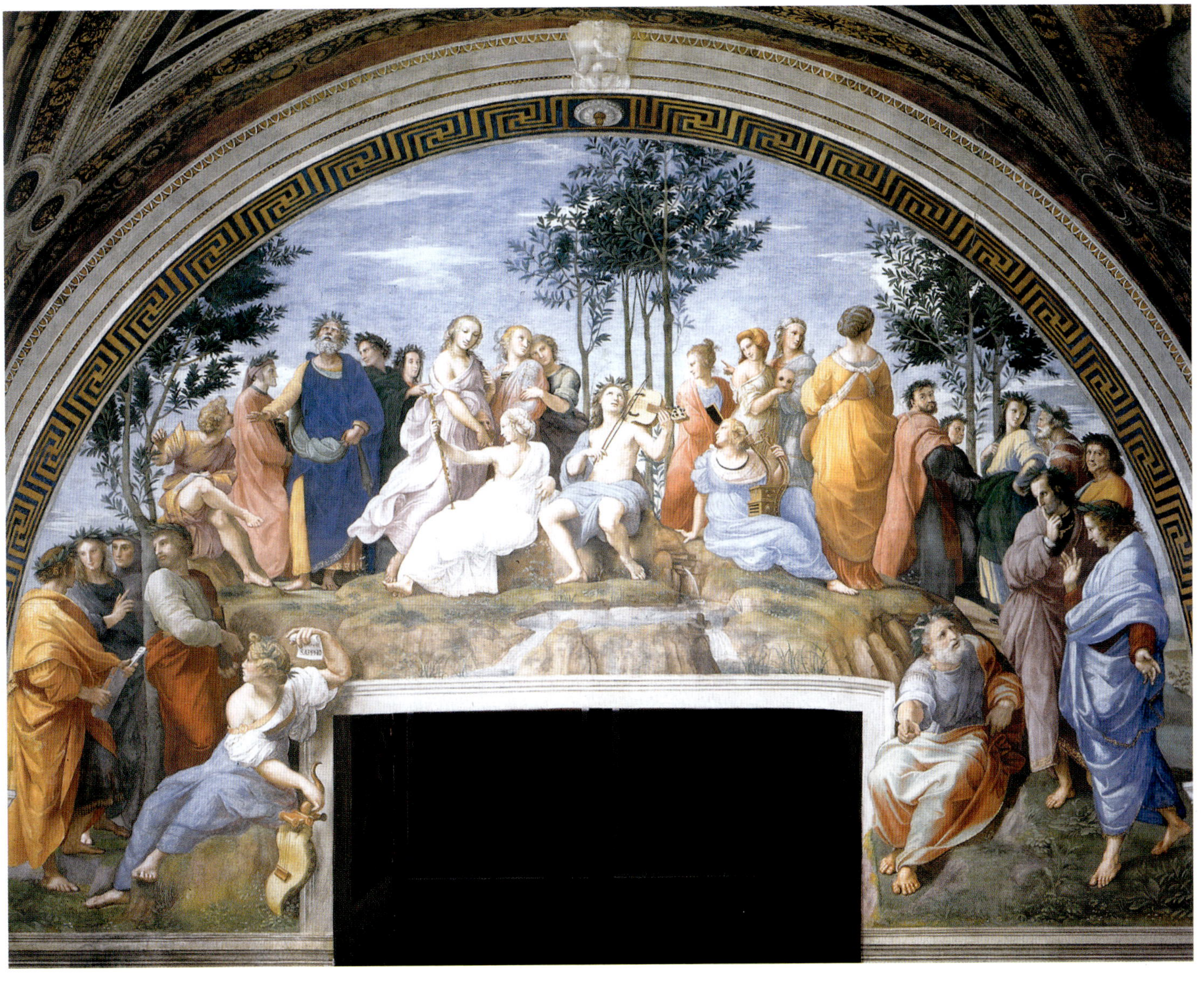

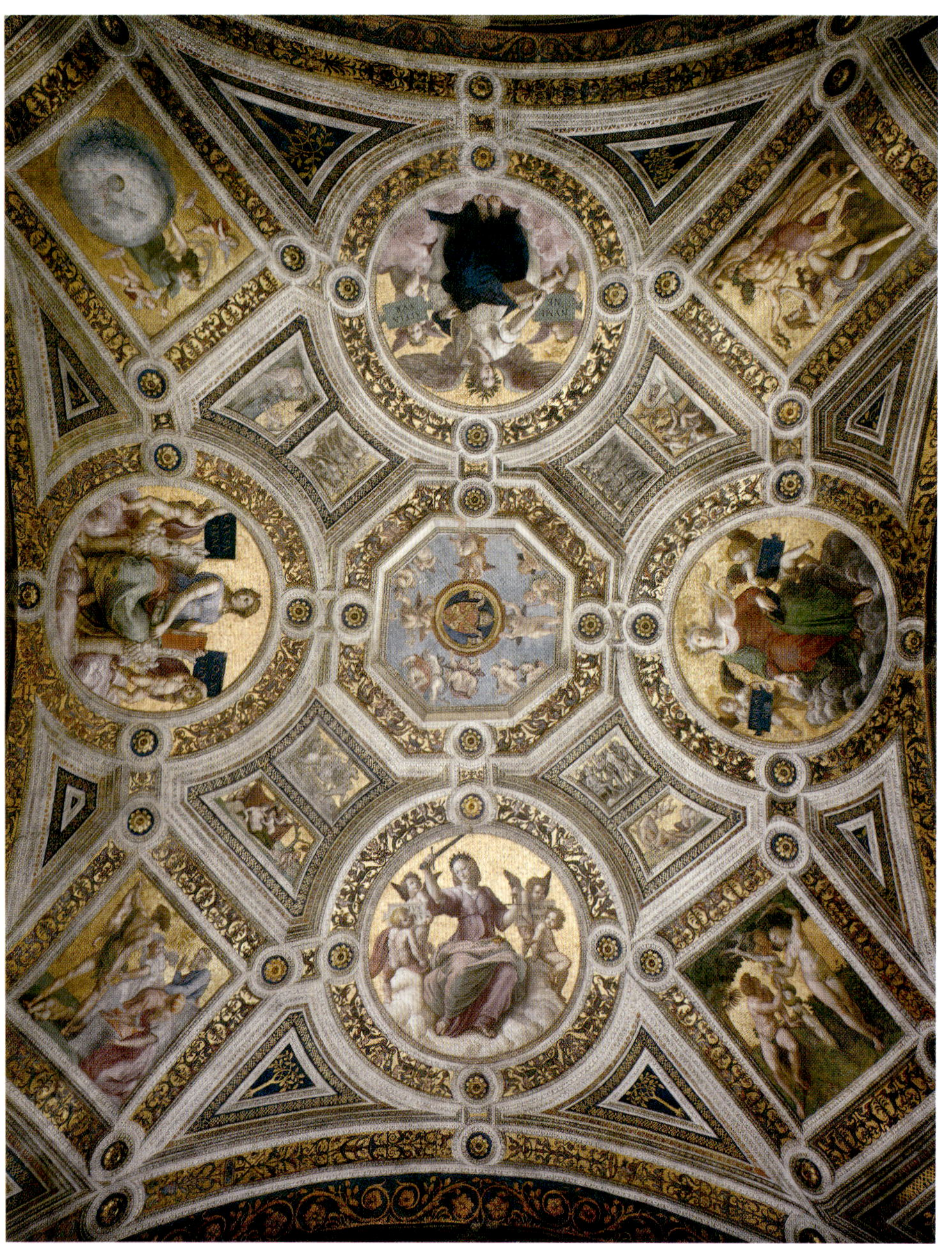

Raphael (Raffaello Sanzio)

Ceiling of the Room of the Signature

The illusionistic architecture of the Room of the Signature's magnificent painted and gilded ceiling provides the setting for various allegorical scenes and scenes from the Old Testament and classical mythology. The frescoes are thought to symbolize the principles of the true, the good, and the beautiful, to which Julius II dedicated his workroom. At the center is the papal coat of arms, floating in the sky supported by four hovering putti that recall Mantegna's famous putti ceiling (ca. 1470) in the ducal palace at Mantua. The number four is a recurring motif, as the most important pictorial fields are the four roundels containing personifications of theology, philosophy, poetry, and justice. These in turn provide the themes for the large wall frescoes as well as the corner fields of the ceiling. Thus *Justice* is framed by two examples of justice from the Old Testament, *Adam and Eve in Paradise* and the *Judgment of Solomon*. The corner field with *Astronomy* is assigned to *Philosophy*, while *Poetry* is accompanied by a depiction of Apollo and Marsyas, who challenged the god of poetry to a musical contest.

Raphael (Raffaello Sanzio), 1483–1520
***Ceiling of the Stanza della Segnatura*, 1508–1511**
Fresco
The Room of the Signature, Raphael Rooms

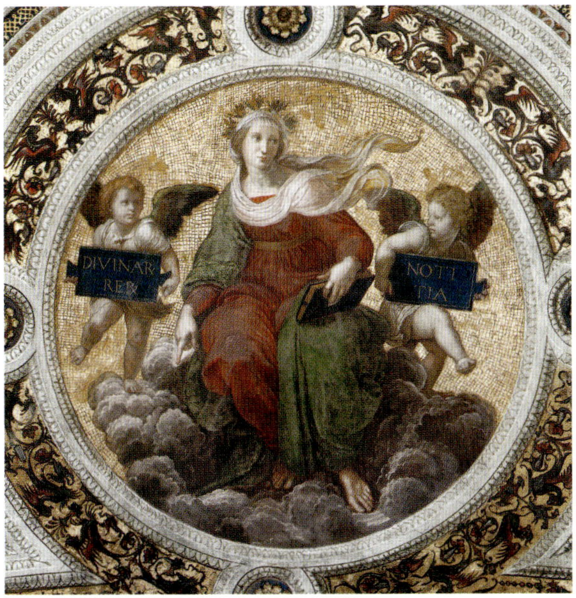

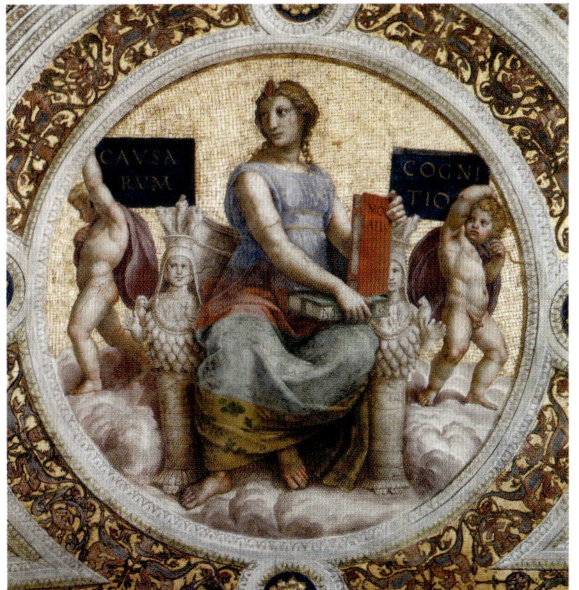

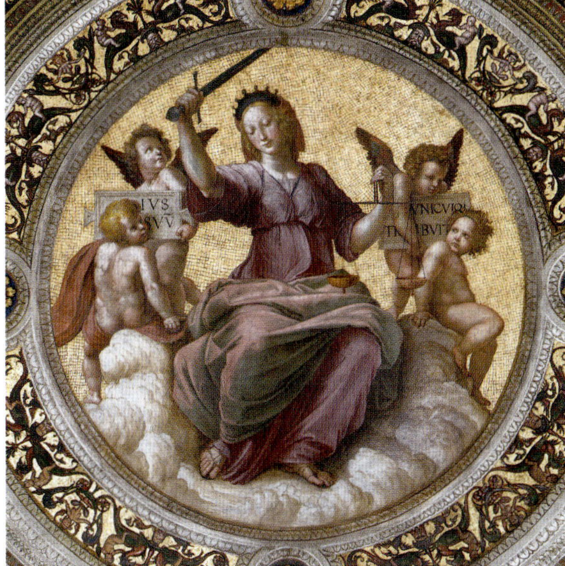

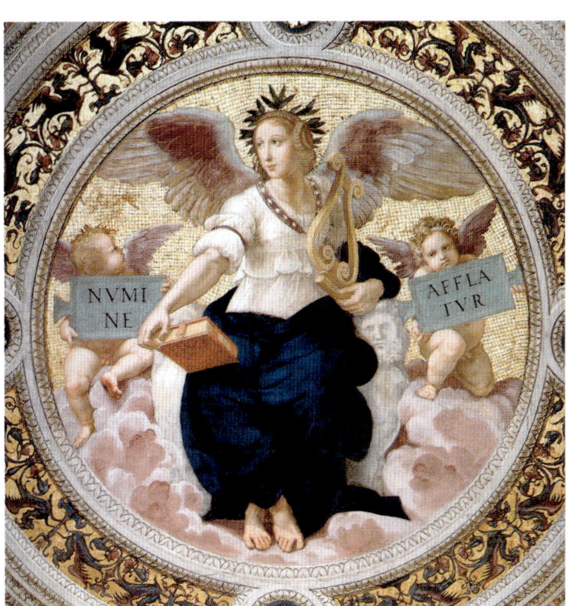

Raphael (Raffaello Sanzio), 1483–1520
Ceiling Detail: ***Allegory of Theology*****, 1508–1511**
Fresco
The Room of the Signature, Raphael Rooms

Raphael (Raffaello Sanzio), 1483–1520
Ceiling Detail: ***Allegory of Philosophy*****, 1508–1511**
Fresco
The Room of the Signature, Raphael Rooms

Raphael (Raffaello Sanzio), 1483–1520
Ceiling Detail: ***Allegory of Justice*****, 1508–1511**
Fresco
The Room of the Signature, Raphael Rooms

Raphael (Raffaello Sanzio), 1483–1520
Ceiling Detail: ***Allegory of Poetry*****, 1508–1511**
Fresco
The Room of the Signature, Raphael Rooms

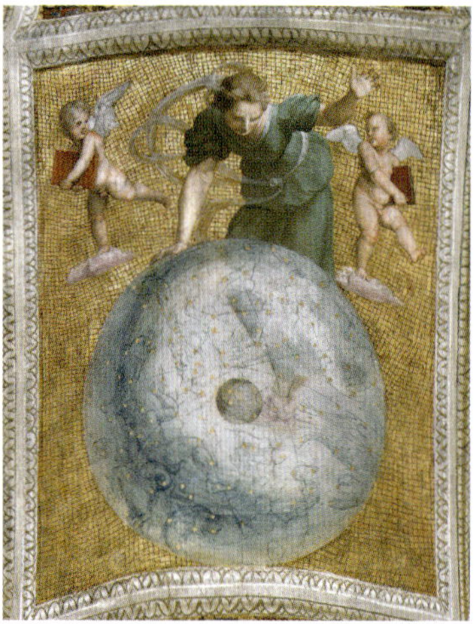

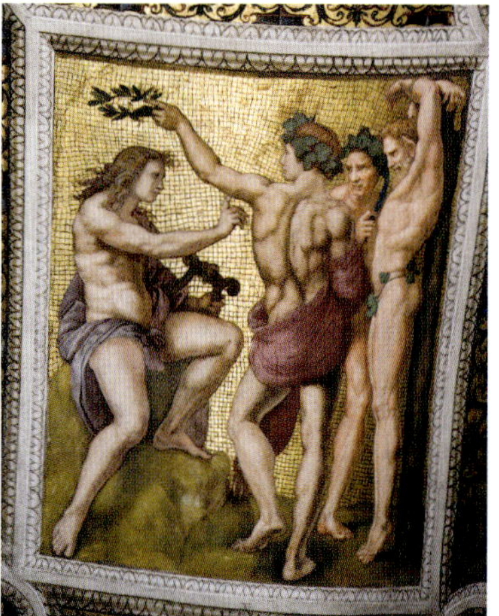

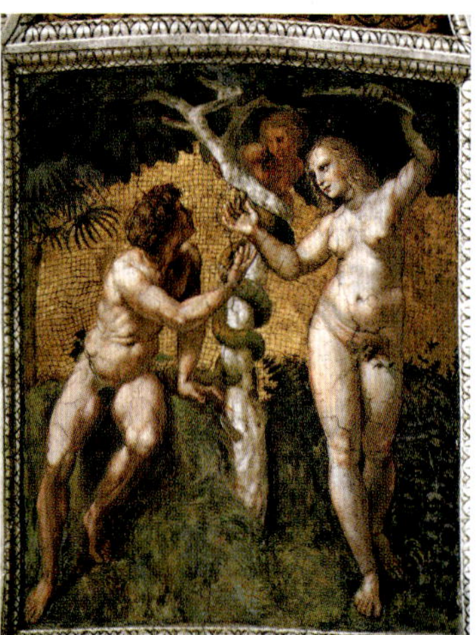

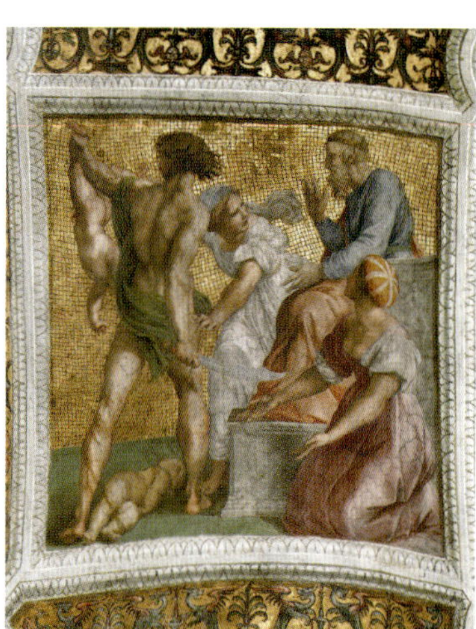

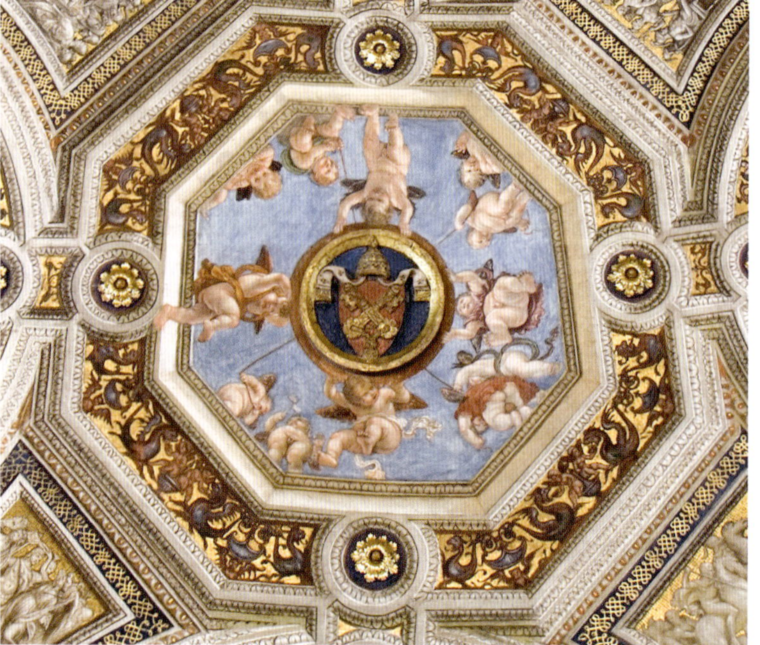

Raphael (Raffaello Sanzio), 1483–1520
Ceiling Detail: ***Creation of the Universe*****, 1508–1511**
Fresco
The Room of the Signature, Raphael Rooms

Raphael (Raffaello Sanzio), 1483–1520
Ceiling Detail: ***Apollo and Marsyas*****, 1508–1511**
Fresco
The Room of the Signature, Raphael Rooms

Raphael (Raffaello Sanzio) , 1483–1520
Ceiling Detail: ***Adam and Eve*****, 1508–1511**
Fresco
The Room of the Signature, Raphael Rooms

Raphael (Raffaello Sanzio), 1483–1520
Ceiling Detail: ***Judgment of Solomon*****, 1508–1511**
Fresco
The Room of the Signature, Raphael Rooms

Raphael (Raffaello Sanzio), 1483–1520
Ceiling Detail: ***Putti Holding the Coat of Arms of Pope Julius II*****, 1508–1511**
Fresco
The Room of the Signature, Raphael Rooms

THE ROOM OF HELIODORUS

Julius II used the neighboring Room of Heliodorus (Stanza di Eliodoro) for private audiences, and its decoration was aimed at reminding the visiting Church, political, and diplomatic dignitaries of the power of God as protector of the Church. The present name of the room derives from the fresco depicting the expulsion of Heliodorus from the Temple, an incident from the Old Testament in which God defends the Church's patrimony. A scene from the New Testament, the *Liberation of St. Peter*, makes explicit reference to God as the protector of the popes, who regard themselves as St. Peter's successors. The *Meeting of Leo the Great with Attila*, set in the early Middle Ages, represents God as the defender of Rome and Christianity against the heathens. Finally the *Mass of Bolsena* depicts the 1263 miracle of the Host, which led Pope Urban IV to institute the feast of Corpus Christi.

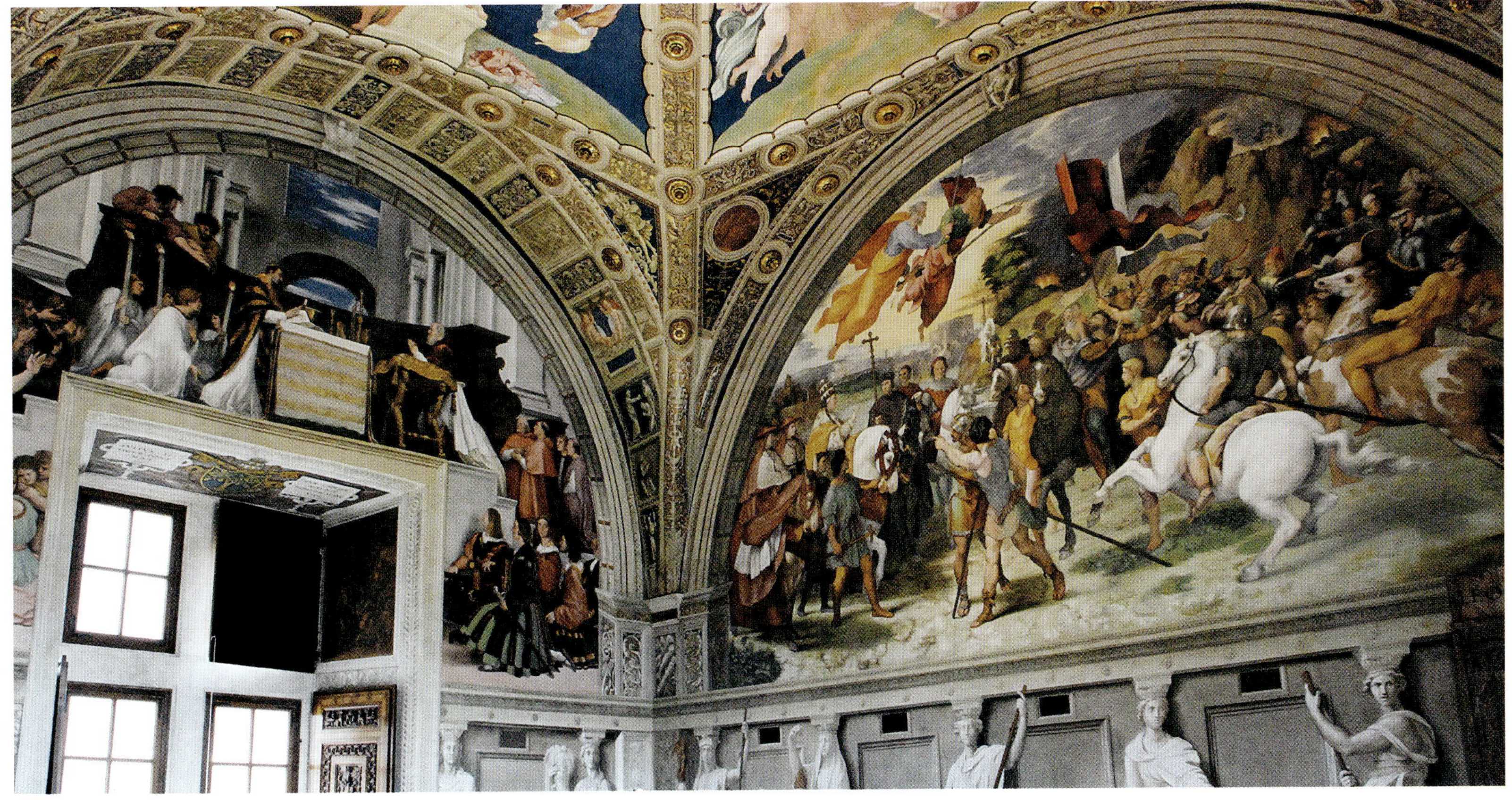

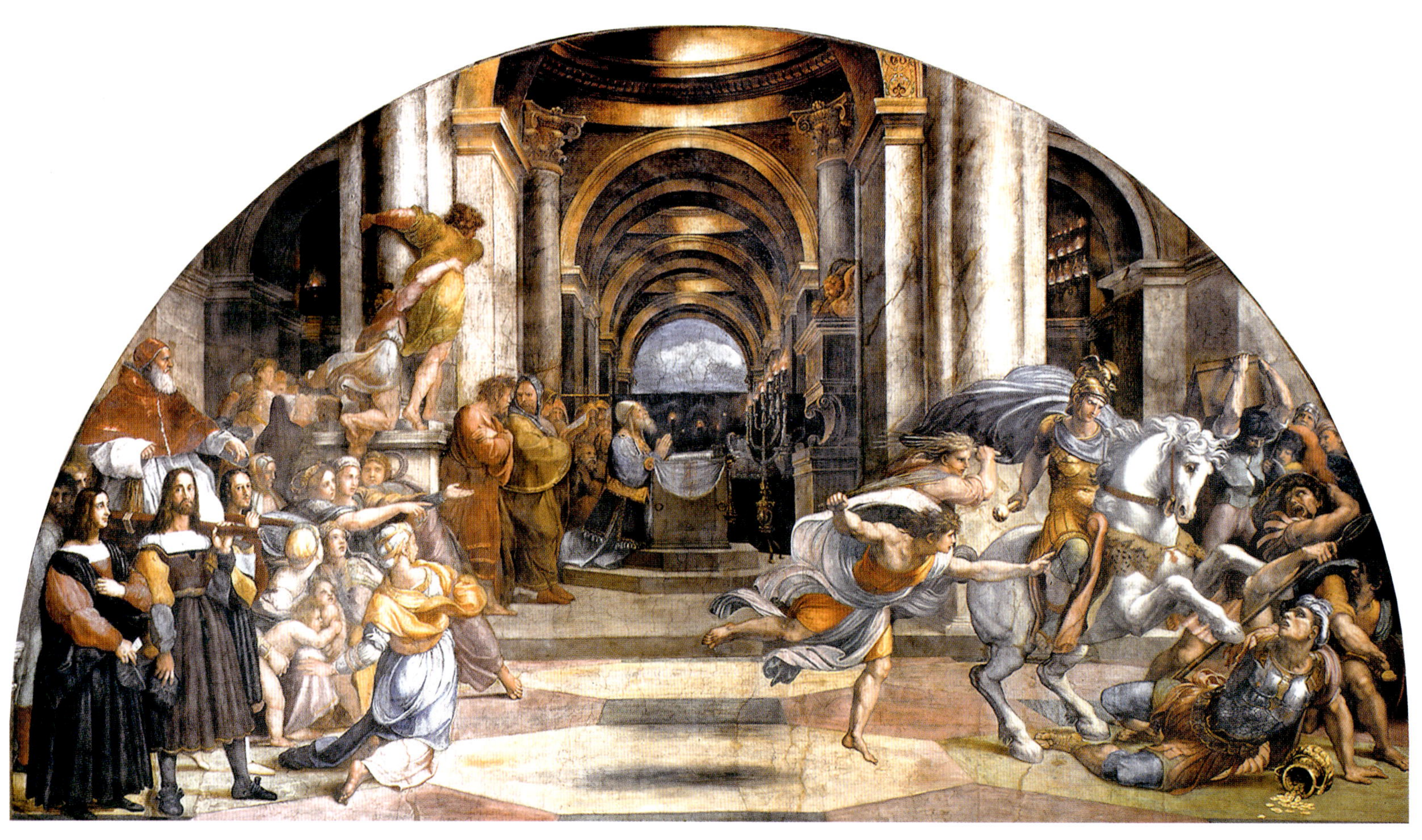

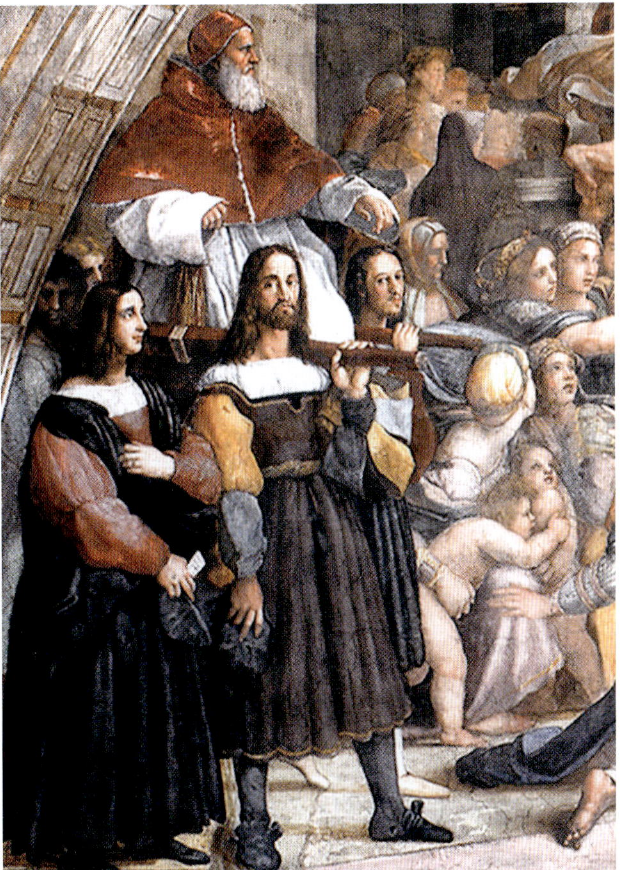

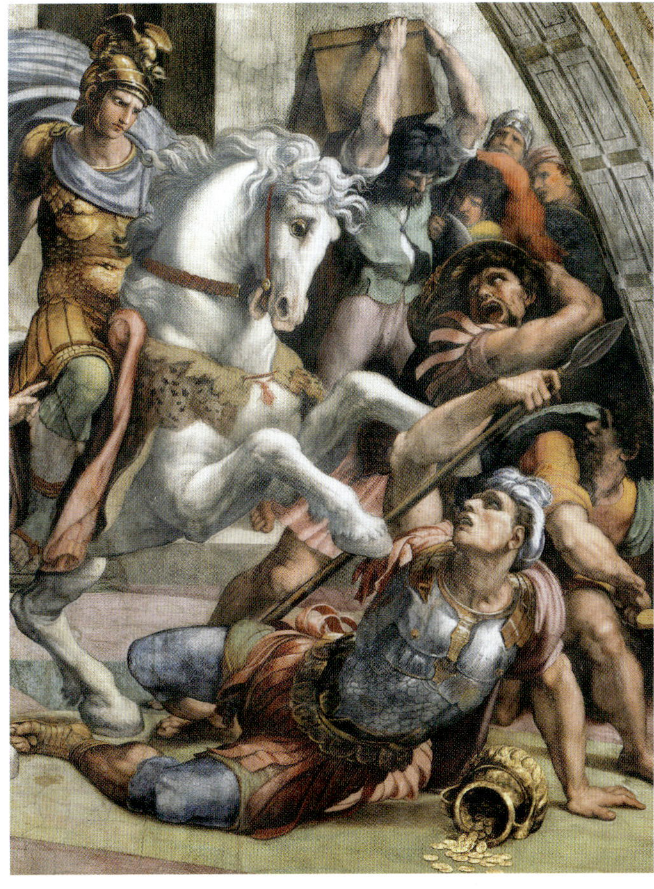

Raphael (Raffaello Sanzio)

The Expulsion of Heliodorus from the Temple

The second book of Maccabees, from the Old Testament, tells of Heliodorus, who was sent by the Seleucid king, the ruler of Israel, to confiscate the treasure of the Temple in Jerusalem (II Maccabees 3). However, as he stood with his soldiers before the treasury, "the Lord of spirits, and the Prince of all power caused a great apparition … An horse with a terrible rider upon him" and two men "notable in strength, excellent in beauty, and comely in apparel" brought Heliodorus to the ground with their blows, and the Temple treasure was saved. Raphael has depicted this moment of high drama with great impact. In the right-hand corner we see Heliodorus lying on the floor, felled by the blows and trampling of the heavenly messengers. In front of him gold coins from the pillaged treasure can be seen rolling out of an amphora. In the background the high priest is shown at the altar beseeching God for help while on the left of the painting the Israeli people observe the battle scene with fascination. Among them is Julius II, enthroned in a sedan chair, who had made the protection of Church patrimony one of his primary aims.

Raphael (Raffaello Sanzio), 1483–1520
***The Expulsion of Heliodorus from the Temple*, 1511–1512**
Fresco
The Room of Heliodorus, Raphael Rooms

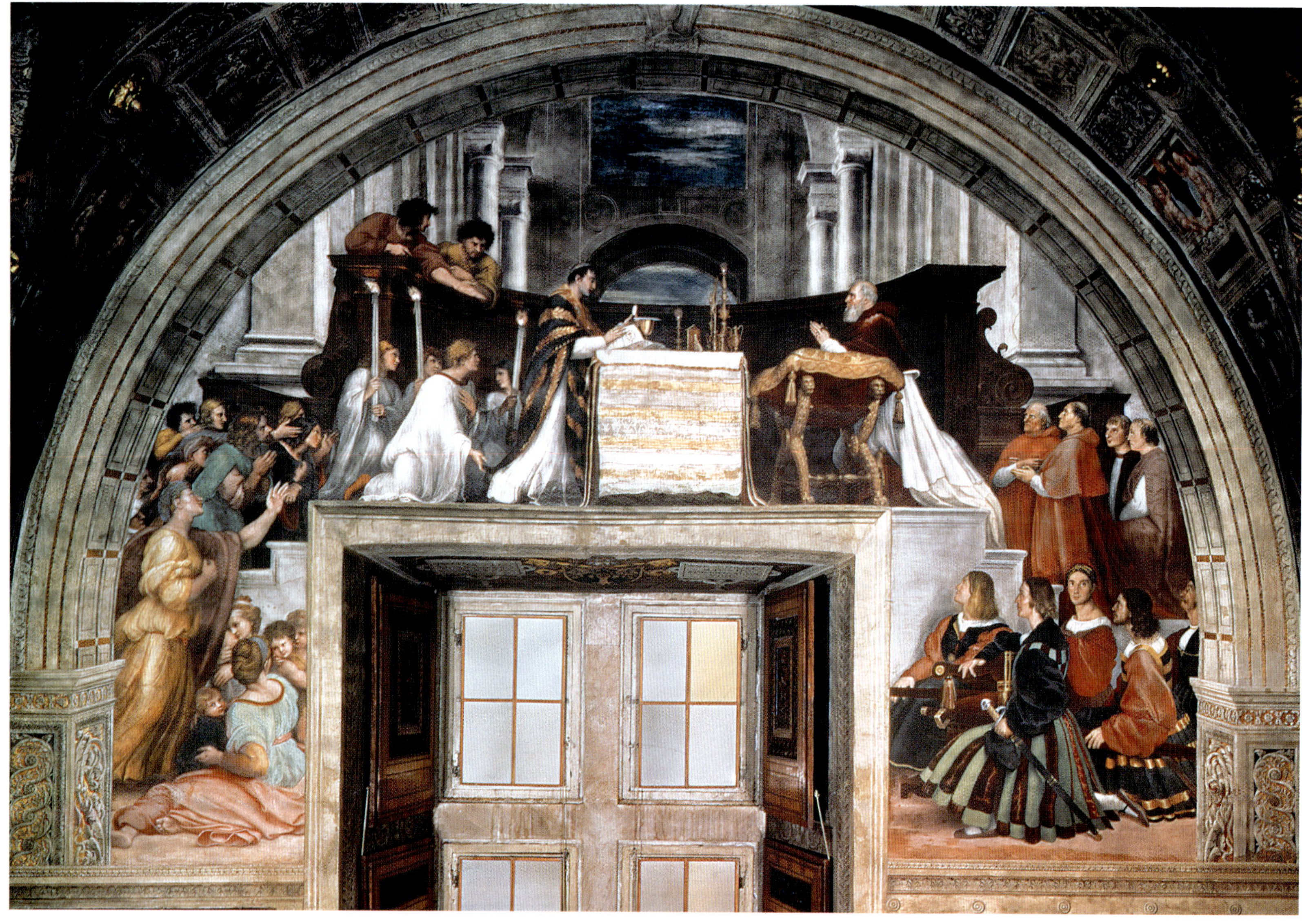

Raphael (Raffaello Sanzio)

The Miracle of Bolsena

This fresco depicts the miracle of the Host, which took place in the church of St. Christina in the central Italian town of Bolsena in 1263. While on a pilgrimage to Rome, a Bohemian priest experienced doubts about the doctrine of transubstantiation as he celebrated Mass, but was converted when blood miraculously began to drip from the Host. The miracle of the Mass of Bolsena led Pope Urban IV to institute the feast of Corpus Christi in 1264. In spite of the intrusive doorway, Raphael created a unified scene by raising the altar area, which has a columned architectural backdrop, and relegating the congregation and the pope's kneeling retinue to the foot of the altar podium. The two levels are linked by glances and gestures, which provide a commentary on the action. The figures also serve as examples to the viewers, calling upon them to be equally moved. In addition to Julius II, other figures have been identified as portraits of contemporary individuals. The male figures right of foreground are of particular interest, as they constitute one of the earliest depictions of the Swiss Guard, which was established by Julius II in 1506.

Raphael (Raffaello Sanzio), 1483–1520
***The Miracle of Bolsena*, 1512–1514**
Fresco
The Room of Heliodorus, Raphael Rooms

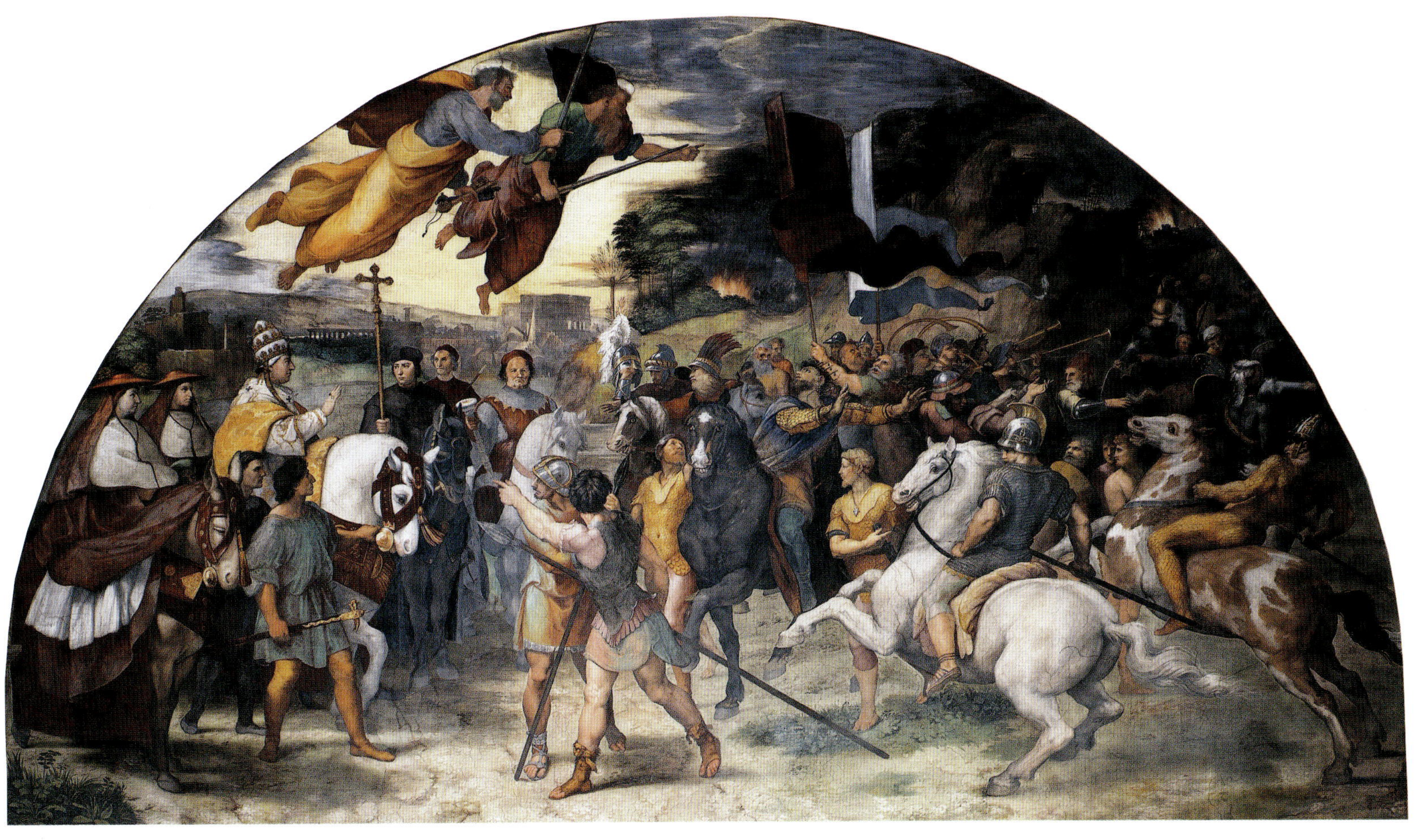

Raphael (Raffaello Sanzio)

The Meeting of Leo the Great with Attila

Raphael (Raffaello Sanzio), 1483–1520
***The Meeting of Leo the Great and Attila*, 1514**
Fresco
The Room of Heliodorus, Raphael Rooms

The subject of this painting is the meeting of Leo I (ca. 400–461, reigned from 440) and Attila, king of the Huns (reigned 434–453), who are shown approaching one another in a hilly landscape. Raphael has located the event, which in reality took place in the vicinity of Mantua, before the gates of Rome—the center of Christendom and the seat of the popes. The Colosseum and other buildings can be made out in the background. The pope bravely approaches the Huns, who, with their weapons pointing at him, are ready for battle and are only able to restrain their rearing horses with some difficulty. However, the focus is Attila, who occupies the precise center of the picture. The king of the Huns leans back on his horse to observe the miraculous appearance of SS. Peter and Paul, who, as Leo I's celestial protection, have raised their swords in readiness to defend the pope. Supported by the might of God, Leo the Great faces up to the superior forces of the Huns without fear and orders them to halt with a simple gesture. Attila acknowledges defeat and holds back his army with outstretched arms. With great skill, Raphael employs painterly means, such as light and dark colors and the contrast between calmness and agitated movement, to emphasize the opposition of good and evil.

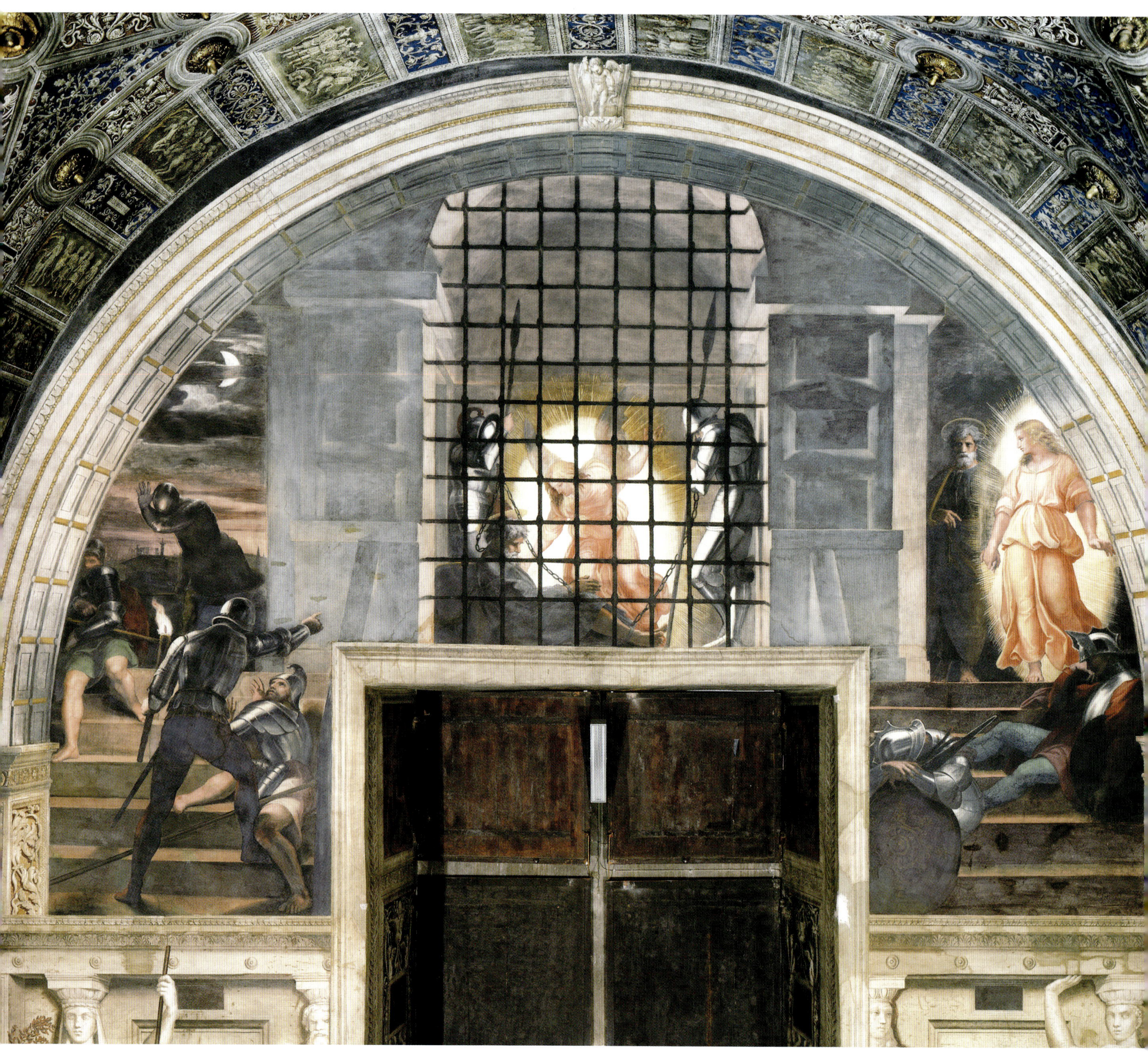

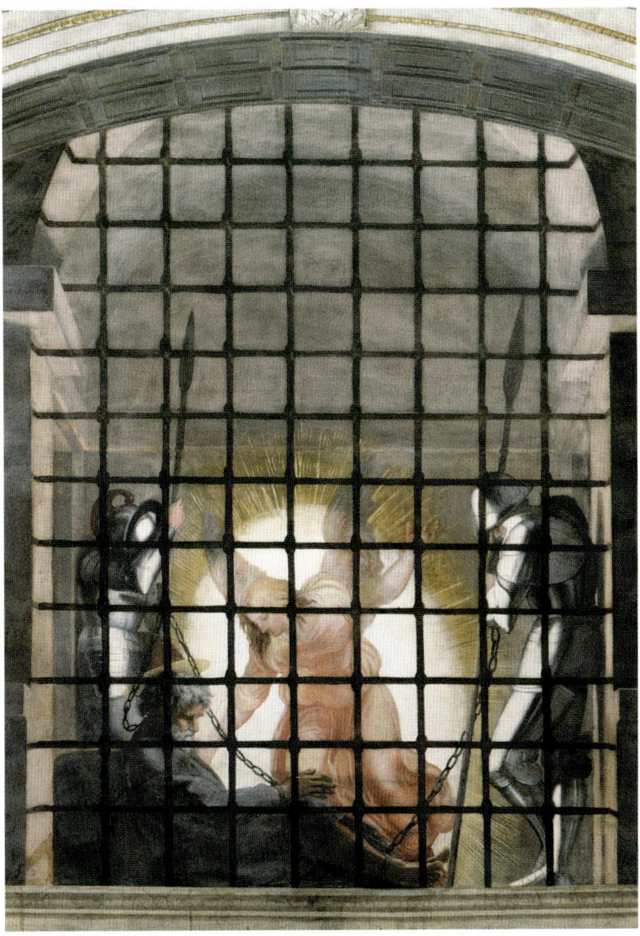

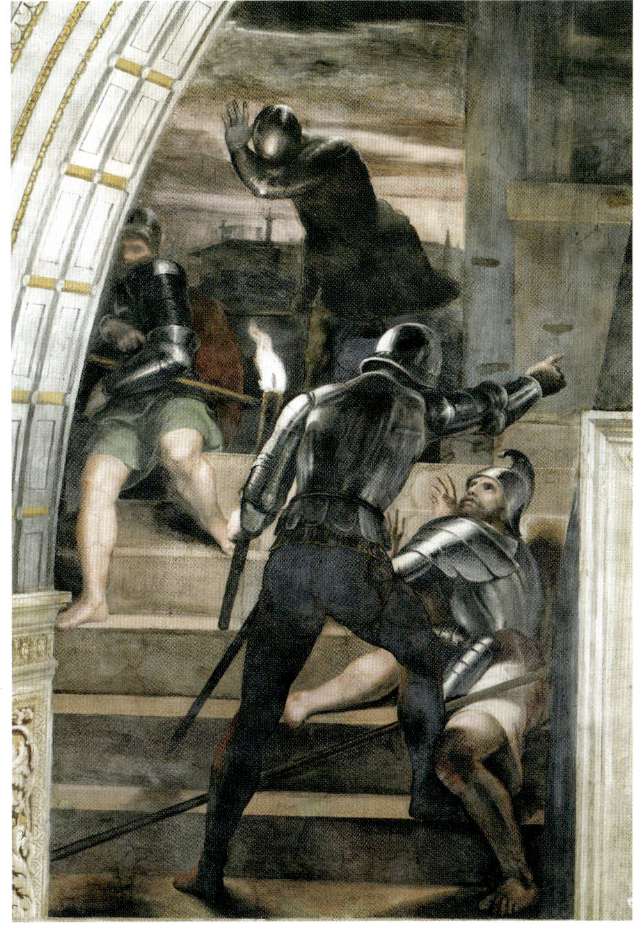

Raphael (Raffaello Sanzio)

The Liberation of St. Peter from Prison

This fresco depicts the liberation of St. Peter from prison, a miraculous event from Acts of the Apostles (Apostles 12:1–19). The king of the Jews, Herod Agrippa I, had Peter thrown in jail and ordered him to be well guarded. But an angel came at night surrounded by a bright light and freed the apostle, leading him out of prison without the guards noticing, even though they were chained to him. This incident offered Raphael an opportunity to demonstrate his skill as a painter of night scenes. He contrasts the gloom of the dungeon with the blazing light of the angel to great effect, emphasizing the unearthly character of the celestial apparition. The fresco presents three moments in the story: In the center we are shown the prison cell with the angel freeing St. Peter from the shackles that attach him to the two sleeping guards. On the right, he leads the saint carefully by the hand past more sleeping soldiers and out of the prison. On the left, we see the soldiers waking up and agitatedly discussing the inexplicable disappearance of their captive. Within the context of the room, this work attests to the miraculous intervention of God on behalf of the faithful, with a special emphasis on St. Peter as the predecessor of the popes.

Raphael (Raffaello Sanzio), 1483–1520
***The Liberation of St. Peter from Prison*, 1514**
Fresco
The Room of Heliodorus, Raphael Rooms

ROOM OF THE FIRE IN THE BORGO

The Room of Fire in the Borgo (Stanza dell' Incendio del Borgo) was the last of the chambers to be decorated by Raphael, painted largely single-handedly between 1513 and 1517. Although he also planned out the adjoining Room of Constantine, his designs were executed by his pupil Giulio Romano and assistant Giovanni Francesco Penni, who had also worked on Room of Fire frescoes. Under Julius II, the Room of Fire served as the meeting place of the highest court of the Curia, but it was transformed by his successor Leo X into a private dining room for the pope and senior state visitors. Leo X tied the iconographical program more strongly to his own papacy by commissioning scenes from the lives of two of his namesakes, Leo III (reigned 795–816) and Leo IV (reigned 847–855), whom he had the painters give his own facial features.

One of the most significant events to have occurred under the pontificate of Leo III was the imperial coronation of Charlemagne in 800, which is depicted on the entrance wall. This scene highlights the close relationship between France and the Papal States, which was renewed by Leo X with the Concordat of Bologna. The *Battle of Ostia* on the opposite wall depicts an episode from the life of Leo IV: the victory of the pope's fleet over the Saracens. Leo X was also confronted by the Turkish threat, and planned a crusade against the Turks. This room's most famous fresco is the *Fire in the Borgo*, from which the room takes its present name. This painting depicts an event that occurred in 847, when Leo IV put out a dangerous fire in the district of Rome located between the Tiber and the Vatican simply by making the sign of the cross from the loggia of St. Peter's. The fresco in the lunette depicts Leo III's oath of purgation, with which the pope refuted various charges leveled against him by claiming that the pontiff is answerable only to God. This principle would underpin the spiritual and secular rule of the popes, justifying the inclusion of this painting in the room's cycle of frescoes.

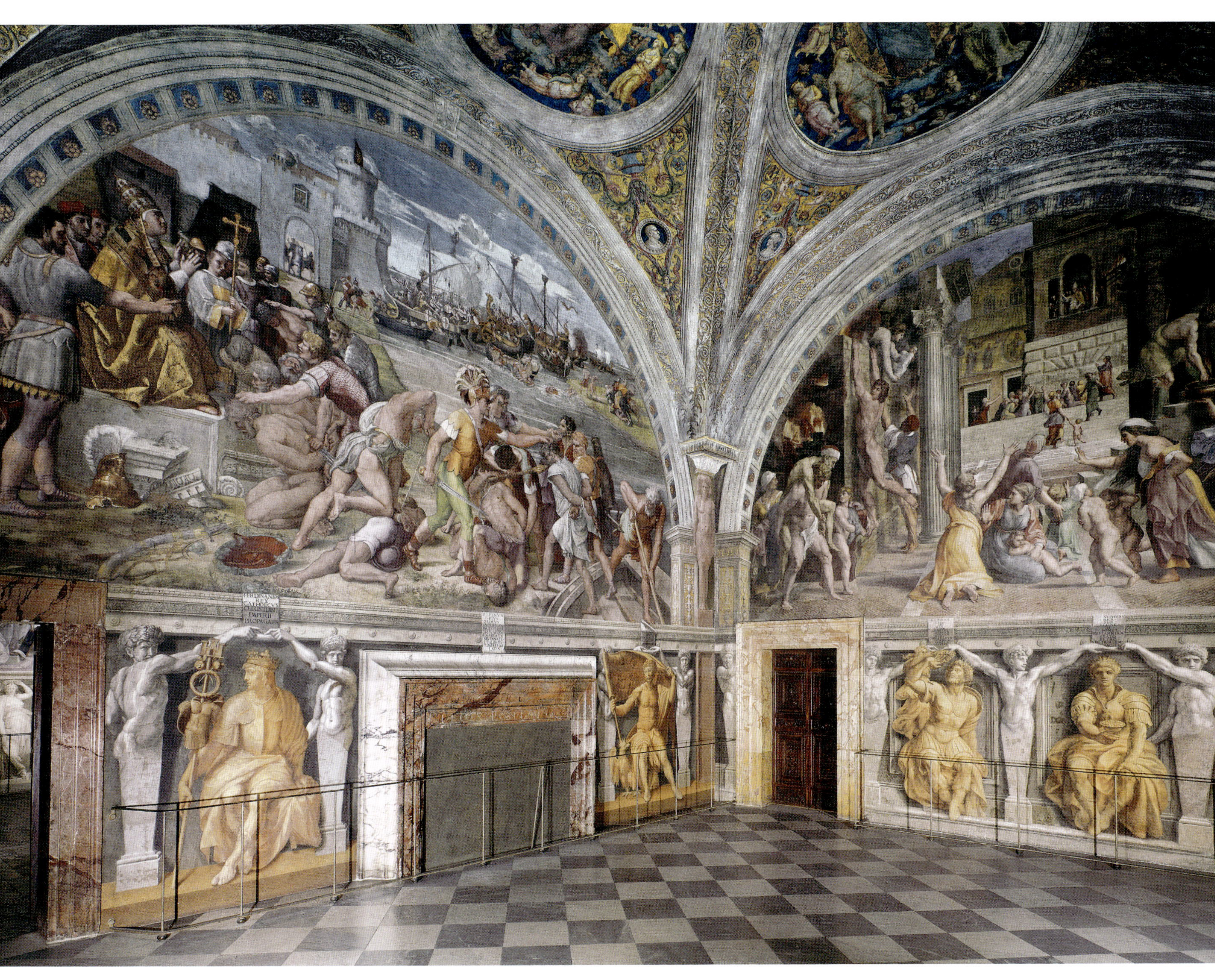

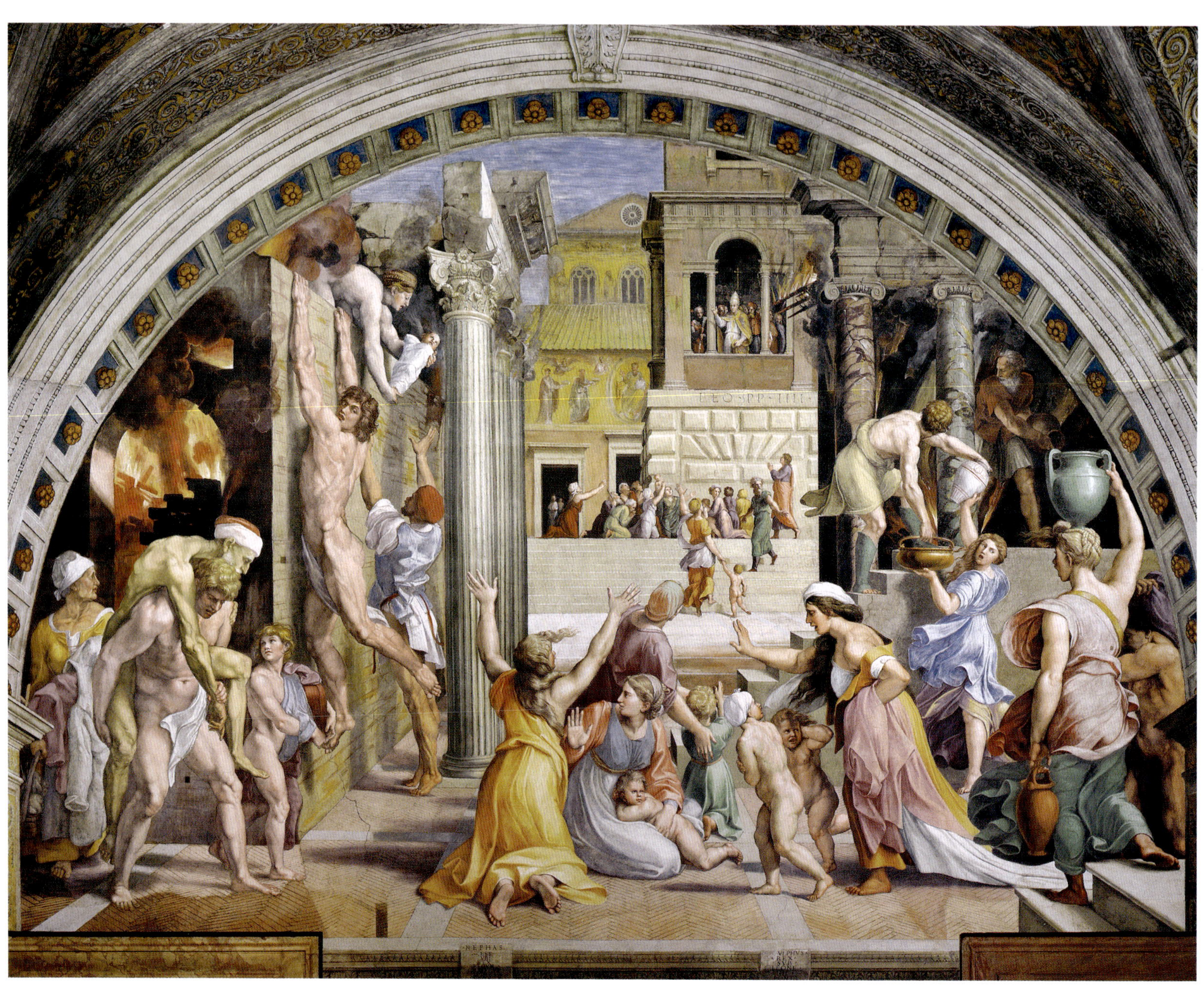

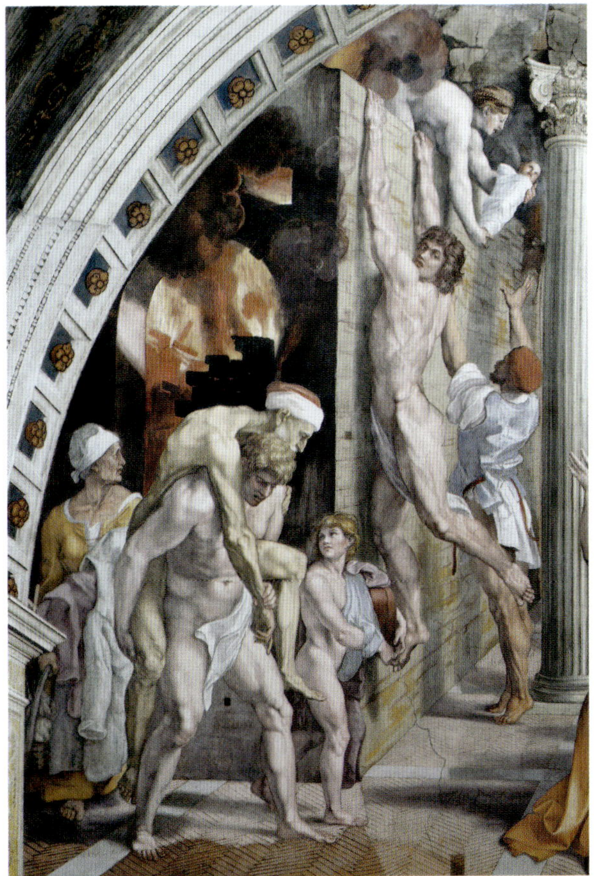
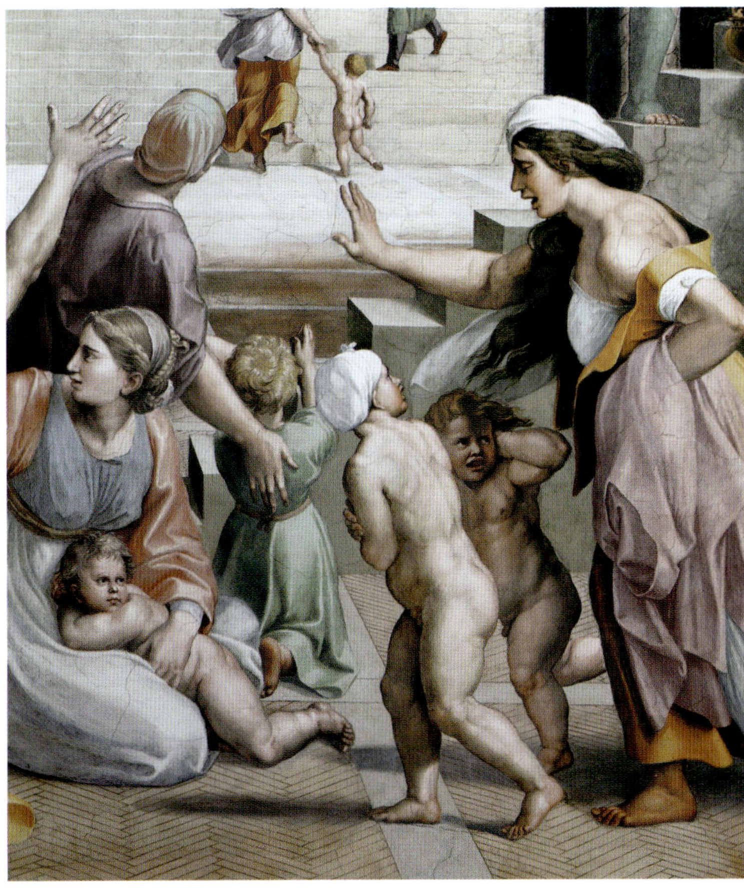

Raphael (Raffaello Sanzio)

The Fire in the Borgo

The dramatic event described in this fresco, from which the whole room takes its name (*incendio* meaning conflagration), is the fire in the Borgo, which took place in 847 during the reign of Leo IV. A vicious fire was threatening to destroy the Borgo, the district of Rome located between the Castel Sant'Angelo and St. Peter's Basilica. In the foreground we see men, women, and children trying desperately to escape the flames by climbing over collapsing walls. On the right-hand side, women are bringing containers of water with which to extinguish the fire. The group of figures in the left foreground alludes to Aeneas, the mythical founder of Rome who carried his father, Anchises, out of burning Troy on his shoulder. In the background we see Leo IV stopping the flames from the loggia of St. Peter's simply by making the sign of the cross. In his depiction of the men, women, and children in the foreground and background, Raphael reveals himself to be a master of emotions. This fresco, which numbers among Raphael's most famous compositions, is also an important architectural document, showing the façade of Old St. Peter's, which was sacrificed to the construction of the new basilica in the sixteenth century.

Raphael (Raffaello Sanzio), 1483–1520
***The Fire in the Borgo*, 1514**
Fresco
The Room of the Fire in the Borgo,
Raphael Rooms

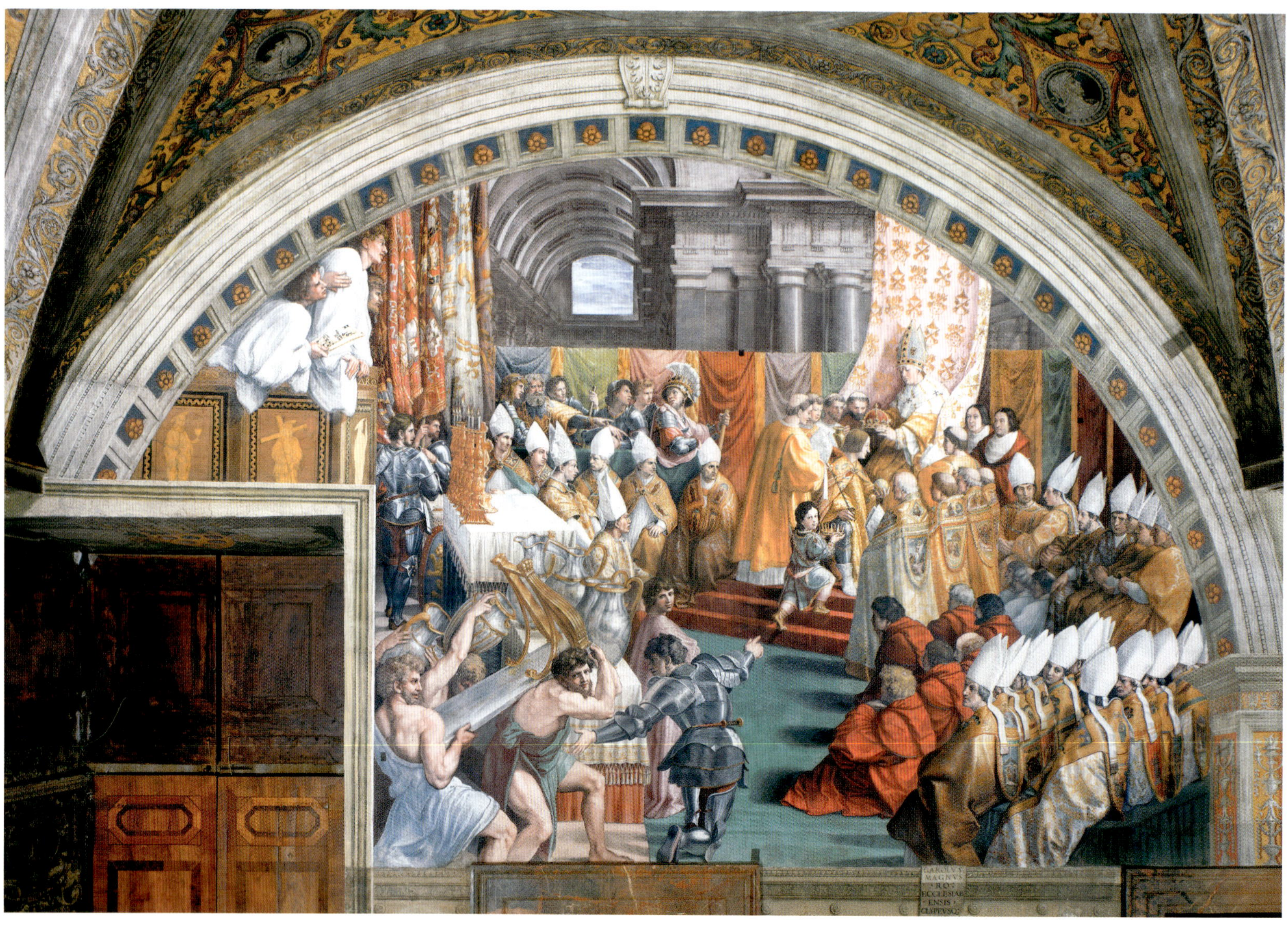

Raphael (Raffaello Sanzio) and Workshop

The Coronation of Charlemagne

The coronation of Emperor Charlemagne in 800 is one of the best-known and most ecclesio-politically important events to have occurred during the pontificate of Leo III (ca. 750–816, reigned from 795). Raphael sets the scene in Old St. Peter's, whose barrel-vaulted nave can be seen in the left background. The actual coronation takes place in the middle ground on the right. The king of the Franks, dressed in a golden dalmatic, kneels before Leo III holding the scepter and orb as the pope places the hoop crown on his head. Leo III has the facial features of Leo X, who was pope at the time of the painting. Around the steps of the papal throne members of the higher clergy are grouped in an open square. In addition to the scarlet-clad cardinals, many bishops and archbishops are also present, identifiable by their gold-embroidered dalmatics and white miters. While the ecclesiastical dignitaries sit there calmly, Charlemagne's entourage comments on the action with excited gestures. The porters and kneeling knight in the foreground form a particular link with the viewer. Like Leo III, Leo X sought an alliance with France, which was duly sealed by the Concordat of Bologna of 1516.

Raphael (Raffaello Sanzio) and Workshop, 1483–1520
***The Coronation of Charlemagne*, 1516–1517**
Fresco
The Room of the Fire in the Borgo, Raphael Rooms

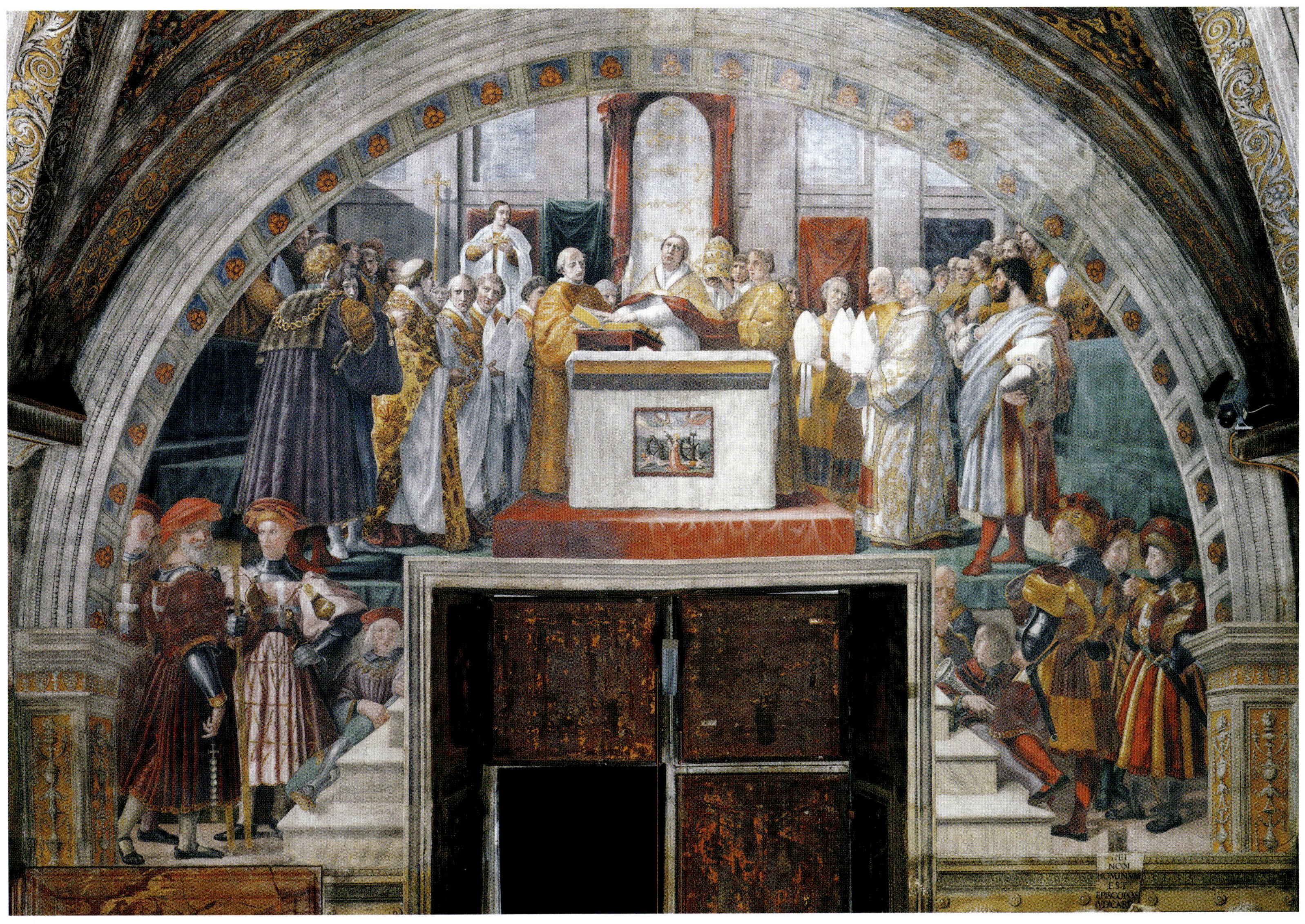

Raphael (Raffaello Sanzio) and Workshop

The Oath of Leo III

The wall space above the window depicts a little-known but nevertheless important event in the life of Leo III, one that is supposed to have happened on the day before Charlemagne was crowned emperor. Leo III had been accused of adultery by the nephews of his predecessor Adrian I. In the presence of Charlemagne, to whom he had appealed for protection, Leo III took an oath of purgation intended to affirm his guiltlessness. In Raphael's fresco, Leo III stands at the precise center of the picture by the altar and professes his innocence with his hands resting on the Bible. In doing so, he established the argument that the pope is answerable for his deeds to God alone, creating an important basis for the spiritual and secular rule of all subsequent popes. The oath of purgation took place in front of countless high-ranking ecclesiastical and secular dignitaries, who are positioned on or at the foot of the altar steps, according to their rank. The knights in the foreground, who serve as a link with the viewers, wear contemporary costume and are therefore historically consistent with Raphael's patron Leo X, who had himself portrayed in the role of Leo III.

Raphael (Raffaello Sanzio) and Workshop, 1483–1520
***The Oath of Leo III*, 1516–1517**
Fresco
The Room of the Fire in the Borgo,
Raphael Rooms

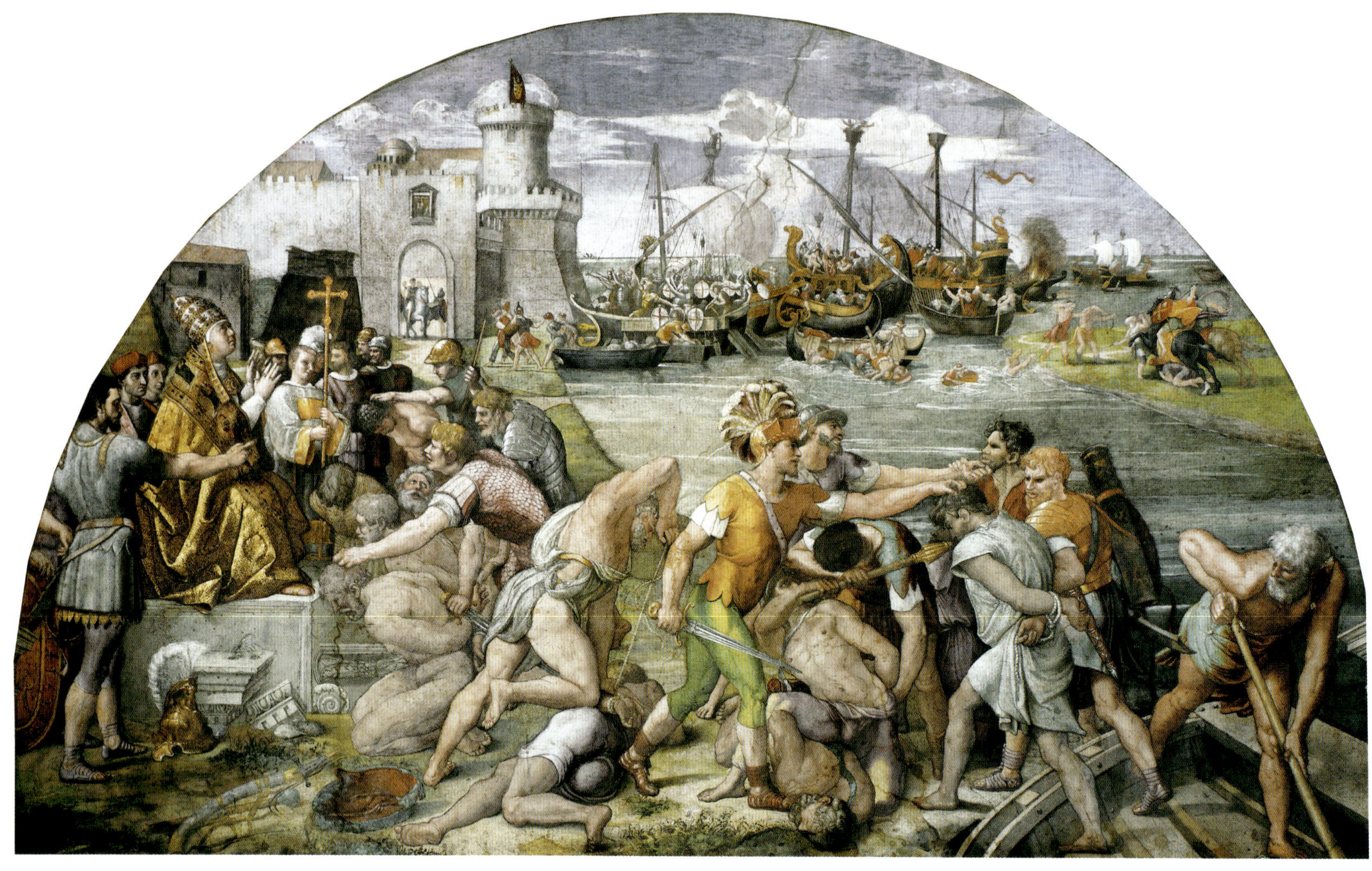

Raphael (Raffaello Sanzio) and Workshop

The Battle of Ostia

Designed by Raphael but executed with the assistance of his pupils Giulio Romano and Giovanni da Udine, who was responsible mainly for the architecture and ships in the background, this fresco depicts an event that occurred during the pontificate of Leo IV. In 849, Saracen pirates appeared off Ostia and threatened to advance up the Tiber estuary to Rome. With the help of galleys from Naples, Amalfi, and Gaeta, the pope's fleet was victorious against the assailants. In the background we see the final phase of the eventful battle, when the Saracens, identifiable by their turbans, are facing defeat, symbolized by the sinking ship in the middle ground. In the foreground, Saracen prisoners are led before Leo IV, enthroned on the left with cardinals and clergymen, who thanks God for His help. The Saracens, shown in contorted positions being treated brutally, are masterpieces of nude painting and demonstrate the talent of the young Giulio Romano. The topical relevance of the fresco was a Turkish threat that Leo X was planning to counter with a crusade.

Raphael (Raffaello Sanzio) and Workshop, 1483–1520
***The Battle of Ostia*, 1514–1515**
Fresco
The Room of the Fire in the Borgo,
Raphael Rooms

Perugino (Pietro di Cristoforo Vannucci)

The Ceiling of the Room of Fire

Perugino's ceiling fresco in the Room of Fire dates from the first phase of decoration of the Rooms under Julius II. According to biographer Giorgio Vasari, Raphael wanted to retain this one part of the old Rooms decorations "in memory of, and out of love for, his master." The four roundels with blue grounds, set in a golden backdrop decorated in the grotesque style, depict scenes from the New Testament and Christian allegories in praise of the glory of God. The choice of program is explained by the original function of the room, which is where the episcopal court, chaired by the pope, once sat. The motif of the administration of justice is made explicit by the roundel showing Christ between personifications of the virtues justice and compassion. The other tondi depict the Trinity and apostles, the enthroned God the Father between angels, and Christ resisting Satan's temptations. These works are distinctive for their balanced composition and harmonious use of color, both of which were prized features of Perugino's style and also that of the young Raphael.

Perugino (Pietro di Cristoforo Vannucci), ca. 1450–1523
The Ceiling of the Room of Fire
Fresco
The Room of the Fire in the Borgo, Raphael Rooms

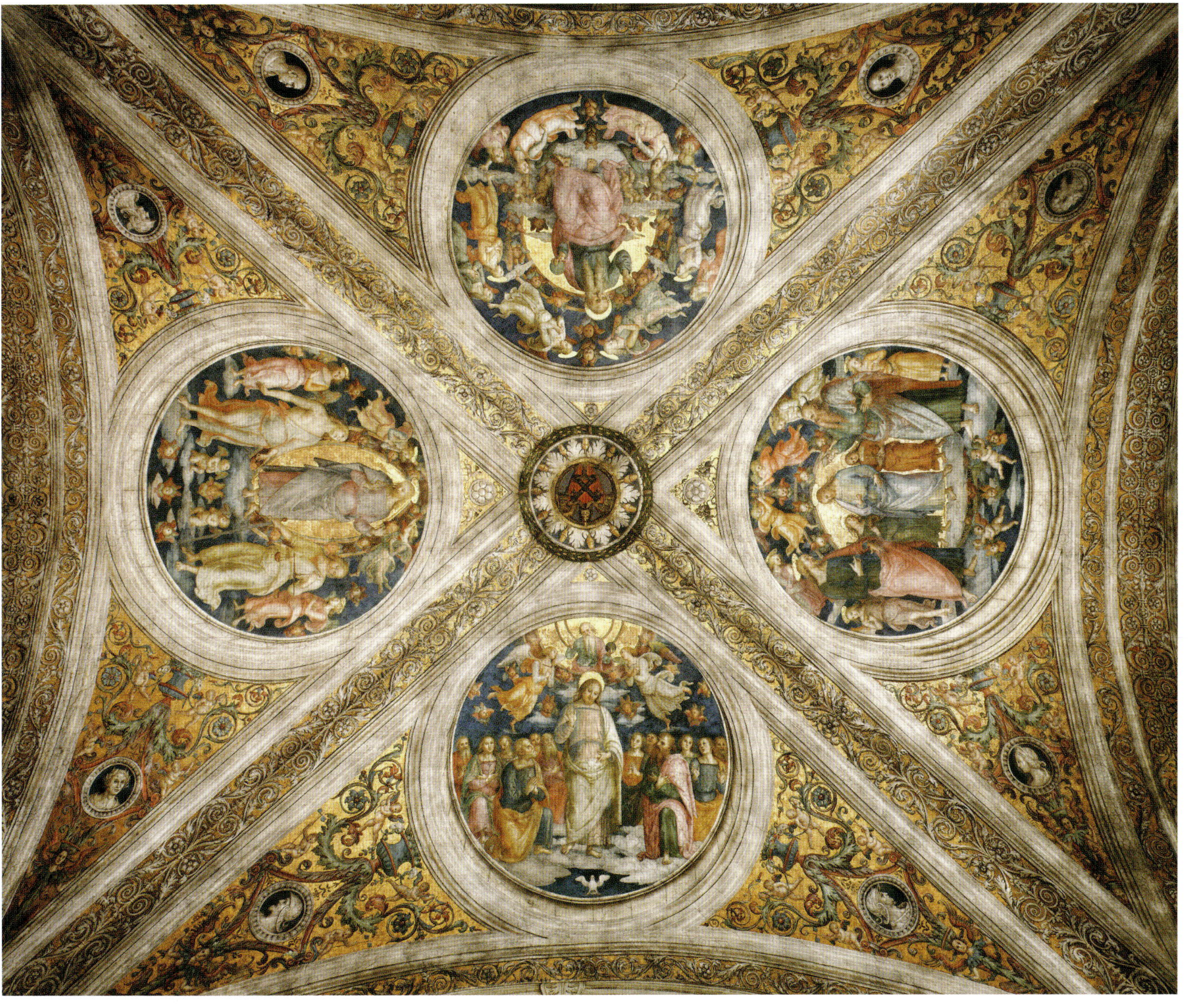

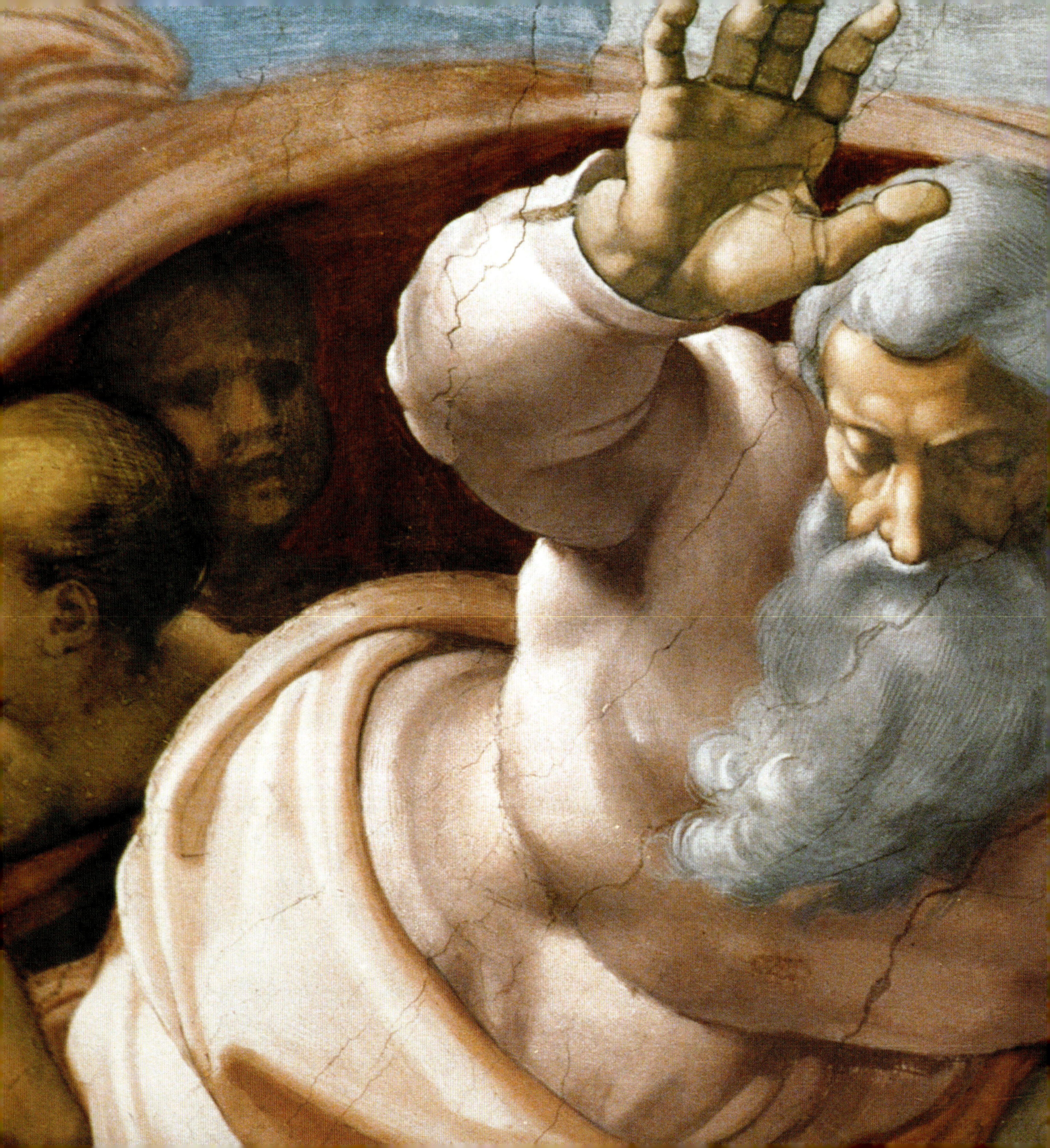

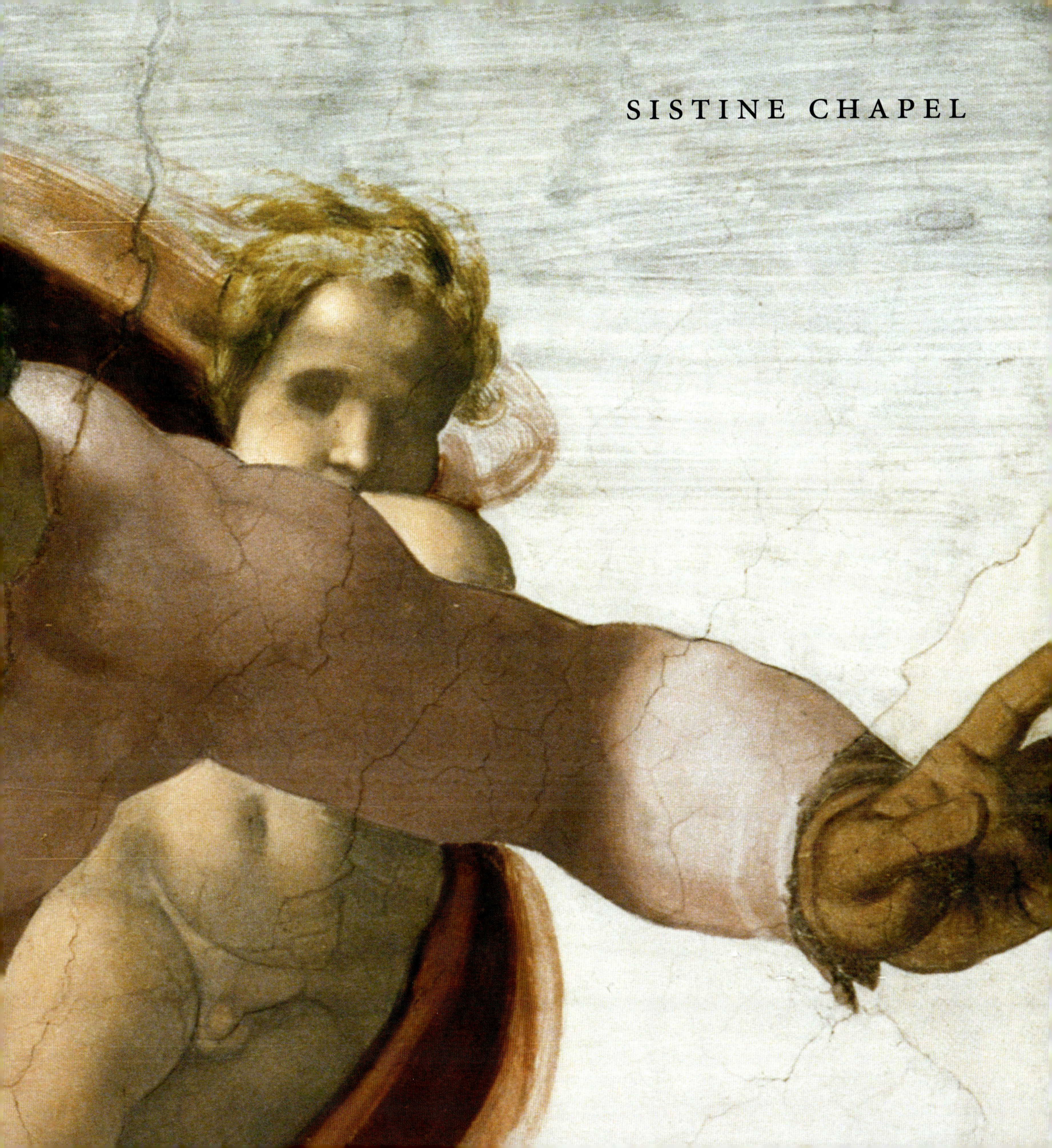

SISTINE CHAPEL

SISTINE CHAPEL

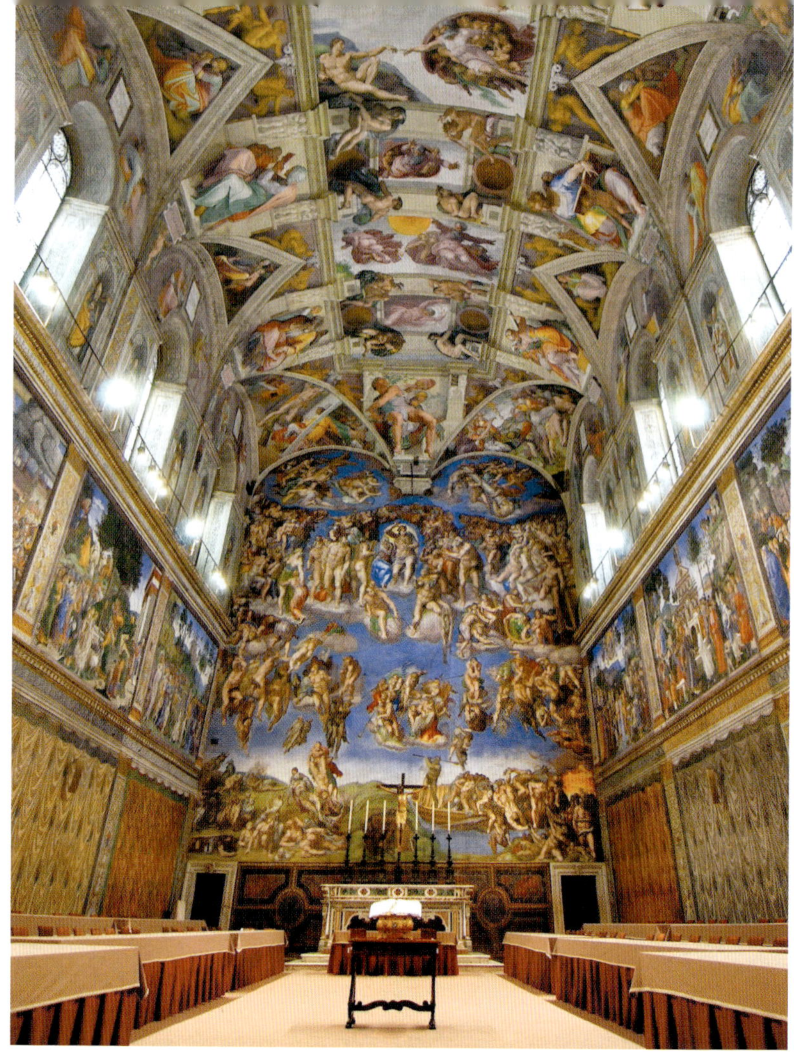

The ceiling of the Sistine Chapel is one of the most famous works in the history of art. Although best known today for its paintings by Michelangelo, the chapel is actually a *Gesamtkunstwerk* (a total work of art) combining architecture, painting, and interior decoration and was the creation of numerous artists over the course of more than a century.

The chapel takes its name from the pontiff who built it, Sixtus IV (1414–1484, pope from 1471). Completed in 1483, the chapel was raised over the foundations of a medieval structure of similar length (40 meters) and breadth (13 meters). The actual chapel space containing Michelangelo's famous frescoes occupies the third floor. In its role as the chapel of the pontifical palace, the Sistine Chapel, dedicated to the Assumption of the Virgin, continues to be used to this day for the celebration of Mass by the pope on important religious holidays, special papal ceremonies and for the election of new popes.

The chapel's liturgical and ceremonial function can be discerned from the division of the space into different functional zones. The most important divider is the marble chancel screen, located at one time in the middle of the room, which separates the lay part of the chapel from the part reserved for the clergy (presbyterium) with its raised sanctuary. The chancel screen designed by the Florentine sculptor Mino da Fiesole (1429–1484) and his workshop dates from the time of the chapel's original construction. Its lower section consists of alternating marble reliefs of Sixtus IV's oak tree coat of arms and garlands of fruit. The individual functional zones are also evident from the floor decoration, whose ornate inlaid marble follows in the tradition of the medieval Cosmati workshop.

Among other models, the decorative scheme conceived by Sixtus IV and his advisers for the walls harks back to Rome's medieval basilicas. This was even more evident in the original chapel decoration than in the renovations that followed in the sixteenth century. Above a high base register, painted with a continuous illusionistic drape in the colors of the family of Sixtus IV della Rovere, the main wall register features large-format frescoes depicting episodes from the lives of Moses and Jesus. These once ran all the way around the chapel. The altar wall originally contained a fresco of the *Assumption of the Virgin*, which was sacrificed in 1536, like all the other frescoes on this wall, for Michelangelo's *Last Judgment*. The window register of the longitudinal walls is decorated with a cycle of full-length portraits of the popes. The original ceiling vault was decorated with golden stars on a blue background and overhung the chapel like a glittering starry sky.

Just a few years after completion, however, static problems occurred that eventually produced cracks in the vault. In addition to taking the necessary structural safety measures, Pope Julius II (1443–1513, reigned from 1503) immediately decided upon a redecoration of the vault and in 1508 commissioned Michelangelo to paint the Sistine Chapel ceiling. The previous starry sky was replaced by a monumental fresco featuring episodes from the Book of Genesis. With Michelangelo's *Last Judgment* on the altar wall, painted between 1536 and 1541, the fresco decoration of the chapel was complete.

The combination of wall frescoes, Michelangelo's ceiling, and the *Last Judgment* create a spectacular *Gesamtkunstwerk* that, following the restoration of the ceiling between 1980 and 1991, shines forth in all its original splendor once more.

These frescos on the central walls are by famous painters of the Tuscan and Umbrian schools of the fifteenth century such as Sandro Botticelli, Pietro Perugino, and Luca Signorelli, each of whom, with the help of their workshops, painted one or more of the pictures. Despite the different styles, the cycle as a whole displays considerable uniformity due to the careful agreement among the painters regarding color scheme, size of the figures, overall composition, and a common horizon line.

The cycle of paintings in this register, which were completed between 1480 and 1483, originally consisted of eight scenes from each of the Old and New Testaments designed to be read as parallel stories. Presented on the North wall (the right-hand wall, as viewed from the altar) are scenes from the life of Jesus, and on the South wall, scenes from the life of Moses, whereby the paintings facing one another form a pair. The choice of episodes may seem strange at first as they are not the scenes from the life of Jesus (extending from birth to Passion) commonly found in other churches. This is due to the need to coordinate the stories of Christ with the stories of Moses. The principle of coupling scenes from the Old Testament with scenes from the New Testament, known as "typology," derives from medieval theology. It understands the Old Testament as prefiguring the New, with the two parts reaching their culmination in the story of Christ's life and suffering. Under this principle, Moses was regarded as an ancestor and precursor of Christ because he led his people out of slavery.

In the choice of some of the scenes from Christ's life, however, the role of the *Sistine* as papal chapel and, most importantly, the desire of Sixtus IV to emphasize the role of the apostles as disseminators of the faith—particularly that of St. Peter as Christ's representative on earth—seem to have been a foremost consideration. As St. Peter's direct successors, the popes themselves played an important part in the story of salvation through Christ. And this role is underlined by the series of papal portraits in the lower window register.

A single aspect often connects the two scenes. In the case of the finding of Moses and the birth of Christ, which once adorned the altar wall, the common element was the miraculous arrival or discovery of a holy or salvation-bringing infant. These two frescoes, destroyed in 1536, were the work of Pietro Perugino, who was also responsible for the altar painting of the *Assumption of the Virgin*. Fortunately the initial painting on each wall, the *Baptism of Christ* and the *Journey of Moses,* survive to bear witness to Perugino's mastery.

The next pair of paintings are by Sandro Botticelli and depict the *Temptations of Christ* and *Scenes from the Life of Moses*. These are followed by the *Calling of the Apostles* by Ghirlandaio and the *Crossing of the Red Sea* by Cosimo Rosselli or Biagio d'Antonio, which are linked compositionally, both featuring a central stretch of water. The same is true of Cosimo Rosselli's *Sermon on the Mount* and *Giving of the Law*, each of which features a large hill in the background. In the following pair of pictures, Perugino's *Christ Giving the Keys to St. Peter* and Botticelli's *Punishment of Korah, Dathan and Abiram*, the background and center are taken up by a large building with round arches. The final two paintings on the side walls are the *Last Supper* by Cosimo Rosselli and the *Testament and Death of Moses* by Signorelli. The entrance wall originally supported Ghirlandaio's *Resurrection* and Signorelli's *Dispute over the Body of Moses,* but these were heavily damaged when the marble architrave above the door collapsed in 1522 and were replaced in 1565 by frescoes of the same subject by Hendrick van den Broeck and Matteo da Lecce.

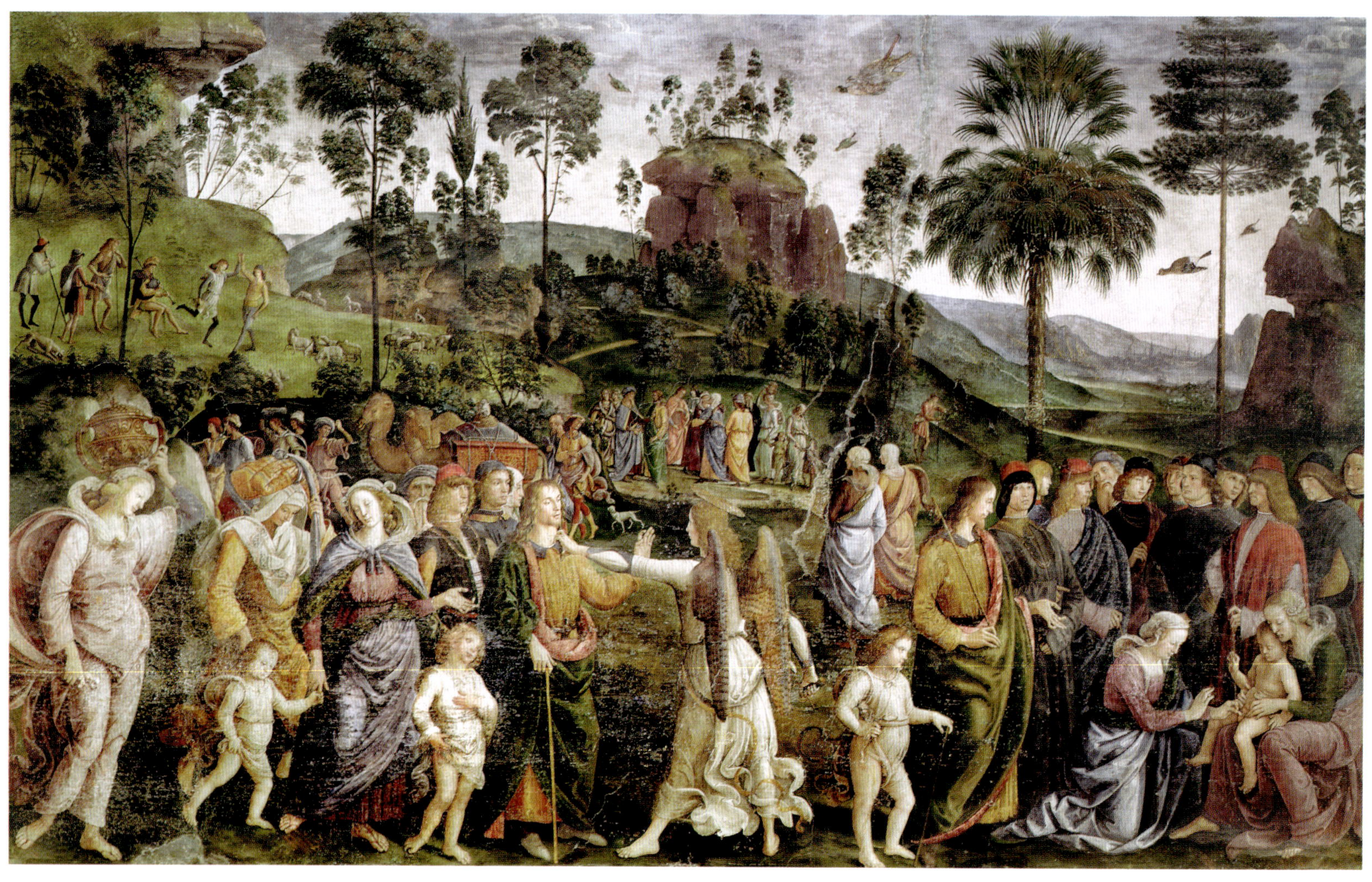

Pietro Perugino (Pietro di Cristoforo Vannucci)

The Journey of Moses

Embedded in a hilly landscape dotted with rocky outcrops and soaring trees, this fresco depicts three episodes that took place during Moses' journey from Midian to Egypt. Beneath the towering outcrop in the background, we see Moses taking leave of his father-in-law, Jethro. The left half of the picture shows Moses—dressed, as throughout the cycle, in green and gold—with his wife, Zippora, their two sons, and a large retinue on the way to Egypt. The colorful procession, incorporating servants, maids, and camels, winds its way through a green plain enlivened by a group of shepherds in the background. At the precise center of the painting an angel in fluttering white robes stops Moses and commands him to have his second son Eliezer circumcised. The circumcision, performed by Zippora, constitutes the third scene and is shown in the right of the painting. Despite consisting of three separate episodes, the impression of an integrated narrative is created thanks to the connecting figure of the angel. Perugino's characteristic warm colors and graceful figures, some of whom seem to be portraits of contemporary personages, contribute to this overall sense of harmony.

Pietro Perugino, ca. 1450–1523
***The Journey of Moses*, 1481–1482**
350 × 572 cm; Fresco
Sistine Chapel, Southern Wall

Pietro Perugino (Pietro di Cristoforo Vannucci)

The Baptism of Christ

The Baptism of Christ, also referred to as a "spiritual circumcision," is the New Testament counterpart to Moses' journey and the circumcision of Eliezer. Witnessed by numerous onlookers, John the Baptist baptizes Christ in the River Jordan. The similarities in the landscape background and in the composition, which emphasizes the main figures at the center, connect this work to its corresponding fresco, *The Journey of Moses*. God the Father appears above Christ in a circle of angels and sends down the dove of the Holy Ghost to his Son. On the right and in the background, other young men can be seen preparing to be baptized. Among the throng of people on the bank are numerous men in contemporary costume who may be portraits of members of the papal court. The city in the background is perhaps Jericho, in whose vicinity John began his work as a preacher. In the middle ground, on either side of the Jordan, Perugino shows two instances of John preaching. Here, as in the Moses fresco, the desert landscape of the Bible has been transformed into a fertile, sylvan meadow against which the colorful clothes of the onlookers and naked figures of those waiting to be baptized stand out strongly.

Pietro Perugino, ca. 1450–1523
***The Baptism of Christ*, 1481–1482**
335 × 540 cm; Fresco
Sistine Chapel, Northern Wall

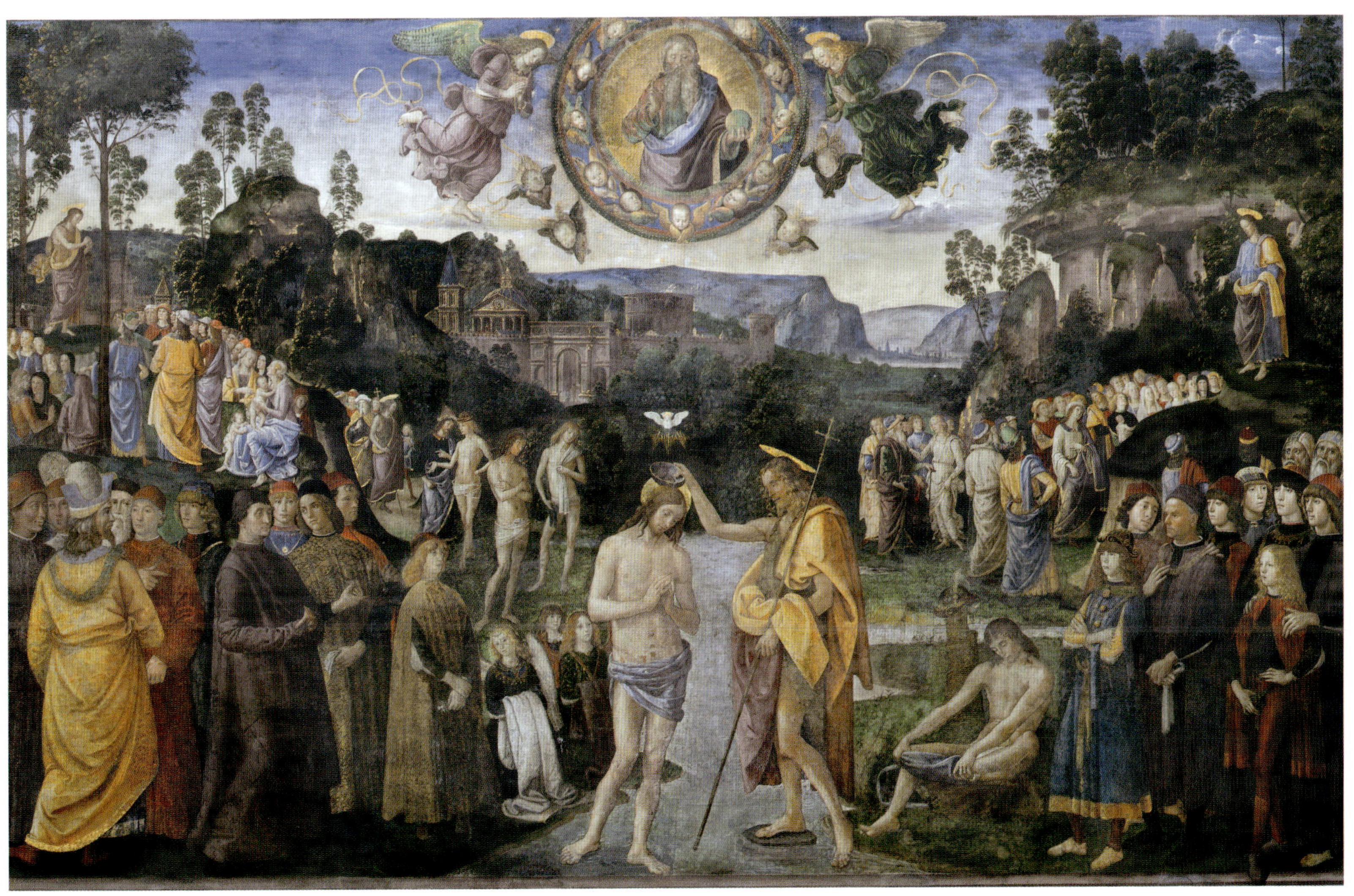

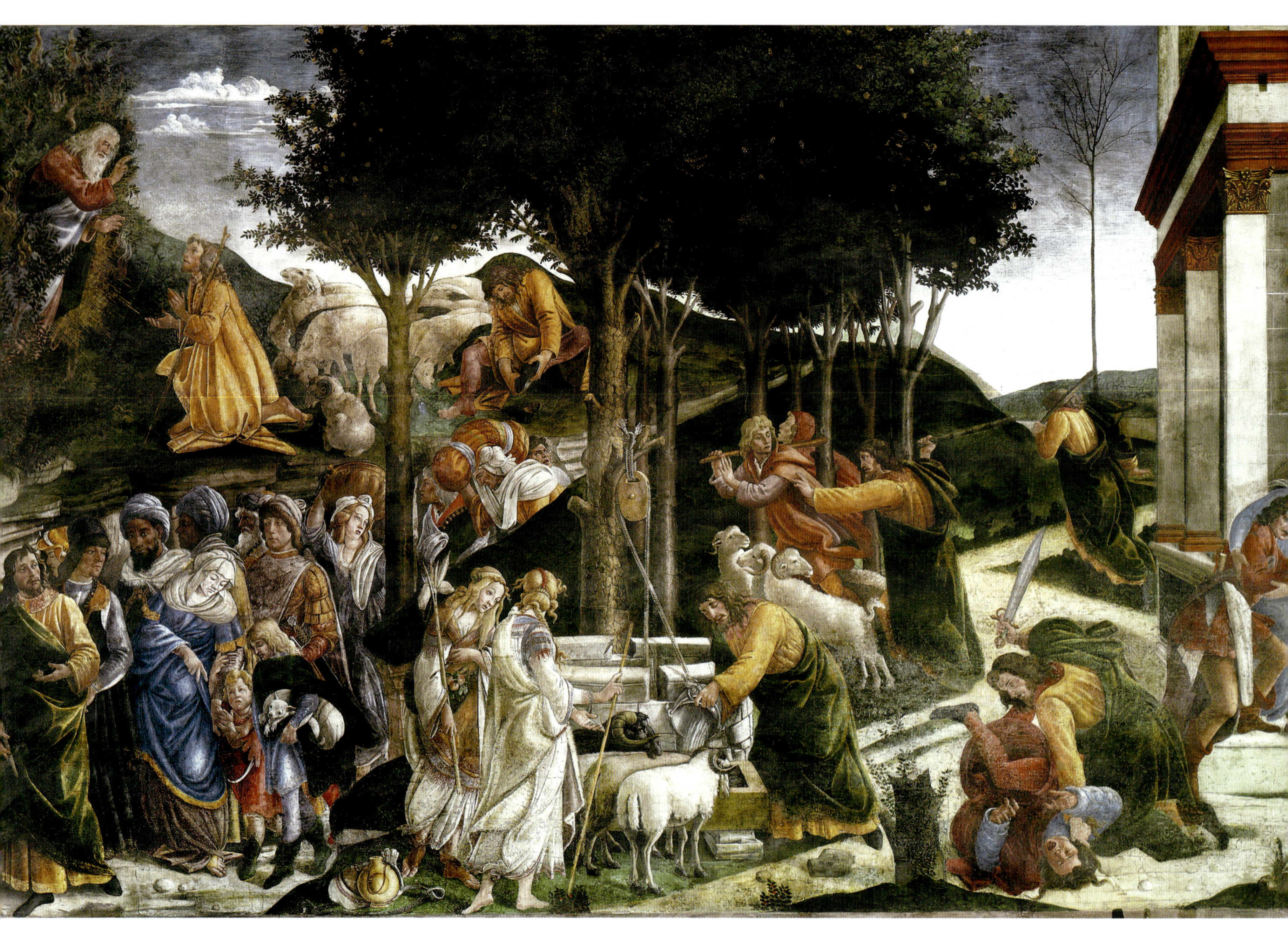

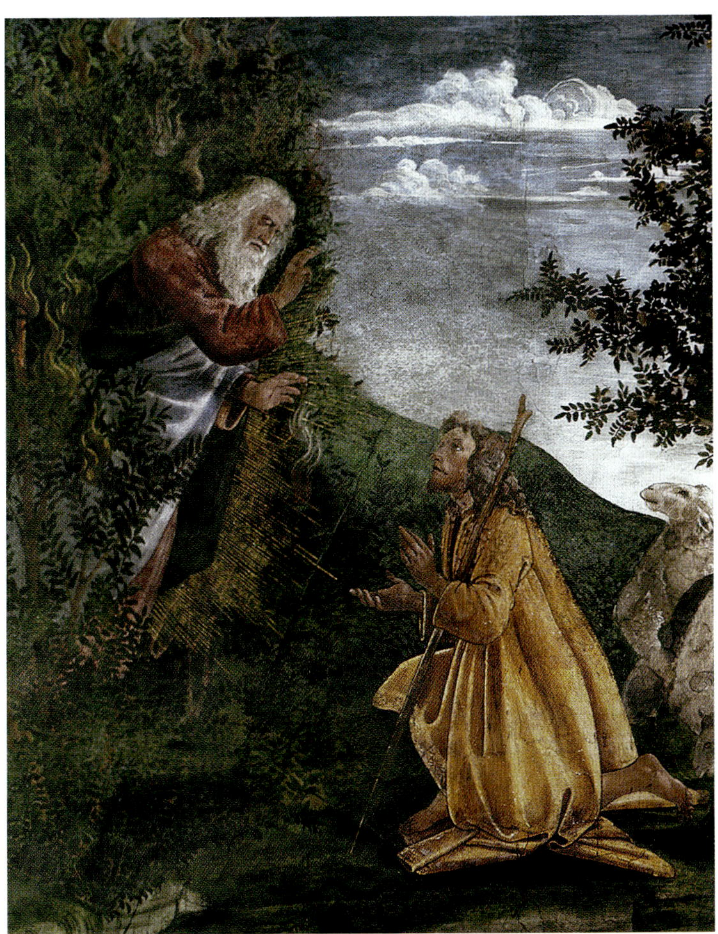

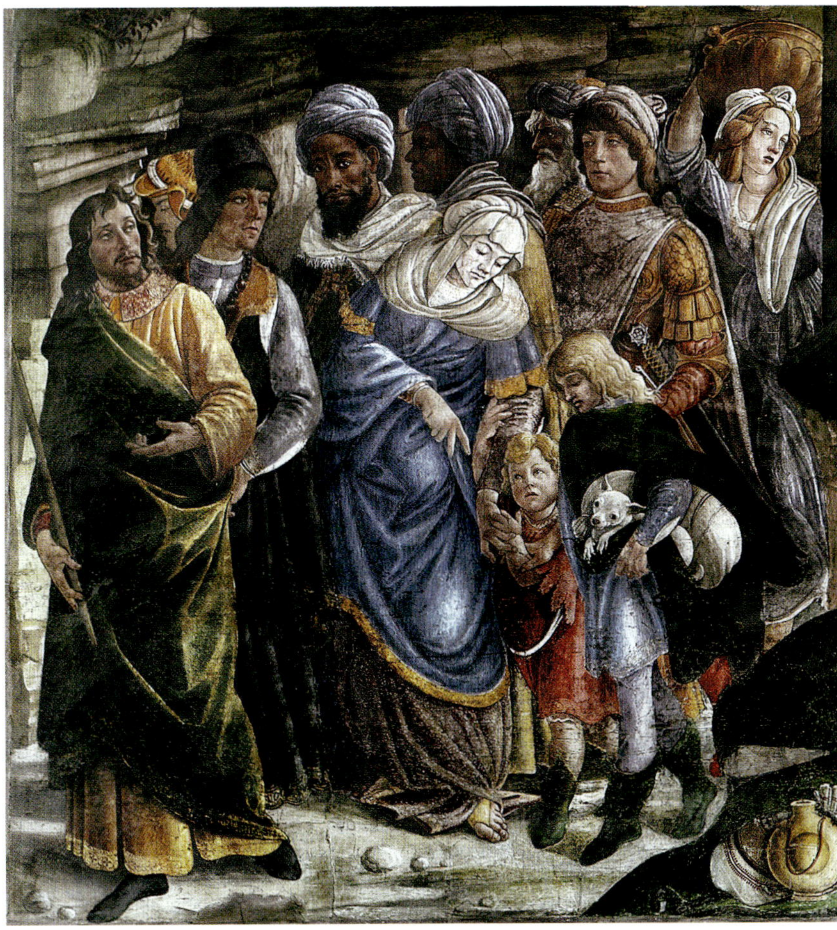

Sandro Botticelli (Alessandro di Mariano Filipepi)

Scenes from the Life of Moses

Sandro Botticelli has included no fewer than seven scenes from the life of Moses in this fresco. The narrative, which covers episodes before and after Moses' journey to Egypt, loops through the picture from right to left, corresponding to the way the work would be viewed from the altar. Right of foreground we see Moses slaying an Egyptian, and behind this he is shown escaping. At the center of the composition, Moses comes to the aid of Jethro's daughters, one of whom is his future wife Zippora, by chasing away troublesome shepherds and then helping the women to draw water. In the background of the left half of the picture, Moses can be seen kneeling before the burning bush on Mount Horeb after removing his shoes on God's instructions and being given the task of leading his people out of Egypt. The exodus is depicted as a long procession extending from the middle ground to the bottom left corner of the picture. Here Botticelli has adopted some of the figures from Perugino's Moses procession, although in keeping with his own style he has made the colors more intense and introduced greater movement into the figures, thereby increasing the tension of individual scenes. The big oak tree alludes to the coat of arms of Sixtus IV, whose place at ceremonies held in the Sistine Chapel was beneath this fresco.

Sandro Botticelli, 1444–1510
***Scenes from the Life of Moses*, 1481–1482**
348.5 × 558 cm; Fresco
Sistine Chapel, Southern Wall

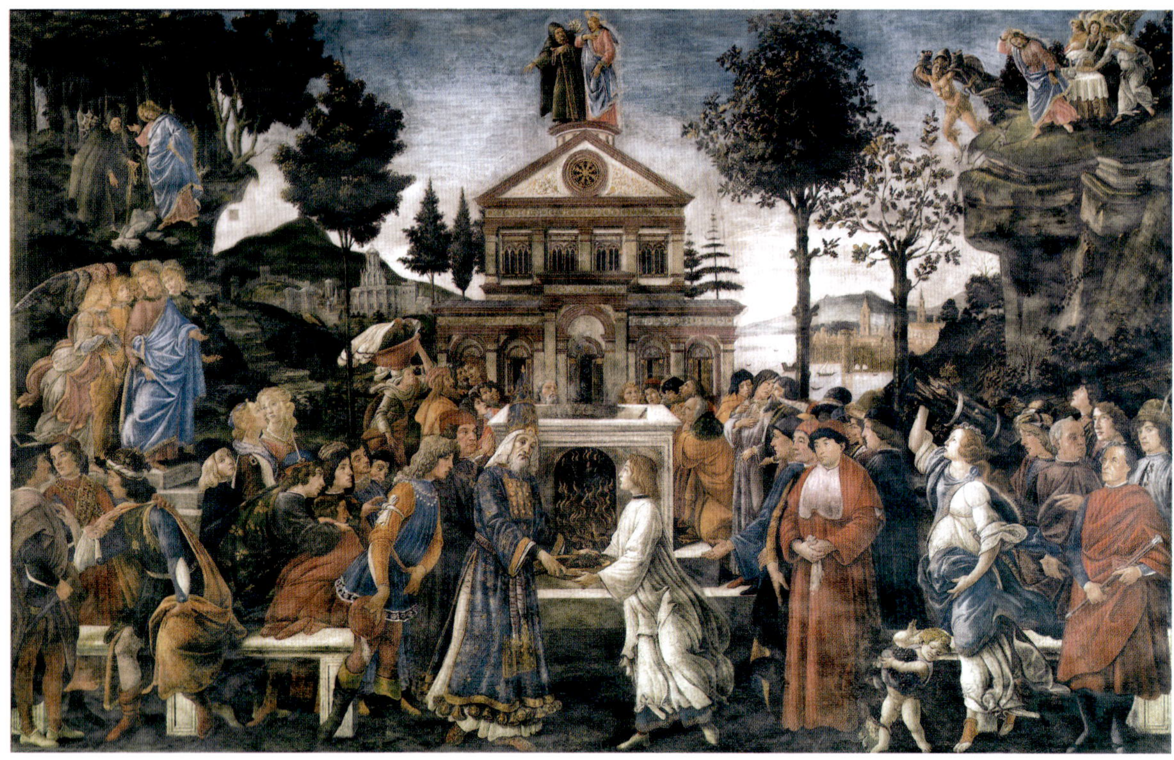

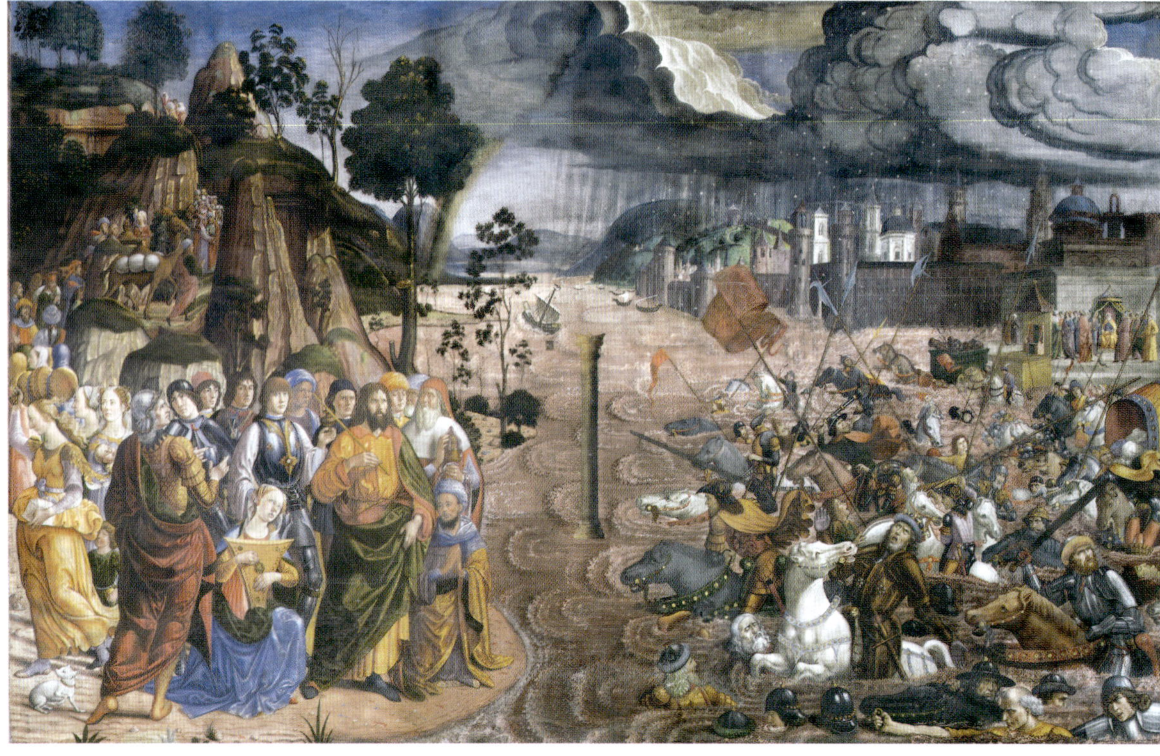

Sandro Botticelli, 1444–1510
***The Temptations of Christ*, 1481–1482**
345.5 × 555 cm; Fresco
Sistine Chapel, Northern Wall

Cosimo Rosselli (or Biagio d'Antonio), 1439–1507
***The Crossing of the Red Sea*, 1481–1482**
350 × 572 cm; Fresco
Sistine Chapel, Southern Wall

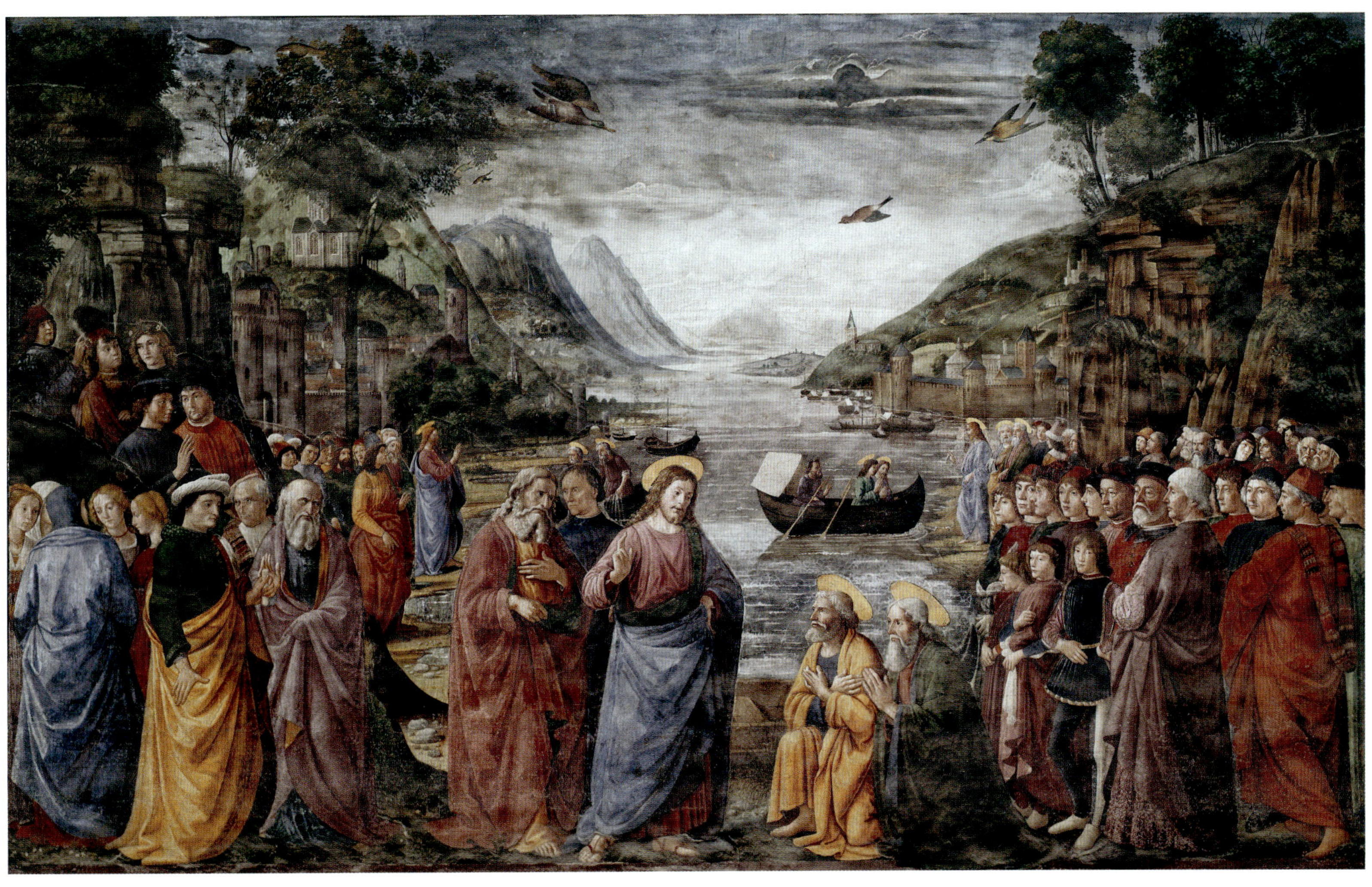

Domenico Ghirlandaio

The Calling of the Apostles

The calling of apostles Peter, Andrew, James, and John takes place before a deep background landscape dominated by the Sea of Galilee. In reality, the lake's precipitous banks are more characteristic of a northern Alpine landscape, such as Domenico Ghirlandaio painted in some of his other works. Jesus is depicted three times in the fresco: in the middle ground on the left at the calling of Simon (Peter) and Andrew, on the right at the calling of James and John, and in the foreground at the blessing of Peter and Andrew. According to the description in the Gospel of Mark (Mark 1:16–19), Jesus came to the Sea of Galilee, where he observed the fisherman Simon and his brother Andrew casting their nets. With the famous words: "Come ye after me, and I will make you to become fishers of men," he called upon them, and also the fishermen James and John, to become his disciples. Peter and Andrew appear again in the foreground, where they receive Christ's blessing. Peter is emphasized through his yellow and gold mantle and proximity to Christ, underscoring his future position as Prince of the Apostles and precursor of the popes. The saints are surrounded by a large crowd of people, among numerous portraits of contemporary figures.

Domenico Ghirlandaio, 1449–1494
***The Calling of the Apostles*, 1481–1482**
349 × 570 cm; Fresco
Sistine Chapel, Northern Wall

Cosimo Rosselli

Descent from Mount Sinai

Cosimo Rosselli's fresco presents three important scenes from the life of Moses: the receiving of the tablets of the law on Mount Sinai, the presentation of the tablets to the people, and the adoration of the golden calf, when the enraged Moses smashes the tablets. At the top of the painting we see Moses, accompanied by his sleeping apprentice Joshua, kneeling at the summit of the mountain in readiness to receive the tablets of the law from the hand of God. Simultaneously, beneath the golden-violet aureole of angels, the Israelites can be seen adoring the golden calf. Left of foreground, Moses, having descended from Mount Sinai, presents the commandments to the people, only to then destroy the tablets out of anger at the Israelites' godlessness. Rosselli draws special attention to the destruction of the tablets through the central positioning of the Moses figure and the power of his raised arm. The two small background scenes show the Israelites' camp (on the left) and the punishing of the idolaters and the handing down of new tablets on the right. On the painted frame beneath the blue-clad dancer in the foreground, Rosselli has signed the work in an original manner: with a dish of red pigment (alluding to his name, the Italian rosso meaning red) and a brush.

Cosimo Rosselli, 1439–1507
***Descent from Mount Sinai*, 1481–1482**
350 × 572 cm; Fresco
Sistine Chapel, Southern Wall

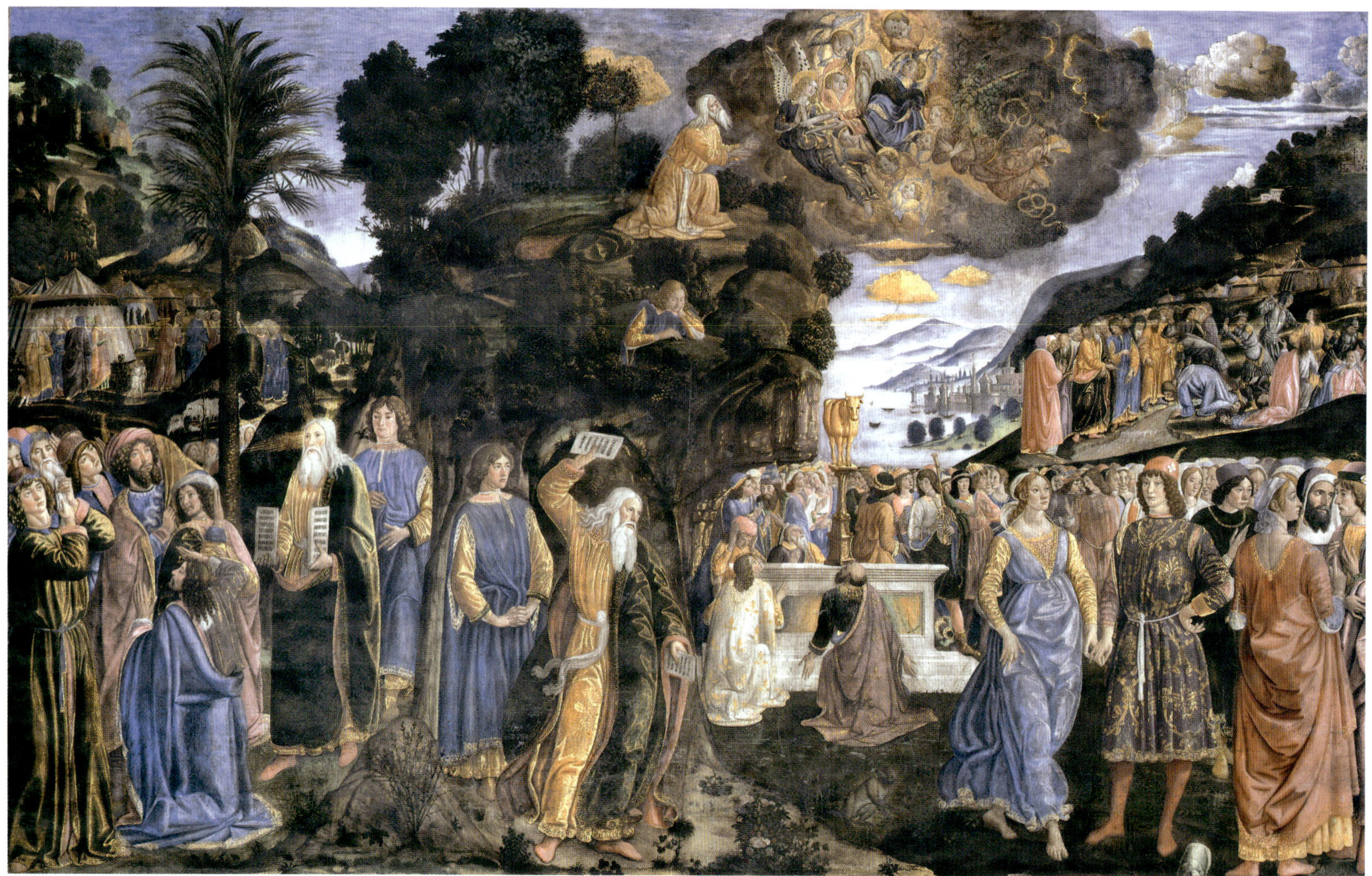

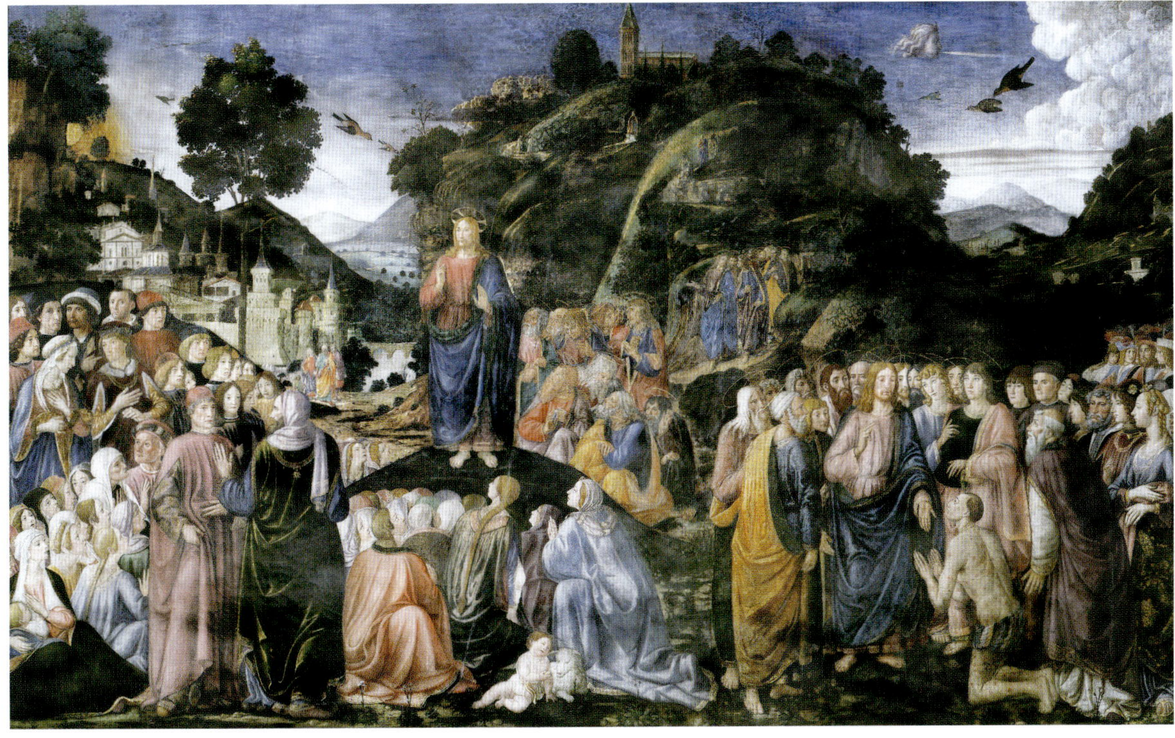

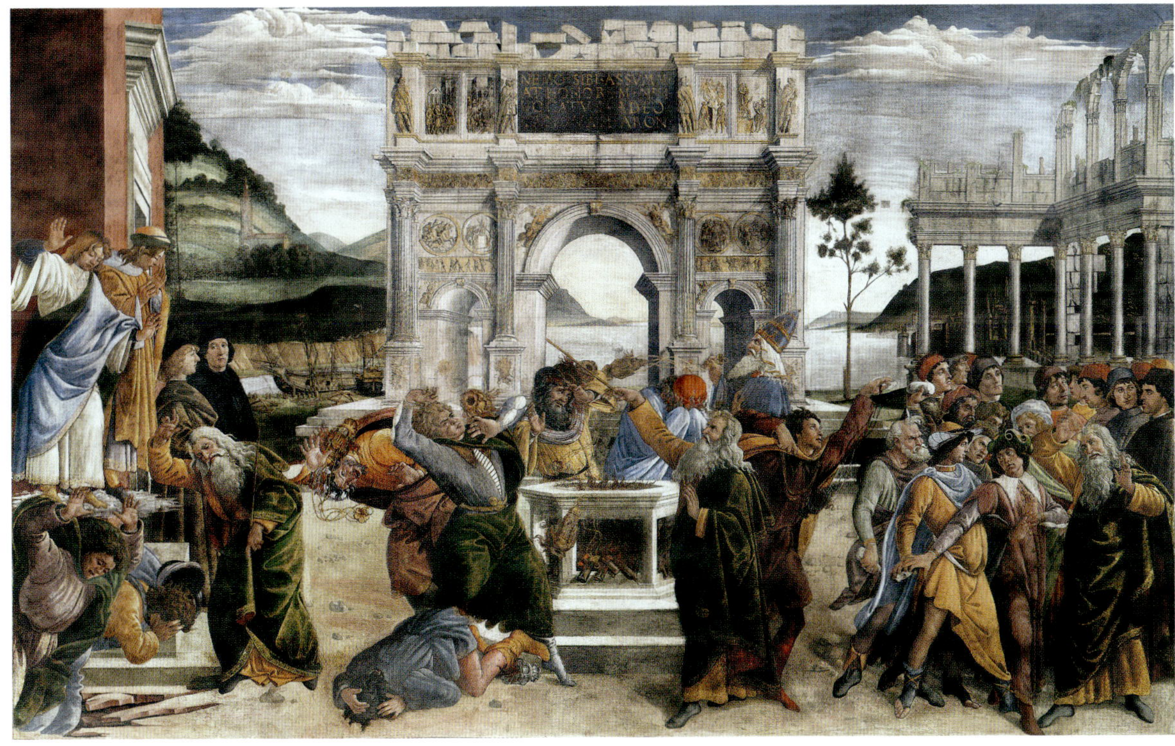

Cosimo Rosselli, 1439–1507
***Sermon on the Mount*, 1481–1482**
349 × 570 cm; Fresco
Sistine Chapel, Northern Wall

Sandro Botticelli, 1444–1510
***Punishment of the Rebels*, 1481–1482**
348.5 × 570 cm; Fresco
Sistine Chapel, Southern Wall

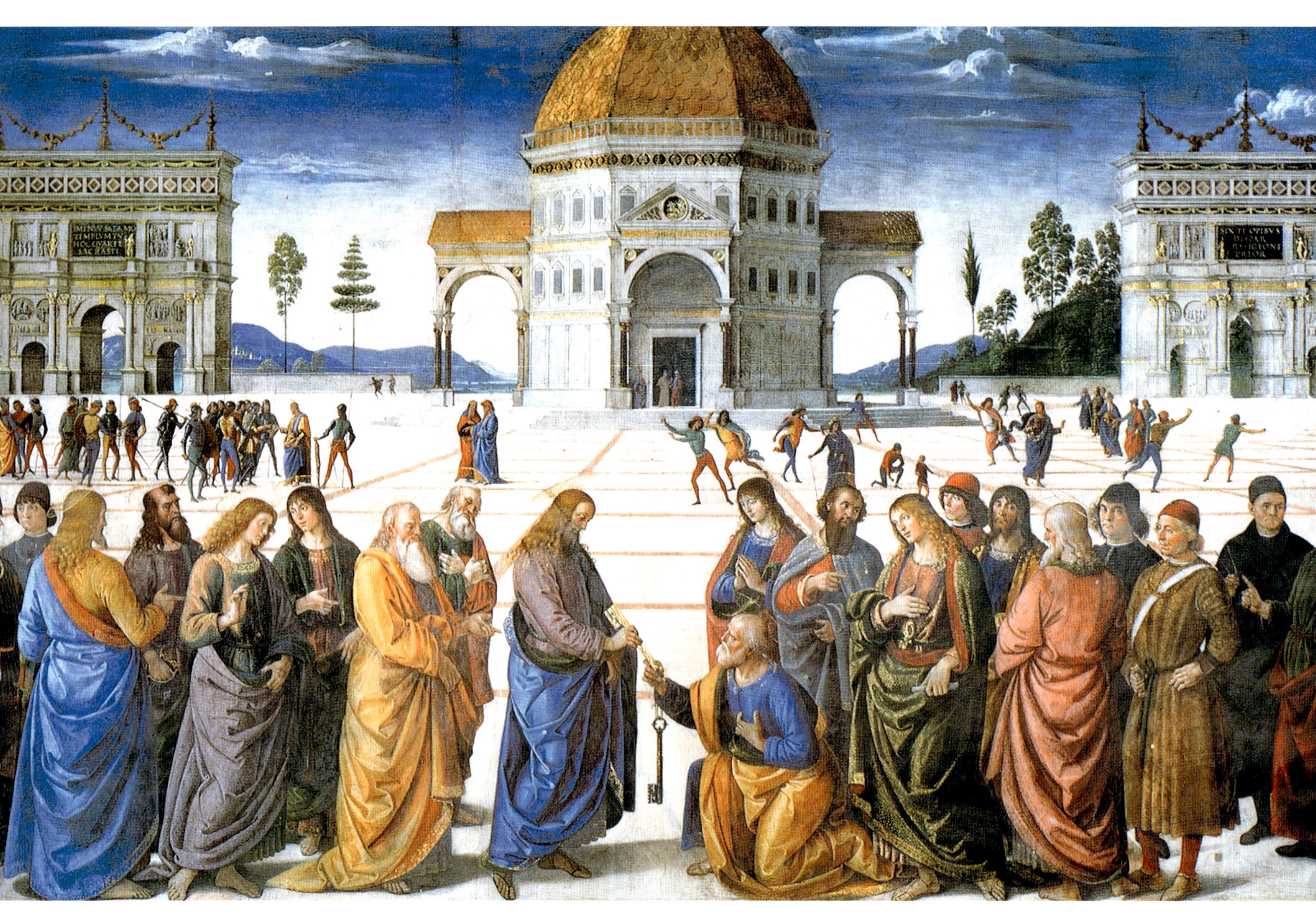

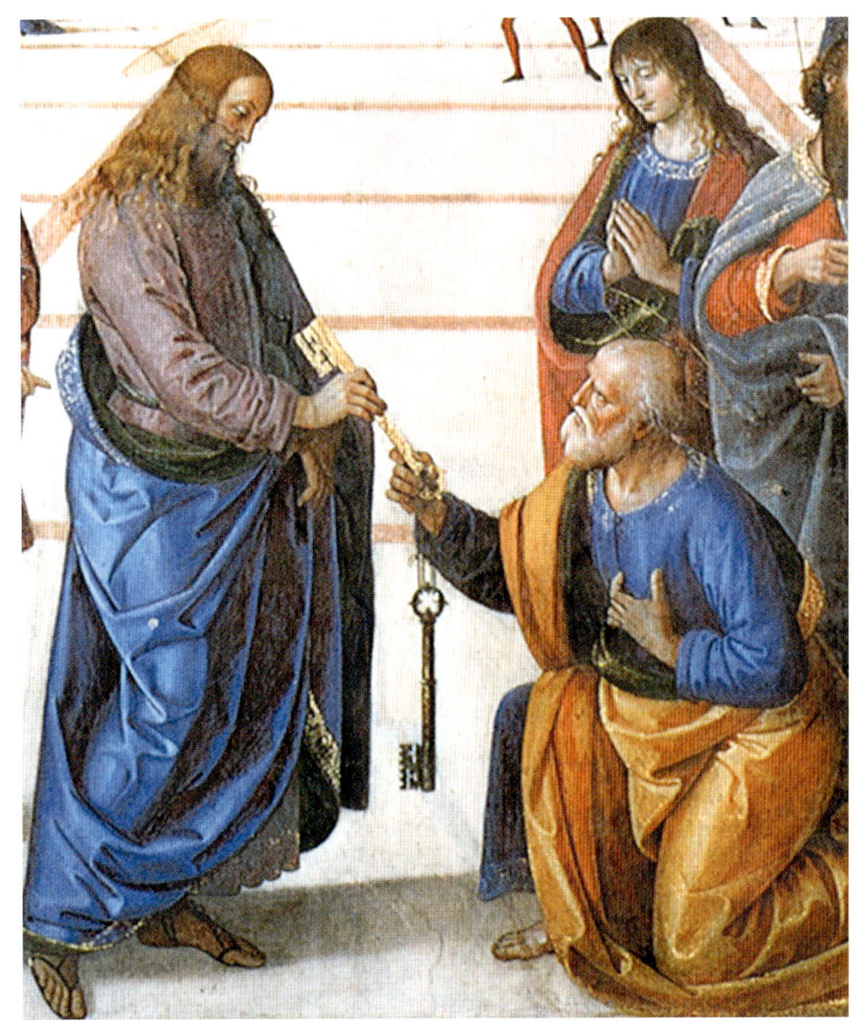

Pietro Perugino (Pietro di Cristoforo Vannucci)

Christ Giving the Keys to St. Peter

Perugino's *Christ Giving the Keys to St. Peter* is widely regarded as the most beautiful fresco in the Sistine Chapel Christ cycle. From the point of view of the popes, it is certainly the most important painting as it places them, as St. Peter's successors, in a direct line with Jesus. According to the Gospel of St. Matthew (Matthew 16:18) the keys represent access to the kingdom of heaven and the power to admit others to it. At the same time, this scene signifies the founding of the papacy, with St. Peter as the rock upon which "I will build my church" (Matthew 16:18). For the depiction of this important event, Perugino has constructed an idealized arena in central perspective with the Temple of Solomon standing as a symbol of the Jewish faith and the two triumphal arches in the background embodying heathen antiquity—both belief systems to be superseded by Christianity. In the foreground we see Christ handing St. Peter, who kneels before him, the two keys, which are precisely aligned with the central axis. Lined up on either side are his disciples and onlookers in contemporary dress, who point to the event with excited gestures. The small scenes in the background show two rarely depicted episodes in the life of Christ: the payment of the tribute money and the attempted stoning of Christ.

Pietro Perugino, ca. 1450–1523
***Christ Giving the Keys to St. Peter*, 1481–1482**
330 × 550 cm; Fresco
Sistine Chapel, Northern Wall

Luca Signorelli

The Testament and Death of Moses

Divided horizontally into two halves, this fresco depicts five concluding events in the life of Moses—two in the foreground and three in the background. The narrative begins in the background on Mount Nebo (in the center of the picture), where God, disguised as an angel, hands the 120-year-old Moses the rod of command. God points to the Promised Land in the background, depicted by Signorelli as a fertile river landscape bordered by mountains. Moses climbs down from the mountain with the rod and on the left hands it to his chosen successor, his apprentice Joshua. On the right we see the prophet speaking to a large crowd of people for the last time. Before him is the open Ark of the Covenant, painted as a still-life, containing the tablets of the law given by God and the manna. Moses sits on a raised seat and reads from the holy book in his hands. Signorelli's depiction of the listeners, conspicuous among whom are two elegant figures viewed from behind, several women with squirming infants, and a naked man who hangs on the prophet's words with rapt attention is noteworthy. In the background on the left a number of his followers are grieving over Moses' body, which can be seen laid out on the ground.

Luca Signorelli, 1445/50–1523
***The Testament and Death of Moses*, 1481–1482**
350 × 572 cm; Fresco
Sistine Chapel, Southern Wall

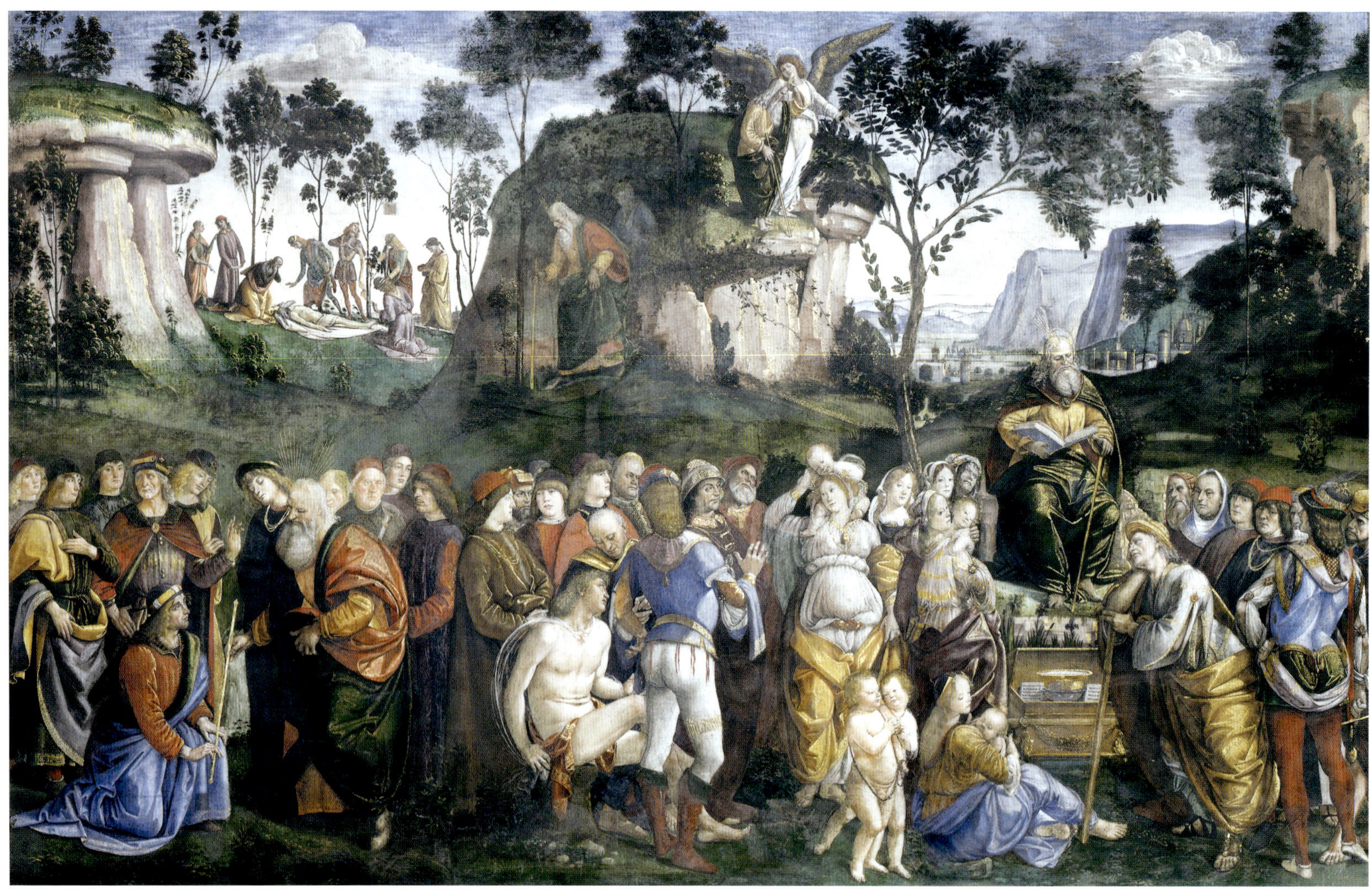

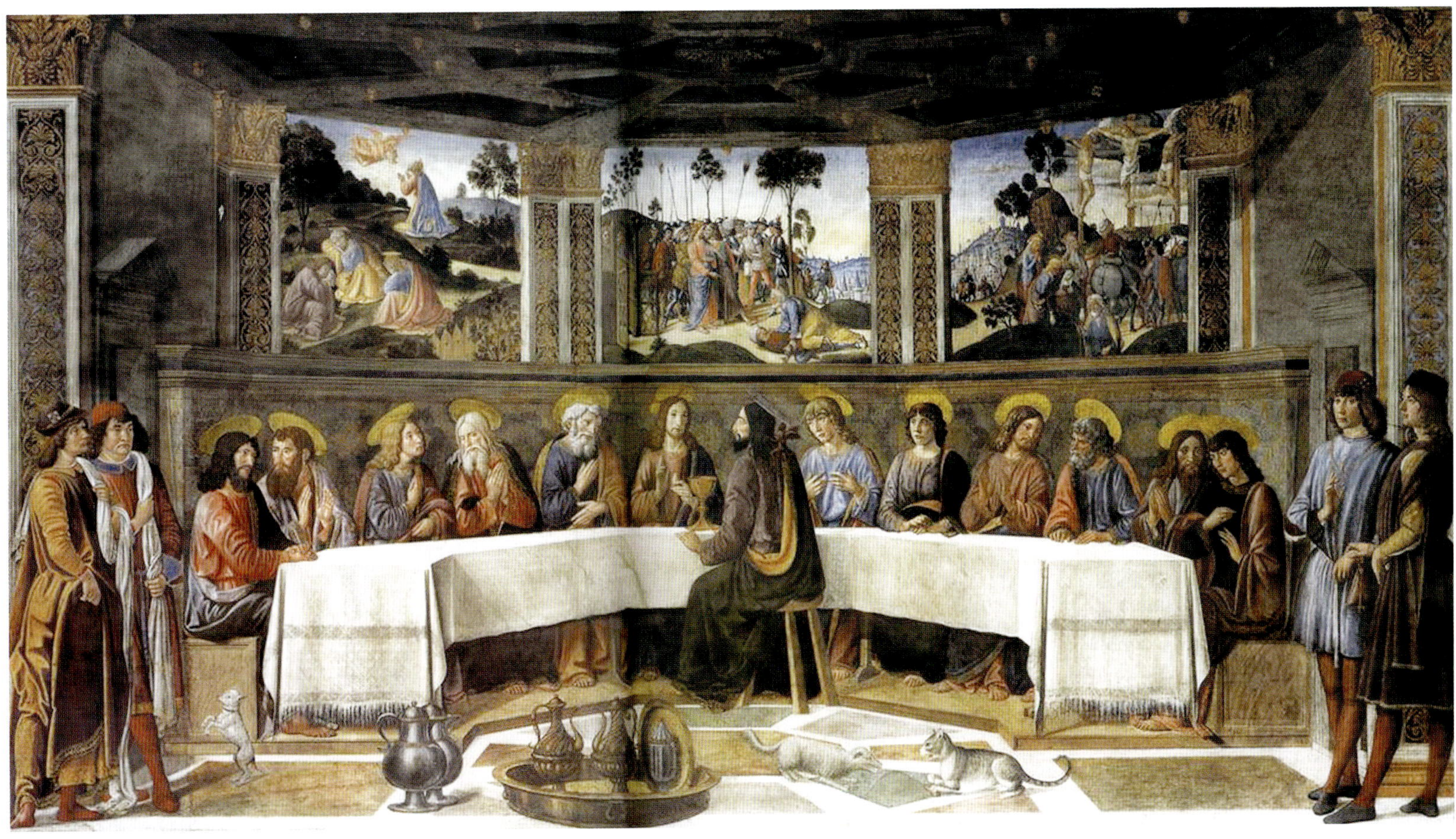

Cosimo Rosselli

The Last Supper

The final fresco in the Christ cycle (side wall) is a collaboration between Cosimo Rosselli and the Florentine Biagio d'Antonio. Jesus is seated with his disciples around a horseshoe-shaped table in a palatial interior. The table is covered by a white cloth and, in contrast to other depictions of the Last Supper, is virtually empty. The only item on the table is the chalice positioned in front of Christ, an allusion, like the Host in his left hand, to the Eucharist. The disciples seated on the outside comment on the news, announced by Jesus, that there is a traitor among them with dramatic gestures. Peter, John, and another disciple have turned to Jesus, who looks at Judas sitting by himself in front of the table. The treacherous role of Judas is underlined by his dark clothing, the small figure of the devil on his back, and the squabbling dog and cat beside his seat. In the foreground is a small still-life of precious jugs and trays, another reference to the Eucharist. The windows in the back wall look out onto three scenes from the Passion of Christ attributed to Biagio d'Antonio: prayers on the Mount of Olives, Christ being taken prisoner, and the crucifixion.

Cosimo Rosselli, 1439–1507
***The Last Supper*, 1481–1482**
349 × 570 cm; Fresco
Sistine Chapel, Northern Wall

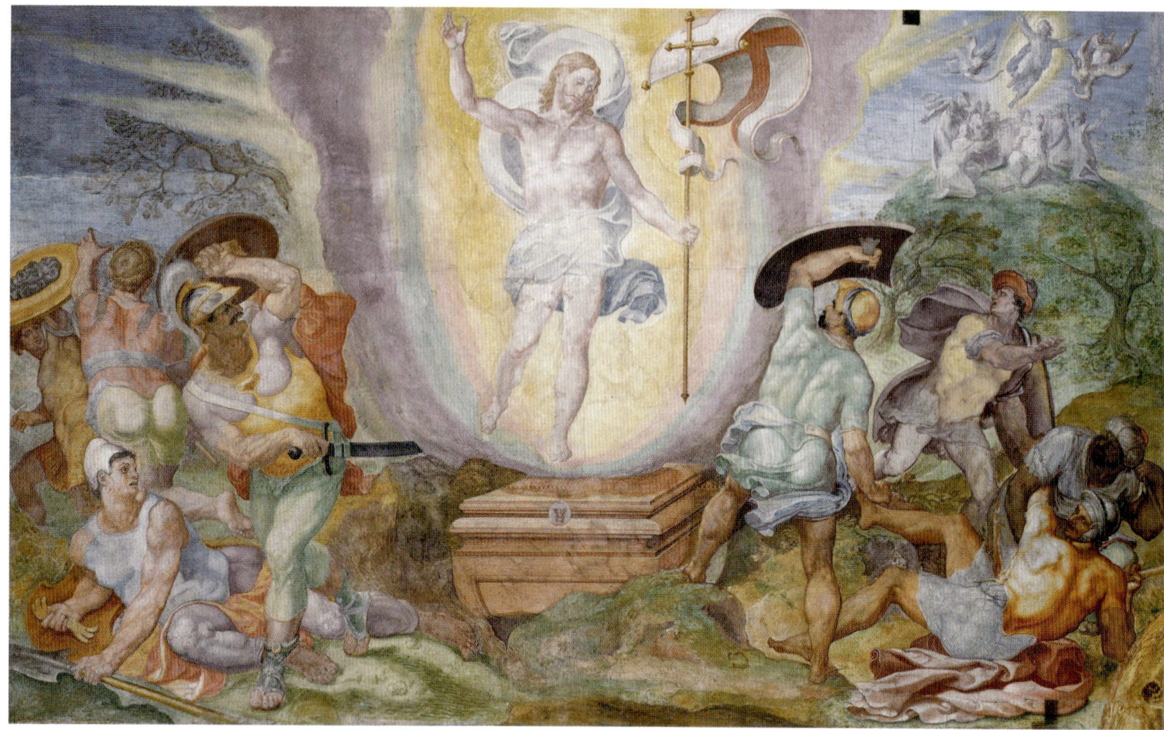

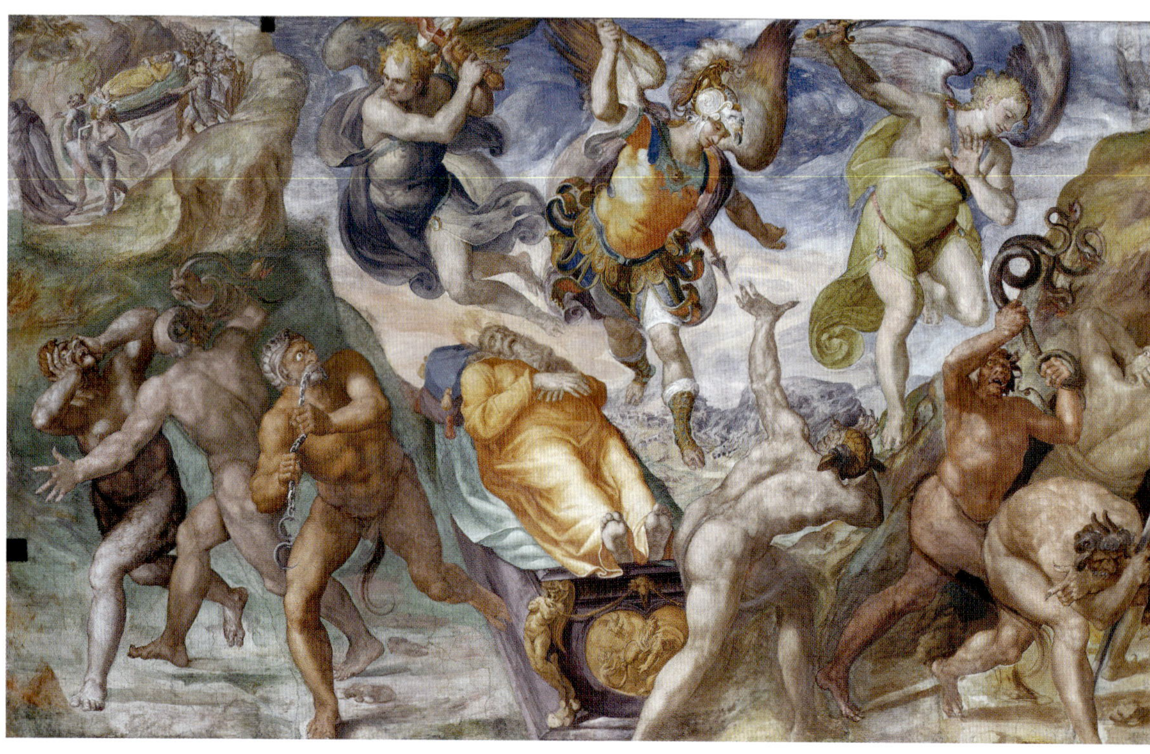

Hendrick van der Broeck, ca. 1522–1600
Resurrection of Christ, 1572
Fresco
Sistine Chapel, Eastern Wall

Matteo da Lecce, 1547–1616
Disputation over Moses' Body, 1572
Fresco
Sistine Chapel, Eastern Wall

SISTINE CHAPEL CEILING

The ceiling of the Sistine Chapel was completed by Michelangelo in 1512 after just four years of work. The concept for his ceiling frescoes was precisely coordinated to fit in with the existing cycles of paintings in the chapel, in particular the large-format motifs from the Old and New Testaments in the central wall register.

Medieval theologians distinguished not only between the Old and New Testaments, but within the Old Testament between the time before and after the Law of Moses (*ante legem* and *sub lege*), when God gave tablets of the law to Moses. With their Christ and Moses cycles, the wall frescoes thus present scenes belonging mainly to the *sub lege* and *sub gratia* periods (the latter referring to the time after the birth of the Savior as a sign of God's grace). By including in the central band of the ceiling scenes relating to the creation of the world up to the drunkenness of Noah, Michelangelo has enriched the iconographical program of the chapel with scenes from the *ante legem*.

In his ceiling for the Sistine Chapel, Michelangelo has created a *Gesamtkunstwerk* of trompe l'oeil architecture, sculpture, reliefs, and different styles of painting that seem to open up the chapel to heaven. What appears at first glance to be a bewildering muddle of individual picture fields and figures, architectural and decorative elements is actually based on a clear thematic and artistic logic. At the highest point is the central band with the nine scenes from Genesis and the story of Noah. In the middle of the sequence are three scenes of Adam and Eve in Paradise with the creation of Eve from Adam's rib at the very center. Unlike the heavily populated history paintings on the walls, the ceiling frescoes focus with very few exceptions on a small number of figures, who come across in consequence as all the more monumental. Adhering to the chronology of the Bible, the sequence begins on the altar wall with the Creation. This is followed by the Fall of Man and ends with four scenes from the life of Noah. However, this was not the order in which Michelangelo worked. As the chapel continued to be used for liturgical purposes, the altar area had to be kept free of scaffolding for as long as possible. According to the latest research, Michelangelo did not paint lying on his back, as was previously believed, but standing with his head tilted back. In spite of this uncomfortable working position, the frescoes have been painted extremely carefully in several layers. Michelangelo applied the top layers of paint very loosely, allowing the layers underneath to show through lending the whole work a delicate quality and fine luster.

Every second picture field in the central band is enclosed on the two outer sides by grisaille medallions designed to simulate reliefs. In the four corners of these fields sit the famous *Ignudi* (male nudes) in almost acrobatic poses. Their significance is primarily ornamental, although they can also be interpreted artistically as variations on the naked Adam, the progenitor of the human race, who occupies the center of the ceiling. These naked figures also allowed Michelangelo, who until this point had been active mainly as a sculptor, to demonstrate his knowledge of anatomy through the medium of painting as well.

In the register below the central band sit the mighty figures of the prophets and the sibyls, who, as representatives of the Old Testament and heathen antiquity, foretold in their writings the coming of Christ and his work. They are shown wearing billowing, brightly colored garments, affording Michelangelo an opportunity to show off his skill as a colorist. The lowest register, making the transition from ceiling to wall, is also Michelangelo's work and depicts Christ's forebears as listed at the beginning of the Gospel of St. Matthew. In the four corners of the end walls are depictions of Old Testament stories, including Judith and Holofernes and the battle of David and Goliath.

The harmony between the deep and light tones and the profusion of varied figures throughout the ceiling lend the work its unusual splendor and vivacity.

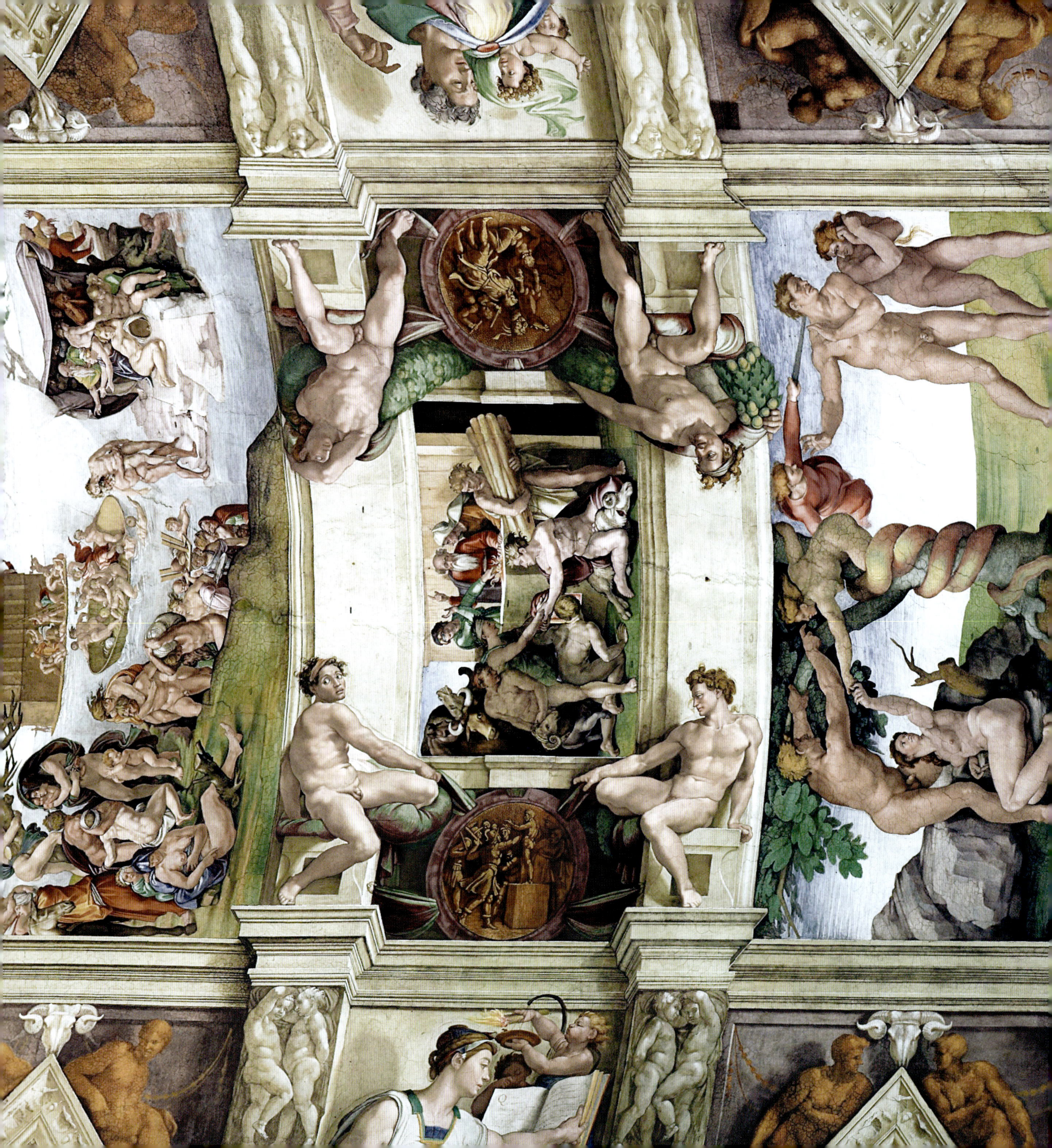

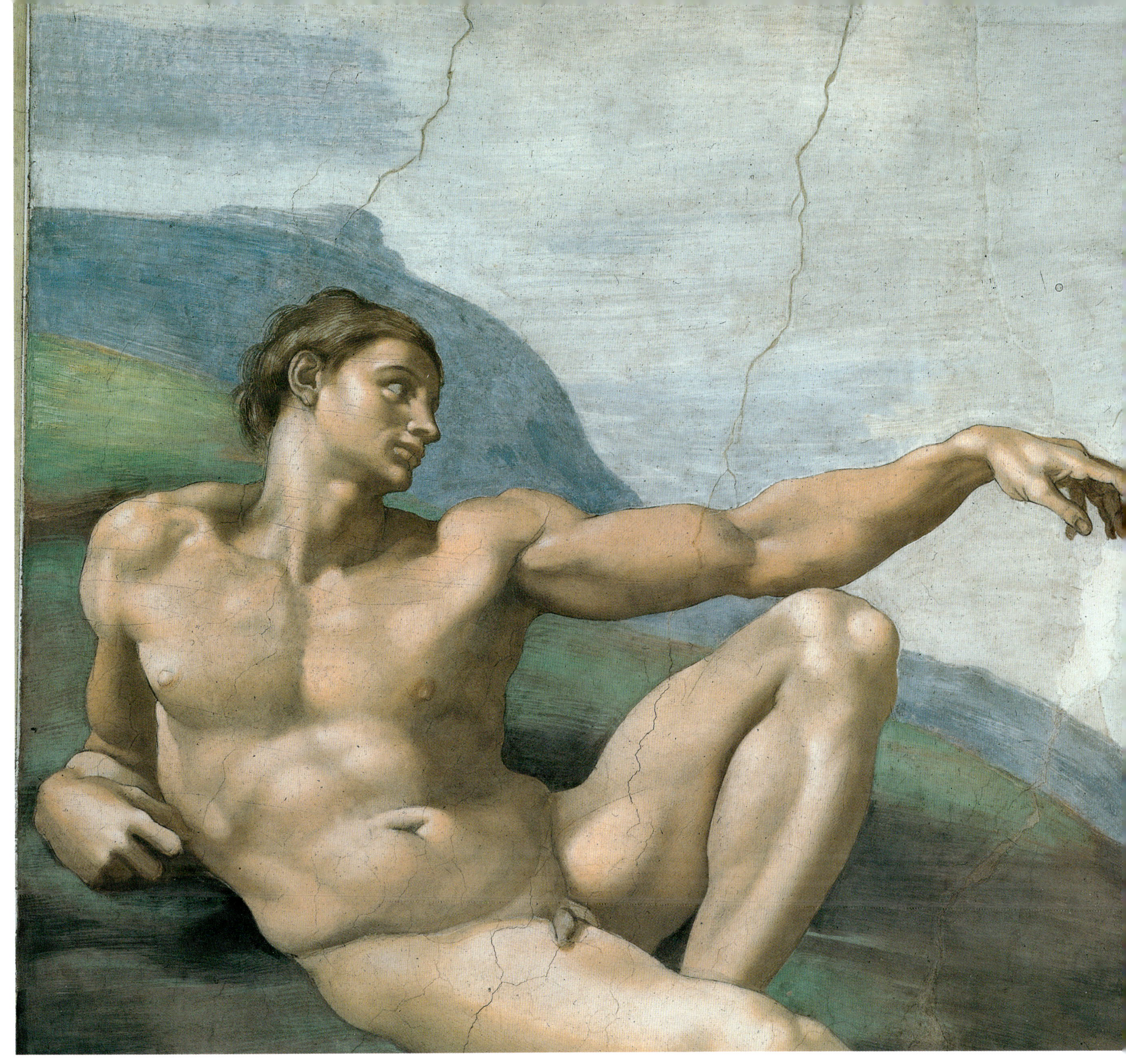

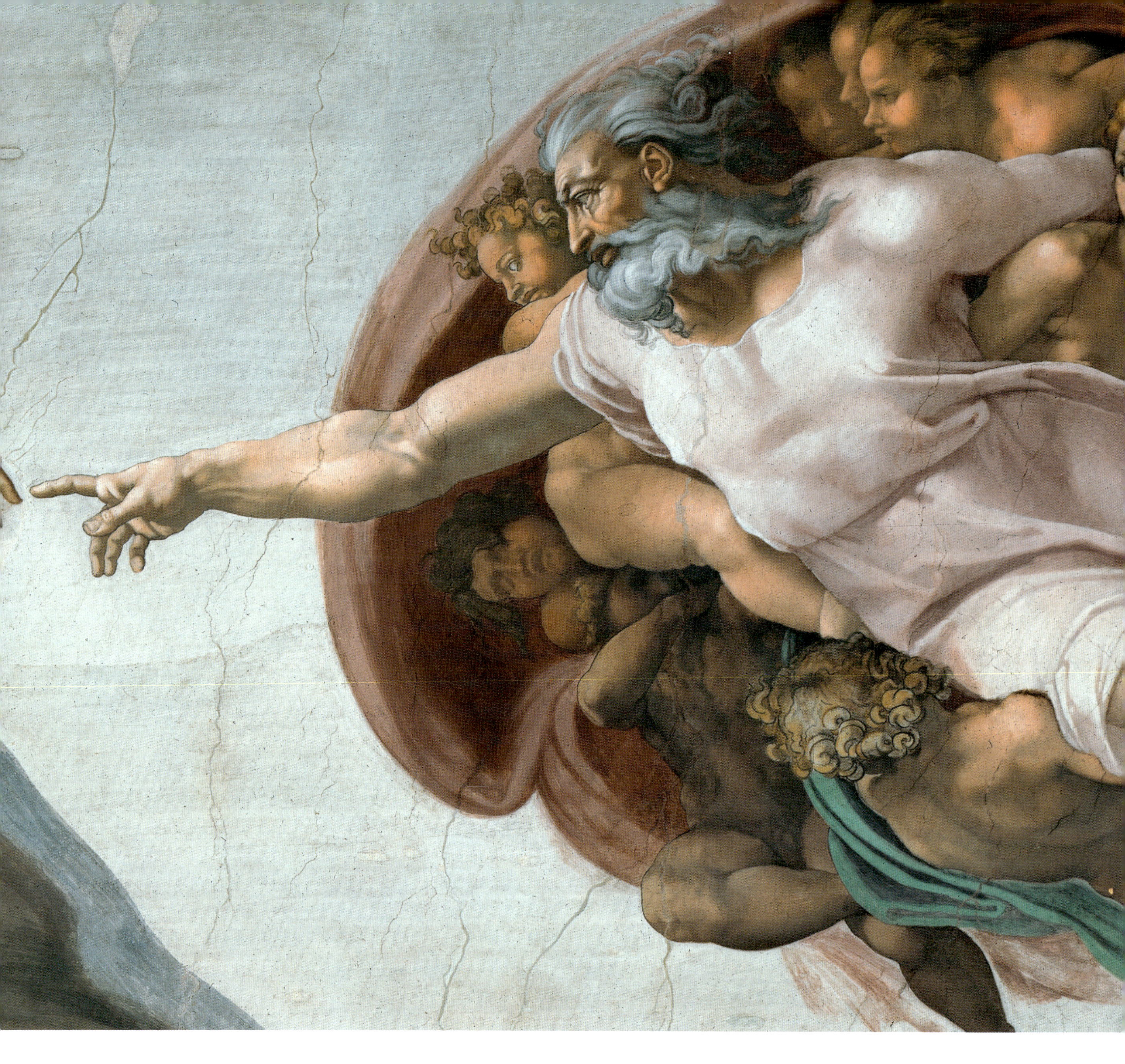

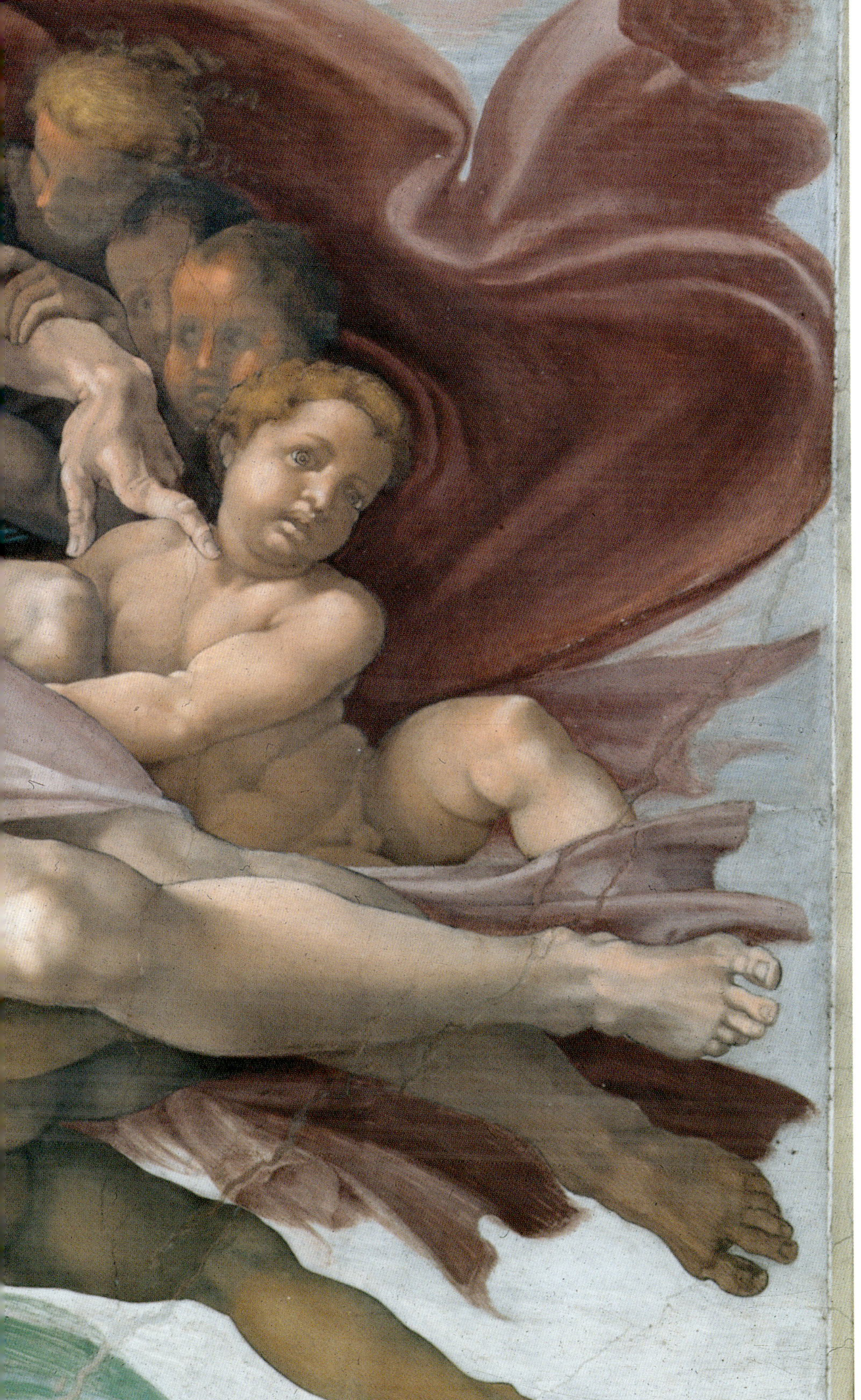

Michelangelo Buonarroti

The Creation of Adam

The Creation of Adam is the most famous scene on the Sistine ceiling. As in the preceding creation frescoes, God is depicted as a flying figure. And as in the scene showing the creation of the sun and the moon, he is accompanied by a host of angels who are enclosed within his mantle as if in a mussel shell. Large and small, male and female, the angels press tightly around him and embrace or support his mighty frame with their bodies. Their attention is directed toward the no less mighty figure of Adam, lying on the earth in the left of the scene with his elbow resting on the knee of his bent leg. In many respects, Adam's posture parallels the God figure's, thereby conveying the idea that man is made in the image of God (Genesis 1:26). This was to become a key aspect of the Renaissance concept of humanity, just as Adam's muscular, naked body came to epitomize masculine beauty. Adam gazes at his creator with a look of devotion in the expectation of receiving his touch, which can be interpreted as the transmission of the life force. This was to become the most famous depiction of the hand of God in the history of art.

Michelangelo Buonarroti, 1475–1564
***The Creation of Adam*, 1508–1512**
Fresco
Sistine Chapel, Ceiling

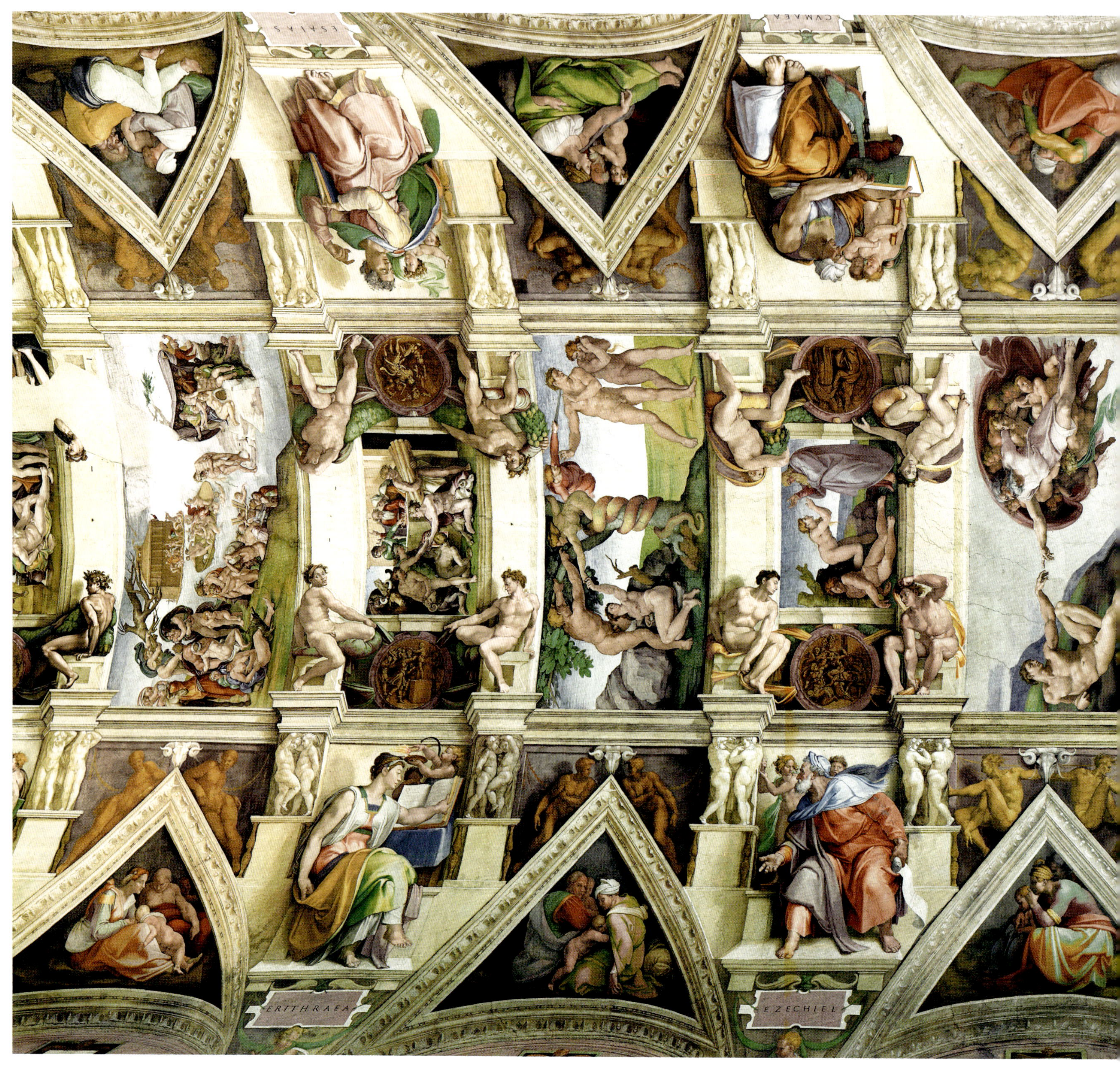
ESAIAS
CVMAEA
ERITHRAEA
EZECHIEL

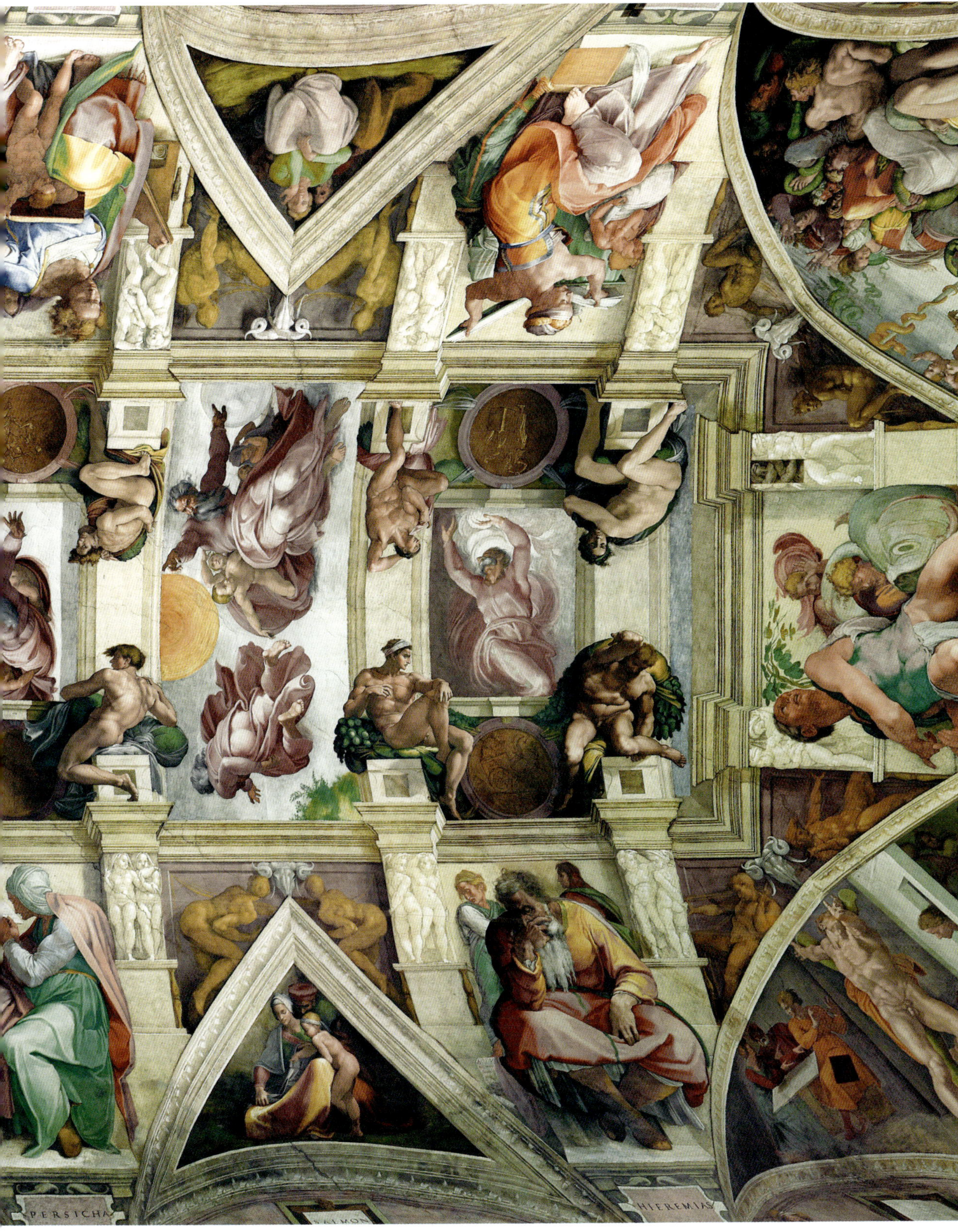

Michelangelo Buonarroti, 1475-1564
Sistine Chapel Ceiling, 1508-1512
40.5 x 14 m; Fresco
Sistene Chapel

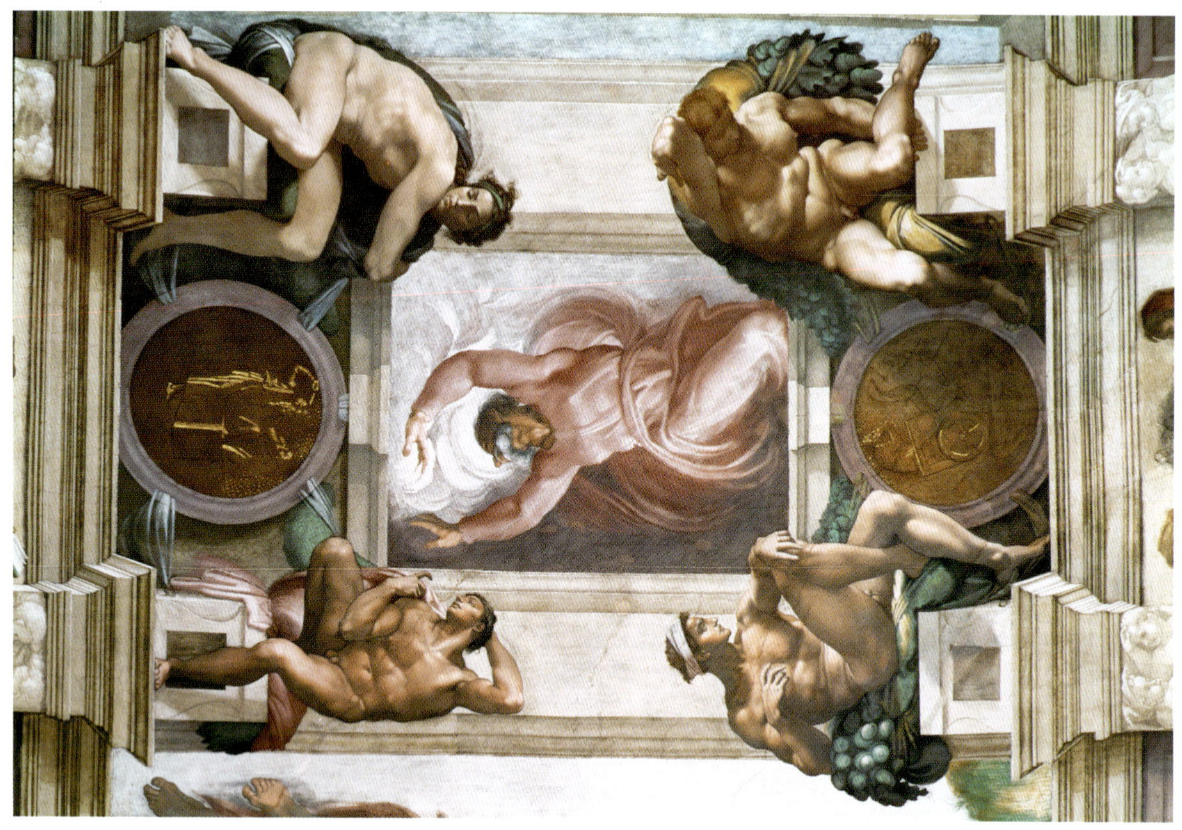

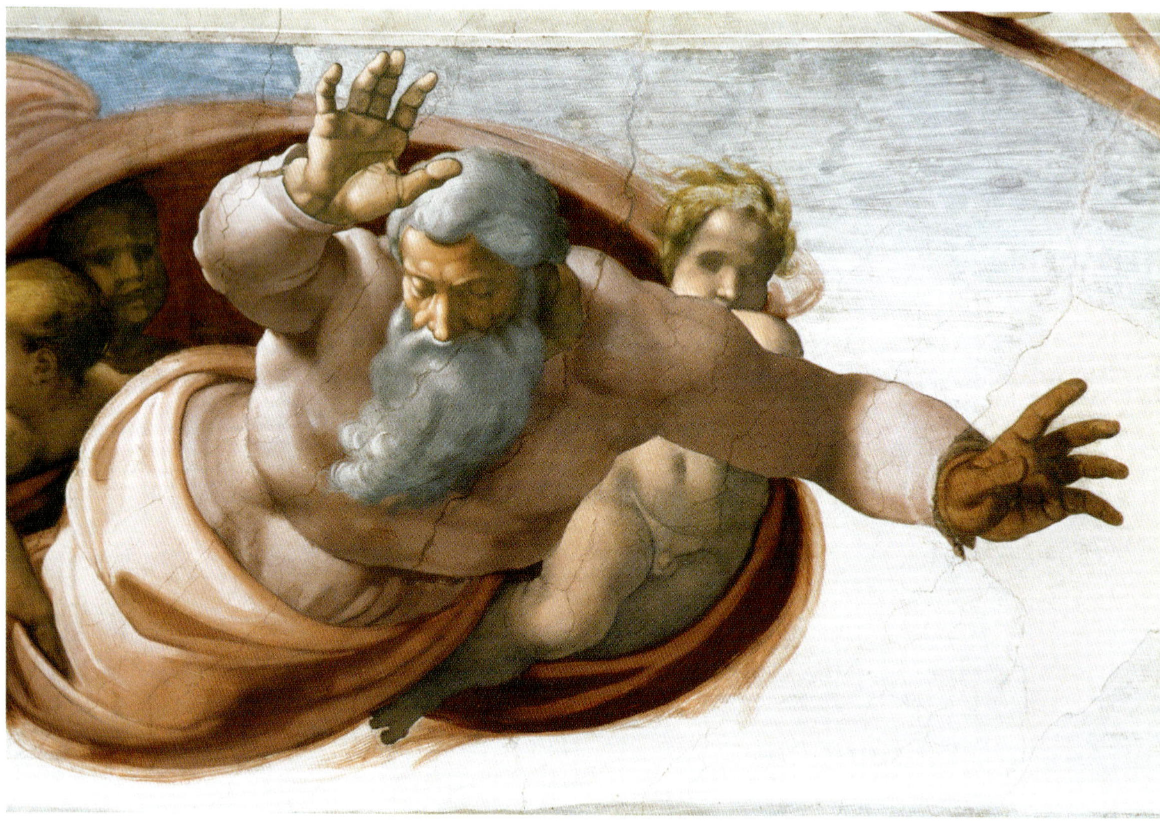

Michelangelo Buonarroti, 1475–1564
***The Separation of Light and Dark*, 1508–1512**
Fresco
Sistine Chapel, Ceiling

Michelangelo Buonarroti, 1475–1564
***Dividing the Waters from the Land*, 1508–1512**
Fresco
Sistine Chapel, Ceiling

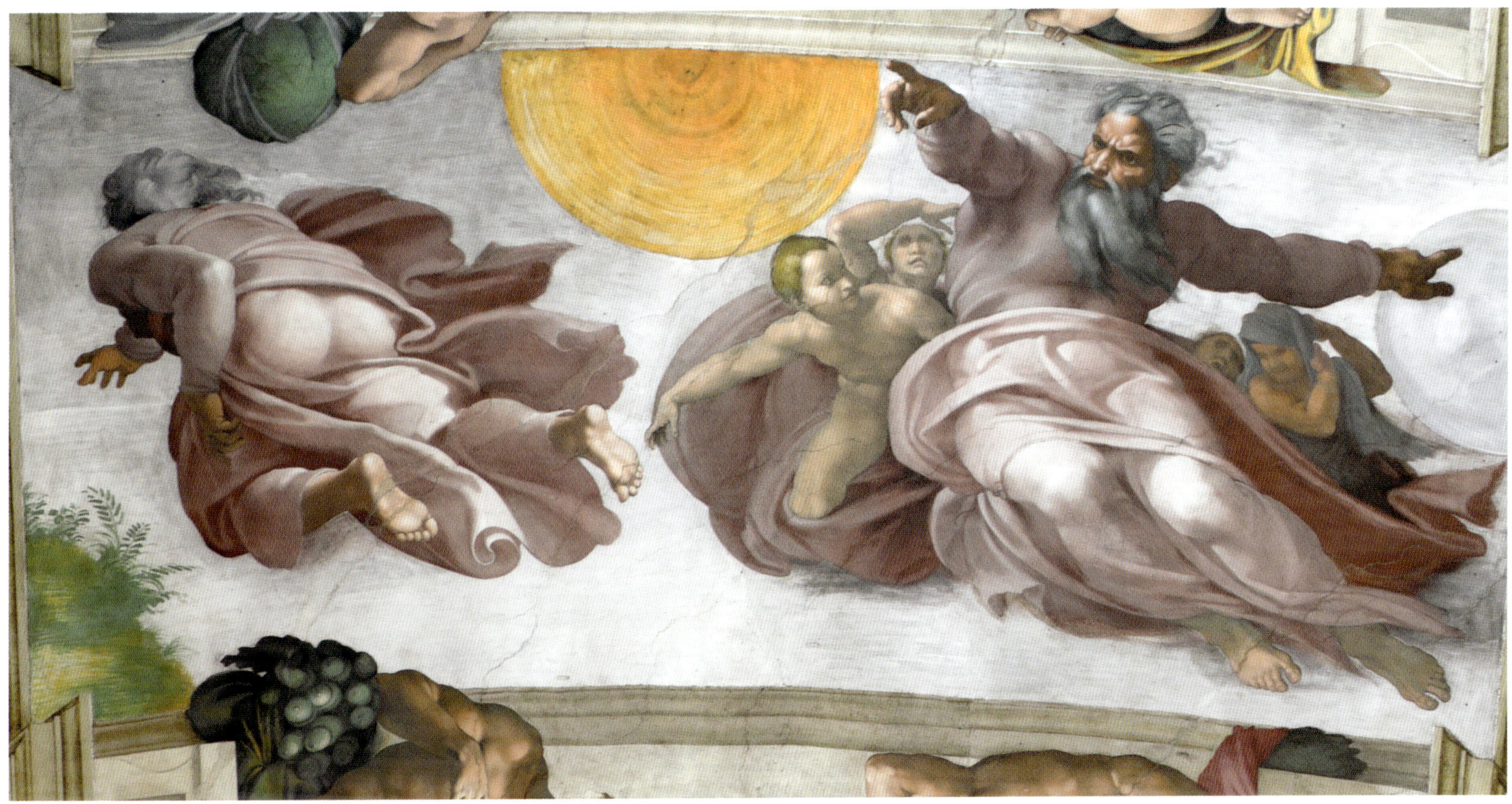

Michelangelo Buonarroti

Creation of the Heavenly Bodies and Vegetation

This fresco sums up the events that took place on the second and third days of creation. On the left we see God creating the plants, as described in Genesis 1:11: "And God said, Let the earth bring forth grass and the herb-yielding seed..." Depicted on the right is the creation of the sun and the moon as reported in Genesis 1:16: "And God made two great lights; the greater light to rule the day, and the lesser light to rule the night..." As in the first scene, which describes the dividing of the light from the darkness, here too God is depicted as a flying figure issuing instructions with imperious gestures. With his resolute gaze, directed toward the sun in the center of the field, and his widespread arms, stretching between the two heavenly bodies, the God figure on the right embodies the idea of an all-powerful God of Creation, the lord of heaven and earth. This figure is accompanied by four angels floating on his fluttering mantle as if on a flying carpet as opposed to the God of the second day of creation, who is shown disappearing into the depths of the picture with his back to the viewer.

Michelangelo Buonarroti, 1475–1564
***Creation of the Heavenly Bodies and Vegetation*, 1508–1512**
Fresco
Sistine Chapel, Ceiling

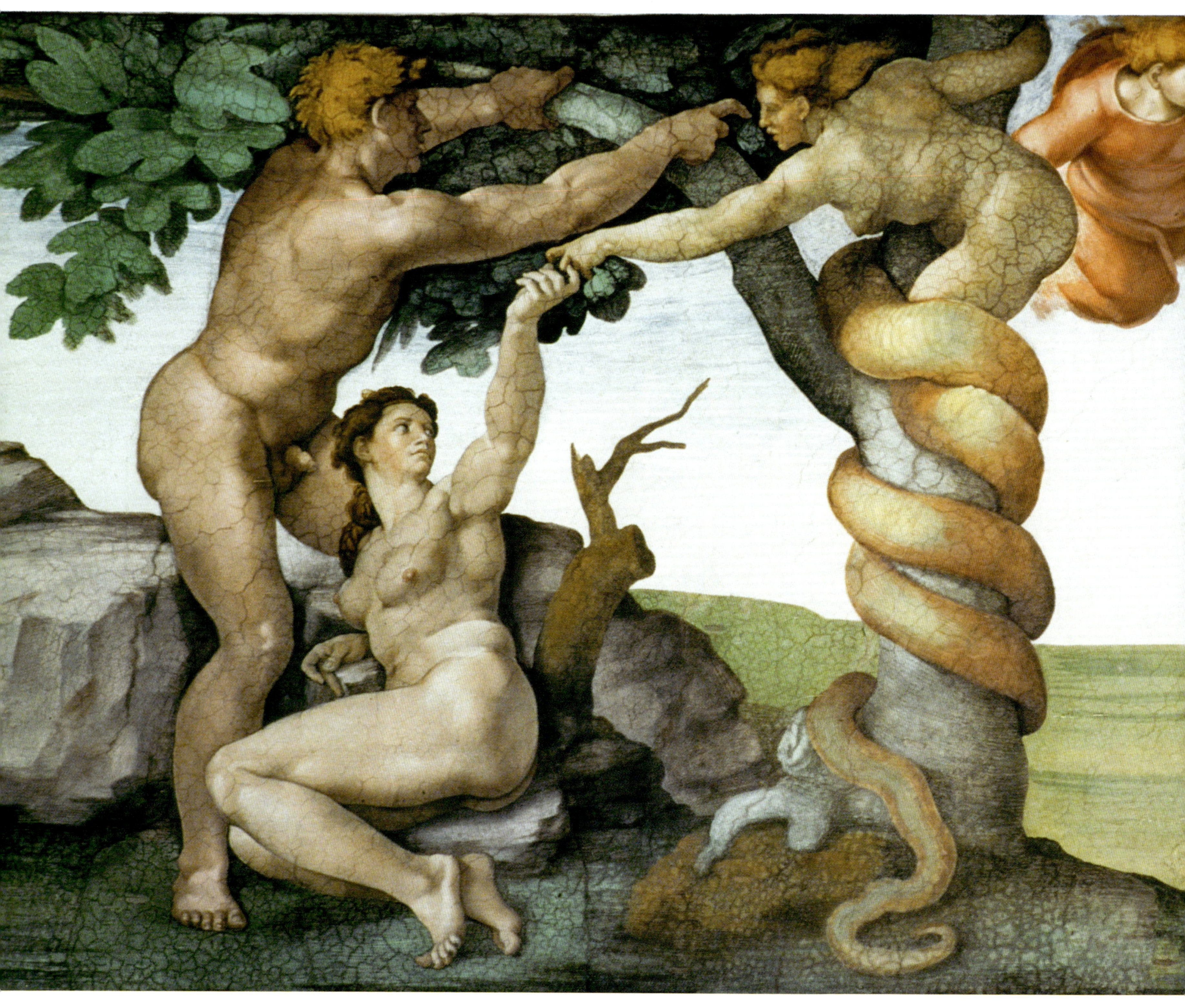

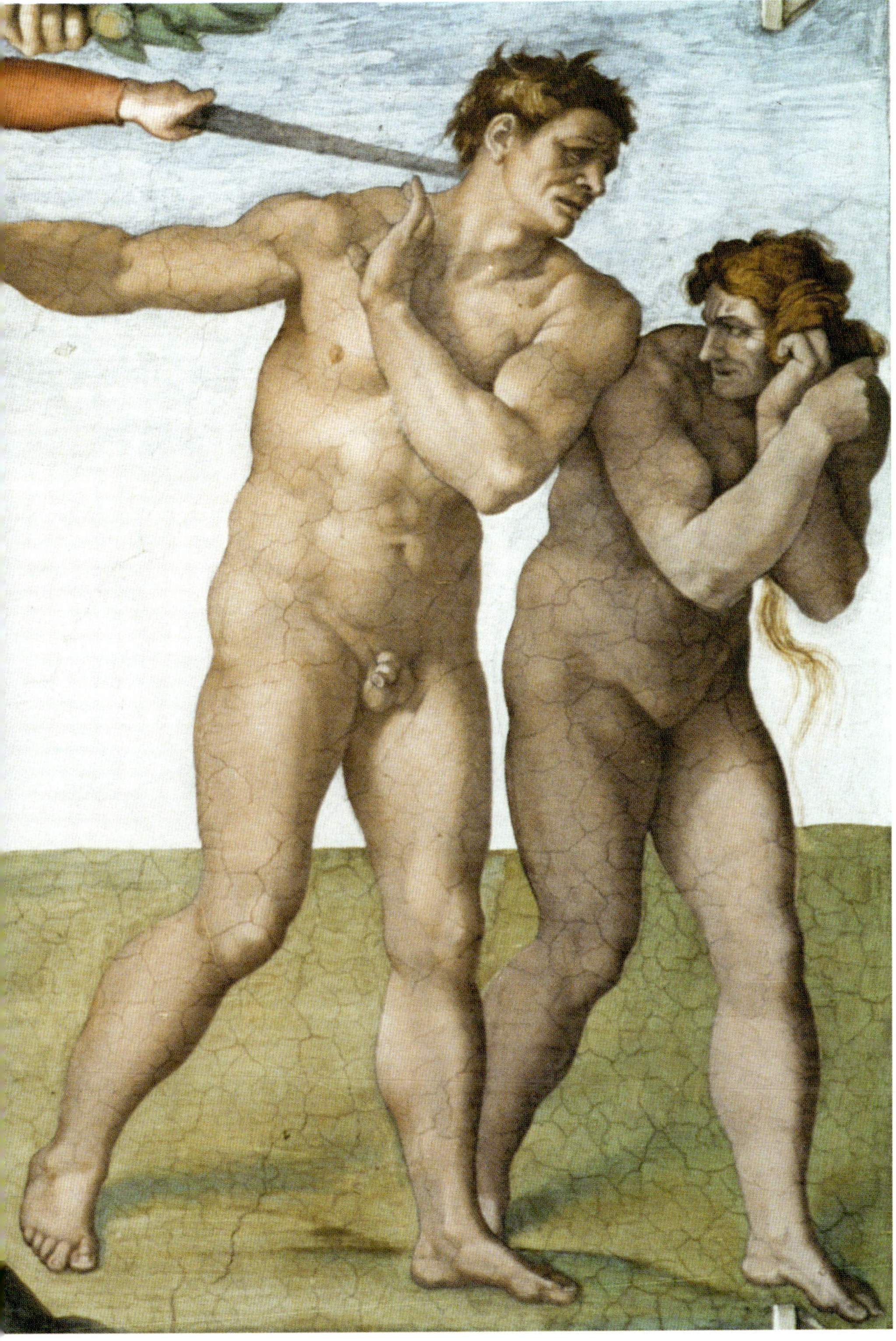

Michelangelo Buonarroti

The Fall and Expulsion

This fresco combines The Fall with The Expulsion of Adam and Eve from Paradise, shown in the right half of the scene. The Tree of Knowledge soars up along the precise central axis. Around it coils the serpent which tempts the first pair of humans to eat the tree's fruit despite God's prohibition. Michelangelo has allocated Adam a far more active role than in most other treatments of the theme. Whereas in the Bible (Genesis 3:6) it is Eve who gives Adam the forbidden fruit after tasting it herself, here she receives the fruit from the serpent as she crouches on the ground while Adam grasps a branch of the tree with both hands as he reaches for the fruit himself. The two progenitors of the human race are distinctive for their muscular bodies, with Eve taking on an almost masculine appearance. The serpent is also depicted as a powerful female form; it is only her long tail coiled around the tree trunk that shows her to be a snake. In contrast with the biblical account, the expulsion of Adam and Eve from the garden is performed not by God himself but by an angel with a sword. Furthermore, in common with most of the other figures in the cycle, Adam and Eve are naked, whereas according to the Bible (Gen 3:21) they should be "clothed" with at least a fig leaf.

Michelangelo Buonarroti, 1475–1564
***The Fall and Expulsion*, 1508–1512**
Fresco
Sistine Chapel, Ceiling

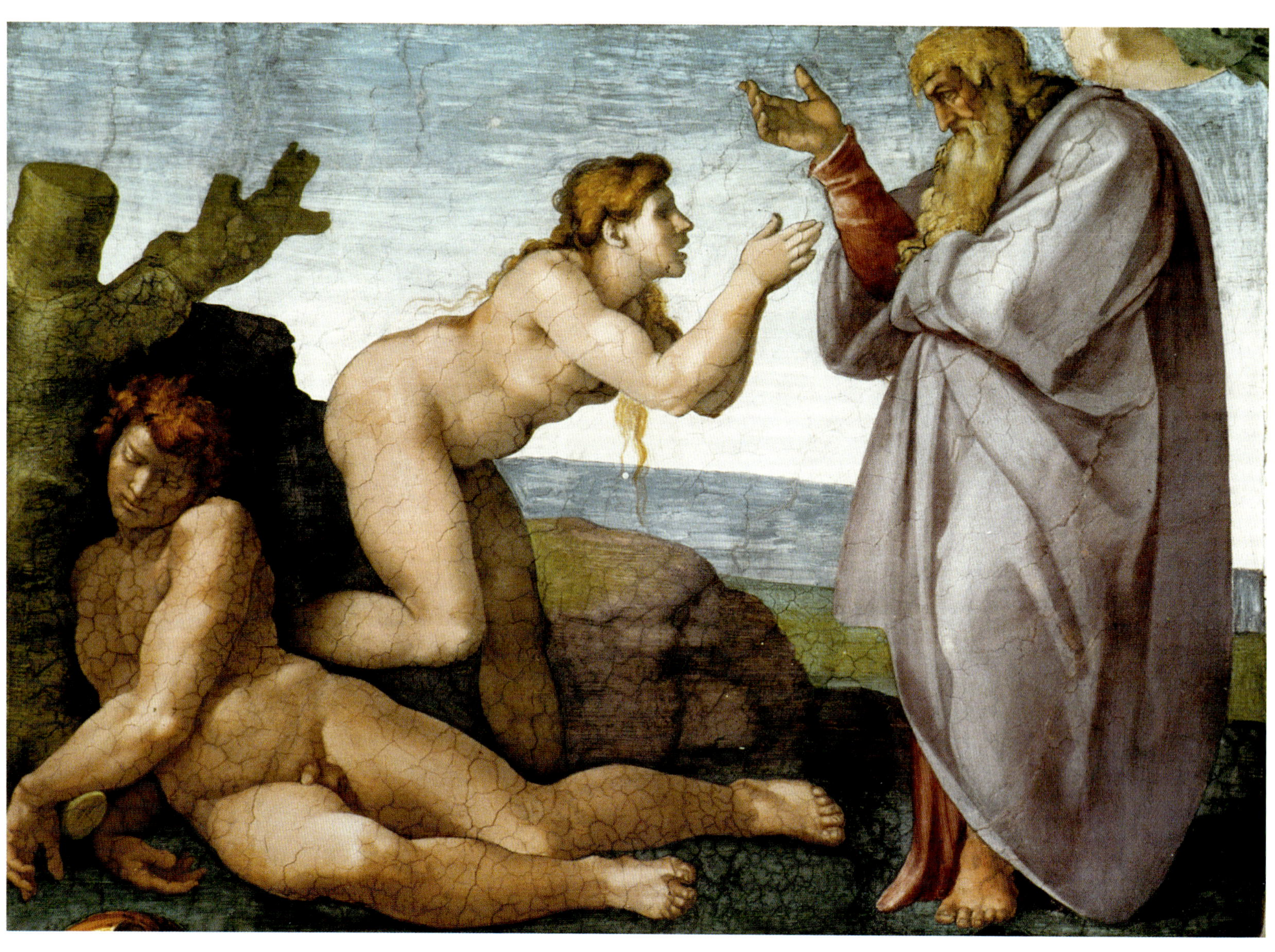

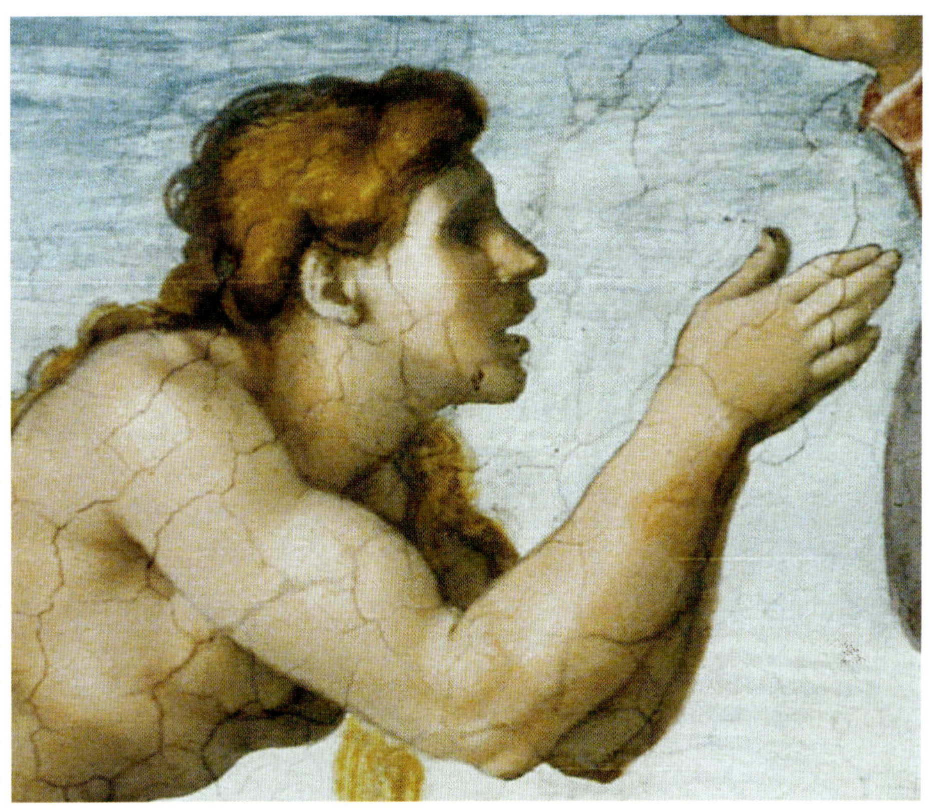

Michelangelo Buonarroti

The Creation of Eve

The scene depicting Eve's creation is located at the center of the Sistine ceiling. In showing her emerging from Adam's side, Michelangelo follows the description in the second chapter of Genesis, in which she is fashioned from a rib taken from the sleeping Adam. As in the scene of his own creation, Adam lies semi-upright on the ground, but is now asleep with his head resting on his shoulder. This allows for a free view of Eve, who is getting to her feet at the center of the picture behind Adam. She seems to be following the upward-motioning hand of God, who stands before her in his gray mantle. The barren landscape focuses attention onto the three protagonists, most importantly Eve and God the Father. This emphasis in the Sistine fresco cycle on the mother of all mankind is theologically motivated. Eve was regarded as a precursor of the Virgin Mary, regarded as the embodiment of the church—whose most senior representatives were the popes. Directly beneath the fresco is the original site of the chancel screen, which marked the division between the lay and clerical parts of the chapel and provided access to the chancel and sanctuary with its depiction of the Assumption of the Virgin.

Michelangelo Buonarroti, 1475–1564
***The Creation of Eve*, 1508–1512**
Fresco
Sistine Chapel, Ceiling

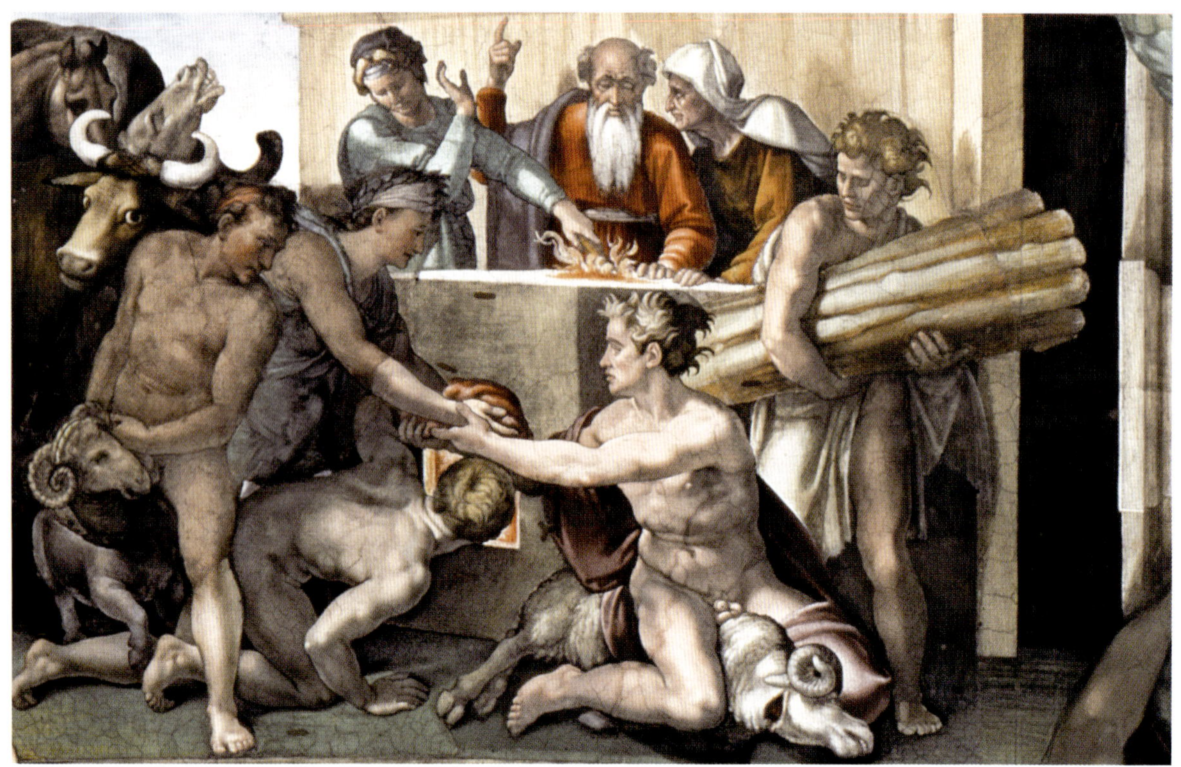

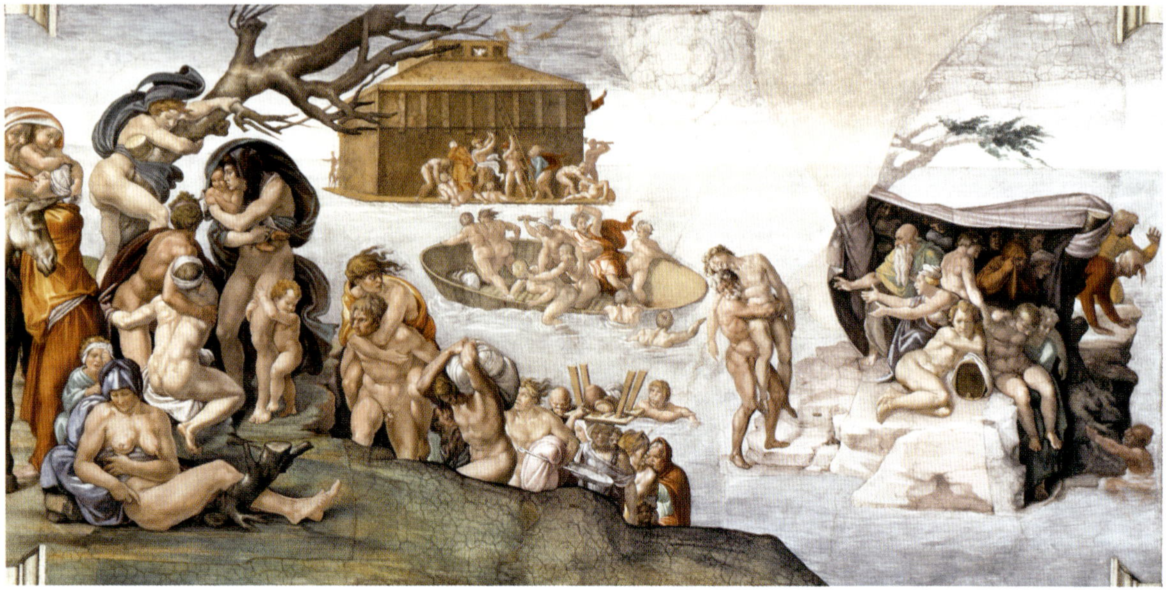

Michelangelo Buonarroti, 1475–1564
***The Sacrifice of Noah*, 1508–1512**
Fresco
Sistine Chapel, Ceiling

Michelangelo Buonarroti, 1475–1564
***The Flood*, 1508–1512**
Fresco
Sistine Chapel, Ceiling

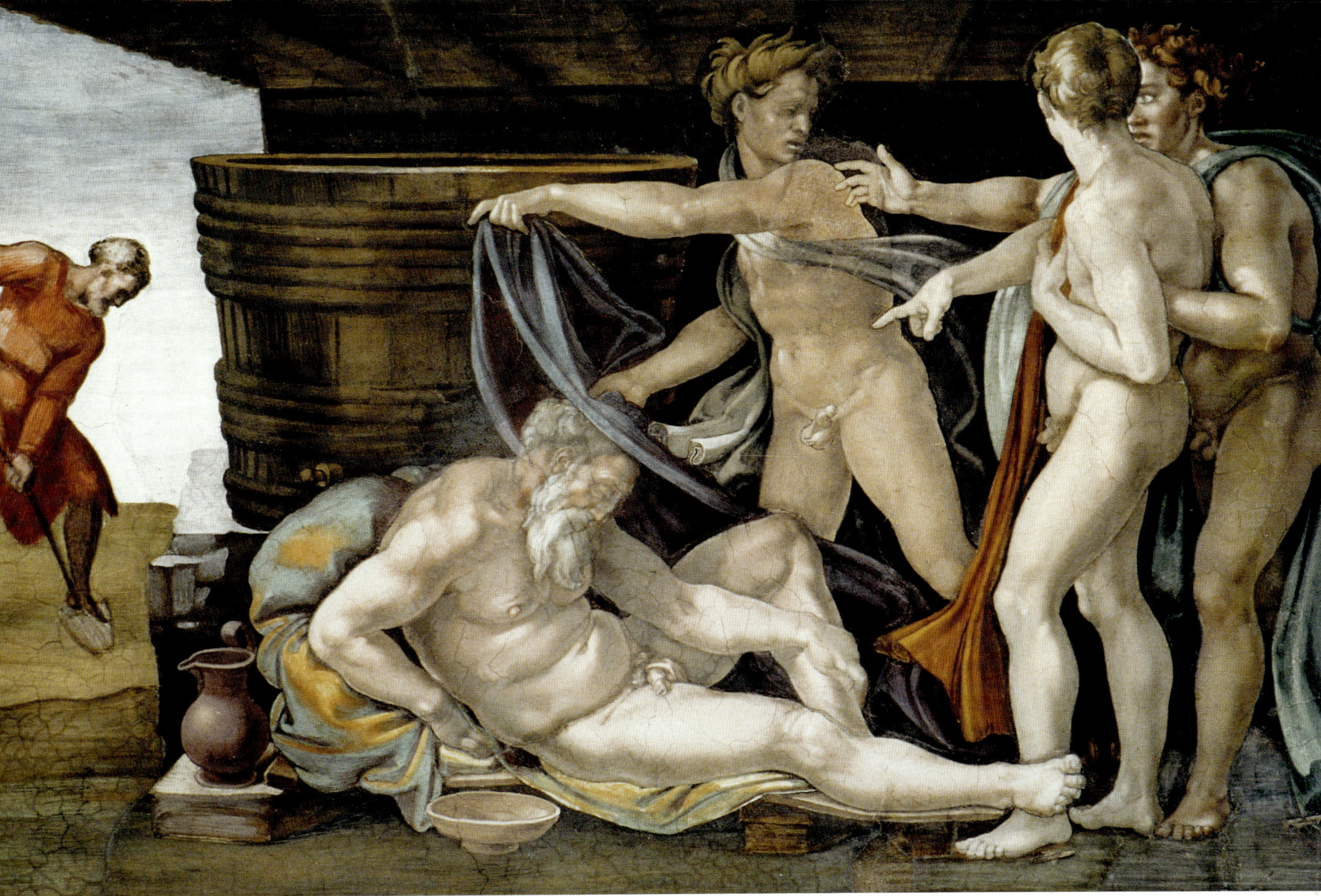

Michelangelo Buonarroti, 1475–1564
***The Drunkenness of Noah*, 1508–1512**
Fresco
Sistine Chapel, Ceiling

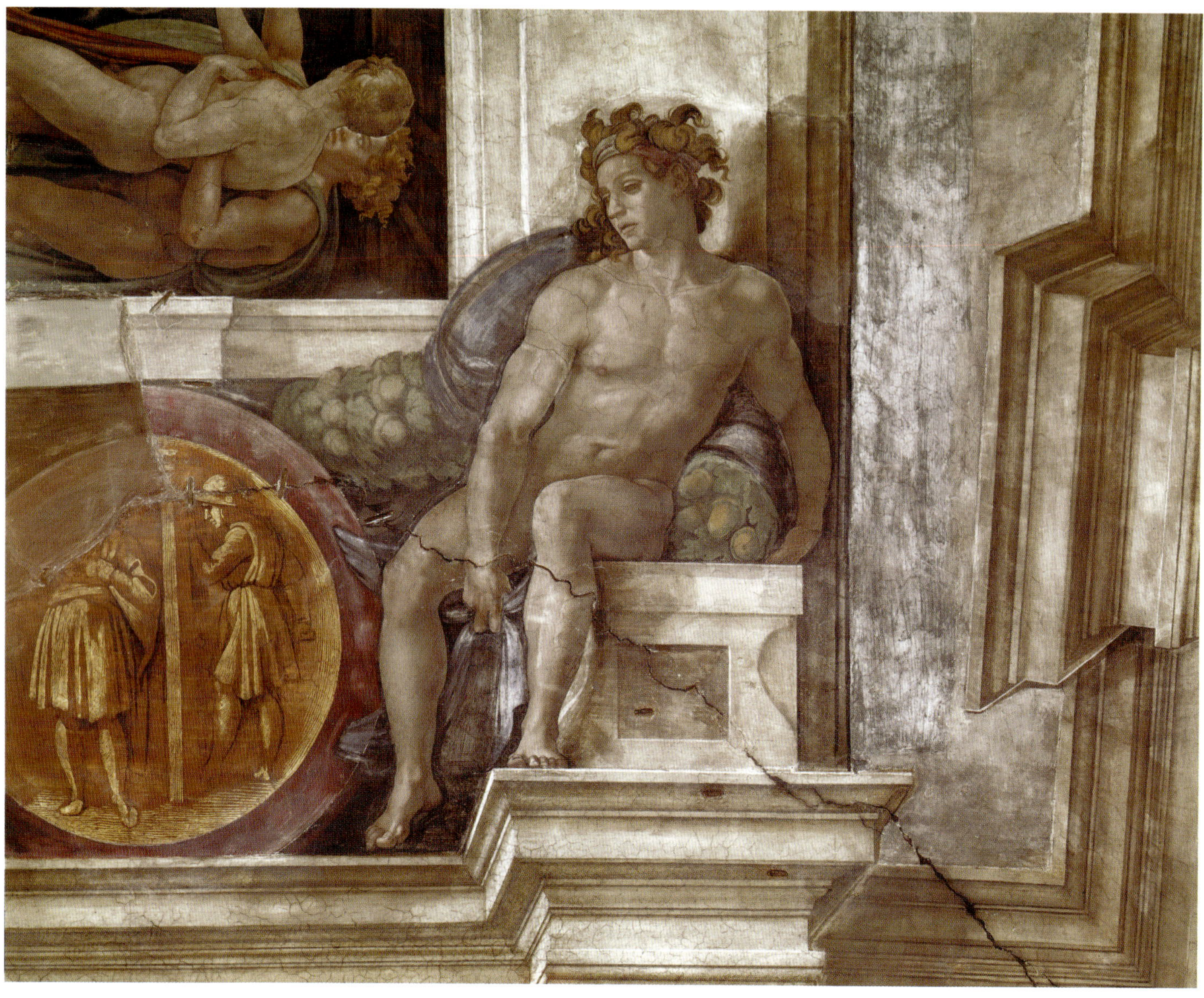

Michelangelo Buonarroti

Ignudo above and to the right of the *Delphic Sybil*

The twenty male nudes that frame the smaller scenes in the Genesis cycle are among the best-known figures of the Sistine ceiling. As an element within the decorative scheme, the *Ignudi* (from *nudo*, Italian for naked) are the invention of Michelangelo, who uses them to demonstrate his mastery of the painted nude. All are athletic young men who show off their bodies in almost acrobatic poses. Twining around these figures, who are seated on marble plinths, are garlands of oak leaves with lush fruits, alluding, in addition to the sexual connotations in the context of the chapel, to the coat of arms of Julius II della Rovere. The *Ignudo* above and to the right of the Delphic Sibyl, next to the *Drunkenness of Noah*, was perhaps the first to have been painted by Michelangelo. In contrast to some of the later *Ignudi*, this one is remarkable for his perfect, regular beauty and the harmonious modeling of his body. His posture mirrors that of the Sibyl below him and at the same time takes account of the framing of the Noah scene. Seen in their entirety, the *Ignudi* seem to multiply the naked figure of Adam and emphasize the importance of this iconographical motif within the context of the ceiling program.

Michelangelo Buonarroti, 1475–1564
***Ignudo* above and to the right of the *Delphic Sybil*, 1508–1512**
Fresco
Sistine Chapel, Ceiling

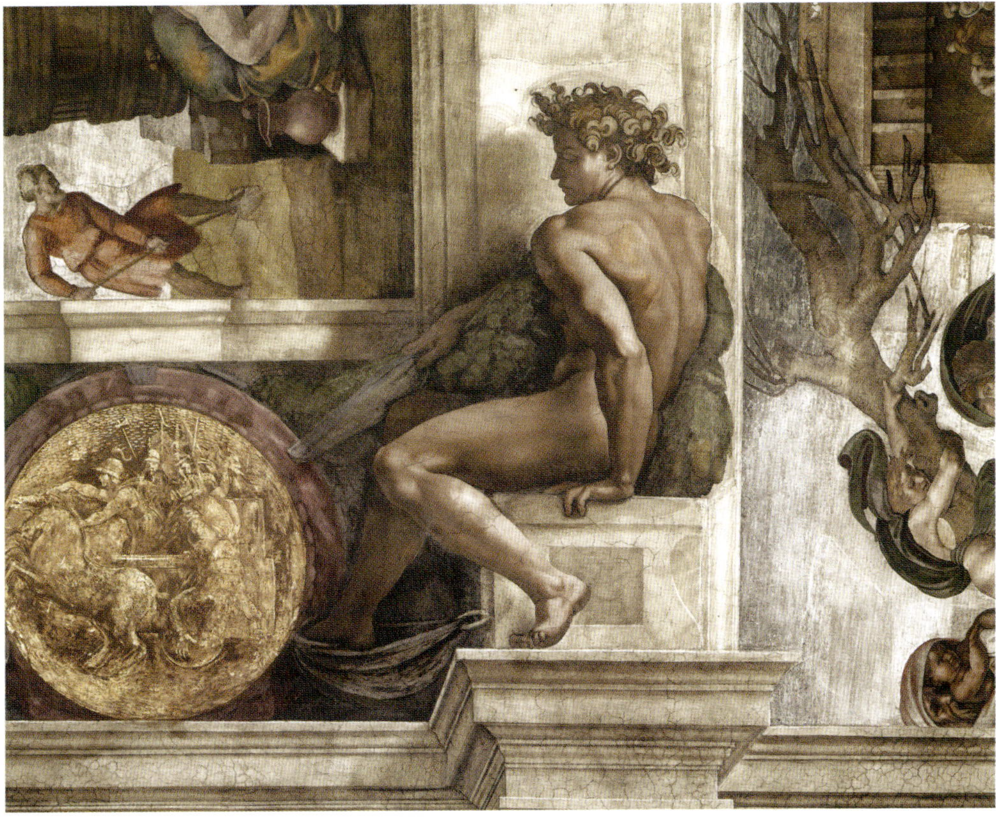

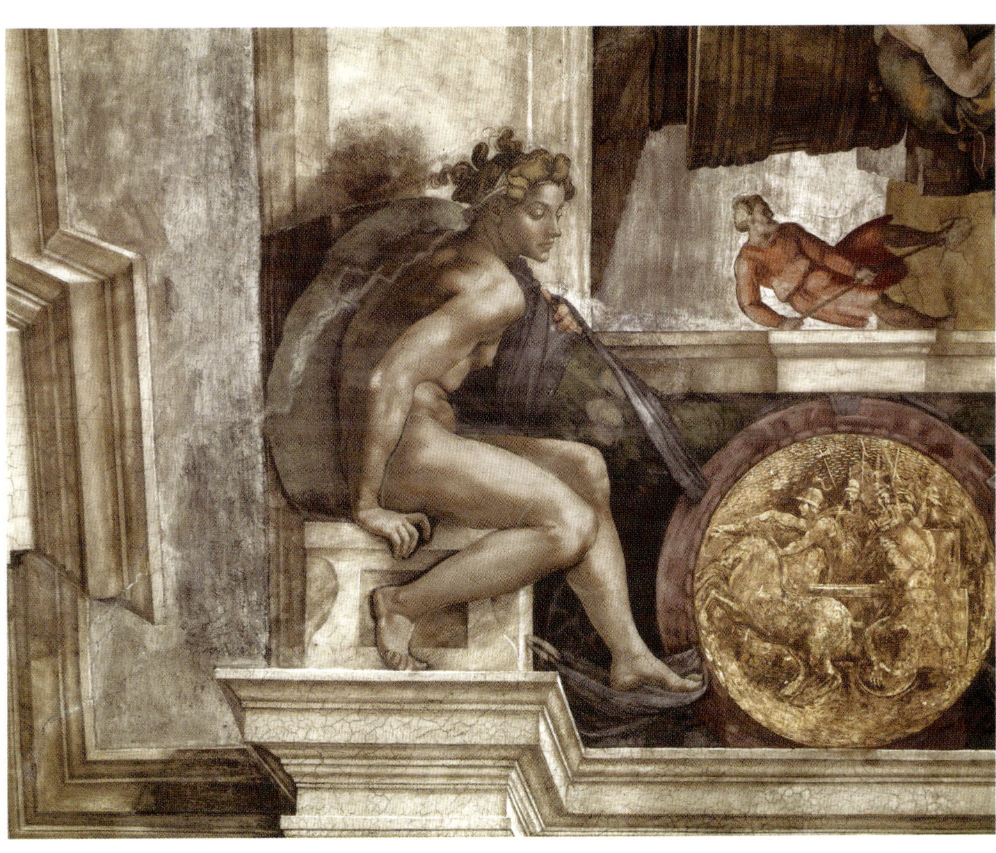

Michelangelo Buonarroti, 1475–1564
***Ignudo* to the upper right of the *Prophet Joel*, 1508–1512**
Fresco
Sistine Chapel, Ceiling

Michelangelo Buonarroti, 1475–1564
***Ignudo* to the upper left of the *Prophet Joel*, 1508–1512**
Fresco
Sistine Chapel, Ceiling

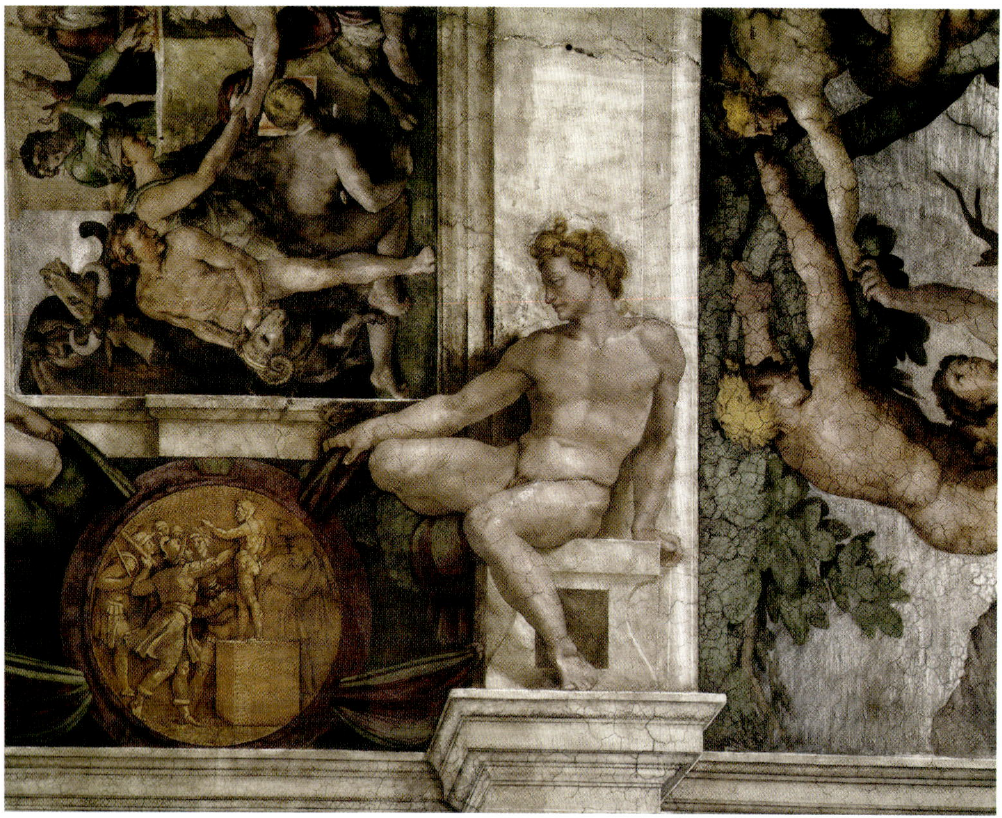

Michelangelo Buonarroti, 1475–1564
***Ignudo* to the upper right of the *Erythraean Sibyl*, 1508–1512**
Fresco
Sistine Chapel, Ceiling

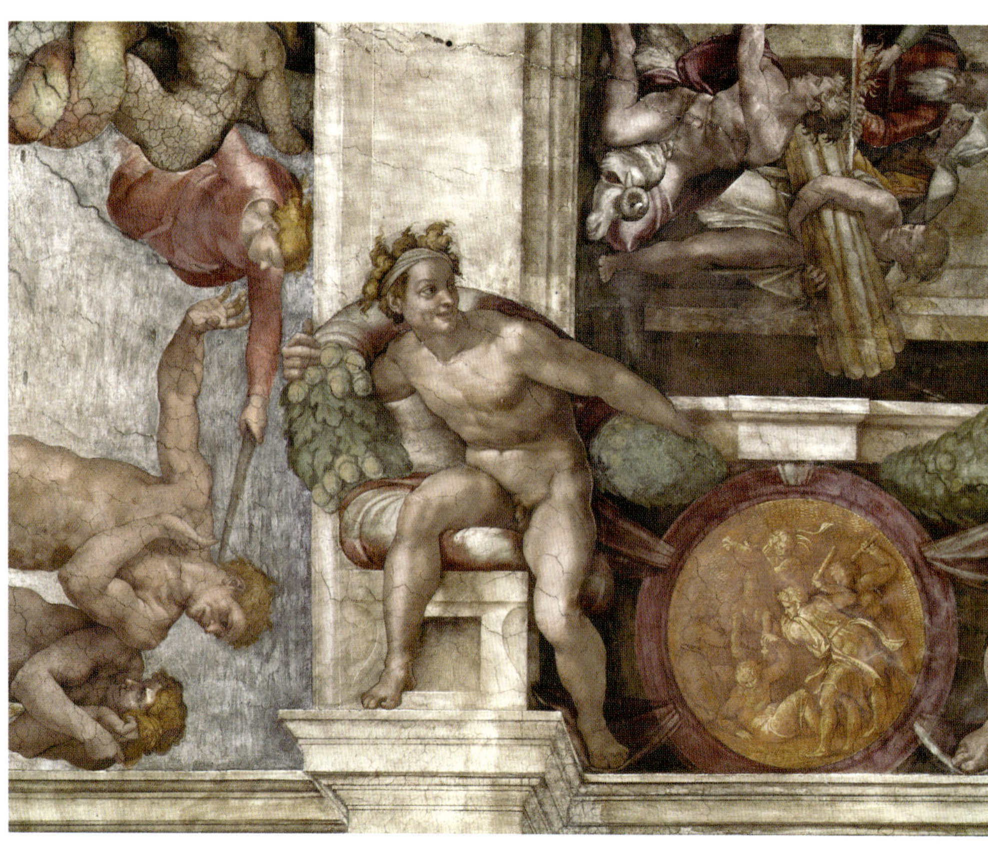

Michelangelo Buonarroti, 1475–1564
***Ignudo* to the upper left of the *Prophet Isaiah*, 1508–1512**
Fresco
Sistine Chapel, Ceiling

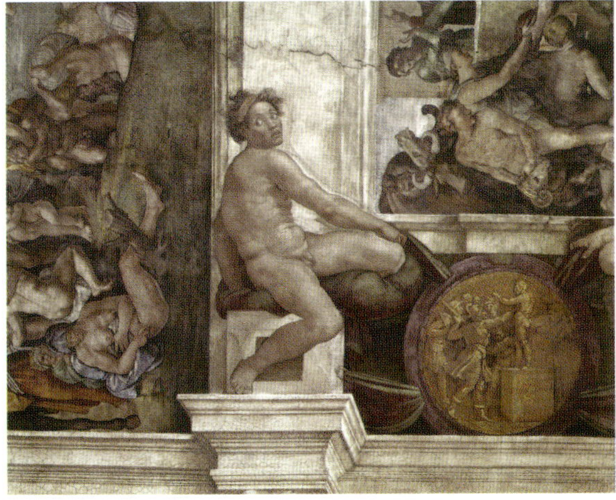
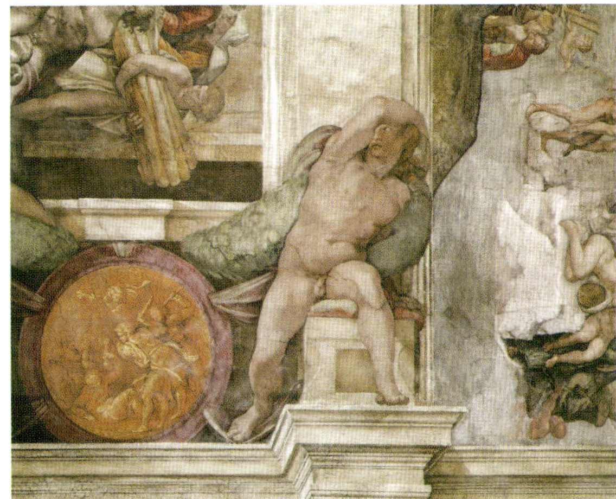
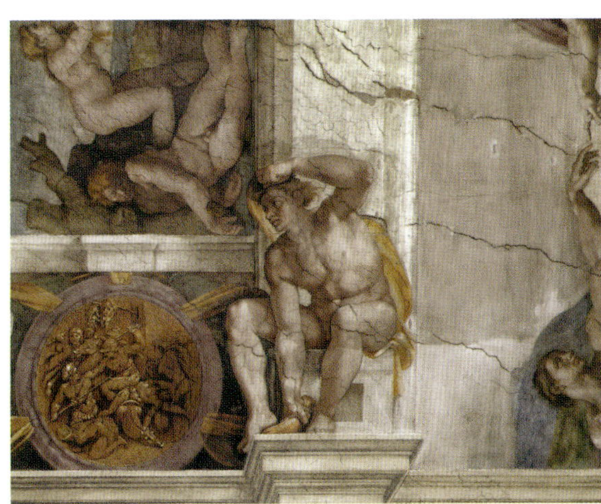
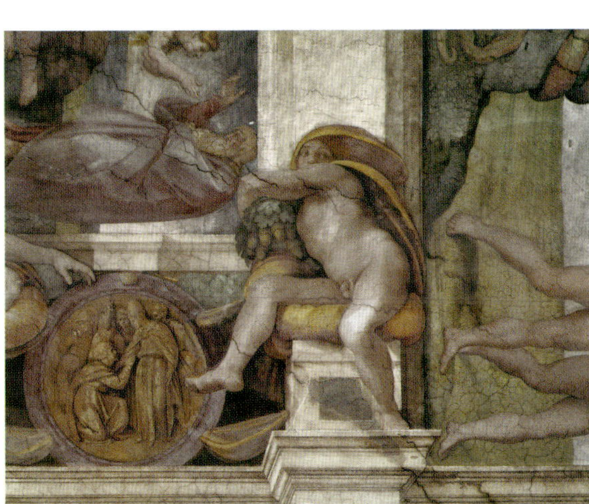
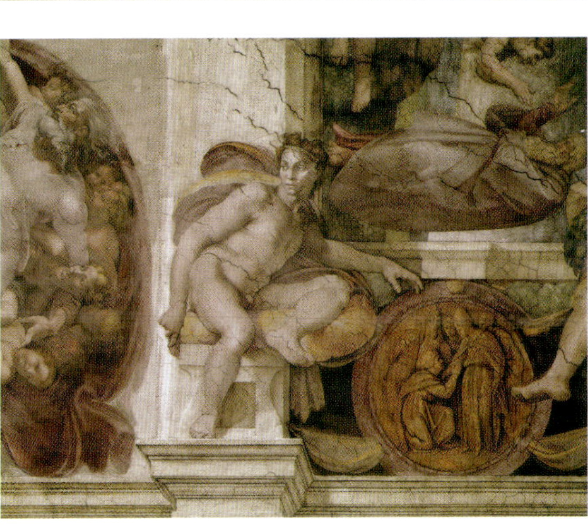

Michelangelo Buonarroti, 1475–1564
Ignudo to the upper left of the *Eritrean Sibyl*, 1508–1512
Fresco
Sistine Chapel, Ceiling

Michelangelo Buonarroti, 1475–1564
Ignudo to the upper right of the *Prophet Isaiah*, 1508–1512
Fresco
Sistine Chapel, Ceiling

Michelangelo Buonarroti, 1475–1564
Ignudo to the upper left of the *Prophet Ezekiel*, 1508–1512
Fresco
Sistine Chapel, Ceiling

Michelangelo Buonarroti, 1475–1564
Ignudo to the upper right of the *Prophet Ezekiel*, 1508–1512
Fresco
Sistine Chapel, Ceiling

Michelangelo Buonarroti, 1475–1564
Ignudo to the upper right of the *Cumaean Sibyl*, 1508–1512
Fresco
Sistine Chapel, Ceiling

Michelangelo Buonarroti, 1475–1564
Ignudo to the upper left of the *Cumaean Sibyl*, 1508–1512
Fresco
Sistine Chapel, Ceiling

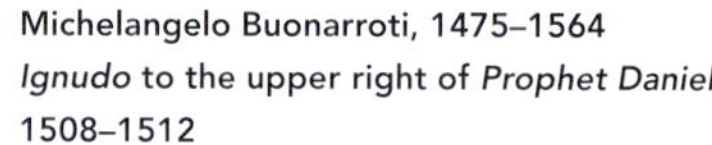

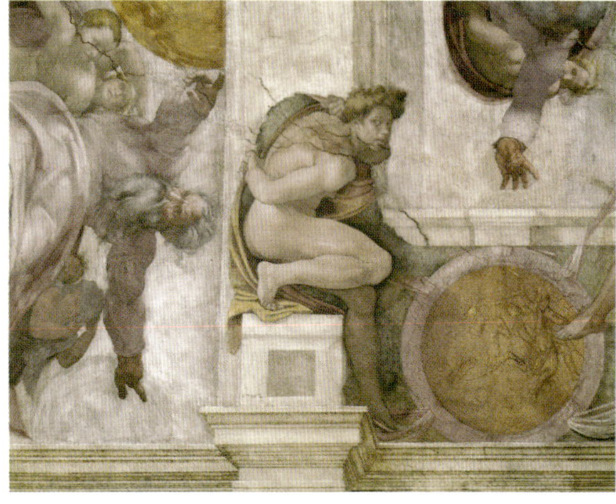

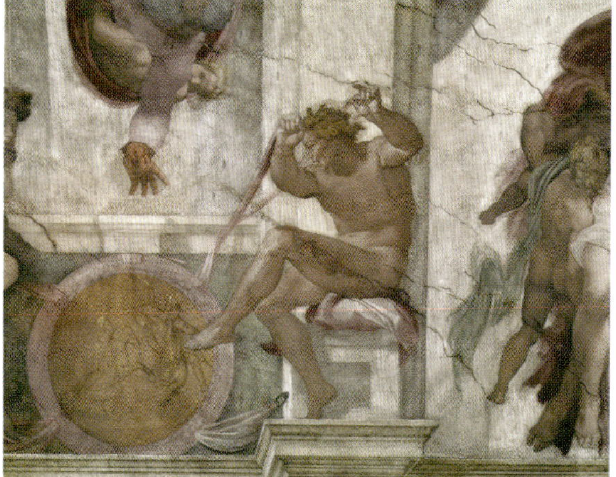

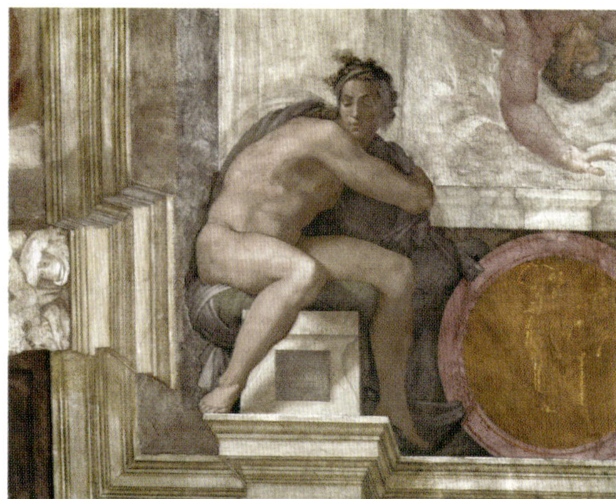

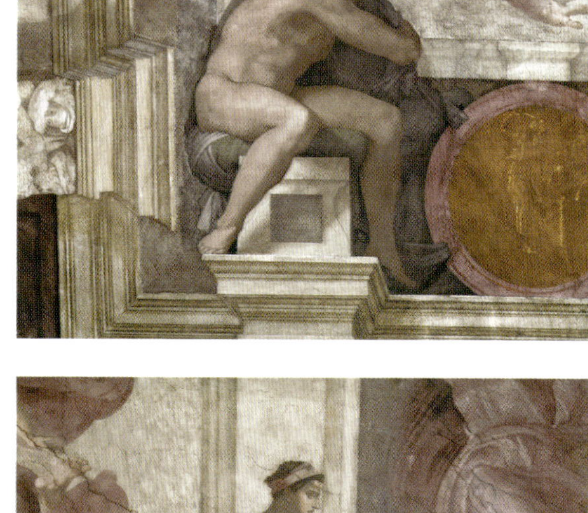

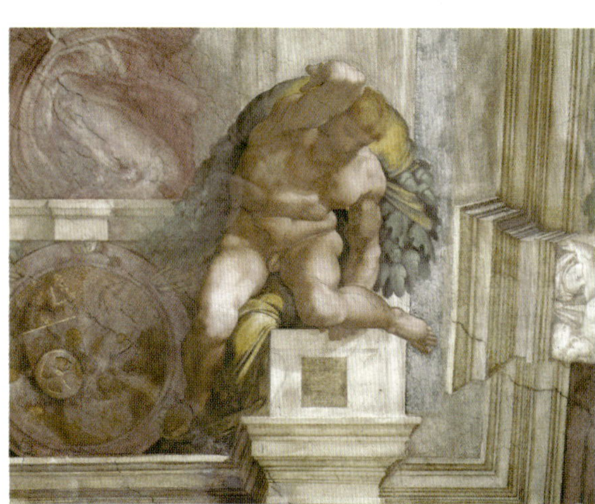

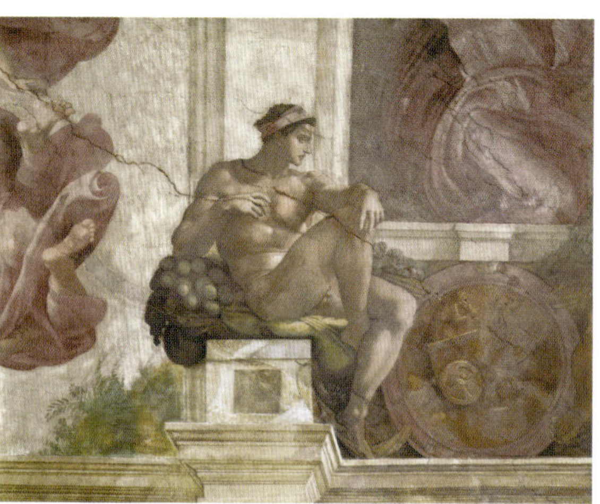

Michelangelo Buonarroti, 1475–1564
Ignudo to the upper right of *Prophet Daniel*, 1508–1512
Fresco
Sistine Chapel, Ceiling

Michelangelo Buonarroti, 1475–1564
Ignudo to the upper right of the *Prophet Daniel*, 1508–1512
Fresco
Sistine Chapel, Ceiling

Michelangelo Buonarroti, 1475–1564
Ignudo to the right of the *Libyan Sibyl*, 1508–1512
Fresco
Sistine Chapel, Ceiling

Michelangelo Buonarroti, 1475–1564
Ignudo to the upper left of the *Libyan Sibyl*, 1508–1512
Fresco
Sistine Chapel, Ceiling

Michelangelo Buonarroti, 1475–1564
Ignudo to the upper right of the *Prophet Jeremiah*, 1508–1512
Fresco
Sistine Chapel, Ceiling

Michelangelo Buonarroti, 1475–1564
Ignudo to the upper left of the *Prophet Jeremiah*, 1508–1512
Fresco
Sistine Chapel, Ceiling

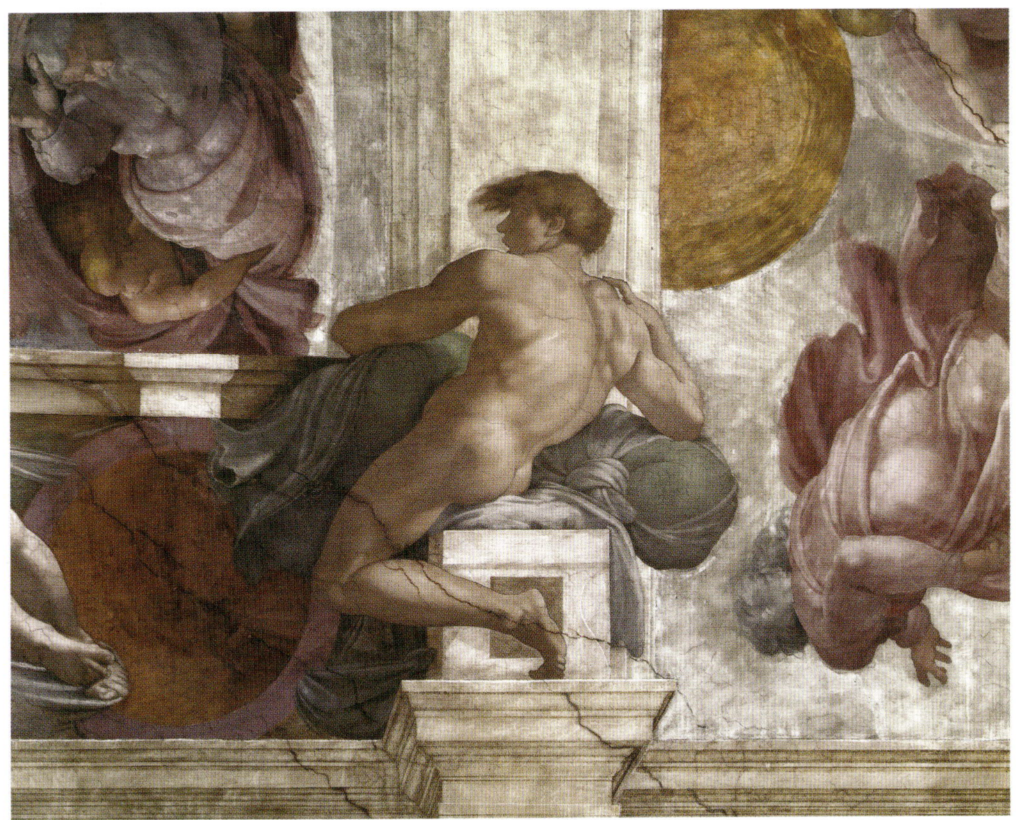

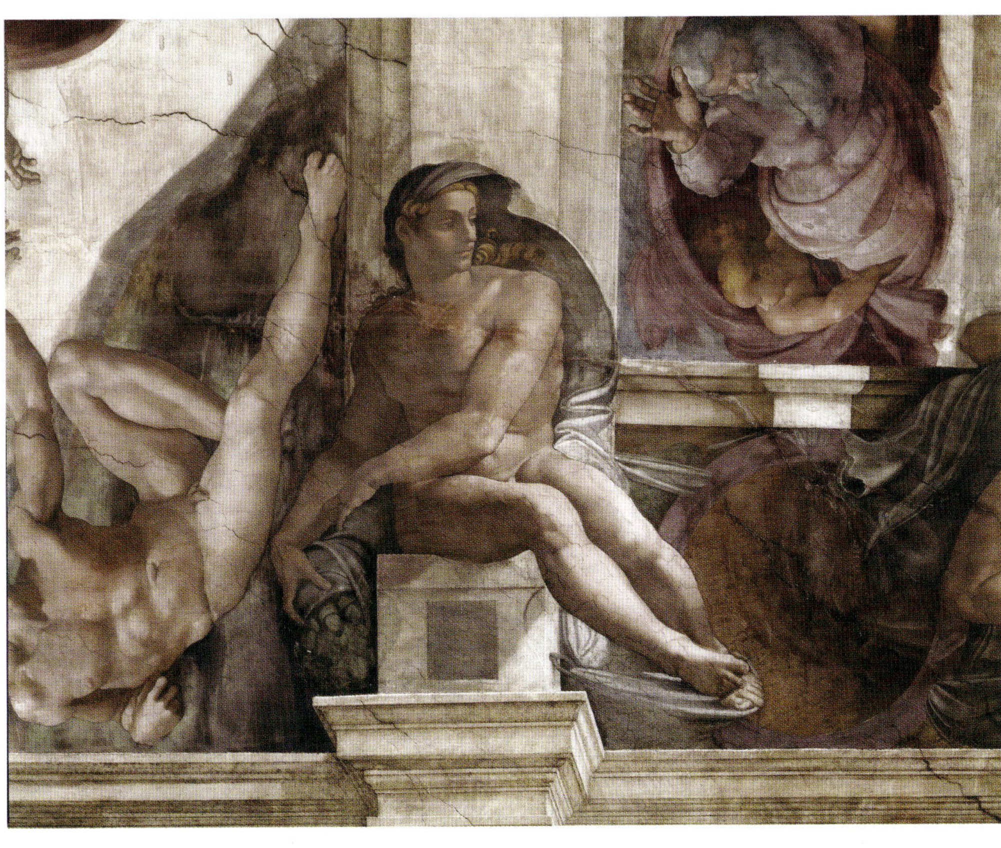

Michelangelo Buonarroti, 1475–1564
***Ignudo* to the upper right of the *Persian Sibyl*, 1508–1512**
Fresco
Sistine Chapel, Ceiling

Michelangelo Buonarroti, 1475–1564
***Ignudo* to the upper left of the *Persian Sibyl*, 1508–1512**
Fresco
Sistine Chapel, Ceiling

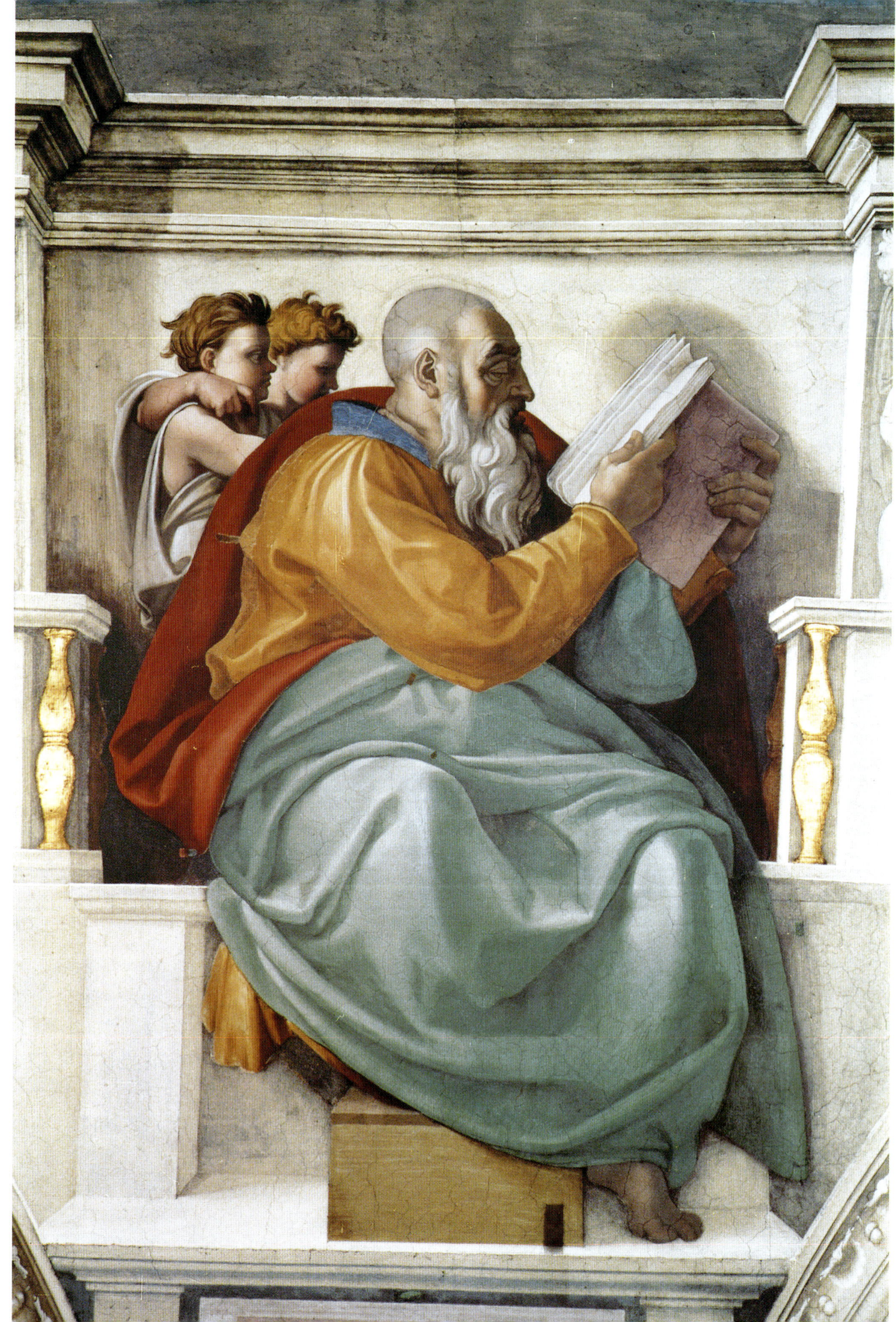

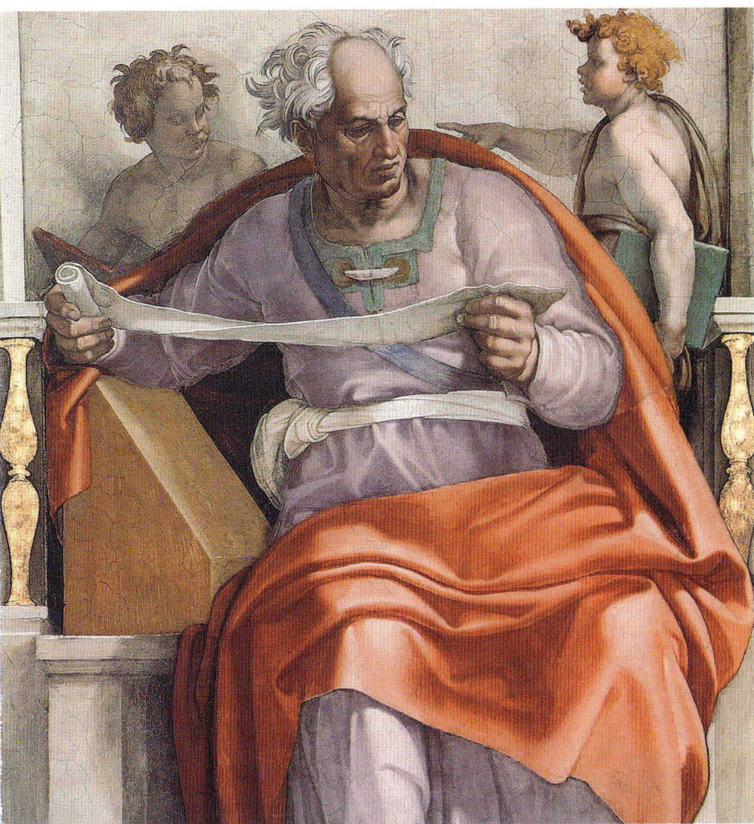

Michelangelo Buonarroti, 1475–1564
***The Prophet Joel*, 1508–1512**
Fresco
Sistine Chapel, Ceiling

Michelangelo Buonarroti

The Prophet Zechariah

Another important element of the ceiling program is the sequence of sibyls and prophets in the second pictorial register. These are almost double the size of the other figures, underlining their importance even in simply formal terms. Among the prophets, Jonah and Zechariah are emphasized by their positions on the two end walls. Zechariah is located on the entrance wall above the sculpted coat of arms of Julius II and a plaque bearing the prophet's name. One of the "minor" prophets of the Old Testament, Zechariah prophesied to the Jewish people the coming of their king, a man "just, and having salvation; lowly, and riding upon an ass, and upon a colt the foal of an ass" (Zechariah 9:9), which is regarded as prefiguring the entry of Jesus into Jerusalem (Mark 1:1–11). Michelangelo has portrayed Zechariah as a wise old man dressed in voluminous red and gold garments, half turned to the side. He is seated on a marble throne and reads from an open book. At his back are two child-angels who imitate him. The profile head of the prophet bears a certain resemblance to Julius II and may be a concealed portrait of Michelangelo's pontifical patron.

Michelangelo Buonarroti, 1475–1564
***The Prophet Zechariah*, 1508–1512**
Fresco
Sistine Chapel, Ceiling

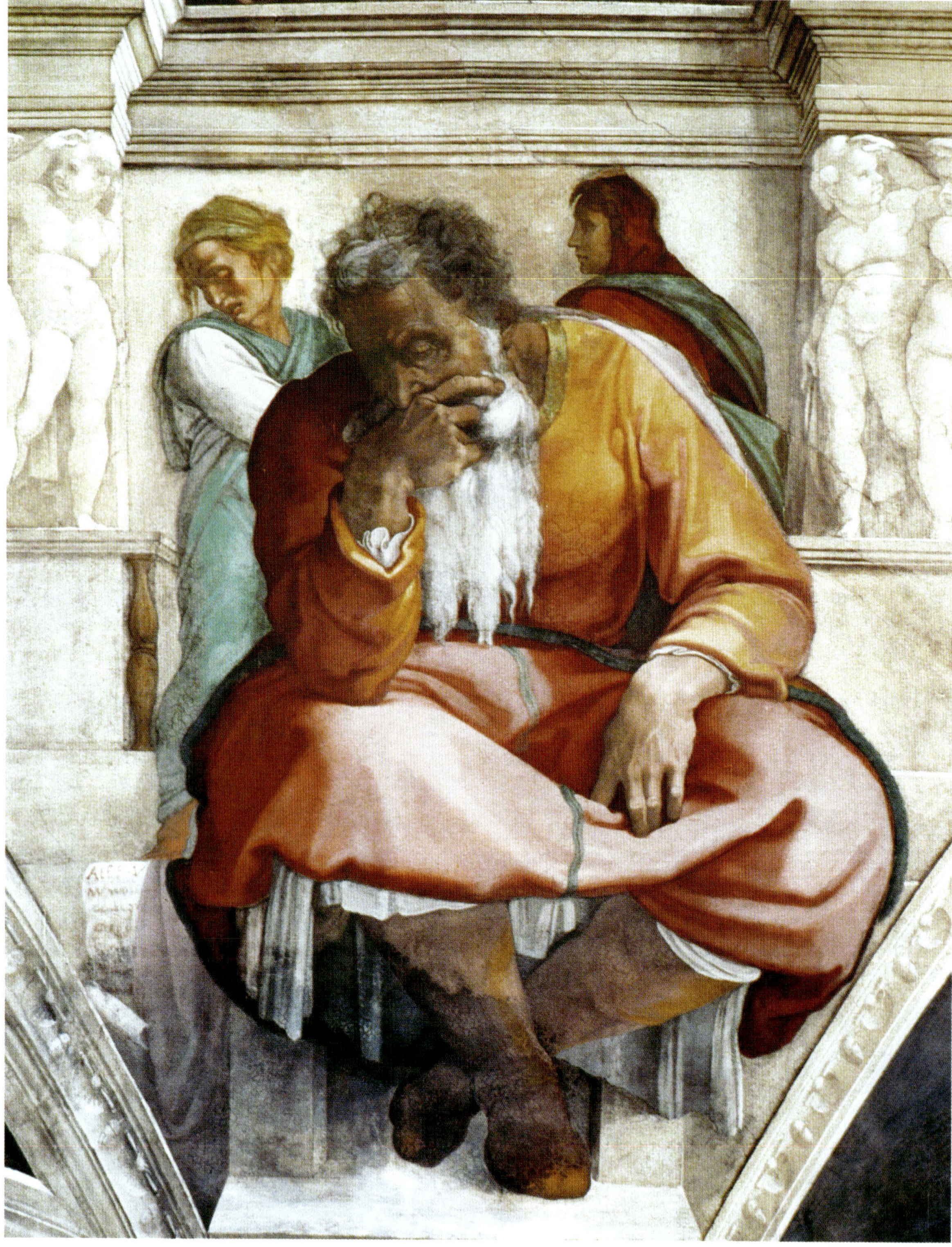

Michelangelo Buonarroti, 1475–1564
***The Prophet Jeremiah*, 1508–1512**
Fresco
Sistine Chapel, Ceiling

Michelangelo Buonarroti, 1475–1564
***The Prophet Ezekiel*, 1508–1512**
Fresco
Sistine Chapel, Ceiling

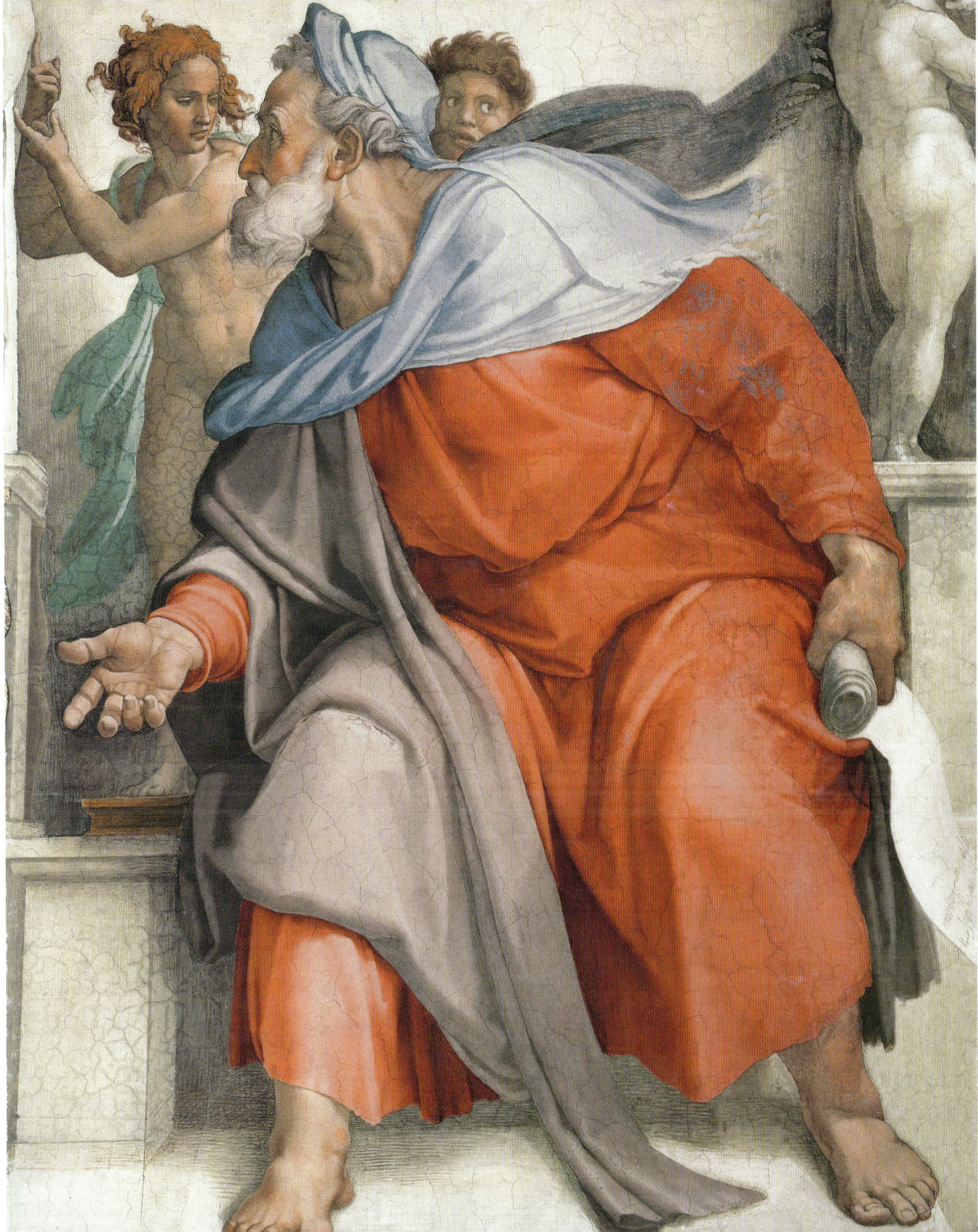

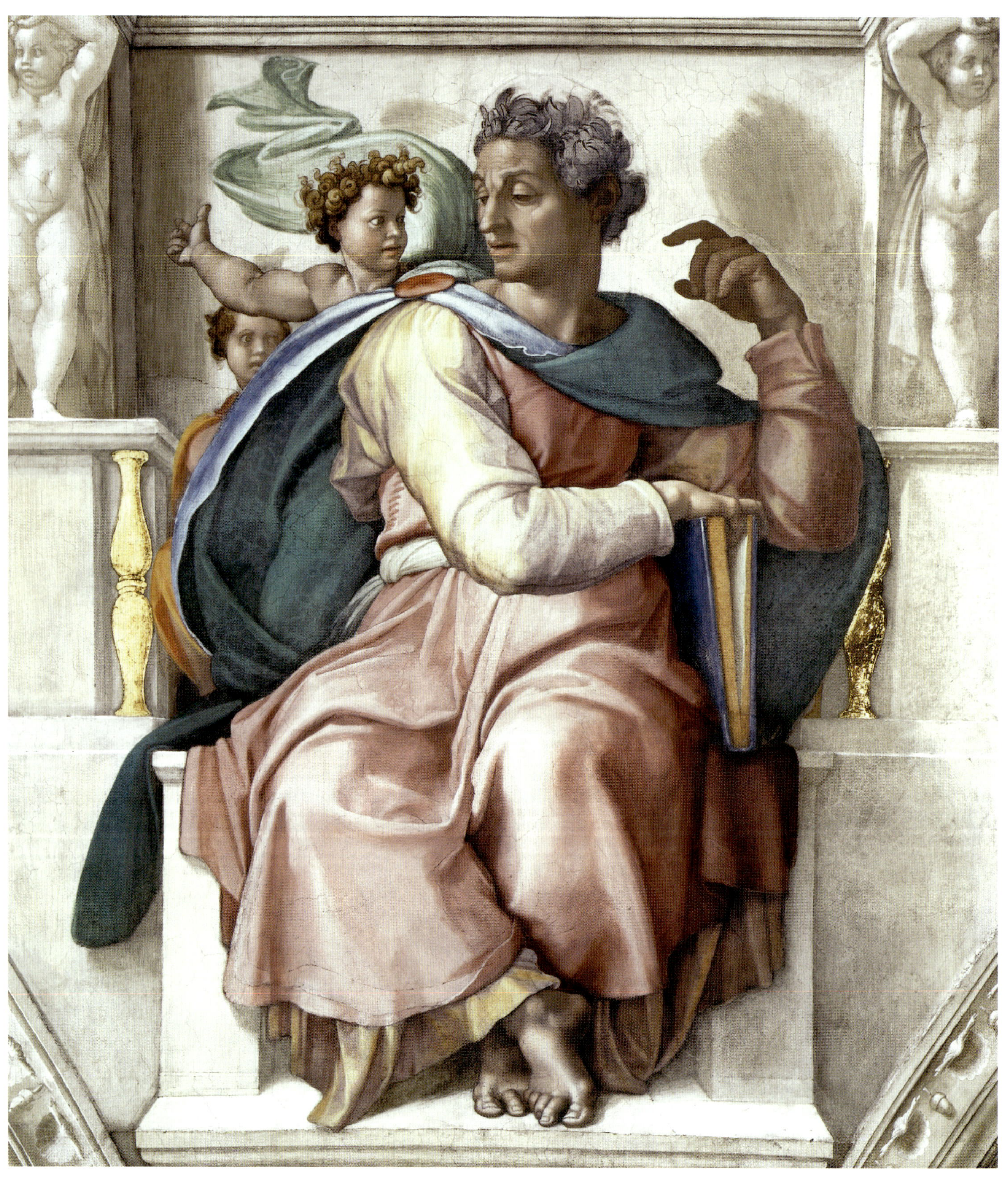

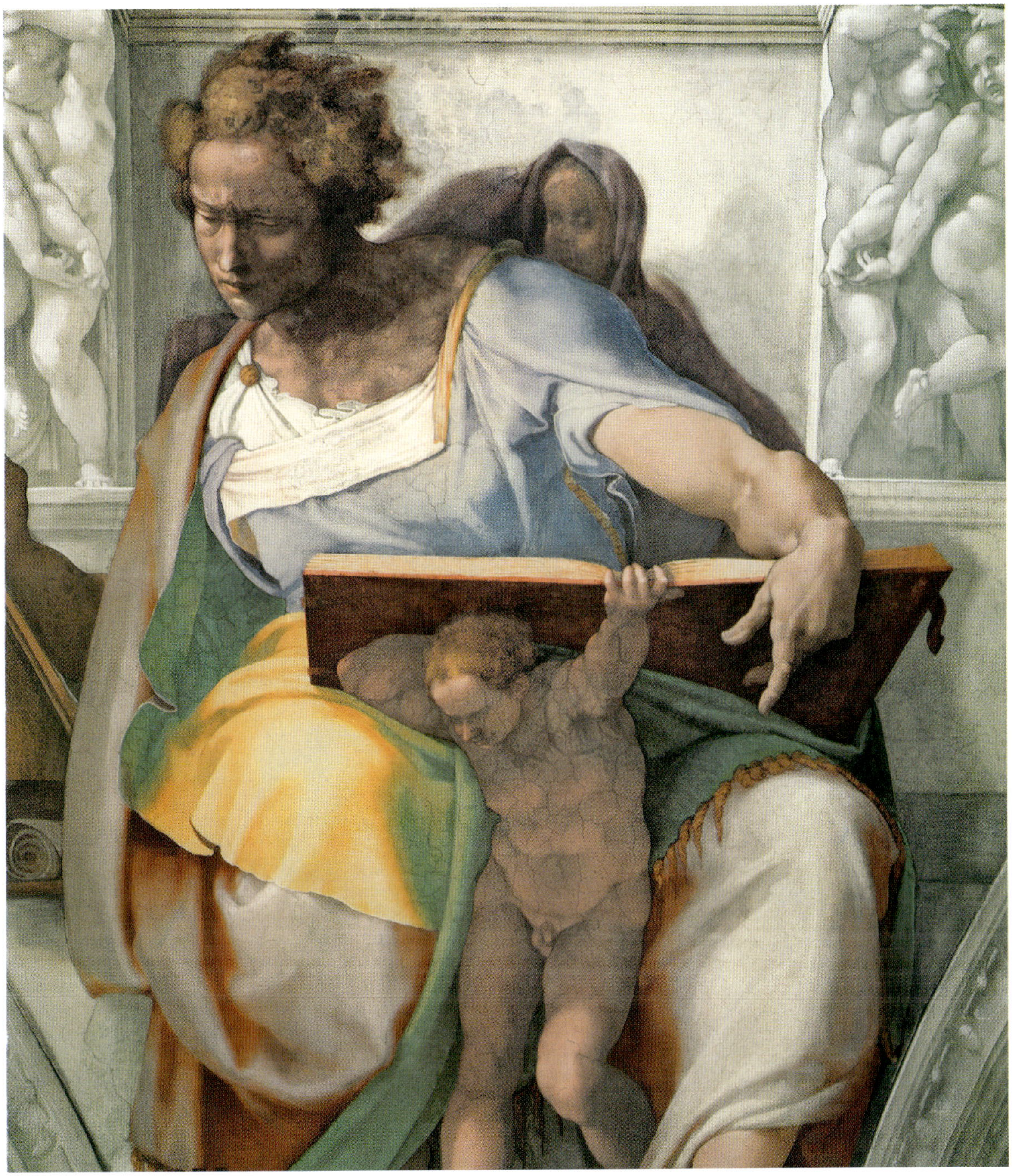

Michelangelo Buonarroti, 1475–1564
***The Prophet Isaiah*, 1508–1512**
Fresco
Sistine Chapel, Ceiling

Michelangelo Buonarroti, 1475–1564
***The Prophet Daniel*, 1508–1512**
Fresco
Sistine Chapel, Ceiling

Michelangelo Buonarroti, 1475–1564
***The Prophet Jonah*, 1508–1512**
Fresco
Sistine Chapel, Ceiling

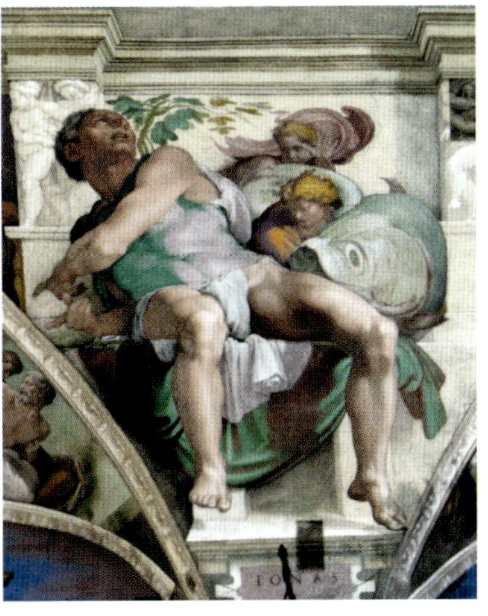

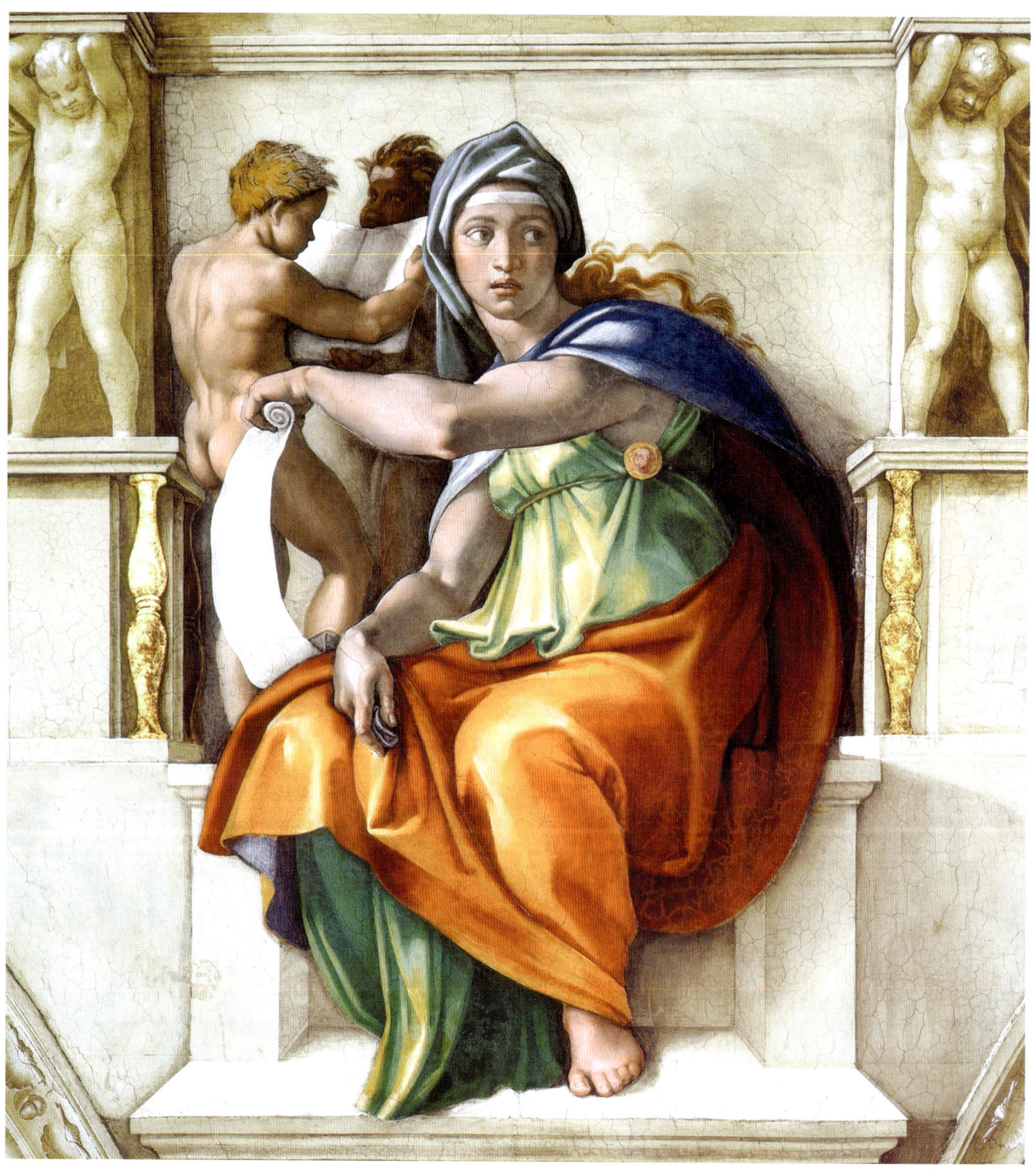

Michelangelo Buonarroti

The Delphic Sybil

The sibyl of Delphi is the youngest and the best known of the five sibyls adorning the Sistine ceiling. She was probably the first sibyl to be painted and, like all the sibyls and prophets, sits on a marble throne, the upper portion of whose side walls are formed of two pairs of sculpted putti. These small figures serve both as a playful form of atlantes, supporting the entablature on which the marble plinths of the *Ignudi* rest. The marble putti are the counterparts of the two child-angels who accompany the sibyls and can be seen here looking with interest at a book. The sibyl, who according to ancient history made her prophecies from a site close to the Delphi oracle, sits on her throne in an artfully contorted posture, with her body twisted to the left (as seen from below), her head facing forward, and her eyes looking to the right. Her clothes—a sleeveless light-green tunic, a red mantle that wraps around her body, and a blue cape—swirl softly around her powerful frame. In her hands she holds a scroll, establishing her identity as an antique prophetess. With her slightly open mouth and wide open eyes, she seems on the verge of announcing a vision, which lends her a mysterious air.

Michelangelo Buonarroti, 1475–1564
***The Delphic Sibyl*, 1508–1512**
Fresco
Sistine Chapel, Ceiling

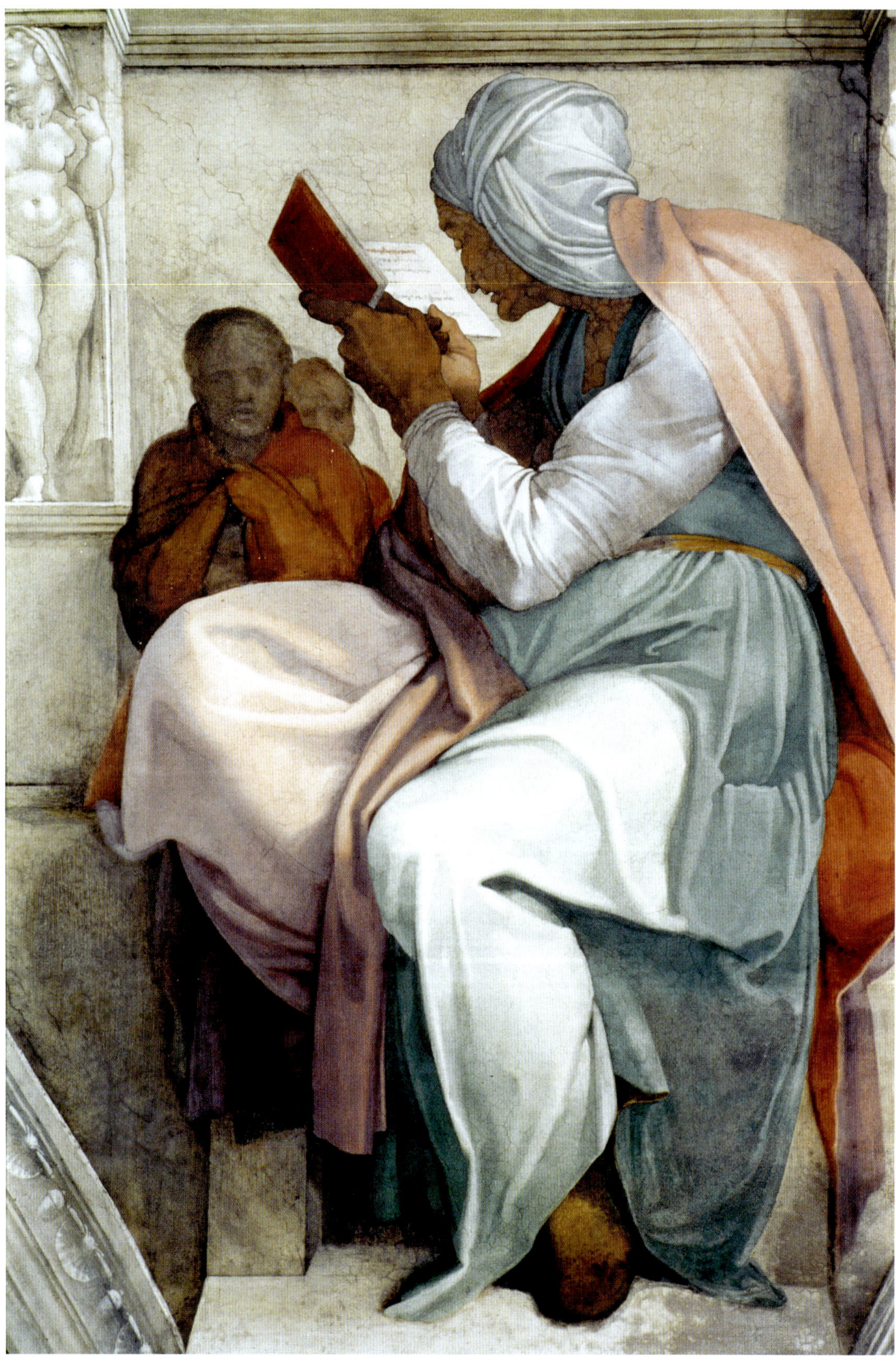

Michelangelo Buonarroti, 1475–1564
***The Persian Sibyl*, 1508–1512**
Fresco
Sistine Chapel, Ceiling

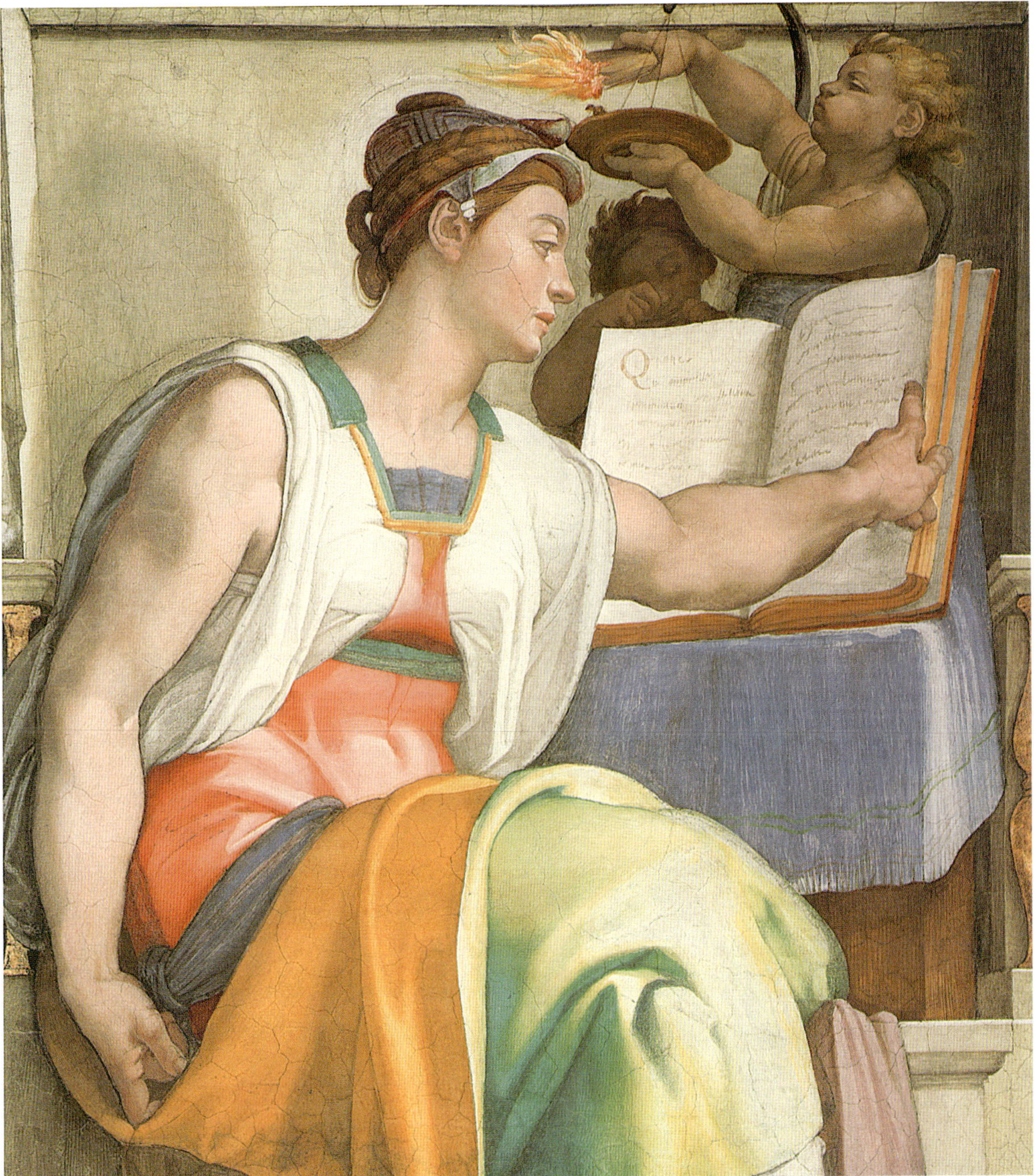

Michelangelo Buonarroti, 1475–1564
***The Erythraean Sibyl*, 1508–1512**
Fresco
Sistine Chapel, Ceiling

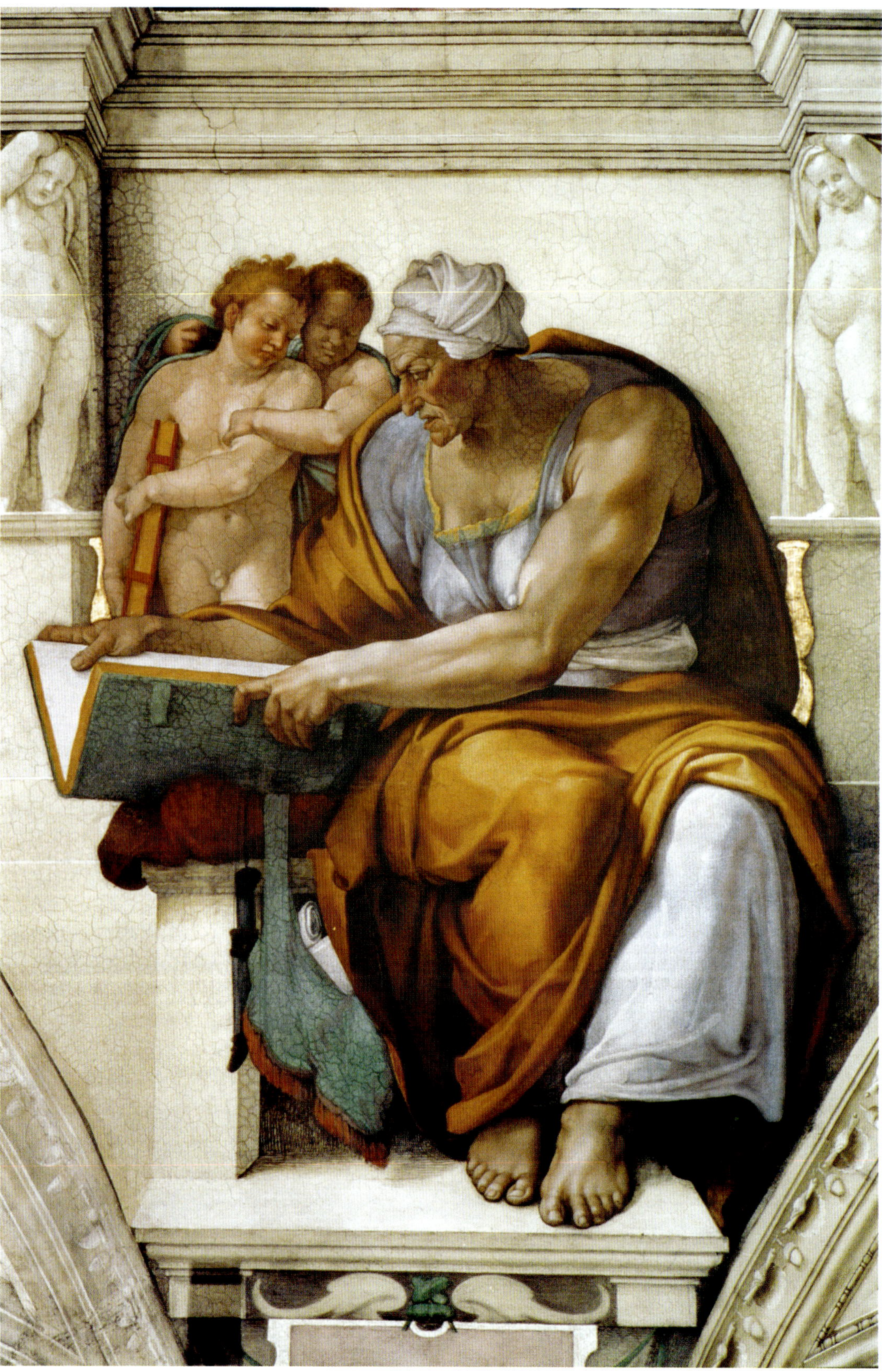

Michelangelo Buonarroti, 1475–1564
***The Cumaean Sibyl*, 1508–1512**
Fresco
Sistine Chapel, Ceiling

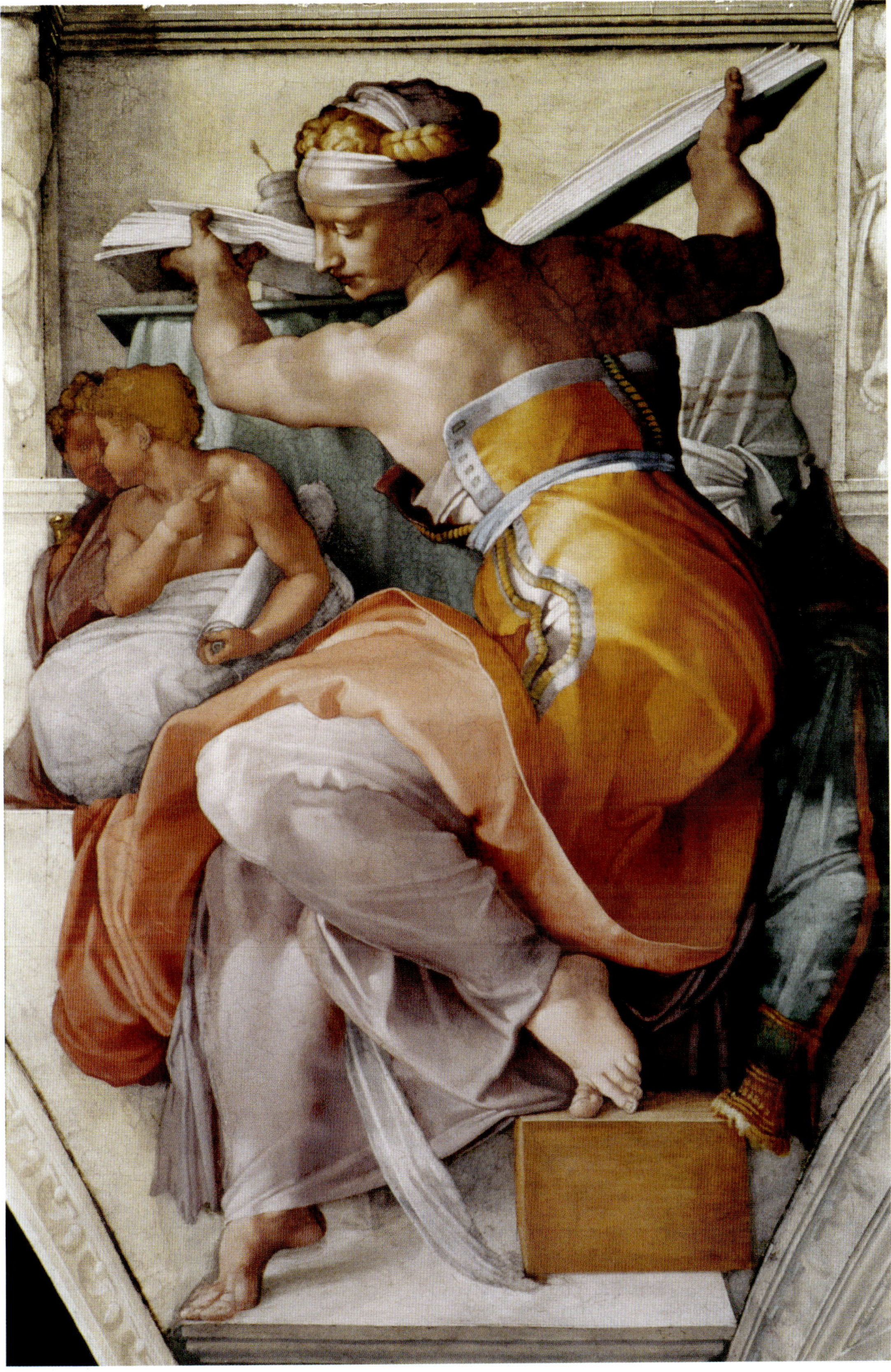

Michelangelo Buonarroti, 1475–1564
***The Libyan Sibyl*, 1508–1512**
Fresco
Sistine Chapel, Ceiling

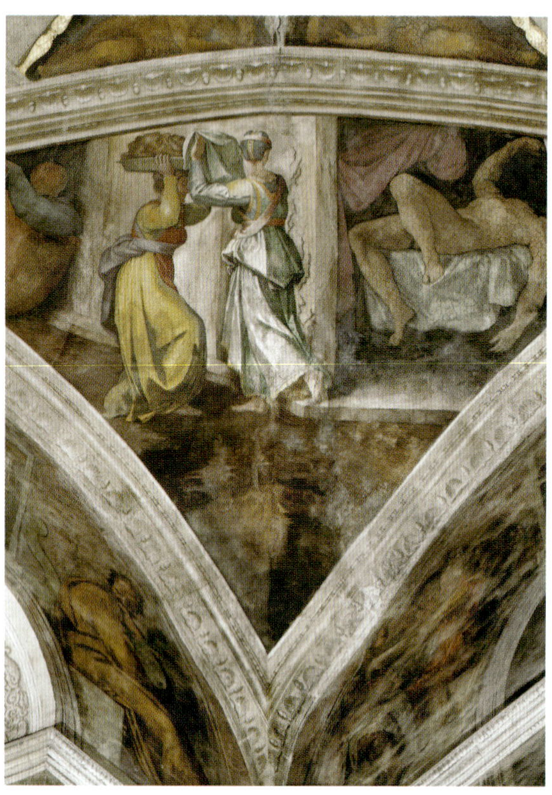

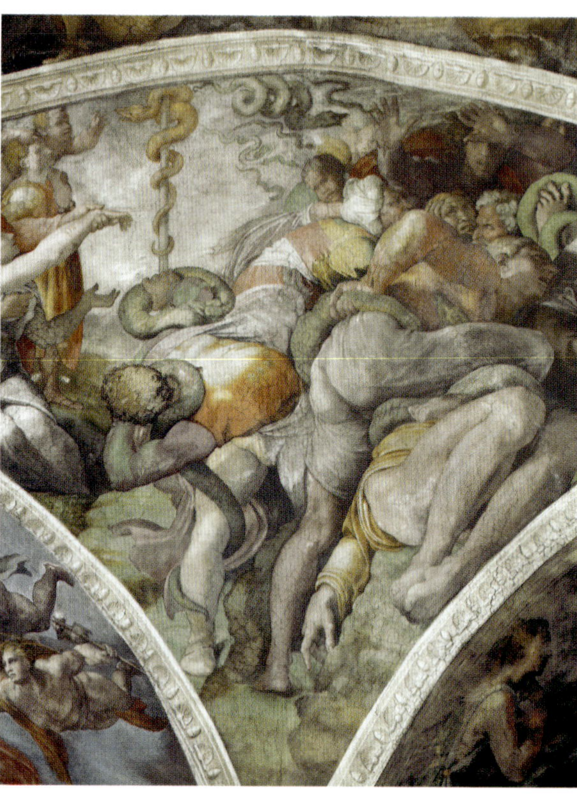

Michelangelo Buonarroti, 1475–1564
***Judith and Holofernes*, 1508–1512**
Fresco
Sistine Chapel, Ceiling

Michelangelo Buonarroti, 1475–1564
***The Brazen Serpent*, 1508–1512**
Fresco
Sistine Chapel, Ceiling

Michelangelo Buonarroti, 1475–1564
***The Punishment of Aman*, 1508–1512**
Fresco
Sistine Chapel, Ceiling

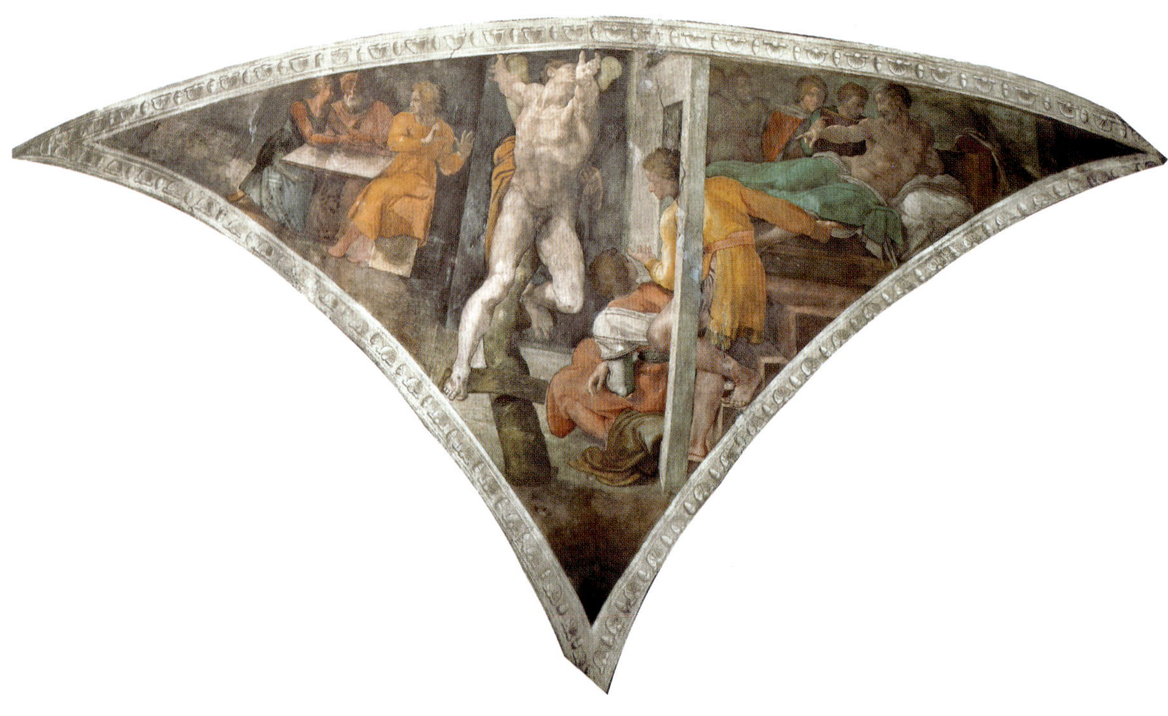

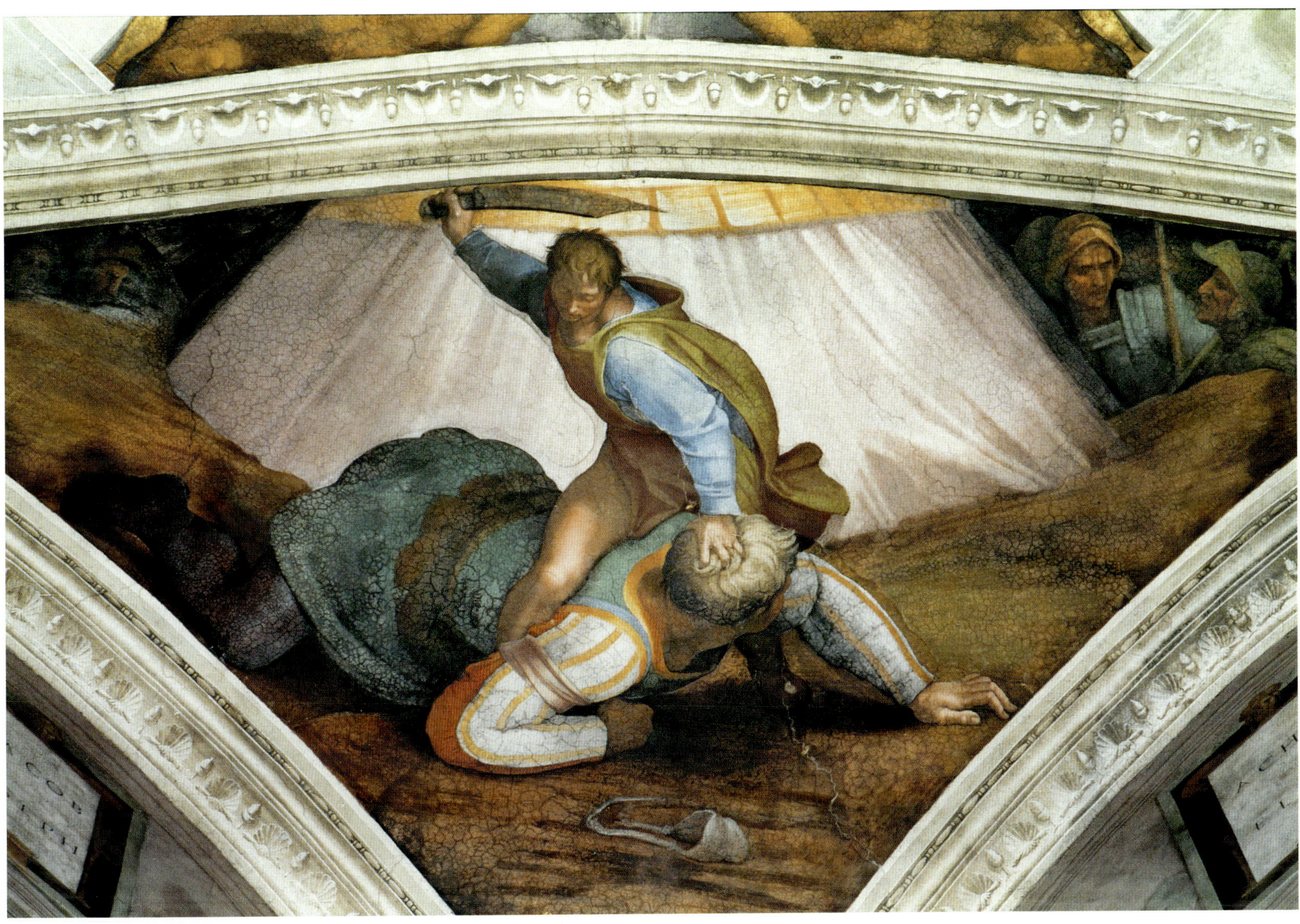

Michelangelo Buonarroti

David and Goliath

The Old Testament story of David's battle against the giant Goliath is seen as an example of the courage of the underdog, which, in conjunction with cunning and trust in God, can lead to victory over evil. In David's case the slaying of Goliath meant the victory of the Israelites over the Philistines, who had attacked and threatened them. David therefore belongs to the sequence of Old Testament heroes whose deeds are celebrated in the corner pendentives of the Sistine ceiling. Michelangelo has focused on the moment of Goliath's decapitation, which he illustrates from an unusual perspective. Seen from the ground, Goliath seems almost to be tumbling head first onto the viewer, while David, sitting on his victim's back, raises the sword of the defeated giant in order to administer the final blow. The slingshot lying in the foreground is the weapon with which the young David brought down the mighty, armor-wearing Goliath, who now rears up beneath his slayer with his last ounce of strength. The tent and the interested spectators observing from behind an earthwork indicate the Israelite camp outside which the battle takes place in the biblical account (I Samuel 17).

Michelangelo Buonarroti, 1475–1564
***David and Goliath*, 1508–1512**
Fresco
Sistine Chapel, Ceiling

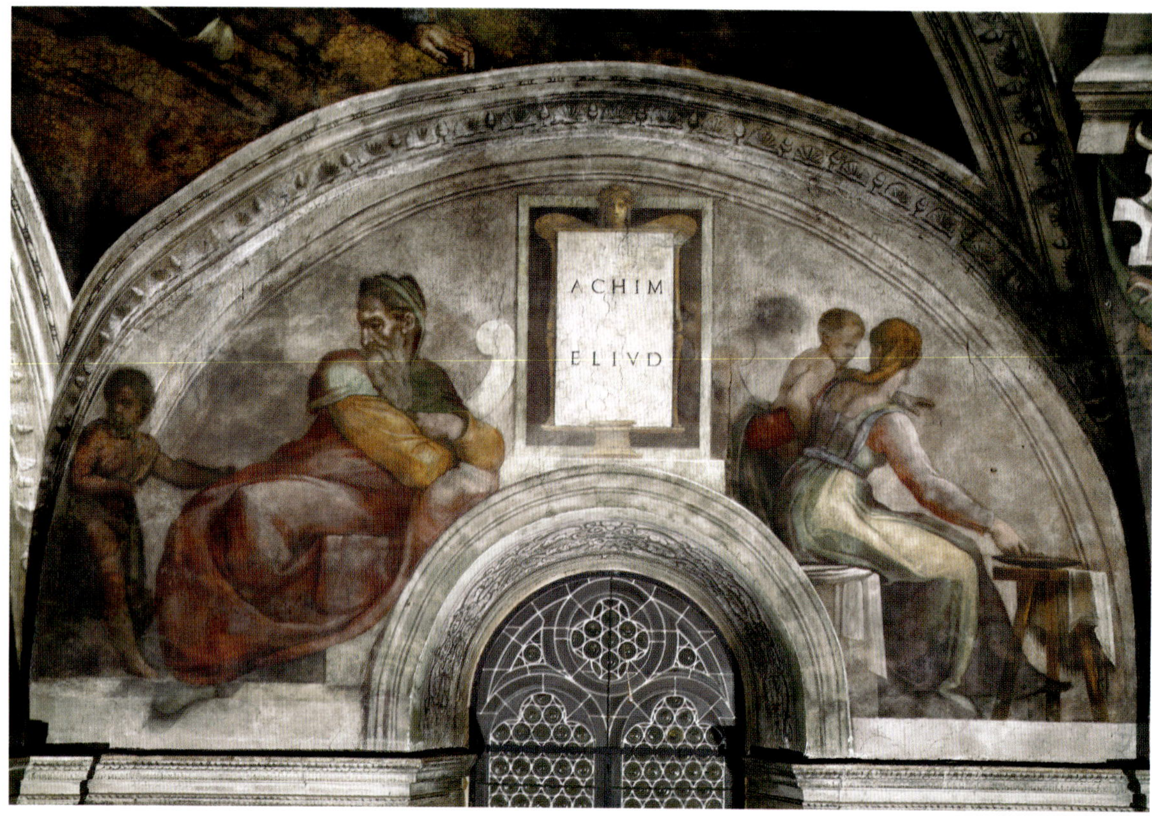

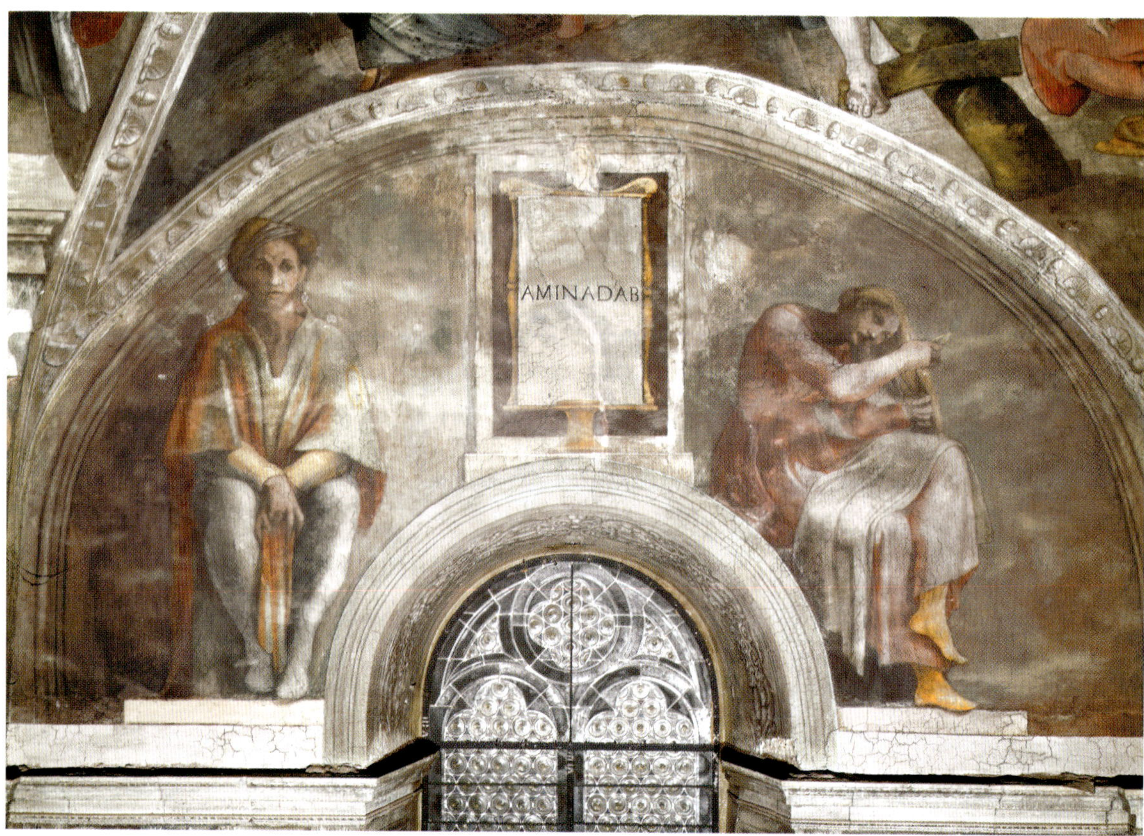

Michelangelo Buonarroti, 1475–1564
***Lunette with Achim and Eliud*, 1508–1512**
Fresco
Sistine Chapel, Ceiling

Michelangelo Buonarroti, 1475–1564
***Lunette with Aminadab*, 1508–1512**
Fresco
Sistine Chapel, Ceiling

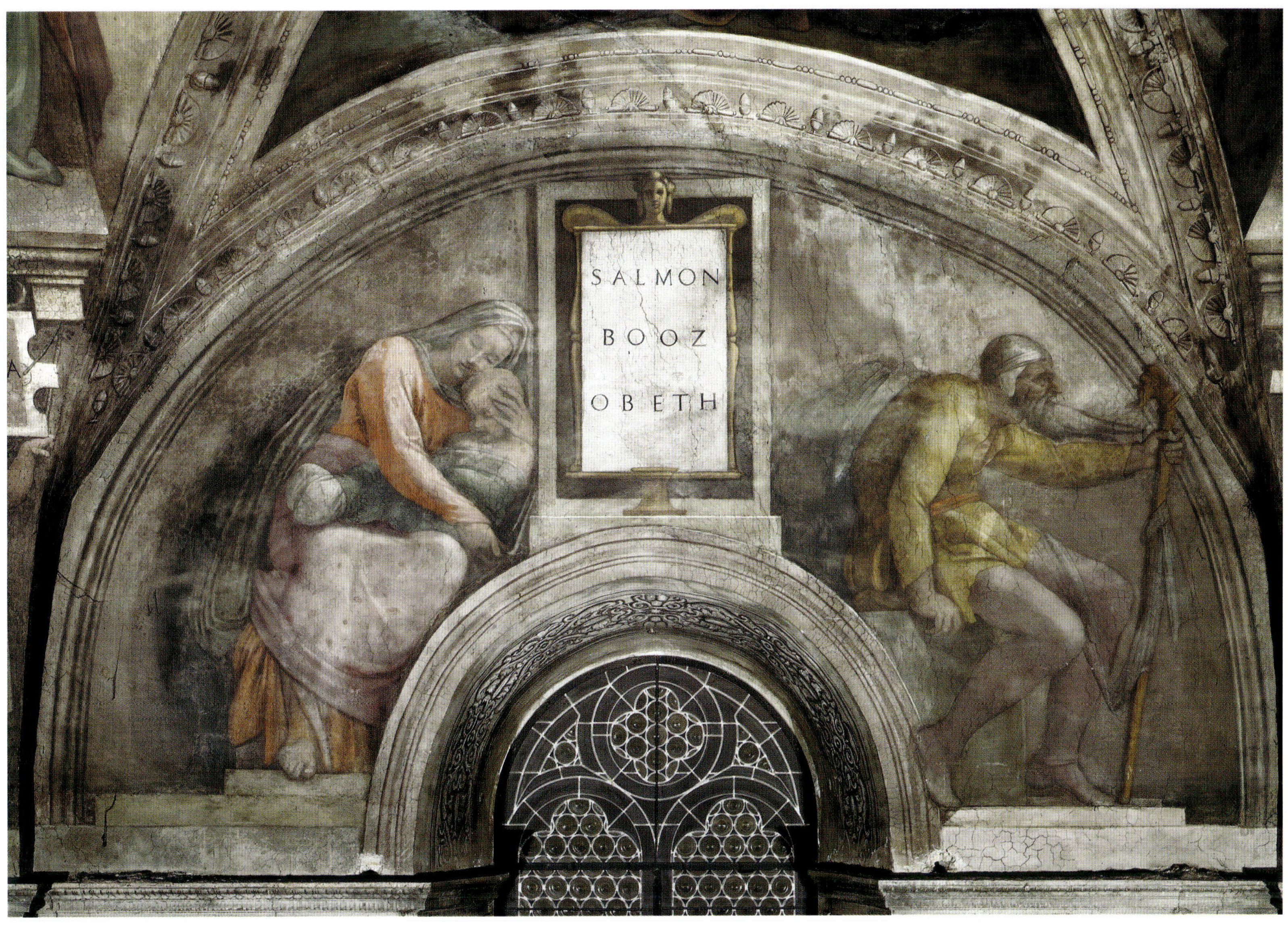

Michelangelo Buonarroti

Lunette: Salmon, Boaz, and Obed

With the most recent restoration, the lunette frescoes, long misinterpreted and for many years extremely dirty, were rediscovered as especially fine examples of Michelangelo's art of painting. They depict Christ's ancestors as named in the first chapter of the Gospel of St. Matthew. Michelangelo shows the spouses on either side of the window arch with their children. According to Matthew 1:5 ("And Salmon begat Booz of Rachab"), the figures in this lunette, named on the plaque as "Salmon, Booz, Obeth" are the family of King David, which is not, however, borne out by the books of the Old Testament. Salmon is depicted as a hunchbacked old man seated on a stone plinth. He is leaning on a gnarled staff whose knob is fashioned like a grotesque head with a pointed beard, which could be a caricature of Salmon himself. Rachab, on the other hand, is depicted with far more dignity as a concerned mother. She tenderly inclines her head to the sleeping child in her lap, placing her arm protectively around it, and with this gesture evokes the Mother of God. The finely graduated chiaroscuro of her clothing reveals Michelangelo's supreme skill in the modeling of colors.

Michelangelo Buonarroti, 1475–1564
***Lunette: Salmon, Boaz, and Obed*, 1508–1512**
Fresco
Sistine Chapel, Ceiling

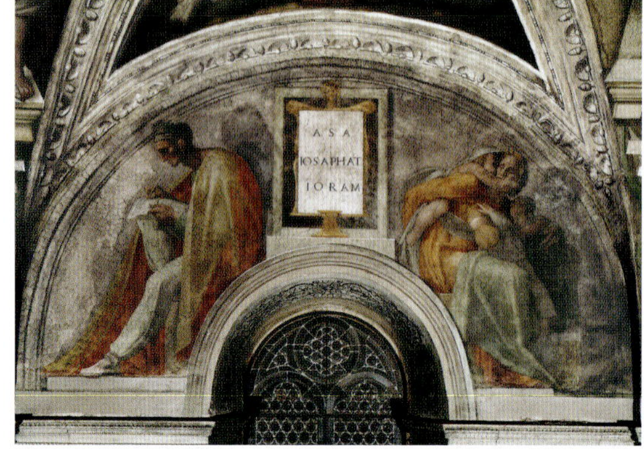

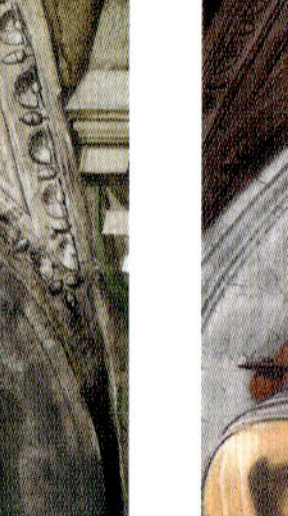

Michelangelo Buonarroti, 1475–1564
***Lunette with Asa, Josephat and Joram,* 1508–1512**
Fresco
Sistine Chapel, Ceiling

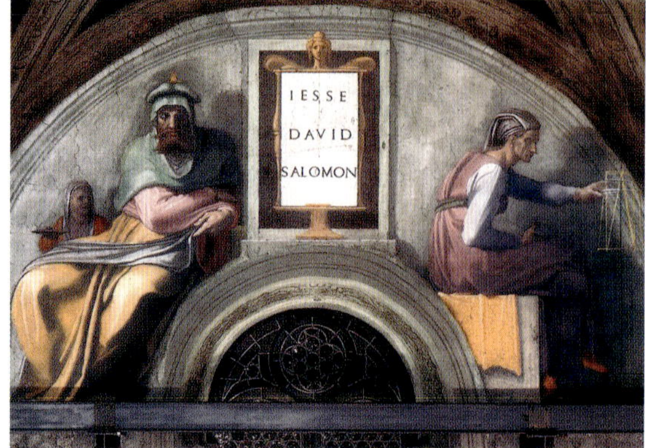

Michelangelo Buonarroti, 1475–1564
***Lunette with Jesse, David, and Salomon,* 1508–1512**
Fresco
Sistine Chapel, Ceiling

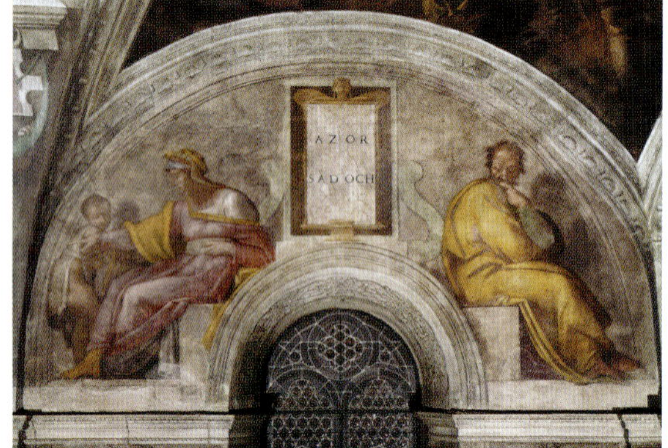

Michelangelo Buonarroti, 1475–1564
***Lunette with Azor and Sadoch,* 1508–1512**
Fresco
Sistine Chapel, Ceiling

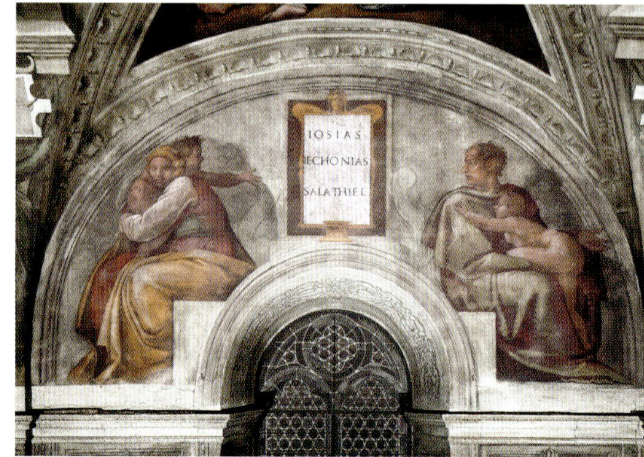

Michelangelo Buonarroti, 1475–1564
***Lunette with Josiah, Jechoniah, and Shealtiel,* 1508–1512**
Fresco
Sistine Chapel, Ceiling

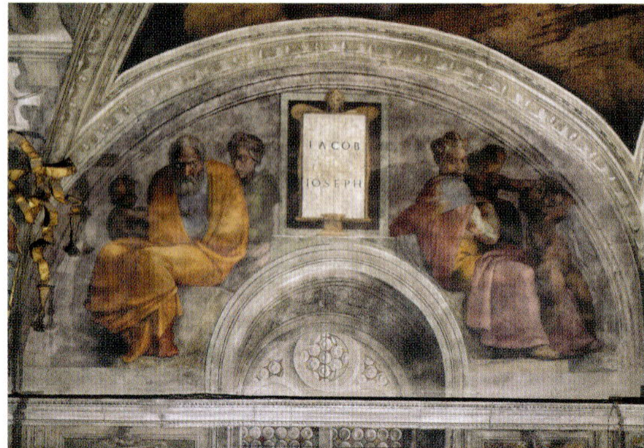

Michelangelo Buonarroti, 1475–1564
***Lunette with Jacob and Joseph,* 1508–1512**
Fresco
Sistine Chapel, Ceiling

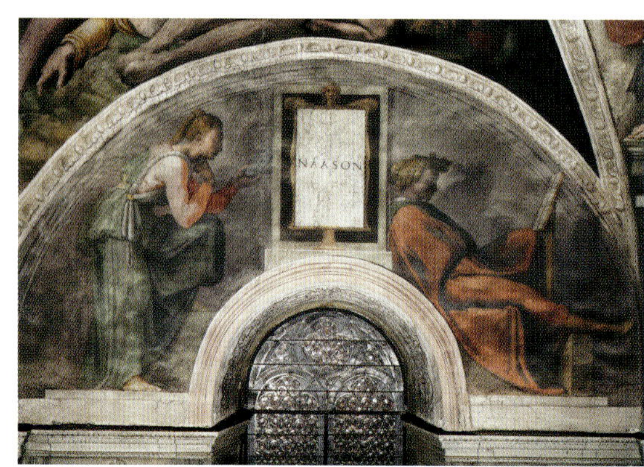

Michelangelo Buonarroti, 1475–1564
***Lunette with Naason,* 1508–1512**
Fresco
Sistine Chapel, Ceiling

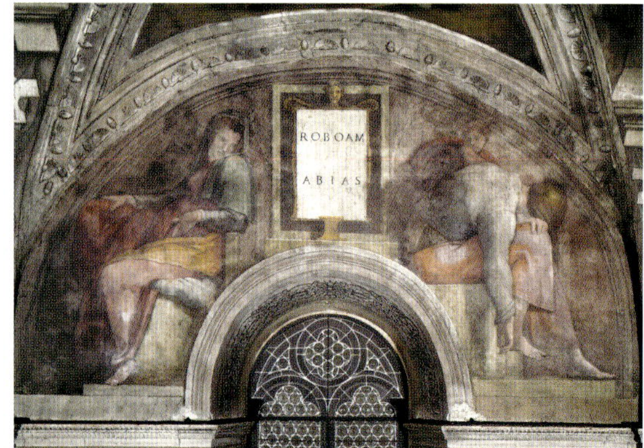

Michelangelo Buonarroti, 1475–1564
***Lunette with Roboam and Abias,* 1508–1512**
Fresco
Sistine Chapel, Ceiling

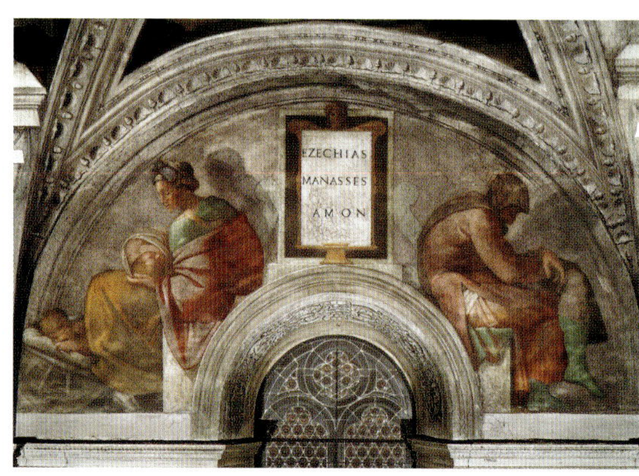

Michelangelo Buonarroti, 1475–1564
***Lunette with Ezechias, Manasses and Amon,* 1508–1512**
Fresco
Sistine Chapel, Ceiling

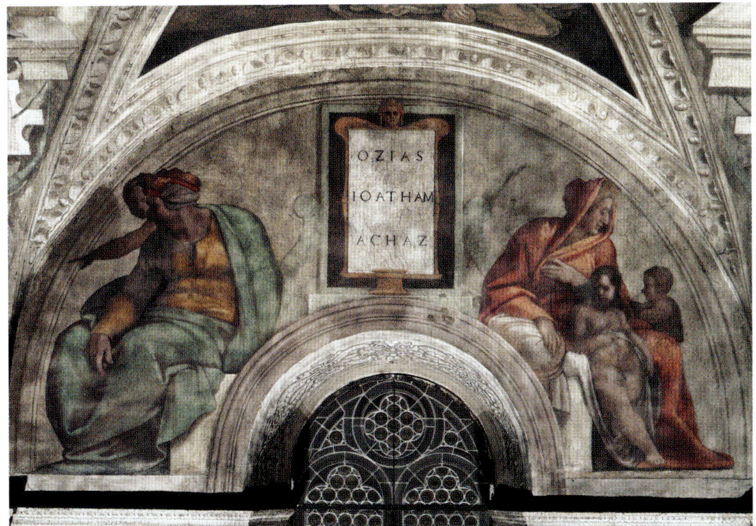

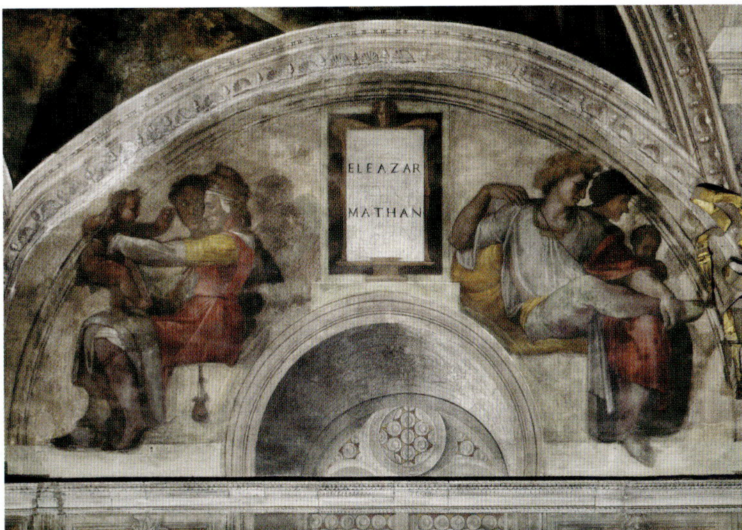

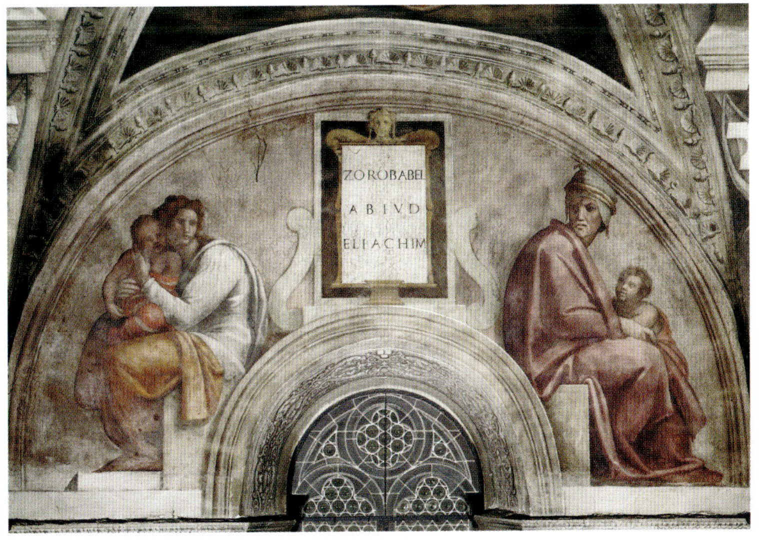

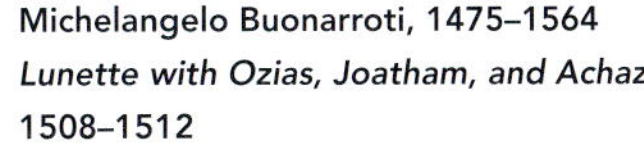

Michelangelo Buonarroti, 1475–1564
***Lunette with Ozias, Joatham, and Achaz,* 1508–1512**
Fresco
Sistine Chapel, Ceiling

Michelangelo Buonarroti, 1475–1564
***Lunette with Eleazar and Mathan,* 1508–1512**
Fresco
Sistine Chapel, Ceiling

Michelangelo Buonarroti, 1475–1564
***Lunette with Zorobabel, Abiud, and Eliachim,* 1508–1512**
Fresco
Sistine Chapel, Ceiling

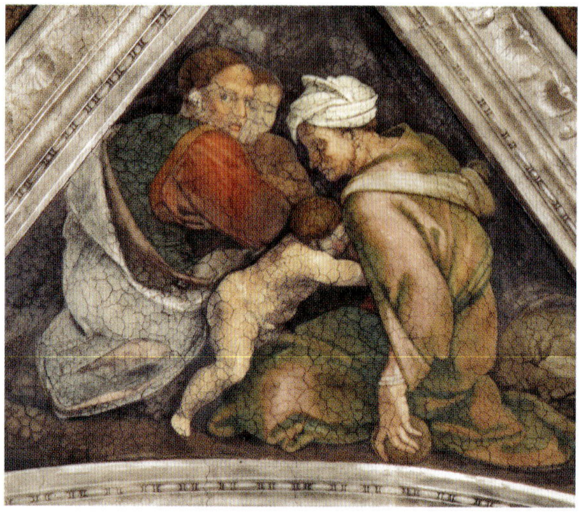

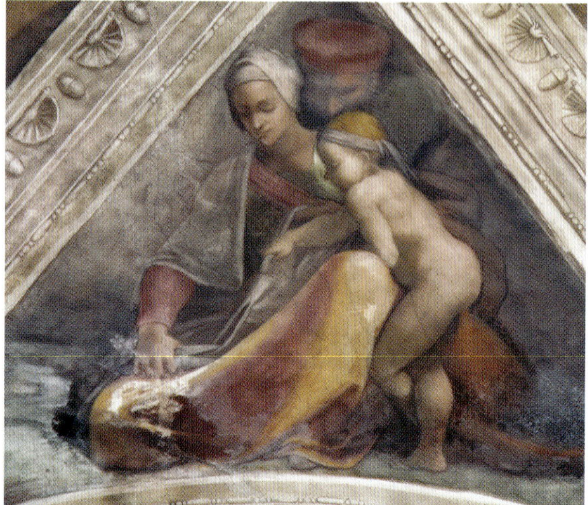

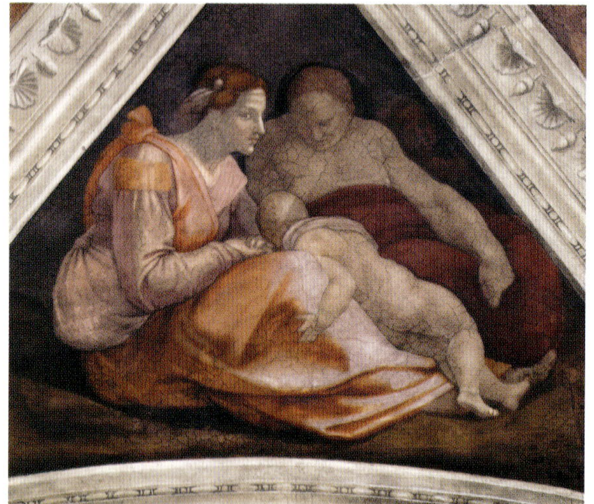

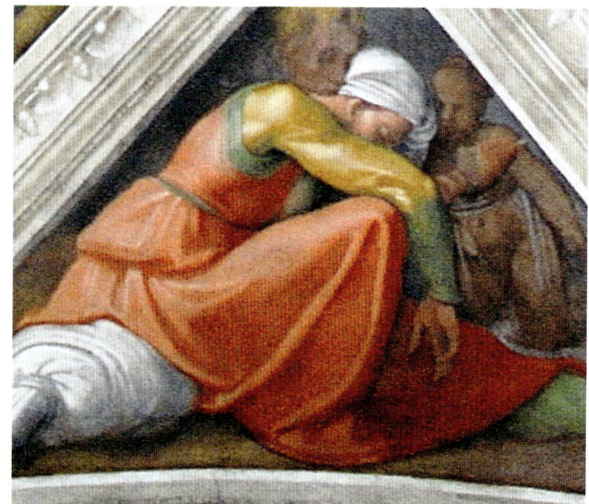

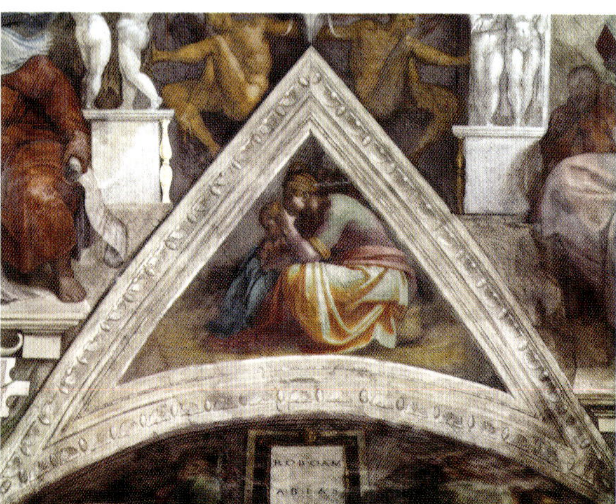

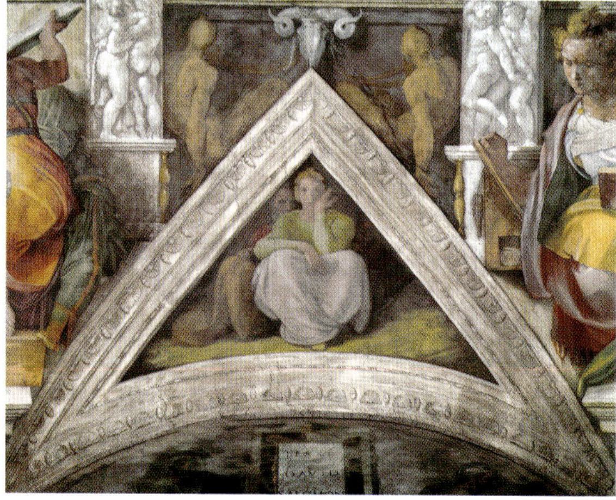

Michelangelo Buonarroti, 1475–1564
Web Lunette with Uzziah, Jotham, Ahaz, 1508–1512
Fresco
Sistine Chapel, Ceiling

Michelangelo Buonarroti, 1475–1564
Web of the Lunette Salmon, Boaz, and Obed, 1508–1512
Fresco
Sistine Chapel, Ceiling

Michelangelo Buonarroti, 1475–1564
Web of the Lunette Zerubbabel, Abiud, and Eliachim, 1508–1512
Fresco
Sistine Chapel, Ceiling

Michelangelo Buonarroti, 1475–1564
Web of the Lunette Asa, Jehoshaphat, and Jehoram, 1508–1512
Fresco
Sistine Chapel, Ceiling

Michelangelo Buonarroti, 1475–1564
Web of the Lunette Rehoboam and Abijah, 1508–1512
Fresco
Sistine Chapel, Ceiling

Michelangelo Buonarroti, 1475–1564
Web of the Lunette Jesse, David, and Solomon, 1508–1512
Fresco
Sistine Chapel, Ceiling

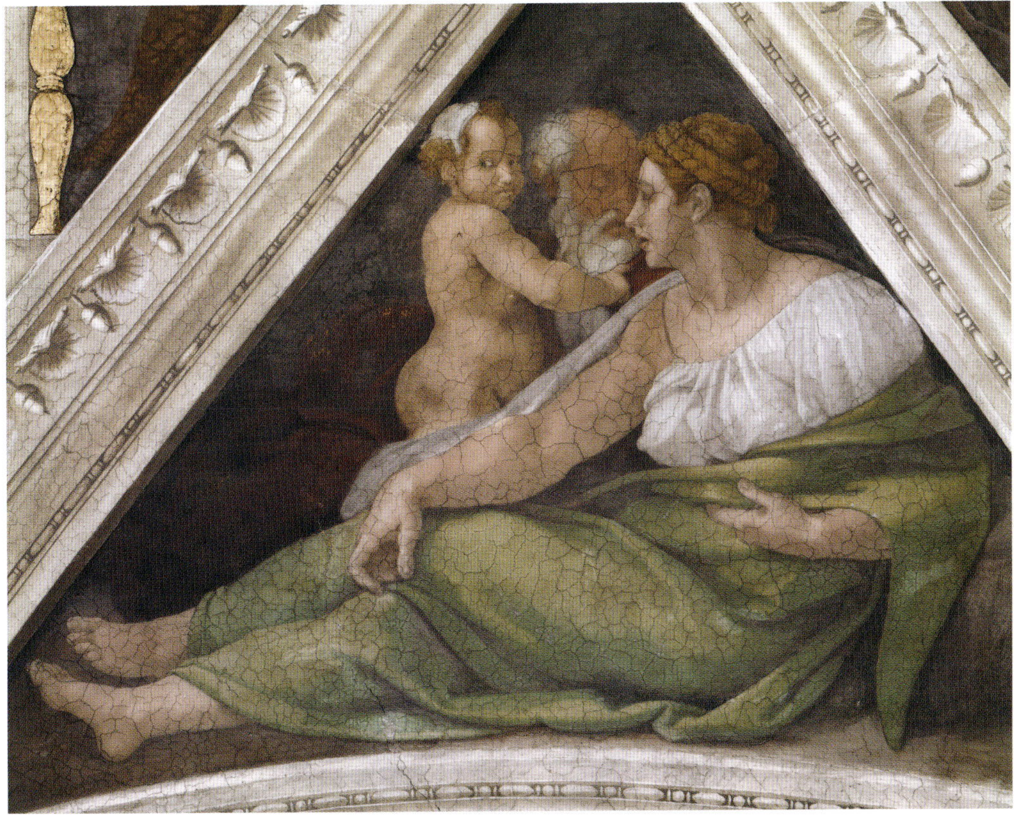

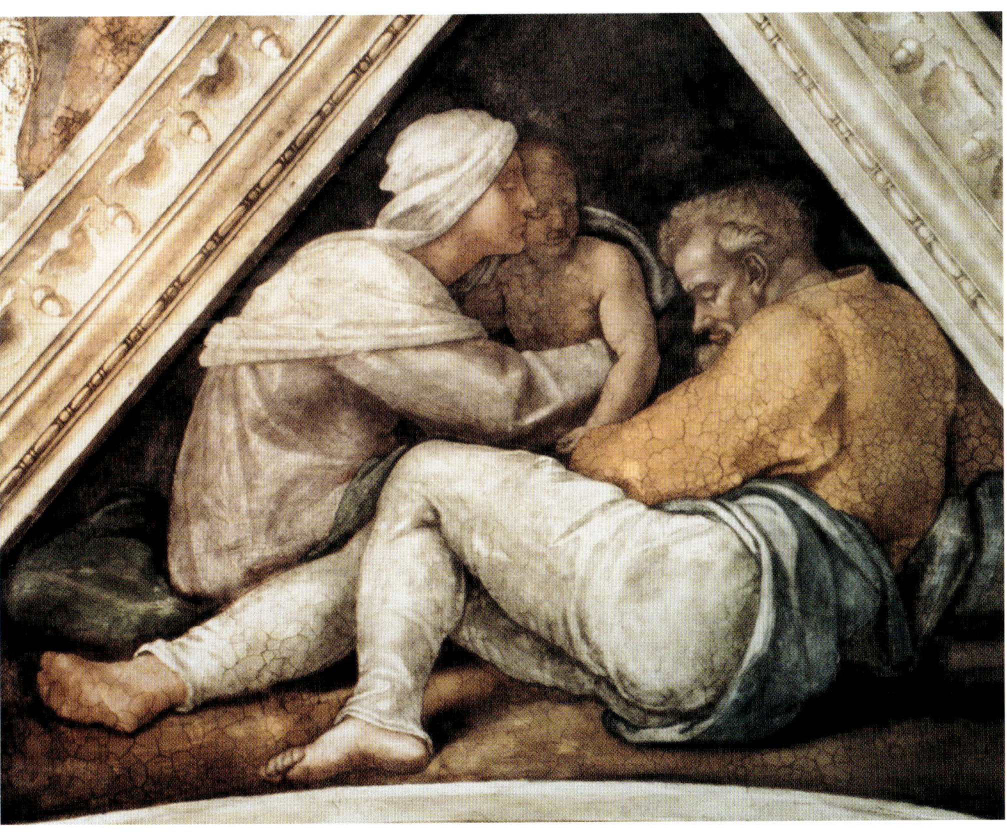

Michelangelo Buonarroti, 1475–1564
Web of the Lunette Ezechias, Manasses, and Amon, 1508–1512
Fresco
Sistine Chapel, Ceiling

Michelangelo Buonarroti, 1475–1564
Web of the Lunette Josiah, Jechoniah, and Shealtiel, 1508–1512
Fresco
Sistine Chapel, Ceiling

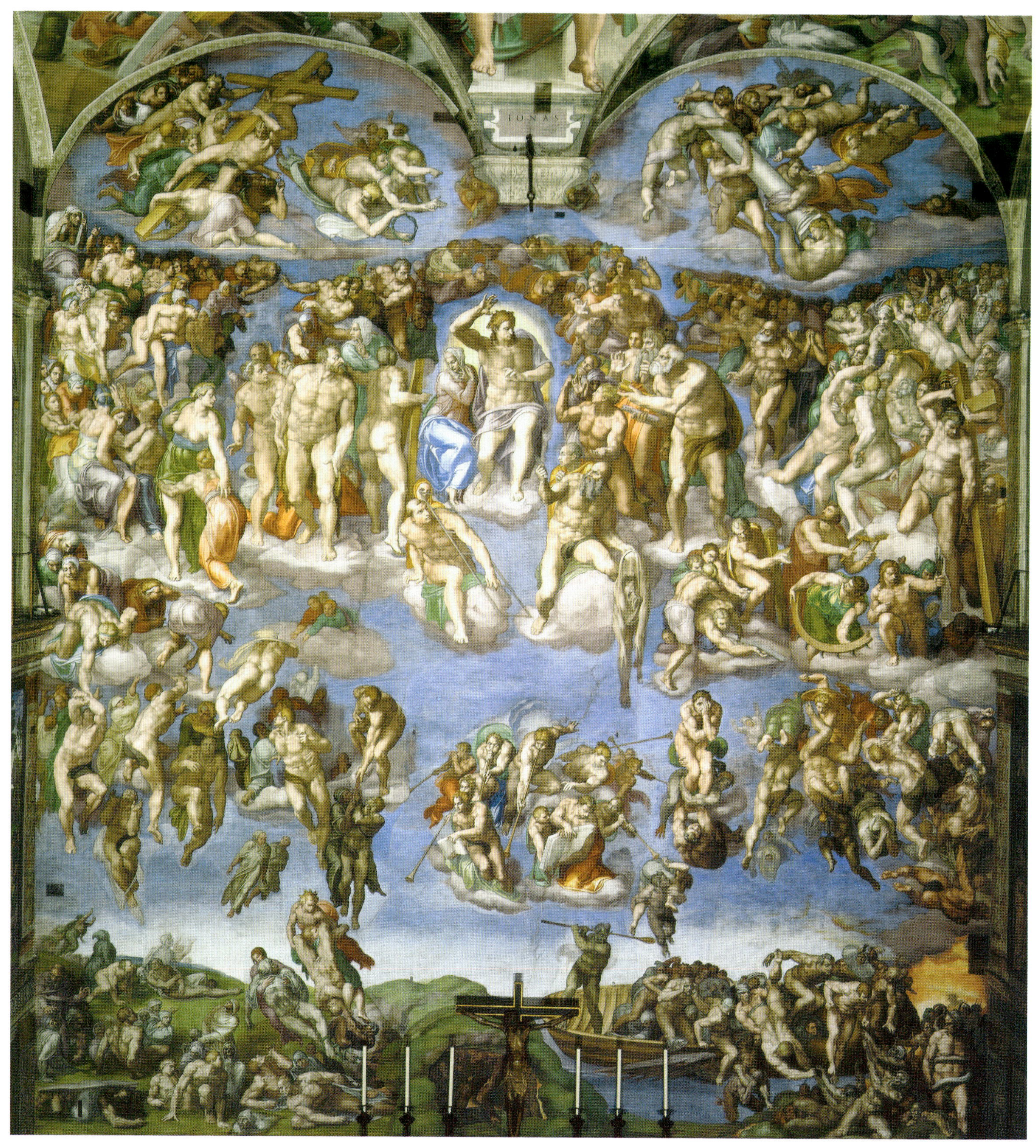
IONAS

Michelangelo Buonarroti

The Last Judgment

"Everything that nature and the art of painting is capable of fashioning from the human figure," wrote Michelangelo's biographer Ascanio Condivi in 1553, was made a reality in the *Last Judgment*. This praise is by no means extravagant. Michelangelo's enormous painting unites some 390 persons around the central Christ figure, and almost all are naked. The work depicts the resurrection of the dead and their separation into the saved and the damned. While the saved souls ascend to heaven on Christ's right-hand side, the side of the "just," the damned descend to hell on his left. Michelangelo has enriched the traditional Last Judgment scene with numerous innovations, many of which gave offense to the artist's contemporaries. These innovations included the teeming nudity of the figures, particularly the saints, which was criticized as blasphemous. The stern theologians at the Council of Trent denounced the fresco and commissioned painter Daniele da Volterra to paint vestments and fig leaves over some of the naked figures in 1565, a year after Michaelango died. These alterations were reversed during the chapel's restoration. In his depiction of the hell scenes, Michelangelo borrowed elements from Dante's *Inferno* (circa 1320), such as the barque of Charon and the figure of Minos, the judge of Hades, in the bottom right-hand corner. The uniform lapis lazuli background lends the work a special luminosity and depth that seems to extend the chapel space to infinity.

Michelangelo Buonarroti, 1475–1564
***The Last Judgment*, 1536-1541**
Fresco
Sistine Chapel

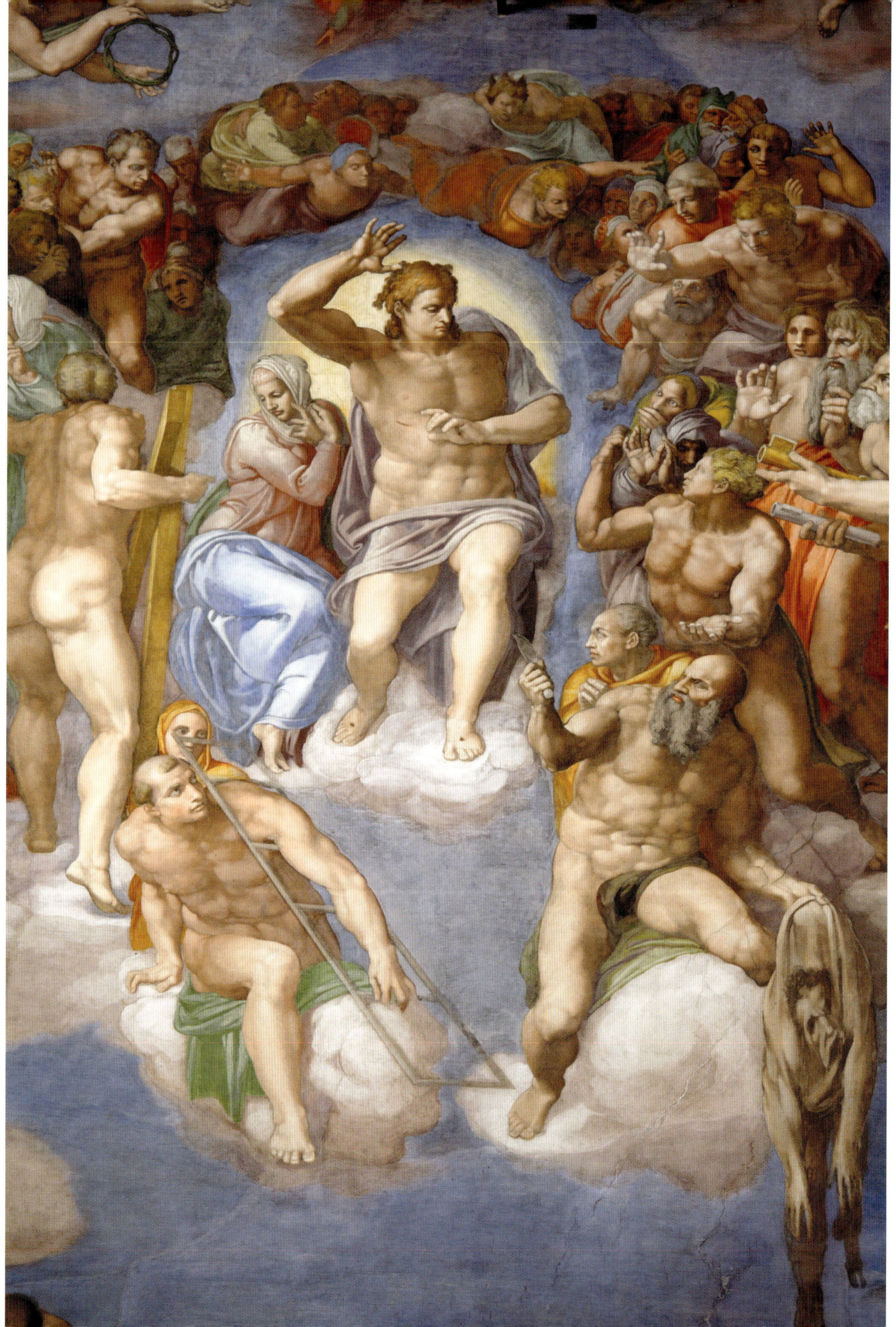

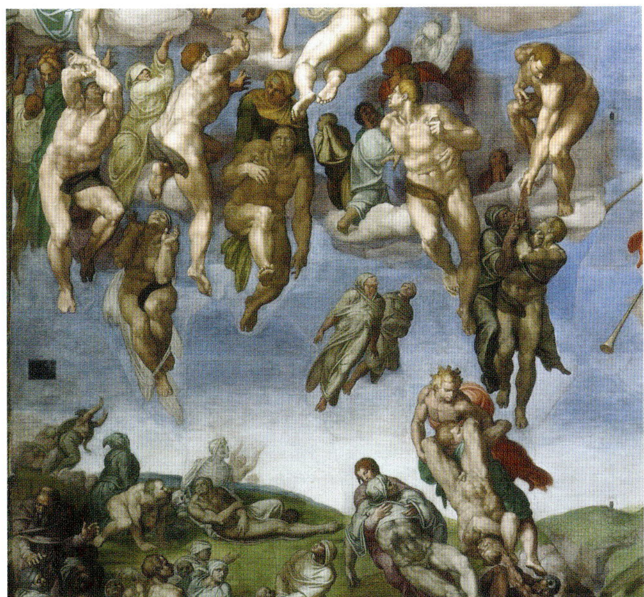

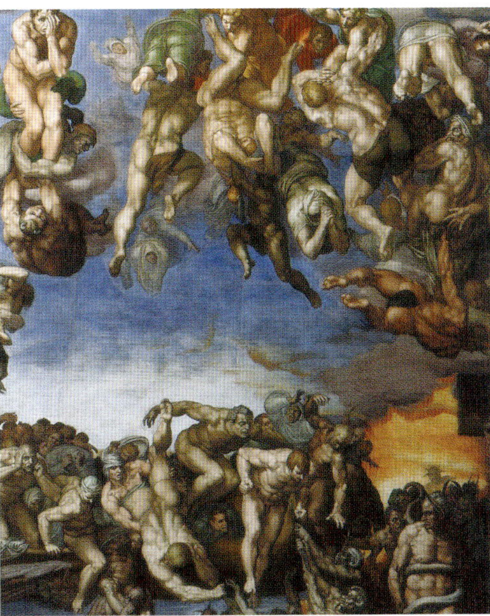

Michelangelo Buonarroti, 1475–1564
***The Last Judgment, Detail: Souls Ascending to Heaven*, 1536-1541**
Fresco
Sistine Chapel

Michelangelo Buonarroti, 1475–1564
***The Last Judgment, Detail: Souls Damned to Hell*, 1536-1541**
Fresco
Sistine Chapel

Michelangelo Buonarroti

The Last Judgment: detail showing Christ, the Virgin Mary, and saints

Among the figures that came in for particular criticism following the unveiling of the *Last Judgment* on October 31, 1541, was the Christ figure for his lack of beard, excessively youthful appearance, and, most importantly, his insufficient dignity. Indeed the muscular body, full facial features, and rippling, curly hair of the Savior are reminiscent less of the suffering Redeemer than of the *Ignudi* on the Sistine ceiling. He floats on a throne of clouds before a yellow and gold aureole and is dressed in a light gray cloak that serves to expose rather than conceal his body. The motion of his arms corresponds to the respective ascending and descending movement of the righteous and the sinners. His gaze is directed toward hell, while the Virgin Mary, seated by his side, casts her eyes toward the saved. She is the only holy figure to be fully clothed. Here Michelangelo is acknowledging her position as the titular patron of the chapel. The saints encircling Christ the Judge, including St. Andrew with his cross, St. Lawrence with his gridiron, and St. Bartholomew, are all depicted virtually naked. Bartholomew is holding onto his flayed skin, a reference to him being skinned alive and crucified upside down in Armenia. His skin is renowned as a possible self-portrait of Michelangelo who often depicted himself in a powerless way.

Michelangelo Buonarroti, 1475–1564
***The Last Judgment: detail showing Christ, the Virgin Mary, and saints*, 1536-1541**
Fresco
Sistine Chapel

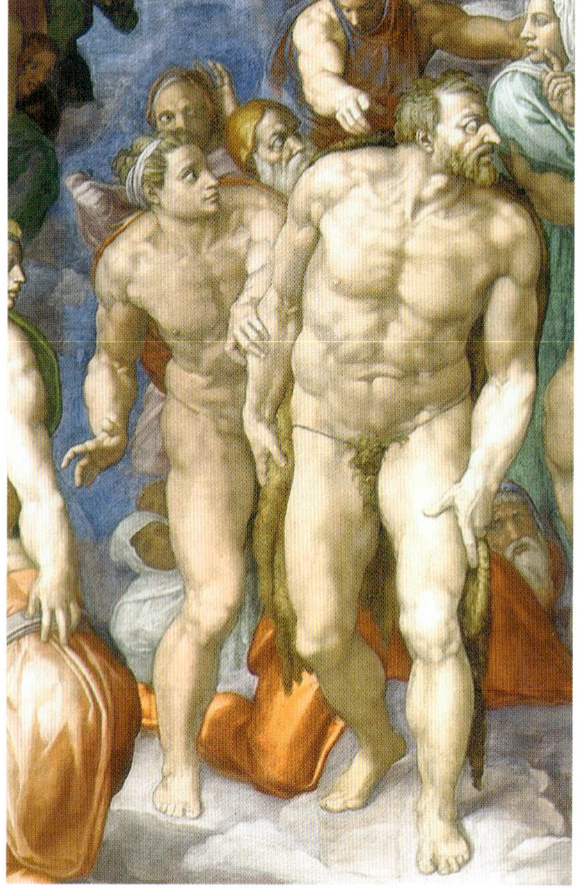

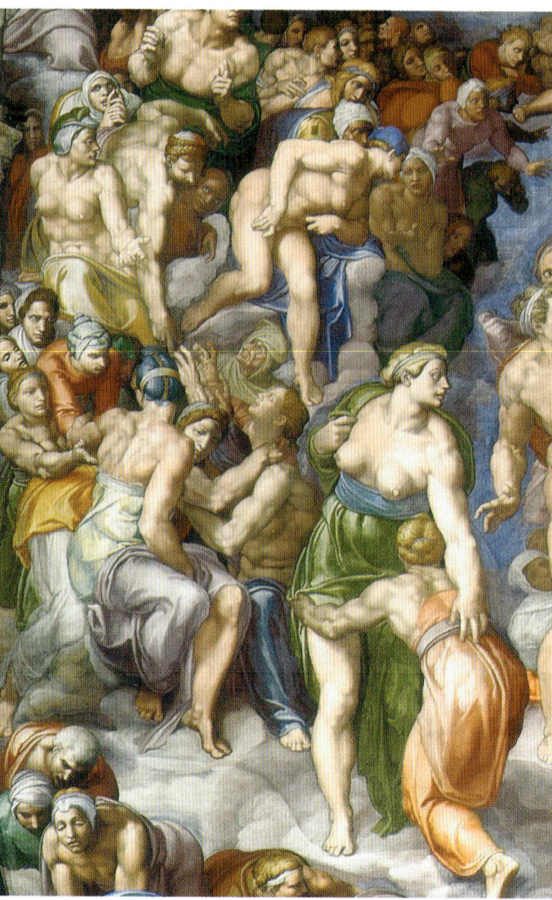

Michelangelo Buonarroti, 1475–1564
***The Last Judgement*, details, 1536-1541**
Fresco
Sistine Chapel

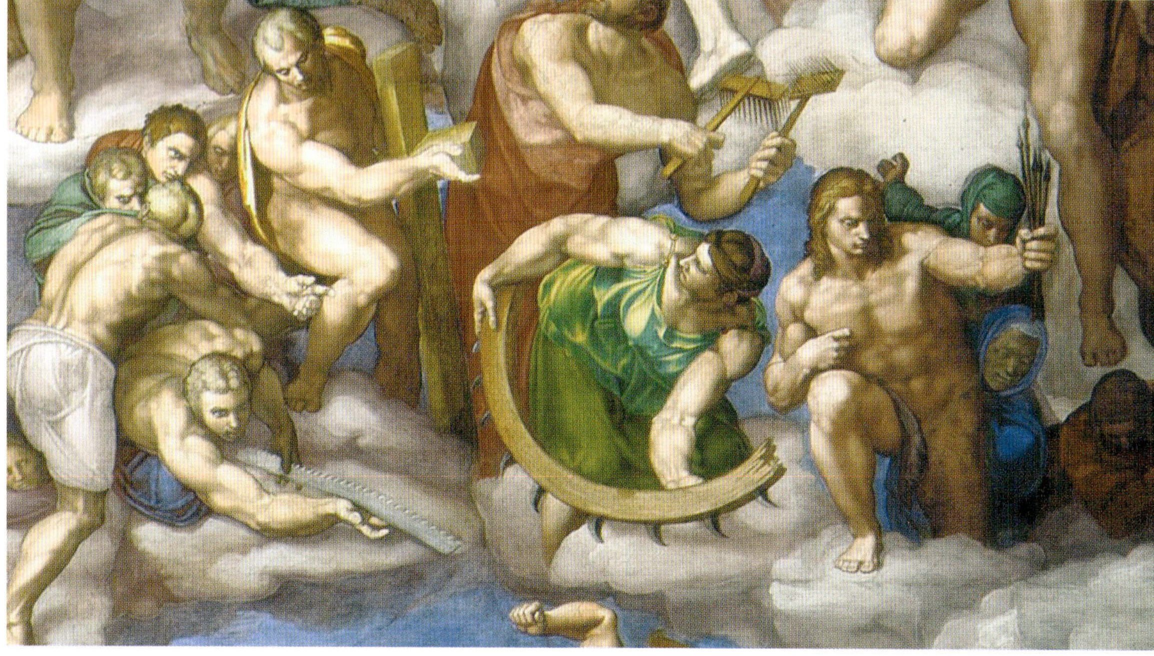

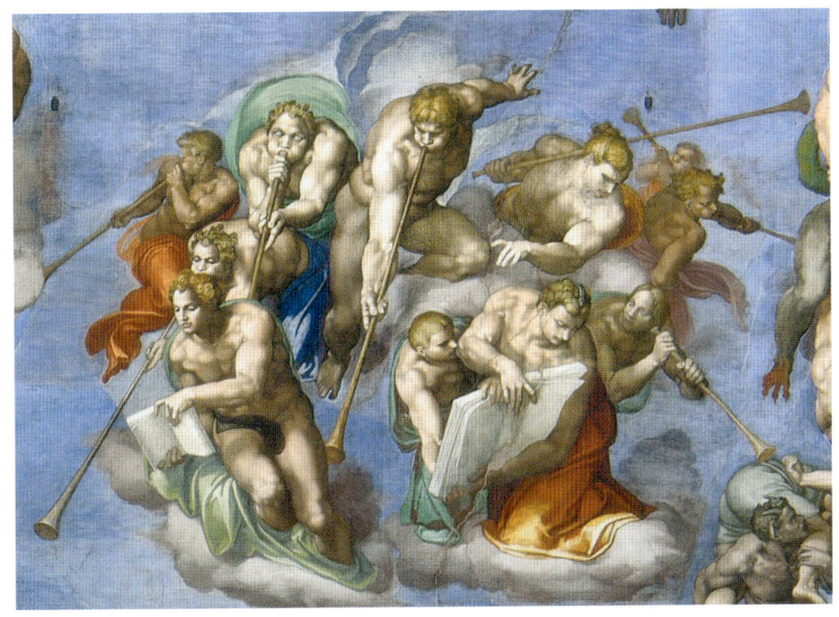

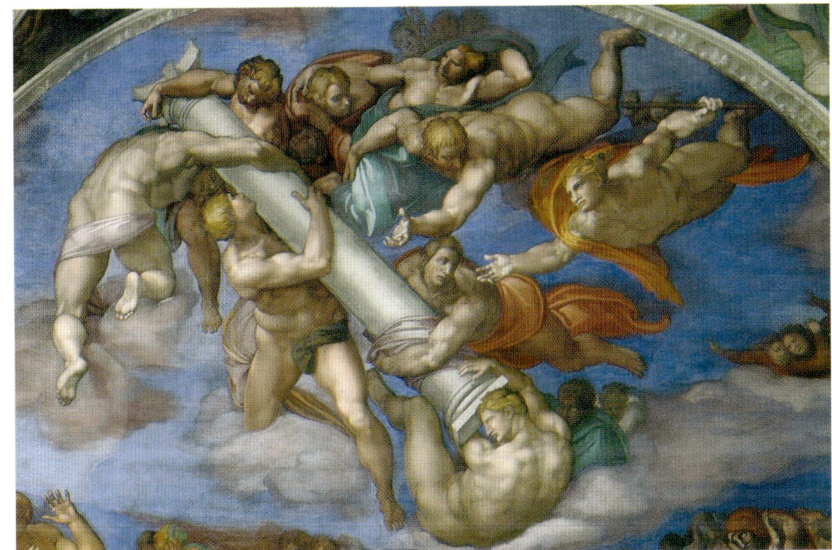

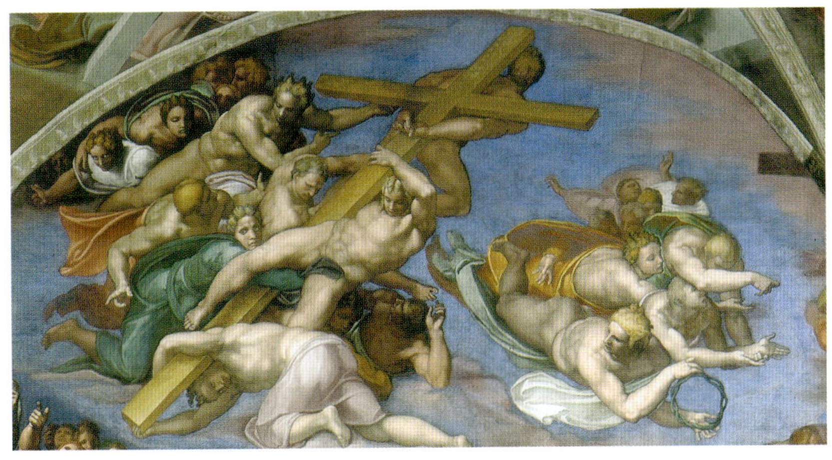

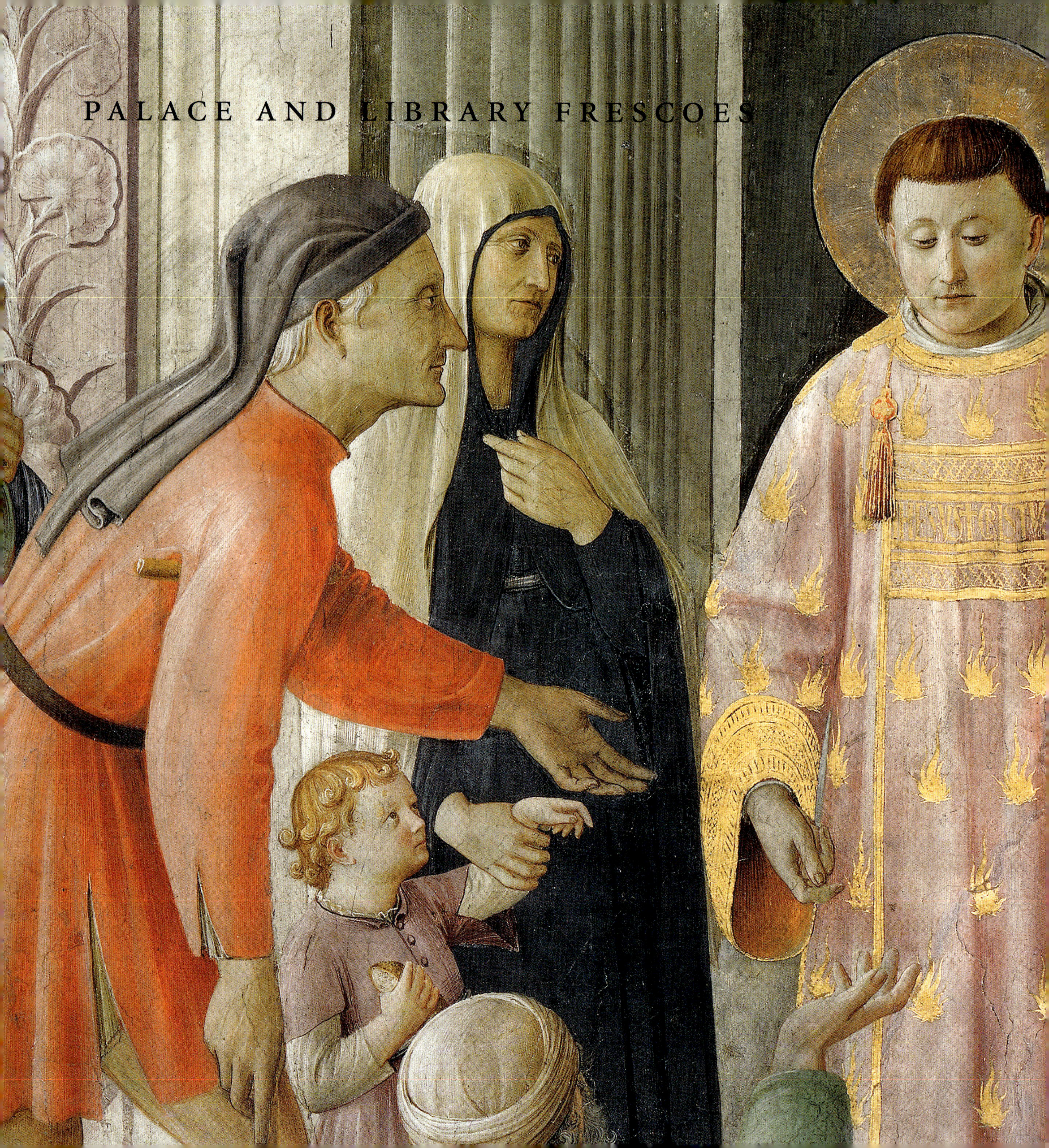

PALACE AND LIBRARY FRESCOES

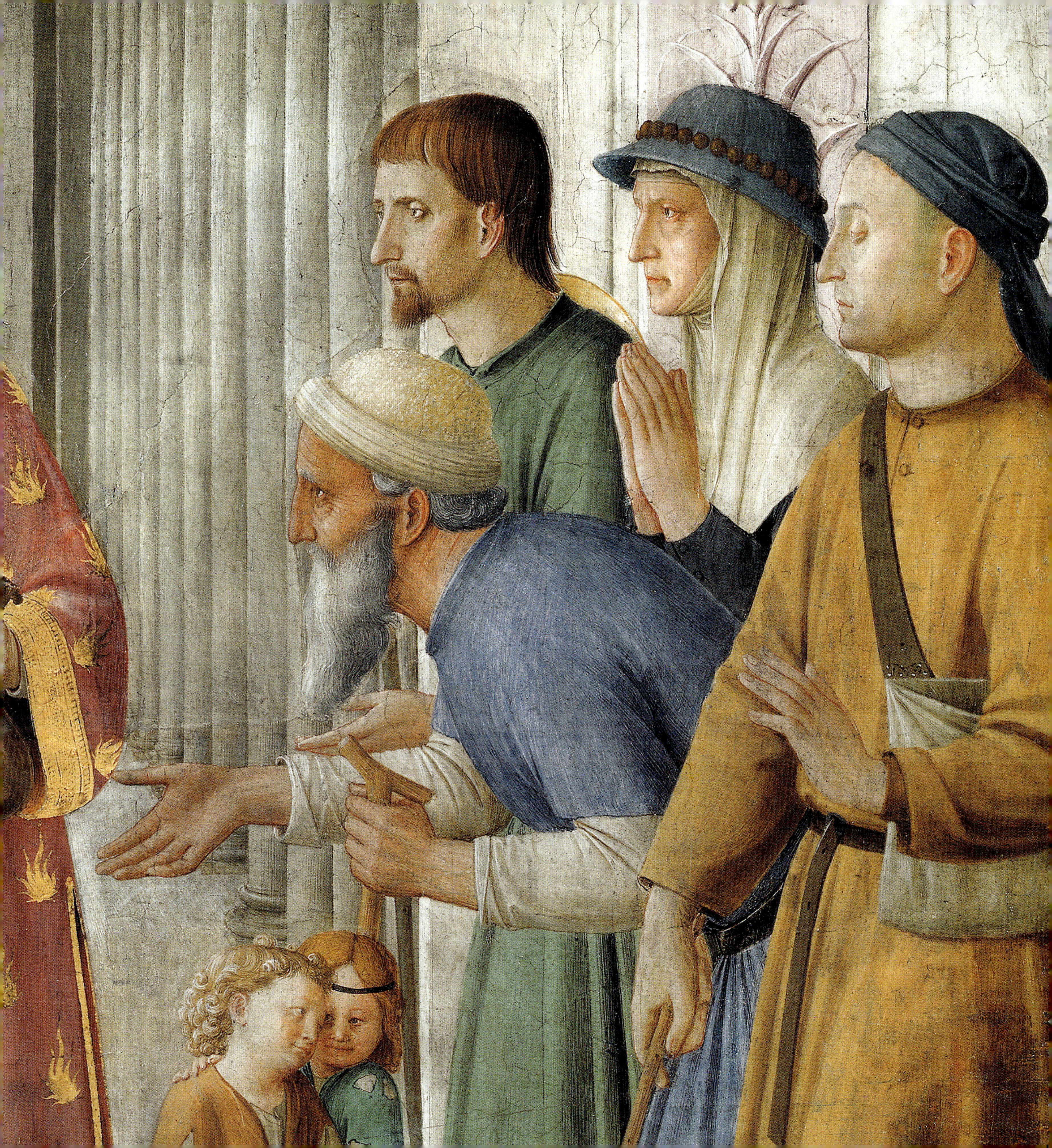

VATICAN PALACES: FRESCOES

In addition to the large cycles in the Sistine Chapel, the Borgia Apartments, and the Raphael Rooms, the Vatican Palace contains numerous other frescoes and paintings from throughout the centuries. They were executed by famous painters commissioned by popes to produce works mainly for their private living quarters. Today, many of these works remain in areas of the Vatican Palace that serve residential or administrative purposes and are therefore inaccessible to the general public. As part of the Vatican's artistic heritage, they are nevertheless worthy of consideration and appreciation.

The current palace complex dates back to the thirteenth century. Of the core structures erected under Nicholas III (ca.1210/20–1280, reigned from 1277) in the vicinity of the Cortile del Pappagallo, only a few remnants of the architecture and frescoes remain due to subsequent rebuilding and refurbishment measures. During the fourteenth century, construction came to an almost complete standstill because from 1309 until the end of the Western Schism in 1417, the majority of the popes resided in Avignon.

The first pontiff to commission extensive building and decoration after the return of the popes was Nicholas V (1397–1455, reigned from 1447). As a humanist, Nicholas V promoted a revival of classical learning in science, art, and architecture. In 1447 he commissioned the Florentine painter Fra Angelico (ca. 1395–1455) to decorate his private chapel. Between 1448 and 1449, Fra Angelico and his workshop frescoed the small chapel with scenes from the lives of SS. Stephen and Lawrence and turned the vault into a starry sky. The radiant colors and golden tendril ornamentation transform the space into a painted jewel box that is one of the most beautiful rooms in the Vatican Palace, and which has lost none of its power to enchant.

The same can be said of the loggia, painted by Raphael (1483–1520) and his workshop in 1518–1519 after a commission by Leo X (1475–1521, reigned from 1513). The Renaissance writer Baldassarre Castiglione describes this space, originally an open gallery, as "perhaps the most beautiful creation to have been seen in Rome since antiquity." The narrow gallery with its thirteen vaulted bays is decorated with fifty-two scenes from the Old and New Testaments and has fittingly been called "Raphael's Bible." The dominant visual element is the extravagant decoration in the grotesque style (from the Italian *grotto*), which covers the walls and vault. The principle of the grotesque lies in the imaginative combining of realistic human figures, animals, and plants with fantasy elements, realistic and stylized architectonic fragments, and decorative, often classicizing forms. This new style of decoration, based on antique models in villas and palaces rediscovered at the end of the fifteenth century, found its first comprehensive expression in the loggia and the *loggetta* of Cardinal Bibbiena, located immediately above. These rooms were to become the model for many more grotesque decorative schemes.

Just as Raphael contributed two important works to the Vatican, so too did Michelangelo (1475–1564), who decorated not only the Sistine Chapel but also the adjoining Pauline Chapel. The chapel and frescoes were commissioned by Paul III (1468–1549, reigned from 1534), who dedicated them to his patron saint, Paul the Apostle. The private chapel of the popes was completed in 1540 by Antonio da Sangallo the Younger and decorated by Michelangelo between 1542 and 1549 with two frescoes on facing walls: the *Conversion of St. Paul* and the *Crucifixion of St. Peter*.

Among Michelangelo's many admirers was the painter and writer on art Giorgio Vasari (1511–1574), who was commissioned between 1571 and 1573 to paint numerous large scenes in the Sala Regia. For the decoration of this reception and audience room, still used as such today, the chosen theme was decisive moments in the history of the Church. Two of the most important scenes are the *Return of Gregory XI from Avignon* and the *Battle of Lepanto*.

Important paintings and fresco cycles continued to be produced in the Vatican in later centuries. Among the most beautiful are Tommaso Conca's (1734–1822) neoclassical wall and ceiling paintings in the Sala delle Muse (Room of the Muses).

Of both historical and art-historical relevance are the fifteen lunette paintings in the Museo Chiaramonti, which also allude to the history of the collection. Among the scenes is the *Return to Rome of Her Stolen Works of Art* painted by Francesco Hayez (1791–1882) in the neoclassical style, whose subject is the 1815 restoration of the works of art plundered from the Vatican by Napoleon in 1797.

Adjacent to the Raphael Rooms are two rooms that assumed their present decoration in the second half of the nineteenth century: the Sala dell'Immacolata ("Room of the Immaculate Conception") and Sala Sobieski. The latter was named after the subject of its main painting, a monumental canvas by the Polish painter Jan Matejko (1838–1893) depicting the victory of Polish king Jan III Sobieski over the Turks outside Vienna in 1683. Matejko completed the painting for the two-hundredth anniversary of the battle, and it was initially exhibited in Krakow. At the artist's request, it was sent to Rome in 1883 as a gift from Poland to Leo XIII, who dedicated an entire room to it.

NICCOLINE CHAPEL

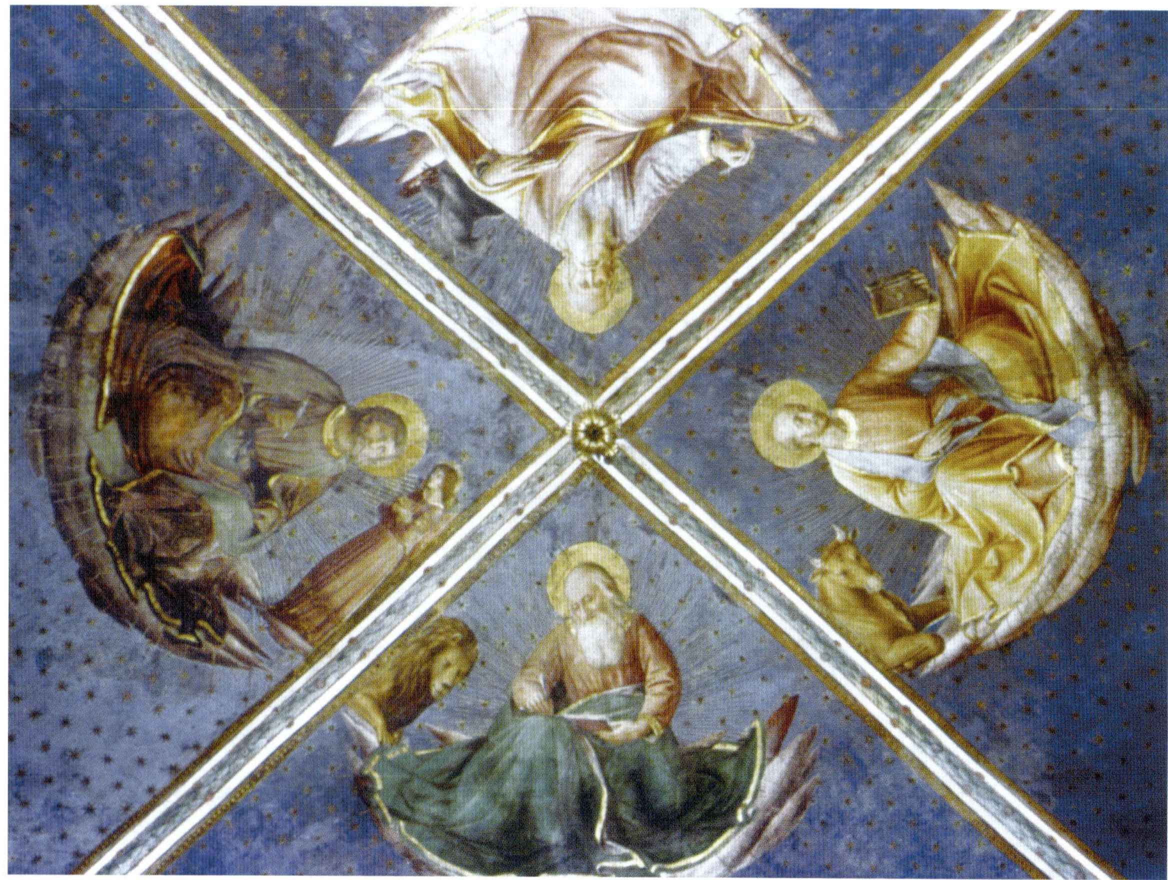

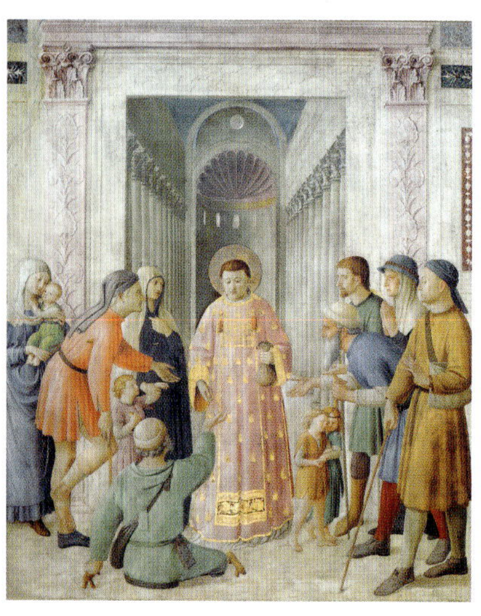

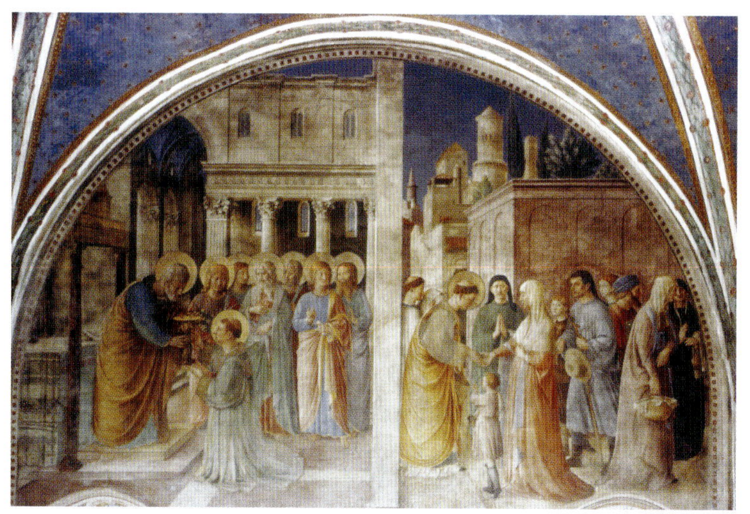

Fra Angelico (Guido di Pietro), 1387–1455
***Ceiling with the Four Evangelists*, 1448–1449**
Fresco
Niccoline Chapel, Vatican Palaces

Fra Angelico (Guido di Pietro), 1387–1455
***Scenes from the Life of St. Lawrence: St. Lawrence Distributing Alms to the Poor*, 1448–1449**
Fresco
Niccoline Chapel, Vatican Palaces

Fra Angelico (Guido di Pietro), 1387–1455
***Scenes from the Life of St. Stephen: St. Stephen Receiving the Diaconate; Distributing Alms*, 1448–1449**
Fresco
Niccoline Chapel, Vatican Palaces

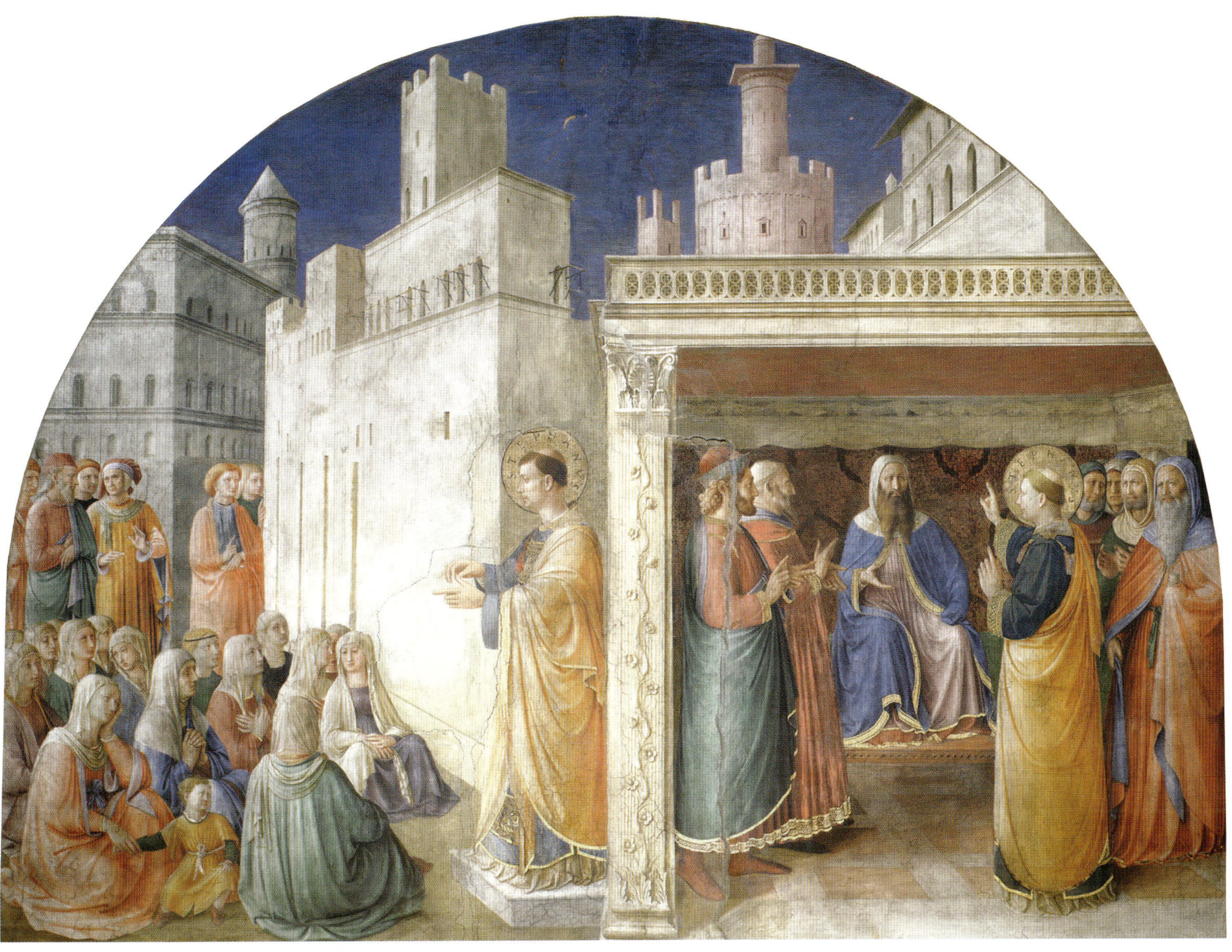

Fra Angelico (Guido di Pietro)

Scenes from the Life of St. Stephen: Preaching of St. Stephen and St. Stephen Addressing the Council

This depiction of two sermons given by St. Stephen is the second in the Niccoline Chapel series on the life of the protomartyr. It is generally regarded as a masterpiece of the mature Fra Angelico. The Acts of the Apostles (Apostles 6–7) tells how as a deacon of the young Christian community in Jerusalem, Stephen spread the word of God and "did great wonders and miracles among the people." He wasn't afraid to engage in scholarly debate with the Jewish doctors, which would eventually lead to him being stoned to death. The preaching fresco shows St. Stephen at the height of his work among the people. On the left we see the saint "full of faith and power" preaching with expressive gestures to the captivated women sitting, and men standing, before him on the square outside the Temple. In the background, a tall building recalls the city palaces of Fra Angelico's native Tuscany. The scene on the right depicts Stephen's disputation with the doctors in the synagogue, whose elegant Renaissance lines make it a masterpiece of architectural representation. The fresco enchants with its well-balanced composition and the harmonious colors of the clothes.

Fra Angelico (Guido di Pietro), 1387–1455
***Scenes from the Life of St. Stephen: Preaching of St. Stephen and St. Stephen Addressing the Council*, 1448–1449**
Fresco
Niccoline Chapel, Vatican Palaces

PAULINE CHAPEL

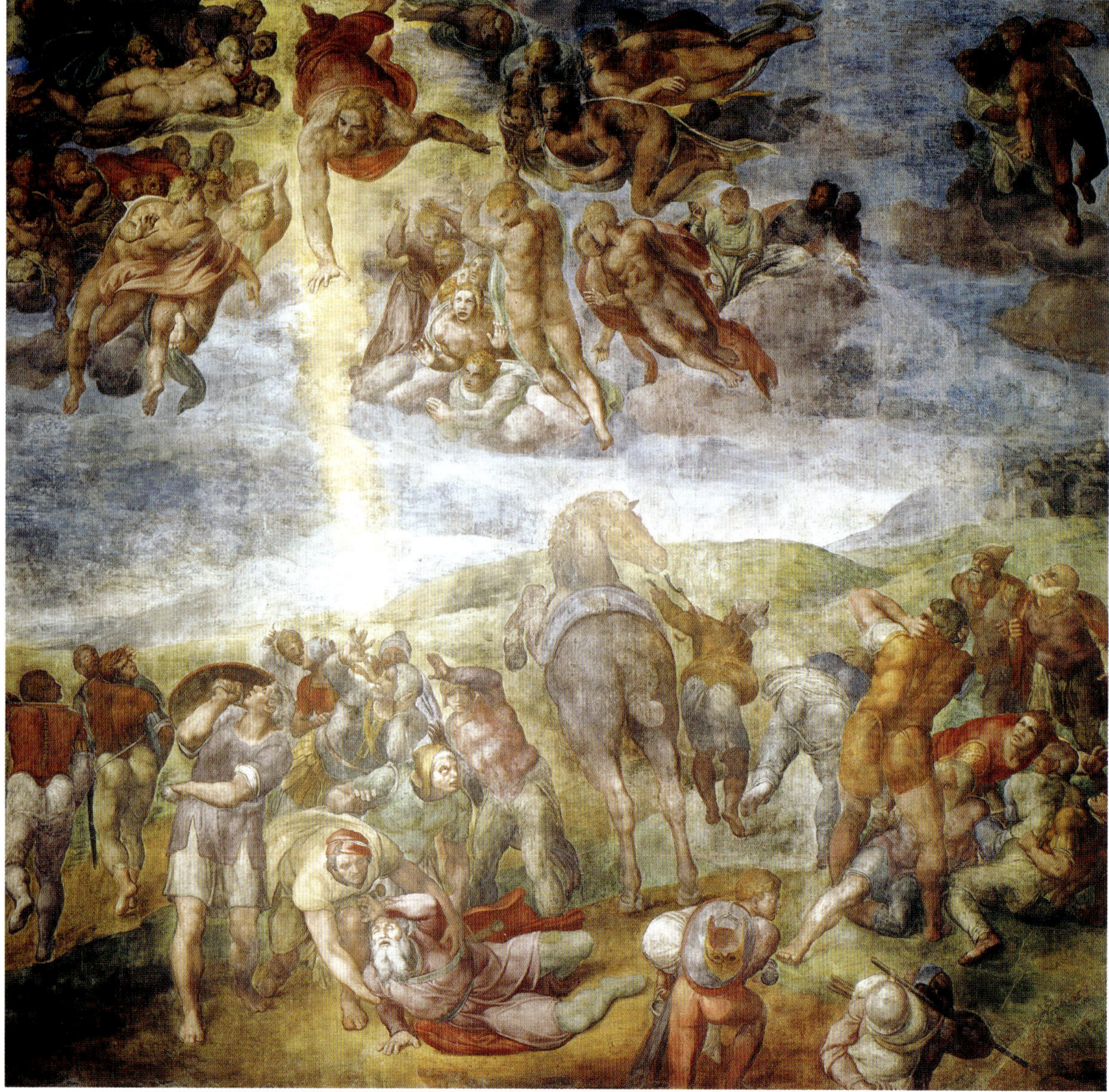

Michelangelo Buonarroti, 1475–1564
***The Conversion of Saul*, 1542–1545**
Fresco
Pauline Chapel, Vatican Palaces

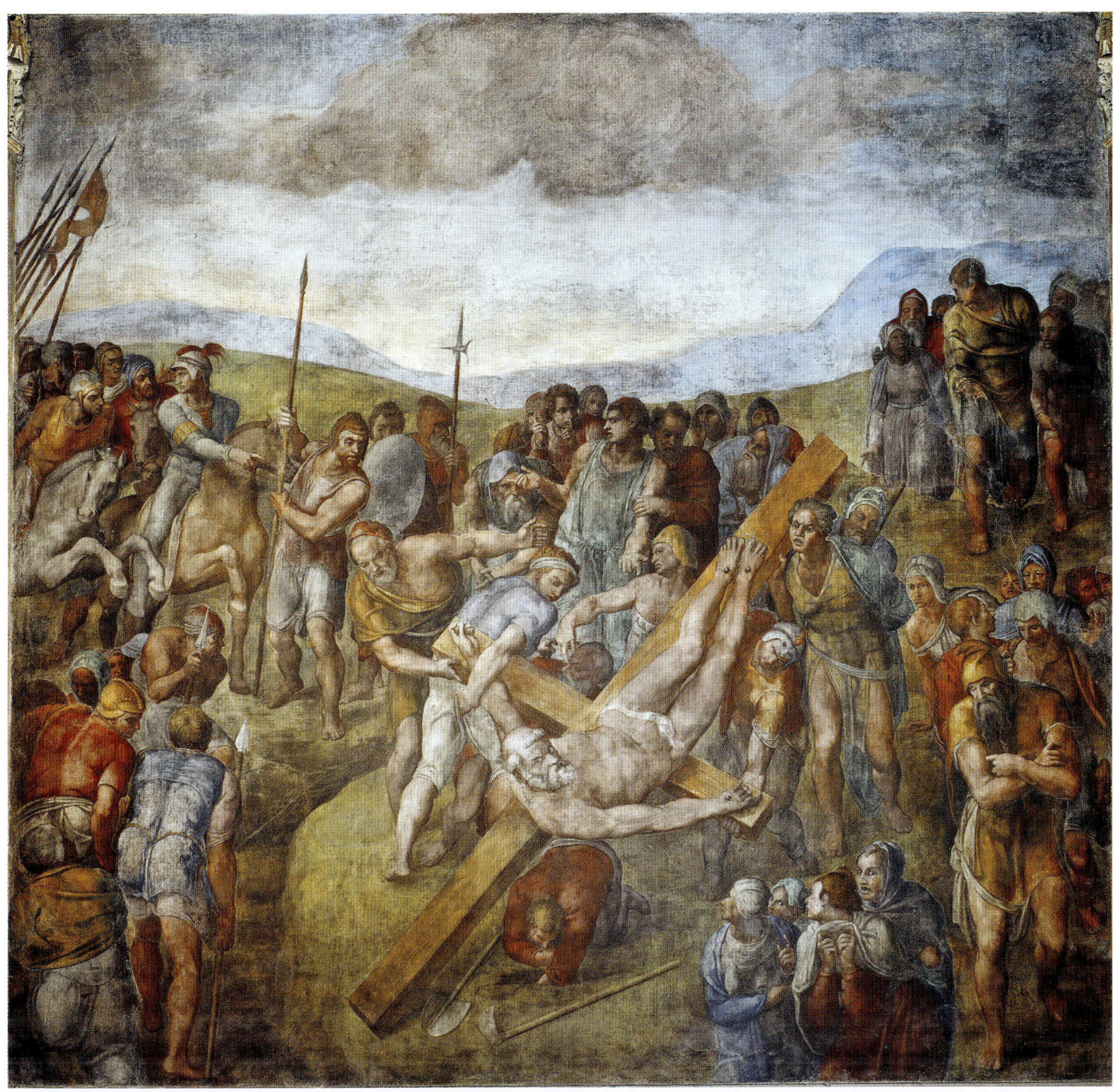

Michelangelo Buonarroti

The Crucifixion of St. Peter

The subject of this almost square picture space is the crucifixion of St. Peter, the name patron of Paul III, who in 1542 commissioned Michelangelo to paint this fresco for his private chapel. Michelangelo has selected the moment when the cross is being erected, an event that has attracted a crowd of soldiers and citizens. According to the legend, the apostle asked to be crucified with his head pointing down because he felt unworthy to suffer the same death as Christ. A total of eight men are trying to set up the enormous cross as the saint appears to slip down it. In the heat of his exertion, the executioner's assistant standing behind the cross to the left almost pokes the man kneeling in front of him in the eye. This may be an allusion to the legendary claim that at the moment of death, St. Peter opened the eyes of hitherto nonbelievers to the glory of God. It is also reported in the legend that St. Peter commanded the people, who had wanted to liberate him, not to prevent his martyrdom. Michelangelo has conveyed the furious and fearful reactions of the onlookers, a number of whom have put their fingers to their lips, presumably as a sign of their silence, with considerable psychological insight.

Michelangelo Buonarroti, 1475–1564
***The Crucifixion of St. Peter*, 1549**
Fresco
Pauline Chapel, Vatican Palaces

LOGGIA

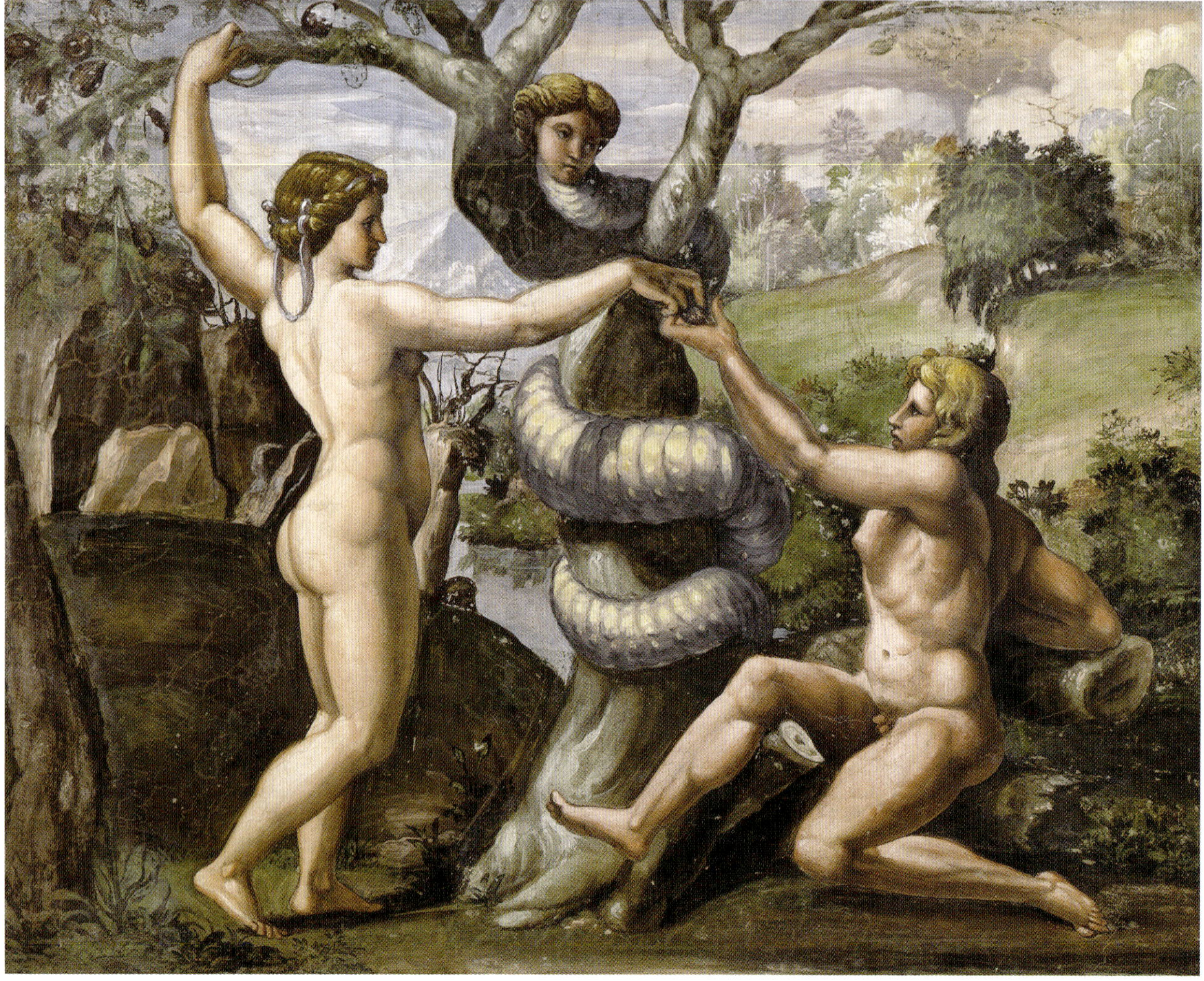

Raphael (Raffaello Sanzio), Workshop of

Story of Adam and Eve: Original Sin

This painting of Adam und Eve's fall adorns the second of the thirteen vaults in the loggia. The Tree of Knowledge, precisely aligned with the central axis, divides the composition into two halves. The left side is taken up by Eve, who is shown in profile standing upright by the tree and handing Adam the forbidden fruit—freshly picked from the tree—with a graceful gesture. Adam sits on the ground to the right of the tree between stumps of branches and accepts the fruit from her with his left hand. He has adopted a complicated sitting position with one leg folded back and his upper body twisted around to reveal his powerful musculature. He is observed by the serpent, who has coiled her mighty, armored body around the trunk of the tree. In her facial features and hairstyle she bears a conspicuous resemblance to Eve, the progenitrix of the human race, thereby embodying Eve's sinfulness and seductive power. The work is clearly inspired by Michelangelo's ceiling frescoes in the Sistine Chapel, although Raphael has switched Adam and Eve's positions and given more weight to the landscape of Paradise.

Raphael (Raffaello Sanzio), Workshop of, 1483–1520
***Story of Adam and Eve: Original Sin*, 1513–1519**
Fresco
Loggia, Vatican Palaces

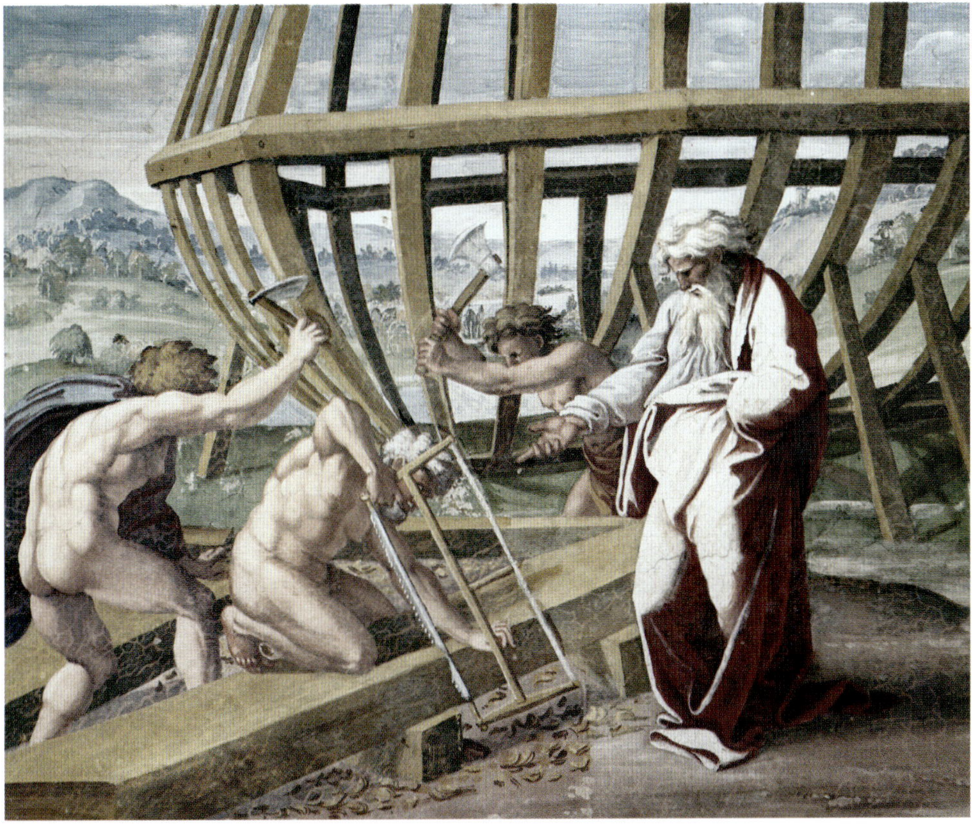

Raphael (Raffaello Sanzio), Workshop of, 1483–1520
***Story of Noah: Construction of the Ark*, 1513–1519**
Fresco
Loggia, Vatican Palaces

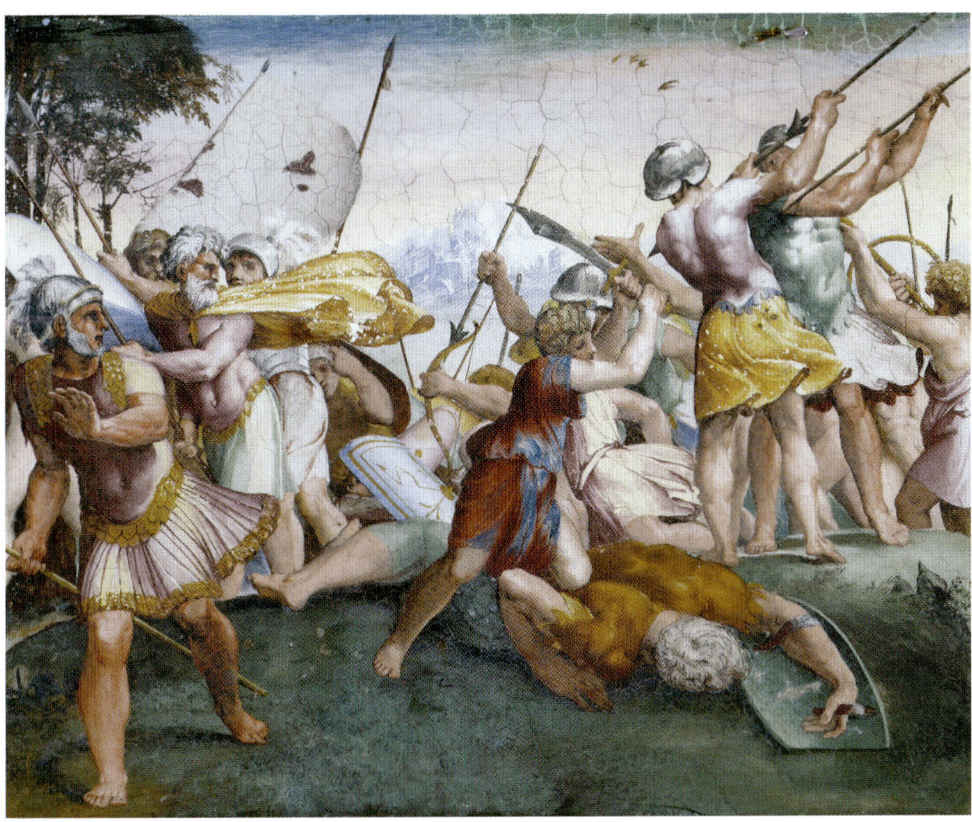

Raphael (Raffaello Sanzio), Workshop of, 1483–1520
***Story of David: David and Goliath*, 1513–1519**
Fresco
Loggia, Vatican Palaces

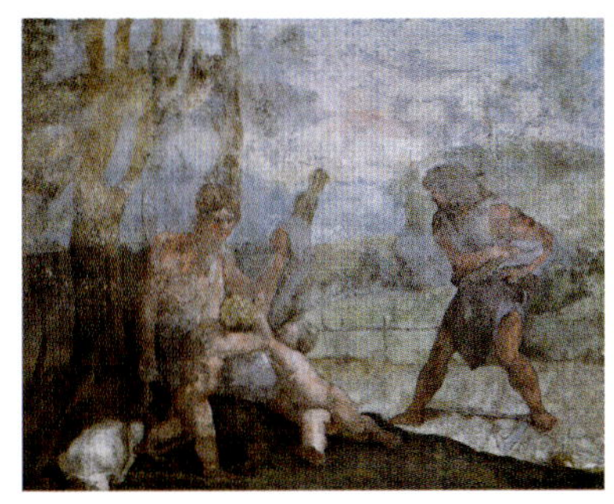

Raphael (Raffaello Sanzio), Workshop of, 1483–1520
***Story of Adam and Eve: Labor of Adam and Eve*, 1513–1519**
Fresco
Loggia, Vatican Palaces

Raphael (Raffaello Sanzio), Workshop of

Story of Moses: The Adoration of the Golden Calf

The adoration of the Golden Calf is one of the key episodes in the story of Moses, occurring immediately after he has received the Ten Commandments (depicted by Raphael in the adjoining vault space). In the Bible it is reported that after Moses has come down from Mount Sinai with Joshua, full of pride and joy over the tablets that bear the law, he sees that the Israelites have gathered to adore the Golden Calf (Exodus 32). Enraged at their godlessness, he first smashes the tablets and then destroys the graven image. Raphael has chosen the moment when Moses, descended from the mountain, discovers the sacrilege and is preparing to destroy the tablets, as shown in the middle ground on the left. The main motif of the fresco, however, is the adoration of the Golden Calf, which Raphael foregrounds. The instigator is Aaron, Moses' brother, who is shown standing behind the altar with raised arms. Around him kneel men, women, and children in trance-like postures, while others dance in ecstasy around the calf. The infatuated mother in the foreground is particularly conspicuous, urging her son to venerate the idol.

Raphael (Raffaello Sanzio), Workshop of, 1483–1520
***Story of Moses: The Adoration of the Golden Calf*, 1513–1519**
Fresco
Loggia, Vatican Palaces

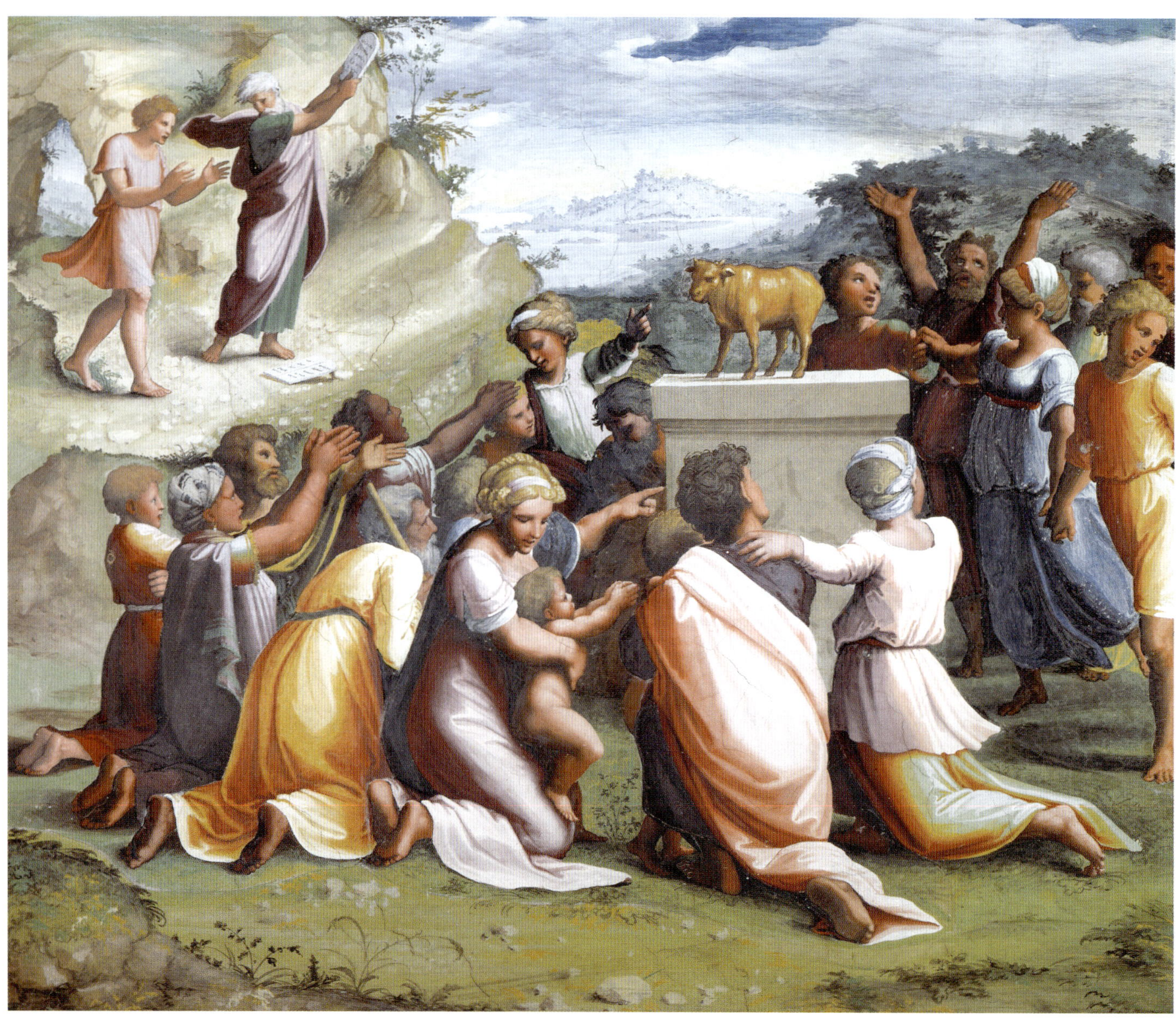

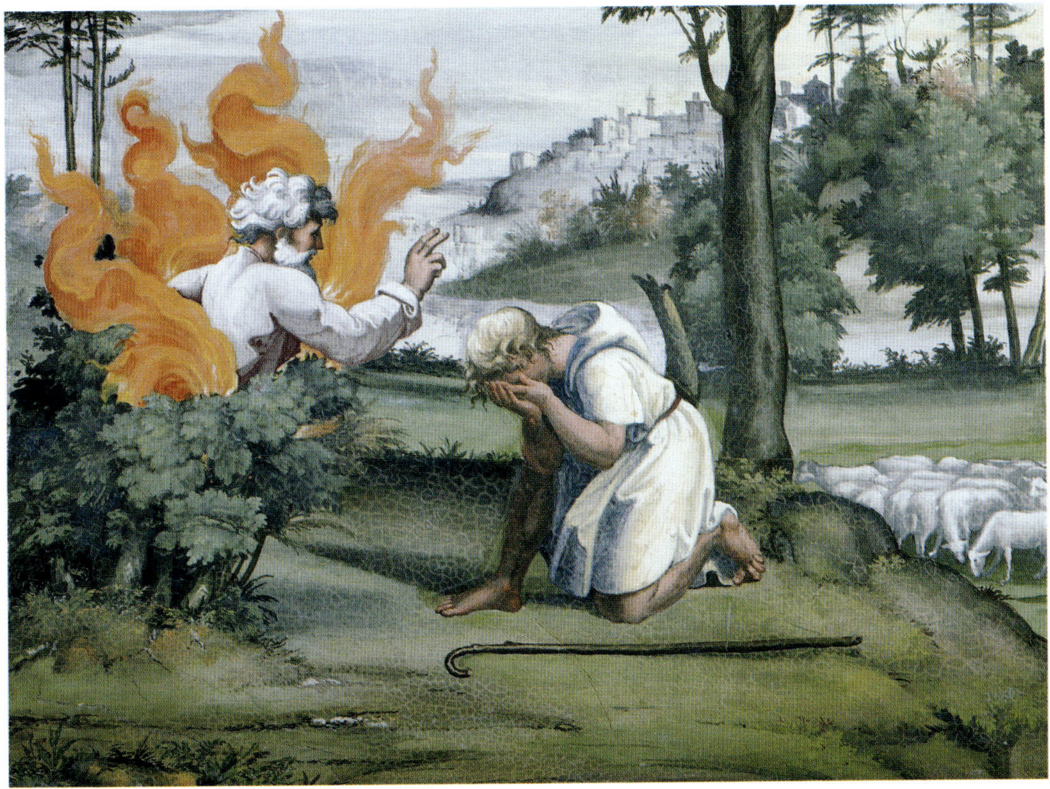

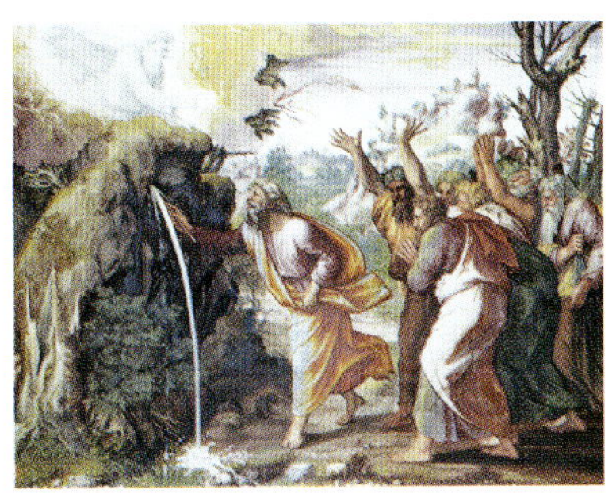

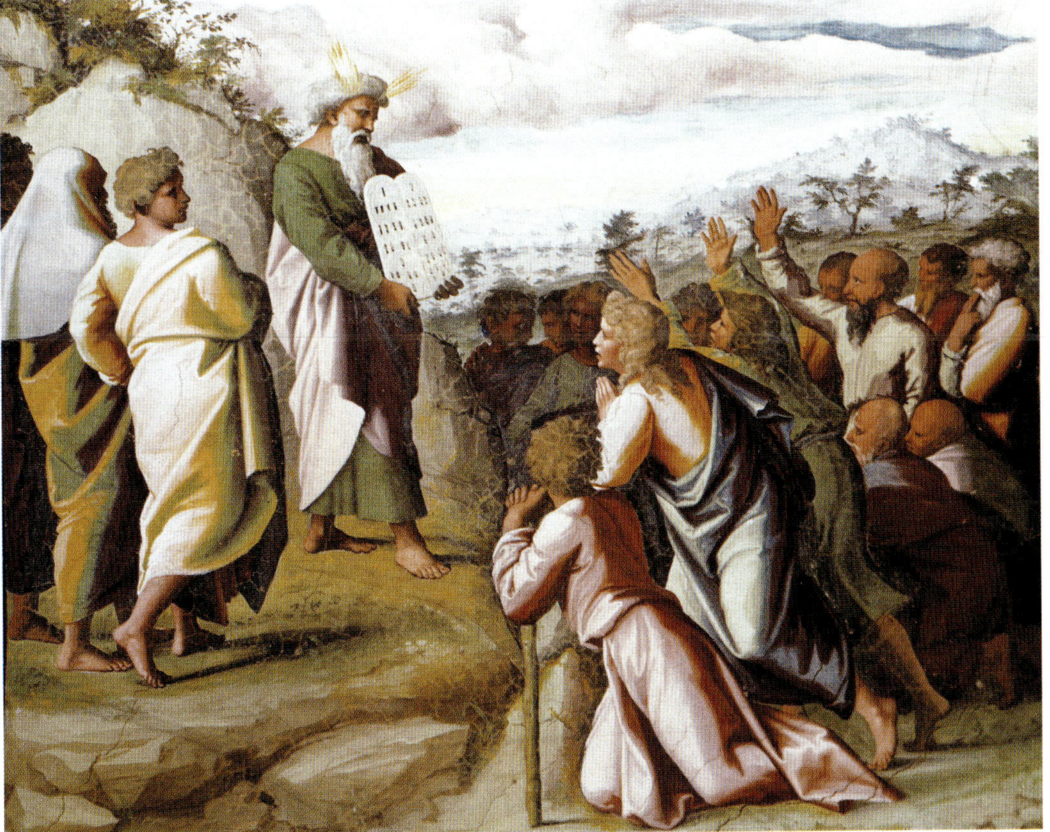

Raphael (Raffaello Sanzio), Workshop of, 1483–1520
***Story of Moses: Moses before the Burning Bush*, 1513–1519**
Fresco
Loggia, Vatican Palaces

Raphael (Raffaello Sanzio), Workshop of, 1483–1520
***Story of Moses: Moses Receiving the Tablets of the Law*, 1513–1519**
Fresco
Loggia, Vatican Palaces

Raphael (Raffaello Sanzio), Workshop of, 1483–1520
***Story of Moses: Moses Striking the Rock*, 1513–1519**
Fresco
Loggia, Vatican Palaces

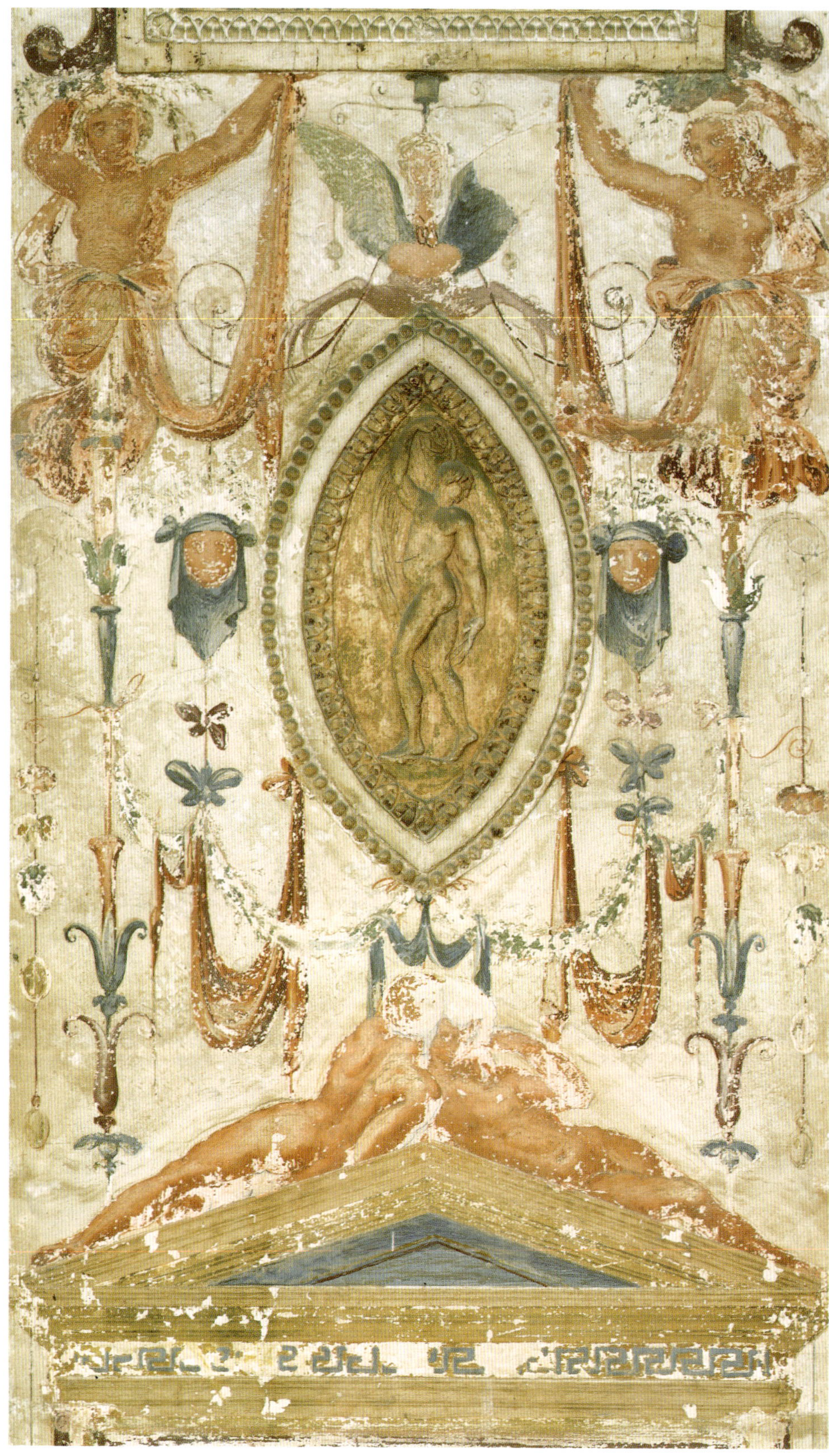

Raphael (Raffaello Sanzio), Workshop of

Wall Decoration with "Grotteschi"

Raphael and his workshop decorated another gallery in the Vatican palace: the loggetta of Cardinal Bibbiena (1470–1520), located one floor above Raphael's famous loggia. The loggetta formed part of the living quarters of the cardinal, who was interested in humanism and who caused a sensation as a writer of comedies. For the gallery that was originally open, Raphael and the young Giovanni da Udine, a pupil of Giorgione, devised a new form of wall painting composed entirely of so-called grotesques, inspired by antiquity. Giovanni da Udine was regarded as a specialist in this style of decoration, with which he had become acquainted when he and Raphael toured the subterranean rooms of the Domus Aurea, the palace of the Roman emperor Nero. During these excursions he also investigated antique frescoing techniques, which he then imitated in the loggetta. The detail shown here presents a typical combination of illusionistic architecture, putti, imaginative garlands and festoons, inscription panels, realistically depicted birds and small animals, flowers, leaf masks, and antique-looking weaponry, which covered the walls and seem to open them up to infinity.

Raphael (Raffaello Sanzio), Workshop of, 1483–1520
***Wall Decoration with "Grotteschi,"* 1513–1519**
Fresco
Loggia, Vatican Palaces

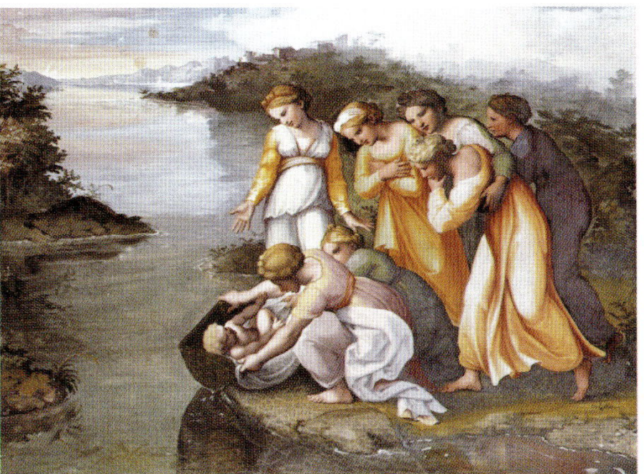

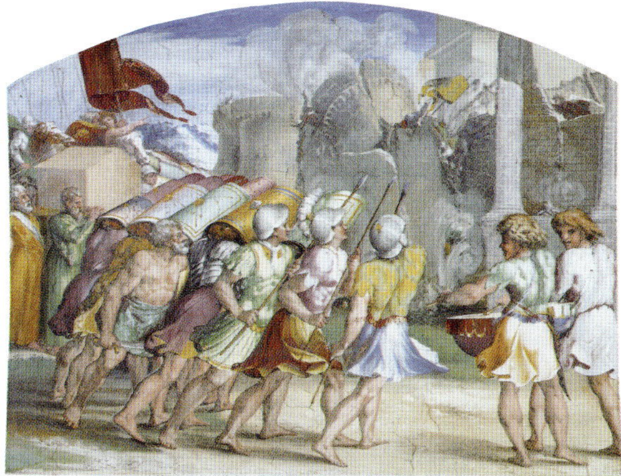

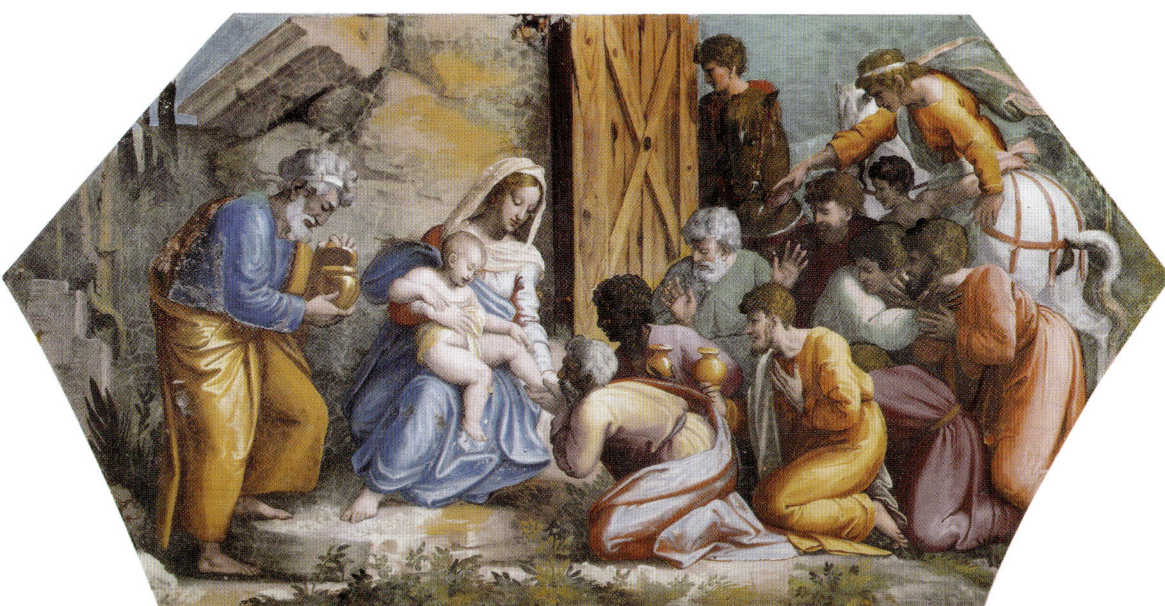

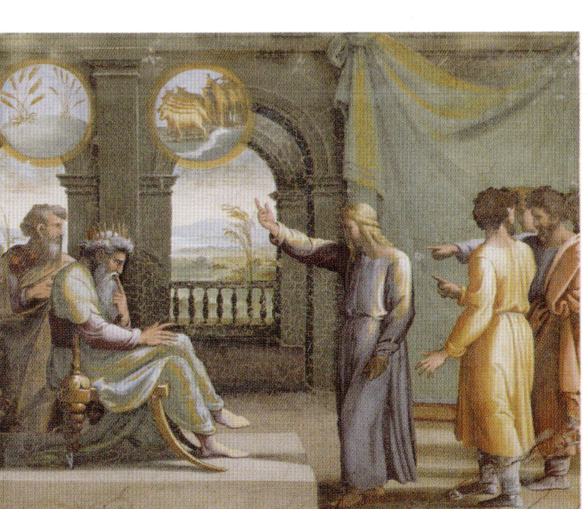

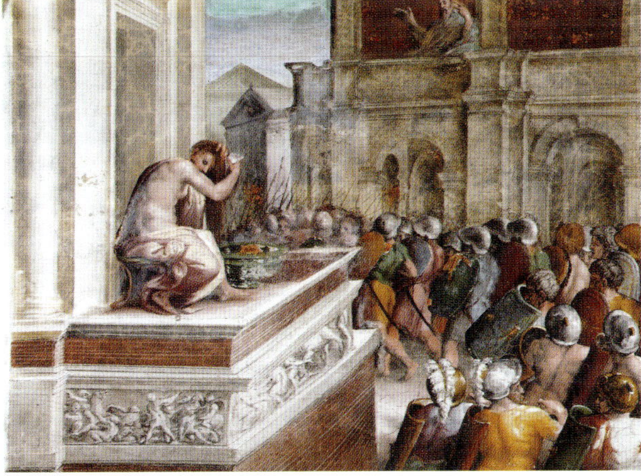

Raphael (Raffaello Sanzio), Workshop of, 1483–1520
***Story of Moses: Moses Rescued from the River*, 1513–1519**
Fresco
Loggia, Vatican Palaces

Raphael (Raffaello Sanzio, Workshop of, 1483–1520
***Story of Joshua: The Fall of Jericho*, 1513–1519**
Fresco
Loggia, Vatican Palaces

Raphael (Raffaello Sanzio), Workshop of, 1483–1520
***Life of Christ: Epiphany*, 1513–1519**
Fresco
Loggia, Vatican Palaces

Raphael (Raffaello Sanzio, Workshop of, 1483–1520
***Story of Joseph: Joseph' s Interpretation of the Pharaoh's Dreams*, 1513–1519**
Fresco
Loggia, Vatican Palaces

Raphael (Raffaello Sanzio, Workshop of, 1483–1520
***Story of David: The Toilet of Bathsheba*, 1513–1519**
Fresco
Loggia, Vatican Palaces

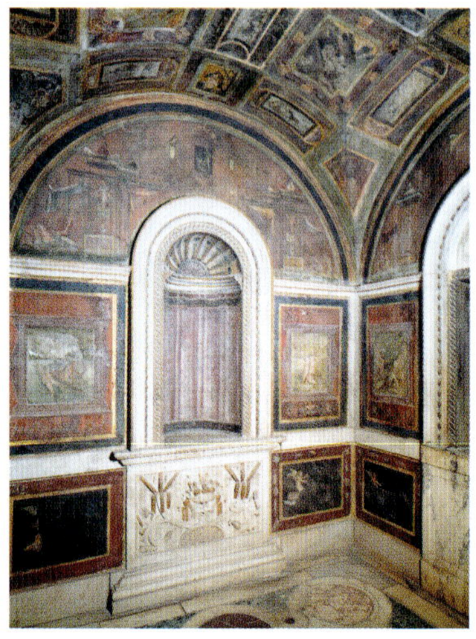

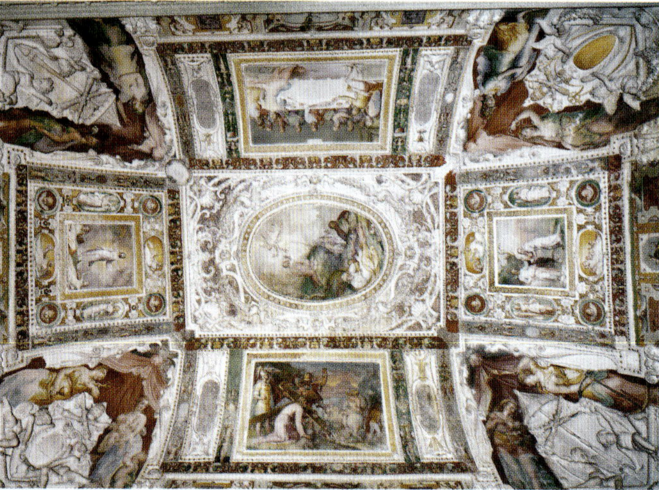

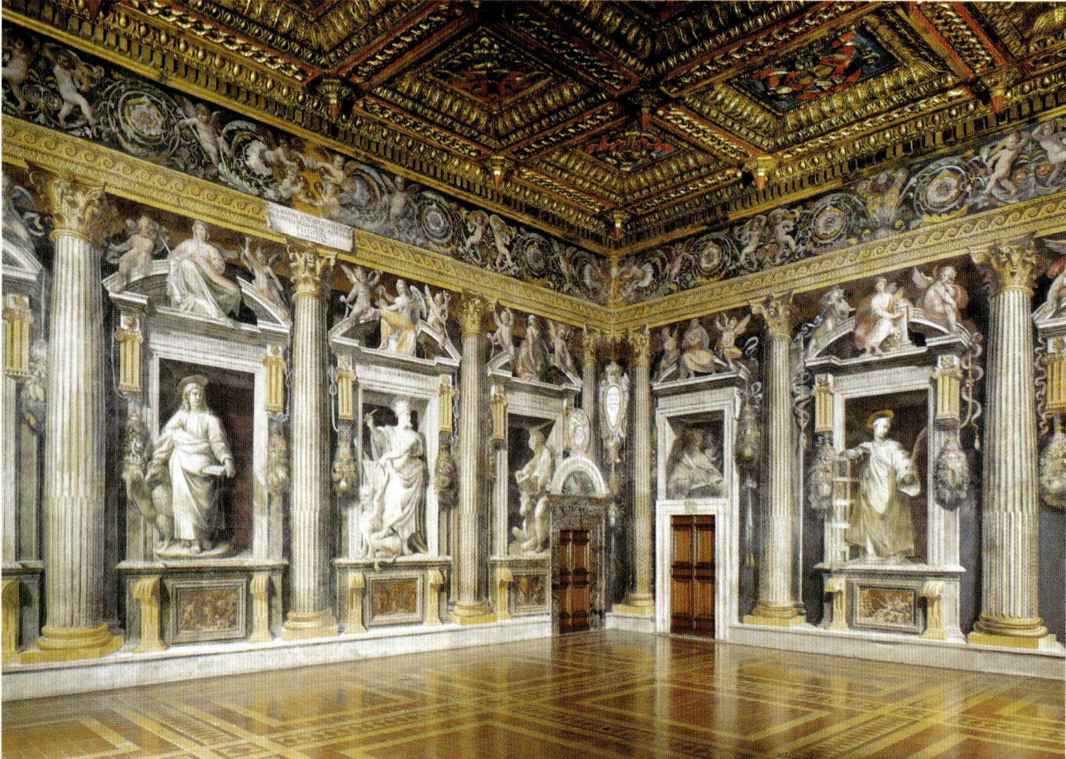

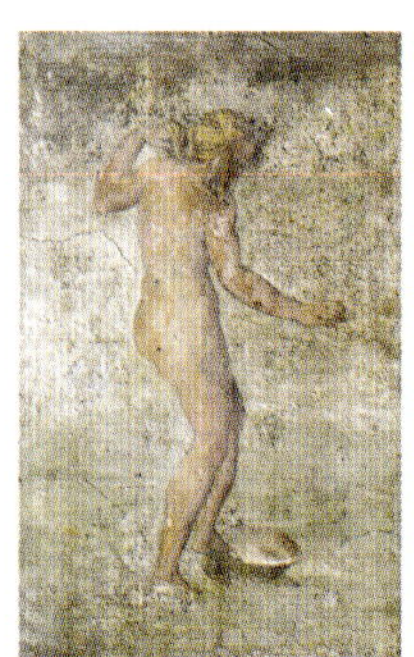

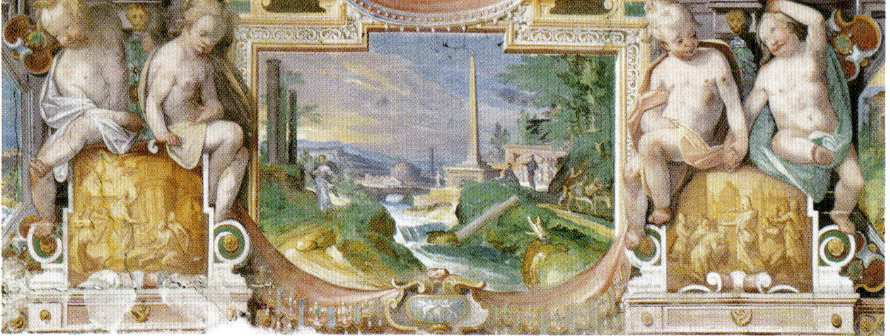

Raphael (Raffaello Sanzio), 1483–1520
***Stufetta del Cardinale Bibbiena (Bathroom of Cardinal Bibbiena)*, 1516**
Fresco
Bathroom of Cardinal Bibbiena,
Vatican Palaces

Federico Zuccari and Workshop, ca. 1540/41–1609
***Frieze with the Story of Moses and Aaron*, ca. 1560**
Fresco
Palazetto del Belvedere, Sala Regolini-Galassi

Zuccari Workshop, ca. 1540/41–1609
***View of the Room with Illusionistic Architecture and Painted Statues*, 1580–1584**
Fresco
Sala dei Palafrenieri (Sala dei Chiaroscuri)

Raphael (Raffaello Sanzio), 1483–1520
***Birth of Venus*, ca. 1516**
Fresco
Bathroom of Cardinal Bibbiena,
Vatican Palaces

Unknown artist, ca. 1609
***Frieze with Landscapes and Ruins*, ca. 1609**
Fresco
Papal Apartments, Library

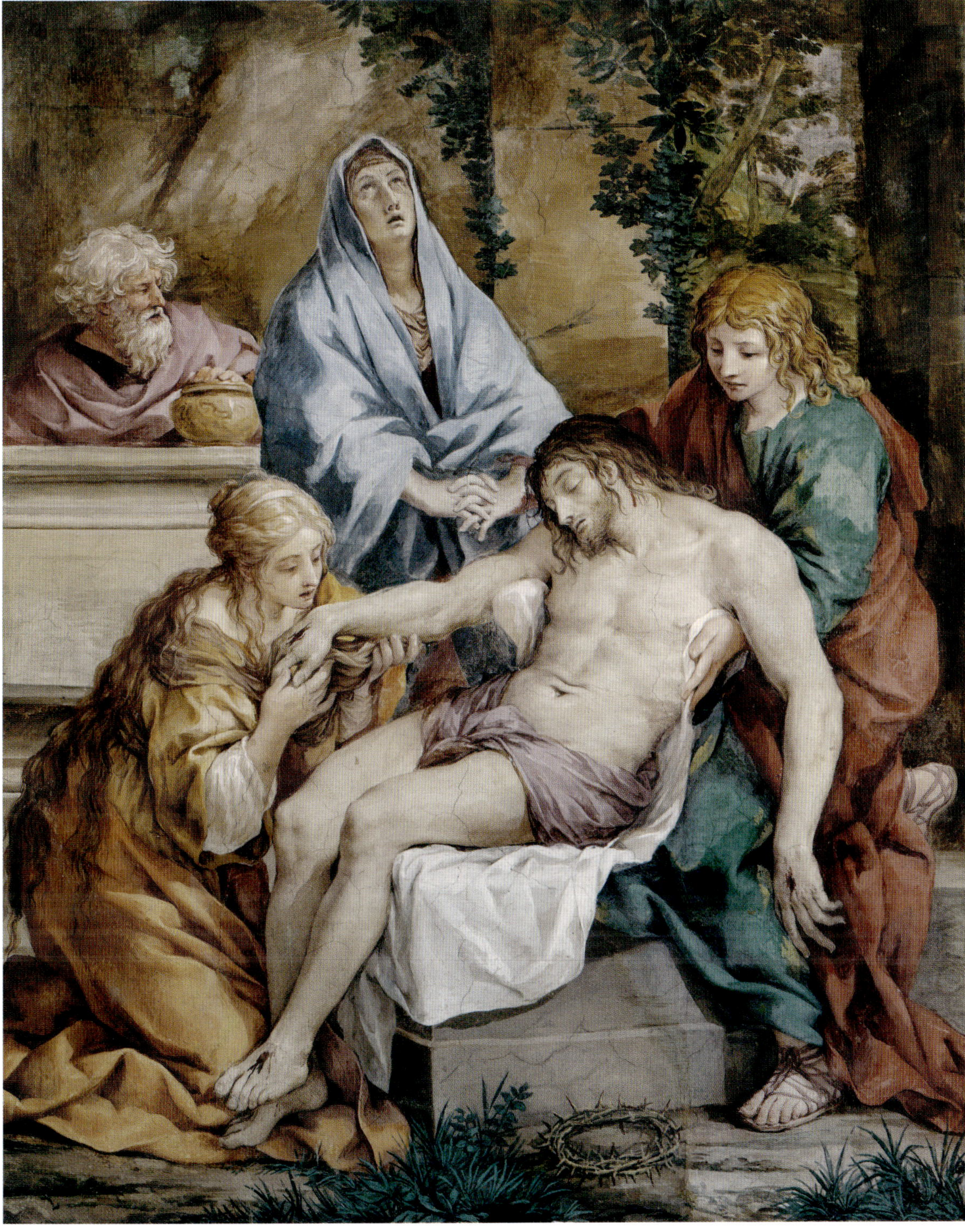

Pietro da Cortona (Pietro Berrettini), 1596–1669
***Pietà*, 1620–1625**
Fresco
Chapel of Urban VIII, Vatican Palaces

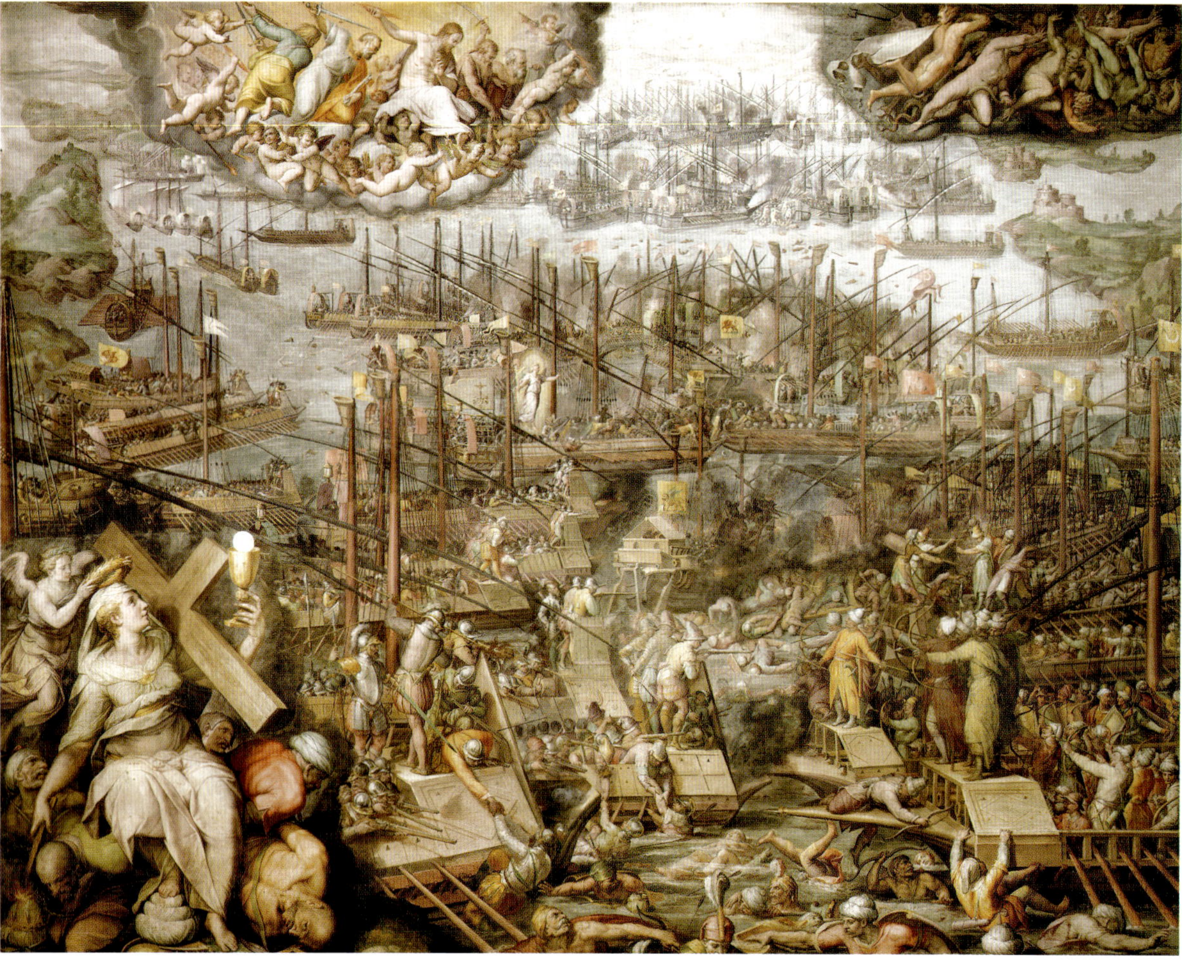

Giorgio Vasari

Battle of Lepanto

The Battle of Lepanto on October 7, 1571, was the most important event to occur in foreign affairs during the pontificate of Pius V (1504–1572, reigned from 1566), who commissioned this fresco. On that day the Holy League, an alliance of Mediterranean Catholic powers under the leadership of the pope, won a victory over the superior forces of the Turkish fleet off the Gulf of Lepanto (Greece) in the Ionian Sea and as a result was able to break the supremacy of the Ottomans in the eastern Mediterranean. The Florentine painter Giorgio Vasari designed and completed this painting in barely two weeks between April 19 and May 2, 1572, working with his usual speed and with such alacrity "that I might have been present myself at the encounter with the Turks." The viewer is presented with a complete panorama of the tumultuous battle as it unfolds under the eyes of the personification of faith and the protection of Christ and the heavenly Host, with a tangle of galleys, Christian soldiers, and Turkish archers shooting at one another, and numerous fighters trying desperately to save themselves from drowning.

Giorgio Vasari, 1511–1574
***Battle of Lepanto*, 1572**
Fresco
Regal Room, Vatican Palaces

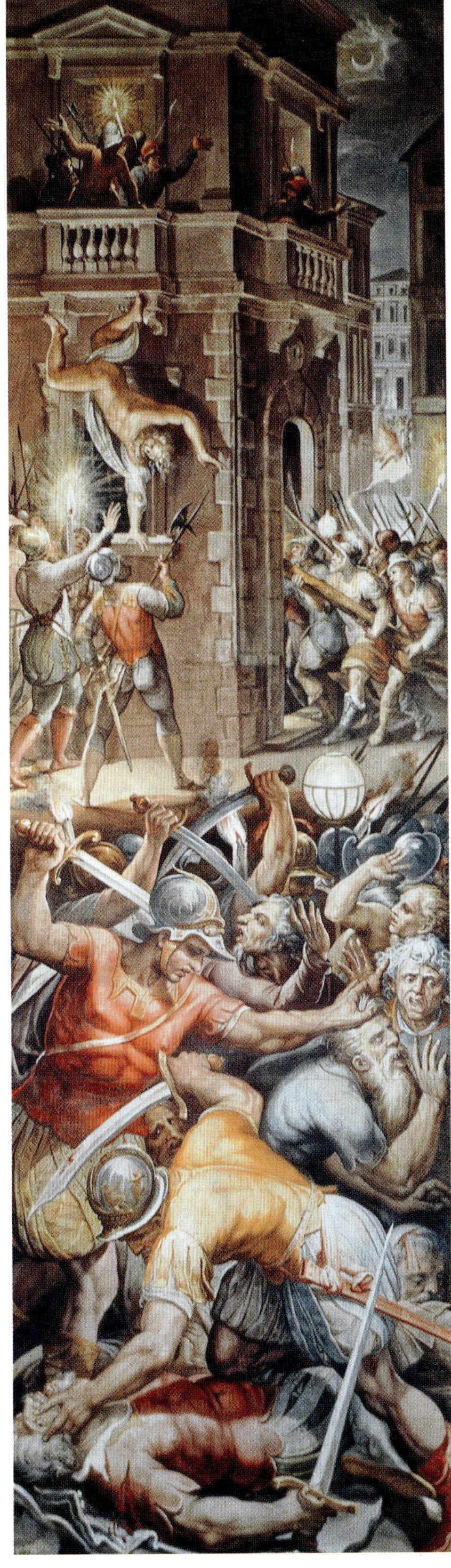

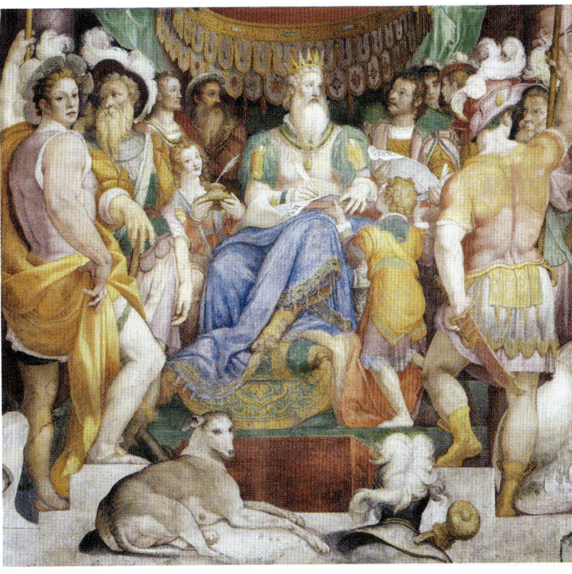

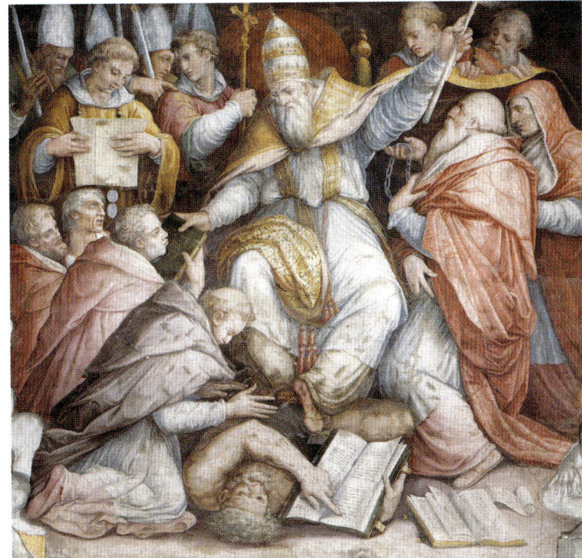

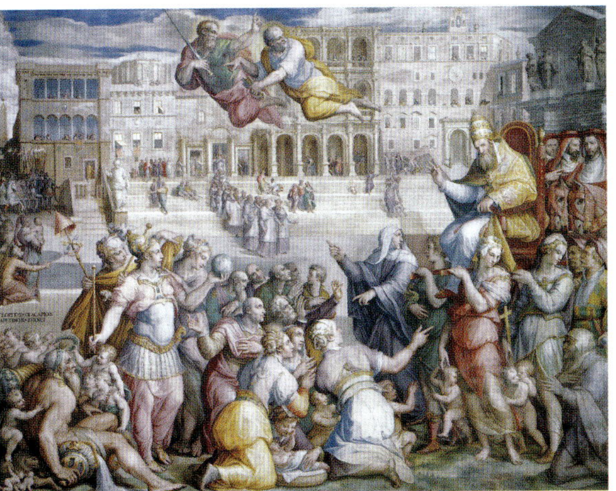

Giorgio Vasari, 1511–1574
***St. Bartholomew's Night: The Massacre of the Huguenots*, 1572–1573**
Fresco
Regal Room, Vatican Palaces

Taddeo Zuccari, 1529–1566
***Charlemagne returns the ancient Patrimony to the Church*, 1564-1565**
Fresco
Regal Room, Vatican Palaces

Giorgio Vasari, 1511–1574
***Gregory IX Excommunicating Frederick II*, 1572–1573**
Fresco
Regal Room, Vatican Palaces

Giorgio Vasari, 1511–1574
***Return of Gregory XI from Avignon*, 1572–1573**
Fresco
Regal Room, Vatican Palaces

SOBIESKI ROOM

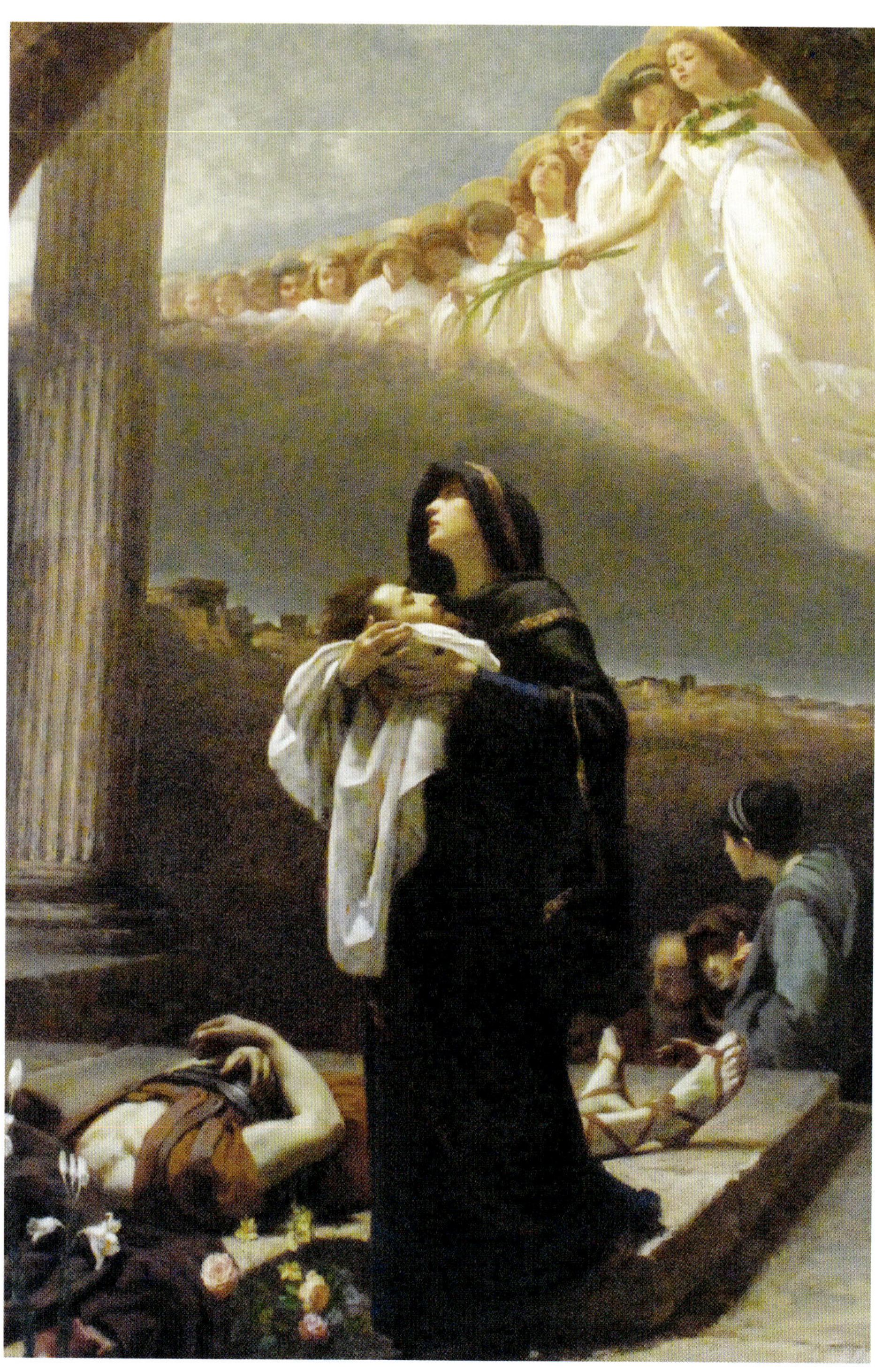

Ponziano Loverini, 1845–1929
***St. Grata with the Relics of St. Alexander*, 1887**
330 x 197 cm; Oil on canvas
Sobieski Room, Vatican Palaces

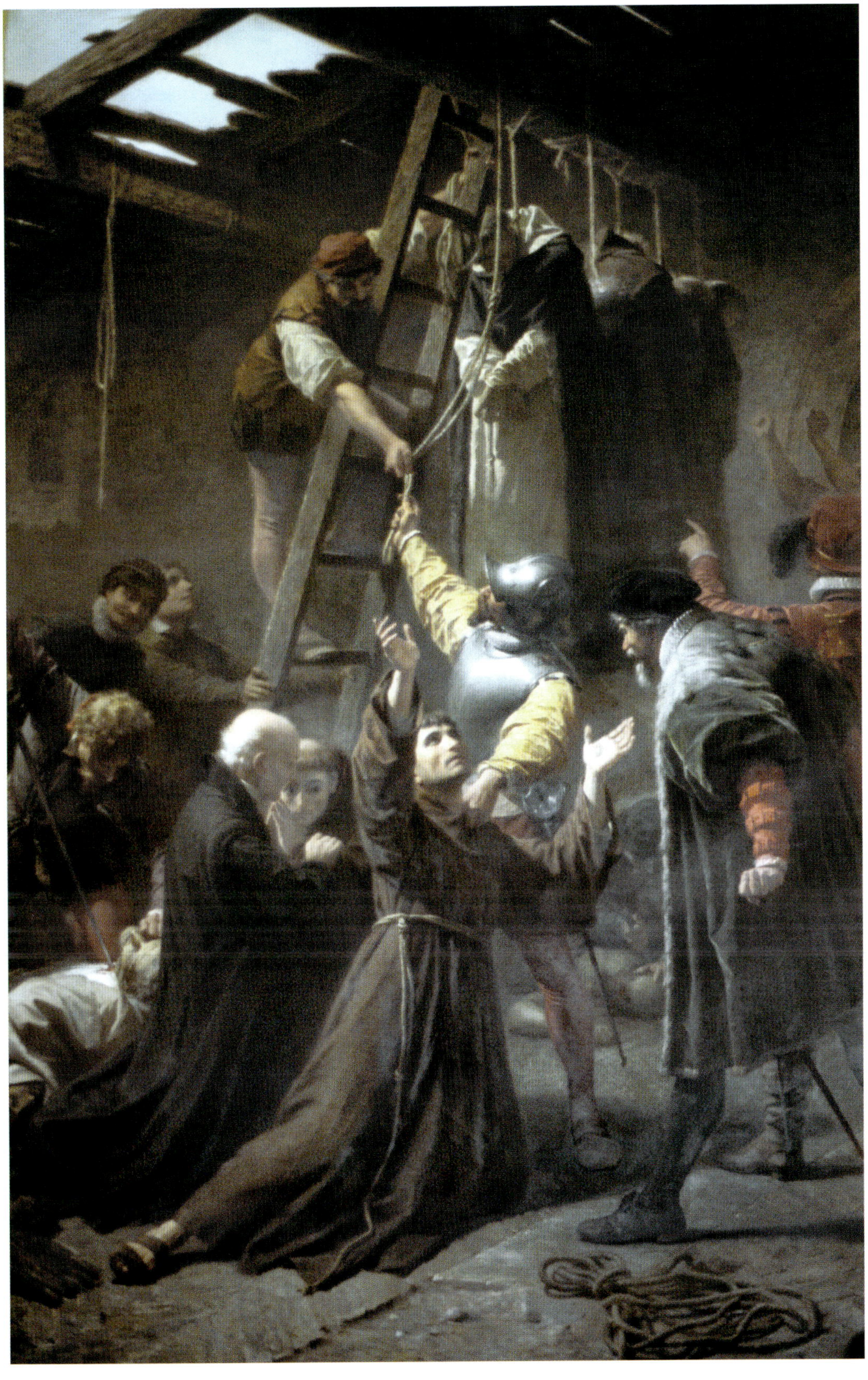

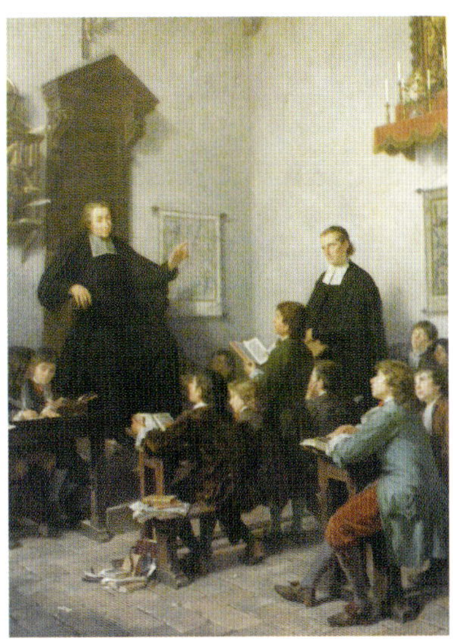

Cesare Fracassini, 1838–1868
***The Martyrs of Gorkum*, 1867**
392 x 289 cm; Oil on canvas
Sobieski Room, Vatican Palaces

Cesare Mariani, 1826–1901
***St. John Baptist de La Salle in School*, ca. 1880**
323 x 210 cm; Oil on canvas
Sobieski Room, Vatican Palaces

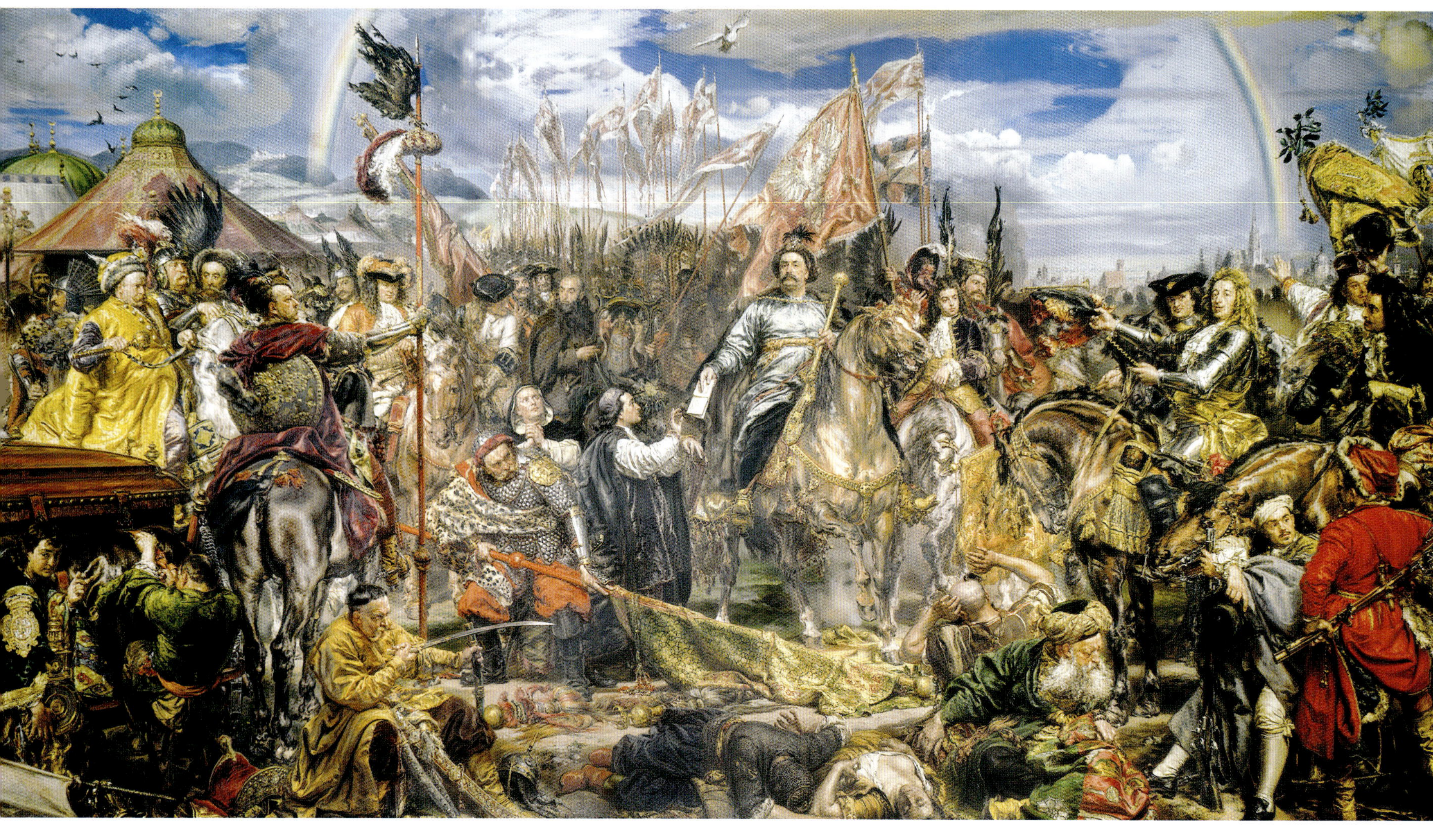

Jan Matejko

Jan Sobieski, King of Poland, defeats the Turks at the Gates of Vienna

This enormous oil painting, which hangs on the north wall of the Sala Sobieski, shows the Polish king Jan III Sobieski (1629–1696) after his victory against the Turks in the Battle of Vienna in 1683. King Sobieski is depicted in the middle of the picture as the resplendent victor on a fiery chestnut horse, surrounded by his own and allied troops. At the precise center, however, is a gleaming white document being handed by the king to a messenger. It is a missive to Innocent XI in which Sobieski informs the pope of the outcome of the battle. This was a victory of immense importance to western Christendom, representing its liberation from the Turkish threat that had been ever-present since the fifteenth century. This was Polish artist Jan Matejko's largest painting, and he presents the victory as a sign from God, as at the end of the flood, which is alluded to by the rainbow and the dove hovering above King Sobieski's head. With the gift of the painting, which he completed in 1883 to mark the two-hundredth anniversary of the victory, Matejko made it an ambassador of the Polish people and a reminder of the important role Poland played in the history of Christianity.

Jan Matejko, 1838–1893
***Jan Sobieski, King of Poland, Defeats the Turks at the Gates of Vienna*, ca. 1883**
Oil on canvas
Sobieski Room, Vatican Palaces

IMMACULATE CONCEPTION ROOM

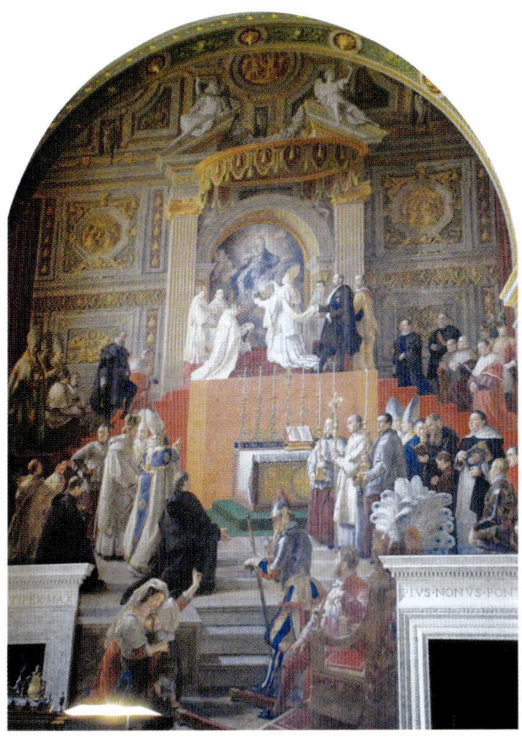

Francesco Podesti, 1800–1895
***The Crowning of Mary*, 1854**
Fresco
Immaculate Conception Room, Vatican Palaces

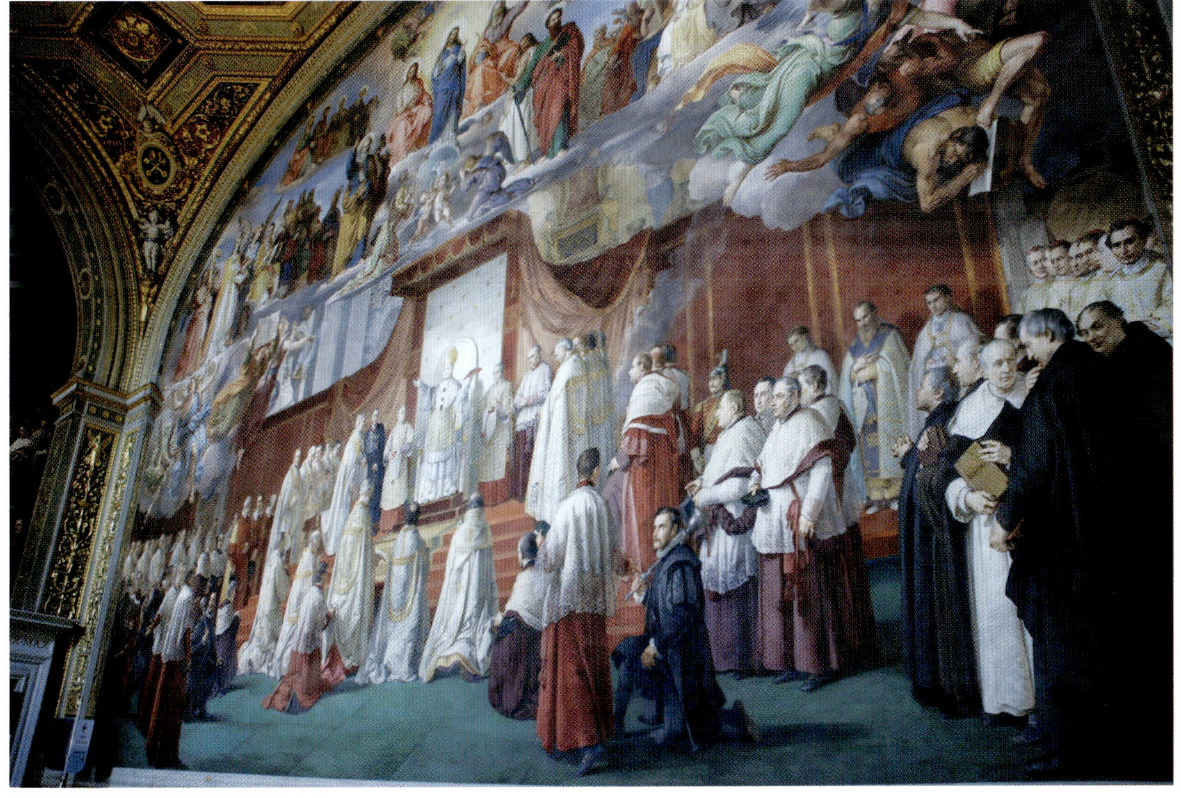

Francesco Podesti, 1800–1895
***Proclamation of the Dogma of the Immaculate Conception*, 1859-1861**
Fresco
Immaculate Conception Room, Vatican Palaces

Francesco Podesti, 1800–1895
***View of Ceiling*, 1854**
Fresco
Immaculate Conception Room, Vatican Palaces

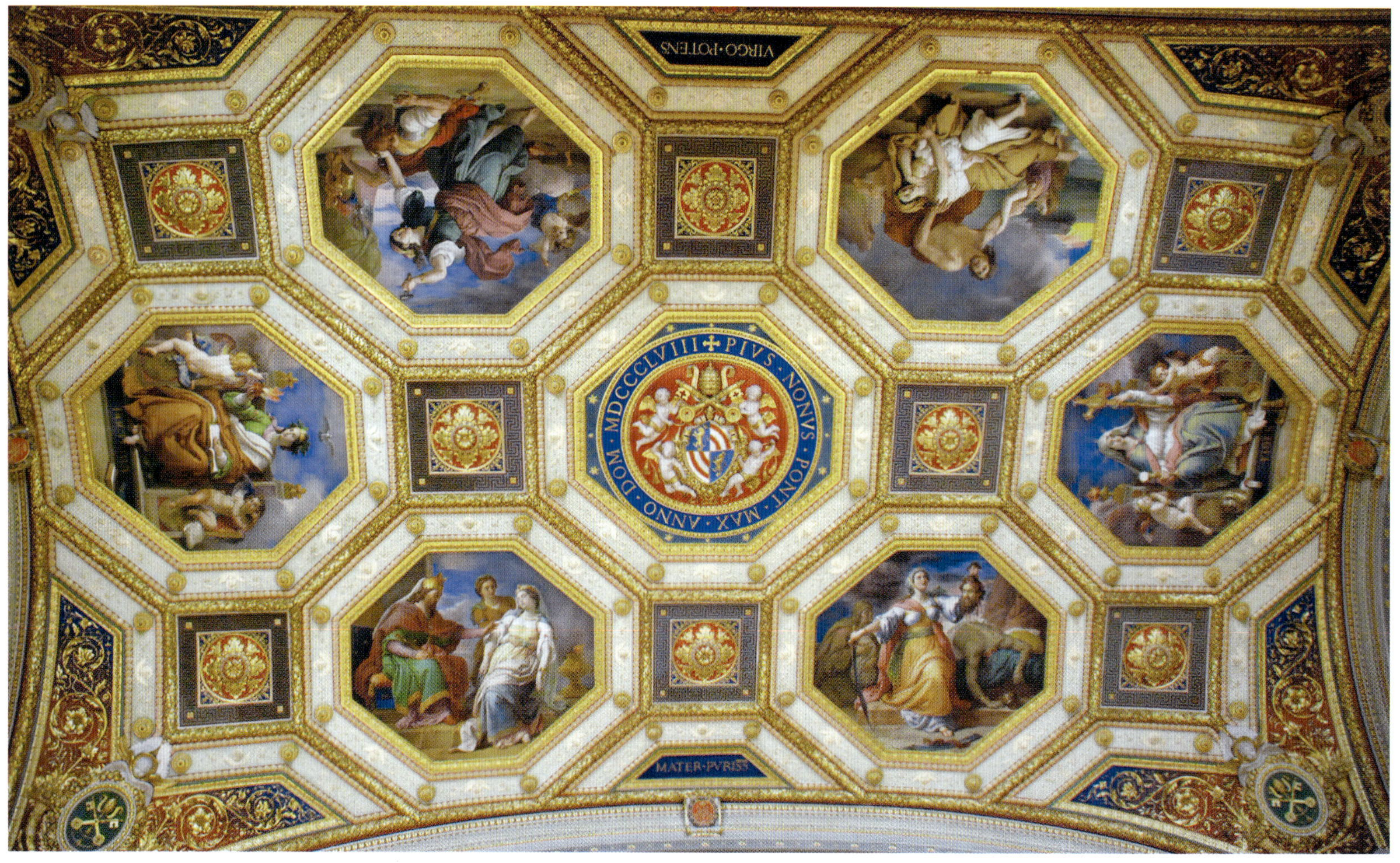

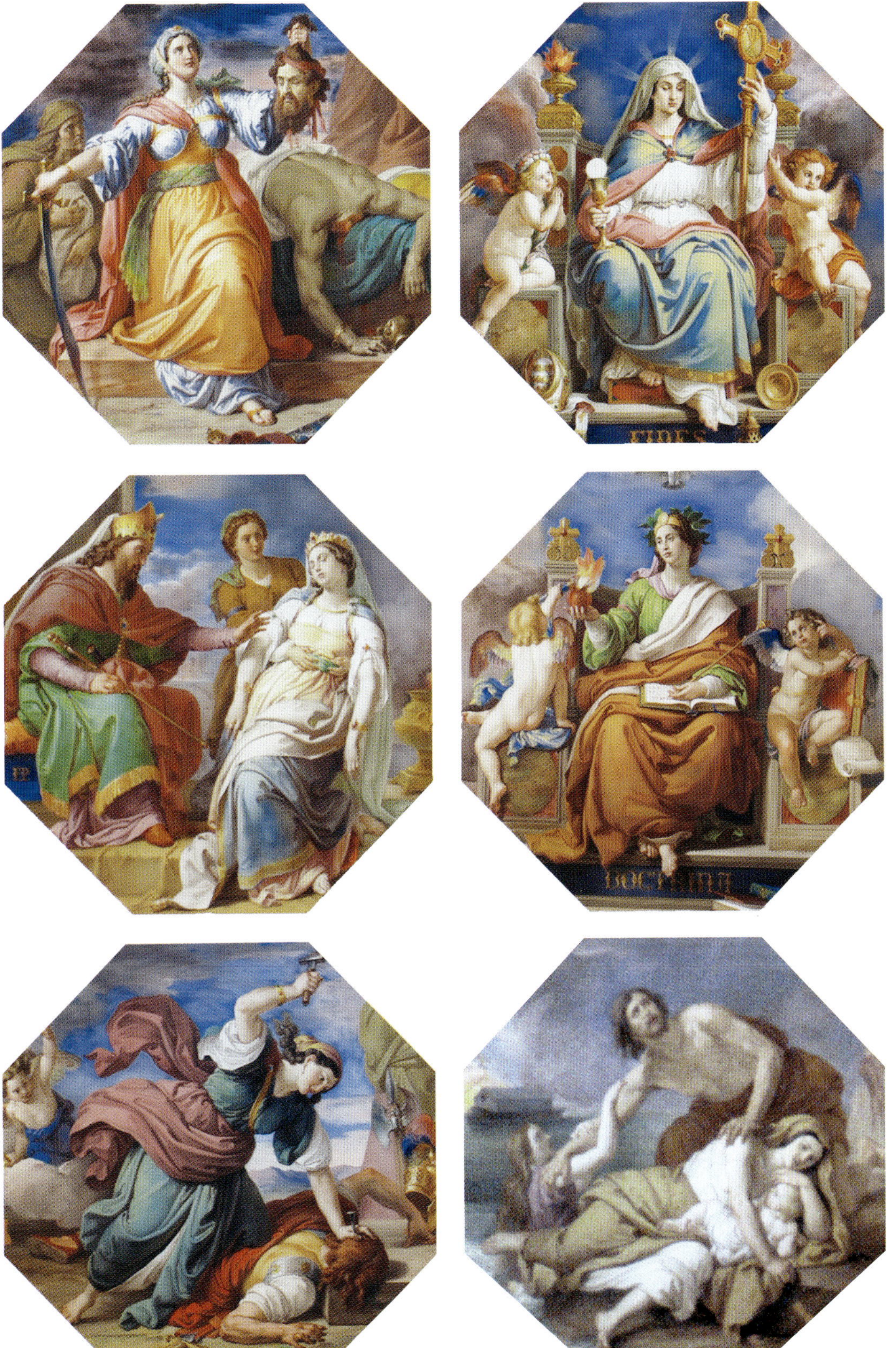

Francesco Podesti, 1800–1895
Judith with the Head of Holofernes, Ceiling, 1854
Fresco
Immaculate Conception Room, Vatican Palaces

Francesco Podesti, 1800–1895
Allegory of Faith, Ceiling, 1854
Fresco
Immaculate Conception Room, Vatican Palaces

Francesco Podesti, 1800–1895
Esther Faints in Front of King Ahasver, Ceiling, 1854
Fresco
Immaculate Conception Room, Vatican Palaces

Francesco Podesti, 1800–1895
Allegory of Theology, Ceiling, 1854
Fresco
Immaculate Conception Room, Vatican Palaces

Francesco Podesti, 1800–1895
Jael Slays Sisera, Ceiling, 1854
Fresco
Immaculate Conception Room, Vatican Palaces

Francesco Podesti, 1800–1895
The Survivors with Noah's Ark in the Background, Ceiling, 1854
Fresco
Immaculate Conception Room, Vatican Palaces

ROOM OF THE MUSES

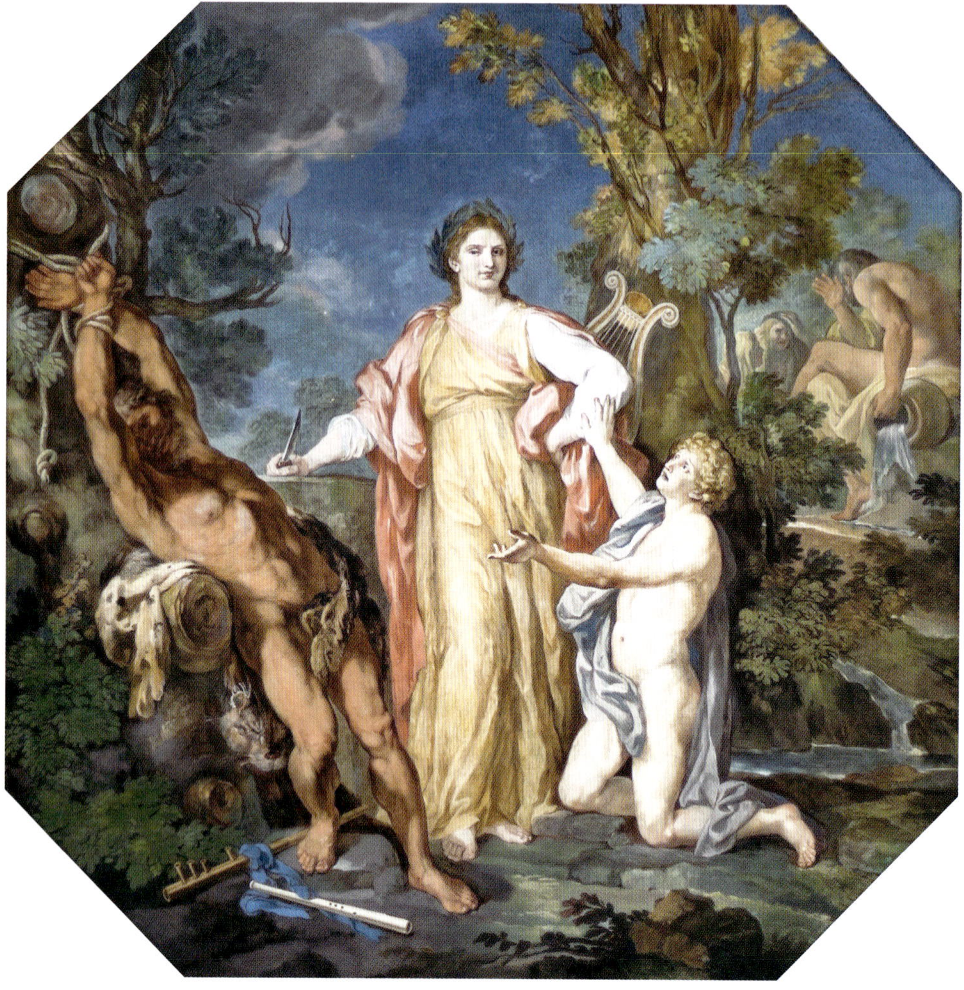

Tommaso Conca

Apollo and Marsyas (ceiling)

The Sala delle Muse, designed to accommodate a series of nine statues of the Muses and a figure of Apollo, is one of the main rooms of the Museo Pio-Clementino, founded by Clement XIV (1705-1774, reigned from 1769) and concluded by Pius VI (1717–1799, reigned from 1775). The octagonal room is surmounted by a vault whose painted illusionistic architecture suggests a cupola open to heaven. It was painted by Tommaso Conca, who trained initially with his famous uncle Sebastiano Conca (1680–1764) in the late Baroque style before turning to classicism. Conca's ceiling of the Sala delle Muse is in the latter style, in keeping with the artworks on display in the room. The central field tells the story of Apollo and Marsyas, who challenges the god of poetry to a musical duel. Though Marsyas plays the double flute given to him by Athena, the Muses adjudge Apollo, with his song and lyre accompaniment, the winner. Thereupon Apollo avenges himself by having Marsyas flayed alive. According to the myth, the river Marsyas, symbolized by the river god in the background, sprang from his spilled blood.

Tommaso Conca, 1734–1822
***Apollo and Marsyas (ceiling)*, 1785–1787**
Fresco
Room of the Muses

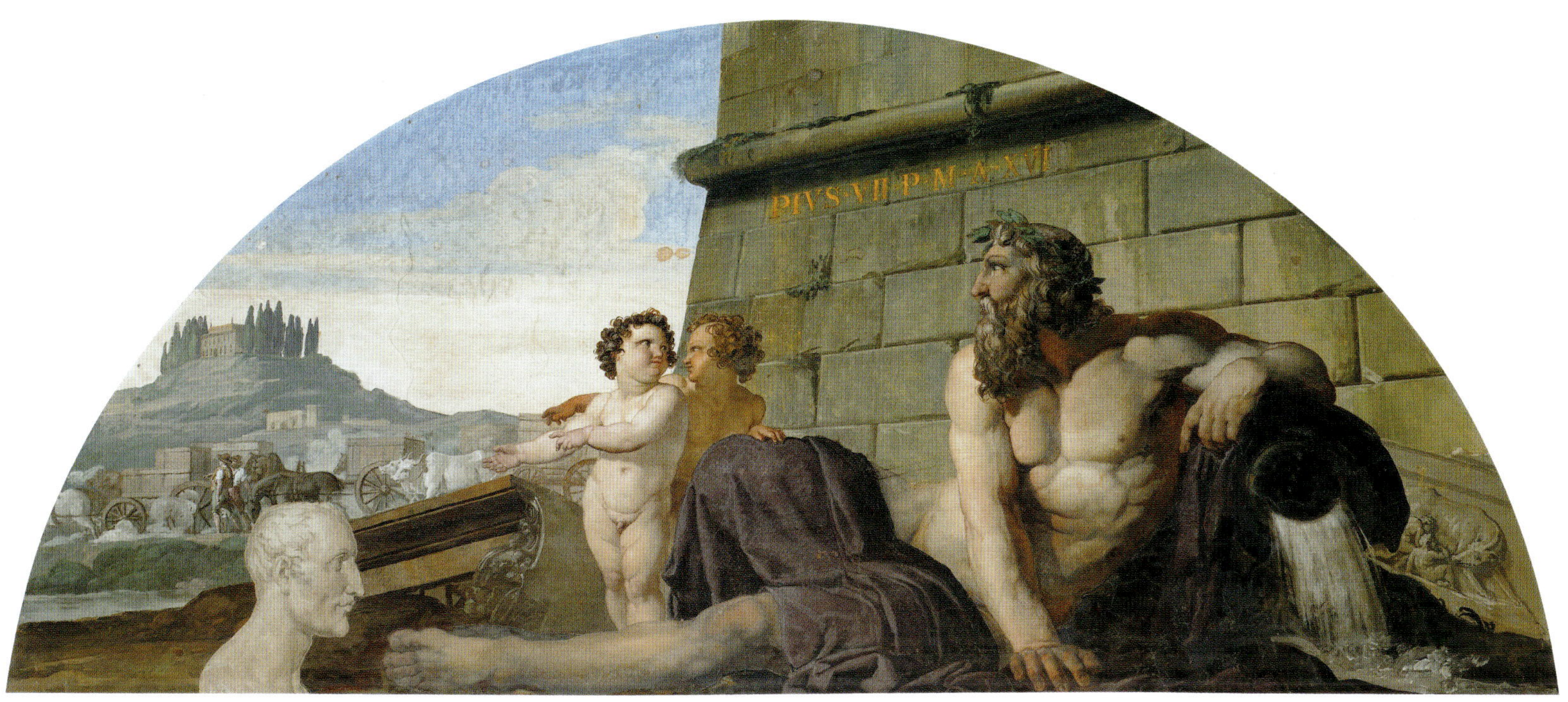

Francesco Hayez

The Return of the Art Works to Rome

One of the darkest events in the history of the Vatican collections was the plundering of art by Napoleon following his occupation of the Vatican in 1797. Over five hundred works, including such treasures as the Laocoön, the Apollo Belvedere, and Raphael's Pala Oddi and Transfiguration, were taken to Paris by the French art commissars in order to enrich the collection of the Louvre. Following the Vienna Congress of 1815, which resolved to have the works of art restored, the sculptor Antonio Canova traveled to France at the behest of Pius VII (1742–1823, reigned from 1800) to supervise the return of the works, which left Paris on October 25, 1815. Hayez completed the lunette in spring 1816, shortly after the arrival of the works in Rome, which is symbolized by the mighty personification of the Tiber before the city gates in the foreground. Two putti point to the long train of horse- and ox-drawn carts laden with crates, making its way in the background through the Roman Campagna. These crates, however, contained only 249 of the 506 plundered works. Of the others, 248 remained in France and nine were claimed to have been lost.

Francesco Hayez, 1791–1882
***The Return of the Art Works to Rome*, 1820**
Fresco
Chiaramonti Museum

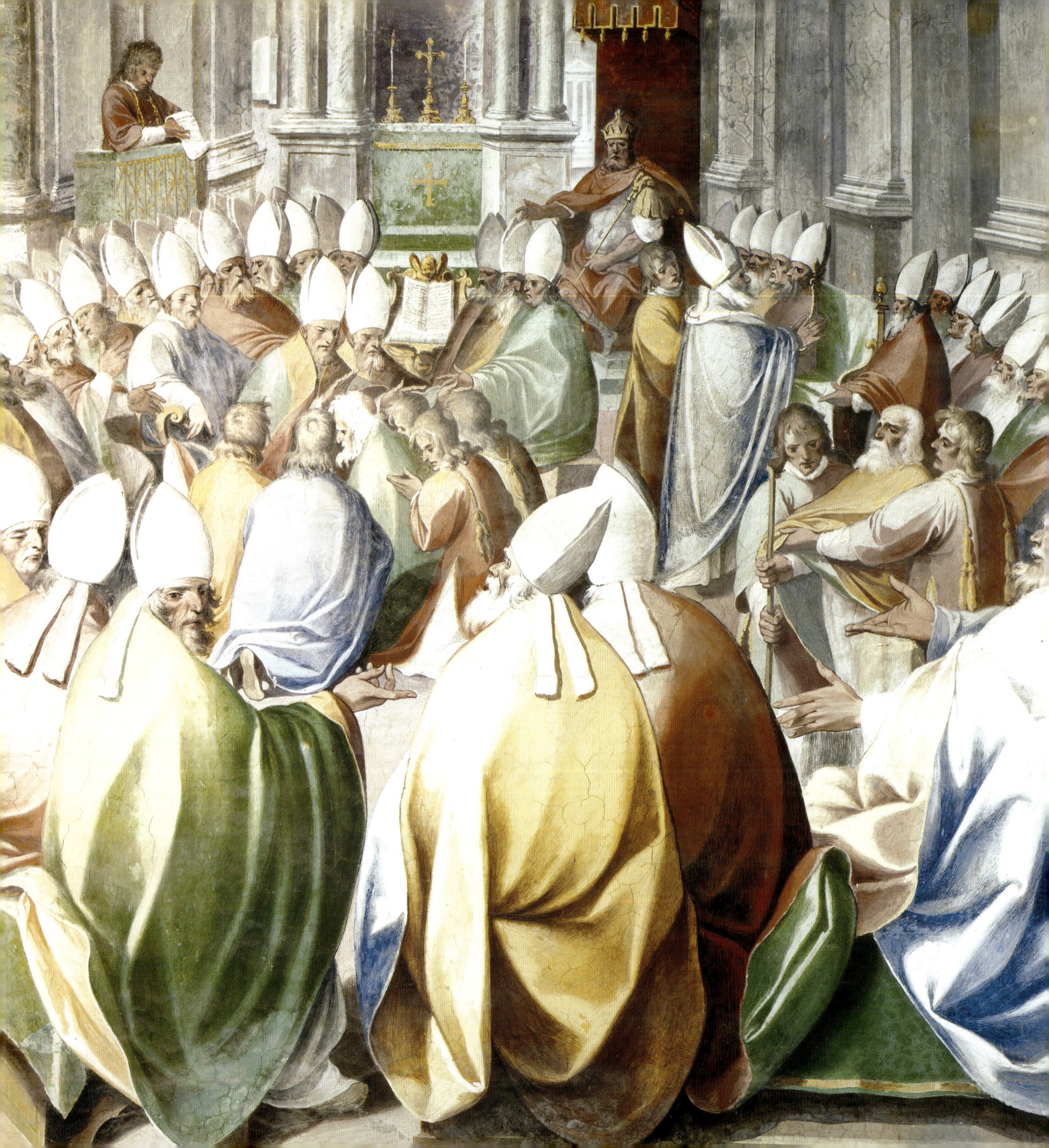

VATICAN LIBRARY: FRESCOES

The papal library is one of the Vatican's oldest institutions and its collections are among the most venerable in the Vatican Museums. Until the invention of letterpress printing in the middle of the fifteenth century, the library consisted exclusively of manuscripts, mainly editions of the Bible, liturgical books, theological writings, and legal texts. Today these manuscripts are some of the most valuable items in the Vatican Library.

The present Biblioteca Apostolica Vaticana was founded on June 15, 1475. On this day Sixtus IV (1414–1484, reigned from 1471) issued the papal bull "Ad decorem militantis Ecclesiae" ("For the adornment of the militant Church"), with which he firmly established the library as an institution. Sixtus specified the library's most important task as being the preservation and dissemination of knowledge and allocated three rooms to it: two publicly accessible reading rooms containing Latin and Greek manuscripts and a private library (the biblioteca secreta). The humanist Bartolomeo Platina was appointed as the first librarian. The act of foundation is recorded in the famous fresco by Melozzo da Forlì, which once graced the library itself but is today housed in the Pinacoteca Vaticana.

In order to ensure public access, the library was established on the ground floor of the palace wing converted by Sixtus IV's predecessor Nicholas V (1397–1455, reigned from 1447) into the Cortile del Belvedere, with an entrance on the Cortile del Pappagallo. Sixtus IV had the rooms decorated by some of the best painters of the day. In addition to Melozzo da Forlì, contributions were also made by Domenico Fontana and Davide Ghirlandaio, who endowed the lunettes of the Biblioteca Latina with depictions of classical and early Christian scholars and Fathers of the Church in an opulent Renaissance-style decorative setting.

In view of the ever-expanding collection of books, Sixtus V (1521–1590, reigned from 1585) decided to create new rooms for the library. Under the direction of the papal architect Domenico Fontana (1543–1607), work started on the new library wing, which still houses the Apostolic Vatican Library, in 1587. The narrow rooms extend along the upper floor of the Cortile del Belvedere and terminate in a smaller courtyard known as the Cortile della Biblioteca. The heart of the library is the Salone Sistino, which was added as a transverse wing on the north side of the Cortile del Belvedere. This room, which measures 70 meters long by 15 meters wide, is divided into two aisles by a row of pillars. Every surface is decorated by frescoes in the late Renaissance style and the Salone Sistino is regarded as one of the world's most beautiful library spaces. With over 180,000 manuscripts and archive items, some 1,600,000 printed books, over 8,600 incunabula, more than 300,000 coins and medals, around 150,000 prints, and over 150,000 photographs, the Apostolic Vatican Library is today one of the largest libraries in the world.

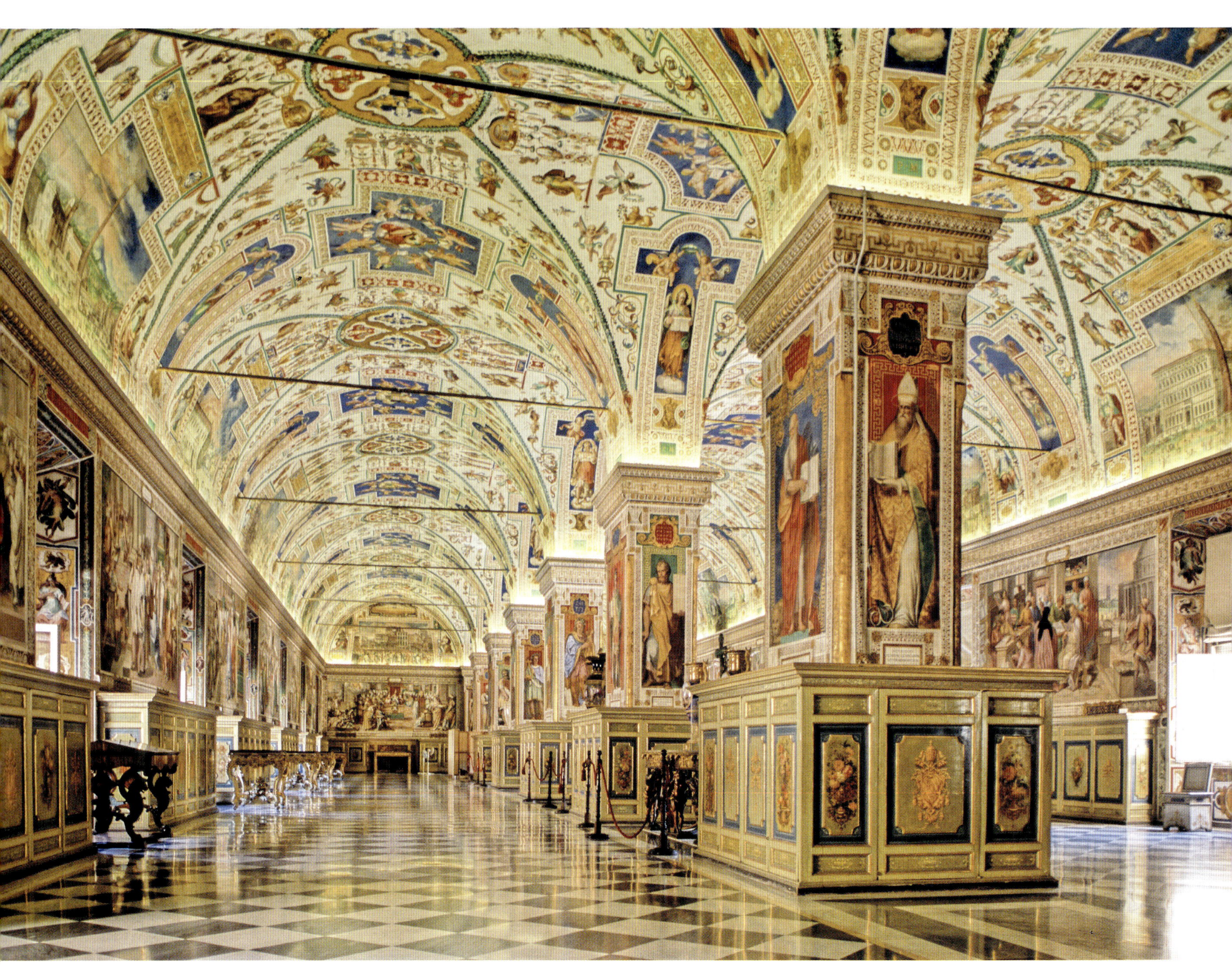

Cesare Nebbia, Giovanni Guerra and Workshop

Sistine Hall (Salone Sistino)

The Salone Sistino is the main room of the Biblioteca Apostolica Vaticana. Construction began in 1587 under the supervision of the papal architect Domenico Fontana, and the frescoes were completed by Cesare Nebbia, Giovanni Guerra, and their workshops between 1588 and 1590. The artists painted the work in record time before the death of their patron, Sixtus V, in 1590. A central row of pillars divides the 70-meter-long, 15-meter-wide room into two aisles, which, in conjunction with the large windows, give the room its structure. The iconographical program, devised by senior library custodian Federico Rainaldi, is dedicated to the glorification of the library and its history. The large rectangular fields on the window wall looking onto the Cortile del Belvedere display views of famous libraries in antiquity. On the opposite window wall are the ecumenical councils that contributed to the interpretation and dissemination of God's word. The lunettes are painted for the most part with views of places and buildings in Rome associated with the urban-planning measures undertaken by Sixtus V. The sides of the rectangular pillars feature biblical characters, antique scholars, and theologians renowned as the inventors of alphabets. The ceiling, with its elaborate decoration in the grotesque style, is entirely in keeping with late Renaissance taste.

Cesare Nebbia, 1536–1614; Giovanni Guerra, 1544–1618, and Workshop
***Sistine Hall (Salone Sistino)*, 16th century**
Fresco
Vatican Library: Frescoes

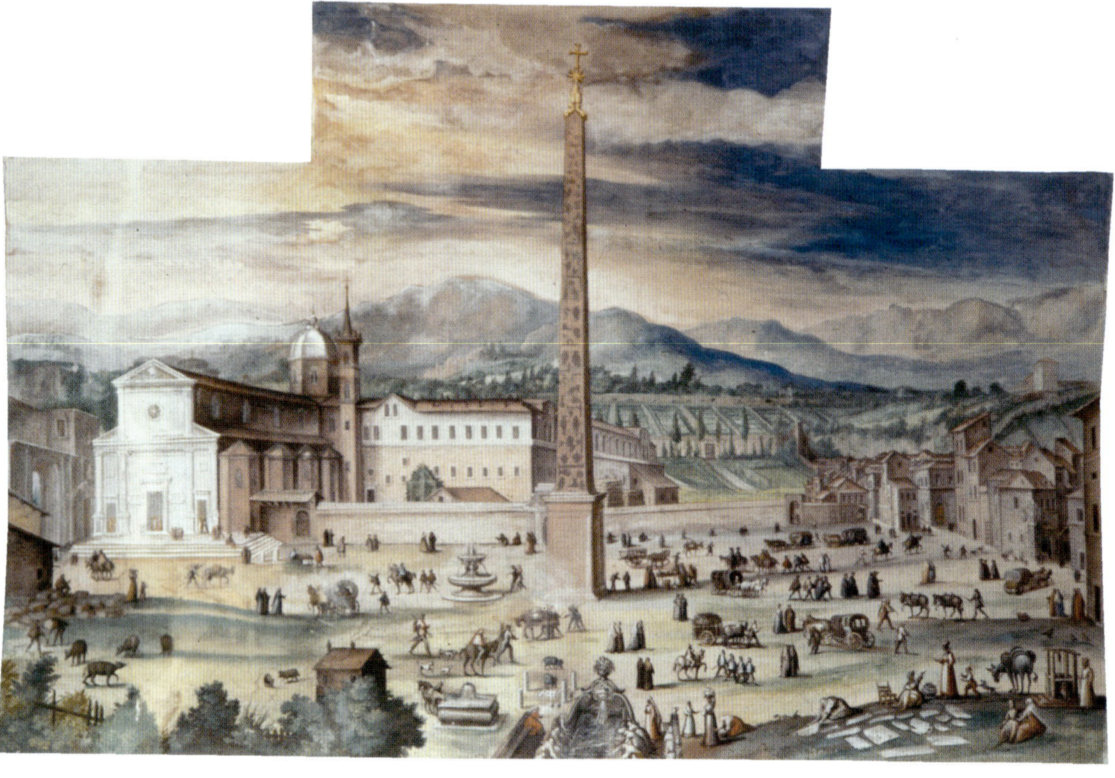

Cesare Nebbia and Workshop

Piazza del Popolo

Sixtus V, who commissioned the Salone Sistino, has gone down in history as one of the keenest builders of all the popes. During his pontificate, which lasted just five years, he also remodeled various squares in Rome and erected obelisks. A particularly prominent example is the Piazza del Popolo, where in 1589 the architect Domenico Fontana raised the Flaminio Obelisk. This fresco, designed by Cesare Nebbia and possibly executed by the Flemish landscape painter Paul Bril, shows a view of the square from the west—the direction of the Vatican. At the precise center of the painting stands the newly erected obelisk, on the left can be seen the façade of the church of Santa Maria del Popolo with the monastery behind, and on the right, between buildings that were pulled down in the nineteenth century, the Via del Corso, Via di Ripetta, and Via Paolina lead out from the square. The silhouette of the Pincian Hill dominates the background. The Piazza del Popolo, which since ancient times had been the entrance to the city for visitors traveling to Rome from the north along Via Flaminia, is shown bustling with people, animals, carriages, and goods, giving a lively impression of contemporary Roman life.

Cesare Nebbia and Workshop, 1536–1614
***Piazza del Popolo*, 16th century**
Fresco
Vatican Library: Frescoes

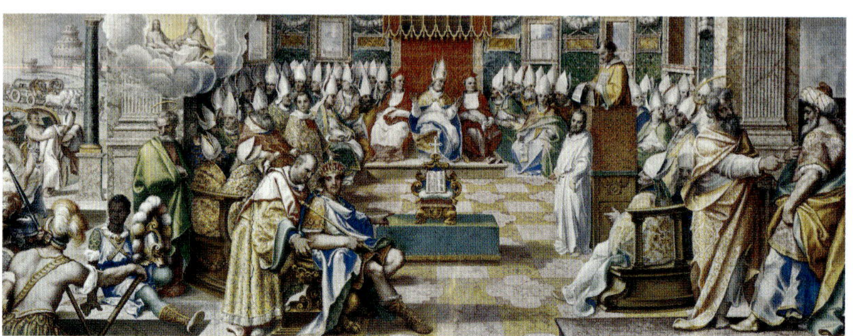

Cesare Nebbia, 1536–1614
***Council of Nicaea*, 16th century**
Fresco
Vatican Library: Frescoes

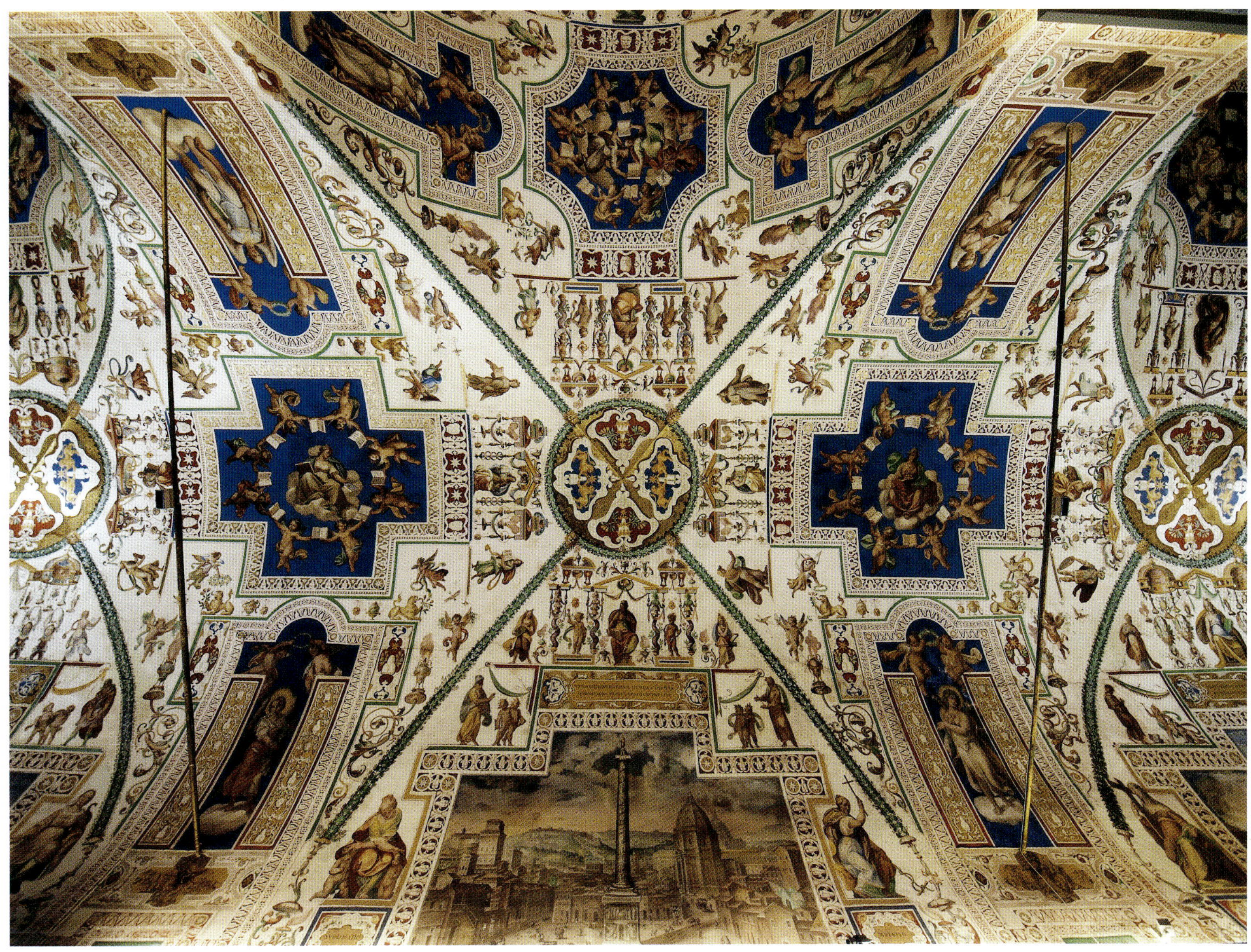

Cesare Nebbia, Giovanni Guerra, and Workshop

Sistine Hall: Ceiling detail

The almost overwhelming visual impact of the Salone Sistino is due in large part to its ceiling frescoes, designed by Cesare Nebbia and Giovanni Guerra and executed in collaboration with numerous assistants in just two years. Behind the multiplicity of forms and figures—bewildering at first glance—is a carefully devised plan that takes its cue from the architecture of the room and transforms the ceiling into a colorful vault of heaven. Images of the saints occupy the blue vertical rectangular fields located precisely above the central pillars with their representations of the inventors of various alphabets. Along the window sides, the wall paintings are surmounted by depictions of libraries and ecumenical councils. Between the images of the saints are Greek crosses, again on blue grounds, filled with rings of angels. The same cross motif can also be found at the center of each vault, framing the painted keystone. Abundant grotesque-style ornament, reminiscent of antique wall paintings, plays over the spaces between the figure fields and the lunette frescoes depicting Roman monuments (prominent among them is Trajan's Column), entirely in keeping with the spirit of the Renaissance.

Cesare Nebbia, 1536–1614; Giovanni Guerra, 1544–1618, and Workshop
***Sistine Hall: Ceiling detail*, 16th century**
Fresco
Vatican Library: Frescoes

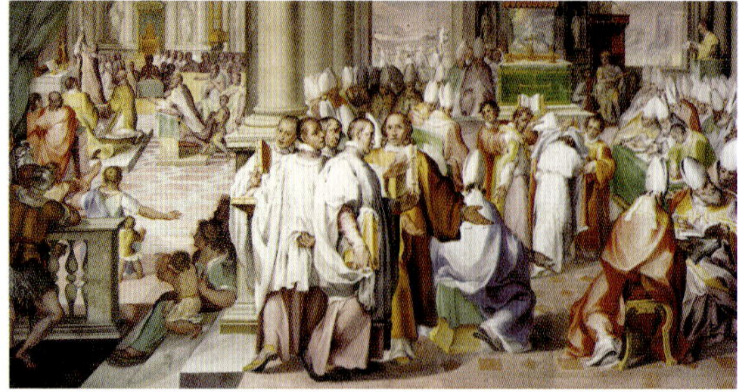
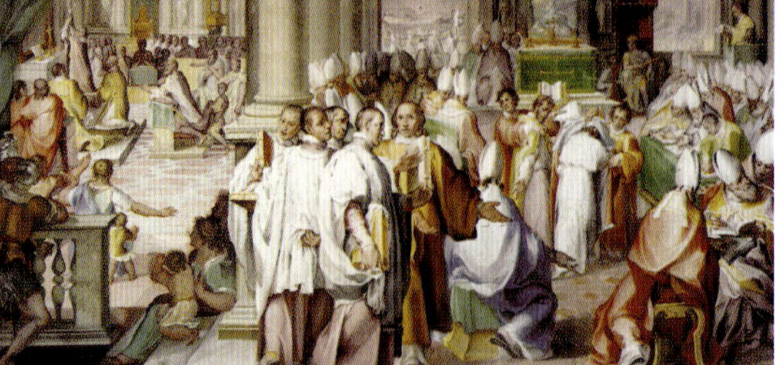
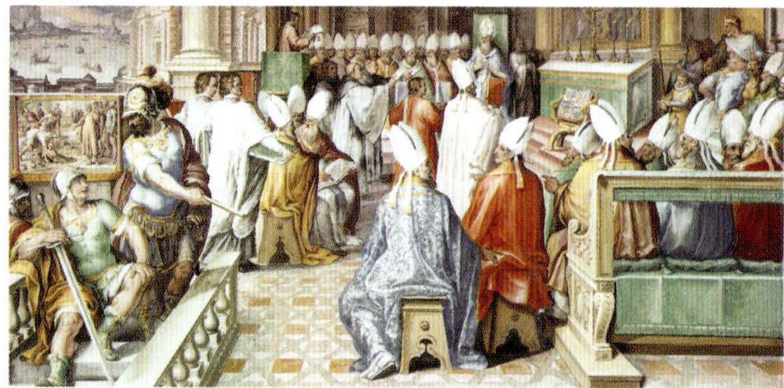
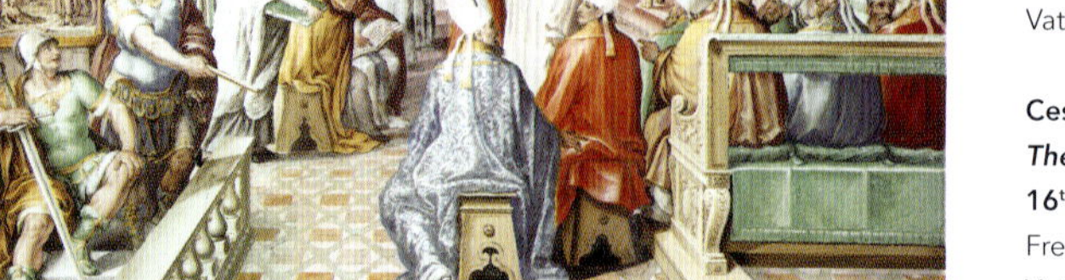
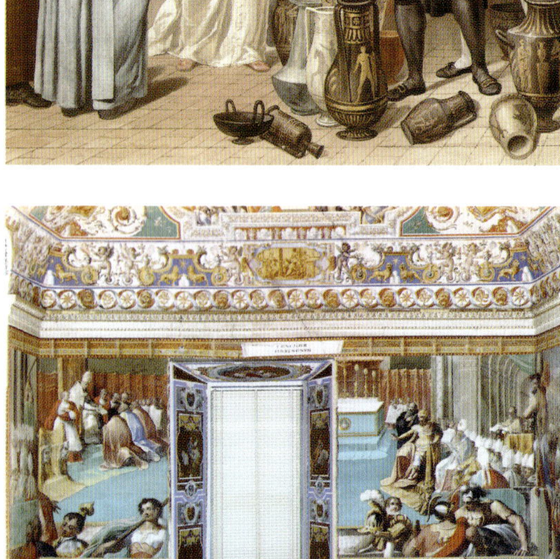
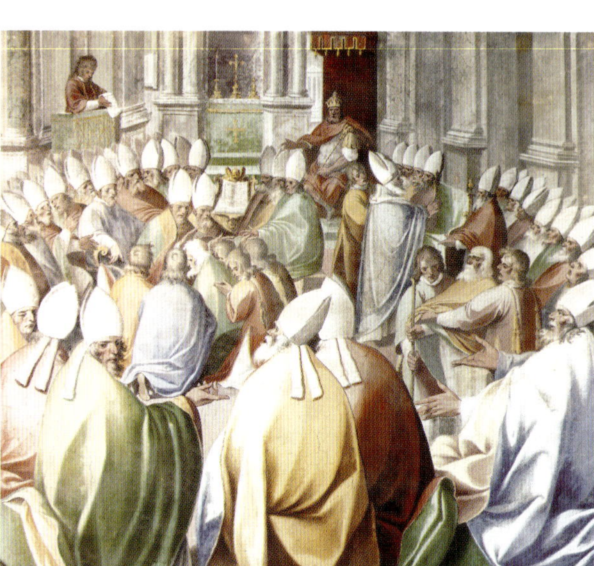
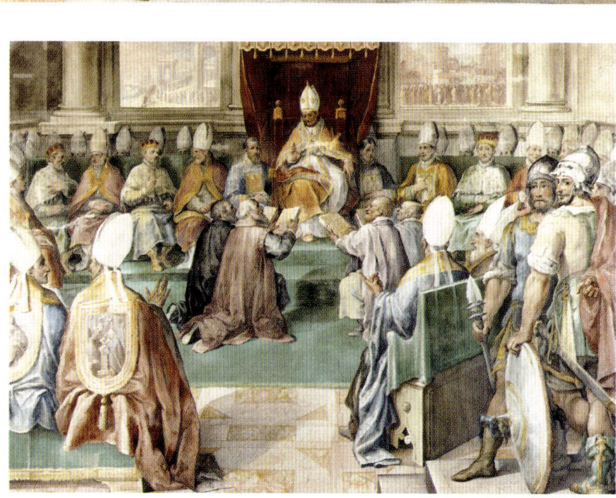

Cesare Nebbia, 1536–1614
***The Third Council of Constantinople (680–681AD)*, 16th century**
Fresco
Vatican Library: Frescoes

Cesare Nebbia, 1536–1614
***The Second Council of Constantinople (553AD)*, 16th century**
Fresco
Vatican Library: Frescoes

Domenico de Angelis, 1736–1804
***Pius VII collects Etruscan Vases in the Library*, 18th century**
Fresco
Vatican Library: Frescoes

Cesare Nebbia, 1536–1614
***The Fourth Council of Constantinople (869–870AD)*, 16th century**
Fresco
Vatican Library: Frescoes

Cesare Nebbia, 1536–1614
***The Council of Florence (1438–1445AD)*, 16th century**
Fresco
Vatican Library: Frescoes

Cesare Nebbia, 1536–1614
***The Council of Vienne (1311–1312AD)*, 16th century**
Fresco
Vatican Library: Frescoes

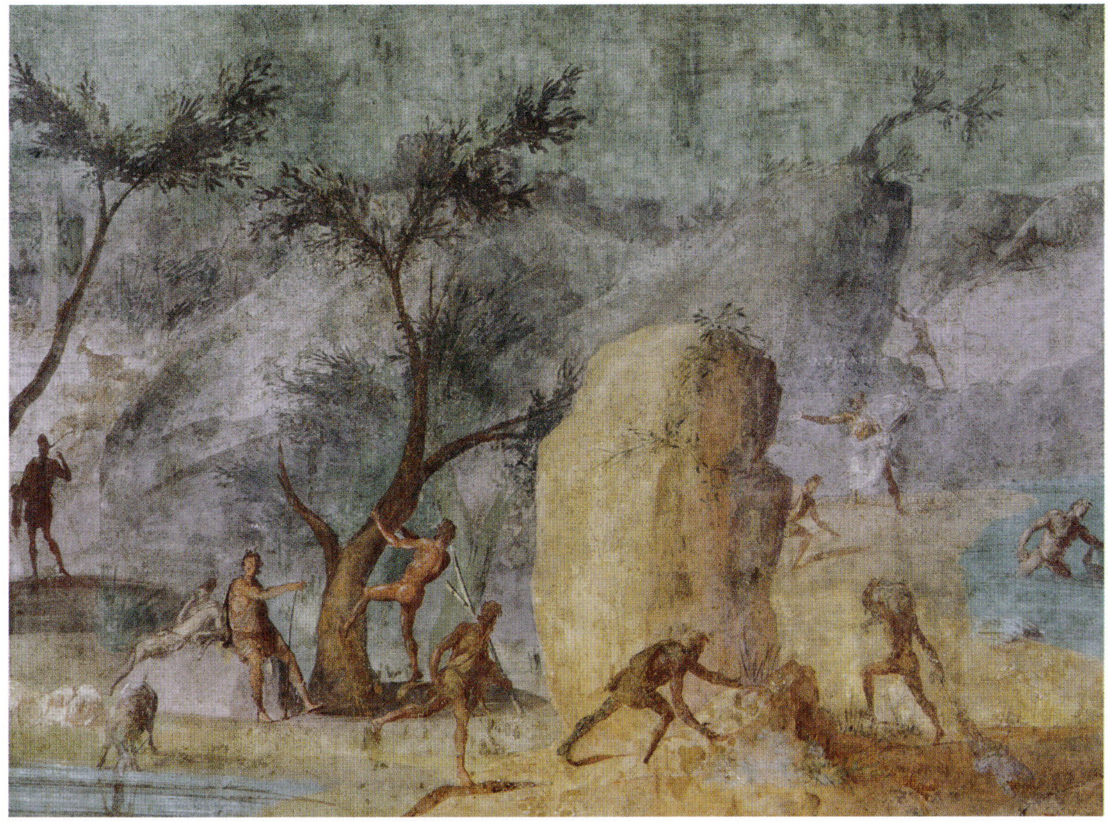

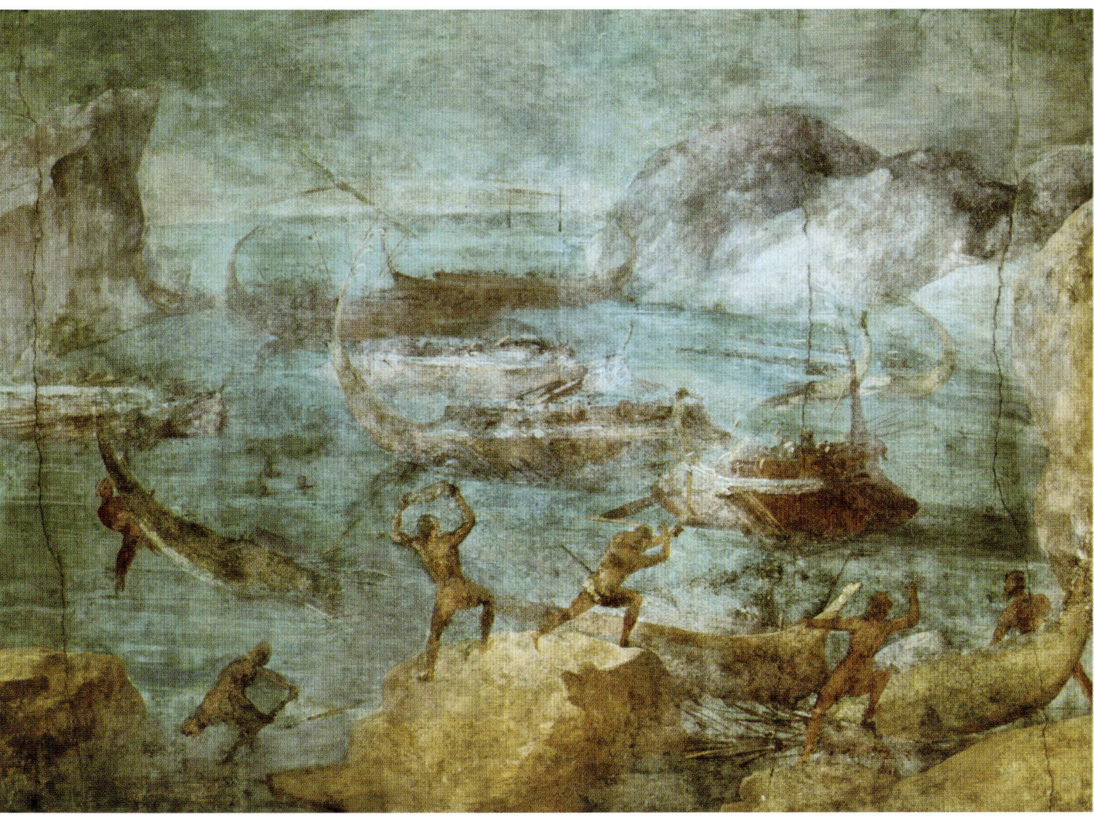

Roman Artist, 1st century BC
***The Laestrygonians and Ulysses*, 1st century BC**
Fresco
Vatican Library: Frescoes

Roman Artist, 1st century BC
***The Laestrygonians at the Fleet of Odysseus*, 1st century BC**
Fresco
Vatican Library: Frescoes

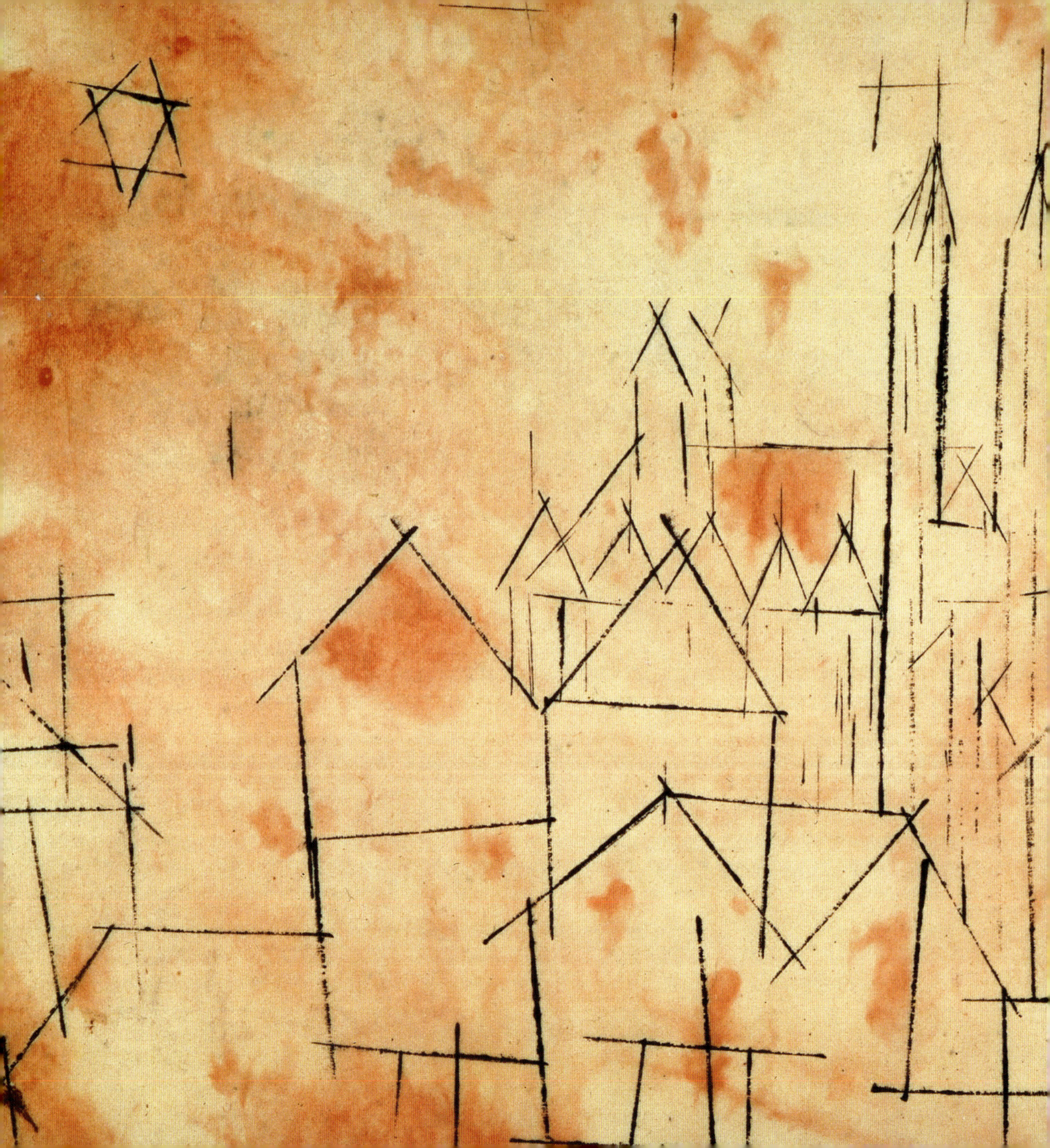

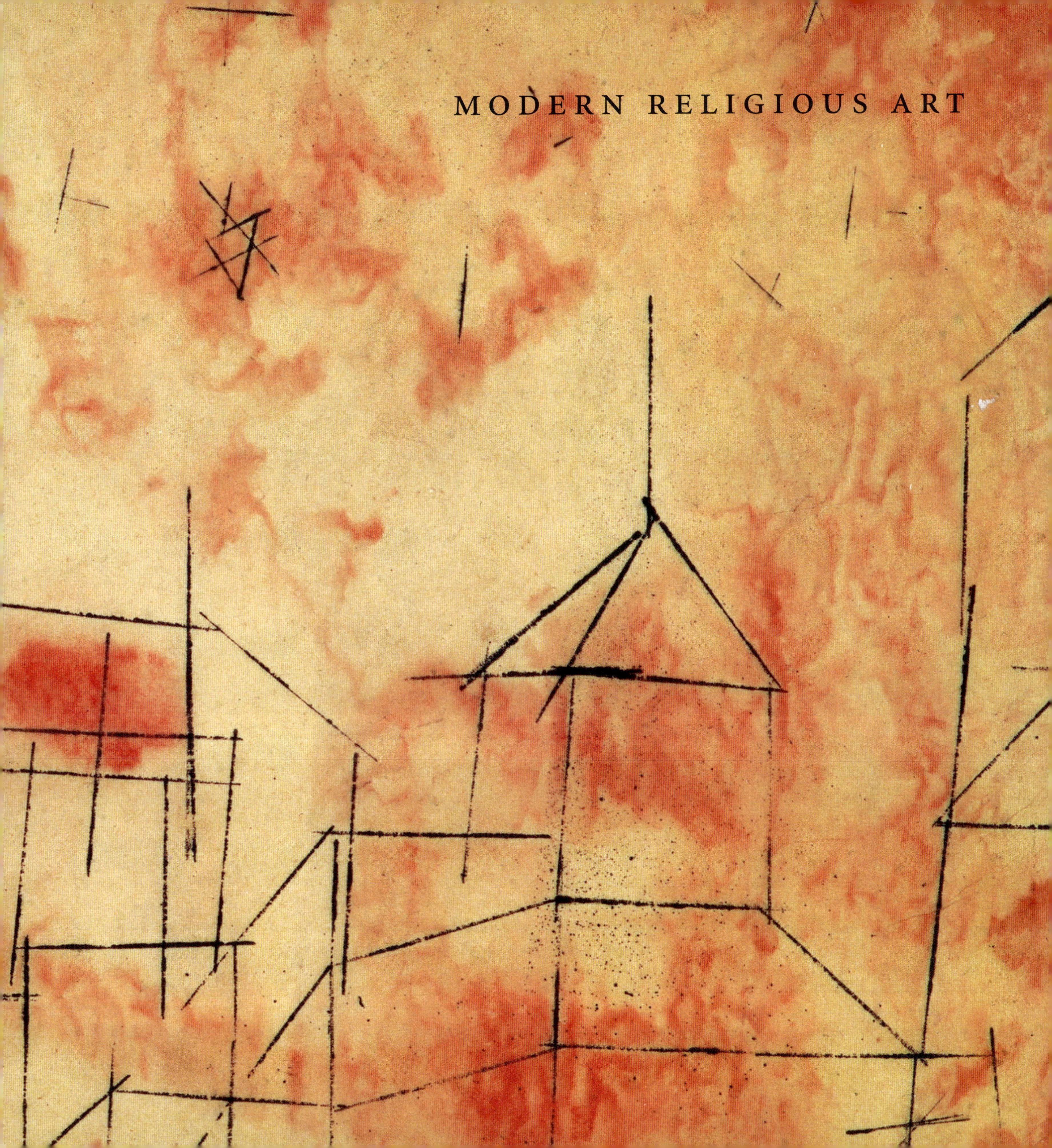
MODERN RELIGIOUS ART

MODERN RELIGIOUS ART

The youngest of the Vatican's museums, the Collection of Modern Religious Art was inaugurated in 1973 by Pope Paul VI (1897–1978, reigned from 1963) with the intention of giving modern art an appropriate forum within the Vatican's historical rooms and collections. Paul VI commissioned numerous works of art—from painters, sculptors, and architects—for the refashioning of different areas of the Vatican Palace and St. Peter's Basilica, and he saw modern art as an expression of piety worthy of promotion and in harmony with the resolutions of the Second Vatican Council (1962–1965). With the opening of the collection on June 23, 1973, he realized his underlying pastoral concept of modern art as "testifying directly to a prodigious capacity to express not merely the human, but the religious and the Christian as well." His successor, John Paul II (1920–2005, reigned from 1978), also called for a stronger inclusion of modern art and engagement with its creators, whose works he saw as an important affirmation of the spirituality of the times.

The Vatican's collection of modern religious art currently numbers more than 800 works by some 250 artists from every continent. Though European and above all Italian artists are in the majority, the collection reflects the presence of the Catholic Church and the Christian faith throughout the world. Virtually all of the works entered the museum as gifts from the artists themselves or their descendants, clerics with an interest in art, Church institutions, or generous collectors. Of the various artistic genres, painting is represented in the largest numbers. However, the museum also possesses numerous sculptures, including two bronzes by Auguste Rodin, and many works from the estate of the Italian sculptor Marino Marini, as well as valuable drawings and prints, with works by Pablo Picasso and Wassily Kandinsky, and designs by the sculptor Henry Moore. The "classic" genres are supplemented by works of textile art by Henri Matisse and others, and stained glass by the likes of Fernand Léger. Newer genres such as photography, media art, and installations, on the other hand, are represented either minimally or not at all.

In terms of period, the Collection of Modern Religious Art ranges from the end of the nineteenth century to the twenty-first, with a particular focus on works of the second half of the twentieth century added under the pontificate of museum founder Paul VI. Thanks to the donation of numerous works by masters of Classic Modernism, however, the museum is able to provide an overview of the development of religious art, and art with a religious theme, over the entire course of the twentieth century. An important criterion here is the engagement of the artist with a Christian subject, rather than the artist's membership in the Catholic Church. Thus Pablo Picasso, who is represented with a number of works, was a professed Communist and Henri Matisse belonged to no specific church. And yet the latter's works for the Chapel of the Rosary at Vence testify to the artist's individual spirituality, reflected in art, which Paul VI saw as the focus of the museum he founded.

The collection of modern and contemporary art complements the Vatican's older art treasures and has been deliberately displayed in the historic rooms. The modern works are exhibited on a changing basis in a total of fifty-five rooms, including many cabinet-like spaces that afford an intimate encounter with the works displayed in them. For reasons of conservation the works on paper, in particular, are only on view for short periods of time. The Borgia Apartments forms the heart of the display, where the modern works enter into an enthralling dialogue with fifteenth-century frescoes.

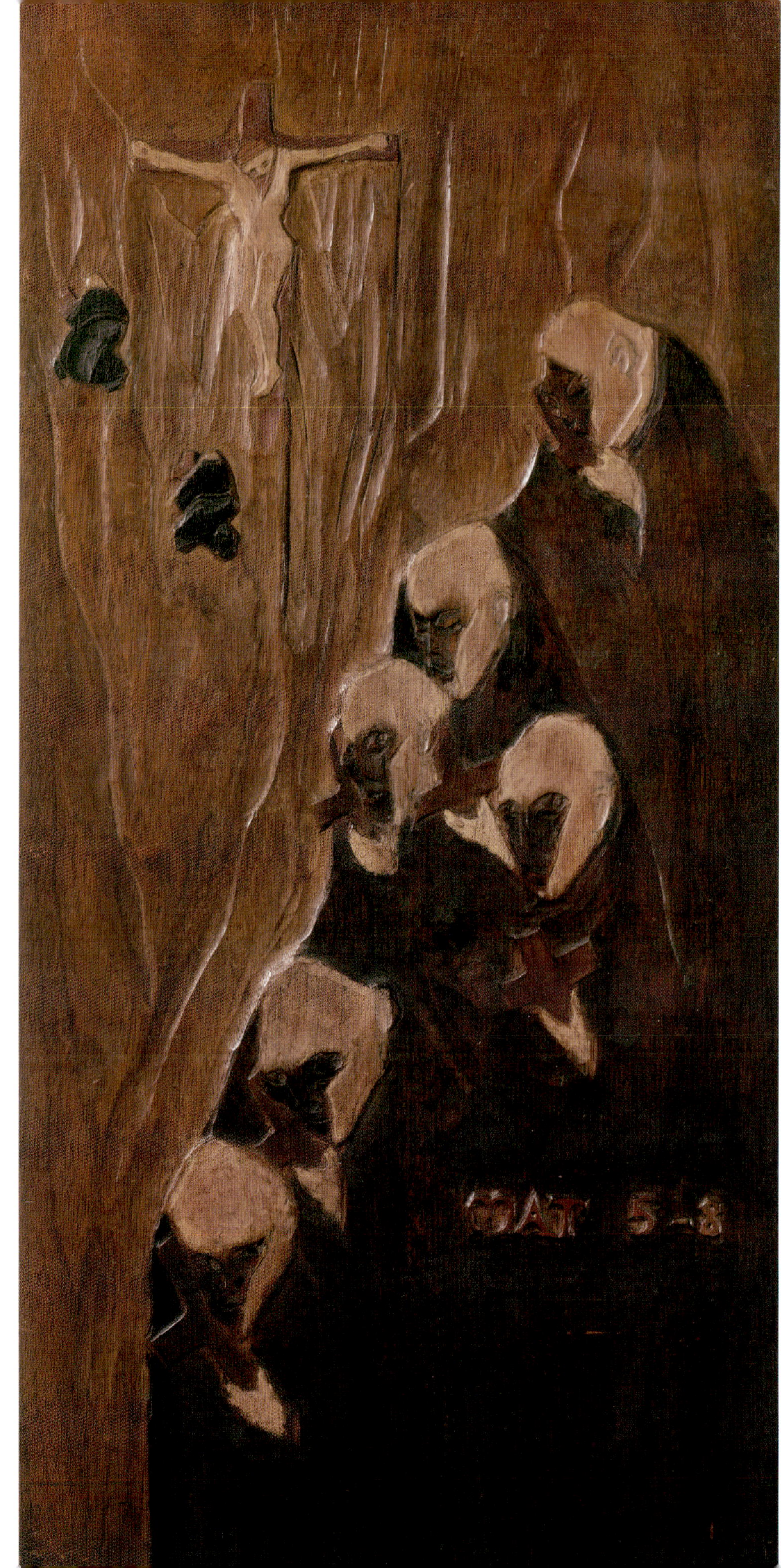
MAT 5-8

Paul Gauguin

Crucifixion

Paul Gauguin saw his colored reliefs, which constitute an independent group of works within his oeuvre, as a form of painting in wood. Exhibiting simple, abstract forms, the reliefs are distinctive for their expressive power, and this is also the source of the peculiar impact of the Crucifixion. The work is divided diagonally into front and rear halves, which are also clearly distinguished from one another by their color. While the front area is taken up by the dark mass of the grieving women, the space behind displays a reddish-brown coloration against which the pale figure of the crucified Christ stands out. This makes Christ's naked body a symbol of purity that connects chromatically with the light-colored bonnets of the women. The mourners are holding large wooden crosses in their hands or against their faces, which are lowered in grief. In terms of subject and style, the relief resembles the works Gauguin produced in Pont-Aven in 1889/1890, in which the artist sought a return to a simpler, more unspoiled and, in his view, truer art through a reduced formal language, renunciation of realism and perspective, and increased ornamentalization.

Paul Gauguin, 1848–1903
***Crucifixion*, ca. 1890**
62 x 31 cm; Wood, carved and painted
Modern Religious Art

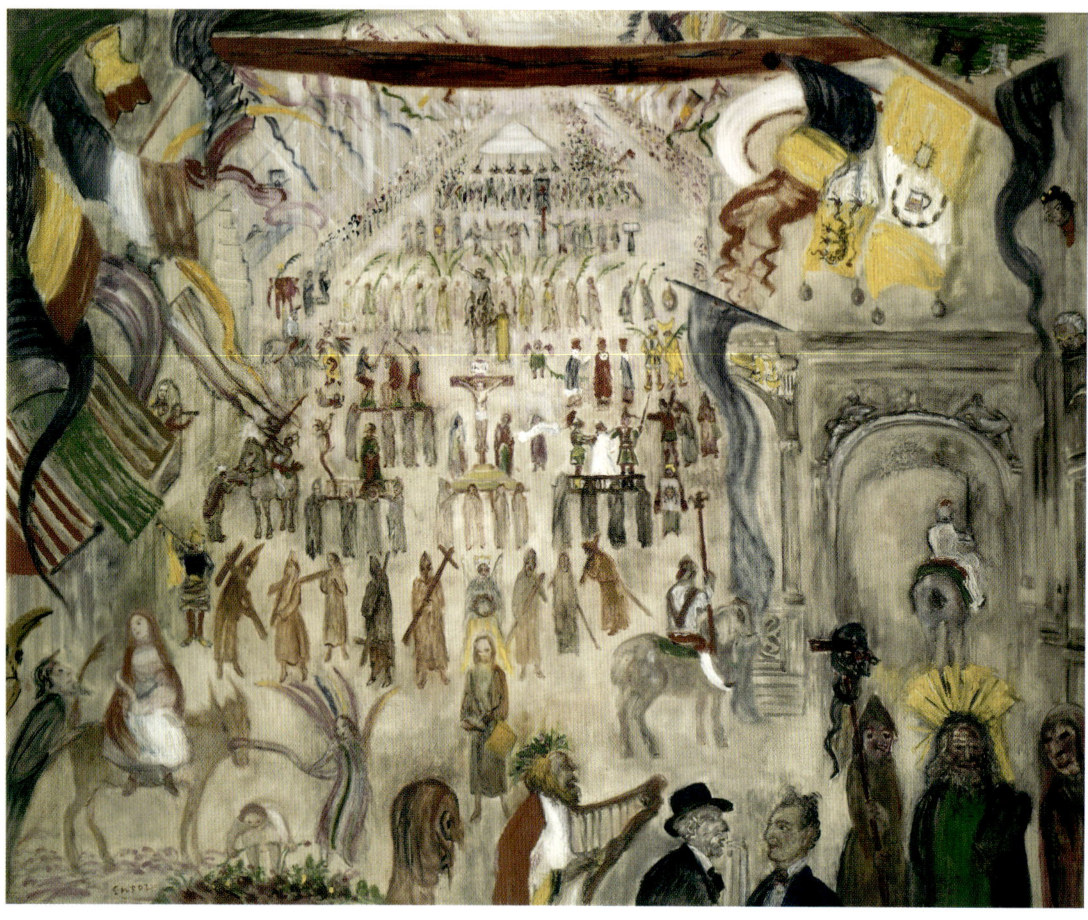

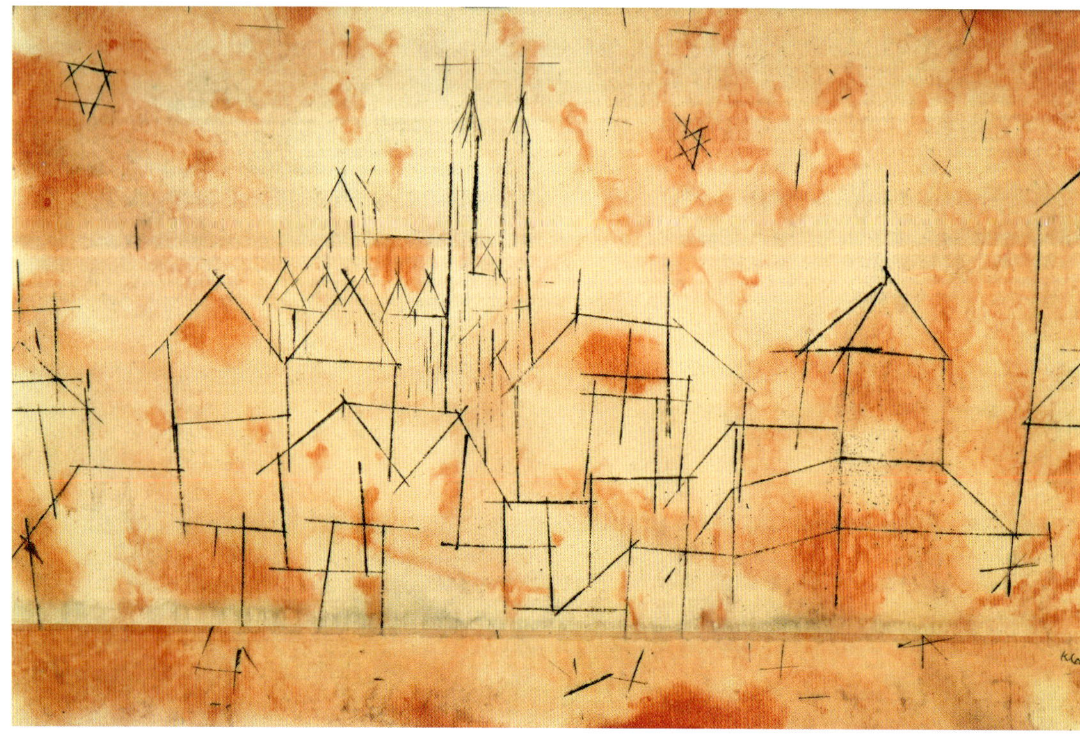

James Ensor, 1860–1949
***Procession of the Penitents of Verne*, 1913**
130 x 162 cm; Oil on canvas
Modern Religious Art

Paul Klee, 1879–1940
***City with a Gothic Cathedral*, ca. 1920**
98 x 74 cm; Oil on canvas
Modern Religious Art

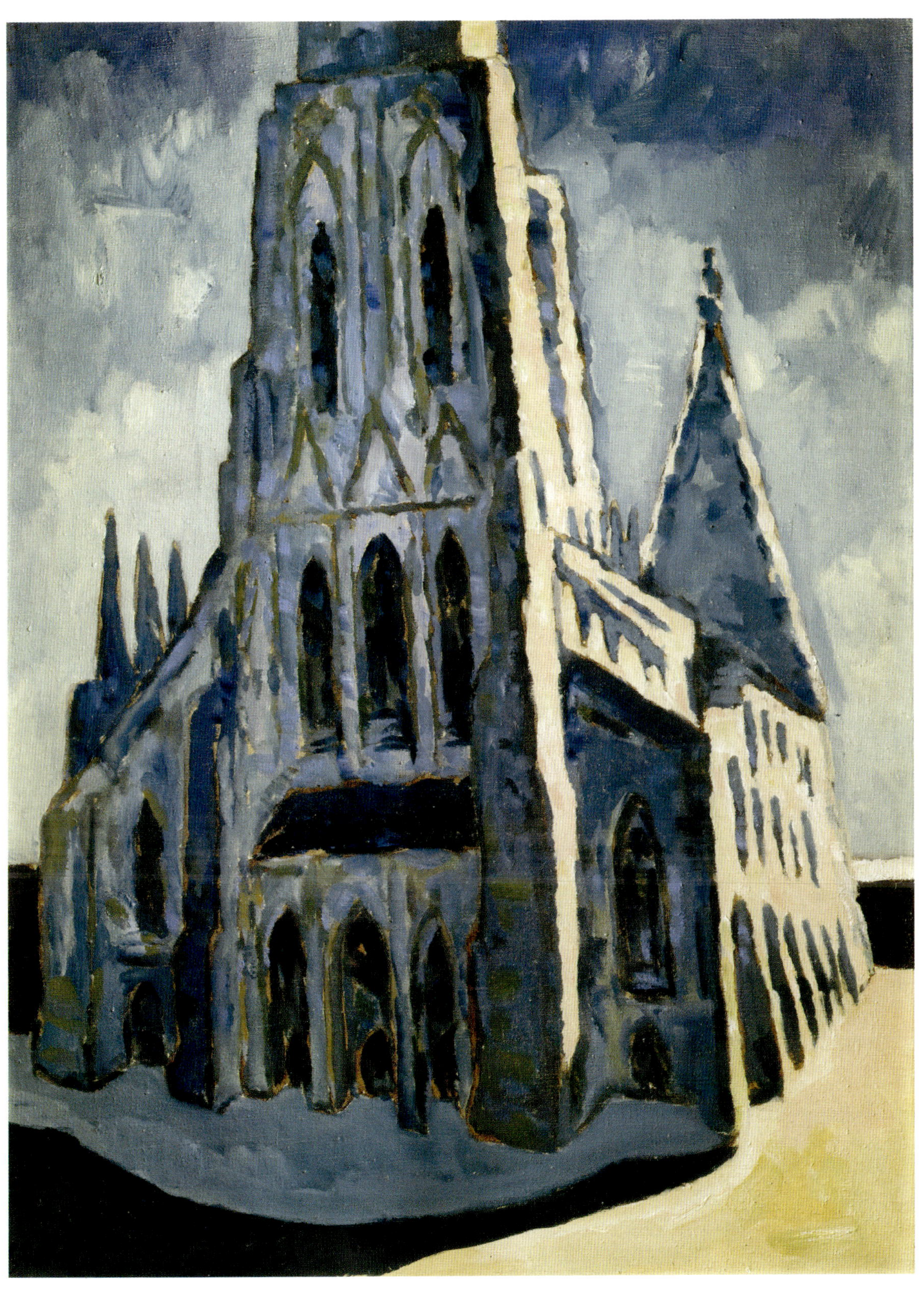

Karl Schmidt-Rottluff, 1884–1976
***Cathedral*, ca. 1910**
27 x 40 cm; Oil on canvas
Modern Religious Art

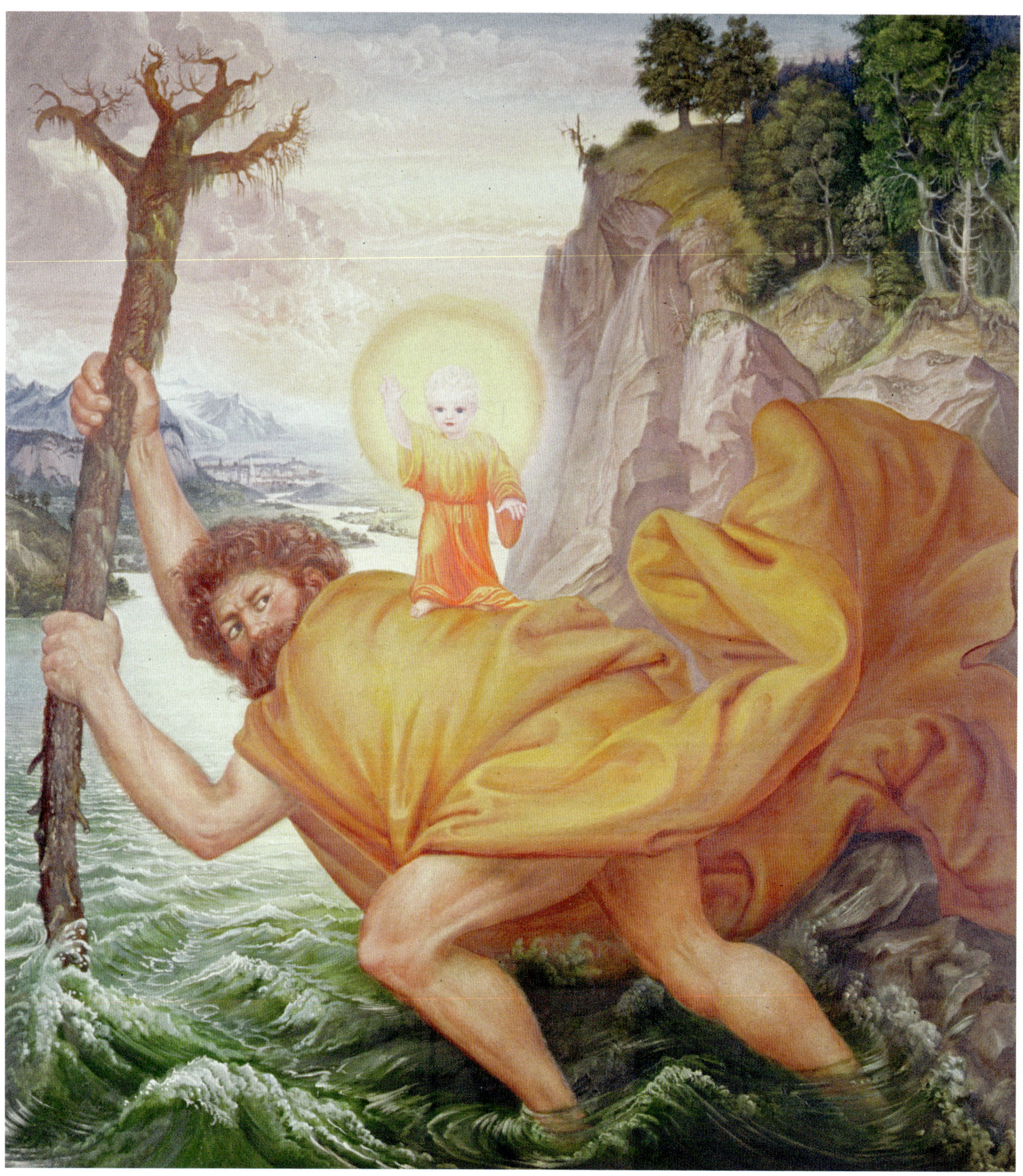

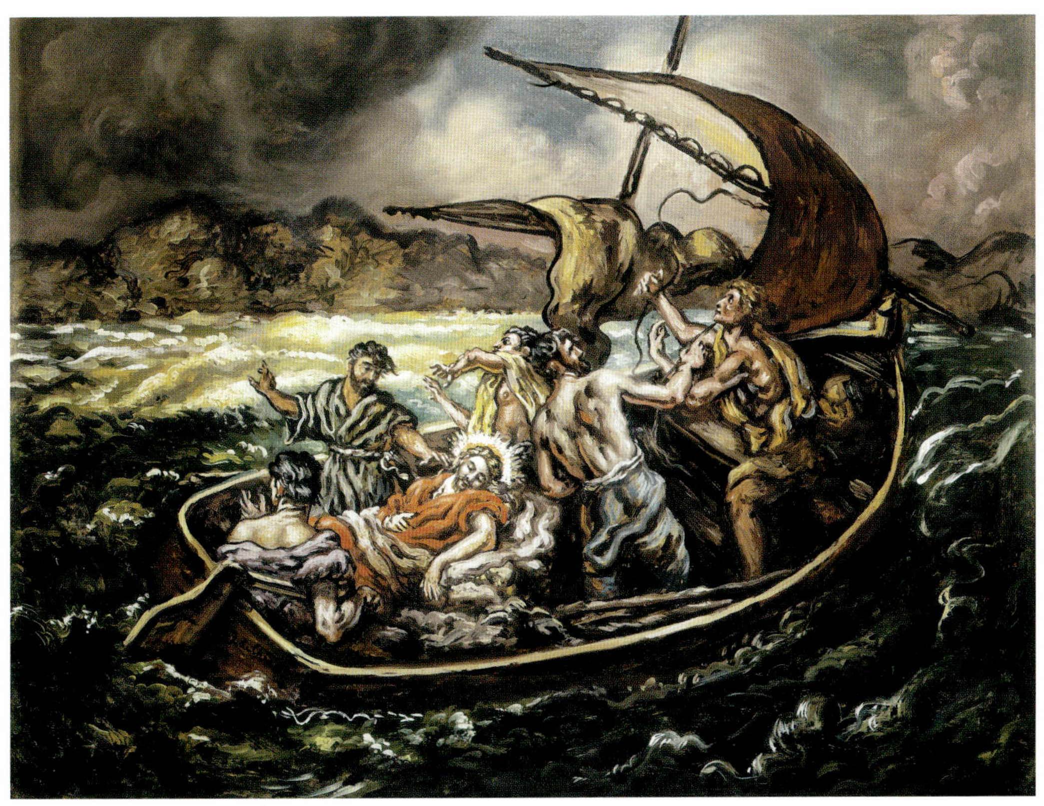

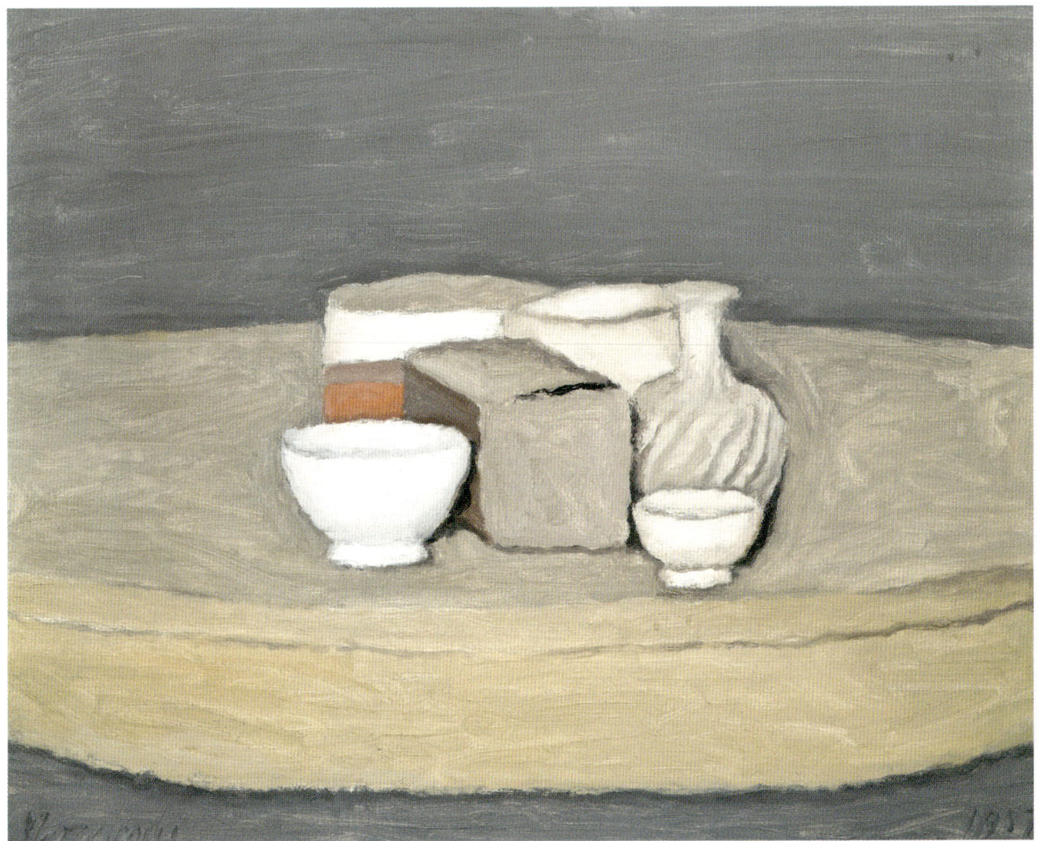

Otto Dix, 1891–1969
***St. Christopher and the Christ Child*, 1938**
135 x 125 cm; Oil on canvas
Modern Religious Art

Giorgio de Chirico, 1888–1978
***Christ and the Tempest*, 1945**
73 x 98 cm; Oil on canvas
Modern Religious Art

Giorgio Morandi, 1890–1964
***Still Life*, ca. 1957**
35 x 45 cm; Oil on canvas
Modern Religious Art

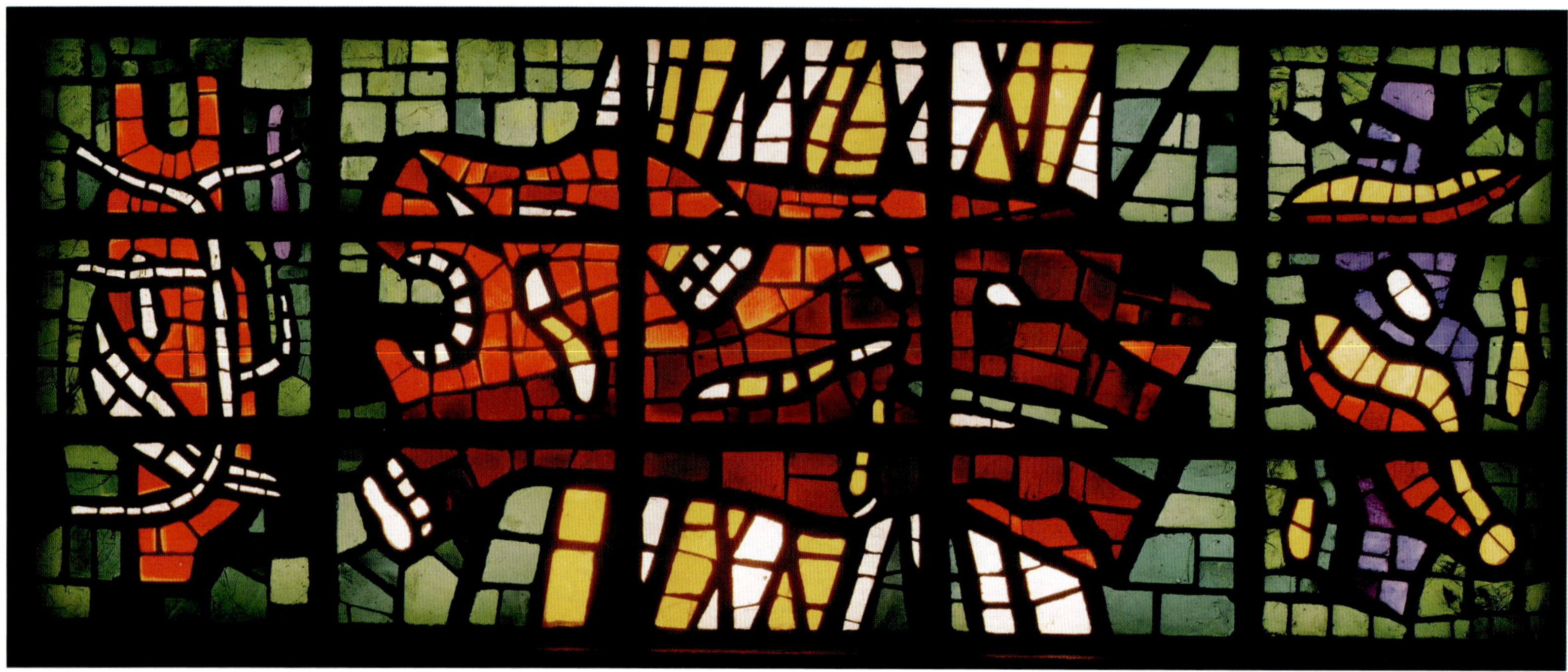

Fernand Léger

The Holy Tunic

Fernand Léger created his stained-glass window *The Holy Tunic* in 1950/1951 as part of a cycle of windows for the church of Sacré-Coeur at Audincourt in Franche-Comté. This cycle consists of fifteen landscape-format windows installed beneath the barrel vault along the walls of the modern church building. The windows tell the story of Christ's Passion through the instruments and objects associated with it, with each window dedicated to a single item. The Léger window in the Vatican is a variant of the corresponding stained-glass window in the church at Audincourt. Christ's red garment lies spread out against a green ground that is presumably intended to indicate the hill of Golgotha. The red color of the tunic alludes to the blood of Christ, symbolizing both suffering and redemption. The white ropes or ties on the left half of the image may represent the belt with which the tunic was fastened. Like their motifs, the colors of Léger's windows, which tend strongly toward abstraction, are partly representational, partly symbolic, and partly decorative. The Audincourt windows were Léger's first stained-glass works and their radiant colors and strong design reveal the painter's fascination with the new medium. They are among Léger's few religious works.

Fernand Léger, 1881–1955
***The Holy Tunic*, 1950-1951**
163 x 425 cm; Stained glass
Modern Religious Art

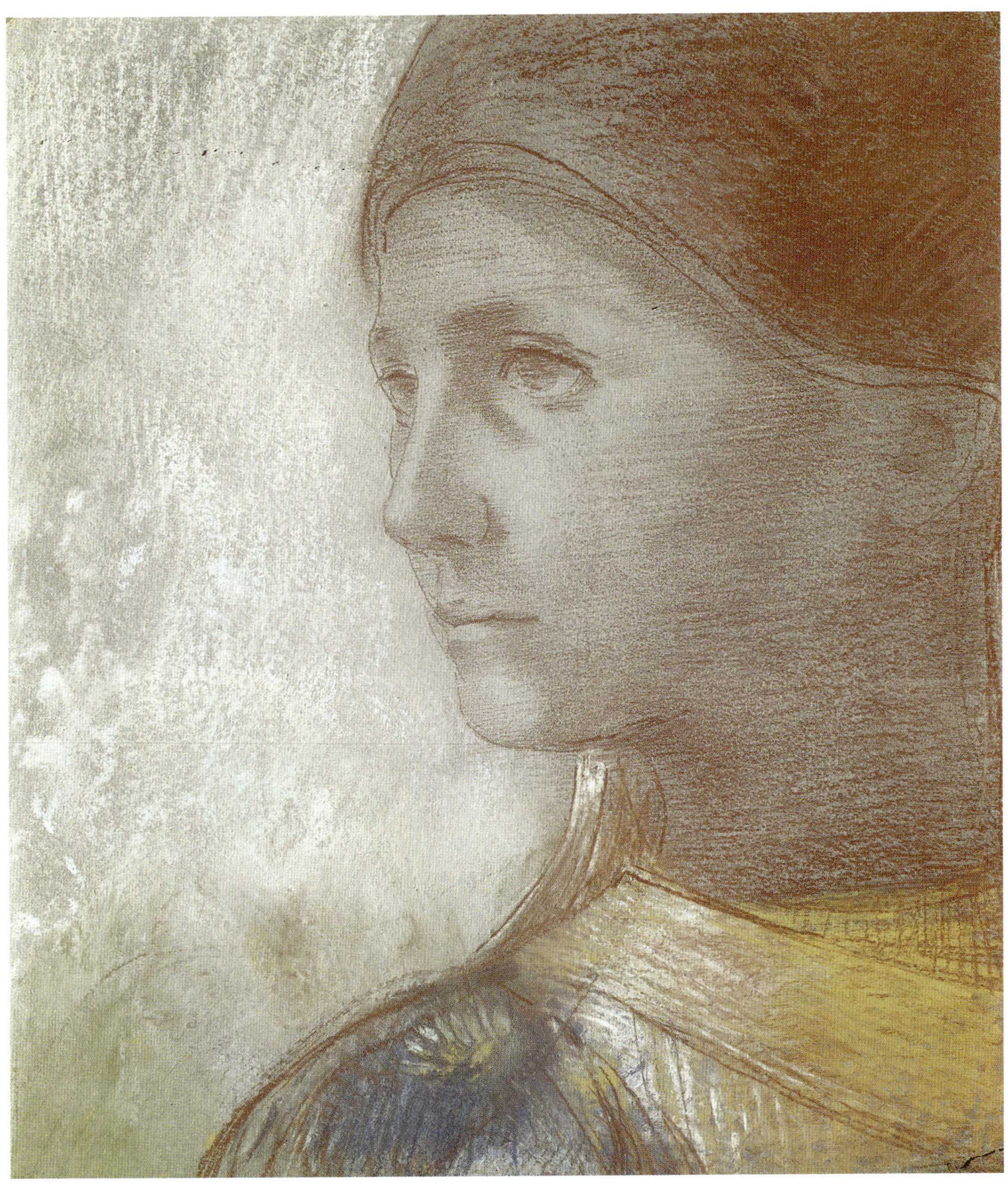

Odilon Redon, 1840–1916
***Joan of Arc*, ca. 1890**
26 x 23 cm; Oil on canvas
Modern Religious Art

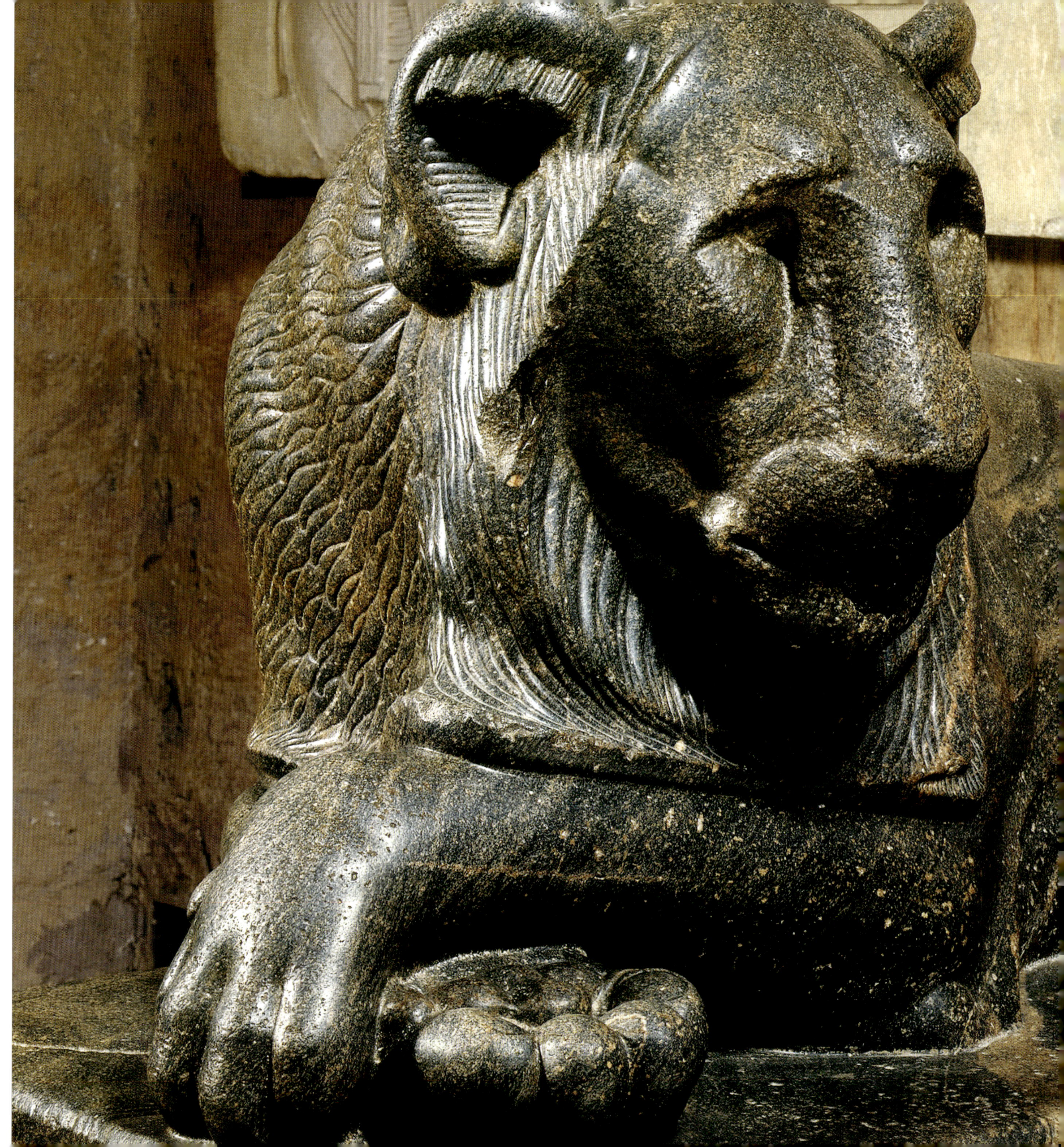

TAPESTRIES, MAPS, SCULPTURE AND ARTIFACTS

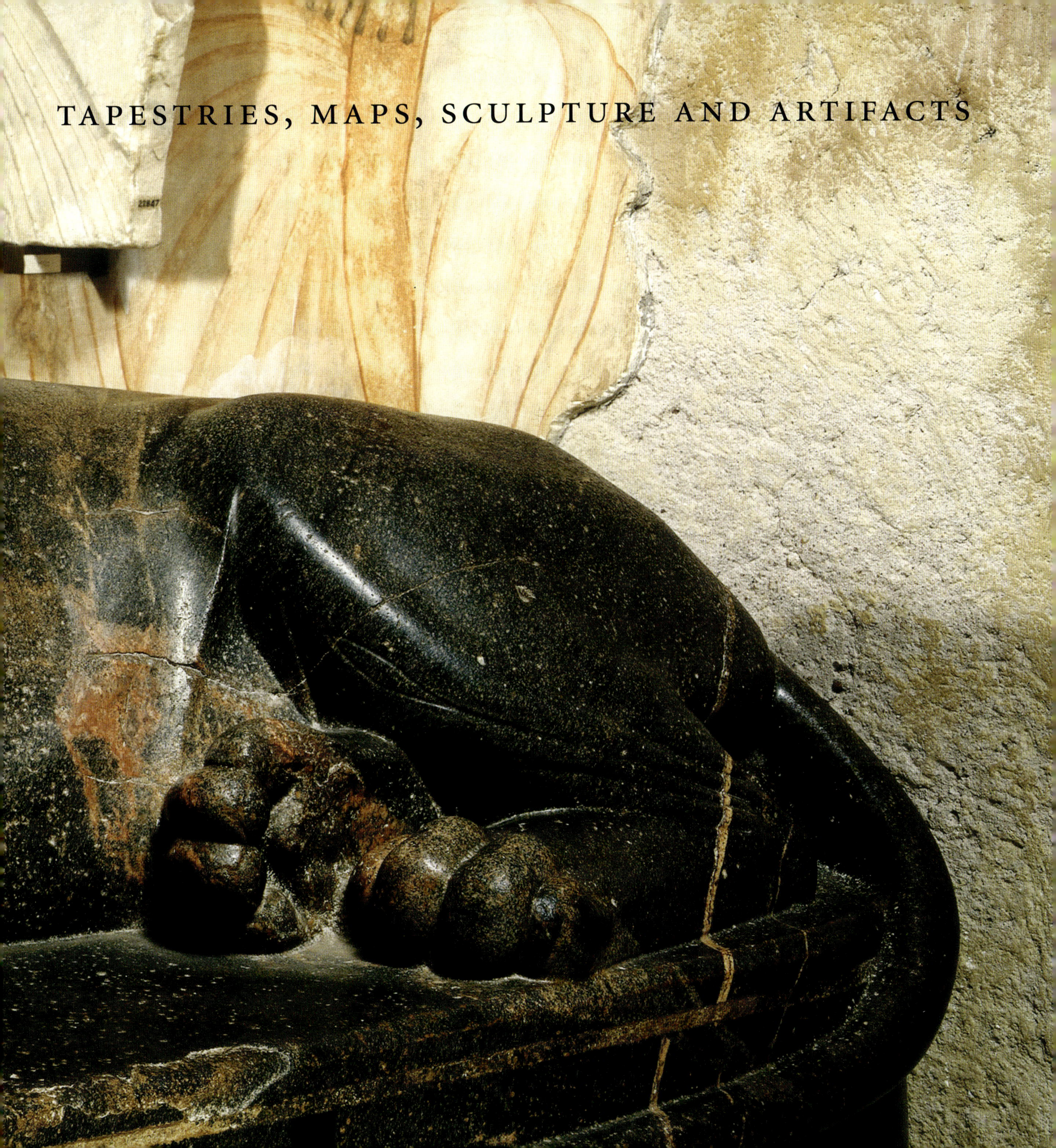

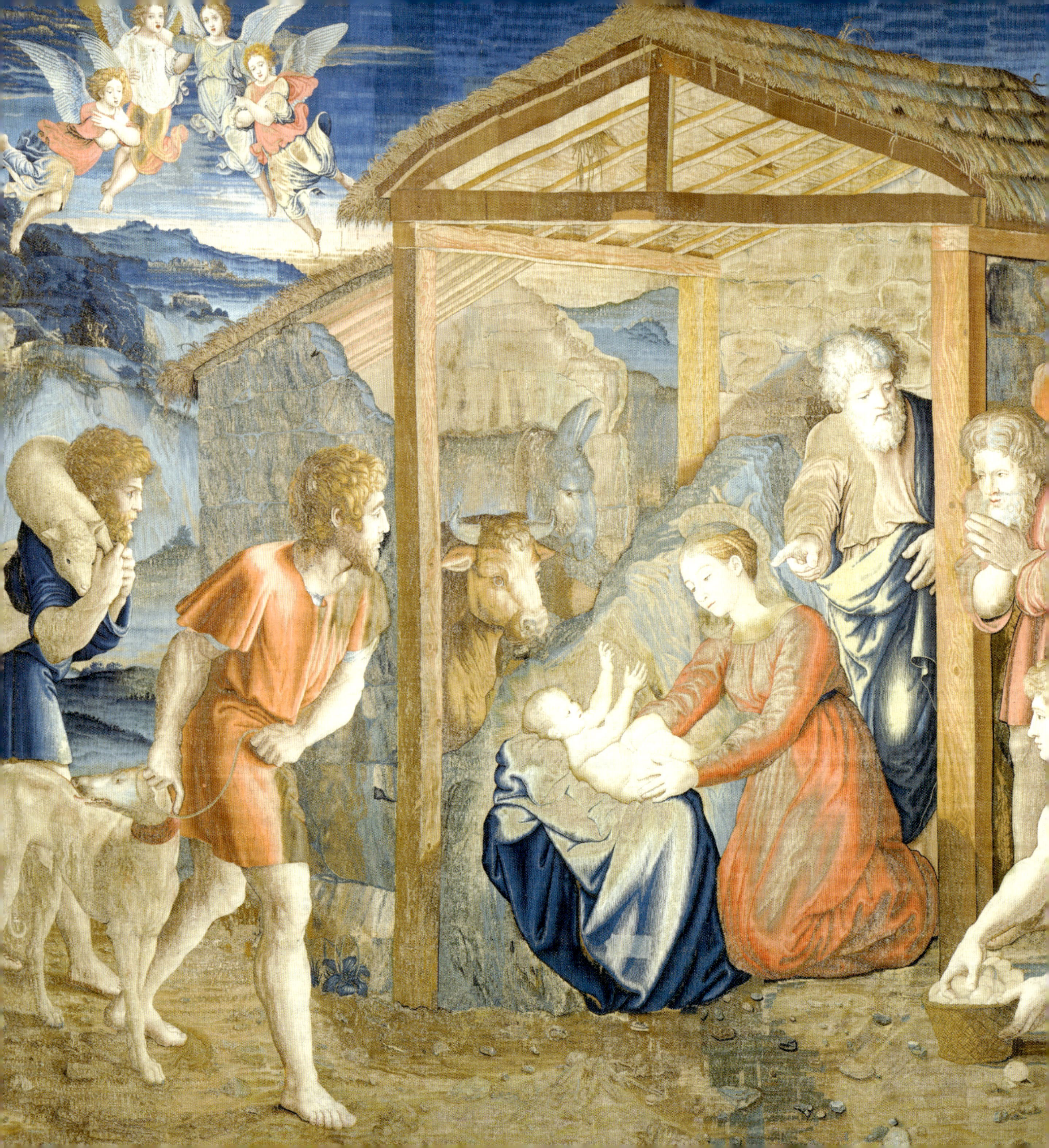

TAPESTRY GALLERY

The Renaissance and Baroque tapestries in the Tapestry Gallery (Galleria degli Arazzi) are among the Vatican's most important treasures. Gregory XVI inaugurated the gallery in 1838 in the long, narrow room preceding the Gallery of Maps. The walls of this room, which was refurbished in the classical style under the lengthy pontificate of Pius VI (1717–1799, reigned from 1775), are almost completely covered by the large tapestries. A number of hangings that had originally adorned the Sistine Chapel and other parts of the papal palace had been moved here in 1814, but it was only in 1838 that the Tapestry Gallery was established on a permanent basis.

Though often dismissed today as "mere textiles," in earlier centuries tapestries were regarded as the most valuable of art objects due to their complex and extremely costly manufacture. Well-known artists produced most of the designs for the scenes depicted in the tapestries—Raphael and important Netherlandish painters, in the case of those in the Tapestry Gallery. These designs were scaled up to full-size templates known as "cartoons" which were then translated into tapestries in specialized weaving mills. During the Renaissance, the best tapestry manufacturers were in Flanders, where between 1518 and 1530 the famous workshop of Pieter van Aelst in Brussels wove the Vatican's two series of tapestries designed by Raphael. The artistry of the weavers lay in translating the monochrome or sparingly colorized designs into colorful textile pictures designed to surpass even frescoes in their vibrancy and three-dimensionality. In addition to woolen threads of different shades, the weavers also used precious gold and silver threads, which made a major contribution to the shimmering surface of the tapestries.

The Tapestry Gallery encompasses works from three different centuries and schools: The oldest tapestries were manufactured in the late fifteenth century in Tournai, a center of Flemish textile production, after designs by early Netherlandish painters depicting scenes from the life of Jesus. The sixteenth century is represented by tapestries from the workshop of Pieter van Aelst after designs by the school of Raphael commissioned by Clement VII (1478–1534, reigned from 1523) for the decoration of the Sistine Chapel, where they were hung in 1531. The cycle comprises various scenes from the life of Christ, from the adoration of the shepherds to the Resurrection. A series of ten scenes from the life of Urban VIII (1568–1644, reigned from 1623) is among the most important examples of Roman textile art of the Baroque era. These tapestries were woven after the designs of an unknown artist by the Barberini Manufactory in Rome, founded in 1627 by Cardinal Francesco Barberini, the nephew of Urban VIII.

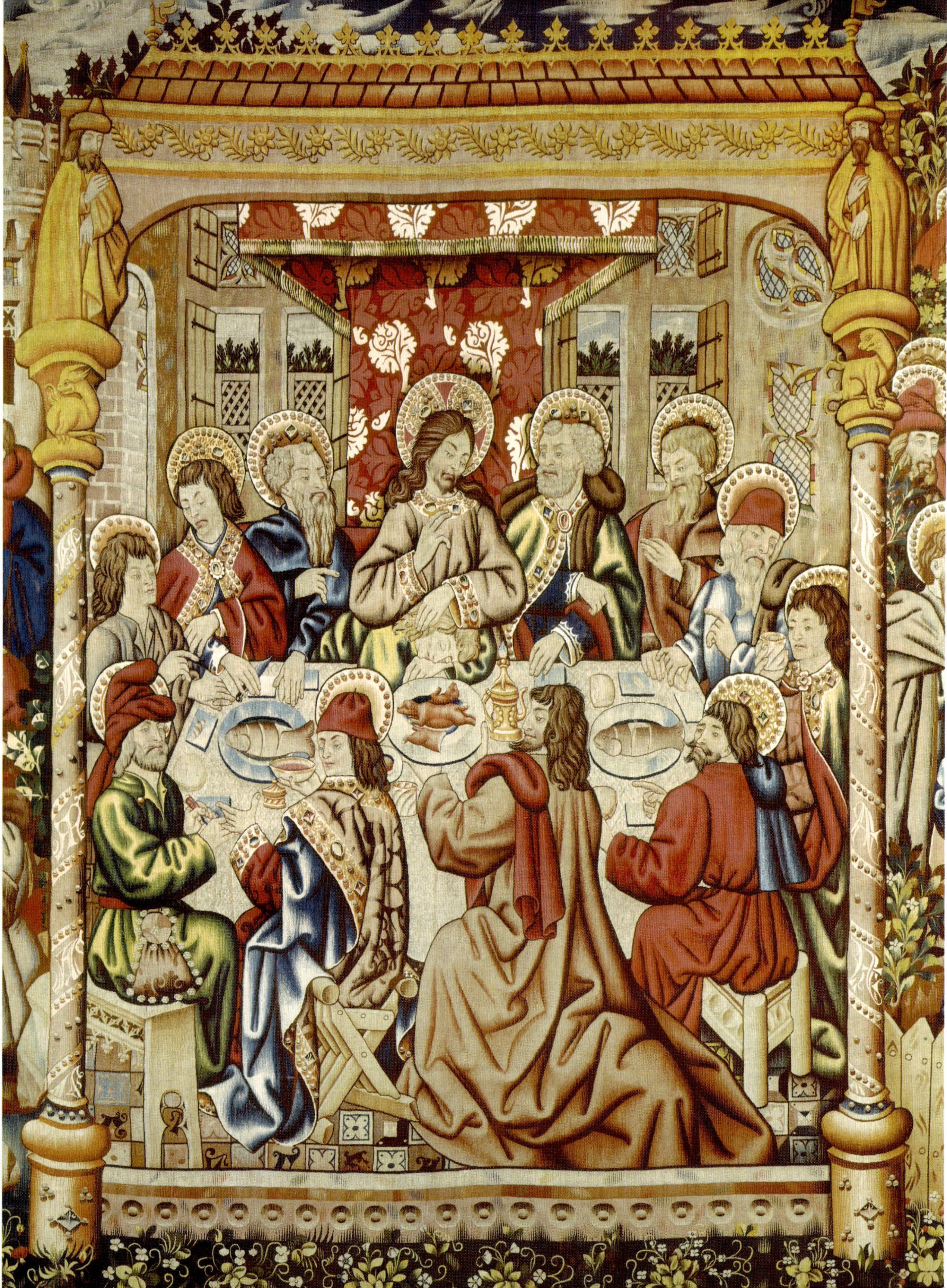

Tournai Workshop

The Last Supper

This tall, rectangular tapestry is almost completely filled with a depiction of the Last Supper. The setting is a late Gothic interior. Christ sits with his twelve disciples around a large rectangular table covered with a finely worked white tablecloth. The dishes being served—lamb, fish, and bread—are symbols of Christ and the Eucharist. Each disciple stands out, with individually designed garments and faces. The older disciple in the foreground is dressed in a particularly conspicuous manner, wearing robes of lustrous green velvet and an artfully knotted red turban and holding an enormous open purse. This figure, who may be the donor of the tapestry, turns to face the viewer. The clothes and the depiction of the room betray a striving for realism that is typical of Netherlandish art. The disciple dressed in brown in the foreground is the traitor Judas, the only member of the company with no halo. The haloes of the other figures are executed in precious gold thread, contributing—like the gold-patterned red baldachino behind Christ—to the resplendence of the tapestry.

Tournai Workshop, late 15th century
***The Last Supper*, ca. 1500**
Wool, silk, gold thread
Tapestry Gallery

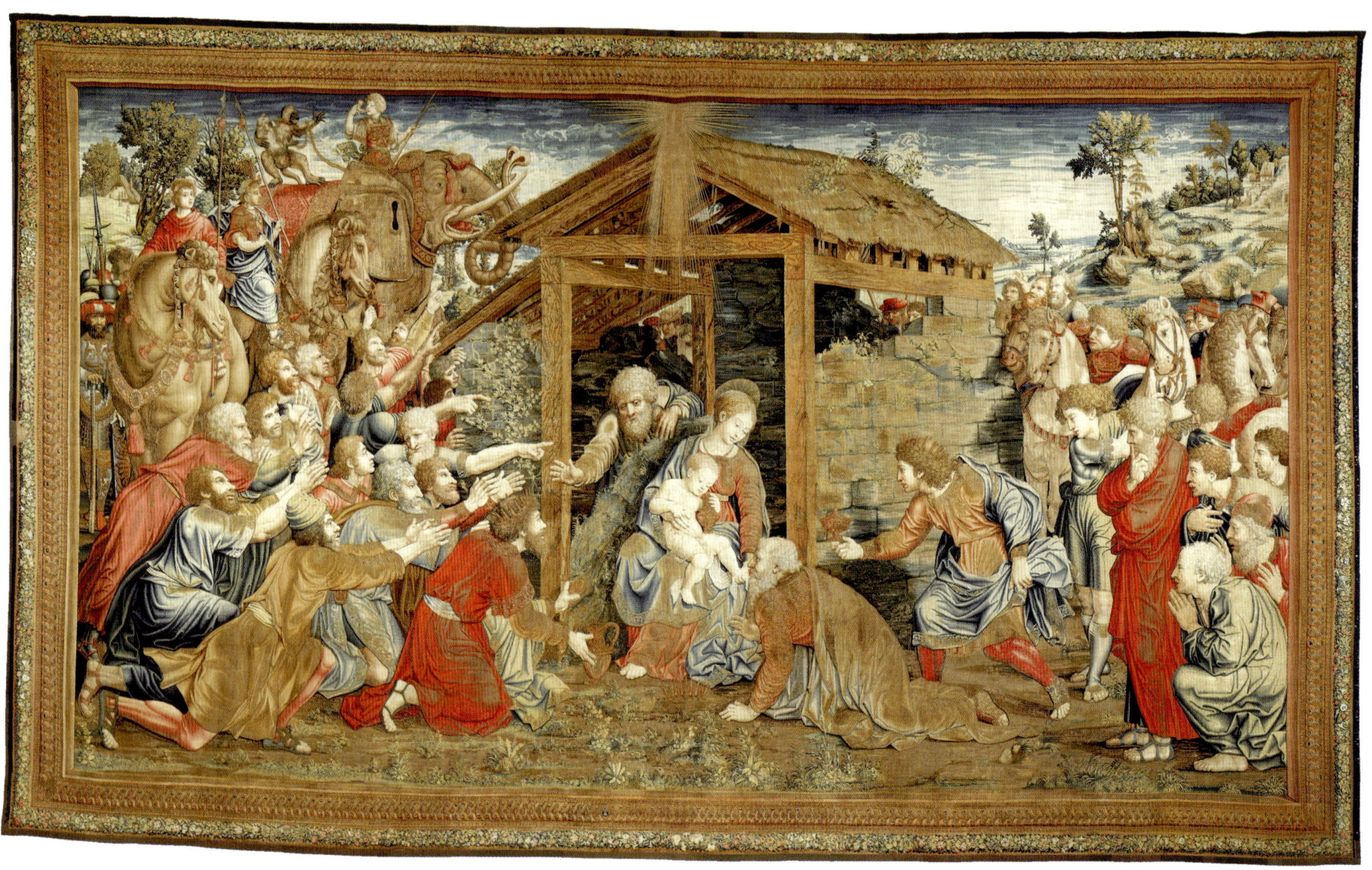

Workshop of Raphael (Raffaello Sanzio) and Pieter van Aelst

Adoration of the Three Magi

Commissioned for the Sistine Chapel, this landscape-format tapestry is one of a series of wall hangings illustrating scenes from the life of Jesus that were manufactured in the Brussels workshop of Pieter van Aelst after designs by the Raphael workshop. The tumultuous scene shows the three kings with their retinue grouped around the stable in Bethlehem. The composition falls into three parts with the center taken up by the Holy Family in front of the stable and the oldest of the kings kneeling before the Virgin and Child and kissing the infant's feet in deep reverence. He is flanked by the other two kings, who proffer their gifts adoringly. Worthy of note is Pieter van Aelst's masterful modeling of light and dark in the clothes of the kings and the fine goldwork of the braiding. Both the dilapidated stable and the background landscape stand out for their high degree of realism. The vibrancy of the scene derives in no small measure from the numerous subsidiary figures and exotic animals that surround the stable building. The star of Bethlehem shines overhead, rendered in precious gold thread.

Workshop of Raphael (Raffaello Sanzio), 1483–1520 and Pieter van Aelst (?–1536)
***Adoration of the Three Magi*, ca. 1525–1530**
Wool, silk, metal thread
Tapestry Gallery

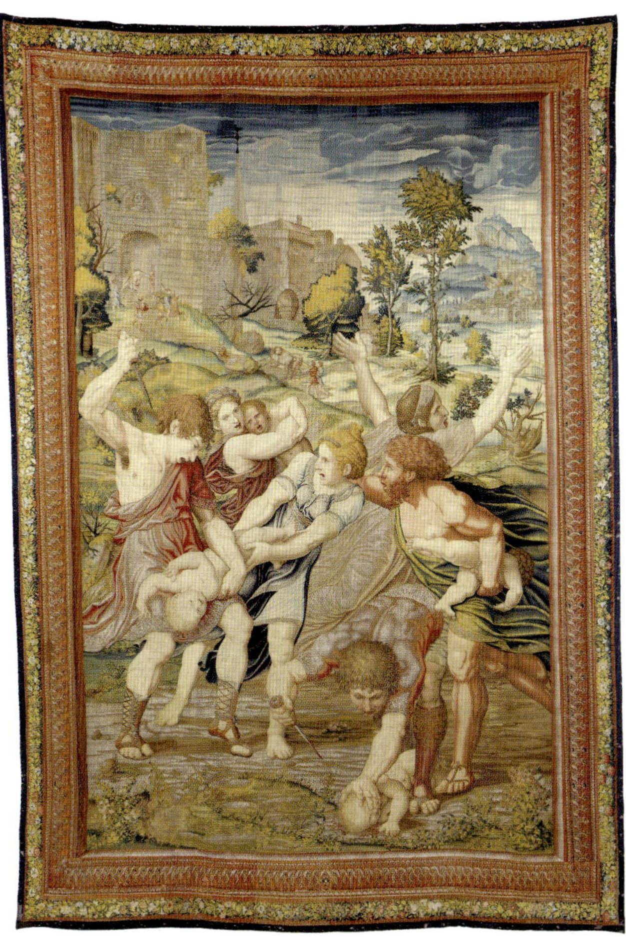

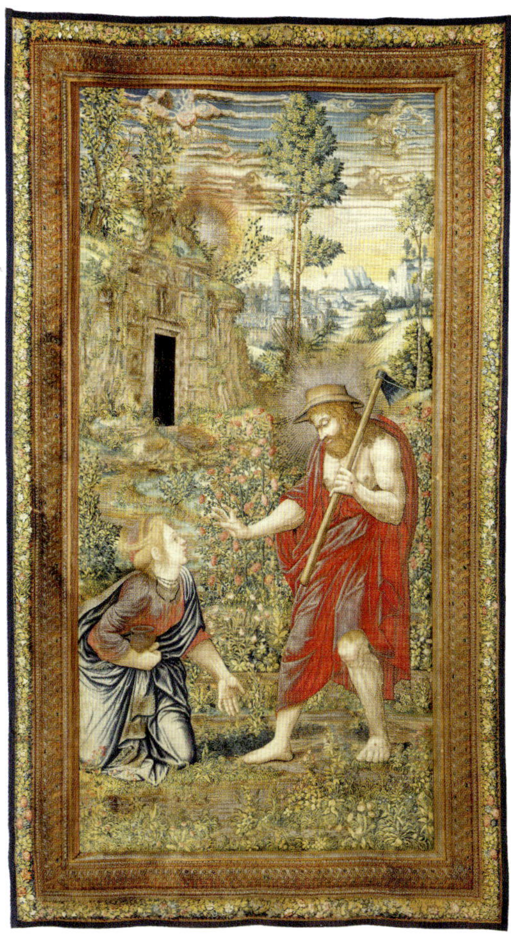

Workshop of Raphael (Raffaello Sanzio), 1483–1520 and Pieter van Aelst (?–1536)
***Slaughter of the Innocents*, ca. 1525–1530**
Wool, silk, metal thread
Tapestry Gallery

Workshop of Raphael (Raffaello Sanzio), 1483–1520 and Pieter van Aelst (?–1536)
***Noli Me Tangere*, ca. 1525–1530**
Wool, silk, metal thread
Tapestry Gallery

Workshop of Raphael (Raffaello Sanzio), 1483–1520 and Pieter van Aelst (?–1536)
***Adoration of the Shepherds*, ca. 1525–1530**
Wool, silk, metal thread
Tapestry Gallery

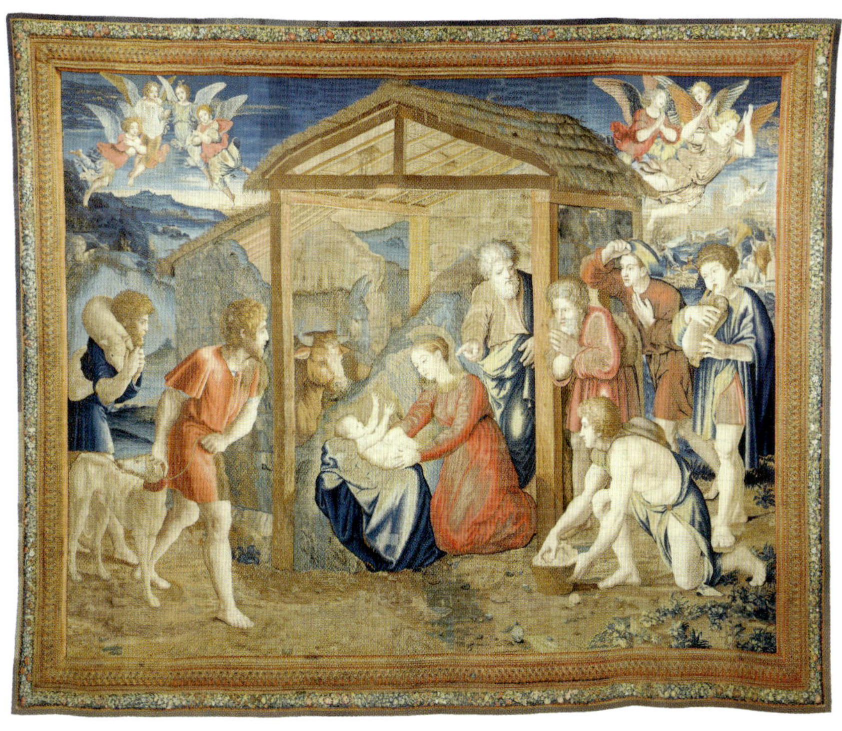

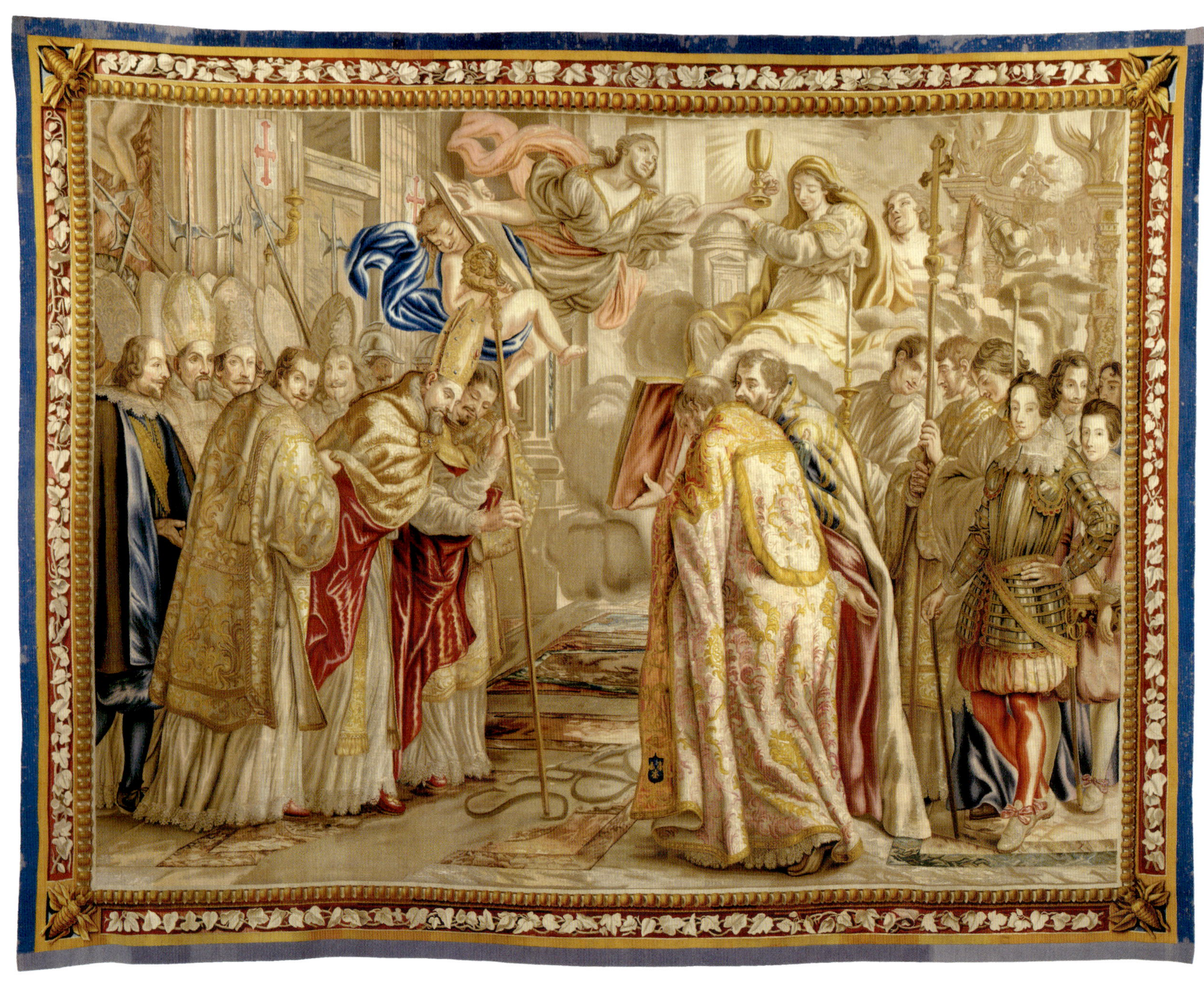

Barberini Manufactory, active 1627–1683
***Pope Urban VIII Consecrates St. Peter's Basilica*, ca. 1671–1673**
40 x 53 cm; Wool, silk, metal thread
Tapestry Gallery

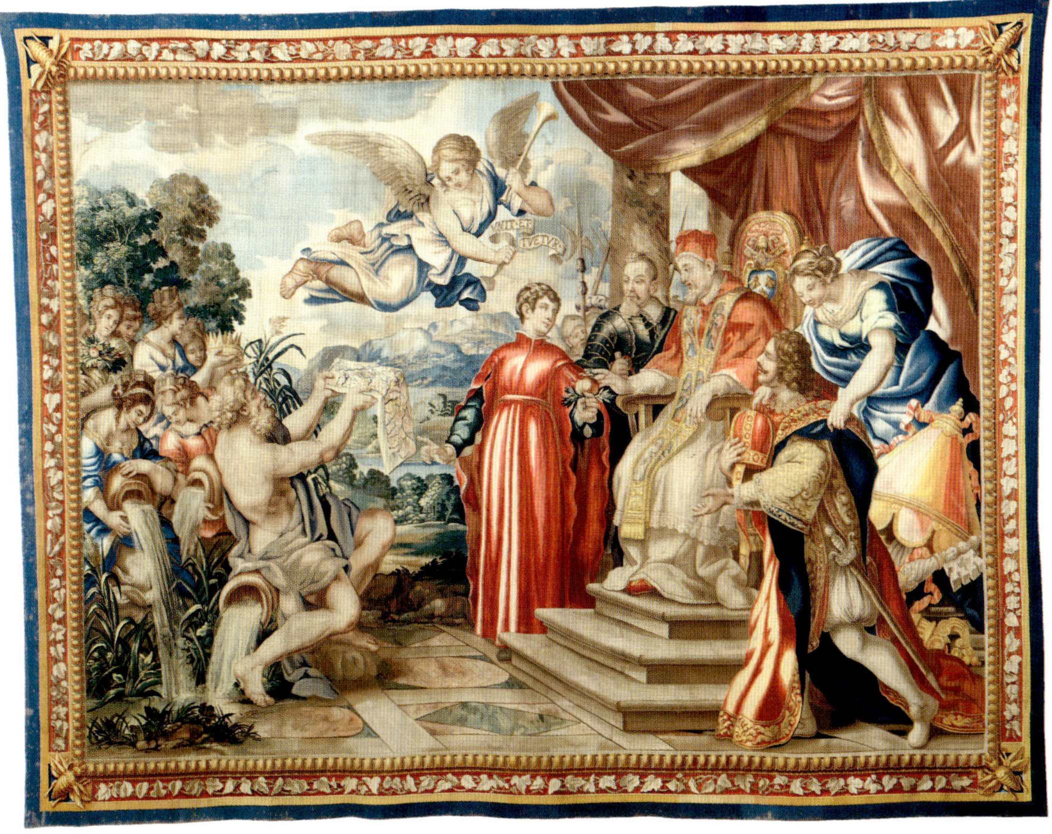

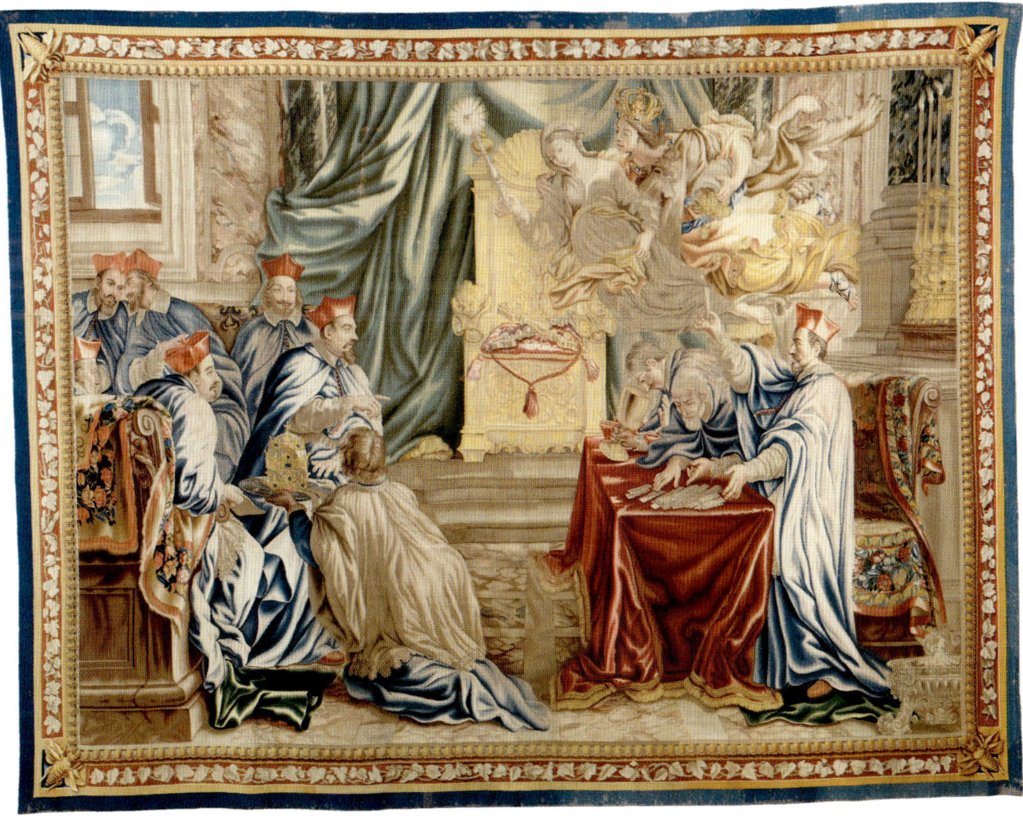

Barberini Manufactory, active 1627–1683
***Tapestries Illustrating the Life of Pope Urban VIII: The Countess Matilda donates her Land to Pope Pascal II*, ca. 1663–1679**
40 x 53 cm; Wool, silk, metal thread
Tapestry Gallery

***Tapestries Illustrating the Life of Pope Urban VIII Maffeo Barberini elected Pope under the Name Urban VIII*, ca. 1663–1679**
40 x 53 cm; Wool, silk, metal thread
Tapestry Gallery

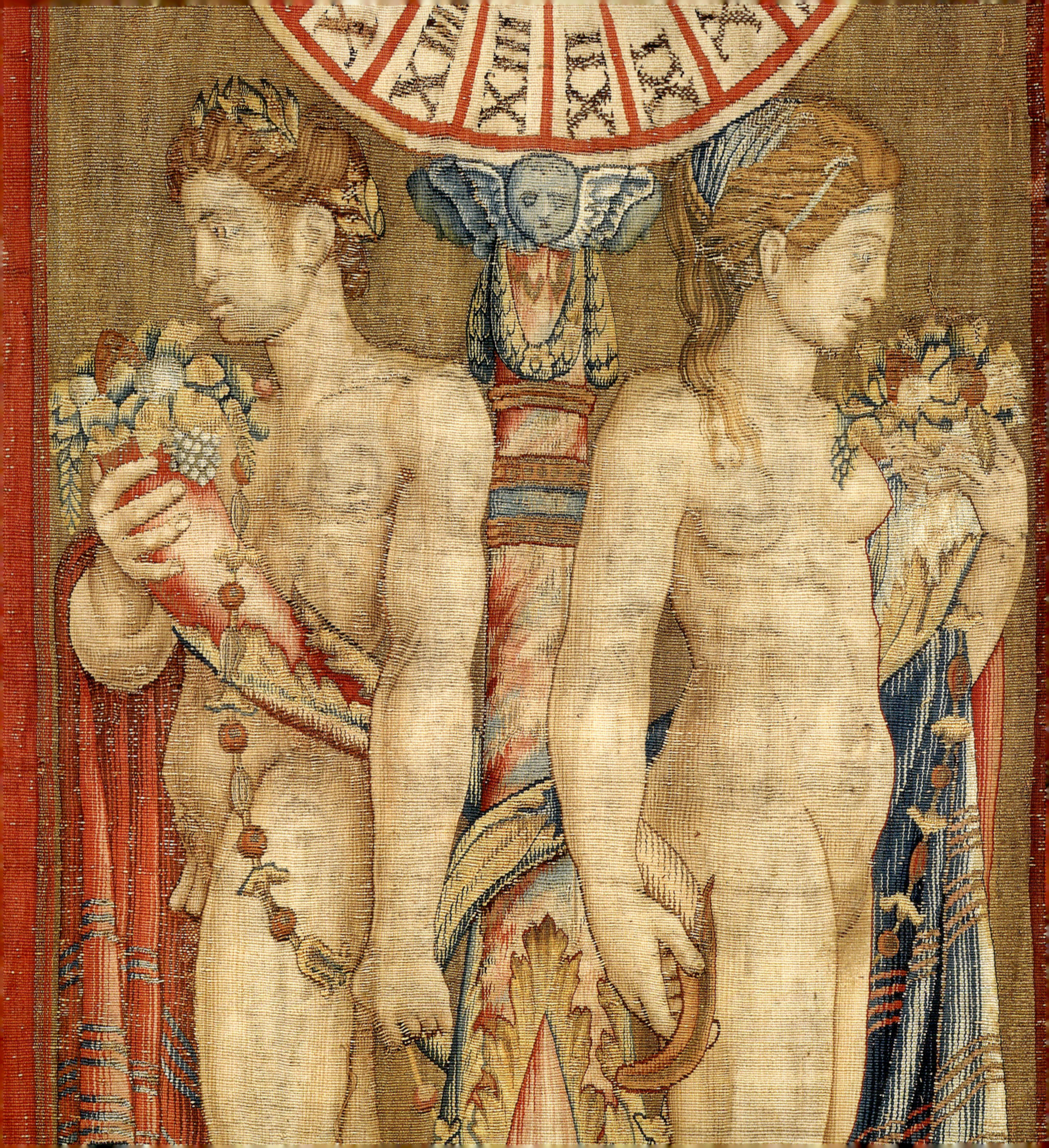

SISTINE CHAPEL TAPESTRIES

In 1515 Pope Leo X (1475–1521, reigned from 1513) commissioned Raphael to produce a series of ten tapestry designs for the Sistine Chapel featuring scenes from the life of SS. Peter and Paul. By 1516 the painter had already completed a set of preliminary full-scale drawings. These designs, or cartoons, were sent off to Brussels to be woven in the workshop of Pieter van Aelst. It was not until 1521 that all ten of the tapestries, which measured (with their borders) almost five meters high and between five and six meters wide, were completed and dispatched to Rome. By the time of Leo X's death in December 1521, only seven of the tapestries had reached the Vatican, and those were pawned in order to cover the cost of the conclave to elect the new pope. Leo X's successor Hadrian VI (1459–1523, reigned from 1522) immediately redeemed the now complete series of tapestries and decorated the Sistine Chapel with them for the festivities marking his assumption of office on August 31, 1522.

Leo X had intended the tapestry cycle to complement the chapel's frescoes, which had been brought to a brilliant, if provisional, culmination under his predecessor Julius II with Michelangelo's Sistine ceiling. The tapestries enabled Leo X to put his own stamp on the chapel. Moreover, the tapestries were many times more valuable than the frescoes: Raphael had received one thousand ducats for his designs and the weaving of each tapestry cost a further fifteen hundred, making the series five times as expensive as Michelangelo's paintings in the Sistine Chapel. As a result, they were only displayed on special occasions.

In terms of content, the tapestries particularly refer to the Moses and Christ cycles adorning the long, narrow walls of the chapel, to which they conform in terms of their size and border decoration. Each of the tapestries was hung below a wall painting, supplementing the Old and New Testament scenes with apostolic ones. The scenes relating to St. Peter were displayed beneath the Moses cycle and those relating to St. Paul beneath the episodes from the life of Christ. After being plundered by Emperor Charles V's troops during the Sack of Rome in 1527 and looted again in 1796 by Napoleon's soldiers, the tapestries were reacquired in 1815 and have been on display in the Pinacoteca Vaticana since 1932.

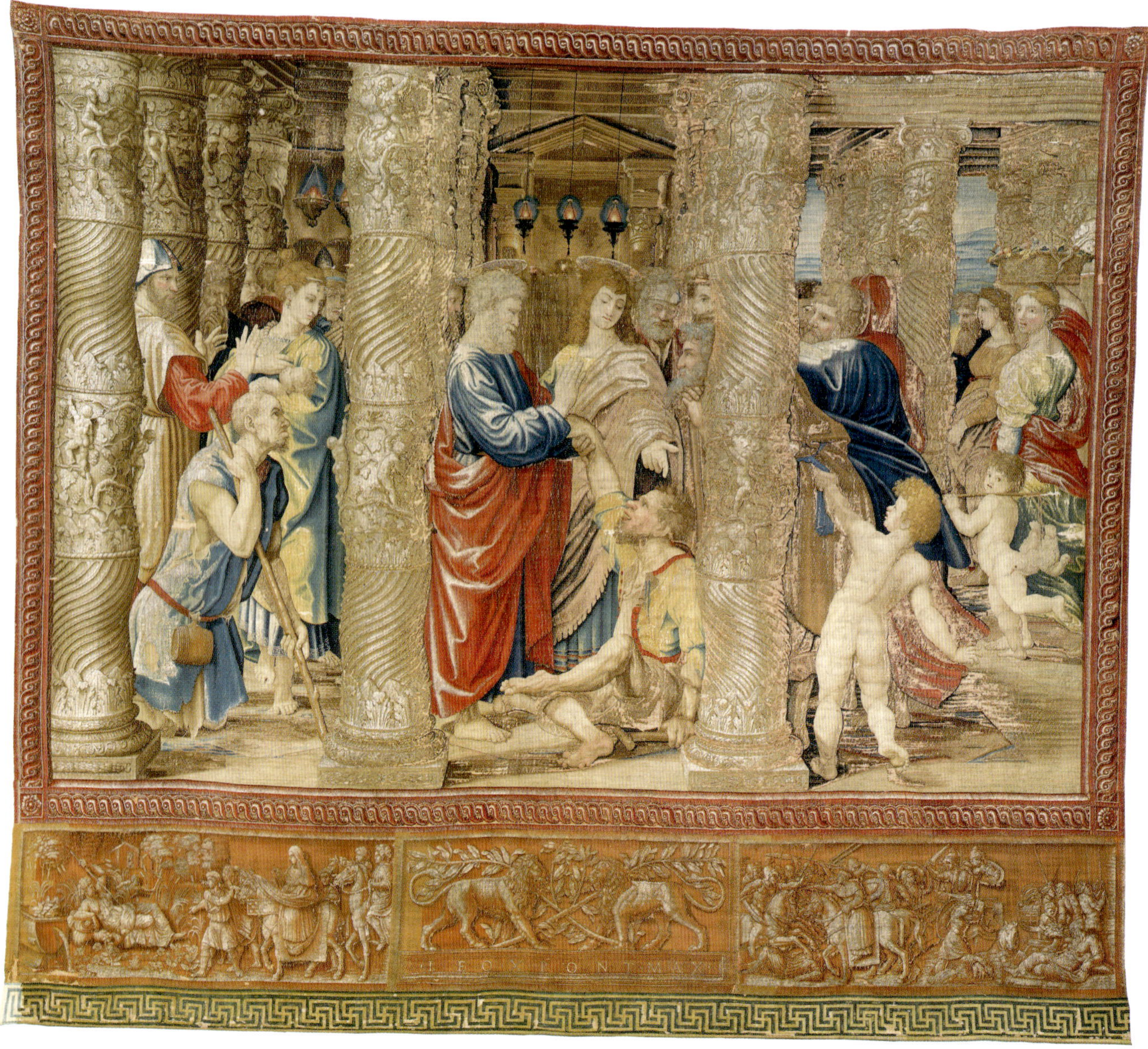

Raphael (Raffaello Sanzio) and Pieter van Aelst

St. Peter Healing a Lame Man

The healing of the lame man was St. Peter's first miracle as an apostle. According to the Acts of the Apostles, St. Peter healed a crippled beggar by the door of the Temple with the simple words: "In the name of Jesus Christ of Nazareth, rise up and walk!" (Acts 3:6). Raphael sets the scene beneath the mighty twisted columns of Solomon's Temple in Jerusalem, whose form and decoration Pieter van Aelst has skillfully translated into tapestry. The columns divide the image into three segments. In the center we see the act of healing taking place, with apostles St. Peter and St. John and the lame man. Raphael has chosen to depict the moment when St. Peter takes the beggar, who is sitting on the floor, by the hand and thereby effects the miracle. Behind him stands St. John, who draws attention to the incident with an outstretched arm. The reactions of the bystanders in the Temple, who witness the miracle from the side colonnades, are depicted with great vivacity. Among them, on the left-hand side, is a standing woman nursing her child and a shabbily dressed shepherd or pilgrim observing the events reverently as he leans on his staff.

Raphael (Raffaello Sanzio), 1483–1520 and Pieter van Aelst (?–1536)
***St. Peter Healing a Lame Man*, ca. 1515–1519**
501 x 566 cm; Wool, silk, silver-gilt thread
Pinacoteca, Room VII

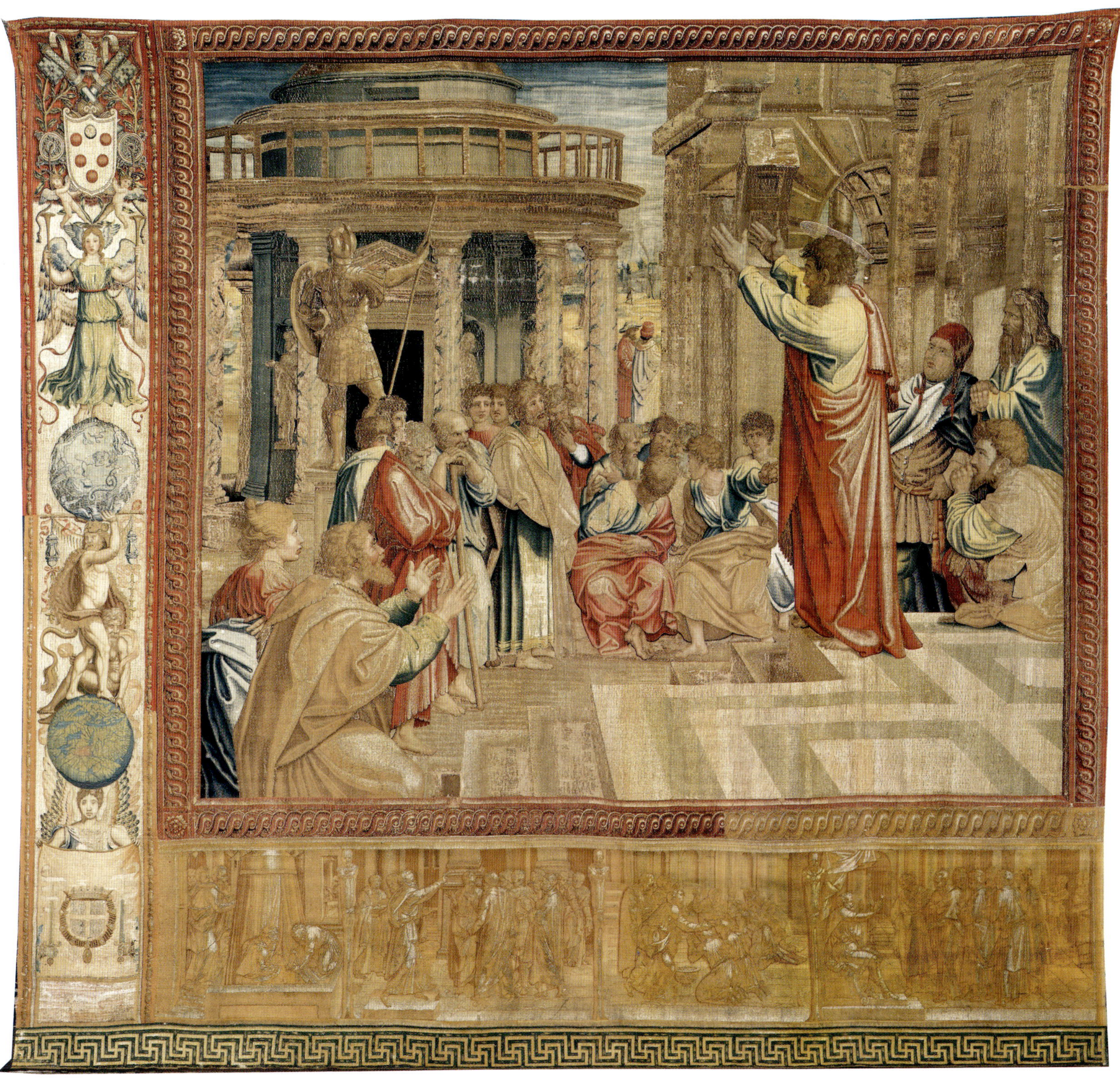

Raphael (Raffaello Sanzio), 1483–1520 and Pieter van Aelst (?–1536)
***St. Paul Preaching in Athens*, ca. 1515–1519**
501 x 566 cm; Wool, silk, silver-gilt thread
Pinacoteca, Room VII

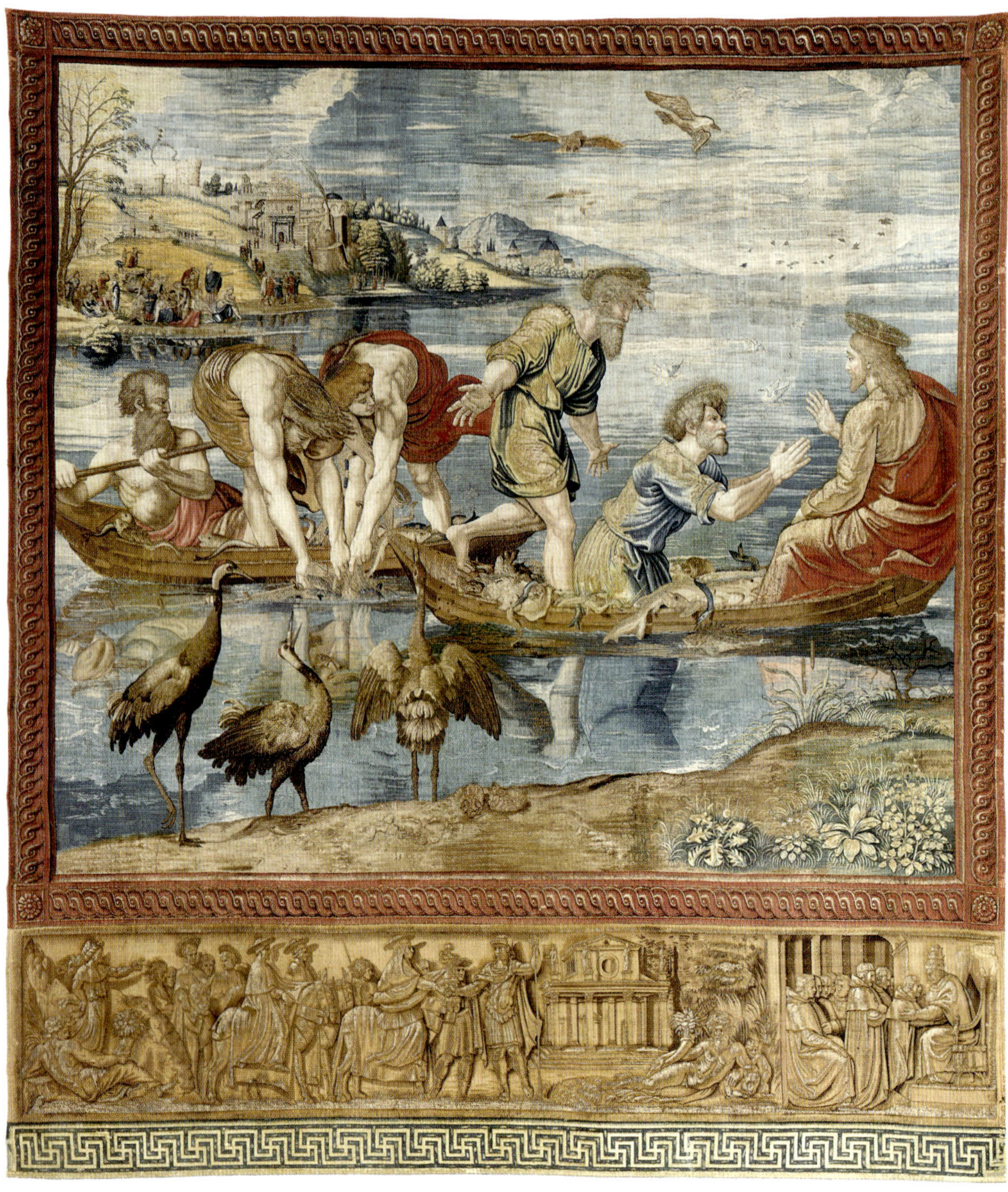

Raphael (Raffaello Sanzio) and Pieter van Aelst

The Miraculous Draught of Fishes

The Miraculous Draught of Fishes, one of the most beautiful tapestries in the Apostle series, depicts the calling of the first disciple, the fisherman Simon Peter. According to the account in the Gospel of St. Luke (Luke; 4-7), Jesus climbed into the boat next to him and commanded him to launch out into the Sea of Galilee to fish. Soon Peter's boat and a second boat that had joined them were so full of fish that they were in danger of sinking. Raphael has chosen to depict the moment of high drama when Simon Peter beseeches Jesus to save them. The Savior called upon them to become his disciples with the famous words: "Fear not; for henceforth thou shalt catch men" (Luke 5:10). Raphael's composition masterfully contrasts calmness and tension, idyll and danger—embodied in the swaying figure of the standing fisherman and the serenely seated Christ. Pieter van Aelst reproduced Raphael's admirably realistic designs for the fish, birds, shore plants, and landscape with supreme mastery. The realistic reflections in the water of the figures and trees also make an important contribution to the work's impact.

Raphael (Raffaello Sanzio), 1483–1520 and Pieter van Aelst (?–1536)
***The Miraculous Draught of Fishes,* ca. 1515–1519**
493 x 440 cm; Wool, silk, silver-gilt thread
Pinacoteca, Room VII

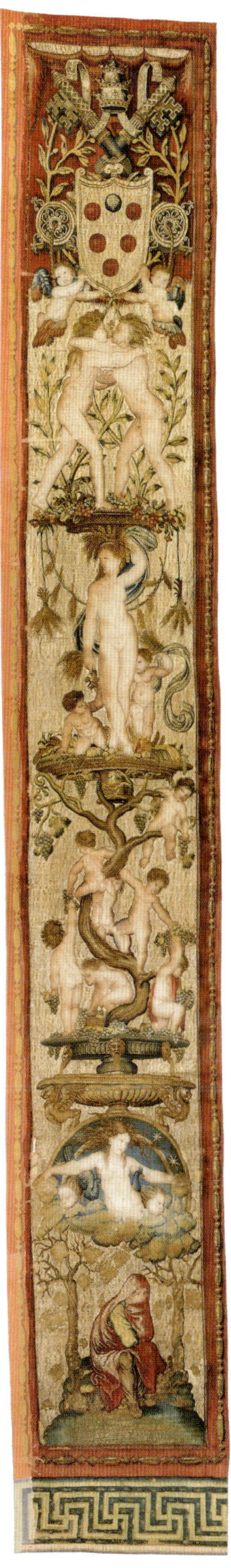

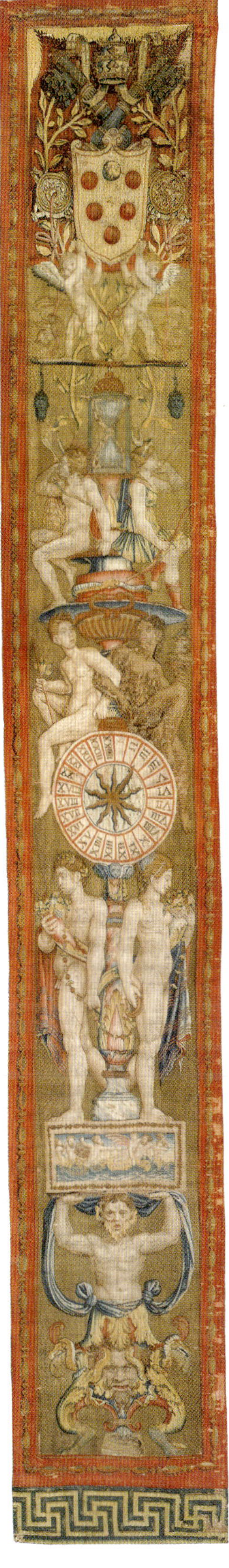

Raphael (Raffaello Sanzio), 1483–1520 and Pieter van Aelst (?–1536)
***Frieze of the Seasons*, ca. 1515–1519**
490 x 80 cm; Wool, silk, silver-gilt thread
Pinacoteca, Room VII

Raphael (Raffaello Sanzio), 1483–1520 and Pieter van Aelst (?–1536)
***Frieze of the Hours*, ca. 1515–1519**
490 x 80 cm; Wool, silk, silver-gilt thread
Pinacoteca, Room VII

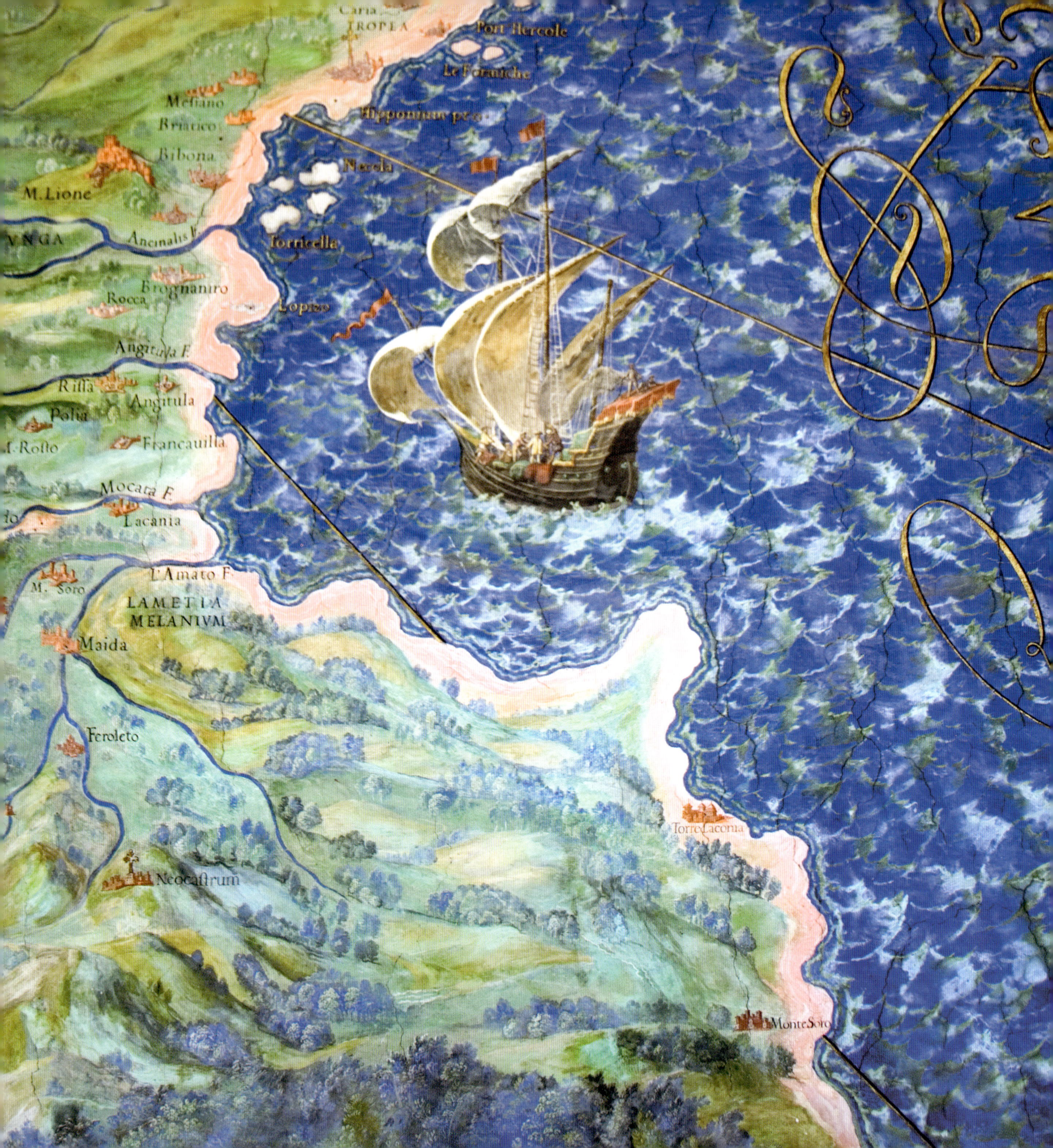

TROPEA
Port Hercole
Meliano
Briatico
Bibona
M. Lione
VNGA
Ancinalis F.
Torricella
Rocca
Angitula F.
Rissa
Angitula
Polia
Francauilla
Mocata F.
Lacania
L'Amato F.
M. Soro
LAMETIA
MELANIVM
Maida
Feroleto
Neocastrum
Torre Laconia
MonteSoro

GALLERY OF MAPS

Extending for 120 meters, the Gallery of Maps houses the largest cycle of geographical pictures ever painted. The gallery, which is also one of the world's oldest, consists of sixteen broad walls between the windows on each of the long sides, plus narrow spaces at the four ends of the long walls and on either side of each short wall. The forty geographical pictures were commissioned by Gregory XIII (1502–1585, reigned from 1572) and completed in an astonishingly short period of time between 1580 and 1581. They depict the various Italian provinces and the territories belonging to the Papal States.

The maps were based on full-sized drawings, or cartoons, by the Dominican monk and cartographer Ignazio Danti (1536–1586) and executed by a large workshop that included the Flemish artist Paul Bril, who specialized in landscapes. Not all the maps have survived in their original condition; the flawless appearance of the majority of the paintings is due to restorations carried out in some cases as long ago as the early seventeenth century.

The gallery begins by juxtaposing maps of antique and contemporary Italy. These are followed by the Italian provinces, the major islands, and the area around the papal seat in Avignon. The gallery itself can be seen as a plan of Italy: the long corridor represents the Apennines while the territories west of the mountain range are depicted on the longitudinal west wall and those to the east of the range on the longitudinal east wall. The narrow spaces on each end wall are filled with depictions of the Italian islands of Tremiti, Elba, Corfu, and Malta at the northern end and Italy's four main ports, Civitavecchia, Ancona, Genoa, and Venice, at the southern end.

Each of the maps is set in a broad rectangular frame with varying ornamentation, topped with a cartouche identifying the location. In some cases smaller inserts with city views are set into the maps. They are executed in an illusionistic manner with frayed edges and apparently curling corners as if a colored copperplate engraving had been glued or tacked to the wall. All the maps are bird's-eye views, so that mountains, rivers, and townships are seen from above and from a slightly diagonal perspective.

The maps locate every place of significance in the history of Italy and the Papal States, and many important events have been worked into the images. For example, the map of Malta refers to the Turkish siege of 1565 and the island of Corfu has been paired with the Battle of Lepanto. To add to the maps' vivacity, they are decorated with white-capped waves and sailing ships, and Neptune, the mythological god of the sea, and other fabulous creatures disport in the water.

The gallery's vaulted ceiling comprises seventeen main pictures, in some cases alternating with smaller images and in others arranged into large, square, symmetrical fields contained within broad stucco frames and identified by Latin inscriptions. The ceiling program embodies the papal claim to secular and spiritual supremacy and includes scenes from the history of Rome and the papacy, beginning with the presumed baptism of Constantine, the legendary donation of Constantine, and the Battle of the Milvian Bridge. Other historical tableaux include the meeting between Emperor Frederick I Barbarossa and Pope Alexander III in Venice (1177), which marked the reconciliation between pope and emperor after some twenty years of enmity. There are also scenes from mythology and the Old Testament, such as the sacrifice of Isaac. The ceiling paintings often refer to the maps in their vicinity. For example, the fresco depicting the founding by St. Romuald of the Camaldolese hermitage near Arezzo is located above the map of Etruria, which roughly corresponds to today's Tuscany. The decoration of the walls and ceiling is therefore governed by a unified overall concept.

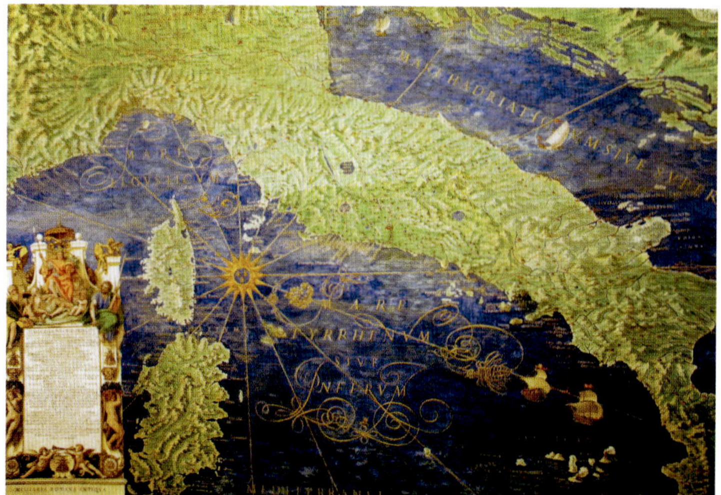

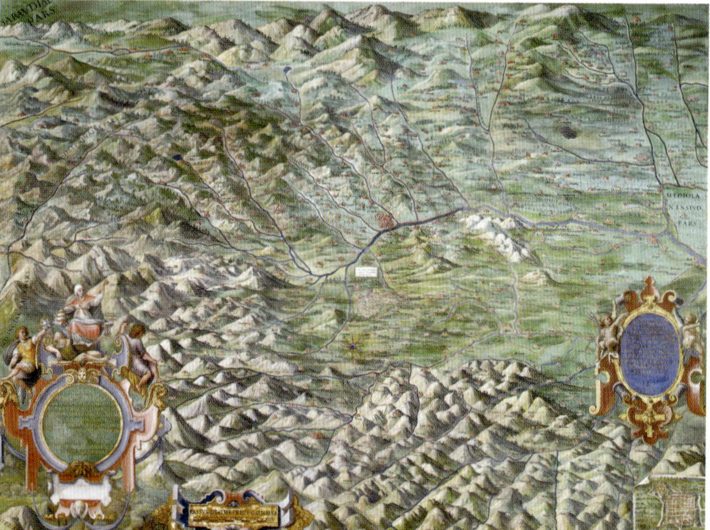

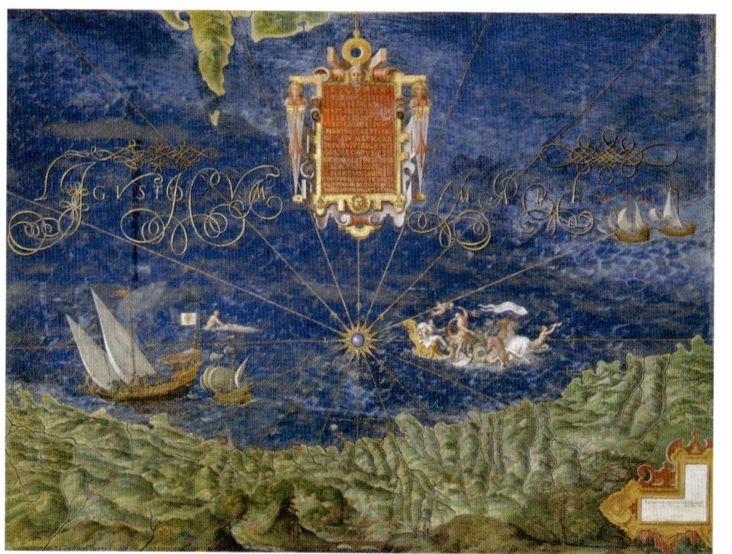

Ignazio Danti, 1536–1586
***Italia Antica*, detail, 1580–1581**
320 x 430 cm; Fresco
Gallery of Maps

Ignazio Danti, 1536–1586
***Piedmont and Monferrato, including a City View of Turin*, 1580–1581**
320 x 430 cm; Fresco
Gallery of Maps

Ignazio Danti, 1536–1586
***Liguria*, 1580–1581**
320 x 430 cm; Fresco
Gallery of Maps

Ignazio Danti, 1536–1586
***View of Genoa*, detail, 1580-1581**
320 x 430 cm; Fresco
Gallery of Maps

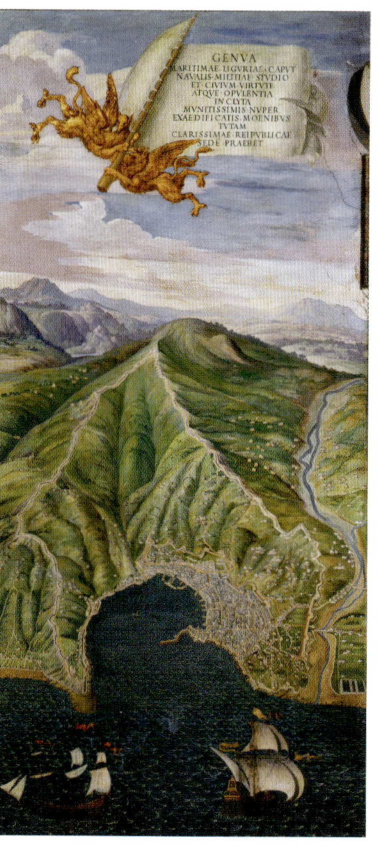

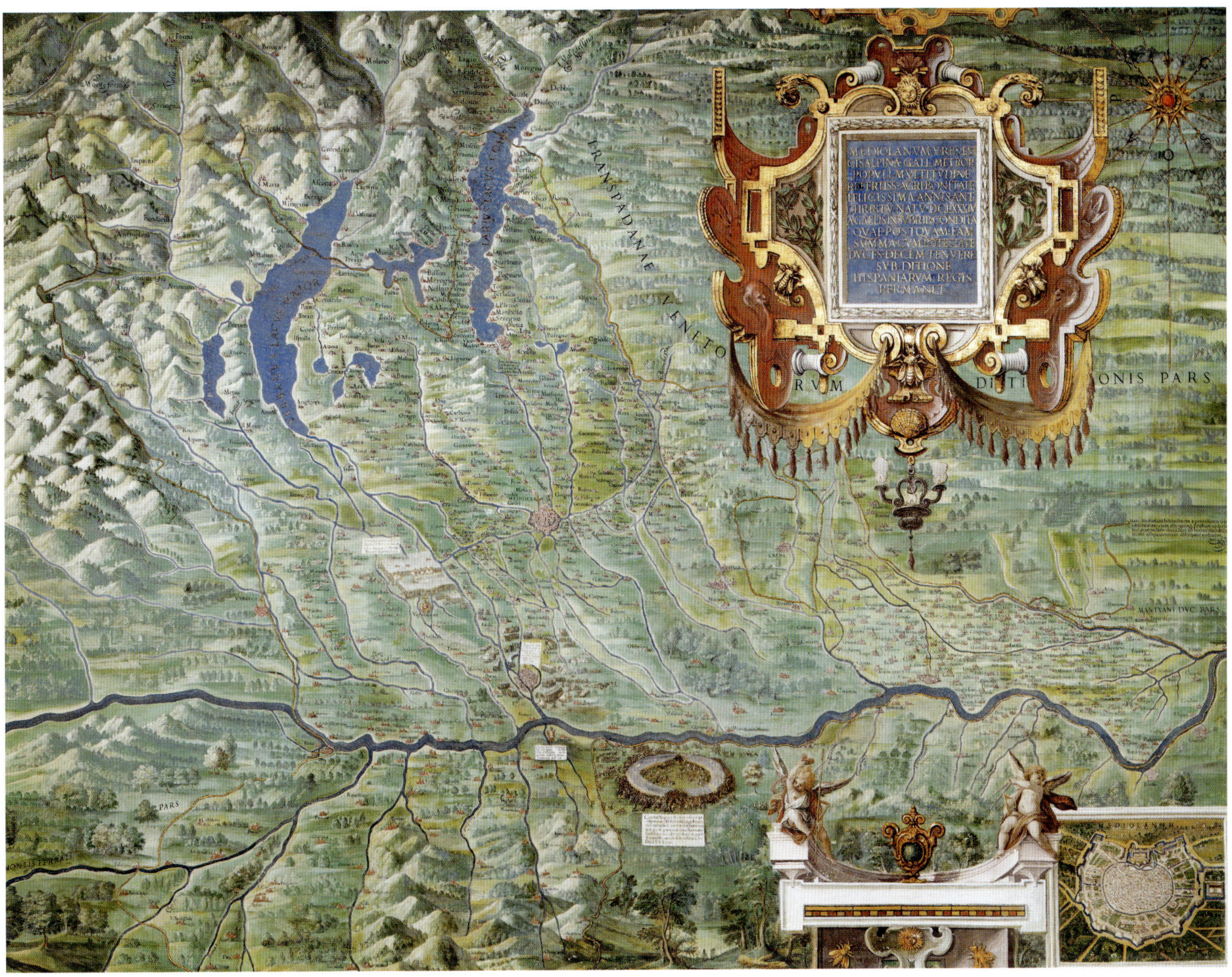

Ignazio Danti and Workshop

Milan

The map of the Duchy of Milan (Mediolanensis Ducatus) shows Lombardy with the Po River cutting through the territory from west to east. The main map, which extends as far north as the lakes in the foothills of the Alps and the Swiss border, is embellished in the foreground with a number of small landscapes. A cartouche richly adorned with arabesque work provides explanation, and a number of historical incidents are also marked. The most striking of these is Hannibal's victorious battle against the Romans by the Ticino River, where he deployed elephants carrying small fortified towers on their backs. There is also the victory of Charlemagne over the Lombards in 774, which led to the incorporation of the Lombard Kingdom into the Frankish Empire. A then-recent event also made its way onto the map, namely the siege of Pavia by the troops of King Francis I of France in 1527. A framed detail view in the foreground shows a bird's-eye view of the city of Milan. It is easy to distinguish the densely built-up medieval city from its newly fortified expansion, which also includes Castello Sforzesco, the castle of the dukes of Milan, and various monasteries with large gardens.

Ignazio Danti and workshop, 1536–1586
***Milan*, 1580–1581**
320 x 430 cm; Fresco
Gallery of Maps

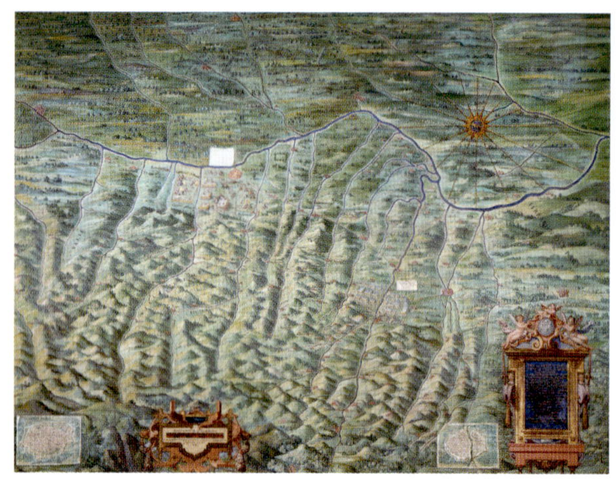

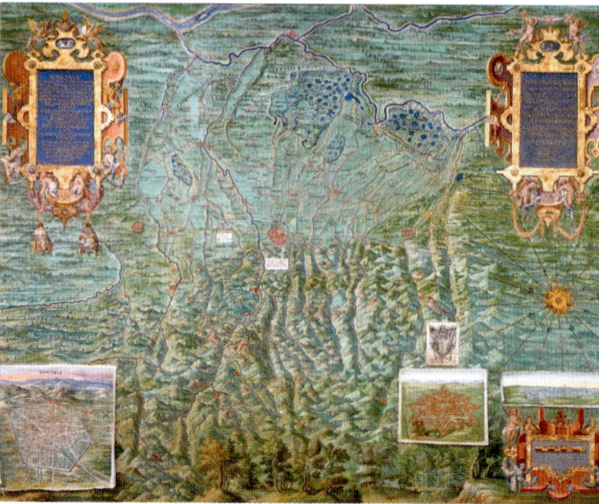

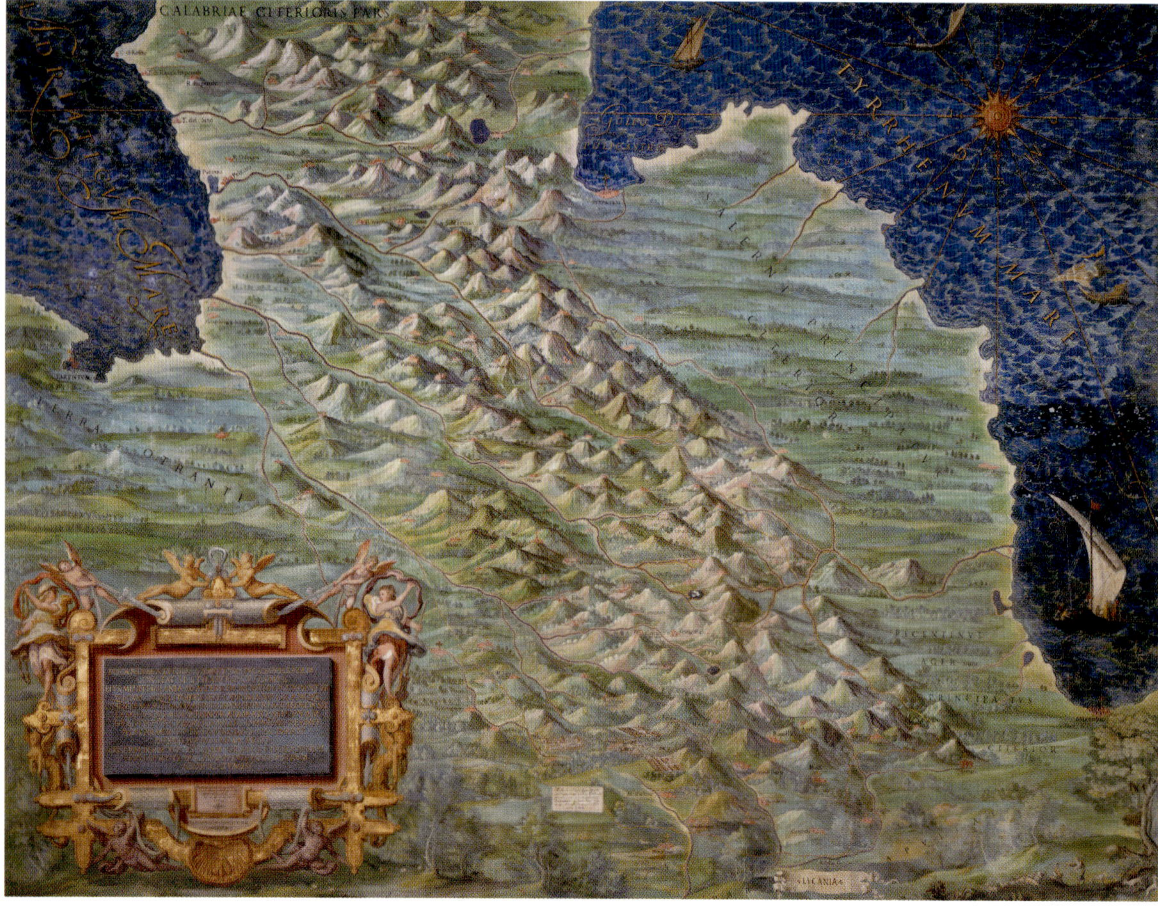

Ignazio Danti, 1536–1586
***Parma and Piacenza*, 1580–1581**
320 x 430 cm; Fresco
Gallery of Maps

Ignazio Danti, 1536–1586
***Territory of Bologna*, 1580–1581**
320 x 430 cm; Fresco
Gallery of Maps

Ignazio Danti, 1536–1586
***Lucania*, 1580–1581**
320 x 430 cm; Fresco
Gallery of Maps

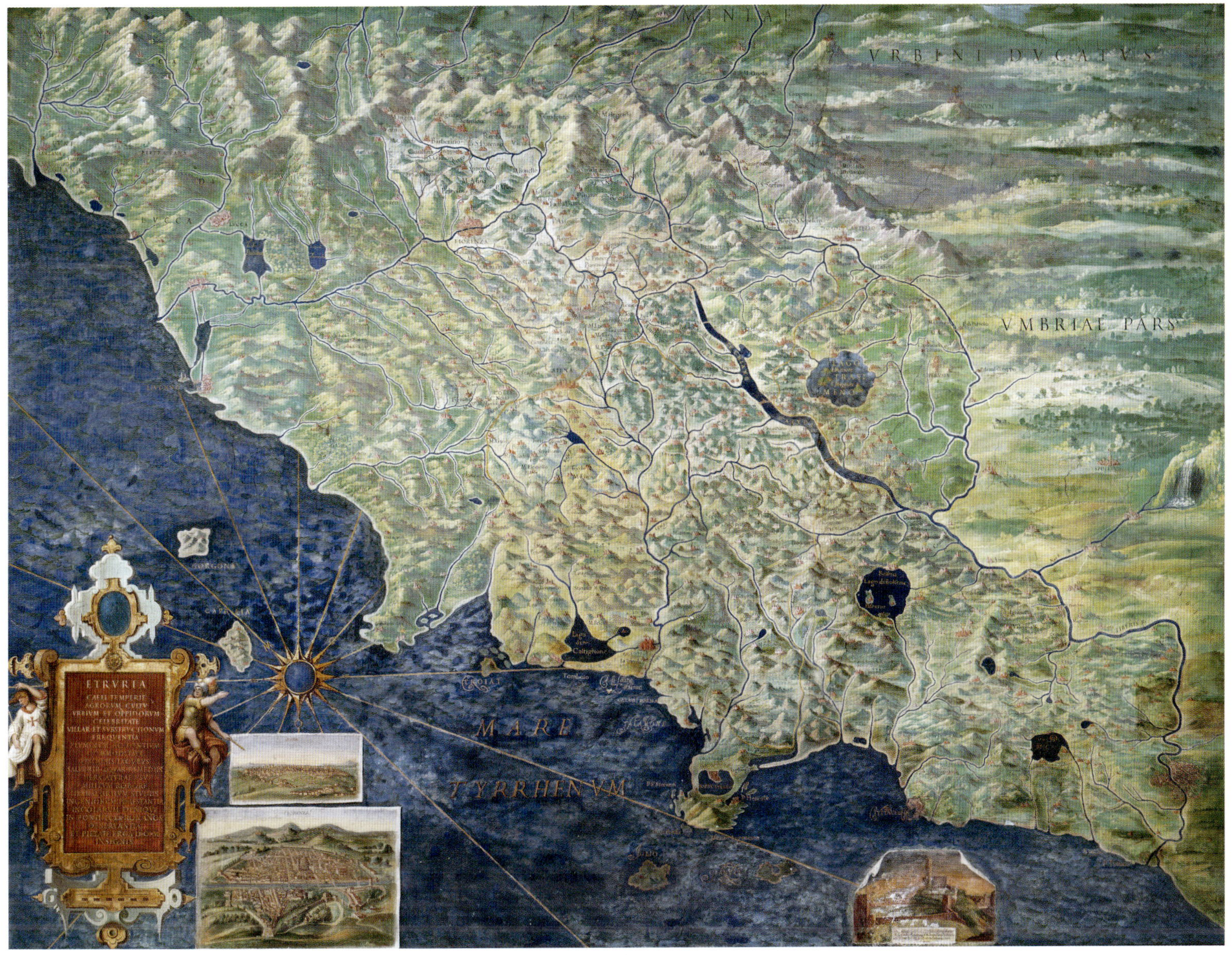

Ignazio Danti and Workshop

Etruria

Etruria covers northern Latium and Tuscany as well as parts of Umbria and the Marches. The main impression conveyed by the map is of a mountainous landscape, depicted by the painter with great precision. A cartouche containing an inscription has been superimposed over the sea, as have a number of detailed views of cities including Siena and Florence. The map is dotted with tiny depictions of towns and castles, all of which are named, just as the tracts of land and rivers have been given their correct geographical designations. Also shown are a number of archaeological sites—depicted by the painter as ruins. On the separate Florence view, we look across the church of San Miniato al Monte and the Arno to the historical heart of the city and the cathedral. Beyond the city walls various smaller settlements can also be made out in the surrounding hills. In the case of Siena, there are outlines of the numerous dynastic towers. A third, badly damaged insert depicts the heavily fortified town of San Miniato, which was ruled by an imperial Statthalter and is dominated by a distinctive castle.

Ignazio Danti and Workshop, 1536–1586
***Etruria*, 1580–1581**
320 x 430 cm, Fresco
Gallery of Maps

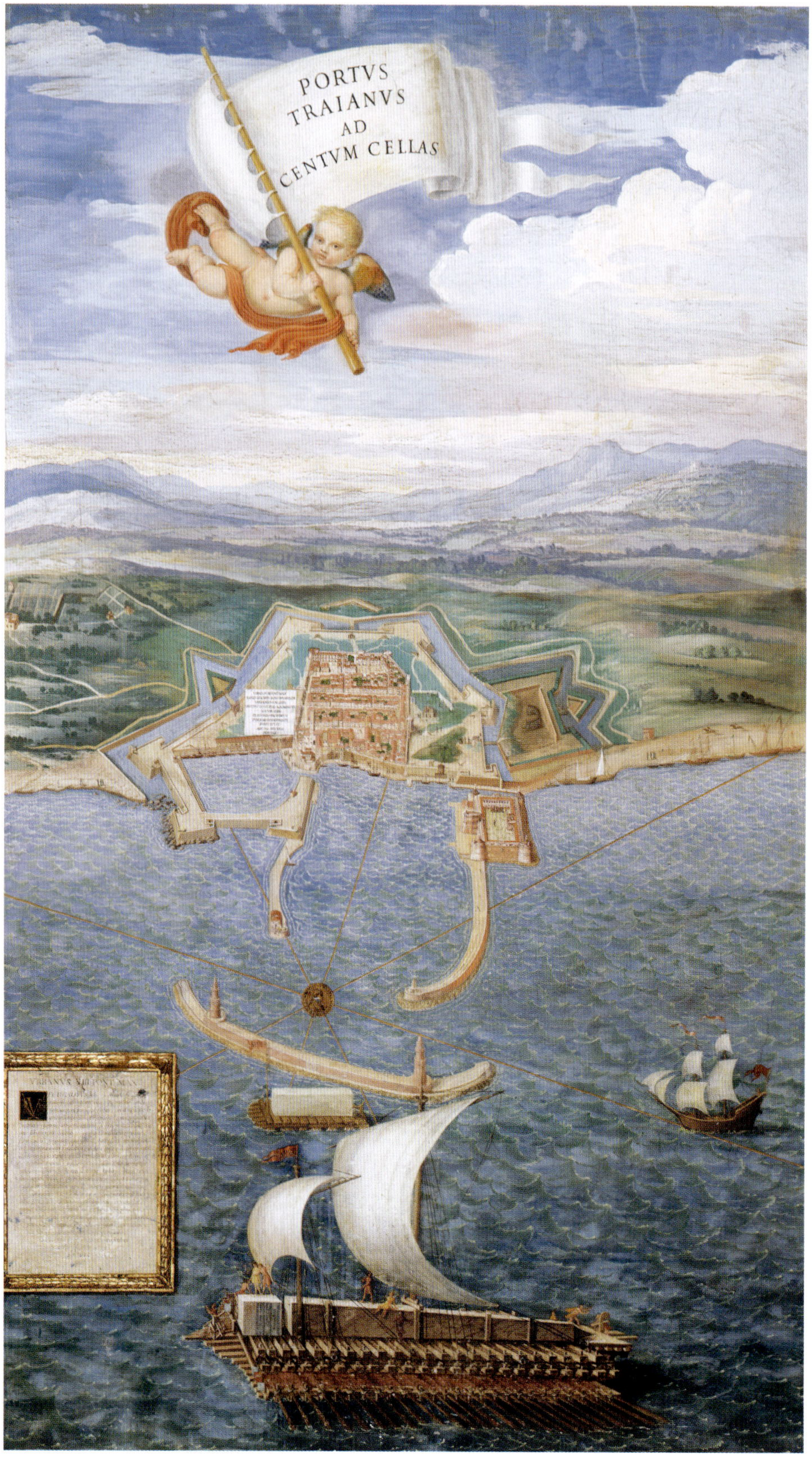

Ignazio Danti, 1536–1586
***Civitavecchia*, 1580–1581**
320 x 430 cm; Fresco
Gallery of Maps

Ignazio Danti, 1536–1586
***Island of Elba*, 1580–1581**
320 x 430 cm; Fresco
Gallery of Maps

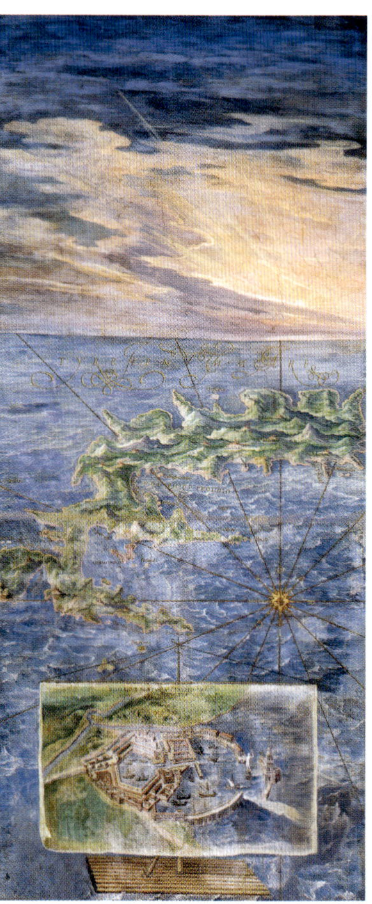

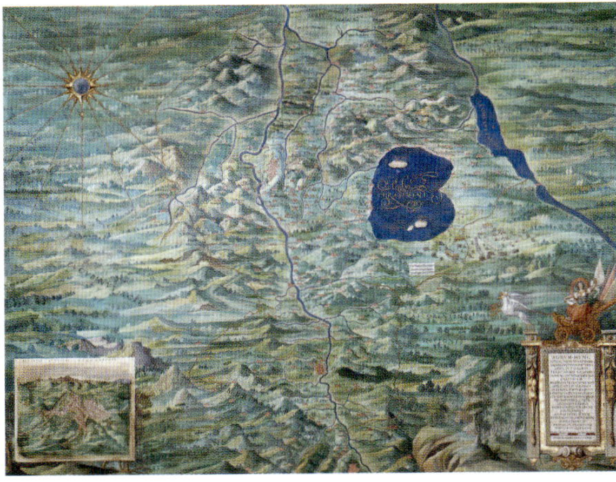

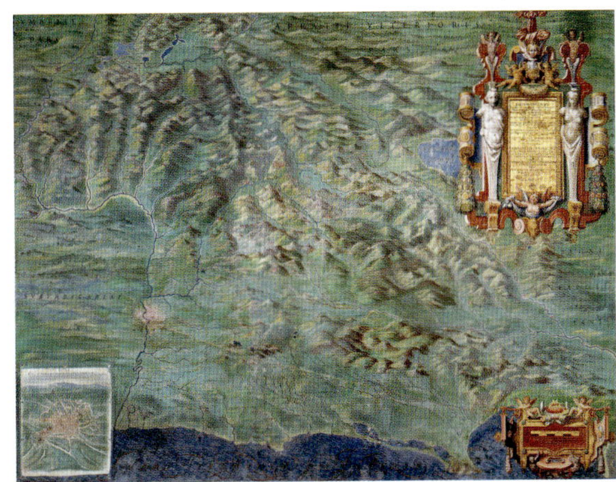

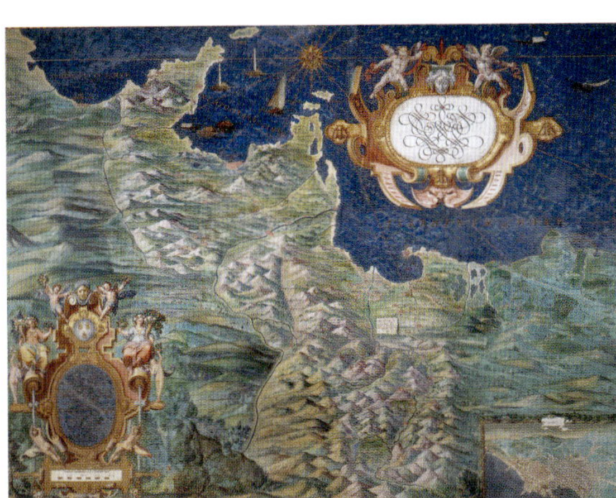

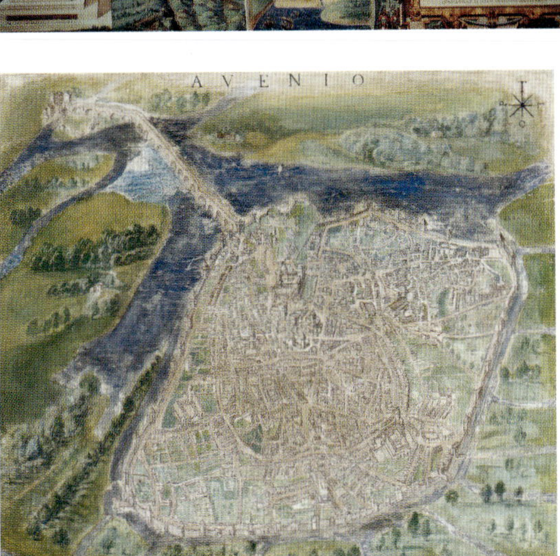

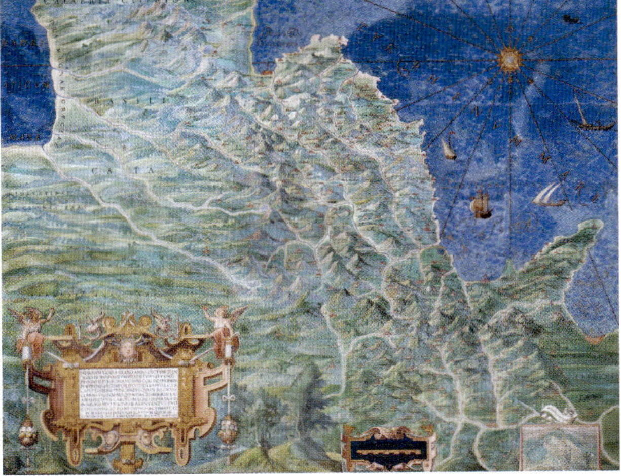

Ignazio Danti, 1536–1586
***Perugia and Citta di Castello*, 1580–1581**
320 x 430 cm; Fresco
Gallery of Maps

Ignazio Danti, 1536–1586
***Latium*, 1580–1581**
320 x 430 cm; Fresco
Gallery of Maps

Ignazio Danti, 1536–1586
***Flaminia from Cattolica to the Walls of Comacchio*, 1580–1581**
320 x 430 cm, Fresco
Gallery of Maps

Ignazio Danti, 1536–1586
***Campania*, 1580–1581**
320 x 430 cm, Fresco
Gallery of Maps

Ignazio Danti, 1536–1586
***City Map of Avignon*, detail, 1580–1581**
320 x 430 cm; Fresco
Gallery of Maps

Ignazio Danti, 1536–1586
***Southern Campania*, 1580–1581**
320 x 430 cm; Fresco
Gallery of Maps

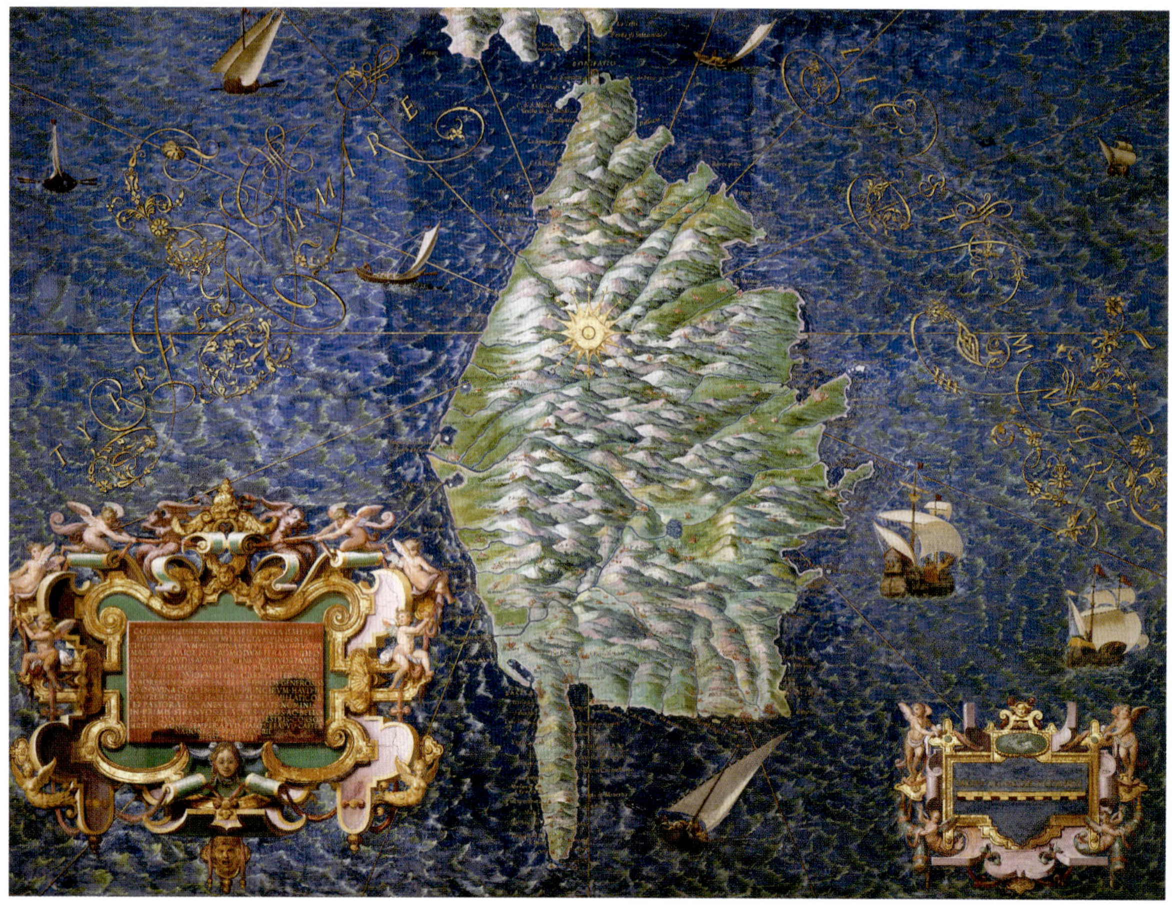

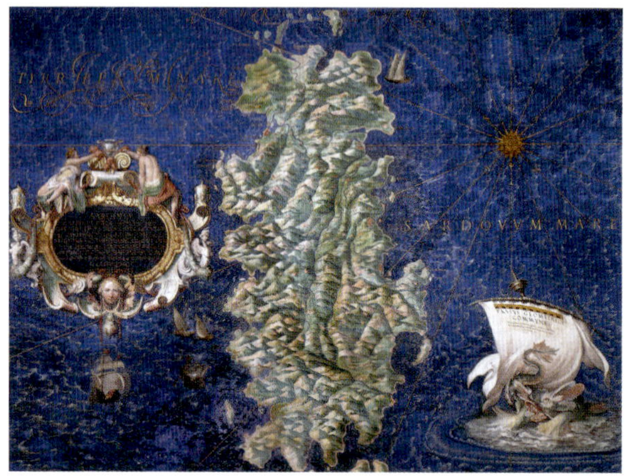

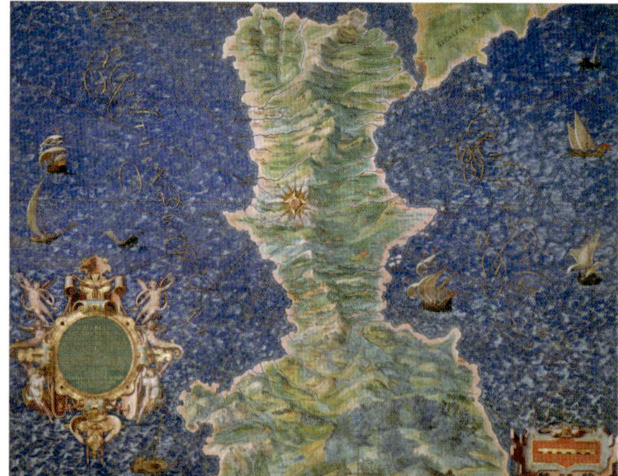

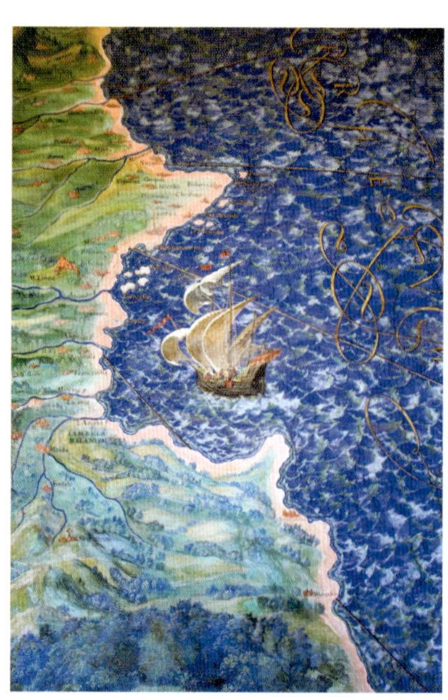

Ignazio Danti, 1536–1586
***Corsica*, 1580–1581**
320 x 430 cm; Fresco
Gallery of Maps

Ignazio Danti, 1536–1586
***Sardinia*, 1580–1581**
320 x 430 cm; Fresco
Gallery of Maps

Ignazio Danti, 1536–1586
***Southern Calabria*, 1580–1581**
320 x 430 cm; Fresco
Gallery of Maps

Ignazio Danti, 1536–1586
***Southern Calabria detail*, 1580–1581**
320 x 430 cm; Fresco
Gallery of Maps

Ignazio Danti and Workshop

Sicily

True to its topography, Sicily is depicted as a mountainous island set in a dark-blue sea whose waves break against the shoreline. The map is supplemented with detailed views of individual cities superimposed on the sea and illusionistically secured with tacks. The largest of these inserts is a view of the city of Syracuse, located on the east coast, and its surrounding landscape. We are shown a bird's-eye view of the old city and harbor and, set somewhat apart, the castle complex dating to the time of Emperor Frederick II (1194–1250, reigned from 1220). The coastline around Syracuse, at that time Sicily's most important city (militarily at least), is punctuated by numerous walls and towers. Alongside is a view of the city of Messina, made to look as if it has been painted on a piece of fraying paper, and a third insert shows Panormus (Palermo). The main map and the detailed views are all aligned with the cardinal points, and the text panel provides geographical information such as the distance to Africa and the circumference of the island.

Ignazio Danti and workshop, 1536–1586
***Sicily*, 1580–1581**
320 x 430 cm, Fresco
Gallery of Maps

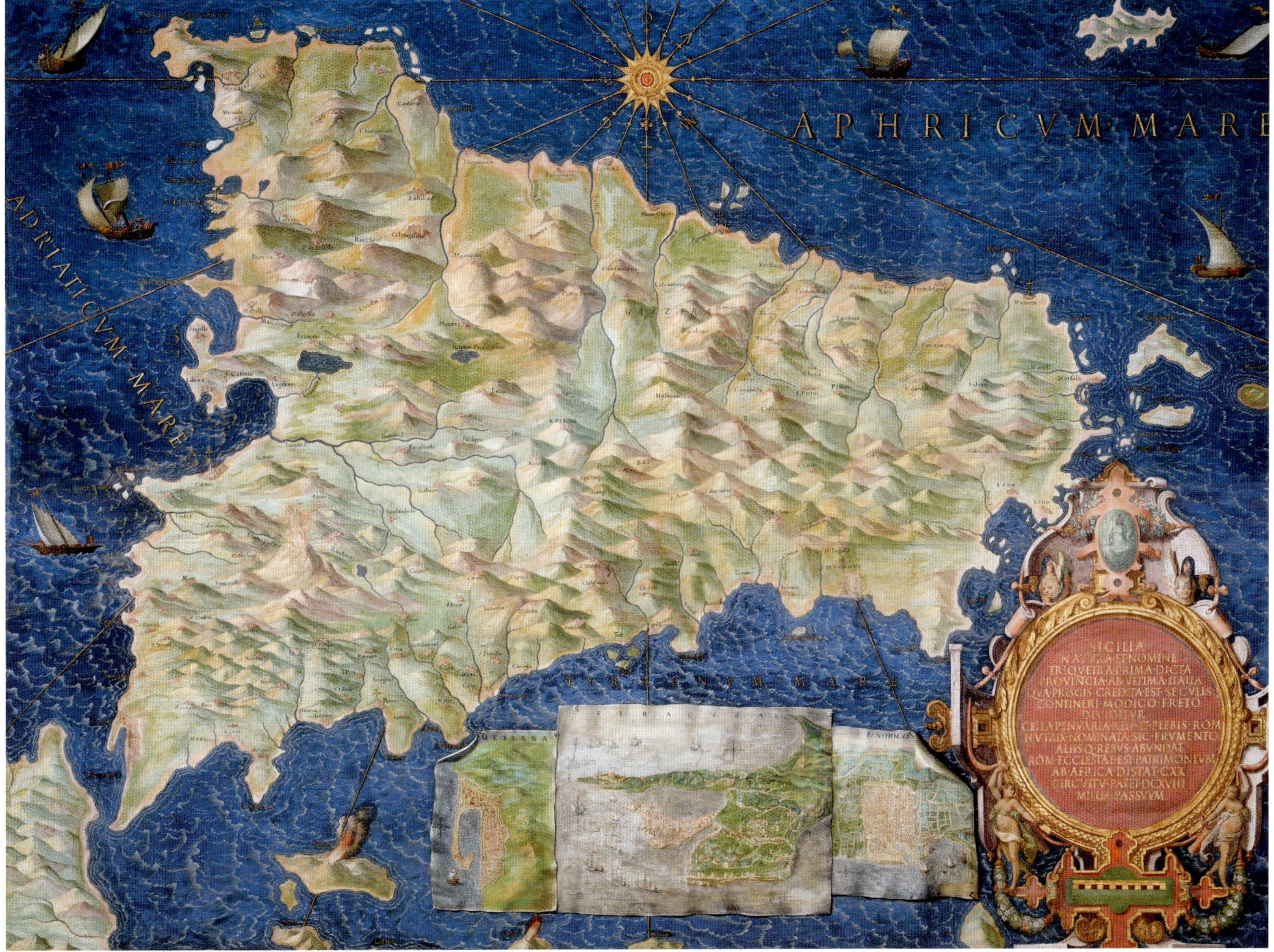

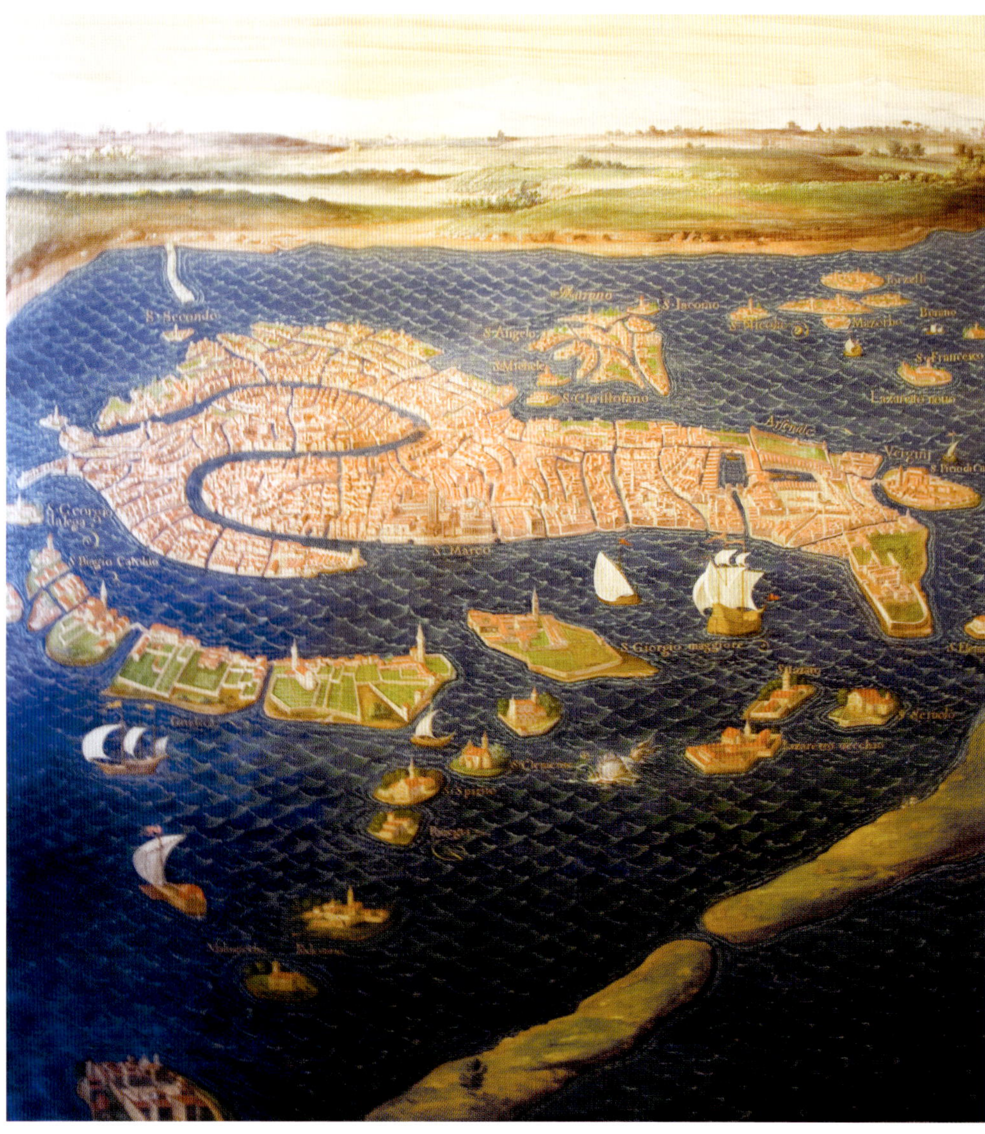

Ignazio Danti and Workshop

Venice

This aerial view of Venice occupies a narrow space on the southern (end) wall of the gallery. Such a perspective called for particular skill as there was no vantage point from where a painter could gain a commanding view of the city. Venice is shown from the south with the long loop of the Grand Canal clearly visible. At the center of the picture we see St. Mark's Basilica with its campanile, St. Mark's Square, and the Doge's Palace. The Rialto Bridge in its earlier wooden incarnation can only just be made out against the dark surface of the water. A few years after the completion of this fresco the Ponte Rialto was replaced by the famous stone bridge that still stands today. The densely built-up main island is contrasted with the gardens of the southern islands, above all La Giudecca. In the distance the hazy outline of the Alps can be made out. As well as depicting buildings such as San Marco and other important landmarks in a realistic manner, the painter has also identified them. The small surrounding islands, with numerous ships sailing between them, have also been furnished with labels.

Ignazio Danti and Workshop, 1536–1586
***Venice, delail*, 1580–1581**
320 x 430 cm; Fresco
Gallery of Maps

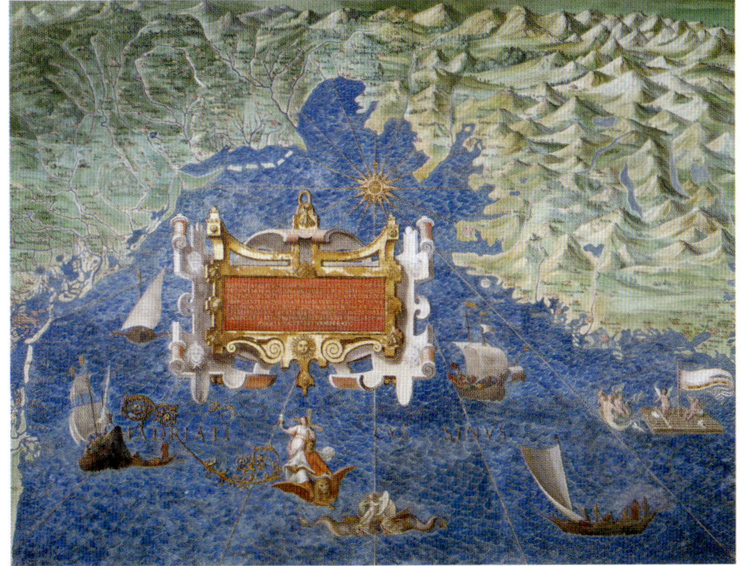

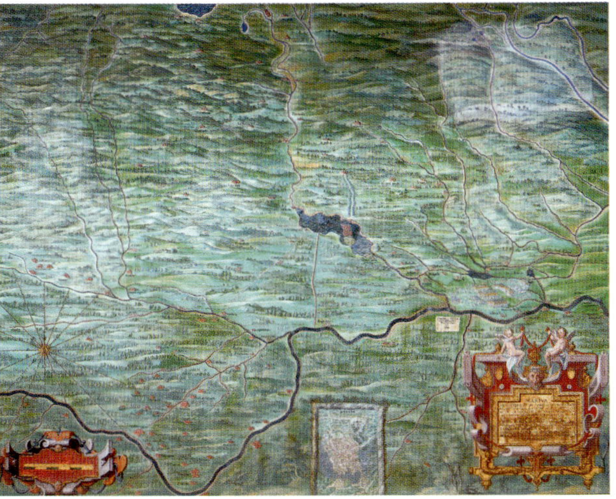

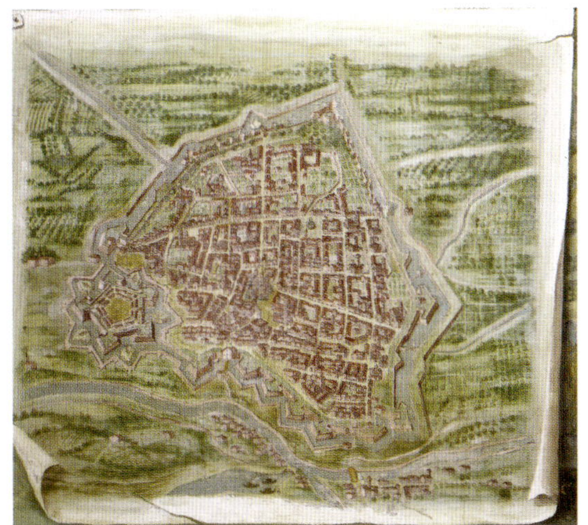

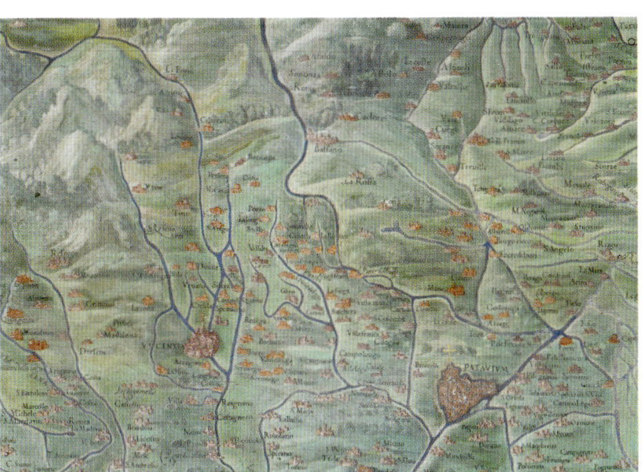

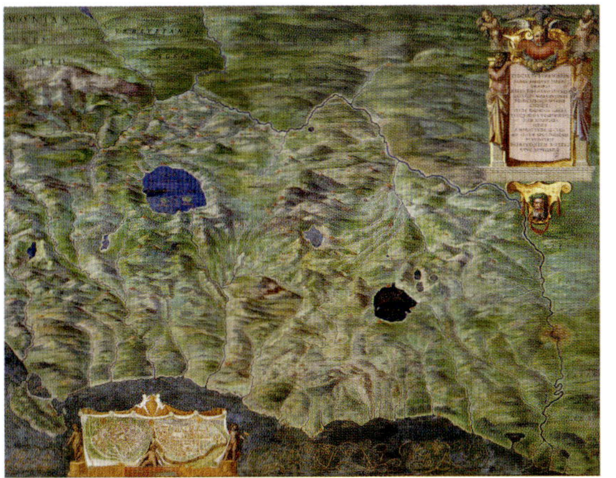

Ignazio Danti, 1536–1586
***Forum Iulii*, 1580–1581**
320 x 430 cm; Fresco
Gallery of Maps

Ignazio Danti, 1536–1586
***The Duchy of Mantua*, 1580–1581**
320 x 430 cm; Fresco
Gallery of Maps

Ignazio Danti, 1536–1586
***Ferrara*, detail, 1580–1581**
320 x 430 cm; Fresco
Gallery of Maps

Ignazio Danti, 1536–1586
***The Mainland Possessions of Venice West of the River Piave*, detail, 1580–1581**
320 x 430 cm; Fresco
Gallery of Maps

Luc Holste, 1596–1661
***Patrimonio di San Pietro (The Papal State): Northern Lazio, including Maps of Viterbo and Orvieto (based on Bellarmato's map "Chorographia Tusciae,"* 1536, 1632–1633**
320 x 430 cm; Fresco
Gallery of Maps

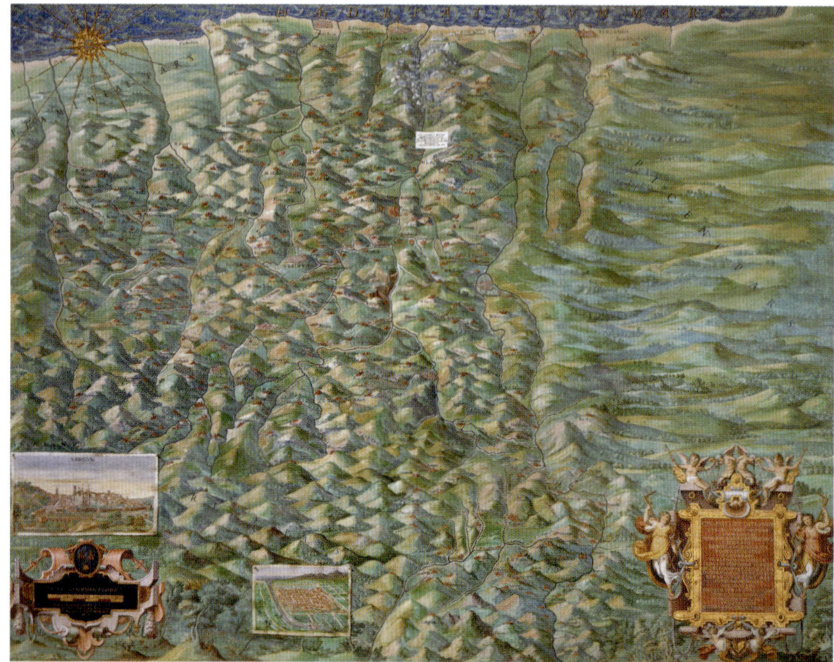

Ignazio Danti, 1536–1586
***Urbino*, 1580–1581**
320 x 430 cm; Fresco
Gallery of Maps

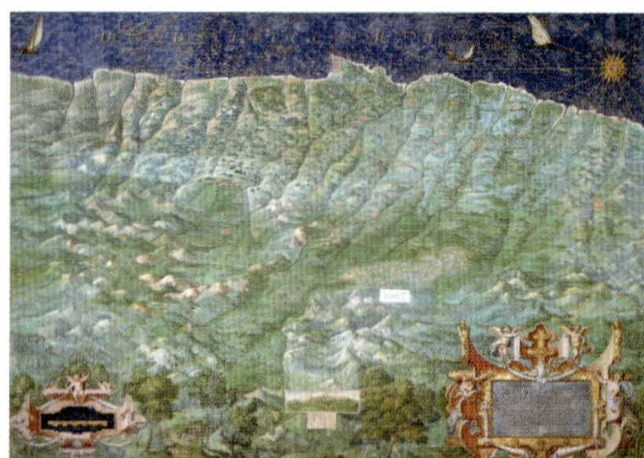

Ignazio Danti, 1536–1586
***Marche*, 1580–1581**
320 x 430 cm; Fresco
Gallery of Maps

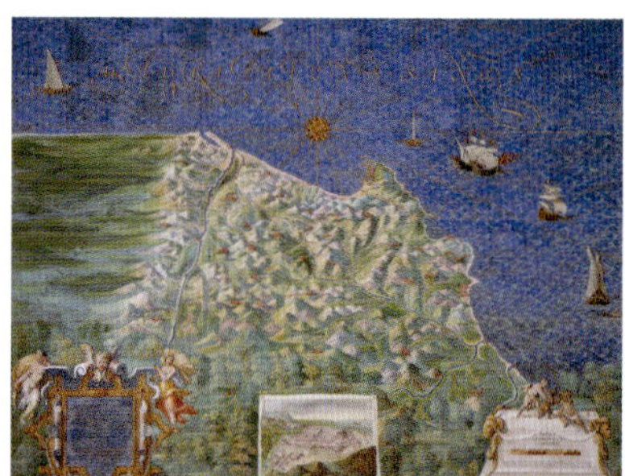

Ignazio Danti, 1536–1586
***Territorio d'Ancona*, 1580–1581**
320 x 430 cm; Fresco
Gallery of Maps

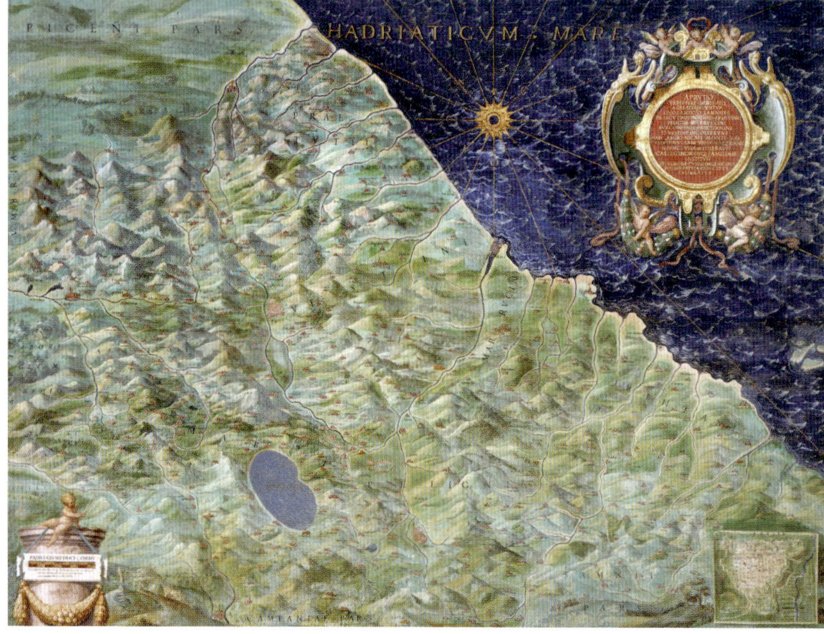

Ignazio Danti, 1536–1586
***Abruzzo*, 1580–1581**
320 x 430 cm; Fresco
Gallery of Maps

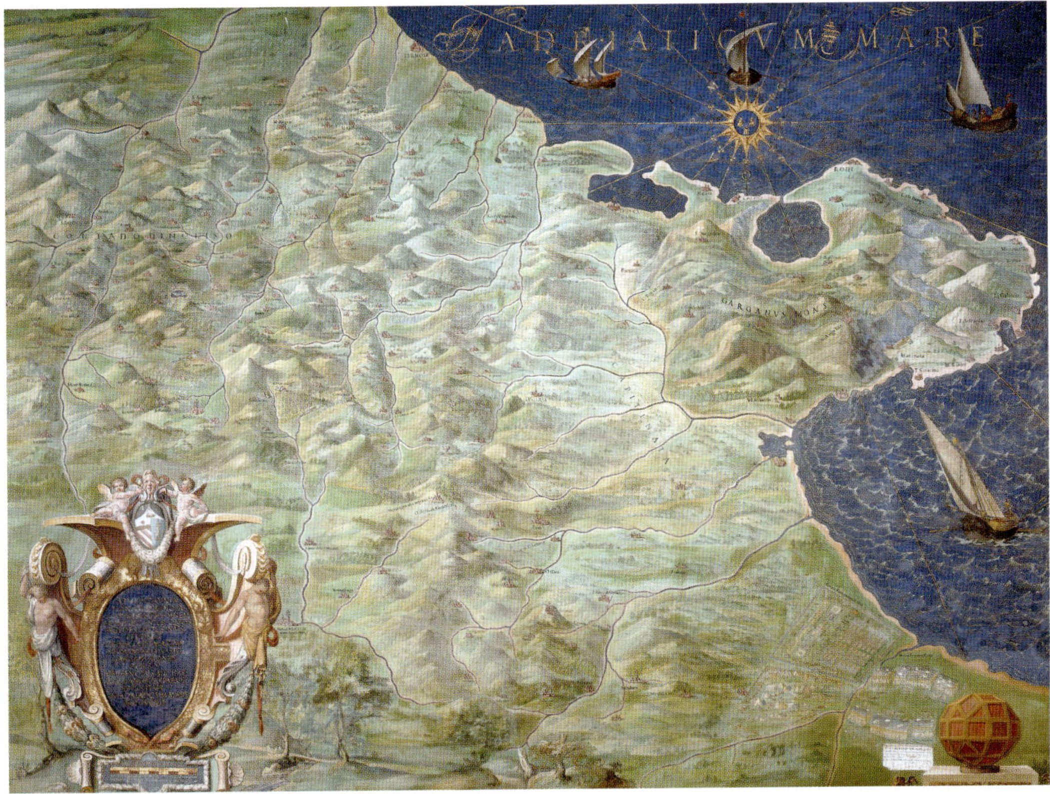

Ignazio Danti, 1536–1586
***Apulia*, 1580–1581**
320 x 430 cm; Fresco
Gallery of Maps

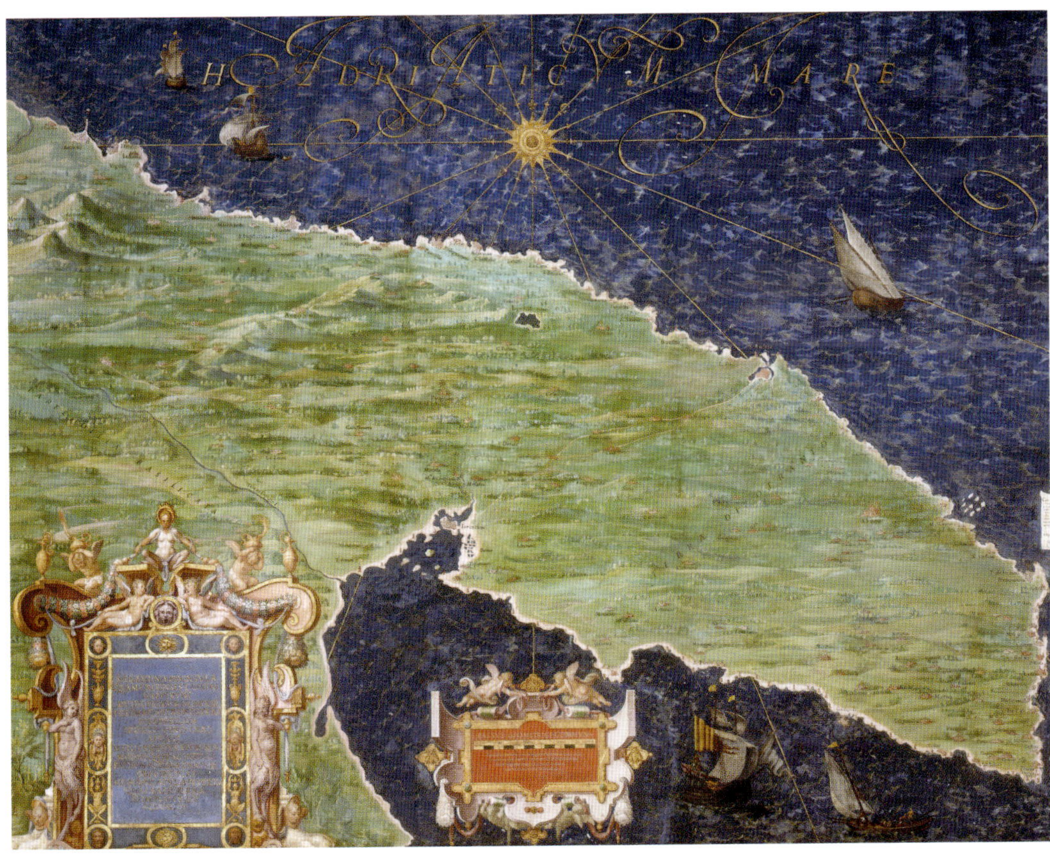

Ignazio Danti, 1536–1586
***Southern Puglia*, 1580–1581**
320 x 430 cm; Fresco
Gallery of Maps

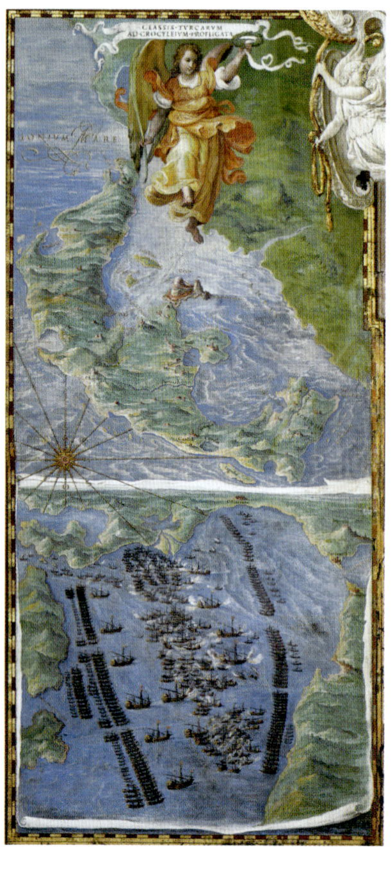

Ignazio Danti, 1536–1586
***Isle of Corfu and Battle of Lepanto (1571)*, 1580–1581**
320 x 430 cm; Fresco
Gallery of Maps

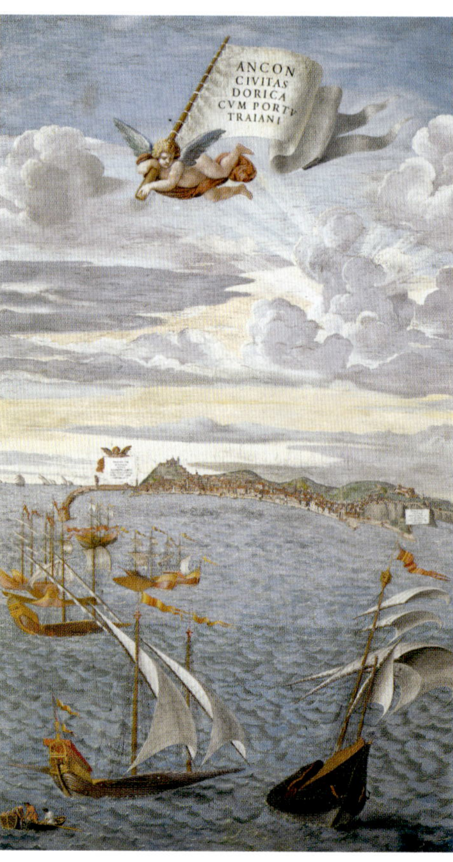

Ignazio Danti, 1536–1586
***Ancona*, 1580–1581**
320 x 430 cm; Fresco
Gallery of Maps

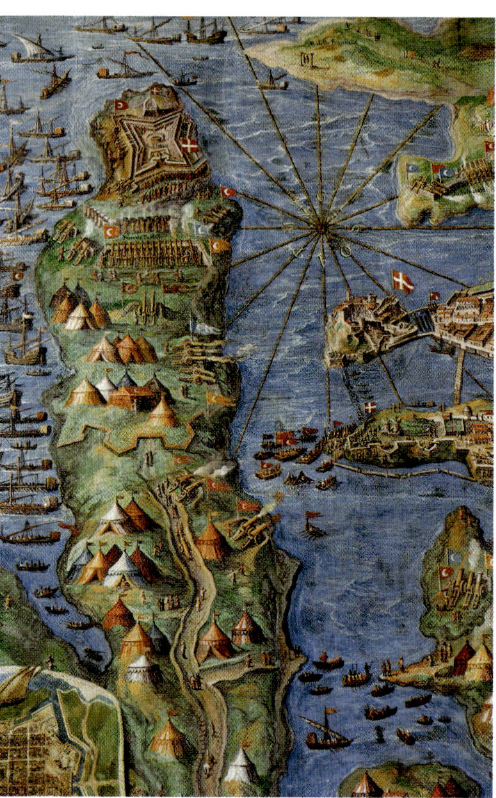

Ignazio Danti, 1536–1586
***The Isle of Malta, (with the Siege of Valletta by the Ottoman Fleet)*, detail, 1565, 1580–1581**
320 x 430 cm; Fresco
Gallery of Maps

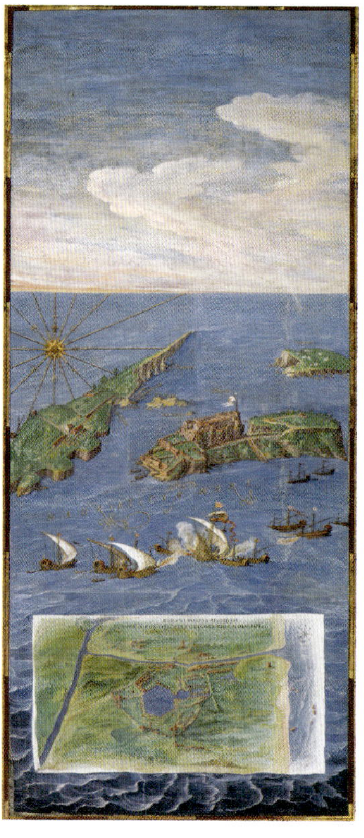

Ignazio Danti, 1536–1586
***Tremiti Islands and a View of Ostia Antica, including a Naval Battle against the Turks (1567)*, 1580–1581**
320 x 430 cm; Fresco
Gallery of Maps

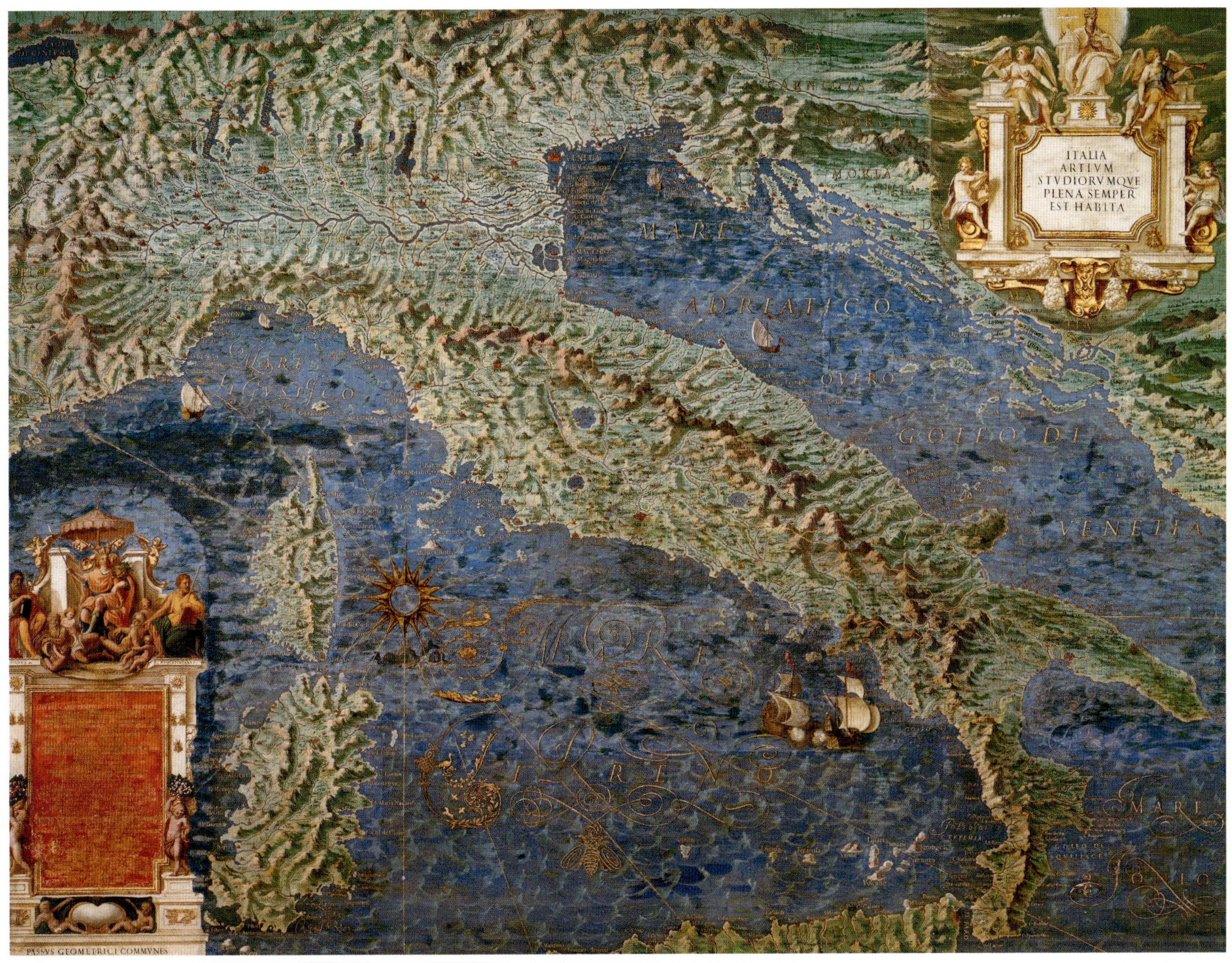

Lukas Holste and Workshop

Modern Italy

Here, the "new" Italy is juxtaposed with the "old" Italy of ancient Rome. Both maps show the "boot" of Italy without Sicily, terminating in the north with the Alps, and stretching from Savoy to the Carnic Alps in Slovenia and beyond the Adriatic to Croatia and Albania. The map was completely repainted in 1632–1633 under the direction of the geographer Lukas Holste (Latin: Lucas Holstenius), a native of Hamburg. Holste, who worked as a librarian in the Vatican from 1636, dispensed with historical events, confining himself to the Italy of around 1600. His fresco demonstrates a high standard of pictorial quality and boasts an abundance of detail. The inscription cartouche is surmounted by an allegory of Italy depicted as a young woman enthroned between the rivers Po and Adige and the historians Flavio Biondo (1392–1463) and Raffaele Maffei da Volterra (1451–1522). The inscription praises Italy, provides geographical data, such as distances and provinces, and lists major historical facts. Italy was only formed in the nineteenth century with the unification of eleven largely independent states and is therefore presented here as a geographical rather than political unit.

Luc Holste and workshop, 1596–1661
***Modern Italy*, 1632-1633**
320 x 430 cm; Fresco
Gallery of Maps

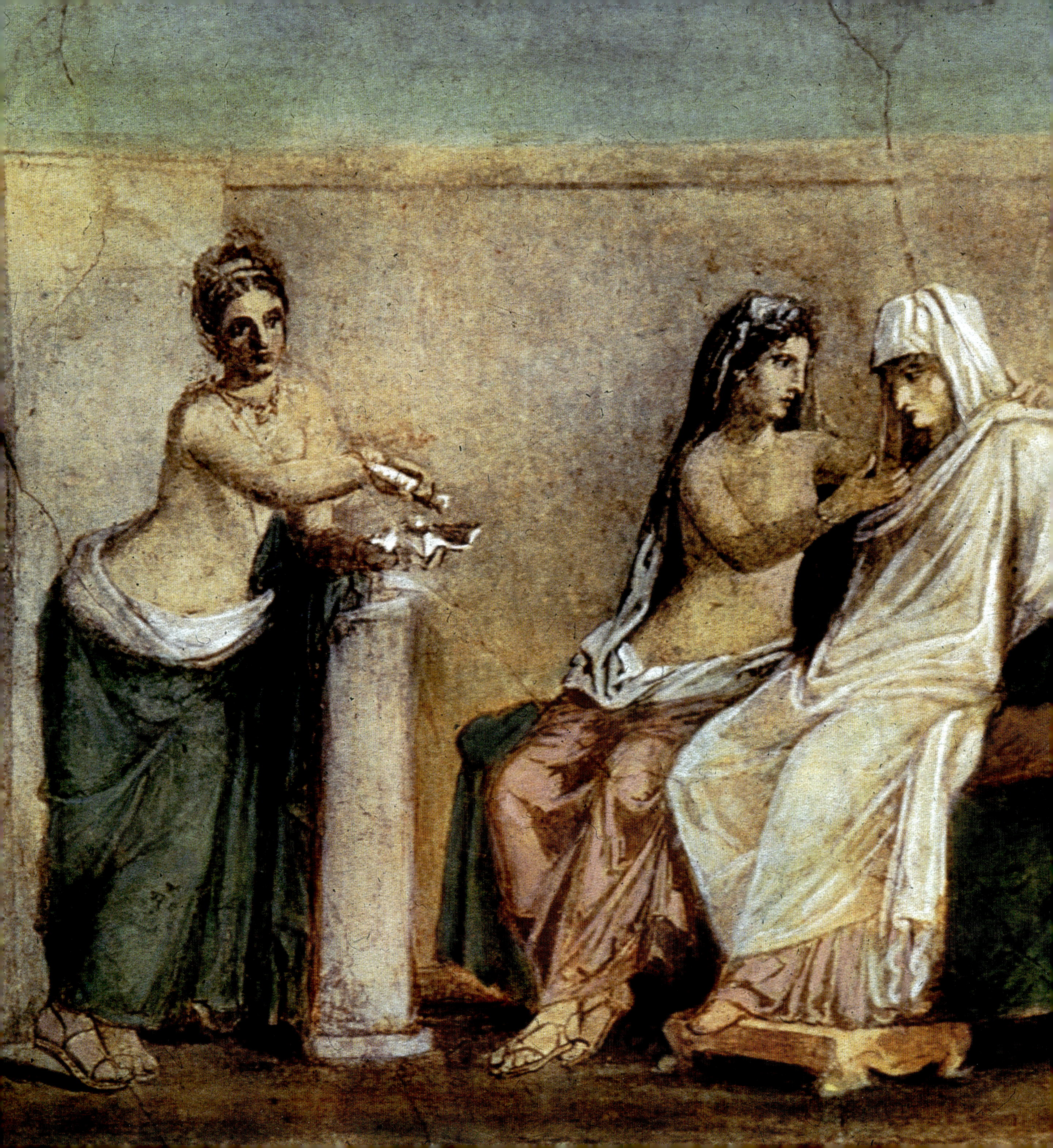

THE SACRED MUSEUM

As early as the Middle Ages, valuable books and precious works of art were given equal prominence in many treasure chambers both sacred and secular. In this sense, the inauguration of the Sacred Museum by Pope Benedict XIV (1675–1758, reigned from 1740) in the rooms of the Biblioteca Apostolica Vaticana in 1756 was part of a long tradition. According to the inscription above the entrance to the museum, Benedict XIV's intention in founding the museum was to "amplify the glory of the city and attest to the truth of religion with holy Christian artifacts."

The objects on display in the library's long galleries are of varied provenance. Some were discovered during the excavation of Roman catacombs and document the early history of Christianity in the city. Some derive from private collections assembled during the Baroque era by clerics with an interest in archaeology, for example the extensive collection of funerary lamps, busts, coins, and medals of Gaspare di Carpegna, Cardinal Vicar of Rome, who died in 1714. From the rich collection of the noble Chigi family, which produced numerous cardinals, came valuable glass vessels, some gilded. The museum also contains artifacts from various Church treasuries, most importantly the popes' Sancta Sanctorum chapel at the Lateran. Items from this chapel, richly endowed with relics, include the golden reliquary cross of Pope Paschal I (ca. 750–824 AD, reigned from 817 AD) and its silver casket, supreme examples of Carolingian metalwork. Many of the items on display, including an extensive collection of precious medieval ivories and enamels, were gifts to the popes from secular and Church dignitaries.

A special section is devoted to valuable liturgical objects and vestments from the treasuries of St. Peter's and the Sistine Chapel. These include the richly embroidered ceremonial vestments given by Ferdinando I de' Medici (1549–1609), grand duke of Tuscany from 1587, to Pope Clement VIII (1536–1605, reigned from 1592) in 1597, which are some of the best-preserved priest's vestments of the late Renaissance period. A separate room, the Sala delle Nozze Aldobrandine, is dedicated to Roman frescoes, in particular the Aldobrandini Wedding, which Pope Pius VII (1742–1823, reigned from 1800) purchased from its private owner in 1818 for the considerable sum of ten thousand scudi.

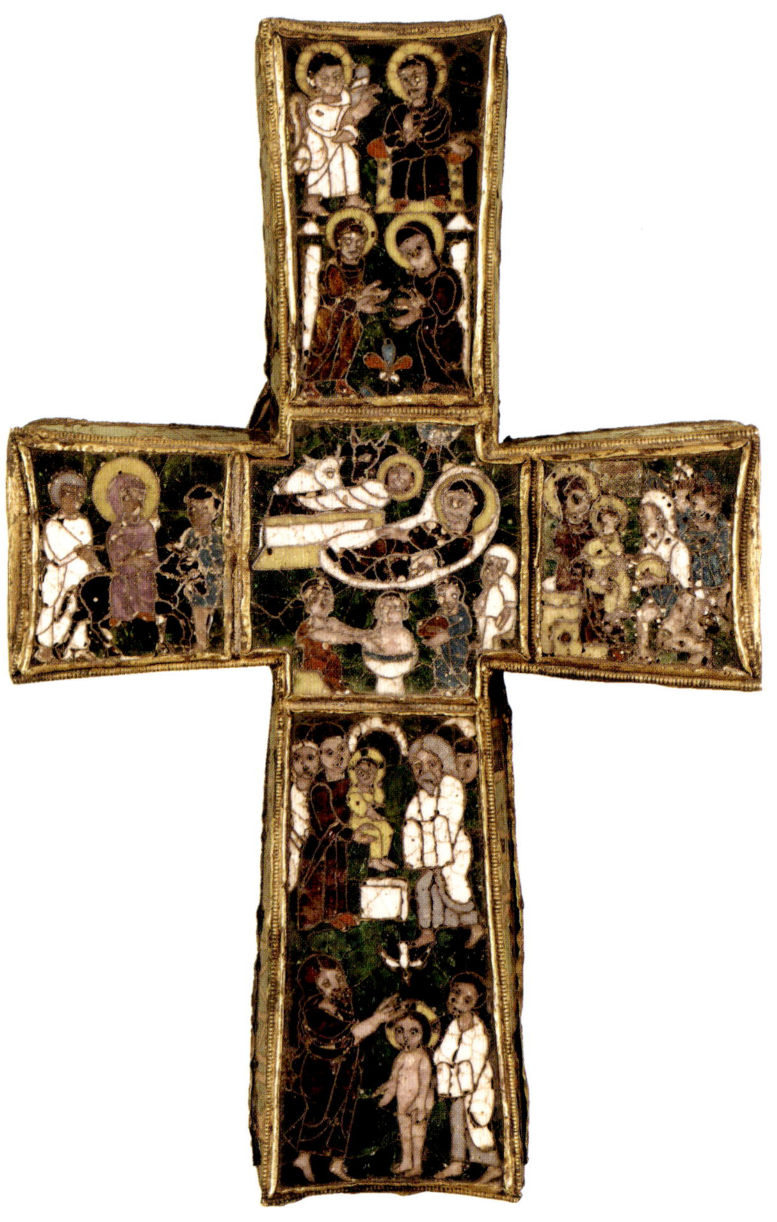

Carolingian goldsmith

Reliquary cross of Pope Paschal I

This reliquary cross decorated with scenes from the life of Jesus Christ is one of the oldest and most valuable items in the Museo Sacro. It once contained fragments of Christ's true cross and according to its inscription was commissioned by Pope Paschal I for the treasury of the Sancta Sanctorum chapel at the Lateran. Along with its silver reliquary casket, it is one of the few medieval treasures to have escaped the subsequent plundering of Rome. The cross is made of fine sheets of gilt copper. The back of the cross, now lost, is thought to have borne enamel work like the front, which is decorated with seven scenes executed in cloisonné bordered by ribbons of small pearls. The scenes depict events from the life of Christ from the Annunciation to his baptism. They are designed to be read from top to bottom, with the birth of Christ occupying the central position, combined with the story of his first bath. The small scenes are distinctive for their vibrant design, and the translucent colors—most prominently green, yellow, red, opal white, and violet—lend the holy scenes an exquisite preciousness and radiance.

Carolingian goldsmith, active early 9th century
***Reliquary cross of Pope Paschal I*, c. 817–824 AD**
27 x 18 x 4 cm; Gilt copper, enamel
The Sacred Museum

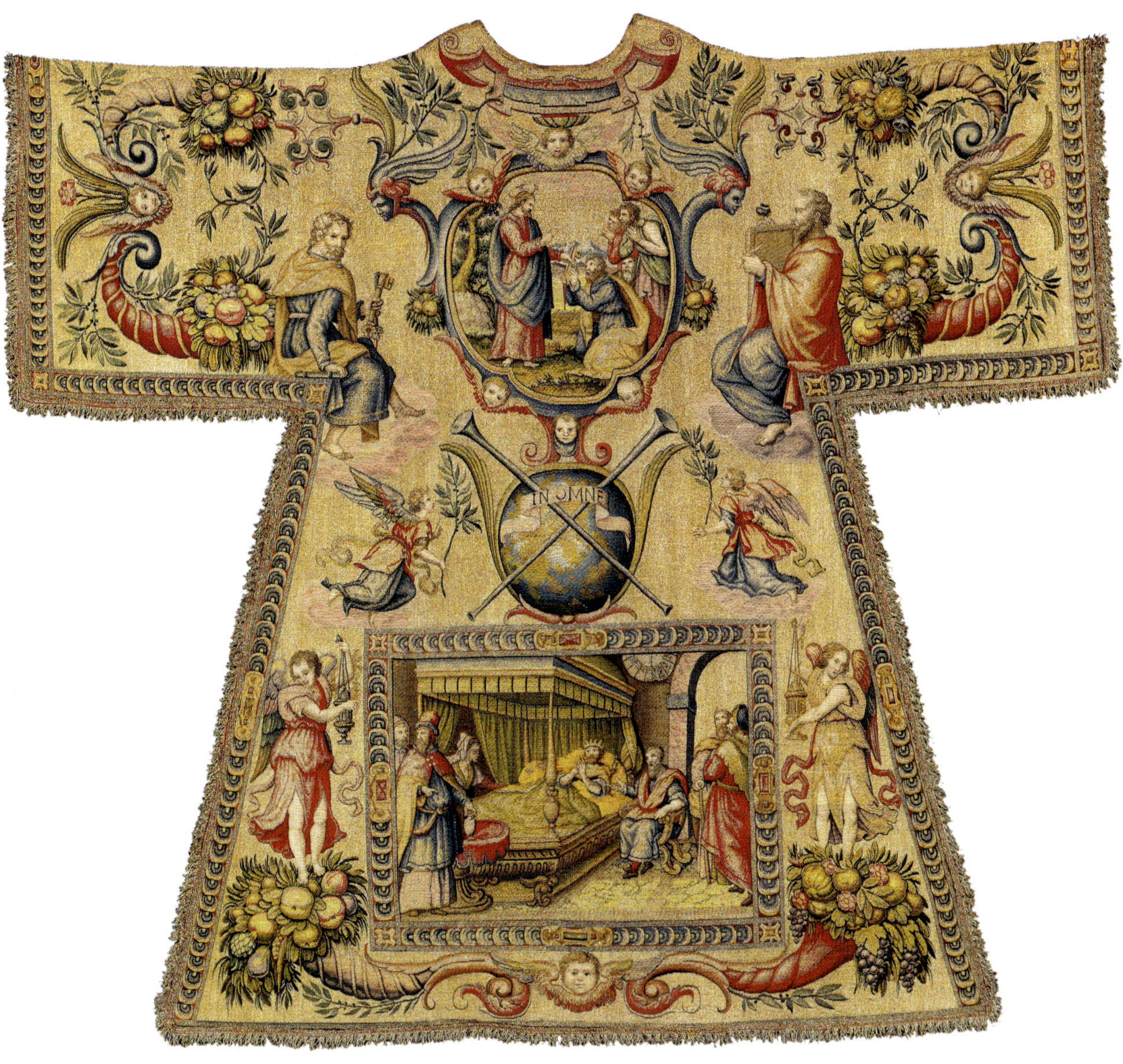

Guasparri di Bartolomeo Papini after a design by Alessandro Allori

Dalmatic Depicting the Consignment of the Keys to St. Peter

Precious textiles were once among the most valuable contents of church treasuries. This dalmatic (the vestment of a deacon) was commissioned by Ferdinando I de' Medici, grand duke of Tuscany, as a gift for Pope Clement VIII. It is made of silk thread woven with gold and silver and is decorated with embroidered figurative scenes and ornaments sewn onto the front and back. The dalmatic is part of a larger set of vestments designed to adorn the Sistine Chapel, particularly during Holy Week. The complex pictorial program, possibly devised by Ferdinando I himself and then executed by craftsmen in the Medici workshops, corresponds to this purpose. Like the cycle of frescoes in the Sistine Chapel, it combines events from the Old and New Testaments. The upper cartouche depicts the consignment of the keys to St. Peter (John 21:15–17), a scene of central importance to the founding of the papacy. The lower scene shows the healing of Hezekiah by the prophet Isaiah (II Kings 20:1–11; Isaiah 38:1–22). Like the handing of the keys to St. Peter, it would have been interpreted as a symbol of God's might.

Guasparri di Bartolomeo Papini, ca.1540–1621
after a design by Alessandro Allori, 1535–1607
***Dalmatic Depicting the Consignment of the Keys to St. Peter*, 1593–1597**
134 x 147 cm; Silk, gold, and silver thread
The Sacred Museum

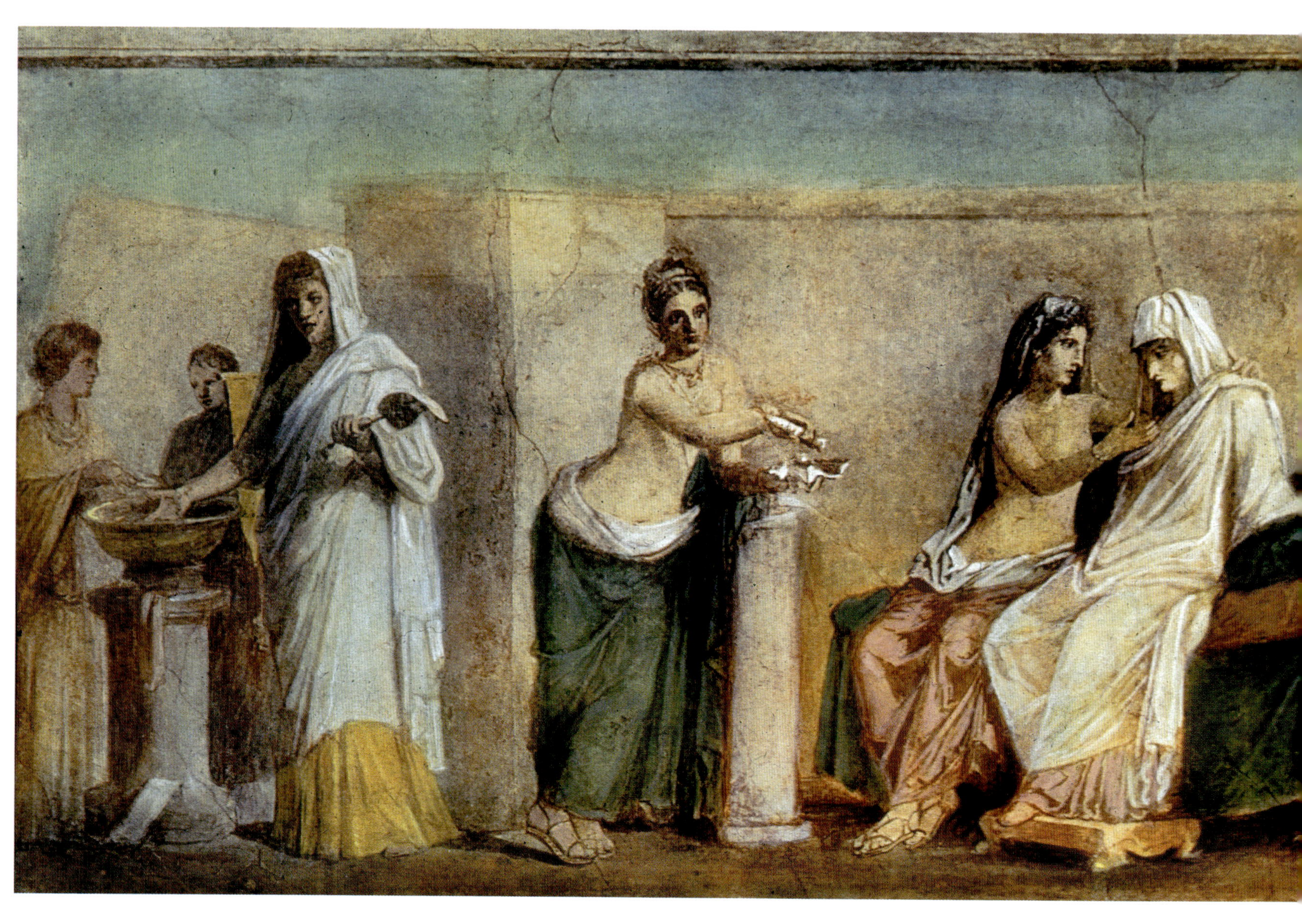

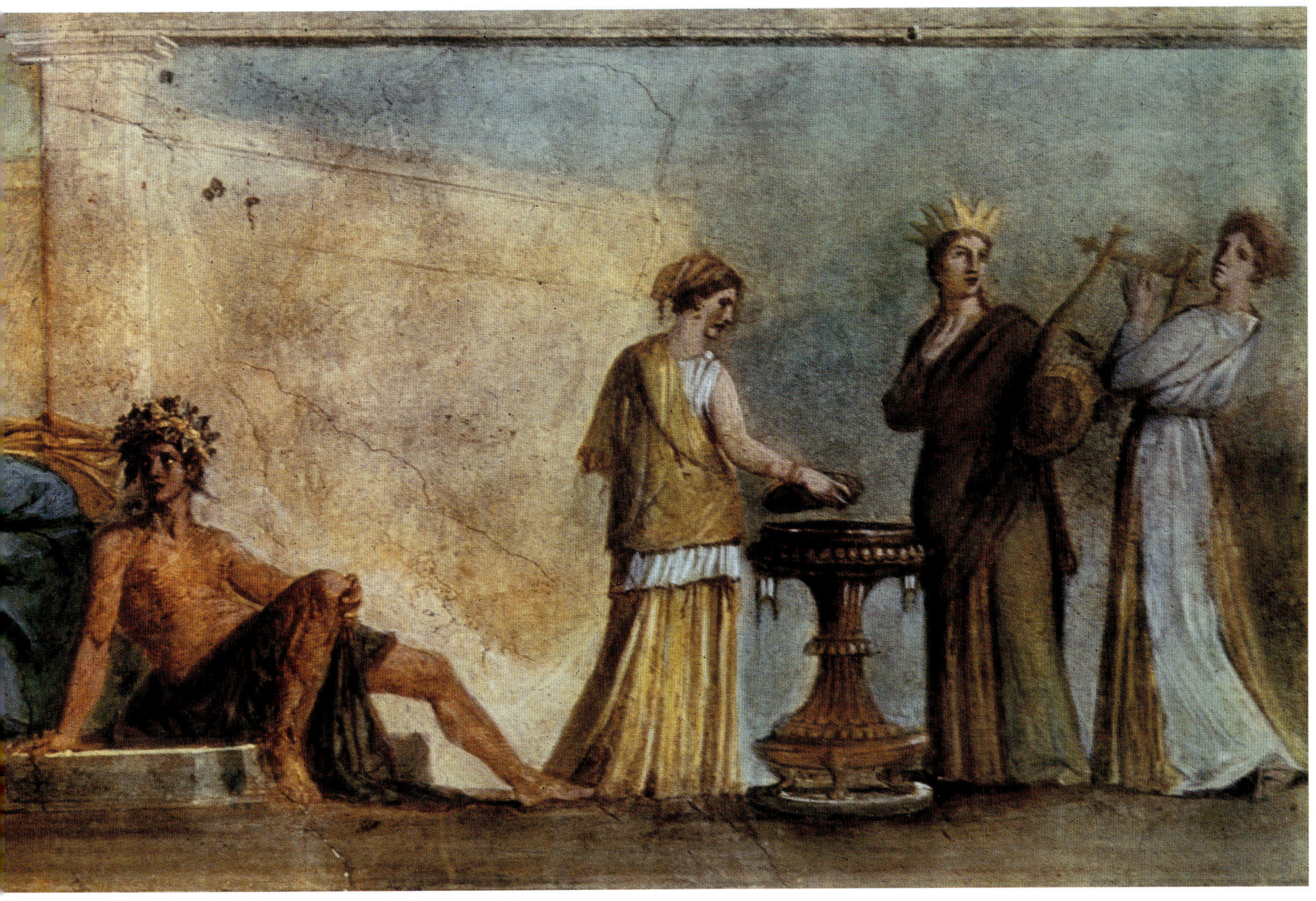

Roman artist

The Aldobrandini Wedding

This Roman fresco from the Augustan era is known as the Aldobrandini Wedding. It was discovered near the church of San Giuliano in Rome in 1601 and acquired soon after by Cardinal Cinzio Aldobrandini. It has been in the Vatican since 1818. From the moment of its discovery, this frieze-like depiction of preparations for a wedding night unleashed a hitherto unknown wave of enthusiasm on the part of artists and the public alike. Copyists and admirers of the work have included Rubens, Poussin, and Pannini as well as the scholar Johann Joachim Winckelmann and the writer Johann Wolfgang von Goethe. The painting shows a bridal chamber resembling a stage set on whose threshold the god of marriage, wearing a crown of leaves, watches the scene. The veiled, hesitant bride sits on a high bed in the company of Venus, who reassures her. A maid enters from the left with a bowl and an ointment vessel in order to prepare the bride for her bath, which awaits her in a side room. The magic of this fresco, painted with extreme sensitivity, is enhanced by the three Muses in the right half of the picture, who provide musical accompaniment to the scene.

Roman artist, active early 1st century
***The Aldobrandini Wedding*, early 1st century**
92 x 242 cm; Fresco
The Sacred Museum

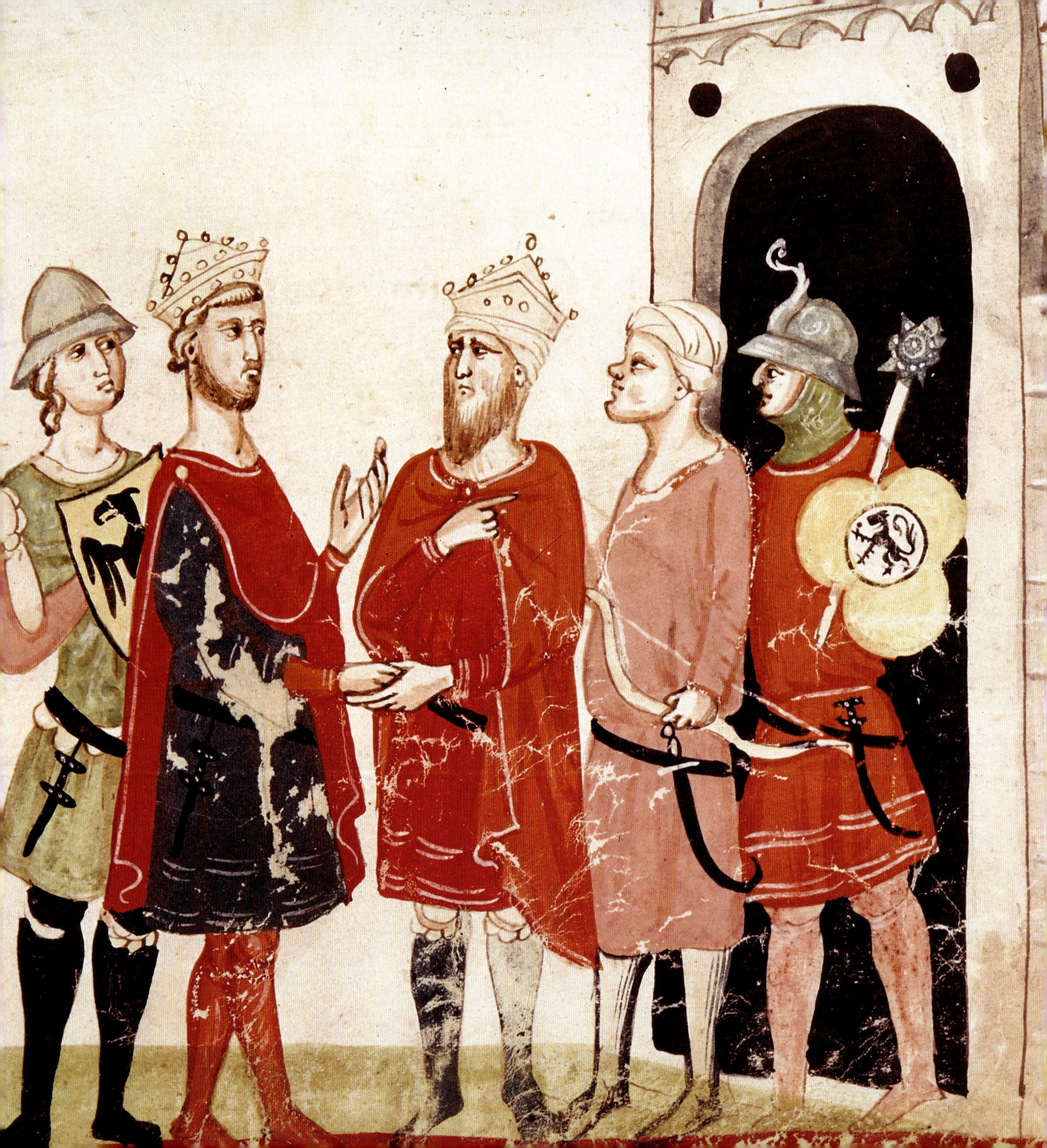

VATICAN LIBRARY: COLLECTIONS

The Apostolic Vatican Library is one of the oldest and most famous libraries in the world. Its collection contains written and printed documents from throughout the history of books, from Egyptian papyri to modern printed and digitized works. It is also one of the largest theological research libraries, used by religious and secular scholars from all over the world.

The history of the Apostolic Vatican Library goes back over fifteen hundred years and has been marked by vicissitudes of various kinds, especially during the early days. It can trace its origins to the beginnings of the papacy in the fourth and fifth centuries, when most of the books were kept not at the Vatican but at the main seat of the popes in the Lateran. The first were mainly liturgical books and Bibles of the kind possessed by every ecclesiastical institution, which were indispensable to the preparation and conducting of church services and religious ceremonies. It can be assumed that these Bible and Mass manuscripts were of an especially high quality in terms of their parchment, script, and illumination as well as the linguistic purity and flawlessness of their texts, which were composed and copied by scholars and trained scribes. Particularly valuable illuminated manuscripts were kept not in the library but in the treasury.

Of the late antique and early medieval book collections of the popes only a few remnants have come down to us. Many items were lost during the plundering of Rome during the Migration period (fourth to sixth centuries AD) and in later eras. Other losses can be explained by negligence, non-return of loaned volumes, and theft. There were also devastating accidents, such as a fire in the papal residence in 1308, and further decimation when the popes left Rome for Avignon in the fourteenth century.

The choice of the Vatican as the main pontifical residence under Nicholas V (1397–1455, reigned from 1447) also marked the beginning of a systematic expansion of the Apostolic Vatican Library as a center of bibliophily and scholarship, a role it retains today. Under Nicholas V, who was interested in humanism, the book collection grew from some 350 Greek and Latin volumes to over 1,200 within just a few years. Many of the Greek manuscripts were from the former imperial library in Constantinople, which was rescued from Turkish plunderers in 1453. Another decisive act in the development of the library was the papal bull "Ad decorem militantis Ecclesiae" ("For the adornment of the militant Church") issued by Sixtus IV (1414–1484, reigned from 1471) in 1475. In it he stipulated that the papal library be maintained as a permanent institution of the Papal States "in order to promote the faith and also for the benefit and honor of scholars and all those who dedicate themselves to the study of the sciences." By 1481 the librarian appointed by Sixtus IV, Bartolomeo Sacchi, known as Platina, was able to produce a detailed catalog of a collection that now ran to thirty-five hundred volumes.

The subsequent popes of the Renaissance and Baroque eras were also noted for their love of books and fostered the expansion of the library through extensive purchasing, by actively commissioning books, and by undertaking building works designed to provide the library with more space. The Library assumed its current physical form under Sixtus V (1521–1590, reigned from 1585). Sixtus was responsible for the building of the new wing (1587–1589) comprising the Salone Sistino, one of the most beautiful library rooms in the world, in order to house what was by then a much augmented collection of manuscripts and printed books.

One of the largest expansions occurred in 1623 with the arrival of the Bibliotheca Palatina, the library of the Elector Palatine, plundered in the Thirty Years War by General Tilly during the conquest of Heidelberg by Catholic troops in 1622. As war booty, it was presented as a gift to Pope Gregory XV by the leader of the Catholic League, Maximilian I of Bavaria.

The Vatican collection was further expanded in the eighteenth through twentieth centuries with the incorporation of the libraries of important noble families. Notable examples include the libraries of the Borgia and Barberini dynasties, both of which entered the Vatican in 1902, as well as the library of bibliophile Giovanni Francesco de Rossi, with its collection of rare manuscripts, which was acquired in 1921. The most recent major accession occurred in 1923 with the gift from the Italian State of the Biblioteca Chigiana, the library of the noble Chigi family. This gift came with a condition: the Library was to be made more accessible to the general public. In recent years the Vatican Library has been satisfying this requirement not only through the creation of modern reading rooms and a lively program of exhibits and publications but also through digitization, by means of which the treasures of the Vatican are able to reach a wide audience.

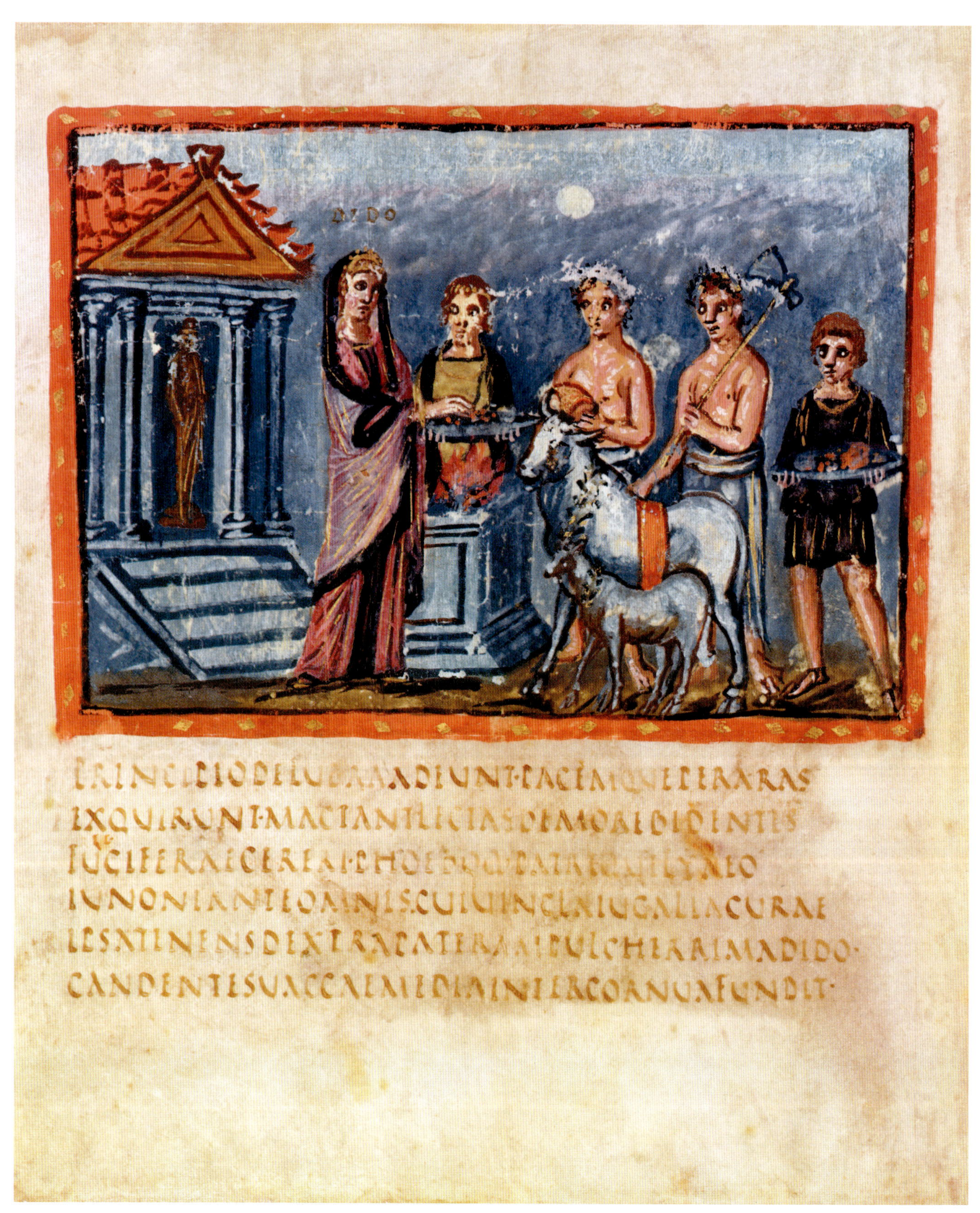
DIDO
PRINCIPIODELUBRAADIUNT·PACEMQUEPERARAS
EXQUIRUNT·MACTANTLECTASDEMOREBIDENTIS
LUCIFERAECERERIPHOEBOQUEPATRIQUELYAEO
IUNONIANTEOMNIS·CUIUINCLAIUGALIACURAE
IPSATENENSDEXTRAPATERAMPULCHERRIMADIDO·
CANDENTISUACCAEMEDIAINTERCORNUAFUNDIT·

Roman book illuminator

Illustration from the Vergilius Vaticanus: "Dido Makes a Sacrifice"

The Vergilius Vaticanus (Vatican Virgil) is one of the most precious examples of late antique book illustration and among the oldest of all illuminated manuscripts. It is dedicated to the works of the Roman poet Virgil (70–19 BC) and is decorated with fifty large-format miniatures in red painted frames. Most of the pictures illustrate *The Aeneid*, which recounts the adventures of Aeneas, the Trojan hero and mythical founder of Rome, during his wanderings around the Mediterranean. One of his stopping points is with Queen Dido in Carthage. Dido falls in love with Aeneas and tries, with the help of the gods, to make him marry her. In this miniature we see Dido making a sacrifice to Hera, the mother of the gods venerated as the guardian of marriage, in front of a temple. Wearing gold-trimmed robes, she stands next to an altar on which a priest has lit a fire. From the right, three servants bring the sacrificial offerings. With its pastel colors and more-or-less realistically proportioned figures and animals, the illustration is reminiscent of late antique wall paintings. The painter has taken great care over details such as the animals' and the servants' wreaths, the exquisite garments, Dido's crown, and the temple with its divine statue. The tense concentration of this sacrificial scene has been rendered with considerable psychological sensitivity.

Roman book illuminator, active 5th century
***Illustration from the Vergilius Vaticanus: "Dido Makes a Sacrifice"*, ca. 400 AD**
35 x 33.5 cm; Illuminated manuscript, body color and gold on parchment
Vatican Library

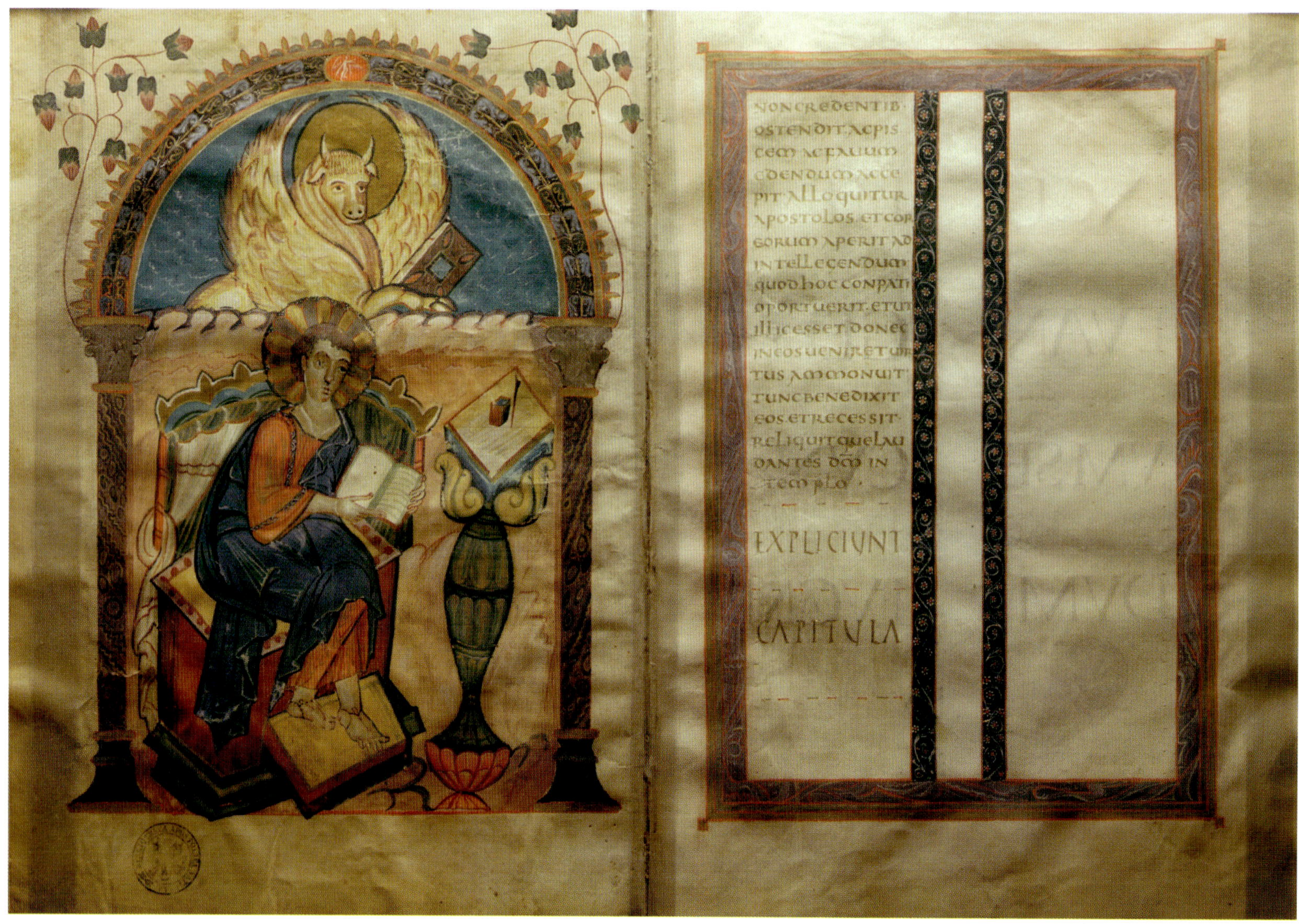

Carolingian artist

Lorsch Gospels: Illustration of St. Luke

The Lorsch Gospels is one of the most beautiful examples of Carolingian book art. It was created around 810–815AD by the Court School of Charlemagne and is known to have arrived at Lorsch Abbey (Hesse, Germany, now a UNESCO World Heritage Site) somewhat later, possibly as part of the Carolingian emperor's endowment. From here it entered the library of the Elector Palatine in Heidelberg and was eventually sent to Rome with the other treasures of the Bibliotheca Palatina in 1623. Written almost entirely in gold, the codex contains the four Gospels, each illustrated with a likeness of its author and an ornamental page marking the beginning of the argument. At some unknown point in time, the codex was split into two parts. In the Vatican volume, the portrait pages are of the evangelists Luke and John. Here, Luke is shown enthroned beneath a richly decorated architectural arch accompanied by his symbolic animal. The pronounced ornamental quality of the garments, figure, and architectural features gives the image an extremely opulent appearance, which was typical of the Court School of Charlemagne.

Carolingian artist, ca. 800-810AD
***Lorsch Gospels: Illustration of St. Luke*, 810**
37 x 27 cm; Illuminated manuscript, body color and gold on vellum
Vatican Library

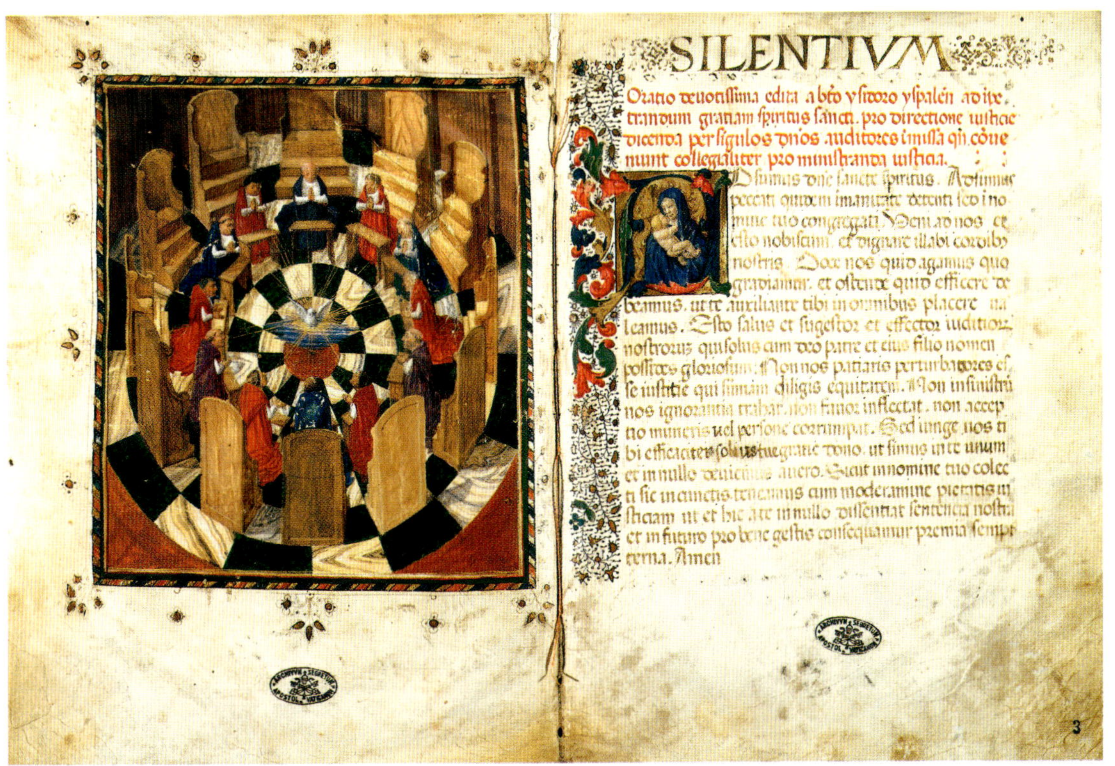

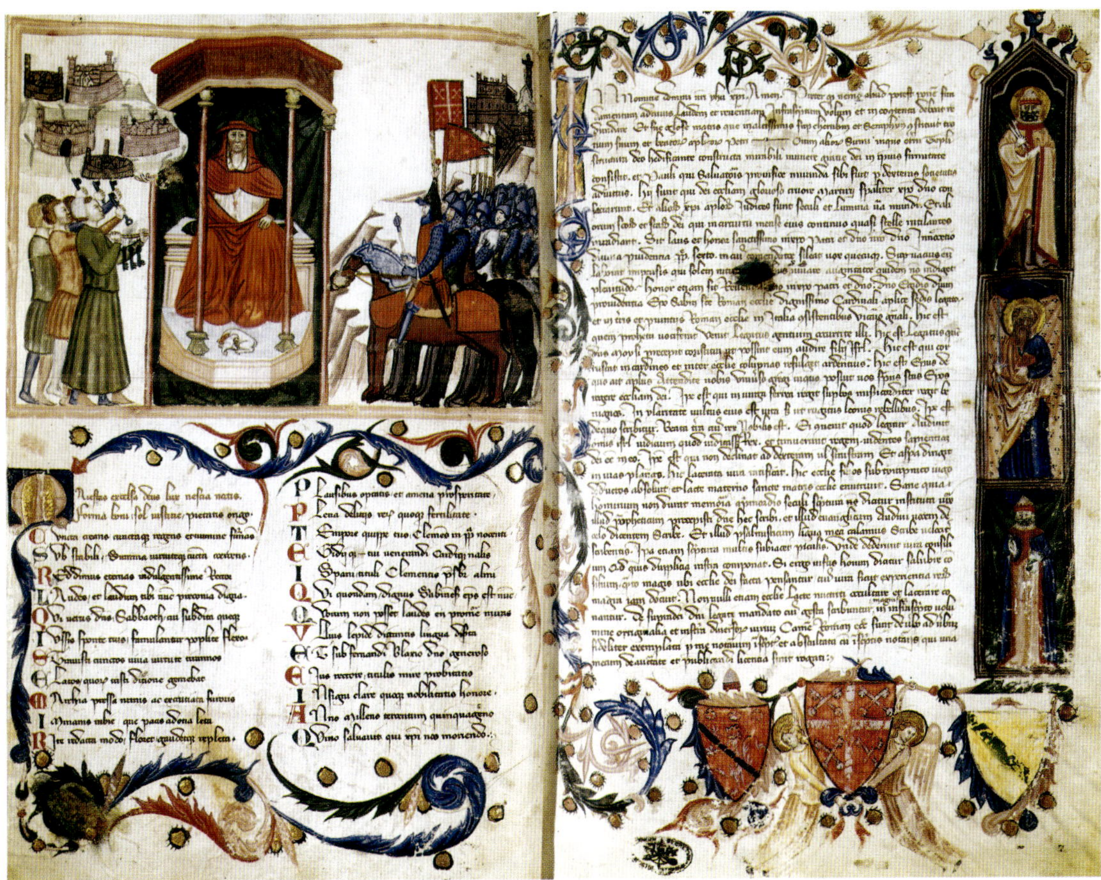

Unknown artist, 14th century
***Seat of the Rota*, 14th century**
Illuminated manuscript
Vatican Library

Unknown artist, 14th century
***Cardinal Albornoz receiving the Keys of the Cities of the Patrimony of St. Peter*, 14th century**
Illuminated manuscript
Vatican Library

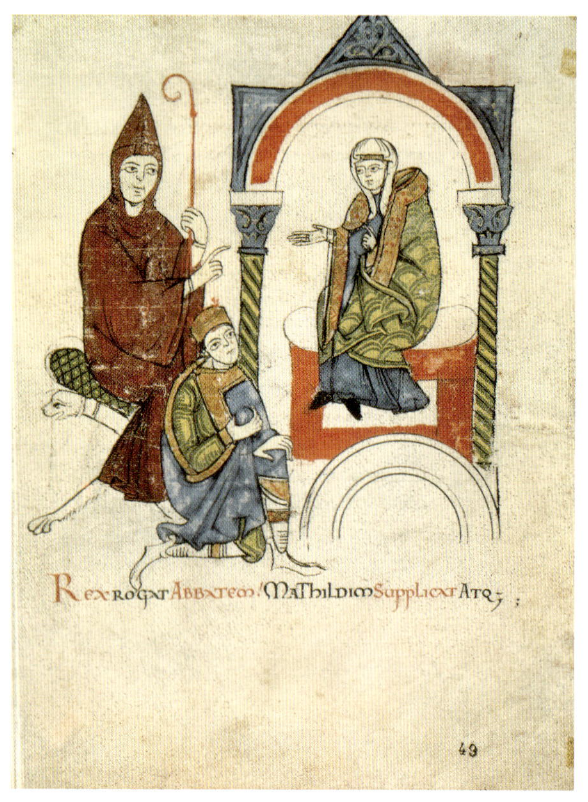

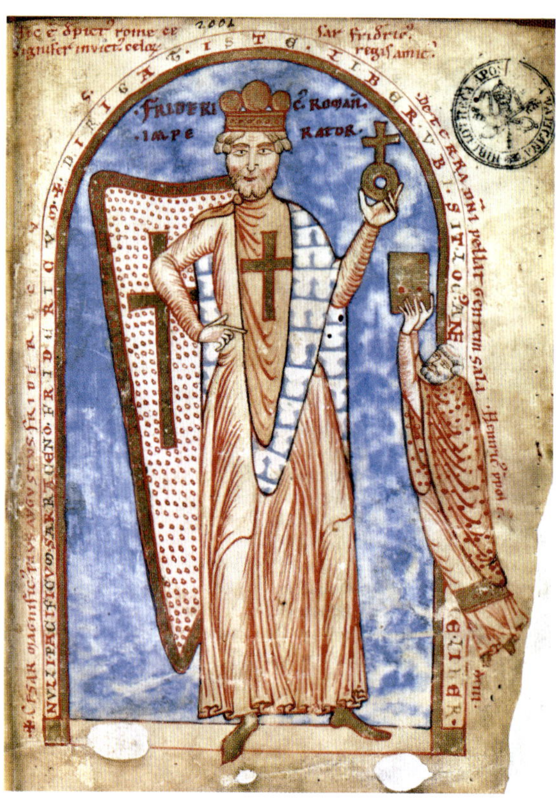

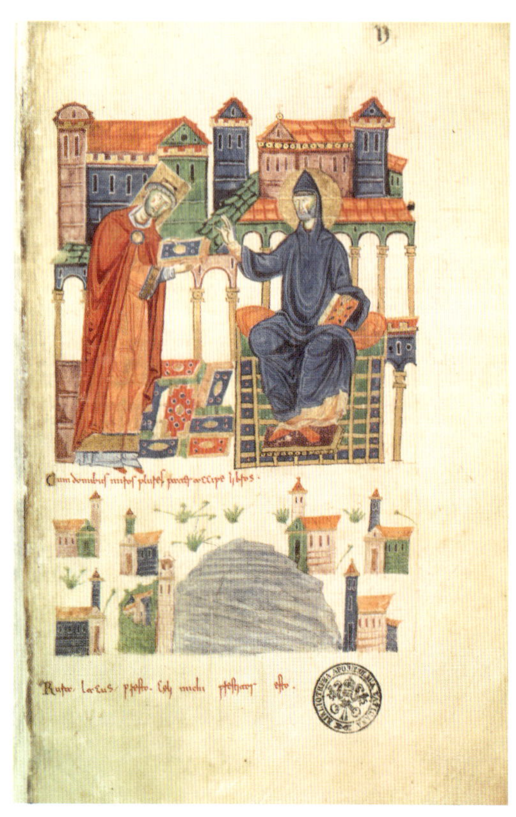

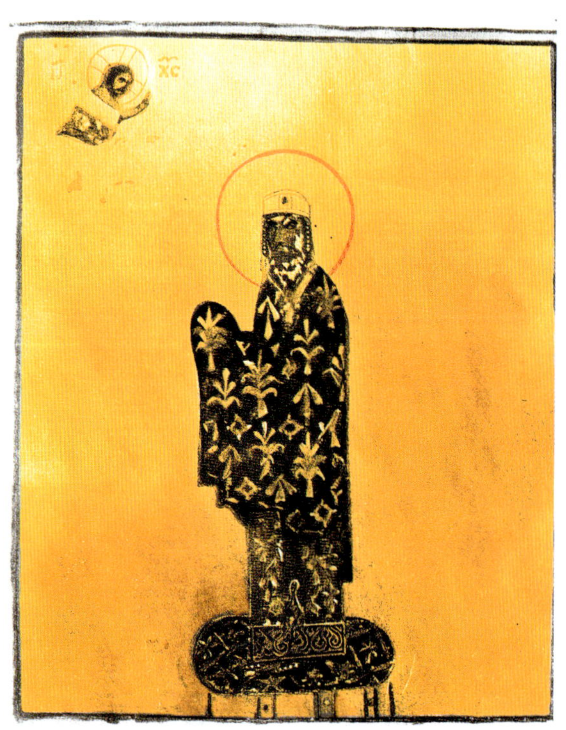

Donizio of Canossa (author) and unknown Italian artist, 12th century
***Vita Matildis (Life of Matilda of Tuscany)*, 1114-1115**
22 x 17 cm; Illuminated manuscript
Vatican Library

Robert de Saint Remy, ca. 12th century
***Miniature of Frederick I (Barbarossa-Red Beard) from "History of the Third Crusade"*, ca. 12th century**
21 x 16 cm; Illuminated manuscript
Vatican Library

Roman artist, date unknown
***Manuscript of Montecassino: The Abbot of Montecassino Offering Codes and Possessions to St. Benedict*, date unknown**
37 x 25 cm; Illuminated manuscript
Vatican Library

Byzantine artist, 12th century
***Alexius I Comnenus (1048–1118)*, 12th century**
33.5 x 24 cm; Illuminated manuscript
Vatican Library

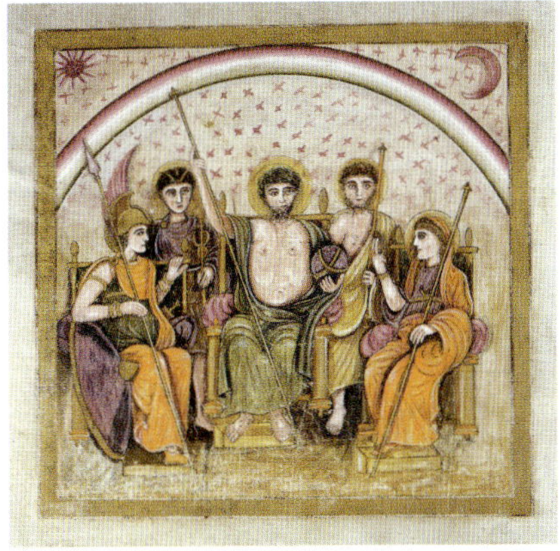

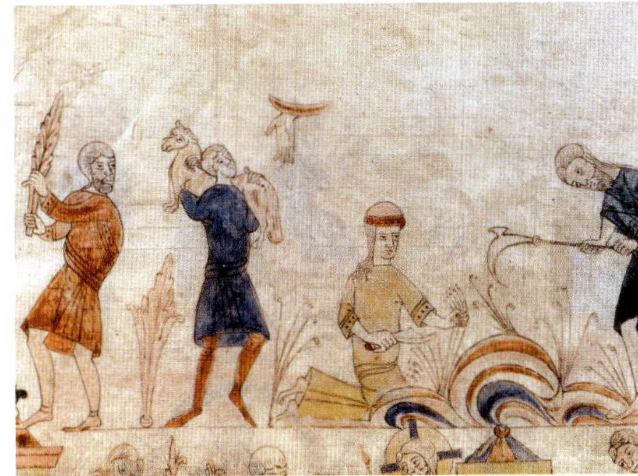

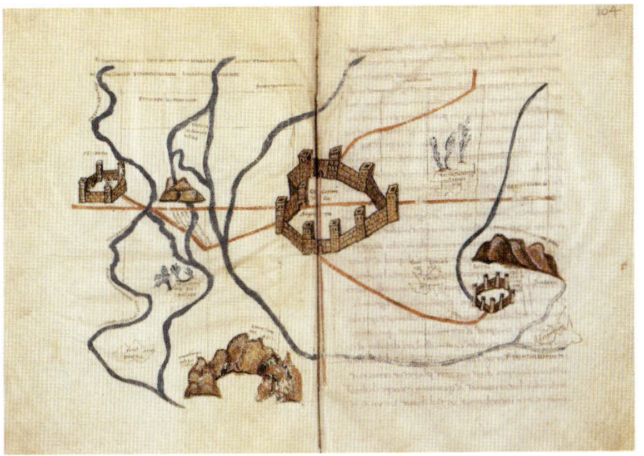

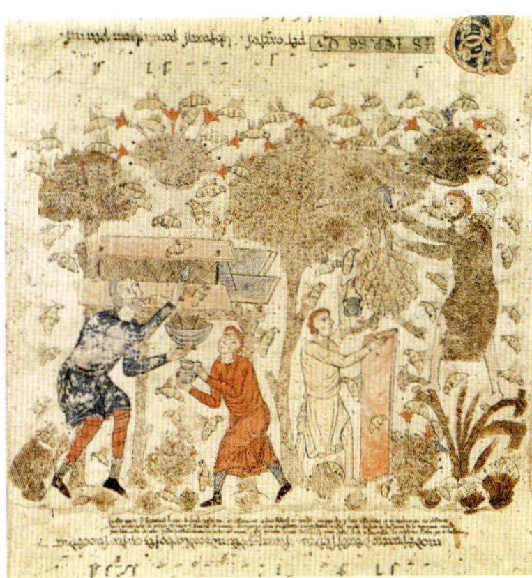

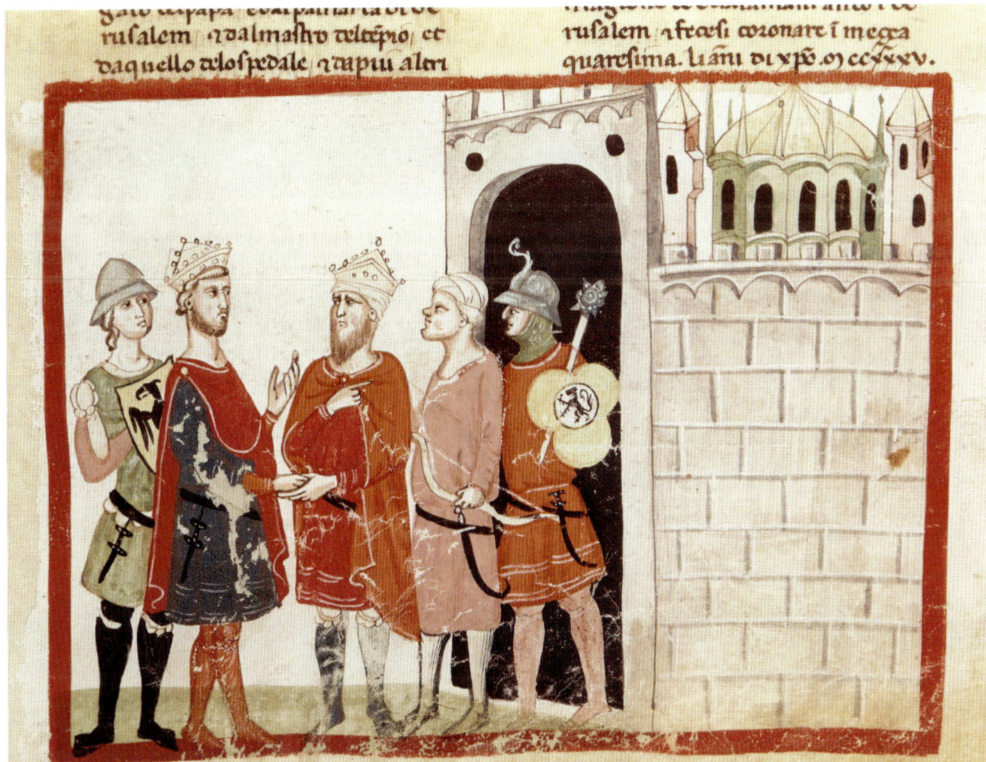

Anonymous, ca. 5th century
***Roman Virgil Manuscript*, ca. 5th century**
35 x 33.5 cm; Illuminated manuscript
Vatican Library

Anonymous, ca. 11th century
***Ripoll Bible: Farmers*, 11th century**
55 x 37 cm; Illuminated manuscript
Vatican Library

Unknown artist, 9th century
***Roman Territory Divided into Centuriae*, 9th century**
27 x 18 cm; Illuminated manuscript
Vatican Library

Unknown artist, ca. 11th–12th century
***Ms Barb Lat. 592, f. 4: Beekeeping*, ca. 11th–12th century**
45 x 31 cm; Illuminated manuscript
Vatican Library

Giovanni Villani (author), Pacino di Bonaguida and workshop (illuminator), 14th century
***Nuova Cronica, detail: Peace agreement between Frederick II and sultan Al-kamil at the gates of Jerusalem (1227)*, 14th century**
37 x 27 cm; Illuminated manuscript
Vatican Library

Mixtec artist

Codex Borgia: The Sun God Tonatiuh

Among the rarities in the Apostolic Vatican Library collection is the Codex Borgia. This is an Mixtec pictorial codex that is thought to have been created in the fifteenth century, prior to the Spanish conquest of Mexico. As with other pre-Columbian manuscripts, it was fabricated as a continuous strip of images, painted on both sides. Measuring more than ten meters in length, it was then folded into concertina format. The content of the "book" comprises various prophecies for specific time spans and for fate in general. Based on the Aztec calendar, "divinatory books" (tonalámatl) were used by priests to determine good and bad omens, for example with respect to the right time to harvest. Page seventy-one depicts the sun god Tonatiuh, one of the most important of Aztec divinities. He is shown seated on an architectural throne drinking the blood of a decapitated sacrificial bird. The boxes that frame the main image contain depictions of the thirteen "birds of the day," each of which corresponds to one of the days of the trecena, the thirteen-day unit of time of the pre-Columbian calendar system. These pictograms, painted in vivid colors, have been objects of fascination ever since the discovery of the codex by Cardinal Stefano Borgia (1731–1804). Some of the images have yet to be decoded.

Mixtec artist, ca. 15th century
***Codex Borgia: The Sun God Tonatiuh*, ca. 1400**
Paint on animal hide
Vatican Library

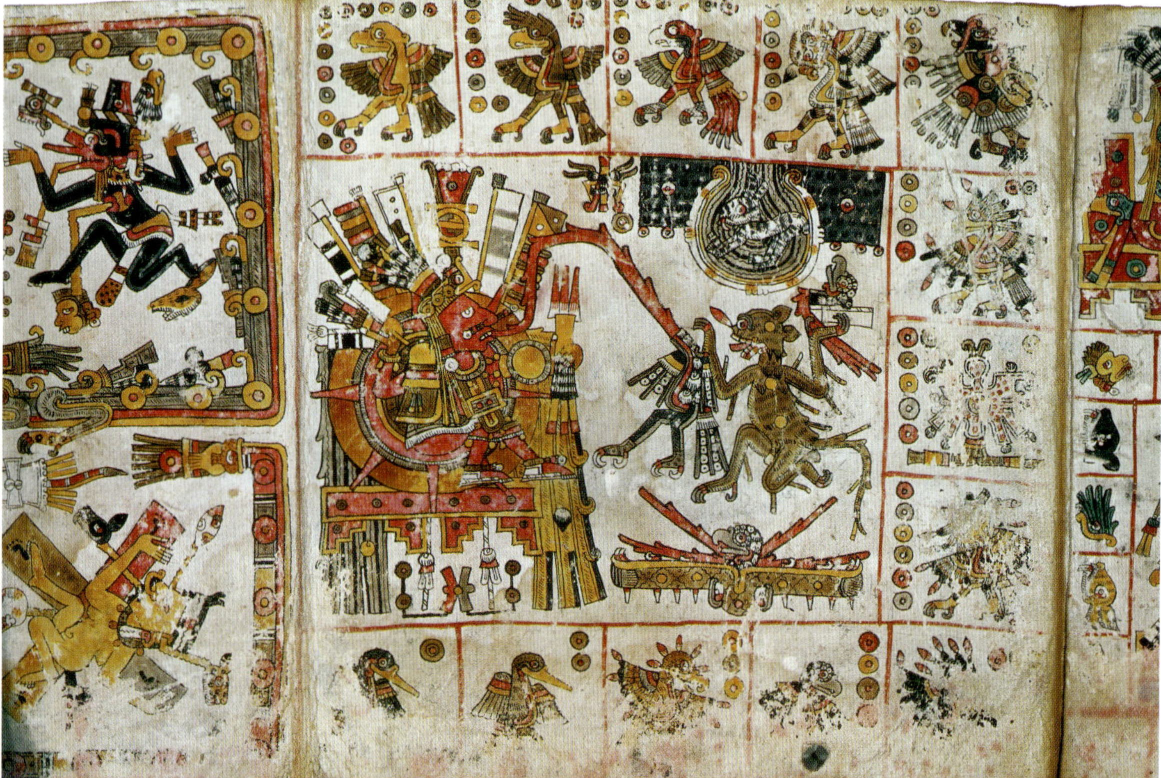

Mixtec artist, ca. 15th century
***Codex Borgianus 1, fol. 30: Aztec Calendar*, ca. 15th century**
Illuminated manuscript
Vatican Library

Mixtec artist, ca. 15th century
***Codex Borgianus: Zoomorphic Form*, ca. 15th century**
Illuminated manuscript
Vatican Library

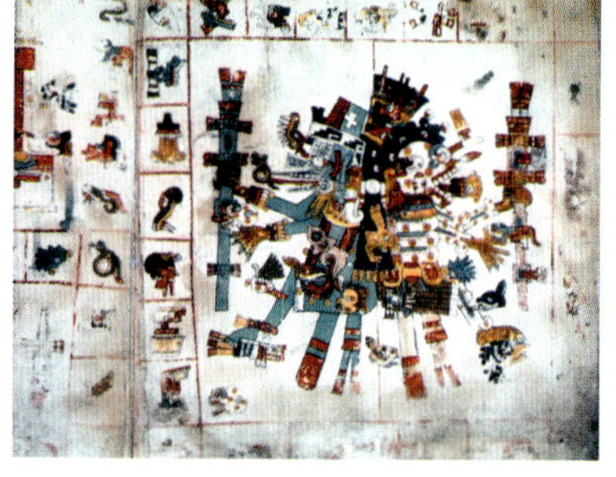

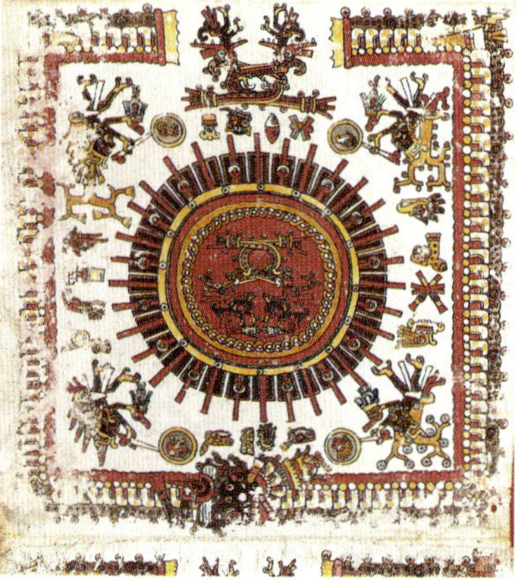

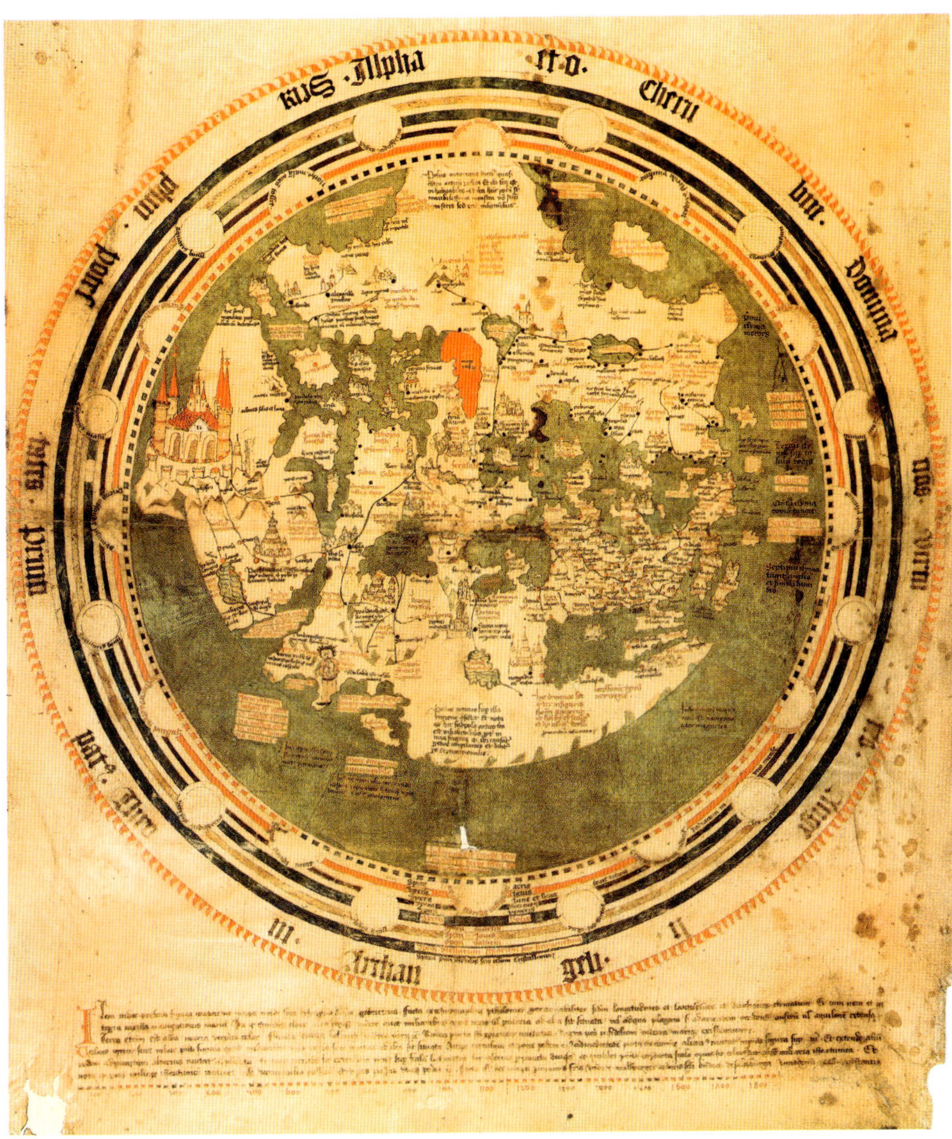

Andreas Walsperger

World Map

In addition to books, the Vatican Library collection also contains important cartographical works. Among them, the world map by Andreas Walsperger, one of the few surviving originals from the Middle Ages, is particularly noteworthy. The creator of this map, made in Constance in 1448, was a Benedictine monk. It is thought to have entered the Biblioteca Apostolica Vaticana in 1623 as part of the Bibliotheca Palatina collections. It is not known where Walsperger acquired his knowledge of cartography. His map represents the earth as a disk. Following the usual medieval practice, the map is oriented with the south at the top, and thus Africa is located in the upper part. The Christian viewpoint is evident in the central positioning of Jerusalem and the red dots indicating Christian cities (black dots denote heathen ones). The large landmass to the left is Asia, which incorporates a vision of paradise as a fortified castle complex. Earth occupies a place at the center of creation, surrounded by the heavenly spheres (the fixed stars and the planets), between which the names of the signs of the zodiac are inscribed. In the legend, Walsperger explains that he has based his map primarily on the Cosmographia of the antique astronomer Ptolemy and gives instructions for measuring distances.

Andreas Walsperger, 15th century
***World Map*, 1448**
58 x 75 cm; Illuminated manuscript, body color on parchment
Vatican Library

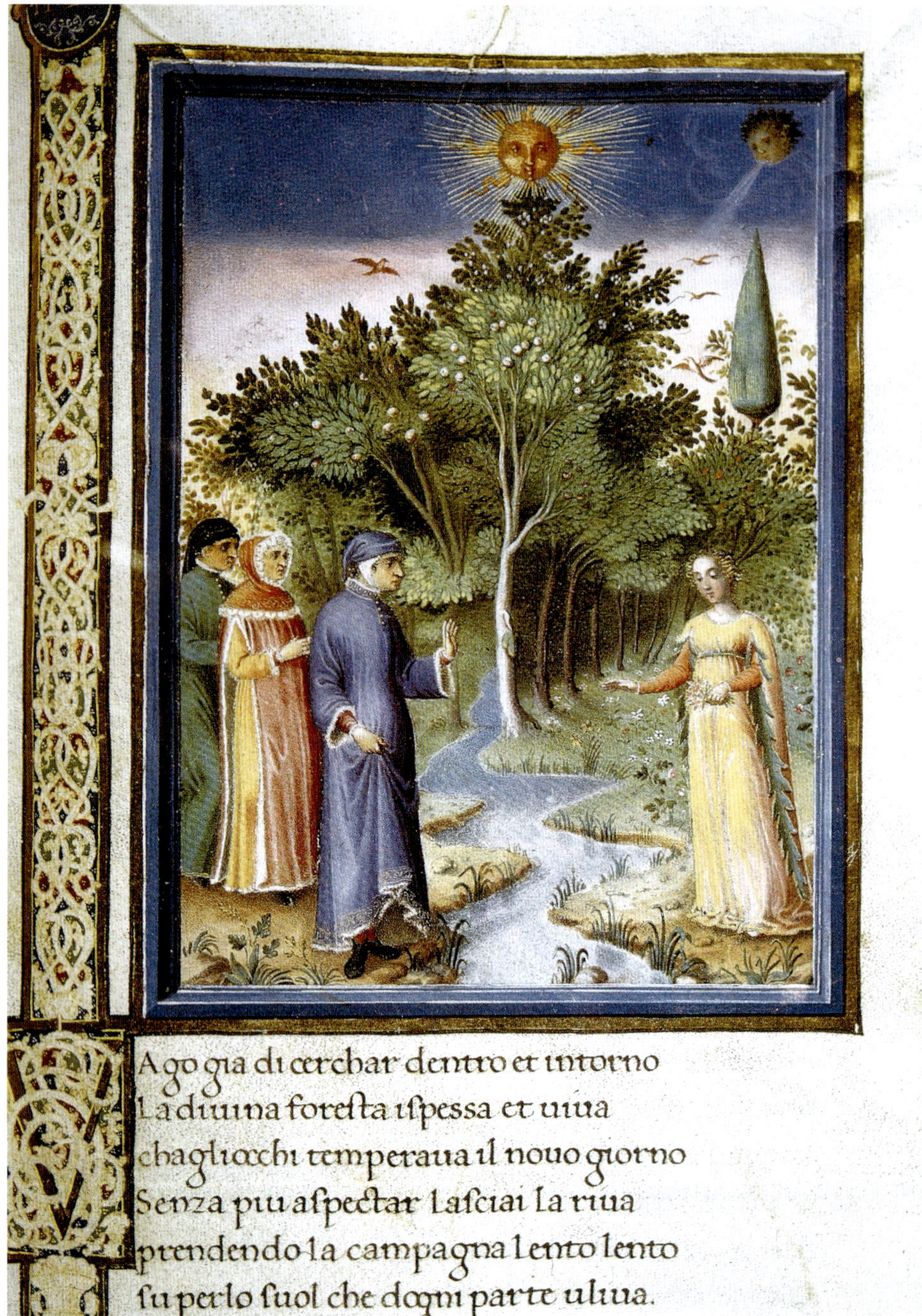

Guglielmo Giraldi and Franco de' Russi

Dante Alighieri, Divina Commedia: Illustration of Purgatorio, Canto 28

In addition to religious works, the Biblioteca Vaticana also holds many secular manuscripts. Among them is this richly illuminated version of Dante's *Divina Commedia* (Divine Comedy), commissioned by Duke Federico da Montefeltro for his library around 1478–1482. The Divine Comedy (ca. 1319/1320) is a classic of Italian literature. The first-person narrator describes his visions of the hereafter, which take him through hell, purgatory, and paradise, in 100 cantos amounting to 14,233 verses. This edition, illuminated by Guglielmo Giraldi and Franco de' Russi, contains 120 miniatures, most of which are positioned at the beginning of a canto and prepare the reader for the events to come. Canto 28 describes the encounter between the narrator and the mysterious Matelda, whose beauty reminds him of Proserpina, the Roman goddess of spring. The magic of this figure is inextricably linked with the idyllic landscape of the earthly paradise, depicted by the miniaturist as a floodplain bathed in light. One can almost smell the flowers and hear the twittering of the birds described by Dante.

Guglielmo Giraldi, active 1445–89, and Franco de' Russi, ca. 15th century
***Dante Alighieri, Divina Commedia: Illustration of Purgatorio, Canto 28*, ca. 1478–82**
38 x 24 cm; Illuminated manuscript
Vatican Library

Italian artist, 15th century
***Dante Divina Commedia: Illustration Inferno XVII (Sodomites)*, 15th century**
38 x 24 cm; Illuminated manuscript, body color and gold on parchment
Vatican Library

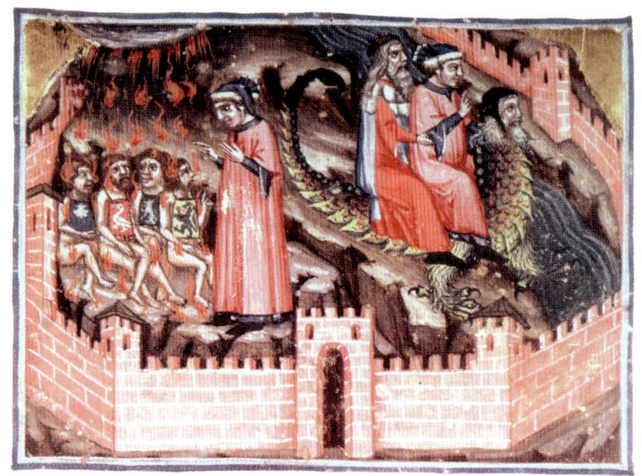

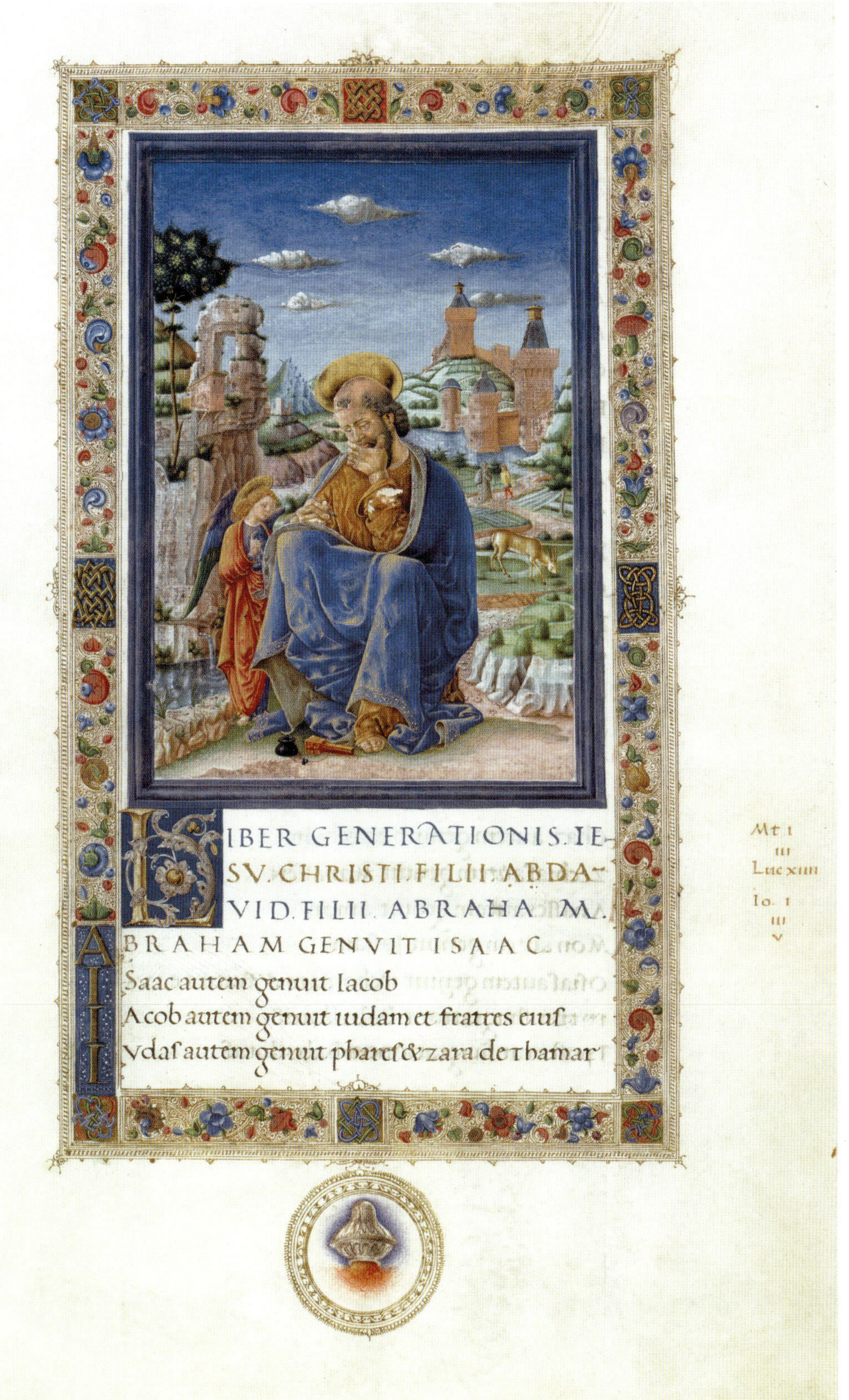

Guglielmo Giraldi and Franco de' Russi

St. Matthew from the Gospels of Federico da Montefeltro

Magnificent miniatures, balanced script, and lavish use of gold and precious colors—these are the characteristic features of the book of Gospels made for Federico da Montefeltro (1422–1482) around 1480. In 1658 this work entered the Vatican with the Renaissance library of the Duke of Urbino. The manuscript contains thirty-four pages of miniatures and ornament, of which the picture of St. Matthew is one of the most beautiful. The evangelist sits in the foreground of a detailed landscape, contemplating the writing of his Gospel. An angel stands at his side dictating the word of God and at his feet is a small inkwell. The background landscape, in which a castle complex on a hill, small walking figures, and a grazing deer can be made out, reveals a similar love of detail. The light colors and fondness for brilliant blues and reds are characteristic of the Ferrarese school of book illumination, of which the miniaturists Guglielmo Giraldi and Franco de' Russi are two of the most important exponents. The neat, minuscule script is by Matteo Contugi, who was also responsible for the duke's renowned Dante manuscript.

Guglielmo Giraldi, active 1445–89, and Franco de' Russi, ca. 15th century
***St. Matthew from the Gospels of Federico da Montefeltro*, ca. 1480**
41 x 26 cm; Illuminated manuscript, body color and gold on parchment
Vatican Library

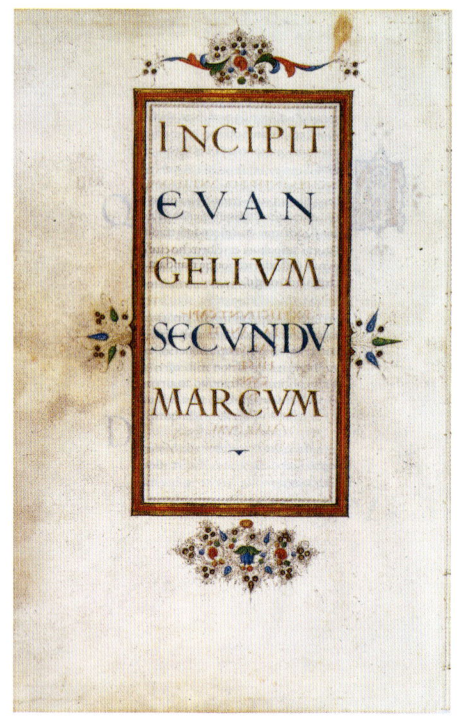

Guglielmo Giraldi, active 1445-1489, and Franco de' Russi, 15th century
***Gospels of Federico da Montefeltro: Beginning of Gospel according to st. Marc*, ca. 1480**
41 x 26 cm; Illuminated manuscript, body color and gold on parchment
Vatican Library

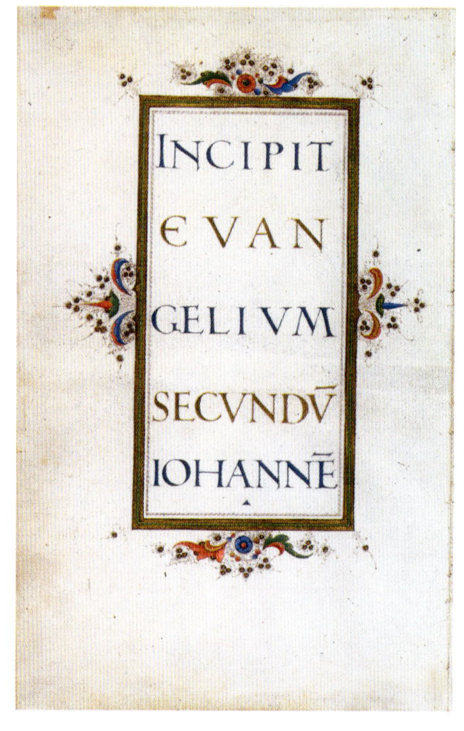

Italian artist, ca. 1480
***Gospel Book, Vatican Council: Beginning of Gospel according to John*, ca. 1480**
41 x 26 cm; Illuminated manuscript
Vatican Library

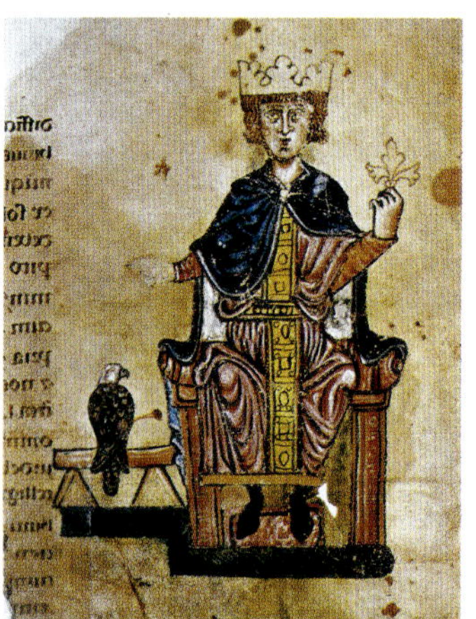

German artist, ca. 1220–1250
***Codex Ms. Pal. Lat 1071: Frederick II, "De arte venandi cum avibus": Miniature of Holy Roman Emperor Frederick II (1194–1250) with an Eagle*, ca. 1220–1250**
24.5 x 36 cm; Illuminated manuscript
Vatican Library

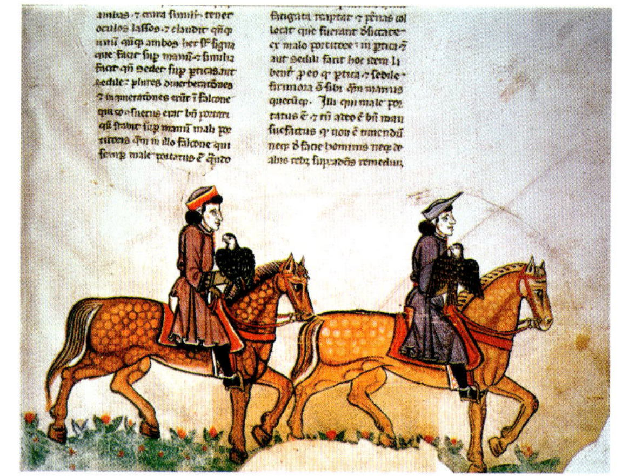

German artist, ca. 1220–1250
***Codex Ms. Pal. Lat 1071: "De arte venandi cum avibus" (Detail): Falconers*, ca. 1220–1250**
24.5 x 36 cm; Illuminated manuscript
Vatican Library

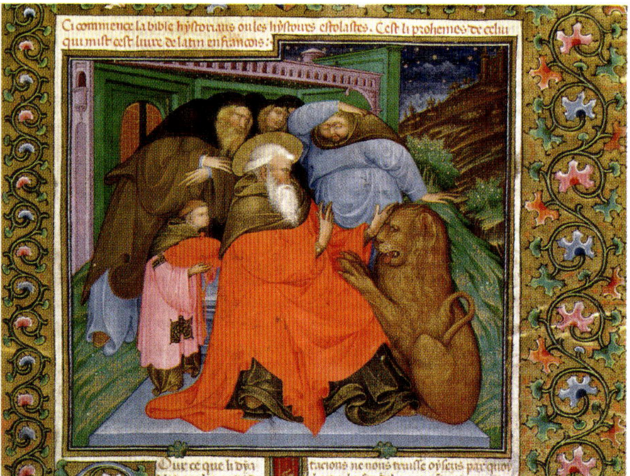

Italian artist, 15th century
***Barberiniano Manuscript (Ms. Lat 613, f.630r): St. Jerome*, 15th century**
38 x 27 cm; Illuminated manuscript
Vatican Library

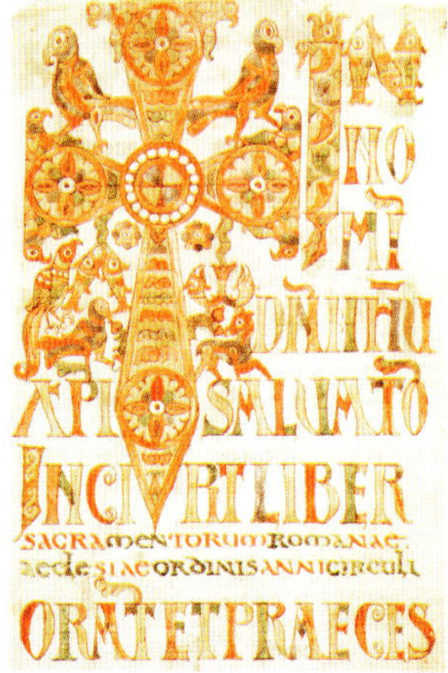

French artist (Abbey of Chelles), ca. 750
***Gelasian Sacramentary (Ms. Reg. Lat. 316 folio 132r): Frontispiece and illuminated Initial Capital Letter*, ca. 750AD**
26 x 17 cm; Illuminated manuscript book
Vatican Library

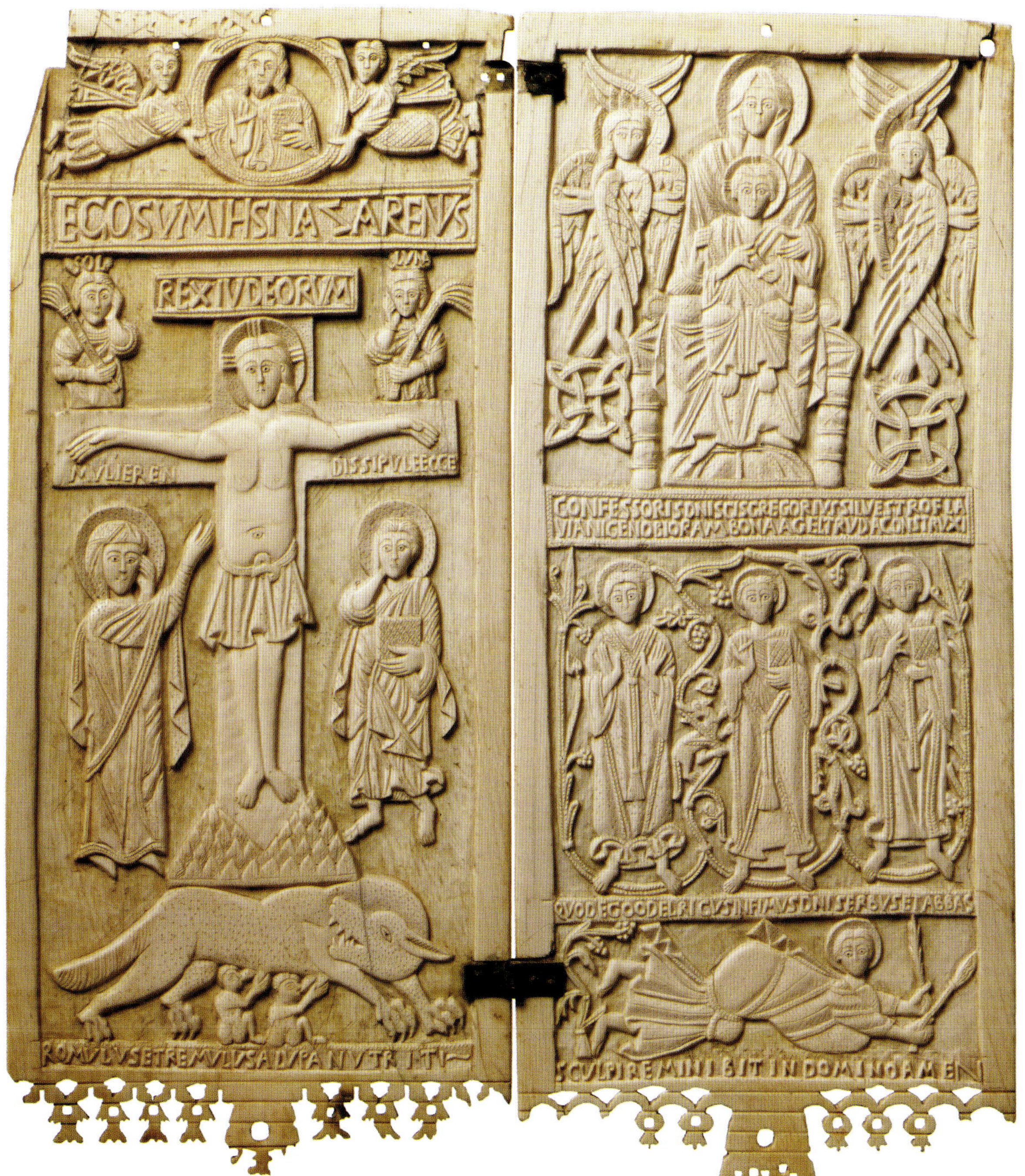

Lombardi artist, ca. 8–9th century
***Rambona Diptych*, ca. 8–9th century**
31 x 27 cm; Ivory
Vatican Library

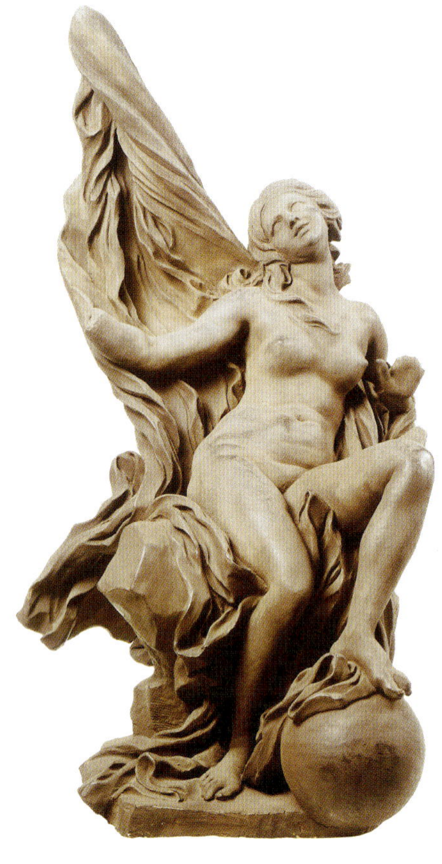

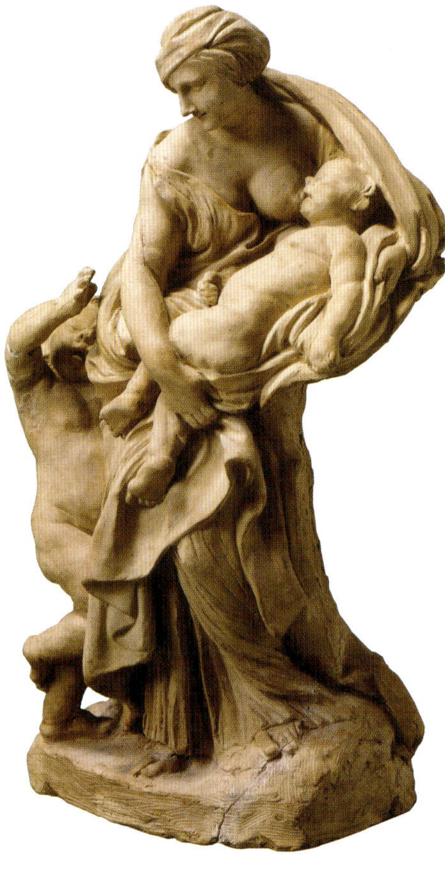

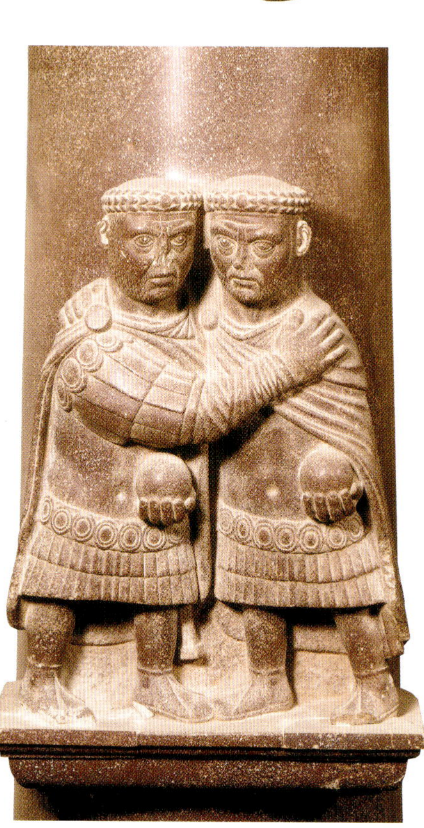

Gian Lorenzo Bernini, 1598–1680
***Truth*, 1645–1652**
Height: 45 cm; Marble
Vatican Library

Gian Lorenzo Bernini, 1598–1680
***Model for Charity*, 1645–1652**
Height 42 cm; Terracotta
Vatican Library

Paolo Taccone, active 1451–1477
***Bust of Pope Pius II*, 15th century**
Marble
Vatican Library

Unknown artist, date unknown
***Relief with Diocletian and Maximian*, date unknown**
385 cm; Porphyry column
Vatican Library

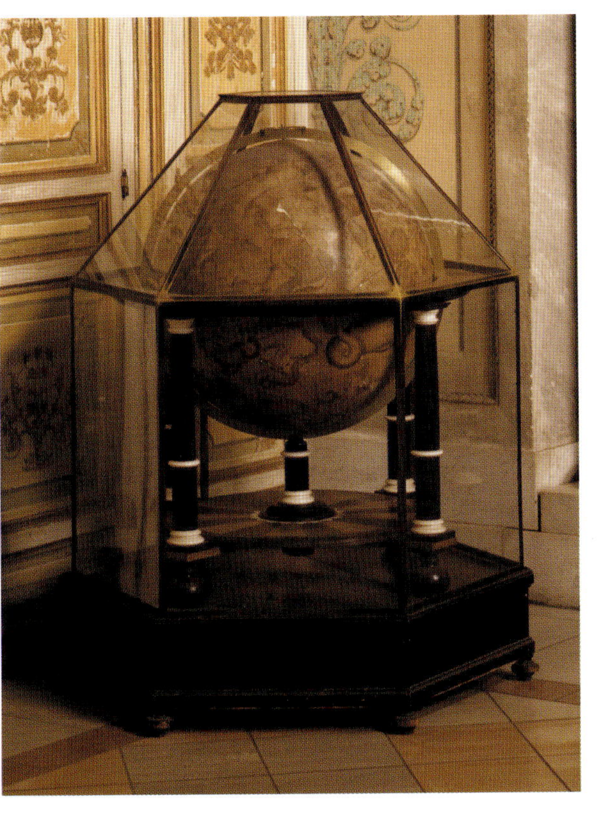

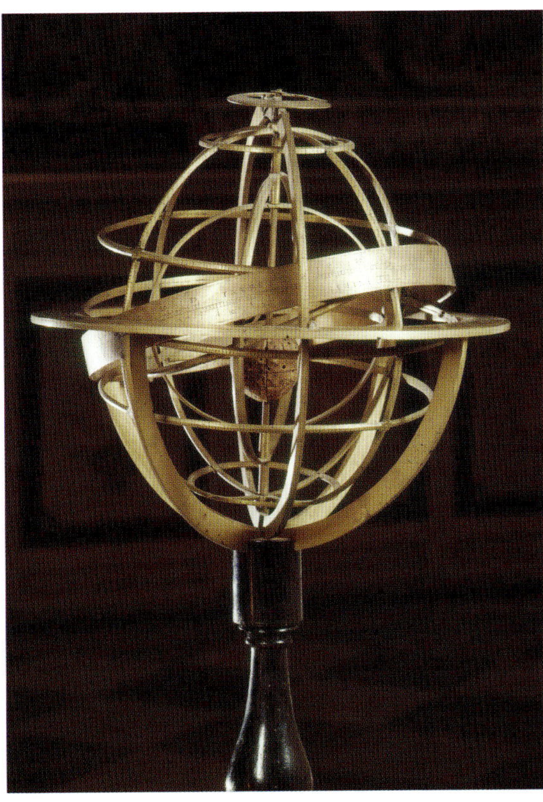

Joan Jan Blaeu, 1596–1673
***Terrestrial Globe*, 17th century**
Globe
Vatican Library

Unknown artist, 17th century
***Armillary Sphere*, 17th century**
Scientific instrument
Vatican Library

Unknown artist, 18th century
***Inlaid table*, 18th century**
Wood
Vatican Library

Unknown artist, 19th century
***Berlin Vase*, 19th century**
Porcelain
Vatican Library

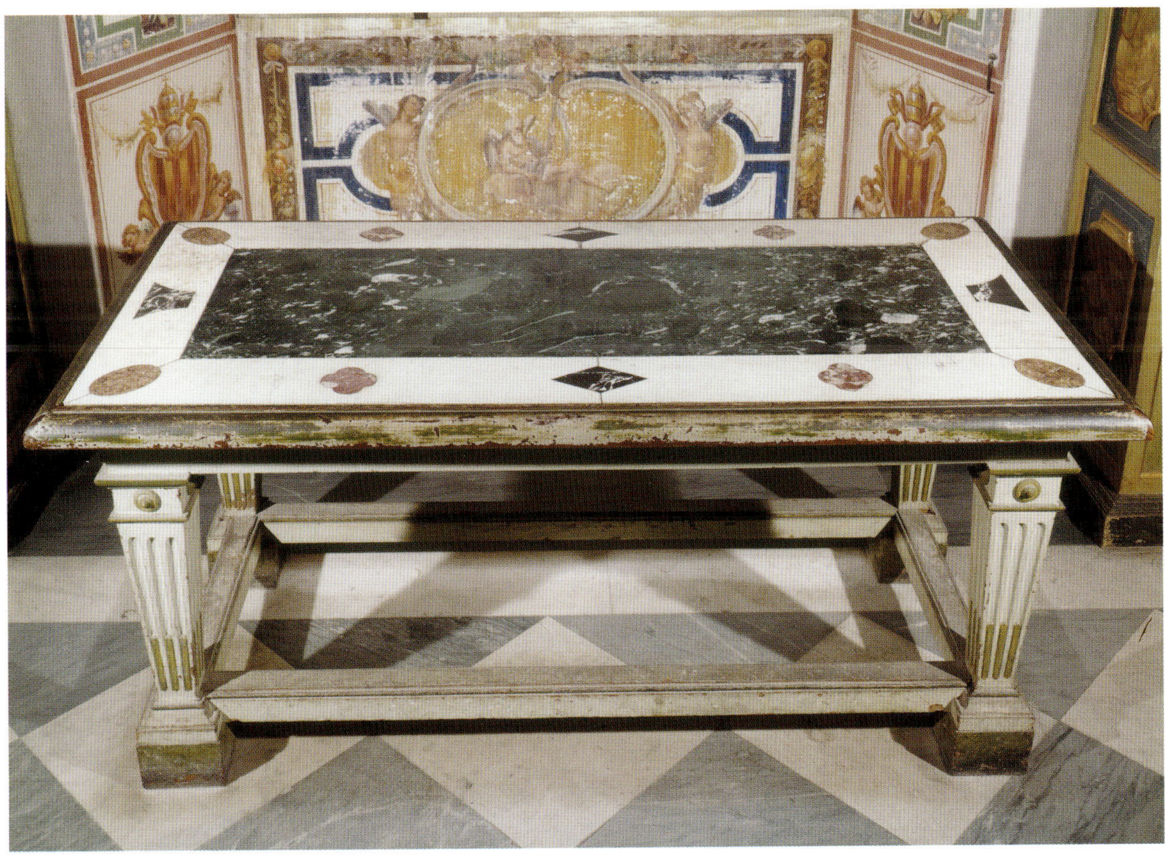

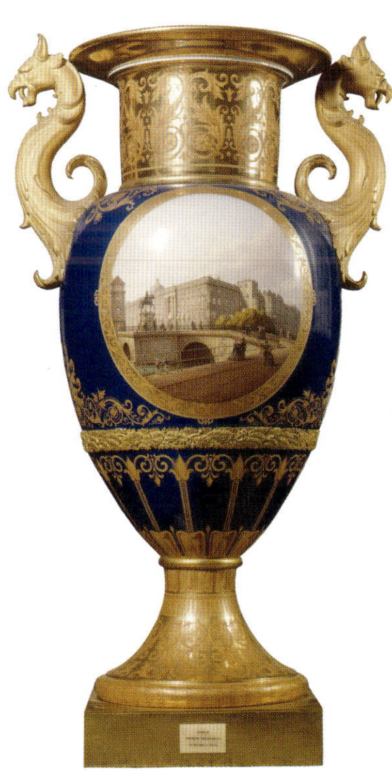

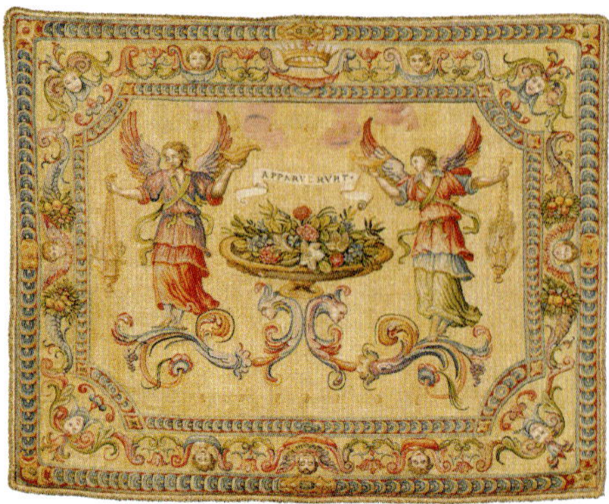

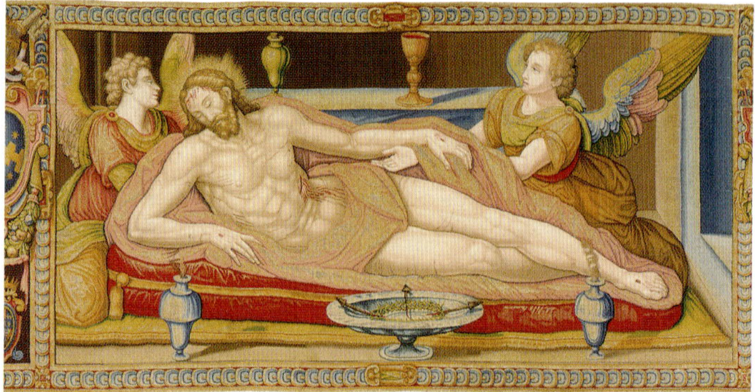

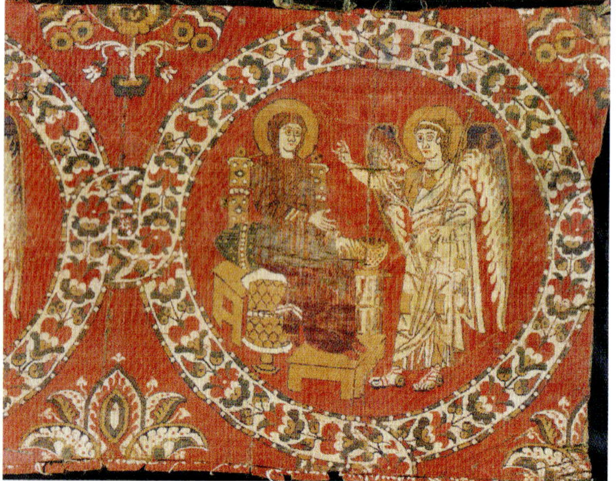

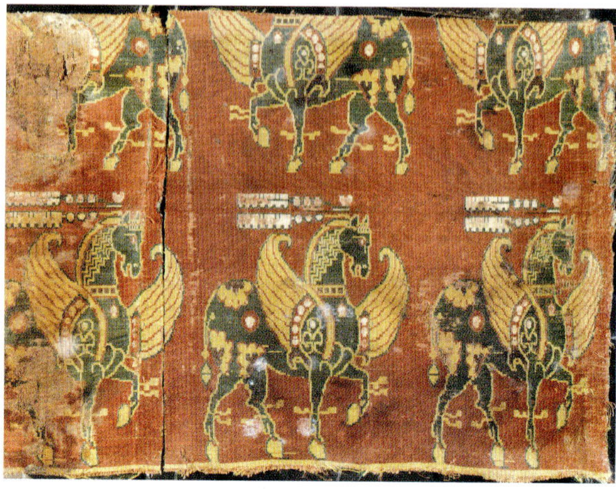

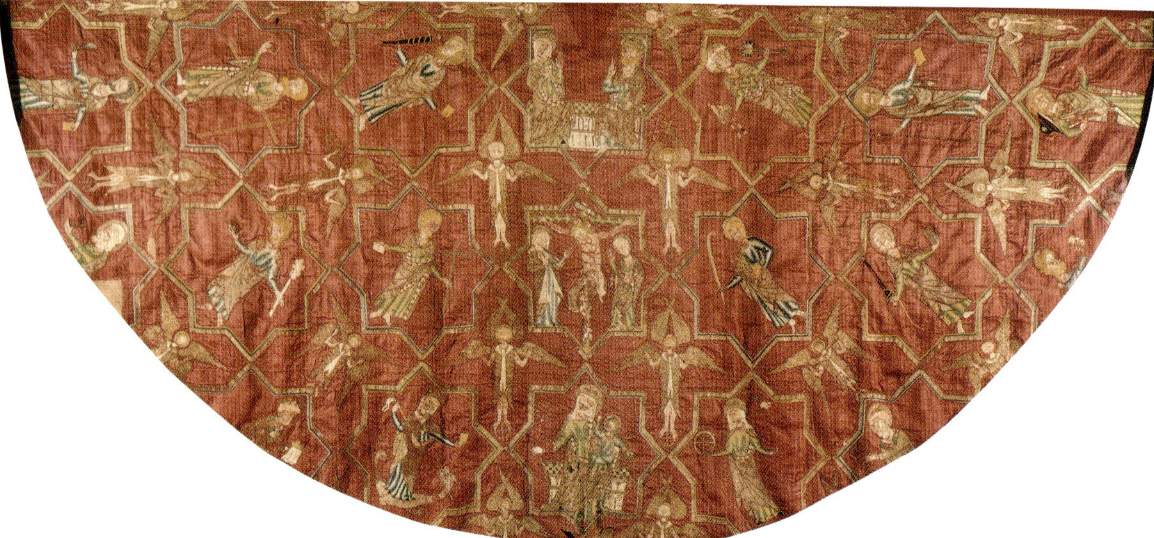

Anonymous, ca. 1535–1607
***Chalice Veil: Two Angels holding Censers*, ca. 1593–1597**
91 x 110 cm; Silk with silver thread
Vatican Library

Unknown artist, 16th century
Antependium (detail) with Dead Christ by Two Angels, 16th century
102 x 371 cm; Silk with silver thread
Vatican Library

Unknown artist, ca. 8th century
***Silk with the Annunciation*, ca. 8th century**
33.7 x 68.6 cm; Silk
Vatican Library

Early Islamic artist, 7th century
***Silk with Winged Horses*, 7th century**
31 x 21 cm; Silk
Vatican Library

English artist, 13th century
***Cape with Scenes from the Life of Christ, the Virgin and Saints*, ca. 1280**
137 x 310 cm; Embroidered silk with silver-gilt and silver threads
Vatican Library

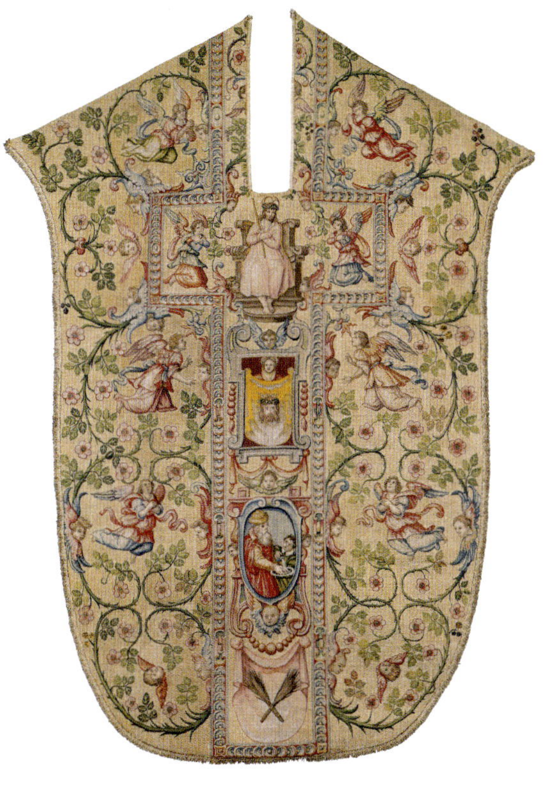

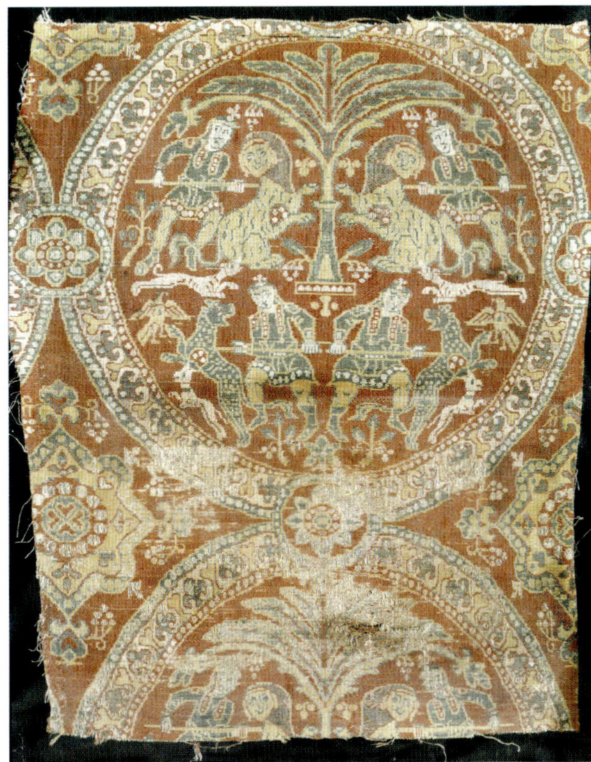

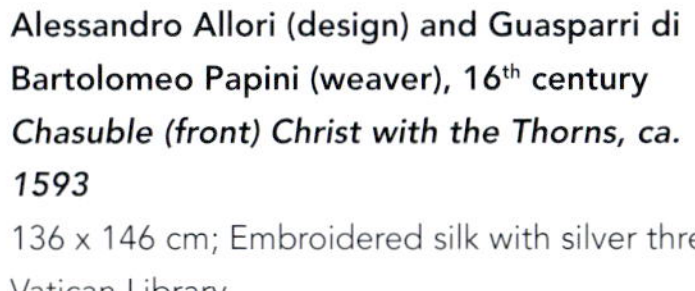

Alessandro Allori (design) and Guasparri di Bartolomeo Papini (weaver), 16th century
Chasuble (front) Christ with the Thorns, ca. 1593
136 x 146 cm; Embroidered silk with silver thread
Vatican Library

Early Islamic artist, date unknown
Silk with Hunting Scene, date unknown
42 x 68 cm; Silk
Vatican Library

Byzantine artist, 8th century
Silk with Lion Motif, 8th Century
13 x 9 cm; Silk
Vatican Library

Benedetto Buglioni, ca. 1461–1521
***Coat of Arms of Innocent VIII Supported by Two Angels*, 1484–1492**
Diameter 121 cm; Glazed terracotta
Vatican Library

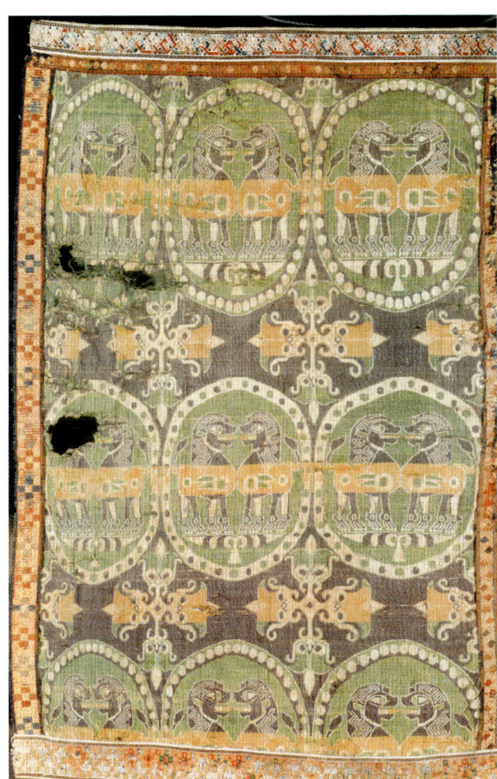

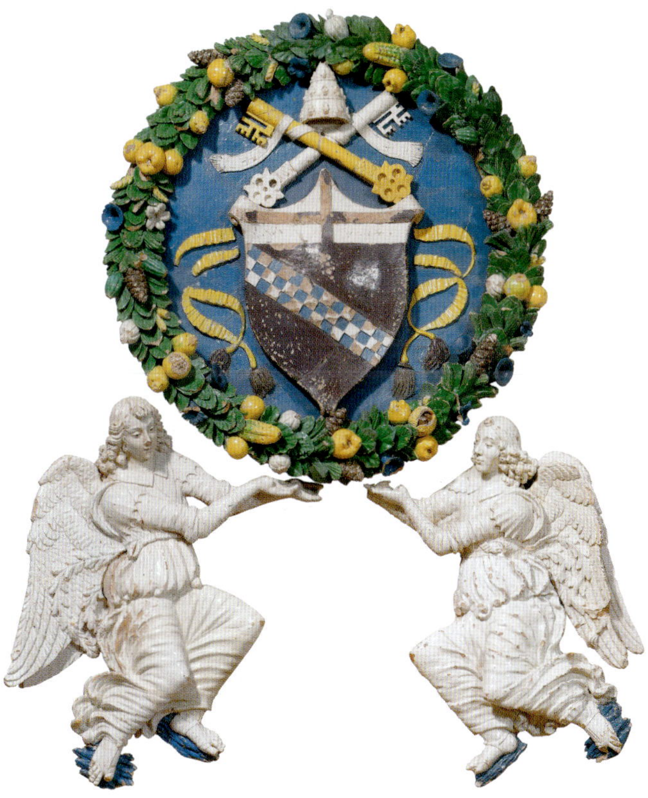

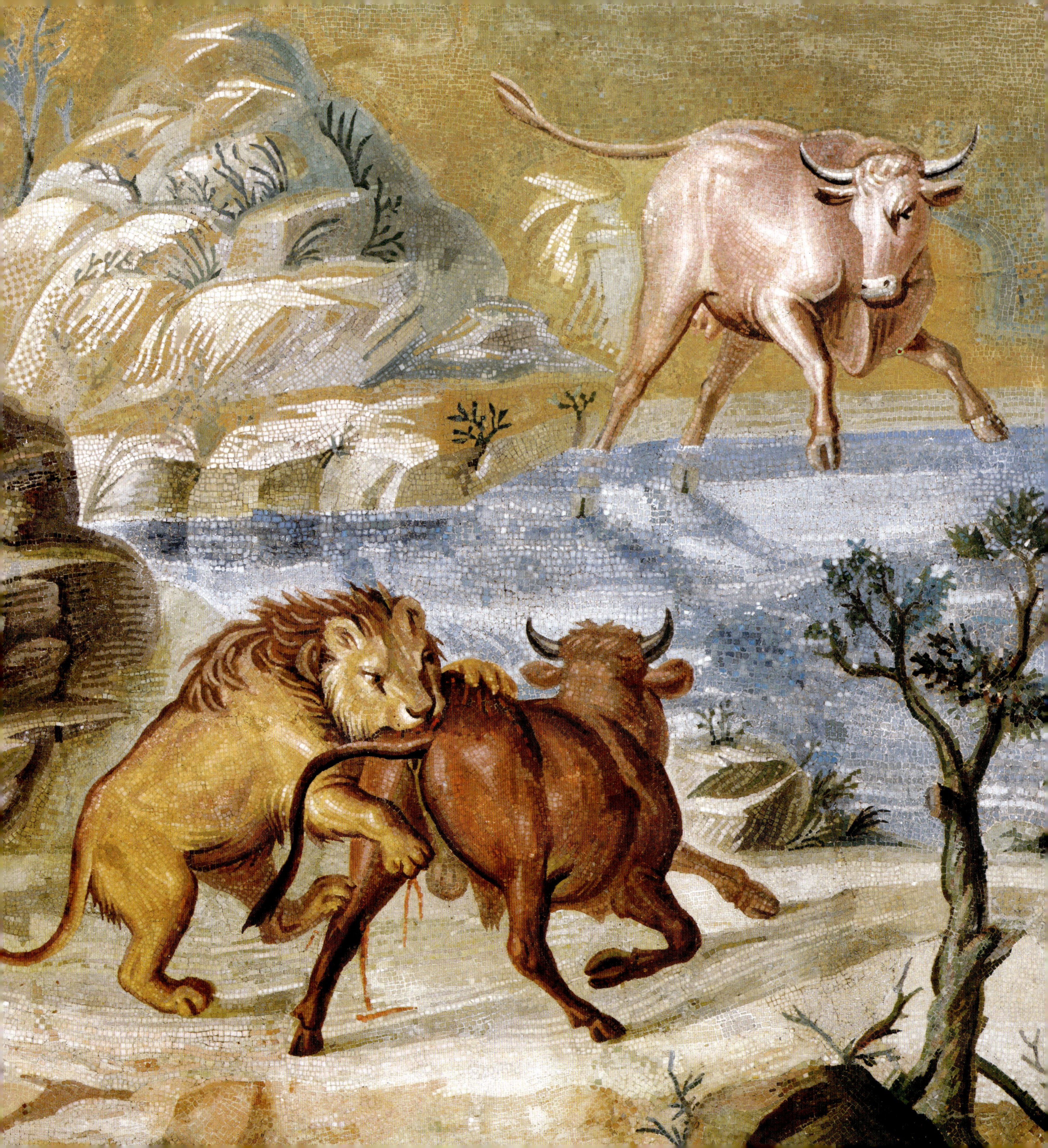

PIO-CLEMENTINO MUSEUM

The Pio-Clementino Museum is the oldest collection complex within the Vatican Museums. The popes began to accumulate the antique sculptures that form the nucleus of the Pio-Clementino Museum as long ago as the sixteenth century. The museum itself was founded in the eighteenth century and it is named after the pontiffs Clement XIV (1705–1774, reigned from 1769) and Pius VI (1717–1799, reigned from 1775), to whose efforts the museum owes its existence. The actual founding father was Clement XIV, whose intention, in the spirit of the Enlightenment, was to promote classical education and classical taste in art. To this end he adapted a number of rooms of the Palazzo del Belvedere, built by Innocent VIII (1432–1492, reigned from 1484), to display his own collection of sculptures. Clement XIV's museum concept was brought to fruition under the long pontificate of Pius VI and the collection was steadily expanded under the subsequent popes. Today the Pio-Clementino Museum is the largest of the four collections of antique art within the Vatican Museums, comprising ten rooms, each dedicated to a single unifying theme.

The heart of the museum is the Cortile Ottagono, which houses some of the most famous statues in the collection. The architectural origins of the courtyard go back to the Cortile delle Statue (Court of Statues), an area of the Palazzo del Belvedere set aside by Julius II (1443–1513, reigned from 1503) for the display of newly discovered antique sculptures. The Renaissance pontiff had been inspired by the idea of reviving the culture of ancient Rome. With the octagonal courtyard, his architect Donato Bramante (1444–1514) had designed an architectural space that was both inspired by classical antiquity and at the same time modern, one that created an appropriate ambience for the display of statues along the walls and in the niches. The first statues known to have been exhibited in the courtyard were the Laocoön and the Apollo Belvedere, which were put on display sometime between 1506 and 1509. They can still be admired here today.

Like most of the other works in the Pio-Clementino Museum, these two works are copies of famous Greek sculptures. Following the Roman conquest of Greece, such copies were made initially by Greek artists and later by Roman sculptors in Rome. Notwithstanding their original cult function, the Roman patrons had the statues copied in order to decorate their palaces and villas and stock their sculpture galleries. Because the originals are in many cases now lost, these copies are today of great value as evidence of the mastery of Greek sculpture. As many of the sculptures were displayed in the open air, durable materials such as marble and bronze were preferred—and these more expensive materials also made the work more imposing and stately. The material of the copies often differed from that of the originals, thus many Greek bronzes, for example, have survived only as Roman marble copies.

Trained by the Greek sculptors, the Roman artists began to create sculptures themselves, above all portrait statues and busts and statues of deities for display in temples, fora, and bath complexes. With the adoption of Christianity as the state religion in the fourth century AD, many of these statues were dismantled or destroyed as "pagan works" and subsequently forgotten. It is thanks to the efforts of the early archaeologists and art lovers of the Renaissance that these ancient works were searched for and excavated and attained a new value as important mementos of the past.

Even in the Renaissance era, antique sculptures were often not left in the condition in which they were found; attempts were made to disguise the works' fragmentary state through restoration in order to make them more presentable for museum display. Particularly in the eighteenth century, it was considered desirable to reconstruct as ideal as possible an image of the antique. During the reorganization of the collection under Clement XIV and above all Pius VI, damaged statues were extensively restored. Many of the works on display in the Cortile Ottagono and the other rooms of the Pio-Clementino Museum therefore embody, no less than the antique art itself, an idealized taste for the antique exemplified by the classicism of the second half of the eighteenth century.

One of the most important neoclassical sculptors in Italy was Antonio Canova (1757–1822), appointed Inspector General of the Vatican Art Treasures in 1802 by Pius VII (1742–1823, reigned from 1800). Canova was responsible for recovering many of the works of art plundered by Napoleon's troops and for reorganizing the museum's collection. His idealized view of the antique is reflected in his marble statue Perseus (ca. 1800), which Pius VII put on display in the Cortile Ottagono, initially on the plinth of the plundered Apollo Belvedere.

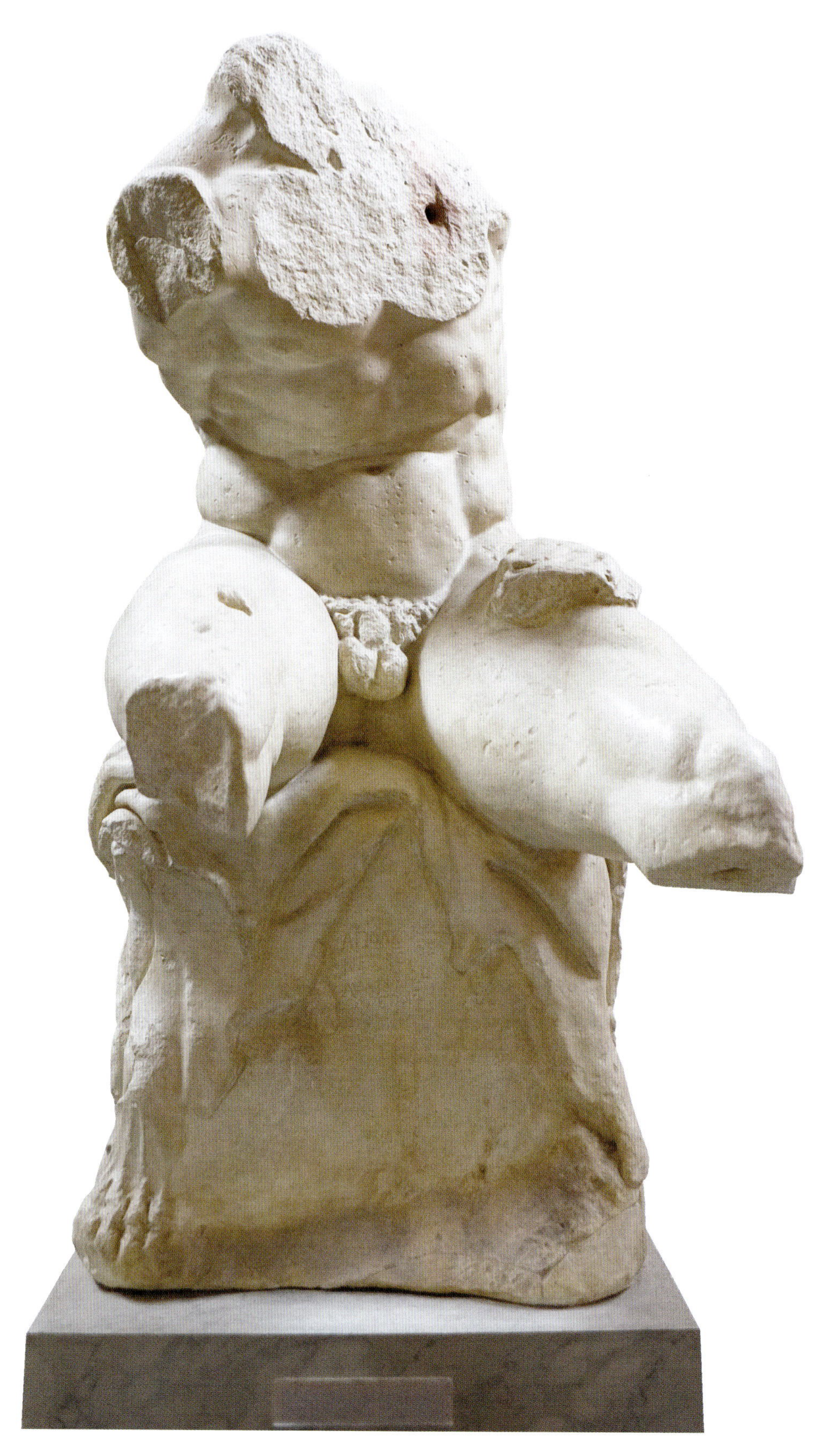

Apollonius of Athens

Belvedere Torso

Though at first glance not an especially prepossessing fragment, the Belvedere Torso derives its significance from the fact that it is one of the few original Greek statues in the collection. Discovered in the fifteenth century, the work entered the Vatican's Court of Statues in around 1530 and immediately attracted the admiration of artists such as Michelangelo. The seated figure, with its muscular upper body inclined slightly to the right, is naked but for an animal hide covering its left hip. The fragmentary condition of the sculpture has given rise to abundant speculation. The right arm may once have rested on the upper thigh, with the left arm raised following the line of vision. At the same time the right leg seems to be stretched out and the left slightly angled. Depending on how the statue is reconstructed, there are various possible identifications. The panther skin could indicate Dionysus, Marsyas, or a satyr. In view of the figure's muscular physique, the Argonaut Philoctetes, Prometheus, Hercules, the Greek hero Ajax contemplating suicide, or a mythical athlete have also been suggested. The front of the plinth bears the signature of the sculptor Apollonius, active in the first century BC.

Apollonius of Athens, 1st century BC
***Belvedere Torso*, 1st century BC**
Height: 159 cm; Marble
Pio-Clementino Museum

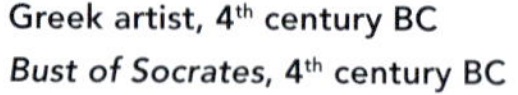

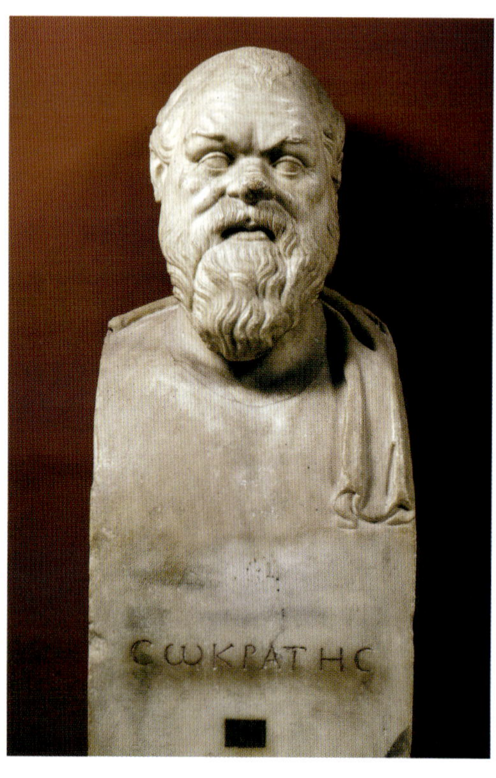

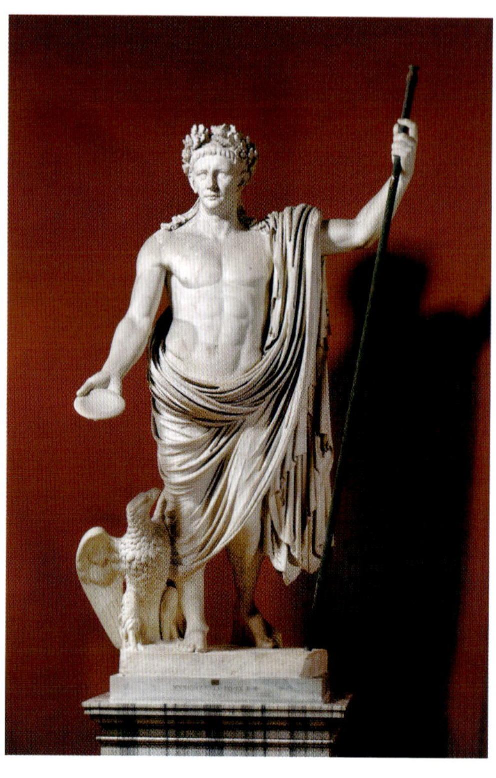

Greek artist, 4th century BC
***Bust of Socrates*, 4th century BC**
Height: 103 cm; Marble
Pio-Clementino Museum

Roman artist, 1st century AD
***Statue of Claudius I*, 1st century AD**
Height: 254 cm; Marble
Pio-Clementino Museum

Roman artist, active 2nd century, after a Greek original by Praxiteles, ca 400–326 BC
***Apollo Sauroctonos*, 2nd century**
Height: 205 cm; Marble
Pio-Clementino Museum

Roman artist, Copy of Lysippos original, 320 BC
***Apoxymenos*, date unknown**
Marble
Pio-Clementino Museum

Roman artist, 250 AD
***Funerary Monument to M. Gratidius Libanus and Gratidia M.L. Carite*, 250 AD**
132 x 252 cm; Marble
Pio-Clementino Museum

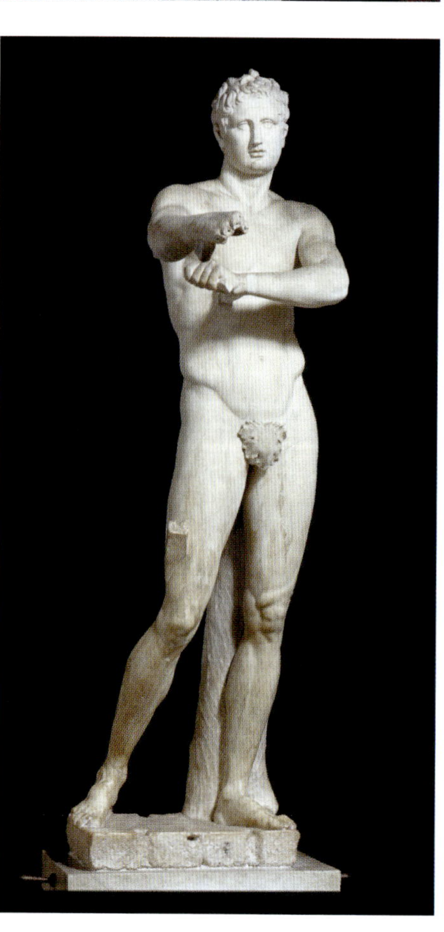

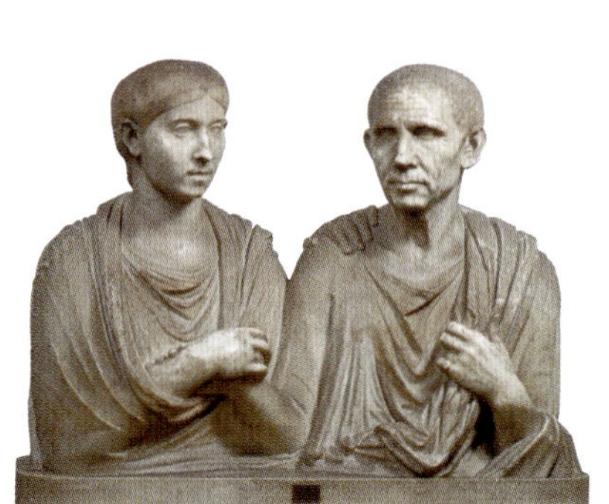

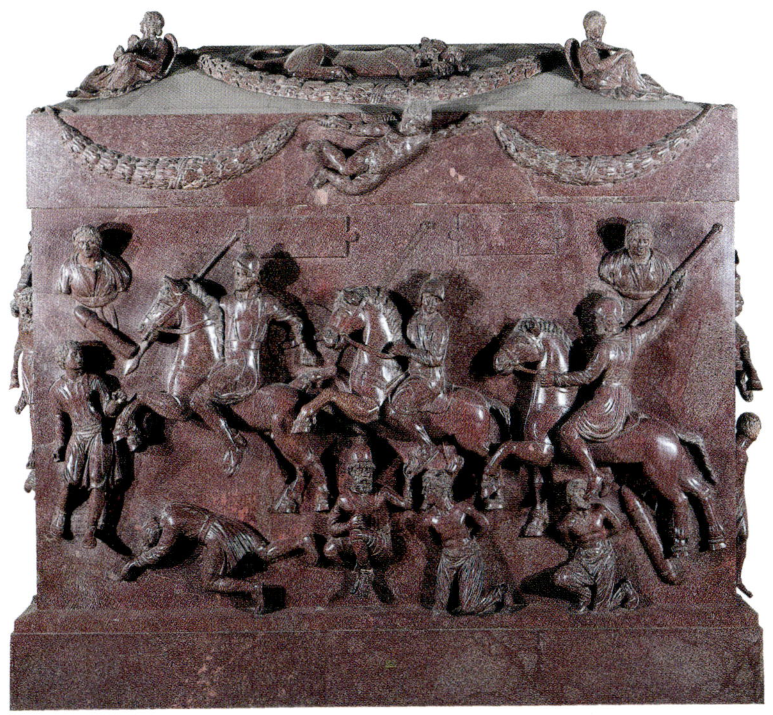

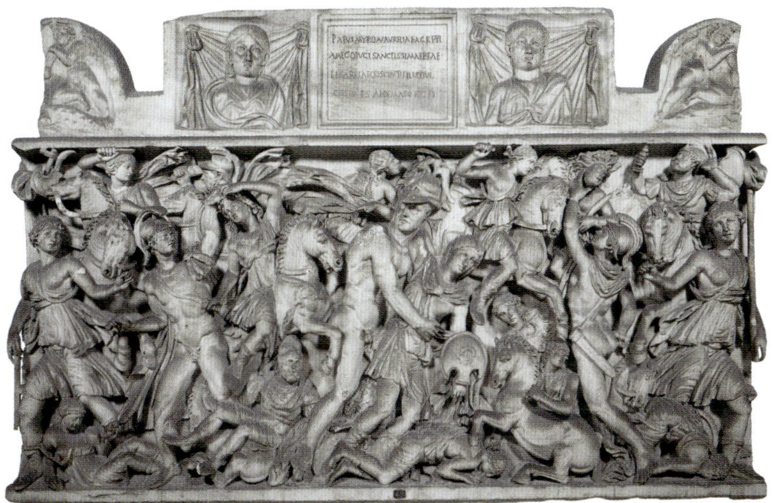

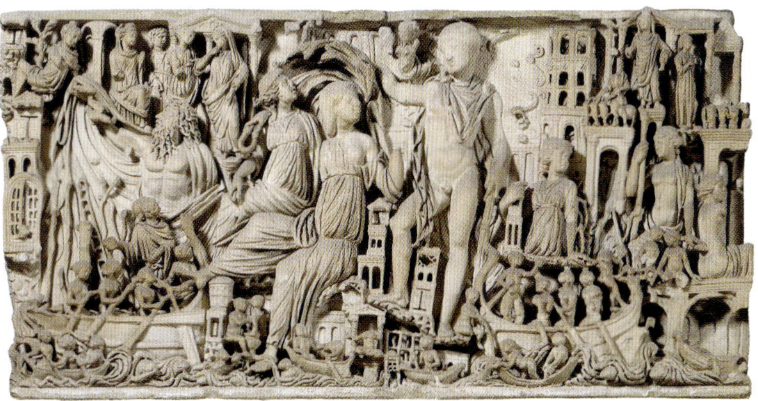

Roman artist, 4th century
***Sarcophagus of Helena*, 4th century**
242 x 184 x 268 cm; Marble
Pio-Clementino Museum

Roman artist, ca. 180–170 BC
***Amazonomachy Sarcophagus (Battle with Achilles)*, ca. 180–170 BC**
119 x 252 x 102 cm; Marble
Pio-Clementino Museum

Roman artist, ca. 250 AD
***View of a Port (Scene from a Roman Sarcophagus)*, ca. 250 AD**
132 x 252 cm; Marble
Pio-Clementino Museum

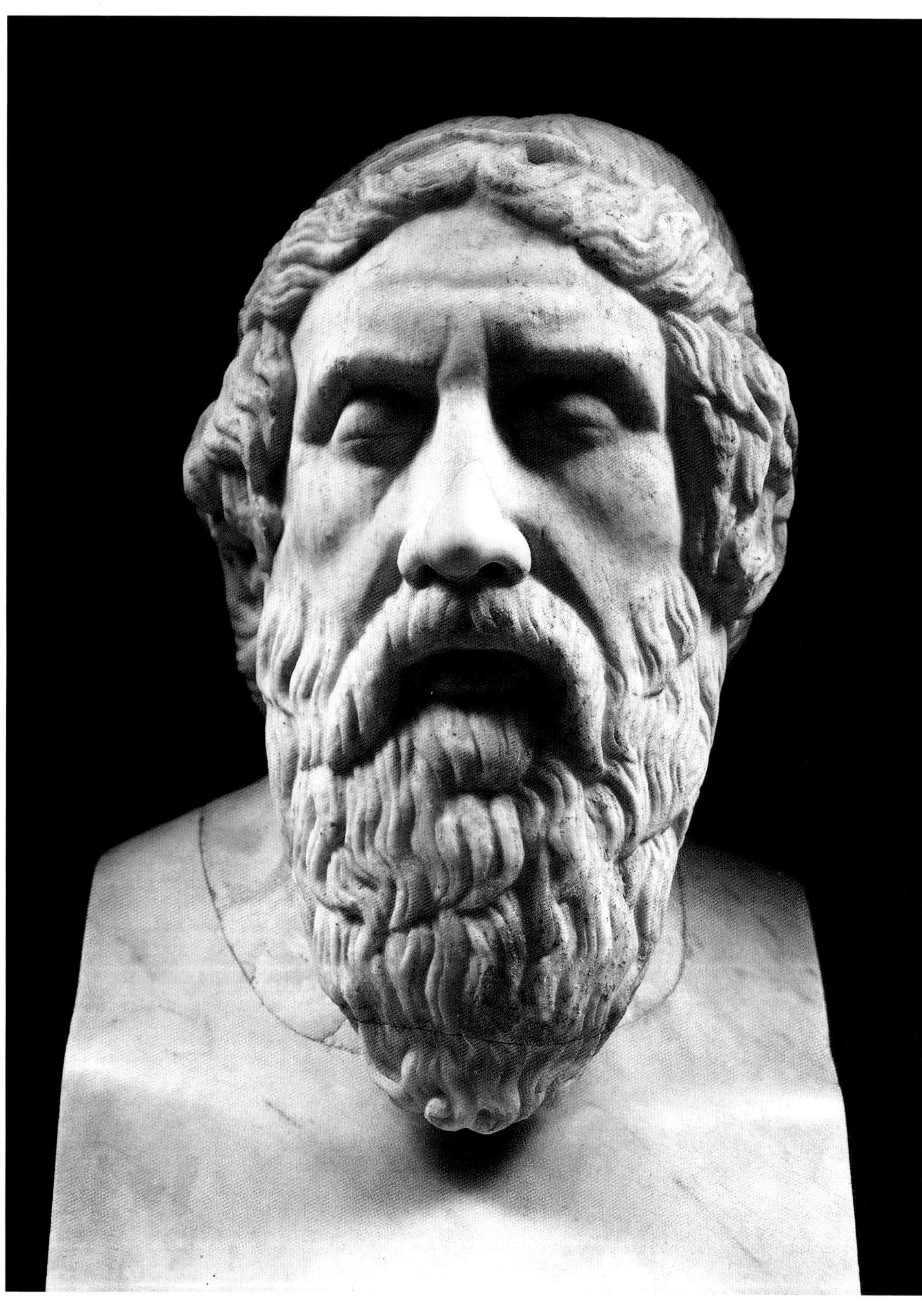

Greek artist, 4th century BC
***Bust of Homer*, 4th century BC**
Height: 33 cm; Marble
Pio-Clementino Museum

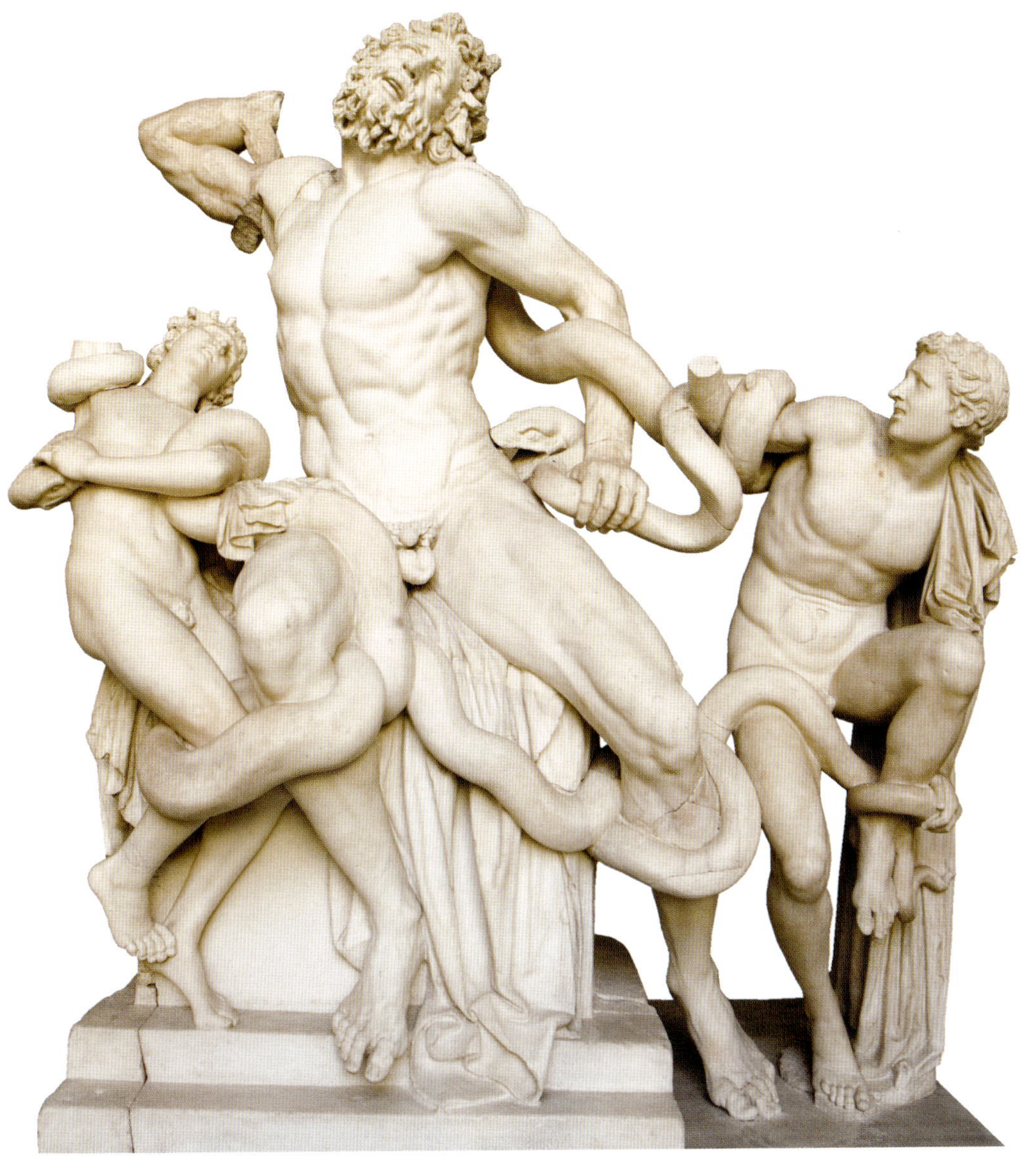

Roman artist after a Greek original

Laocoön

In early 1506 a large marble sculptural group was discovered in the Esquiline vineyards. The group had caused a sensation in the ancient Roman art world centuries before. In his *Natural History*, the classical author Pliny the Elder (ca. 23–79 AD) describes the Laocoön as a work that is "to be preferred to all other works of painting and sculpture." This sculptural group, acquired by Julius II in 1506, was one of the earliest works to be exhibited in the Cortile Ottagono and it remains among the most famous of all antique sculptures. Thought to have been made after a Greek bronze original, the group depicts the gruesome death of the Trojan priest Laocoön after warning his fellow citizens of the deception involving the Trojan Horse. As punishment, the goddess Athena, who was favorably disposed to the Greeks, sent two sea serpents to throttle Laocoön and his two sons. Laocoön is regarded as embodying the tragic figure who tries to rebel against preordained fate and is cruelly punished for it. Among other aspects, artists such as Michelangelo admired the realistic depiction of the play of muscles, shown here at the point of their greatest exertion, and the convincing facial expressions and gestures of figures in the throes of death.

Roman artist, active early 1st century, after a Greek original from 2nd century BC
***Laocoön*, early 1st century**
Height: 225 cm; Marble
Pio-Clementino Museum

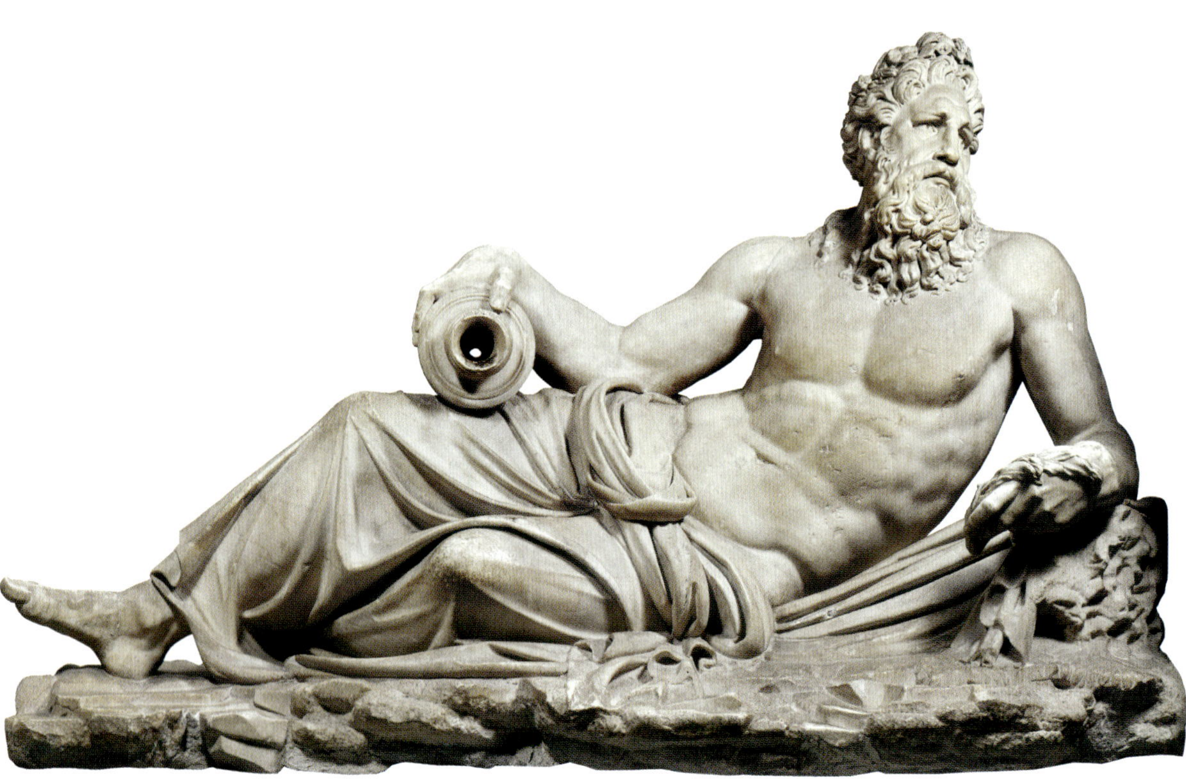

Roman artist after a Hellenistic model

A River God (Representing the Tigris or the Arno)

This marble sculpture, believed to have been created in the late Hadrianic period, is of an unidentified river god. The deity has been represented as a powerfully built older man with a luxuriantly curly beard and head of hair who reclines on his left side, propped up on his arm. (The expressive head is a restoration by a Renaissance sculptor.) His arms and raised upper body are distinctive for their well-defined musculature. The lower part of his body, below the hips, is concealed by a loosely draped cloth beneath which the outline of his limbs can be made out. The god holds a vase in his right hand, symbolizing a river's flowing water. The realistic depiction of body, musculature, and garments is typical of Hellenistic sculpture of the fourth to third centuries BC. This work continued to exert its influence as late as the Roman Empire. In view of the Medici emblem carved onto the vase, this marble statue seems to have entered the Vatican collections under Leo X (1475–1521, reigned from 1513), a member of the Medici family. It was initially thought to have been a personification of the Arno River, but was later reinterpreted as a representation of the Tigris. It served for many years as part of a fountain whose basin was a sarcophagus decorated with scenes of battling Amazons.

Roman artist, active 2nd century after a Hellenistic model
A River God (Representing the Tigris or the Arno), **2nd century**
Height: 248 cm; Marble
Pio-Clementino Museum

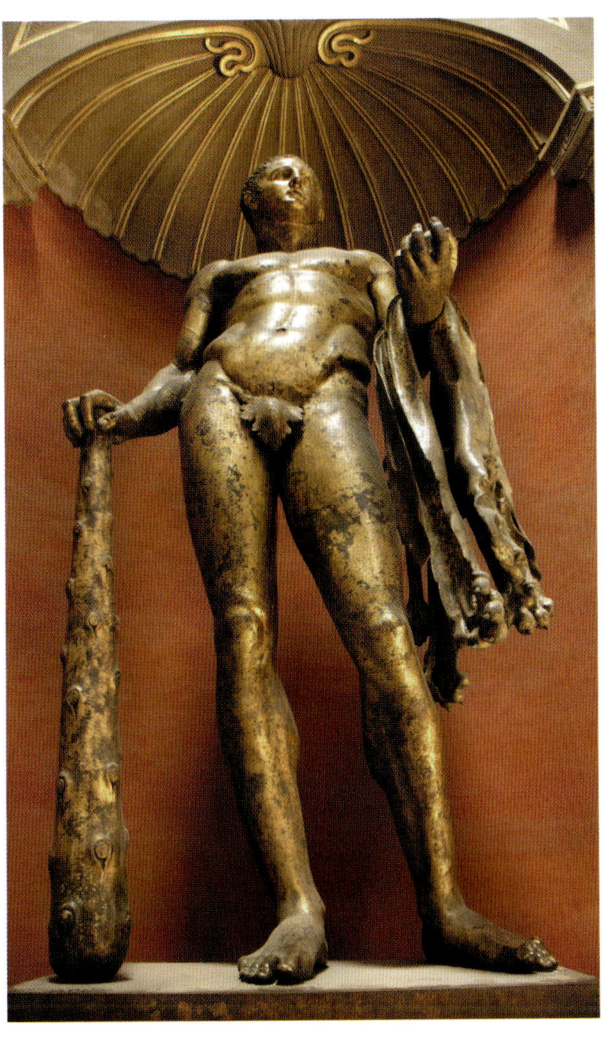

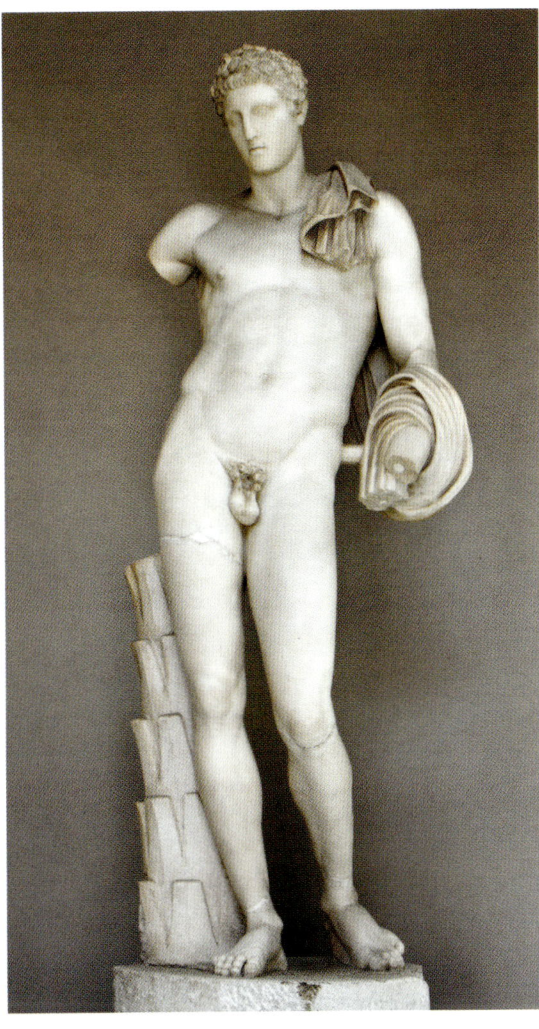

Roman artist, 2nd century
***Colossal Statue of Hercules*, 2nd century**
383 cm; Gilded bronze
Pio-Clementino Museum

Roman artist, 2nd century, Copy of Praxiteles original, 4th century BC
***Hermes (Mercury)*, 2nd century**
165 cm; Marble
Pio-Clementino Museum

Roman artist, 2nd century
***Jupiter/Zeus*, 2nd century**
231 cm; Marble
Pio-Clementino Museum

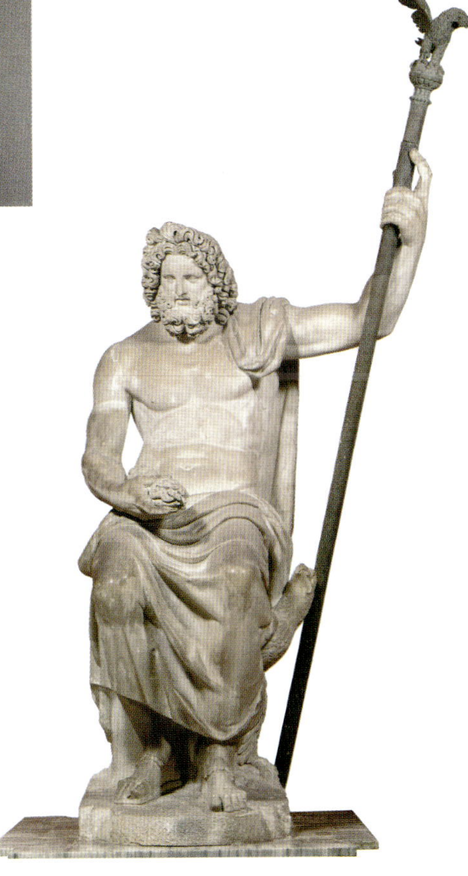

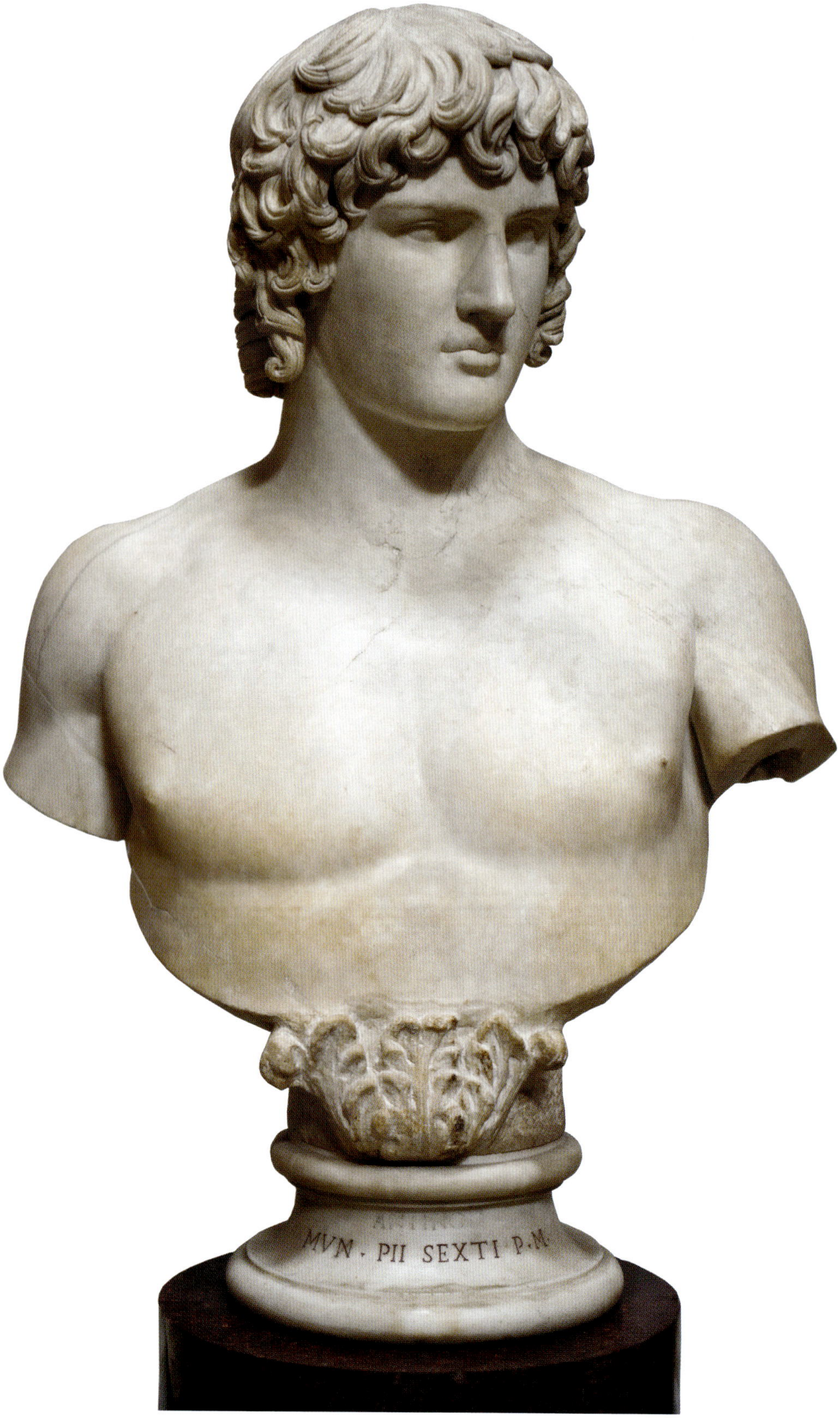

Roman artist

Bust of Antinous

Antinous (ca. 110/115–130 AD) was the youthful favorite of the Roman emperor Hadrian. Tradition has it that Antinous was around twelve years old when Hadrian met the beautiful boy, fell madly in love with him, and made him his constant companion. After the tragic premature death of the youth, who drowned in the Nile before the eyes of the emperor, Hadrian proclaimed him a god. Within a short space of time numerous Antinous statues and busts had been made for the various cult sites, including this bust that has been on display in the Sala dei Busti since 1770. Its representation of the youth conforms to the official portrait type, which shows him as a god or hero with naked torso. Antinous can be identified from his pensive expression and lowered eyes, the soft, classical-idealized facial features, and the full, sensuous lips. His abundant, curly hair plays around his forehead and temples. The bust entered the Museo Chiaramonti after being presented as a gift by Cardinal Federico Marcello Lantes to Clement XIV in 1770. Its provenance is thought to be Villa Adriana, the countryseat of Emperor Hadrian.

Roman artist, active 2nd century
***Bust of Antinous*, ca. 130–140 AD**
Height: 90 cm; Marble
Pio-Clementino Museum

Hadrianic artist, ca. 120 AD
***Satyrical Mask*, ca. 120 AD**
Height: 90 cm; Marble
Pio-Clementino Museum

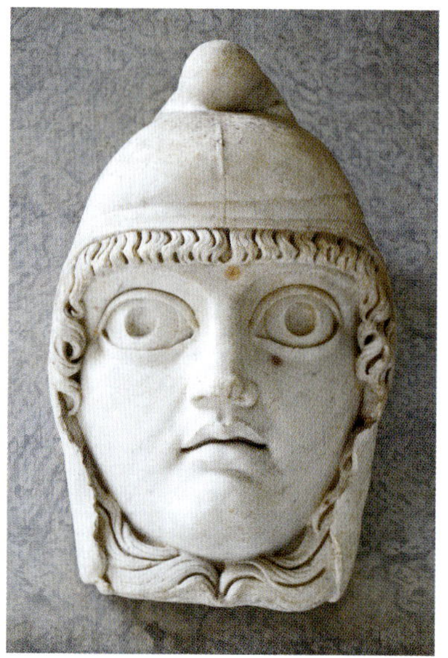

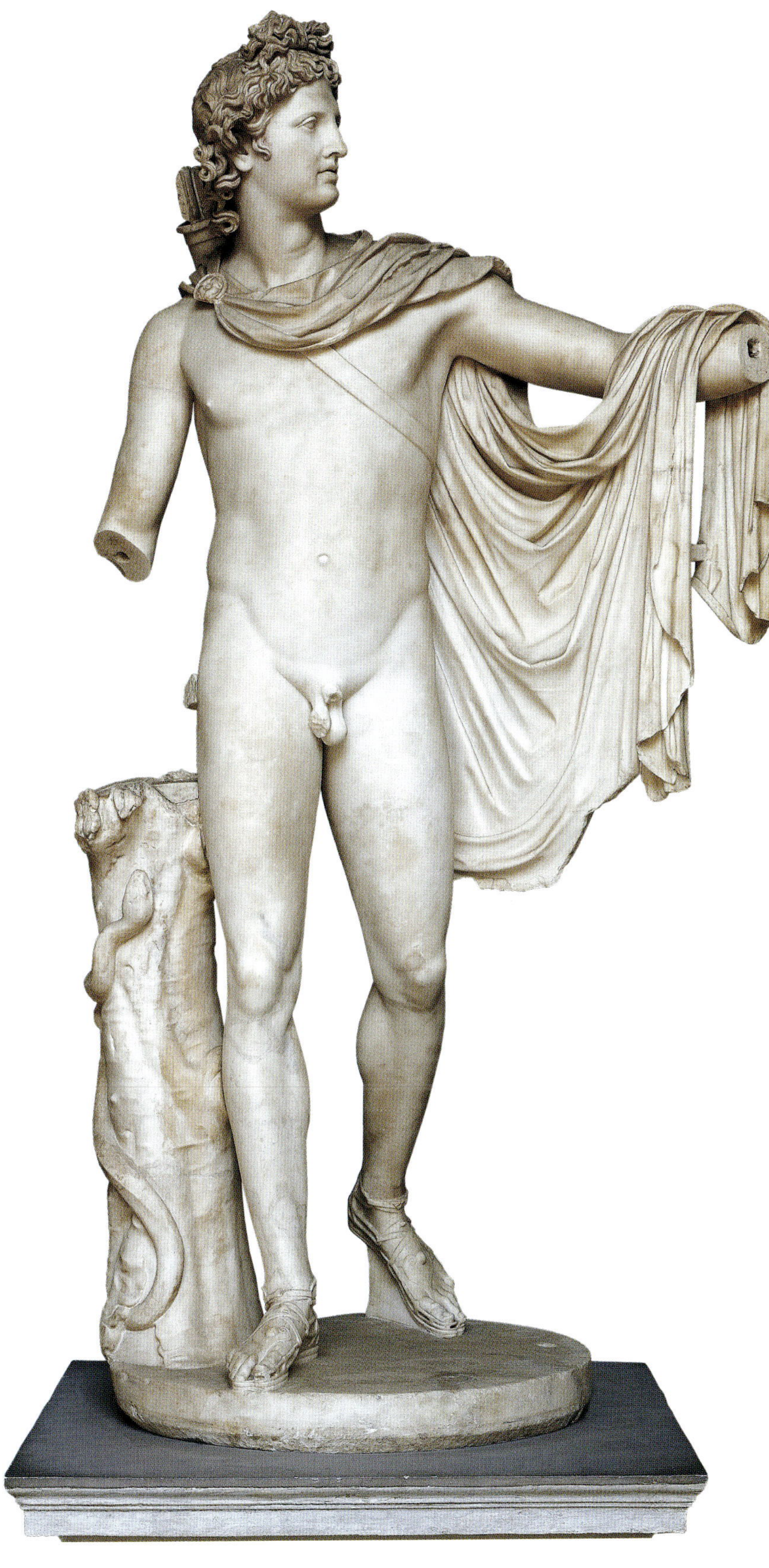

Roman artist

Apollo Belvedere

The Apollo Belvedere is perhaps the most famous statue in the Vatican Museums and indeed one of the best-known sculptures in the history of art. This figure of the antique god of the Muses and of war was discovered virtually undamaged at the end of the fifteenth century and put on display by Julius II in the Belvedere courtyard by 1508 at the latest. It is generally regarded as a Roman copy of a Greek bronze made around 330–320 BC and attributed to the Athenian sculptor Leochares, who was renowned for his balanced forms. The larger-than-life-size statue depicts Apollo not as the art-loving god of the Muses holding a lyre, but instead in a more martial pose. He is shown stepping forward on his right foot and glancing to his left with his upper body inclined slightly in that direction. The original forearms are missing but the recently restored position of the arms reveals that he has just shot an arrow from the quiver slung over his shoulder. The mantle draped over his back and upper left arm exposes to view his well-proportioned, muscular upper body. Disseminated in numerous reproductions, the sculpture has been regarded as the epitome of classical beauty ever since it was put on display in the Cortile Ottagono. The antiquarian Johann Joachim Winckelmann praised it in the middle of the eighteenth century as representing "the highest artistic ideal of all the works of antiquity."

Roman artist, active 2nd century,
after a Greek original attributed to Leochares, 4th century BC
***Apollo Belvedere*, ca. 130–140 AD**
Height: 224 cm; Parian marble
Pio-Clementino Museum

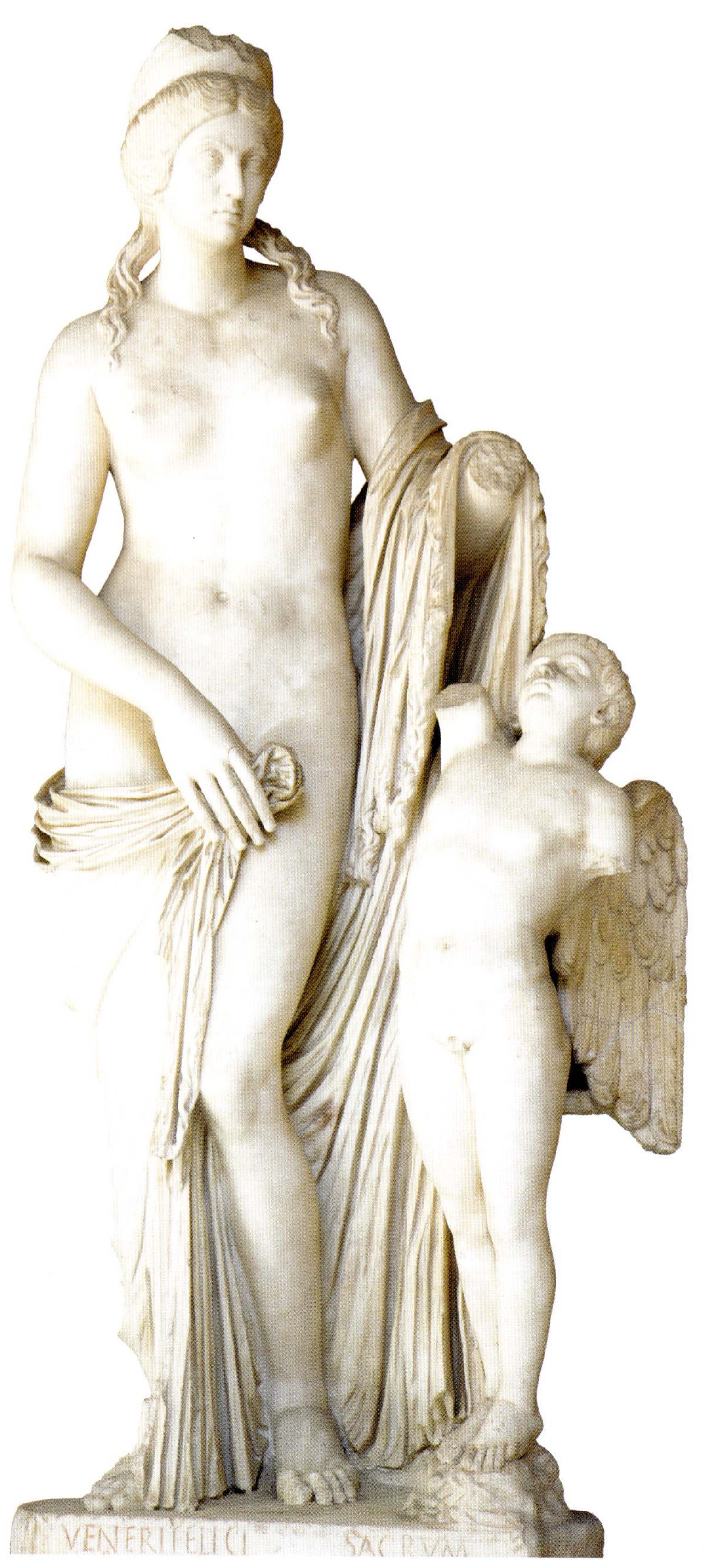

Roman artist

Venus Felix

The Venus Felix (Venus of Good Fortune) is a work of classical beauty and balance. The figure stands in a contrapposto stance with a finely folded cloth draped loosely around her lower body. The inscription on the plinth indicates that the figure was a votive offering from the Roman matron Sallustia and Helpidius, who was possibly her son. The latter is perhaps portrayed as the winged Cupid figure standing next to Venus on a small mound of earth and reaching up to the deity, probably originally in order to hold up a looking glass for her. The Venus figure is modeled on the Cnidian Aphrodite by the Greek sculptor Praxiteles, regarded as the first life-sized, realistically modeled female nude in classical Greek art and described by numerous classical writers. The characteristic of this figure type is the positioning of her right hand in front of her pudenda as a sign of virginity. The Roman creator of this Venus Felix has doubled this gesture with the gathered tip of her garment, which the goddess holds with considerable grace. Her gentle smile conforms to the statue's function as a votive figure, no doubt once displayed in one of Rome's temples dedicated to Venus.

Roman artist, active 2nd century after Praxiteles, 4th century BC
***Venus Felix*, 2nd century**
Height: 214 cm; Marble
Pio-Clementino Museum

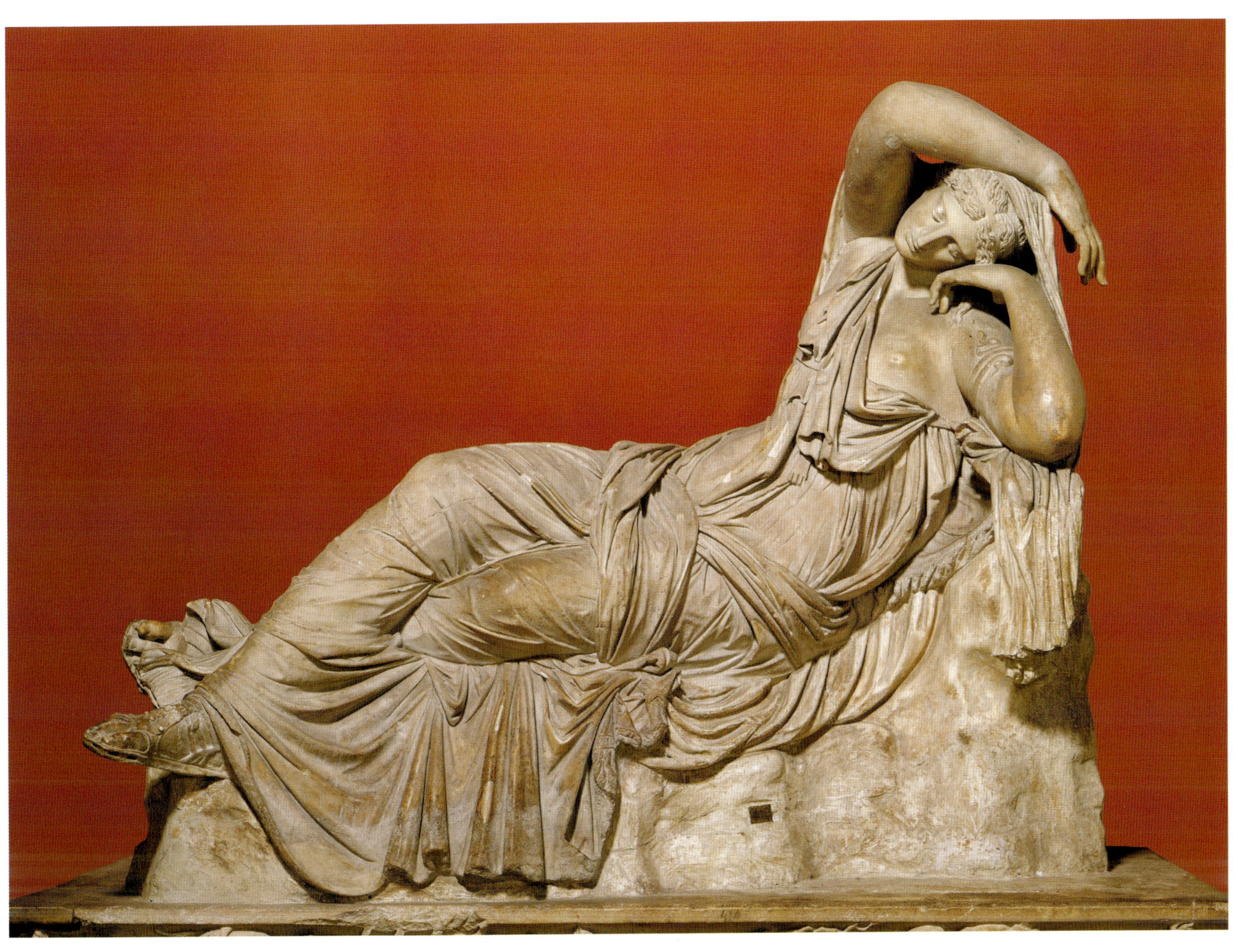

Roman artist, active 2nd century after an original of the Pergamon school, 240 BC
***Sleeping Ariadne*, 2nd century**
161 x 195 cm; Marble
Pio-Clementino Museum

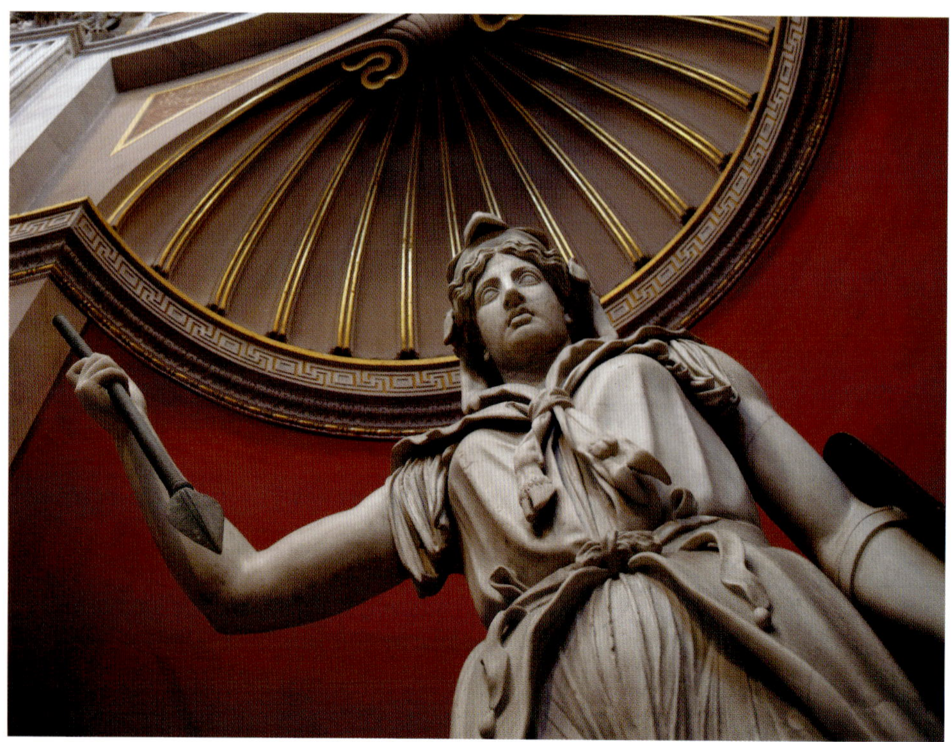

Roman artist, 2nd century
***Juno Sospita*, 2nd century**
Height: 305 cm; Marble
Pio-Clementino Museum

Roman artist, active 2nd century after Praxiteles, 4th century BC
***Venus*, 2nd century**
Height: 100 cm; Marble
Pio-Clementino Museum

Roman artist, 2nd century
***Calliope, Chief of the Muses and Muse of Epic and Heroic Poetry*, 2nd century**
Marble
Pio-Clementino Museum

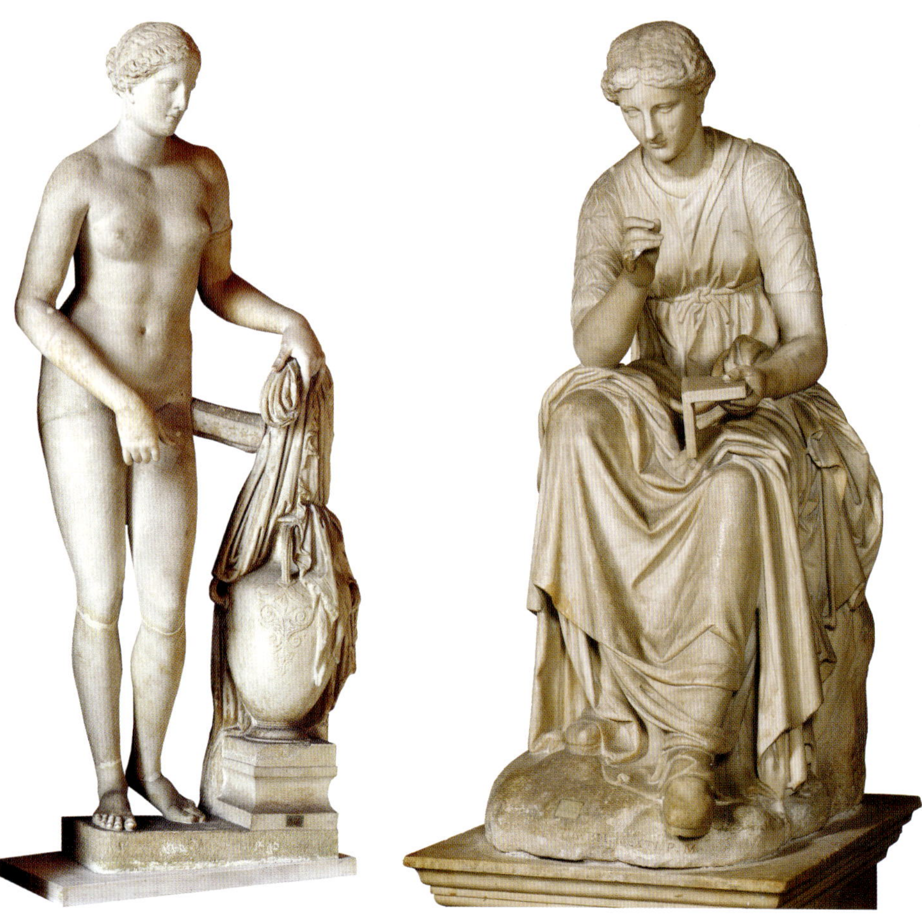

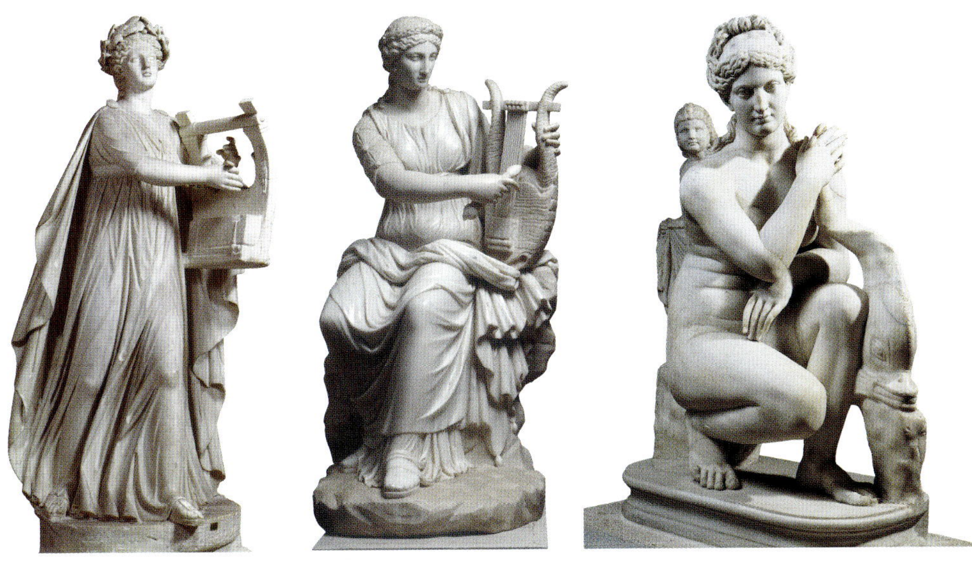

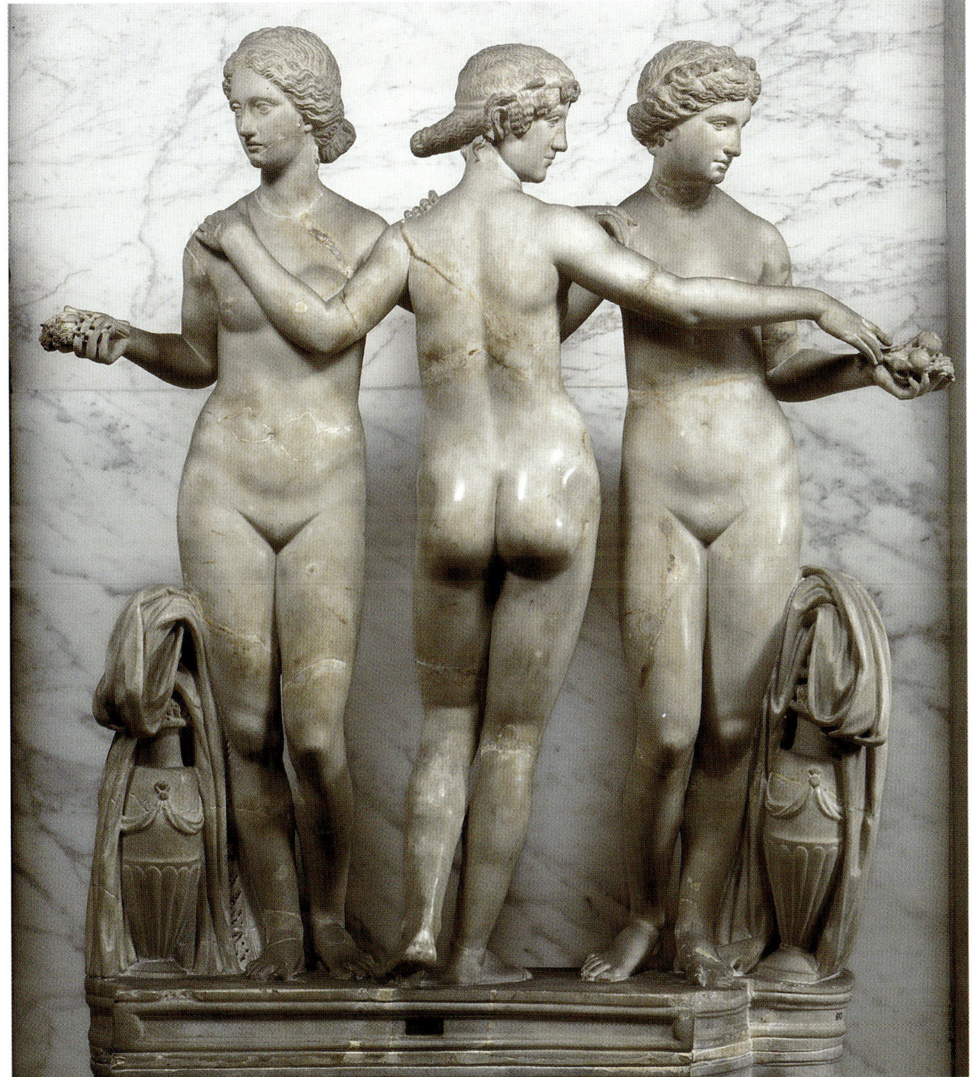

Hadrianic artist, ca. 120 AD
***Apollo Citharoedus*, ca. 120 AD**
Height: 203 cm; Marble
Pio-Clementino Museum

Roman artist, 2nd century
***Terpsichore, Muse of Choral Song and Dance*, 2nd century**
Marble
Pio-Clementino Museum

Roman artist, 3rd century copy of a Doidalsas original, 3rd century BC
***Crouching Aphrodite*, 3rd century**
Height: 53 cm; Marble
Pio-Clementino Museum

Roman artist, ca. 2nd century
***The Three Graces*, 2nd century**
Height: 133 cm; Marble
Pio-Clementino Museum

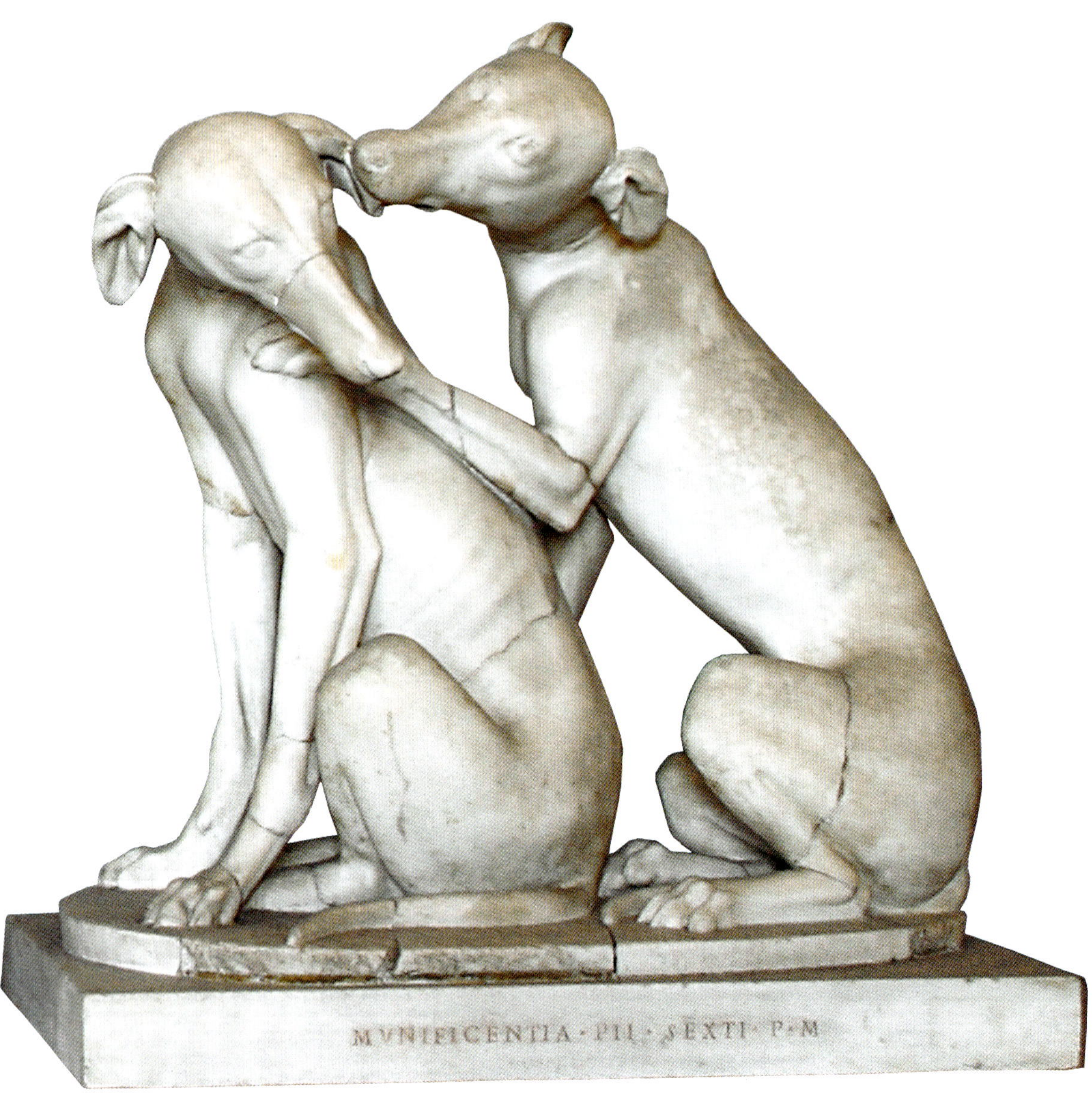

Roman artist

Two Greyhounds Playing

This charming animal statue depicts two greyhounds, probably a dog and a bitch, at play. They are sitting one behind the other on their hind legs with their bodies supported by their forelegs. The dog, in front, is sitting calmly and has turned his head around toward his female companion. Almost tenderly the bitch has laid her left paw on the dog's shoulder, beneath his muzzle, and is nibbling at his left ear. The heads and bodies have been depicted in a realistic manner, with the individual features of the more powerful male and more delicate female carefully drawn out of the marble. Particularly in the case of the dog, the ribs and sinewy musculature can be discerned beneath the smooth surface of the coat. In the female, more attention is given to the thicker folds around the neck, wrinkled with exertion. The fleshy, partly pointed, partly floppy ears also contribute to the extremely lifelike impression created by this pair of what are most likely saluki greyhounds, which were very popular in the ancient world. This sculpture, restored with considerable restraint, was found on Monte Cagnolo in Rome in 1774 with another almost identical group now conserved in the British Museum.

Roman artist, active 1st–2nd century
***Two Greyhounds Playing*, 1st–2nd century**
Height: 60 cm; Marble
Pio-Clementino Museum

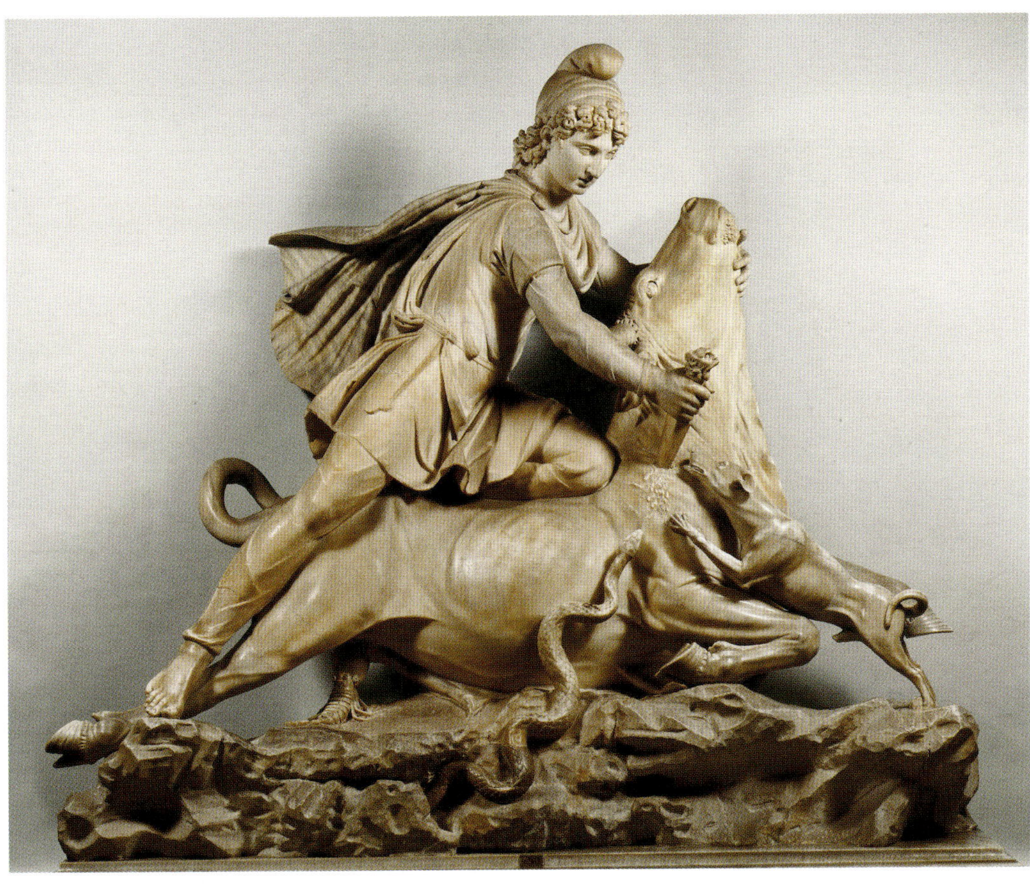

Roman artist, ca. 2nd century
***Mithras Tauroctonos*, ca. 2nd century**
152 x 180 cm; Marble
Pio-Clementino Museum

Roman artist, copy of a Greek original attributed to Skopas, ca. 490 AD
***Meleager with a Dog*, ca. 490 AD**
Height: 280 cm; Marble
Pio-Clementino Museum

Roman artist, date unknown
***Molossus Attacking a Stag*, date unknown**
Height: 67 cm; Marble
Pio-Clementino Museum: Room of the Animals

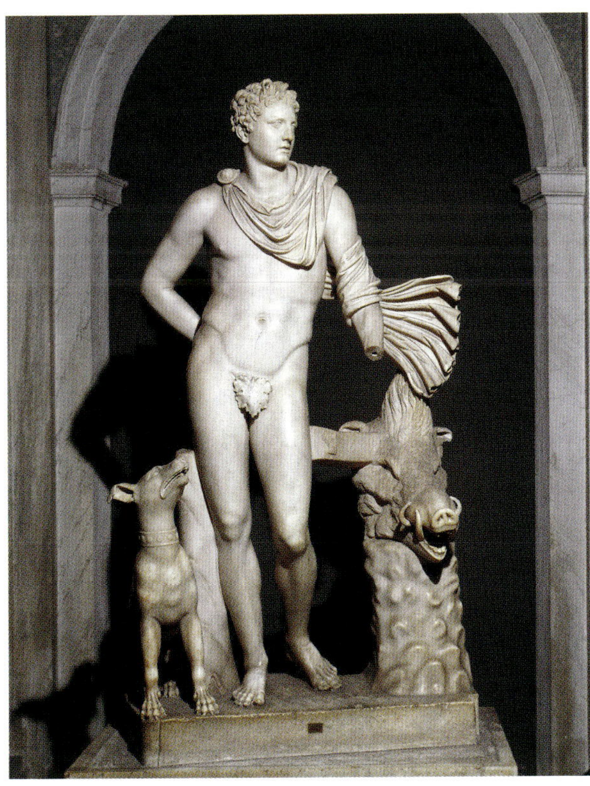

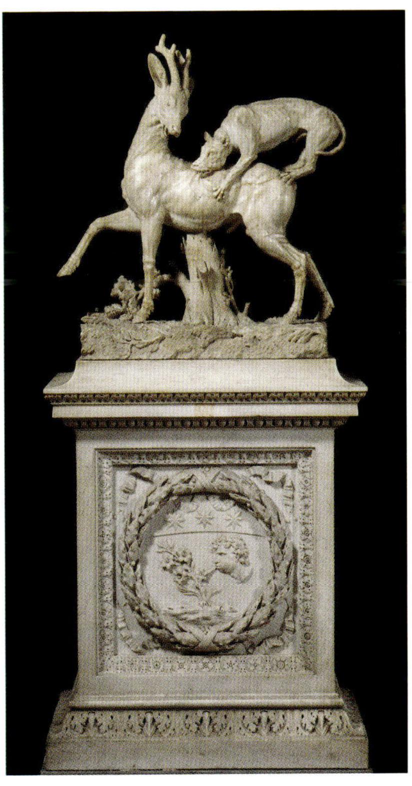

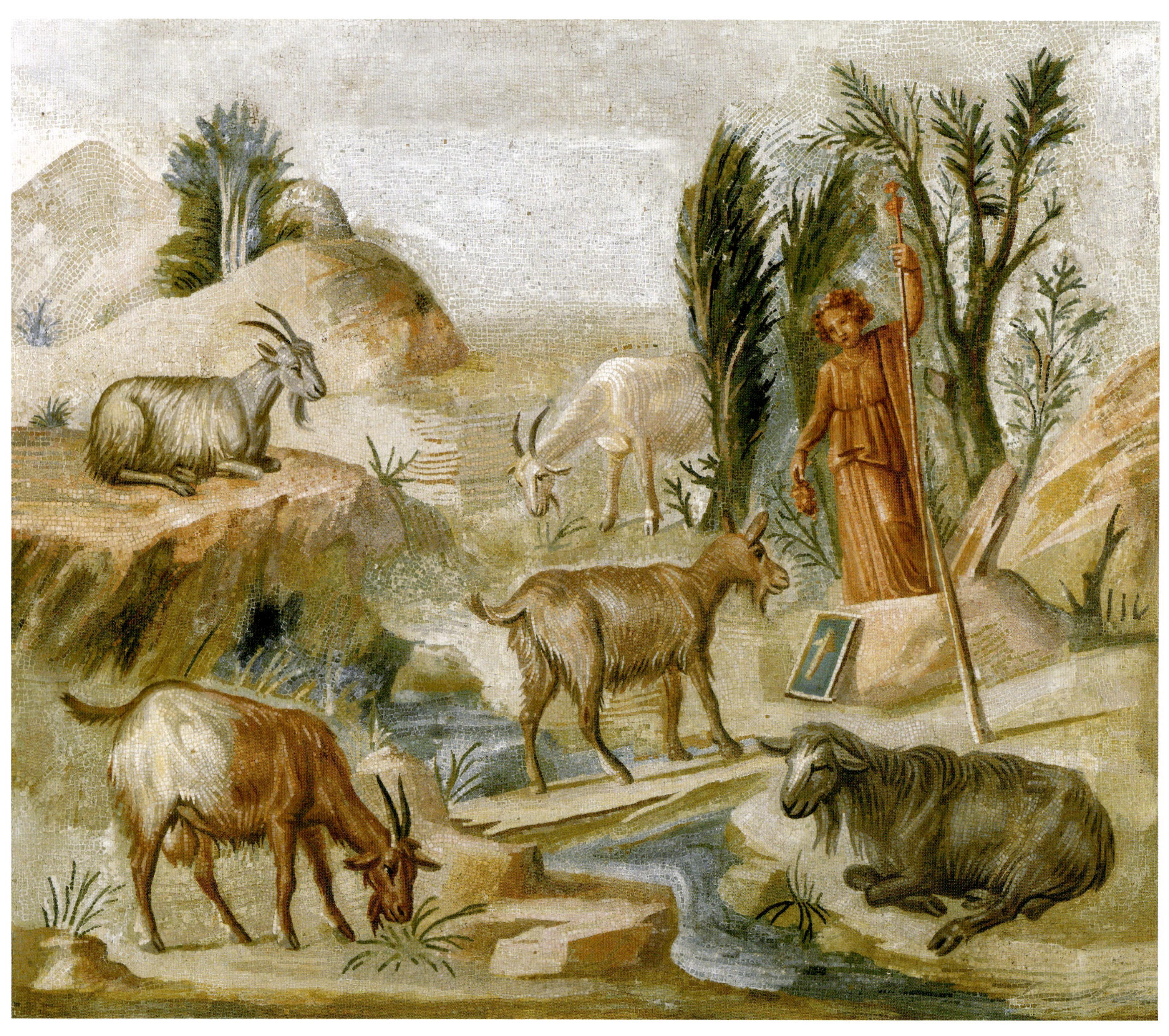

Roman artist, date unknown
***Bucolic Scene with Goats Resting by a Creek with Dionysos as a Shepherd*, date unknown**
Mosaic
Pio-Clementino Museum: Room of the Animals

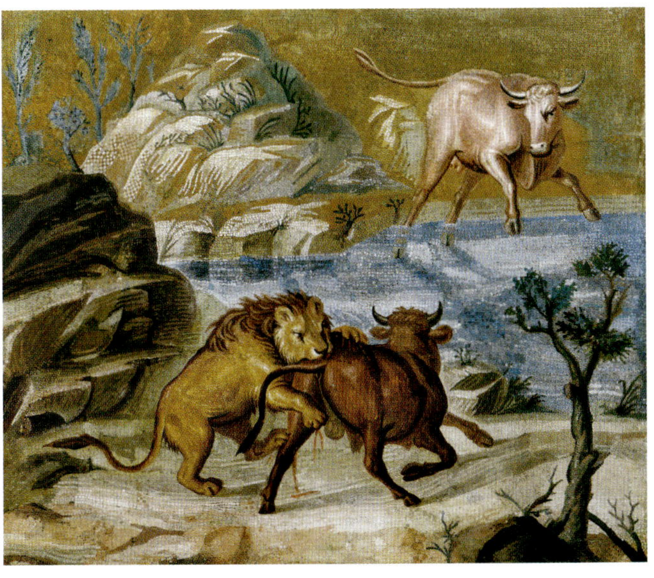

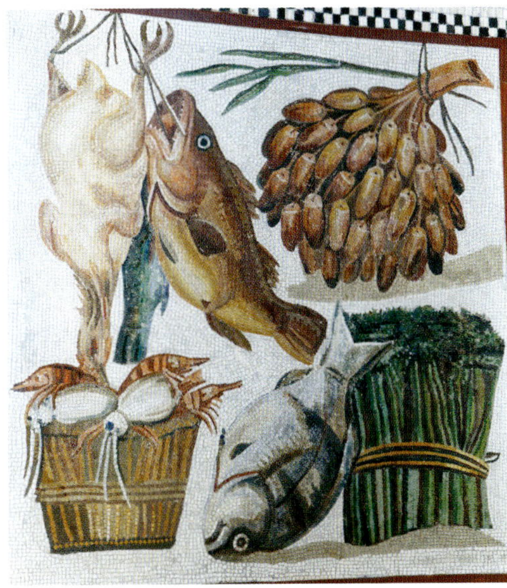

Roman artist, date unknown
***Lion Attacking a Bull*, date unknown**
Mosaic
Pio-Clementino Museum: Room of the Animals

Roman artist, date unknown
***Still-life with Cuttlefish and Lobster*, date unknown**
Mosaic
Pio-Clementino Museum: Room of the Animals

Roman artist, ca. 2nd century
***Mosaic Floor with Basket of Flowers*, ca. 2nd century**
Mosaic
Pio-Clementino Museum

Roman artist, ca. 2nd century
***Rodeo-type Circus Game of a Horseman Chasing a Bull*, ca. 2nd century**
Mosaic
Pio-Clementino Museum: Room of the Animals

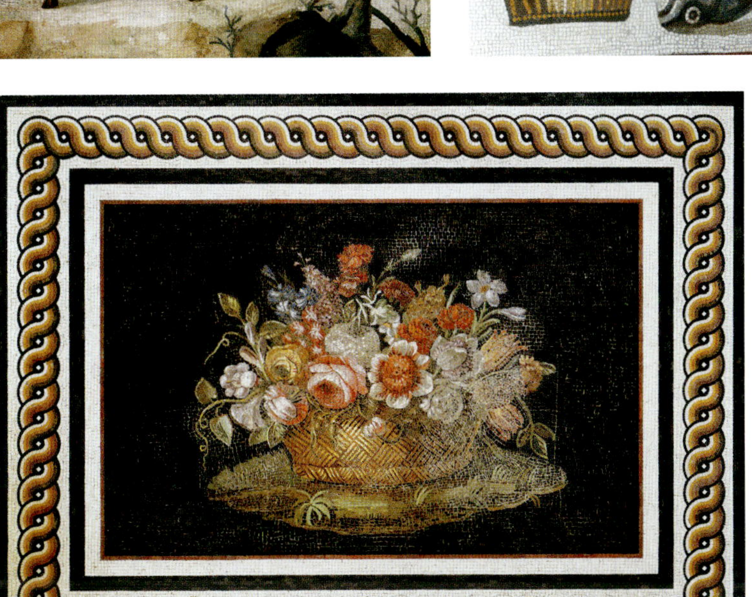

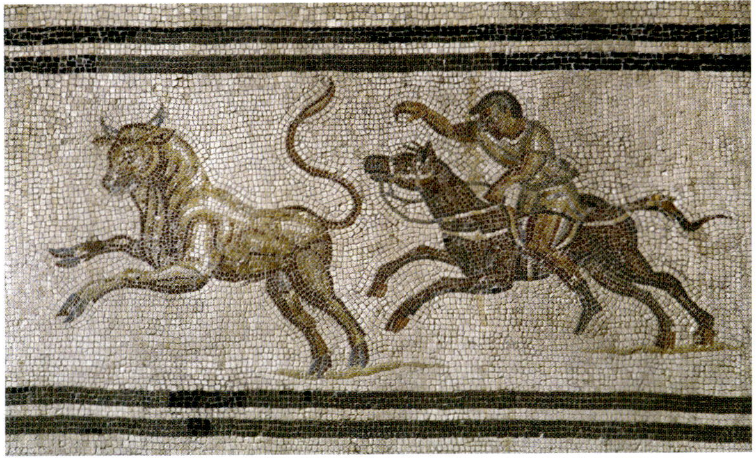

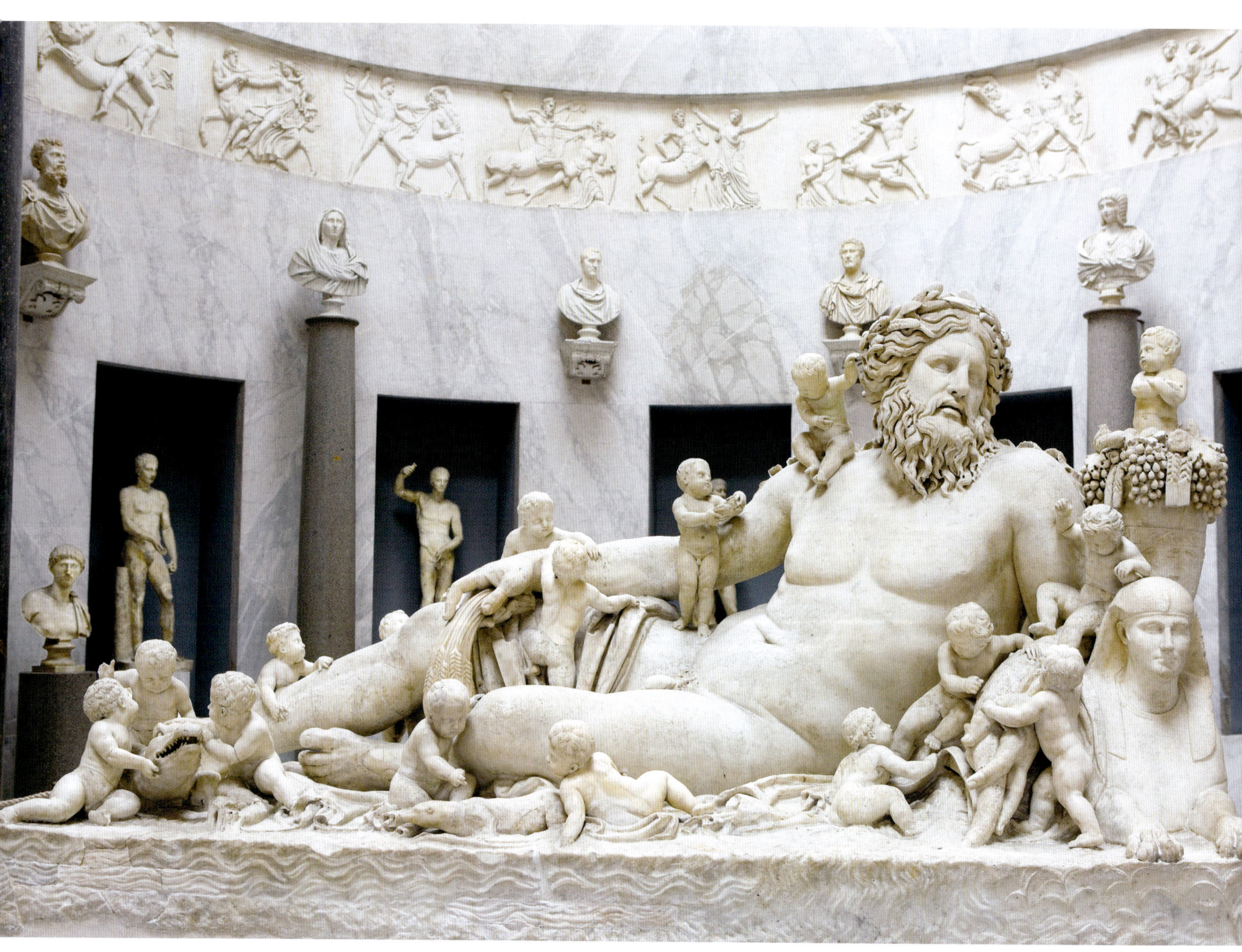

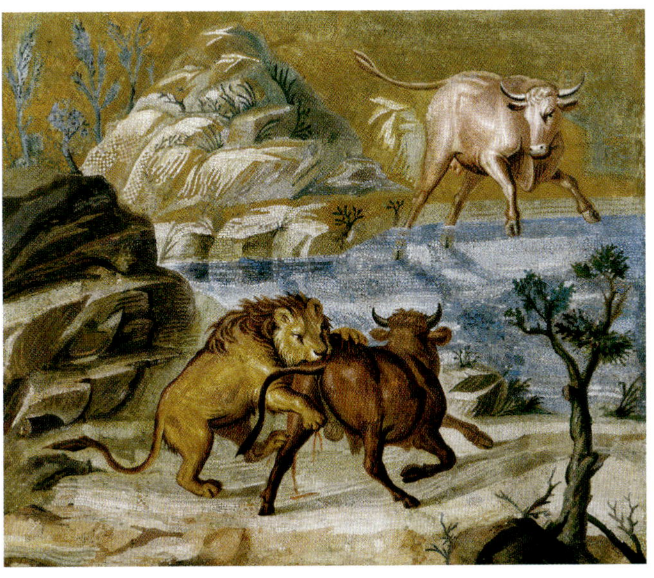

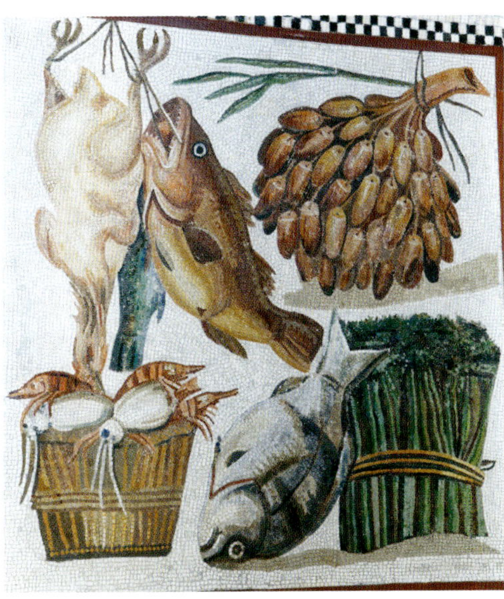

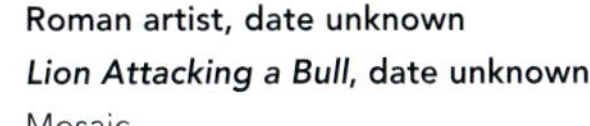

Roman artist, date unknown
***Lion Attacking a Bull*, date unknown**
Mosaic
Pio-Clementino Museum: Room of the Animals

Roman artist, date unknown
***Still-life with Cuttlefish and Lobster*, date unknown**
Mosaic
Pio-Clementino Museum: Room of the Animals

Roman artist, ca. 2nd century
***Mosaic Floor with Basket of Flowers*, ca. 2nd century**
Mosaic
Pio-Clementino Museum

Roman artist, ca. 2nd century
***Rodeo-type Circus Game of a Horseman Chasing a Bull*, ca. 2nd century**
Mosaic
Pio-Clementino Museum: Room of the Animals

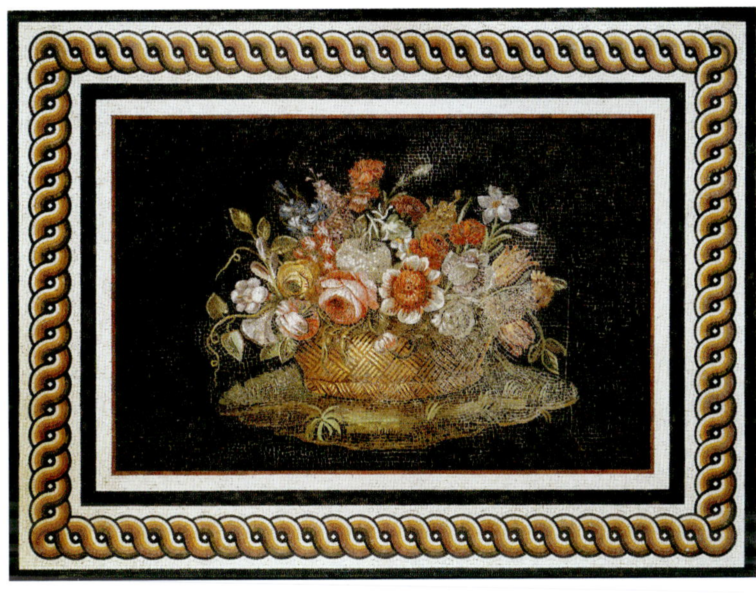

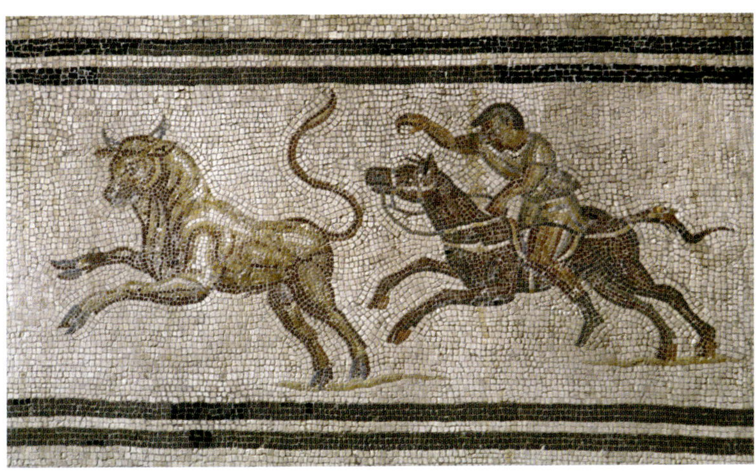

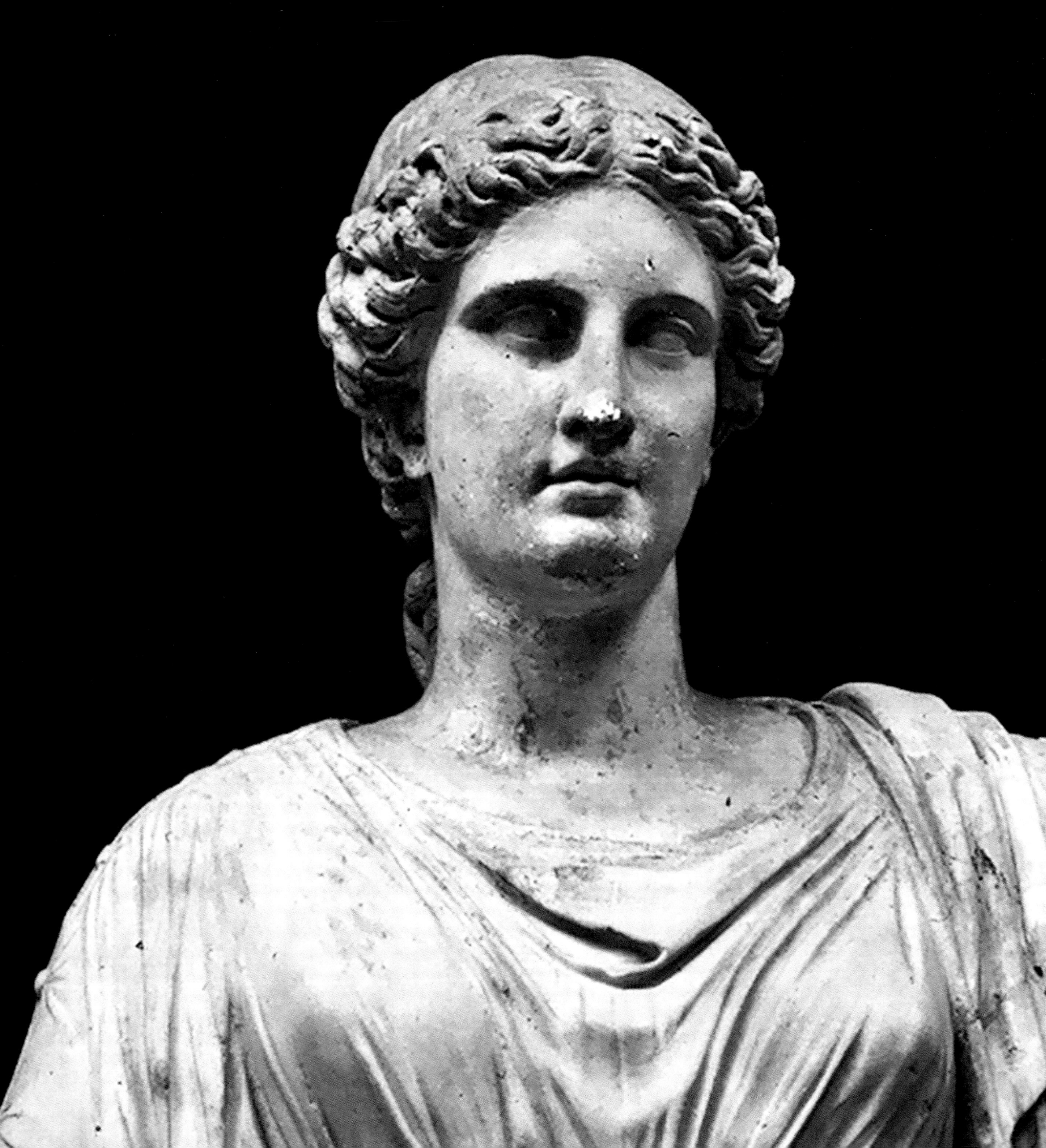

CHIARAMONTI MUSEUM (BRACCIO NUOVO)

Though its collection is no less important, the Chiaramonti Museum is not as well known as the Pio-Clementino Museum. It is named after its founder, Pius VII (1742–1823, reigned from 1800), who was born Count Luigi Barnaba Niccolò Maria Chiaramonti. When Pius VII acceded to the papal throne three months after the death of Pius VI (1717–1799, reigned from 1775), many of the Vatican's art treasures, including key pieces from the Pio-Clementino Museum such as the Apollo Belvedere, were being held in France as Napoleon's spoils of war. Pius VII apparently desired to follow in the footsteps of his predecessors Clement XIV (1705–1774, reigned from 1769) and Pius VI by founding a museum of antique art.

The Chiaramonti Museum was curated from 1807 onward by the neoclassical sculptor Antonio Canova (1757–1822), appointed Inspector General of the Vatican collections by Pius VII in 1802. The pope was himself taken prisoner by Napoleon in 1806 and held at Fontainebleau, only returning to Rome after the fall of the emperor in 1814. The location chosen for the new museum was the long gallery on the ground floor of the papal palace that leads from the Palazzetto del Belvedere to the Borgia Apartments. A large portion of the thousand or so ancient Roman sculptures, above all portrait busts, statues of deities, and reliefs, were displayed along its walls. In 1822, shortly before his death, Pius VII inaugurated the Braccio Nuovo (New Wing), a connecting wing on the south side of the Cortile della Pigna designed in the neoclassical style by the Roman architect Raffaele Stern (1770–1820). This wing connects the gallery on the east side of the courtyard with the gallery on the west side that housed the Apostolic Vatican Library. On display in the Braccio Nuovo are mainly larger statues, including the colossal figure of the River Nile.

The Chiaramonti Museum also includes an extensive collection of epigraphs. The so-called Galleria Lapidaria is located in the southern part of the gallery and contains over three thousand pagan and early Christian inscription stones, gravestones, and assorted monuments, mainly tablets, steles, vases, urns, altars, and sarcophagi. The collection was assembled for the most part in the eighteenth century and organized and installed by the archaeologist and epigraph expert Luigi Gaetano Marini at the beginning of the nineteenth century. It is the largest collection of its kind in the world but is generally only accessible by appointment for purposes of academic research.

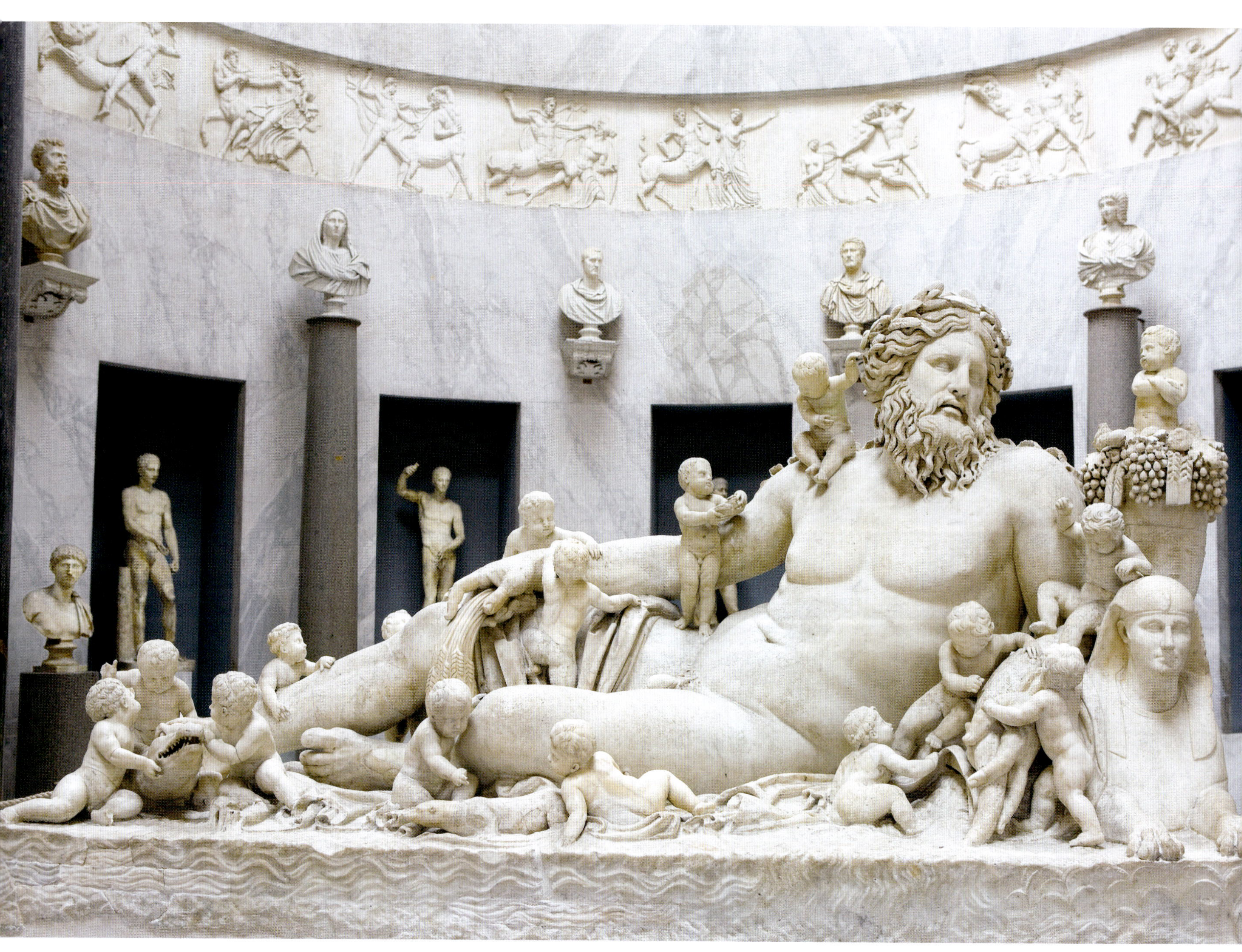

Roman artist after a Greek original

The River Nile

This mighty allegory of the Nile is one of the largest sculptures in the Vatican Museums. The Egyptian river is represented in the customary manner of antique personification of rivers as a naked, bearded man reclining on a substructure of waves with his upper body propped up on a statue of a sphinx. On his head he wears a wreath of wheat, reeds, and lotus blossoms, symbolizing the fertility bestowed by the Nile. What is unusual about this sculpture, discovered near the church of Santa Maria sopra Minerva in the vicinity of the Pantheon in 1513 and brought to the Vatican in 1523, are the sixteen putti and small animal figures playing next to and clambering on the Nile figure. They represent the sixteen cubits (7.3 m) by which the level of the river needs to rise each year in order to flood the Nile Valley and render it fertile. This is symbolized by the different levels at which the putti are depicted, with the highest standing in the cornucopia denoting fertility. Typical Nile dwellers include the crocodile and the Egyptian mongoose, depicted in the foreground. Other creatures, including a hippopotamus, are represented on the base.

Roman artist, after a Greek original
***The Nile River*, 1st century AD**
Height: 162 cm; Marble
Chiaramonti Museum: Braccio Nuovo Gallery

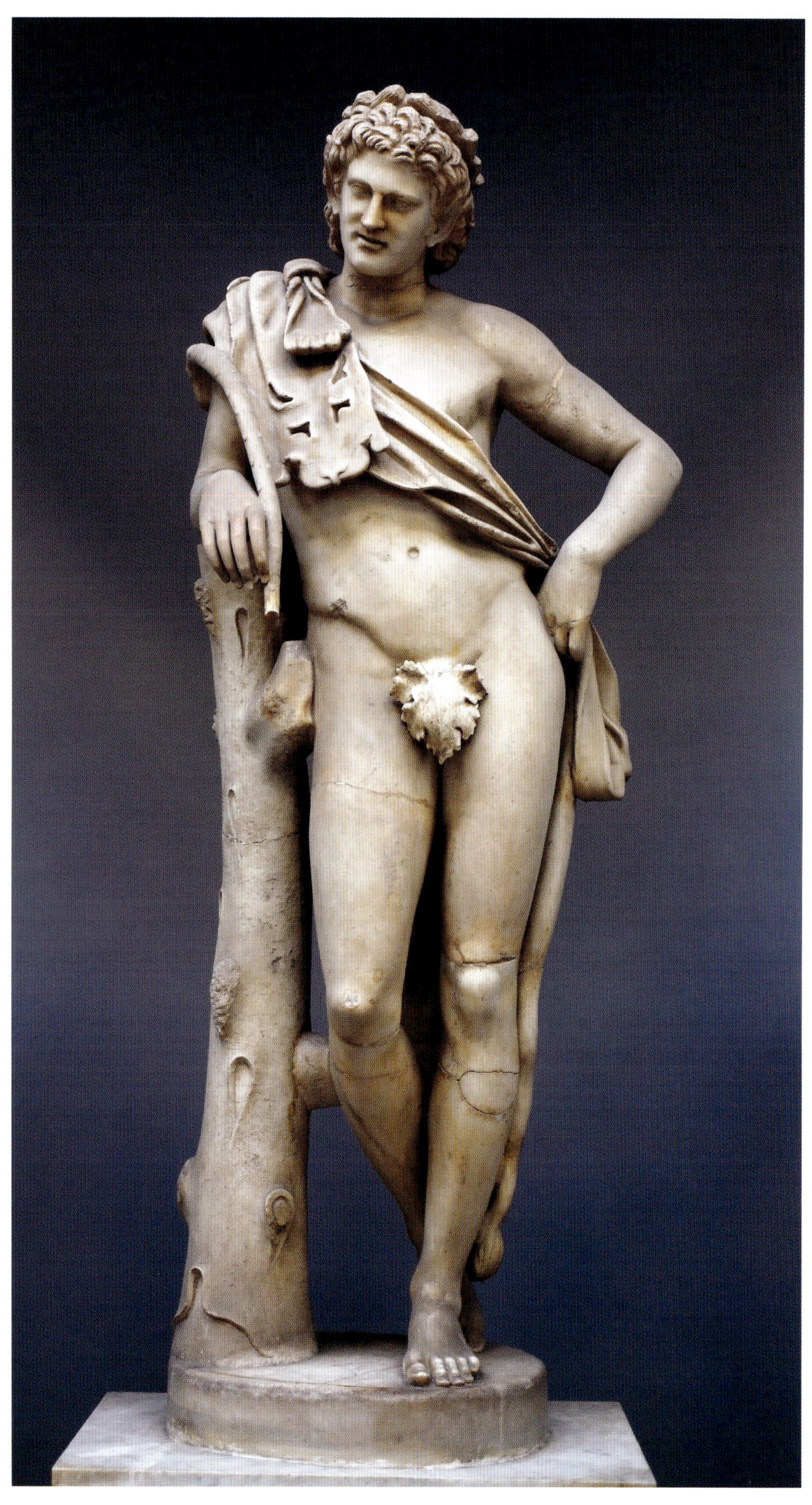

Roman copy of a 5th century BC Athens Altar
***Resting Satyr*, ca. 130 AD**
Height 189 cm; Marble
Chiaramonti Museum: Braccio Nuovo Gallery

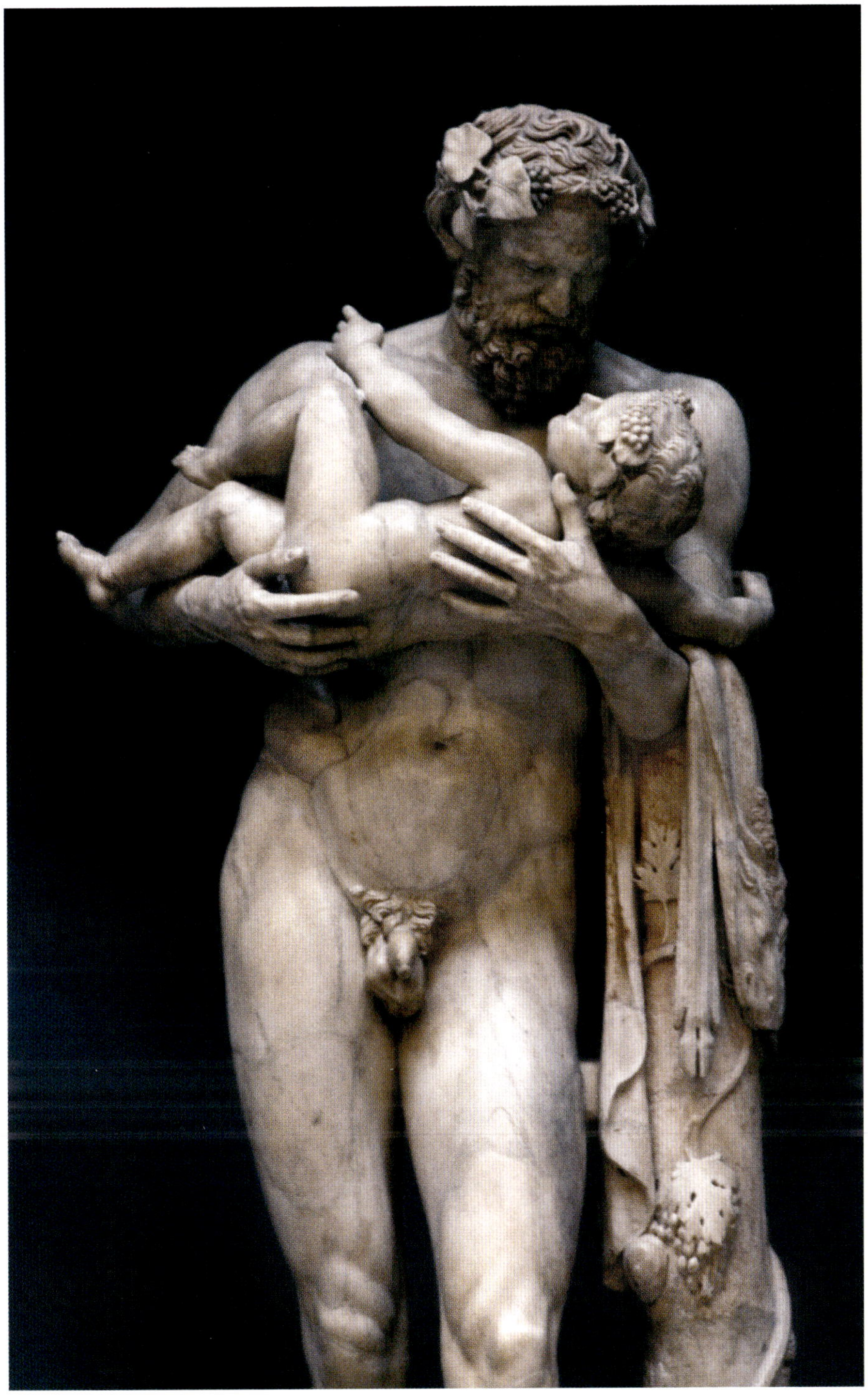

Roman copy of a Greek original
***Silenus with Infant Dionysus*, 4th century BC**
Height: 191 cm; Marble
Chiaramonti Museum: Braccio Nuovo Gallery

Roman, based on a Greek original from late 5th–early 4th century BC
***Athena (Athena Giustiniani)*, 2nd century AD**
Height: 225 cm; Marble
Chiaramonti Museum: Braccio Nuovo Gallery

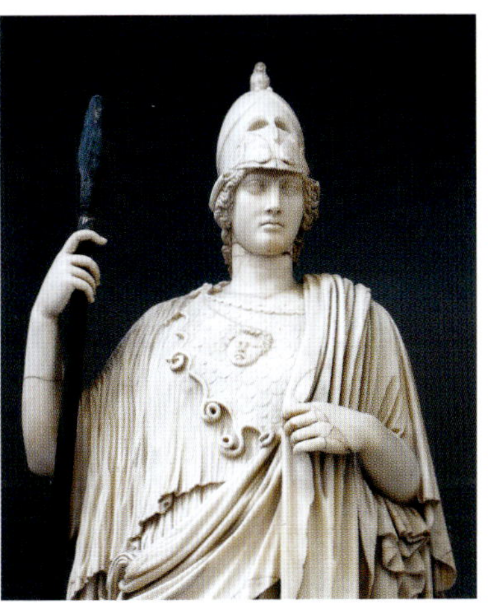

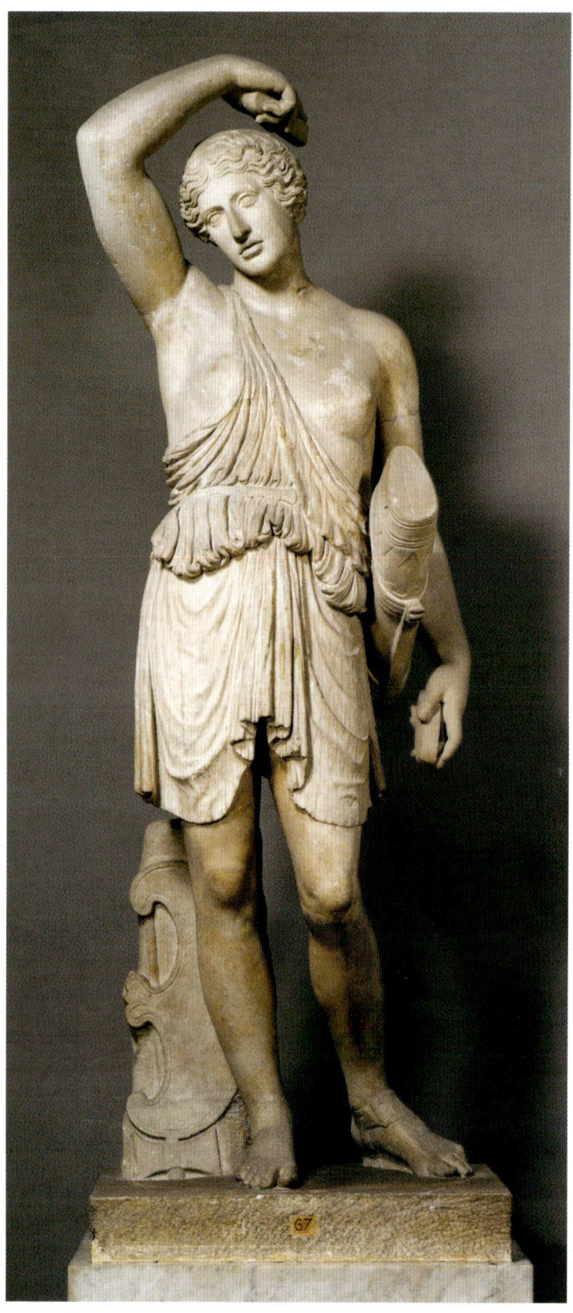

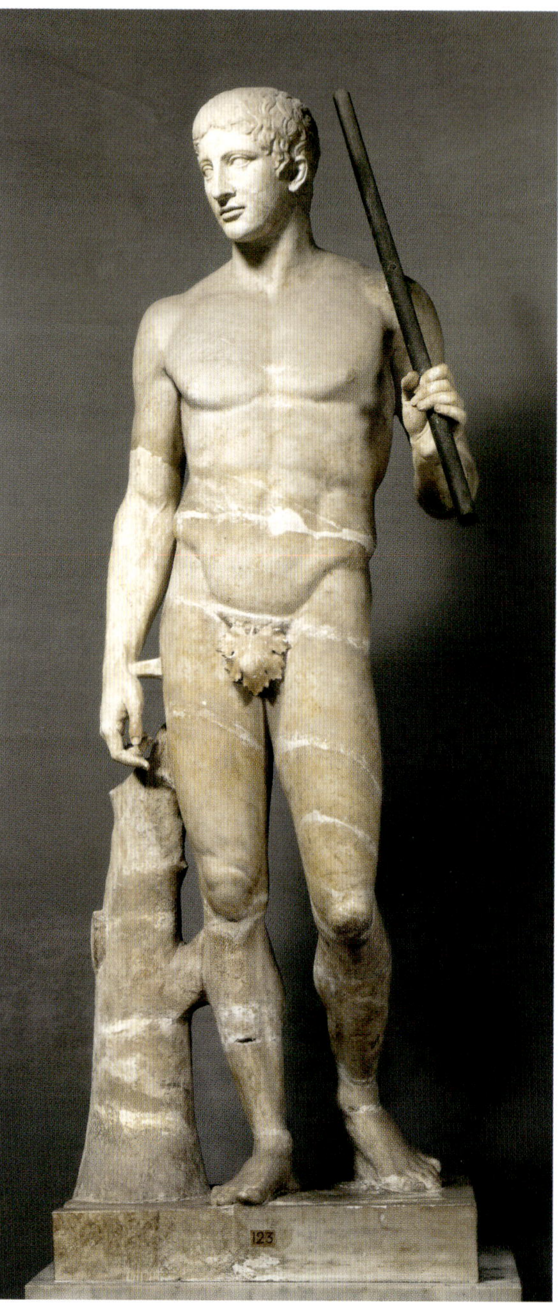

Roman, copy of a statue by Kresilas, 430 BC
***Wounded Amazon*, unknown**
Height: 186 cm; Marble
Chiaramonti Museum: Braccio Nuovo Gallery,

Roman artist, copy of a bronze original by Polykleitos, 5th century BC
***Spearbearer*, 5th century BC**
Marble
Chiaramonti Museum: Braccio Nuovo Gallery

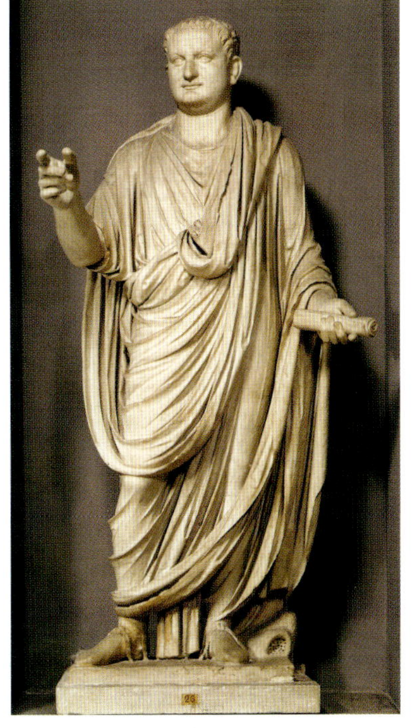

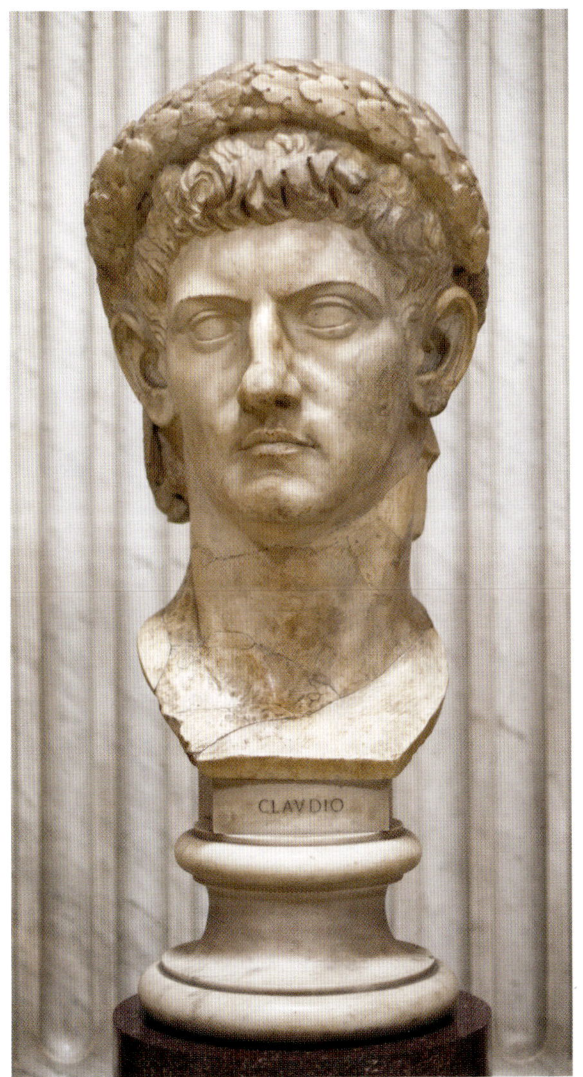

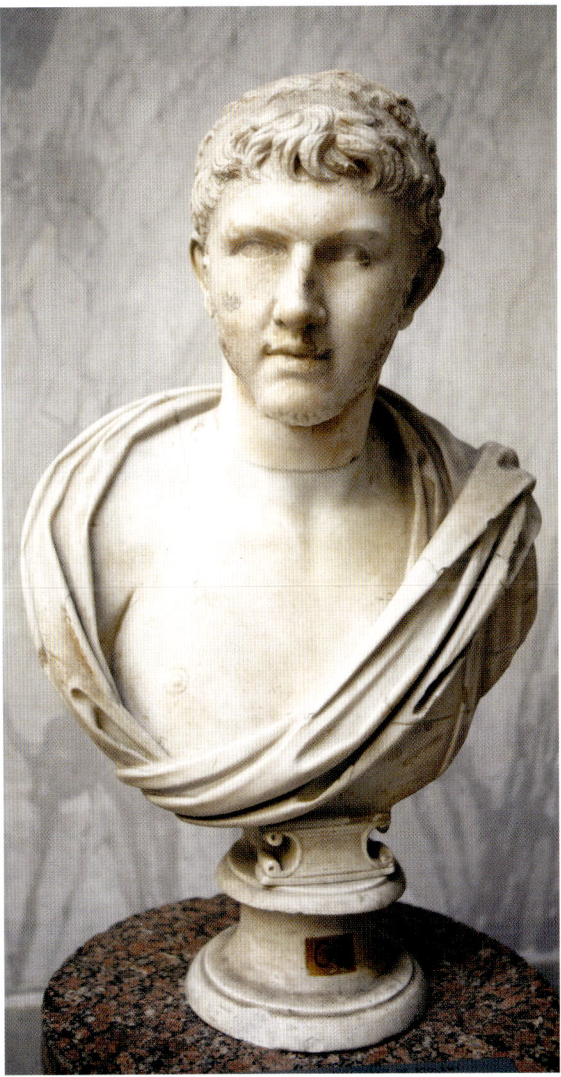

Roman copy of a work by Praxiteles, 4th century BC
***Claudius*, 1st century AD**
Height: 293 cm; Marble
Chiaramonti Museum: Braccio Nuovo Gallery

Roman artist, 1st Century AD
***Ptolemy, King of Numidia (20–40 AD)*, 1st century AD**
Height: 72 cm; Marble
Chiaramonti Museum: Braccio Nuovo Gallery

Hellenistic artist, unknown
***Statue of Titus wearing a Toga*, unknown**
Height: 196 cm; Sculpture
Chiaramonti Museum: Braccio Nuovo Gallery

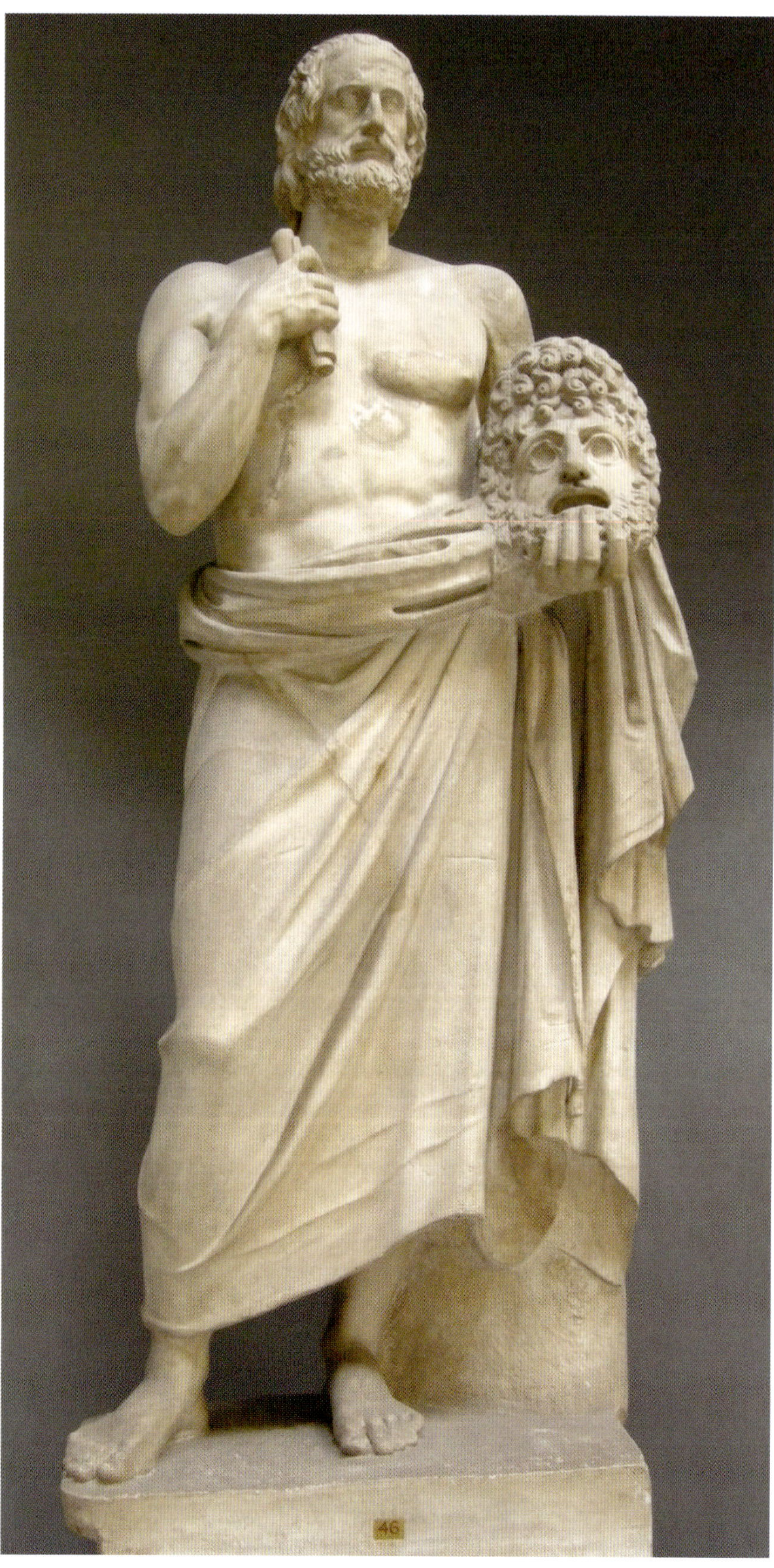

Roman artist, date unknown
***Euripides*, date unknown**
Height: 234 cm; Marble
Chiaramonti Museum: Braccio Nuovo Gallery

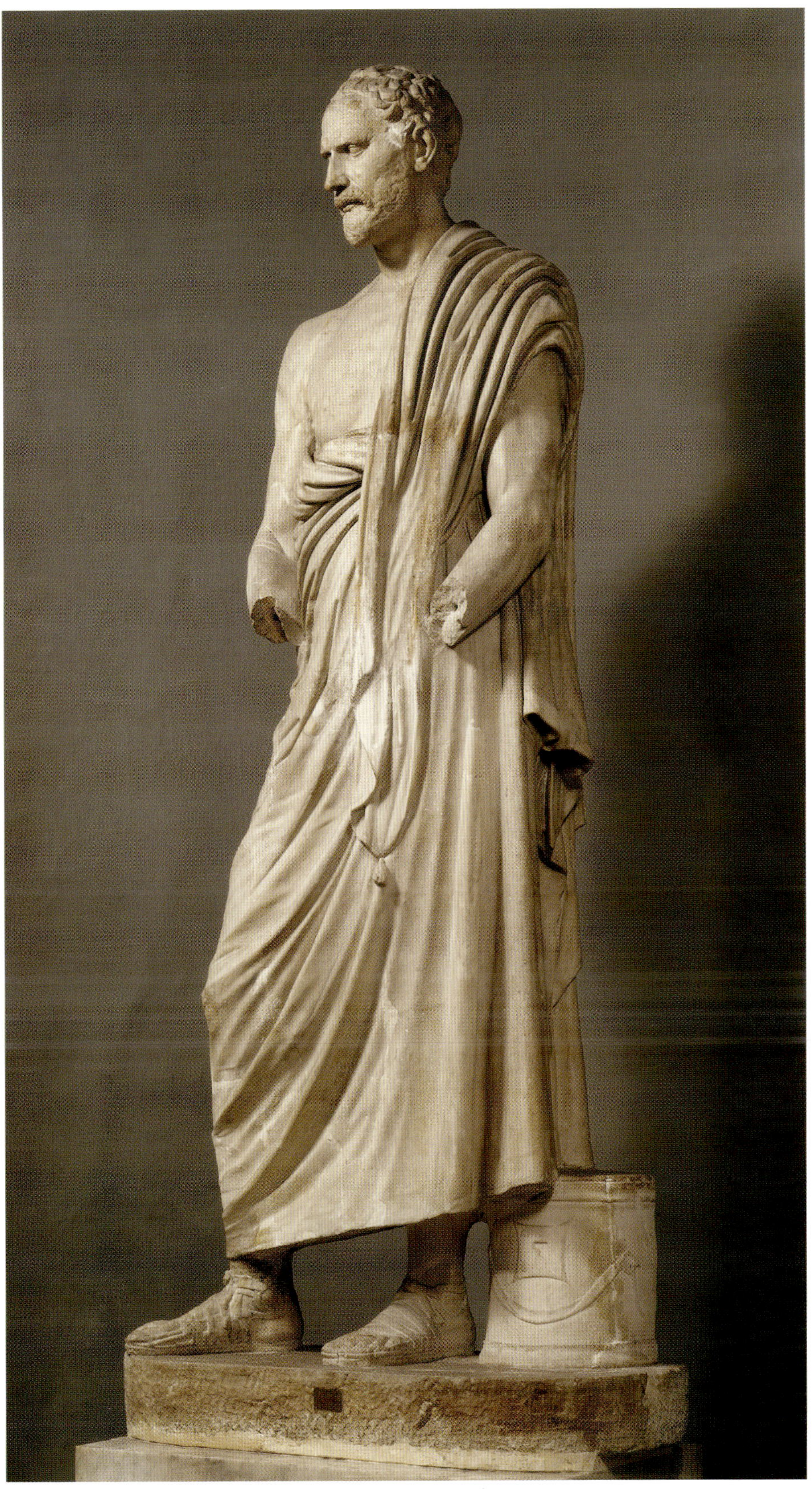

Roman, copy of a bronze original by Polyeuktos, 280 BC
***Statue of Demosthenes*, date unknown**
Height: 207 cm; Marble
Chiaramonti Museum: Braccio Nuovo Gallery,

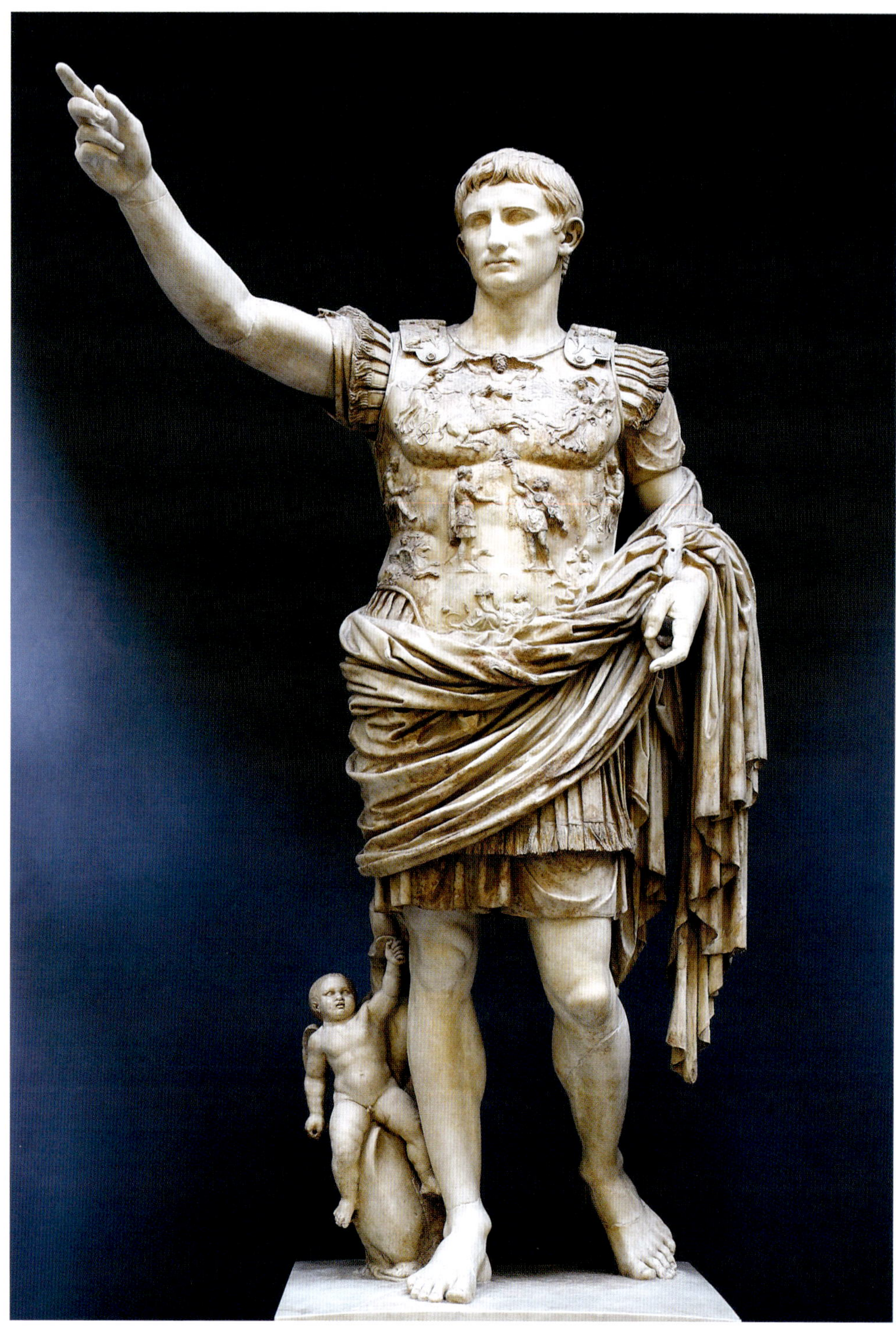

Roman artist

Augustus Prima Porta

This statue discovered in the district of Prima Porta in the north of Rome depicts the Roman emperor Augustus Caesar (63 BC–14 AD, reigned from 30 BC). He is represented stepping forward on his right foot, accompanied by a putto, and has raised his right arm in an appeal for quiet. With his left hand he gathers his cloak (*paludamentum*) around him at hip level. The emperor's richly decorated breastplate marks him as a military commander, shown here addressing his troops (*adlocutio*). The facial features of the separately worked head correspond to the well-known, consistently idealized portraits of Augustus, whose status as a resolute leader is underscored by the overall posture of his athletic figure. This larger-than-life-size sculpture is distinctive for its cuirass, whose reliefs can be read as an allegory of Augustus's imperial claims. The scene at the center has been interpreted as the return of the Roman standard to Augustus by the Parthian king, a sign of his subjugation. The female figures on either side are intended to signify the empire's two provinces, while the heavenly and earthly gods in the upper and lower portions of the breastplate present Augustus in a cosmic context.

Roman artist, 15 AD
***Augustus Prima Porta*, 15 AD**
Height: 219 cm, Marble
Chiaramonti Museum: Braccio Nuovo Gallery, Inv. 2290

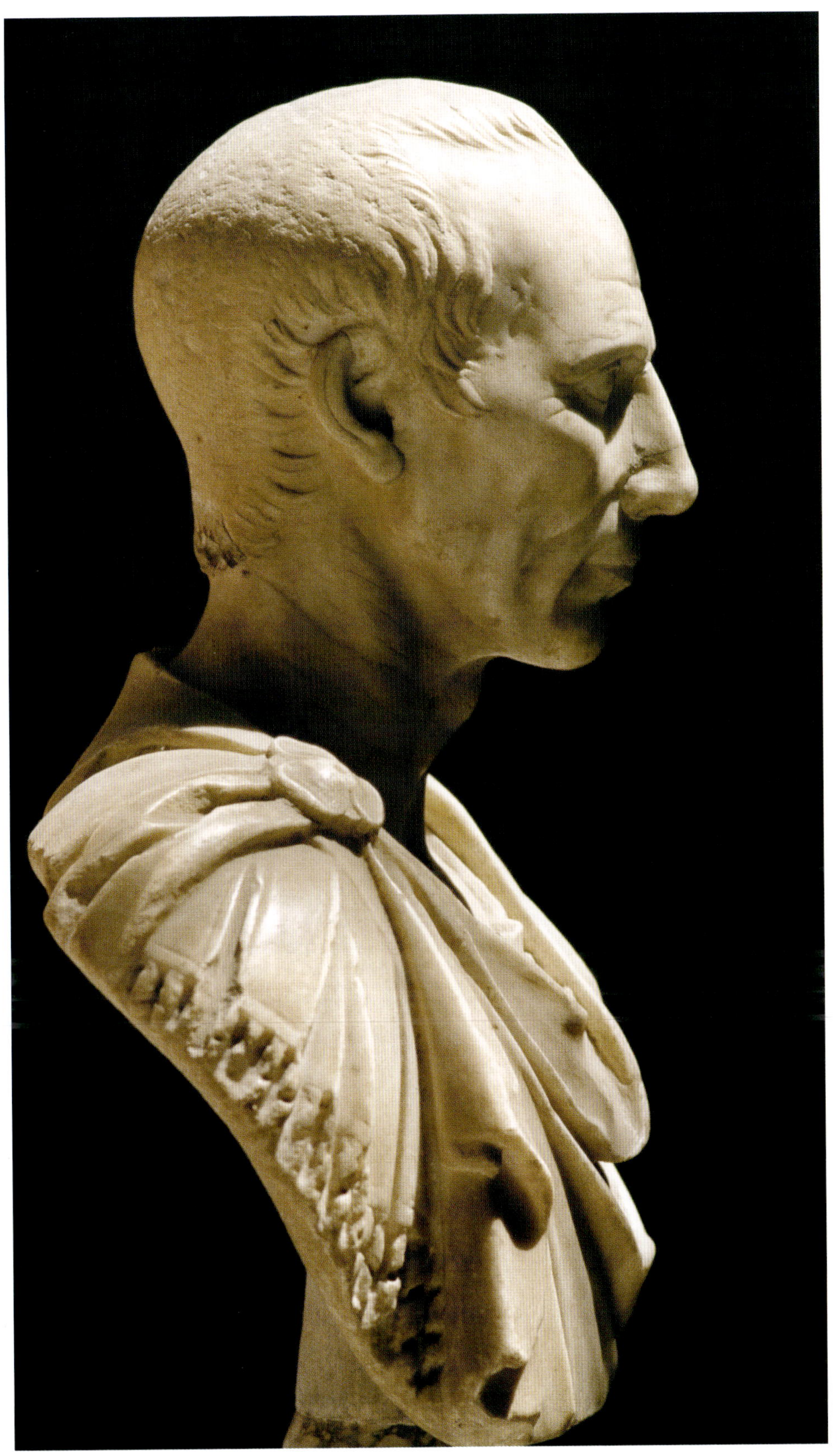

Roman, copy of a Greek statue, ca. 30–20 BC
***Bust of Julius Caesar*, ca. 30–20 BC**
Marble
Chiaramonti Museum: Braccio Nuovo Gallery

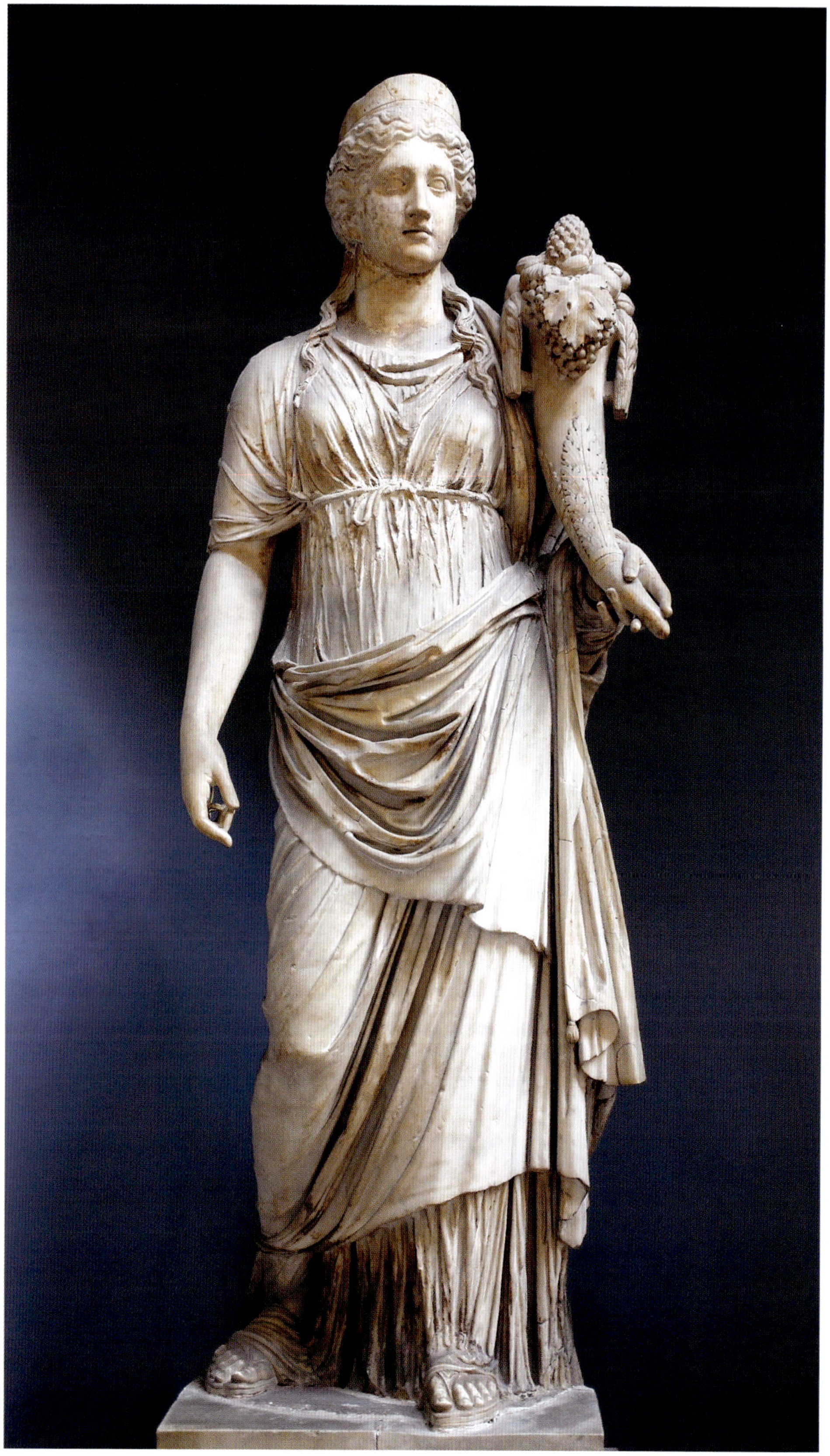

Roman copy of a Greek original
***Personification of Fortune with Cornucopia*, date unknown**
Height: 219 cm; Marble
Chiaramonti Museum: Braccio Nuovo Gallery

Roman, 2nd century AD
***Peacock from the Mausoleum of Hadrian*, 2nd century AD**
Height: 106 cm; Gilt bronze
Chiaramonti Museum: Braccio Nuovo Gallery

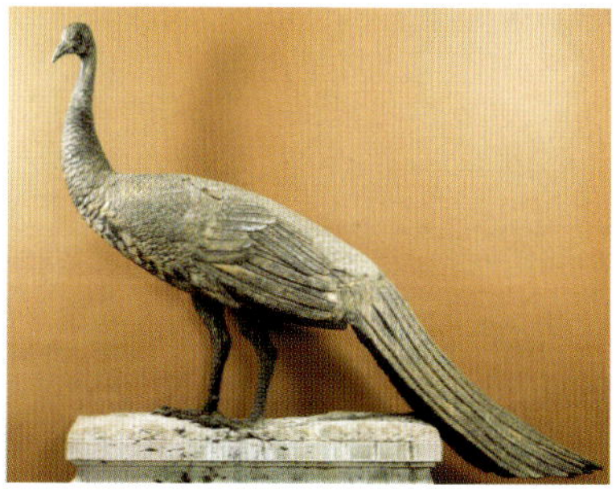

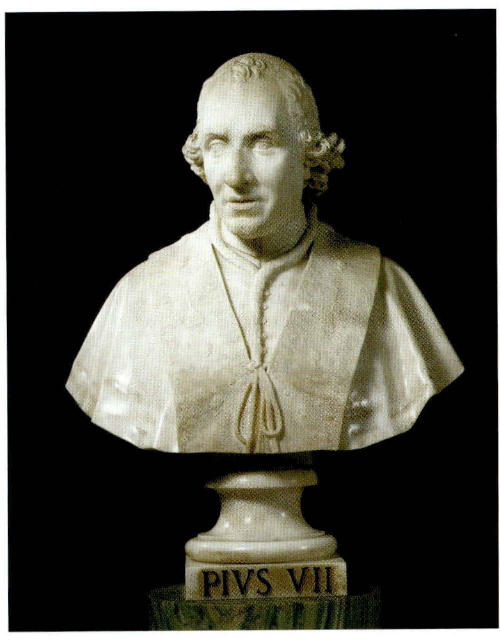

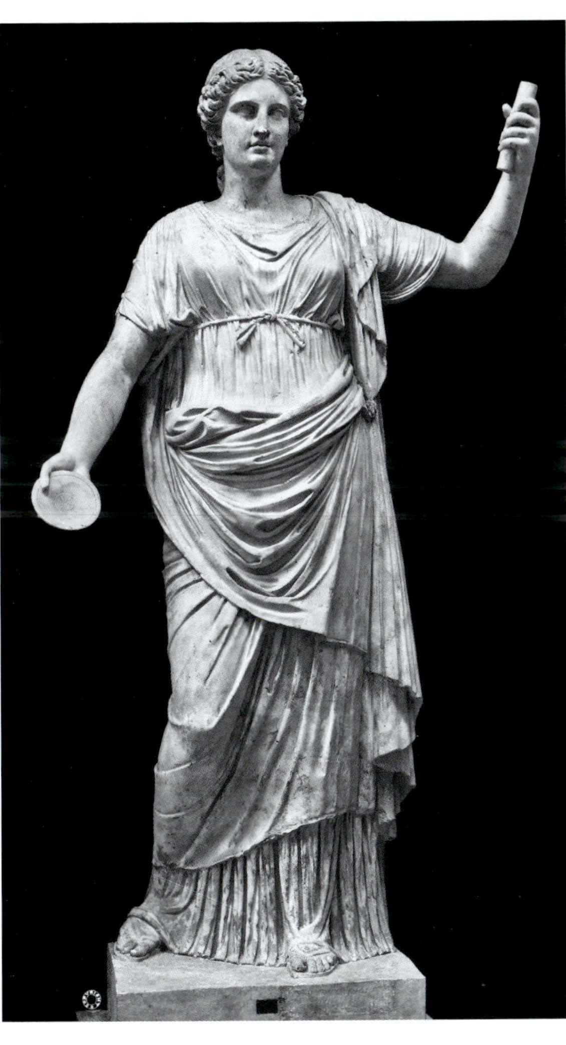

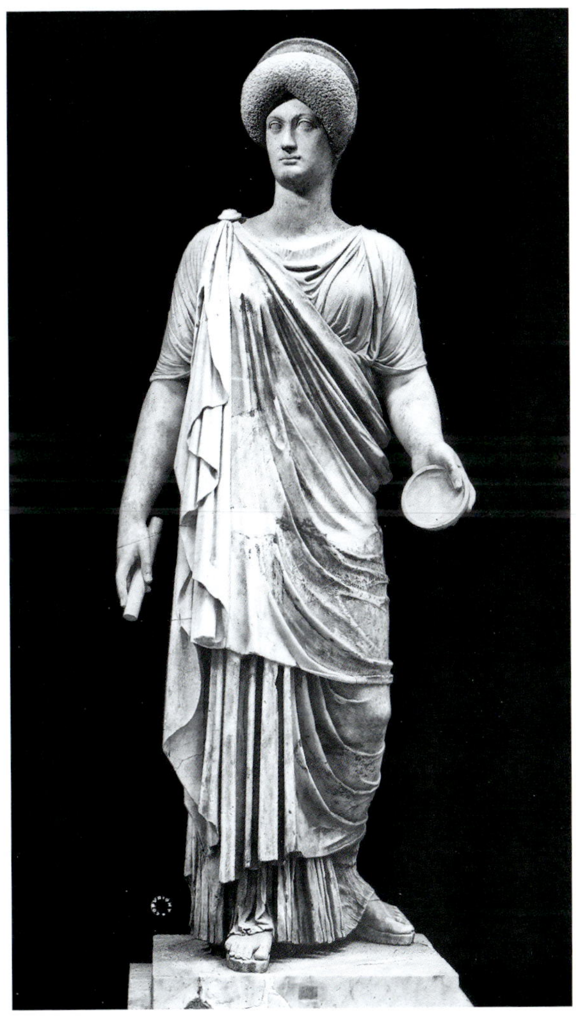

Antonio Canova, 1757–1822
***Portrait Bust of Pope Pius VII*, ca. 1820**
Height: 74 cm; Marble
Chiaramonti Museum: Braccio Nuovo Gallery

Roman copy of a Greek original
***Personification of Clemency*, date unknown**
Height: 218 cm; Marble
Chiaramonti Museum: Braccio Nuovo Gallery

Roman copy of a Greek original
***Personification of Mercy*, date unknown**
Height: 218 cm; Marble
Chiaramonti Museum: Braccio Nuovo Gallery

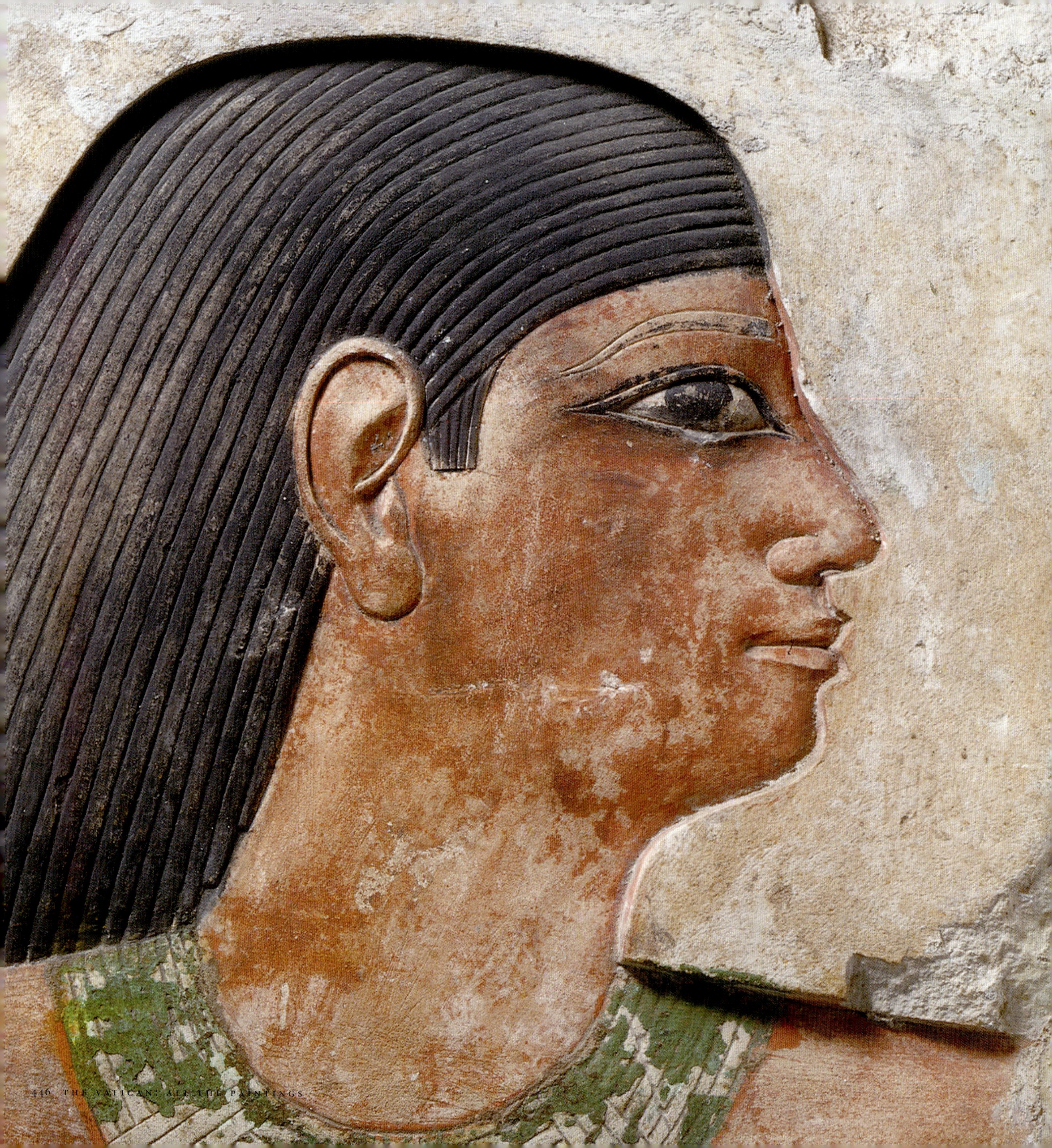

GREGORIAN EGYPTIAN MUSEUM

The Gregorian Egyptian Museum owes its existence to Gregory XVI (1765–1846, reigned from 1831) and his passion for Egypt. Even before being made pontiff, during his time as a cardinal and prefect of the Congregation for the Evangelization of Peoples, Gregory XVI engaged intensively with the scientific debate surrounding research into the hieroglyphs and culture of ancient Egypt. This debate began around 1800 and reached an early climax in 1818 with the deciphering of the Rosetta Stone by Jean-François Champollion (1790–1832). In 1825 the French scholar was invited by Leo XII (1760–1829, reigned from 1823) and the prefect of the Vatican Library, Angelo Mai (1782–1854), to examine the newly acquired collection of rare papyrus manuscripts.

Following his founding of the Gregorian Etruscan Museum in 1837, Gregory XVI announced his intention to establish a similar museum for Egyptian antiquities. Suitable artifacts first needed to be collected. The pope commissioned the renowned Egyptologist Father Luigi Maria Ungarelli (1779–1845) to set up the new museum. The exhibits were drawn mainly from various Roman and Italian collections such as those from the Villa Borghese, the Villa Farnesina, and the Biblioteca Casanatense, as well as from private collections abroad. In addition to these new acquisitions, statues and other objects that had found their way to Rome during the first and second centuries AD, and had been rediscovered during the excavation of Roman sites during the eighteenth century, were transferred from the various papal collections. The best known of these sites was Villa Adriana at Tivoli, the countryseat of Emperor Hadrian, who had a particular admiration for Egyptian culture.

The Gregorian Egyptian Museum was officially opened on February 2, 1839, the anniversary of Gregory XVI's accession to the papal throne. In response to critics who feared an excessive presence of pagan cultures at the seat of the Catholic Church, Gregory XVI argued that the study of Egyptian and other Near Eastern cultures would contribute to a better understanding of biblical events and the history of early Christianity. The next few popes also subscribed to this view and encouraged the expansion of the museum, which now occupies nine rooms.

The museum is organized thematically. The first two rooms are dedicated to funerary practices and the commemoration of the dead. In addition to sarcophagi, richly decorated tomb steles, and typical funerary equipment, there are also two mummies. Based on the examples of the Villa Adriana and other excavation sites, the next two rooms highlight the vogue for things Egyptian in ancient Rome. Masterpieces of ancient Egyptian sculpture, including many large statues of divinities, are displayed in the adjoining semicircular room. The final rooms contain smaller bronzes and clay sculptures and reliefs, which give expression to the wealth of Egyptian art and culture. Most of the bronzes were donated by Carlo and Nedda Grassi in 1952 in memory of their son who fell at El Alamein. Two small rooms are dedicated to reliefs and other finds from ancient Mesopotamia and the Syrian-Palestinian region.

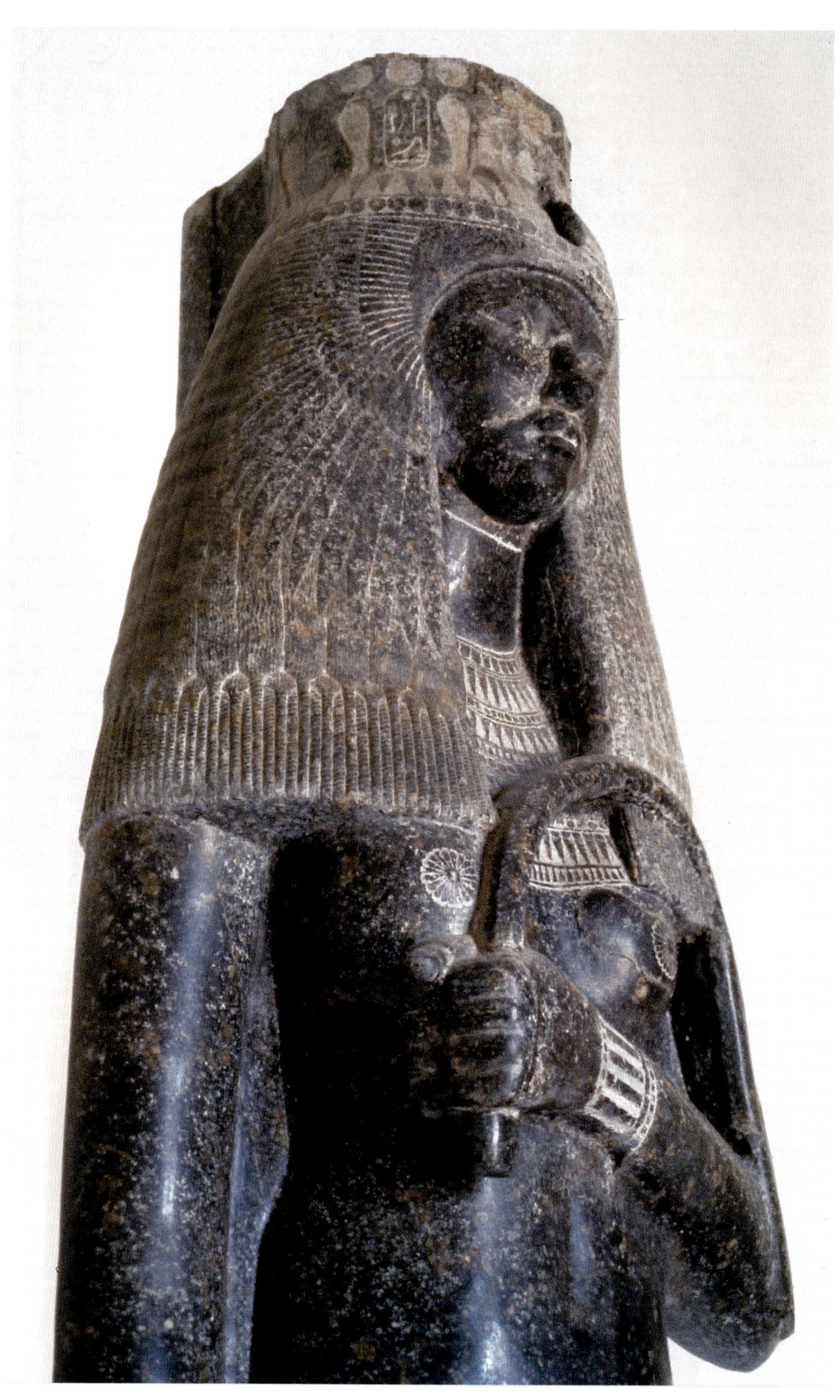

Egyptian artist

Colossal Statue of Queen Tuya

This colossal statue from the so-called Ramesseum in Thebes is of Queen Tuya (also known as Mut-Tuya, c. 1325–1258 BC), the consort of Pharaoh Seti I (c. 1323–1279 BC, reigned from 1294 BC). Tuya was the mother of the renowned Pharaoh Ramses II (c. 1303–1213 BC, reigned from 1279 BC), from whose long reign this sculpture dates. This statue of Tuya, whose dark granite material lends it a particular expressiveness, testifies to the great blossoming of architecture and art under Ramses II. The queen stands upright, facing the viewer, with one foot slightly in front of the other. She wears a long, close-fitting gown beneath which her shapely, slender body is well delineated. The garment is richly decorated around the neck and cuffs and on the breasts in a manner designed to suggest opulent gold trimming. The royal crown sits atop the queen's long hair, which frames her head and shoulders. In her angled left hand, raised to her breast, she holds a short whip, a relic from nomadic times that alludes to the pharaoh's status as the supreme shepherd. In her right hand she holds a papyrus scroll, symbolizing nobility.

Egyptian artist, ca. 1279–1213 BC
***Colossal Statue of Queen Tuja*, ca. 1279–1213 BC**
Height 227 cm; Granite
Gregorian Egyptian Museum

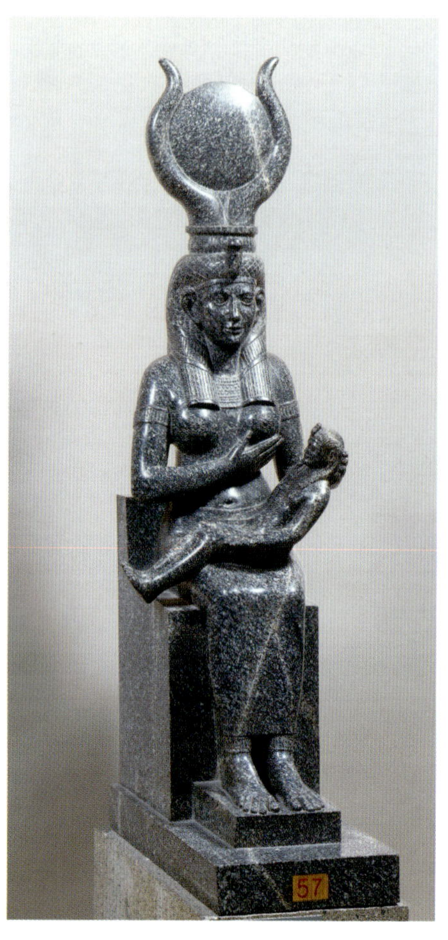

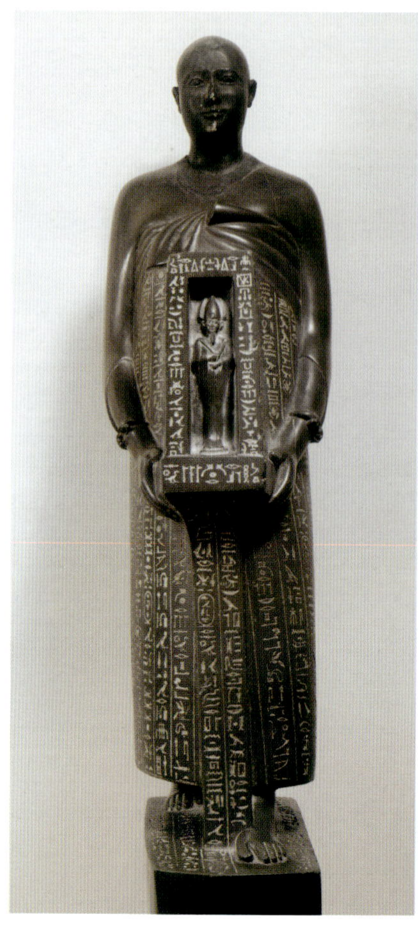

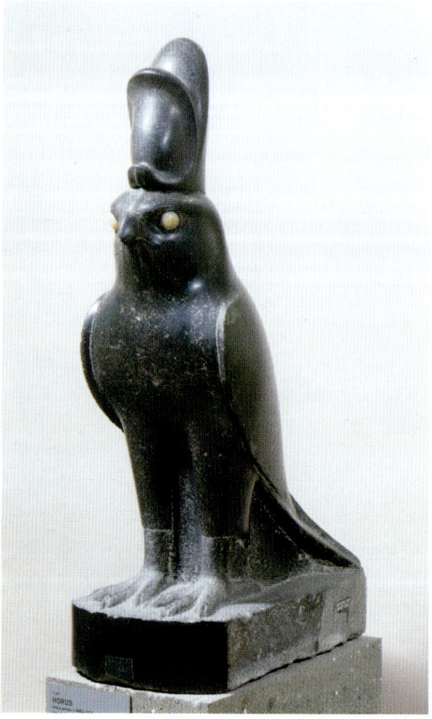

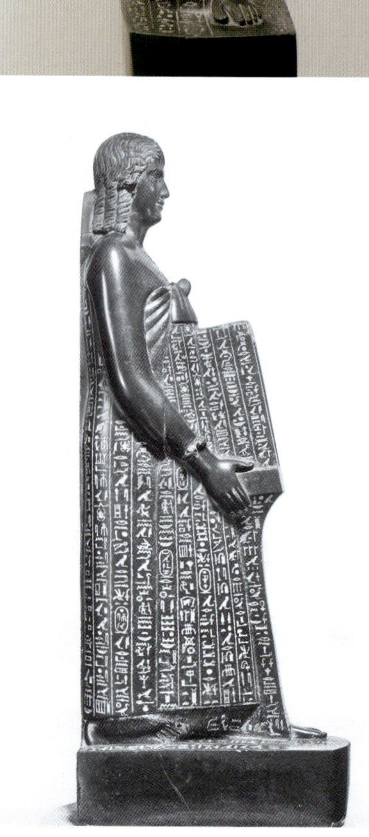

Egyptian artist, 1st century BC
***Isis Suckling Horus*, 1st century BC**
Granite
Gregorian Egyptian Museum

Persian artist, 519 BC
***Statue of a Man Carrying a Temple (Naophoros) so-called Priest Ugiahorresne*, 27th Persian dynasty, 3rd year of reign of Darius 519 BC**
Height: 69 cm; Granite
Gregorian Egyptian Museum

Egyptian artist, 664–332 BC
***The God Horus as a Falcon*, 664–332 BC**
Granite
Gregorian Egyptian Museum

Ptolemaic artist, 332–330 BC
***Statue of the Priestess Utahorresenet*, 332–330 BC**
Granite
Gregorian Egyptian Museum

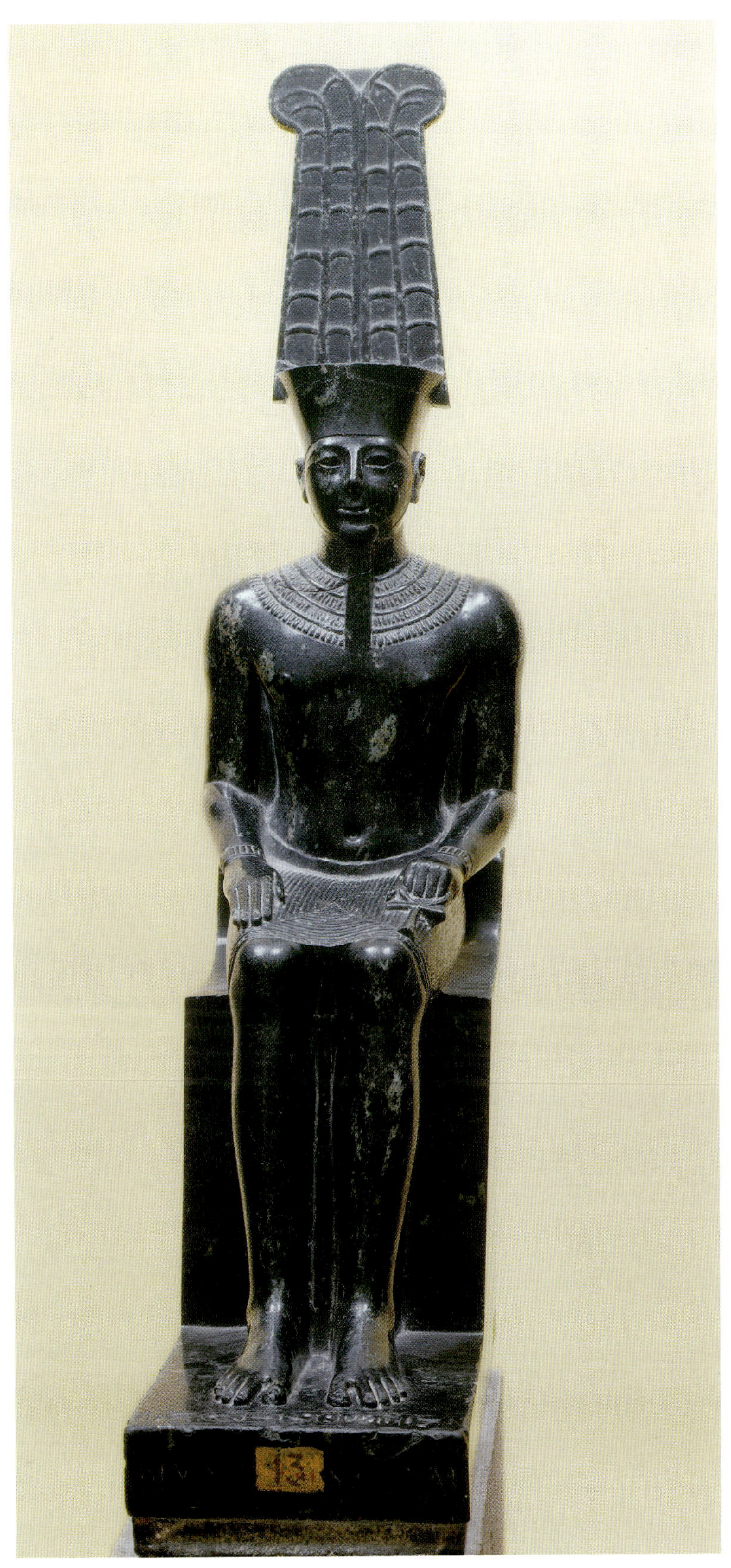

Egyptian artist, 1290–1279 BC
***Seated Amon-Ra*, 1290–1279 BC**
Granite
Gregorian Egyptian Museum

Egyptian artist, 380–343 BC
***Lion*, 380–343 BC**
72 x 185 cm; Grey granite
Gregorian Egyptian Museum

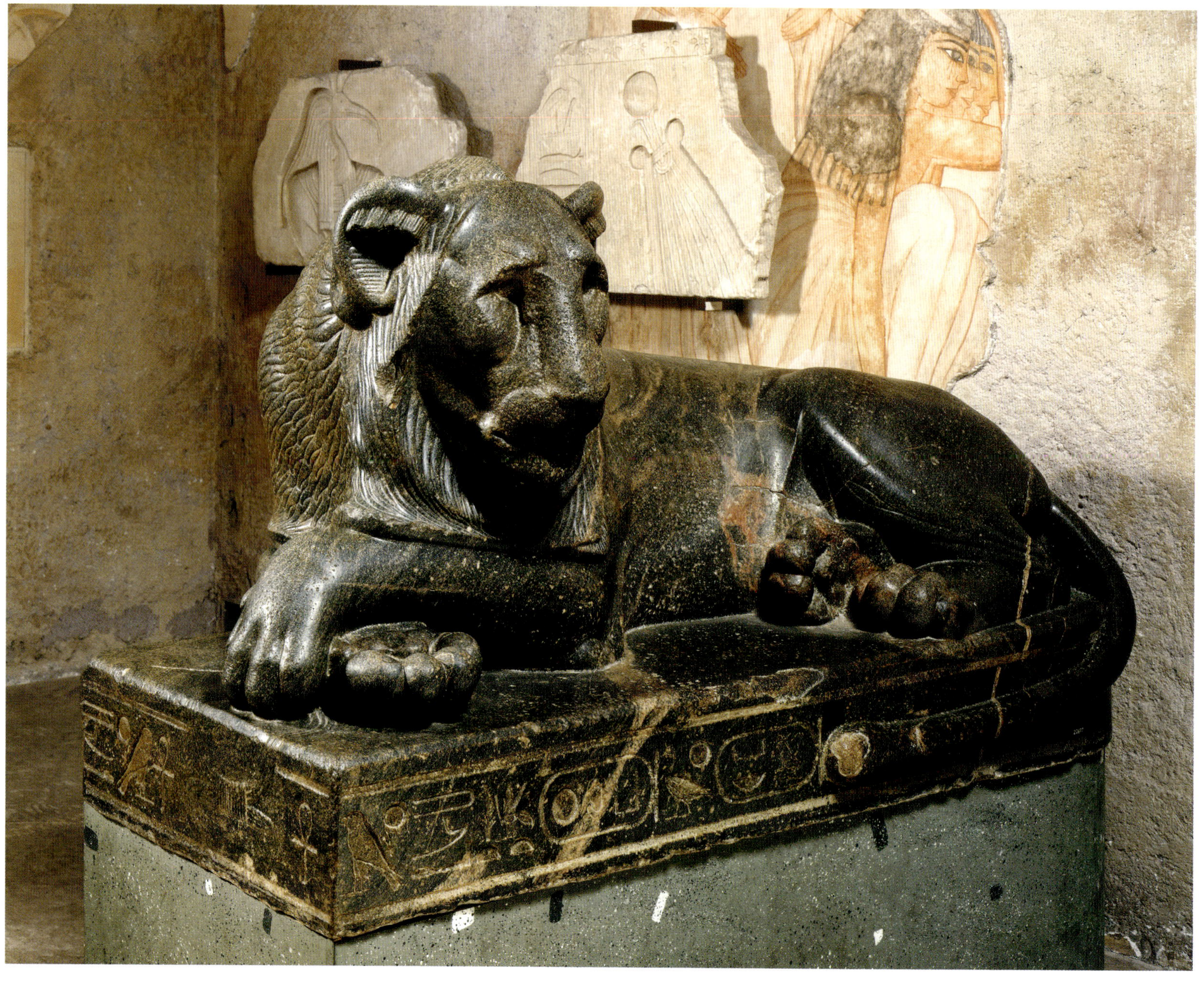

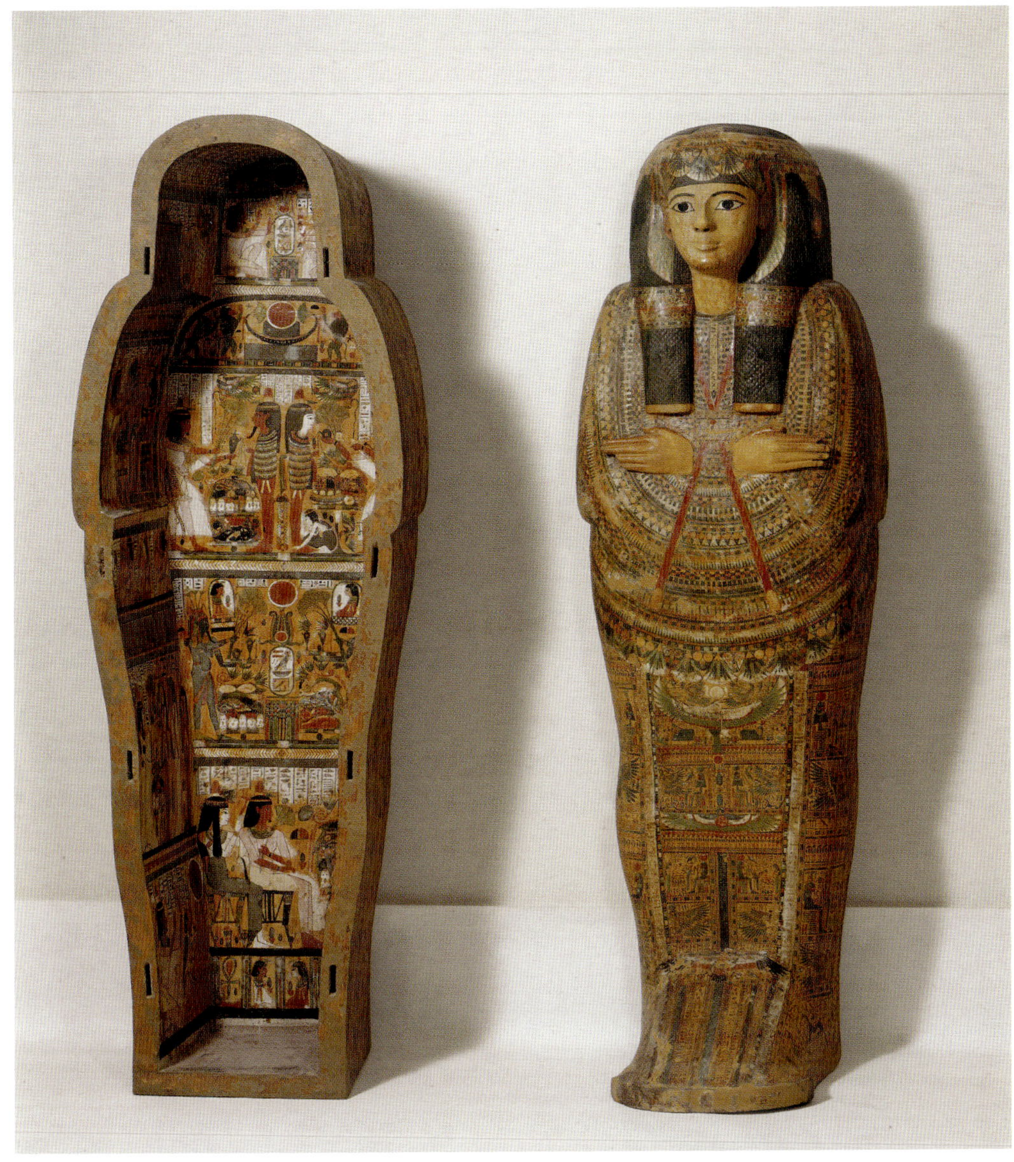

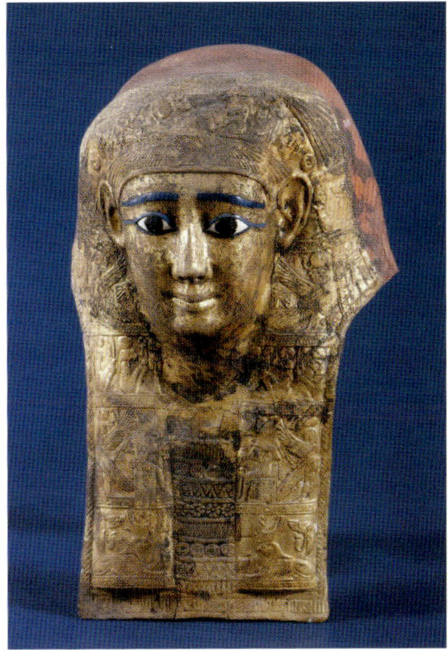

Ptolemaic artist, 332–330 BC
***Golden Mask of a Sarcophagus*, 332–330 BC**
Painted wood
Gregorian Egyptian Museum

Egyptian artist

Sarcophagus and Lid of Djet-Mut

Priestess Djet-Mut's painted wooden sarcophagus is a particularly well-preserved example of what are among the most splendid manifestations of ancient Egyptian funerary culture. Wooden sarcophagi were used to hold the mummy of the deceased; this example, made one thousand years before Christ, is painted within and without. The mainly mineral-based pigments symbolize the elements of the Egyptian landscape, such as earth, desert, and water. Adapted from the form of the male body and distinctive for its richly painted decoration, Djet-Mut's sarcophagus is typical of the design of the Third Intermediate Period. Figures, ornament, and inscriptions mingle with images of the afterlife of the deceased. The sarcophagus is therefore simultaneously a receptacle for the dead body and a symbol of the deceased's resurrection and victory over hostile powers in the hereafter. Djet-Mut herself is described in an inscription as the "wet nurse of the god Montu," the Egyptian god of war. The sarcophagus is from the Deir el-Bahari necropolis north of Thebes, a burial place mainly for members of the Egyptian upper and middle classes.

Egyptian artist, 1187–1064 BC
***Sarcophagus and Lid of Djet-Mut*, 1000 BC**
Height: 202 cm; Painted wood
Gregorian Egyptian Museum

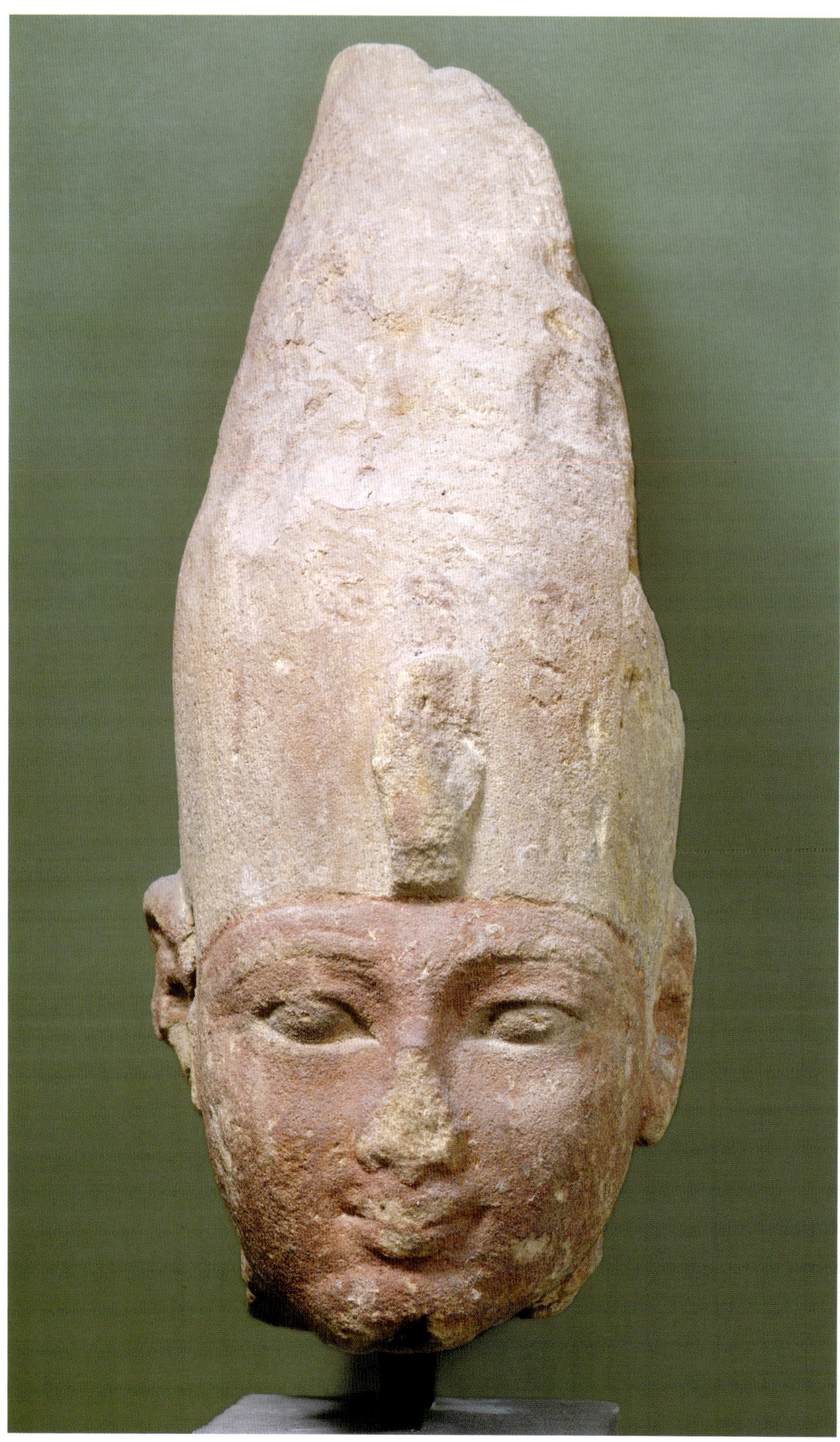

Egyptian artist

Head of Pharaoh Mentuhotep II

This head of Pharaoh Mentuhotep II (c. 2010–1998 BC) of the eleventh dynasty is one of the oldest works in the Gregorian Egyptian Museum. It has been identified on the basis of an inscription located on its back and is thought to have been part of a full-length, possibly seated, statue of the pharaoh. Stylistically, the head, which is remarkably well preserved for its age, can be dated to the end of Mentuhotep II's fifty-one-year reign. The realistic execution and lifelike facial expression make the larger-than-life-size head an outstanding example of monumental ancient Egyptian ruler portraiture. As with other Egyptian statues, the red paint on the face is designed to reproduce the skin color. The eyes are lacking the white detailing of the pupils and the brows would have originally been painted black. The pharaoh wears the tall white crown (*hedjet*) of the rulers of upper Egypt. The sculpture is originally from Thebes, Mentuhotep II's seat of government and a place of architectural vitality where art was actively fostered. Standing and seated sandstone statues of the pharaoh once lined the road through the forecourt of his burial temple at Deir el-Bahari, north of Thebes.

Egyptian artist, ca. 2050 BC
***Head of Pharaoh Mentuhotep II*, ca. 2000 BC**
Height: 62 cm; Painted limestone
Gregorian Egyptian Museum

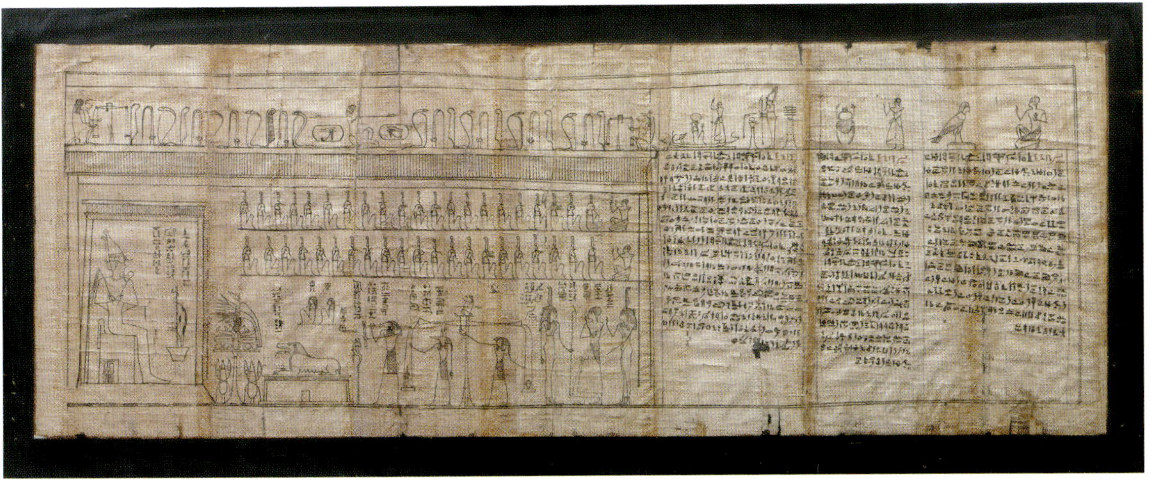

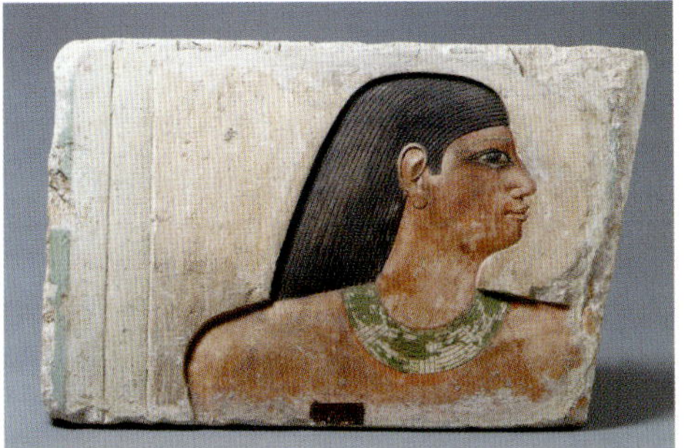

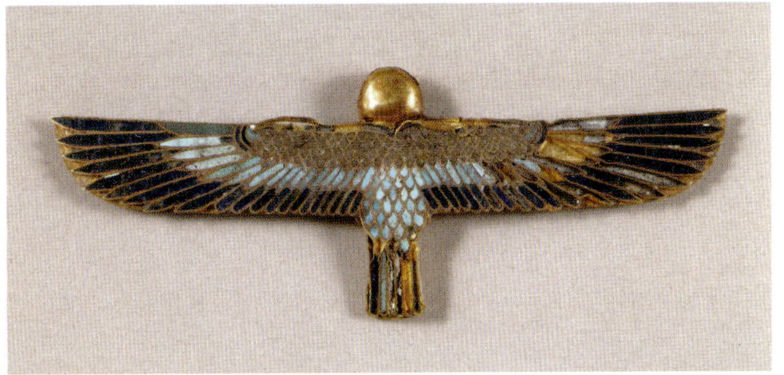

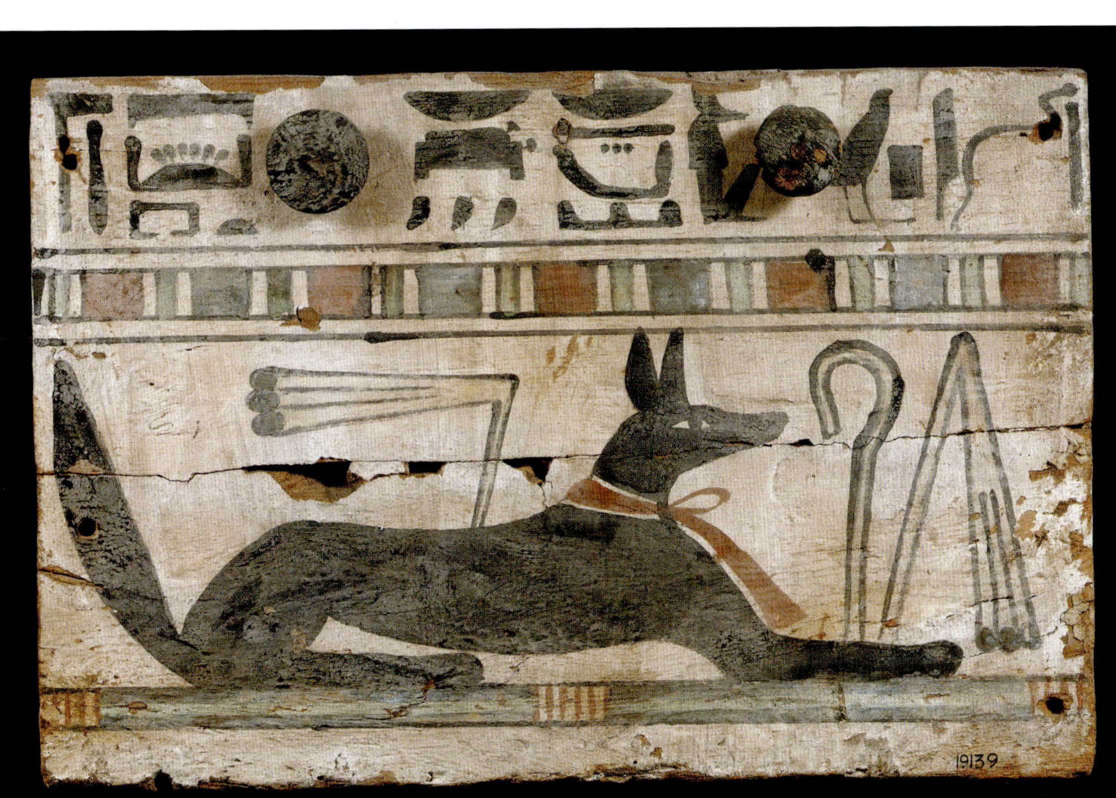

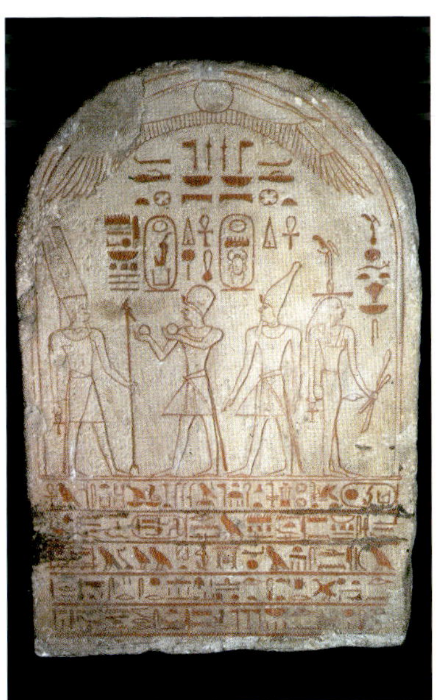

Egyptian artist, 720–332 BC
***Book of the Dead*, 720–332 BC**
33 x 72 cm; Papyrus, painted
Gregorian Egyptian Museum

Egyptian artist, 2585–2235 BC
***Head of a Man*, 2585–2235 BC**
29 x 48 cm; Basalt
Gregorian Egyptian Museum

Egyptian artist, 4th century BC
***Falcon, Symbol of the God Horus*, 4th century BC**
Gold
Gregorian Egyptian Museum

Egyptian artist, 10th–8th century BC
***The God Anubis*, 10th–8th century BC**
Painted wood
Gregorian Egyptian Museum

Egyptian artist, 1475–1468 BC
***Stele of Queen Hatshepsut*, ca. 1450 BC**
Height: 115 cm; Yellow sandstone
Gregorian Egyptian Museum

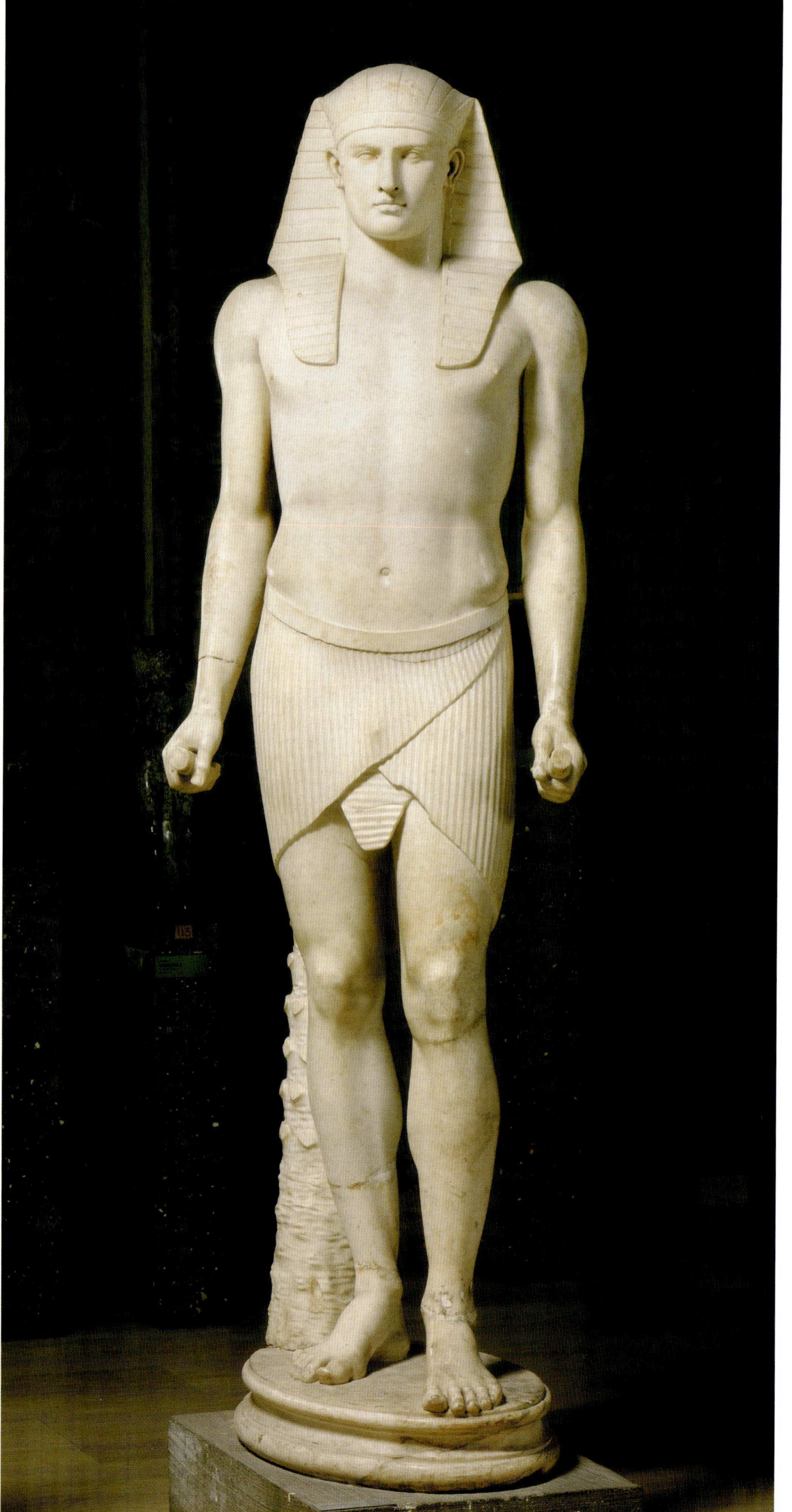

Roman artist, 2nd century AD
***Antinous (in Egyptian Dress), from Hadrian's Villa*, 131–138 AD**
Height: 241 cm; Marble
Gregorian Egyptian Museum

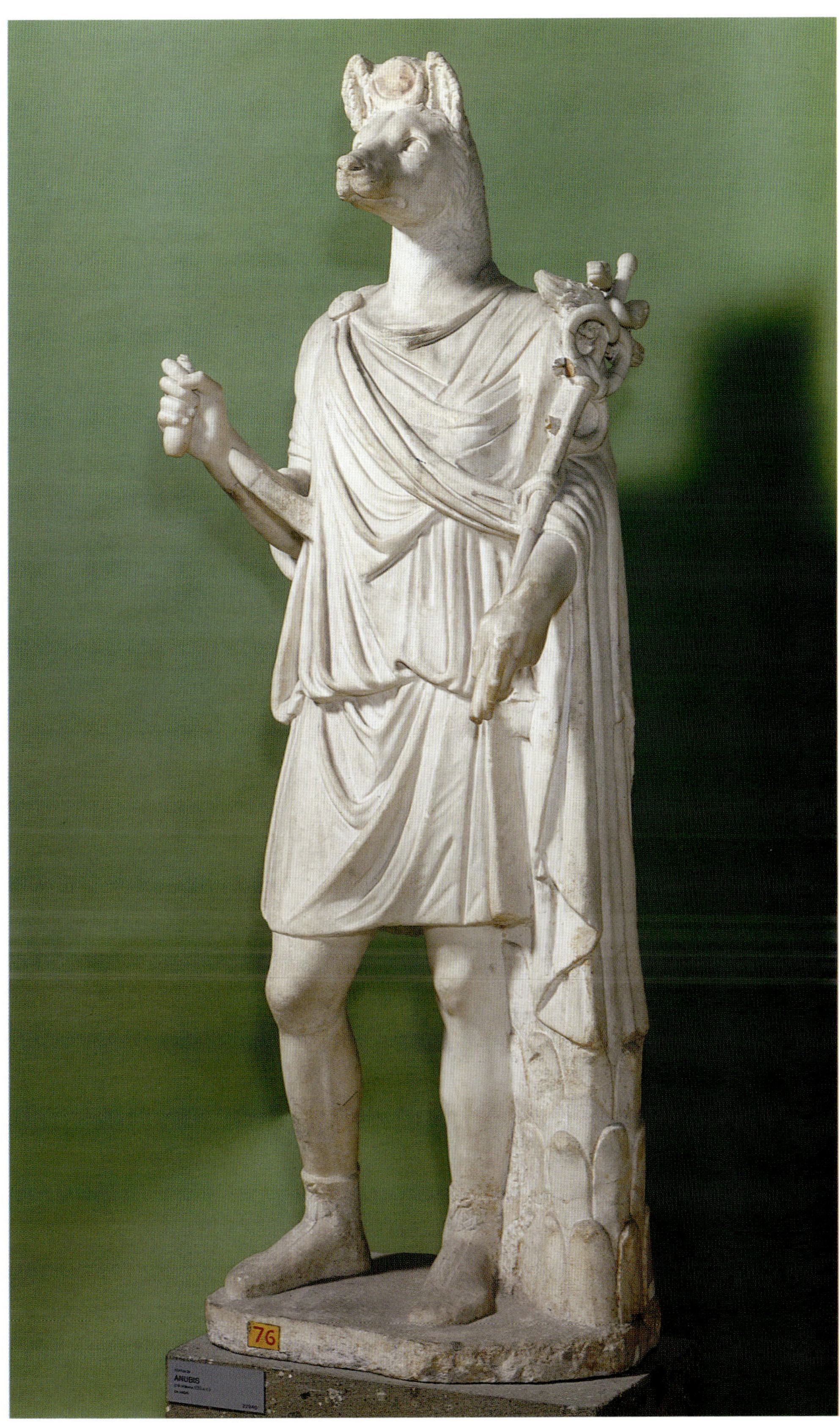

Roman artist

The God Anubis with the Attributes of Hermes

Anubis is the Egyptian god of funerary rites and embalming and also guides the deceased into the kingdom of the dead. He is always depicted as either a jackal or a man with a jackal's head. The statue of the deity in the Gregorian Egyptian Museum is a Roman copy of an Egyptian statue of Anubis, endowed by the later artist with the attributes of the Greek god Hermes. The Roman character of the figure is underlined by the toga fastened with a large fibula on the right shoulder. The characteristic attribute of Hermes, the messenger of the gods, is his wand of two entwined snakes (the caduceus), which had the power to induce sleep and with which the god also indicated the route to Hades. The rattle (sistrum) in his right hand, however, is of ancient Egyptian origin. The intermingling of the two deities can be explained by the fact that in Greco-Roman mythology one of the roles of Hermes/Mercury was to guide dead souls to the underworld. The Hermes-Anubis figure was discovered, along with various other finds from the Roman period, on the grounds of the Villa Pamphili in Rome. It exemplifies a vogue in Roman art for Egyptian culture, which reached its climax under Emperor Hadrian at the beginning of the second century AD.

Roman artist, 1st to 2nd century AD
***The God Anubis with the Attributes of Hermes*, 1st–2ND century AD**
Height: 155 cm; Marble
Gregorian Egyptian Museum

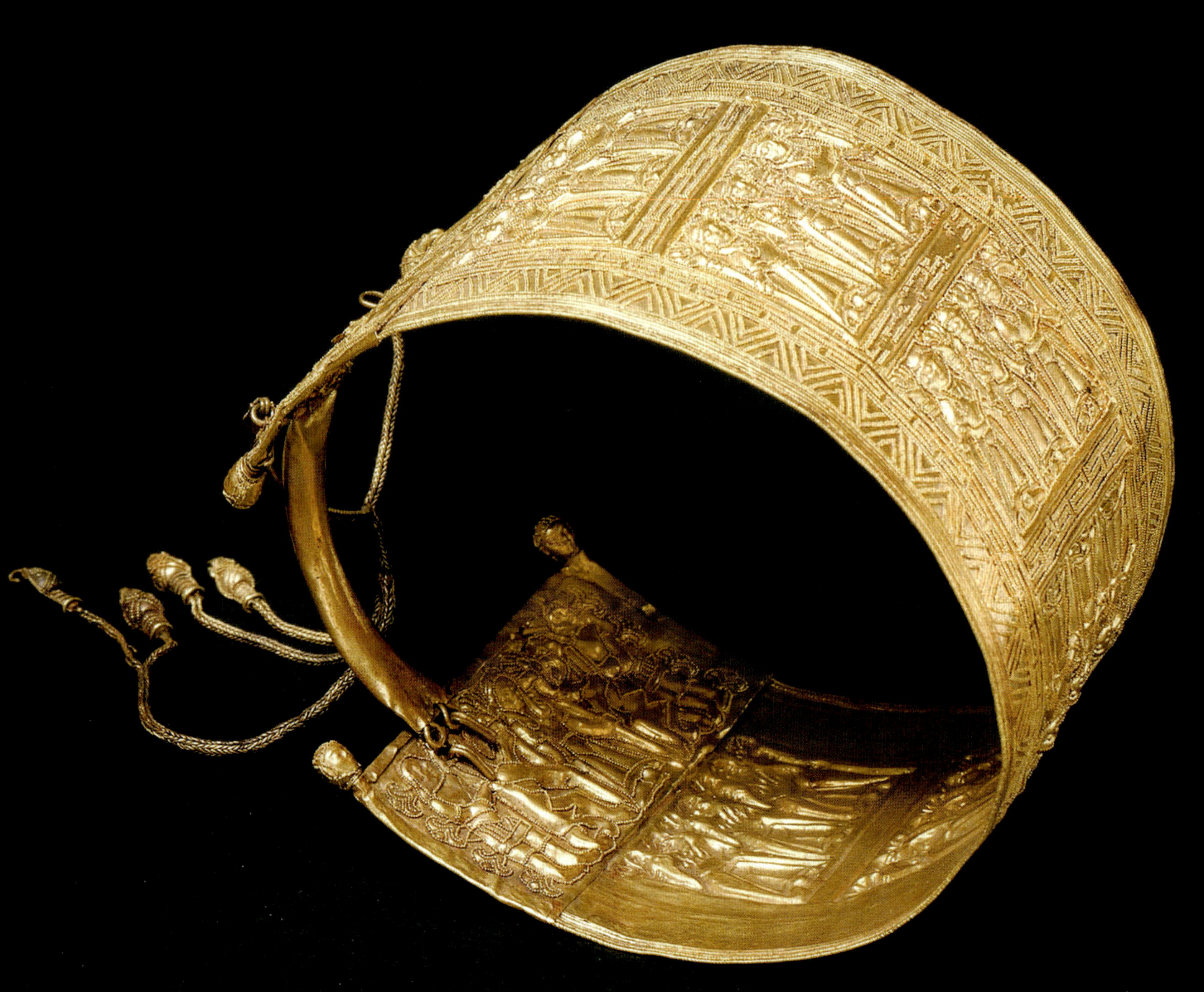

GREGORIAN ETRUSCAN MUSEUM

The Gregorian Etruscan Museum was the first museum to be inaugurated by Gregory XVI (1765–1846, reigned from 1831), following in the footsteps of his art-loving predecessors Clement XIV (1705–1774, reigned from 1769), Pius VI (1717–1799, reigned from 1775), and Pius VII (1742–1823, reigned from 1800), who had distinguished themselves as founders of the Pio-Clementino Museum and the Chiaramonti Museum. The Gregorian Etruscan Museum opened on February 2, 1837, the sixth anniversary of the accession of Gregory XVI. The museum connects the Scala Simonetti, from where it is entered, to the rooms of the Pio-Clementino Museum, remodeled not long before under Pius VI.

There are also historical connections between the two collections, although the Gregorian Etruscan Museum, comprising Etruscan works of art, showcases the rich culture that was dominant on the Italian peninsula prior to the development of the Roman Empire, which it decisively influenced. While the buildings of Roman antiquity had continually been excavated and researched since the Renaissance, interest in Etruscan culture only developed at the beginning of the nineteenth century. The Vatican played a key role in Etruscan research as large parts of southern Etruria lay within the territory of the Papal States. In 1820 the edict of Cardinal Bartolomeo Pacca (1756–1844), who did much for the protection of cultural assets, stipulated how the Vatican was to proceed in excavating Etruscan sites and how the discovered art treasures were to be handled. One of the most important outcomes of the edict was the founding of the Gregorian Etruscan museum.

Today the museum is one of the Vatican's most extensive collections in terms of number of items. It affords a comprehensive overview of the history of Etruscan art and culture from the Villanovan culture of the ninth and eighth centuries BC, via the Orientalizing period in the seventh century BC and the Archaic and Classical periods of the sixth and fifth centuries BC, all the way to the Hellenistic era beginning in the fourth century BC. The Orientalizing period, whose name derives from the multiple influences absorbed by Etruria from the art of the eastern Mediterranean and the Near East during this time, is regarded as the golden age of the Etruscan Empire. The prosperity attained through manifold trading contacts is also reflected in the materials used in the artworks, above all the use of precious metals such as gold and bronze rather than the iron used in Villanovan culture. Bronze also dominates the sculpture of the Archaic and Classical periods, whose realism is in no way inferior to the sculpture being produced in Greece at the same time. An extremely close relationship with Greek art is also evinced by the museum's collection of vases, one of the most extensive in the world. With their scenes from mythology, the theater, banquet culture, and everyday life, these beautifully painted vessels in a wide variety of shapes constitute perhaps the most vibrant testimony of all to the flowering of Etruscan culture.

Arkesilas painter, 6th century BC
Black-figure Kylix: Atlas and the Punishment of Prometheus, 560-550 BC
Diameter: 20.2 cm; Ceramics
Gregorian Etruscan Museum

Greek artist, 6th century BC
Red-Figure Pelike with Theseus and the Minotaur, late 6th century BC
Height: Approx. 50 cm; Ceramics
Gregorian Etruscan Museum

Athenian artist, 6th century BC
Tyrrhenian Amphora from Vulci Hercules Atruggles with the Centaur (above), Animal Scenes (below), 6th century BC
Height: Approx 50 cm; Ceramics
Gregorian Etruscan Museum

Greek artist, date unknown
Attic Goblets in the Shape of Human Heads, unknown
Height: 19 cm, 20 cm; Ceramics
Gregorian Etruscan Museum

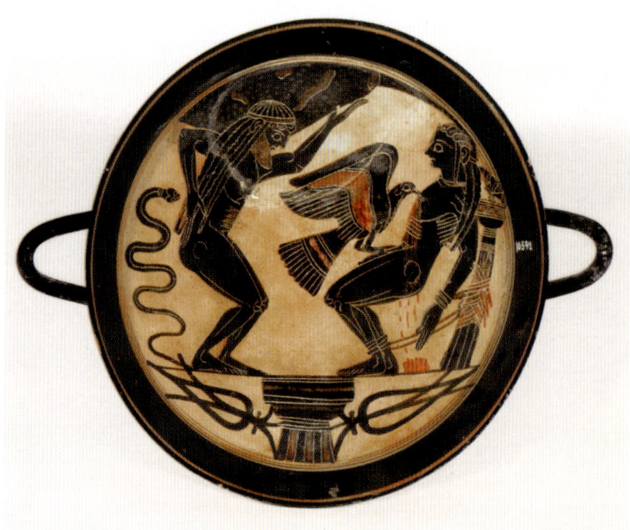

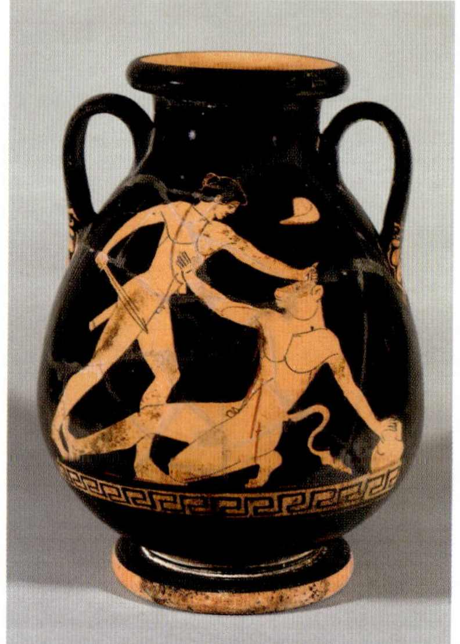

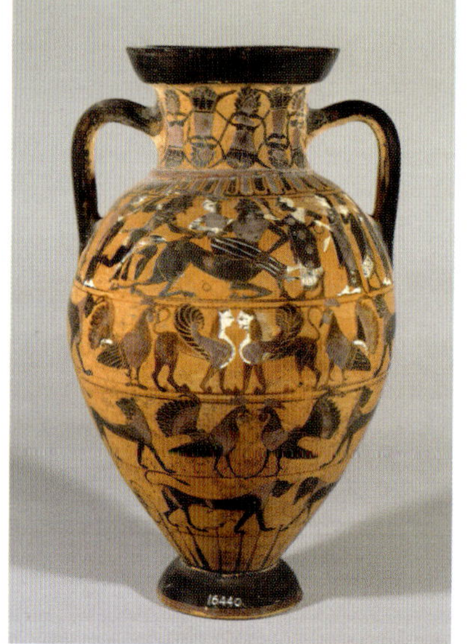

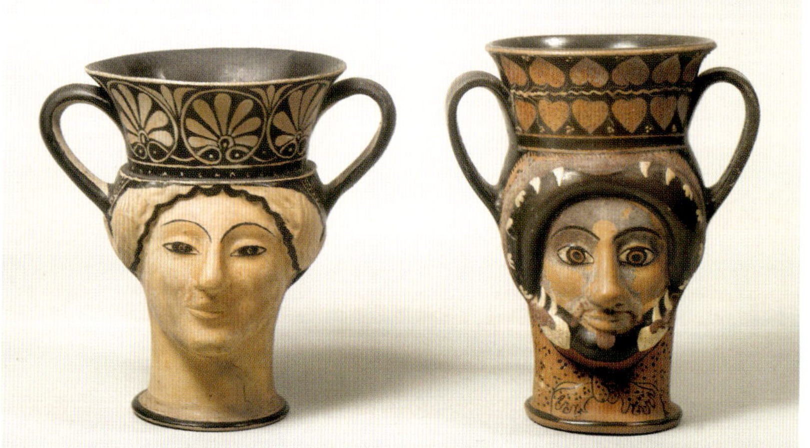

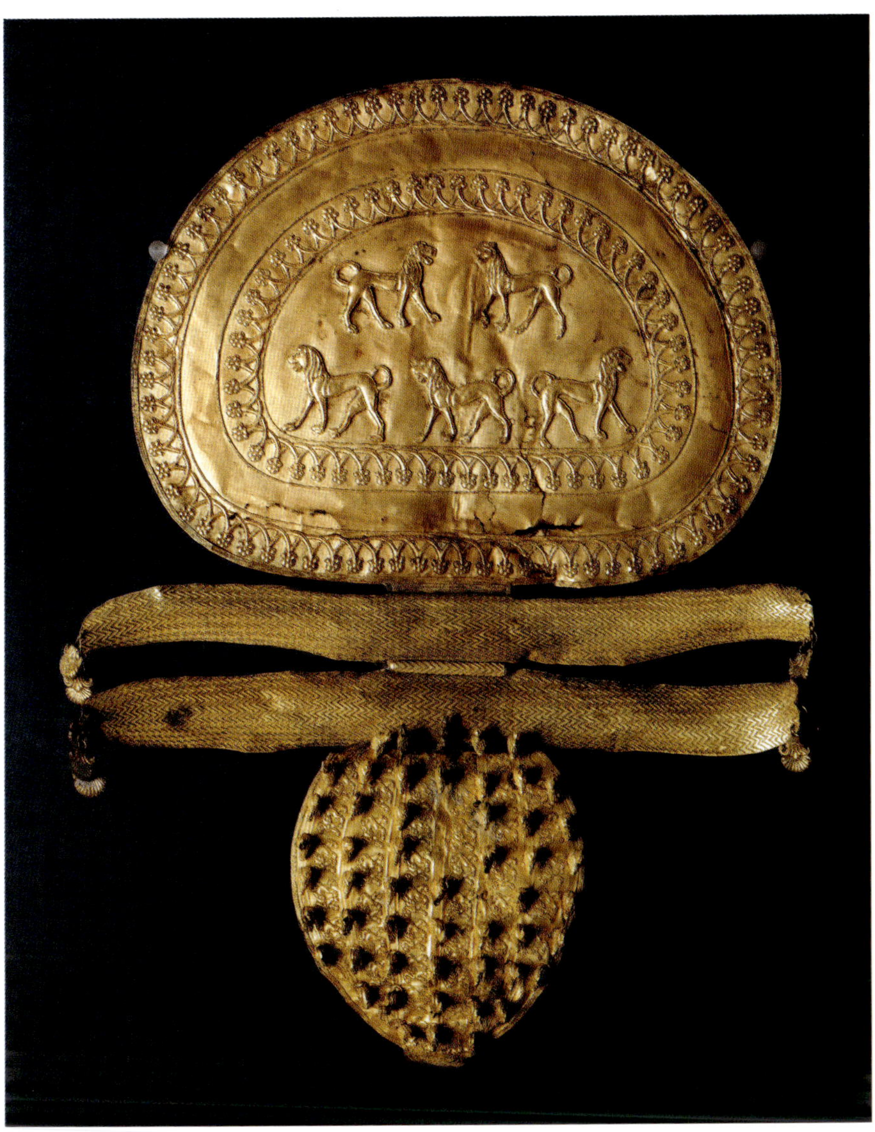

Etruscan Goldsmith

Large Golden Fibula

This large solid-gold fibula is one of the most precious objects in the Gregorian Etruscan Museum. It was found in the so-called Regolini-Galassi tomb, named after its two excavators Archpriest Alessandro Regolini and General Vincenzo Galassi, in a previously undisturbed necropolis at Cerveteri in 1836. Together with other richly decorated gold items that also found their way into the Vatican, the clasp formed part of the ceremonial dress of the deceased, who must have been a member of the highest aristocracy or even the royal family. Weighing 173 grams, the fibula was used to fasten its owner's robes at the shoulder, and in view of its magnificent form and size, would have been a symbol of power and wealth. The extremely delicate Regolini-Galassi fibula is distinctive for its artistic and technical sophistication. The upper part consists of an almost oval plate in repoussé work with five striding lions in profile at the center, ringed by a double border of rosette-crowned arcs.
The outlines and interior lines are emphasized by fine granulation and profiling. The pendant below the transverse bars is decorated with rows of tiny soldered ducks sculpted in the round, along with other animal motifs typical of the Orientalizing style of the period.

Etruscan Goldsmith, 7th century BC
***Large Golden Fibula*, 7th century BC**
32 cm long; Gold
Gregorian Etruscan Museum

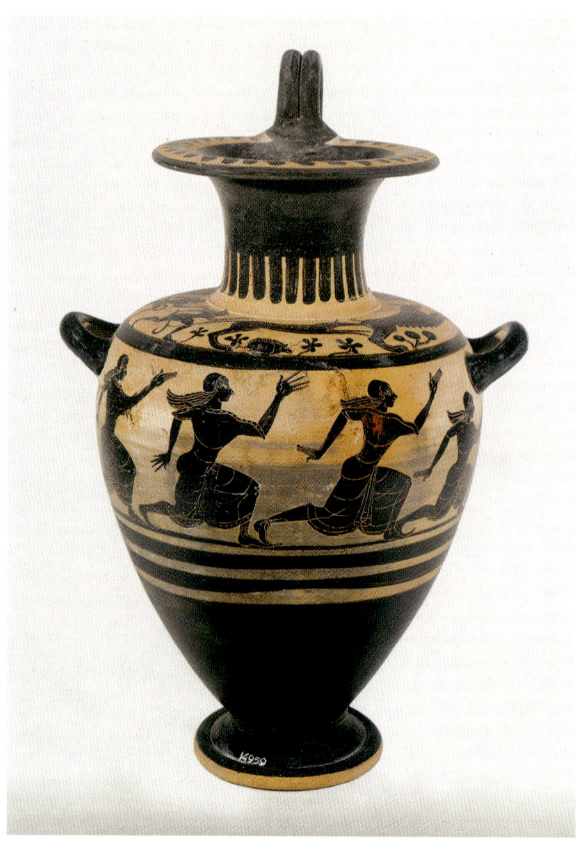

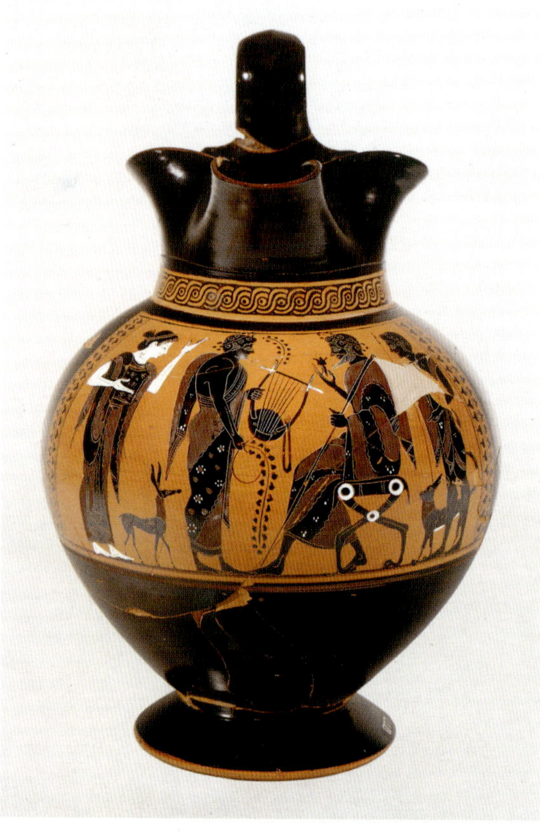

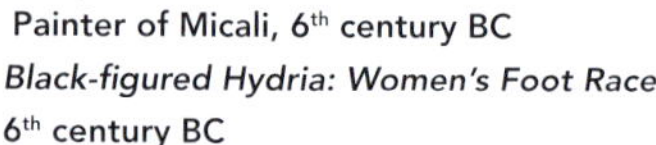

Painter of Micali, 6th century BC
Black-figured Hydria: Women's Foot Race,
6th century BC
Height: 52 cm; Ceramics
Gregorian Etruscan Museum

Amasis painter, 6th century BC
Attic Black Figure Oinochoe: Seated Man and a Youth with a Lyre,
6th century BC
Height: 31 cm; Ceramics
Gregorian Etruscan Museum

Greek artist, 7th century BC
Corinthian Olpe Decorated with Wild Animals,
7th century BC
Height: Approx. 30 cm; Ceramics
Gregorian Etruscan Museum

Boston Phiale painter, from Vulci, 440–430 BC
Polychrome Attic Krater with Hermes Entrusting Dionysus to Silenus, **440–435 BC**
Height: 32.8 cm; Ceramics
Gregorian Etruscan Museum

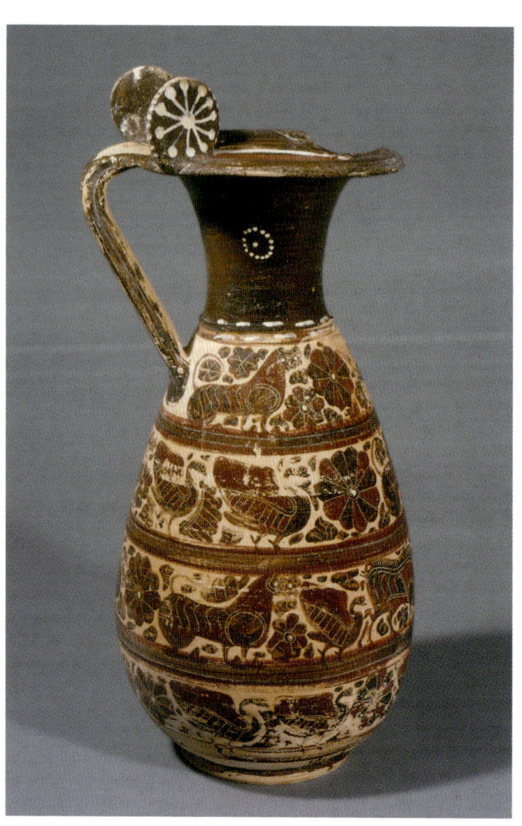

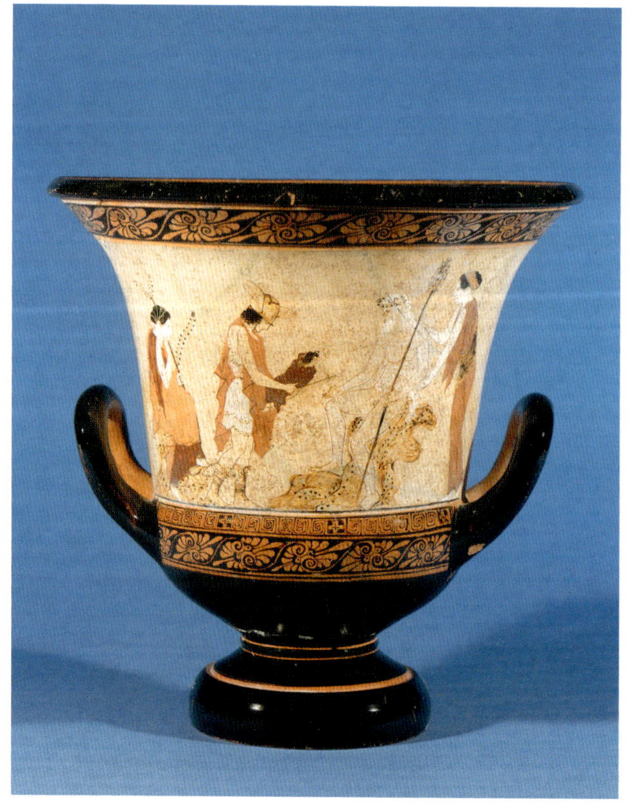

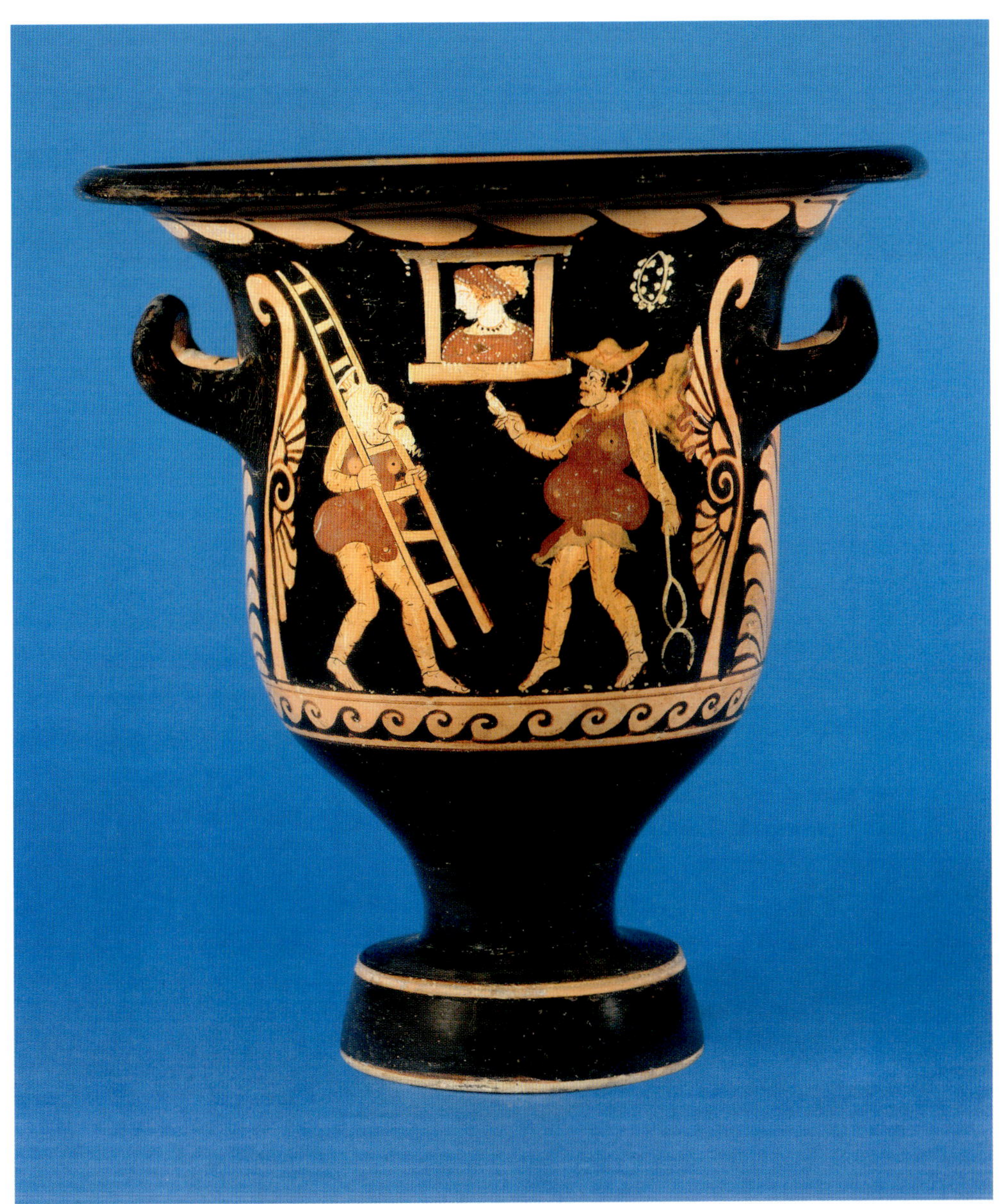

Asteas artist, attributed to

Krater from Paestum

This vase-like vessel with two side handles is of a type known as a krater (from the Greek "to mix"), a vessel used in Greek antiquity for the mixing of water and wine. It is distinctive for its unusual painted decoration in the red-figure style, parodying a scene from Greek mythology: Zeus, the father of the gods, preparing to pay court to Alcmene, the wife of Amphitryon. According to the myth, Zeus adopted the outward appearance of Amphitryon, depicted here as a short, portly old man. Even more corpulent is the usually youthful messenger of the gods, Hermes, shown standing on the right-hand side dressed in a comedy costume with his snake wand pointing downward. In his right hand Hermes holds a small lamp with which he indicates the way to the window, where Alcmene appears in her finery. Scenes from Greek comedy such as this enjoyed great popularity in the Etruscan Empire of the fourth century. The Paestan painter Asteas, one of the few Etruscan artists known by name, was also influenced by Greek culture and, for stylistic reasons, the krater is attributed to him.

Asteas artist, attributed to, late 4th century
***Krater from Paestum*, ca. 360–330 BC**
Height: 37 cm; Ceramic, painted
Gregorian Etruscan Museum

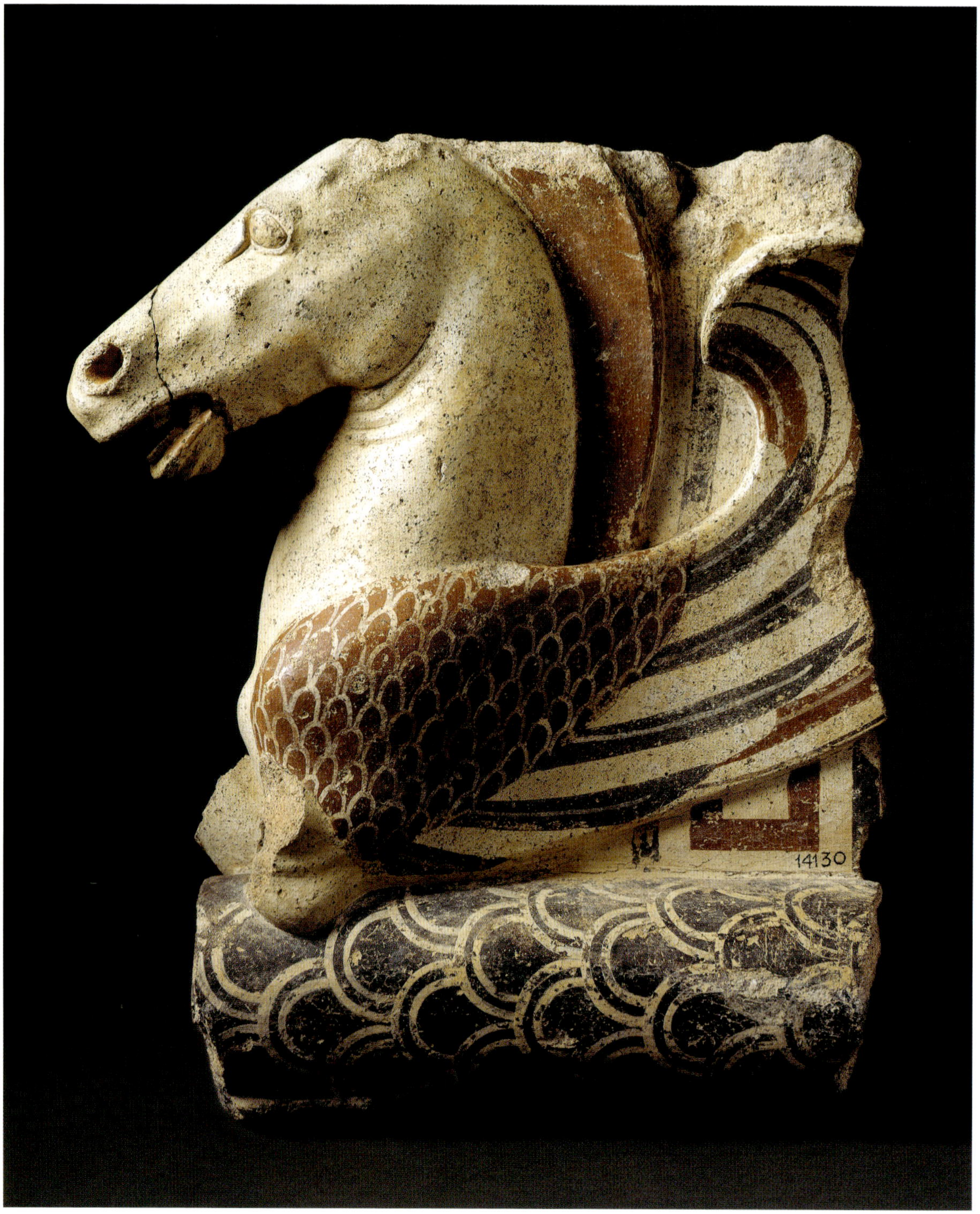

Etruscan artist, 450–430 BC
***Head of Pegasus*, 450–430 BC**
46 x 40.5 cm; Terracotta
Gregorian Etruscan Museum

Etruscan artist, 5th century BC
***Back of Mirror with Eos*, 470 BC**
17 cm; Bronze
Gregorian Etruscan Museum

Etruscan artist, 3rd century BC
***Portrait of a Woman (votive Bust from Cerveteri)*, 3rd century BC**
Terracotta
Gregorian Etruscan Museum

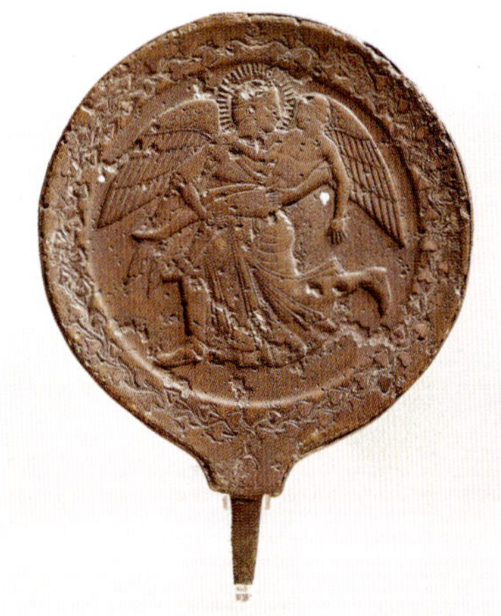

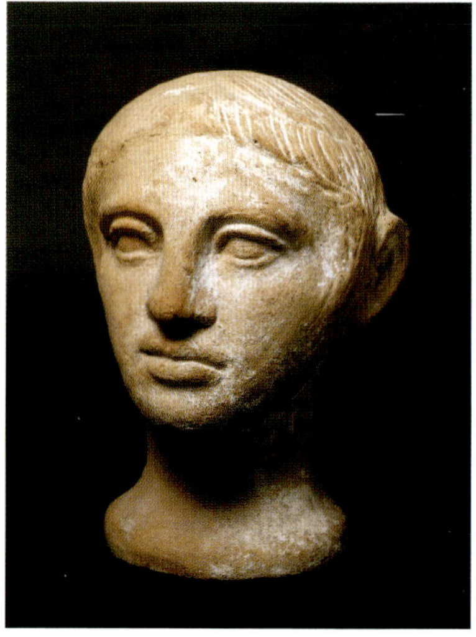

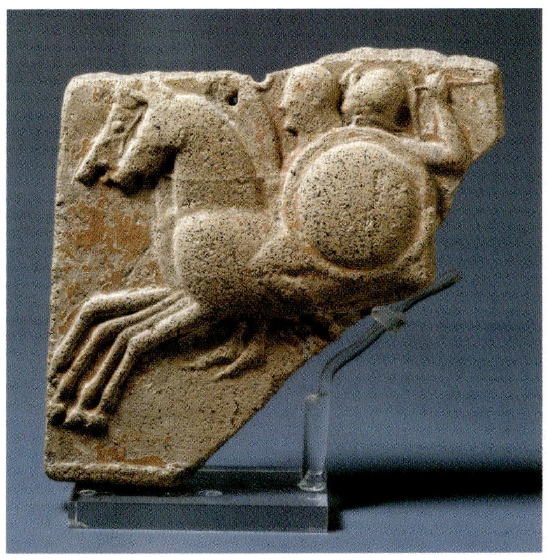

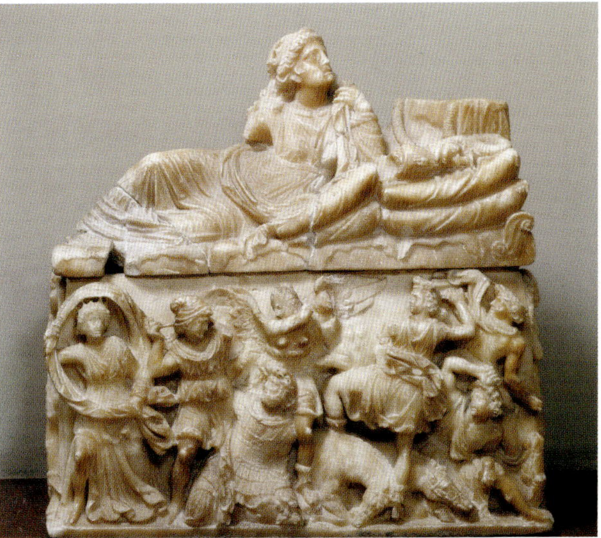

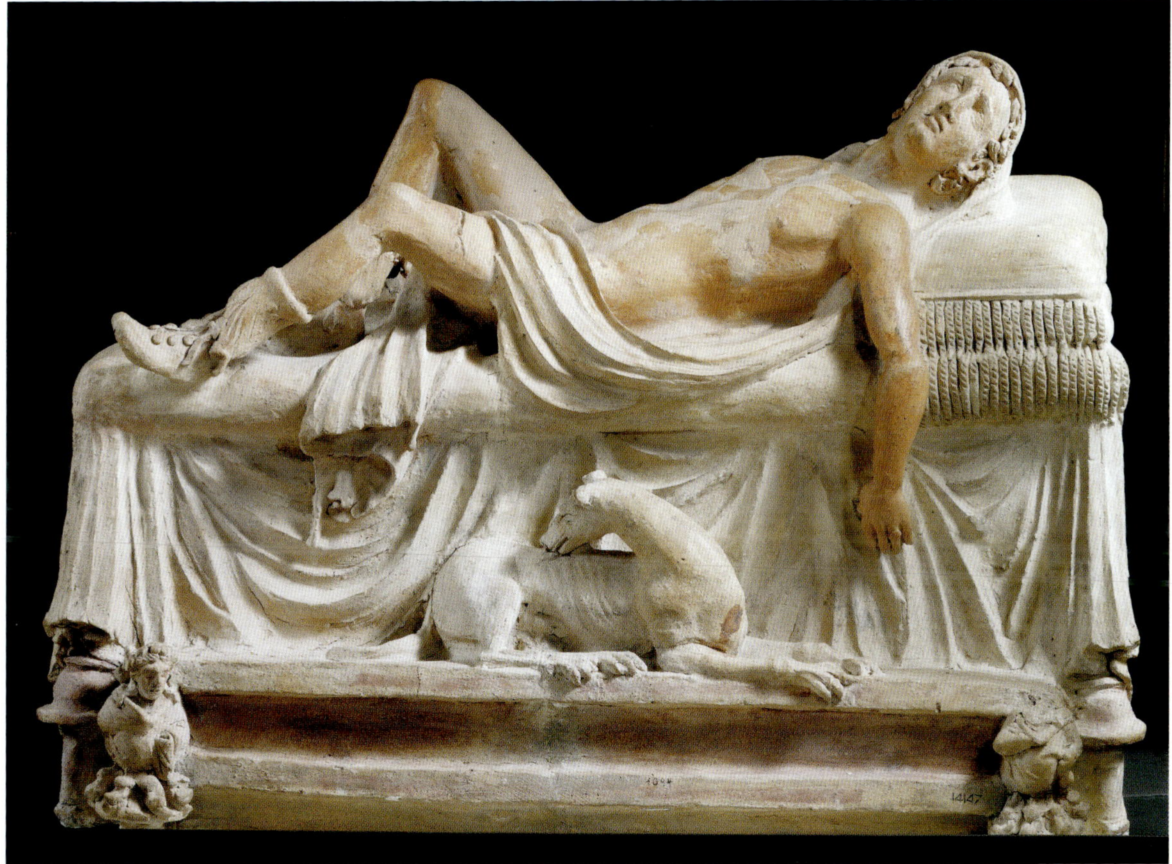

Etruscan artist, 1st century CE
***Slab with Horsemen*, 1st century CE**
Ceramics
Gregorian Etruscan Museum

Etruscan artist, 2nd century BC
***Cinerary Urn from Volterra*, early 2nd century BC**
84 x 85 x 29 cm; Alabaster
Gregorian Etruscan Museum

Etruscan artist, 3rd century BC
***Monument of Adonis*, late 3rd century BC**
62 x 89 x 40 cm; Terracotta
Gregorian Etruscan Museum

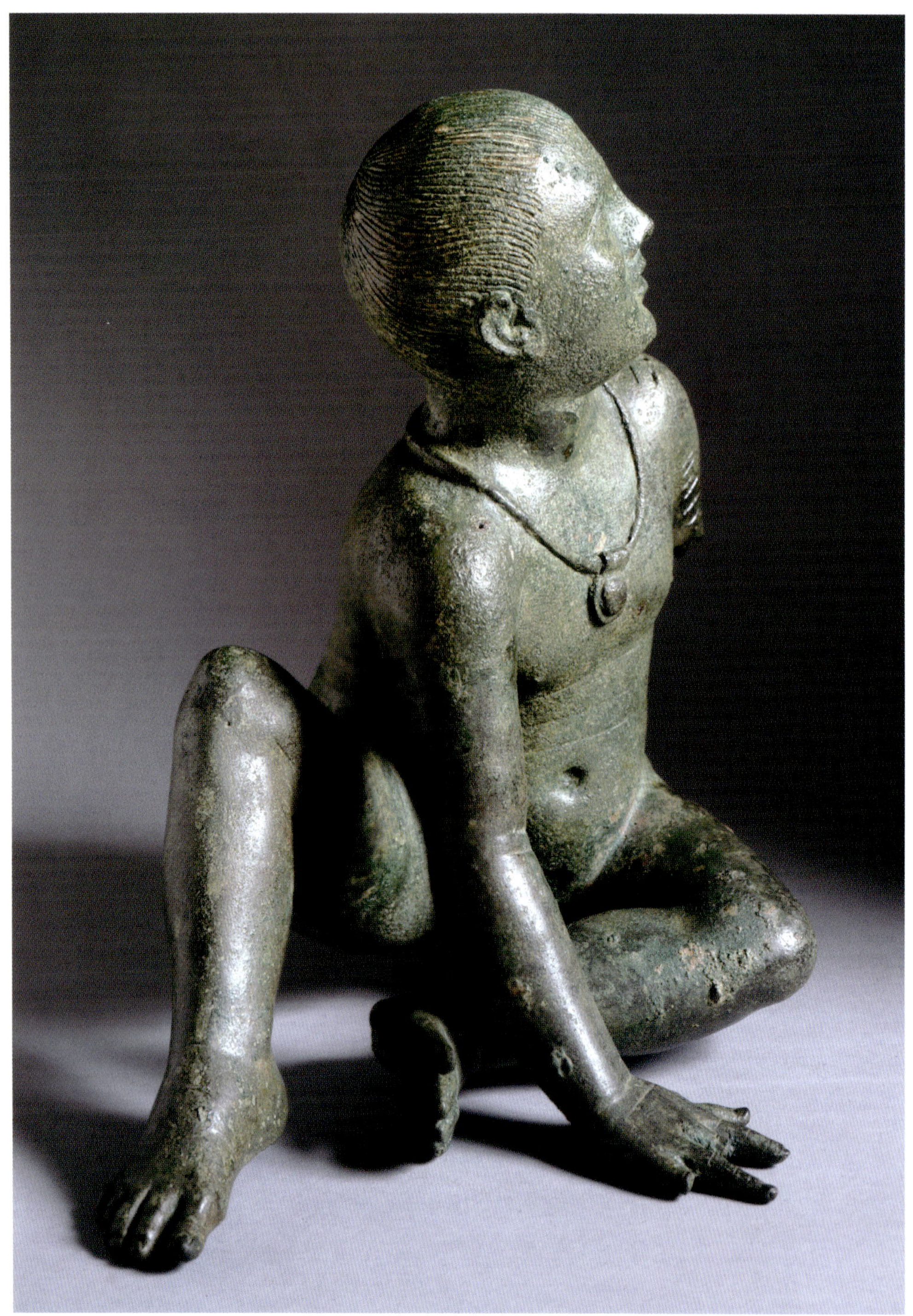

Etruscan artist

Sitting Child (Putto)

This figure of a seated naked boy is one of the most famous bronzes of the Etruscan era. It is distinctive for its outstanding realism, which makes the child seem almost alive. It was excavated in 1770 in Tarquina, one of the oldest and most important of Etruscan cities, by Monsignor Francesco Carrara and donated by him to the Vatican the following year. Like similar statues of boys from the Etruscan period, the sculpture served as a votive figure (ex-voto). More precisely, according to the inscription on the left upper arm it was a votive offering to the forest god Silvanus, from whose destructive power children required protection. The chain with the pendent (bulla) indicates that the "son of Vel," as the child is named in the inscription, was of free birth. The figure, whose left arm and two fingers of his right hand are missing, originally sat on a plinth. It adopts a complicated seating position, with the twisted body and upward gaze contributing decisively to the lifelike impression. It is possible that with his missing left hand the figure was originally making an offering to the deity. The childishly plump body of the boy contrasts strongly with its significantly more mature face, which argues against the statue being a portrait of a specific child.

Etruscan artist, 3rd century BC
***Sitting Child (Putto)*, 3rd century BC**
Height: 32.7 cm; Bronze
Gregorian Etruscan Museum

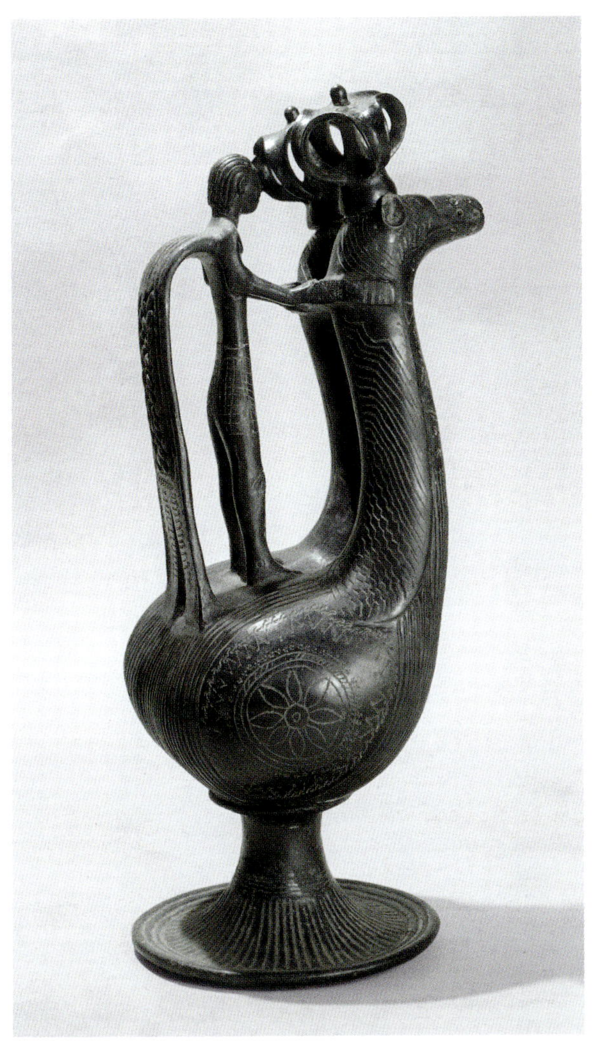

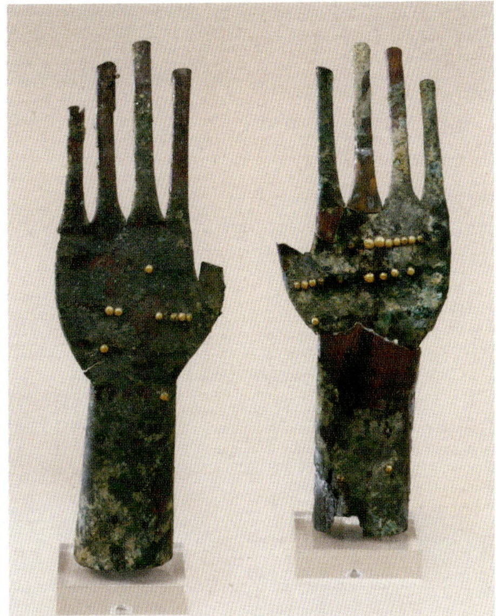

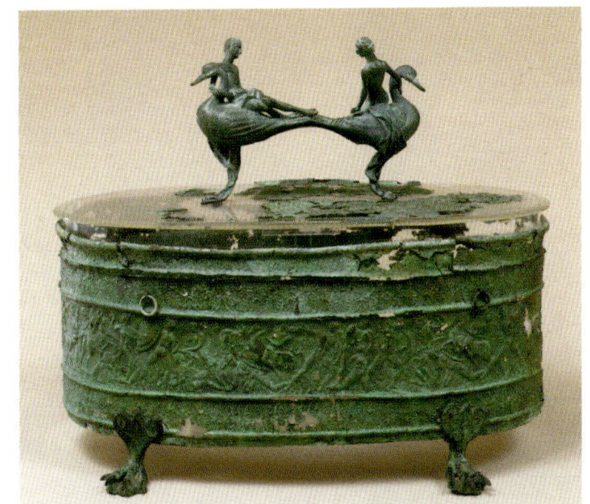

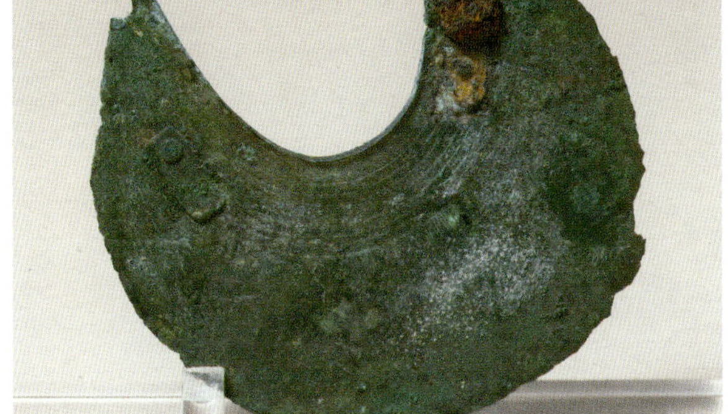

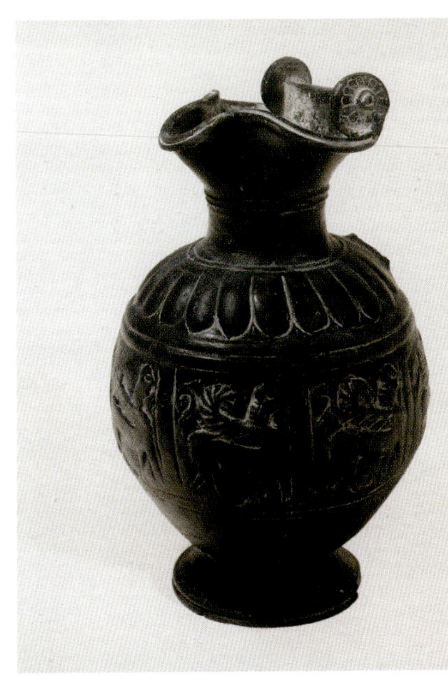

Etruscan artist, 7th century BC
***Askos in the Shape of a Charioteer*, 7th century BC**
Height: 30 cm; Bucchero
Gregorian Etruscan Museum

Etruscan artist, 7th century BC
***Bronze Hands with Gold Studs*, 7th century BC**
Bronze
Gregorian Etruscan Museum

Etruscan artist, late 4th century BC
***Oval Bin from Vulci with Figures*, late 4th century BC**
Length: 49 cm; Bronze
Gregorian Etruscan Museum

Etruscan artist, 6th century BC
***Half-moon in Bronze*, 6th century BC**
Bronze
Gregorian Etruscan Museum

Etruscan artist, 7th century BC
***Heavy Oinochoe*, late 7th century BC**
Bucchero
Gregorian Etruscan Museum

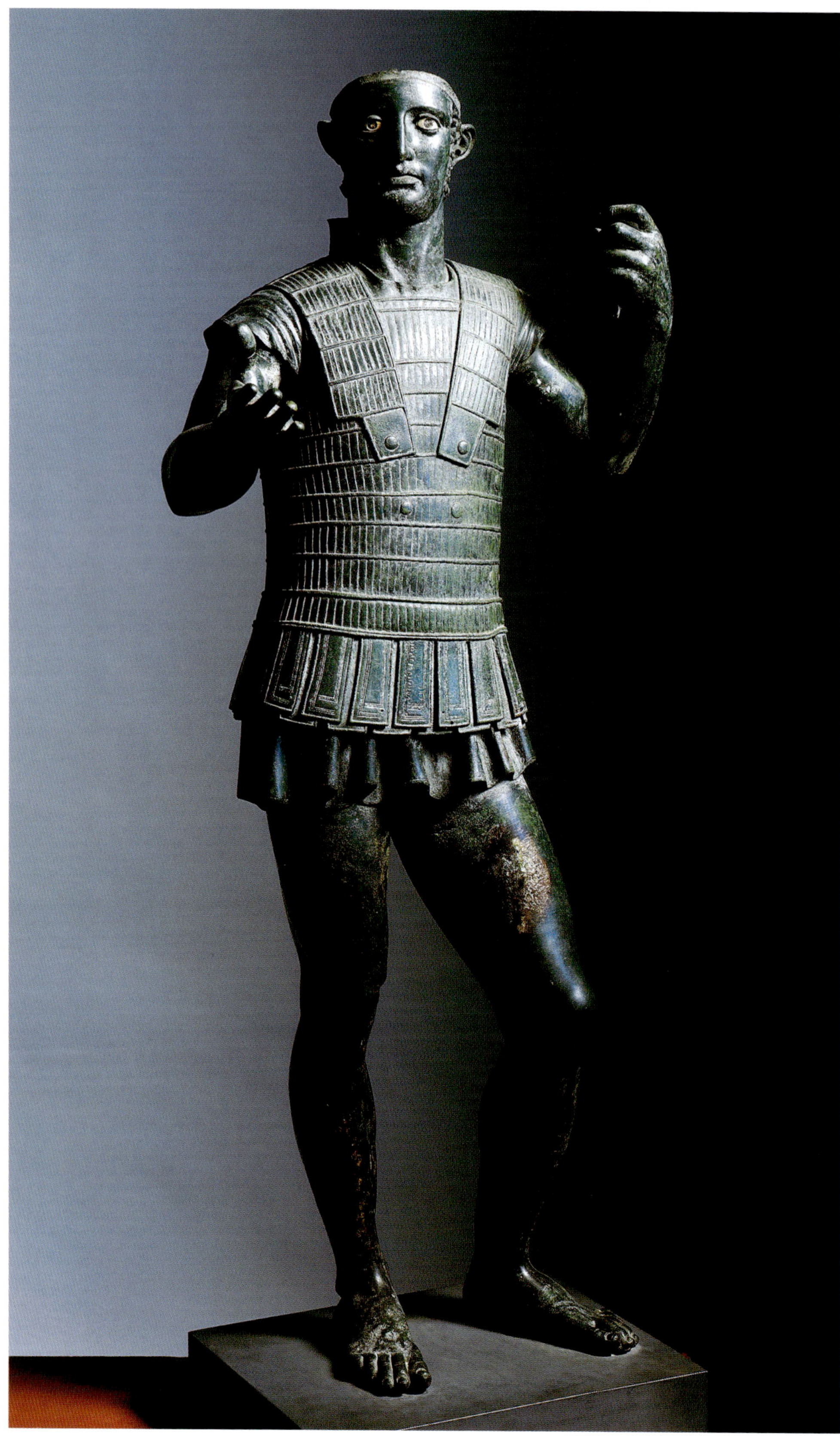

Etruscan artist

Mars of Todi

This bronze statue is of a warrior in armor. Dating from the end of the fifth century BC, it is distinctive for its unusually lifelike quality. The figure has been portrayed in a classical contrapposto stance, with his weight resting on his right leg and his free left leg slightly angled. Although presenting himself frontally to the viewer, the soldier's head is inclined slightly to the right, in the direction of his raised right hand, which once contained a shallow bowl (*patera*), now housed in its own vitrine. The slightly tilted position of the hand indicates that the soldier is in the process of pouring a libation before his first battle. Also exhibited separately is the iron spear originally held in the soldier's left hand. The statue was made using the hollow cast method and is one of the largest surviving bronze figures from the Etruscan period; aside from the missing helmet, it is also extraordinarily well preserved. The incredibly realistic rendering of the musculature, the surface structure of the skin, the facial features, which seem almost to be in the act of speaking, and the individual sections of the slatted armor indicate that this is the work of an outstanding sculptor who may well have trained in Greece. The dedicatory inscription on the middle strip of the leather *pteryges* indicates that the figure, discovered beneath blocks of travertine during excavations on Monte Santo in Todi in 1835, was intended as a votive statue.

Etruscan artist, 5th century BC
***Mars of Todi*, 5th century BC**
Height: 141 cm; Bronze
Gregorian Etruscan Museum

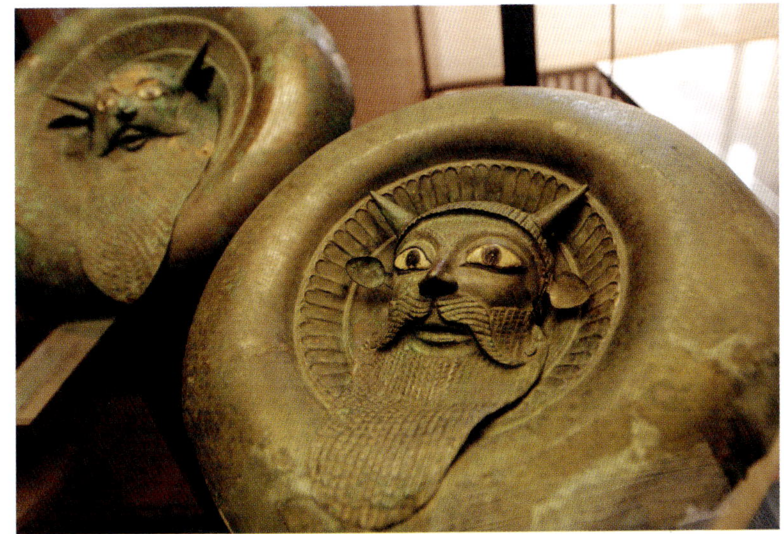

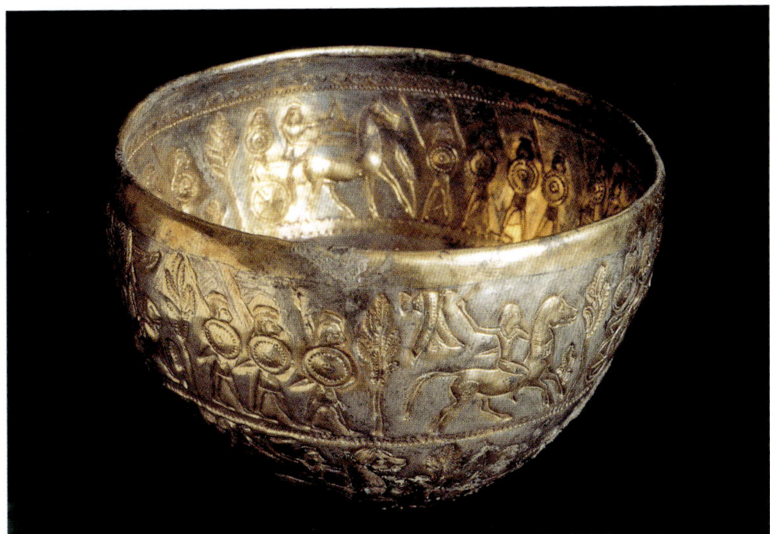

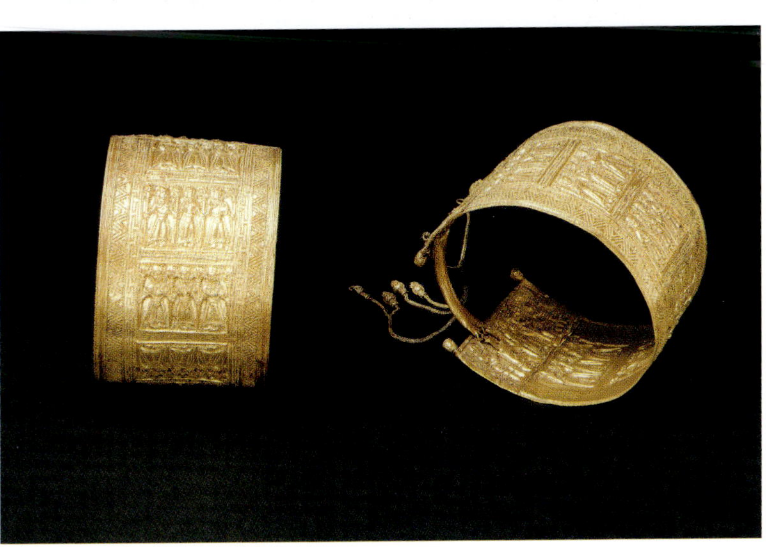

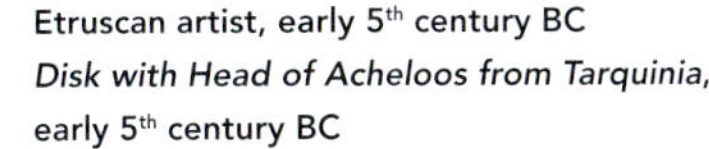

Etruscan artist, early 5th century BC
***Disk with Head of Acheloos from Tarquinia,* early 5th century BC**
Diameter: 40 cm; Bronze
Gregorian Etruscan Museum

Etruscan artist, ca. 470 BC
***Cup with Procession of Warriors and other Scenes,* ca. 470 BC**
Diameter: 17 cm; Gilded silver
Gregorian Etruscan Museum

Etruscan artist, ca. 650 BC
***Pair of Armbands,* ca. 650 BC**
Diameter: 10 cm; Gold
Gregorian Etruscan Museum

Etruscan artist, 4th century BC
***Gold Laurel Wreath, Necklace with Pendants and Cluster Earrings,* 4th century BC**
Gold
Gregorian Etruscan Museum

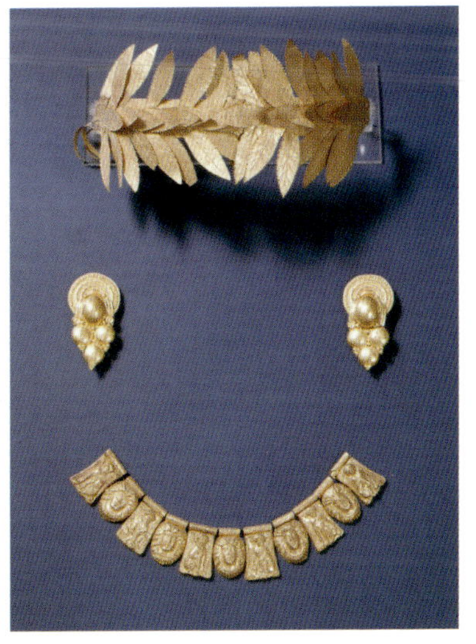

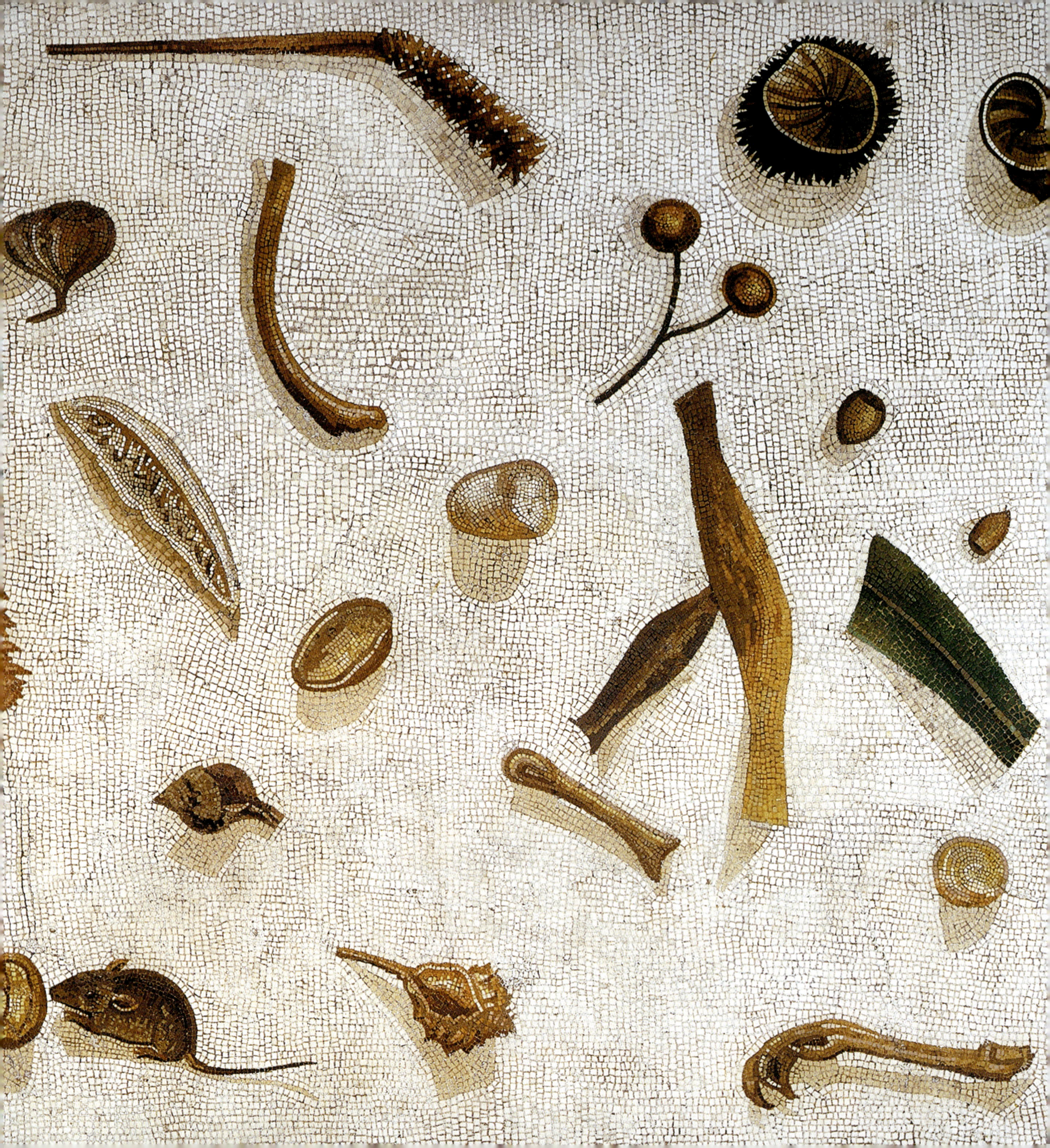

GREGORIANO PROFANO MUSEUM

The Gregoriano Profano Museum was inaugurated by Pope Gregory XVI (1765–1846, reigned from 1831). Like the Pio-Christian Museum, it was initially housed in the Lateran Palace before being transferred to the Vatican under Pope Paul VI (born 1897, reigned 1963–1978) in 1970. Both collections are now displayed in a new wing purpose-built by the architecture firm Studio Passarelli, and the two complement each other in terms of content. Whereas the Pio-Christian Museum is concerned with the art and culture of early Christianity in Rome, the Gregoriano Profano Museum emphasizes Roman antiquity with a particular focus on objects from the worlds of politics and everyday culture.

Both the Pio-Christian Museum and the Gregoriano Profano Museum result from the intensive excavations conducted during the first half of the nineteenth century. Almost all the exhibits are finds from Rome or Roman sites located within the territory of the Vatican State. They can be classified into five thematic groups, which are reflected in their presentation: The first group mainly comprises sculptures and reliefs of Greek origin from the fifth and fourth centuries BC, most of which have survived in a fragmentary state. The second consists of copies and imitations of Greek originals from the Roman Empire (first to third centuries AD). Particularly noteworthy is the Athena-Marsyas group of sculptures, copies of originals by the Greek sculptor Myron (active 480-440 BC). The third section comprises Roman sculptures from the first and early second centuries AD, representing originals by Roman sculptors. These works are mainly busts and altars or altar fragments, including the Altar of the Vicomagistri (ca. 30–40 AD), perhaps the best known among them. The display of objects in this section is chronological, allowing both Roman history and the history of art to be followed literally step by step. The fourth part is the gallery of sarcophagi, organized thematically, while the final section presents Roman sculptures of the second and third centuries AD. Jewish inscription stones, including 137 objects in Greek and Latin from the Monteverde Catacomb, dating from the first to the third centuries AD, are in a section of their own.

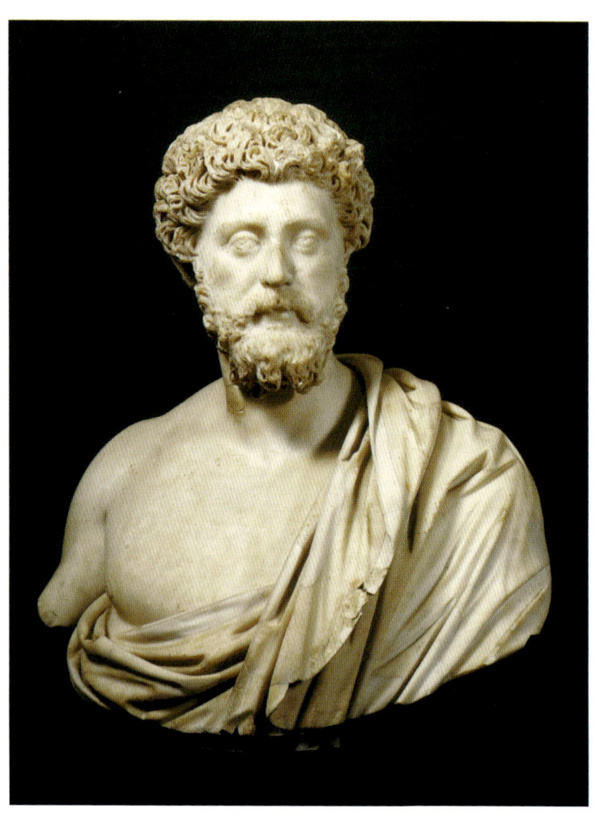

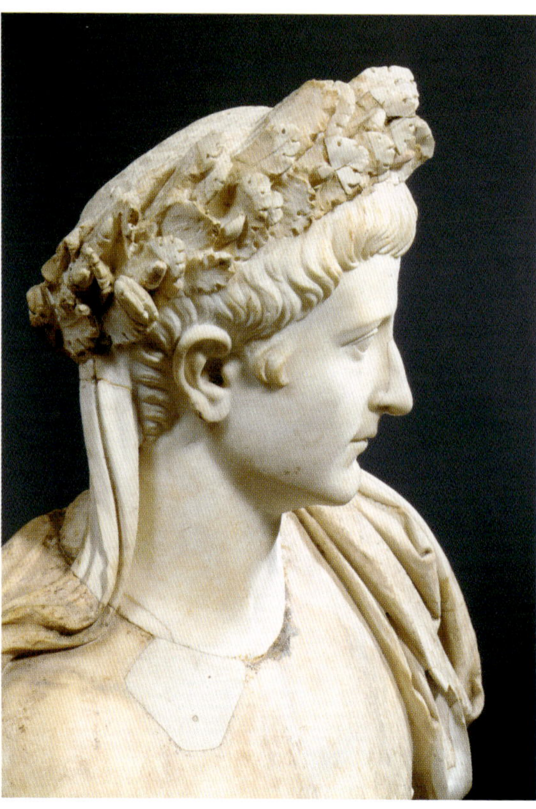

Roman artist, active ca. 170 AD
***Bust of Marcus Aurelius*, ca. 170 AD**
Height: 31 cm; Marble
Gregoriano Profano Museum

Roman artist, active mid-1st century
***Sitting Statue with Head of Tiberius*, mid-1st century**
Height: 20 cm; Marble
Gregoriano Profano Museum

Roman artist, active 14–37 AD
***Tiberius Claudius Drusus*, 14–37 AD**
Height: 140 cm; Marble
Gregoriano Profano Museum

Roman artist, copy of a Greek original, 2nd century
***Minerva and Marsyas*, 2nd century**
Height: 171 cm; Marble
Gregoriano Profano Museum

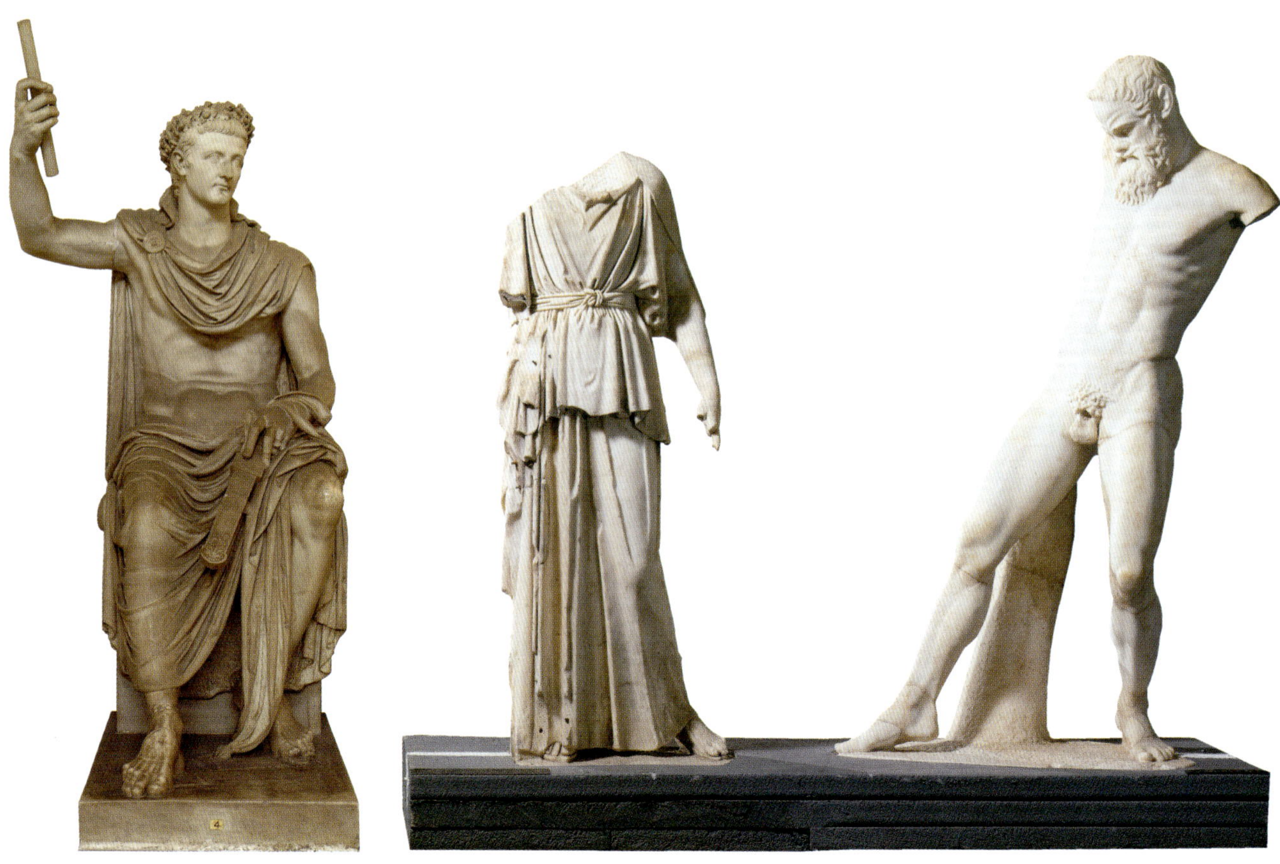

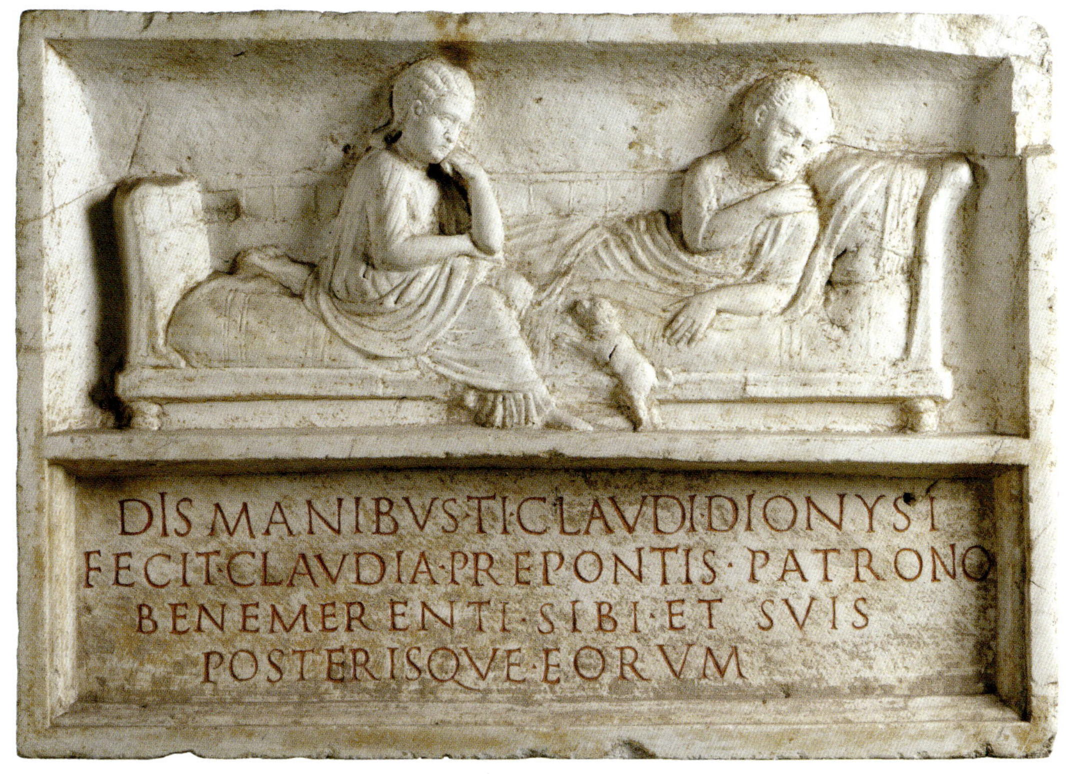

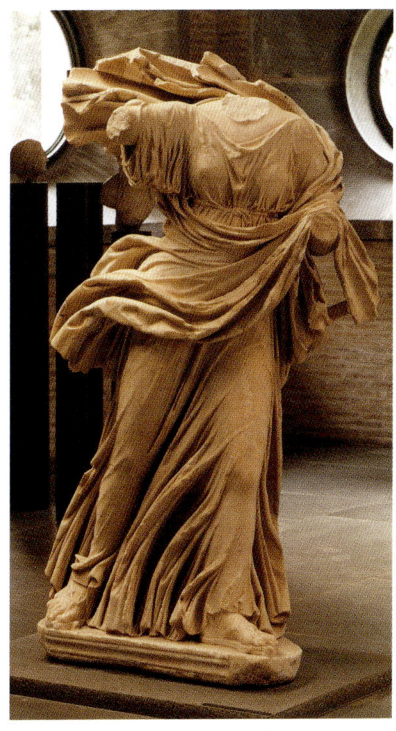

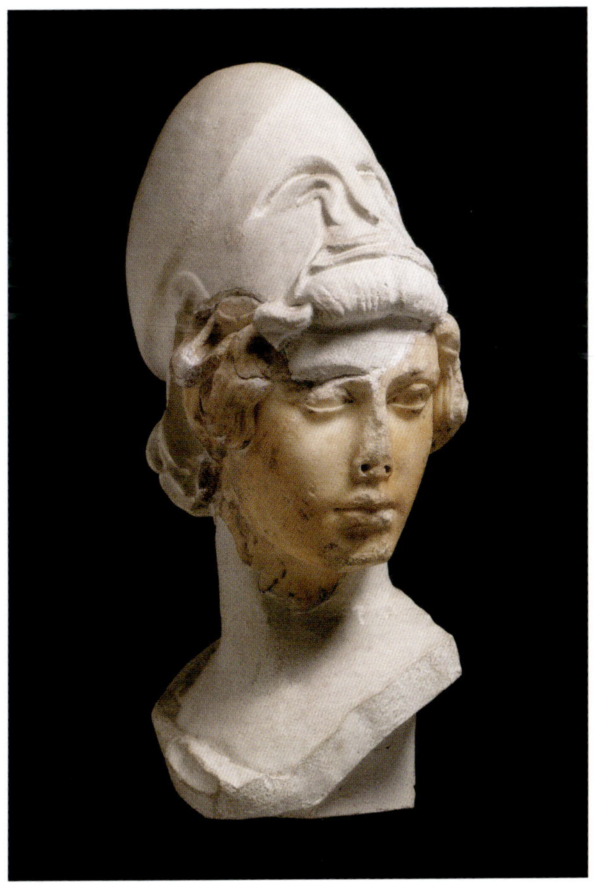

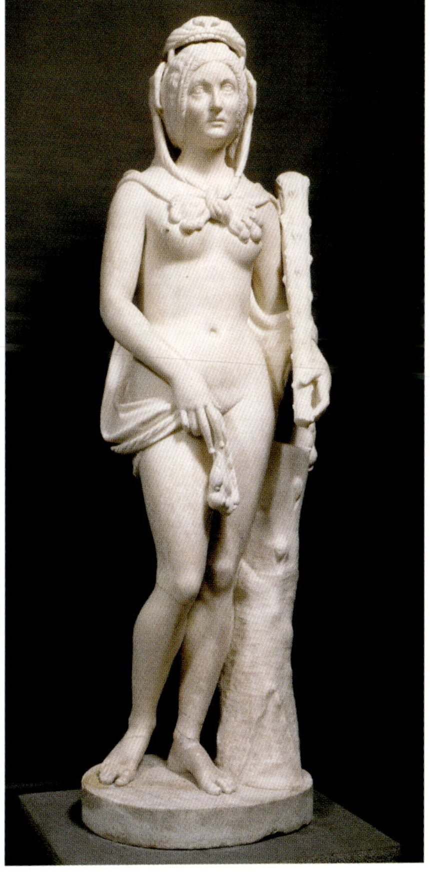

Roman artist, active 1st century
***Funeral Relief of Claudius Dionisius*, 1st century**
62 x 89 cm; Marble
Gregoriano Profano Museum

Roman copy of a Greek original
***Chiaramonti Niobid*, 3rd century BC**
Height: 176 cm; Marble
Gregoriano Profano Museum

Greek artist, 2nd century BC
***Head of Athena*, 2nd century BC**
Height: 17 cm; Marble
Gregoriano Profano Museum

Roman artist, 2nd century
***Statue of Omphale*, 2nd century**
Height: 174 cm; Marble
Gregoriano Profano Museum

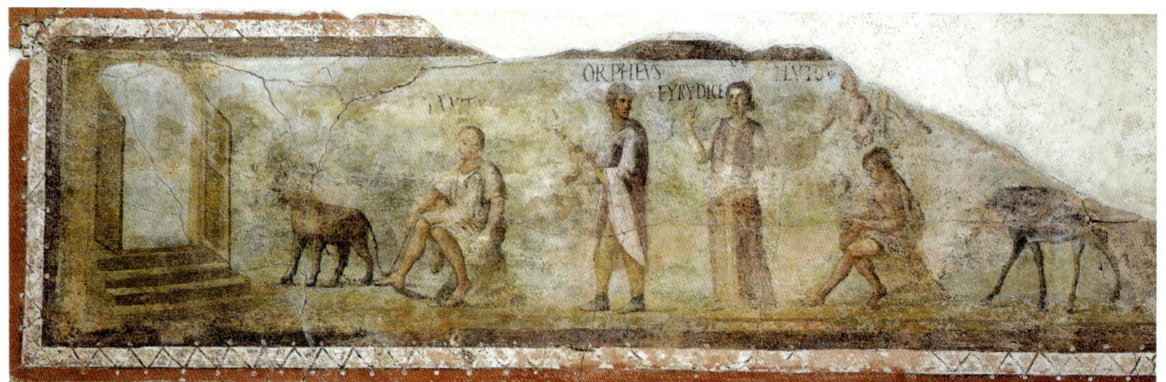

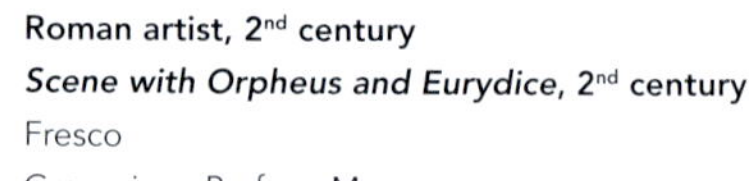

Roman artist, 2nd century
***Scene with Orpheus and Eurydice*, 2nd century**
Fresco
Gregoriano Profano Museum

Heracleitus (Roman artist), 2nd century
***Theatre Mask*, 2nd century**
Colored stone, glass
Gregoriano Profano Museum

Heracleitus (Roman artist), 2nd century
***Unswept Floor*, 2nd century**
Colored stone, glass
Gregoriano Profano Museum

Roman artist, 2nd century
***Scene from a Tragedy*, 2nd century**
Fresco
Gregoriano Profano Museum

Roman artist, 3rd century
***Mosaic Floor*, 3rd century**
Colored stone, glass
Gregoriano Profano Museum

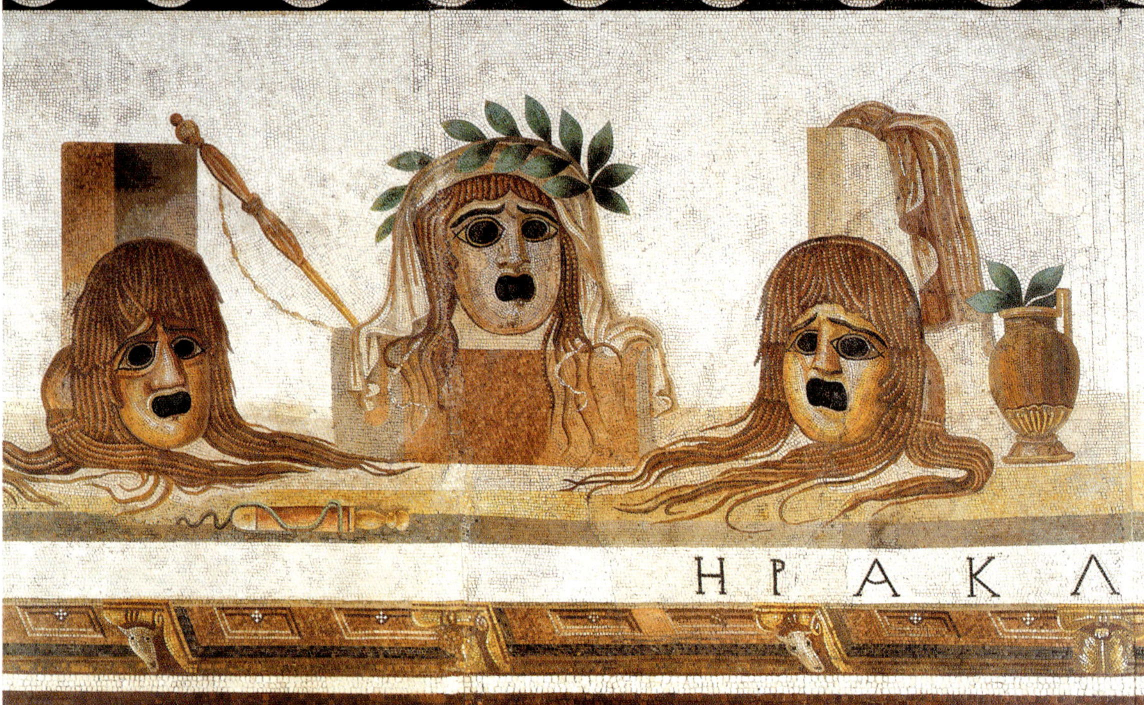

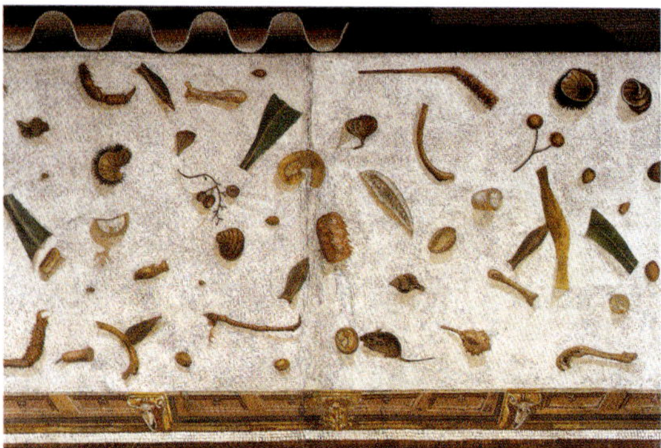

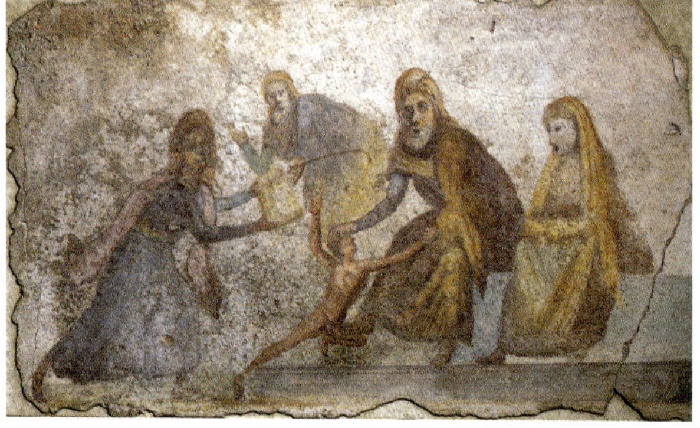

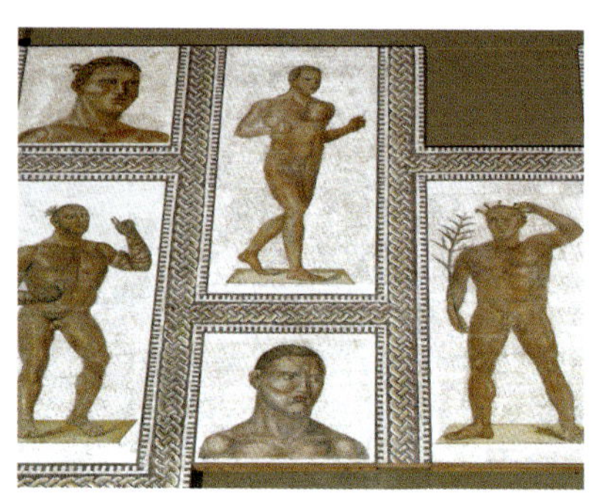

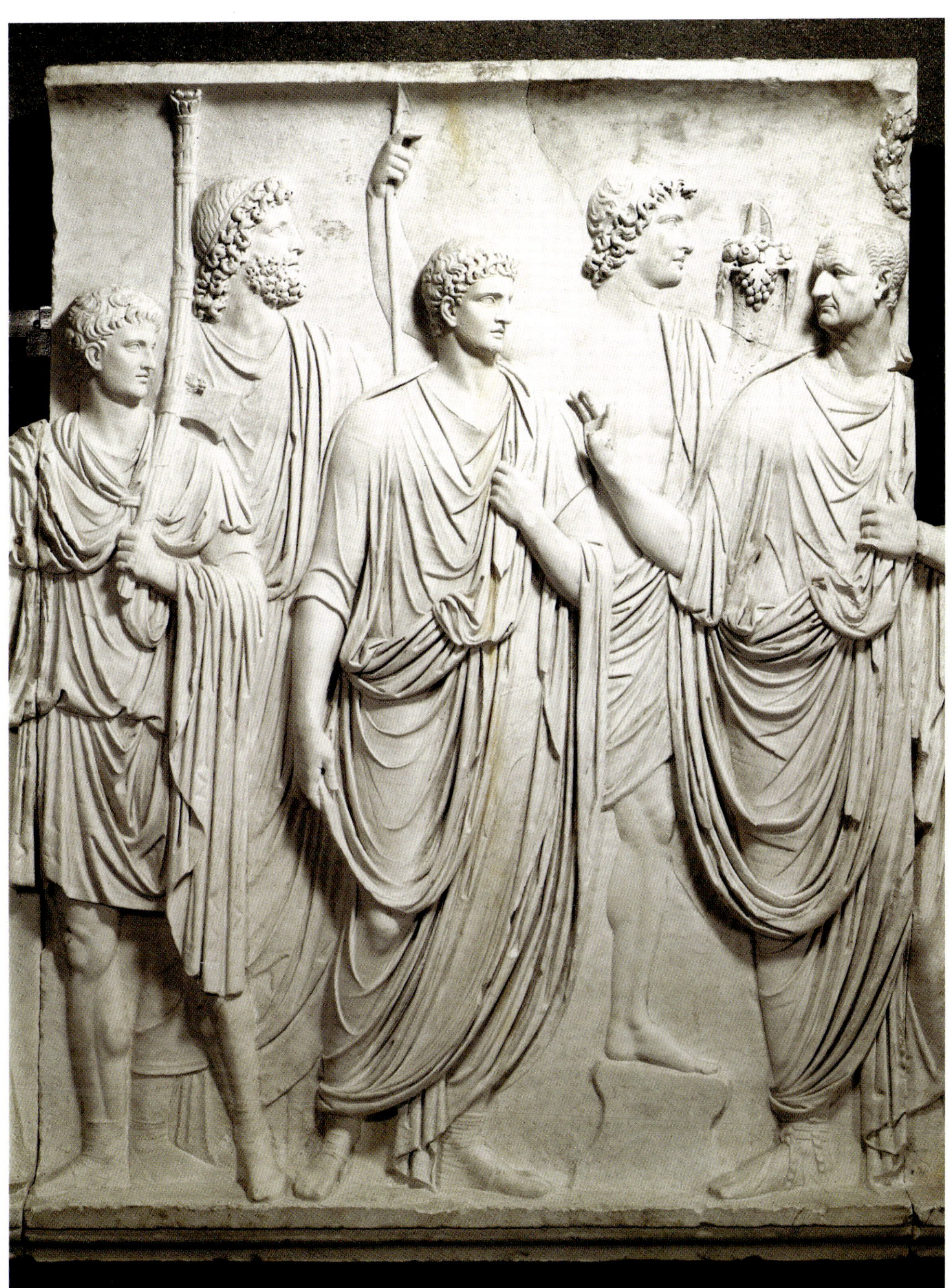

Roman artist

Relief from the Cancelleria: The Adventus of Emperor Vespasian

In ancient Rome, the adventus, or entry of a ruler into a city, was always a special event. This work, so-called Relief B of the Cancelleria Reliefs, depicts the return of Vespasian (9–79 AD, emperor from 69 AD) to Rome from Palestine after the Jewish War (66–70 AD), which also marked his official proclamation as emperor. Ringed by soldiers, Vespasian is shown graciously saluting members of the Senate, distinctive in their long togas. Behind Vespasian a supporter holds aloft a cornucopia filled with fruit, a symbol of fertility and prosperity. The Cancelleria Reliefs (A and B) are named after the Palazzo della Cancelleria in Rome, underneath which they were discovered in 1930. In view of the prominent depiction of Emperor Domitian (51–96 AD, emperor from 81 AD), the son of Vespasian, particularly on Relief A, it is believed that the two reliefs were commissioned by the later emperor in order to celebrate the achievements of the Flavian dynasty in the service of the empire. The works are examples of the blossoming of the Roman historical relief during the first and second centuries AD, and an enduring Augustan influence is clearly discernible in their classical-monumental style.

Roman artist, active late 1st century
Relief from the Cancelleria: The Adventus of Emperor Vespasian,
ca. 93–95 AD
Height: 206 cm; Marble
Gregoriano Profano Museum

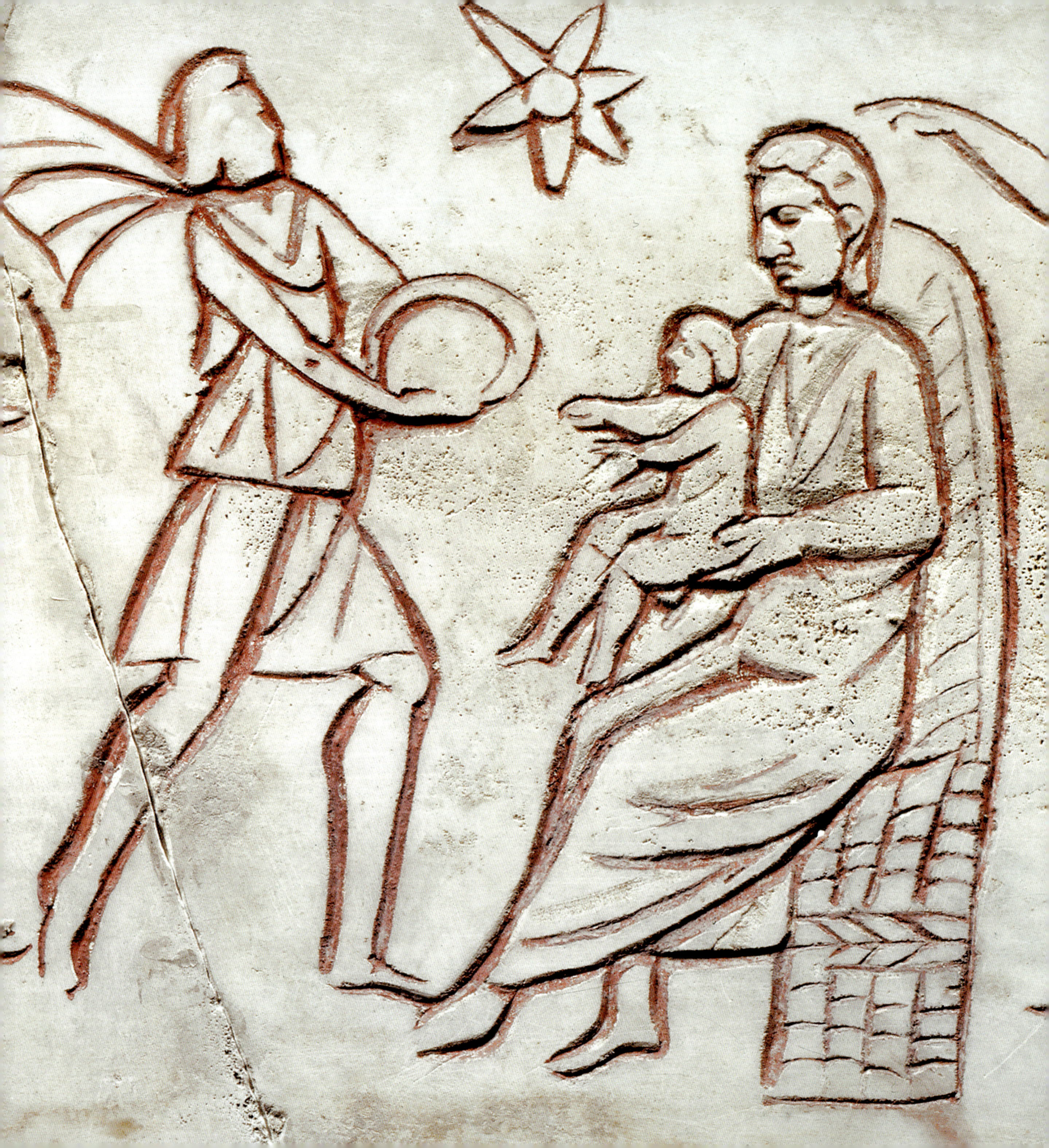

PIO CHRISTIAN MUSEUM

The Pio Christian Museum is one of the papal museums that were originally housed in the Lateran Palace. By installing a museum in the Lateran, its founder Pius IX (1792–1878, reigned from 1846) was following the lead of his predecessor Gregory XVI (1765–1846, reigned from 1831), who had founded the Gregoriano Profano Museum. The Pio Christian Museum opened in 1854, two years after the Commission of Sacred Archaeology was established with the chief purpose of excavating and preserving the early Christian catacombs in and around Rome. Most of the artworks in the Pio Christian Museum can be traced back to these campaigns of excavation. The majority were objects considered too conservationally at risk to remain at their respective sites. In 1963, John XXIII (1881–1963, reigned from 1958) decided to move the museum to the Vatican, where it reopened in 1970 in the new building designed by Studio Passarelli.

The items in the Pio Christian Museum can be divided into two main groups: The first comprises architectural fragments, mosaics, and sculptures dating to the first few centuries after the birth of Christ, including numerous sarcophagi. The second consists of epigraphical memorials, above all inscription plaques, classified by age and theme. This historically important section of the collection is only accessible by appointment to specialists.

Some of the museum's most prominent items were discovered during earlier excavations carried out under the direction of the popes from the sixteenth century onwards. Some of the early Christian finds, including the sculpture known as the Good Shepherd and sarcophagi from the necropolises beneath and around St. Peter's, had already been incorporated by Benedict XIV (1675–1758, reigned from 1740) into the Museo Sacro that he opened in 1756. They were later transferred to the Pio Christian Museum, where they bear witness to the golden age of late antique art during the early years of Christianity.

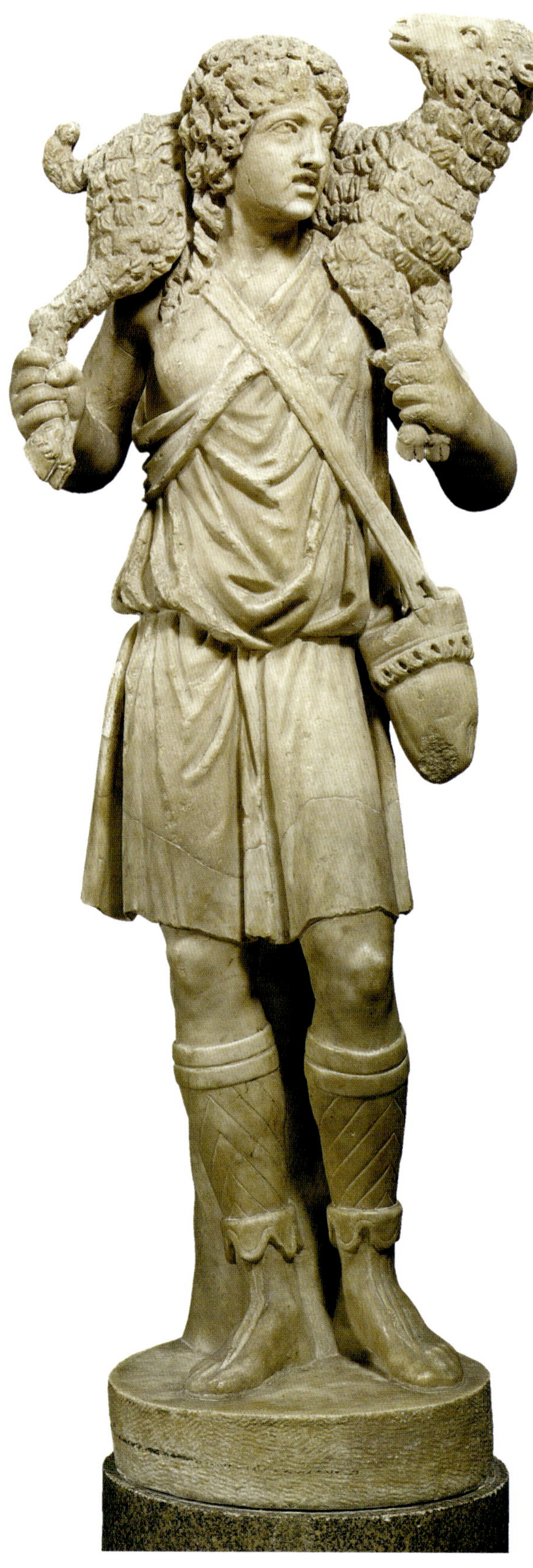

Early Christian artist

The Good Shepherd

This statue, heavily repaired and restored in the eighteenth century, represents a young shepherd carrying a sheep on his shoulders. In 1757 it was put on display at the entrance to what was then the Museo Sacro before being moved to the Lateran Palace after the founding of the Pio Christian Museum. The youth wears the typical dress of a shepherd, consisting of a short tunic-like garment (exomis) belted at the hips, with his knees and right shoulder left bare. A sheepskin pouch, slung diagonally over his right shoulder on a long strap, hangs against his left side. His long, thick curly hair falls freely onto his shoulders, terminating in corkscrew curls. In contrast to this stylized mass of hair, the extremely lifelike face, which gives the impression that the shepherd boy is about to speak, appears smooth and soft. The sculpture's realism is reinforced by the natural-looking folds of the tunic. The provenance and original purpose and location of this masterfully executed sculpture are unclear. Evidently the sculptor used an even older sculpture of a shepherd as the model for his work, which was reinterpreted within the Christian context as Christ in the guise of the "good shepherd" (John 10:11).

Early Christian artist, late 3rd century
***The Good Shepherd*, late 3rd century**
Height: 100 cm; Marble
Pio Christian Museum

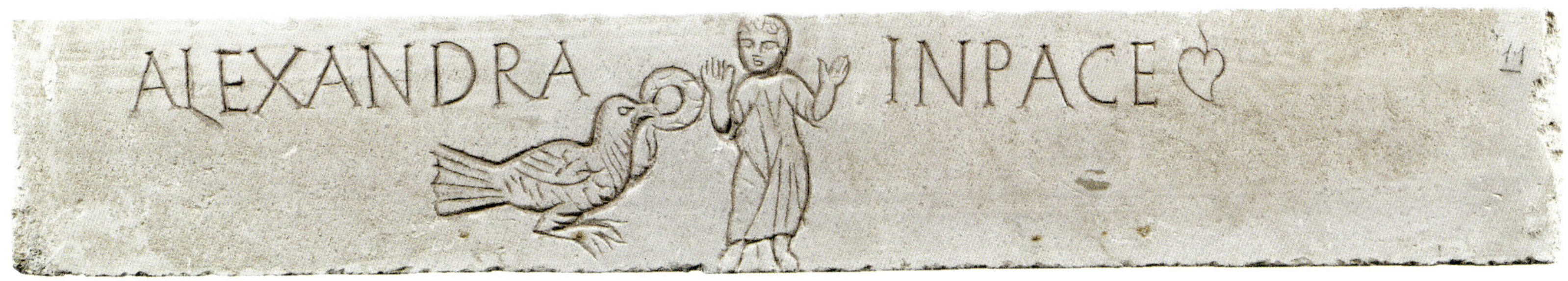

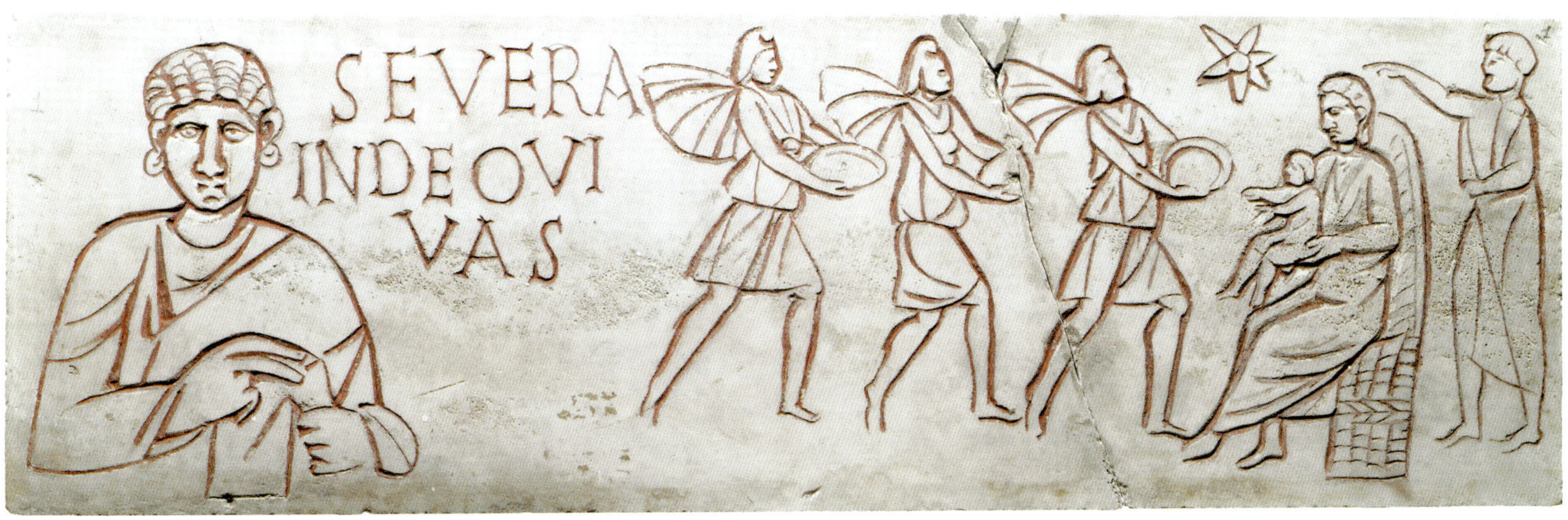

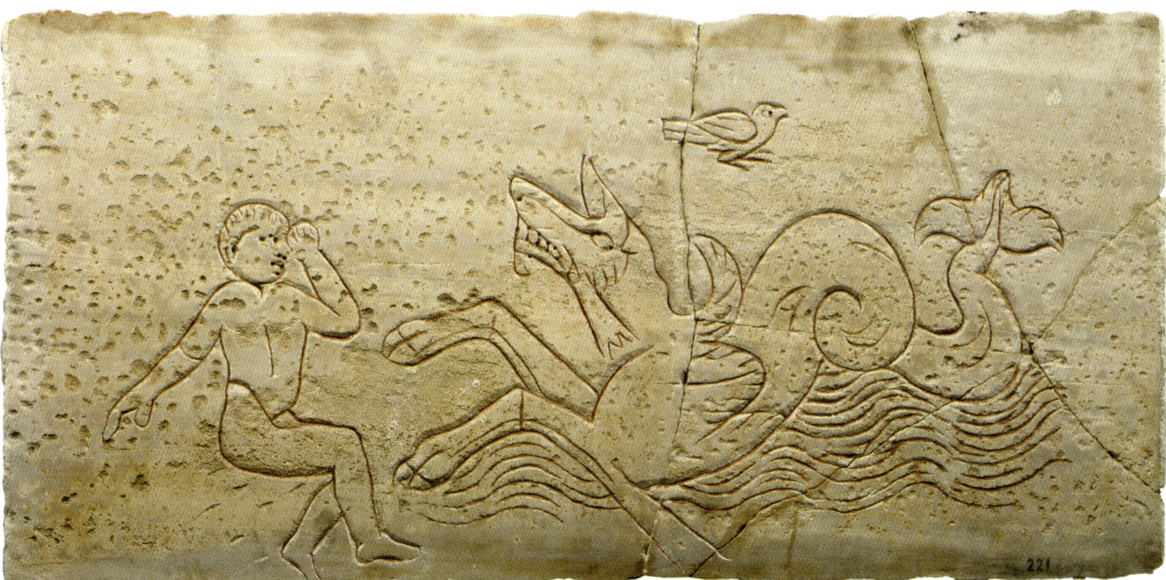

Early Christian artist, 4th century
***Gravestone of Alexandra with Orante*, 4th century**
32 x 102 x 25 cm; Marble
Pio Christian Museum

Early Christian artist, early 4th century
***Gravestone of Severa Adoration of the Magi*, early 4th century**
32 x 102 cm; Marble
Pio Christian Museum

Early Christian artist, ca. 300 AD
***Gravestone Depicting Jonah and the Whale*, ca. 300AD**
43 x 90 cm; Marble
Pio Cristiano Museum

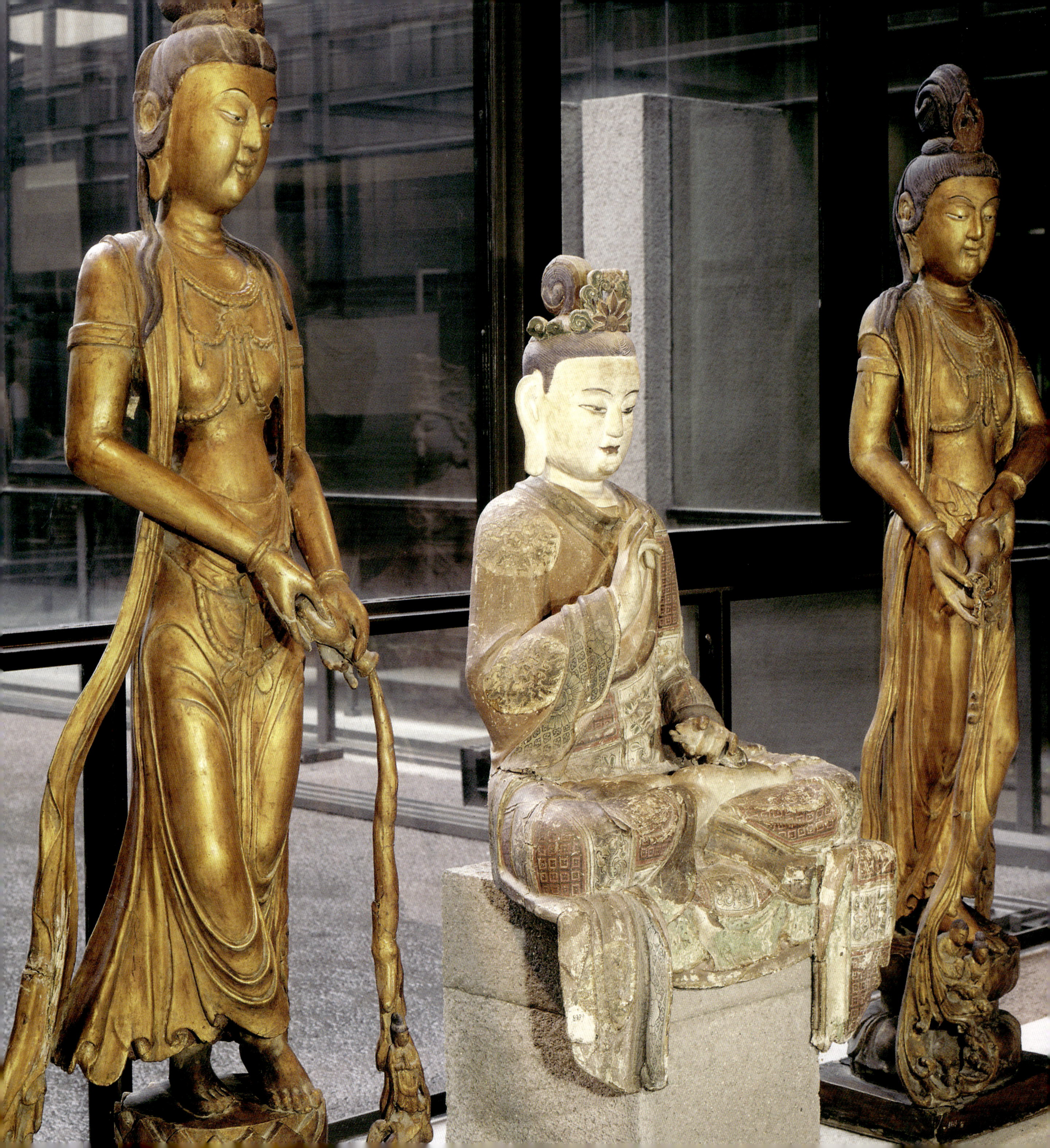

ETHNOLOGICAL MUSEUM

To the surprise of many visitors, the Vatican also has extensive holdings of non-European, and in many cases non-Christian, artwork. Since 1926/1927 this collection has been housed in the Pontificio Museo Entological Museum, founded by Pope Pius XI (1857–1939, reigned from 1922) with the intention of perpetuating the Missionary Exhibition (Esposizione Missionaria) initiated by him in 1925. The Ethnological Museum can be seen as the counterpart of the secular colonial museums being established by many European nations at the end of the nineteenth century and beginning of the twentieth. Notwithstanding the interest in foreign cultures, the museum's view of the rest of the world is from a distinctly Western Christian perspective. Today, more so than at the time of its inauguration, the Museo Missionario Etnologico has to face the challenge of increasing globalization.

The African, Asian, and South American works in the museum testify to the sophistication of indigenous cultures before and after the beginning of colonization. Some objects entered the Vatican collections during the course of the first major missionary campaigns of the popes under the aegis of the Congregation for the Evangelization of Peoples (Propaganda Fide) as early as the late seventeenth century. They include items from the collection of Cardinal Stefano Borgias (1731–1804), the prefect of Propaganda Fide. Most of the artifacts, however, were collected in the nineteenth and twentieth centuries.

The Entological Museum was initially housed in the Lateran Palace. In 1973 it became the last of the Lateran museums to be transferred to the Vatican. During the reinstallation, an attempt was made to take into account the resolution of the Second Vatican Council (1962–1965) regarding missionary work in the Third World, which called for greater respect for local cultures. As a result, objects unconnected to Christianity were also presented. Today the museum comprises well over sixty-one thousand items, of which some ten thousand are from Africa, ten thousand from the Americas, twenty thousand from Asia, and six thousand from Oceania, as well as over fifteen thousand prehistoric artifacts. Only a small portion of the holdings is permanently on display.

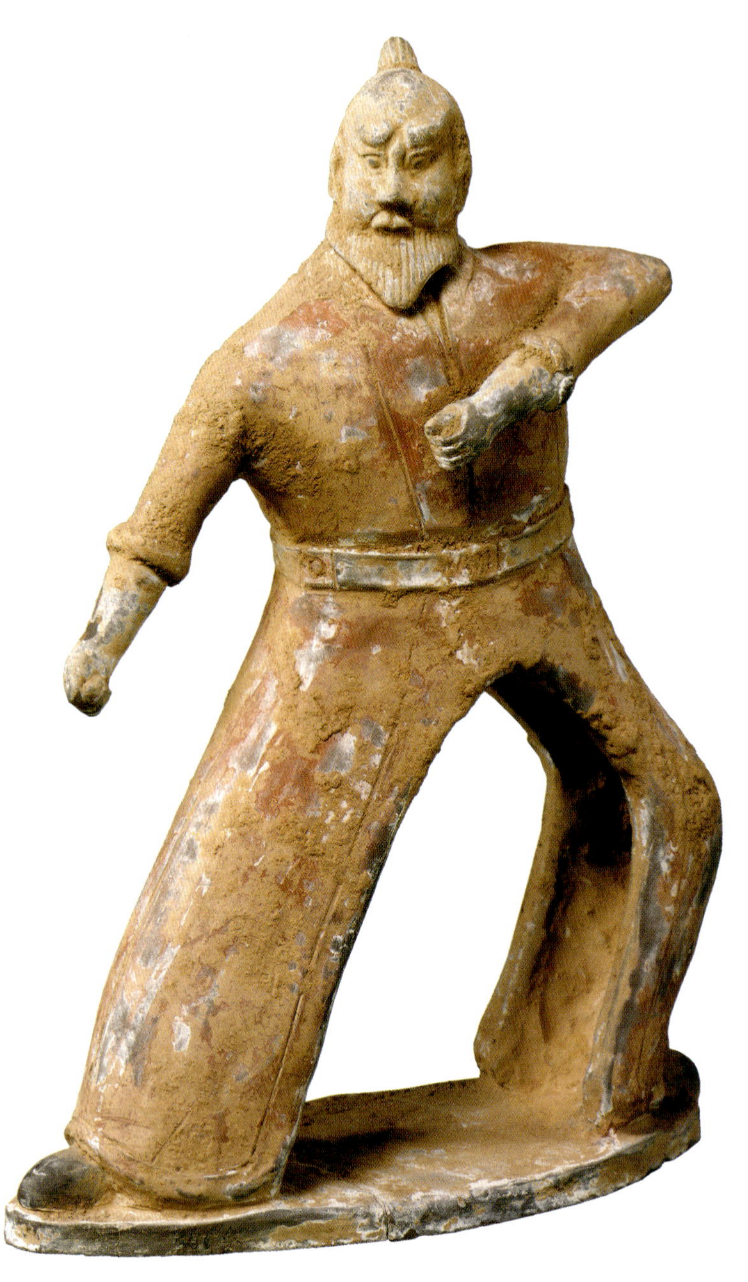

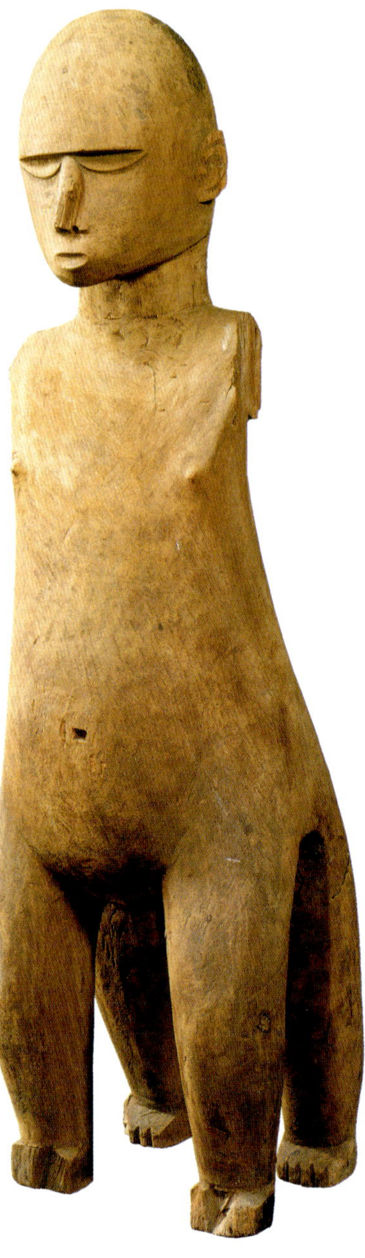

Qin Dynasty, 221–206 BC
***Guardian*, 221–206 BC**
Polychrome terracotta
Ethnological Museum

Gambier Islands, Polynesia, before 1835
***The God Tu*, before 1835**
113 x 28 cm; Wood
Ethnological Museum

Ming Dynasty, 1368–1644
***Buddha Vairochana*, 1368–1644**
Wood
Ethnological Museum

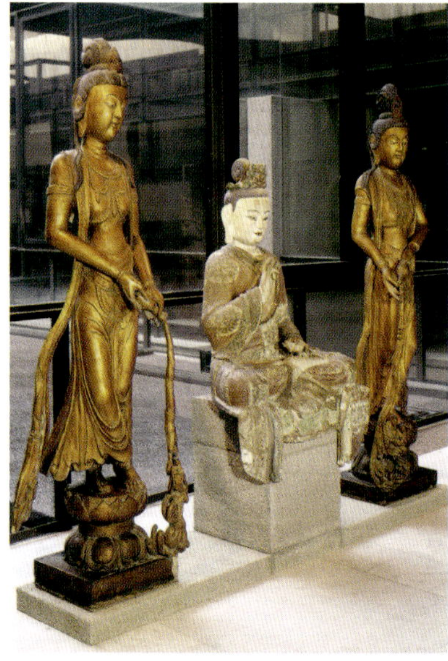

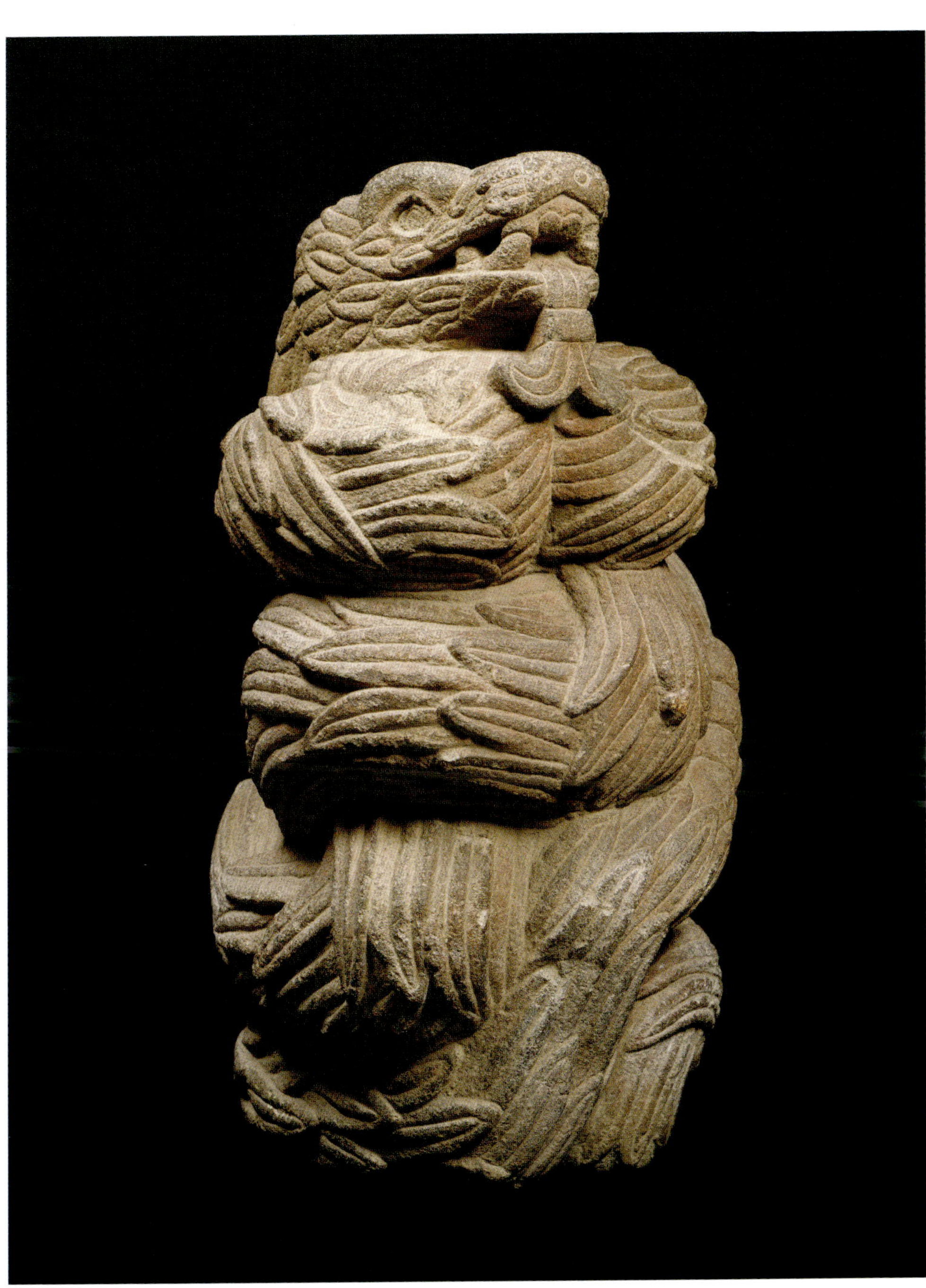

Aztec artist

Quetzalcoatl

This sculpture, which from a distance looks like woven stone, represents Quetzalcoatl, the "plumed serpent," shown in an upright position. The skin of the serpent, whose squat form resembles that of an otter or large guinea pig, is completely covered with feathers. They are arranged in broad, overlapping bands—horizontally, vertically, and to some extent diagonally—around its body. Its head is covered with shorter feathers, lending the mythical beast an eagle-like appearance. The serpent has opened its mouth, and its forked tongue, whose end bears the shape of a lily, protrudes downward, giving the figure a threatening appearance typical of many Aztec deities. Quetzalcoatl was the god of the wind, as evidenced by its thick coat of feathers, and its speed was equated with that of a snake. Stylistically the figure, with its expressive physiognomy, can be attributed to the Classical period of Aztec art. The circumstances of the sculpture's discovery and function are unknown. It entered the Vatican with the Museo Borgiano di Propaganda Fide.

Aztec artist, active 15th century
***Quetzalcoatl*, 15th century**
51 x 26 x 26 cm; Stone
Ethnological Museum

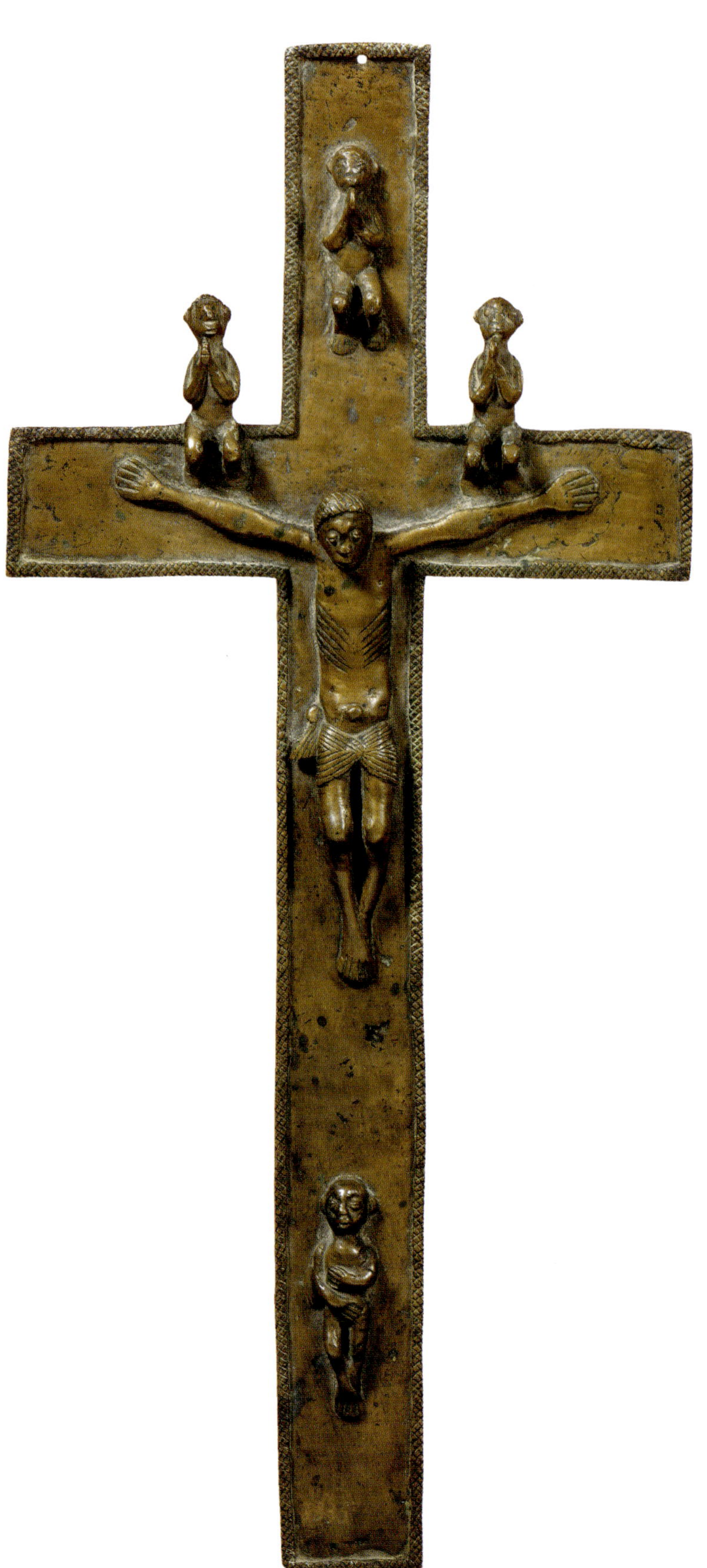

Congolese artist

Crucifix

The first sustained contact between Europeans and the people of the Congo occurred in the late fifteenth century, when the Portuguese established bases on the Congolese coast during the course of their African expeditions. The Congo is one of the African regions in which Christianity gained an early foothold. Although at first liturgical objects were mainly imported from Europe, during the sixteenth century they were increasingly made locally, with the craftsmen taking their cues from works produced by their European contemporaries, as this crucifix demonstrates. This bronze cross, an extremely rare example of its type, depicts Christ in the final moments of his life. He is naked but for a loincloth and has lowered his pain-filled gaze. On the arms of the cross grieving figures are shown worshipping or praying for the Savior. Conspicuous here is the strong "Africanization" of Christ, who, like the worshippers, clearly bears central-African facial features.

Congolese artist, active 17th century
***Crucifix*, 17th century**
40 x 19 cm; Bronze
Ethnological Museum

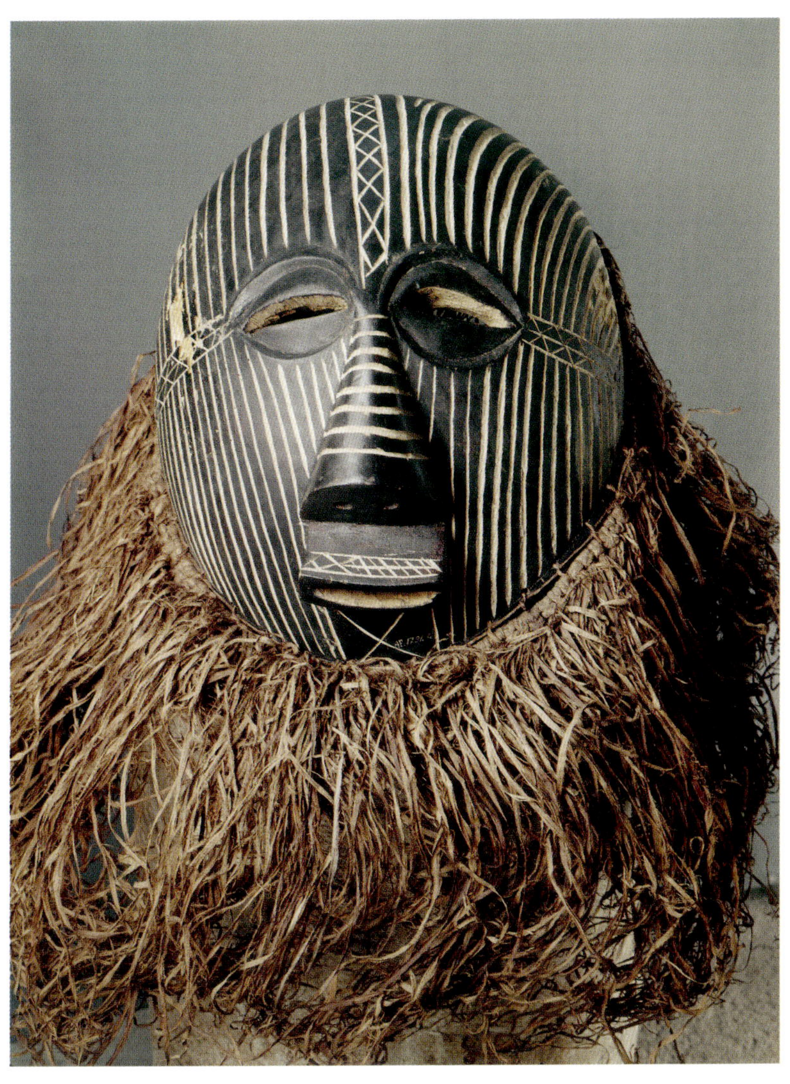

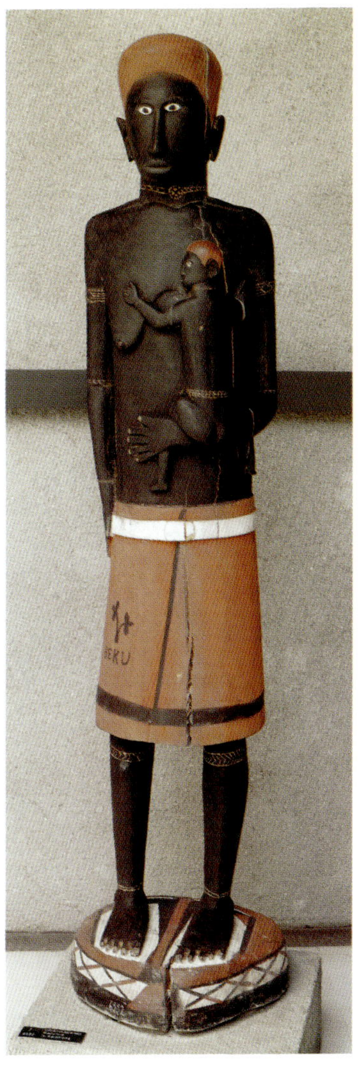

African artist, undated
***Mask*, undated**
Carved wood
Ethnological Museum

Solomon Islands, undated
***Madonna and Child*, undated**
Carved wood
Ethnological Museum

Papua New Guinea, early 19th century
***Tymban Hook*, early 19th century**
150 x 23 cm; Carved wood
Ethnological Museum

Papua New Guinea (Kaminimbit village), 18th century
***Wooden Panel Carved with Water Deities*, 18th century**
127 x 35 cm; Carved wood
Ethnological Museum

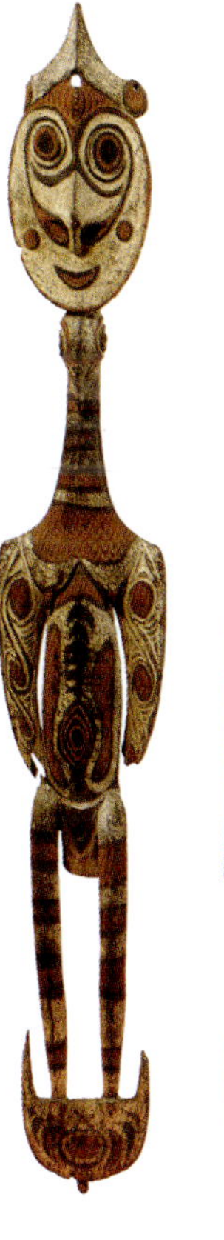

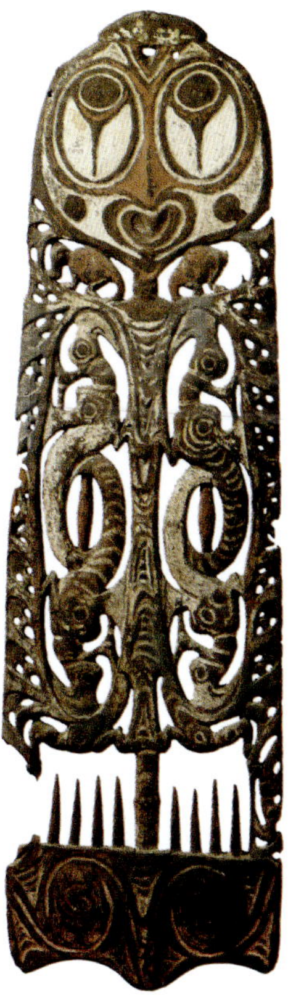

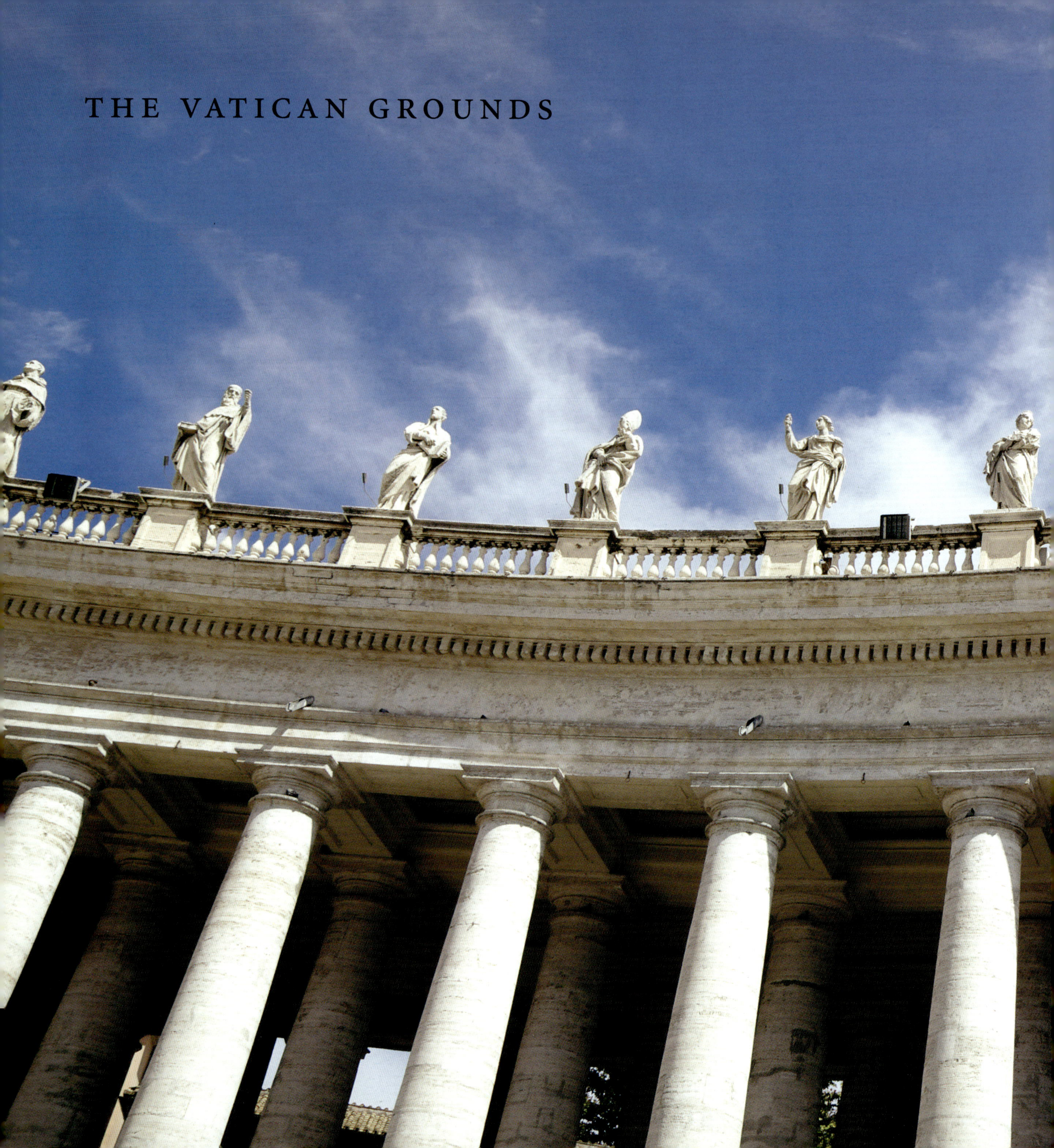

THE VATICAN GROUNDS

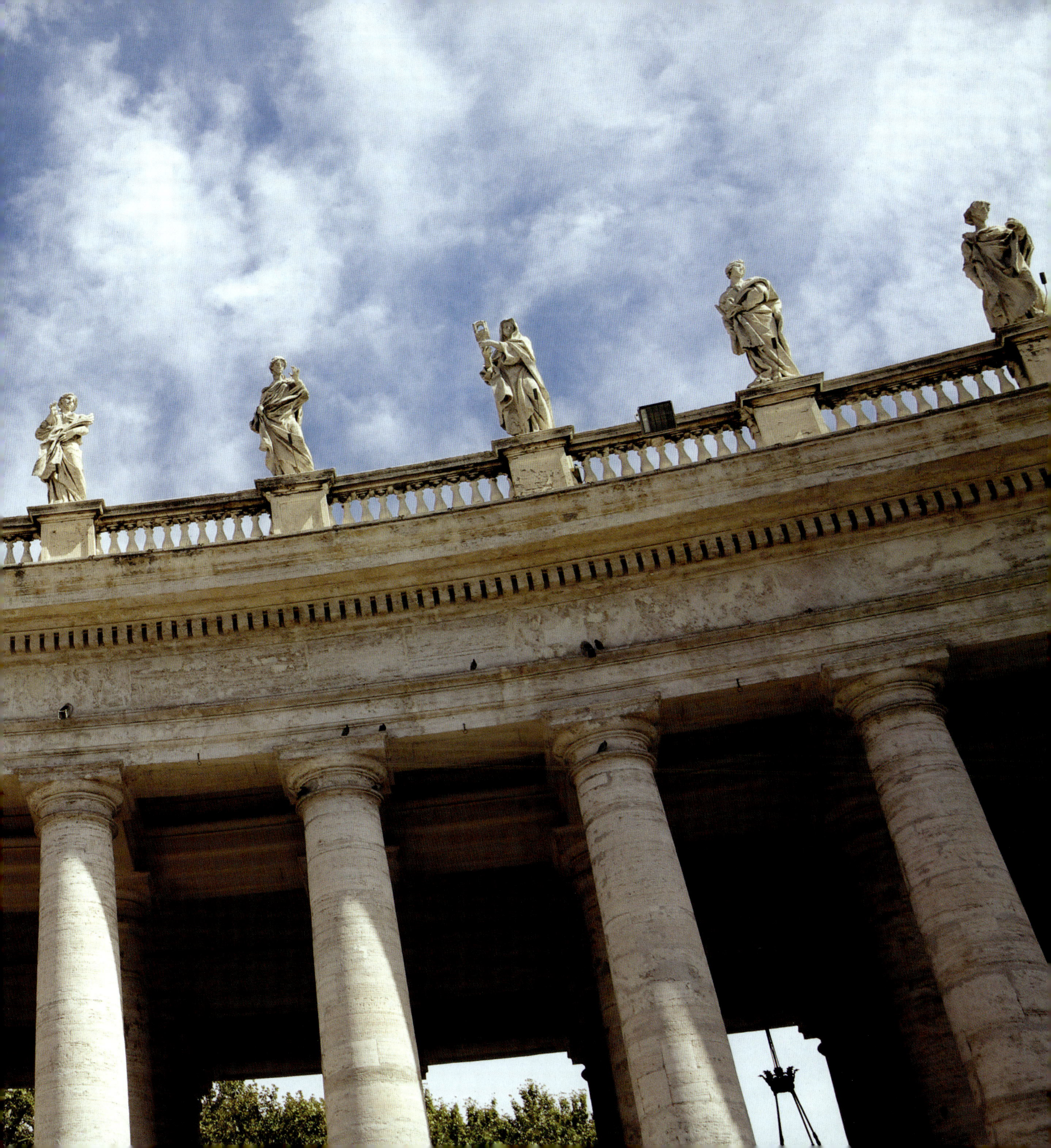

ST. PETER'S BASILICA AND PIAZZA

St. Peter's Basilica, with its magnificent colonnaded piazza, is the center of Catholicism. It is here that the pope celebrates Mass on the most important dates in the Church calendar and from here that he offers his blessing to the faithful gathered on the square below. The basilica is the main church of the Vatican City State, and with a capacity of twenty thousand people, it is the largest and most important of the pontifical basilicas in Rome. With a length of 211.5 meters and a transept width of 187 meters, it has one of the largest floor areas of any church building in the world. The interior is not only large but also extremely imposing. The vault of the 132.5-meter-high structure is supported by some eight hundred columns, and the basilica contains a total of forty-five altars and around 450 large statues.

St. Peter's may be one of the oldest churches in Rome, but its current architecture and the piazza in front of it date only to the sixteenth and seventeenth centuries. To allow the vast new church to be constructed, its late antique predecessor, Old St. Peter's, erected under Emperor Constantine the Great (ca. 270/288–337 AD, reigned from 306 AD) and consecrated in 326 AD, had to be pulled down in stages. Vestiges of the old Constantinian basilica—one of the largest places of worship of the Middle Ages, with five aisles, a length of 119 meters and a width of 64 meters—have been preserved beneath the current church. However, despite containing the tomb of St. Peter, Old St. Peter's was not the main papal church in Rome, and neither is the current St. Peter's. Since the time of Constantine, the pontifical cathedral has been the basilica of San Giovanni in Laterano. And throughout the entire Middle Ages, the neighboring Lateran Palace was the seat of the popes, for whom the Vatican was merely a secondary residence. Not until the end of the Great Schism, following the Council of Constance (1414–1418), and most importantly under the pontificate of Nicholas V (1397–1455, reigned from 1447), was the Vatican expanded and transformed into the principal seat of the popes.

In 1506, Pope Julius II (1443–1513, reigned from 1503) made the decision to completely rebuild St. Peter's Basilica. The venerable Constantinian basilica was allegedly found to be unsafe but it is thought that the art-loving but also ambitious and acclaim-seeking pope wanted a more modern and imposing building. Julius II laid the foundation stone for the new St. Peter's on April 18, 1506. However, it would be 120 years before the new church was completed. It was finally consecrated by Pope Urban VIII (1568–1644, reigned from 1623) on November 18, 1626. Because the program of church services needed to be maintained during construction, Old St. Peter's was demolished step-by-step as building work progressed, with parts of it surviving into the seventeenth century. Several frescoes and other works of art dating from the Renaissance and Baroque periods now conserved in the Vatican Palace and Vatican Museums convey a vivid impression of what Old St. Peter's looked like.

Construction and demolition went hand in hand—not only

as the old church was pulled down to make room for the new but also as the result of continual modifications to the plans, which necessitated the demolishing and rebuilding of parts of the new structure. The first architect, Donato Bramante (1444–1514), was commissioned to draw up plans for a new basilica by Julius II in 1505/1506. The challenge he faced was to preserve the spirit of the old Constantinian basilica—the burial place of St. Peter and thus closely associated with the origins of the Catholic Church—while at the same time developing a modern concept that would satisfy the Renaissance popes' need for showpiece architecture. Instead of a longitudinal basilica, Bramante designed a centrally planned building in the shape of a Greek cross, surmounted by a dome. During the course of realizing the plans, however, Bramante was confronted by numerous, mainly static, problems because the pillars he designed were unable to support the weight of the enormous cupola. As an alternative, he came up with a new plan based on the Latin cross. By the time the architect died in 1514, however, neither of his two designs had been realized. Modified alternative designs that strove to combine Bramante's two ground plans were submitted by Bramante's assistant and successor Antonio da Sangallo (1448–1546), in conjunction with Baldassare Peruzzi (1481–1536), and also by Raphael (1483–1520), who was engaged by Leo X (1475–1521, reigned from 1513), but neither was implemented.

Following Sangallo's death, Pope Paul III (1468–1549, reigned from 1534) appointed Michelangelo Buonarroti (1475–1564) as the new architect. After securing assurances of total freedom, Michelangelo submitted a model in 1547 based on Bramante's concept of a centralized structure with a high cupola over the ground plan of a Greek cross. By the time of Michelangelo's death, construction of the dome area and aisles had progressed to the point where his successor Jacopo Barozzi da Vignola (1507–1573) was able to complete the erection of the dome with a few minor modifications. The final architect to work on the project (from 1607) was Carlo Maderno (ca. 1556–1629), who extended Michelangelo's centrally planned church by adding the current nave, partly, no doubt, in order to provide more space for the numerous processions held in the church and the streams of pilgrims visiting St. Peter's tomb.

It was the Baroque sculptor, painter, and architect Gianlorenzo Bernini (1598–1680), however, who exerted the decisive influence over the almost overpowering impression created by the interior of the basilica, not least through his inlaid marble and sculptural decoration. Not only were he and his workshop responsible for the central baldachino, numerous popes' tombs, the Cathedra Petri, and the monumental sculptures on the crossing piers, but in 1656–1667 Bernini completed his largest work with the design of the piazza in front of St. Peter's. With its mighty colonnades crowned by 140 statues of saints, Piazza San Pietro is rightly considered one of the most beautiful public squares in the world.

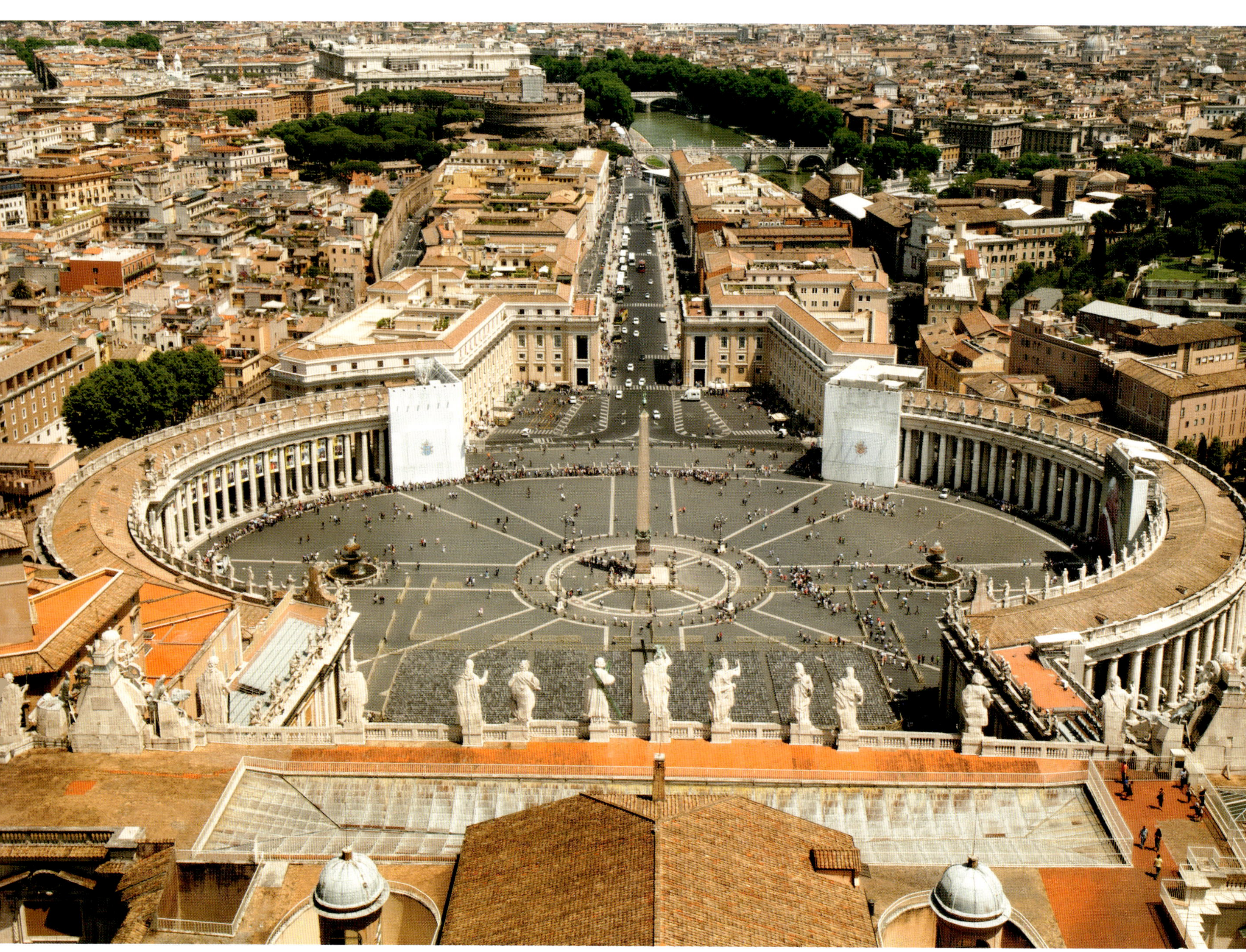

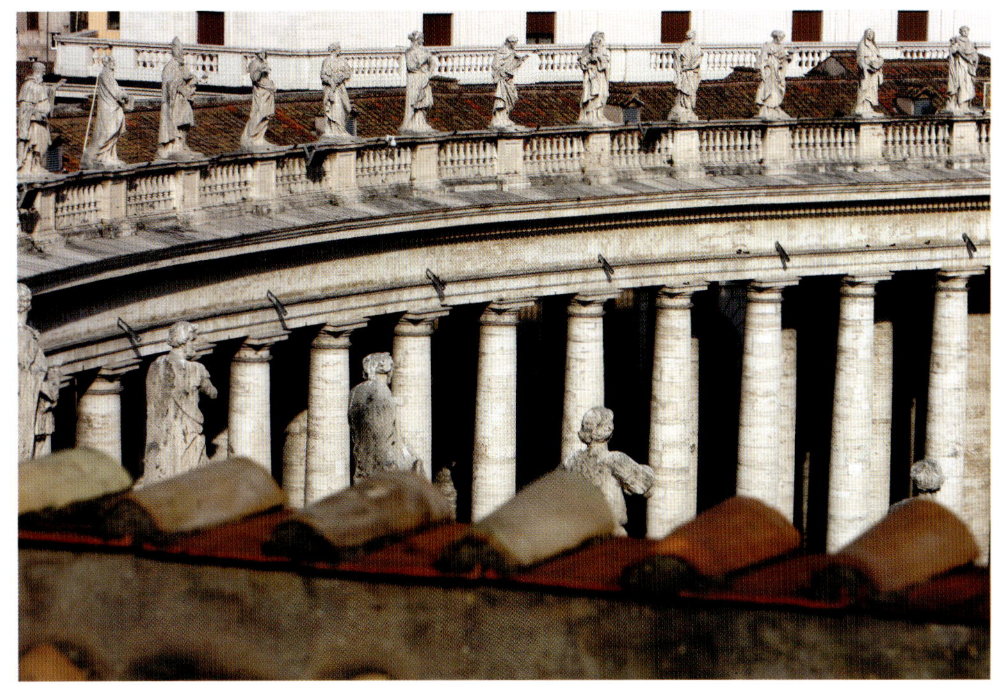

Gian Lorenzo Bernini and Workshop

St. Peter's Square with Colonnades

In 1656, Pope Alexander VII (1599–1667, reigned from 1655) commissioned Bernini to design St. Peter's Square, thereby presenting the sculptor and architect with perhaps the biggest challenge of his career. The work would only be completed under Clement X (1590–1676, reigned from 1670). Prior to Bernini's intervention, St. Peter's Square was an imposing empty space with an obelisk at its center. Bernini transformed it into an enclosed piazza whose bordering colonnades embrace the space like arms while at the same time creating a link with St. Peter's Basilica. The tension between closed and open form is also a feature of the monumental colonnaded walkways around the edges, comprising 284 Doric columns in four ranks. Bernini and his assistants also created the 140 large statues of saints that line the edges of the colonnade roofs on the inner, piazza side, attending the faithful as they make their way to the basilica like spectators observing a procession.

Gian Lorenzo Bernini and Workshop, 1598–1680
***St. Peter's Square with Colonnades*, 1656–1672**
Width: 240 m; Marble

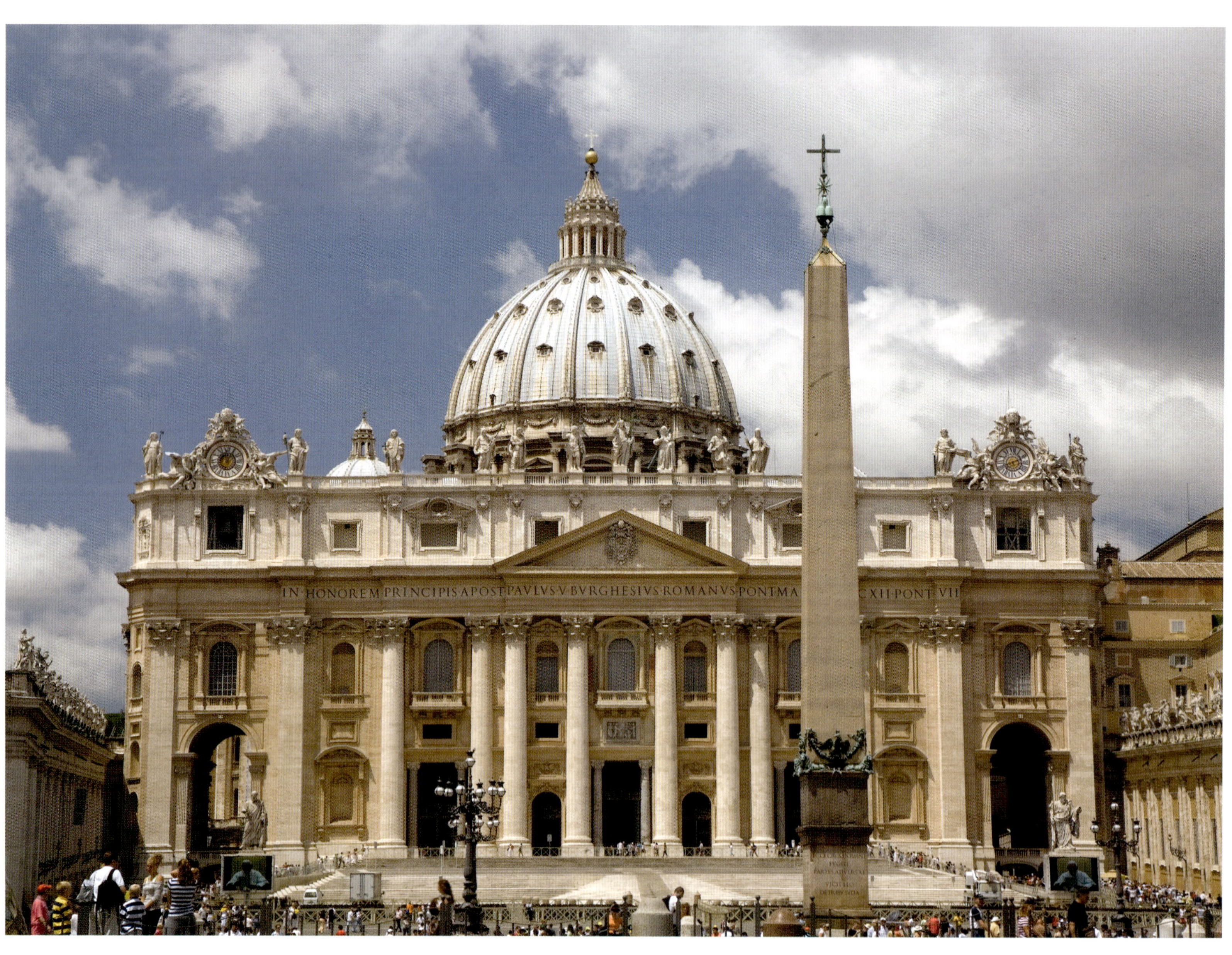
IN HONOREM PRINCIPIS APOST PAVLVS V BVRGHESIVS ROMANVS PONT MA
CXII PONT VII

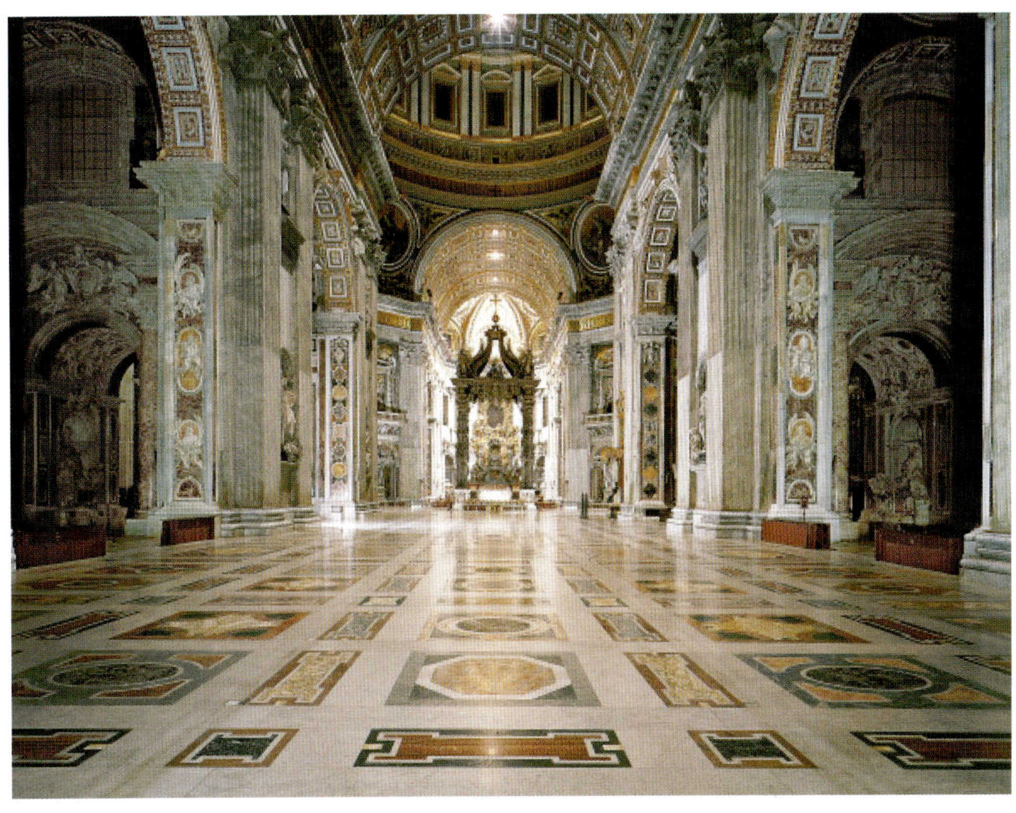

Donato Bramante, Michelangelo Buonarroti, Giacomo Barozzi da Vignola, Giacomo della Porta, Carlo Maderno, and other architects

St. Peter's Basilica

The façades and enormous dome of St. Peter's Basilica rise majestically above the colonnades of the piazza. The current basilica was constructed between 1504 and 1626 and is the work of numerous artists and well-known architects. Throughout the many years it took to build, there were repeated design changes provoked by the popes' changing tastes, financial constraints, and static problems. The decision to demolish Old St. Peter's was taken during the pontificate of Pope Julius II. His architect Donato Bramante envisaged a domed, centrally planned building, which was realized on a significantly more monumental scale by Michelangelo from 1547 onward. At the beginning of the seventeenth century it was decided to extend the centralized structure through the addition of a nave, whose construction was overseen by Carlo Maderno between 1603 and 1626. Maderno was also responsible for the church's columned portico. Urban VIII was finally able to consecrate the papal basilica, which is also the sepulchral church of St. Peter, on November 18, 1626. With a floor area of 15,160 square meters and space for twenty thousand worshippers, St. Peter's Basilica is one of the world's largest sacred buildings.

Donato Bramante (1444–1514), Michelangelo Buonarroti (1475–1564), Giacomo Barozzi da Vignola (1507–1573), Giacomo della Porta (ca. 1532–1602), Carlo Maderno (ca. 1556–1629), and other architects
***St. Peter's Basilica*, 1504–1626**
Length: 211.5 m, width: 138 m, height: 132.5 m

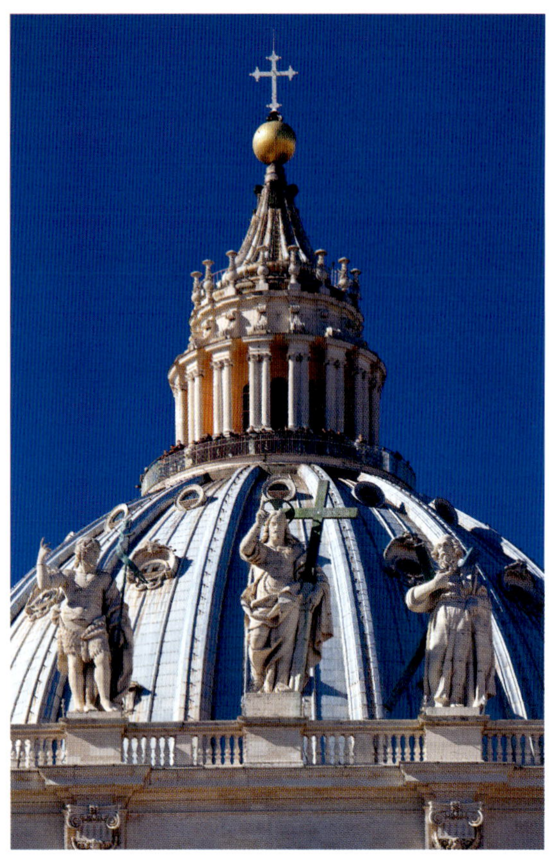

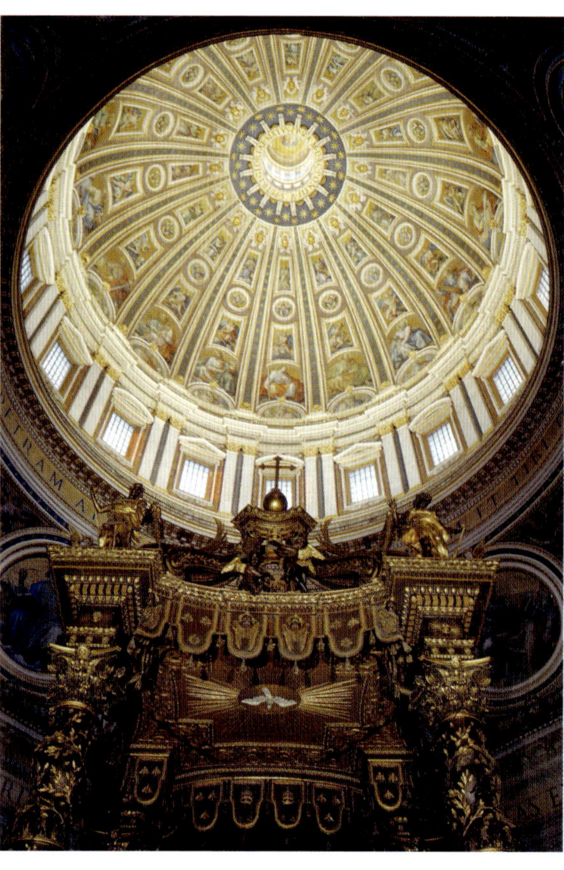

Donato Bramante (1444–1514), Michelangelo Buonarroti (1475–1564), Giacomo Barozzi da Vignola (1507–1573), Giacomo della Porta (ca. 1532–1602), Carlo Maderno (ca. 1556–1629), and other architects
Dome of St. Peter's Basilica
Height: 136.57 m; internal diameter: 41.47 m

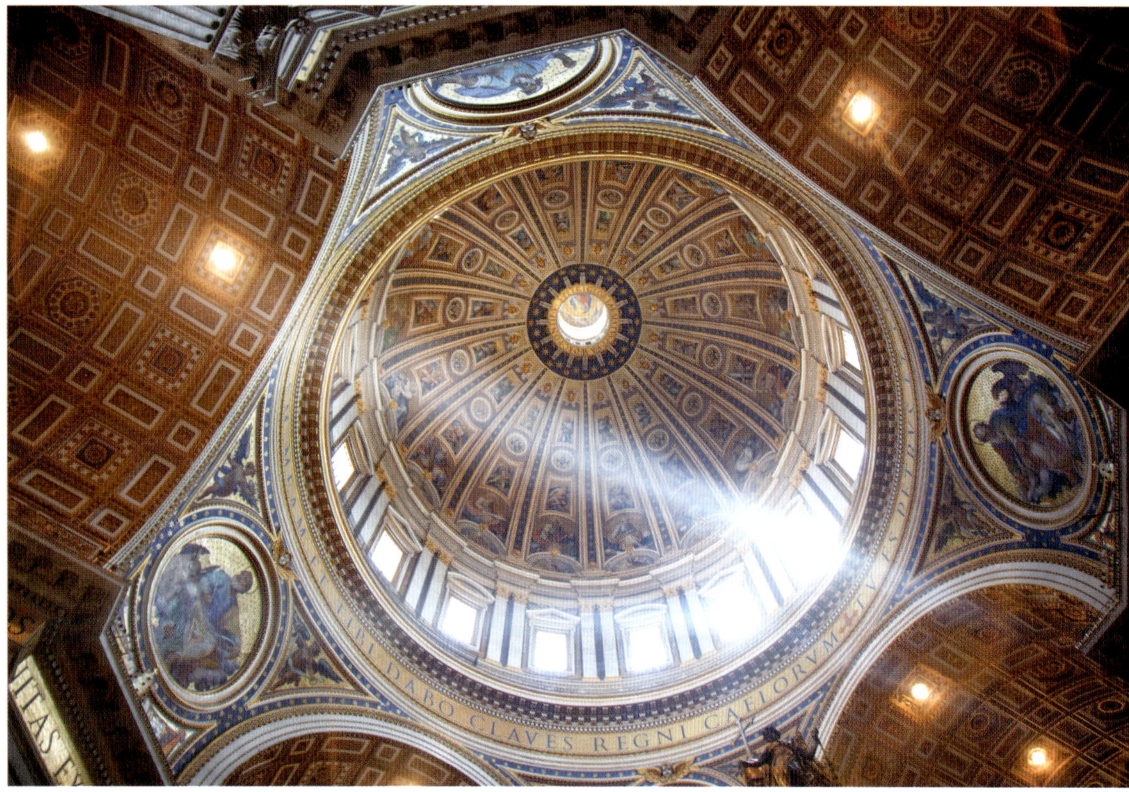

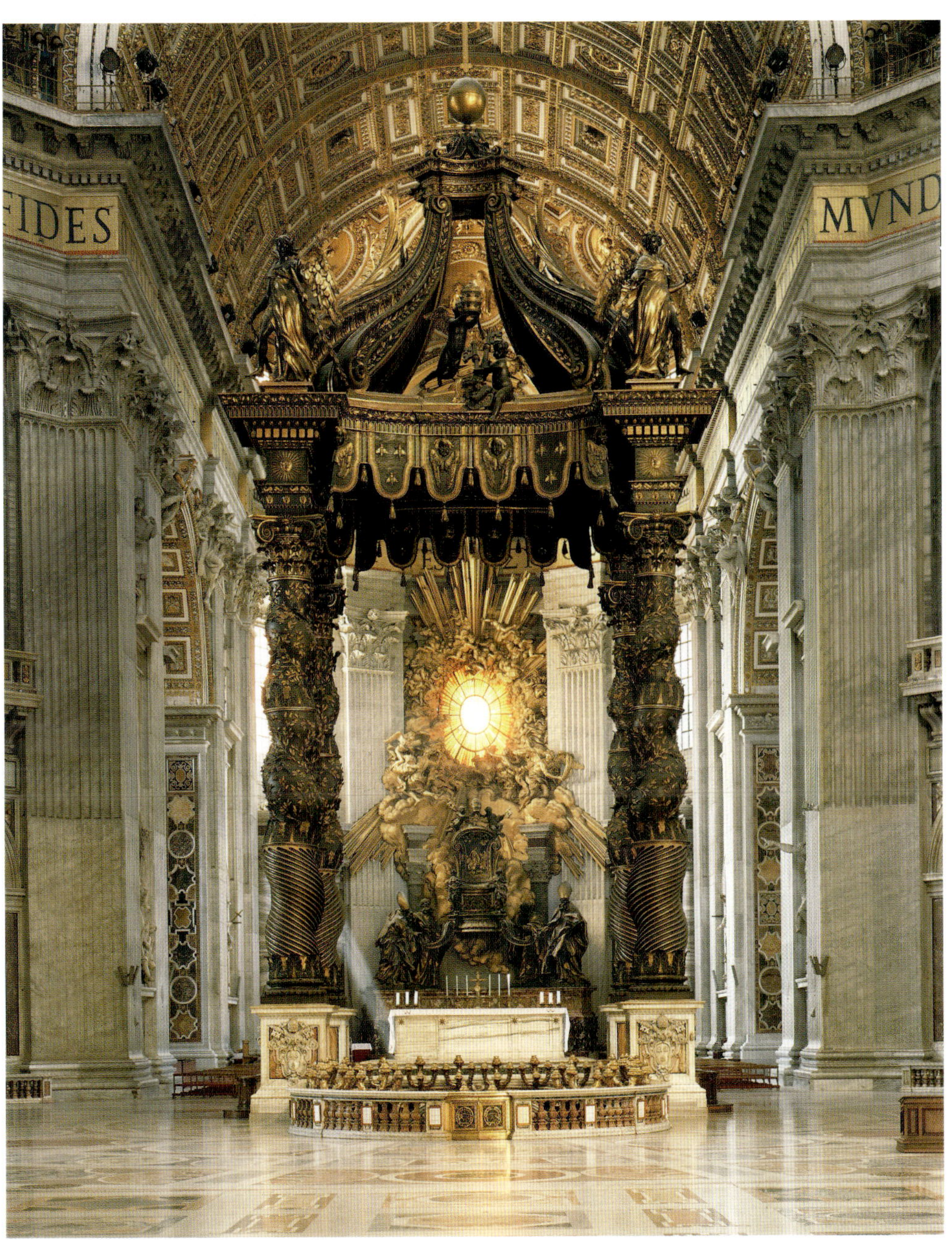

Gian Lorenzo Bernini

Baldachino (St. Peter's Canopy)

The bronze baldachino was the first piece of work undertaken by the young Bernini for St. Peter's Basilica. Commissioned by Pope Urban VIII (1568–1644, reigned from 1623), it is positioned at the center of the crossing and crowns the papal altar erected over the tomb of St. Peter. Half architecture, half sculpture, the baldachino consists of four tall spiral columns supporting an entablature hung with a fringed bronze canopy. This is in turn crowned by a voluted superstructure at whose corners rise four angels, extending the columns even further upward. At its center the voluted crown supports a golden orb surmounted by a cross. Bernini's enormous masterpiece contains many symbolic allusions: The supporting columns recall the spiral columns of the Temple of Jerusalem. The exuberant putti above the entablature hold the papal emblems, the tiara and the key of St. Peter, while two other pairs of putti hold the saint's attributes. The bees on the baldachino represent the heraldic animal of Pope Urban VIII. To provide the vast amount of bronze required for the baldachino, the pope instructed that the antique bronze entablature of the porch of the Pantheon be melted down. Although this act attracted criticism, the dissenting voices were by and large silenced by the splendor of the finished baldachino.

Gian Lorenzo Bernini, 1598–1680
***Baldachino (St. Peter's Canopy)*, 1624–1633**
Height: 28.5 m; Bronze, partly gold-plated
St. Peter's Basilica

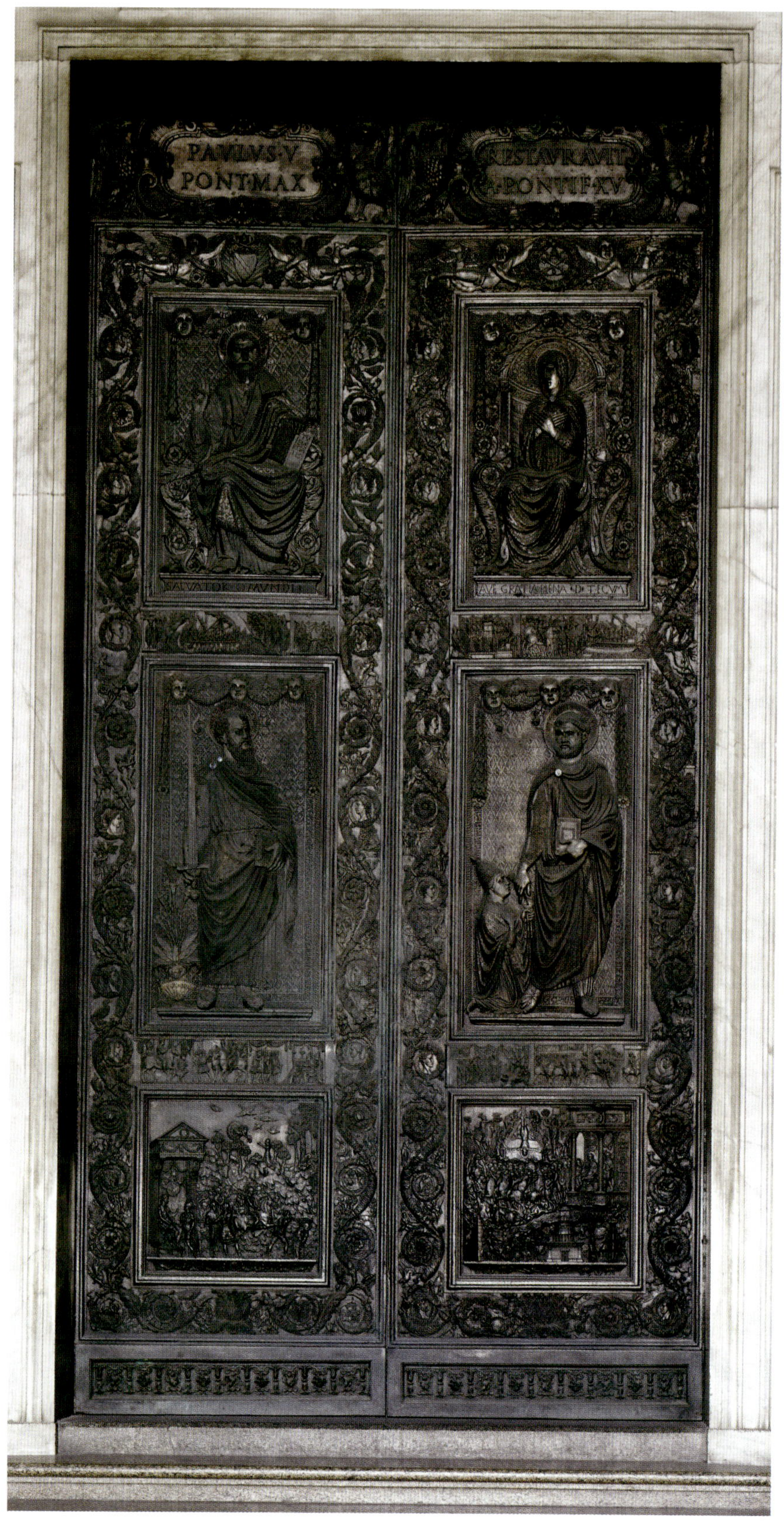

Filarete (Antonio Averlino) and Workshop

Bronze Doors

The basilica's bronze doors were commissioned from the Florentine sculptor Filarete and his workshop by Eugene IV (1383–1447, reigned from 1431) and are among the few surviving furnishings from Old St. Peter's. Executed in the early Renaissance style between 1433 and 1445, the double doors were incorporated as the central portal of the new building. They are completely covered with reliefs and were probably originally partly enameled. The doors' larger fields depict holy figures while the narrow panels interspersed between them describe scenes from the life of Pope Eugene IV. In addition to Christ and the Virgin Mary, the two saints of greatest significance to the basilica, SS. Peter and Paul, are shown in the large panels along with scenes of their martyrdom. The four large figures greet the faithful at the entrance to the church. Of particular note among the narrow panels depicting events from the pontificate of Eugene IV are, top left, the coronation of Holy Roman Emperor Sigismund of Luxembourg (1368–1437, reigned from 1433), the procession of the pope and the emperor to Castel Sant'Angelo, and the Council of Florence of 1438. The frieze running around the panels features figures from classical mythology and is entirely in keeping with the spirit of the Renaissance. Filarete signed his work above the martyrdom of St. Paul and included a small self-portrait alongside it.

Filarete (Antonio Averlino) and Workshop, 1400–1469
***Bronze Doors*, 1433–1445**
635 x 179 cm (each door); Bronze
St. Peter's Basilica

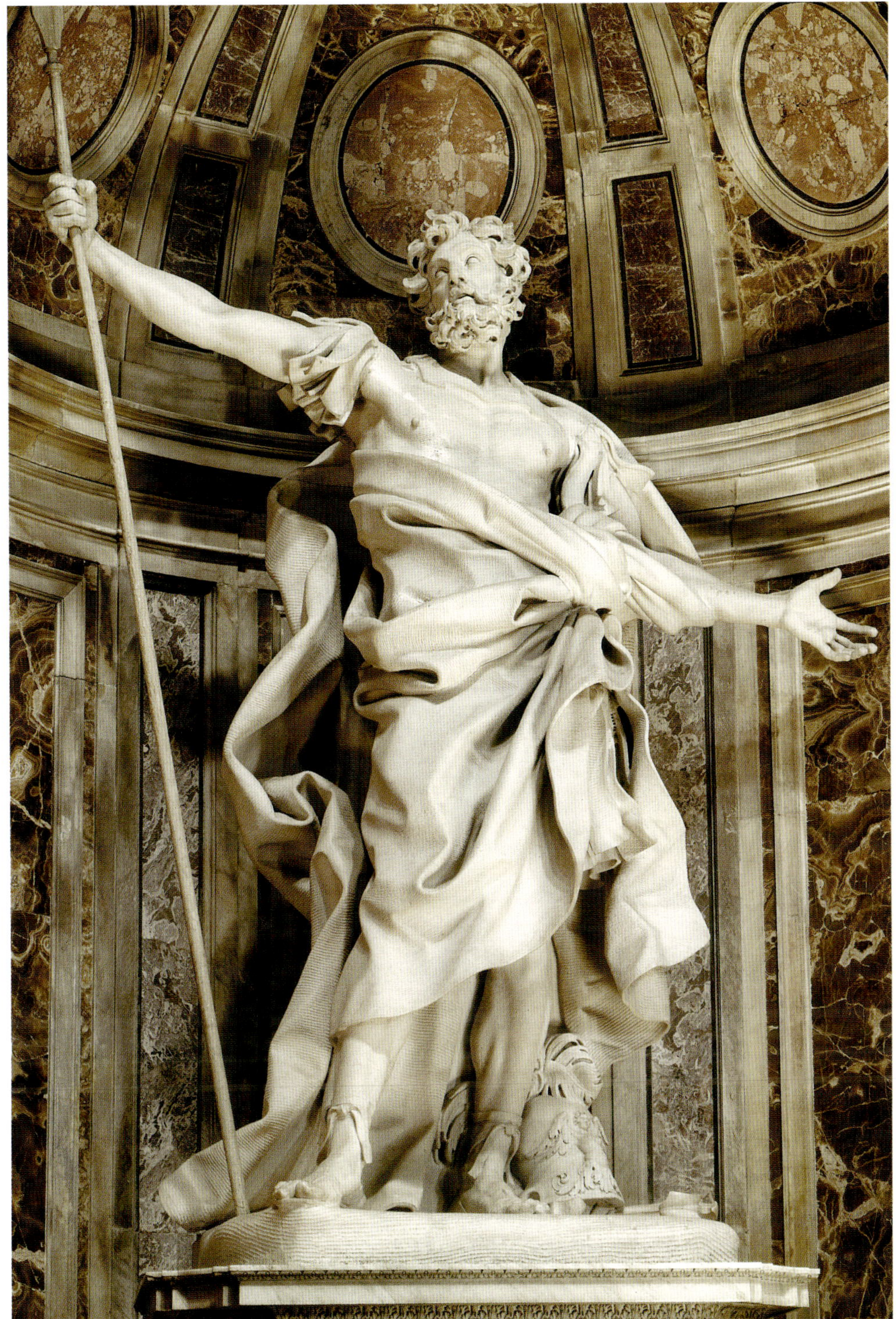

Gian Lorenzo Bernini

St. Longinus

According to Christian legend, St. Longinus was the soldier who pierced the side of Christ on the cross with his spear (John 19:34). He is also identified with the Roman captain described in the Gospel of St. Mark as having acknowledged Christ's divinity after seeing him die: "Truly this man was the son of God!" (Mark 15:39). Longinus, who later died a martyr's death, was the subject of great veneration as the first pagan convert in the Catholic Church. His spear is one of the four main relics preserved in the crossing piers of St. Peter's Basilica. Bernini sculpted the colossal statue of the saint, one of his most famous creations, for the Longinus pier between 1628 and 1638. St. Longinus stands in a contrapposto stance with widespread arms, symbolizing his readiness to embrace the Christian faith. In his outstretched right hand he holds his attribute, the holy spear, thereby rendering visible to the faithful the relic concealed within the pier. The emotion and excitement of the saint at the moment of recognizing God is revealed through his ecstatic, upward gaze and the agitated folds of his mantle, which are also examples of Bernini's mastery.

Gian Lorenzo Bernini, 1598–1680
***St. Longinus*, 1628–1638**
Height: 440 cm; Marble
St. Peter's Basilica

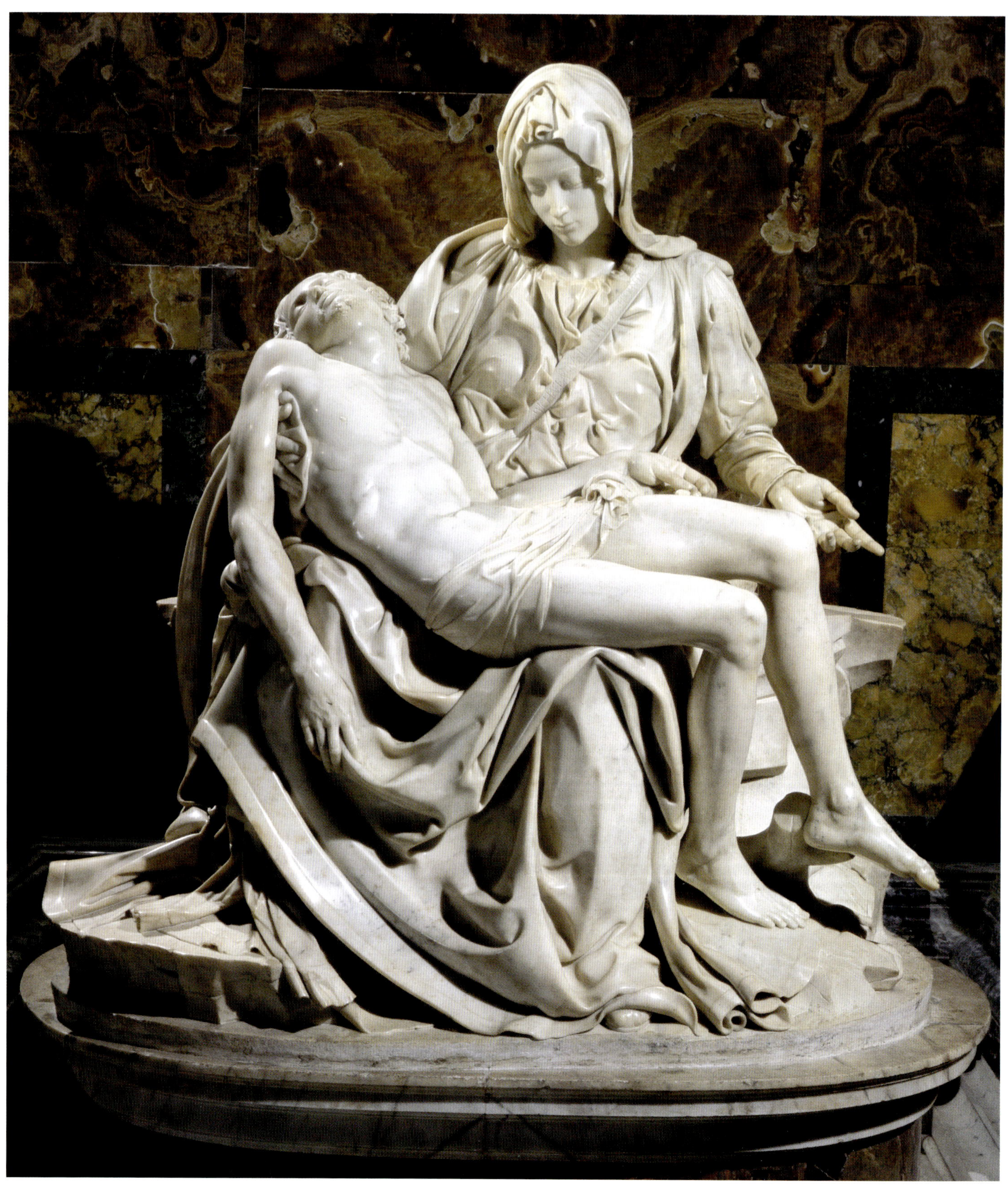

Michelangelo Buonarroti

Pietà

One of the most famous works in St. Peter's Basilica is Michelangelo's life-size Pietà, located in the chapel of the Pietà to the right of the main entrance. This is an early masterpiece created by Michelangelo at around twenty-five years of age for the French cardinal legate Jean de Bilhère. The figural group is carved from a single block of Carrara marble and with its lifelike realism testifies to Michelangelo's supreme skill as a sculptor. Christ's corpse lies limply in the lap of his mother, who supports his slack upper body with her right arm. Christ appears to rest on a white sea of winding sheet and mantle, on whose folded drapery Michelangelo has inscribed his signature at chest height. Mary has lowered her eyes in grief and submits humbly and composedly to her God-given fate. Her submissiveness is also expressed by her open left hand, held palm upward behind the body of her son. The composition radiates an immense concentration and harmony, which gives dignified expression to the grief of the Mother of God.

Michelangelo Buonarroti, 1475–1564
***Pietà*, ca. 1498–1500**
Height: 174 cm; Marble
St. Peter's Basilica

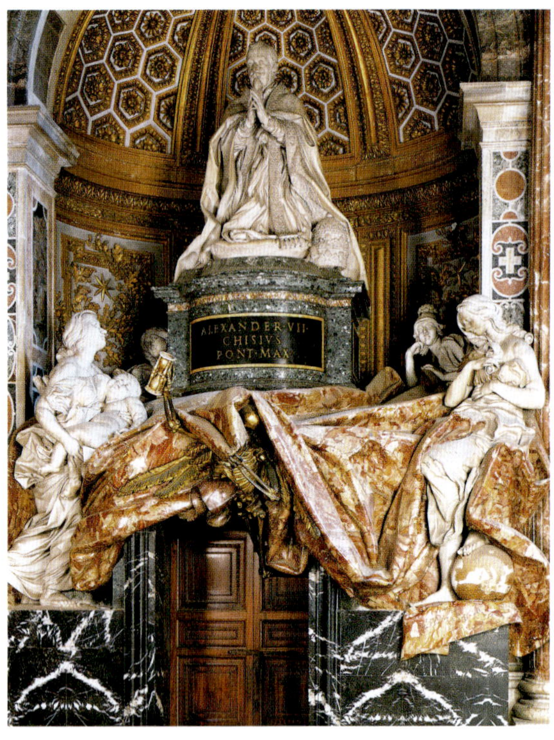

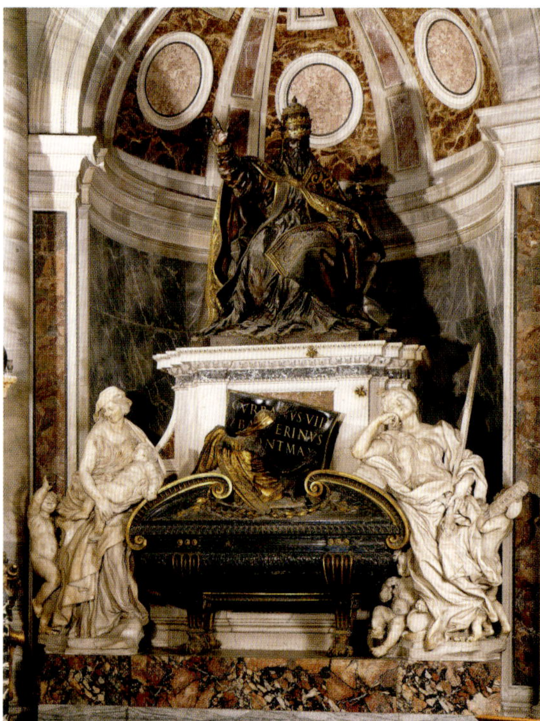

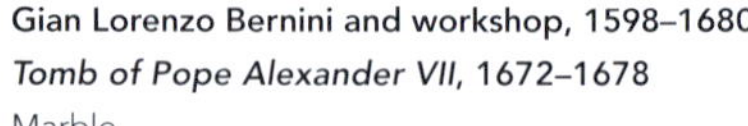

Gian Lorenzo Bernini and workshop, 1598–1680
***Tomb of Pope Alexander VII*, 1672–1678**
Marble
St. Peter's Basilica

Gian Lorenzo Bernini and workshop, 1598–1680
***Tomb of Pope Urban VIII*, 1628–1647**
Marble
St. Peter's Basilica

Francesco Mochi, 1580–1654
***Statue of St. Veronica*, 1629**
Marble
St. Peter's Basilica

Andrea Bolgi, 1605–1656
***St. Helena*, 1635**
Height: 450 cm; Marble
St. Peter' s Basilica

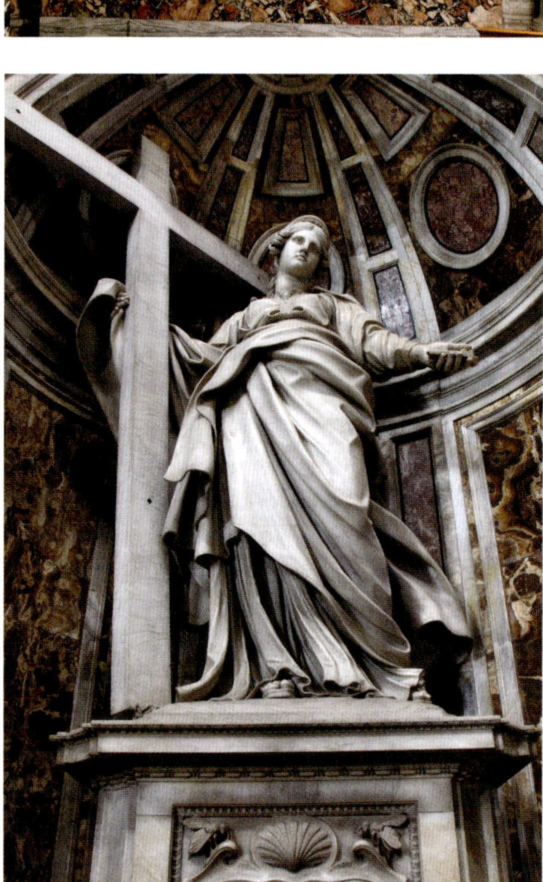

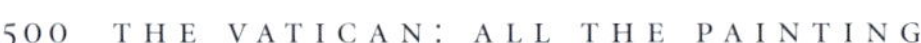

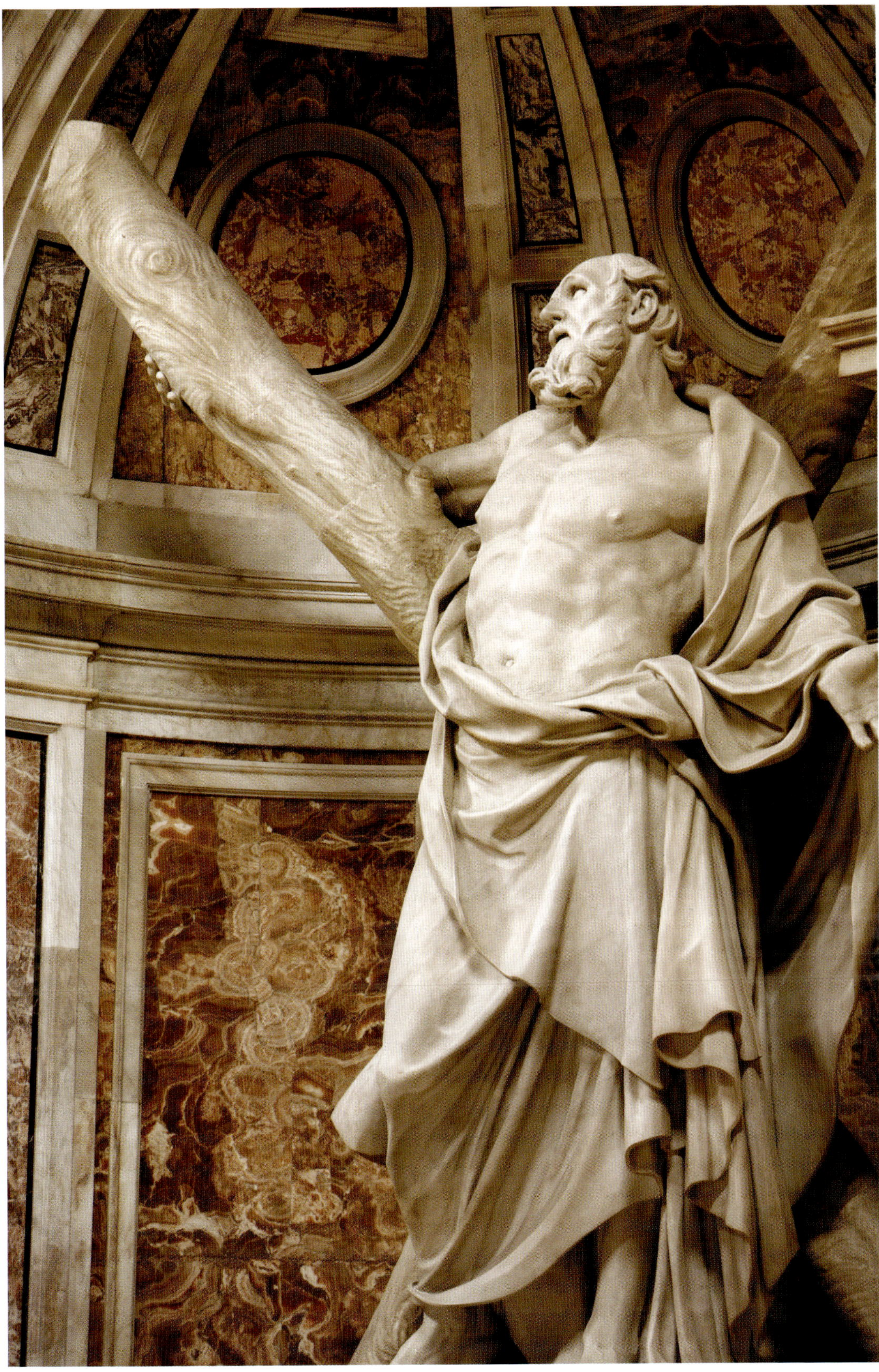

Francois Duquesnoy, 1597–1643
***St. Andrew*, 1633**
Height: 450 cm; Marble
St. Peter's Basilica

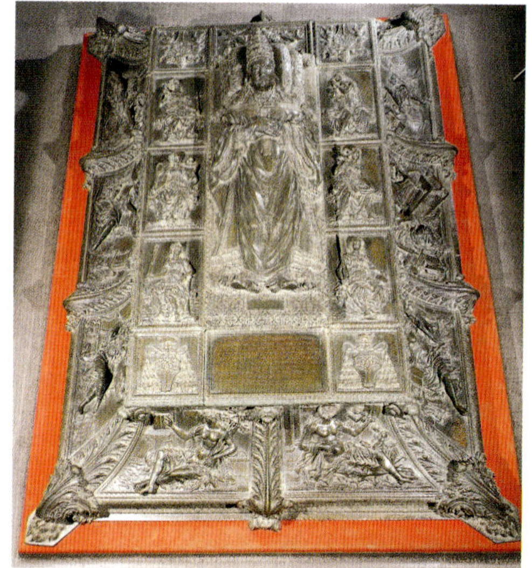

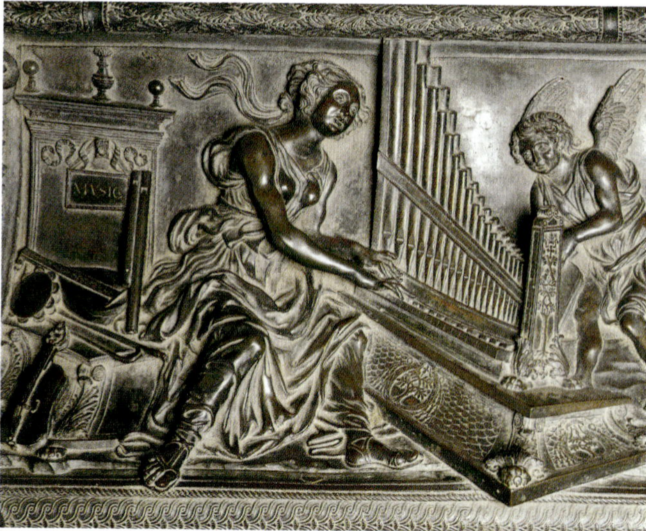

Antonio Pollaiuolo, 1432–1498
***Tomb of Pope Sixtus IV*, 1484–93**
Length: 445 cm; Bronze
St. Peter's Basilica

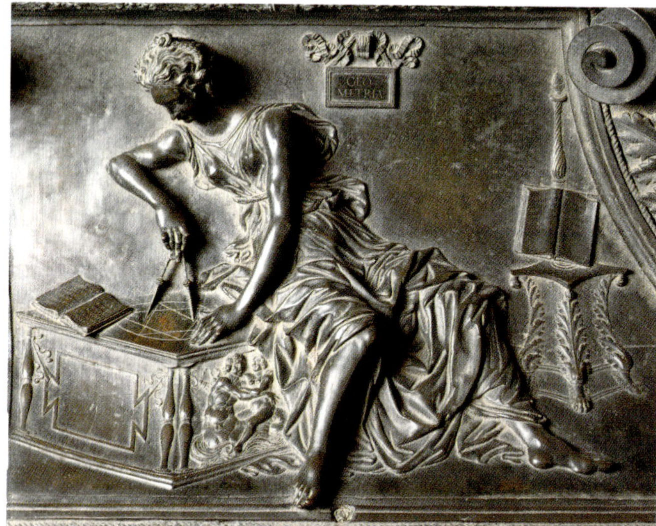

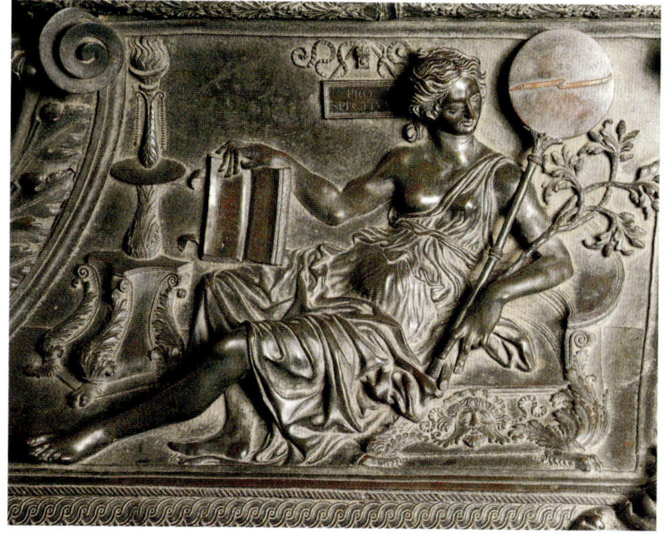

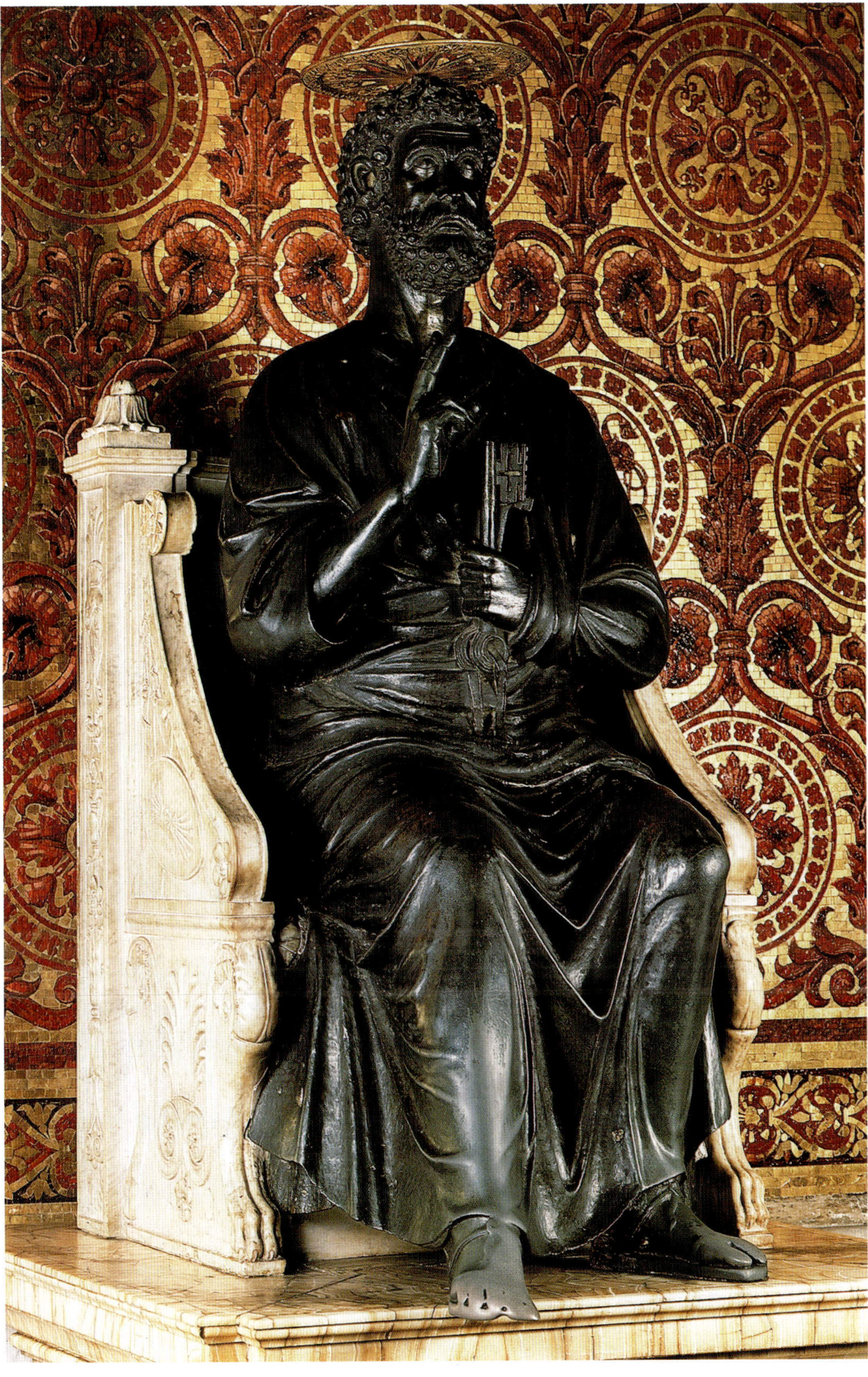

Arnolfo di Cambio, ca. 1240–1302/1310
***Bronze Statue of St. Peter*, 14th century**
Bronze
St. Peter's Basilica

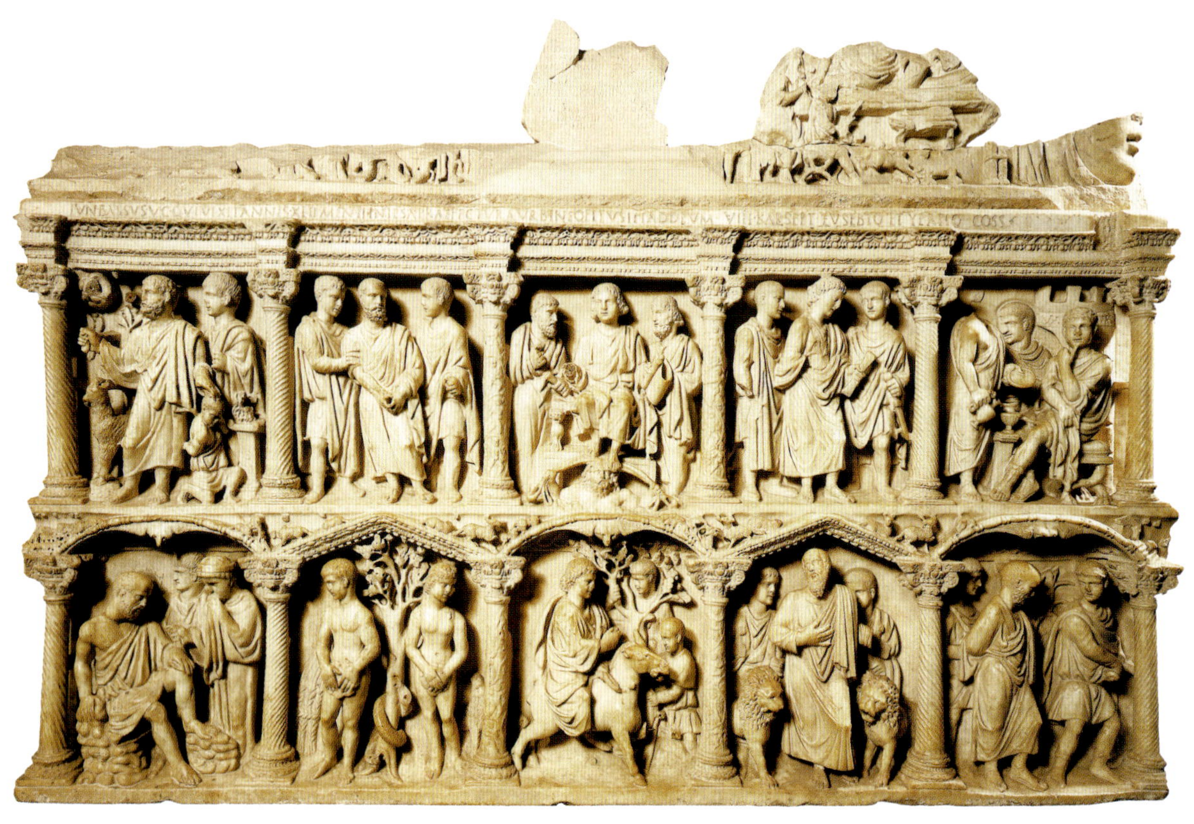

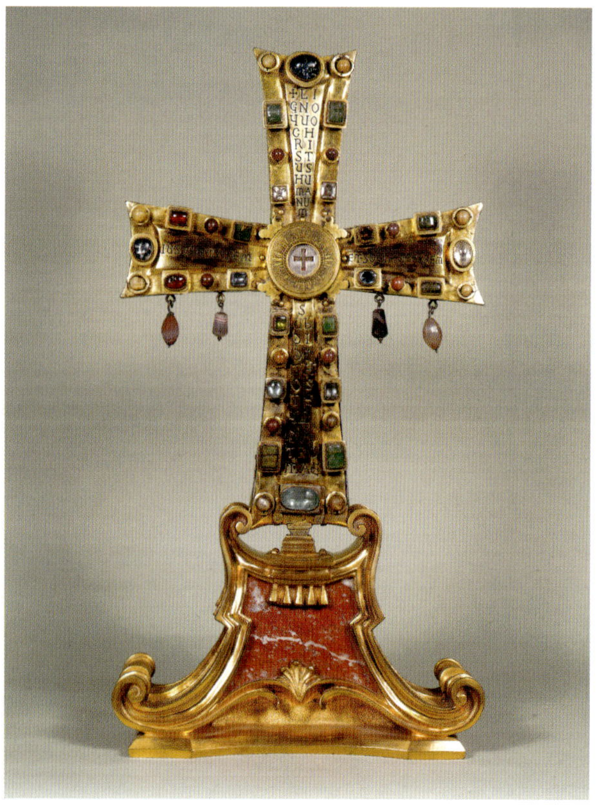

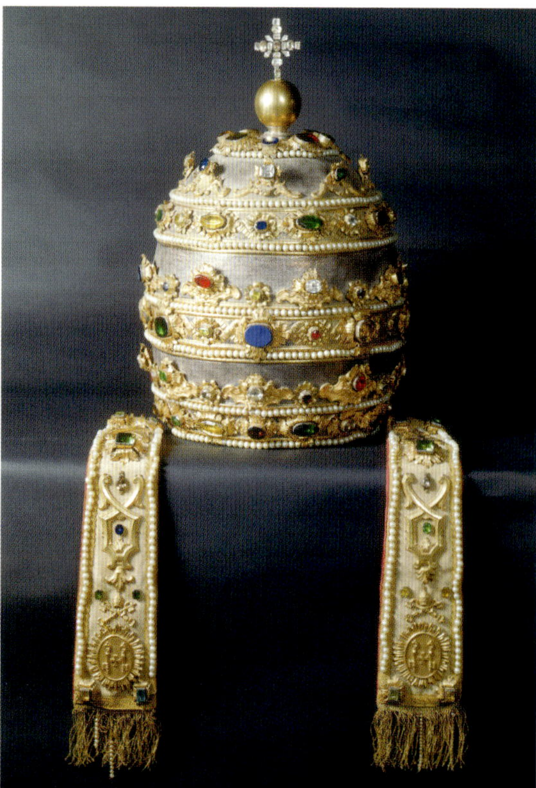

Late Roman, 4th century
***Sarcophagus of Junius Bassus*, 4th century**
122 x 244 x 122 cm; Marble
St. Peter's Basilica, Treasury Museum

Anonymous, 6th century
***Cross of Justin II*, 6th century**
40 x 30 cm; Silver and gold with pearls and inlaid gems
St. Peter's Basilica, Treasury Museum

Anonymous, 16th century
***Tiara of the Bronze Statue of St. Peter*, 16th century**
Silver with pearls and previous gems
St. Peter's Basilica, Treasury Museum

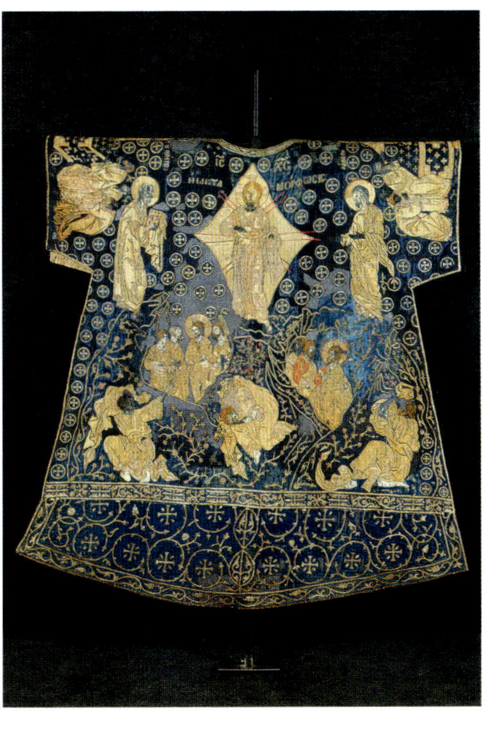

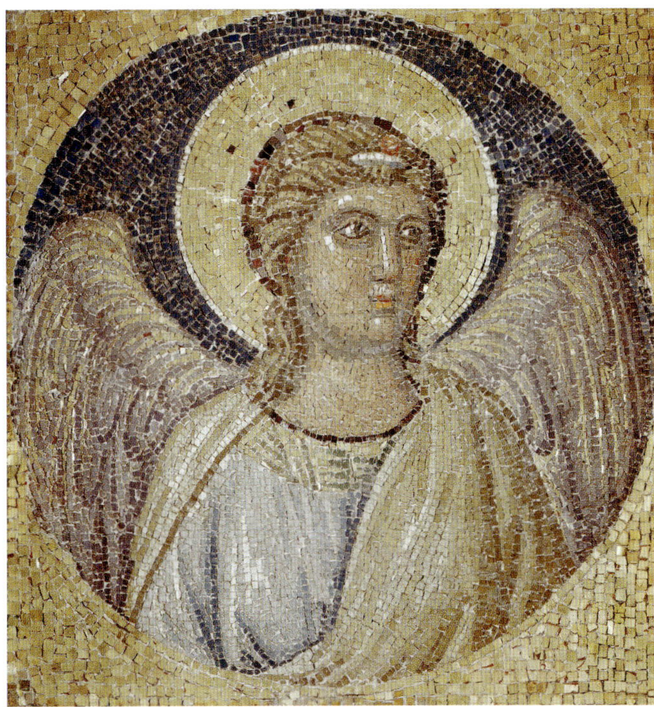

Byzantine era, 14th–15th century
***Dalmatic of Charlemagne*, 14th–15th century**
Textile
St. Peter's Basilica, Treasury Museum

Giotto di Bondone, 1266–1336
***Angel*, 14th century**
Mosaic
St. Peter's Basilica, Sacred Grottoes

Anonymous, ca. 2nd–3rd century
***Colonna Santa*, ca. 2nd-3rd century**
Marble
St. Peter's Basilica, Treasury Museum

Antonio Pollaiuolo, 1432–1498
***Tomb of pope Innocent VIII*, 1492 Bronze**
St. Peter's Basilica, Treasury Museum

Anonymous, 9th century
***Throne of Charles the Bald known as St. Peter's Throne*, 9th century**
Height: 145 cm; Wood
St. Peter's Basilica, Treasury Museum

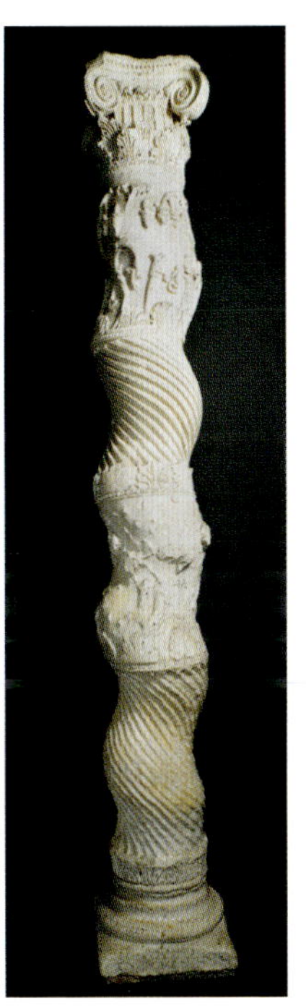

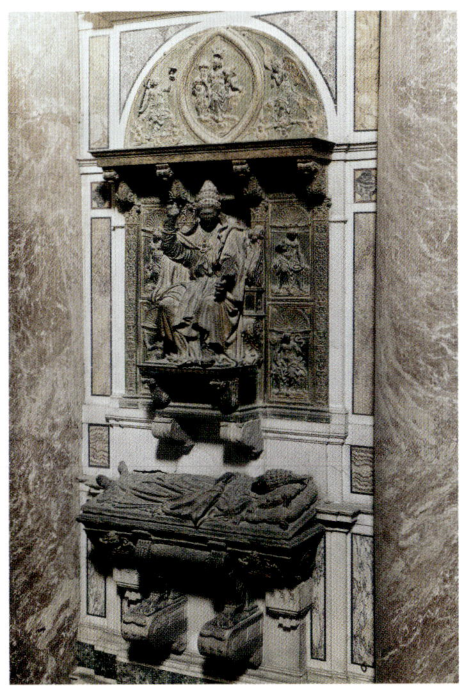

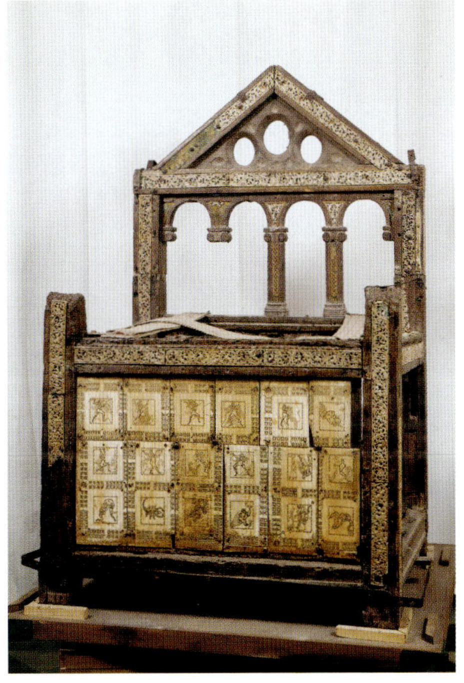

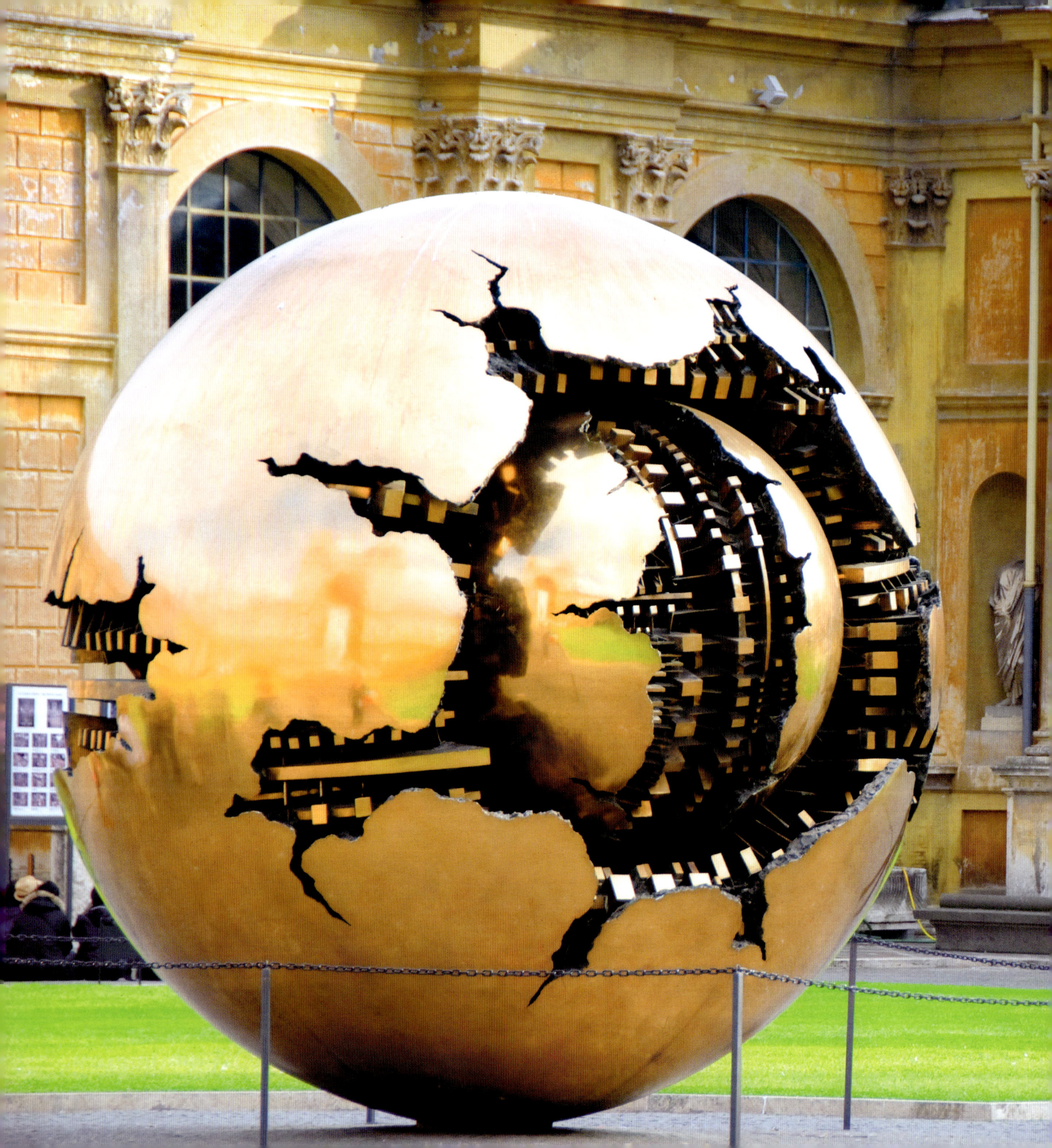

VATICAN STAIRCASES AND COURTYARDS

At first glance the Vatican strikes the visitor as a bewildering maze of buildings dating from many different periods and interspersed with courtyards, passages, and gardens. However, when one recalls that this is an independent state with all the different functions that entails, the abundance of buildings and facilities no longer seems so extraordinary. The Vatican is built on a hill—a challenge for earlier architects—so the individual building volumes are situated on different levels. Those original planners nevertheless made a virtue out of necessity and produced imposing designs for courtyards and staircases that continue to inspire admiration today.

Of the courtyards, the two most worthy of mention are the Cortile del Belvedere and the Cortile della Pigna, created out of the former Belvedere Garden. Both now form part of the Vatican Museums complex. In the neighboring Belvedere Palace, one of Donato Bramante's (1444–1514) most formidable creations has survived in the form of his large spiral staircase. Left unfinished at the time of the architect's death, the stair once served not only to connect the various stories, but also to bridge the height differential between the palace and the neighboring gardens. The significant difference in height between street level and the Vatican Hill also posed a major logistical problem for the designers of the Vatican Museums. One of the most elegant solutions was the double spiral staircase constructed by Giuseppe Momo (1875–1940) in 1932 as the visitor entrance to the museums. During the course of alterations undertaken within the context of Holy Year 2000, it was replaced as the entrance by a new, oval-shaped stairway and now serves as an exit.

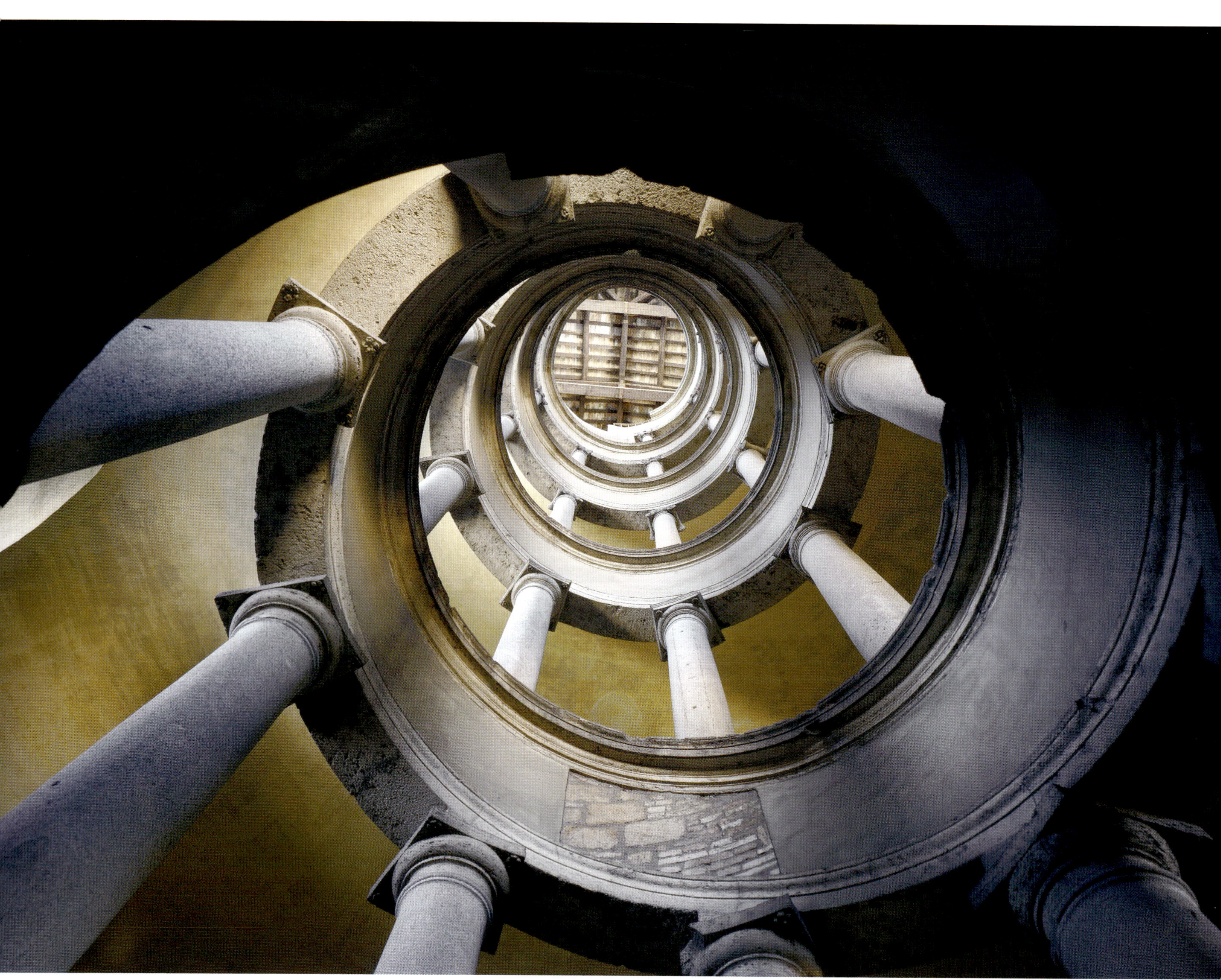

Donato Bramante

Spiral Staircase

Somewhat hidden away in the Vatican Museums is Donato Bramante's spiral staircase, a masterpiece of Renaissance architecture. This was once the main means of access to the various levels of the Palazzo del Belvedere, at the center of which Bramante had already created the Cortile Ottagono in 1504–1505. It is also assumed that the staircase connected the palace with the neighboring, slightly lower-lying section of garden. The different stages of the spiral staircase are structured on the basis of the classical architectural order, as seen, for example, in the Colosseum. The lower level is governed by the Doric order, the middle level by the Ionic order, and the top, or noblest, level by the Corinthian order. The materials were chosen to match the function of the staircase, which was in part to impress visitors. The supporting columns are made of granite, which makes for a charming color contrast with the pale stone of the balustrades and entablature. The steps are conspicuously shallow and wide, ensuring an easy climb. The staircase was unfinished at the time of Bramante's death and was completed under Pius IV (1499–1565, reigned from 1559) by Pirro Ligorio (1514–1583).

Donato Bramante, 1444–1514
***Spiral staircase*, 1511–1514**
Stone, granite columns
Vatican Staircases and Courtyards

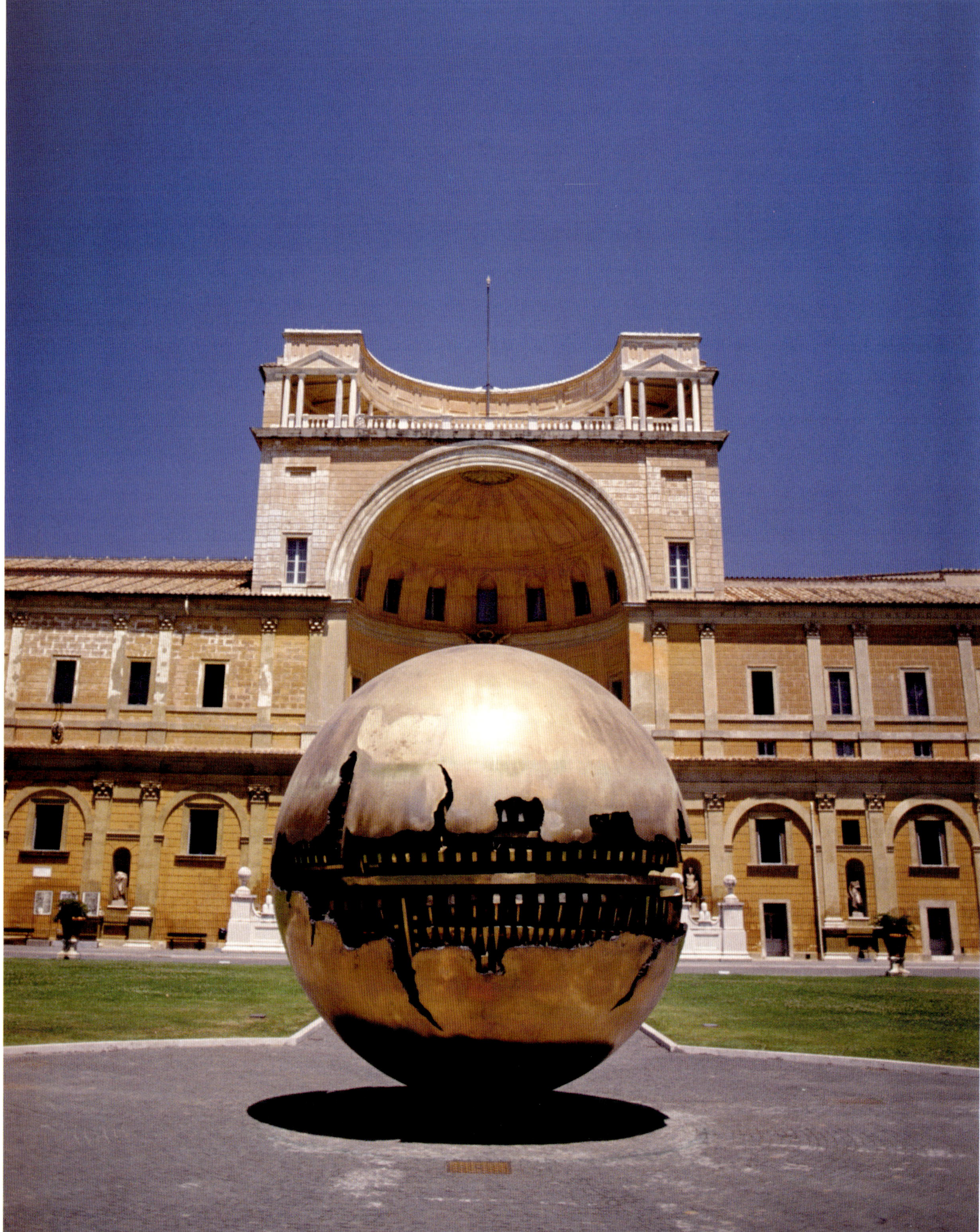

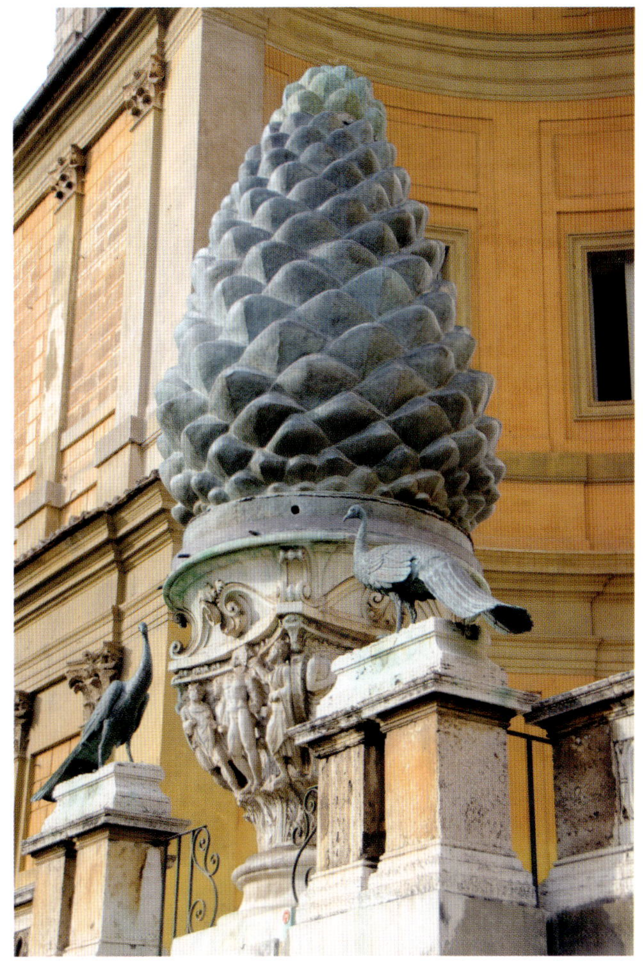

Pirro Ligorio, Michelangelo Buonarroti, and other architects

Cortile della Pigna

The Cortile della Pigna (Court of the Pine) is the upper part of the extensive Belvedere gardens laid out by Pope Innocent VIII (1432–1492, reigned from 1484). It is here that Innocent's successor Julius II (1443–1513, reigned from 1503) had his architect Bramante erect the Belvedere Palace (begun 1504) with its famous Cortile Ottagono for the display of antique statuary. During the pontificate of Pius IV, in 1560–1565, the architect Pirro Ligorio replaced the architectural recess (exedra) designed by Bramante as a shady place from which to survey the garden with a colossal niche; in 1608, an antique sculpture of a pinecone (first century AD) was installed in front of it, giving the courtyard its name. The bronze sculpture has been in the Vatican since the Middle Ages and was celebrated by Dante Alighieri in his Divine Comedy. It is raised slightly to form part of a fountain ensemble (Fontana della Pigna) and is flanked by two bronze peacocks, based on originals that once decorated the tomb of Emperor Hadrian (76–138 AD). The steps were installed by Michelangelo in 1551. The sculpture Sphere within Sphere (1990) by the Italian sculptor Arnaldo Pomodoro (born 1926) stands at the center of the courtyard, providing visitors with delightful sightlines.

Pirro Ligorio, 1514–1583, Michelangelo Buonarroti, 1475–1564, and other architects
***Cortile della Pigna*, 1565**
Vatican Staircases and Courtyards

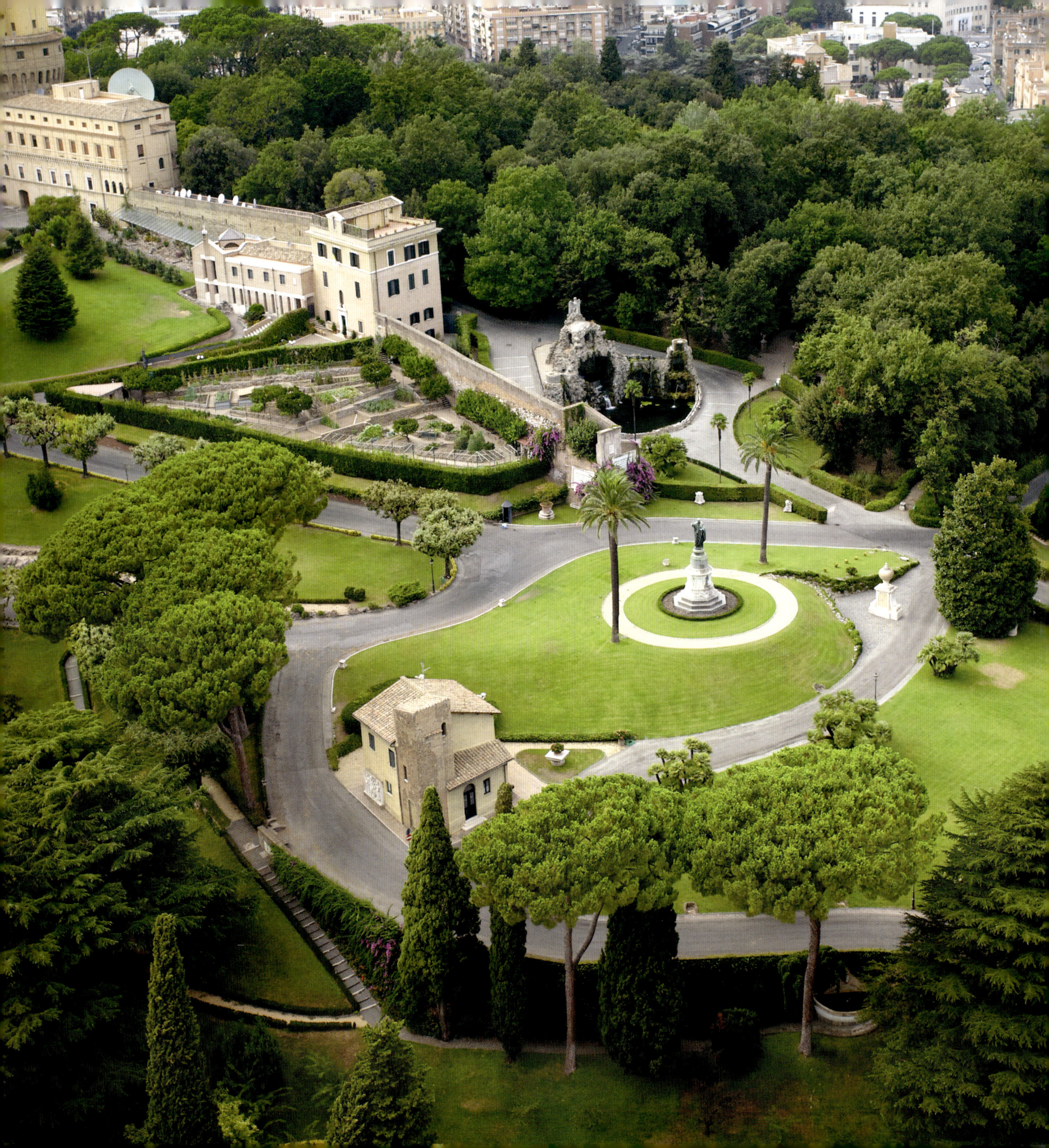

VATICAN GARDENS

Gardens have been an integral part of the papal palace complex since its earliest days. However, today's Vatican Gardens have little in common with the garden areas that existed on the Vatican site following the return of the popes to Rome in year 1417. Pictures and written descriptions record that in the fifteenth and sixteenth centuries the main garden extended between the south side of the present Cortile del Belvedere and the north side of the Cortile della Pigna, which had not yet been divided by the wing erected at the end of the sixteenth and beginning of the nineteenth centuries.

The original papal gardens extended from the heart of the old papal palace with the Sistine Chapel and so-called Borgia Tower to the rise in the land by the north wall of the Vatican. Innocent VIII (1432–1492, reigned from 1484) had a loggia built on the original gardens, after designs by the Florentine Renaissance painter Antonio del Pollaiuolo (1433–1498), as a resting place and viewing point during his walks. This was the beginning of what was subsequently transformed by the architect Donato Bramante (1444–1514) into the Palazzo del Belvedere under Julius II (1443–1513, reigned from 1503). It was part of a tripartite terrace complex that connected the various elevations of the land from the papal palace to the Belvedere Hill. The Belvedere Garden, laid out in the Renaissance style, served not only as a place of recuperation for the pope but also as a backdrop for court festivities, for example the double wedding in 1565 of two nephews of Pius IV (1499–1565, reigned from 1559).

The architectural changes to the Belvedere courtyard described above also meant that at the end of the sixteenth century the gardens needed to be moved. Furthermore, new garden styles emerged during the Baroque and Rococo periods. One of the first innovations was the Villa or Casino of Pius IV, erected by the architect and landscape gardener Pirro Ligorio (1514–1583) between 1559 and 1562 as a garden pavilion for the pope. A conspicuous feature of the parklike gardens, which are planted with a wide variety of trees and hedges, are the numerous fountains and monuments that punctuate the twenty-three-hectare terrain, forming eye-catching focal points.

Palace of the Governorate of Vatican City State (center) and the Mater Ecclesiae Monastery (right)
Vatican Gardens

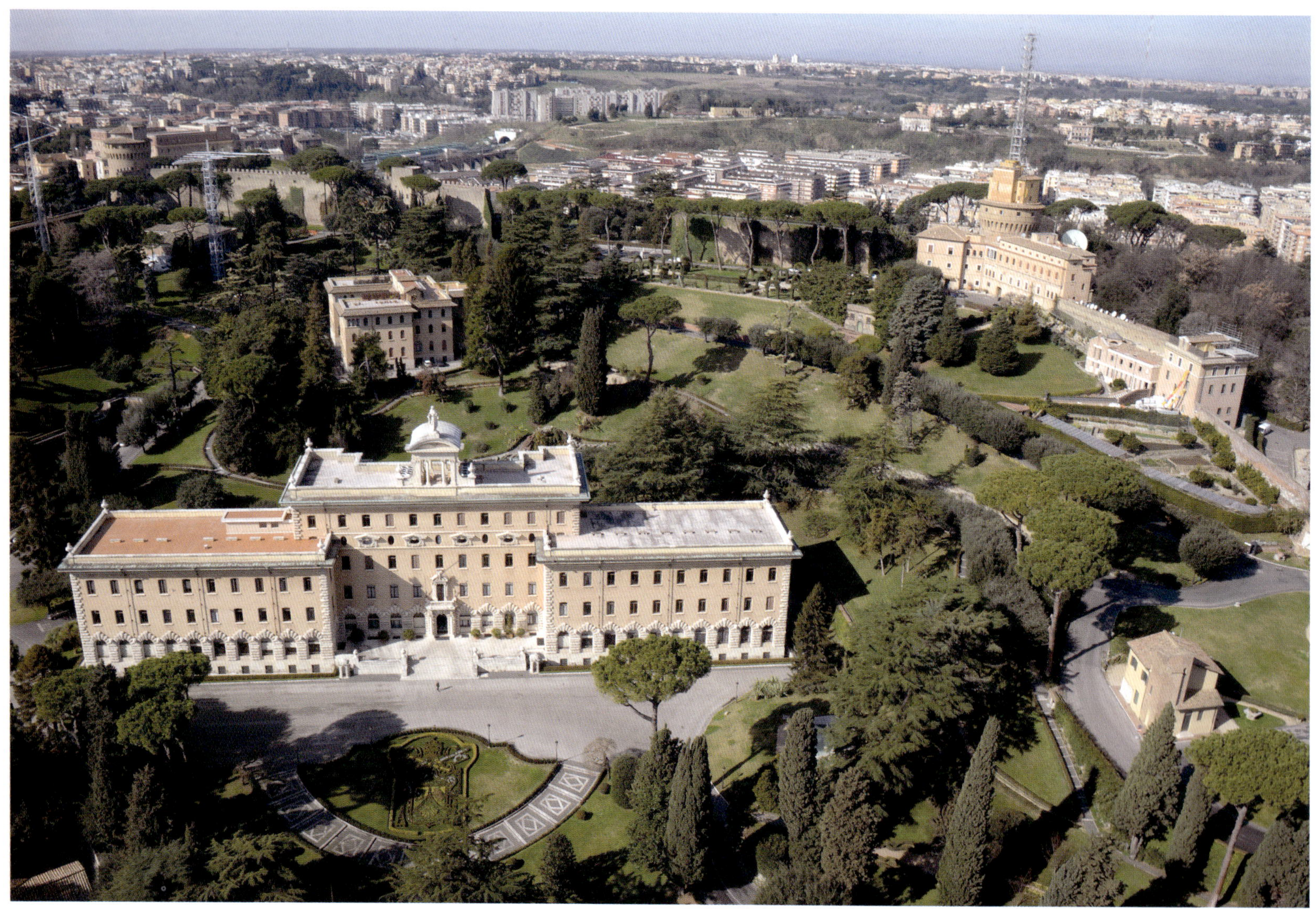

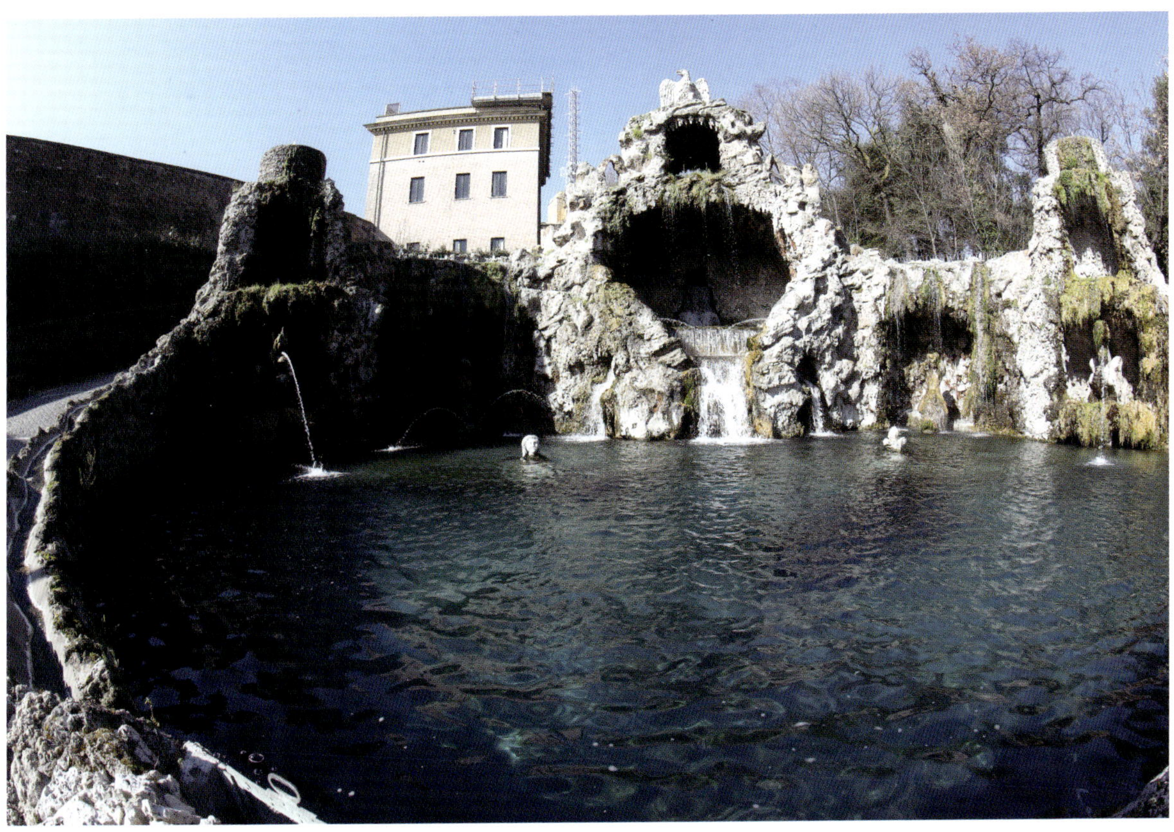

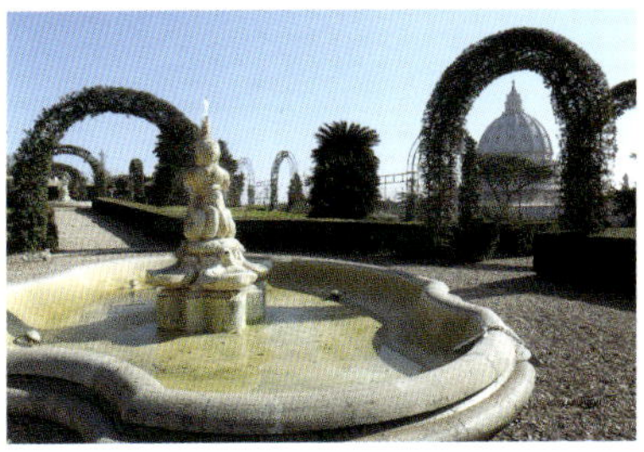

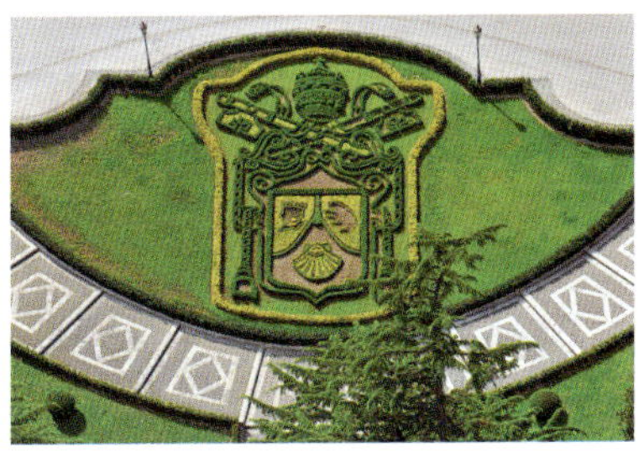

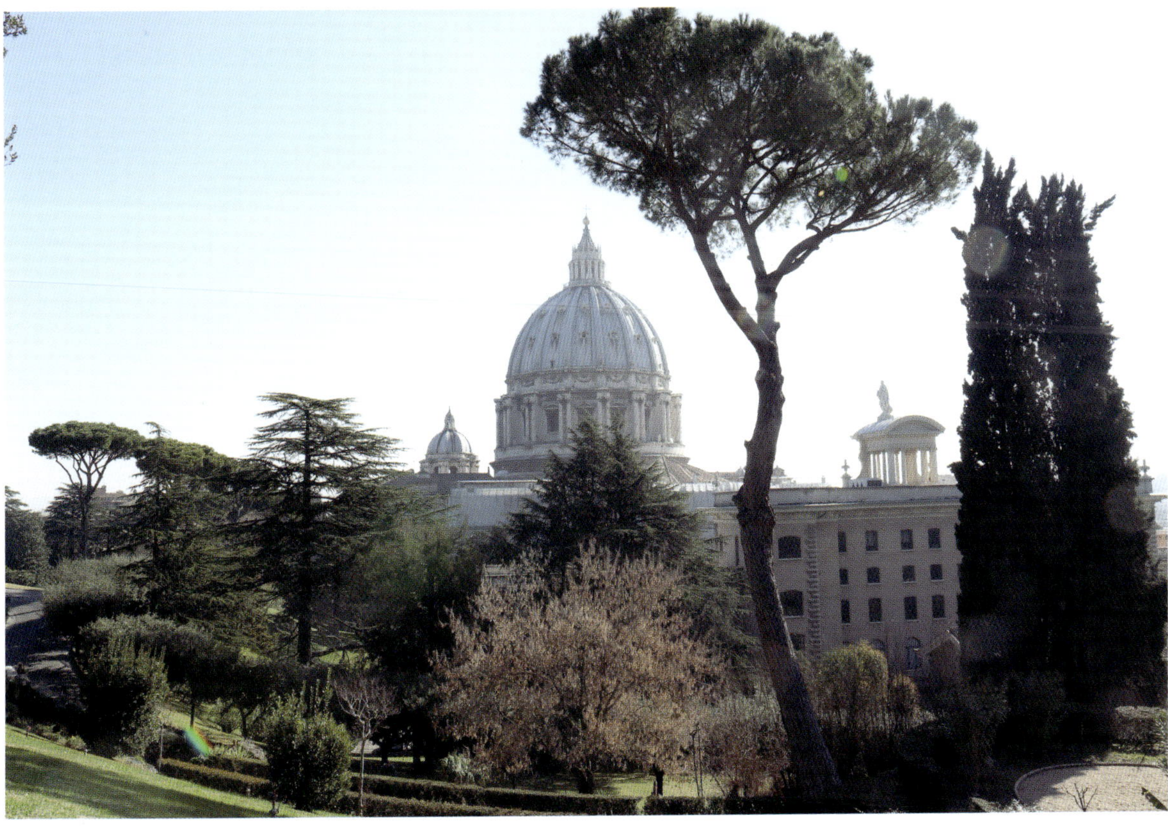

Vasanzio (Jan van Santen), 1550–1621
Fountain of the Eagle, 1620
Vatican Gardens

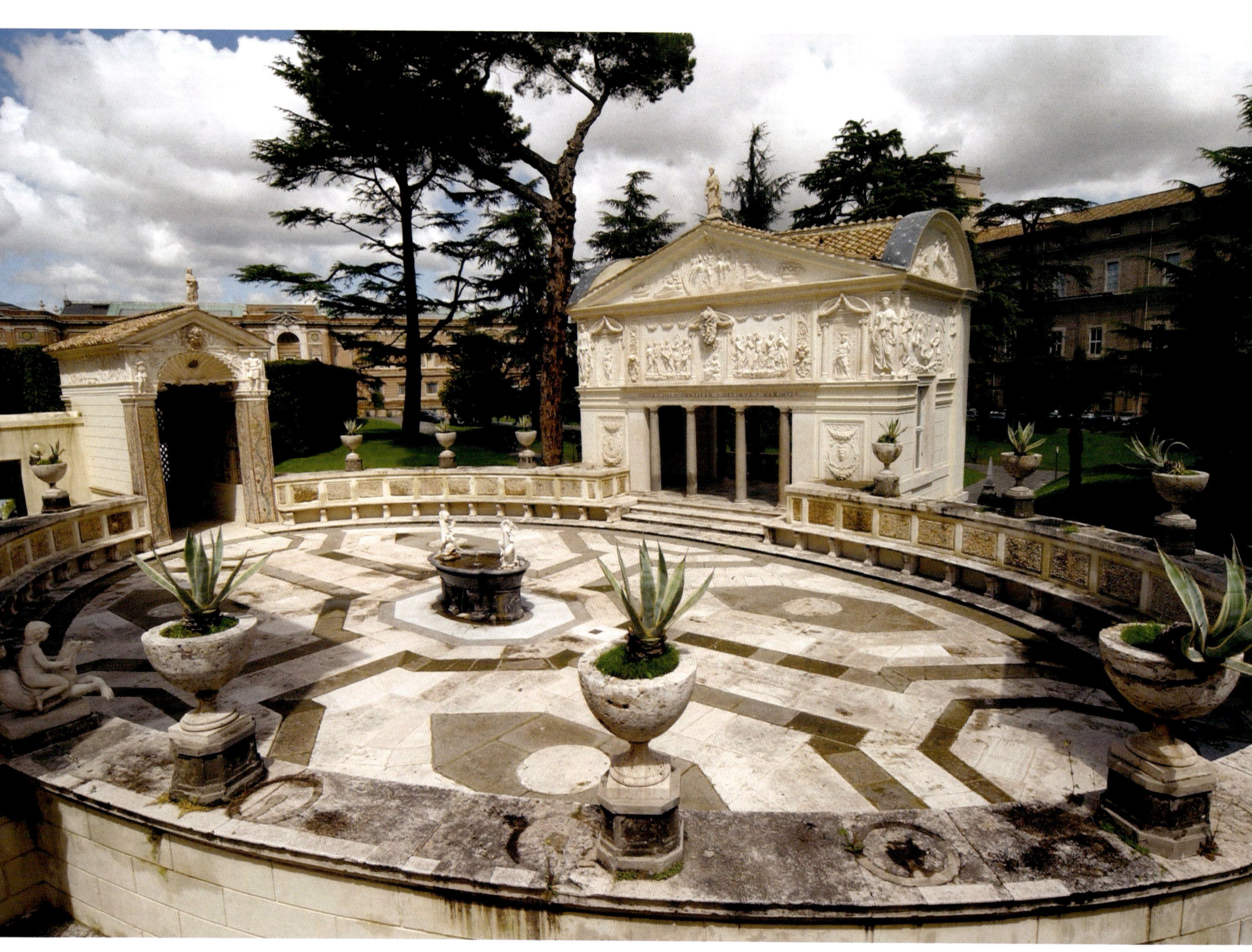

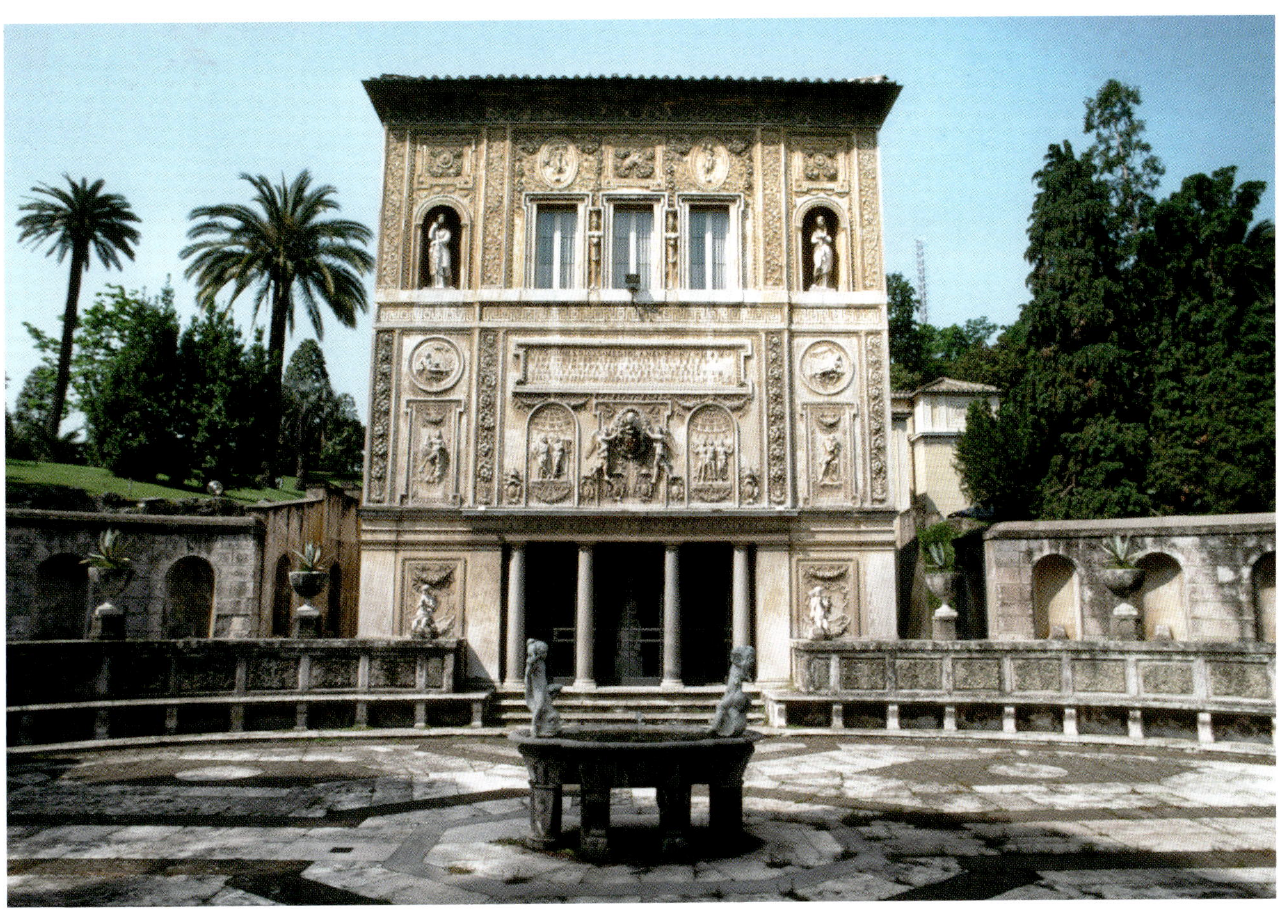

Pirro Ligorio

Casino of Pius IV

Like many Renaissance popes, Pius IV indulged in a somewhat worldly lifestyle and had a liking for fine art. Shortly after taking office in 1559, he took up the project of his predecessor, Paul IV (1476–1559, reigned 1555-1559), to build a garden house on the western side of the papal palace and the Cortile del Belvedere. The villa designed in the Mannerist style by the painter, architect, and landscape gardener Pirro Ligorio was used by the pope for the purpose of relaxation. It was somewhere to take refreshment while out on his walks and also somewhere to entertain small groups of people. The complex comprises two smaller freestanding buildings, the villa itself, and a loggia positioned before it, where views of the Belvedere and St. Peter's could once be enjoyed. Between the two parts of the building is a small oval courtyard. In keeping with Mannerist taste, Pius's summerhouse was adorned with lavish stucco work, frescoes of mythological scenes, Roman statues, and shell decoration, lending the place an antique ambience. Today the villa and a new building in the classical style erected in front of it house the Pontifical Academy of Sciences.

Pirro Ligorio, 1514–1583,
***Casino of Pius IV*, 1559–1562**
Vatican Gardens

INDEX OF ARTISTS

INDEX OF ARTWORKS

IMAGE CREDITS

(t:top; l:left; m:middle; r:right; b:bottom)

akg-images: 218-9, 264-5, 338t, 354©DACS, 398, 405, 406tl, 406tr, 427tm, 431b / Erich Lessing: front cover, 244-245, 268, 270-1, 272-3, 275, 282, 284, 290, 293, 294b, 402l

Alinari: 177

Bridgeman Art Library: 350©DACS 2013; 396, 400br, 401mr, 404r, 406mr

DP: 17tr, 17mr, 17br, 19ml (1), 19ml (2), 19mr (1), 19mr (2), 19b, 20br, 34tl, 39tr, 39br, 47t (3), 47tr, 48, 50tr, 50br, 51, 52, 70tr, 70ml, 71tl, 71mr, 71b, 88tl, 108tl, 108tr, 108ml, 108mr, 115tl, 120mr, 121tr, 124bc, 124br, 136tr, 136ml, 139tr, 139mr, 139bl, 142tr, 142mr, 144ml, 144mr, 152mc, 152mr, 152bl, 153tl, 153tr, 153ml, 153mr, 155r, 156, 157, 172ml, 172bl, 172br, 173, 198, 209t, 209b, 227, 326, 327r, 329tr, 329b, 330, 331

Getty Images: 494b, 500br, 510/ AFP: 514; **age fotostock:** 136tl, 226tr, 269, 283, 285, 287, 291, 300mr, 304, 332, 339, 355tr, 419, 421l, 421tr, 422, 424, 428, 429t, 437tr, 437b, 438r, 439l, 439m, 444l, 500bl; **Alinari:** 16, 70bl, 70mr, 90tr, 131, 226ml, 238, 388, 392-3, 406ml, 432, 441r, 445bl, 445br, 448; **Altrendo:** 208, 216-7, 414; Apic: 212; **Beanstock Images:** 486; **Bridgeman:** 136bl, 248, 292; **Marco Brivio:** back cover; **De Agostini** 8tl, 22, 24-25, 42t, 42bl, 63, 68, 69, 71ml, 74-5, 78, 98-99, 107bl, 125, 132, 133, 134bc, 231, 320, 325l, 379ml, 394, 400tl, 400bl, 401tl, 401ml, 401b, 402tr, 403r, 406br, 416bl, 416bc, 417t, 418, 423, 426bl, 427tr, 429bl, 461, 464tr, 464l, 466, 468, 469m, 470, 472bl, 474, 485tl, 493, 494tr, 495, 500tl, 500tr, 502, 503, 504t, 505bc; E+: 512; **Gamma-Rapho:** 246, 434, 516: hemis.fr: 494b; **Image Bank:** 262-3, 266-7, 490; **Imagno:** 403l; **Franco Origlia:** 515tl, 515tr, 515b, 591; **Superstock:** 1-2, 21, 70tl, 71tr, 94br, 126, 147l, 174, 178, 213, 225br, 226b, 228, 229l, 230, 256-7, 259, 274, 286, 288, 317t, 319tl, 319bl, 321tl, 341, 372, 374t, 380br, 382, 498, 506, 511; UIG: 102, 155l, 214-5, 233l, 250-1, 252t, 253, 255b, 302, 305, 306-7, 312br, 400tr, 401tr, 402br, 442, 492; **Roger Viollet:** 517

iStockphoto: 2

Scala Archives: 348t©DACS 2013; 349©DACS 2013; 351t©DACS 2013; 351b©DACS 2013; 352© ADAGP, Paris and DACS, London 2013; 355b ©Lucio Fontana/SIAE/DACS, London 2013; 5, 6, 7, 8tr, 8b, 9, 10, 12, 13, 14, 15, 17l, 18, 19t, 20tl, 20tr, 20bl, 23, 26, 27, 28, 29, 30, 31, 32, 33, 34bl, 34tr, 34br, 35, 36, 37, 38, 39bl, 39tl, 40, 41, 42br, 43, 44, 45, 46, 47tl, 47t(2), 47ml, 47mr, 47b, 49, 50tl, 50ml, 50mr, 50bl, 52tl, 52ml, 52mc, 52mr, 52b, 53, 54, 56, 57, 58, 59, 60, 61, 62, 64, 66, 67, 70br, 72, 73, 76, 77, 80, 81, 82, 83, 84, 85, 86, 87, 88tr, 88b, 89, 90tl, 90b, 91, 92, 93, 94tl, 94tr, 94ml, 94mr, 94bl, 95, 96, 97, 100, 101, 103, 104, 106, 107tl, 107m, 107r, 108b, 109, 110, 111, 112, 113, 114, 115tr, 115bl, 115br, 116, 117, 118, 119, 120tl, 120tr, 120tc, 120ml, 120mc, 120bl, 120bc, 120br, 121tl, 121b, 122, 123, 124tl, 124tr, 124bl, 128, 129, 130, 134tl, 134tr, 134bl, 134br, 135, 136mr, 136br, 137, 138, 139tl, 139tc, 139ml, 139br, 140, 141, 142tl, 142ml, 142b, 143, 144tl, 144tr, 144bl, 144br, 145, 146, 147r, 148, 149, 150, 151, 152t, 152ml, 152br, 153tc, 153bl, 153br, 154, 158-9, 163, 164-5, 166, 167, 168, 169, 170-1, 172t, 175, 176, 179, 180-1, 182-3, 184-5, 186, 187, 188, 190, 191, 192, 193, 194, 195, 196, 197, 199, 203, 204, 205, 206, 207, 209m, 211, 220, 221, 222, 224, 225tl, 225tr, 225bl, 226tl, 226mr, 229r, 232, 233r, 237, 239, 240, 241, 242, 243, 249, 252b, 254, 255t, 258, 260, 276, 277, 278, 279, 280, 281, 294tl, 294tr, 295, 296, 297, 298, 299, 300tl, 300tr, 300ml, 300br, 301t, 308-9, 312t, 312bl, 313, 314, 315, 316, 317bl, 317br, 318, 319tl, 321tr, 321m, 321bl, 321br, 322, 323, 324, 325tr, 325mr, 325br, 327l, 328, 329tl, 333, 334, 338b, 340, 342-3, 346, 348b, 349, 351, 353, 355tl, 356-7, 358, 360, 362, 363, 364, 365, 366, 368, 369, 370, 371, 374ml, 374b, 374r, 375, 376, 377, 378, 379tl, 379tr, 379mr, 379bl, 379br, 380, 381, 383, 384, 385, 386, 387, 390, 391, 399, 407, 408, 409tr, 409bl, 409br, 410, 411, 412, 416tl, 416tr, 416br, 417m, 417b, 420, 421r, 425, 426t, 426br, 427tl, 427b, 429br, 430, 431tl, 431m, 436, 437tl, 438l, 438m, 439r, 440, 441l, 444r, 445t, 446, 450tl, 450tr, 450bl, 451, 452, 453, 454, 455t, 455ml, 455mr, 455bl, 456, 457, 458, 460, 462, 463, 464br, 465, 467, 469bl, 469br, 472tl, 472tr, 473, 474br, 475, 476, 478, 479, 480, 482, 483, 484, 485tr, 485bl, 485br, 496, 497, 501r, 504bl, 504br, 505, 508

Superstock: 200-1, 234-5, 301b, 336, 404l, 409tl, 431tr, 443, 469t, 496, 501l, 515br